ESSENTIALS OF UNDERSTANDING PSYCHOLOGY

ESSENTIALS OF UNDERSTANDING PSYCHOLOGY

ROBERT S. FELDMAN
University of Massachusetts at Amherst

McGRAW-HILL BOOK COMPANY

NEW YORK ST. LOUIS SAN FRANCISCO AUCKLAND BOGOTÁ CARACAS
COLORADO SPRINGS HAMBURG LISBON LONDON MADRID MEXICO MILAN
MONTREAL NEW DELHI OKLAHOMA CITY PANAMA PARIS SAN JUAN
SÃO PAULO SINGAPORE SYDNEY TOKYO TORONTO

This book was set in Times Roman by Waldman Graphics, Inc.
The editors were James D. Anker and David Dunham;
the designer was Joan E. O'Connor; the production
supervisor was Diane Renda.
The photo editor was Inge King.
Cover illustration was drawn by Cathy Hull.
The drawings were done by J & R Services, Inc.
Von Hoffman Press, Inc. was printer and binder.

**ESSENTIALS OF
UNDERSTANDING PSYCHOLOGY**

Copyright © 1989 by McGraw-Hill, Inc. All rights reserved. Printed in the United States of America. Except as permitted under the United States Copyright Act of 1976, no part of this publication may be reproduced or distributed in any form or by any means, or stored in a data base or retrieval system, without the prior written permission of the publisher.

1234567890 VNHVNH 89321098

ISBN 0-07-020457-8

Library of Congress Cataloging-in-Publication Data

Feldman, Robert S. (Robert Stephen), (date).
The essentials of understanding psychology
Robert S. Feldman. p. cm.
Abridged ed. of: Understanding psychology. © 1987
Bibliography: p.
Includes indexes.
ISBN 0-07-020457-8
1. Psychology. I. Feldman, Robert S.
(Robert Stephen), (date).
Understanding psychology. II. Title.
BF121.F34 1989
150—dc19 88-19679

To
Jonathan, Joshua, Sarah,
and Kathy, with love

REVIEWERS

I am grateful to the following people, who reviewed all or part of the manuscript.

Phillip L. Ackerman
University of Minnesota
Robert C. Beck
Wake Forest University
Brenda Bennett
Vincennes University
David Berg
Community College of Philadelphia
Allen E. Bergin
Brigham Young University
Tom Bind
Thomas Nelson Community College
Donald Bowers
Community College of Philadelphia
Allen R. Branum
South Dakota State University
David Brodzinsky
Rutgers University
Peter Burzynski
Vincennes University
Jay S. Caldwell
California State University, Chico
Bernardo J. Carducci
Indiana University—Southeast
Stephen S. Coccia
Orange County Community College
Mary C. Comden
Oakland Community College
Helen J. Crawford
University of Wyoming
William O. Dwyer
Memphis State University
Marsha Epstein
Middlesex Community College
William F. Ford
Bucks County Community College
Marvin Goldstein
Rider College
David A. Griesé
S.U.N.Y. at Farmingdale
Earl Harper
Bunker Hill Community College
Lynn Hasher
Temple University
Donna Hummel
Trinity College
Janet Hyde
Denison University
Carroll E. Izard
University of Delaware
Don Kaesser
Des Moines Area Community College
Harold Mansfield
Ft. Lewis College
Kevin D. McCaul
North Dakota State University
Fay-Tyler Norton
Cuyahoga Community College
Frances O'Keefe
Tidewater Community College
Joseph J. Palladino
University of Southern Indiana
Holly A. Pennock
Hudson Valley Community College
James S. Perry
East Tennessee State University
Richard B. Powers
Utah State University
Richard Rasor
American River College
Richard M. Ryckman
University of Maine-Orono
Valerie J. Sasserath
Chatham Township Schools
Joyce Schaeuble
Sacramento City College
Luella M. Snyder
Parkland College
Robert D. Sorkin
Purdue University
Robert Stern
Pennsylvania State University
Alfred W. Stone
Edinboro University of Pennsylvania
John R. Suler
Rider College
Robert Thompson
Hunter College
Carol Vitiello
Kirkwood Community College
Charles Weichert
San Antonio College
Fred Wright
John Jay College of Criminal Justice

Robert S. Feldman

CONTENTS IN BRIEF

PART ONE

THE SCIENCE OF PSYCHOLOGY 1

CHAPTER 1 INTRODUCTION TO PSYCHOLOGY 3

PART TWO

THE BIOLOGICAL FOUNDATIONS OF PSYCHOLOGY 41

CHAPTER 2 THE BIOLOGY UNDERLYING BEHAVIOR 43
CHAPTER 3 SENSATION AND PERCEPTION 77

PART THREE

LEARNING AND THINKING ABOUT THE WORLD 123

CHAPTER 4 LEARNING 125
CHAPTER 5 MEMORY 163
CHAPTER 6 COGNITION AND LANGUAGE 187
CHAPTER 7 INTELLIGENCE 209

PART FOUR

FEELING AND EXPERIENCING THE WORLD 235

CHAPTER 8 MOTIVATION AND EMOTION 237
CHAPTER 9 STATES OF CONSCIOUSNESS 281

PART FIVE

THE PERSON DEVELOPS AND DIFFERENTIATES 311

CHAPTER 10 DEVELOPMENT 313
CHAPTER 11 PERSONALITY 359

PART SIX

ABNORMAL BEHAVIOR AND TREATMENT 389

CHAPTER 12 ABNORMAL BEHAVIOR 391
CHAPTER 13 TREATMENT OF ABNORMAL BEHAVIOR 431

PART SEVEN

THE SOCIAL FOUNDATIONS OF BEHAVIOR 463

CHAPTER 14 SOCIAL PSYCHOLOGY: THE INDIVIDUAL IN A SOCIAL WORLD 465
CHAPTER 15 SOCIAL PSYCHOLOGY: INTERACTING WITH OTHERS 489

APPENDIX

GOING BY THE NUMBERS: STATISTICS IN PSYCHOLOGY 517

ACKNOWLEDGMENTS A-1
REFERENCES R-1
GLOSSARY G-1
INDEXES
- Name Index I-1
- Subject Index I-7

CONTENTS

PART ONE
THE SCIENCE OF PSYCHOLOGY 1

CHAPTER 1 **INTRODUCTION TO PSYCHOLOGY** 3

PROLOGUE 4
LOOKING AHEAD 4

The common link among psychologists: The study of behavior and mental processes 4

Try It! How Much Psychology Do You Already Know? 5

PSYCHOLOGISTS AT WORK 7

Studying the biological foundations of psychology: Biopsychologists 8

Sensing, perceiving, learning, and thinking about the world: Experimental psychologists 8

Understanding change and individual differences: Developmental and personality psychologists 8

Studying and caring for people's physical and mental health: Health, clinical, and counseling psychologists 9

Understanding the social world: Social, industrial-organizational, and environmental psychologists 10

Emerging areas of study 10

Here, there, everywhere: Where do psychologists work? 11

The Cutting Edge. Pushing the Limits of Psychology: Psychology in Outer Space 12

Recap and Review I 13

A SCIENCE EVOLVES: SURVEYING THE PAST AND FORETELLING THE FUTURE OF PSYCHOLOGY 14

The roots of psychology: Historical perspectives 15

Blood, sweat, and fears: Biological approaches 16

Understanding the inner person: Psychodynamic approaches 17

Understanding understanding: Cognitive approaches 17

Understanding the outer person: Behavioral approaches 17

The special qualities of *homo sapiens:* Humanistic approaches 18

A final word about models 18

Psychology at Work. Buckling Up—with Psychology—to Save Lives 19

The future of psychology 20

Recap and Review II 20

ASKING THE RIGHT QUESTIONS AND GETTING THE RIGHT ANSWERS: THEORY AND RESEARCH IN PSYCHOLOGY 21

Asking the right questions: Theories and hypotheses 21

Getting the right answers: Research in psychology 22

Studying one person to learn about many: The case study 23

Studying the records: Archival research 23

Studying what is there already: Naturalistic observation 23

Asking for answers: Survey research 23

Determining cause-and-effect relationships: Experimental research 26

Knowing what's right: The ethics of research 31

The informed consumer of psychology: Distinguishing good psychology from bad psychology 32

Recap and Review III 33

Psychology looks toward the 1990s. On the frontlines of an epidemic: AIDS and psychology 34

LOOKING BACK 36

KEY TERMS AND CONCEPTS 37

FOR FURTHER STUDY AND APPLICATION 38

PART TWO THE BIOLOGICAL FOUNDATIONS OF PSYCHOLOGY 41

CHAPTER 2 THE BIOLOGY UNDERLYING BEHAVIOR 43

PROLOGUE 44

LOOKING AHEAD 44

THE BASICS OF BEHAVIOR: THE NEURONS AND THE NERVOUS SYSTEM 46

Beginning with the basics: The neuron 46

The smoking gun: Firing the neuron 49

Recap and Review I 50

Bridging the gap: Where neuron meets neuron 50

STRINGING NEURONS TOGETHER: THE NERVOUS SYSTEM 52

The near and the far: The central and peripheral nervous systems 53

Emergency! Activating the autonomic nervous system 55

Recap and Review II 56

TYING IT ALL TOGETHER: THE BRAIN 56

The Cutting Edge. Looking at the Brain—from the Outside In 57

Exploring and mapping the brain: Discovering the old brain and the new 58

Of chemicals and glands: The endocrine system 60

Passing the border between the old brain and the new: The limbic system 61

Recap and Review III 62

THE NEW BRAIN: THE CEREBRAL CORTEX 63

The motor area of the brain 63

The sensory area of the brain 64

The association area of the brain 64

The Cutting Edge. The Brain Transplant: Solving Old Problems—and Creating New Ones? 66

TWO BRAINS OR ONE?: THE SPECIALIZATION OF THE HEMISPHERES 67

Try It! Using Your Left and Right Brains 68

Psychology at Work. Probing the Brain on Madison Avenue 69

Understanding the two hemispheres: Split-brain patients 69
The informed consumer of psychology: Learning to control your heart—and brain—through biofeedback 70
Try It! Biofeedback on Your Own 72
Recap and Review IV 73
Psychology looks toward the 1990s. Using the brain as a diagnostic device: neurometrics 73

LOOKING BACK 74
KEY TERMS AND CONCEPTS 75
FOR FURTHER STUDY AND APPLICATION 75

CHAPTER 3 SENSATION AND PERCEPTION 77

PROLOGUE 78

LOOKING AHEAD 78

SENSING THE WORLD AROUND US 80
Is the light really there or are we in the dark?: Absolute thresholds 81
Comparing apples with apples: Just noticeable differences 83
Becoming accustomed to stimulation: Sensory adaptation 84
Recap and Review I 86

THE FIVE + SENSES 86
The eyes have it: Seeing the world 87
Try It! Find Your Blind Spot 90
Recap and Review II 96
Hearing and moving about the world: The sense of sound and balance 96
The Cutting Edge. It's All in the Astronaut's Head: Curing Space Sickness 99
Psychology at Work. Replacing a Sense Organ: An Electronic Ear Implant for the Deaf 101
Making sense of the other senses: Smell, taste, and the skin senses 102
The informed consumer of psychology: How do you spell relief—from pain? 104
Recap and Review III 106

VIEWING THE WORLD AS IT SEEMS: PERCEPTION 106
Creating wholes from parts: The gestalt laws of organization 107
Where 1 + 1 equals more than 2: The whole is greater than the sum of its parts 108
Translating 2-D to 3-D: Depth perception 109
Is the cup half full or half empty?: Figuring the figure from the ground 109
Sorting out the auditory world: Selective attention 111

PERCEPTION IN EVERYDAY LIFE 112
Misperceptions of the eye: Visual illusions 114
Recap and Review IV 116
Psychology looks toward the 1990s. Computer versions of vision 116

LOOKING BACK 118
KEY TERMS AND CONCEPTS 119
FOR FURTHER STUDY AND APPLICATION 120

PART THREE
LEARNING AND THINKING ABOUT THE WORLD 123

CHAPTER 4 LEARNING 125

PROLOGUE 126

LOOKING AHEAD 126

PAVLOV'S DOGS AND THE GOLDEN ARCHES: CLASSICAL CONDITIONING 128
Canine conditioning: Pavlov's dogs 128
Classical conditioning is not just for the dogs: Applying conditioning principles to human behavior 131
Unlearning what you have learned: Extinction 132
The return of the conditioned response: Spontaneous recovery 132
A rose is a rose is a rose: Generalization and discrimination 133
When a CS becomes a UCS: Higher-order conditioning 133
Recap and Review I 134

THE REWARDS OF REINFORCEMENT: OPERANT CONDITIONING 135
Cat-in-a-box: Thorndike's law of effect 136
From cat-in-a-box to Skinner box: The basics of operant conditioning 137
Try It! Using Positive Reinforcement to Change Behavior 139
Recap and Review II 141
Timing life's rewards: Schedules of reinforcement 141
Learning the right stimulus from the wrong: Discrimination and generalization in operant conditioning 144
Superstitious behavior 145
Reinforcing what doesn't come naturally: Shaping 146
The Cutting Edge. A Pigeon Posse: Saving Lives with Operant Conditioning 147
The informed consumer of psychology: Using computer-assisted programmed instruction to shape your own behavior 148
Discriminating between classical and operant conditioning: The difference is not always clear 149
Recap and Review III 150

THE THINKING PERSON'S LEARNING THEORY: COGNITIVE APPROACHES TO LEARNING 151
Learning by copying: Observational learning 152
Accepting the unacceptable: Learned helplessness 153
The unresolved controversy: Cognitive learning theory in perspective 154

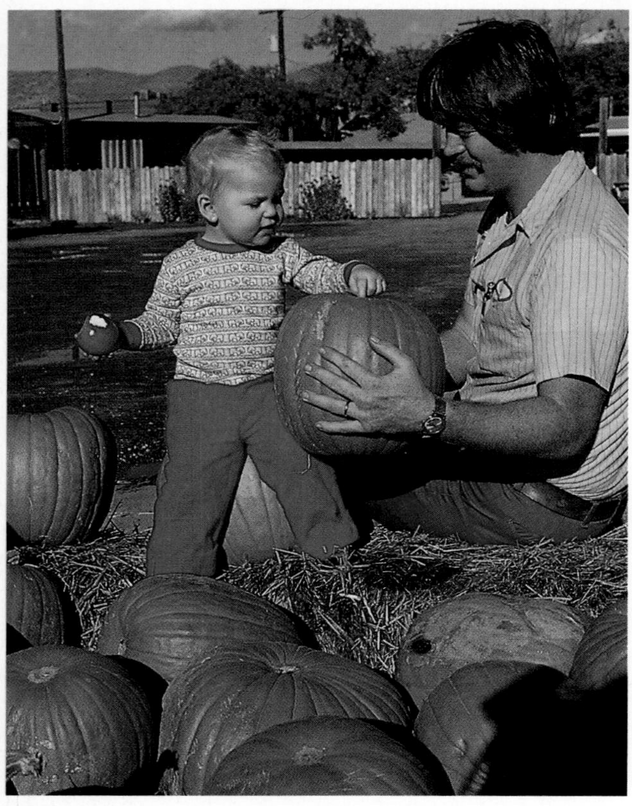

Levels of processing 171
Recap and Review I 172

IT'S THERE SOMEWHERE—THE TRICK IS FINDING IT: REMEMBERING WHAT IS STORED IN LONG-TERM MEMORY 172

Flashbulb memories 174
Building memories: Constructive processes in memory 175
Psychology at Work. The Witness: Memory in the Courtroom 176
Recap and Review II 177

WHEN MEMORY FAILS: FORGETTING WHAT YOU HAVE REMEMBERED 178

The before and after of forgetting: Proactive and retroactive interference 179
The Cutting Edge. Locating Memory in the Brain: Searching for the Biological Bases of Memory 180
The informed consumer of psychology: Improving your memory 181
Recap and Review III 183
Psychology looks toward the 1990s. Mapping memory: The search for the engram 183

LOOKING BACK 184
KEY TERMS AND CONCEPTS 185
FOR FURTHER STUDY AND APPLICATION 185

BEHAVIOR ANALYSIS AND BEHAVIOR MODIFICATION 154

Psychology at Work. Safety on the Job: Preventing Accidents by Changing Human Behavior 155
The informed consumer of psychology: Using behavior-modification techniques to manage your time 156
Recap and Review IV 157
Psychology looks toward the 1990s. Computers learn to learn 158

LOOKING BACK 159
KEY TERMS AND CONCEPTS 160
FOR FURTHER STUDY AND APPLICATION 161

CHAPTER 5 MEMORY 163

PROLOGUE 164

LOOKING AHEAD 164

THE THREE R'S OF REMEMBERING: RECORDING, RETAINING, AND RETRIEVING INFORMATION 165

The initial encounter: Sensory memory 165
Our working memory: Short-term memory 167
Try It! Impress Yourself with Your Own Memory 168
The final repository: Long-term memory 168

CHAPTER 6 COGNITION AND LANGUAGE 187

PROLOGUE 188

LOOKING AHEAD 188

COGNITIVE PROCESSES IN PROBLEM SOLVING 189

Thinking and problem solving 190
Recap and Review I 193

HINDRANCES TO PROBLEM SOLVING: BIASES IN JUDGMENT 193

What is obvious may not be right: Functional fixedness 194
When it's wrong to follow the rules: Biases in algorithms and heuristics 194
Try It! Problems to Ponder 195
The informed consumer of psychology: Solving problems creatively 196
Psychology at Work. Teaching College Students to Think 197
Recap and Review II 198

COMMUNICATING OUR THOUGHTS: LANGUAGE 198

The language of language: Grammar 198
Developing a way with words: Language development 199
The roots of language: Understanding language acquisition 201

The Cutting Edge. Exploring Human Language—by Communicating with Animals 202
Does language determine thought—or does thought determine language? 203
Categorizing the world: Using concepts 204
Recap and Review III 205
Psychology looks toward the 1990s. Capturing the complexities of common sense 205

LOOKING BACK 206
KEY TERMS AND CONCEPTS 207
FOR FURTHER STUDY AND APPLICATION 207

INTELLIGENCE 209

PROLOGUE 210

LOOKING AHEAD 210

BEING SMART ABOUT INTELLIGENT BEHAVIOR: DEFINING INTELLIGENCE 211
Separating the intelligent from the unintelligent: Measuring intelligence 213
The IQ measuring sticks: Stanford-Binet, Wechsler, et al. 214
IQ tests don't tell all: Alternate formulations of intelligence 217
Does information processing equal intelligence?: Contemporary approaches to understanding intelligence 218
Psychology at Work. Is Work Intelligence Different from School Intelligence? 219
The informed consumer of psychology: Can you learn to do better on standardized tests? 220
Recap and Review I 221

ABOVE AND BELOW THE NORM: VARIATIONS IN INTELLECTUAL ABILITY 222
Falling below the norm: Mental retardation 222
The other end of the spectrum: The intellectually gifted 224
The Cutting Edge. High Intelligence, Low Intelligence, . . . and Now, Artificial Intelligence 225
Recap and Review II 227

INDIVIDUAL DIFFERENCES IN INTELLIGENCE: HEREDITY, ENVIRONMENT—OR BOTH? 227
Try It! A Culture—*Un*fair Intelligence Test 228
The basic controversy: Heredity versus environment 229
Neither heredity nor environment: Putting the question in perspective 231
Recap and Review III 231
Psychology looks toward the 1990s. Establishing intelligence: The earliest signs of IQ 232

LOOKING BACK 232
KEY TERMS AND CONCEPTS 233
FOR FURTHER STUDY AND APPLICATION 233

PART FOUR
FEELING AND EXPERIENCING THE WORLD 235

CHAPTER 8 **MOTIVATION AND EMOTION** 237

PROLOGUE 238

LOOKING AHEAD 238

THE PRIMARY DRIVES 239
Eating your needs away: Hunger 240
The facts of life: Human sexual motivation 244
The informed consumer of psychology: Dieting and losing weight successfully 248
Recap and Review I 249

HUMAN STRIVING: ACHIEVEMENT, AFFILIATION, AND POWER MOTIVATION 249
Striving for success: The need for achievement 250
Striving for friendship: The need for affiliation 252
Striving for impact on others: The need for power 252

COMBINING HUMAN MOTIVES 252
Homeostasis is not enough: Theories of motivation 253
The Cutting Edge. For Money or Love? Rewarding Intrinsic Motivation 254

Try it! Do you seek out sensation? 256
Ordering motivational needs: Maslow's hierarchy 259
Recap and Review II 261

UNDERSTANDING EMOTIONAL EXPERIENCES 261
What emotions do for us: Understanding the functions of emotions 263
Labeling our feelings: Determining the range of emotions 264

KNOWING HOW WE FEEL: UNDERSTANDING OUR OWN EMOTIONS 265
Do gut reactions equal emotions?: The James-Lange theory 266
Physiological reactions as the result of emotions: The Cannon-Bard theory 267
Emotions as labels: The Schachter-Singer theory 268
Summing up the theories of emotion 269
Psychology at Work. The Truth about Lies: Using Emotional Responses to Separate the Honest from the Dishonest 269
Recap and Review III 270

EXPRESSING EMOTIONS: THE ROLE OF NONVERBAL BEHAVIOR 271
If you met some New Guineans, would you know what they were feeling?: Universality in emotional expressivity 271
Smile, though you're feeling blue: The facial-feedback hypothesis 273
The informed consumer of psychology: Can you ''read'' others' nonverbal behavior? 274
Recap and Review IV 275
Psychology looks toward the 1990s. Understanding the link between diet and exercise 275

LOOKING BACK 276
KEY TERMS AND CONCEPTS 278
FOR FURTHER STUDY AND APPLICATION 279

CHAPTER 9 STATES OF CONSCIOUSNESS 281

PROLOGUE 282

LOOKING AHEAD 282

LIFE IS BUT A DREAM . . . : SLEEP AND DREAMS 284
Awakening our knowledge about sleep: The stages of sleep 284
Try It! Testing Your Knowledge of Sleep and Dreams 285
Is sleep necessary? 287
The reality of dreams: The function and meaning of dreaming 288
Dreams without sleep: Daydreams 290
Slumbering problems: Sleep disturbances 290
The informed consumer of psychology: Sleeping better 291
Recap and Review I 292

ALTERED STATES OF CONSCIOUSNESS: HYPNOSIS AND MEDITATION 293
You are under my power—or are you?: Hypnosis 293
Regulating your own state of consciousness: Meditation 294
Psychology at Work. Using Hypnosis Outside the Laboratory 295
Recap and Review II 296

THE HIGHS AND LOWS OF CONSCIOUSNESS: DRUG USE 297
Drug highs: Stimulants 298
Drug lows: Depressants 301
Flying high while staying on the ground: Hallucinogens 302
The Cutting Edge. Discovering the Secrets of Alcoholism 303
The informed consumer of psychology: Dealing with drug and alcohol problems 305
Recap and Review III 306
Psychology looks toward the 1990s. Looking for a ''sober'' pill 306

LOOKING BACK 307
KEY TERMS AND CONCEPTS 308
FOR FURTHER STUDY AND APPLICATION 309

PART FIVE
THE PERSON DEVELOPS AND DIFFERENTIATES 311

CHAPTER 10 DEVELOPMENT 313

PROLOGUE 314

LOOKING AHEAD 314

NATURE VERSUS NURTURE: A FUNDAMENTAL DEVELOPMENTAL QUESTION 315
Try It! Nature or Nurture—That's the Question 316
Addressing the Nature-Nurture Question 317
The start of life: Conception and beyond 318
Recap and Review I 322

HOW WE DEVELOP PHYSICALLY AND SOCIALLY 323
Growth after birth 324
Taking in the world: Development of perception 325
Forming relationships: Social development 326
Psychology at Work. Who Is Taking Care of the Children?: Determining the Effects of Day-Care 329
Recap and Review II 331

OUR MINDS: HOW WE DEVELOP COGNITIVELY 332
Stages of understanding: Piaget's theory of cognitive development 333

The informed consumer of psychology: Maximizing cognitive development 337
The Cutting Edge. Raising a Superstar Child: How Is Talent Nurtured? 338
Recap and Review III 339

BECOMING AN ADULT: ADOLESCENCE 339
The changing adolescent: Physical development 340
Distinguishing right from wrong: Moral and cognitive development 341
Searching for identity: Psychosocial development 343

THE MIDDLE YEARS OF LIFE: EARLY AND MIDDLE ADULTHOOD 345
The peak of health: Physical development 346
Working at life: Social development 346

THE LATER YEARS OF LIFE: GROWING OLD 347
Physical aging: Physical changes during old age 348
Thinking about—and during—old age: Cognitive changes in the elderly 348
Facing Death 351
Recap and Review IV 351
Psychology looks toward the 1990s. Keeping smart: Avoiding intellectual declines in old age 352

LOOKING BACK 354
KEY TERMS AND CONCEPTS 355
FOR FURTHER STUDY AND APPLICATION 356

CHAPTER 11 PERSONALITY 359

PROLOGUE 360

LOOKING AHEAD 360

EXPLAINING THE INNER LIFE: PSYCHOANALYTIC THEORIES OF PERSONALITY 361
What you see is *not* what you get: Freud's psychoanalytic theory 362
Revising Freud: The neo-Freudian psychoanalysts 368
Recap and Review I 369

IN SEARCH OF PERSONALITY: TRAIT, LEARNING, AND HUMANISTIC APPROACHES 370
Labeling personality: Trait theories 370
The Cutting Edge. Is Personality a Myth?: Personality versus Situational Factors 373
Explaining the outer life, ignoring the inner life: Learning theories of personality 373
Understanding the self: Humanistic theories of personality 375
Try It! Assessing Your Real Self-Concept and Your Ideal Self-Concept 377
Answering the old question: Which theory is right? 377
Recap and Review II 378

DETERMINING WHAT MAKES YOU SPECIAL: ASSESSING PERSONALITY 379
The keys to assessing personality: Reliability and validity 380
Asking a little to learn a lot: Self-report measures of personality 381
Looking into the unconscious: Projective methods 382
Psychology at Work. Assessment Comes to the Personnel Office 383
The informed consumer of psychology: Assessing personality assessments 383
Recap and Review III 384
Psychology looks toward the 1990s. The roots of personality: The inheritance of traits 384

LOOKING BACK 385
KEY TERMS AND CONCEPTS 387
FOR FURTHER STUDY AND APPLICATION 387

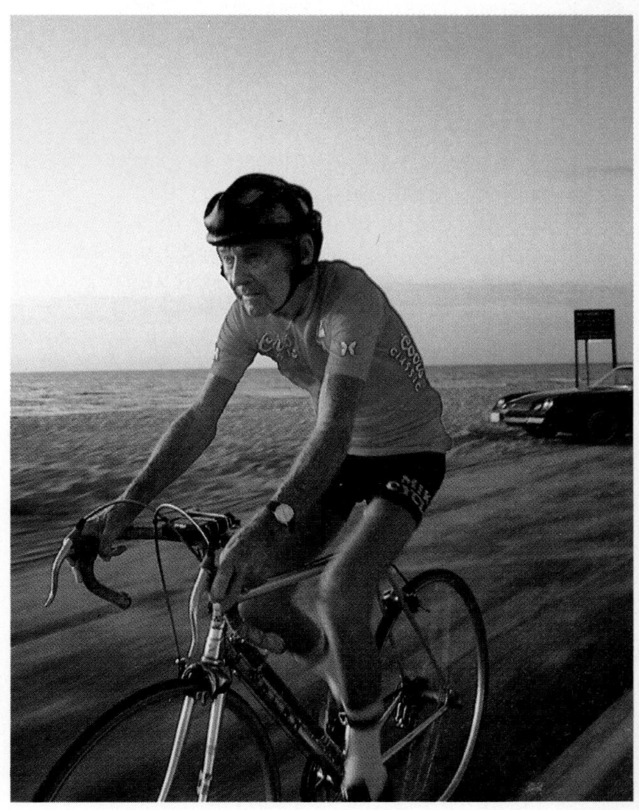

PART SIX
ABNORMAL BEHAVIOR AND TREATMENT 389

CHAPTER 12 ABNORMAL BEHAVIOR 391

PROLOGUE 392

LOOKING AHEAD 393

NORMAL VERSUS ABNORMAL: MAKING THE DISTINCTION 393

Try It! Separating Normal from Abnormal 395

Approaches to abnormality 395

The Cutting Edge. The Mental State of the Union: A Census of Mental Disorder 397

Drawing the line on abnormality: The continuum of abnormal and normal behavior 397

Recap and Review I 398

MODELS OF ABNORMALITY: FROM SUPERSTITION TO SCIENCE 398

Abnormal behavior as a biological disease: The medical model 400

Conflicting causes of abnormal behavior: The psychoanalytic model 400

When behavior itself is the problem: The behavioral model of abnormal behavior 401

Putting the person in control: The humanistic model of abnormal behavior 402

Society as the cause of abnormal behavior: The sociocultural model 403

Applying the models: The case of John Hinckley 404

Psychology at Work. When Law and Psychology Mix: The Insanity Defense 405

The informed consumer of psychology: Do you feel abnormal? 405

Recap and Review II 406

THE ABC's OF DSM-III: CLASSIFYING TYPES OF ABNORMAL BEHAVIOR 407

THE MAJOR DISORDERS 408

Anxiety without reason: Anxiety disorders 408

When the physical leads to the psychological: Somatoform disorders 411

One becomes two (or more): Dissociative disorders 412

Recap and Review III 413

The mood is wrong: Affective disorders 414

Psychology at Work. The Special Problems of College Students 415

When reality is lost: Schizophrenia 416

The Cutting Edge. Schizophrenia: A Behavioral or a Biological Problem? 420

Lacking distress: Personality disorders 421

The informed consumer of psychology: Deciding when you need help 422

Recap and Review IV 423

Psychology looks toward the 1990s. The psychology of health and stress 424

LOOKING BACK 426
KEY TERMS AND CONCEPTS 427
FOR FURTHER STUDY AND APPLICATION 428

CHAPTER 13 TREATMENT OF ABNORMAL BEHAVIOR 431

PROLOGUE 432

LOOKING AHEAD 432

PSYCHOTHERAPY: PSYCHOLOGICAL APPROACHES TO TREATMENT 433

Beyond the therapy-room couch: Psychodynamic treatment 434

Learning the good and unlearning the bad: Behavioral approaches to treatment 437

Try It! Learning to Relax 440

Psychology at Work. When Being Your Own Therapist Works: Self-Management through Behavior Modification 442
Recap and Review I 443
Helping people to help themselves: Humanistic approaches to therapy 444
Evaluating psychotherapy 447
Recap and Review II 450

THE MEDICAL MODEL AT WORK: BIOLOGICAL TREATMENT APPROACHES 450
Medicine for mental disturbances: Drug therapy 451
Shocking abnormal behavior away: Electroconvulsive therapy (ECT) 453
Cutting out the bad: Psychosurgery 454
Can abnormal behavior be cured?: Biological treatment in perspective 455
The informed consumer of psychology: Choosing the right therapist 455
The Cutting Edge. Focus on Prevention: The Campus Crisis Center 456
Recap and Review III 457
Psychology looks toward the 1990s. In search of new treatments 457

LOOKING BACK 458
KEY TERMS AND CONCEPTS 459
FOR FURTHER STUDY AND APPLICATION 460

PART SEVEN
THE SOCIAL FOUNDATIONS OF BEHAVIOR 463

CHAPTER 14 **SOCIAL PSYCHOLOGY: THE INDIVIDUAL IN A SOCIAL WORLD** 465

PROLOGUE 466

LOOKING AHEAD 466

ATTITUDES, BEHAVIOR, AND PERSUASION 467
Forming and maintaining attitudes 467
Fitting attitudes and behavior together: Cognitive consistency approaches 468
Psychology at Work. Professional Persuasion: The Rules Advertisers Follow 469
Recap and Review I 472

UNDERSTANDING OTHERS: SOCIAL COGNITION 473
Understanding what others are like: Social cognition 473
Try It! Are You Susceptible to Stereotyping? 475
Recap and Review II 477

UNDERSTANDING THE CAUSES OF BEHAVIOR: ATTRIBUTION PROCESSES 478
We all make mistakes: Biases in attribution 479
Understanding our own behavior: Self-perception theory 480
The Cutting Edge. Improving Your Grades by Improving Your Attributions 481
The informed consumer of psychology: Forming more accurate impressions 481
Recap and Review III 483
Psychology looks toward the 1990s. Imitating the Japanese: Changing the attitudes on the job 484

LOOKING BACK 485
KEY TERMS AND CONCEPTS 486
FOR FURTHER STUDY AND APPLICATION 486

CHAPTER 15 **SOCIAL PSYCHOLOGY: INTERACTING WITH OTHERS** 489

PROLOGUE 490

LOOKING AHEAD 490

SOCIAL INFLUENCE 491
Doing what others do: Conformity 491
Doing what others tell us to do: Compliance 493
The informed consumer of psychology: Strategies for maintaining your own point of view 494
Recap and Review I 496

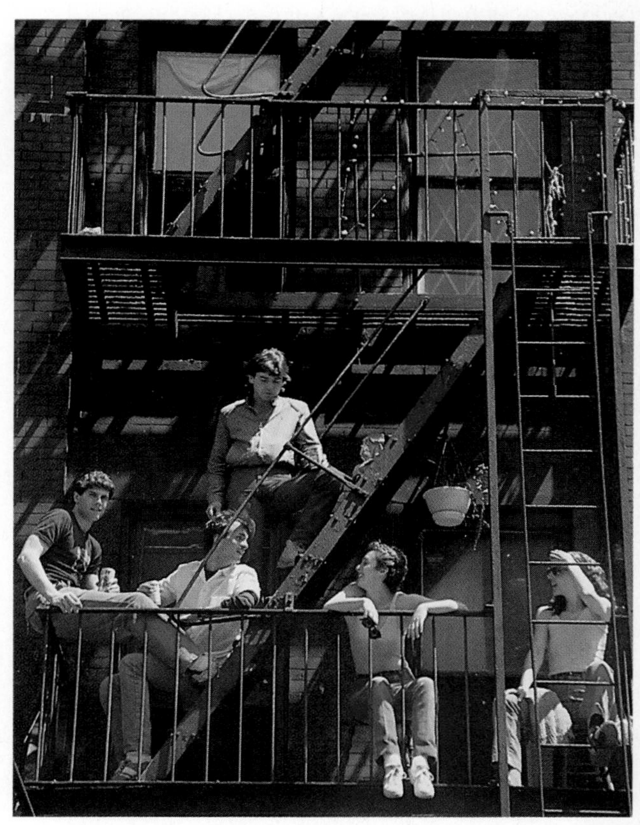

LIKING AND LOVING: INTERPERSONAL ATTRACTION AND THE DEVELOPMENT OF RELATIONSHIPS 496

How do I like thee? Let me count the ways 496

How do I love thee? Let me count the ways 498

The rise and fall of liking and loving: Understanding the course of relationships 500

Recap and Review II 503

HURTING AND HELPING OTHERS: AGGRESSION AND PROSOCIAL BEHAVIOR 503

Hurting others: Aggression 504

Try It! Is This Aggression? 505

The Cutting Edge. Does It Hurt to Watch TV?: Media Aggression 507

Psychology at Work. Should Pornography Be Banned?: The Link between Pornography and Violence toward Women 509

Helping others: The brighter side of human nature 510

The informed consumer of psychology: Learning to be helpful 511

Recap and Review III 512

Psychology looks toward the 1990s. Hot flashes: Environmental psychology 513

LOOKING BACK 515

KEY TERMS AND CONCEPTS 515

FOR FURTHER STUDY AND APPLICATION 515

APPENDIX GOING BY THE NUMBERS: STATISTICS IN PSYCHOLOGY 517

PROLOGUE 518

LOOKING AHEAD 518

DESCRIPTIVE STATISTICS 518

Finding the average: The mean 521

Finding the middle: The median 521

Finding what is most frequent: The mode 522

Comparing the three M's: Mean versus median versus mode 522

Recap and Review I 523

MEASURES OF VARIABILITY 524

Highest to lowest: The range 524

Differences from the mean: The standard deviation 524

Recap and Review II 526

USING STATISTICS TO ANSWER QUESTIONS: INFERENTIAL STATISTICS AND CORRELATION 526

Measuring relationships: The correlation coefficient 528

The informed consumer of psychology: Evaluating statistics 529

Recap and Review III 531

LOOKING BACK 531

KEY TERMS AND CONCEPTS 532

FOR FURTHER STUDY AND APPLICATION 532

ACKNOWLEDGMENTS A-1

REFERENCES R-1

GLOSSARY G-1

INDEXES

Name Index I-1

Subject Index I-7

PREFACE

The human behavior that we find in the world defies easy explanation. There is behavior which is good and there is that which is bad; there is the sensible, and there is the irrational; there is cooperation, and there is violent competition among the world's peoples. How to explain these extremes of behavior, and the countless forms of behavior that lie in between, represents the challenge of the science of psychology.

Essentials of Understanding Psychology, which is designed to meet the challenges presented by the field of psychology, is a condensed and updated version of the 21-chapter *Understanding Psychology,* published by McGraw-Hill. *Essentials of Understanding Psychology* preserves the basic features of the original text, but in a shorter form, concentrating on the fundamentals of the field while still making clear the relevance of psychology to people's everyday lives.

Essentials of Understanding Psychology was written to accomplish three major goals. First, it is meant to provide effective coverage of the major areas of the field of psychology, introducing readers to its theories, research, and applications. Second, it is intended to foster an appreciation for the scientific basis of the field, as well as providing an impetus for readers to begin to think as scientific psychologists even after their recall of specific content has waned. Finally, it is designed to be engaging and interesting, a book in which readers' intellectual curiosity about the world is aroused and manifested in an appreciation of the discipline of psychology.

These goals, of course, are interdependent. In fact, I would argue that if the text is successful in accurately communicating the nature of psychology, understanding and interest regarding the field will follow naturally. To that end, the writing style of this book has received considerable attention. The style of the book is intended to provide as close a facsimile to two people sitting down and discussing psychology as can be conveyed with the written word. When I use "we," I am referring to the two of us—me, the author, and you, the reader.

Moreover, the book has features in every chapter that are designed to involve you (Try It! questionnaires and demonstrations), challenge you (Cutting Edge inserts with the latest findings), demonstrate the everyday relevance of psychology (Psychology at Work boxes), and improve the quality of your own life (Informed Consumer of Psychology sections). In addition, in a feature new to this version of the text, each chapter ends with a section called "Psychology Looks toward the 1990s," which suggests where the discipline is headed as we move into the last decade of the twentieth century.

Essentials of Understanding Psychology is also a book that has been carefully designed to promote learning. Material is presented in rational, manageable chunks, followed by a succinct summary (called a "Recap") and a set of questions on the material (a "Review"). Readers who answer these questions—and then check the answers, which are provided on a following page—will be able to assess their degree of mastery of the material, as well as having a head start on long-term recall of the information.

In sum, *Essentials of Understanding Psychology* is, as I reiterate in the first chapter, designed to be "user-friendly." It is a book that not only exposes you to the content—and promise—of psychology, but does so in a way that will bring alive the excitement of the field and keep that excitement alive long after you have completed your introduction to the discipline.

THE CONTENT OF *ESSENTIALS OF UNDERSTANDING PSYCHOLOGY*

Essentials of Understanding Psychology contains seven parts, divided into 15 chapters. Part One opens with an overview of the field, examining its theoretical, historical, and methodological underpinnings. We then turn, in Part Two, to the ways in which the biological structures and functions of the body affect behavior, considering the nervous system, brain, and sensation and perception.

Part Three presents the fundamental principles of learning and thinking, and we focus on learning, memory, thinking and reasoning, and intelligence. Part Four and Part Five describe the ways in which people experience the world, and here we consider motivation, emotions, and states of consciousness, as well as the development and differentiation of individuals. We explore the course we all travel through life, beginning at birth and ending at old age and death. We also consider personality here, including both the characteristics that differentiate one person from another and the degree of uniformity an individual displays in behavior in different situations.

Finally, in Part Six and Part Seven, we turn to mental health and the social world in which we live. We focus on the various forms of psychological disturbance and the treatments that psychologists have devised for them. We then consider how our attitudes about others develop and function and the influence that others have on us. We also examine some of the fundamental forms of social behavior in human life: liking and loving, aggression, and helping behavior.

As this brief overview suggests, *Essentials of Understanding Psychology* emphasizes the traditional topical areas of psychology, including the biological foundations of behavior, sensation and perception, learning, memory, cognition, human development, personality, abnormal behavior, and social psychological foundations of behavior. Notably, however, it also includes material that focuses on applications of psychological theory and research in nonlaboratory, field settings.

The flexibility of this organizational structure is considerable. Because chapters are self-contained, this book can be used in either biologically oriented or socially oriented introductory psychology courses by choosing only the relevant chapters. Moreover, the material on applications is well-integrated throughout the chapters that cover the most traditional, theoretical topics, successfully conveying the relevance of psychology to readers.

Overall, then, the book includes a combination of traditional core topics and contemporary applied subjects, presenting the fundamentals of psychology in a readable, involving format. It should be apparent that this book is neither an applied psychology text nor a theories-oriented text. Instead, it draws from theoretical and applied approaches and integrates them with presentations of research that illustrate how the science of psychology has evolved and grown. Indeed, *Essentials of Understanding Psychology* exemplifies the view that a theory-application dichotomy is a false one. Applications are not presented as devoid of theory; instead, they are placed in a theoretical context, grounded in research findings. Likewise, when theoretical material is presented, practical implications are drawn from it.

An example can illustrate this approach. If you turn to the material on sensation and perception (Chapter 3), you will find that it includes the traditional material on hearing and the sense of balance in the ear. But the text moves beyond a mere recitation of the various parts of the ear and explanations of hearing and balance; it also explores current work involving an electronic ear implant in the cochlea to help the deaf, as well as NASA's attempts to solve the problem of astronauts' space sickness. By providing a theoretical context for understanding the sense of hearing and balance, then, the text demonstrates how applications grow out of the theoretical and research base of the field.

In its integration of theory, research, and applications, *Essentials of Understanding Psychology* emphasizes the presentation of knowledge and theories in an objective, eclectic manner. At the same time, the complexities of the analytical underpinnings of the field of psychology, as well as divergent and controversial findings, are included, but they are summarized and synthesized in a way that makes them accessible. Moreover, no single theoretical position or point of view is supported. Rather, the goal is to present theories, research, and applications in a rational, logical, and orderly manner—views that are representative of the field.

LEARNING AIDS AND FEATURES OF *ESSENTIALS OF UNDERSTANDING PSYCHOLOGY*

Essentials of Understanding Psychology has been designed with its ultimate consumer—the student—in mind. As you can see from the following list of elements that are common to every chapter, this book incorporates educational features, based on learning and cognitive instructional design theory and research, that make it an effective learning device and, at the same time, enticing and engaging:

■ *Chapter Outline*. Each chapter opens with an outline of the chapter structure. Not only does the outline provide a means of understanding the interrelationships of the material within the chapter, but it serves as a form of chapter organizer, helping to bridge the gap between what a reader already knows and the subsequent chapter content.

■ *Prologue*. Every chapter starts with an account of a real-life situation that involves major aspects of the topics in the chapter. These openers are used to demonstrate the relevance of basic principles and concepts of psychology to everyday issues and problems. For example, the chapter on learning starts with a description of how the behavior of an Olympic gold medalist is affected by learning processes; one chapter on social psychology begins with an account of a campus referendum; and the chapter on intelligence describes a profoundly retarded individual who produces internationally acclaimed paintings.

■ *Looking Ahead*. A chapter overview follows the introduction. It presents the key themes, issues, and questions and a set of chapter objectives. The chapter objectives pinpoint material on which to focus.

■ *Psychology at Work*. Each chapter includes a boxed insert that illustrates an application of psychological theory and research findings to a real-world problem. For example, the chapter on the biological bases of behavior discusses how advertisers use findings regarding brain hemispheric specialization to prepare advertisements, the memory chapter includes a discussion of eyewitness identification in judicial settings, and the chapter on personality presents assessment procedures used by business firms.

■ *The Cutting Edge*. Each chapter contains a box that describes a contemporary research program that is in the forefront of the discipline—suggesting where the field of psychology is heading. This feature helps provide a sense of the growing and developing status of the science of psychology. For instance, the memory chapter presents work on the biochemical basis of memory, and the intelligence chapter discusses artificial intelligence.

■ *The Informed Consumer of Psychology*. Every chapter includes information designed to make readers more informed consumers of psychological information and knowledge by giving them the ability to critically evaluate what the field of psychology offers. For example, this feature includes ways of dealing with drugs and alcohol (states of consciousness chapter), evaluating computer-assisted instructional programs (learning chapter), personality/vocational testing (personality chapter), and evaluating psychological therapy (treatment chapter).

■ *Try It!* In order to promote involvement in the chapter content, each chapter contains a "Try It!" box. Material in this kind of box presents a demonstration that readers can carry out themselves. For instance, the chapter on the biology underlying behavior provides a biofeedback demonstration.

■ *Recap and Review*. Research is clear in indicating the importance of stressing the organization of textual material, learning material in relatively small chunks, and actively reviewing material. Consequently, each chapter is divided into three or four sections, each of which concludes with a Recap and Review. The Recaps summarize the key points of the previous section, and the Reviews present a series of questions for students to answer. There are a variety of types of questions, including multiple-choice, fill-in, short answer, and matching, in order to test both recall and higher-level understanding of the material.

■ *Running Glossary*. Key terms are defined in the margin of the text, along with a pronunciation guide for difficult words. There is also an end-of-book Glossary.

■ *Looking Back*. To facilitate the review of the material covered in each chapter and to aid in the synthesis of the information covered, there is a numbered summary at the end of every chapter. The summary emphasizes the key points of the chapter.

■ *Key Terms and Concepts*. A list of key terms and concepts, keyed to page numbers where they are first introduced, is at the end of each chapter.

■ *For Further Study and Application*. An annotated bibliography is appended to each chapter. This bibliography contains two types of selections—books and articles which deal with theory, and others that are more oriented toward applications.

■ *Psychology Looks toward the 1990s*. Each chapter ends with a feature new to this edition of the book: Psychology Looks toward the 1990s. This section highlights advances in the field and suggests ways in which the discipline will evolve and is apt to grow during the last decade of the century. For example, the chapter on learning discusses the search for computer models of learning and the chapter on personality discusses evidence that is just now unfolding regarding the genetic components of personality.

■ *A full-color graphic design*. To support the instructional design features of the text, a graphic design structure was developed to enhance the pedagogy of the text. For example, all Try It! boxes are in green, Cutting Edge boxes in magenta, and Psychology at Work boxes in blue. Moreover, parts and chapters are color-keyed on every page, making the structure of the book more explicit. The beautiful design and photos make the text inviting and a book from which it is easy to learn.

ANCILLARY MATERIALS

Essentials of Understanding Psychology is accompanied by an extensive ancillary package that enhances the value of the text as a teaching and learning tool. The *Study Guide,* by Valerie J. Sasserath, includes an introductory section on how to study and how to use the Guide effectively with the text. Following this material are chapters (corresponding to each text chapter) which include chapter outlines and overviews, learning objectives, more than one thousand questions in a variety of formats, and application exercises. *Micro Study Guide,* a computerized version, is also available for use with the Apple and IBM PC computers.

There are two test files in this package, which together offer close to 3,000 multiple-choice and true-false questions that test both factual recall and higher-order understanding. These questions are keyed to the learning objectives in the text and are arranged under the major text headings. Answers and text page references are included for all questions. Test File A was prepared by David Arnold of St. Lawrence University, Linda Baker of the University of Maryland, Baltimore Campus, Frank McAndrew of Knox College, John Rosenkoetter of Southwest Missouri State University, Thomas Thieman of the College of St. Catherine, and William Zachry of the University of Tennessee at Martin. Test

File B was developed by William O. Dwyer of Memphis State University. Both test files are available in computerized formats for use with mainframe and microcomputers.

The *Instructor's Manual,* prepared by the authors of Test File A, offers chapter overviews, lecture objectives and topics, key terms, discussion topics, "Take a Stand" sections (which outline issues for debate), demonstrations and projects, essay questions with answers, and an annotated bibliography of audiovisual resources.

In addition to the print supplements described above, the ancillary package includes a set of fifty overhead transparencies of illustrations in the text. These transparencies can be used in conjunction with the 110 generic overheads in the *McGraw-Hill Introductory Psychology Overhead Transparency Set.* The *McGraw-Hill Introductory Psychology Slide Set,* consisting of 110 slides which duplicate the generic overheads, McGraw-Hill/CRM Films, and a series of videotapes covering the major areas of psychology are also available to adopters.

Psychworld by John C. Hay of the University of Wisconsin in Milwaukee is an acclaimed generic software package that contains fourteen simulations of classic psychology experiments. Professors can use it in the classroom and students can use it in the lab. In addition, *MacLaboratory for Psychology* by Douglas L. Chute of Drexel University and Robert S. Daniel of the University of Missouri is available for use on Apple Macintosh computers. This software consists of thirteen projects that convert the computer into various pieces of laboratory equipment. Your local McGraw-Hill sales representative can explain the details of *Psychworld* and *MacLaboratory for Psychology.*

Each of these features is designed to achieve the goals of introducing you to psychology's theories, research, and applications, fostering your appreciation of the scientific basis of the field, and doing so in an engaging and interesting manner. If, after reading this book, you feel that psychology can provide answers to your curiosity about the world and improve the quality of your life and the lives of others, I will feel satisfied that these goals have been met.

ACKNOWLEDGMENTS

As the long list of reviewers on page vi attests, this book involved the efforts of many psychologists. They lent their expertise to evaluate all or parts of the manuscript, providing an unusual degree of quality control. Their careful work and thoughtful suggestions have improved the manuscript many times over from its first-draft incarnations. I am grateful to every one of them for their comments.

My thinking has been shaped by many teachers along the way. My first introduction to psychology came at Wesleyan University, where several committed and inspiring teachers—and in particular Karl Scheibe—made the excitement and relevance of the field clear to me. Although the nature of the University of Wisconsin, where I did my graduate work, could not have been more different from the much smaller Wesleyan, the excitement and inspiration were similar. Once again, a nucleus of excellent teachers—led, especially, by the late Vernon Allen—molded my thinking, and by the time I left Wisconsin to begin teaching I could envision no other career but that of psychologist.

There are several students at the University of Massachusetts who make the pleasures of being a professor particularly salient; among them are Bob Custrini, Pierre Philippot, and Lee Rosen. My colleagues at the university provide ongoing intellectual stimulation and friendship, and I thank them for making the university a very good place to work. Several people also provided extraordinary research and editorial help: Carolyn Dash, Richard Fleming, Kate Ward, Janice Rose, and Kate Schildauer. Finally, the initial inspiration for this book came from David Serbun, whose good advice and friendship I continue to value.

Anyone who reads this book owes a debt of gratitude to Rhona Robbin, senior developmental editor at McGraw-Hill. Her adept editing, insightful questioning, and—when necessary—prodding and pushing resulted in a level of quality that could not have otherwise been attained. Jim Anker provided the impetus for this book; and his insight, savvy, and friendship brought the book to fruition. Other people at McGraw-Hill were instrumental in producing this book; these include David Dunham, Alison Meerschaert, Phil Butcher, Joan O'Connor, and Inge King. I am proud to be a part of this first-class team.

Finally, I am, as always, indebted to my family. The love and support of my parents, Leah Brochstein and the late Saul D. Feldman, remain a bedrock of my life. Other family members also play a central role in my life; these people include, more or less in order of age, my nieces and nephews, my brother, various brothers- and sisters-in-law, Ethel Radler, Harry Brochstein, and the late Mary Vorwerk, whose unconditional positive regard I especially miss.

Ultimately, my children, Jonathan, Joshua, and Sarah, and my wife, Katherine, are the focal point of my life. I thank them, with fondness and love.

Robert S. Feldman

ABOUT THE AUTHOR

Robert S. Feldman is Professor of Psychology at the University of Massachusetts at Amherst. A former Fulbright Senior Research Scholar and Lecturer, he is a Fellow of the American Psychological Association and author of more than seventy scientific articles, book chapters, and papers. He has also written or edited five books, including *Social Psychology: Theories, Research, and Applications* (McGraw-Hill, 1985). A committed teacher, Professor Feldman has taught the introductory psychology course for fifteen years. His spare time is most often devoted to serious cooking and earnest, inelegant (but improving) piano playing. He lives with his wife, also a psychologist, and three children in Amherst, Massachusetts.

USING *ESSENTIALS OF UNDERSTANDING PSYCHOLOGY:* STRATEGIES FOR EFFECTIVE STUDY

Essentials of Understanding Psychology has been written with the reader in mind, and it therefore includes a number of unique features that will allow you to maximize your learning of the concepts, theories, facts, and other kinds of information that make up the field of psychology. To take advantage of these features, there are several steps that you should take when reading and studying this book. Among the most important:

■ Familiarize yourself with the logic of the book's structure. Begin by reading the Table of Contents. It provides an overview of the topics that will be covered and gives a sense of the way the various topics are interrelated. Next, review the Preface, which describes the book's major features. Note how each chapter is divided into three or four self-contained units; these provide logical starting and stopping points for reading and studying. Also note the major landmarks of each chapter: a chapter opening outline, a Prologue, a Looking Ahead section that includes chapter objectives, Recaps and Reviews of key information following each of the major units, and—at the end of every chapter—a Looking Back section, Key Terms and Concepts, and a Further Study and Application section. Because every chapter is structured in the same way, you are provided with a set of familiar landmarks as you chart your way through new material, allowing you to organize the chapter's content more readily.

■ Use a study strategy. Although we are expected to study and ultimately learn a wide array of material throughout our schooling, we are rarely taught any systematic strategies that permit us to study more effectively. Yet, just as we wouldn't expect a physician to learn human anatomy by trial and error, it is the unusual student who is able to stumble upon a truly effective studying strategy.

Psychologists, however, have devised several excellent—and proven—techniques for improving study skills. By using these procedures—known by the initials "SQ3R" and "MURDER"—you can raise your ability to learn and retain information, not just in psychology but in all academic subjects.

The SQ3R method includes a series of five steps, having the initials S-Q-R-R-R. The first step is to *survey* the material by reading the chapter outlines, chapter headings, figure captions, recaps, and Looking Ahead and Looking Back sections, providing yourself with an overview of the major points of the chapter. The next step—the "Q" in SQ3R—is to *question*. Formulate questions—either aloud or in writing—prior to actually reading a section of the material. For instance, if you had first surveyed this section of the book, you might jot down in the margin, what do "SQ3R" and "MURDER" stand for? The reviews that end each section of the chapter are also a good source of questions. But it is important not to rely on them entirely; making up your own questions is critical. *Essentials of Understanding Psychology* has wide margins in which you can write out your own questions. Such questioning helps you to focus in on the key points of the chapter, while putting you in an inquisitive frame of mind as well.

It is now time for the next, and most traditional, step: to *read* the material. Read carefully and, even more important, actively. For instance, while you are reading, answer the questions you have asked yourself. You may find yourself coming up with new questions as you read along; that's fine, since it shows you are reading inquisitively and paying attention to the material.

The next step—the second "R"—is the most unusual. This "R" stands for *recite,* in which you look up from the book and describe and explain to yourself, or to a friend, the material you have just read and answer the questions you have posed earlier. Do it aloud; this is one time when talking to yourself is nothing to be embarrassed about. The recitation process helps you to clearly identify your degree of understanding of the material you have just read. Moreover, psychological research has shown that communicating material to others (even imaginary others, if you are reciting aloud to yourself and not a friend) aids you in learning it in a different—and deeper—way than material which you do not intend to communicate. Hence, your recitation of the material is a crucial link in the studying process.

The final "R" refers to *review*. As we will discuss in Chapter 5, reviewing is a prerequisite to fully learning and remembering material you have studied. Look over the information; reread the Recaps and Looking Back summaries; answer in-text review questions; and use any ancillary materials you may have available. (There is both a traditional and a computerized student study guide available to accompany *Essentials of Understanding Psychology*.) Reviewing should be an active process, in which you consider how different pieces of information fit together and develop a sense of the overall picture.

An alternative approach to studying—although not altogether dissimilar to SQ3R—is provided by the MURDER system of Dansereau (1978). Despite the unpleasant connotations of its title, the MURDER system is a useful study strategy.

In MURDER, the first step is to establish an appropriate **m**ood for studying by setting goals for a study session and choosing a time and place in which you will not be distracted. Next comes reading for **u**nderstanding, in which careful attention is paid to the meaning of the material being studied. **R**ecall is an immediate attempt to recall the material from memory, without referring to the text. **D**igesting the material comes next; you should correct any recall errors, and attempt to organize and store newly learned material in memory.

You should work next on **e**xpanding (analyzing and evaluating) new material, and try to apply it to situations that go beyond the applications discussed in the text. By incorporating what you have learned into a larger information network in memory, you will be able to recall it more easily in the future. Finally, the last step is **r**eview. Just as with the SQ3R system, MURDER suggests that systematic review of material is a necessary condition for successful studying.

Both the SQ3R and MURDER systems provide a proven means of increasing your study effectiveness. It is not necessary, though, to feel tied to a particular strategy; you might want to combine other elements into your own system. If a study system results in your full mastery of new material, stick with it.

■ The last aspect of studying that warrants mention is that *when* and *where* you study are in some ways as important as *how* you study. One of the truisms of the psychological literature is that we learn things better, and are able to recall them longer, when we study material in small chunks over several study sessions, rather than massing our study into one lengthy period. This implies that all-night studying just prior to a test is going to be less effective—and a lot more tiring—than employing a series of steady, regular study sessions. If you have always had trouble with deadlines and have difficulty scheduling regular study sessions, you should also investigate formal time management techniques, discussed in Chapter 4.

In addition to carefully timing your studying, you should seek out a special location to study. It doesn't really matter where it is, as long as it has minimal distractions and is a place that you use *only* for studying. Identifying a special "territory" allows you get in the right mood for study as soon as you begin.

A final comment

By using the proven study strategies presented above, as well as by making use of the pedagogical tools integrated in the text, you will maximize your understanding of this book, and, more importantly, the field of psychology. It is worth the effort: the excitement, challenge, and promise that psychology holds for you is immense.

PART ONE

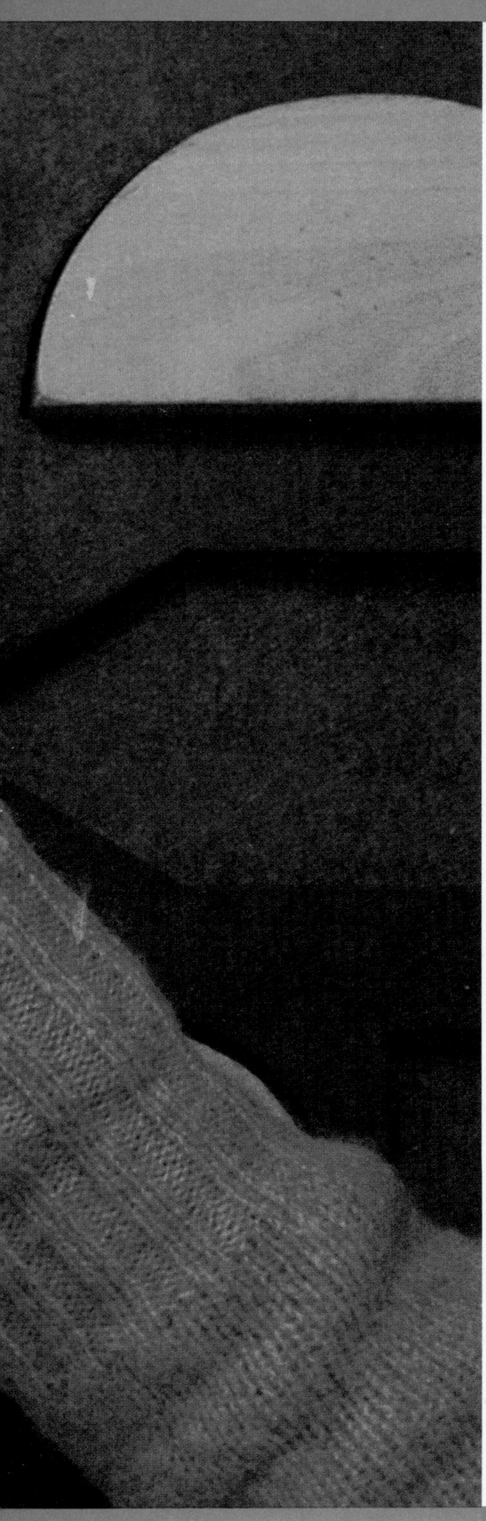

THE SCIENCE OF PSYCHOLOGY

In this introductory part of the book, we will meet some people living near a nuclear plant who must cope with a radioactive gas leak. We will also encounter a group of people who hear the screams of terror of a woman being attacked—and do not even bother to call the police. And we will consider how the science of psychology plays a role in everyone's life.

This part of the book provides an introduction to psychology. We will learn what psychology is, and we will look at the diverse topics that psychologists study. After examining the places in which psychologists are employed, we will consider how psychologists solve scientific—and practical—problems by carrying out research. Finally, we will examine how we can be informed consumers of psychology.

In Chapter 1, then, the focus is on the science of psychology, encompassing its past, present, and future.

CHAPTER 1

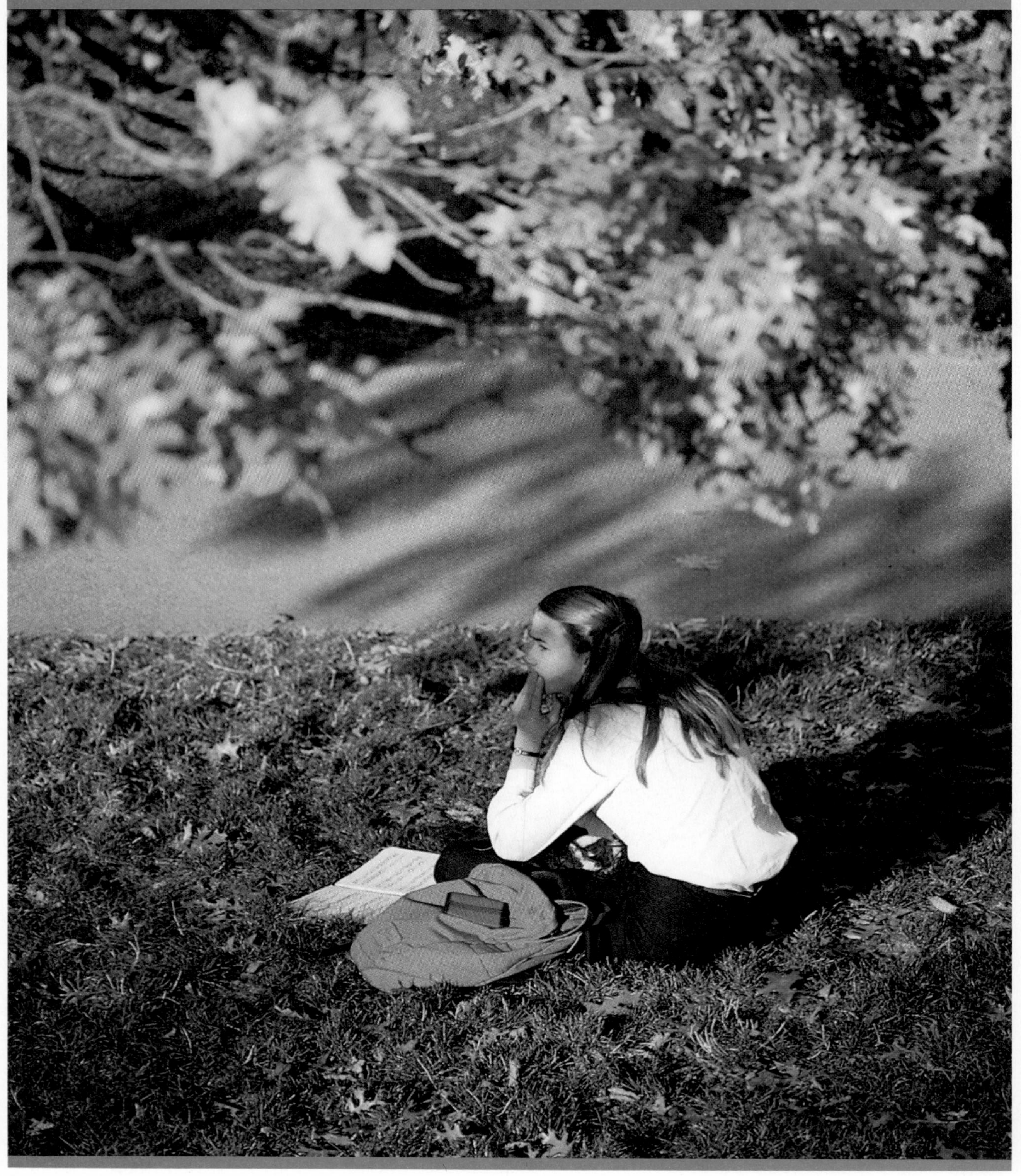

INTRODUCTION TO PSYCHOLOGY

PROLOGUE

LOOKING AHEAD

TRY IT! How Much Psychology Do You Already Know?
The common link among psychologists: The study of behavior and mental processes

PSYCHOLOGISTS AT WORK

Studying the biological foundations of psychology: Biopsychologists
Sensing, perceiving, learning, and thinking about the world: Experimental psychologists
Understanding change and individual differences: Developmental and personality psychologists
Studying and caring for people's physical and mental health: Health, clinical, and counseling psychologists
Understanding the social world: Social, industrial-organizational, and environmental psychologists
Emerging areas of study
Here, there, everywhere: Where do psychologists work?
THE CUTTING EDGE. Pushing the Limits of Psychology: Psychology in Outer Space
Recap and review I

A SCIENCE EVOLVES: SURVEYING THE PAST AND FORETELLING THE FUTURE OF PSYCHOLOGY

The roots of psychology: Historical perspectives
Blood, sweat, and fears: Biological approaches
Understanding the inner person: Psychodynamic approaches
Understanding understanding: Cognitive approaches
Understanding the outer person: Behavioral approaches
The special qualities of *homo sapiens:* Humanistic approaches
A final word about models
PSYCHOLOGY AT WORK. Buckling Up—with Psychology—to Save Lives
The future of psychology
Recap and review II

ASKING THE RIGHT QUESTIONS: THEORIES AND HYPOTHESES

Getting the right answers: Research in psychology
Studying one person to learn about many: The case study
Studying the records: Archival research
Studying what is there already: Naturalistic observation
Asking for answers: Survey research
Determining cause-and-effect relationships: Experimental research
Knowing what's right: The ethics of research
THE INFORMED CONSUMER OF PSYCHOLOGY. Distinguishing Good Psychology from Bad Psychology
Recap and review III
PSYCHOLOGY LOOKS TOWARD THE 1990s. On the frontlines of an epidemic: AIDS and psychology

LOOKING BACK

KEY TERMS AND CONCEPTS

FOR FURTHER STUDY AND APPLICATION

PROLOGUE

It began with a loud bang in the middle of the night.

To the residents of Harrisburg, Pennsylvania, the sudden noise was nothing new, since the Three Mile Island nuclear plant that was situated at their doorsteps regularly made all sorts of sounds.

But this time things were different. Inside, warning lights were flashing and an electronic alarm was ringing. As the small night-shift crew desperately tried to figure out what was happening, there was a serious leak of radioactive steam. More leaks occurred several times over the next few days as the plant hovered near the brink of an even greater disaster: a nuclear "meltdown" of the sort that occurred at Chernobyl nuclear plant in the Soviet Union, in which radioactive material was released in such great quantities that the damage was catastrophic.

As it turned out, however, no one was hurt by the accident at the Three Mile Island plant—at least in terms of the immediate toll. But some experts warned of the possibility of eventual cancer, genetic deformities, and other long-term outcomes from the radiation that did escape. For those consequences, though, the residents of Harrisburg would have to wait.

LOOKING AHEAD

In an age when disaster occurs with alarming regularity, the nuclear accident at Three Mile Island is not unique. Yet what does this accident of a purely technological nature have to do with psychology? Quite a bit, it turns out:

- To psychologists who specialize in studying the biology underlying human behavior, it provided an opportunity to examine changes in the responsiveness of the nervous system following exposure to low-level doses of radioactivity.
- To psychologists specializing in the study of learning and memory, it offered a chance to investigate the kinds of details concerning accidents that people are most apt to learn about and later recall.
- To health psychologists, the accident provided an opportunity to examine how a person's health is affected by stress.
- To psychologists who are interested in social interaction, the rumors that followed in the wake of the accident provided a good basis for studying human behavior under conditions of severe threat.
- To psychologists who engage in psychological counseling, the disaster brought about a sharp increase in the number of clients who complained of feelings of anxiety.

The Common Link among Psychologists: The Study of Behavior and Mental Processes

Psychology: *The scientific study of behavior and mental processes*

The common link among these people is that all are specialists in the general area of study called psychology. **Psychology** is the scientific study of behavior and mental processes.

This definition, while clear-cut and accurate, is also deceptively simple. For in order to encompass the breadth of the field, "behavior and mental processes" must be understood to mean many things: The term includes not just what people

TRY IT!

HOW MUCH PSYCHOLOGY DO YOU ALREADY KNOW?

To test your knowledge of psychology, try answering the following questions:

1. Babies love their mothers primarily because their mothers fulfill their basic biological needs, such as providing food. True or false? ____

2. People who are geniuses generally have poor social adjustment. True or false? ____

3. The best way to make sure that a desired behavior will continue after training is completed is to reward that behavior every single time it occurs during training, rather than rewarding it only periodically. True or false? ____

4. A schizophrenic is someone with at least two distinct personalities. True or false? ____

5. If you are having trouble sleeping, the best way to get to sleep is to take a sleeping pill. True or false? ____

6. Children's IQ scores have very little to do with how well they do in school. True or false? ____

7. Frequent masturbation can lead to mental illness. True or false? ____

8. Once people reach old age, their leisure activities change radically. True or false? ____

9. Most people would refuse to give painful electric shocks to other people. True or false? ____

10. One of the least important factors affecting how much we like another person is that person's physical attractiveness. True or false? ____

Scoring This Try It! is easy to score: As you will learn as you read this book, psychologists have proved each of the items false. If you have a low score, though, don't despair; these items were chosen because they represent some of the most common myths among students who enter introductory psychology classes (based on Lamal, 1979). In other words, they were designed to fool you. After you have read this text, you will understand why these statements are myths and how psychologists systematically and scientifically find answers to questions such as these.

do, but also their thoughts, their feelings, their perceptions, their reasoning processes, their memories, and even, in one sense, the biological activities that keep their bodies functioning.

When psychologists speak of "studying" behavior and mental processes, their interests are equally broad. To psychologists, it is not enough to simply describe behavior. As with any science—and psychologists clearly consider their discipline a science—its goals are to explain, predict, modify, and ultimately improve the lives of people and the world in which they live.

Psychologists seek to achieve these goals by taking a scientific approach. They do not consider it sufficient to rely on intuition, insight, and logic to study behavior; too often, people are simply wrong in their guesses about human behavior. (To prove this for yourself, answer some of the questions in the accompanying Try It! box.) Instead, psychologists have developed well-controlled, methodical techniques, employing both humans and animals as subjects, to find answers to their questions.

And what a variety of questions about human behavior there are. Consider these examples: How do we see colors? What is intelligence? Can abnormal behavior be cured? Is a hypnotic trance the same as sleep? Is aging inevitable? How does stress affect us? What is the best way to lose weight? What is normal sexual behavior?

These questions provide just a hint of the range of topics that will be presented in this book as we explore the field of psychology. Our discussions will take us

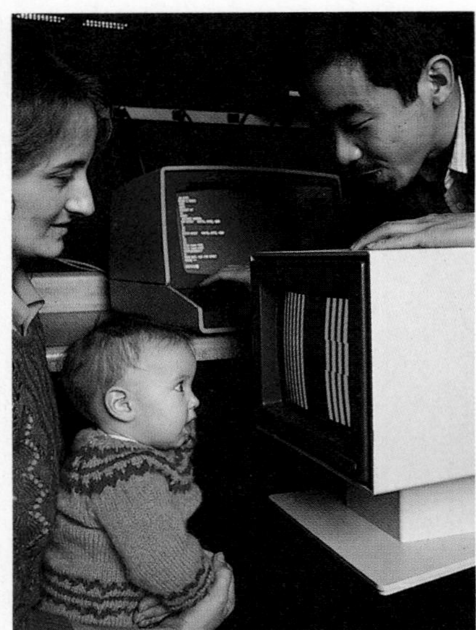

A psychologist interested in perceptual development uses sophisticated technology to investigate the visual capabilities of infants. (*Enrico Ferorelli/DOT*)

Is the sign language Roger Fouts uses to communicate with the chimp Lucy similar in sophistication to the language used when human beings converse? As discussed in Chapter 7, the answer is controversial. (*Paul Fusco/Magnum*)

across the spectrum of what is known about behavior and mental processes. At times, we will leave the realm of humans and explore animal behavior, since many psychologists study nonhumans in order to determine general laws of behavior that pertain to *all* organisms, and since animal behavior can provide important clues to answering questions about human behavior. But we will always return to the usefulness of psychology in helping to solve the everyday problems that confront all human beings.

In this introductory chapter, we cover a number of topics that are central to an understanding of psychology. We begin by introducing the different types of psychologists and the roles they play. Next, we discuss the major approaches and models that are used to guide the work psychologists do. Finally, we describe the research methods psychologists employ in their search for the answers to questions that will help them to better understand behavior.

In covering this introductory material, we also introduce the text itself. This book is intended to provide as close a facsimile to two people sitting down and discussing psychology as one can convey with the written word; when I write "we," I am talking about the two of us—reader and writer. To borrow a phrase from the folks who spend most of their time with computers, the book is meant to be "user-friendly."

You will find, then, material that is meant to involve and challenge you (Try It! boxes), material to demonstrate the ways in which psychologists apply what they have learned to everyday life (Psychology at Work boxes), and material to show you what the future of psychology holds (Cutting Edge boxes). There are also sections in each chapter that are intended to make you a more informed consumer of psychological information by enhancing your ability to critically evaluate the contributions psychologists offer society. These sections, called The Informed Consumer of Psychology, will include concrete recommendations for incorporating psychology into your life.

The book itself is designed to make it easier for you to learn the material we discuss. Based on the principles that psychologists who specialize in learning and memory have developed, information is presented in relatively small chunks, with each chapter including three or four major sections. Following each of these sections, there is a Recap and Review which lists the key points that have been covered and asks a series of questions. (Answers to these questions are provided on the page following the review.) This kind of quick review will help you in learning, and later recalling, the material.

In sum, this chapter has a number of major objectives. After reading and studying it, you will be able to

- Define the science of psychology and outline the reasons for studying it
- Identify the different kinds of psychologists and understand the roles they play
- Describe each of the major models that psychologists employ to guide their work
- Explain how theory and research are used by psychologists to answer questions of interest
- Discuss the different forms of research and the ways in which they are carried out
- Understand the major features of this book
- Define and apply the key terms and concepts listed at the end of the chapter

PSYCHOLOGISTS AT WORK

Wanted: Industrial/Organizational Psychologist. Ph.D. required. Psychologist will work with other psychologists who are responsible for generating accurate job descriptions, developing and administering training programs, designing performance evaluation systems, and developing and implementing a program for the early identification of managerial talent within the company.

* * *

Wanted: Counseling Psychologist. Ph.D. required, including internship and experience relevant to understanding both college student development and higher education environments. Responsibilities include counseling/therapy with individuals and groups, and consultation with campus units. Innovation in devising new counseling methods and developing new programs is encouraged.

* * *

Wanted: Psychology Instructor, Community College. Master's degree required. Instructor will teach one to three sections of introductory psychology and two to four classes from interest areas including family relations, child and adult development, educational psychology, personality, social psychology, and experimental psychology. Additional duties will include advising entering and first-year students (American Psychological Association, 1980).

Many people mistakenly believe that almost all psychologists analyze and treat abnormal behavior. However, as the actual job descriptions reprinted above indicate, the range and scope of the field of psychology are much broader than this common misconception would suggest. We can examine the major branches and specialty areas of psychology by describing them in the general order in which they are discussed in this book. (Figure 1-1 displays the percentage of psychologists who are engaged in each of the major specialty areas.)

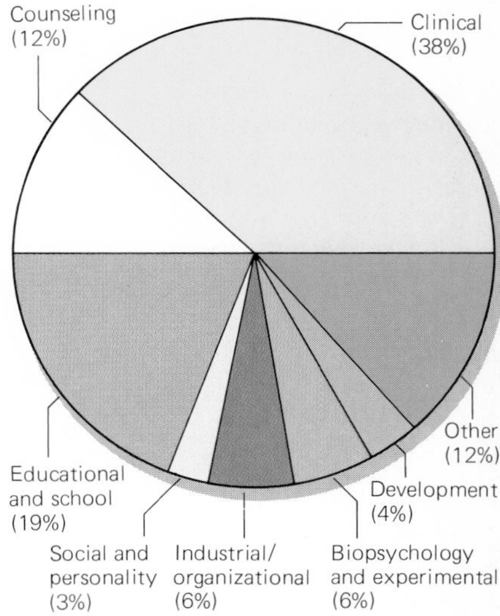

Figure 1-1
The major specialties within the field of psychology. (*Adapted from Stapp, Tucker, & VandenBos, 1985 (table 2), p. 1324.*)

Studying the Biological Foundations of Psychology: Biopsychologists

Biopsychology: *The branch of psychology that studies the biological basis of behavior*

About a year and a half after the Three Mile Island accident, a team of psychologists studied the urine of people who lived near the damaged nuclear plant. Why would psychologists be interested in urine? The answer, it turns out, is that research done in the field of **biopsychology**, the branch that specializes in the biological bases of behavior, has shown that long-term stress results in the excretion of certain chemicals that are not ordinarily found in large quantities. In order to understand the nature of stress at Three Mile Island, then, it was important to search for the presence of such chemicals—which were, in fact, found in abnormally large quantities in people living near the Three Mile Island nuclear plant seventeen months after the accident (Baum, Gatchel, & Schaeffer, 1983).

Biopsychologists study a broad range of topics with a focus on the biological foundations of the brain and nervous system. For example, they may investigate the ways in which specific sites in the brain are related to disorders such as Parkinson's disease (as we discuss in Chapter 2), or they may attempt to determine how bodily sensations are related to emotion (see Chapter 8).

Sensing, Perceiving, Learning, and Thinking about the World: Experimental Psychologists

Experimental psychology: *The branch of psychology that studies the processes of sensing, perceiving, learning, and thinking about the world*

If you have ever wondered how acute your vision is, how you experience pain, or how you can most effectively study, you have raised a question that is most appropriately answered by an experimental psychologist. **Experimental psychology** is the branch of psychology that studies the processes of sensing, perceiving, learning, and thinking about the world.

The work of experimental psychologists overlaps that done by biopsychologists, as well as that done in other branches of psychology. Actually, the term "experimental psychologist" is somewhat misleading, since psychologists in every branch use experimental techniques, and experimental psychologists do not limit themselves to only experimental methods.

Cognitive psychology: *The branch of psychology that considers higher mental processes including thinking, language, memory, problem solving, knowing, reasoning, judging, and decision making*

Several subspecialties have grown out of experimental psychology and have become central parts of the field in their own right. For example, **cognitive psychology** is the branch of psychology that specializes in the study of higher mental processes including thinking, language, memory, problem solving, knowing, reasoning, judging, and decision making. Covering a wide swath of human behavior, cognitive psychologists have, for instance, identified more efficient ways of remembering and better strategies for solving problems.

Understanding Change and Individual Differences: Developmental and Personality Psychologists

A baby producing its first smile . . . taking its first step . . . saying its first word. These events, which can be characterized as universal milestones in development, are also singularly special and unique for each person. Developmental psychologists, whose work we will discuss in Chapter 10, trace these changes throughout people's lives.

Developmental psychology: *The branch of psychology that studies how people grow and change throughout their lives*

Developmental psychology is the branch of psychology that studies how people grow and change throughout the course of their life span. Another branch,

Many veterans faced psychological difficulties after returning from the war in Vietnam. Clinical and counseling psychologists (such as the one in the white sweater) often used a treatment technique with them that consisted of weekly discussions with other veterans. (*J. P. Laffont/Sygma*)

personality psychology, attempts to explain both consistency and change in a person's behavior over time, as well as the individual traits that differentiate the behavior of one person from another when each confronts the same situation. The major issues relating to the study of personality will be considered in Chapter 11.

Personality psychology: *The branch of psychology that studies consistency and change in people's behavior and the characteristics that differentiate people*

Studying and Caring for People's Physical and Mental Health: Health, Clinical, and Counseling Psychologists

If you have difficulties getting along with others, continual unhappiness with your life, or a fear that prevents you from carrying out your normal activities, you might consult one of the psychologists who devote their energies to the study of physical or mental health: health psychologists, clinical psychologists, and counseling psychologists.

Health psychology is the branch of psychology that explores the relationship between psychological factors and physical ailments or disease. For instance, health psychologists are interested in how long-term stress (a psychological factor) can affect physical health, as we saw in the example of Three Mile Island. They are also concerned with identifying ways of promoting behavior related to good health (such as increased exercise) or in discouraging unhealthy behavior such as smoking.

Health psychology: *The branch of psychology that explores the relationship of physical and psychological factors*

For clinical psychologists, the focus of activity is on the treatment and prevention of psychological disturbance. **Clinical psychology** is the branch of psychology that deals with the study, diagnosis, and treatment of abnormal behavior. Clinical psychologists are trained to diagnose and treat problems ranging from the everyday crises of life—such as grief due to the death of a loved one—to more extreme conditions such as loss of touch with reality. Some clinical psychologists also conduct research, investigating issues that range from identifying the early signs of psychological disturbance to studying the relationship between family communication patterns and psychological disorder.

Clinical psychology: *The branch of psychology that studies diagnosis and treatment of abnormal behavior*

As we will see when we discuss abnormal behavior and its treatment in

Chapter 12, the kinds of activities carried out by clinical psychologists are varied indeed. It is the clinical psychologist who administers and scores psychological tests and who provides psychological services in community mental-health centers. Even sexual problems are often treated by the clinical psychologist.

Counseling psychology: *The branch of psychology that focuses on educational, social, and career adjustment issues*

Counseling psychology is the branch of psychology that focuses on educational, social, and career adjustment problems. Almost every college has a counseling center staffed with counseling psychologists, where students can get advice on the kinds of jobs they might be most suited for, on methods of studying effectively, and on strategies for resolving everyday difficulties, from problems with roommates to concerns about a specific professor's grading practices.

Educational psychology: *The branch of psychology that considers how the educational process affects students*

School psychology: *The branch of psychology that considers the academic and emotional problems of elementary and secondary school students*

Two close relatives of counseling psychology are educational psychology and school psychology. **Educational psychology** considers how the educational process affects students; it is, for instance, concerned with ways of understanding intelligence, developing better teaching techniques, and understanding teacher-student interaction. **School psychology**, in contrast, is the specialty devoted to assessing children in elementary and secondary schools who have academic or emotional problems and to developing solutions to such problems.

Understanding the Social World: Social, Industrial-Organizational, and Environmental Psychologists

None of us lives in isolation; rather, we are all part of a complex network of interrelationships. These networks with other people and with society as a whole are the focus of study of a number of different kinds of psychologists.

Social psychology: *The branch of psychology that studies how people's thoughts, feelings, and actions are affected by others*

Social psychology, as we will see in Chapters 14 and 15, is the study of how people's thoughts, feelings, and actions are affected by others. Covering a broad area, social psychologists focus on such diverse topics as understanding human aggression, learning why people form relationships with one another, and determining how we are influenced by advertisements.

Industrial-organizational psychology: *The branch of psychology that studies the psychology of the workplace, considering productivity, job satisfaction, and related issues*

Industrial-organizational psychology is concerned with the psychology of the workplace. Such questions as "How do you increase productivity and worker accuracy?" "How can you select the right person for a job?" and "Are there ways an employee's job satisfaction can be increased?" are asked by industrial and organizational psychologists.

Environmental psychology: *The branch of psychology that considers the relationship between people and their physical environment*

If you were interested in designing an inner-city apartment building that wouldn't be prone to vandalism, you might turn to an environmental psychologist. **Environmental psychology** considers the relationship between people and the physical environment. Environmental psychologists have made important advances in understanding how a person's physical environment affects his or her life on a number of fundamental levels.

Emerging Areas of Study

Forensic (for EN sik) **psychology**: *The branch of psychology that studies insanity and other legal issues related to psychology*

Consumer psychology: *The branch of psychology that considers our buying habits and the effects of advertising on buyer behavior*

As the field of psychology matures, the number of specialty areas increases. For example, **forensic psychology** focuses on legal issues, such as deciding what criteria indicate that a person is legally insane and whether larger or smaller juries make fairer decisions. **Consumer psychology** is oriented toward understanding the factors underlying consumers' buying habits and the ways in which

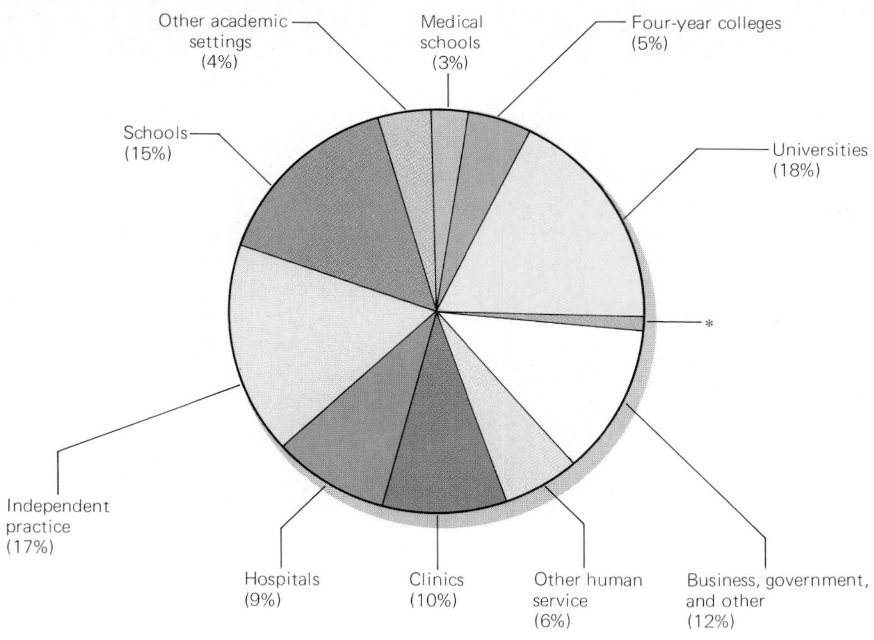

Figure 1-2
Where psychologists work: the major settings in which psychologists are employed. (*Adapted from Stapp, Tucker, & VandenBos, 1985 (table 4), pp. 1326–1327.*)

people respond to advertisements. Psychologists interested in **program evaluation** also constitute a growing body; they focus on assessing large-scale programs, usually run by the government, to determine whether they are effective in meeting their goals. For example, psychologists specializing in evaluation have examined the effectiveness of such governmental social services as the Head Start day-care program and Medicaid.

Program evaluation: *The assessment of large-scale programs to determine their effectiveness in meeting their goals*

Here, There, Everywhere: Where Do Psychologists Work?

Given the diversity of roles that psychologists play, it is not suprising that they are employed in a variety of settings. As you can see in Figure 1-2, the primary employers are institutions of higher learning: universities, two- and four-year colleges, and medical schools. The next-most-frequent employment settings are hospitals, clinics, community mental-health centers, and counseling centers. A substantial number of psychologists are also employed in private practice. Other settings include human-services organizations, research and consulting firms, and business and industry.

Why are so many psychologists found in academic settings? The primary reason is that the three major roles played by psychologists in society—teacher, scientist, and professional—are easily carried out in such an environment. Very often professors of psychology are also actively involved in research or in serving clients. Whatever their particular job setting, however, all psychologists share a commitment to better both individual lives and society in general, and the topics they explore range from a person's inner life to the far reaches of outer space (see the Cutting Edge box).

THE CUTTING EDGE

PUSHING THE LIMITS OF PSYCHOLOGY:

Psychology in Outer Space

As the rocket headed into space after takeoff, the astronauts unstrapped themselves from their seats to begin the mission tasks. The first order of business: meeting with the crew psychologist, whose job it was to ensure the psychological adjustment of the astronauts and to keep their performance at a high level.

Although there has yet to be a psychologist aboard a space mission, the scenario described above may well become a reality in the future. This prediction is based on the arguments of a growing number of experts, who suggest that psychological problems among astronauts are likely to increase as space exploration becomes more common.

For example, social psychologist Robert L. Helmreich (1986) provides several reasons for psychologists to play a critical role in space exploration:

- As space flight becomes more common and safe, flying in a rocket will have little more significance than flying in an airplane. Parades and White House visits for astronauts will be a thing of the past. As these kinds of rewards for space flight diminish, the costs—in terms of isolation and crowding—will take on greater significance to space voyagers. It is likely, then, that psychological problems will become more common.
- Because crews on early space flights were relatively homogeneous in terms of background and experience, there was a relatively low chance of friction among crew members. But as the crews grow in diversity, the possibility of conflict will grow. In fact, it may become necessary to carry out even more rigorous psychological screening of crew members than NASA currently does.
- Groups that are isolated are subject to poor decision making, a phenomenon called "groupthink" (Janis & Mann, 1976). Consequently, attention must be paid to ensure the soundness of decisions made by astronauts.
- As the duration of space flights increases, the lack of leisure activities will likely assume greater importance. Work carried out by psychologists in other settings—such as in undersea laboratories—suggests that leisure and recreational needs must be met in order for the crew to work effectively (Nowlis, 1972). The need for privacy and the possibility of sexual tensions in mixed-gender crews must also be taken into account.

The realization that psychological issues will play an important role in space flight suggests, then, that psychologists may come to play an increasing part in the space-exploration program. Indeed, perhaps psychology texts of the future will include "space psychology" among the branches of the field.

If the dangers of spaceflight are overcome and space travel becomes more frequent, psychologists are likely to play an increasing role in dealing with the psychological problems of astronauts. (*NASA*)

RECAP AND REVIEW I

Recap

- Psychology is the scientific study of behavior and mental processes.
- Among the major kinds of psychologists are biopsychologists; experimental psychologists; cognitive psychologists; developmental and personality psychologists; health, clinical, and counseling psychologists; educational and school psychologists; and environmental psychologists. Other emerging areas include forensic psychology, consumer psychology, and the psychology of program evaluation.
- Most psychologists are employed by institutions of higher learning, while others are employed by hospitals, clinics, and community health centers or are engaged in private practice.

Review

1. Which of the following is the most accurate definition of psychology?
a. Psychology is the scientific study of behavior and mental processes. **b.** Psychology is ''mental medicine,'' the major purpose of which is to treat mental problems. **c.** Psychology is the study of the mind's interaction with the environment. **d.** Psychology is the scientific study of human thought.

2. Most of present-day psychology has its foundation in
a. Intuition **b.** Observation and experimentation **c.** Trial and error **d.** Metaphysics

3. Match each branch of psychology with the issues or questions posed below.
a. ____ Biopsychology
b. ____ Experimental psychology
c. ____ Cognitive psychology
d. ____ Developmental psychology
e. ____ Personality psychology
f. ____ Health psychology
g. ____ Clinical psychology
h. ____ Counseling psychology
i. ____ Educational psychology
j. ____ School psychology
k. ____ Social psychology
l. ____ Industrial psychology
m. ____ Consumer psychology

1. Joan, a college freshman, is panicking. She needs to learn better organizational skills and study habits to cope with the demands of college.
2. At what age do children generally begin to acquire an emotional attachment to their fathers?
3. It is thought that pornographic films that depict violence against women may prompt aggressive behavior in some men.
4. What chemicals are released in the human body as a result of a stressful event? What are their effects on behavior?
5. John is fairly unique in his manner of responding to crisis situations, with an even temperament and a positive outlook.
6. The general public is more apt to buy products that are promoted by attractive and successful actors.
7. Eight-year old Jack's teachers are concerned that he has recently begun to withdraw socially and to show little interest in school work.
8. Janet's job is demanding and stressful. She wonders if this lifestyle is leaving her more prone to certain illnesses such as cancer or heart disease.
9. A psychologist is intrigued by the fact that some people are much more sensitive to painful stimuli than others.
10. A strong fear of crowds leads a young woman to seek treatment for her problem.
11. What mental strategies are involved in solving complex word problems?
12. What teaching approaches most effectively motivate elementary school students to successfully accomplish academic tasks?
13. Jessica is asked to develop a management strategy that will encourage safer work practices in an assembly plant.

(Answers to review questions are at the bottom of page 14.)

A SCIENCE EVOLVES: SURVEYING THE PAST AND FORETELLING THE FUTURE OF PSYCHOLOGY

Some half-million years ago, primitive peoples assumed that psychological problems were caused by the presence of evil spirits. To allow these spirits to escape, an operation called trephining was performed. Trephining consisted of chipping away at the skull with crude stone instruments until a hole was cut through the bone. Because archeologists have found skulls with signs of healing around the opening, we can assume that patients sometimes survived the cure.

* * *

The famous Greek physician Hippocrates thought that personality was made up of four temperaments: sanguine (cheerful and active), melancholic (sad), choleric (angry and aggressive), and phlegmatic (calm and passive). These temperaments were influenced by the presence of "humors," or fluids, in the body. For instance, a sanguine person was thought to have relatively more blood than other people.

* * *

According to the philosopher Descartes, nerves were hollow tubes through which "animal spirits" conducted impulses in the same way that water is transmitted through a tube. When people put a finger too close to a fire, then, the heat was transmitted via the spirits through the tube, directly into the brain.

While these "scientific" explanations sound farfetched to us, at one time they represented the most advanced thinking regarding what might be called the psychology of the era. Even without knowing much about modern-day psychology, it is probably clear to you that our understanding of behavior has advanced tremendously since these earlier views were formulated. Yet most of the advances have occurred relatively recently, for, as sciences go, psychology is one of the newcomers on the block.

Although its roots can be traced back to the ancient Greeks and Romans, and though philosophers have argued for several hundred years about some of the same sorts of questions that psychologists grapple with today, the formal beginning of psychology is generally set at 1879. In that year, the first laboratory devoted to the experimental study of psychological phenomena was established in Germany by Wilhelm Wundt; at about the same time, the American William James set up his laboratory in Cambridge, Massachusetts.

Models: *Systems of interrelated ideas and concepts used to explain phenomena*

Throughout its some 110 years of formal existence, psychology has led an active life, developing gradually into a true science. As part of this evolution, it has produced a number of conceptual **models**—systems of interrelated ideas and concepts used to explain phenomena—that have guided the work being carried out. Some of these models have been discarded—just as have the views of Hippocrates and Descartes—but others have been developed and elaborated on and provide a set of maps for psychologists to follow.

Each of the models provides a different perspective, emphasizing different factors. Just as we may employ not one but many maps to find our way around

ANSWERS TO REVIEW QUESTIONS

Review I: **1.** a **2.** b **3.** a.-4, b.-9, c.-11, d.-2, e.-5, f.-8, g.-10, h.-1, i.-12, j.-7, k.-3, l.-13, m.-6

Wilhelm Wundt, in the center of this photo, established the first laboratory to study psychological phenomena in 1879. (*Archives of the History of American Psychology*)

a given geographical area—one map to show the roads, one the major landmarks, and one the topography of the hills and valleys—psychologists also find that more than one approach may be useful in understanding behavior. Given the range and complexity of behavior, no single model will invariably provide an optimal explanation—but together, the models provide us with a means to explain the extraordinary breadth of behavior.

The Roots of Psychology: Historical Perspectives

When Wilhelm Wundt set up the first psychological laboratory in Leipzig, Germany, in 1879, he was interested in studying the building blocks of the mind. To do this, he developed a model that came to be known as structuralism. **Structuralism** focuses on the fundamental elements that underlie thinking and other significant mental activities.

Structuralism: *An early approach to psychology which focused on the fundamental elements underlying thoughts and ideas*

Introspection: *A method in which subjects are asked to describe in detail their thoughts and feelings*

Wundt and other structuralists used a procedure called introspection to study the structure of the mind. In **introspection**, people were asked to describe, in great detail, what they were experiencing as they were exposed to various material. Wundt argued that psychologists could come to understand the structure of the mind through the reports the subjects made of their reactions.

Wundt's structuralism did not stand the test of time, however. People had difficulty describing their inner experiences, and there was little way that an outside observer could verify the accuracy of the introspections the subjects did make. Such drawbacks led to the evolution of new models.

The next major model, which largely supplanted structuralism, was called functionalism. Rather than focusing on the mind's components, **functionalism** concentrated on the functions of mental activities. Functionalists asked what roles behavior played in allowing people to better adapt to their environments. Led by the American psychologist William James, the functionalists, rather than raising the more abstract questions concerning the processes of mental behavior, examined the ways in which behavior allows people to satisfy their needs.

Functionalism: *An early approach to psychology that considered the role of mental activity in adapting to one's environment*

Gestalt (geh SHTALLT) **psychology**: *An approach to psychology that focuses on the organization of perception and thinking in a "whole" sense, rather than on the individual elements of perception*

Another reaction to structuralism was the development of gestalt psychology. **Gestalt psychology** is a model of psychology focusing on the study of how

William James, one of the first American psychologists, rejected structuralism and promoted the model of functionalism. (*Library of Congress*)

perception is organized. Instead of considering the individual parts that make up thinking, gestalt psychologists took the opposite tack, concentrating instead on how individual elements are considered as units or wholes. Their credo was "the whole is greater than the sum of its parts," by which they meant that the elements of perception taken together produce something greater and more meaningful than those individual elements alone. As we shall see in Chapter 3, the contributions of gestalt psychologists to the understanding of perception were substantial.

Today, several major models have evolved from the roots of structuralism, functionalism, and gestalt psychology, each of them emphasizing different aspects of behavior. These include the biological, psychodynamic, cognitive, behavioral, and humanistic models.

Each of these models varies in a number of critical dimensions, as summarized in Table 1-1. One theory may have a basically positive and optimistic view of human nature, focusing on the potential for good in people's behavior, while another may be more oriented toward the negative aspects of human behavior such as selfishness and aggression. The models may also differ in the degree of emphasis placed on mental processes, with some essentially ignoring thought processes and focusing on observable behavior, and others placing primary emphasis on thinking. Finally, some theories consider environmental causes as predominant, while others base their explanations more on the nature of the individual.

As we discuss each of the models, it is important to keep in mind how they differ in these major dimensions.

Blood, Sweat, and Fears: Biological Approaches

Biological model: *The psychological model that views behavior in terms of biological functioning*

When you get down to the basics, behavior is carried out by living creatures made of skin and guts. According to the **biological model**, the behavior of both

TABLE 1-1

Comparison of the major models of psychology

MODEL	CONCEPTUAL FOCUS	VIEW OF HUMAN NATURE	IMPORTANCE OF MENTAL PROCESSES	EMPHASIS: ENVIRONMENT OR PERSON
Biological	Biological functions as basis of behavior	Neutral	Moderate	Person
Psychodynamic	Unconscious determinants of behavior	Negative	Maximum (for unconscious)	Person
Cognitive	Nature of thought processes and understanding of world	Neutral	Maximum	Both
Behavioral	Observable behavior	Neutral	Minimum	Environment
Humanistic	Human desire to reach potential	Positive	Maximum	Person

people and animals should be considered from the perspective of their biological functioning: how the individual nerve cells are joined together, how the inheritance of certain characteristics from parents and other ancestors influences behavior, how the functioning of the body affects hopes and fears, what behaviors are due to instincts, and so forth. Even more complex kinds of behaviors—emotional responses such as fear, for example—are viewed as having critical biological components by psychologists using the biological model.

Because every behavior can at some level be broken down into its biological components, the biological model has broad appeal. Psychologists who subscribe to this model have contributed important advances in the understanding and bettering of human life, advances that range from suggesting cures for deafness to identifying drugs to help people with severe mental disorders.

Sigmund Freud, a Viennese physician, developed the psychodynamic model in which people's behavior was considered to be determined by unconscious processes. (*Bettmann Archive*)

Understanding the Inner Person: Psychodynamic Approaches

To many people who have never taken a psychology course, psychology begins and ends with the **psychodynamic model**. Proponents of the psychodynamic perspective believe that behavior is brought about by inner forces over which the individual has little control. Dreams and slips of the tongue are viewed as indications of what a person is truly feeling within a seething caldron of subconscious psychic activity.

Psychodynamic (sy ko dy NAM ik) **model**: *The psychological model based on the belief that behavior is brought about by unconscious inner forces over which an individual has little control*

The psychodynamic view is intimately linked with one individual: Sigmund Freud. Freud was a Viennese physician in the early 1900s, whose ideas about unconscious determinants of behavior had a revolutionary effect on twentieth-century intellectual thinking, not just in psychology but in related fields as well. Although many of the basic principles of psychodynamic thinking have been roundly criticized, the model that has grown out of Freud's work has provided a means not only for treating mental disorders, but for understanding everyday phenomena such as prejudice and aggression.

Understanding Understanding: Cognitive Approaches

The route to understanding behavior leads some psychologists straight into the mind. Evolving in part from structuralism, which, as we noted earlier, was concerned with identifying the various parts of the mind, the **cognitive model** focuses on how people know, understand, and think about the world. The emphasis, though, has shifted away from learning about the structure of the mind itself to how people understand and represent the outside world within themselves.

Cognitive model: *The psychological model that focuses on how people know, understand, and think about the world*

Psychologists relying on this model ask questions ranging from whether a person can watch television and study a book at the same time (the answer is ''probably not'') to how anyone can figure out the causes of human behavior. The common element that links cognitive approaches is the emphasis on how people understand the world.

Understanding the Outer Person: Behavioral Approaches

While the biological, psychodynamic, and cognitive approaches look inside the organism to determine the causes of its behavior, the behavioral model takes a very different approach. The **behavioral model** grew out of a rejection of psychology's early emphasis on the inner workings of the mind, suggesting instead that observable behavior should be the focus of the field.

Behavioral model: *The psychological model that suggests that observable behavior should be the focus of study*

Rejecting psychology's initial emphasis on the inner workings of the mind, John B. Watson proposed a behavioral approach in which the focus was on observable behavior. (*Culver Pictures*)

The first major American psychologist who championed a behavioral approach, John B. Watson, was firm in his view that a full understanding of behavior could be obtained by studying and modifying the environment in which people operated. In fact, he believed rather optimistically that by properly controlling a person's environment, any desired sort of behavior could be obtained, as his own words make clear: "Give me a dozen healthy infants, well-formed, and my own specified world to bring them up in and I'll guarantee to take any one at random and train him to become any type of specialist I might select—doctor, lawyer, artist, merchant-chief, and, yes, even beggar-man and thief, regardless of his talents, penchants, tendencies, abilities, vocations and race of his ancestors" (Watson, 1925).

As we will see, the behavioral model crops up along every byway of psychology. Along with the influence it has had in the area of learning processes—much of our understanding of how people learn new behaviors is based on the behavioral model—its influence can also be found in such diverse areas as the treatment of mental disorders, the curbing of aggression, the solution of sexual problems, and even the prevention of littering.

The Special Qualities of Homo Sapiens: Humanistic Approaches

Humanistic model: *The psychological model that suggests that people are in control of their lives*

Free will: *The human ability to make decisions about one's own life*

Although it emerged in the 1950s and 1960s, the **humanistic model** is still considered the newest of the major approaches. Rejecting the views that behavior is largely determined by automatic, biological forces or unconscious processes, it instead suggests that people are in control of their lives. Humanistic psychologists maintain that people are naturally inclined to develop toward higher levels of functioning and that, if given the opportunity, they will strive to reach their full potential. The emphasis, then, is on **free will**, the human ability to make decisions about one's life.

More than any other approach, the humanistic model stresses the role of psychology in enriching people's lives and helping them to achieve self-fulfillment. While not as all-encompassing as some of the other general models, the humanistic perspective has had an important influence on the thinking of psychologists, reminding them of their commitment to the individual person and society.

A Final Word about Models

You may be wondering about how the five major models of psychology we have just discussed relate to the different branches of psychology that were presented earlier. The models and branches of psychology actually present two separate and independent ways of approaching the science. Thus a psychologist from any given branch might choose to employ any one, or more, of the major models. (See Table 1-2.) For example, a developmental psychologist might subscribe to a psychodynamic model *or* a behavioral model *or* any of the other models. Although some kinds of psychologists are more or less likely to adhere to a particular model, as the table indicates, in theory at least each of the models is available to any psychologist who chooses to employ it. And don't let the abstract qualities of the models fool you: They each have very practical implications, implications that will concern us throughout this book. (See, for instance, the accompanying Psychology at Work box.)

TABLE 1-2

Major models of psychology as used by different kinds of psychologists. Models that are used most frequently by a particular type of psychologist are checked.

	Models				
TYPE OF PSYCHOLOGIST	**BIOLOGICAL**	**PSYCHODYNAMIC**	**COGNITIVE**	**BEHAVIORAL**	**HUMANISTIC**
Biopsychologist	√			√	
Experimental	√		√	√	
Cognitive			√		
Developmental	√	√	√	√	√
Personality	√	√	√	√	√
Health	√		√	√	
Clinical	√	√	√	√	√
Counseling		√		√	√
Educational			√	√	√
School			√	√	√
Social			√	√	√
Industrial-organizational			√	√	
Environmental	√		√	√	

PSYCHOLOGY AT WORK

BUCKLING UP—WITH PSYCHOLOGY—TO SAVE LIVES

What do seat belts and psychology have to do with each other?

Quite a bit, in the eyes of E. Scott Geller, an experimental psychologist who is leading a nationwide campaign to get people to use the seat belts in their automobiles. According to government statistics, auto accidents are responsible for over 30,000 deaths and 500,000 injuries each year—but the rates for each could be cut in half if more people wore seat belts. Still, despite massive publicity efforts, only about 15 percent of the drivers in the United States wear seat belts.

Enter psychologist Geller, who has developed a number of strategies for increasing seat-belt use, all based on psychological principles. For starters, he examined popular television programs, where he observed that less than 5 percent of our television heroes use seat belts. Because psychological research has shown that TV actors can exert a powerful influence on

A nationwide campaign, based on psychological principles, is helping to increase the use of seat belts in automobiles. (*Richard Hutchings/Photo Researchers, Inc.*)

viewers, Geller has started a drive aimed at getting television characters to buckle up—a drive that has begun to show some results. (Watch what happens now when Mr. T. gets into his car!)

Even more successful have been efforts, using principles derived from the behavioral model of psychology, aimed at directly providing rewards for people who use seat belts when driving. For example, in one surprisingly simple but effective experiment, every driver who approached an outdoor bank window wearing a seat belt was given a number for a community bingo game. Seat-belt usage rates doubled. Another project has been a "flash-for-life" program whereby a passenger in a car holds a large flash card to the window; the card says "Please buckle up—I care." If a rider in another car buckles up as a result of seeing the sign, the "flasher" turns over the card, which says on the other side, "Thank you for buckling up." This simple technique, based on psychological research on rewards and learning, produced compliance in more than one-fifth of nonusers who saw the sign (Geller & Streff, 1984; Rudd & Geller, 1985).

As the promising results of these strategies reveal, psychology *is* at work—and *does* work. As we will see throughout this book in other Psychology at Work boxes, the basic principles of the science of psychology are providing both the potential and the realization of meaningful and significant improvement in the quality of people's lives.

The Future of Psychology

Where is psychology heading? Although crystal balls looking into the future of scientific disciplines are notoriously cloudy, a few trends can be safely foretold:

- Psychologists will become increasingly specialized. In a field in which practitioners must be experts on such diverse topics as the intricacies of the transmission of electrochemical impulses across nerve endings and the communication patterns of employees in large organizations, no one person can be expected to master the field entirely. It is likely, then, that there will be increased specialization as psychologists delve into new areas.
- New models will emerge. As a growing, evolving science, psychology will produce new models to supplant the ones we now have. Moreover, older models may be merged to form new ones. We can be certain, then, that as psychologists accumulate more knowledge they will become increasingly sophisticated in their understanding of behavior and mental processes.
- There will be increasing emphasis on applications of psychological knowledge. As you will see, this book is a testament to the fact that the knowledge acquired by psychologists can be applied to the betterment of the human condition.

RECAP AND REVIEW II

Recap

- The foundation of today's major models rests on the earlier models of structuralism, functionalism, and gestalt psychology.
- The dominant contemporary conceptual models of psychology encompass biological, psychodynamic, cognitive, behavioral, and humanistic approaches.
- In the future, psychologists are likely to become more specialized, new models will emerge, and there will be increasing emphasis on applications of psychological knowledge.

Review

1. An experimental psychology lab was established in Germany in 1879 by
   a. Descartes **b.** Freud **c.** James **d.** Wundt
2. Although the major models of psychology differ in some details, the underlying assumptions they hold about the nature and causes of human behavior are identical. True or false?

3. Jeanne's therapist asks her to recount a violent dream she recently experienced in order to gain insight into the unconscious forces affecting her behavior. Jeanne's therapist is working from a ______________ model.
4. "It is behavior that can be observed which should be studied, not the suspected inner workings of the mind." This statement was most likely made by someone following the perspective of a
   a. Cognitive model **b.** Biological model **c.** Humanistic model **d.** Behavioral model
5. Recent studies of schizophrenia have identified peculiar arrangements of nerve cells, possibly inherited, as a suspected cause of that mental illness. Research such as this is typical of a ______________ model.
6. "My therapist is wonderful! She always points out my positive traits. She dwells on my uniqueness and strength as an individual. I feel much more confident about myself—as if I'm really growing and reaching my potential." The therapist referred to above probably practices from a ______________ model.

(Answers to review questions are at the bottom of page 22.)

ASKING THE RIGHT QUESTIONS AND GETTING THE RIGHT ANSWERS: THEORY AND RESEARCH IN PSYCHOLOGY

> It took her killer some thirty minutes to finish the job. When Kitty Genovese was first attacked, she managed to free herself and run toward a police call box into which she screamed, "Oh, my God, he stabbed me. Please help me!" In the stillness of the night, her screams were heard by no fewer than thirty-eight neighbors. Windows opened and lights went on. One couple pulled chairs up to the window and turned off their lights so they could see better. Someone yelled, "Let that girl alone." But shouts were not enough to scare off the killer. He chased Kitty, stabbing her eight more times and sexually molesting her before leaving her to die.

And how many of the thirty-eight witnesses came to her aid? Not one.

The Kitty Genovese case remains one of the most horrifying and dismaying cases of "bad Samaritanism." Both the general public and psychologists found it difficult to explain how so many people could stand by without coming to the aid of an innocent victim whose life might well have been saved had there been any active intervention on the part of even one bystander.

Social psychologists in particular puzzled over the problem for many years, and they finally reached a strange conclusion: Kitty Genovese might well have been better off had there been far fewer than thirty-eight people who heard her cries. In fact, had there been just one bystander present, the chances of that person intervening might have been fairly high. For it turns out that the *fewer* witnesses present in a situation such as this one, the better the victim's chances of getting help.

But how could anyone come to such a conclusion? After all, logic and common sense would clearly suggest that more bystanders would mean a greater likelihood that someone would help a person in need. This seeming contradiction—and the way psychologists resolved it—illustrates the crux of a challenge central to the field of psychology: the challenge of asking and answering questions of interest.

Asking the Right Questions: Theories and Hypotheses

This challenge has been met through reliance on the joint use of theory and research to guide psychologists in searching for answers to questions that con-

Theories: *Broad explanations and predictions concerning phenomena of interest*

cern them. **Theories** are broad explanations and predictions concerning phenomena of interest. Although all of us carry around our own theories of human behavior—such as "people are basically good" or "human behavior is usually motivated by self-interest"—psychologists develop more formal and focused ones.

For example, social psychologists Bibb Latané and John Darley responded to the Kitty Genovese case by developing a theory based on a phenomenon they called diffusion of responsibility (Darley & Latané, 1968; Latané & Darley, 1970). According to their theory, the greater the number of bystanders or witnesses to an event that calls for human intervention, the more the responsibility for helping is felt to be shared by all the bystanders. Because of this sense of shared responsibility, then, the more people present in an emergency situation, the less personally responsible each person will feel—and the less likely it is that any single person will come forward to help.

Developing Hypotheses While such a theory makes sense, these psychologists could not stop there. Their next step was to devise a way of testing whether their reasoning was correct. To do this, they needed to derive a hypothesis. **Hypotheses** are predictions stated in a way that allows them to be tested. Just as we have broad theories about the world, we also make up hypotheses (ranging from why our English professor dresses so eccentrically to the best way to study for a test). Although we rarely test them systematically, we do try to determine if they are right or not. Perhaps we might try cramming for one exam but studying over a longer period of time for another. By assessing the results, we have created a way to compare the two methods.

Hypothesis (hy POTH eh sis): *A prediction that can be tested experimentally*

Latané and Darley's hypothesis was a straightforward derivation from their more general theory: The more people who witness an emergency situation, the less likely it is that help will be given to a victim. They could, of course, have chosen another hypothesis (for instance, that people with greater skills related to emergency situations will not be affected by the presence of others); but their initial derivative seemed to offer the most direct test of the theory.

There are several reasons why psychologists use theories and hypotheses. For one thing, these postulations allow sense to be made of individual observations, by placing them together within a framework that organizes and summarizes them. In addition, they offer psychologists the opportunity to move beyond facts that are already known about the world and to make deductions about phenomena that have not yet been explained. In this way, theories and hypotheses provide a reasonable guide to the direction that future investigation ought to take.

In sum, then, theories and hypotheses help psychologists to ask the right questions. But how do they answer such questions? The answers come from psychological **research**, systematic inquiry aimed at the discovery of new knowledge.

Research: *Systematic inquiry aimed at discovering knowledge*

Getting the Right Answers: Research in Psychology

Just as we can derive several theories and hypotheses to explain particular phenomena, there are a considerable number of alternate ways to carry out research. The way that is chosen to test the hypothesis is known as operationalization.

ANSWERS TO REVIEW QUESTIONS

Review II: **1.** d **2.** False **3.** Psychodynamic **4.** d **5.** Biological **6.** Humanistic

Operationalization refers to the process of taking a hypothesis and translating it into the particular procedures that are used in the experiment. There is no single way to go about doing this; instead, it depends on logic, the equipment and facilities available, and the ingenuity of the researcher. We will consider several of the major weapons in the psychologist's research arsenal.

Operationalization: *The process of translating a hypothesis into experimental procedures*

Studying One Person to Learn about Many: The Case Study

When Kitty Genovese's killer was identified, many people found themselves asking what it was in his background that might have led to his behavior. In order to answer this question, a psychologist might conduct a **case study**, an in-depth interview of a single individual. In a case study, psychologists might well include psychological testing, in which a carefully designed set of questions is used to gain some insight into the personality of the person being studied. In using case studies as a research technique, the goal is often not only to learn about the individual, but to use the insights gained to better understand people in general.

Case study: *An in-depth interview of an individual in order to better understand that individual and to make inferences about people in general*

Studying the Records: Archival Research

If you were interested in finding out more about emergency situations in which bystanders did not provide help, you might start by examining historical records. In **archival research**, existing records are examined to confirm a hypothesis. By using newspaper accounts, for example, we might find support for the notion that a decrease in helping behavior accompanies an increase in the number of bystanders.

Archival (ar KY vul) **research**: *The examination of written records for the purpose of understanding behavior*

Studying What Is There Already: Naturalistic Observation

Although archival research allows us to test a hypothesis for which data already exist, researchers typically aren't lucky enough to find sufficient appropriate data intact. They often turn instead to naturalistic observation to carry out their research.

In **naturalistic observation**, the investigator simply observes some naturally occurring behavior and does not intervene in the situation. For example, a researcher investigating helping behavior might turn to a high-crime area of a city and observe there the kind of help that is given to victims of crime. The important point about naturalistic observation is that the researcher is passive and simply meticulously records what occurs.

Naturalistic observation: *Observation without interference, in which the researcher records information about a naturally occurring situation in a way that does not influence the situation*

While the advantage of naturalistic observation is obvious—we get a sample of what people do in their "natural habitat"—it also has an important drawback: the inability to control any of the factors of interest. For example, we might find so few naturally occuring instances of helping behavior that we would be unable to draw any conclusions. Because naturalistic observation prevents researchers from making changes in a situation, they must wait until appropriate conditions occur. Similarly, if people know that they are being watched, they may react in such a way that the behavior observed is not truly representative of the group in question.

Asking for the Answers: Survey Research

There is no more direct way of finding out what people think, feel, and do than by asking them directly. For this reason, survey research is an important research

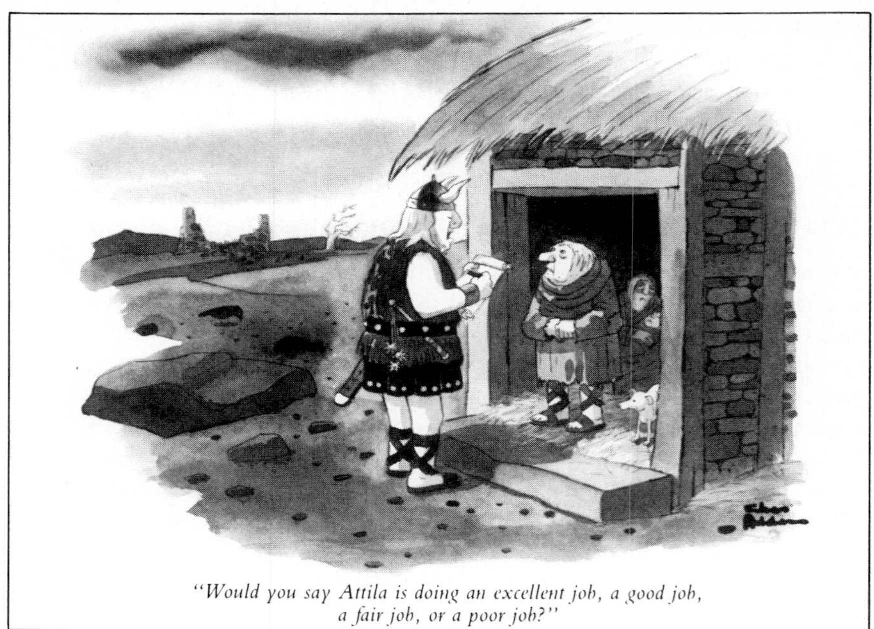
"Would you say Attila is doing an excellent job, a good job, a fair job, or a poor job?"

Although survey techniques are considerably more sophisticated than this view would indicate, the basic idea of asking people directly about their opinions is accurate. (*Drawing by Charles Addams; © 1982 The New Yorker Magazine, Inc.*)

Survey research: *Sampling a group of people by assessing their behavior, thoughts, or attitudes, then generalizing the findings to a larger population*

method. In **survey research**, people chosen to represent some larger population are asked a series of questions about their behavior, thoughts, or attitudes (Fink & Kosecoff, 1985). Survey methods have become so sophisticated that even using a very small sample is sufficient to infer with great accuracy how a larger group would respond. For instance, sampling just a few thousand voters is sufficient to predict within one or two percentage points who will win a presidential election—if the sample is chosen with care.

Researchers interested in helping behavior might conduct a survey asking people their reasons for not wanting to come forward to help. Similarly, researchers concerned with sexual behaviors have carried out surveys to learn which sexual practices are common and which are not, and to chart the changes in sexual morality that have occurred as time has passed.

Although asking people directly about their behavior in some ways seems like the most straightforward approach to understanding what people do, survey research has several potential drawbacks. For one thing, people may give inaccurate information because of lapses of memory or because they don't want to let the researcher know what they really feel. Moreover, people sometimes make responses they think the researcher wants to hear—or, in just the opposite instance, responses they think the researcher *doesn't* want to hear.

Correlational Research One of the possibilities available to researchers using the survey method as well as the other forms of research we have discussed is to determine the relationship between two behaviors, or between responses to two questions. For instance, we might want to find if people who report that they attend religious services also report that they are more helpful to strangers in emergency situations. If we did find such a relationship, we could say that there was a correlation between attendance at religious services and being helpful in emergencies.

Correlational research: *Research to determine whether there is a relationship between certain behaviors and responses*

In research that is **correlational**, the relationship between two sets of factors is examined to determine if they are associated, or "co-related." The strength of a relationship is represented by a mathematical score ranging from +1.0 (a perfect positive relationship) to −1.0 (a perfect negative relationship). Although actual correlations are rarely perfect, the closer the correlation is to +1.0 or −1.0, the stronger the relationship. (You can read more about the concept of correlation, and how statistics in general are used by psychologists, in the appendix at the end of the book.)

Although correlational techniques cannot tell us whether one factor *causes* changes in another, they can indicate if knowing the value of one variable allows us to predict the value of another variable. We may not be able to tell, then, if attending religious services *causes* people to be helpful in emergencies, but correlational procedures will tell us if knowing that specific people attend religious services will help us to predict how they will behave in an emergency situation.

Another example can illustrate the critical point that correlations tell us nothing about cause and effect but only provide a measure of the strength of a relationship between two factors. For instance, we might find that children who watch a lot of television programs having aggressive content are apt to demonstrate a relatively high degree of aggressive behavior, while those who watch few television shows that portray aggression are apt to exhibit a relatively low degree of such behavior (see Figure 1-3). We cannot say that the aggression is *caused* by the TV viewing, since it is just as likely to be caused by some other factor. For example, we may learn that children of low socioeconomic status watch more programs having aggressive content *and* are more aggressive. Factors relating to a family's socioeconomic status, then, may be the true cause of the children's higher incidence of aggression. In fact, there may be several factors that underlie both the aggressive behavior and the television viewing. It is even possible that people who show high aggressiveness choose to watch shows with high aggressive content *because* they are aggressive. It is clear, then, that any number of causal sequences are possible—none of which can be ruled out by correlational research.

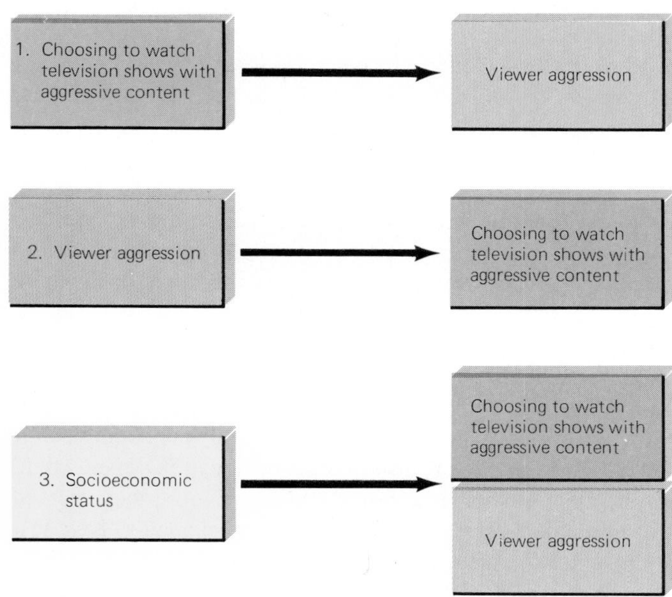

Figure 1-3
If we find that a frequent viewing of television programs having aggressive content is associated with high levels of aggressive behavior, we might cite several possible causes, as suggested above. Correlational findings, then, do not permit us to determine causality.

The inability of correlational research to answer questions of a cause-and-effect nature is a crucial drawback. There is, though, an alternative technique that establishes causality: the experiment.

Determining Cause-and-Effect Relationships: Experimental Research

Experiment: *A study carried out to investigate the relationship between two or more factors in order to establish causality*

Experimental manipulation: *The intentional alteration of factors in an experiment to affect responses or behaviors*

Variable: *A behavior or event that can be changed*

The *only* way that psychologists can establish cause-and-effect relationships through research is by carrying out an experiment. In a formal **experiment**, the relationship between two (or more) factors is investigated by deliberately producing a change in one factor and observing the effect that change has upon other factors. The change deliberately produced is called the **experimental manipulation**. The factors that are changed are called **variables**, behaviors or events that are capable of change.

There are several steps in carrying out an experiment, but the process typically begins with the development of one or more hypotheses for the experiment to test. Recall, for example, the hypothesis derived by Latané and Darley to test their theory of helping behavior: The more people who witness an emergency situation, the less likely it is that help will be given to a victim. We can trace how they developed an experiment to test this hypothesis.

The first step was to operationalize the hypothesis by translating it into actual procedures that could be used in an experiment. Operationalizing their hypothesis required that Latané and Darley take into account the fundamental principle of experimental research that we mentioned earlier: There must be a manipulation of at least one variable in order to observe what effects the manipulation has on another variable. But this manipulation cannot be viewed in isolation; if a cause-and-effect relationship is to be established, the effects of the manipulation must be compared with the effects of no manipulation or a different manipulation.

Treatment: *The manipulation implemented by the experimenter to influence results in a segment of the experimental population*

Treatment group: *The experimental group receiving the treatment, or manipulation*

Control group: *The experimental group receiving no treatment*

Experimental research requires, then, that at least two groups be compared with each other. One group will receive some special **treatment**—the manipulation implemented by the experimenter—while another group receives either no treatment or a different treatment. The group receiving the treatment is called the **treatment group**, while the other group is called the **control group**. (In some experiments, however, there are multiple treatment and control groups, each of which is compared with another.)

By employing both a treatment and a control group in an experiment, researchers are able to rule out the effects of factors not associated with the experimental manipulation as a source of any changes seen in the experiment. If we didn't have a control group, we couldn't be sure that some other factor—such as the temperature at the time we were running the experiment or the mere passage of time—wasn't causing the changes observed. Through the use of control groups, then, researchers can be sure that the causes of effects are isolated—and cause-and-effect inferences can be drawn.

To Latané and Darley, a means of operationalizing their hypothesis, based on the requirement of having more than one treatment group, was readily available. They decided they would create a bogus emergency situation which would require the aid of a bystander. As their experimental manipulation, they decided to vary the number of bystanders present. They could have decided to have just an experimental group with, for instance, two people present, and a control group for comparison purposes with just one person present. Instead, they settled on a more complex procedure in which there were three groups that could be compared with one another, consisting of two, three, and six people.

Latané and Darley now had identified what is called the experimenter's **independent variable**: the variable that is manipulated. In this case, it was the variation in the number of people present. The next step was to decide how they were going to determine what effect varying the number of bystanders had on subjects' behavior. Crucial to every experiment is the **dependent variable**, which is the variable that is measured and is expected to change as a result of changes caused by the experimenter's manipulation. Experiments have, then, both an independent and a dependent variable. (To remember the difference, you might recall that a hypothesis predicts how a dependent variable *depends* on the manipulation of the independent variable.)

Independent variable: *The variable that is manipulated in an experiment*

Dependent variable: *The variable that is measured and is expected to change as a result of experimenter manipulation*

How, then, should the dependent measure be operationalized for Latané and Darley's experiment? One way might have been to use a simple "yes"-or-"no" measure of whether a subject helped or didn't help. But the two investigators decided they wanted a measure that provided a finer-grained analysis of helping behavior, so they settled on the amount of time it took for a subject to provide help.

Latané and Darley now had all the components of an experiment. The independent variable, manipulated by them, was the number of bystanders present in an emergency situation. The dependent variable was the time it took for the bystanders in each of the groups to provide help. *All* true experiments in psychology fit this straightforward model (see Figure 1-4.)

The Final Step: Random Assignment of Subjects to Treatments There was only one remaining crucial step to make the experiment a valid test of the hypothesis: properly assigning subjects to a specific treatment condition. Why should this step be so important?

The reason becomes clear when we examine various alternative procedures. For example, the experimenters might have considered the possibility of assigning just males to the group with two bystanders, just females to the group with three bystanders, and both males and females to the group with six bystanders. Had they done so, however, it would have become clear that any differences they found in responsive behavior could not be attributed to the group size alone, but might just as well be due to the composition of the group. A more reasonable procedure would be to ensure that each group had the same composition in terms of sex; then they would be able to make comparisons across groups with considerably more accuracy.

It is clear that subjects in each of the treatment groups ought to be comparable, and it is easy enough to create similar groups in terms of sex. The problem becomes a bit more tricky, though, when we consider other subject characteristics. How can we ensure that subjects in each treatment group will be equally intelligent, extroverted, cooperative, and so forth, when the list of characteristics—any one of which may be important—is potentially endless?

The solution to the problem is a simple but elegant procedure called **random assignment to condition**. In random assignment, subjects are assigned to different experimental conditions on the basis of chance and chance alone. The experimenter might, for instance, put the names of all potential subjects into a hat, and draw names to make assignments to specific groups. The advantage of this technique is that subject characteristics have an equal chance of being distributed across the various conditions or groups. By using random assignment, the experimenter can be confident that each of the groups will have approxi-

Random assignment to condition: *The assignment of subjects to given conditions on a chance basis alone*

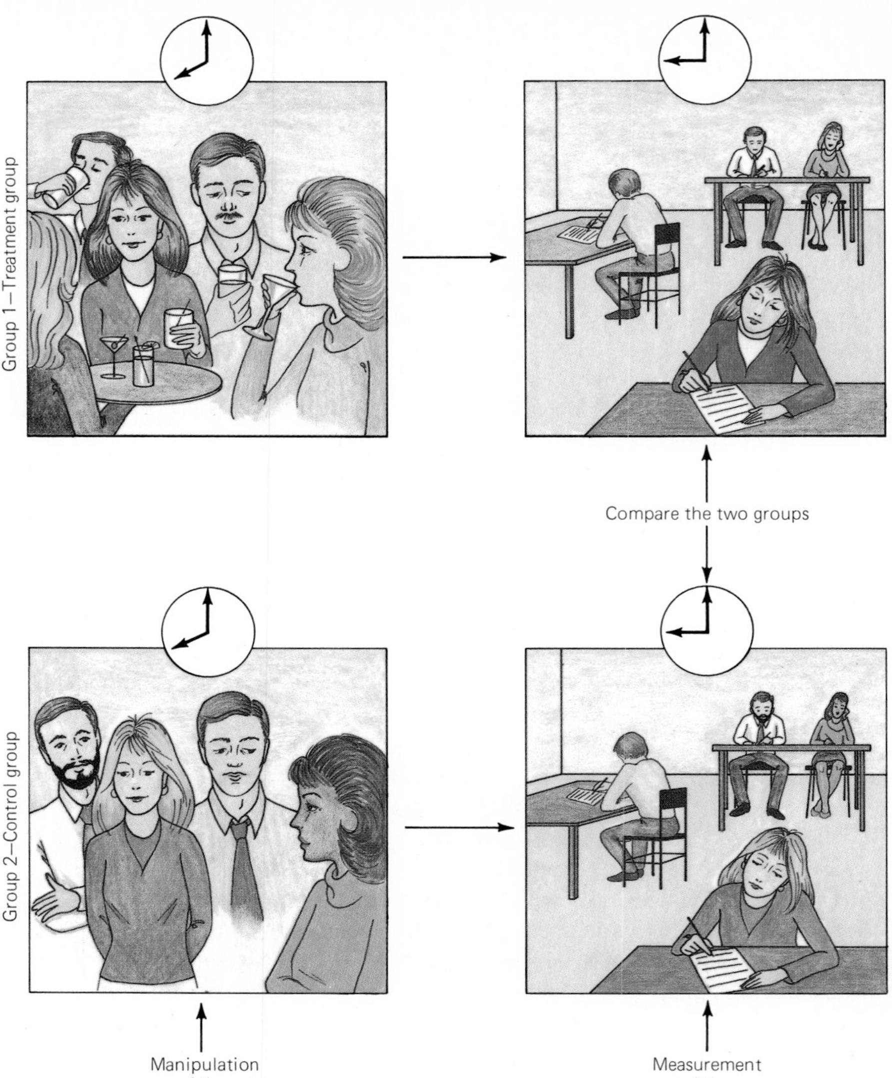

Figure 1-4
The basics of an experiment are represented in this figure. A group of people—who become the subjects of the experiment—are randomly assigned to one of two groups. Subjects in group 1 are given the treatment—a dose of alcohol to learn its effects on performance—while subjects in group 2, the control group, do not receive the alcohol. The administration of alcohol is the independent variable. Later, the performance of subjects in each group is measured, and the performance of the two groups is compared. The variable that is measured—subject performance—is the dependent variable.

mately the same proportion of intelligent people, cooperative people, extroverted people, males and females, and so on.

Experimental bias: *Factors that could lead an experimenter to an erroneous conclusion about the effect of the independent variable on the dependent variable*

Experimenter expectations: *An experimenter's unintentional message to a subject about results expected from the experiment*

Threats to Experiments: Experimenter and Subject Expectations You're probably thinking that by this point Latané and Darley ought to have been ready to run their experiment. But there were a few further considerations that they had to take into account to avoid **experimental bias**—factors that could mislead them into concluding that the independent variable alone effected changes in behavior.

One problem that they had to avoid was **experimenter expectations**, whereby an experimenter unintentionally transmits cues to subjects about the way they are expected to behave in a given experimental condition. The danger is that these expectations will bring about an "appropriate" behavior—one that may not have otherwise occurred. For example, if Latané and Darley had behaved toward subjects in the two-bystander condition as if they expected them to help, but let on that they had low expectations for helping in the six-person bystander condition, such variations in experimenter behavior—no matter how unintentional—might have affected the results.

A related problem is **subject expectations** about what is appropriate behavior for them. If you have ever been a subject in an experiment, you know that you quickly develop ideas about what is expected of you, and it is typical for people to develop their own hypothesis about what the experimenter hopes to learn from the study. If these expectations influence a subject's behavior, it becomes a cause for concern, since it is no longer the experimental manipulation producing an effect, but rather the subject's expectations.

Subject expectations: *A subject's interpretation of what behaviors or responses are expected in an experiment*

To guard against the problem of subject expectations biasing the results of an experiment, the experimenter may disguise the true purpose of the experiment. Subjects who are unaware that helping behavior is being studied, for example, are more likely to act in an unbiased manner than if they are told the purpose of the experiment is to study their helping behavior. Latané and Darley decided to tell their subjects, then, that the actual purpose of the experiment was to hold a discussion among college students about their personal problems. In doing so, they expected that their subjects would not suspect the true purpose of the experiment.

In some experiments, it is impossible to hide the true purpose of the research. In cases such as these, other techniques are available. For example, suppose you were interested in testing the ability of a new drug to alleviate the symptoms of severe depression. If you simply gave the drug to half your subjects and not to the other half, subjects given the drug might report feeling less depressed merely because they knew they were getting a drug. Similarly, the subjects who got nothing might report feeling no better because they knew that they were in a no-treatment control group.

To solve this problem, psychologists typically use a procedure in which subjects in the control group do receive treatment, sometimes in the form of a pill called a placebo. A **placebo** is a "sugar pill," without any significant chemical properties. Because members of both groups are kept in the dark as to whether they are getting a real or a bogus pill, any differences that are found can be attributed to the quality of the drug and not to the possible psychological effects of being administered a pill.

Placebo (pla SEE bo): *A biologically ineffective pill used in an experiment to keep subjects, and sometimes experimenters, from knowing whether or not the subjects have received a behavior-altering drug*

But there is still one more thing that a careful researcher must do in an experiment such as this. In order to overcome the possibility that experimenter expectations will affect the subject, the person who administers the drug shouldn't know whether it is actually the true drug or the placebo. By keeping both the subject and the experimenter who interacts with the subject "blind" as to the nature of the drug that is being administered—a method known as the **double-blind procedure**—the effects of the drug can be more accurately assessed.

Double-blind procedure: *The technique by which both the experimenter and the subject are kept from knowing which subjects received a drug, making any observed behavior variations more reliable*

Were Latané and Darley Right?: The Data Answer By now, you must be wondering whether Latané and Darley were right when they hypothesized that increasing the number of bystanders present in an emergency situation would lower the degree of helping.

The answer is simple: According to the results of the experiment they carried out, their hypothesis was right on target. In their test of the hypothesis, they used a laboratory setting in which subjects were told that the purpose of the experiment was to hold a discussion about personal problems associated with college over an intercom in order to avoid the embarrassment of face-to-face contact. This was not, of course, the true purpose of the experiment, but one used to keep subjects' expectations from biasing their behavior. (Consider how they would have been affected if they had been told that their helping behavior in emergencies was being tested. The experimenters could never have gotten an accurate assessment of what the subjects would actually do in an emergency; by definition, emergencies are rarely announced in advance.)

The sizes of the discussion groups were two, three, and six people, which constituted the manipulation of the independent variable of group size. Subjects were randomly assigned to one of these three conditions upon their arrival at the laboratory.

Confederate (kon FED er it): *A participant in an experiment who has been instructed to behave in ways that will affect the responses of other subjects*

As the subjects in each group were holding their discussion, they suddenly heard one of the other participants (in reality a trained **confederate** of the experimenters) lapse into what sounded like an epileptic seizure:

> I-er-um-I think I-I need-er-if-if- could-er-er-somebody er-er-er-er-er-er-er give me a little-er-give me a little help here because-er-I-er-I'm-er-er-h-h-having a-a-a real problem-er-right now and I-er-if somebody could help me out it would-it-would-er-er s-s-sure be-sure be good . . . because-er-there-er-er-a cause I-er-I-uh-I've got a-a one of the-er-sei---er-er-things coming on and-and-and I could really-er-use some help so if somebody would-er-give me a little h-help-uh-er-er-er-er-er c-could somebody-er-er-help-er-us-us-us [choking sounds]. . . . I'm gonna die-er-er-I'm . . . gonna die-er-help-er-er-seizure-er-[choking sounds, then silence] (Latané and Darley, 1970, p. 379).

The subjects' behavior was now what counted. The dependent variable was the time that elapsed from the start of the "seizure" to the time a subject began trying to help the "victim." If six minutes went by without a subject offering help, the experiment was ended.

The results? If you look at Figure 1-5, you can see that the size of the group had a large effect on whether a subject went to help the victim (Latané & Darley, 1970). In the two-person group (in which subjects thought they were alone with the victim), average elapsed time was fifty-two seconds; in the three-person group (the subject, the victim, and one other person), the average elapsed time was ninety-three seconds; and in the six-person group (the subject, victim, and four others), the average time was 166 seconds. Looking at a "yes"-or-"no" measure of whether help was given confirms the elapsed-time pattern. When group size was two, 85 percent helped; when it was three, 62 percent helped;

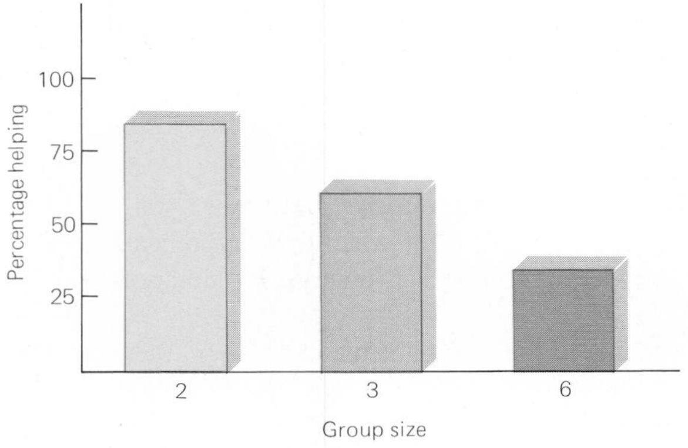

Figure 1-5
The results of the Latané and Darley experiment showed that as the size of the group witnessing an emergency increased, helping decreased. (*Based on Latané & Darley, 1968.*)

and when it was six, 31 percent responded. It is clear, then, that the hypothesis was confirmed: As the number of bystanders increased, helping behavior decreased.

The Latané and Darley study contains all the elements of an experiment: an independent variable, a dependent variable, random assignment to conditions, and multiple treatment groups. Because it does, we can say with some confidence that group size *caused* changes in the degree of helping behavior.

Of course, one experiment alone does not resolve forever the question of bystander intervention in emergencies. Psychologists require that findings be **replicated**, or repeated, using other procedures and in other settings, before full confidence can be placed in the validity of any single experiment. [In this case, the experiment has stood the test of time: In a review of some fifty studies that were carried out in the ten years following their study, the finding that an increase in bystanders leads to decreased helping has been replicated in numerous other studies (Latané & Nida, 1981).]

Replication: *The repetition of an experiment in order to verify the results of the original experiment*

Knowing What's Right: The Ethics of Research

If you were to put yourself in the place of one of the subjects in the Latané and Darley experiment, how would you feel when you learned that the person who you thought was having a seizure was in reality a confederate of the experimenter?

Although at first you might experience relief that there was no real emergency, you might also feel some resentment that you were deceived by the experimenter. And you might also experience concern that you were placed in an unusual situation in which, depending on how you behaved, you may have had a blow to your self-esteem.

Most psychologists argue that the use of deception is sometimes necessary in order to avoid having subjects influenced by what they think is the study's true purpose. (If you knew the Latané and Darley study was actually concerned with your helping behavior, wouldn't you be tempted to intervene in the emergency?) In order to avoid such behavior, researchers sometimes must use deception.

Because research has the potential to violate the rights of participants, psychologists adhere to a strict set of ethical guidelines aimed at protecting subjects (American Psychological Association, 1981). These guidelines advocate the protection of subjects from physical and mental harm, the right of subjects to privacy regarding their behavior, the assurance that participation in research is completely voluntary, and the necessity of informing the subjects about the nature of procedures prior to participation in the experiment. Although the guidelines do allow the use of deception, the experiment must be reviewed by an independent panel prior to its use—as must all research that uses human beings as subjects (Ceci, Peters, & Plotkin, 1985; Keith-Spiegel & Koocher, 1985).

Psychologists carrying out research on animals have their own set of guidelines to ensure that animals do not suffer. Moreover, there are federal regulations specifying how animals are to be housed, fed, and maintained. Because some research with important implications for solving human suffering—such as devising techniques for saving mentally disturbed patients who would otherwise starve themselves to death or finding new drugs and procedures to alleviate human pain and depression—cannot be ethically carried out on humans, guidelines permit the use of animals in such cases where the potential benefits clearly outweigh the costs (Gallup & Suarez, 1985; Miller, 1985b). Still, there are stringent regulations that prohibit researchers from inflicting unnecessary pain.

The Informed Consumer of Psychology: Distinguishing Good Psychology from Bad Psychology

Penetrate the Minds of Others—with Mind Prober! Psychologists agree that most of us conceal our fears, hopes, and inner desires from our closest friends, and even from ourselves! Now you can use the power of your personal computer to unlock those hidden truths about anyone in your life. With Mind Prober software, you'll gain useful, accurate insight into anyone you choose as a subject, and be able to use that information to improve your relationships. . . . Mind Prober is equally useful in your social and business lives. There is no limit to the number of people you may analyze. If you'd like to reveal hidden truths about people you know (or think you know), order Mind Prober today!

* * *

''Hello, this is Dr. Joy Browne on WITS,'' says the agreeable voice on the Boston radio station. ''Today we're having an open-line program. You can call in with any problem on any topic.'' The first call comes from Steve, who opens with ''Hi, Dr. Joy,'' and tells about his fainthearted attempts to re-establish contact with an old flame, now married. Dr. Joy analyzes Steve's problem as ''a classic case of approach-avoidance,'' advises him to stop being ''so tentative'' and to go ahead and ''play it by ear.'' She asks him to call back to ''let me know what happens.''

Jan, 19, calls to talk about her struggle with overeating, and to ask why her psychiatrist keeps probing her past relationships. Dr. Joy defends the traditional psychiatric approach, telling Jan, ''The issue may not be just your eating behavior, but your feelings about yourself.'' She leaves Jan with a cheerful ''don't give up on therapy, kid.''

The program breaks for commercials for Heinz ketchup and Kava instant coffee (Rice, 1981, p. 39).

* * *

To the left side of your brain, Saab turbocharging is a technological feat that retains good mileage while increasing performance.

To the right side of your brain, Saab turbocharging is what makes a Saab go like a bat out of hell . . .

The left side of your brain is your mother telling you that a Saab is good for you . . .

The right side of your brain guides your foot to the clutch, your hand to the gears, and listens for the ''zzzooomm.''

While con artists no longer sell magic elixirs and snake oil from the backs of horse-drawn carriages, their modern-day counterparts are still in business. This time though, rather than selling waters from the fountain of youth and the like, they are often hawking the secrets of psychology.

From advertisements to talk shows, we are bombarded daily by the media with information and misinformation about the field of psychology. We are told how to become smarter, happier, and better adjusted, and how to improve our lives by learning psychology's secrets.

Yet all psychology—and all psychologists—are not alike, and the quality of advice that psychologists and self-styled "experts" give varies widely. For this reason, there are several points to keep in mind when you evaluate information dispensed by people who claim to be representing the field:

- There's no free ride. If a way to actually learn while you sleep had already been invented, don't you think it would be in widespread use and not advertised in the back pages of magazines? If you could, in fact, buy a computer program that would really "unlock the hidden truths" about others, wouldn't you have heard about it already? And if your problems could be assessed, analyzed, and resolved in five minutes of radio air time, don't you think people would be clogging the phone lines with their calls, rather than spending thousands of dollars on treatment for their problems? The point is that difficult problems require complex solutions, and you should beware of simple, glib responses on how to resolve major difficulties.
- If advice that is dispensed by psychologists is accepted by a consumer, the consequences of following that advice should be critically monitored, evaluated, and—if necessary—modified to ensure that it is producing desirable effects. In the case of talk-show psychology, this almost never occurs; it is rare that we discover how well the advice that was dispensed in a given case worked. Both the people with the problems *and* the other listeners and viewers may be getting bad advice—but they never have any way of knowing without follow-up.
- No single psychologist or psychological method can solve all problems. The range of difficulties bound up with the human condition is so broad that no person can be an expert in all areas, and any individual or any method that purports to resolve all problems is making an inappropriate claim.

What Psychology Can Do for You Despite these cautions, the field of psychology has produced a wealth of important information that can be drawn upon for suggestions about every phase of people's lives. As we explained earlier in this chapter, one of the major goals of this book is to make you a more informed consumer of psychological knowledge by enhancing your ability to evaluate what psychologists have to offer. Ultimately, this book should provide you with the tools you need to critically evaluate the theories, research, and applications that psychologists have developed. In doing so, you will be able to appreciate the contributions that the field of psychology has made in improving the quality of human life.

RECAP AND REVIEW III

Recap

- Psychologists use theories and hypotheses to guide their research.
- In correlational research, the relationship between two variables is examined to determine whether or not they are associated, although cause-and-effect associations cannot be established.
- In a formal experiment—which is the only means of determining cause-and-effect associations—the relationship between factors is investigated by deliberately producing a change in one factor and observing change in the other.
- Threats to valid experiments include experimenter expectations and subject expectations.

Review

1. If we wanted to test our hunch that students who underline chapters as they read retain the information better than those who do not, we would first have to state this prediction in testable terms, that is, develop
   a. An experiment **b.** A theory **c.** A hypothesis **d.** A hunch

2. In our experiment on retention, we might want to deliberately produce a change in students' study habits to see if the change does have an effect on how long they remember facts. This process is known as the ______________________ ______________________.
3. We decide to perform our experiment on a large scale, with two groups. We arrange for one group to change their study habits; this group is called the ______________________ group. We arrange for another group to study as they always have; this group is called the ______________________ group.
4. The variable being measured in our experiment—retention of factual information—is called the ______________________ variable.
5. What if the students we assign to one group happen to be more intelligent or more motivated than those of the other group? That would certainly cloud our comparison. What procedure should we use to avoid such a problem?
6. We are concerned that some of the researchers we employ in our study might give subtle cues to subjects about how they should respond. This type of experimental bias is known as
   a. Experimenter expectations **b.** Subject expectations **c.** Demand characteristics **d.** The placebo effect
7. An experimenter knowingly administers a sugar pill to subjects in a control group so that both groups think they are being treated. This is called a double-blind procedure. True or false?
8. Other types of research are often conducted in psychology. Match each example at the right with the type of research it describes.

a. ____ Archival research

b. ____ Survey research

c. ____ Naturalistic observation

d. ____ Case study

1. Distributing a questionnaire to a group representing a larger population to assess attitudes on abortion

2. Interviewing a mass murderer and conducting psychological tests to determine the causes of such behavior

3. Reviewing existing records to confirm a hypothesis about the behavior of terrorists

4. Watching the interactions of young children in various nursery school settings to determine differences in social behavior

(Answers to review questions are on page 36.)

Psychology Looks Toward the 1990s
On the Frontlines of an Epidemic: AIDS and Psychology

It is 8 o'clock on the evening of November 21, 1991, and the president of the United States is on television. His mood is somber. "My fellow Americans," he says, "I want to talk to you tonight about one of the most dangerous public-health problems this nation has ever known—the disease we call AIDS. As you know, the AIDS epidemic is now killing nearly 60,000 Americans a year, placing enormous burdens on our system of medical care and creating tragic and bitter divisions in our society. Nearly a decade of intensive effort by medical science has failed to produce a preventive vaccine or a cure—and though we must not give up hope, we must now confront the growing threat of AIDS courageously and decisively.

Tomorrow I will ask Congress for new legislation to combat this national emergency. My program will include a substantial increase in funding for scientific and medical research. It will call for comprehensive reform of the structure and financing of the nation's health-care system. And it will confer wider legal authority on the National Commission on AIDS—specifically, the power to test the blood of any person believed to be afflicted with this dreadful disease. (Morganthau, 1986, p. 30).

No one can foretell whether this chilling scenario will become a reality. However, with no simple cure on the immediate horizon, acquired immune deficiency syndrome (AIDS) threatens not only to produce the greatest public health crisis in the 1990s, but potentially in the entire twentieth century. Transmitted only through sexual contact or by exposure to infected blood, AIDS has no cure and is ultimately fatal to those afflicted with it.

Psychologists working on several fronts have joined the battle against AIDS. Among the most important thrusts:

- Biopsychologists are considering drugs that may alleviate the symptoms of AIDS, lengthen the lives of those afflicted with the disease, prevent its spread, and, ultimately, cure it.
- Health psychologists have focused on ways in which sexual practices can be changed, fostering ''safe sex'' as a means of preventing the transmission of AIDS.
- Clinical and counseling psychologists are dealing with AIDS victims in several arenas. Some deal with the psychological difficulties associated with a disease that is viewed as incurable and invariably fatal and that often strikes people in the prime of their lives. Others deal with the distress brought about by the fears of people who are concerned that they will contract the disease from AIDS virus carriers and with the harsh measures that have been proposed to isolate AIDS victims. Still other clinical and counseling psychologists work with individuals who know from blood tests that they carry the virus, but have not yet acquired the disease itself. For these people, the uncertainty of whether they will actually contract the disease can be debilitating.
- Developmental psychologists are working with some of the most tragic cases of AIDS—infants and children who are victims of a virus that they contracted from mothers who had the disease. The problems of such children are usually compounded by the poverty of their families, which have often already broken apart due to drug abuse. In many cases, the mothers of children with AIDS die first, leaving the children to be cared for by relatives, hospitals, and foster mothers.
- Social psychologists are dealing with changing people's attitudes regarding AIDS. Their concerns range from modifying attitudes about sexual practices to fostering more accurate and realistic attitudes about the lack of danger in interacting with AIDS victims.

As yet, no definitive cure for AIDS has been found. However, there have been noticeable changes in sexual practices associated with the spread of the disease. People are less likely to engage in casual sex with new acquaintances, and the use of condoms during sexual intercourse has increased (Adler, 1985; McKusick, Horstman, & Coates, 1985).

Still, the magnitude of the AIDS epidemic makes it defy easy solution. United States experts project that by the end of 1991, the total number of cases of AIDS will reach 270,000, with 179,000 deaths occurring unless more effective treatments are found. In 1991 alone, some 54,000 deaths are likely to occur. And these figures are just for the United States: Worldwide, some 10 million people may already be infected, and by 1992, as many as 100 million people could be infected (Eckholm, 1987).

Looking into the 1990s, it appears that the only way to deal with the problem of AIDS is through the adoption of preventative measures. Because most cases of AIDS are related to sexual activity, psychologists and other health professionals have suggested ways for people to engage in safer sexual practices. Among the most important:

- Know your sexual partner—*well*. Sexual activity with someone whose sexual history is unfamiliar to you is risky. Before you enter into a sexual relationship with someone, be aware of his or her background.
- Avoid having multiple sexual partners or partners whose activities (such as drug addiction) put them into a high-risk group.
- Avoid the exchange of bodily fluids, particularly semen. Most experts recommend the avoidance of anal intercourse. The AIDS virus can spread through small tears in the rectum, making anal intercourse without using condoms particularly dangerous.
- Use condoms. Condoms are the most reliable means of preventing transmission of the AIDS virus.
- Consider the benefits of monogamy. People who are in long-term, monogamous relationships are not at risk (with the exception of intravenous drug users or those who have received a transfusion of blood that may have been contaminated).

Until a cure is found for AIDS, it will continue to have a profound effect on the world of the 1990s. And psychologists will remain at the forefront of the battle against the disease.

LOOKING BACK

1. Although the definition of psychology—the scientific study of behavior and mental processes—is clear-cut, it is also deceivingly simple, since ''behavior'' encompasses not just what people do, but their thoughts, feelings, perceptions, reasoning, memory, and biological activities.

2. Psychology has a number of major areas in which psychologists specialize. Biopsychologists focus on the biological basis of behavior, while experimental psychologists study the processes of sensing, perceiving, learning, and thinking about the world. Cognitive psychology, an outgrowth of experimental psychology, considers the study of higher mental processes, including thinking, language, memory, problem solving, knowing, reasoning, judging, and decision making.

3. The branches of psychology that study change and individual differences are developmental and personality psychology. Developmental psychologists study how people grow and change throughout their life span. Personality psychologists consider the consistency and change in an individual's behavior as he or she moves through different situations, as well as the individual differences that distinguish one person's behavior from another's when each is placed in the same situation.

4. Health, clinical, and counseling psychologists are primarily concerned with promoting physical and mental health. Health psychologists study psychological factors that affect physical disease, while clinical psychologists consider the study, diagnosis, and treatment of abnormal behavior. Counseling psychologists focus on educational, social, and career adjustment problems.

5. Educational psychologists investigate how the educational process affects students, while school psychologists specialize in assessing and treating children in elementary and secondary schools who have academic or emotional problems.

6. Social psychology is the study of how people's thoughts, feelings, and actions are affected by others. Industrial-organizational psychologists focus on how psychology can be applied to the workplace, while environmental psychologists explore the relationship between people and their physical environment.

7. Psychologists are employed in a variety of settings. Although the primary employment sites are universities and colleges, many psychologists are found in hospitals, clinics, community mental-health centers, and counseling centers. Many also have practices in which they treat patients privately.

ANSWERS TO REVIEW QUESTIONS

Review III: **1.** c **2.** Experimental manipulation **3.** Treatment, control **4.** Dependent **5.** Random assignment to condition **6.** a **7.** False **8.** a.-3, b.-1, c.-4, d.-2

8. Psychology was begun by Wundt in Germany. Early conceptual models that guided the work of psychologists were structuralism, functionalism, and gestalt psychology. Structuralism focused on identifying the fundamental elements of the mind, largely by using introspection. Functionalism concentrated on the functions played by mental activities, while gestalt psychology focused on the study of how perception is organized into meaningful units. Modern-day psychologists rely primarily on five models: the biological, psychodynamic, cognitive, behavioral, and humanistic models.

9. The biological model focuses on the biological functioning of people and animals, reducing behavior to its most basic components. The psychodynamic model takes a very different approach; it suggests that there are powerful, unconscious inner forces about which people have little or no awareness and which are primarily determinants of behavior.

10. Cognitive approaches to behavior consider how people know, understand, and think about the world. Growing out of early work on introspection and later work by the gestaltists and functionalists, cognitive models study how people understand and represent the world within themselves.

11. Behavioral models deemphasize internal processes and concentrate instead on observable behavior. They suggest that an understanding and control of a person's environment is sufficient to fully explain and modify behavior.

12. Humanistic models are the newest of the major models of psychology. They emphasize that humans are uniquely inclined toward psychological growth and higher levels of functioning, that human beings will strive to reach their full potential.

13. Three major trends seem to be emerging in terms of the future of psychology. Psychology will become increasingly specialized, new models will emerge, and there will be increasing emphasis on applications of psychological knowledge.

14. Research in psychology is guided by theories (broad explanations and predictions of phenomena of interest) and hypotheses (derivations of theories that are predictions stated in a way that allows them to be tested).

15. The case study represents an in-depth interview and examination of one person, while archival research uses existing records such as old newspapers or other documents to confirm a hypothesis. In naturalistic observation, the investigator mainly acts as an observer, making no change in a naturally occurring situation. In survey research, people are asked a series of questions about their behavior, thoughts, or attitudes. These techniques rely on correlational studies, which describe associations between various factors but cannot determine cause-and-effect relationships.

16. In a formal experiment, the relationship between factors is investigated by deliberately producing a change—called the experimental manipulation—in one of them and observing the change in the other. The factors that are changed are called variables, behaviors or events that are capable of change and can take on two or more levels. In order to test a hypothesis, it must be operationalized: The abstract concepts of the hypothesis are translated into the actual procedures used in the study.

17. In an experiment, at least two groups must be compared with each other in order to assess cause-and-effect relationships. The group receiving the treatment (the special procedure devised by the experimenter) is the treatment group, while the second group (which receives no treatment) is the control group. There also may be multiple treatment groups, each of which is subjected to a different procedure and can then be compared with the others. The variable that is manipulated is the independent variable; the variable that is measured and expected to change as a result of manipulation of the independent variable is called the dependent variable.

18. In a formal experiment, subjects must be assigned to treatment conditions randomly. This allows subject characteristics to be evenly distributed across the different treatment conditions.

19. Experiments are subject to a number of threats, called experimental bias. Experimenter effects occur when an experimenter unintentionally transmits cues to subjects about his or her expectations regarding their behavior in a given experimental condition. Subject expectations can also bias an experiment. To help eliminate bias, researchers use placebos and double-blind procedures.

20. Informed use of psychology requires that consumers be aware that answers to psychological problems are complex, that advice offered by psychologists should be monitored and evaluated, and that no single method is a cure-all for every difficulty.

KEY TERMS AND CONCEPTS

psychology (p. 4)
biopsychology (p. 8)
experimental psychology (p. 8)
cognitive psychology (p. 8)
developmental psychology (p. 8)
personality psychology (p. 9)
health psychology (p. 9)
clinical psychology (p. 9)
counseling psychology (p. 10)
educational psychology (p. 10)
school psychology (p. 10)
social psychology (p. 10)
industrial-organizational psychology (p. 10)
environmental psychology (p. 10)
forensic psychology (p. 10)
consumer psychology (p. 10)
program evaluation (p. 11)
models (p. 14)
structuralism (p. 15)
introspection (p. 15)
functionalism (p. 15)
gestalt psychology (p. 15)
biological models (p. 16)
psychodynamic models (p. 17)
cognitive models (p. 17)
behavioral models (p. 17)
humanistic models (p. 18)
free will (p. 18)
theories (p. 22)
hypotheses (p. 22)
research (p. 22)
operationalization (p. 23)
case study (p. 23)
archival research (p. 23)
naturalistic observation (p. 23)

survey research (p. 24)
correlational research (p. 24)
experiment (p. 26)
experimental manipulation (p. 26)
variable (p. 26)
treatment (p. 26)
treatment group (p. 26)
control group (p. 26)
independent variable (p. 27)
dependent variable (p. 27)
random assignment to condition (p. 27)
experimental bias (p. 28)
experimenter expectations (p. 28)
subject expectations (p. 29)
placebo (p. 29)
double-blind procedure (p. 29)
confederate (p. 30)
replication (p. 31)

FOR FURTHER STUDY AND APPLICATION

American Psychological Association. (1980). *Careers in psychology.* Washington, DC: American Psychological Association.

This booklet, which can be obtained free of charge by writing to the American Psychological Association at 1200 17th Street, N.W., Washington, DC 20036, provides a clear overview of the many roles that psychologists play. It also discusses some of the possibilities for students who are interested in pursuing a career in psychology.

Schultz, D. (1981). *A history of modern psychology* (3rd ed.). New York: Academic Press.

This is a well-written, comprehensive view of the background of modern psychology.

Martin, D. W. (1985). *Doing psychology experiments* (2nd ed.). Monterey, CA: Brooks/Cole.

This is a fine introduction to the ins and outs of doing research in psychology. After reading this book, you should be in a position to carry out simple psychological experiments on your own.

Grash, A. F. (1983). *Practical applications of psychology.* Boston: Little, Brown.

This volume is devoted to taking the theories and research of psychology and applying them to everyday life. By looking through this book you can get a feel for the many contributions that psychology has made.

PART TWO

PART TWO

THE BIOLOGICAL FOUNDATIONS OF PSYCHOLOGY

This part of the book takes us into many worlds. We encounter a 35-year-old man who suffers from tremors that rack his body five times a second and his surgeon who is about to carry out a pioneering operation on the man's brain. And we will be led into the lives of a woman racked with excruciating pain and of a boy who is incapable of experiencing any pain at all.

As you will find in the next two chapters, psychologists have explored how the biological structures and functions of the body affect behavior. We will see how the brain and nervous system work together to affect every aspect of our psychological lives. We will find out how the body takes in information through its sense organs, and how such information is understood and interpreted.

In Chapter 2, the focus is on the relationship between behavior and the brain, the nervous system, and other biological structures.

In Chapter 3, we discuss how our bodies are able to incorporate and use outside stimuli and information, and then we turn to the ways in which we perceive and organize the world.

CHAPTER 2

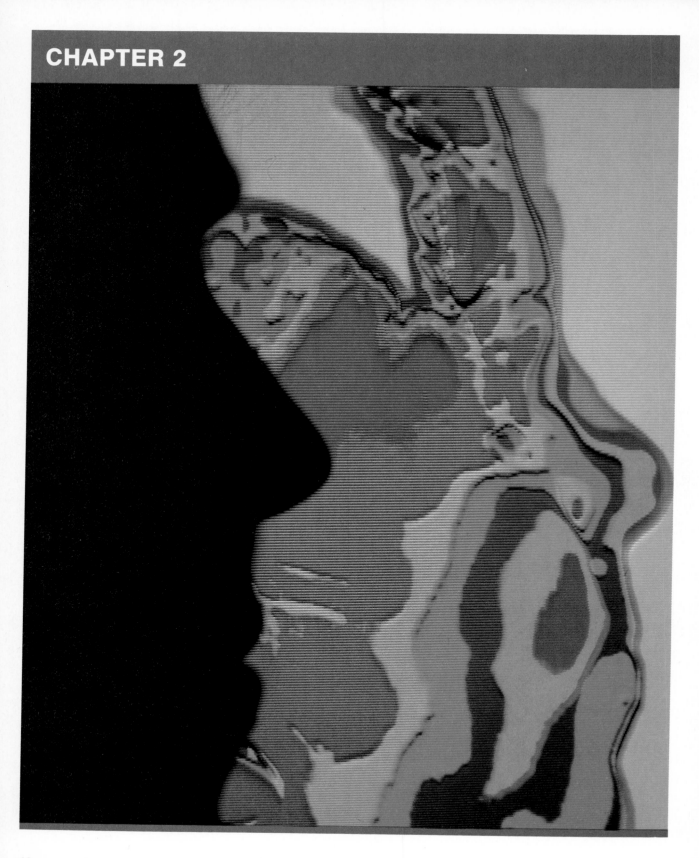

THE BIOLOGY UNDERLYING BEHAVIOR

PROLOGUE

LOOKING AHEAD

THE BASICS OF BEHAVIOR: THE NEURONS AND THE NERVOUS SYSTEM
Beginning with the basics: The neuron
The smoking gun: Firing the neuron
Recap and review I
Bridging the gap: Where neuron meets neuron

STRINGING NEURONS TOGETHER: THE NERVOUS SYSTEM
The near and far: Central and peripheral nervous systems
Emergency!: Activating the autonomic nervous system
Recap and review II

TYING IT ALL TOGETHER: THE BRAIN
THE CUTTING EDGE. Looking at the Brain—from the Outside In
Exploring and mapping the brain: Discovering the old brain and the new brain
Of chemicals and glands: The endocrine system
Passing the border between the old brain and the new brain: The limbic system
Recap and review III

THE NEW BRAIN: THE CEREBRAL CORTEX
The motor area of the brain
The sensory area of the brain
THE CUTTING EDGE. The Brain Transplant: Solving Old Problems—and Creating New Ones?
The association area of the brain

TWO BRAINS OR ONE?: THE SPECIALIZATION OF THE HEMISPHERES
TRY IT ! Using Your Left and Right Brains
PSYCHOLOGY AT WORK. Probing the Brain on Madison Avenue
Understanding the two hemispheres: Split-brain patients
The informed consumer of psychology: Learning to control your heart—and brain—through biofeedback
TRY IT! Biofeedback on Your Own
Recap and review IV
PSYCHOLOGY LOOKS TOWARD THE 1990s. Using the brain as a diagnostic device: Neurometrics

LOOKING BACK

KEY TERMS AND CONCEPTS

FOR FURTHER STUDY AND APPLICATION

PROLOGUE

He was like a caged bird, flapping his wings in a futile effort to escape his entrapment. But Raymond Walker was a 35-year-old man who suffered from what seemed to be an incurable case of Parkinson's disease.

The symptoms had first appeared when he was 19 years old and had now progressed to the stage in which his arms and legs shook rhythmically at a rate of five times a second. He had almost no voluntary control of his muscles. His movements were so severe that his hospital bed—which, with its sides constantly up to keep Walker from heaving himself to the floor, acted like a kind of prison—shook violently along with his diseased body.

On rare occasions, though, he was able to move voluntarily. When overcome by strong emotion, his shaking temporarily stopped. Walker used these unusual occasions to attempt suicide, once thrusting his head through a window and trying to cut his throat on the broken glass.

Was there any hope for this unfortunate man? After trying all other standard treatments, such as the use of drugs, neurosurgeon Irving Cooper saw only one possibility left. What had caused Walker's problem in the first place was a virus that had fed on certain nerve cells in his brain. Acting first on just a few cells and later spreading to more and more, the virus short-circuited critical cells that controlled Walker's muscles. In the words of Cooper, "The information the diseased nerve cells passed on to other nerve centers became either deficient or erroneous. By the time the messages from these centers reached Raymond's muscles, they were hopelessly distorted. The transmission of information to his muscles became like static on a telephone cable. To the muscles, the nerves said, 'Contract, contract, contract,' and they endlessly contracted, locking Raymond into his own body" (Cooper, 1976, p. 51).

Cooper's cure was based on this premise: If the blood supply to the diseased area of the brain could be terminated, the rampaging, out-of-control cells would die, and the body could potentially return to its normal means of functioning, free of tremors and shaking.

In a series of operations that had never before been performed, he opened Walker's skull, cut into his brain, and severed two tiny vessels—the anterior choroidal arteries—each less than one-sixteenth of an inch in diameter. This seemingly simple procedure brought dramatic results. At the conclusion of the operations, Walker's trembling stopped completely; he was able to control his movements; his facial expressions, which had previously been frozen into a cadaverlike pose, returned to normal. As the result of two minute cuts within the brain, Walker became, literally, a new man. Within a few weeks of his discharge from the hospital, this person who had been institutionalized for some fifteen years had found a job and had begun to reclaim his life.

LOOKING AHEAD

The results of the operation performed on Raymond Walker are no less than miraculous. But the greater miracle rests on the object of the surgical procedure: the brain itself. As we shall see in this chapter, the brain, an organ roughly half the size of a loaf of bread, controls our behavior through every waking and sleeping moment. The brain and its pathways extending throughout the body compose the human **nervous system**. Our movements, thoughts, hopes, aspirations, dreams—the very awareness that we are human—are all intimately related to this system.

Nervous system: *The brain and its pathways extending throughout the body*

Because of the importance of the nervous system in controlling behavior and because of the fact that when we consider human beings at their most basic level we are considering biological entities, psychologists have paid special attention to the biological underpinnings of behavior. One group of psychologists—known as **biopsychologists**—specialize in considering the ways in which the biological structures and functions of the body affect behavior. Biopsychologists seek to answer questions such as these: What are the bases for voluntary and involuntary operation of the body? How are messages communicated from one part of the body to another? What is the physical structure of the brain, and how does this structure affect behavior? Can the causes of psychological disorders be traced to biological factors, and how can such disorders be treated?

Biopsychologists: *Psychologists who study the ways biological structures and body functions affect behavior*

These questions and others are addressed in this chapter, which focuses on those biological structures of the body that are most closely related to the interests of biopsychologists. Initially, we discuss nerve cells, called neurons, and the nervous system, which allow messages to travel from one part of the body to another. We will see that through their growing knowledge of neurons and the nervous system, psychologists are increasing their understanding of human behavior and are uncovering important clues in their efforts to cure certain kinds of diseases. The structure and main divisions of the nervous system are then presented, with explanations of how they work to control voluntary and involuntary behaviors and how the various parts of the nervous system operate together in emergency situations to produce life-saving responses to danger.

Next, we consider the brain itself, examining its major structures and the ways in which these affect behavior. We see how the brain controls movement, the five senses, and our thought processes. We also consider the fascinating notion that the two halves of the brain may operate independently of each other.

As we discuss the biological characteristics that are of interest to biopsychologists, it is important to keep in mind the basic rationale for doing so: Our understanding of human behavior cannot be complete without knowledge of the fundamentals of the brain and the rest of the nervous system. As we shall see, much of our behavior—our moods, motivations, goals, and desires—has a good deal to do with our biological makeup.

In sum, after reading and studying this chapter you will be able to

- Describe the basic element of the nervous system, the neuron
- Explain how neurons are activated, and how they pass electrical and chemical messages from one to another
- Identify ways in which understanding the nervous system has applications in the relief of disease and pain
- Describe how neurons are tied together into the larger structures of the nervous system, and identify those structures
- Identify the major parts of the brain and the behaviors for which the parts are responsible
- Describe how the two halves of the brain may operate independently, and discuss evidence regarding similarities and dissimilarities in their functioning
- Define and apply the key terms and concepts listed at the end of the chapter

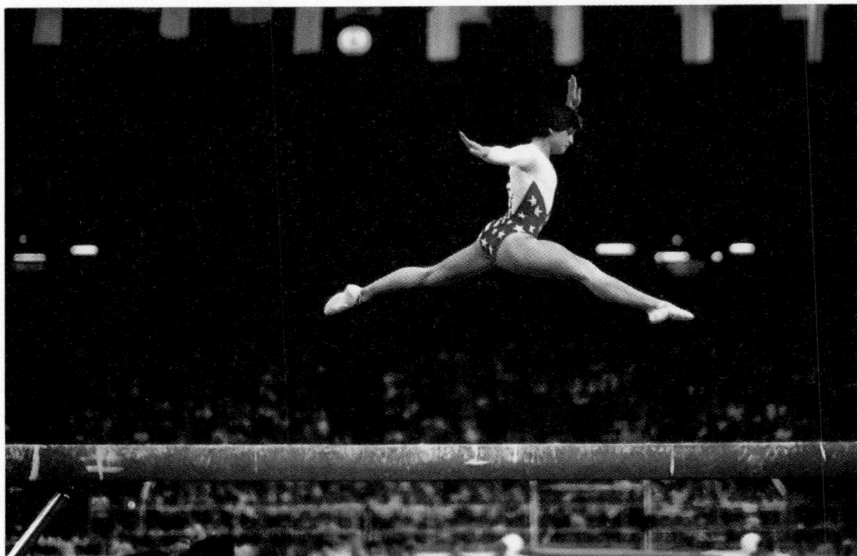

The sophistication of the human nervous system allows Olympic star Mary Lou Retton to carry out complex maneuvers flawlessly. (*G. Rancinan/Sygma*)

THE BASICS OF BEHAVIOR: THE NEURONS AND THE NERVOUS SYSTEM

When Olympic-gold-medal-winner Mary Lou Retton carries out the "Retton flip," a series of somersaults and handstands on the uneven parallel bar, she knows that one small deviation from her careful routine is enough to bring her crashing to the ground, introducing the possibility of a crippling injury or even death. Yet time after time she is able to carry out the dangerous maneuvers flawlessly, as her muscles shape and power her body into the exact position necessary to carry them out.

The precision with which Mary Lou Retton is able to move is a testament to the complexity—and wondrous abilities—of the human nervous system. To understand how the nervous system is able to provide such precise control over the body, we must begin by describing the most basic parts of the nervous system and consider the way in which nerve impulses are transmitted throughout the human body.

Beginning with the Basics: The Neuron

While the ability to throw a discus, run a mile, or hit a tennis ball depends, at one level, on muscle coordination, if we consider *how* the muscles involved in such activities are activated, we see that there are also more basic processes involved. It is necessary for the body to be able to provide messages to the muscles in order to coordinate them and produce the complex movements that characterize successful physical activity.

Neurons (NOOR onz): *The basic elements of the nervous system that carry messages*

Such messages are passed through specialized cells called **neurons**, the basic elements of the nervous system. Their quantity is staggering; there are between 100 billion and 200 billion neurons in the brain alone. Although there are several types of neurons, each has a similar basic structure, as illustrated in Figures 2-1 and 2-2 (Levy, Anderson, & Lehmkuhle, 1984).

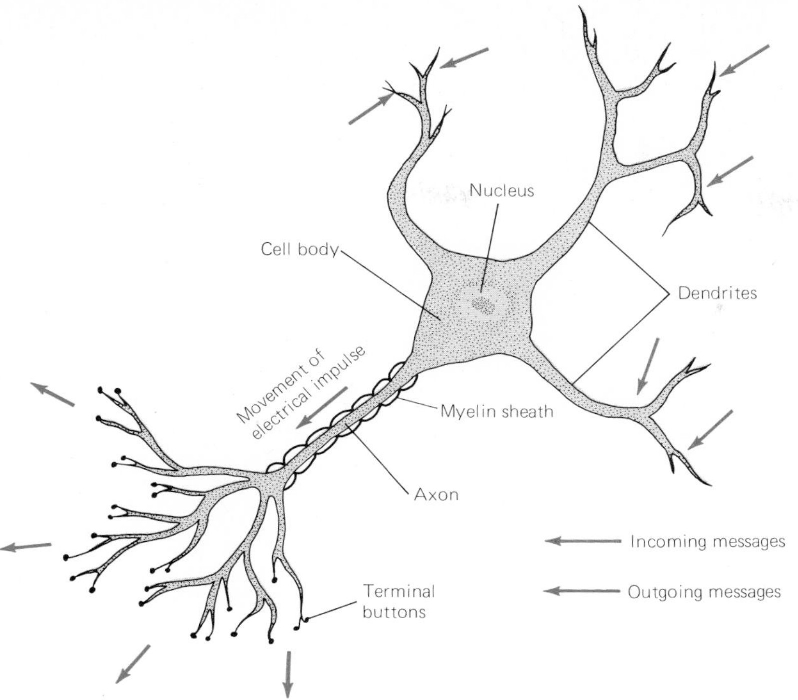

Figure 2-1
The primary components of the specialized cell called the neuron, the basic element of the nervous system.

Unique among all the body's cells, neurons have a distinctive feature: the ability to communicate with other cells. As you can see in Figure 2-1, neurons have a cluster of fibers called **dendrites** at one end; it is from these fibers, which look like the twisted branches of a tree, that they receive messages from other neurons. At the opposite end, neurons have a long, slim, tubelike extension called an **axon**, which carries messages destined for other cells through the neuron. As you can see, the axon is considerably longer than the rest of the neuron; most are 1 to 2 inches long, though some may reach 3 feet in length. In contrast, the remainder of the neuron is only a fraction of the size of the axon. (The scale drawing of the neuron in Figure 2-3 illustrates the relative proportions of the various parts.) Finally, at the end of the axons are small

Dendrites: *Fibers at one end of a neuron that receive messages from other neurons*

Axon: *A long, slim, tubelike extension from the end of a neuron that carries messages*

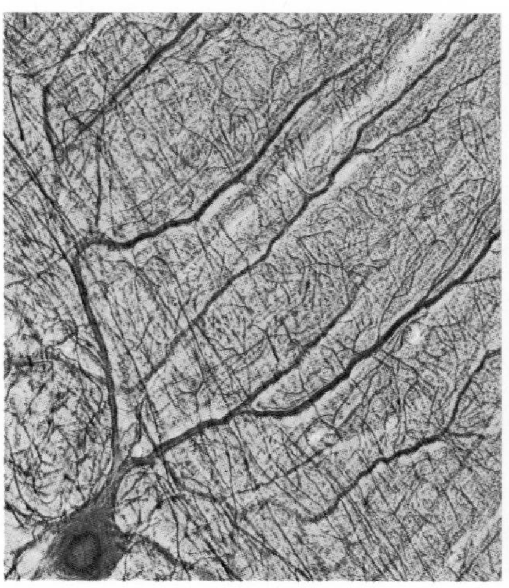

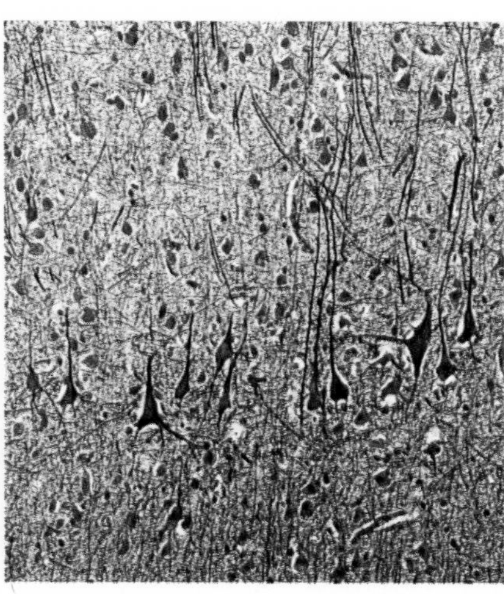

Figure 2-2
These two photographs, made with an electron microscope, show (*a*) a single neuron and (*b*) a group of interconnected neurons in the cerebral cortex, a part of the brain. [(*a*) *Manfred Kage/ Peter Arnold, Inc.*; (*b*) *Michael Abbey/ Photo Researchers, Inc.*]

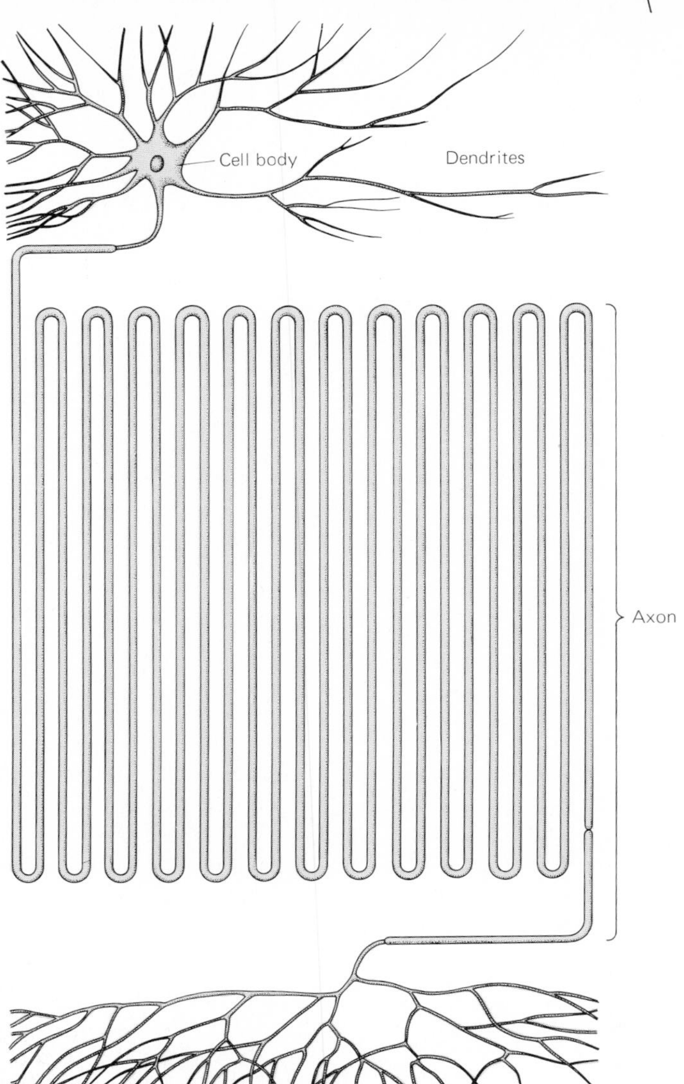

Figure 2-3
This drawing of a neuron, enlarged 250 times, shows the proportions of its various parts. As you can see, the axon, which is folded so that it can fit within the diagram, is considerably longer than the other parts of the neuron. (*Stevens, 1979, p. 56.*)

Terminal buttons: *Small branches at the end of an axon that relay messages to other cells*

branches called **terminal buttons** through which messages are relayed to other cells.

The messages that travel through the neuron are electrical in nature. They generally move across neurons as if they were traveling on a one-way street, following a route that begins with the dendrites, continuing in the cell body, and leading ultimately down the tubelike extension, the axon.

Myelin sheath (MY uh lin SHEETH): *An axon's protective coating, made of fat and protein*

In order to prevent messages from short-circuiting one another, it is necessary for the axons to be insulated in some fashion (analogous to the way electric wires must be insulated). In most cases, this is done with a protective coating known as the **myelin sheath**, made up of a series of specialized cells of fat and protein that wrap themselves around the axon. The critical nature of the myelin sheath is illustrated by the severe sensory and movement difficulties encountered by people who suffer from multiple sclerosis, a disease in which there is a loss of myelin cells. People with the disease may be unable to walk, have vision difficulties, and show general muscle impairment.

Although the electric impulse always moves across the neuron in a dendrite-to-cell body-to-axon sequence, recent research shows that substances travel within parts of the neuron in the opposite direction (Schmeck, 1984). For instance, axons allow a reverse flow toward the cell body, whereby chemical substances needed for the nourishment of the cell are brought into the cell nucleus. Certain diseases, such as amyotrophic lateral sclerosis (ALS), or Lou Gehrig's disease (named for its most famous victim), may be caused by the inability of the neuron to transport vital materials in this reverse direction, eventually causing the neuron to figuratively die from starvation. Similarly, rabies is caused by the transmission of the rabies poison by reverse flow along the axon from the terminal buttons.

The movement of material along the dendrite is also multidirectional; rather than always transmitting information from other neurons to the cell body, the dendrites sometimes "leak" information away from the neuron. In fact, scientists now suspect that epilepsy, the disorder in which a person suffers from periodic convulsions, may be caused by leakage from the neurons, making the neurons prone to discharging built-up electric energy in an uncontrolled manner.

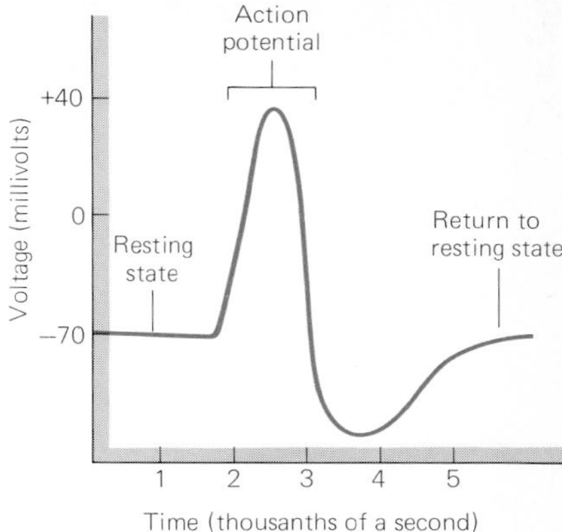

Figure 2-4
Changes in the electrical charge of a neuron during the passage of an action potential. In its normal resting state, a neuron has a negative charge of around −70 millivolts. When an action potential is triggered, however, the cell charge becomes positive, increasing to about +40 millivolts. Following the passage of the action potential, the charge becomes even more negative than its typical state. It is not until the charge returns to its resting potential that the neuron will be fully ready to be triggered once again.

The Smoking Gun: Firing the Neuron

Just as with the action of a gun, a neuron either fires or doesn't fire; there is nothing in between. Pulling harder on the trigger is not going to make the bullet travel faster or more surely. Similarly, neurons follow an **all-or-nothing law**: they are either on or off; once triggered beyond a certain point, they will fire. When they are off—that is, in a **resting state**—there is a typical electric charge of about −70 millivolts within the neuron (a mullivolt is one-thousandth of a volt). This charge is caused by the presence of more negatively charged ions or molecules within the neuron than outside it. You might think of the neuron as one of the poles of a miniature battery, with the inside of the neuron representing the negative pole and the outside of the neuron the positive pole.

However, when a message arrives from another neuron, the cell walls allow the entry of positively charged ions, which in turn permits the charge within that part of the cell to change momentarily from negative to positive. When the charge reaches a critical level, the "trigger" is pulled, and an electric nerve impulse, known as an **action potential**, then travels down the neuron (see Figure 2-4).

All-or-nothing law: *The principle governing the state of neurons, which are either on (firing) or off (resting)*
Resting state: *The nonfiring state of a neuron when the charge equals about −70 millivolts*
Action potential: *An electric nerve impulse that travels through a neuron when it is set off by a "trigger," changing the cell's charge from negative to positive*

The action potential moves from one end of the neuron to the other like a flame moves across a fuse toward an explosive. As the impulse moves toward the end of the neuron, the movement of ions causes a sequential change in charge from positive to negative along the cell (see Figure 2-5). After the passage of the impulse, positive ions are pumped out of the neuron, and the neuron charge returns to negative.

Just after an action potential has passed, the neuron cannot be fired again—it is in its **absolute refractory period**. It is as if the gun has to be reloaded after each shot. There is also a **relative refractory period** in which it is more difficult than usual to fire the neuron. During this period, although an impulse can pass through the neuron, it takes a stronger stimulus to set it off than if the neuron had been given sufficient time to reach its normal resting potential. Eventually, though, the neuron returns to its resting state and is ready to be fired once again.

Absolute refractory period: *The period following the triggering of a neuron in which the neuron recovers and prepares for another impulse*
Relative refractory period: *The period during which a neuron, not yet having returned to its resting state, requires more than the normal stimulus to be set off*

These complex events occur at speeds that vary with the function and structure of the neuron. Some neurons can fire as many as 500 times per second, while

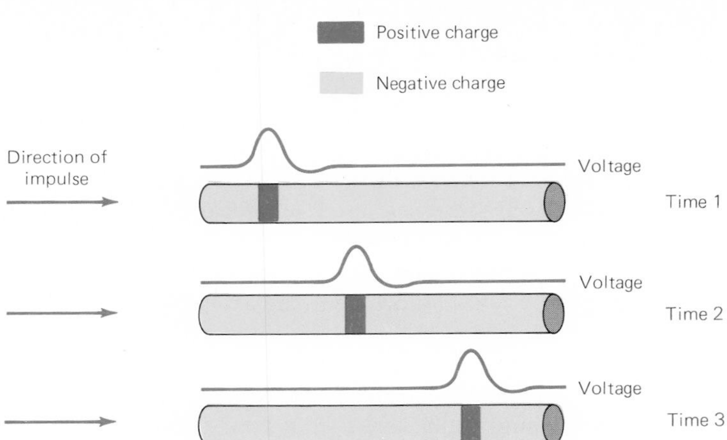

Figure 2-5
Movement of an action potential across a neuron can be seen in this series of three drawings. Just prior to time 1, positively charged ions enter the cell walls, changing the charge within that part of the cell from negative to positive. The action potential is thus triggered, traveling down the neuron, as illustrated in the changes occurring from time 1 to time 3 (from top to bottom in these drawings). Following the passage of the action potential, positive ions are pumped out of the neuron, restoring its charge to negative. The change in voltage illustrated at the top of each neuron is better seen in the more detailed graph in Figure 2-4.

others take longer. The speed at which impulses travel is a function of the size of the neuron; neurons with small diameters carry impulses at about 8 feet per second, while longer and thicker ones can average speeds that are forty times faster.

RECAP AND REVIEW I

Recap

- Neurons are the basic elements of the nervous system; they allow the transmission of messages that coordinate the complex activities of the human body.
- All neurons have a similar basic structure: They receive messages through the dendrites and transmit them through the axon to other neurons.
- Neurons fire according to an all-or-nothing law; they are either firing or resting.

Review

1. The specialized cells that function as the basic element of the nervous system are called ______.
2. Clusters of fibers transmitting messages to the neuron are called ______.
3. As if delivering a letter from the hand of the mail carrier to the recipient, the ______ ______ make the final relay of messages to other cells.
4. The sensory movement disabilities suffered by individuals with multiple sclerosis are due to a loss of cells in the
a. Axon **b.** Dendrite **c.** Myelin sheath **d.** Terminal buttons
5. Electric impulses and chemical substances both travel through the neuron in a dendrite-cell body-axon sequence. True or false? ______
6. The electric nerve impulse which travels down a neuron is called a(n) ______ ______.
7. Electric movement through the neuron is analogous to a light which can be dimmed or intensified by a wall switch; that is, the charge may fluctuate in intensity. True or false?
8. A stronger stimulus than usual is needed to set off an electrical impulse in the neuron during the
a. Relative refractory period **b.** Action potential period **c.** Absolute refractory period **d.** Resting state

(Answers to review questions are on page 53)

Bridging the Gap: Where Neuron Meets Neuron

Have you ever put together a radio kit? If you have, you probably remember that the manufacturer supplied you with wires that had to be painstakingly connected to one another or to some other component of the radio; every piece had to be physically connected to something else.

The human body is considerably more sophisticated than a radio; it has evolved a neural transmission system in which there is sometimes no need for a structural connection between its parts. Instead, it relies on a chemical connection to bridge the gap—known as a *synapse*—between two neurons (see Figure 2-6). When a nerve impulse comes to the end of the axon and reaches a terminal button, it secretes a chemical called a **neurotransmitter**. Neurotransmitters carry various sorts of chemical messages across the synapse to the dendrite of a receiver neuron. Although messages travel in electrical form *within* neurons, they move *between* neurons using a chemical transmission system.

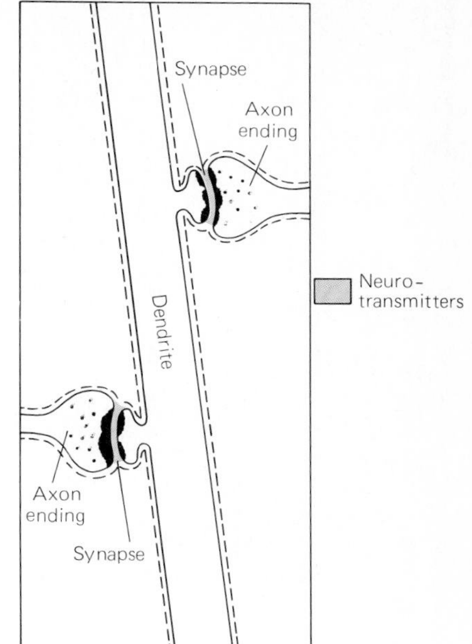

Figure 2-6
A typical synapse, the junction between an axon and dendrite. The gap between the axon and dendrite is bridged by chemicals called neurotransmitters.

The chemical message arriving from a neuron is basically one of two types: excitatory or inhibitory. An **excitatory message** "tells" the receiving neuron to fire, thereby making it more likely that an action potential will travel down the axons. An **inhibitory message**, in contrast, does just the opposite; it prevents or decreases the likelihood that the receiving neuron will fire.

Because the dendrites of a neuron receive many messages simultaneously, some of which are excitatory and some inhibitory, the neuron must integrate the messages in some fashion. It does this through a kind of summation process; if the number of excitatory messages outweighs the number of inhibitory ones, an action potential will occur. On the other hand, if the number of inhibitory messages outweigh the excitatory ones, nothing will happen. The neuron will remain in its resting state.

Varieties of Neurotransmitters There are many different sorts of neurotransmitters that produce excitation of inhibition at different rates and different strengths. Moreover, at any given synapse there may be more than one type of neurotransmitter signaling to other neurons.

Neurotransmitter (noor o TRANZ mit tur): *A chemical, secreted when a nerve impulse comes to the end of an axon, that carries messages between neurons*
Excitatory message: *A chemical secretion that "tells" a receiving neuron to fire*
Inhibitory message: *A chemical secretion that prevents a receiving neuron from firing*
Acetylcholine (a see tul KO leen) **(ACh)**: *A common neurotransmitter that produces contractions of skeletal muscles*

One of the most common neurotransmitters is **acetylcholine**, usually called by its chemical symbol, **ACh** (Blusztajn & Wurtman, 1983). ACh produces contractions of skeletal muscles—accounting for the deadliness of the black widow spider, whose venom causes the continuous release of ACh, eventually killing the victim through muscle spasms. ACh is also related to the drug called curare, used by South American Indians in their poison arrows. Curare blocks reception of ACh, thereby paralyzing the skeletal muscles and ultimately producing death by suffocation, since the victim is unable to breathe. On the brighter side, the study of ACh has helped provide knowledge regarding such medical conditions as myasthenia gravis, a disease in which there is gradual loss of muscle control. Specifically, treatments have been devised in which drugs can be administered to prevent the destruction of ACh by the body, thereby allowing the normal transmission of impulses across the synapses.

Dopamine (DOPE uh meen) **(DA)**: *A common neurotransmitter that inhibits certain neurons and excites others*

Another major neurotransmitter is **dopamine (DA)**, which has an inhibitory effect on some neurons and an excitatory effect on others, such as those of the heart. The ingestion of certain drugs has a marked effect on dopamine release, and this has led to the development of effective treatments for a wide variety of both physical and mental ailments. For instance, Parkinson's disease (the severe medical problem of Raymond Walker, whose case was discussed at the start of the chapter) seems to be caused by a deficiency of dopamine in the brain. Drugs have been developed to stimulate the production of dopamine, and they have proved highly effective in reducing the symptoms of Parkinson's in many patients. Similarly, researchers have hypothesized that certain mental disturbances, such as schizophrenia, are affected or perhaps even caused by the

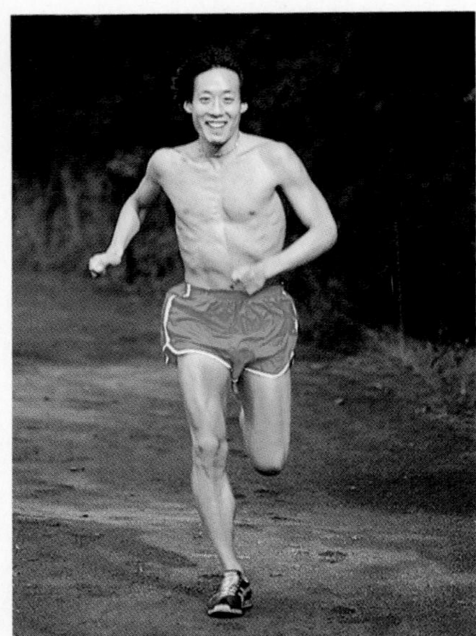

A "runner's high" may occur from the release of endorphins, a kind of natural painkiller, in the brain. (© *Jim Anderson/ Woodfin Camp & Assoc.*)

overproduction of dopamine, and drugs that suppress dopamine production have been successful in reducing abnormal behavior in people diagnosed as schizophrenic—as we will discuss further when we consider abnormal behavior and its treatment in Chapters 12 and 13.

Stopping the Pain and Feeling Good: Endorphins

Unless he was jogging, David Bartlett was a quiet, unassuming person. Most people who knew him tended to think of him as an introvert. But when he jogged, a noticeable change seemed to come over David. By the time he finished his daily 5- or 6-mile run he was excited, happy—even euphoric at times—and talkative. Anyone who was with David after a run noticed the change. In fact, some of his friends joked about it, saying that he acted as if he were "high" on something he had taken while he was out running.

What happened to David Bartlett when he was jogging? Given our current discussion, you might suspect that his behavior related to a neurotransmitter—an explanation that appears well founded.

The specific neurotransmitter involved is likely to be an endorphin. **Endorphins** are chemicals produced by the body that interact with a particular kind of neuron called an **opiate receptor**. Opiate receptors act to reduce the experience of pain, and in fact many painkilling drugs, such as morphine, are used to activate the opiate receptors. Endorphins are a kind of "natural" morphine produced by the body to reduce pain. For instance, people who are afflicted with diseases that produce long-term, severe pain often develop large concentrations of endorphins in their brains—suggesting an attempt by the body to control the pain (Watkins & Mayer, 1982).

Endorphins (en DOR fins): *Chemicals produced by the body that interact with an opiate receptor to reduce pain*

Opiate (O PEE ut) **receptor**: *A neuron that acts to reduce the experience of pain*

Endorphins, mimicking the effects of morphine and other opiates, may go even further than mere pain reduction: They may also produce the kind of euphoric feelings that jogger David Bartlett experienced after running. It is possible that the amount of exercise and perhaps even the pain involved in a long run stimulate the production of endorphins—ultimately resulting in what has been called a "runner's high" (Hathaway, 1984).

Endorphin release may also explain other phenomena that have long puzzled psychologists, such as the reasons that acupuncture and placebos—pills that contain no actual drugs but which patients *believe* will make them better—are sometimes effective in reducing pain (Bolles & Fanselow, 1982). Specifically, it is possible that acupuncture and placebos both act to release endorphins, thereby bringing about positive results. The study of endorphins may also help biopsychologists to develop new, more effective painkillers based on the natural functions of the body. This work, now in progress, clearly illustrates the relevance of fundamental biological processes to everyday behavior, and demonstrates why psychologists must consider explanations of behavior that range from the biological to the social.

STRINGING NEURONS TOGETHER: THE NERVOUS SYSTEM

Given the complexity of individual neurons and the neurotransmission process, it should come as no surprise that the structures formed by the neurons are likewise complicated in their own right. However, there is a certain logic—even

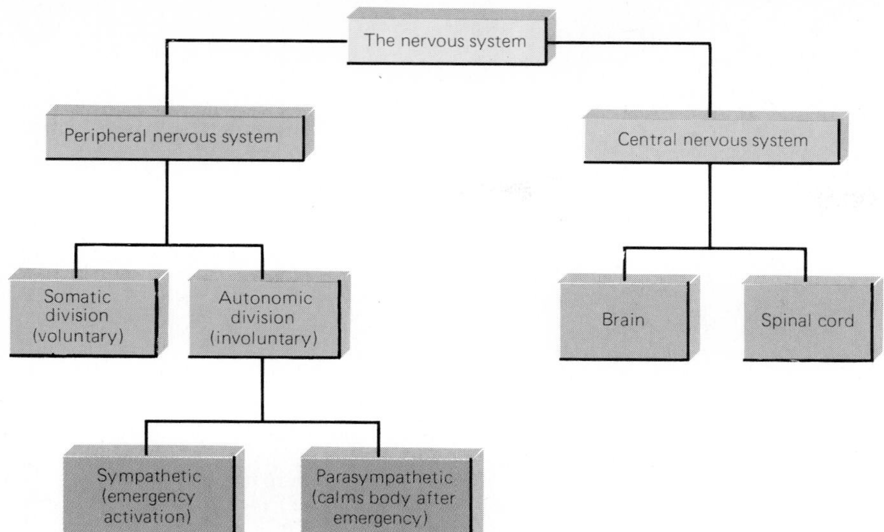

Figure 2-7
A schematic diagram of the relationship of the parts of the nervous system.

an elegance—to the human nervous system. To see this, consider Figure 2-7, which offers a general overview of the system.

The Near and Far: The Central and Peripheral Nervous Systems

As you can see from the figure, the nervous system is divided into two main parts: the central nervous system and the peripheral nervous system. The **central nervous system (CNS)** is composed of the brain and spinal cord. The **spinal cord** is a bundle of nerves, about the thickness of a pencil, that leaves the brain and runs down the length of the back (see Figure 2-8). It is the main means for transmitting messages between the brain and the body.

Central nervous system (CNS): *The system that includes the brain and the spinal cord*

Spinal cord: *A bundle of nerves running along the spine, carrying messages between the brain and the body*

The importance of the spinal cord is illustrated by cases in which the cord is severed in an accident. In the resulting injury, **paraplegia**, a person is unable to voluntarily move any muscles in the lower half of the body. However, even though the cord is severed, the undamaged area of the spinal cord is still able to produce some simple reflex actions, if stimulated appropriately. For instance, if a paraplegic's knee is tapped lightly, the lower leg will jerk slightly forward. The reason this capability remains is that the spinal cord itself is responsible for simple reflex movements—called **spinal reflexes**—without any input from the brain. There are other functions that are controlled by the spinal cord as well. For instance, if a male paraplegic's genitals are stimulated, he is capable of having an erection and ultimately an ejaculation. However, with a damaged spinal cord, the paraplegic would not experience the sensations that are normally a part of sexual experiences and, in fact, would not even be aware of his arousal.

Paraplegia (pair uh PLEE ja): *The inability, as a result of injury to the spinal cord, to move any muscles in the lower half of the body*

Spinal reflexes: *Simple reflex movements carried out by the spinal cord without input from the brain*

As suggested by its name, the **peripheral nervous system** includes all parts of the nervous system other than the brain and spinal cord. The peripheral

Peripheral (pur IF er ul) **nervous system**: *All parts of the nervous system* except *the brain and the spinal cord (includes somatic and autonomic divisions)*

ANSWERS TO REVIEW QUESTIONS

Review I: **1.** Neurons **2.** Dendrites **3.** Terminal buttons **4.** c **5.** False **6.** Action potential **7.** False **8.** a

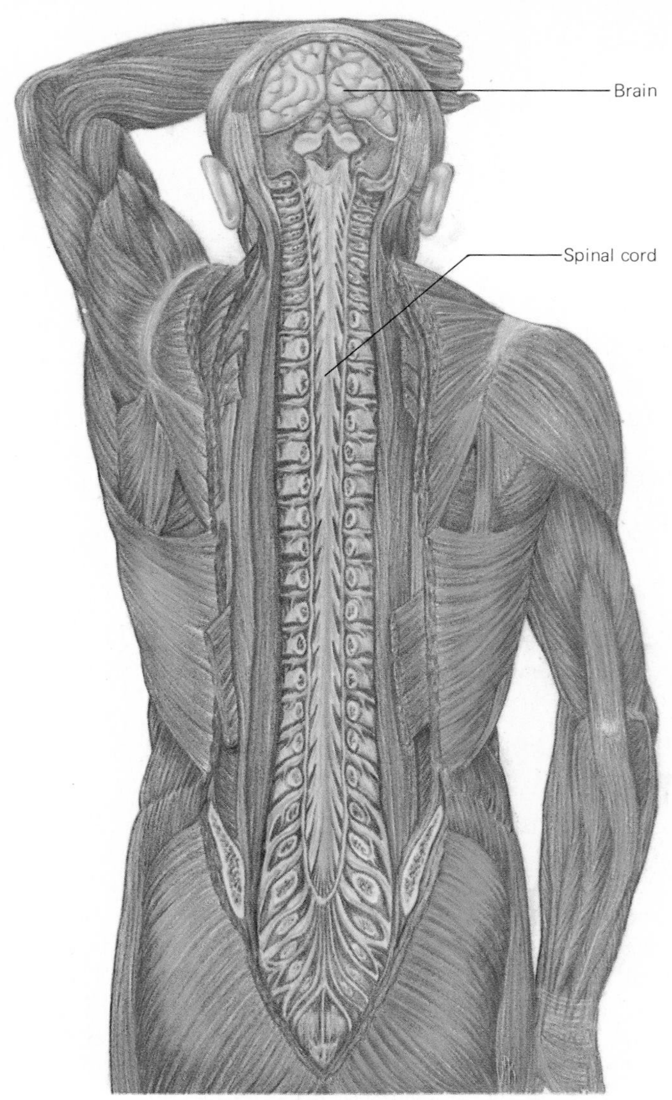

Figure 2-8
The central nervous system consists of the brain and spinal cord. (*Gruppo Editorial Fabbri/Milano.*)

nervous system branches out from the spinal cord and brain and reaches every portion of the body. There are two major divisions, the somatic division and the autonomic division, both of which connect the central nervous system with the sense organs, muscles, glands, and other organs. The **somatic division** specializes in controlling the voluntary movements of the skeletal muscles—such as the movement of the eyes to read this page or of the hand to turn this page—and the communication of information to and from the sense organs. On the other hand, the **autonomic division** is concerned with the parts of the body that keep us alive—the heart, blood vessels, glands, lungs, and other organs that function involuntarily without our awareness. As you are reading along right now, the autonomic division of the peripheral nervous system is pumping the blood through your body, pushing your lungs in and out, overseeing the digestion of the meal you had a few hours ago, and so on—all without a thought or care on your part.

Somatic (so MA tik) **division**: *The part of the nervous system that controls voluntary movements of the skeletal muscles*

Autonomic (ott uh NOM ik) **division**: *The part of the nervous system that controls involuntary movement (the actions of the heart, glands, lungs, etc.)*

Emergency!: Activating the Autonomic Nervous System

The autonomic division plays a particularly crucial role during emergency situations. Suppose as you are reading along you suddenly sense that there is a stranger watching you through the window. As you look up, you see the glint of something that just might be a gun. As confusion races through your mind and fear overcomes your attempts to think rationally, what happens to your body? If you are like most people, you react immediately on a physiological level: Your heart rate increases, you begin to sweat, and you develop goose bumps all over your body (see Figure 2-9).

The physiological changes that occur result from the activation of one part of the autonomic division: the sympathetic division. The **sympathetic division** acts to prepare the body in stressful emergency situations, engaging all the organism's resources to respond to a threat, a response that often takes the form of "fight or flight." In contrast, the **parasympathetic division** acts to calm the body after the emergency situation is resolved. When you find, for instance, that the stranger at the window is actually your roommate who has lost his keys and is climbing in the window to avoid waking you, your parasympathetic division begins to predominate, lowering your heart rate, stopping your sweating, and returning your body to the state it was in prior to your fright. The parasympathetic division also provides a means for the body to maintain storage of energy sources such as nutrients and oxygen. The sympathetic and parasympathetic divisions work together to regulate many functions of the body. For instance, sexual arousal is controlled by the parasympathetic division, while sexual orgasm is a function of the sympathetic division.

Sympathetic division: *The part of the autonomic division of the peripheral nervous system that prepares the body to respond in stressful emergency situations*

Parasympathetic (pair uh SIMP uh thet ik) **division**: *The part of the autonomic division of the peripheral nervous system that calms the body, bringing functions back to normal after an emergency has passed*

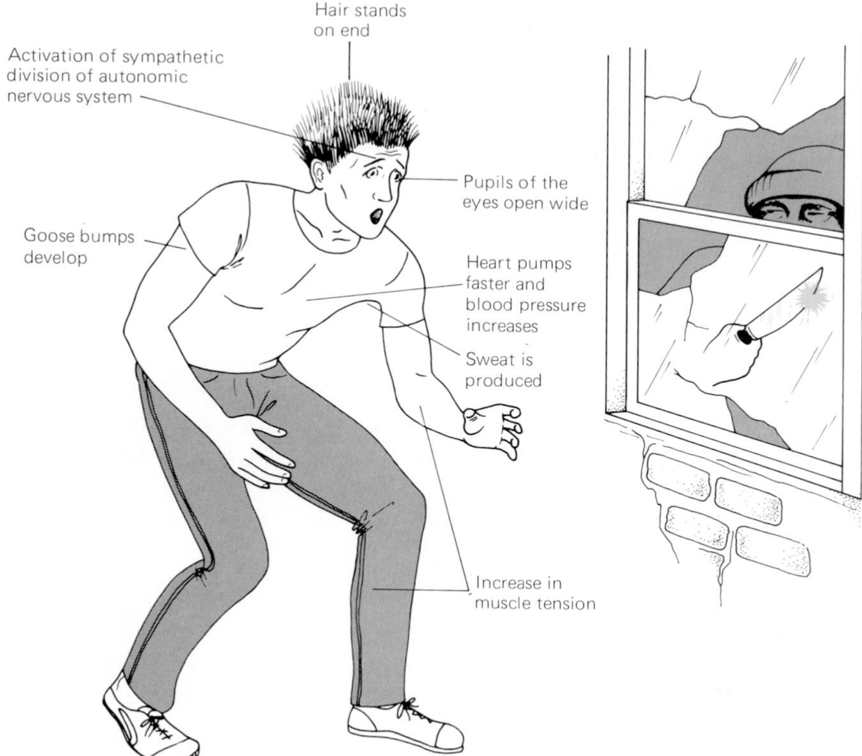

Figure 2-9
The activation of the sympathetic division of the autonomic nervous system prepares the body for emergency, "fight-or-flight" situations.

RECAP AND REVIEW II

Recap

- The specific site of transmission from one neuron to another is called the synapse. Messages moving across synapses are chemical in nature, although they travel within neurons in an electrical form.
- Neurotransmitters are the specific chemicals that make the chemical connection at the synapse; these act either to excite other neurons into firing or to inhibit neurons from firing.
- The central nervous system (CNS) is made up of the brain and spinal cord, a thick bundle of nerves running from the brain down the length of the back. The spinal cord provides the major route for transmission of messages between the brain and the rest of the body.
- The peripheral nervous system includes all parts of the nervous system other than the brain and spinal cord. It has two major parts: the somatic division (for voluntary movements) and the autonomic division (for involuntary movements).
- The autonomic division, which has two parts (sympathetic and parasympathetic divisions), plays a major role during emergency situations.

Review

1. The chemical connection which bridges the gap in neurotransmission is called a(n) ____________ ; the chemical itself is called a(n) ____________.

2. It is more likely that the action potential will travel down the axons of a neuron when it has received a(n) ____________ message.

3. Match the description in the right-hand column with the neurotransmitter whose release most likely explains the effect given.

a. ___ Dopamine	1. The poison had the effect of paralyzing the individual's muscles, thereby causing death by suffocation.
b. ___ Endorphins	2. Medications have helped sufferers of mental illness by regulating the production of a neurotransmitter.
c. ___ Acetylcholine	3. Sharon finished her longest run yet, pushing herself well beyond the discomfort stage. As a result she felt a "runner's high."

4. The brain and spinal cord compose the ____________ nervous system, whereas the ____________ nervous system branches out from the brain and spinal cord.

5. Barbara saw a young boy run into the street and get hit by a car. When she got to the fallen child, she was in a state of panic. She was sweating and her heart was racing. Her physiological state resulted from the activation of what division of the autonomic nervous system?

a. Parasympathetic **b.** Somatic **c.** Peripheral **d.** Sympathetic

6. Opiate receptors act to reduce pain. True or false?

(Answers to review questions are on page 58.)

TYING IT ALL TOGETHER: THE BRAIN

> When you come right down to it, it is not a very pretty sight. Soft, spongy, mottled, and pinkish-gray in color, one could hardly say that it possesses much in the way of physical beauty. Despite its physical appearance, however, it ranks as the greatest natural marvel that we know and possesses a kind of beauty and sophistication all its own.

The object to which this description applies is, as you might guess, the brain. The brain is responsible for our loftiest thoughts—and our most primitive urges. It is the overseer of the intricate workings of the human body. If one were to attempt to design a computer to mimic the capabilities of the brain, the task would be nearly impossible; in fact, it has proved difficult to even come close. Just the sheer quantity of nerve cells in the brain—numbering many billions—

located in a structure weighing just 3 pounds in the average adult is enough to daunt even the most ambitious computer engineer. However, it is not the number of cells that is the most astounding thing about the brain but its ability to allow human intellect to flourish as it guides our behavior and thoughts.

THE CUTTING EDGE

LOOKING AT THE BRAIN—FROM THE OUTSIDE IN

The brain has always posed a challenge to those wishing to study it. For most of history, it could be examined only after a person was dead—for only then was it possible to open up the skull and cut into the brain tissue without causing serious risk to the patient.

Today, however, the story is different. Investigators have discovered a variety of methods to study the brain without the need for surgical intrusion into the skull (Turkington, 1985). Probably the most important advances that have been made in the study of the brain concern the use of the **brain scan**, a technique by which a picture of the internal workings of the brain can be taken without having to surgically cut into a patient's skull. The main kinds of scanning techniques are illustrated in Figure 2-10 and are listed below.

Brain scan: *A method of "photographing" the brain without opening the skull*

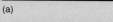

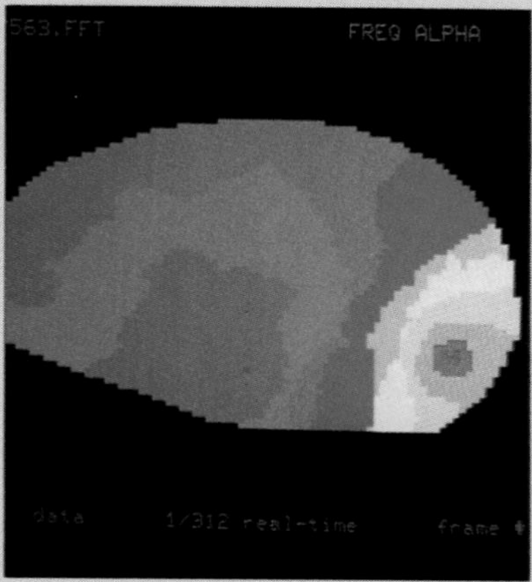

(a)

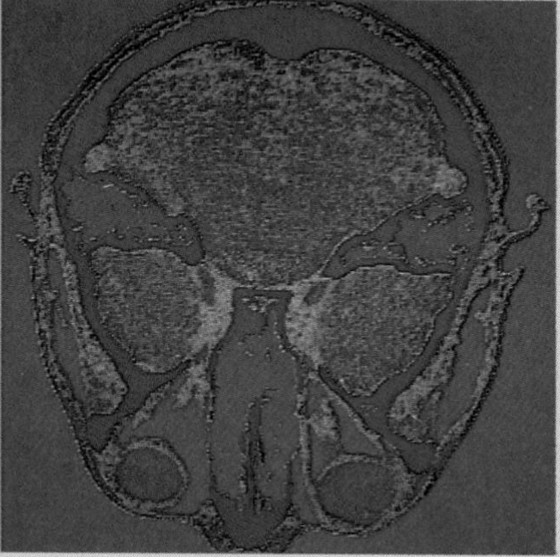

(b)

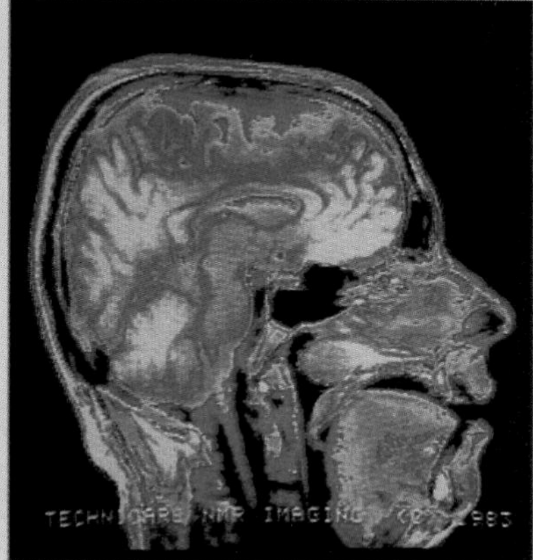

(c)

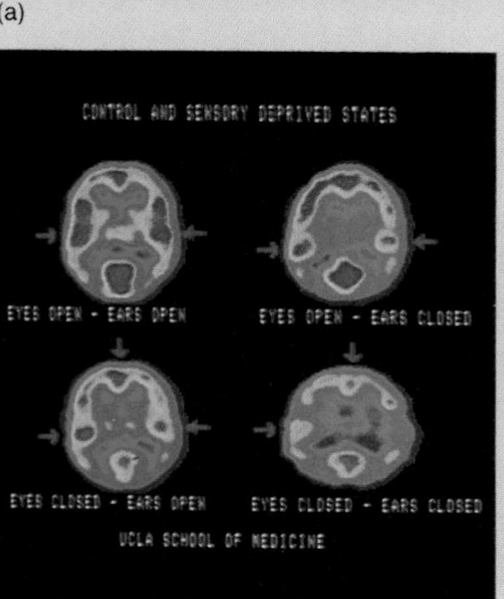

(d)

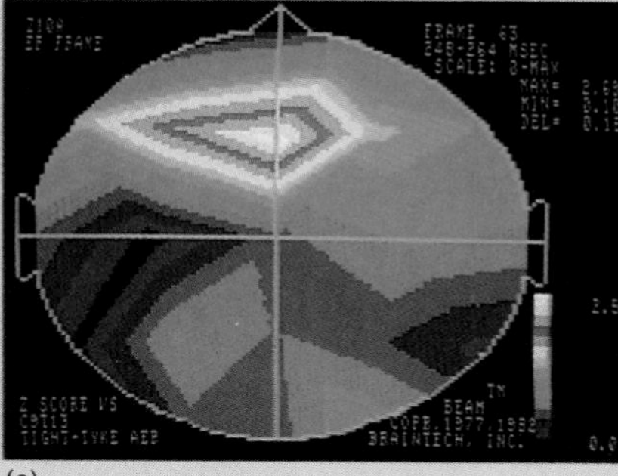

(e)

Figure 2-10
Brain scans produced by different techniques: (*a*) A computer-produced EEG image along with the more traditional pattern of waves. (*b*) The CAT scan shows the structures of the brain. (*c*) The NMR scan uses a magnetic field to detail the parts of the brain. (*d*) PET scans display the functioning of the brain at a given moment in time and are sensitive to the person's activities. (*e*) The BEAM scan provides a "map" of electrical activity in the brain. [(*a*) Dr. Richard Coppola/NIH; (*b*) © *Dan McCoy/Rainbow;* (*c*) Technicare Corp.; (*d*) *Courtesy of J. C. Mazziotta and M. E. Phelps, UCLA School of Medicine;* (*e*) © *Alexander Tsiaras/Medichrome.*]

■ The **electroencephalogram**, or **EEG**, records the electrical signals being transmitted inside the brain through the use of electrodes placed on the outside of the skull. Although traditionally the EEG could produce only a graph of electrical wave patterns, new techniques are able to transform the brain's electrical activity into moment-by-moment maps. This method allows diagnosis of such problems as epilepsy and learning disabilities.

■ The **computerized axial tomography,** or **CAT**, scan uses a computer to construct an image of the brain by combining thousands of separate x- rays taken at slightly different angles. It is most useful for showing abnormalities in the structure of the brain; it does not provide information about brain activity.

■ The **nuclear magnetic resonance**, or **NMR**, scan produces a powerful magnetic field to provide a computer-generated image of the brain which is even more detailed than that possible through CAT scans. Although still considered experimental, it is becoming the scan of choice because of the wealth of detail that can be constructed.

■ The **positron emission tomography**, or **PET**, scan is able to indicate how the brain is functioning at a given moment in time. By injecting radioactive sugar into a patient, a computer that measures radiation in the brain is able to show whether the brain is functioning normally.

■ **Brain electrical activity mapping**, or **BEAM**, provides a computerized map of electrical activity within the brain. BEAM machines can be used to diagnose subtle brain injuries in infants whose problems might otherwise go undetected.

Each of these techniques provides exciting possibilities for the diagnosis and treatment of brain injuries—as well as providing the opportunity for an increased understanding of the functioning of the brain.

Electroencephalogram (ee LEK tro en SEF uh lo gram) **(EEG)**: *A technique that records the brain's electrical activity*

Computerized axial tomography (AX ee ul toe MOG rah fee) **(CAT) scan**: *A scanning procedure that shows the structures within the brain*

Nuclear magnetic resonance (NMR) scan: *A scan produced by a magnetic field which shows brain structures in great detail*

Positron emission tomography (POS ih tron ee MISH on toe MOG rah fee) **(PET) scan**: *A scan technique which indicates how the brain is functioning at a given moment*

Brain electrical activity mapping (BEAM): *A computerized scan technique that indicates electrical activity within the brain*

Exploring and Mapping the Brain: Discovering the Old Brain and the New Brain

Central core: *The "old brain," which controls breathing, eating, sleeping, etc., and is common to all vertebrates*

Medulla (meh DOO lah): *The part of the central core of the brain that controls many important body functions such as breathing and the heartbeat*

Pons: *The part of the brain that joins the halves of the cerebellum, transmitting motor information to coordinate muscles and integrate movement between the right and left sides of the body*

While the capabilities of the human brain far exceed those of the brain of any other species, it is not surprising that the basic functions that we share with other, more primitive animals—such as breathing, eating, and sleeping—are directed by a relatively primitive part of the brain. A part of the brain known as the **central core** (see Figure 2-11) is quite similar to that found in all vertebrates (species with backbones). The central core is often referred to as the "old brain" because it is thought to have evolved relatively early in the development of the human species.

If you were to move up the spinal cord from the base of the skull to locate the structures of the central core of the brain, the first part you would come to would be the medulla (see Figure 2-12). The **medulla** controls a number of important body functions, the most important of which are breathing and maintenance of heartbeat. The pons comes next, joining the two halves of the cerebellum, which lies just adjacent to it. Containing large bundles of nerves, the **pons** acts as a transmitter of motor information, permitting the coordination of

ANSWERS TO REVIEW QUESTIONS

Review II: **1.** Synapse, neurotransmitter **2.** Excitatory **3.** a.2; b.3; c.1 **4.** Central, peripheral **5.** d **6.** True muscles and the integration of movement between the right and left halves of the body.

The **cerebellum** is found just above the medulla and behind the pons. Without the help of the cerebellum we would be unable to walk a straight line without staggering and lurching forward, for it is the job of the cerebellum to control bodily balance. It constantly monitors feedback from the muscles to coordinate their placement, movement, and tension. In fact, drinking too much liquor seems to depress the activity of the cerebellum, leading to the unsteady gait and movement characteristic of drunkenness.

So far our description of the parts of the brain has suggested that it is made up of a series of individual, well-defined separate structures. However, the complexity of the brain is shown by the fact that its parts do not simply follow each other in a sequential order but are found both within and between other structures. An example of this is the **reticular formation**, which extends from the medulla through the pons. The reticular formation is made up of a group of nerve cells that serves as a kind of guard that immediately activates other parts of the brain to cause a general arousal of the body. If, for example, you are startled by a loud noise, your reticular formation is likely to engage your body in immediate vigilance, prompting a heightened state of awareness to determine if a response is necessary. In addition, it serves a different function when we

Figure 2-11
The major divisions of the brain: the "new brain," the cerebral cortex, and the "old brain," the central core.

Cerebellum (ser rah BELL um): *The part of the brain that controls bodily balance*

Reticular (reh TIK u lar) **formation**: *A group of nerve cells in the brain that arouses the body to prepare it for appropriate action and screens out background stimuli*

Figure 2-12
(*a*) A three-dimensional view of the structures within the brain. (*Nauta & Feirtag, 1979.*)
(*b*) In this view, we can see the inside of a brain that has been cut in half; we are viewing the inner surface of the right side. (From *Thompson, 1967.*)

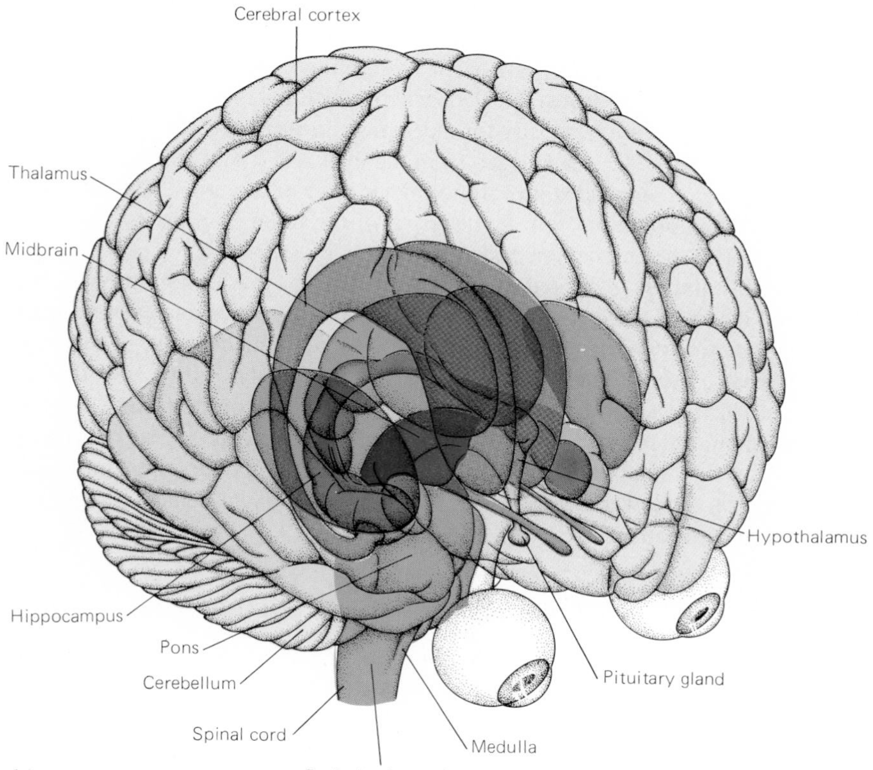

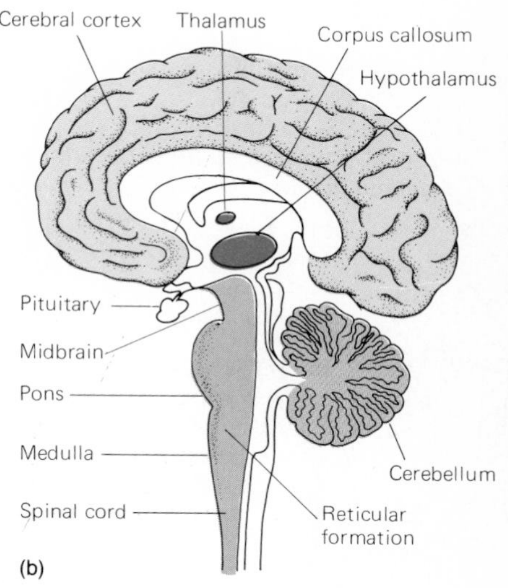

The uncoordinated behavior that makes this man appear drunk is brought about by a reduction in the activity of the brain's cerebellum due to alcohol. (*Van Bucher/ Photo Researchers, Inc.*)

are sleeping, seeming to screen out background stimuli to allow us to sleep undisturbed.

Thalamus (THAL a muss): *The part of the brain's central core that transmits messages from the sense organs to the cerebral cortex and from the cerebral cortex to the cerebellum and medulla*

The final structures that are part of the "old brain" are the thalamus and the hypothalamus. The **thalamus**, located centrally within the "old brain," acts primarily as a relay station, mostly for messages concerning sensory information (Casey & Morrow, 1983). Messages from the eyes, ears, and skin travel to the thalamus to be communicated upward to higher parts of the brain. The thalamus also integrates information from higher parts of the brain, sorting it out so that it can be sent to the cerebellum and medulla.

Hypothalamus (hy po THAL a muss): *Located below the thalamus of the brain, its major function is to maintain homeostasis*

Homeostasis (ho mee o STAY sis): *The process by which an organism tries to maintain an internal biological balance or steady state*

The **hypothalamus** is located just below the thalamus. Although tiny—about the size of the tip of a finger—the hypothalamus plays an inordinately important role in the functioning of the body. One of its major functions is to maintain **homeostasis**, a steady internal environment for the body; as we will discuss further in Chapter 8, the hypothalamus helps provide a constant body temperature and monitors the amount of nutrients stored in the cells. A second major function is equally important: It produces and regulates behavior that is important to the basic survival of the species—eating, drinking, sexual behavior, fighting, and nurturance of offspring.

Endocrine (EN doe krin) **system**: *A chemical communication network that sends messages throughout the nervous system and secretes hormones that affect body growth and functioning*

Hormones: *Chemicals that circulate throughout the blood and affect the functioning and growth of parts of the body*

Of Chemicals and Glands: The Endocrine System

As we move upward through the brain, we need to pause a moment and consider the **endocrine system**, a chemical communication network that sends messages throughout the nervous system. Although not a structure of the brain itself, the endocrine system is intimately involved with the hypothalamus. The job of the endocrine system is to secrete **hormones**, chemicals that circulate through the blood and affect the functioning or growth of other parts of the body (Crapo, 1985).

The major component of the endocrine system is the **pituitary gland**, found near—and regulated by—the hypothalamus. The pituitary gland is sometimes called the master gland because it controls the functioning of the rest of the endocrine system. But the pituitary gland is more than just the taskmaster of other glands; it has important functions in its own right. For instance, hormones secreted by the pituitary gland control growth, keeping a person's size within the appropriate range. Extremely short people—dwarfs—and extremely large ones—giants—usually have pituitary gland deficiencies. Figure 2-13 shows the location and function of the major endocrine glands.

Pituitary (pih TOO ih tair ee) **gland**: *The "master gland," the major component of the endocrine system, which secretes hormones that control growth*

Passing the Border between the Old Brain and the New Brain: The Limbic System

After a fight with his girlfriend Bill felt he needed something to make himself feel better. He took out his battery pack, attached it to the electrode that had been implanted in his brain at the legal age of 18, and set the timer to deliver a tiny shock to his brain's "pleasure center" every three seconds for the next thirty minutes. "Ah," he thought to himself as the waves of pleasure began flooding his body, "it never fails to make me feel better."

This bizarre view of the future, while seemingly farfetched, is not altogether unthinkable, given what we know about a part of the brain known as the **limbic system**. Located just outside the "new brain," the limbic system consists of several different structures which together control a variety of basic functions, such as eating and reproduction.

Limbic system: *The part of the brain located outside the "new brain" that controls eating and reproduction*

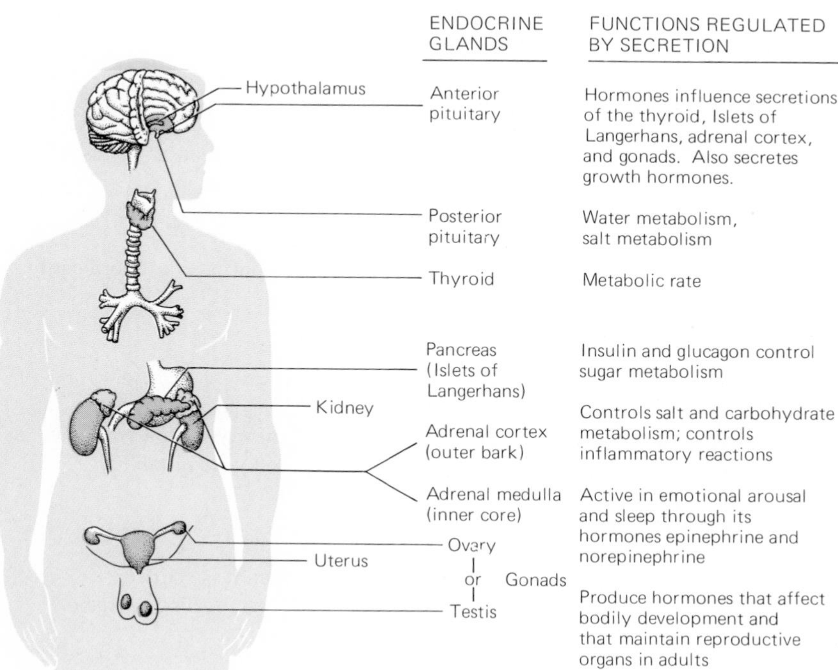

ENDOCRINE GLANDS
FUNCTIONS REGULATED BY SECRETION
Hypothalamus
Anterior pituitary
Hormones influence secretions of the thyroid, Islets of Langerhans, adrenal cortex, and gonads. Also secretes growth hormones.
Posterior pituitary
Water metabolism, salt metabolism
Thyroid
Metabolic rate
Pancreas (Islets of Langerhans)
Insulin and glucagon control sugar metabolism
Kidney
Adrenal cortex (outer bark)
Controls salt and carbohydrate metabolism; controls inflammatory reactions
Adrenal medulla (inner core)
Active in emotional arousal and sleep through its hormones epinephrine and norepinephrine
Uterus
Ovary
or
Gonads
Testis
Produce hormones that affect bodily development and that maintain reproductive organs in adults

Figure 2-13
Location and function of the major endocrine glands. (*Source: Rosenzweig & Leiman, 1982.*)

Injury to the limbic system can produce marked changes in behavior. Animals that are usually docile and tame will turn into belligerent savages. Conversely, those that are usually wild and uncontrollable may become meek and obedient (Fanelli, Burright, & Donovick, 1983).

Probably the most thought-provoking finding to come out of the study of the limbic system comes from research that has examined the effects of mild electric shocks to certain parts of the system (Olds & Milner, 1954). In one experiment, rats with an electrode implanted in their limbic systems were given the opportunity to pass an electric current through the electrode by pressing a bar. Even starving rats on their way to food would stop to press the bar as many times as they could. In fact, if allowed to do so, the rats would stimulate their limbic systems literally thousands of times an hour—until they collapsed with fatigue (Routtenberg & Lindy, 1965).

The extraordinarily pleasurable quality of certain kinds of limbic-system stimulation has also been found in humans, who have—usually as part of some treatment for brain dysfunction—received electrical stimulation to certain areas of the limbic system. Although they are at a loss to describe just what it feels like, these people report the experience to be intensely pleasurable—similar in some respects to sexual orgasm.

Whether self-stimulation of the limbic system to produce feelings of pleasure is just a bizarre futuristic fantasy or a probable reality is hard to guess. But given the nature of the limbic system, such a scenario does seem within the realm of possibility.

RECAP AND REVIEW III

Recap

- The central core of the human brain—sometimes referred to as the "old brain"—is similar to the brains found in all vertebrates.
- If we trace the CNS from the top of the spinal cord up into the brain, the first structure we find is the medulla, which controls such functions as the heartbeat. Next is the pons, which acts to transmit motor information, while the cerebellum is involved in the control of motion.
- The reticular formation, extending from the medulla and through the pons, arouses and activates the body, but also censors outside stimulation during sleep.
- The thalamus acts primarily as a sensory-information relay center, while the hypothalamus maintains homeostasis, a steady internal environment for the body.
- The endocrine system, a chemical communication network that sends messages throughout the nervous system, secretes hormones, chemicals that affect the function and growth of the body.
- Eating and reproductive behavior are controlled to a large extent by the limbic system, which also produces an extraordinarily pleasurable experience when electrically stimulated.

Review

1. Breathing is one function controlled by that part of the central core of the brain known as the ____________.
2. "I was staggering drunk!" Jeff exclaimed. "Let me state it more technically," his roomate offered snidely. "You consumed an excess of liquor, which served to depress the activity of your ____________ , which caused your instability."
3. The structure of the brain which maintains the body's homeostasis is called the
   a. Reticular formation **b.** Hypothalamus **c.** Thalamus **d.** Pons
4. Hormones which control growth are secreted by the ____________ gland.
5. The ____________ ____________ activates the body into a state of arousal when it is startled.
6. Experimental evidence has demonstrated that stimulating the limbic system produces extremely unpleasant feelings. True or false?

(Answers to review questions are on page 64.)

THE NEW BRAIN: THE CEREBRAL CORTEX

As we have moved up the spinal cord and into the brain, our discussion has centered on the areas of the brain that control functions similar to those found in lower, less sophisticated organisms. But where, you may be asking, are the parts of the brain that allow humans to do the things they do best, things that distinguish humankind from all other animals? Those unique features of the human brain—indeed the very capabilities that allow you to come up with such a question in the first place—are embodied in the ability to think and remember. And the central location of these abilities, along with many others, is the **cerebral cortex**.

Cerebral cortex (suh REE brul KOR tex): *The "new brain," responsible for the most sophisticated information processing in the brain; contains the lobes*

The cerebral cortex—called the "new brain" because of its relatively recent evolution—is a mass of deeply folded, rippled, convoluted tissue. Although it is only about one-twelfth of an inch thick, if flattened out it would cover a $2\frac{1}{2}$-foot-square area. This physical configuration allows the surface area of the cortex to be considerably higher than if it were more loosely and smoothly packed into the skull. It also allows the neurons within the cortex to be intricately connected to one another, permitting the highest level of integration within the brain, and therefore the most sophisticated processing of information.

There are four major structures within the cortex, called lobes. The **frontal lobes** lie at the front center of the cortex, and the **parietal lobes** lie behind it. The **temporal lobes** are on either side of the brain, with the **occipital lobes** lying behind them. Within these lobes are specialized areas associated with specific functions and areas of the body (see Figure 2-14). Three major areas have been discovered: the motor area, the sensory area, and the association area.

Frontal lobes: *The brain structure, located at the front center of the cortex, that contains major motor and speech and reasoning centers*
Parietal (puh RY uh tul) **lobes**: *The brain structure to the rear of the frontal lobes; the center for bodily sensations*
Temporal lobes: *The portion of the brain located on either side of the cortex*
Occipital (ox SIP ih tul) **lobes**: *The structures of the brain lying behind the temporal lobes*
Motor area: *One of the major areas of the brain, responsible for voluntary movement of particular parts of the body*

The Motor Area of the Brain

If you look at the frontal lobe in Figure 2-14, you will see a shaded portion labeled the **motor area**. This part of the brain is largely responsible for voluntary

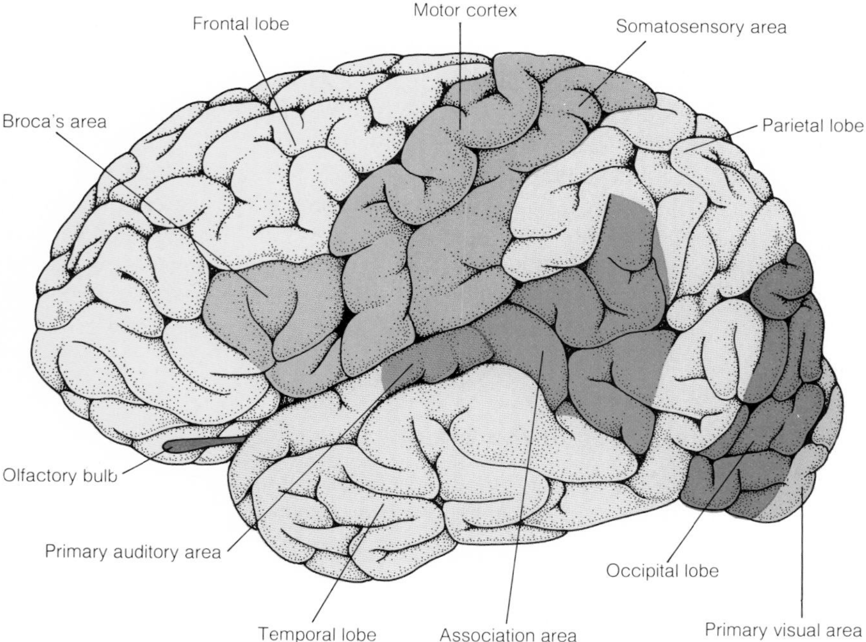

Figure 2-14
The major structures of the cerebral cortex. (*Stevens, 1979, p. 186.*)

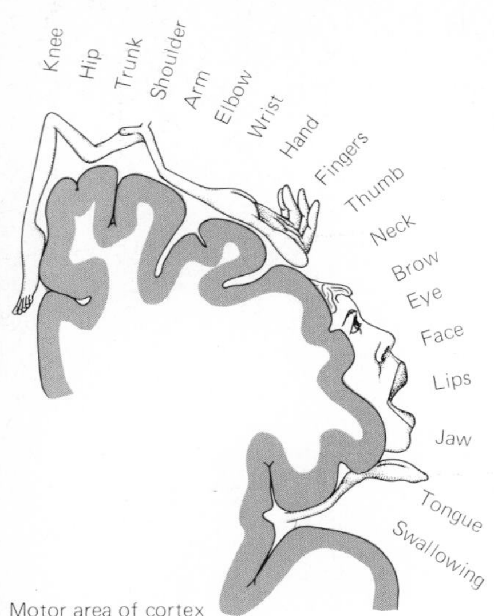

Figure 2-15
The correspondence between the amount and location of tissue in the brain's motor area and the specific body parts where movement is controlled by that tissue. *(Penfield & Rasmussen, 1950.)*

Sensory area: *The site in the brain of the tissue that corresponds to each of the senses, the degree of sensitivity relating to amount of tissue*

Somatosensory (so mat o SEN sor ee) **area**: *See sensory area*

movement of particular parts of the body. In fact, every portion of the motor area corresponds to a specific locale within the body. If we were to insert an electrode into a particular part of the motor area of your brain and apply mild electrical stimulation, there would be involuntary movement in the corresponding part of the body (Kertesz, 1983). If we moved to another part of the motor area and stimulated it, a different part of the body would move.

The motor area has been so well mapped that it is possible to devise the kind of schematic representations shown in Figure 2-15. This weird-looking model illustrates the amount and relative location of cortical tissue that is used to produce movement in specific parts of the human body. As you can see, the control of body movements that are relatively large-scale and require little precision—such as movement of a knee or a hip—is centered in a very small space in the motor area. On the other hand, movements that must be precise and delicate—such as facial expressions or the use of the fingers—are controlled by a considerably larger portion of the motor area. In sum, the brain's motor area provides a clear guide to the degree of complexity and the importance of the motor capabilities of specific parts of the body.

The Sensory Area of the Brain

Given the one-to-one correspondence between motor area and body location, it is not surprising that scientists have found a similar relationship between a specific portion of the brain and the senses. If you look at Figure 2-16 you can see that within the **sensory area** of the cortex—also called the **somatosensory area**—there are specific locations that are associated with the ability to perceive touch in a specific area of the body. As with the motor area, the amount of brain tissue related to a specific body part determines the degree of sensitivity of that part: The greater the space within the brain, the more sensitive the part. As you can see from the figure, then, areas such as the fingers, which are related to proportionally more space in the sensory areas, are the most sensitive.

The other senses are also represented in specific areas of the cerebral cortex. There is an auditory area located in the temporal lobe that is responsible for our sense of hearing. If the auditory area is stimulated electrically, a person will hear sounds such as clicks or humming. It also appears that particular locations within the auditory areas correspond to the specific pitch of sound.

The visual center in the brain operates analogously to the other sensory areas; stimulation by electrodes produces the experience of flashes of light or colors, suggesting that the raw sensory input of images from the eyes is received in this area of the brain and transformed into meaningful stimuli. The visual area also provides another example of how areas of the brain are intimately related to specific areas of the body: Particular areas of the eye are related to a particular part of the brain—with, as you might guess, more space in the brain given to the most sensitive portions of the eye.

The Association Area of the Brain

Twenty-five-year-old Phineas Gage, a railroad employee, was blasting rock one day in 1848 when an accidental explosion punched a 3.5-foot-long spike,

ANSWERS TO REVIEW QUESTIONS

Review III: **1.** Medulla **2.** Cerebellum **3.** b **4.** Pituitary **5.** Reticular formation **6.** False

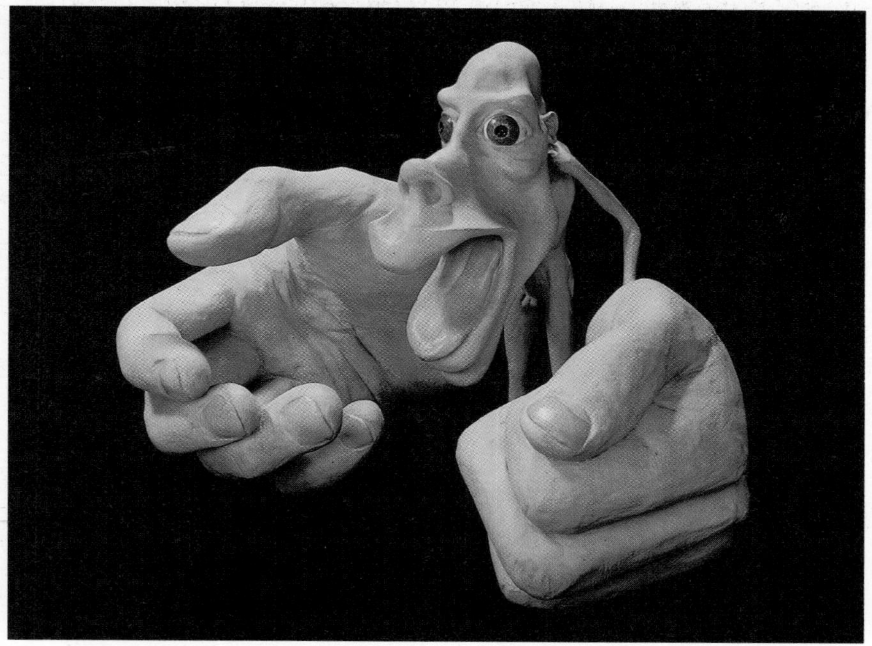

Figure 2-16
If the parts of our bodies reflected proportionally the space that the brain gives to the body parts' sensations, we might look like this strange creature. (*British Museum of Natural History*.)

about an inch in diameter, completely through his skull. The spike entered just under his left cheek, came out the top of his head, and flew into the air. He immediately suffered a series of convulsions, yet a few minutes later was talking with rescuers. In fact, he was able to walk up a long flight of stairs before receiving any medical attention. Amazingly, after a few weeks his wound healed, and he was physically close to his old self again. Mentally, however, there was a difference: once a careful and hard-working person, Phineas now became enamored with wild schemes and was flighty and often irresponsible. As one of his physicians put it, "Previous to his injury, though untrained in the schools, he possessed a well-balanced mind, and was looked upon by those who knew him as a shrewd, smart businessman, very energetic and persistent in executing all his plans of operation. In this regard his mind was radically changed, so decidedly that his friends and acquaintances said he was 'no longer Gage' " (Harlow, 1869, p. 14).

What had happened to the old Gage? Although there is no way of knowing for sure—science being what it was in the 1800s—we might speculate that the accident may have injured the association area of Gage's cerebral hemisphere.

If you return one last time to our diagram of the cerebral cortex (Figure 2-14), you will find that the motor and sensory areas take up a relatively small portion of the cortex; the remainder contains the association area. The **association area** is generally considered to be the site of higher mental processes such as thinking, language, memory, and speech. Most of our understanding of the association area comes from patients who have suffered some brain injury—from natural causes such as a tumor or a stroke, either of which would block certain blood vessels within the cerebral cortex, or, as in the case of Phineas Gage, from accidental causes. Damage to this area can result in unusual behavioral changes, indicating the importance of the association area to normal functioning.

Association area: *One of the major areas of the brain, the site of the higher mental processes such as thought, language, memory, and speech*

THE CUTTING EDGE

THE BRAIN TRANSPLANT:

Solving Old Problems—and Creating New Ones?

With heart transplants becoming almost routine and other organs being replaced on a regular basis, there is one possibility that has yet to become reality: the brain transplant. Although it sounds like something out of a science fiction movie, researchers are taking some tentative first steps toward making such an eerie prospect come true.

In 1976 scientists successfully performed an essential first step in the brain-transplant process (White, 1976). They removed the brain of a chimpanzee and kept it alive for more than twenty-four hours by supplying it with oxygen and other essential nutrients. Researchers have also found preliminary evidence that small parts of the brain damaged by an accident or disease might be replaced. For example, research conducted in Sweden on patients with Parkinson's disease suggests that the introduction of undamaged tissue into impaired areas of a patient's brain may help repair damaged brain cells (Sullivan, 1984). In their work, the investigators took cells from an adrenal gland near the kidney of a Parkinson's patient and inserted them into the area of the brain that was damaged, hoping to stimulate dopamine production. Because the adrenal gland produces dopamine, the researchers reasoned it would alleviate the symptoms of Parkinson's—a hypothesis that was supported when at least one patient regained a degree of muscular control that had previously been lost to Parkinson's.

Such work is promising, raising the possibility that damaged areas of the brain might someday be repaired by the introduction of compatible, healthy cells. However, the ultimate possibility of an actual brain transplant raises a set of psychological and ethical issues that transplants of other organs do not. One issue concerns the distinction between the mind and body, an ancient philosophical question (Pribram, 1986). If we assume that the mind is separate from the body, whose mind will be in charge of the recipient's body—the donor's or the recipient's? If we reject the separation of body and mind—as most psychologists do—we have a hard-to-imagine situation: a new mind taking control of an old body.

The situation holds out even more complexities. Because others frequently react to us on the basis of our physical appearance (as we shall see in Chapter 15), a brain inhabiting someone else's body would have to adjust to a whole new set of reactions from others. Who would this new brain-in-a-body be? While these issues may not be of immediate concern, they do have serious implications.

Apraxia (uh PRAX ee uh): *The inability to perform activities in a logical way*

Consider, for instance, the condition known as **apraxia**. Apraxia occurs when a person is unable to integrate activities in a rational or logical manner. For example, a patient asked to get a soda from the refrigerator might go to the refrigerator and open and close the door repeatedly, or might take bottle after bottle of soda out of the refrigerator, dropping each to the floor. Similarly, a person with apraxia who is asked to open a lock with a key may be unable to do so in response to the request—but, if simply left alone in a locked room, wishing to leave, will be able to unlock the door (Lechtenberg, 1982).

Apraxia is clearly not a muscular problem, since the person is capable of carrying out the individual components of the overall behavior. Moreover, if asked to perform the individual components of a larger behavioral pattern one at a time, a patient is often quite successful. It is only when asked to carry out a sequence of behaviors requiring a degree of planning and foresight that the patient shows deficits. It appears, then, that the association area may act as a kind of "master planner," that is, the organizer of actions.

Aphasia (uh FAYZH ee uh): *A disorder resulting in problems with verbal expression due to brain injury*

Broca's (BRO kaz) **aphasia**: *A syndrome involving verbal expression*

Other difficulties that arise because of injury to the association area of the brain relate to the use of language. Problems with verbal expression, known as **aphasia**, can take many forms. In **Broca's aphasia** (caused by damage to the part of the brain first identified by a French physician, Paul Broca), speech becomes halting and laborious. The speaker is unable to find the right words—

in a kind of tip-of-the-tongue phenomenon that we all experience from time to time, except that in the case of the person with aphasia, it happens almost constantly. Patients with aphasia also speak in "verbal telegrams"; a phrase like "I put the book on the table" comes out as "I . . . put . . . book . . . table" (Lechtenberg, 1982).

In another type of aphasia, there are difficulties with the understanding of language rather than with its production. This is called **receptive aphasia**. In this case, the patient's speech is fluent—but it makes no sense, since he or she has misunderstood what was said initially.

Receptive aphasia: *A syndrome involving problems with understanding language, resulting in fluent but nonsensical speech*

TWO BRAINS OR ONE?: THE SPECIALIZATION OF THE HEMISPHERES

In a 1984 movie, Steve Martin plays a lawyer whose brain becomes inhabited by another person—an unhappy Lily Tomlin—who has been mistakenly transferred there by a well-meaning but inept swami. The movie revolves around Martin's attempts to rid himself of Tomlin, who struggles with him to take control of his body, illustrating a bizarre situation in which there are separate brains in the same body.

The movie is interesting not just for its hilarious premise, but because of the fact that it mirrors more of reality than its creators may have been aware when they wrote the script. For it turns out that the one major feature of the brain that we have not yet discussed is that it has symmetrical left and right halves, or **hemispheres**, which permit the brain to function at times almost as if there were indeed two separate brains within the same body.

Hemispheres: *Symmetrical left and right halves of the brain*

Specifically, the brain structure can be divided into two roughly similar mirror-image halves—just as we have two arms, two legs, and two lungs. Because of the way nerves are connected from the brain to the rest of the body, the left hemisphere of the brain generally controls the right side of the body, and conversely the right hemisphere controls the left side of the body. Damage to the right side of the brain, then, is typically indicated by functional difficulties in the left side of the body.

Yet the structural similarity between the two hemispheres of the brain is not reflected in all aspects of its functioning; it appears that certain activities are more likely to occur in one hemisphere than in the other. Early evidence for the functional differences between halves of the brain came from studies of people with aphasia; researchers found that people with the speech difficulties characteristic of aphasia tended to have physical damage to the left hemisphere of the brain. In contrast, physical abnormalities in the right hemisphere of the brain tended to produce far fewer problems with language (Corballis & Beales, 1983). The conclusion? Language is **lateralized**, or located more in one hemisphere than the other—in this case, in the left side of the brain.

Lateralization: *The dominance of one hemisphere of the brain in specific functions*

It now seems clear that the two hemispheres of the brain specialize in different functions. The left hemisphere is best at tasks that require verbal strength, such as speaking, reading, thinking, and reasoning. The right hemisphere has its own strengths, particularly in nonverbal areas, such as spatial understanding, recognition of patterns and drawings, mathematical skills, music, and emotional expression (Gazzaniga, 1983; Levy, 1983). (To get a hint of how the two hemispheres operate individually, see the accompanying Try It! box.)

TRY IT!

USING YOUR LEFT AND RIGHT BRAINS

You can easily demonstrate which half of the brain is processing information by noting the direction in which a person's eyes move when he or she is thinking of the answer to a question.

To do this, ask someone the questions below and watch to see in what direction his or her eyes move. If they move to the right, it suggests that this person is using the left half of the brain; if they move to the left, it suggests that the individual is using the right half. (This will work only if your subject is right-handed; left-handed people show great variability.)

1. Think of what your mother looked like the last time she got angry with you.
2. Use a sentence with the words "brain" and "behavior."
3. Describe the last sunset you saw.
4. Define the word "lateralization."

Because questions 1 and 3 call upon primarily spatial and emotional abilities, most people use right hemisphere processing, and therefore they will probably look toward the left when answering. In contrast, the second and fourth questions call for verbal skills, resulting in left-hemisphere processing; people usually look to the right when responding to questions of this nature (Schwartz, Davidson, & Maer, 1975).

Is the functioning of one hemisphere more important than the other? The fact that language and formal reasoning capabilities are two of the primary functions that distinguish humans from other species might seem to suggest that the left hemisphere is of greater importance. The issue, however, is really a matter of values. In our computerized western culture, a brain that operates in a logical, sequential fashion might be preferred. But there are many cultures in which thinking proceeds in a less direct and less logical fashion and is organized pictorially rather than mathematically and verbally. In cultures such as these, a strong right hemisphere might be preferable (Annett, 1985).

Luckily, none of us has to choose between the two hemispheres of our brains; unless there is brain damage, both halves will be intact and will function together (Best, 1985). Moreover, people (especially young children) who suffer brain damage to the left side of their brain and lose linguistic capabilities often recover the ability to speak—because the right side of the brain pitches in and takes over some of the functioning of the left side (Weiderhold, 1982). The brain, then, is remarkably adaptable and can modify its functioning—to some extent at least—in respect to adverse circumstances (McConnell, 1985; Beaton, 1986).

Our understanding of the differences between the hemispheres of the brain remains incomplete. For instance, there are differences between right- and left-handed people in hemispheric functioning, although the nature of these differences has not yet been fully identified (Gazzaniga, 1985; Beaton, 1986).

Still, the differences in hemispheric functioning at least suggest the possibility that there may be individual differences in the strengths of each hemisphere. For example, we might speculate that a talented writer has a brain in which the left side is particularly dominant, while an artist or architect might have more strength in the right hemisphere. What we do best in life, then, may be a function of which side of our brain has the greater strengths. (For another view of how differences between the hemispheres of the brain might affect us, see the accompanying Psychology at Work box.)

PSYCHOLOGY AT WORK

PROBING THE BRAIN ON MADISON AVENUE

When he wanted to find out why a new television commercial was not very successful, Herbert Krugman, manager of public opinion research at General Electric, thought of a less-than-obvious culprit: the right hemisphere of the brain. Perhaps, he reasoned, the commercial was so visually appealing that it evoked right-hemispheric processing of the information, and the verbal message was lost along the way.

To test his hunch, he hooked up a series of brain probes to a group of viewers while they were watching the commercial, and found, without exception, that the right hemispheres of the viewers' brains were considerably more active electrically than their left hemispheres. His conclusion: The commercial appealed more to the emotional, artistic, and visual right hemisphere—and the commercial's verbal message was being missed by the rational left side of the brain.

Krugman's method of measuring brain activity in order to predict or account for viewer reaction to commercials has become one of a number of important tools used by advertisers eager to ensure the success of their commercials (Golman, 1979; Weinstein, 1984). In one case, for instance, an agency showed the same commercial over and over again to the same people and measured their physiological responses to see how well the commercial would retain a viewer's interest after repeated showings. In addition, physiological measures have been used to choose an actor for a spot in a commercial. By showing observers a series of film clips of several actors the agency was able to determine who produced the greatest physiological response in the brain—presumably giving that person an edge in the selection process.

Some advertisers have begun to use measures of brain activity routinely as they search for the best way to get a product's message across. When watching a commercial in what you might think of as a mindless state, contemplate just what *is* happening inside your brain.

Understanding the Two Hemispheres: Split-Brain Patients

When the seizures first started, Cindy Gluccles thought her physician would be able to give her a drug that would prevent their recurrence. Her physician and her neurologist were both optimistic, maintaining that in most cases seizures could be controlled with the proper drugs. But the seizures got worse and more frequent, and no drug treatment seemed to help. Further examination revealed that the seizures were caused by remarkably large bursts of electrical activity that were starting in one hemisphere and moving to the other. Finally, her doctors prescribed a last-ditch measure: surgically cutting the bundle of nerves that connected the two hemispheres to each other. Almost magically, the seizures stopped. The operation was clearly a success—but was Cindy the same person she had been before the operation?

That issue has evoked a great deal of interest on the part of brain researchers, and, in fact, has earned a Nobel Prize for Roger Sperry. Sperry, with a group of colleagues, explored the behavior of patients who had had the links between the two hemispheres of the brain surgically cut. The research team found that, in most ways, there were no major changes in either personality or intelligence.

On the other hand, patients like Cindy Gluccles, called **split-brain patients**, did occasionally display some unusual behavior. For instance, one patient reported pulling his pants down with one hand and simultaneously pulling them up with the other. In addition, he mentioned grabbing his wife with his left hand and shaking her violently, while his right hand tried to help his wife by bringing his left hand under control (Gazzaniga, 1970).

Split-brain patient: *A person who suffers from independent functioning of the two halves of the brain, as a result of which the sides of the body work in disharmony*

Interest in this occasional curious behavior, however, was peripheral to the rare opportunity that split-brain patients provided for research in the independent functioning of the two hemispheres of the brain, and Sperry developed a number of ingenious techniques for studying how each hemisphere operated (Sperry, 1982). In one experimental procedure, blindfolded subjects were allowed to touch an object with their right hand and were asked to name it. Because the right side of the body is connected to the left side of the brain—the hemisphere that is most responsible for language—the split-brain patient was able to name it. But if the blindfolded subject touched the object with his or her left hand, naming it aloud was not possible. However, the information had registered: If the blindfold was taken off, the subject could choose the object that he or she had touched. Information can be learned and remembered, then, using only the right side of the brain. (By the way, this experiment won't work with you—unless you have had a split-brain operation—since the nerves connecting the two halves of a normal brain immediately transfer the information from one half of the brain to the other.)

It is clear from experiments such as this that the right and left hemispheres of the brain specialize in handling different sorts of information. At the same time, it is important to realize that they are both capable of understanding, knowing, and being aware of the world—although in somewhat different ways. The two hemispheres, then, should be seen as different in terms of the efficiency with which they process certain kinds of information, rather than viewed as two entirely separate brains. Moreover, in people with normal, nonsplit brains, the hemispheres work interdependently to allow the full range and richness of thought of which humans are capable.

The Informed Consumer of Psychology: Learning to Control Your Heart—and Brain—through Biofeedback

When her blood pressure rose to unacceptably high levels, Carla Lewitt was first given the option of undergoing a standard treatment with drugs. When she asked if there was any alternative, her physician suggested an approach that would entail her learning to control her blood pressure voluntarily. Although Carla didn't think she was capable of controlling something she wasn't even aware of, she agreed to give it a try. Within three weeks, her blood pressure had come down to normal levels.

* * *

Bill Jackson had experienced excruciatingly painful headaches all his life. No drug seemed to stop them, and they were often accompanied by a loss of appetite and vomiting. When a friend suggested he try a new procedure designed to enable him to voluntarily control the headaches by learning to control the constriction of muscles in his head, he laughed. "I've been trying to learn to stop these headaches all my life," he said, "and it's never worked." Convinced by his friend that it was worth a try, though, he went to a psychologist specializing in biofeedback—and in four weeks had put an end to his headaches.

We typically think of our heart, respiration rate, blood pressure, and other bodily functions as under the control of innate biological factors. But, as the cases above illustrate, psychologists are finding that what were once thought of as entirely involuntary biological responses are proving to be susceptible to

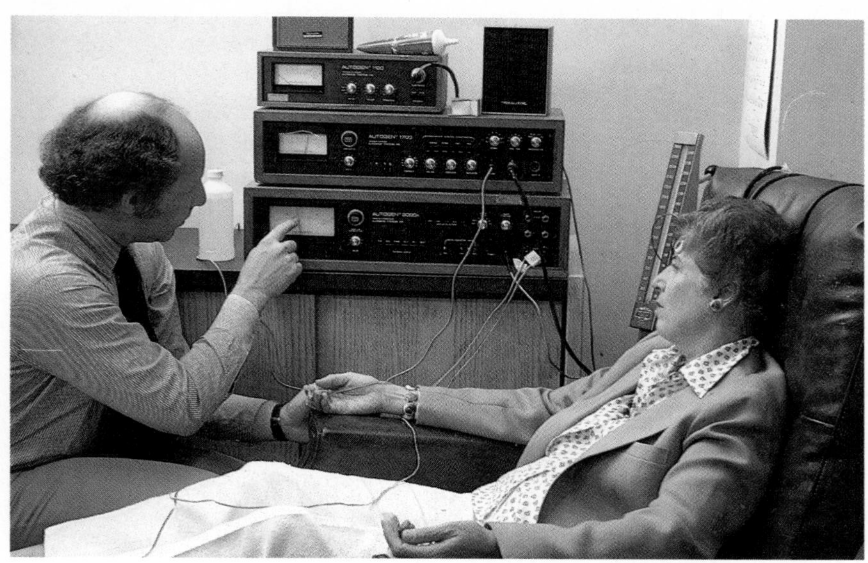

Using biofeedback, this woman learns to control her blood pressure. (*David Attie/ Medichrome*)

voluntary control—and, in the process, they are learning about important treatment techniques for a variety of ailments.

The technique that both lowered Carla Lewitt's blood pressure and stopped Bill Jackson's headaches was the same: biofeedback. **Biofeedback** is a procedure in which a person learns to control internal physiological processes such as blood pressure, heart rate, respiration speed, skin temperature, sweating, and constriction of certain muscles (Yates, 1980).

Biofeedback: *The control of internal physiological processes through conscious thought*

How can people learn to voluntarily control such responses, which are typically considered "involuntary"? The answer is that such learning is possible after training with electronic devices that provide continuous feedback on the physiological response in question. For instance, a person interested in controlling her blood pressure might be hooked up to an apparatus that constantly monitors and displays her blood pressure. As she consciously thinks about altering the pressure, she receives immediate feedback as to the measure of her success. In this way she can eventually learn to bring her blood pressure under control. Similarly, if an individual wanted to control headaches through biofeedback, he might have electronic sensors placed on certain muscles in his head and thereby learn to control the constriction and relaxation of those muscles. Then, when he felt a headache coming on, he could relax the relevant muscles and abort the pain. (See the accompanying Try It! box.)

While the control of physiological processes through the use of biofeedback is not easy to learn, results in a number of areas have been employed with success in a variety of ailments, including emotional problems (such as anxiety, depression, phobias, tension headaches, insomnia, and hyperactivity); medical problems with a psychological component (such as asthma, high blood pressure, ulcers, muscle spasms, migraine headaches, and menstrual distress); and physical problems (such as nerve-muscle injuries due to stroke, cerebral palsy, and—as we see in Figure 2-17—curvature of the spine).

Given that biofeedback is still experimental, we cannot assume that treatment is going to be successful in every case (Roberts, 1985). What is certain, however, is that learning through biofeedback has opened up a number of exciting

TRY IT!

BIOFEEDBACK ON YOUR OWN

You can easily demonstrate to yourself how biofeedback works by trying this procedure for raising the temperature of your finger (Brown, 1977).

First purchase an ordinary thermometer, about 6 to 8 inches long and filled with red mercury, at a drugstore or hardware store. Tape the bulb end of the thermometer to the pad of your middle finger with masking tape, making sure that it is not so tight that circulation is impeded.

After about five minutes of sitting quietly with your eyes closed, see what the temperature reading is. Then, while still sitting quietly, say these phrases to yourself:

"I feel relaxed and warm."
"My hand feels heavy."
"My arm feels heavy."
"My hand feels warm."
"My hands feel warm and relaxed."
"I feel calm and relaxed."

Say each of these phrases slowly, and then go through the series again. Every five to ten minutes check your finger temperature.

After ten or twenty minutes, most people begin to show a rise in finger temperature—some just a few degrees, and some as many as 10 degrees.

possibilities for treating people with physical and psychological problems. Moreover, some psychologists speculate that the use of biofeedback may become a part of everyday life one day in the future.

For instance, one researcher has suggested that students whose minds wander during studying might be hooked up to apparatus that gives them feedback as to whether they are paying attention to the information they are studying (Ornstein, 1977). If they stop paying attention, the computer will alert them—putting them back on the right track.

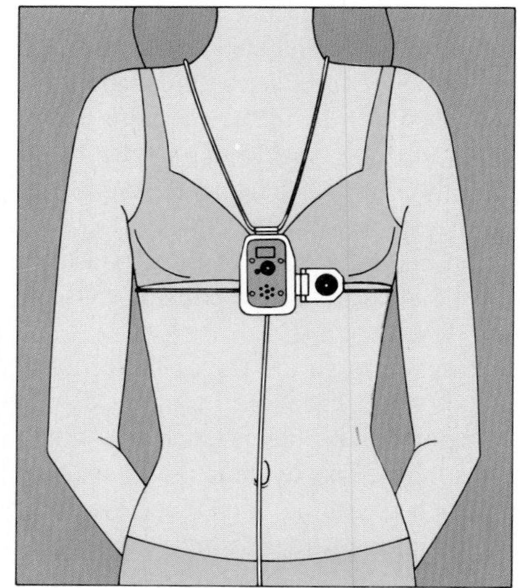

Figure 2-17
The traditional treatment for curvature of the spine employs an unsightly, cumbersome brace. In contrast, biofeedback treatment for the disability employs an unobtrusive set of straps attached to a small electronic device that produces tonal feedback when the patient is not standing straight. The person learns to maintain a position that gradually decreases the curvature of the spine until the device is no longer needed. [*Miller, 1985(a).*]

RECAP AND REVIEW IV

Recap

- The cerebral cortex—the "new brain"—contains three major areas: the motor, sensory, and association areas. The three areas of the cortex control voluntary movement, the senses, and higher mental processes (including thought, language, memory, and speech), respectively.
- The two halves, or hemispheres, of the brain are structurally similar, but they seem to specialize in different functions. The left side of the brain is most closely related to language and verbal skills, the right side to nonverbal skills such as mathematical and musical ability, emotional expression, pattern recognition, and the processing of visual information.
- Biofeedback is a procedure in which a person learns to control certain internal physiological processes, thereby bringing relief to a variety of specific ailments.

Review

1. Surprisingly, fine motor movements are controlled by a larger portion of the motor area of the cerebral cortex than are gross motor movements. True or false?
2. Touch, sight, and hearing are associated with what area within the cerebral cortex?
3. As a result of an injury to the association area of the brain, the patient was subsequently unable to understand language. This condition is labeled
   a. Broca's aphasia **b.** Receptive aphasia **c.** Apraxia **d.** Broca's apraxia
4. Marcy demonstrated strong academic skills in reading, writing, and powers of reasoning. We might say these strengths are associated with the ________________ side of her brain.
5. Research with split-brain patients has shown that even in normal individuals the left and right hemisphere function quite independently. True or false?
6. Biofeedback can be used in the treatment of
   a. Migraine headaches **b.** Muscle spasms **c.** Emotional problems **d.** All of the above

(Answers to review questions are on page 74.)

Psychology Looks Toward the 1990s
Using the Brain as a Diagnostic Device: Neurometrics

A new technological innovation is promising to revolutionize the diagnosis of subtle kinds of brain dysfunction that previously might have gone overlooked. Called *neurometrics*, this technique quantifies and statistically analyzes electrical activity in the brain of an individual and compares it to results from "normal" individuals. Early results show that specific kinds of deviations from average patterns can be used to infer not only that an individual is suffering from some kind of psychological or medical problem but also the particular nature of the problem (John, Prichep, Fridman, & Easton, 1988).

Major advances in neurometrics have come from the development of an innovative technique for comparing electrical activity in the brains of normal people to that of people who suffer from some psychological or medical problem. By matching BEAM (brain electrical activity mapping) scans, specific patterns of brain electrical activity have emerged. For example, Figure 2-18 shows average BEAM scans for a group of individuals suffering from several kinds of problems.

The diagnostic possibilities implicit in neurometrics are extraordinary. For

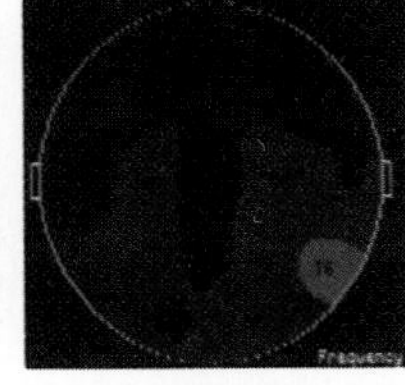

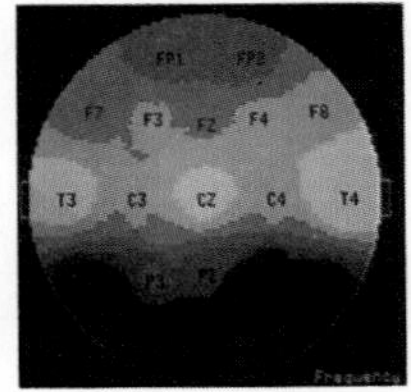

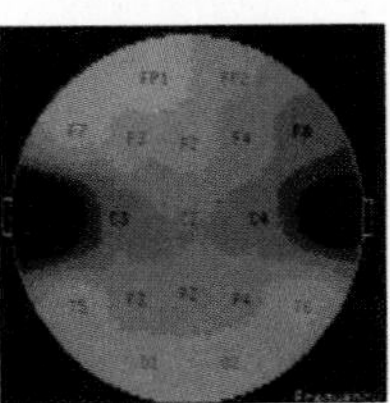

Figure 2-18
These are average BEAM scans for groups of people who have been diagnosed as normal, depressive, and schizophrenic. The color coding corresponds to the degree of deviation, with red showing excess and blue showing deficiency.

example, even when patients display identical symptoms, scientists who use neurometrics may be able to detect that the underlying problems causing the symptoms are actually quite different. In turn, this may lead to more individualized treatments.

Even more interesting is the possibility of identifying psychological difficulties before any overt symptoms have emerged. In this way, psychological problems can be prevented from disrupting people's lives before they occur—a true advance in the field of psychology.

LOOKING BACK

1. In this chapter we have seen that understanding human behavior requires knowledge of the biological influences underlying that behavior. This chapter reviews what biopsychologists (psychologists who specialize in studying the effects of biological structures and functions on behavior) have learned about the human nervous system.

2. Neurons, the most basic elements of the nervous system, allow nerve impulses to pass from one part of the body to another. Information generally enters a neuron through its dendrite, is passed on to other cells via its axon, and finally exits through its terminal buttons.

3. Each neuron is protected by a coating called the myelin sheath. When a neuron receives a message to fire, it releases an action potential, an electric charge that travels through the cell. Neurons operate according to an all-or-nothing law: They are either at rest or an action potential is moving through them. There is no in-between state, then; a neuron is either firing or at rest.

4. Once a neuron fires, nerve impulses are carried to other neurons through the production of chemical substances, neurotransmitters, which actually bridge the gaps—known as synapses—between neurons. Neurotransmitters may either be excitatory, telling other neurons to fire, or inhibitory, preventing or decreasing the likelihood of other neurons firing. Among the major neurotransmitters are acetylcholine (ACh), which produces contractions of skeletal muscles, and dopamine, which has been linked to Parkinson's disease and certain mental disorders such as schizophrenia.

5. Endorphins, another type of neurotransmitter, are related to the reduction of pain. By interacting with opiate receptors—specialized neurons that reduce the experience of pain—they seem to produce a natural kind of morphine, and are probably responsible for producing the kind of euphoria that joggers sometimes experience after running.

6. The nervous system is made up of the central nervous system (the brain and spinal cord) and the peripheral nervous system (the remainder of the nervous system). The peripheral nervous system is made up of the somatic division, which controls voluntary movements and the communication of information to and from the sense organs, and the autonomic division, which controls involuntary functions such as those of the heart, blood vessels, and lungs.

7. The autonomic division of the peripheral nervous system is further subdivided into the sympathetic and parasympathetic divisions. The sympathetic division prepares the body in emergency situations, and the parasympathetic division helps the body return to its typical resting state.

8. The central core of the brain is made up of the medulla (which controls such functions as breathing and the heartbeat), the pons (which coordinates the muscles and the two sides of the body), the cerebellum (which controls balance), the reticular formation (which acts to heighten awareness in emergencies), the thalamus (which communicates messages to and from the brain), and the hypothalamus (which maintains homeostasis, or body equilibrium, and regulates basic survival behaviors). The functions of the central core structures are similar to those found in other vertebrates; this part of the brain is sometimes referred to as the "old brain."

9. The endocrine system secretes hormones, allowing the brain to send messages throughout the body. Its major component is the pituitary gland, which affects growth. The limbic system, found on the border of the "old" and "new" brains, is associated with eating, reproduction, and the experiences of pleasure and pain.

10. The cerebral cortex—the "new brain"—has areas that control voluntary movement (the motor area); the senses (the somatosensory area); and thinking, reasoning, speech, and memory (the association area). It is divided into two halves, or hemispheres, each of which generally controls the opposite side of the body from that in which it is located. However, each hemisphere can be thought of as specialized in the functions it carries out: The left is best at verbal tasks, such as logical reasoning, speaking, and reading; the right is best at nonverbal tasks, such as spatial understanding, pattern recognition, mathematics, and emotional expression.

11. Biofeedback is a procedure in which a person learns to control internal physiological processes. By controlling what were previously considered involuntary responses, people are able to relieve a variety of specific psychological and physical problems, including anxiety, tension, migraine headaches, and a wide range of other problems.

ANSWERS TO REVIEW QUESTIONS

Review IV: **1.** True **2.** Somatosensory area (or sensory area) **3.** b **4.** Left **5.** False **6.** d

KEY TERMS AND CONCEPTS

nervous system (p. 45)
biopsychologist (45)
neuron (46)
dendrite (47)
axon (47)
terminal button (48)
myelin sheath (48)
all-or-nothing law (49)
resting state (49)
action potential (49)
absolute refractory period (49)
relative refractory period (49)
neurotransmitter (51)
excitatory message (51)
inhibitory message (51)
acetylcholine (51)
dopamine (51)
endorphin (52)
opiate receptor (52)
central nervous system (53)
spinal cord (53)
paraplegia (53)
spinal reflexes (53)
peripheral nervous system (53)
somatic division (54)
autonomic division (54)
sympathetic division (55)
parasympathetic division (55)
brain scan (57)
electroencephalogram (EEG) (58)
computerized axial tomography (CAT) scan (58)
nuclear magnetic resonance (NMR) scan (58)
positron emission tomograph (PET) scan (58)
brain electrical activity mapping (BEAM) (58)
central core (58)
medulla (58)
pons (58)
cerebellum (59)
reticular formation (59)
thalamus (60)
hypothalamus (60)
homeostasis (60)
endocrine system (60)
hormones (60)
pituitary gland (61)
limbic system (61)
cerebral cortex (63)
frontal lobes (63)
parietal lobes (63)
temporal lobes (63)
occipital lobes (63)
motor area of the brain (63)
sensory area of the brain (64)
somatosensory area (64)
association areas of the brain (65)
apraxia (66)
aphasia (66)
Broca's aphasia (66)
receptive aphasia (67)
hemisphere (67)
lateralization (67)
split-brain patient (69)
biofeedback (71)

FOR FURTHER STUDY AND APPLICATION

Carlson, N. R. (1985). *Physiology of behavior* (3rd ed.). Boston: Allyn & Bacon.

Levinthal, C. F. (1983). *Introduction to physiological psychology* (2nd ed.). Englewood Cliffs, NJ: Prentice-Hall.

These texts provide a comprehensive view of the physiological underpinnings of human behavior while remaining readable and straightforward.

Netter, F. H. (1953). *The Ciba collection of medical illustrations (Vol. 1: Nervous system).* Summit, NJ: Ciba Pharmaceutical Co.

Although some aspects of these illustrations are dated, they are for the most part the best drawings we have of the human nervous system. The drawings convey a sense of the intricacies and marvels underlying the operation of our bodies.

Wiederhold, W. C. (Ed.). (1982). *Neurology for non-neurologists.* New York: Academic Press.

This volume provides a series of chapters, written by experts but designed for the nonexpert, on various disorders of the nervous system and on methods of treatment.

Corballis, M. C., & Beale, I. L. (1983). *The ambivalent mind: The neuropsychology of left and right.* Chicago: Nelson-Hall.

This book presents an interesting view of left and right dominance in the brain, as well as left and right dominance in other parts of the body.

Gardner, H. (1974). *The shattered mind: The person after brain damage.* New York: Random House.

This fascinating book discusses a number of case histories of individuals who have suffered brain damage in light of what their difficulties might suggest about normal brain function.

Baskin, Y. (1983, August). Interview with Roger Sperry. *OMNI,* pp. 68–73, 98–100.

An insightful interview with one of the pioneers and leading experts on the brain, this article summarizes his accomplishments and discusses where work on the brain is heading.

Penfield, W. (1975). *The mystery of the mind.* Princeton, NJ: Princeton University Press.

Written by an expert on the brain, this book provides fascinating glimpses into the operation and mysteries of the mind.

CHAPTER 3

SENSATION AND PERCEPTION

PROLOGUE

LOOKING AHEAD

SENSING THE WORLD AROUND US

Is the light really there or are we in the dark? Absolute thresholds

Comparing apples with apples: Just noticeable differences

Becoming accustomed to stimulation: Sensory adaptation

Recap and review I

THE FIVE+ SENSES

The eyes have it: Seeing the world

TRY IT! Find Your Blind Spot

Recap and review II

Hearing and moving about the world: The sense of sound and balance

THE CUTTING EDGE. It's All in an Astronaut's Head: Curing Space Sickness

PSYCHOLOGY AT WORK. Replacing a Sense Organ: An Electronic Ear Implant for the Deaf

Making sense of the other senses: Smell, taste, and the skin senses

The informed consumer of psychology: How do you spell relief—from pain?

Recap and review III

VIEWING THE WORLD AS IT SEEMS: PERCEPTION

Creating wholes from parts: The gestalt laws of organization

Where 1 + 1 equals more than 2: The whole is greater than the sum of its parts

Translating 2-D to 3-D: Depth perception

Is the cup half full or half empty?: Figuring the figure from the ground

Sorting out the auditory world: Selective attention

PERCEPTION IN EVERYDAY LIFE

Misperceptions of the eye: Visual illusions

Recap and review IV

PSYCHOLOGY LOOKS TOWARDS THE 1990S. Computer Versions of Vision

LOOKING BACK

KEY TERMS AND CONCEPTS

FOR FURTHER STUDY AND APPLICATION

PROLOGUE

The alarm rings at 7, and she reaches for the pillbox. It is the first act of her day. Her suffering, like the box itself, is divided into four spaces, each with its allotments of pink, white, brown and blue pills. "The pain is always there," she says; "there are just different levels of it." First there is the "daily, hard, getting-around pain." This constant pain of rheumatoid arthritis has been with Maureen Hemmis, 37, since she was 18 years old. Then there is the variable pain; spots of acute, stabbing sensations that change location each day. Worst of all are the arthritic flare-ups when each joint rages and burns, hot to the touch. "The pain is everywhere. You can't be moved or touched. It's very much like being on fire" (Wallis, 1984, p. 58).

* * *

The twelve-year-old boy's sweet smile makes a poignant contrast to his otherwise pitiful appearance. His arms and legs are deformed and bent, as though he had suffered from rickets. Several fingers are missing. A large open wound covers one knee, and the smiling lips are bitten raw. He looks for all the world like a battered child, but only nature is to blame for his condition. He was born with an extremely rare genetic defect that makes him insensitive to pain. His fingers were crushed or burned because he did not pull his hand away from things that were hot or dangerous. His bones and joints are misshapen because he pounded them too hard when he walked or ran. His knee had ulcerated from crawling over sharp objects that he could not feel. Should he break a bone or dislocate a hip, he would not feel enough to cry out for help (Wallis, 1984, pp. 58, 60).

LOOKING AHEAD

Luckily, few of us suffer from the unfortunate conditions that afflict these two individuals. Yet they illustrate clearly the profound effect that our bodily sensations can have on our behavior. In the first case we see a woman overwhelmed by excruciating pain—pain so intense that it becomes the focal point of her life. In the second example we see a young boy with a rare genetic disorder, whose inability to experience pain leads to a life every bit as painful, in its own way, as the woman's.

These two cases illustrate dramatically how people's sensations shape their experiences in a fundamental way. But of course it is not just pain to which we are responsive; we react also to light, sound, tastes, smells, and a variety of other stimulation that comes from the world around us.

Sensation: *The process by which an organism responds to a stimulus*

Perception: *The sorting out, interpretation, analysis, and integration of stimuli from our sensory organs*

In this chapter we focus on the area of psychology concerned with the nature of information our body takes in through its sense organs and the way we interpret such information. We will be concerned both with **sensation,** the process by which an organism responds to physical stimulation from the environment, as well as **perception,** the sorting out, interpretation, analysis, and integration of stimuli by our sense organs. To a psychologist who is interested in understanding the causes of behavior, sensation and perception are fundamental topics, since our behavior is so much a reflection of how we react to and interpret stimuli from the world around us. Indeed, questions such as how we identify the fundamentals of vision and hearing, how we know whether sugar or lemon is sweeter, and how we distinguish one person from another all fall into the realms of sensation and perception.

Although perception is clearly an outgrowth of sensation, it is sometimes difficult to distinguish the two. (Indeed, psychologists—and philosophers, as well—have argued for years over the distinction.) The primary difference is that sensation can be thought of as an organism's first encounter with a raw sensory stimulus, while perception is the process by which it is interpreted, analyzed, and integrated with other sensory information. For instance, if we were considering sensation, we might ask how bright a stimulus appears; if we were to consider perception, we might ask whether someone recognizes the stimulus and what its meaning is to them.

The chapter begins with a discussion of the relationship between the nature of a physical stimulus and the kinds of sensory responses that are made to it. The sensitivity of the senses to various kinds of stimuli is considered, and the degree to which different levels of stimulation can be differentiated from one another is discussed. We will see how the nature of the specific kinds of stimuli to which we, as humans, are capable of responding has important effects on every aspect of our behavior.

The chapter then moves to a discussion of the particular senses. It starts with vision, explaining the physical aspects of light and how the eye uses it to see. The structure of the eye is presented, as are the mechanisms by which the eye transforms light into messages that can be used by the brain. Next, the sense of hearing and its relationship to motion and balance are considered as we discuss the ear. Beginning with the physical structure of sound, we trace its movement through the ear and learn how it is modified from a physical stimulus into something usable by the brain. We also discuss some of the remaining senses: smell, taste, and the skin senses, which include touch and the experience of pain.

Next, the chapter discusses a number of issues relating to perception. We begin by discussing the way we organize the stimuli to which our sense organs are exposed in an effort to actively make sense of our environment. Then we consider vision, focusing on how we are able to perceive the world in three dimensions when our retinas are only capable of sensing two-dimensional images. Finally, we discuss visual illusions, which provide us with important clues for understanding our general perceptual mechanisms.

In sum, after reading and studying this chapter, you will be able to:

- Describe the relationship between the physical nature of a stimulus and a person's response to it
- Identify the major senses and understand the fundamentals of how they operate
- Explain how the physical aspects of light and sound are transformed and used by the structures of the eye and ear, and identify those structures
- Summarize the operation of the smell, taste, and skin senses
- Describe the major principles of perceptual organization, and explain how we are able to perceive images in three dimensions
- Identify the predominant visual illusions and discuss their causes
- Understand and use the key terms and concepts listed at the end of this chapter

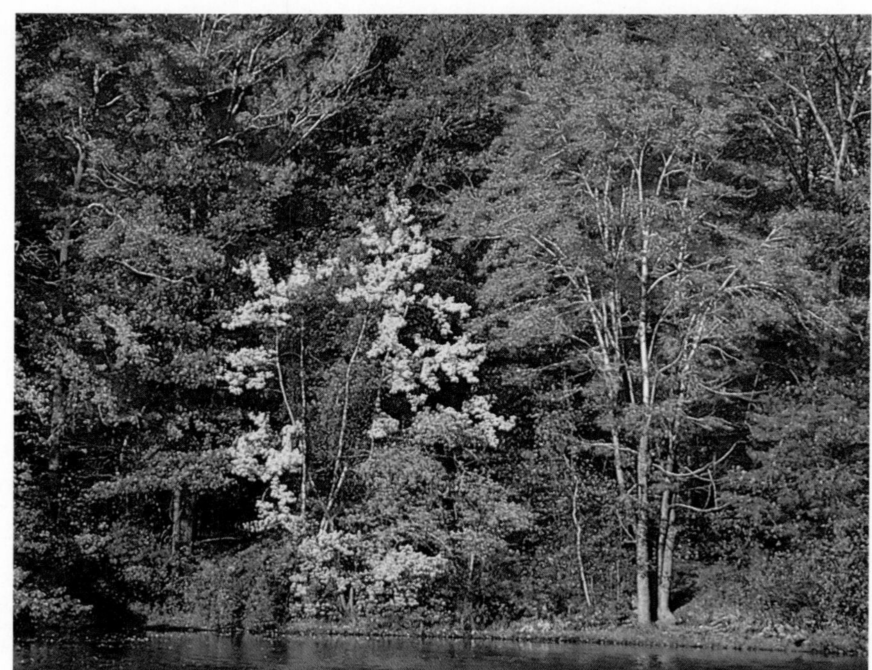

This tranquil scene is actually clogged with stimuli, most of which cannot be sensed by the human sensory system. *(James M. Crump III/The Picture Cube)*

SENSING THE WORLD AROUND US

It was a quiet, sunny afternoon, and Rich thought it was a good time to do a little studying. He got in his car and drove to Puffers Pond, probably the most scenic spot in town. When he got there, he spread a blanket on the shore, lay down, and got out some books. Although the wind made a softly rustling sound through the leaves, all else was quiet—so quiet, in fact, that Rich was lulled into drowsiness after only a short time. As he drifted off to sleep, he thought to himself that the world needed a lot more serene, isolated spots where one could have total peace and quiet and be left completely alone.

Although to Rich the pond's shoreline represented a refuge from the sights and sounds of a busy world, he was making a mistake to assume that little activity was occurring there. For instance, for other species it would have been a challenge to sort out the many stimuli that were actually present—stimuli that Rich could not, because of the limitations of the human body, detect through his senses. To a dog wandering by, the pond would have unleashed an enticing set of smells, a symphony of random sounds, and a bustling scene of swarming insects and other tiny organisms. In fact, the area abounded with other examples of physical energy, of which neither Rich, nor the dog, nor any other living organism, for that matter, could be aware: radio waves, ultraviolet light, and tones extremely high or low in pitch.

Stimulus: *A source of physical energy that activates a sense organ*

To understand how a psychologist would analyze the scene at the pond, we first need a basic working vocabulary. In formal terms, if any passing source of physical energy activates a sense organ, the energy is known as a **stimulus**. A stimulus, then, is energy that produces a response in a sense organ. The term sensation is used to describe the process by which an organism responds to the stimulus. Sensation is concerned with a person's first moment of contact with and response to the stimulus. Hence stimuli are the sources of sensations.

Stimuli vary in both kind and strength. Different kinds of stimuli activate different sense organs. For instance, we can differentiate light stimuli, which activate our sense of sight and allow us to see the colors of a tree in autumn, from sound stimuli, which permit us to hear the sounds of an orchestra through our sense of hearing.

Each sort of stimulus that is capable of activating a sense organ can also be considered in terms of its strength, or **magnitude**. For instance, how bright does a light stimulus have to be before it is capable of being detected? The issue of the nature of the relationship between the magnitude of a stimulus and sensory response has been investigated in a branch of psychology known as psychophysics. **Psychophysics** is the study of the relationship between the physical nature of stimuli and a person's sensory responses to them.

Magnitude: *The strength of a stimulus*

Psychophysics: *The study of the relationship between the physical nature of stimuli and a person's sensory responses to them*

Is the Light Really There or Are We in the Dark?: Absolute Thresholds

It is obvious that people are not capable of detecting all physical stimuli that are present in the environment, as we mentioned in our earlier example of the seemingly quiet pond. Just when does a stimulus become strong enough to be detected by our sense organs? The answer to this question requires an understanding of the concept of absolute thresholds. An **absolute threshold** is the smallest amount of physical intensity of a stimulus that must be present for it to be detected. Although we previously compared the sensory capabilities of humans unfavorably with those of dogs, in fact, absolute thresholds in human

Absolute threshold: *The smallest amount of physical intensity by which a stimulus can be detected*

Sight
Candle flame seen from a distance of 30 miles

Hearing
Ticking of a watch in a room 20 feet away

Taste
One teaspoon sugar dissolved in 2 gallons of water

Smell
One drop of perfume in a three-room house

Touch
The wing of a bee falling on your cheek from a distance of 1 centimeter

Figure 3-1
The extraordinary sensitivity of our senses is illustrated in these examples of absolute thresholds.

The noise in this bar is not just auditory; the crowded conditions produce noise that affects the senses of vision, smell, taste, and touch as well. *(Ken Regan/Camera 5)*

sensory organs are quite extraordinary. Consider, for instance, those examples of absolute thresholds for the various senses (see Figure 3-1):

- Sight: A candle flame can be seen 30 miles away on a dark, clear night.
- Hearing: The ticking of a watch can be heard 20 feet away under quiet conditions.
- Taste: Sugar can be discerned when 1 teaspoon is dissolved in 2 gallons of water.
- Smell: Perfume can be detected when one drop is present in a three-room apartment.
- Touch: A bee's wing falling from a distance of 1 centimeter can be felt on a cheek (Galanter, 1962).

As you can see, such thresholds permit a wide range of sensory stimulation to be detected by the human sensory apparatus. In fact, the capabilities of our senses are so fine-tuned that we might have problems if they were any more sensitive. For instance, if our ears were just slightly more sensitive, we would be able to hear the sound of air molecules in our ears knocking into each other—something that would surely prove distracting and might even prevent us from hearing sounds outside our bodies as well.

Noise: *Background stimulation that interferes with the perception of other stimuli*

Of course, the absolute thresholds we have been discussing are measured under ideal conditions; normally our senses cannot detect stimulation quite so well because of the presence of noise. **Noise**, as defined by psychophysicists, is background stimulation that interferes with the perception of other stimuli. Hence noise does not refer just to auditory stimuli, the most obvious examples, but also to those stimuli that affect the other senses. Picture a talkative group of people crammed into a small, crowded, smoke-filled room at a party. The smoke makes it difficult to see, the din of the crowd makes it hard to hear individual voices, and even tasting the food becomes difficult because of all the smoke in the room. In this case, the smoke and crowded conditions would be considered ''noise'' since they are preventing sensation at more discriminating and sensitive levels.

In addition to noise, other factors that may influence our sensitivity to stimulation are our expectations about whether a stimulus is present and our assumptions about the kind of stimulus it might be (Schiffman, 1982). For instance, if you as a batter know when a pitcher is likely to throw a curve ball, you will be better prepared to track the incoming pitch—and ultimately to hit it—than if you do not know what kind of pitch to expect.

Finally, the motivation of an observer to detect a stimulus will influence response sensitivity. For example, a physician whose aim is to detect a heart abnormality when examining a patient would likely be highly motivated to detect any stimuli indicating a problem. Consequently, the likelihood of finding an abnormality would probably be greater than if motivation were lower.

Signal detection theory To systematically understand how a person's sensations are affected by factors such as noise, expectations about whether a stimulus is present or absent, and motivation, psychologists have developed an approach to psychophysics known as signal detection theory (Swets & Pickett, 1982).

Signal detection theory goes a step beyond the question of whether a person is able to detect a stimulus when it is actually present—as in classical psychophysics; in addition, it considers cases in which there is a question of whether any stimulus is actually present at all. The theory acknowledges that observers may err in either of two ways: in reporting that a stimulus is not present when it is not, or in reporting that a stimulus is not present when it actually is. For instance, imagine the consequences of a physician who mistakenly thinks she hears a heart abnormality when listening to your chest—and orders heart surgery for you. The error may be just as costly as if she listens to your heart and fails to detect an abnormality that is actually there.

Signal detection theory: *The theory that addresses the questions of whether a person can detect a stimulus and whether a stimulus is actually present at all*

Difference threshold: *The smallest detectable difference between two stimuli*
Just noticeable difference: *(See difference threshold)*

Signal detection theory, then, is able to provide an understanding of how errors in judgment, as well as such factors as observer expectations and motivation, affect our judgments of sensory stimuli. It also allows us to increase the reliability of our predictions about which conditions will cause observers to be most accurate in their judgments.

Comparing Apples with Apples: Just Noticeable Differences

Suppose a shopkeeper said you could choose six apples from a barrel of apples, and you wanted to compare them in a number of aspects to see which half dozen were best—which were bigger, which were redder, which tasted sweeter. One approach to this problem would be to systematically compare one apple with another until you were left with a few so similar that you could not tell the difference between them (see Figure 3-2).

Psychologists have discussed this problem in terms of the **difference threshold**, the smallest detectable difference between two stimuli—also known as a **just noticeable difference**. They have found that the stimulus value that constitutes a just noticeable difference depends on the initial intensity of the stimulus. For instance, you may have noticed that the light change which comes in a three-way bulb when you switch from 75 to 100 watts appears greater than when you switch from 100 to 125 watts, even though the wattage increase is the same in both cases. Similarly, when the moon is visible during the late afternoon, it appears relatively dim—yet against a dark night sky, it seems quite bright.

Figure 3-2
One way of choosing six apples from a barrel would be to systematically compare one apple with another.

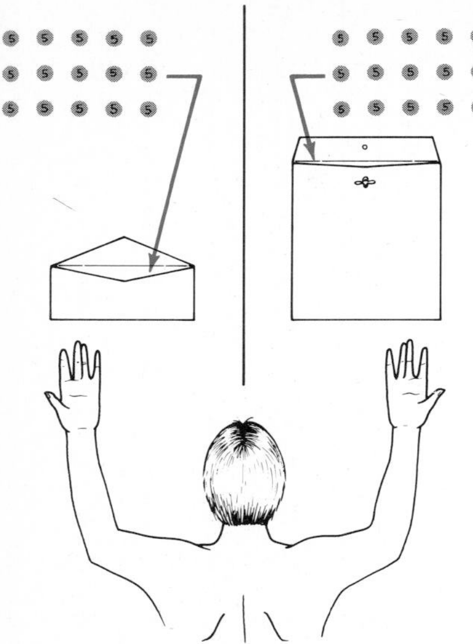

Figure 3-3
To determine the effects of context on judgments of sensory stimuli, try this simple experiment in which you place fifteen nickels in two envelopes of differing sizes. If you then compare the weight of the two envelopes, it will seem that the nickels in the smaller envelope weigh more—demonstrating that the context of one stimulus (the envelope size) modifies responses to another stimulus (the envelope weight).

The relationship between changes in the original value of a stimulus and the degree to which the change will be noticed forms one of the basic laws of psychophysics: Weber's law. **Weber's law** states that a just noticeable difference is a constant proportion of the magnitude of an initial stimulus. Therefore, if a 10-pound increase in a 100-pound weight produces a just noticeable difference, it would take a 1000 pound increase to produce a noticeable difference if the initial weight were 10,000 pounds. In both cases, the increase necessary to produce a just noticeable difference is proportionally identical—1:10 (10:100 = 1000:10,000). (Actually, Weber found the true proportion increase in weight that produces a just noticeable difference to be between 2 and 3 percent.) Similarly, the just noticeable difference distinguishing changes in loudness between sounds is larger for sounds that are initially loud than for sounds that are initially soft—as exemplified by the fact that a person in a quiet room is more apt to be startled by the ringing of a telephone than a person in a room that is already noisy. In order to produce the same amount of reaction in a noisy room, a telephone ring might have to approximate the loudness of cathedral bells.

Weber's law seems to hold for all sensory stimuli, although its predictions are less accurate at extremely high or extremely low levels of stimulation. Moreover, the law helps explain psychological phenomena that lie beyond the realm of the senses. For example, imagine that you own a house you would like to sell for $85,000. You might be satisfied if you received an offer of $80,000 from a potential buyer, even though it was $5000 less than the asking price. On the other hand, if you were selling your car and asking $10,000 for it, an offer of $5000 less than your asking price would probably not make you happy. Although the absolute amount is the same in both cases, the psychological value of the $5000 is very different.

Weber's law: *The principle that states that the just noticeable difference is a constant proportion of the magnitude of an initial stimulus*

Becoming Accustomed to Stimulation: Sensory Adaptation

In an old television commercial for a room deodorizer, a woman walks into someone's house, takes a sniff, and whispers to a companion, "Oh, I can tell they had fish for dinner." Meanwhile, the hapless occupants of the house are blithely unaware of their malodorous house.

* * *

As the circus strongman carries a group of five acrobats across the circus tent, someone asks him if they aren't awfully heavy. He replies, "Not if you've just been carrying an elephant."

Adaptation: *An adjustment in sensory capacity following prolonged exposure to stimuli*

Both of these cases illustrate the phenomenon of **adaptation**, an adjustment in sensory capacity following prolonged exposure to stimuli. Adaptation occurs as people get used to stimuli and change their frame of reference. Consequently, they do not respond to the stimulus in the way they did earlier.

Probably the clearest example of adaptation is the decrease in sensitivity to sensory stimulation that occurs after repeated exposure to a stimulus. If, for example, you were to repeatedly hear a loud tone, it would begin to sound softer after a while. Similarly, if you were forced to enter a room that had a lingering fish odor from the occupants' evening meal, you would soon be unaware of the smell (although, if you were to believe the commercial described earlier, your evening might be spoiled nonetheless).

The apparent decline in sensitivity to sensory stimuli is due to the inability of the sensory nerve receptors to constantly fire off messages to the brain. Because these receptor cells are most responsive to *changes* in stimulation,

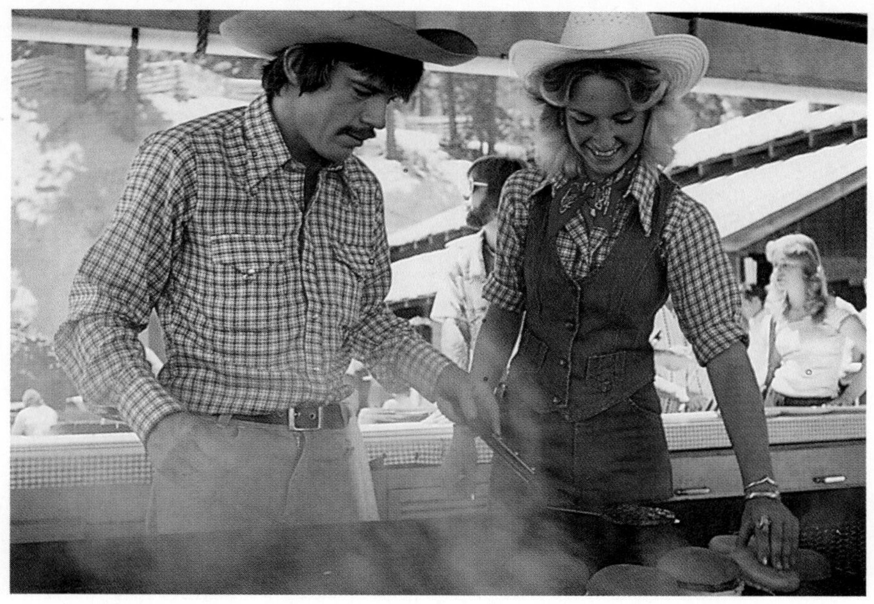

Unlike these people, who have habituated to the smell of smoke and grease, a person coming upon this scene might well find the situation less than tolerable. *(Arthur Sirdofsky/The Stock Shop)*

constant stimulation is not effective in producing a reaction. In fact, most receptor cells are incapable of constant firing, and their reaction to unvarying stimulation is a steady decline in the rate at which impulses are communicated. For instance, a fishy smell in a room initially produces a high rate of firing of sensory neurons, but this rate cannot be sustained, and constant firing eventually tapers off. In addition, there seems to be a depletion of certain chemicals in the receptor cells, making them less sensitive to stimulation.

Similar adaptation occurs with the other senses. For example, if you were able to stare unblinkingly at the exact same spot on this page for a long period of time—something that is impossible to do because of minute, involuntary movements of the eye—the spot would eventually disappear as the visual neurons lost their ability to fire.

Judgments of sensory stimuli are also affected by the context in which the judgments are made. Just as carrying five trapeze artists seems like nothing to the strongman after carting an elephant around the tent, judgments are not made in isolation from other stimuli but in terms of preceding sensory experience. You can demonstrate this for yourself by trying a simple experiment.

Take two envelopes, one large and one small, and put fifteen nickels in each. Now lift the large envelope, put it down, and lift the small one (see Figure 3-3). Which seems to weigh more?

Most people report that the small one is heavier—although, as you know, the weights are identical. The reason for this misconception is that the physical context of the envelope interferes with the sensory experience of weight; adaptation to the context of one stimulus (the size of the envelope) alters responses to another stimulus (the weight of the envelope) (Coren, Porac, & Ward, 1984).

Sensory-adaptation phenomena provide another illustration that a person's reaction to sensory stimuli is not always an accurate representation of the physical stimuli that brought it about. This point will become even more apparent as we move from consideration of sensation—which is the direct response of an organism to physical stimuli—and begin to discuss the specific senses of the human body.

RECAP AND REVIEW I

Recap

- Sensation occurs when an organism responds to a stimulus, which is any form of energy that activates a sense organ, while perception is the sorting out, interpretation, analysis, and integration of stimuli by our sense organs. The branch of psychology called psychophysics studies the relationship between the physical nature of stimuli and the sensory responses that are made.
- An absolute threshold is the smallest amount of physical intensity by which a stimulus can be detected. The level of the absolute threshold is affected by noise—background interference from other stimuli—and by a person's expectations and motivation.
- Signal detection theory is used to predict the accuracy of sensory judgments. An observer may err in two ways: by reporting the presence of a stimulus when there is none or by reporting the absence of a stimulus when there actually is one.
- Difference threshold or just noticeable difference refers to the smallest detectable difference between two stimuli. According to Weber's law, a just noticeable difference is a constant proportion of the size of an initial stimulus.
- Sensory adaptation occurs when people are exposed to a stimulus for so long that they become used to it and therefore no longer respond to it.

Review

1. The initial contacts and responses to stimuli are known as
a. Psychophysics **b.** Sensations **c.** Noises **d.** Stimuli

2. A researcher is investigating the effects of noise levels on human sensory responses. The area of psychology she is working in is known as ______________________.

3. Match the descriptive statements in the right column with the appropriate label in the left column:

a. ____ Noise	1. The minimum amount of magnitude of a stimulus needed for it to be detected
b. ____ Absolute threshold	2. Background stimuli which interfere with and impede sensory discrimination
c. ____ Adaptation	3. The smallest detectable difference between two stimuli
d. ____ Just noticeable difference	4. Adjustment of our sensory capacity following extended exposure to a stimulus

4. Signal detection theory takes into account the specific kinds of errors that are made by people who are judging whether a stimulus is present. True or false?

5. ____ states that the difference threshold is a constant proportion of the magnitude of the initial stimulus.
a. Psychophysics **b.** Sensory adaptation **c.** Weber's law **d.** Signal detection theory

(Answers to review questions are on page 88.)

THE FIVE + SENSES

As she sat down to Thanksgiving dinner, Rhona reflected on how happy she was to leave dormitory food behind—at least for the long holiday weekend. She was just plain tired of seeing and smelling the same monotonous cafeteria food. Even chewing the stuff was distasteful—it all felt like mush. ''In fact,'' she thought to herself, ''If I have to eat toast covered with chipped beef one more time, I may never eat again.'' But this thought was soon interrupted when she saw her father carry in the turkey on a tray and place it squarely in the center of the table. The noise level, already high from the talking and laughter of the family members, grew still louder. As she picked up her fork, the smell of the turkey reached her and she felt her stomach growl hungrily. With the sight and sound of her family around the table—not to speak of the smell and taste of all that food—she felt more relaxed than she had since she had left for college in the fall. ''Ah, home, sweet home,'' she thought.

Put yourself in this scene and consider how different it might be if any one of your senses were not functioning. What if you were blind and unable to see the faces of your family—or the welcome shape of the succulent turkey? What if you had no sense of hearing and could not listen to the family's talk, or were

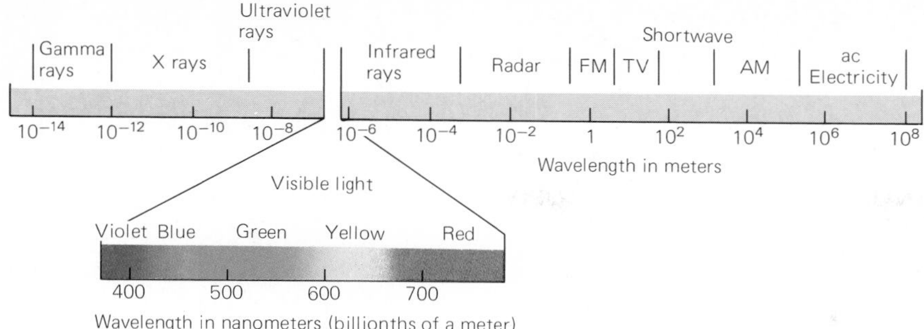

Figure 3-4
The visual spectrum—the range of wavelengths to which people are sensitive—represents only a small part of the wavelengths present in our environment.

unable to feel your stomach growl, or smell the dinner, or taste the food? Clearly, an important dimension of the situation would be lacking, and no doubt the dinner would evoke a very different experience for you than it would for someone whose sensory apparatus was intact.

Moreover, the sensations mentioned above barely scratch the surface of sensory experience. Although most of us have been taught at one time or another that there are just five senses—sight, sound, taste, smell, and touch—this enumeration is far too modest, since human sensory capabilities go far beyond the basic five senses. It is well established, for example, that we are sensitive not merely to touch, but to a considerably wider set of stimuli—pain, pressure, temperature, vibration, and more. In addition, the ear is responsive to information that not only allows us to hear but to keep our balance as well.

Although all of the senses, alone and in combination with one another, play a critical role in determining how we experience the world, most psychological research has focused on vision and hearing—the two modes on which we will concentrate here.

The Eyes Have It: Seeing the World

To consider how our sense of vision allows us to view the world, we must first begin outside the body and consider the nature of the stimulus that produces vision—**light**. Although we are all familiar with light, having all our lives basked in the sun or its artificial equivalent, its underlying physical qualities are less apparent.

Light: *The stimulus that produces vision*

The stimuli that register as light in our eyes are actually electromagnetic radiation waves to which our bodies' visual apparatus happens to be sensitive and capable of responding. As you can see in Figure 3-4, electromagnetic radiation is measured in wavelengths, with the size of the wavelength corresponding to different sorts of energy. The range of wavelengths that humans are sensitive to—called the **visual spectrum**—is actually relatively small, but the differences among wavelengths within that spectrum are sufficient to allow us to see a range of all the colors, running from violet at the low end of the visual spectrum to red at the top. Colors, then, are associated with a particular wavelength within the visual spectrum.

Visual spectrum (SPEK trum): *The range of wavelengths to which humans are sensitive*

Light waves coming from some object outside the body (imagine the light reflected off the face of the Mona Lisa, as in Figure 3-5) first encounter the only organ that is capable of responding to the visual spectrum: the eye. Strangely enough, most of the eye is not concerned with reacting directly to light and transforming it into a message that can be sent to the brain via nerve cells, but with shaping the entering image into something that can be used by the neurons

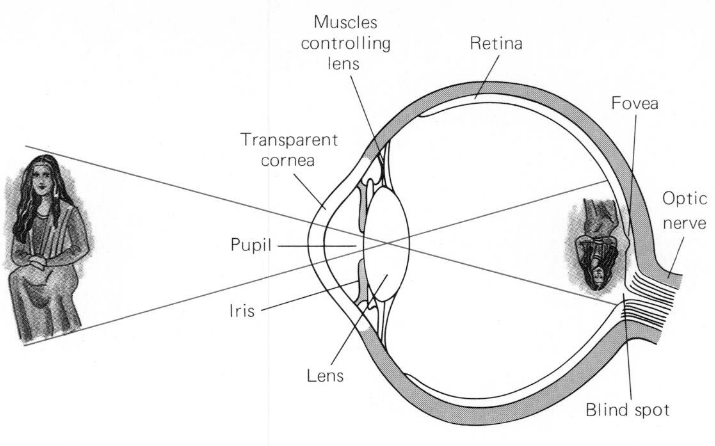

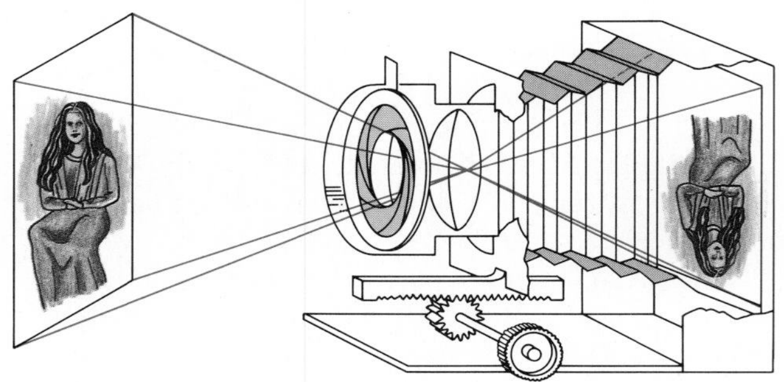

Figure 3-5
Although human vision is far more complicated than the most sophisticated camera, in some ways basic visual processes are analogous to those used in photography.

that will serve as messengers. The neurons themselves take up a relatively small percentage of the total eye. In other words, most of the eye is a mechanical device, analogous in many respects to a camera without film, as you can see in Figure 3-5. (It is important to realize, though, the limitations of this analogy: Vision involves processes that are far more complex and sophisticated than any camera is capable of mimicking.)

Cornea (CORN ee uh): *A transparent, protective window into the eyeball*

Pupil: *A dark hole in the center of the eye's iris which changes size as the amount of incoming light changes*

Iris: *The colored part of the eye*

Illuminating the Structure of the Eye The ray of light we are following as it is reflected off the Mona Lisa first travels through the **cornea**, a transparent, protective window that is constantly being washed by tears, keeping it moist and clean. After moving through the cornea, the light traverses the pupil. The **pupil** is a dark hole found in the center of the **iris**, the colored part of the eye, which ranges in humans from a light blue to a dark brown. The size of the pupil opening depends on the amount of light in the environment: The dimmer the surroundings, the more the pupil opens in order to allow more light to enter.

Why shouldn't the pupil be maximally opened all the time, thereby allowing the greatest amount of light into the eye? The answer to that question has to do with the basic physics of light. A small pupil greatly increases the range of distances at which objects are in focus; with a wide-open pupil, the range is relatively small, and details are harder to discern. (Camera buffs know this in terms of the aperture or f-stop setting that they must adjust on their cameras.)

ANSWERS TO REVIEW QUESTIONS

Review I: **1.** b **2.** Psychophysics **3.** a.2; b.1; c.4; d.3 **4.** True **5.** c

The eye takes advantage of bright light by decreasing the size of the pupil and thereby becoming more discerning; in dim light the pupil expands in order to enable us to view the situation better—but at the expense of visual detail. Perhaps one reason that candlelight dinners are often thought of as romantic may be that the dimness of the light prevents one from seeing the details of a lover's flaws.

Once light passes through the pupil, it enters the **lens**, which is located directly behind the pupil. The lens acts to bend the rays of light coming from the Mona Lisa so that they are properly focused on the rear of the eye. The lens focuses the light by changing its own thickness, a process that is called **accommodation**. The kind of accommodation that occurs depends on the location of the object in relation to the body. Distant objects require a relatively flat lens; in this case, the muscles controlling the lens relax, allowing the fluid within the eye to flatten the lens. In contrast, close objects are viewed best through a rounded lens. Here, then, the muscles contract, taking tension off the lens—and making it rounder.

Having traveled through the pupil and lens, our image of the Mona Lisa is finally able to reach its ultimate destination in the eye—the **retina**—where the electromagnetic energy is converted into messages that the brain can use. It is important to note that—again because of the physics of light—the image has reversed itself as it traveled through the lens, and it reaches the retina upside down (relative to its original position). Although you might think this would cause major difficulties in understanding and moving about the world, it turns out not to be a problem. Because we see *everything* upside down, we have long since adjusted to this orientation. In fact, if we were ever to put on mirrored glasses that righted the image, we would have a hard time, because everything would look upside down to us—although eventually we would adjust to the new orientation.

The retina is actually a thin layer of nerve cells at the back of the eyeball (see Figure 3-6). There are two kinds of light-sensitive receptor cells found in

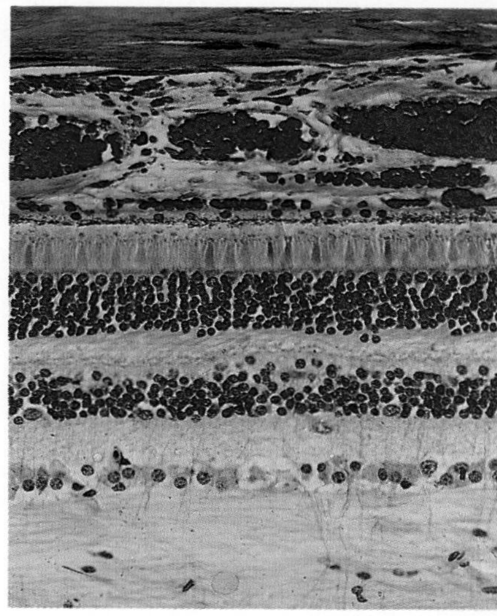

This microscopic photo of the rods and cones of the eye clearly reveals their distinctive shapes. *(Manfred Kage/Peter Arnold, Inc.)*

Lens: *The part of the eye located behind the pupil that bends rays of light to focus them on the retina*

Accommodation: *The ability of the lens to vary its shape in order to focus incoming images on the retina*

Retina (RET in uh): *The part of the eye that converts the electromagnetic energy of light into useful information for the brain*

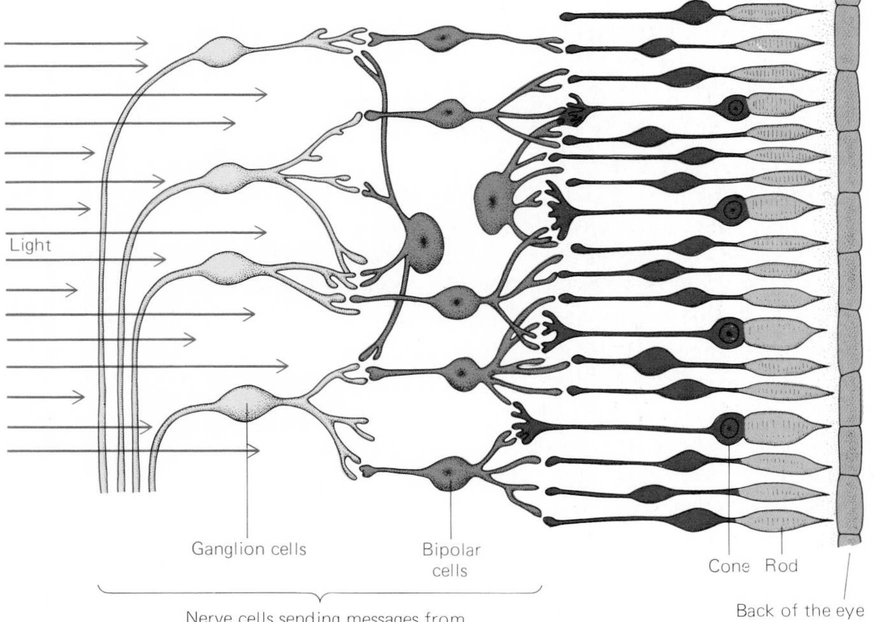

Figure 3-6
The basic cells of the eye. Light entering the eye travels through the ganglion and bipolar cells and strikes the light-sensitive rods and cones. The rods and cones then transmit nerve impulses to the brain via the bipolar and ganglion cells. (*Coren, Porac, & Ward, 1984.*)

Rods: *Long, cylindrical, light-sensitive receptors in the retina that perform well in poor light but are largely insensitive to color and small details*

Cones: *Cone-shaped, light-sensitive receptor cells in the retina that are responsible for sharp focus and color perception, particularly in bright light*

Fovea (FOVE ee uh): *A very sensitive region of the retina that aids in focusing*

the retina, and the names they have been given describe their shapes: **rods**, which are long and cylindrical, and **cones**, which are short, thick, and tapered. The rods and cones are distributed unevenly throughout the retina, with the greatest concentration of cones on the part of the retina called the **fovea** (refer back to Figure 3-5). The fovea is a particularly sensitive region of the retina; if you want to focus in on something of particular interest, you try to center the image from the lens onto the area of the fovea.

The farther away on the retina from the fovea, the smaller the number of cones becomes. Conversely, there are no rods in the fovea—but the number increases rapidly toward the edges of the eye. Because the fovea covers only a small portion of the eye, there are fewer cones (about 7 million) than there are rods (about 125 million).

Peripheral (pur IF er ul) **vision**: *The ability to see objects behind the eyes' main center of focus*

The rods and cones are not only structurally dissimilar, but they play distinctly different roles in vision (Cohen & Lasley, 1986). Cones are primarily responsible for the sharply focused perception of color, particularly in brightly lit situations, while rods are related to vision in dimly lit situations and are largely insensitive to color and to details as sharp as those the cones are capable of recognizing. The rods are used for **peripheral vision**—seeing objects that are outside the main center of focus—and for night vision. In both cases, the level of detail that can be discerned is far lower when the rods come into play than when the cones are activated—as you know from groping your way across a dark room at night. Although you may just dimly see the outlines of furniture, it is almost impossible to distinguish color and the other details of obstacles in

TRY IT!

FIND YOUR BLIND SPOT

Because the area where the optic nerve leaves the retina has no nerve cells, you are blind in that particular spot. To prove this to yourself, try this: Close your right eye and look at the haunted house in Figure 3-7 with your left eye. You will see the ghost on the periphery of your vision. Now, while staring at the house, move the page toward you. When the book is about a foot from your eye, the ghost will disappear. At this moment, the image of the ghost is falling on your blind spot.

But also notice how, when the page is at that distance, not only does the ghost seem to disappear, but the line seems to run continuously through the area where the ghost used to be. This shows how we automatically compensate for missing information by using nearby material to complete what is unseen. That's the reason you never notice the blind spot: What is missing is replaced by what is seen next to the blind spot.

Figure 3-7
Is there a ghost near this haunted house? The ghost disappears when its image falls on your blind spot.

your path. You may also have noticed that you can improve your view of an object at night by looking slightly away from it. The reason? If you shift your gaze off-center, the image from the lens falls not on the relatively night-blind foveal cones, but moves toward the more light-sensitive rods.

Shedding Light on Vision: Sending the Message from the Eye to the Brain What happens when light energy strikes the retinal receptors is partially dependent on whether it strikes a rod or a cone. Rods contain **rhodopsin**, a complex, reddish-purple substance that changes chemically when energized by light, thereby setting off a chemical reaction. The substance involved in cone receptors is different, but the principles seem similar: Stimulation of the nerve cells in the eye triggers a neural response that is transmitted to other nerve cells leading to the brain. These are called bipolar cells and ganglion cells.

Rhodopsin (ro DOP sin): *A complex, reddish-purple substance that changes when energized by light, causing a chemical reaction*

Bipolar cells connect directly with the rods and lead to the **ganglion cells**, which collect and summarize information that comes from the rods. The visual information is gathered and moved out of the back of the eyeball through a bundle of ganglion axons called the **optic nerve**.

Bipolar (by PO lur) **cells**: *Nerve cells leading to the brain that are triggered by nerve cells in the eye*

Ganglion (GANG lee yon) **cells**: *Nerve cells that collect and summarize information from rods and carry it to the brain*

Optic nerve: *A bundle of ganglion axons in the back of the eyeball that carry visual information to the brain*

Because the opening for the optic nerve pushes through the retina, there are no rods or cones in the area, which creates a blind spot. Normally, however, this absence of nerve cells does not interfere with vision, because you automatically compensate for the missing part of your field of vision. (To find your blind spot, see the accompanying Try It! box.)

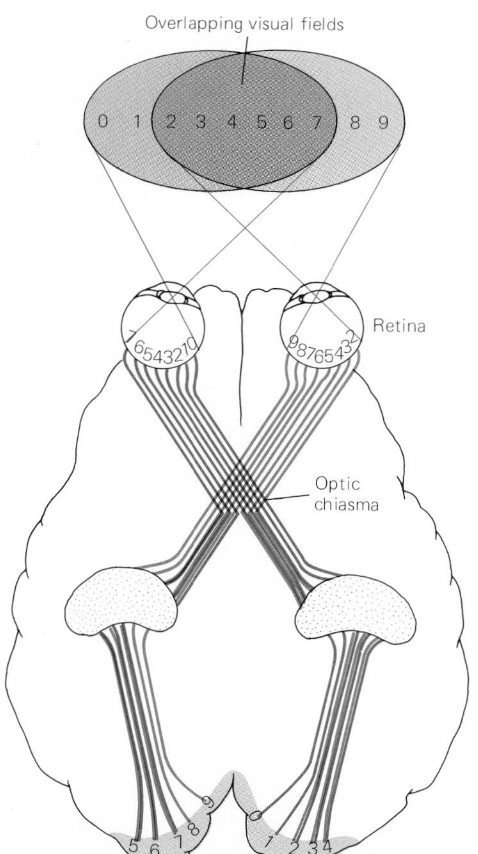

Figure 3-8
Because the optic nerve coming from each eye splits at the optic chiasma, the image to a person's right is sent to the left side of the brain, and the image to the person's left is transmitted to the right side of the brain. (*Based on Lindsay & Norman, 1977.*)

Optic chiasma (ky AZ muh): *A point between and behind the eyes at which nerve impulses from the optic nerves are reversed and "righted" in the brain*

Once beyond the eye itself, the image of the Mona Lisa we have been following moves through the optic nerve. As the optic nerve leaves the eyeball, its path does not take the most direct route to the part of the brain right behind the eye. Instead, the optic nerves from each eye meet at a point roughly between the two eyes—called the **optic chiasma**—where each optic nerve then splits.

When the optic nerve splits, the nerve impulses coming from the right half of each retina are sent to the right side of the brain, and the impulses arriving from the left half of each retina are sent to the left side of the brain. Because the image on the retina is reversed and upside down, however, those images coming from the right half of the retina are actually included in the field of vision to the left of the person, and images coming from the left half of the retina represent the field of vision to the right of the individual (see Figure 3-8). In this way, our nervous system ultimately produces the phenomenon we discussed first in Chapter 2, in which each half of the brain is associated with the functioning of the opposite side of the body.

Glaucoma (glaw KO muh): *A dysfunction of the eye in which fluid pressure builds up and causes a decline in visual acuity*

Tunnel vision: *An advanced stage of glaucoma in which vision is reduced to the narrow circle directly in front of the eye*

One of the most frequent causes of blindness is related to the transmission of impulses across the optic nerve. **Glaucoma**, which strikes between 1 and 2 percent of those over age 40, occurs when pressure in the fluid of the eye begins to build up, either because it cannot be properly drained or because it is overproduced. When this first begins to happen, the nerve cells that communicate information about peripheral vision are constricted, leading to a decline in the ability to see anything outside of a narrow circle directly ahead. This problem is called **tunnel vision**. Eventually, the pressure can become so great that all the nerve cells are contracted, leading to total blindness.

From Light to Dark: Adaptation Have you ever walked into a movie theater on a bright, sunny day and stumbled into your seat, barely being able to see at all? Do you also recall later getting up to buy some popcorn and having no trouble navigating your way up the aisle?

Light adaptation: *The eye's temporary insensitivity to light dimmer than that to which it has become accustomed (as when entering a movie theater)*

Dark adaptation: *A heightened sensitivity to light resulting from being in low-level light*

Your initial trouble seeing in the dimly lit theater was due to **light adaptation**, a phenomenon in which the eye grows insensitive to light that is dimmer than the level to which it has been most recently exposed. In contrast, the fact that you were later able to see relatively well is due to **dark adaptation**, a heightened sensitivity to light that results from being in relative dimness.

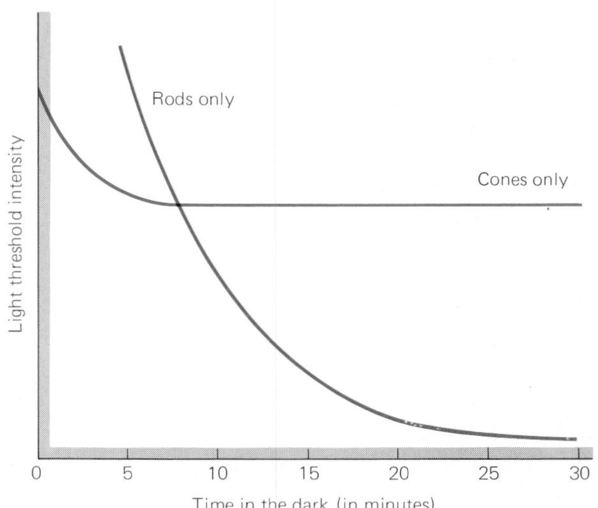

Figure 3-9
Dark adaptation—the heightened sensitivity to light that occurs after moving to a dimmer environment—occurs at different rates for rods and cones. As this graph shows, the visual threshold (the lowest amount of light needed to be detected) is lower for rods than for cones after about thirty minutes in a dimly lit environment. (*Adapted from Cornsweet, 1970.*)

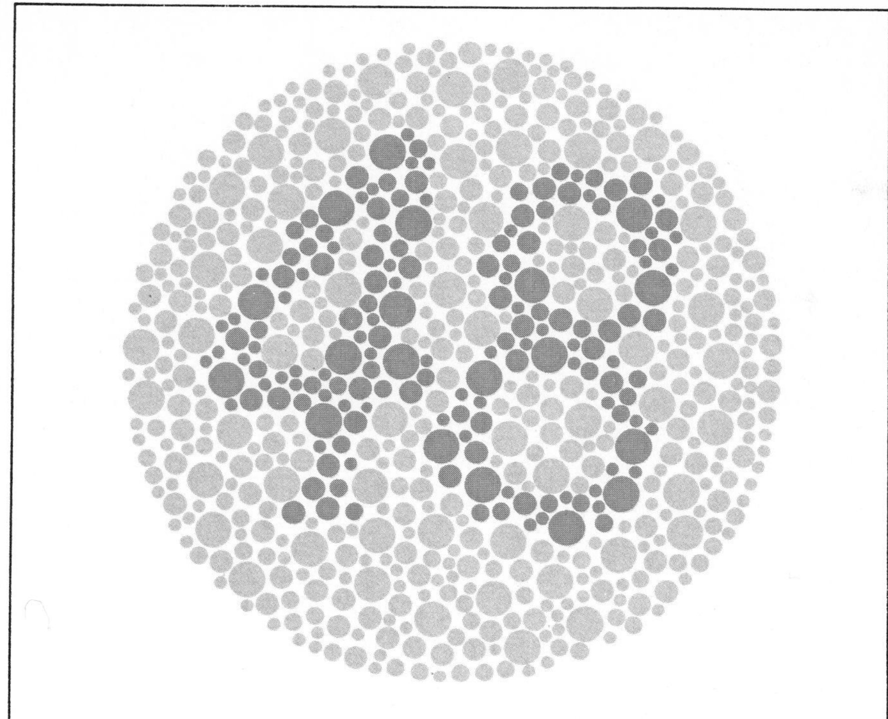

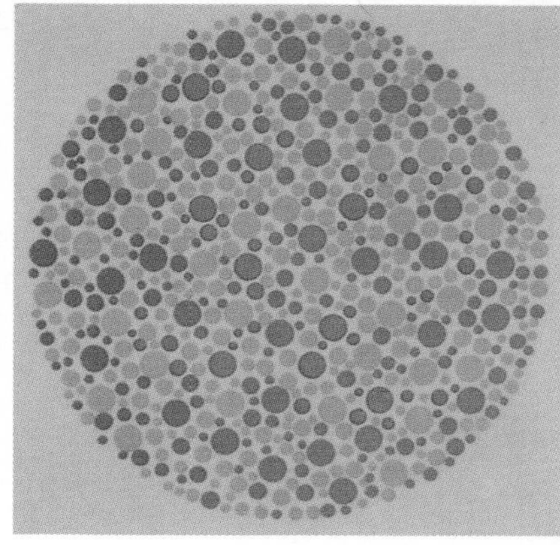

Figure 3-10
Although people who are color-blind are able to easily see the "48," they cannot detect the presence of the figure "32" within these designs. (*Reproduced by permission from the* Dvorine Color Vision Test. *Copyrights assigned to the Psychological Corporation 1977. All rights reserved.*)

The speed at which both dark and light adaptation occur is a function of the rate at which changes occur in the chemical composition of the rods and cones. As you can see in Figure 3-9, the changes occur at different speeds for the two kinds of cells, with the cones reaching their greatest level of adaptation in just a few minutes, but the rods taking close to thirty minutes to reach the maximum level. On the other hand, the cones never reach the level of visual acuity that the rods attain. When considered jointly, though, dark adaptation is complete in a darkened room in about half an hour.

The 7-Million-Color Rainbow: Color Vision and Color Blindness Although the range of wavelengths to which humans are sensitive is relatively narrow, at least in comparison to the entire electromagnetic spectrum, the range to which we are capable of responding still allows us great flexibility in sensing the world. Nowhere is this clearer than in terms of the colors we can discern: A person with normal color vision is capable of distinguishing no less than 7 million different colors (Bruce & Green, 1984).

Although the variety of colors that people are generally able to distinguish is vast, there are certain individuals whose ability to perceive color is quite limited—the color-blind. Interestingly, the condition of these individuals has provided some of the most important clues for understanding how color vision operates (Nathans et al., 1986).

Look, for a moment, at the designs shown in Figure 3-10. If you cannot see any numbers or designs embedded within the dots, you probably are one of the 2 percent of men (and 2 out of 10,000 women) who are color-blind.

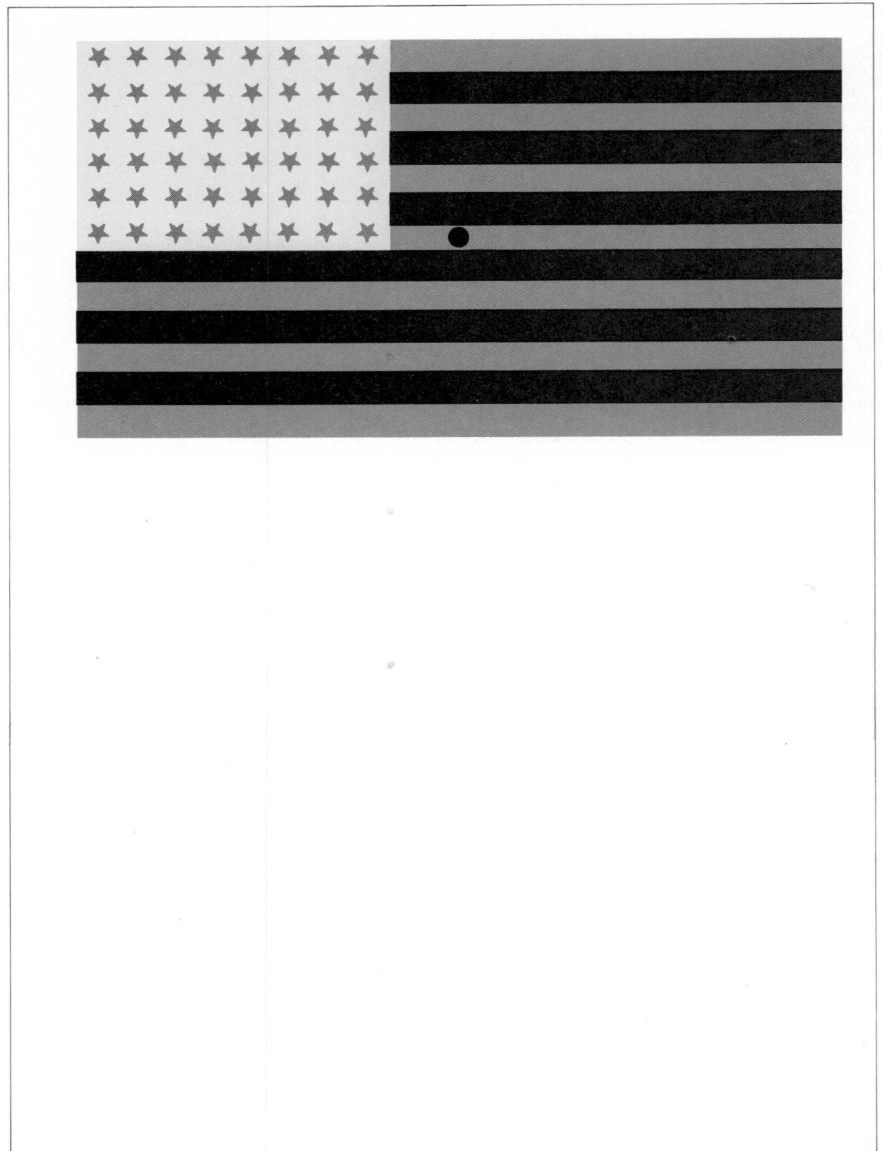

Figure 3-11
If you stare at the dot in this flag for about a minute and then look at the white space below, the afterimage phenomenon will make a traditional red, white, and blue flag appear.

For most people who are color-blind, the world probably looks quite dull: Red fire engines look yellow, green grass looks yellow, and the three colors of a traffic light all look yellow. In fact, in the most common form of color blindness, all red and green objects are seen as yellow. There are other forms of color blindness as well, but they are quite rare. In yellow-blue blindness, people are unable to tell the difference between yellow and blue, and in the most extreme case an individual perceives no color at all: The world to such a person looks something like the picture on a black-and-white television set.

To understand why some of us are color-blind, it is necessary to understand the basics of color vision. There appear to be two processes involved. The first process is based on what has been labeled the **trichromatic theory**. It suggests that there are three kinds of cones in the retina, each of which responds primarily to a specific range of wavelengths. One is most responsive to blue-violet colors, one to green, and the other to yellow-red (Brown & Wald, 1964). According to trichromatic theory, perception of color is influenced by the relative strength with which each of the three kinds of cones is activated. If, for instance, we see a blue sky, the blue-violet cones are primarily involved, while the others show less activity. The trichromatic theory provides a straightforward explanation of color blindness: It suggests that one of the three cone systems malfunctions, and colors covered by that range are perceived improperly.

Trichromatic (try kro MAT ik) **theory of color vision**: *The theory that suggests that the retina has three kinds of cones, each responding to a specific range of wavelengths, perception of color being influenced by the relative strength with which each is activated*

However, there are phenomena that the trichromatic theory is less successful at explaining. For instance, it cannot explain why pairs of colors can combine to form gray, and it does not explain what happens after you stare at something like the flag shown in Figure 3-11 for about a minute. Try this yourself, and then move your eyes to the white space below. You will see an image of the traditional red, white, and blue American flag. Where there was yellow, you'll see blue, and where there were green and black, you'll see red and white.

The phenomenon you have just experienced is called an **afterimage**, and it occurs because activity in the retina continues even when you are no longer staring at the original picture. However, it also demonstrates that the trichromatic theory does not explain color vision completely: Why should the colors in the afterimage be different from those in the original?

Afterimage: *The image appearing when you move your eyes from a certain image to a blank object*

Because trichromatic processes do not provide a full explanation of color vision, another theory, the **opponent-process theory**, has been proposed. According to the theory, members of pairs of different receptor cells are linked together to work in opposition to each other. Specifically, there is a blue-yellow pairing, a red-green pairing, and a black-white pairing. If an object reflects light that contains more blue than yellow, it will stimulate the firing of the blue receptors, simultaneously discouraging or inhibiting the firing of yellow receptors—and the object will appear blue. If, on the other hand, a light contains more yellow than blue, the yellow receptors will be stimulated to fire while the blue ones are inhibited, and the object will appear yellow.

Opponent-process theory of color vision: *The theory that suggests that members of pairs of different receptor cells are linked together to work in opposition to each other*

The opponent-process theory allows us to explain afterimages very directly. When we stare at the yellow in the figure, for instance, our receptor cells for the yellow component of the yellow-blue pairing begin to get fatigued and will be less able to respond to yellow stimuli. On the other hand, the blue part of the pair is not tired, since it is not being stimulated. When we look at a white surface, the light reflected off it would normally stimulate both the yellow and the blue receptors equally. But the fatigue of the yellow receptors prevents this; they temporarily do not respond to the yellow, which makes the white light appear to be blue. Since the other colors in the figure do the same thing relative to their specific opponents, the afterimage produces the opponent colors—for a while, at least. Of course, the afterimage lasts only a short time, since the fatigue of the yellow receptors is soon overcome, and the white light begins to be perceived more accurately.

Most psychologists assume that both opponent processes and trichromatic mechanisms are at work to allow us to see colors, although they operate in different parts of the visual sensing system. It seems most likely that trichromatic processes work within the retina itself, while opponent processes operate at a later stage of neuronal connections and processing (Beck, Hope, & Rosenfeld, 1983).

RECAP AND REVIEW II

Recap

- Although people have traditionally thought in terms of five senses, psychologists studying sensation have found that the number is actually far greater.
- The eyes are sensitive to electromagnetic radiation waves of certain wavelengths; these waves register as light.
- As light enters the eye, it passes through the cornea, pupil, iris, lens, and ultimately reaches the retina, where the electromagnetic energy of light is converted into nerve impulses usable by the brain. These impulses leave the eye via the optic nerve.
- The retina is composed of nerve cells called rods and cones, which play differing roles in vision and are responsible for dark and light adaptation.
- Humans are able to distinguish around 7 million colors. Color vision involves two processes: trichromatic mechanisms and an opponent-processing system.

Review

1. The visual spectrum can best be described as:
a. The existing wavelengths of the universe **b.** The stimulation of the retina by a variety of wavelengths **c.** The wavelengths not visible by the naked eye **d.** The range of wavelengths to which human beings are sensitive

2. Match each definition in the right column with the correct word in the left column. All words relate to the structure or function of the eye.

a. ____ Lens	1. Keep moist by tears, this part of the eye could be considered a protective window.
b. ____ Accommodation	2. The action performed by the lens, which serves to focus the light passing through it.
c. ____ Iris	3. The colored part of the eye, ranging from light blue to dark brown in humans.
d. ____ Retina	4. The dark hole centered in the colored part of the eye.
e. ____ Cornea	5. This feature of the eye bends rays of light so they are focused on the rear of the eye.
f. ____ Pupil	6. The site where the visual image is transformed into messages that the brain can use.

3. Perception of the myriad colors visible at the beach on a sunny day is the responsibility of the receptor cells of the eye known as ____________. On the other hand, discriminating features in a dimly lit restaurant is the job of the ____________.

4. The area on the retina containing the greatest concentration of cones is the
a. Fovea **b.** Optic chiasma **c.** Rhodospin **d.** Optic nerve

5. ____________ is a disease in which pressure in the fluid of the eye begins to build up, resulting in a decline in peripheral vision known as ____________ ____________.

6. John was to meet his girlfriend in the movie theater. As was typical, he was late and the movie had begun. He stumbled down the aisle, barely able to see because of ____________ adaptation. Unfortunately, the woman he sat down beside and attempted to put his arm around was not his girlfriend. He sorely wished he had given his eyes a chance and waited for ____________ adaptation to occur.

7. ____________ theory suggests that there are three kinds of cones in the retina, each of which responds primarily to a specific range of wavelengths.
a. Opponent process **b.** Afterimage **c.** Trichromatic **d.** Color blindness

(Answers to review questions are on page 98.)

Hearing and Moving about the World: The Sense of Sound and Balance

The blast-off was easy compared to what he was experiencing now: space sickness. The constant nausea and vomiting were enough to make him consider calling Mission Control and asking to return to base. Even though he had been warned that there was a 50 percent chance that his first experience in space would cause such sickness, he wasn't prepared for how terribly sick he really felt. How can he ever go on to live and work on the space station for the next three months feeling like this?

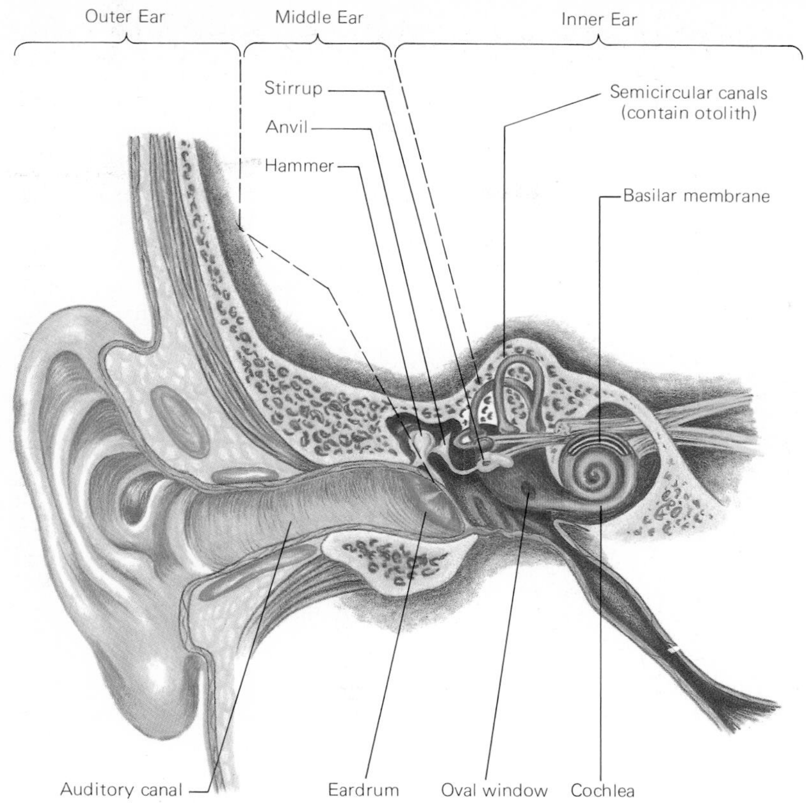

Figure 3-12
The ear.

Whether or not our mythical astronaut turns his rocket around and heads back to earth, his experience—which is a major problem for space travelers—is related to a basic sensory process that is centered in the ear: the sense of motion and balance, which allows people to navigate their bodies through the world and maintain an upright position without falling. Along with hearing, the process by which sound waves are translated into understandable and meaningful forms, the sensing of motion and balance represent the two major functions of the ear.

The Site of Sound and Balance: The Ear While many of us think only of the **outer ear** when we consider hearing, this part is little more than a reverse megaphone, designed to collect and bring sounds into the internal portions of the ear, illustrated in Figure 3-12. **Sound** is the movement of air molecules brought about by the vibration of an object. Sounds travel through the air in wave patterns similar to those made by a stone thrown into a still pond.

Once sounds, which arrive in the form of wave vibrations, have been herded into the **auditory canal**, a tubelike passage, they reach the **eardrum**. The eardrum is aptly named because it operates like a miniature drum, vibrating when sound waves hit it. The louder the sound, the more it vibrates. These vibrations are then transmitted into the **middle ear**, a tiny chamber containing just three bones, called, because of their shapes, the **hammer**, the **anvil**, and the **stirrup**. These bones have one function: to transmit vibrations to the **oval window**, a thin membrane leading to the inner ear. Because of their shape, the hammer, anvil, and stirrup do a particularly effective job not only transmitting vibrations but actually increasing their strength, since they act as a set of levers.

Outer ear: *The visible part of the ear that acts as a sound collector*
Sound: *The movement of air molecules brought about by the vibration of an object*
Auditory canal: *A tubelike passage in the ear through which sound moves to the eardrum*
Eardrum: *The part of the ear that vibrates when sound waves hit it*
Middle ear: *A tiny chamber containing three bones—the hammer, the anvil, and the stirrup—which transmit vibrations to the oval window*
Hammer: *A tiny bone in the middle ear that transfers vibrations to the anvil*
Anvil: *A tiny bone in the middle ear that transfers vibrations to the stirrup*
Stirrup: *A tiny bone in the middle of the ear that transfers vibrations to the oval window*
Oval window: *A thin membrane between the middle ear and the inner ear that transmits vibrations while increasing their strength*

Moreover, since the opening into the middle ear is considerably larger than the opening out of it, the force of sound waves on the smaller area becomes amplified. The middle ear, then, acts as a tiny mechanical amplifier, making us aware of sounds that would otherwise go unnoticed.

Inner ear: *The interior structure that changes sound vibrations into a form that can be transmitted to the brain*

Cochlea (KOKE lee uh): *A coiled tube filled with fluid that receives sound via the oval window or through bone conduction*

Basilar (BAZ ih lar) **membrane**: *A structure dividing the cochlea into an upper and a lower chamber*

Hair cells: *Tiny cells covering the basilar membrane that, when bent by vibrations entering the cochlea, activate sensory receptor cells*

The Inner Sanctum: The Inner Ear The **inner ear** is the portion of the ear that actually changes the sound vibrations into a form that allows them to be transmitted to the brain. It also contains the organs that allow us to locate our position and determine how we are moving through space. When the sound enters the inner ear through the oval window, it moves into the **cochlea**, a coiled tube filled with fluid that looks something like a snail. Inside the cochlea is the **basilar membrane**, a structure that runs through the center of the cochlea, dividing it into an upper and a lower chamber (see Figure 3-12). The basilar membrane is covered with **hair cells**. When these hair cells are bent by the vibrations entering the cochlea, sensory receptor cells are activated.

Although sound typically enters the cochlea via the oval window, there is an additional method of entry: bone conduction. Because the ear rests on a maze of bones within the skull, the cochlea is able to pick up subtle vibrations that travel across the bones from other parts of the head. For instance, one of the ways you hear your own voice is through bone conduction, which explains why you sound different to yourself than to other people who hear your voice. (Listen to yourself on a tape recorder sometime to hear what you *really* sound like!) The sound of your voice reaches you both through the air and via bone conduction, and therefore sounds richer to you than to everyone else.

Semicircular canals: *Part of the inner ear containing fluid that moves when the body moves to control balance*

Otoliths: *Structure in the semicircular canals that sense body acceleration*

Balancing the Ups and Downs of Life The ear has several other structures that are more related to our sense of balance than to our hearing. The **semicircular canals** of the inner ear consist of three tubes containing fluid that sloshes through them when the head moves, signaling rotational or angular movement to the brain. The pull on our bodies caused by the acceleration of forward, backward, or up-and-down motion, as well as the constant pull of gravity, is sensed by the **otoliths**, motion-sensitive organs within the semicircular canals. The actual sense of acceleration is caused by the movement of tiny crystals within each otolith, which shift like sands on a windy beach when we move. The otolith's inexperience with the weightlessness of space is the cause of the space sickness experienced by the astronaut in our earlier example—a problem that is actually quite common among space travelers. (For a discussion of work on a possible cure for space sickness, see the Cutting Edge box.)

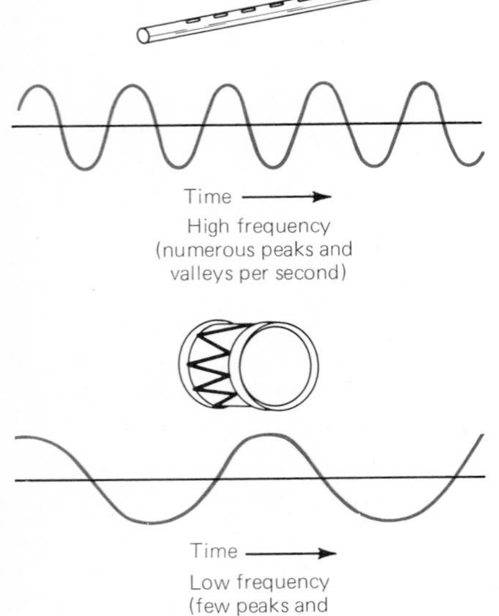

Figure 3-13
The waves produced by different stimuli are transmitted—usually through the air—to our ear.

Hearing about Sound: The Physical Aspects As we mentioned earlier, what we refer to as sound is actually the physical movement of air molecules in regular, wavelike patterns caused by the vibration of an object (see Figure 3-13). Sometimes it is even possible to view these vibrations, as in the case of a stereo speaker that has no enclosure. If you have ever seen one, you know that, at least when the lowest notes are playing, you can see the speaker moving in and out. What is less obvious is what happens next: The speaker pushes air molecules into waves with the same pattern as its movement. These wave pat-

ANSWERS TO REVIEW QUESTIONS

Review II: **1.** d **2.** a.5; b.2; c.3; d.6; e.1; f.4 **3.** Cones, rods **4.** a **5.** Glaucoma, tunnel vision **6.** Light, dark **7.** c

THE CUTTING EDGE

IT'S ALL IN AN ASTRONAUT'S HEAD

Curing Space Sickness

If NASA goes ahead with its plans to build a permanently staffed orbiting space station in the early 1990s, one of the first problems it is going to have to solve is the riddle of space sickness. Although rarely talked about in public (NASA tries hard to present just the positive side of space exploration), it presents a difficulty that has to be resolved before people can begin to shuttle routinely back and forth between earth and space. Already, the tight schedules of a number of missions have been severely disrupted because of the space sickness of crew members (Joyce, 1984).

Although the reason for space sickness has not been completely determined, most psychologists believe the source of the problem lies in the inner ear, where our sense of balance and control of motion are located. According to Charles Oman, associate director of the Man-Vehicle Laboratory at the Massachusetts Institute of Technology, who has done much of the work on space sickness, "When you move your body, the brain has learned what sensory signals to expect. . . . It compares the expected to the actual. When it sees a difference, it says to itself, 'Ah, something is new here,' and it triggers corrective movements" (Joyce, 1984, p. 34).

The problem arises when the body is floating in zero-gravity space; the lack of gravity confuses the ear's otoliths. Even though the semicircular canals are still able to accurately interpret the movement and rotation of the head, the discrepancy between information coming from the otoliths and from the semicircular canals produces two messages to the brain that don't fit together. The result: space sickness.

Although the effects of space sickness eventually wear off as astronauts become accustomed to the effects of zero gravity, valuable time can be lost before normal functioning begins. To provide a quicker cure, psychologists such as Patricia Cowings at NASA's Ames Research Center in California are working to develop better techniques to prevent the onset of space sickness. One method now being tried is biofeedback (discussed in Chapter 2), a technique that teaches astronauts to focus attention on specific parts of their body in order to bring them under their conscious control. More specifically, they learn to control some twenty physiological functions relating to space sickness, such as heart rate, breathing, and muscle relaxation. During biofeedback training, they are hooked up to a measuring device that gives them constant readouts of their physiological state, and they learn from the feedback how to bring the function under control. By focusing on psychologically controlling the physiological symptoms of space sickness, they are able to control the effects of the mismatched signals arriving in the brain from the sense organs.

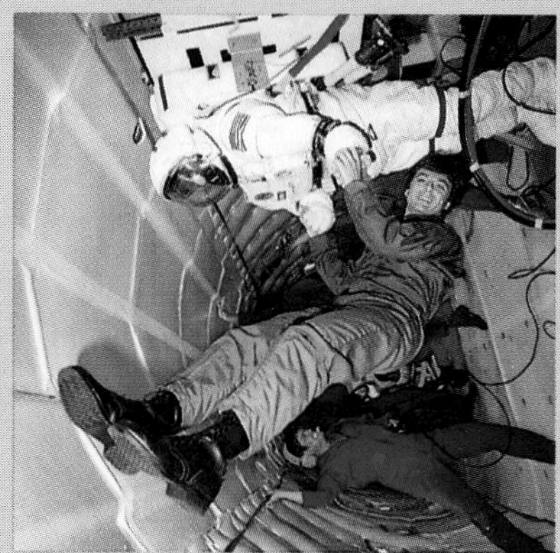

The inexperience of the ear's otolith with weightlessness can produce space sickness in astronauts. *(NASA)*

Biofeedback techniques seem promising, and they will be tested in upcoming space flights. Whether they can help astronauts to overcome space sickness completely remains to be seen, but such methods of prevention may become part of the standard training for astronauts if the early research is borne out.

terns soon reach your ear, although their strength has been weakened considerably during their travels. All other stimuli that produce sound work in essentially the same fashion, setting off wave patterns that move through the air to the ear. Air—or some other medium such as water—is necessary to make the vibrations of objects reach us; there can be no sound in a vacuum.

Frequency: *The number of wave crests occurring each second in any particular sound*

We are able to see the speaker moving when low notes are played because of a primary characteristic of sound called frequency. **Frequency** is the number

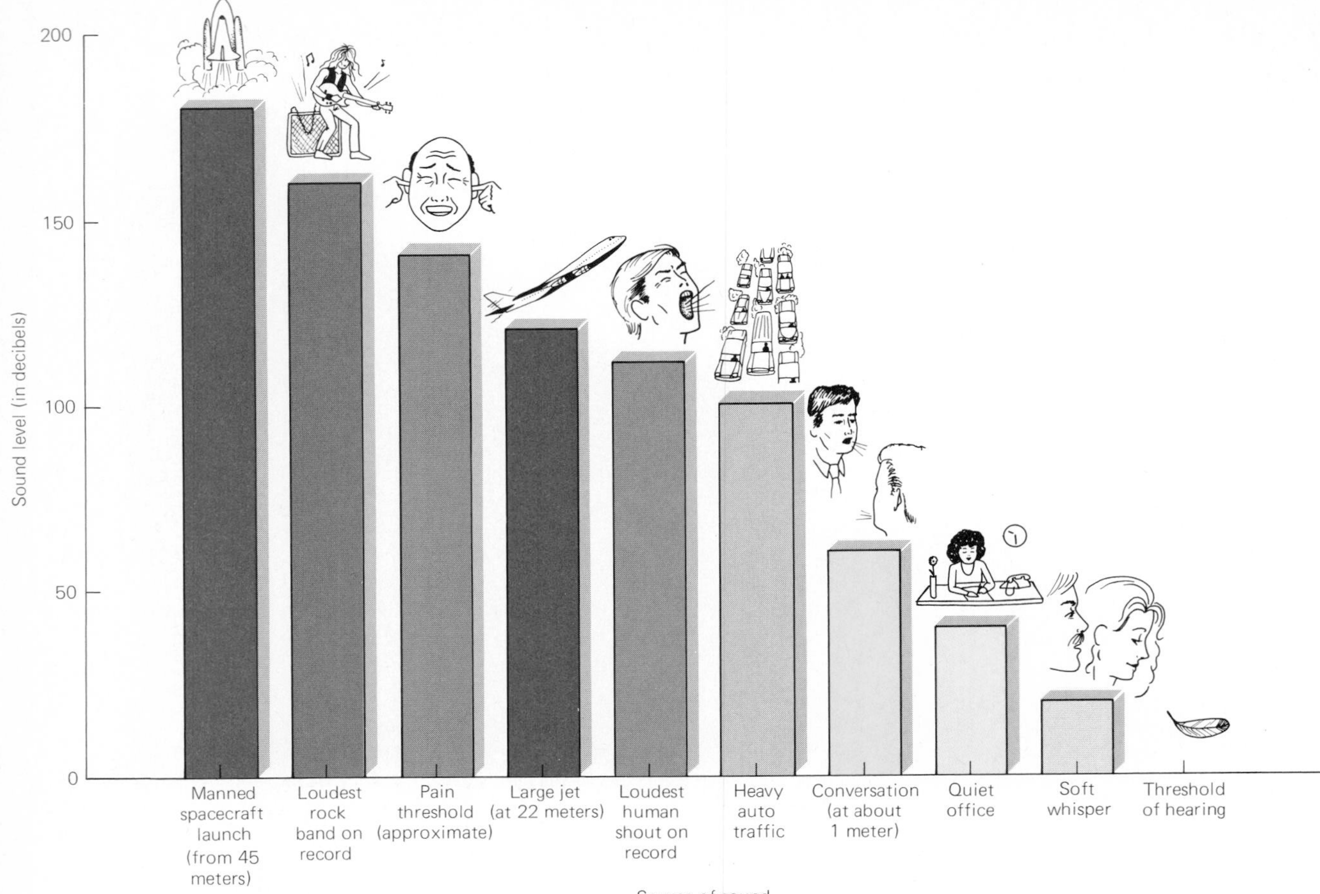

Figure 3-14
Illustrations of decibel levels (measures of sound intensity).

of wave crests that occur in a second. With very low frequencies there are relatively few, and therefore slower, up-and-down wave cycles per second—which are visible to the naked eye as vibrations in the speaker. Low frequencies are translated into a sound that is very low in pitch. (**Pitch** is the characteristic of sound by which it can be described as "high" or "low.") For example, the lowest frequency that humans are capable of hearing is 20 cycles per second. Higher frequencies translate into higher pitch; at this end of the sound spectrum, people can detect sounds with frequencies as high as 20,000 cycles per second.

Pitch: *The "highs" or "lows" in sound*

While sound frequency allows us to enjoy the sounds of the high notes of a piccolo and the bass notes of a tuba, **intensity** is a feature of wave patterns that allows us to distinguish between loud and soft passages. Intensity refers to the difference between the peaks and valleys of air pressure in a sound wave as it travels through the air. Waves with narrow peaks and valleys produce soft sounds, while those that are relatively wide produce loud sounds.

Intensity: *A feature of wave patterns that allows us to distinguish between loud and soft passages*

We are sensitive to a broad range of sound intensity: The loudest sounds we are capable of hearing are about 10 million times as intense as the very weakest sound that we can hear. This range is measured in **decibels**, which can be used to place everyday sounds along a continuum (see Figure 3-14). When sounds get higher than 120 decibels, they become painful to the human ear, and long-term exposure to such high levels eventually leads to a permanent hearing loss—a phenomenon all too familiar to many rock musicians (and some of their fans).

Decibels (DES ih bells) *Individual measures of sound intensity*

PSYCHOLOGY AT WORK

REPLACING A SENSE ORGAN:
An Electronic Ear Implant for the Deaf

What appeared just a few years ago to be science fiction has become a reality, potentially enabling some 60,000 to 200,000 deaf people in the United States to hear sounds such as automobile horns and doorbells for the first time. The device allowing this advance is an electronic ear implant which is connected directly to the cochlea.

The device works in certain cases of deafness in which the hair cells in the cochlea are damaged and unable to convert vibrations into the electric impulses that the brain is able to use. Instead, a tiny microphone outside the ear is used to pick up sound, which is then converted into an electronic signal and sent to a coil behind the ear. This coil transmits a radio wave to a receiver implanted inside the skull, which is connected by a short wire directly to the cochlea (see Figure 3-15). The receiver emits electronic signals that stimulate the cochlea, sending a message to the brain that sound is being heard (Molotsky, 1984).

Although the device does not allow people to understand words distinctly, it enables them to detect changes in tone of voice and volume. Moreover, as the technology continues to improve, it is likely that the sounds will be made more distinct, and perhaps one day the implant will approach the sensitivity of the ear itself.

Although not all forms of deafness can be treated using this technique, the artificial ear offers real hope to thousands of deaf people (Loeb, 1985). Moreover, the possibility exists that the electronic ear implant may be just the first in a series of artificial sense organs.

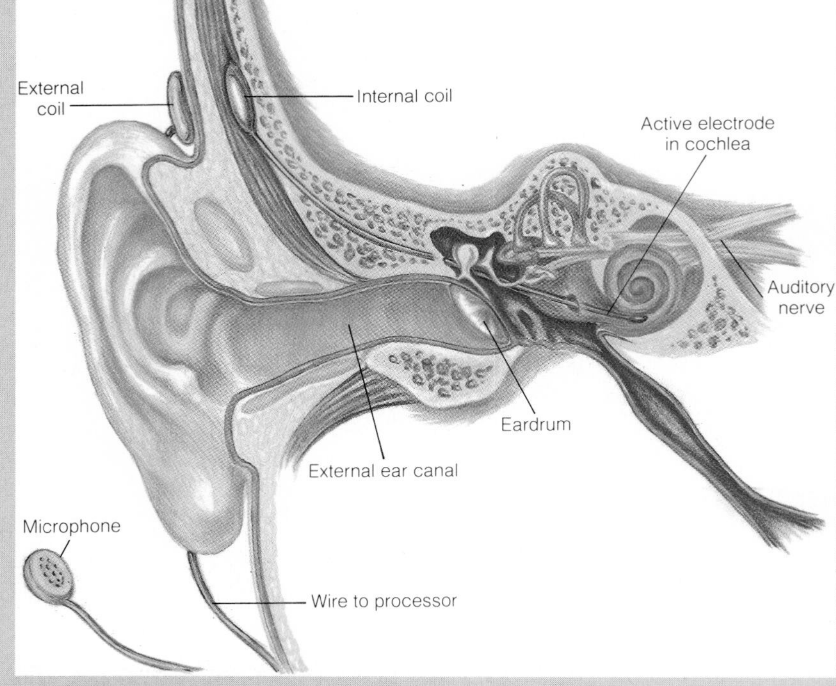

Figure 3-15
A cochlear implant. (*New York Times, November 30, 1984.*)

How are our brains able to sort out wavelengths of different frequencies and intensities? One clue comes from studies of the basilar membrane, the area within the cochlea that translates physical vibrations into neutral impulses. It turns out that sounds affect different areas of the basilar membrane, depending on the frequency of the wave. The part of the basilar membrane nearest the oval window is most sensitive to high-frequency sounds, while the part nearest the cochlea's inner edge is most sensitive to low-frequency sounds. This finding has led to the **place theory of hearing**, which says that different areas of the basilar membrane respond to different frequencies.

Place theory of hearing: *The theory that states that different frequencies are responded to by different areas of the basilar membrane*

Frequency theory of hearing: *The theory that suggests that the entire basilar membrane acts like a microphone, vibrating in response to sound*

On the other hand, other mechanisms are also involved. The **frequency theory of hearing** suggests that the entire basilar membrane acts like a microphone,

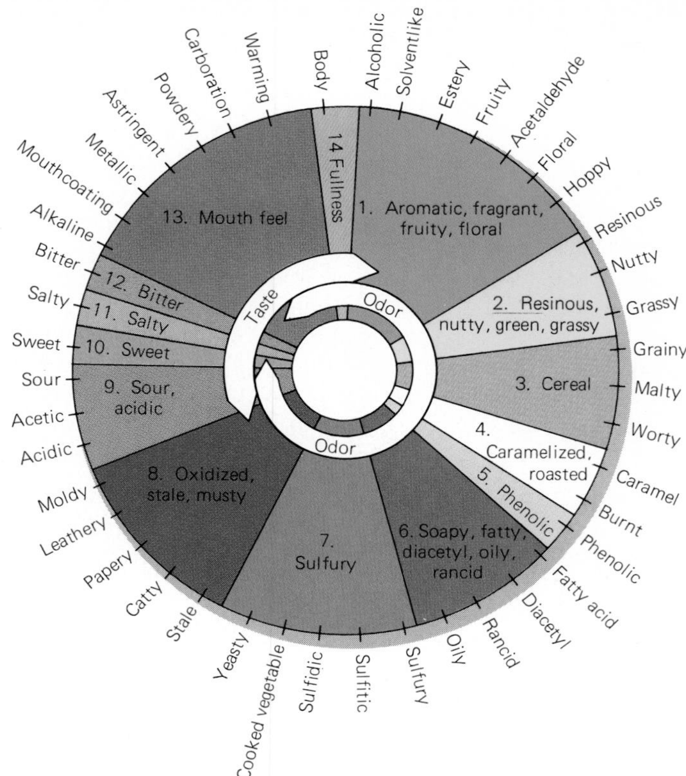

Figure 3-16
The beer industry has devised the set of descriptive terms in this flavor wheel to help in the production and quality control of beer. Both odors and tastes are included in the wheel. (*American Society of Brewing Chemists.*)

vibrating as a whole in response to a sound. In this system, the nerve receptors send out signals that are tied directly to the frequency to which the person is exposed. Our sense of hearing operates, then, using both place and frequency systems. (To learn about the latest attempts at helping people with hearing problems, see the accompanying Psychology at Work box.)

Making Sense of the Other Senses: Smell, Taste, and the Skin Senses

When Audrey Warner returned home after a day's work, she knew that something was wrong the minute she opened her apartment door. The smell of gas—a strong, sickening smell that immediately made her feel weak—permeated the apartment. She left her apartment, ran to the pay phone across the street, and called the gas company. As she was explaining what she smelled, Audrey heard a muffled explosion and then saw flames begin to shoot out of her apartment window. She knew at that moment that her life had been saved by her ability to smell the gas.

Although there are few instances in which the sense of smell provides such drama, it is clear that our lives would be considerably less interesting if we could not smell freshly mowed hay, sniff a bouquet of flowers, or smell an apple pie baking. Like our senses of vision and hearing, each of the remaining senses that we now consider—smell, taste, and the skin senses—plays an important role in our lives.

Smell and Taste Although many animals have keener abilities to detect odors than we do—a point reflected by the fact that a greater proportion of their brains is related to the sense of smell than ours is—we are still able to detect a wide range of smells. People can be trained to make sophisticated, complex judgments of smells; there are even professions in which the major task is to continually assess the quality of the odor of a manufactured product. For instance, the beer industry has developed the odor wheel (see Figure 3-16), which is used during the production of beer as part of quality-control checks.

Results of "sniff tests" have shown that women generally have a better sense of smell than do men and that a nonsmoker's sense of smell is better than a smoker's. In addition, there are changes in the sense of smell with age: Sensitivity to smells is greatest between the ages of 30 and 60, declining from age 60 on (Doty, 1986).

We know considerably less about the mechanisms underlying smell than we do about those concerning sight and sound. It is clear that the sense of smell comes into play when molecules of a substance enter the nasal passages and meet **olfactory cells**, the receptor cells of the nose. Each of these cells has hairlike structures that stick out into the air and are capable of transforming the passing molecules into nerve impulses that can be used by the brain.

Olfactory (all FAK tor ee) **cells**: *The receptor cells of the nose*

More is understood about the sense of taste, which is intimately related to smell. There are only four fundamental sensations responsible for the myriad tastes that we experience: sweet, sour, salty, and bitter. Every other taste is simply a combination of these four basic qualities.

The receptor cells for taste are located in **taste buds**, which are distributed across the tongue. However, the distribution is uneven, and certain areas of the tongue are more sensitive to certain of the fundamental tastes than are others (Bartoshuk, 1971). As we can see in Figure 3-17, the tip of the tongue is most sensitive to sweetness; in fact, a granule of sugar placed on the rear of the tongue will hardly seem sweet at all. Similarly, only the sides of the tongue are very sensitive to sour tastes, and the rear specializes in bitter tastes.

Taste buds: *The receptor cells of the tongue*

Of course, the sense of taste does not operate simply through the tongue, as anyone with a stuffy nose can confirm. The smell, temperature, texture, and even the appearance of food all affect our sense of taste. Moreover, some people are more sensitive to certain tastes than are others, and the ability to taste certain substances runs in some families. Our sense of taste is indeed complex.

Skin senses: *The senses that include touch, pressure, temperature, and pain*

Senses of the Skin: Touch, Pressure, Temperature, and Pain For the two people whose conditions were described at the beginning of this chapter, pain—or lack of it—is the central aspect of their lives. Although the experience of pain is never pleasant, the consequences of a complete lack of sensitivity can be just as tragic. If, for example, you were insensitive to pain, instead of recoiling when your arm brushed against a hot teapot, you might lean against it, not noticing that you were being severely burned. Similarly, without the warning sign of stomach pain that typically accompanies an inflamed appendix, your appendix might rupture, spreading a fatal infection through your body. Such examples underscore the vital importance of our sense of pain.

In fact, all of our **skin senses**—touch, pressure, temperature, and pain—play an important role in survival, making us aware of potential danger to our bodies. Most of these senses operate through nerve receptor cells located at various depths throughout the skin, although they are not evenly distributed. When we consider receptors sensitive to pressure, for example, some areas—such as the fingertips—have many more cells and are therefore more sensitive to pressure than others—such as the middle of the back.

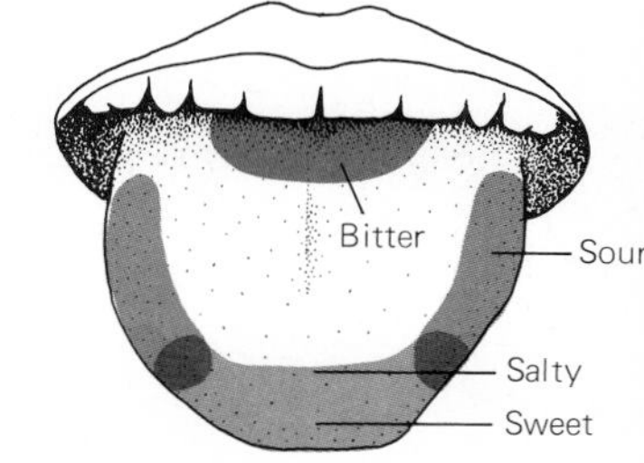

Figure 3-17
Particular portions of the tongue are sensitive to tastes that are bitter, sour, sweet, or salty.

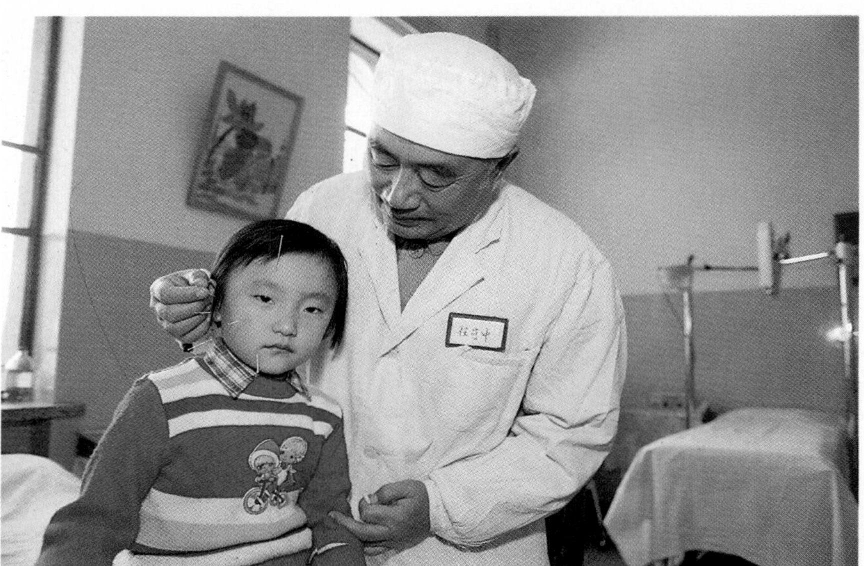

The gate-control theory of pain may explain the effectiveness of acupuncture, in which sharp needles inserted into the skin produce pain relief. *(J. P. Laffont/Sygma)*

The Informed Consumer of Psychology: How Do You Spell Relief—from Pain?

Probably the most extensively researched skin sense is pain, and with good reason: People consult physicians and take medication for pain more than for any other symptom or condition. Nearly one-third of the population of the United States has problems with persistent or recurrent pain—and many of these individuals are disabled to the point of being unable to function normally in society.

Until fairly recently, little was understood about the biology and psychology of pain—and even less about how to treat it. Today, however, the major theory relating to the experience of pain, called the gate-control theory, is providing us with new clues for understanding how we can control pain. The **gate-control theory** suggests that particular nerve receptors lead to specific areas of the brain related to pain (Melzack & Wall, 1965). When these receptors are activated because of some injury or problem with a part of the body, a ''gate'' to the brain is opened, allowing the sensation of pain to be experienced.

Gate-control theory of pain: *The theory that suggests that particular nerve receptors lead to specific areas of the brain related to pain; when these receptors are activated by an injury or bodily malfunction, a ''gate'' to the brain is opened and pain is sensed*

However, another set of neural receptors close the ''gate'' to the brain when stimulated, thereby reducing the experience of pain. What this suggests is that if one can stimulate the nerves associated with shutting the gate, pain can be eliminated. The gate-control theory may explain the effectiveness of **acupuncture**, an ancient Chinese technique still in use today, in which sharp needles are inserted into various parts of the body (see Figure 3-18). The sensation from the needles may close the gateway to the brain, reducing the experience of pain. It is also possible that the body's own painkillers, the endorphins (which we discussed in Chapter 2), as well as positive and negative emotions, may play a role in opening and closing the gate.

Acupuncture (a kew PUNK shur): *A Chinese technique of relieving pain through specific placement of needles in the body*

Searching for Pain Relief: The Pain Clinic The most comprehensive approach to relieving pain is found in pain clinics, which number about 150 worldwide. Designed for people who suffer from lingering, chronic pain that has resisted previous treatment, pain clinics offer a multidisciplinary approach to the relief of pain (Holzman & Turk, 1985). In the typical clinic, the patient is first evaluated thoroughly by a team of health practitioners, including physicians, psychologists, and various medical specialists, and then a treatment is prescribed. Among the major antipain weapons in the arsenal of the pain clinic are the following:

- Drugs: Drugs remain the most popular treatment in fighting pain. Drugs range from those that treat the source of the pain—such as reducing swelling in painful joints—to those that work on the symptom of the pain.
- Hypnosis: Some 15 to 20 percent of the people who can be hypnotized can achieve a major degree of pain relief.
- Biofeedback: As we discussed in the previous chapter, biofeedback is a process in which people learn to control such ''involuntary'' functions as heartbeat and respiration. If the pain involves muscles, such as in tension headaches or back pain, biofeedback can be helpful (Dolce & Raczynski, 1985).
- Nerve and brain stimulation: Low-voltage electric current passed through painful parts of the body in a process called **transcutaneous electrical nerve stimulation (TENS)** can sometimes bring pain relief. In extreme cases, electrodes can be surgically implanted into the brain, and a handheld battery pack can stimulate nerve cells to provide direct relief.

Transcutaneous (tranz kew TANE ee us) **electrical nerve stimulation**: *A method of providing relief from pain by passing a low-voltage electric current through parts of the body*

- Relaxation techniques: People can be trained to systematically relax their bodies, thereby decreasing the pain caused by tension.
- Surgery: One of the most extreme methods, surgery can be used to cut certain nerve fibers carrying pain messages to the brain. Still, because there is a danger that other functions of the body will be affected, surgery is a treatment of last resort.
- Psychological counseling: In cases where pain cannot be successfully treated (it is important to keep in mind that there are no ''miracle cures''), psychological counseling is employed to help a patient cope more effectively with the experience of pain.

When should you consider using a pain clinic? If you have severe, long-term pain, the first place to go is to your own physician. If the physician is unable to determine the cause of the pain and the pain lingers and begins to affect your

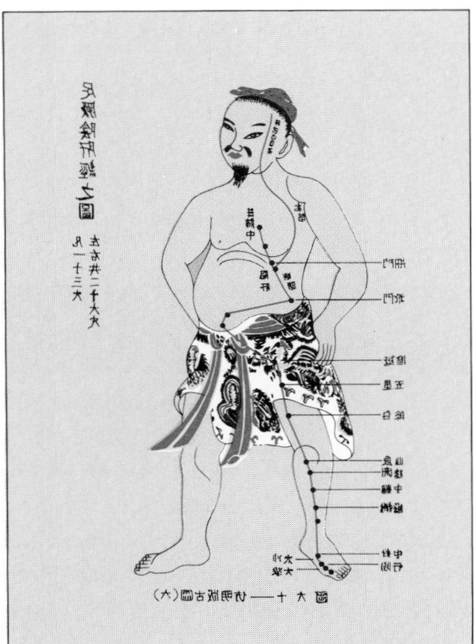

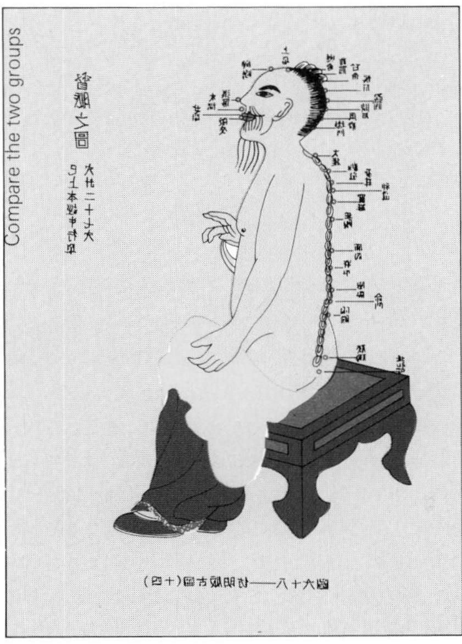

Figure 3-18
Acupuncture has been in existence for centuries. These Ming dynasty charts from around the fourteenth century illustrate locations in which needles are to be inserted. (*British Museum.*)

daily life, then a pain clinic may be the next reasonable stop. You can find a pain clinic by checking with a local hospital or medical center; chances are there is one nearby if you live near a major city. There may be a waiting list, and costs can run as high as $10,000, although insurance may help pick up the tab.

Is it worth it? To a person suffering from chronic pain, very often the truth is that no amount of money is too much. As one patient said, "Any reduction in pain level, any improvement in my quality of life, is beneficial" (Stark, 1985, p. 36).

RECAP AND REVIEW III

Recap

- The senses of hearing, motion, and balance are centered in the ear.
- The major parts of the ear are the outer ear (which includes the auditory canal and eardrum), the middle ear (with the hammer, anvil, and stirrup), and the oval window leading to the inner ear. The inner ear contains the cochlea, basilar membrane, and hair cells.
- The sense of balance is centered in the ear's semicircular canals and otoliths.
- The physical aspects of sound include frequency and intensity. Both place and frequency processes are involved in the transformation of sound waves into the experience of sound.
- Less is known about the senses of smell, taste, and the skin senses (touch, pressure, temperature, and pain) than about vision and hearing. One major focus has been on understanding the causes of pain and devising ways to alleviate it, often by using treatments including drugs, hypnosis, biofeedback, nerve and brain stimulation, relaxation techniques, surgery, and psychotherapy.

Review

1. Trace the path of sound through an ear by ordering, from the outside in, the following structures: eardrum, auditory canal, outer ear, middle ear, inner ear, oval window.
2. The hammer, anvil, and stirrup are tiny bones contained in the
   a. Outer ear **b.** Middle ear **c.** Inner ear **d.** Oval window
3. The process by which the cochlea picks up subtle vibrations moving across the skull is known as bone conduction. True or false?
4. The structure of the ear that senses the constant pull of gravity is the
   a. Basilar membrane **b.** Semicircular canal **c.** Otolith **d.** Eardrum
5. High- and low-pitched sounds are characterized by waves of different ________________, whereas loud and soft sounds are characterized by waves of different ________________.
6. Our sense of smell is activated through contact with the ________________ ________________.
7. The sour taste of a lemon is most distinct when exposed to what part of the tongue?
   a. Tip **b.** Underside **c.** Sides **d.** Rear

(Answers to review questions are on page 108.)

VIEWING THE WORLD AS IT SEEMS: PERCEPTION

Look, for a moment, at the shapes in Figure 3-19. Most of us would report that we saw a figure on a horse in Figure 3-19*a,* a set of brackets in Figure 3-19*b,* rows of circles and squares in Figure 3-19*c,* and a circular figure and a square intersecting in Figure 3-19*d*. But are these the only interpretations that could be given? A reasonable person could argue that there are a series of unrelated blotches in Figure 3-19*a,* ten lines with two protrusions coming off each line in Figure 3-19*b,* seven columns of alternating circles and squares in Figure 3-19*c,* and in Figure 3-19*d,* three distinct enclosed areas.

(a)

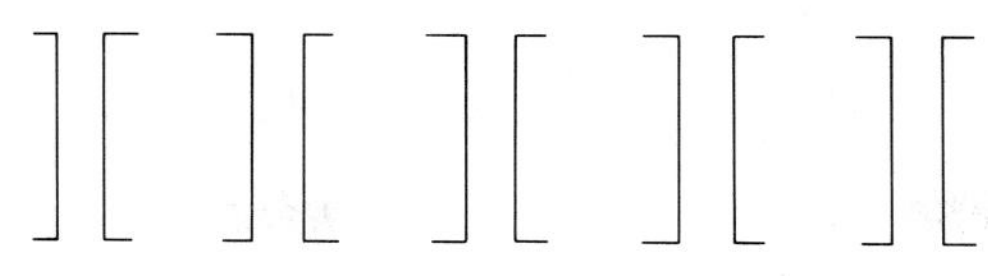

(b)

(c)

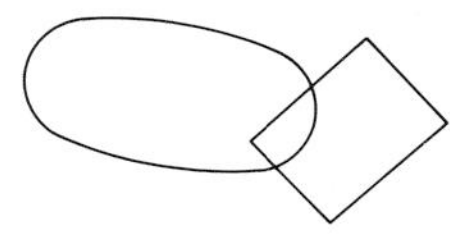

(d)

Figure 3-19
Perceptual organization at work: Although the figure in (*a*) can be seen as a series of unrelated splotches, (*b*) as lines with protrusions at top and bottom, (*c*) as columns of alternating circles and squares, and (*d*) as three separate shapes, most of us see in (*a*) a horse and rider, in (*b*) a series of brackets, in (*c*) rows of circles and squares, and in (*d*) an overlapping oval and square. [*(a) Mednick, Higgins, & Kirschbaum, 1975.*]

The fact that most of us are apt to interpret the shapes as meaningful wholes illustrates some of the basic processes of perception at work: We try to simplify the complex stimuli presented to us by the environment. If we did not reduce the complex into something understandable, the world would present too much of a challenge for us to function, and—unless we lived as hermits in drab, colorless, silent caves—we would spend all our time just sorting through its myriad stimuli. Perception, then, allows us to take stimuli and form meaningful representations of the environment.

Creating Wholes from Parts: The Gestalt Laws of Organization

The most basic perceptual processes operate according to a series of principles that describe how we organize bits and pieces of information into meaningful wholes. These are known as **gestalt laws of organization**, named for a group of German psychologists who studied patterns—or **gestalts**—in the early 1900s (Wertheimer, 1923). Among the most important principles they discovered are the following:

Gestalt (geh SHTALLT) **laws of organization**: *A series of principles which describe how we organize pieces of information into meaningful wholes; they include closure, proximity, similarity, and simplicity*
Gestalts: *Patterns studied by the gestalt psychologists*

- **Closure**—Groupings tend to be made in terms of enclosed or complete figures rather than open ones. We tend to ignore the breaks, then, in Figure 3-19*a* and *b* and concentrate on the overall forms.
- **Proximity**—Elements that are closer together are grouped together. Because of this, we tend to see pairs of dots rather than a row of single dots below.

. .   . .

- **Similarity**—Elements that are similar in appearance are grouped together. We see, then, horizontal rows of circles and squares in Figure 3-19*c* instead of vertical mixed columns.
- **Simplicity**—In a general sense, the overriding gestalt principle is one of simplicity: When we observe a pattern, we perceive it in the most basic, straightforward manner that we can (Hochberg, 1978). For example, Figure 3-19*d* is

Closure (KLO zhur): *The tendency to group according to enclosed or complete figures rather than open or incomplete ones*
Proximity: *The tendency to group together those elements that are close together*
Similarity: *The tendency to group together those elements that are similar in appearance*
Simplicity: *The tendency to perceive a pattern in the most basic, straightforward, organized manner possible—the overriding gestalt principle*

Figure 3-20
Although at first it is difficult to distinguish anything in this drawing, you probably will eventually be able to discern the figure of a dog.

seen as an interlocking of the simpler two figures, rather than as two separate forms. If we have a choice in interpretations we generally opt for the simpler one.

Where 1 + 1 Equals More Than 2: The Whole Is Greater Than the Sum of Its Parts

If someone were to try to convince you that 1 plus 1 equals more than 2, you would think that person needed to brush up on some basic arithmetic. Yet the idea that two objects considered together form a whole that is greater than the simple combination of the objects was a fundamental principle of the gestalt psychologists. They argued—quite convincingly, in fact—that perception of stimuli in our environment goes well beyond the individual elements that we sense, and represents an active, constructive process carried out within the brain, where bits and pieces of sensations are put together to make something greater—and more meaningful—than the individual elements separately.

Consider, for instance, Figure 3-20. As you examine the black patches, it is likely that you will perceive the form of a dog. The dog represents a gestalt, or perceptual whole. Although we can see the individual parts that make up the figure, putting each of them together forms something greater than these individual parts. The whole, then, is greater than the sum of the individual elements.

Perceptual constancy: *The phenomenon by which physical objects are perceived as unvarying despite changes in the appearance of the object or the surrounding environment*

One outgrowth of the active perceptual processing that we carry out relates to **perceptual constancy**, a phenomenon in which physical objects are perceived as unvarying and consistent, despite changes in the physical environment or in the appearance of objects being viewed. For instance, consider what happens as you finish a conversation with a friend and she begins to walk away from

ANSWERS TO REVIEW QUESTIONS

Review III: **1.** Outer ear; auditory canal; eardrum; middle ear; oval window; inner ear **2.** b **3.** True **4.** c **5.** Frequency, intensity **6.** Olfactory cells **7.** c you. As you watch her walk down the street, the image on your retina becomes smaller and smaller. Yet you do not think she is shrinking, despite this change in sensory experience. Instead, because you factor into your thinking the knowledge that she is also getting farther away, the phenomenon of perceptual size constancy compensates for the change in retinal image, and you ultimately perceive her as the same size no matter how far away she moves.

Translating 2-D to 3-D: Depth Perception

As sophisticated as the retina is, the images that are projected onto it are flat and two-dimensional. Yet the world around us is three-dimensional, and we perceive it that way. How do we make the transformation from 2-D to 3-D?

The ability to view the world in three dimensions and to perceive distance—an ability known as **depth perception**—is largely due to the fact that we have two eyes. Because there is some distance between the eyes, a slightly different image reaches each retina, and the brain integrates them into one composite view. But it does not ignore the difference in images, which is known as **binocular disparity**; the disparity allows our brains to estimate the distance of an object from us.

Generally speaking, the closer the object, the greater the disparity between the two images. You can see this for yourself. Hold a pencil at arm's length and look at it first with one eye and then with the other. There is little difference between the two views relative to the background. Now bring the pencil just 6 inches away from your face, and try the same thing. This time you will perceive a greater difference between the two views. The fact that the discrepancy between the two eyes varies according to object distance provides you with a means of determining distance: Greater discrepancies are interpreted to mean that an object is closer, while smaller discrepancies are interpreted to mean that an object is farther away.

It is not always necessary to use two eyes to perceive depth, however; certain cues allow us to obtain a sense of depth and distance with just one eye (Burnham, 1983). These cues are known as **monocular cues**. For example, one monocular cue—**motion parallax**—is the relative movement of objects as you move your head from side to side. When this movement causes changes in the image of an object on the retina, your brain is able to calculate the relative distance of the object by the amount of change in the retinal image. Similarly, experience has taught us that if two objects are the same size, the one that makes a smaller image on the retina is perceived to be farther away than the one that provides a larger image—an example of the monocular cue of **relative size**.

Finally, anyone who has ever seen railroad tracks that seem to join together in the distance knows that distant objects appear to be closer together than nearer ones, a phenomenon called **linear perspective** (see Figures 3-21, 3-22, and 3-23). People use linear perspective as a monocular cue in estimating distance, allowing the two-dimensional retinal image to register the three-dimensional world (Bruce & Green, 1984).

Is the Cup Half Full or Half Empty?: Figuring the Figure from the Ground

Look at the drawing in Figure 3-24. Do you see white cup on a black background, or do you see two black faces staring at each other across a white background?

Depth perception: *The ability to view the world in three dimensions and to perceive distance*

Binocular disparity (by NOCK you lur dis PAIR ih tee): *The difference between the images that reach the retina of each eye; this disparity allows the brain to estimate distance*

Monocular (mon OCK u lar) **cues**: *Signals that allow us to perceive distance and depth with just one eye*

Motion parallax (PAIR uh lax): *The relative movement of objects as your head moves*

Relative size: *The phenomenon by which, if two objects are the same size, the one that makes a smaller image on the retina is perceived to be farther away*

Linear perspective: *The phenomenon by which distant objects appear to be closer together than nearer objects*

Figure 3-21
It appears that these railroad tracks come closer together as they move away from the observer, illustrating the depth cue of linear perspective. (*©Ellis Herwig/Stock, Boston.*)

Figure 3-22
Artists are trained to use linear perspective to promote the feeling of distance in their work, as this van Gogh painting illustrates. [*Van Gogh, Vincent.* Hospital Corridor at Saint Rémy. (1889) *Collection, The Museum of Modern Art, New York. Abby Aldrich Rockefeller Bequest.*]

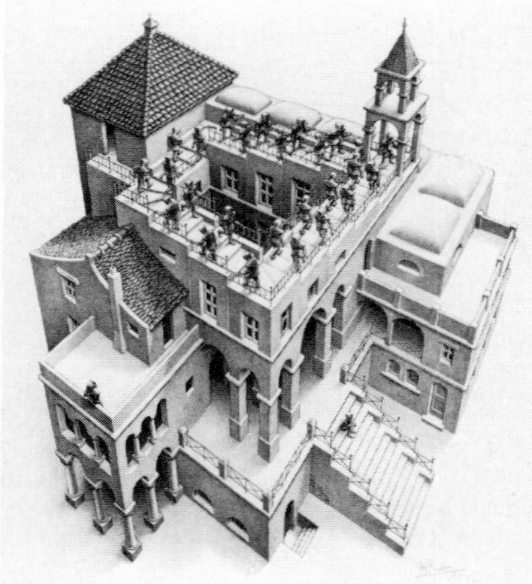

Figure 3-23
Clever use of linear perspective cues in this M. C. Escher painting creates an impossible scene, as monks walk along a staircase that never ends. (Ascending and Descending. *© M.C. Escher Heirs c/o Cordon Art, Baarn, Holland. Courtesy Haags Gemeentemuseum*)

Figure/ground: *Figure refers to the object being perceived, whereas ground refers to the background of or spaces within the object*

Chances are that you first saw one, but then very soon after perceived the other. Most people, in fact, shift back and forth between these two interpretations. The difficulty we face is that because the figure is two-dimensional, the usual means we employ for distinguishing the **figure** (the object being perceived) from the **ground** (the background or spaces within the object) do not work.

The fact that we can look at the same figure in either of two ways illustrates an important point, first emphasized by the gestalt psychologists: We do not just passively respond to visual stimuli that happen to fall on our retinas. Instead, we actively try to organize and make sense of what we see (see Figure 3-25). Perception, then, is typically a constructive process by which we go beyond the stimuli that are presented to us and attempt to construct a meaningful situation (Haber, 1983).

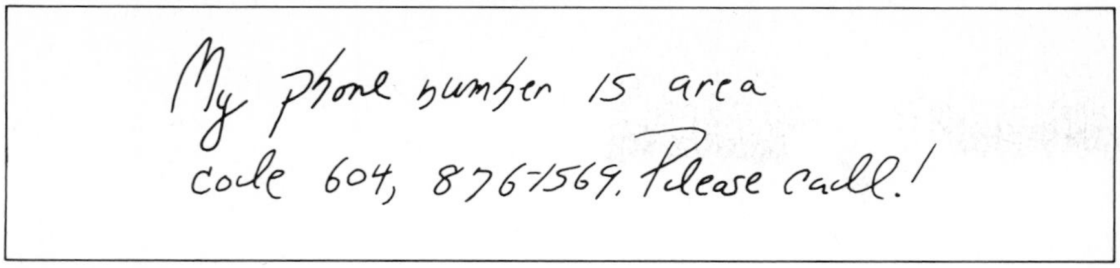

My phone number is area code 604, 876-1569. Please call!

Figure 3-25
What does this message say? You probably read it as "My phone number is area code 604, 876–1569. Please call!" If you did, however, you were being affected by the context of the message in the way you perceived it. Look more carefully at it, and you'll notice that the word "is" and the number "15" are written identically. You'll also note that the "h" in the word "phone" and the "b" in the word "number" are the same, and that the "d" in the word "code" and the "l" in the word "please" are identical. You probably had no trouble in sorting these similarities out, though, because of your prior experience and because of the context that the message provided. (*Coren, Porac, & Ward, 1979.*)

Figure 3-24
Do you see a cup—or is it two faces staring at one another? Most people can shift their attention back and forth between the two interpretations, illustrating the use of figure and ground cues. (*Boring, Langfeld, & Weld, 1948, p. 277.*)

Sorting Out the Auditory World: Selective Attention

The scene: a crowded, noisy party. As the guy who has latched on to you drones on about his new car, you suddenly hear snatches of conversation from behind you about your friend Susan, who seems to have left the party with some fellow she had just met earlier in the evening. Straining to hear what is being said by the person behind you, you lose track of what the guy is saying about his car—until suddenly you realize he has asked a question that requires a response. Brightly you say, ''Pardon me—I just didn't hear what you said with all the noise.''

Anyone who has been stuck listening to a bore go on and on about something trivial is probably familiar with situations similar to the one described above. Psychologists interested in perception are also familiar with circumstances such as this one in which there are many stimuli to pay attention to simultaneously, although the psychologist's interest lies primarily in the question of how people are able to sort out and make sense of the many stimuli the world presents to them.

Selective attention is the perceptual process of choosing which stimulus to pay attention to. To study the phenomenon, a procedure has been developed, called **dichotic listening**, whereby a person wears earphones through which a different message is sent to each ear at the same time. The individual is asked to repeat one of the messages aloud as it comes into one ear—a procedure known as **shadowing**, since the listener's voice acts as a verbal ''shadow'' of the message being received.

Selective attention: *The perceptual process of choosing a stimulus to attend to*

Dichotic (dy KOT ik) **listening**: *A procedure in which an individual wears earphones through which different messages are sent to each ear at the same time*

Shadowing: *A technique used during dichotic listening in which a subject is asked to repeat one of the messages aloud as it comes into one ear*

The question of interest is not so much whether the person is able to shadow the message adequately (most people can do so fairly easily); instead, it revolves around the effects of the message coming into the other ear. It turns out that although the content of the second message typically cannot be recalled, certain characteristics of the message can be remembered (Cherry, 1953). For instance, listeners accurately report whether the speaker was a man or a woman and whether the sex of the speaker changed during the course of the message. About one-third of the time, they can also report hearing whether their names were spoken.

Pickle mustard/JUMPED OVER THE LAZY DOG
THE QUICK BROWN FOX/rye pastrami
Person told to shadow the message from this ear
THE QUICK BROWN FOX JUMPED OVER THE LAZY DOG

Figure 3-26
A shadowing experiment. Subjects are told to shadow—or repeat—only the message being heard in their right ear, as the two messages shown in the captions are heard simultaneously. Although subjects are unaware that they are doing it, if the message switches to the opposite ear, they will typically begin to shadow that message, despite the experimenter's instructions.

One factor that seems particularly important is the meaningfulness of the message being shadowed. If a message that is being shadowed from one ear suddenly switches to the other, subjects generally "follow" the message to the second ear and begin to shadow from the second ear, even though they have been specifically instructed to shadow only what is being heard in the first ear (see Figure 3-26). Moreover, they are usually not even aware that they have made the switch (Treisman, 1960).

Experiments such as these suggest that although people may fully concentrate on only one message at a time, they still pay attention on some level to other information. This explains our ability, then, to eavesdrop on one conversation at a party, but know when it is time to make a response to someone we are supposedly listening to at the same time.

PERCEPTION IN EVERYDAY LIFE

Consider this recreated conversation, which starts off with an actual quote from Vitruvius, a famous Greek architect who lived around 30 B.C.

VITRUVIUS: For sight follows gracious contours, and unless we flatter its pleasure by proportionate alternations of these parts (so that by adjustment we offset the amount to which it suffers illusions) an uncouth and ungracious aspect will be presented to the spectators.
ASSISTANT: Huh? I wish you would speak more clearly.
VITRUVIUS: All right. I merely said that when we build something, we've got to remember that people do not always see the world accurately, and that we must consider how people's eyes and brains will perceive buildings when they are finished. For example, take the Parthenon, our most famous building. While it looks true and straight to the eye, it was actually built with a bulge in one side. This bulge fools viewers into thinking it is straight. If it didn't have that bulge—and quite a few other tricks like it, such as columns that incline inward—it would look as if it were crooked and falling down.

In fact, Vitruvius was right: As anyone who has ever seen the Parthenon (the famous ancient Greek temple) knows, it appears to be completely upright, with the lines straight and with right angles at every corner. However, careful measurement of the building would show this to be merely an example of a **visual illusion**, a physical stimulus that consistently produces errors in perception—judgments that do not match the physical reality of the stimulus (Coren, Porac, & Ward, 1984).

Visual illusion: *A physical stimulus that consistently produces errors in perception (often called an optical illusion)*

As you can see in Figure 3-27, if the building were completely square it would seem to be sagging, since there is a common visual illusion that makes angles placed above a line give the line the appearance of being bent (as seen in Figure 3-27*b*). If this had not been compensated for, the Parthenon would have looked as it does in Figure 3-27*c*. Therefore, the Parthenon was built with a slight upward curvature (as seen in Figure 3-27*d*). Such insights did not stop with the Greeks; modern-day architects also take such visual distortions into account in their designs (see Figure 3-28).

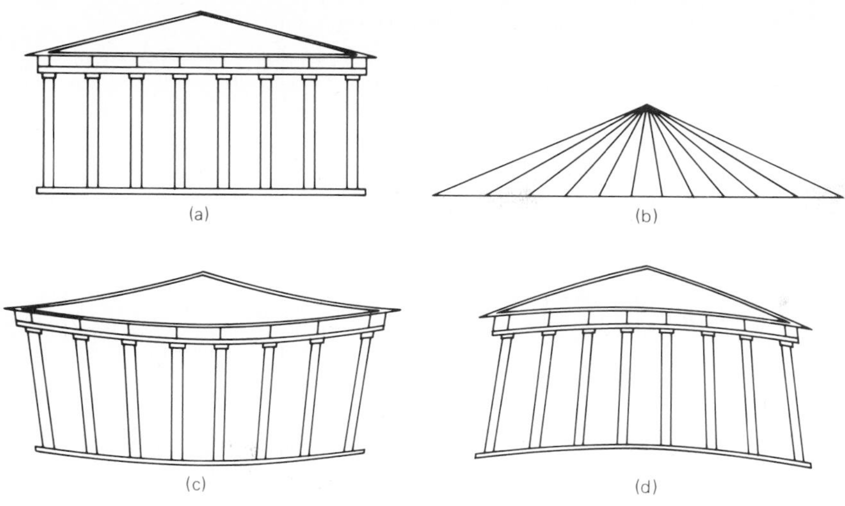

Figure 3-27
In building the Parthenon, the Greeks constructed an architectural wonder that looks perfectly straight and true as in (*a*). However, the visual illusion illustrated in (*b*) would have made it look as it appears in (*c*) if it actually had been built with true right angles. To compensate for this illusion, the Parthenon was designed to have a slight upward curvature, as shown in (*d*). (*Coren, Porac, & Ward, 1979, p. 6.*)

Figure 3-28
In order to make it appear that the yard of this house in Houston was longer, architects designed a small pool with a tapered shape. The wider end of the pool is closest to the house. (*Timothy Hursley*)

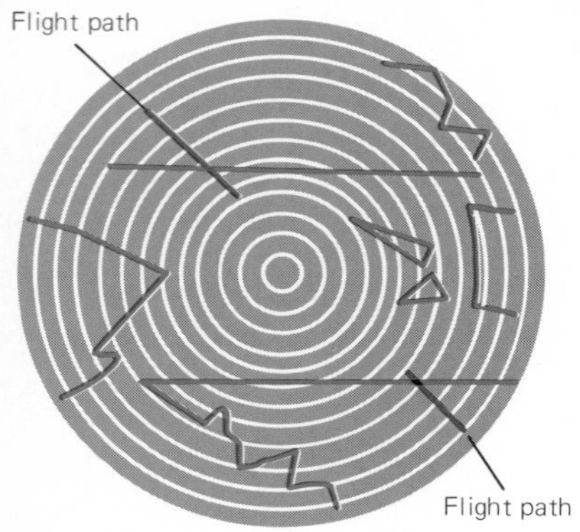

Figure 3-29
Put yourself in the shoes of a flight controller and look at the flight paths of the two planes on this radar screen. A first glance suggests that they are headed on different courses and will not hit each other. But now take a ruler and lay it along the two paths. Your career as a flight controller might well be terminated prematurely if you were guiding the two planes and allowed them to continue without a change in course. (*Coren, Porac, & Ward, 1979, p. 7.*)

Misperceptions of the Eye: Visual Illusions

The implications of visual illusions go beyond the attractiveness of buildings, however. For instance, suppose you were an air traffic controller watching a radar screen like the one shown in Figure 3-29. You might be tempted to sit back and relax as the two planes, whose flight paths are indicated in the figure, drew closer and closer together. If you did, however, you might end up with an air disaster: Although it looks as if the two planes will miss each other, they are headed for a collision. In fact, investigation has suggested that some 16 percent of all airplane accidents are caused by misperceptions of one sort or another (Kraft & Elworth, 1969).

The flight-path illustration (Figure 3-29) provides an example of a well-known visual illusion called the **Poggendorf illusion**. As you can see in Figure 3-30, the Poggendorf illusion, when stripped down to its basics, gives the impression that line X would pass *under* line Y if it were extended through the pipelike figure, instead of heading directly toward line Y as it actually does.

The Poggendorf illusion is just one of many illusions that consistently fool the eye (Perkins, 1983). Another, called the **Müller-Lyer illusion**, is illustrated in Figure 3-30*b*. Although the two lines are the same length, the one with the arrows pointing inward appears to be longer than the one with the arrows pointing outward.

Although all kinds of explanations for visual illusions have been suggested, most concentrate either on the eye's visual sensory apparatus itself or on the interpretation that is given a figure by the brain (Schiffman, 1982). Visual explanations for the Müller-Lyer illusion suggest, for example, that eye movements are greater when the arrows face inward, making it look longer than when they face outward.

Poggendorf (POG en dorf) **illusion**: *An illusion involving a line that passes diagonally through two parallel lines (see Figure 3-30a)*

Müller-Lyer (MEW lur LY ur) **illusion**: *An illusion where two lines of the same length appear to be of different lengths because of the direction of the arrows at the ends of each line; the line with arrows pointing out appears shorter than the line with arrows pointing in (see Figure 3-30b)*

Other evidence, however, suggests that the cause of the illusion rests on the brain's interpretive errors. For instance, one hypothesis to explain the Müller-Lyer illusion assumes that its occurrence is a result of the meaning we give to each of the lines (Gregory, 1978). When we see the bottom line, we tend to perceive it as if it were the outside corner of a building; when we view the line with the arrows facing inward, we perceive it as the inside corner of a room (as illustrated in Figure 3-31). Previous experience leads us to assume that the outside corner is closer than the inside corner, and we make the further assumption that the inside corner must be larger.

Although it may seem that there are so many assumptions being made that it is unlikely the explanation is correct, in fact there is a good degree of convincing evidence for it. One of the most telling pieces of support comes from cross-cultural studies that show that people raised in areas where there are few right angles—such as the Zulu in Africa—are much less susceptible to the illusion than people who grow up where most things are built using right angles and rectangles (Segall, Campbell, & Herskovits, 1966).

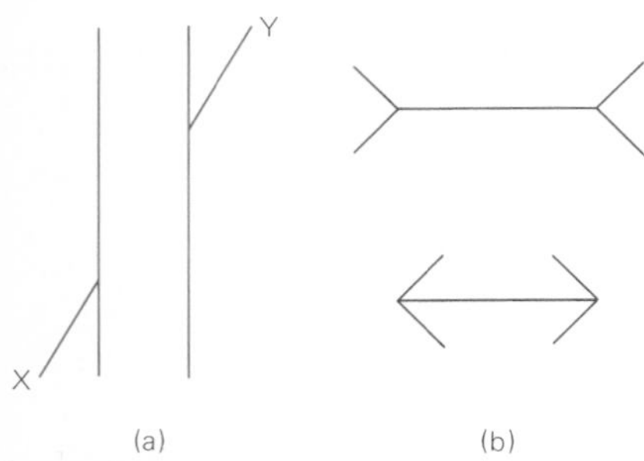

Figure 3-30
(*a*) The Poggendorf illusion in which the two diagonal lines appear as if they would not meet if extended toward one another; (*b*) the Müller-Lyer illusion in which the upper horizontal line appears longer than the lower one.

There are actually several kinds of cultural factors that affect the ways in which we perceive the world. Consider, for example, the drawing in Figure 3-32. Sometimes called the "devil's tuning fork," it is likely to produce a mind-boggling effect, as the center tine of the fork alternates between appearing and disappearing.

Now try to reproduce it on a piece of paper. Chances are that the task is nearly impossible for you—unless you are a member of an African tribe with little experience with western cultures. For such individuals, the task is simple; they have no trouble in reproducing the figure. The reason seems to be that western people automatically interpret the drawing as something that cannot exist in three dimensions, and they are therefore inhibited from reproducing it. The African tribal members, on the other hand, do not make the assumption that the figure is "impossible," and instead view it in two dimensions, which enables them to copy the figure with ease (Deregowski, 1973).

Cultural differences are also reflected in depth perception. A western viewer of Figure 3-33 would interpret the drawing as one in which the hunter is trying to spear the antelope in the foreground while an elephant stands under the tree in the background. A member of an isolated African tribe, however, interprets the scene very differently by assuming that the hunter is aiming at the elephant. Westerners use the difference in sizes between the two animals as a cue that the elephant is farther away than the hunter (Hudson, 1960).

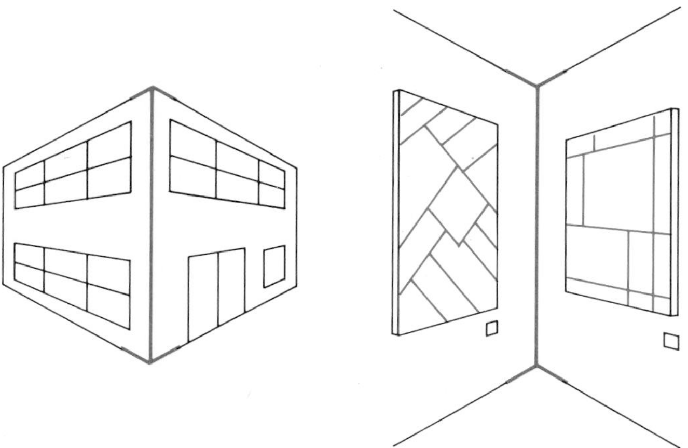

Figure 3-31
An explanation for the Müller-Lyer illusion suggests that the line with outward-pointing arrows is interpreted as the relatively close end of a rectangular object extended out toward us (as in the building corner), while the line with inward-pointing arrows is viewed as the inside corner of a rectangle extending away from us (as in the room corner). Our previous experience with distance cues leads us to assume that the outside corner is closer than the inside corner and that the inside corner must therefore be larger.

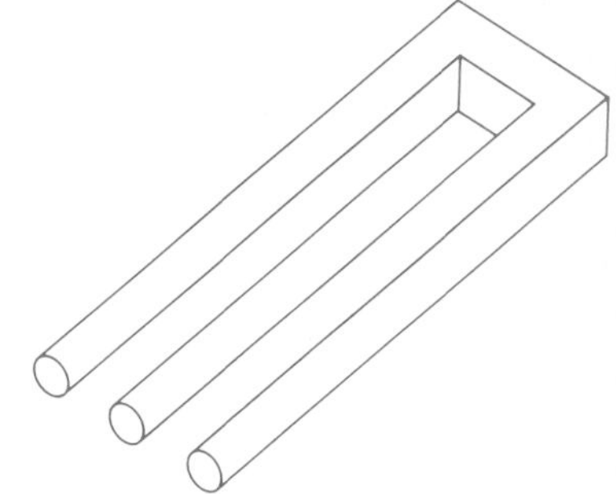

Figure 3-32
The "devil's tuning fork" has three prongs . . . or does it have just two?

Our misinterpretations of visual images are ultimately due, then, to errors in both fundamental visual processing and in the way the brain processes this information (Coren & Porac, 1983). But illusions also illustrate something fundamental about perception, and thus go beyond being mere psychological curiosities. There seems to be a basic connection between a person's past experience and the way in which he or she perceives and understands the world. Our prior knowledge, needs, motivations, and expectations about how the world is put together influence the way we perceive it. Each of us, then, perceives the world in a way that is unique and special—a fact that allows each of us to make our own special contribution to the world.

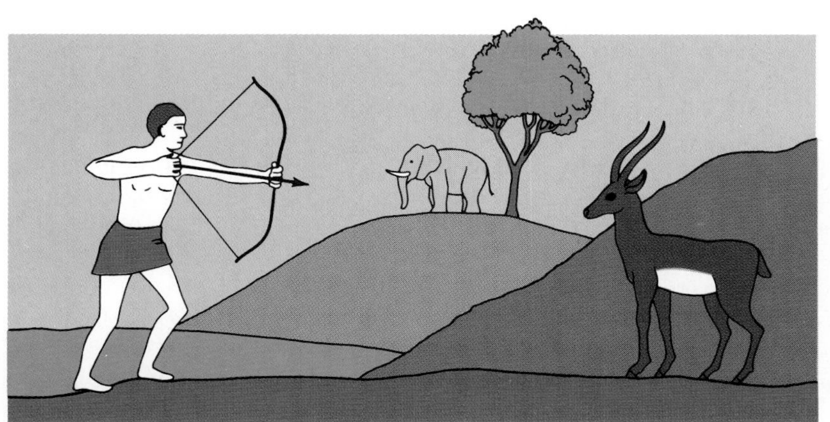

Figure 3-33
Is the man about to spear the elephant or the antelope? Westerners assume that the differences in size between the two animals indicates that the elephant is farther away, and therefore the man is aiming for the antelope. On the other hand, members of some African tribes, not used to depth cues in two-dimensional drawings, assume that the man is aiming for the elephant. (*Based on Deregowski, 1973.*)

RECAP AND REVIEW IV

Recap

- Among the gestalt laws of organization are closure, proximity, similarity, and simplicity.
- Because objects and elements are perceived not in isolation from one another, but as parts of a larger whole, the perception of a group of elements considered together is typically greater than the sum of the individual elements.
- Depth perception occurs because of binocular disparity, motion parallax, and relative size of images on the retina.
- Selective attention is the perceptual process of choosing which stimulus to pay attention to.
- Visual illusions are physical stimuli that consistently produce errors in perception. Illusions occur both in visual processing and in the way the brain interprets this information.

Review

1. Two principles of the gestalt laws of organization are:
a. closure and similarity **b.** proximity and complexity **c.** comparability and similarity **d.** comparability and complexity

2. Seeing objects as consistent and invariant is known as ____________________.

3. Match each term with its definition by placing the appropriate number in each blank.

a. ____Depth perception — 1. The difference in images received by our retinas
b. ____Binocular disparity — 2. A monocular cue relating near and far objects
c. ____Monocular cues — 3. The phenomenon by which two parallel lines appear to converge in the distance
d. ____Motion parallax — 4. The means by which we can obtain a sense of depth with just one eye
e. ____Relative size — 5. The relative movement of objects as one's head moves from side to side
f. ____Linear perspective — 6. Our ability to view the world in three dimensions and discriminate distance
g. ____Selective attention — 7. A clue to depth through only one eye
h. ____Dichotic listening — 8. The relative movement of objects as one moves one's head from side to side

4. Physical stimuli that produce consistent errors in perception are known as visual ____________________.

5. An American views a familiar figure as three-dimensional and proceeds to try to reproduce it in a drawing. A member of an African tribe is given the same figure to sketch; it is a totally unknown object to her. You would expect the American to be more successful at accurately sketching the figure. True or false?

(Answers to review questions are at the bottom of page 118.)

Psychology Looks Towards the 1990s
Computer Versions of Vision

Can a computer be taught to see?

Not yet, although important breakthroughs seem to be just over the horizon. After twenty-five years of research and great strides in our understanding of both vision and computer processes, experts have finally reached a point where they can design computers that recognize and distinguish simple objects. Yet they are still far from recreating the capacity to respond to the complex recognition challenges that the human eye meets with ease.

The difficulties psychologists face in reaching the elusive goal of mimicking human visual capabilities illustrate the complexities of vision and the perceptual processes that underlie it (Grossberg & Stone, 1986). Consider, for example, the photo in Figure 3-34. Although to us the task of identifying the form of the basketball player is straightforward, a computer viewing the scene through the lens of a television camera has a considerably more difficult time. It is able to see only a jumble of lines, as the crude reproduction in Figure 3-34 reveals. As you might guess, it is difficult for the computer to recognize the figure as a human being.

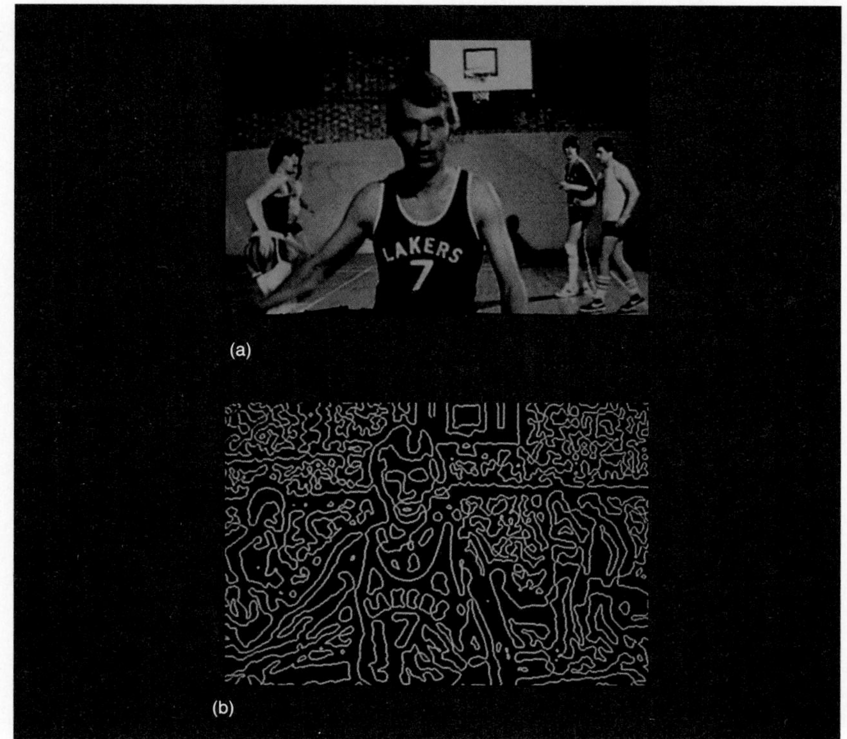

Figure 3-34
(*a*) It is easy for people to see that there is a basketball player here. (*b*) On the other hand, a computer trying to simulate human vision using a television camera ends up with this primitive, incomplete image. (*Dan McCoy/Rainbow*)

The major reason for these difficulties is the complexity of perception. The brain gives meaning to forms and fills in patterns with missing pieces (see Figures 3-35 and 3-36). The retina of the eye alone is capable of some 10 billion calculations per second, far exceeding the ability of any existing computer (Broad, 1984).

Recently, however, scientists have made some important strides toward the goal of mimicking human vision with computers. For instance, several types of computer programs have been developed that more closely mimic the information processing approaches used by the brain. The program recognizes simple stimuli, and has had some initial success in identifying airplanes from photographs. Furthermore, some programs are able to look at a high-contrast scene and compare it with one stored in memory, noting any discrepancies. Such programs can be used on assembly lines to check on the shape of completed products. The difficulty, though, is that conditions need to be almost perfect in

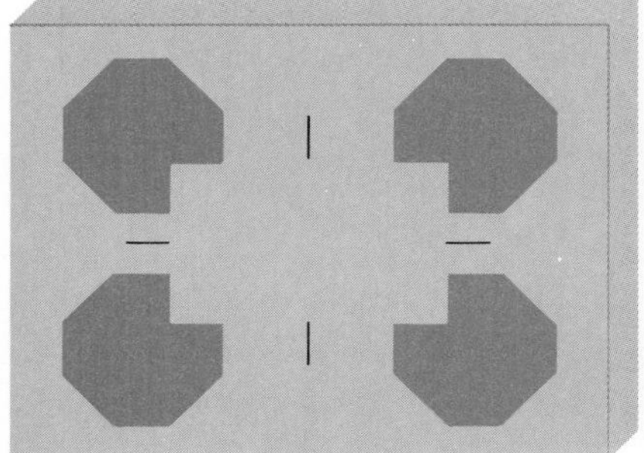

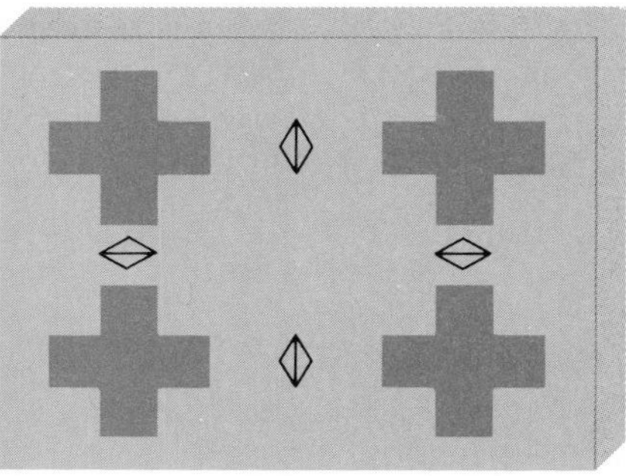

Figures 3-35 and 3-36
There appears to be a rectangle in Figure 3-35, while in Figure 3-36 no rectangle is apparent. In reality both figures contain a rectangular space in the center. This kind of perceptual problem presents difficulties when trying to "teach" a computer to see. (*Broad, 1984.*)

order for the system to work accurately, and only major discrepancies can be identified.

Work continues, though, and the promise of computer-simulated vision is real. Most researchers agree that a computer program must be able to identify surfaces, textures, colors, and shadings before it moves on to identifying particular objects (Marr, 1982; Grossberg & Mingolla, 1985). It will take advances, then, both in our understanding of the perceptual processes of vision and in the sophistication of computers in order to build a visual system that is as adept as the human eye.

LOOKING BACK

1. This chapter has examined how our senses respond to the world around us. It has focused on sensation, which concerns our initial contact with stimuli (forms of energy that activate a sense organ), and perception, the way in which we experience and respond to such stimuli.

2. The study of sensation has traditionally been investigated by the branch of psychology called psychophysics, which studies the relationship between the physical nature of stimuli and the sensory responses of people to the stimuli. Among the major areas of psychophysics is the study of absolute thresholds, the smallest amount of physical intensity of a stimulus that can be detected. Although under ideal conditions absolute thresholds are extraordinarily sensitive, the presence of noise (background stimuli that interfere with the other stimuli) reduces detection capabilities. Moreover, factors such as an individual's expectations about a stimulus and motivations affect the success of detection. Signal detection theory is now used to predict success and accuracy of judgments by systematically taking into account the kind of errors made by observers, which may be of two kinds: reporting the presence of a stimulus when it is not present, or reporting the absence of a stimulus when it actually is present.

3. Difference thresholds relate to the smallest detectable difference between two stimuli, a difference known as a just noticeable difference. According to Weber's law, a just noticeable difference is a constant proportion of the magnitude of an initial stimulus. This means that if an initial stimulus is relatively small, it takes only a small increase in that stimulus to produce a just noticeable difference; but if the initial stimulus is large, it takes a larger increase to produce a just noticeable difference.

4. Sensory adaptation occurs when we become so used to a constant stimulus that we change our frame of reference and evaluate new stimuli in terms of their relationship to the initial stimulus. Moreover, the repeated exposure results in an apparent decline in sensitivity to the original stimulus.

5. Human sensory experience goes well beyond the traditional five senses, although most is known about just two: vision and hearing. Vision depends on sensitivity to light, electromagnetic waves that are reflected off objects outside the body. The eye shapes the light into an image that is transformed into nerve impulses and interpreted by the brain.

6. When light first enters the eye, it travels through the cornea and then traverses the pupil, a dark hole in the center of the iris. The size of the pupil opening adjusts according to the amount of light entering the eye. Light then enters the lens, which acts to focus light rays onto the rear of the eye using a process called accommodation. On the rear of the eye is the retina, which is composed of light-sensitive nerve cells called rods and cones. The rods and cones are unevenly spaced over the retina, with the greatest concentration in an area called the fovea.

7. The visual information gathered by the rods and cones is transferred via bipolar and ganglion cells through the optic nerve, which leads to the optic chiasma—the point where the optic nerve splits. Because the image on the retina is reversed and upside down, images from the right half of the retina are actually from the field of vision to the left of the person, and vice versa. Moreover, because of the phenomenon of adaptation, it takes time to adjust to situations that are either measurably lighter or measurably darker than the previous environment.

8. Color vision operates on the basis of two processes described by the trichromatic theory and the opponent-process theory. The trichromatic theory suggests that there are three kinds of cones in the retina, each of which is responsive to a certain range of colors. The opponent-process theory describes how there are pairs of different types of cells in the eye. These cells work in opposition to each other so that if one is activated, the other is inhibited or prevented from firing.

9. Sound, motion, and balance are centered in the ear. Sounds, in the form of vibrating air waves, enter through the outer ear and auditory canal until they reach the eardrum. The vibrations of the eardrum are transmitted into the middle ear, consisting of three bones, the hammer, the anvil, and the stirrup. These bones transmit vibrations to the oval window, a thin membrane leading to the inner ear. In the inner ear, vibrations move into the cochlea, which encloses the basilar membrane. Hair cells on the

ANSWERS TO REVIEW QUESTIONS

Review IV: **1.** a **2.** Perceptual constancy **3.** a. 6; b. 1; c. 4; d. 5; e. 2; f. 3 **4.** illusions **5.** False basilar membrane change the mechanical energy into nerve impulses which are transmitted to the brain. In addition to sound, the ear serves as the site of the organs that sense balance and motion through the semicircular canals and otoliths.

10. Sound has a number of important characteristics. One is frequency, the number of wave crests that occur in a second. Differences in frequency of sound waves are related to sounds of different pitches. Another aspect of sound is intensity, the variations in pressure produced by a wave as it travels through the air. Intensity is measured in decibels. The place theory of hearing and the frequency theory of hearing explain the processes involved with how sounds of varying frequencies and intensities are distinguished.

11. Considerably less is known about smell, taste, and the skin senses than vision and hearing. Still, it is clear that smell employs the olfactory membranes (the receptor cells of the nose), and that taste is centered in the tongue's taste buds, which are capable of sensing combinations of sweet, sour, salty, and bitter flavors.

12. The skin senses are responsible for the experiences of touch, pressure, temperature, and pain. We know the most about pain, which is explained by the gate-control theory. The theory suggests that particular nerve receptors lead to specific areas of the brain related to pain. When these receptors are activated, a "gate" to the brain is opened, allowing the sensation of pain to be experienced. In addition, there is another set of receptors that, when stimulated, close the gate, thereby reducing the experience of pain. Endorphins, internal painkillers, may also affect the gate's operation.

13. In cases of severe, long-term pain, pain clinics can sometimes offer relief. Among the current techniques used to alleviate pain are drugs, hypnosis, biofeedback, nerve and brain stimulation, relaxation techniques, surgery, and psychotherapy.

14. Perception is the process by which we sort out, interpret, analyze, and integrate stimuli to which our senses are exposed. Perception follows the gestalt laws of organization. These laws provide a series of principles by which we organize bits and pieces of information into meaningful wholes, known as gestalts. Among the most important laws are those of proximity, similarity, and—most importantly—simplicity.

15. The gestalt psychologists demonstrated convincingly that perception follows the general rule: "The whole is greater than the sum of its parts." Moreover, work on figure-ground distinctions shows that perception is a constructive process in which people go beyond the stimuli that are physically present and try to construct a meaningful situation.

16. Depth perception is the ability to perceive distance and to view the world in three dimensions, even though the images projected on our retinas are two-dimensional. We are able to judge depth and distance due to binocular disparity (the difference in images as seen by each of the two eyes) and monocular cues, such as motion parallax (the apparent movement of objects as one's head moves from side to side), the relative size of images on the retina, and linear perspective.

17. Selective attention is the perceptual process of choosing which stimulus to pay attention to. Psychologists study attention using a dichotic listening procedure, in which a message is presented in each ear and the person is asked to repeat, or shadow, one of the messages.

18. Visual illusions are physical stimuli that consistently produce errors in perception, causing judgments that do not accurately reflect the physical reality of a stimulus. Among the best-known illusions are the Poggendorf illusion and the Müller-Lyer illusion. Most evidence suggests that visual illusions are a result of errors in the brain's interpretation of visual stimuli.

KEY TERMS AND CONCEPTS

sensation (78)
perception (78)
stimulus (80)
magnitude (81)
psychophysics (81)
absolute threshold (81)
noise (82)
signal detection theory (83)
difference threshold (83)
just noticeable difference (83)
Weber's law (84)
adaptation (84)
light (87)
visual spectrum (87)
cornea (88)
pupil (88)
iris (88)
lens (89)
accommodation (89)
retina (89)
rods (90)
cones (90)
fovea (90)
peripheral vision (90)
rhodopsin (91)
bipolar cells (91)
ganglion cells (91)
optic nerve (91)
optic chiasma (92)
glaucoma (92)
tunnel vision (92)
light adaptation (92)
dark adaptation (92)
trichromatic theory (95)
afterimage (95)
opponent-process theory (95)
outer ear (97)
sound (97)
auditory canal (97)
eardrum (97)
middle ear (97)
hammer (97)
anvil (97)
stirrup (97)
oval window (97)
inner ear (98)
cochlea (98)
basilar membrane (98)
hair cells (98)
semicircular canals (98)
otoliths (98)
frequency (99)
pitch (100)
intensity (100)
decibels (100)
place theory of hearing (101)
frequency theory of hearing (101)

olfactory cells (103)
taste buds (103)
skin senses (103)
gate-control theory of pain (104)
acupuncture (104)
transcutaneous electrical nerve stimulation (TENS) (105)
gestalt laws of organization (107)
gestalts (107)
closure (107)
proximity (107)
similarity (107)
simplicity (107)
perceptual constancy (108)
depth perception (109)
binocular disparity (109)
monocular cues (109)
motion parallax (109)
relative size (109)
linear perspective (109)
figure/ground (110)
selective attention (111)
dichotic listening (111)
shadowing (111)
visual illusion (112)
Poggendorf illusion (114)
Müller-Lyer illusion (114)

FOR FURTHER STUDY AND APPLICATION

Schiffman, H. R. (1982). *Sensation and perception* (2nd ed.). New York: Wiley.

Goldstein, E. B. (1984). *Sensation and perception* (2nd ed.). Belmont, CA: Wadsworth.

These are fine general overviews of sensation and the senses, including a broad and balanced treatment of theories, principles, and findings.

Gregory, R. L. (1978). *The psychology of seeing* (3rd ed.). New York: McGraw-Hill.

This volume focuses on the operation of the eye and the nature of human sight.

Fairley, P. (1980). *The conquest of pain*. New York: Charles Scribner.

Hendler, N. H., Long, D. M., & Wise, T. N. (1982). *Diagnosis and treatment of chronic pain.* Boston: J. Wright.

These books provide a layperson's view of treatments and strategies for pain reduction.

Coren, S., & Girgus, J. S. (1978). *Seeing is deceiving: The psychology of visual illusions.* Hillsdale, NJ: Erlbaum.

This book provides a fascinating glimpse at visual illusions and a clear understanding of them, along with a repertoire of visual tricks that will amuse your friends.

PART THREE

PART THREE

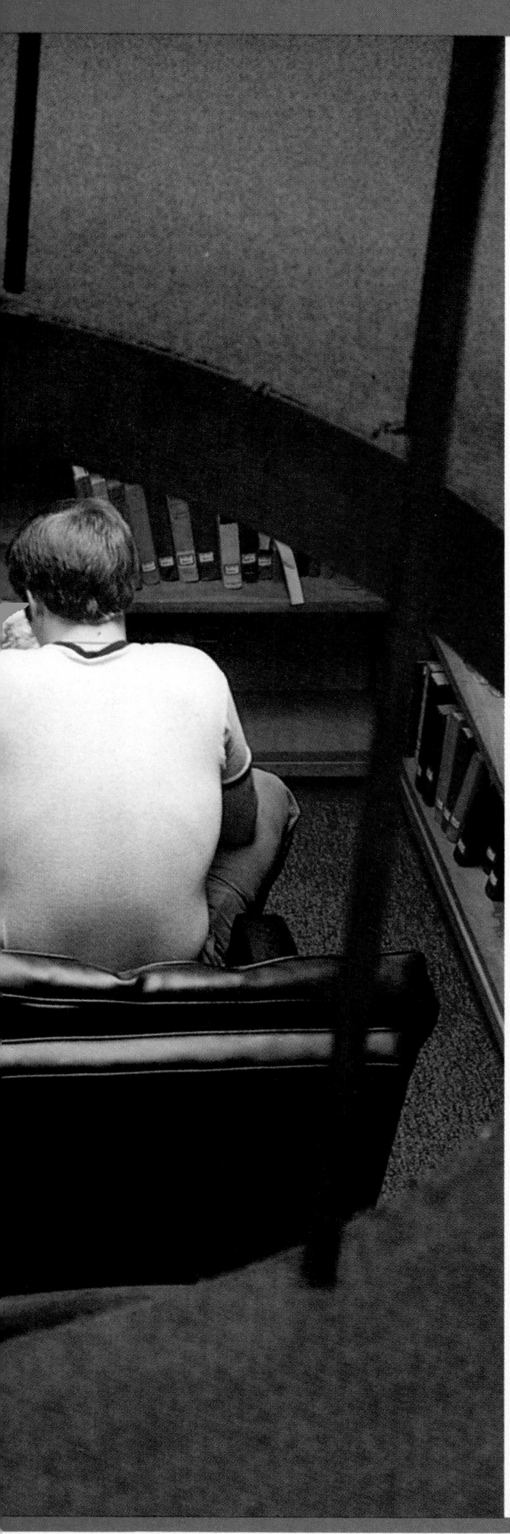

LEARNING AND THINKING ABOUT THE WORLD

In this part of the book, we focus on the way in which we learn and remember. We encounter an Olympic star, honing his skills to such a sharp edge that he wins a gold medal, and we find a group of pigeons trained to save lives. We meet a man who can remember almost everything to which he is exposed—and someone who remembers almost nothing of the past.

These topics are tied together by the fundamental principles identified by psychologists as learning and memory. We will see how the basic principles of learning, developed largely from animal research, can account for human mastery of the most complex material. And we will find how we are able to remember obscure details from our past, but may still forget the names of people to whom we have just been introduced.

In Chapter 4, then, the focus is on learning, ranging from the most simple to the most complex.

In Chapter 5, the discussion turns to memory, and how it is structured and operates.

In Part III, our basic thinking processes are also examined, along with ways in which language provides a vehicle for communication and thought. We discuss differences in intellectual capabilities, ranging from the highest to the lowest, and the effects such capabilities have on behavior.

In Chapter 6, we will consider the processes that underlie our abilities to think, to reason about the world, and to use language.

In Chapter 7, we turn to a consideration of intelligence and the abilities of which it is comprised.

CHAPTER 4

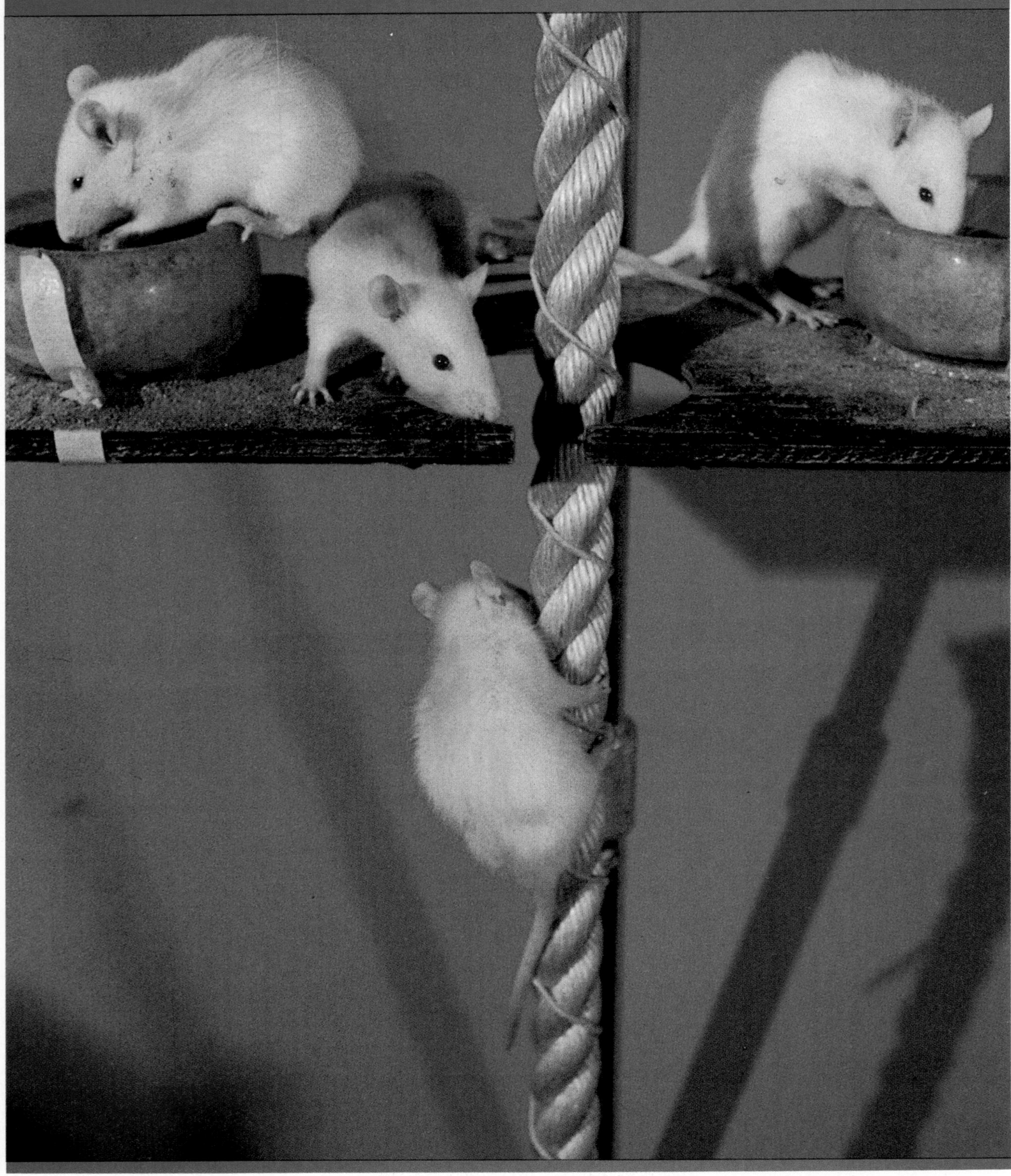

LEARNING

PROLOGUE

LOOKING AHEAD

PAVLOV'S DOGS AND THE GOLDEN ARCHES: CLASSICAL CONDITIONING

Canine conditioning: Pavlov's dogs
Classical conditioning is not just for the dogs: Applying conditioning principles to human behavior
Unlearning what you have learned: Extinction
The return of the conditioned response: Spontaneous recovery
A rose is a rose is a rose: Generalization and discrimination
When a CS becomes a UCS: Higher-order conditioning
Recap and review I

THE REWARDS OF REINFORCEMENT: OPERANT CONDITIONING

Cat-in-a-box: Thorndike's law of effect
From cat-in-a-box to Skinner box: The basics of operant conditioning
TRY IT! Using Positive Reinforcement to Change Behavior
Recap and review II
Timing life's rewards: Schedules of reinforcement
Learning the right stimulus from the wrong: Discrimination and generalization in operant conditioning
Superstitious behavior
Reinforcing what doesn't come naturally: Shaping
THE CUTTING EDGE. A Pigeon Posse: Saving Lives with Operant Conditioning
The informed consumer of psychology: Using computer-assisted programmed instruction to shape your own behavior
Discriminating between classical conditioning and operant conditioning: The difference is not always clear
Recap and review III

THE THINKING PERSON'S LEARNING THEORY: COGNITIVE APPROACHES TO LEARNING

Learning by copying: Observational learning
Accepting the unacceptable: Learned helplessness
The unresolved controversy: Cognitive learning theory in perspective

BEHAVIOR ANALYSIS AND BEHAVIOR MODIFICATION

PSYCHOLOGY AT WORK. Safety on the Job: Preventing Accidents by Changing Human Behavior
The informed consumer of psychology: Using behavior-modification techniques to manage your time
Recap and review IV
PSYCHOLOGY LOOKS TOWARD THE 1990s. Computers Learn to Learn

LOOKING BACK

KEY TERMS AND CONCEPTS

FOR FURTHER STUDY AND APPLICATION

PROLOGUE

Finally the time had come. After devoting years of his life to rigorous training, which had taken its toll on both his social life and his studies, Greg Louganis knew that his participation in the Summer Olympics represented the culmination of his efforts.

As he walked to the end of the diving board, many thoughts ran through the mind of the young diver from California. At first he sang to himself, as he often did during competition. ''It's usually 'Believe in Yourself' from 'The Wiz' that I sing,'' said Louganis afterward. ''You're up there 33 feet above the water with not a whole lot on, and seven people are judging you. It's a very vulnerable position. You've got to have a lot of confidence in yourself.''

Then, just before the dive, he blotted out all but the most relevant thought: the image of a diver executing a perfect three-and-a-half-somersault dive into the water. He replayed the image that had gone through his mind so often, concentrating on nothing else.

Who was the diver in this mental picture? It was Louganis himself. After the years of training, the exacting dive itself was almost second nature to him. For Louganis it was important to ignore the thought that a gold medal—the ultimate reward for any Olympian—depended on how well he executed this particular dive, and to exercise sheer concentration on the dive itself. Every diver knows what trainer Dennis Golden had been telling Louganis and the other American divers: Diving is ''almost 100 percent mental,'' and you must mentally experience the performance you want to achieve.

For Louganis, this meant rehearsing his dives over and over in his mind, sometimes from the perspective of an observer and sometimes from his own perspective as a diver, until he could blot out every distracting stimulus in the environment. Having done so repeatedly had enabled him to associate particular bodily feelings and visual cues with a perfect dive. During training he had also learned to remind himself of his past successes, thereby helping himself to overcome those low moments that afflict every athlete.

Now the critical moment had arrived. As Louganis sprang off the board the years of work came together. With power and grace, he carried out the risky dive (which the previous year had killed a Russian diver during pre-Olympic competition). He knew he had completed a beautiful dive, and when the judges' scores were announced he let a feeling of elation overcome him: He had clinched the gold medal by earning a world-record-breaking score. Later, as he stood at the awards ceremony with the medal draped around his neck and heard the band playing the ''Star-Spangled Banner,'' he felt a rush of emotion wash over him. His years of effort had paid off.

LOOKING AHEAD

The same processes that allowed Greg Louganis to harness and shape his physical talents into a gold-medal-winning performance are at work in each of our lives, whether we are reading a book, driving a car, playing poker, studying for a test, or performing any of the many other activities important to us. Like Louganis, each of us must acquire and then hone our skills and abilities through the basic phenomenon of learning.

A fundamental subject for psychologists, learning underlies many of the diverse topics discussed throughout this book. For example, a psychologist studying perception might ask, "How do we learn that people who look small from a distance are just far away and not simply tiny?"; a developmental psychologist might inquire, "How do babies learn to discriminate their mothers from other people?"; a clinical psychologist might wonder, "Why do some people learn to be afraid when they see a spider?"; and a social psychologist might ask, "How do we learn to feel that we are in love?" Each of these questions, although drawn from very different fields of psychology, can be answered only with reference to learning processes. In fact, learning plays a central role in almost every topic of interest to psychologists.

What do we mean by the term "learning"? Although psychologists have identified a number of different types of learning, a general definition encompasses them all: **Learning** is a relatively permanent change in behavior brought about by experience. What is particularly important about this definition is that it permits us to distinguish between performance changes due to **maturation** (the unfolding of biologically predetermined patterns of behavior due simply to getting older) and those that are brought about by experience. For instance, children become better tennis players as they grow older partially because they gain greater strength with their increase in size—a maturational influence. Such maturational changes need to be distinguished from improvements due to learning, which are a consequence of experience.

Figure 4-1
After years of training, Greg Louganis begins his 3½ somersault dive to capture the Olympic Gold Medal in diving. (*Focus on Sports*)

Learning: *A relatively permanent change in behavior brought about by experience*
Maturation: *The unfolding of biologically predetermined patterns of behavior due to aging*

Similarly, we must distinguish between short-term changes in behavior that are due to factors other than learning, such as declines in performance due to fatigue or lack of effort, and performance changes due to actual learning. For example, if Greg Louganis dives poorly one day because of tension or fatigue, this does not mean he has not learned to dive correctly or has forgotten how.

The distinction between learning and performance is critical, and yet is not always easy to make. Learning is an *inferred* process; we cannot see it happening directly, and we can assume that it has occurred only by observing changes in performance. This fact makes the learning psychologist's task a difficult one, since there is not always a one-to-one correspondence between learning and performance—as those of us who have done poorly on an exam because we were tired can well understand. Poor performance, then, does not necessarily indicate an absence of learning.

In this chapter, we examine basic learning processes. We begin by discussing classical conditioning, a type of learning that underlies many emotional responses. We see how responses as diverse as a dog salivating at the sound of its owner's footsteps and Greg Louganis's emotional response to the sound of the national anthem are examples of classical conditioning. We also consider some of the basic principles of classical conditioning, explaining how learned responses may disappear and how new responses can be learned by linking them to older ones.

Next we focus on operant conditioning, another major type of learning. Operant conditioning not only helps to explain why people such as Louganis strive for gold medals, it also underlies more commonplace behaviors such as working for good grades, money, and praise from others.

We next examine how patterns of reinforcement bring about and maintain desired behavior. We then tackle the issue of using punishment to modify behavior, considering both the pros and cons as identified by psychologists.

Our discussion proceeds with an explanation of the principles of generalization and discrimination as related to operant conditioning, and then we look at some of the differences between classical and operant conditioning. We also examine

Ivan Pavlov, a Russian physiologist, was the first to recognize the importance of the learning processes represented in classical conditioning. *(Culver Pictures)*

a third major learning theory, one that considers the social and cognitive aspects of learning.

Finally, we discuss ways of formally analyzing behavior, and techniques for modifying and controlling it. Some practical methods for bringing about behavior change are presented, and we end the chapter by discussing strategies based on learning principles which informed consumers of psychology can use to better manage their time.

In sum, after reading and studying this chapter you will be able to

- Explain the basic principles of classical and operant conditioning
- Distinguish between different forms of rewards, or reinforcement
- Identify and describe the effects of different schedules of reinforcement
- Define punishment as psychologists use the term, and understand the positive and negative results of its use
- Differentiate between operant and classical conditioning
- Describe cognitive approaches to learning
- Understand how behavior analysts use behavior-modification principles
- Define and apply the key terms and concepts listed at the end of the chapter

PAVLOV'S DOGS AND THE GOLDEN ARCHES: CLASSICAL CONDITIONING

PERRY: This has been a nice drive, but I think I'm ready to get back. Let's take the coast highway.
JILL: That's fine. Oh, what's that ahead?
PERRY: Ah, the golden arches. Y'know, I just see them and my mouth begins to water and I get hungry.
JILL: I know what you mean. Let's stop. I'm beginning to get hungry, too.

What does people getting hungry at the sight of McDonald's golden arches have to do with learning? Quite a bit, according to a major model of learning called classical conditioning. The processes that underlie classical conditioning explain such diverse phenomena as crying at the sight of a bride walking down the aisle, fear of the dark, or falling in love with the girl next door.

Canine Conditioning: Pavlov's Dogs

Ivan Pavlov, a Russian physiologist, never intended to do psychological research. In 1904 he won the Nobel Prize for his work on digestion, testimony to his contribution to that field. Yet Pavlov is remembered not for his physiological research, but for his experiments on basic learning processes—work that he began quite accidentally.

Pavlov had been studying the secretion of stomach acids and salivation in dogs in response to the ingestion of varying amounts and kinds of food. While doing so, he observed a curious phenomenon: Sometimes stomach secretions and salivation would begin when no food had actually been eaten; the mere sight of a food bowl, the individual who normally brought the food, or even the sound of the footsteps of that individual was enough to produce a physiological response in the dogs. Pavlov's genius was his ability to recognize the implications of this rather basic discovery. He saw that the dogs were responding not only on the basis of a biological need (hunger), but also as a result of learning—or, as it came to be called, classical conditioning. In **classical conditioning**, an organism learns a response to a stimulus that normally does not bring about that response.

Classical conditioning: *A kind of learning in which a response is made to a previously neutral stimulus that would not naturally bring about that response*

To demonstrate and analyze classical conditioning, Pavlov ran a series of experiments (Pavlov, 1927). In one, he attached a tube to the salivary gland of a dog, allowing him to measure precisely the amount of salivation that occurred. He then sounded a tuning fork and, just a few seconds later, presented the dog with meat powder. This pairing, carefully planned so that exactly the same amount of time elapsed between the presentation of the sound and the meat, occurred repeatedly. At first the dog would salivate only when the meat powder itself was presented, but soon it began to salivate at the sound of the tuning fork. In fact, even when Pavlov stopped presenting the meat powder, the dog still salivated after hearing the sound. The dog had been classically conditioned to salivate to the tone.

As you can see in Figure 4-2, the basic processes of classical conditioning underlying Pavlov's discovery are straightforward, although the terminology he chose has a technical ring to it. Consider first the diagram in Figure 4-2*a*. Prior to conditioning, we have two unrelated stimuli: the sound of a tuning fork and meat powder. We know that the sound of a tuning fork leads not to salivation but to some irrelevant response such as perking of the ears or, perhaps, a startle reaction. The sound in this case therefore is called the **neutral stimulus** because it has no effect on the response of interest. We also have meat powder, which, because of the biological makeup of the dog, naturally leads to salivation, the particular response that we are interested in conditioning. The meat powder is considered an **unconditioned stimulus**, or **UCS**, because food placed near a dog's mouth automatically causes salivation to occur. The response that the meat powder produces is called an **unconditioned response**, or **UCR**—a response that is not associated with previous learning. Unconditioned responses are natural and innate responses that need no training, and they are always brought about by unconditioned stimuli.

Neutral stimulus: *A stimulus that, before conditioning, has no effect on the desired response*

Unconditioned stimulus (UCS): *A stimulus that brings about a response without having been learned*

Unconditioned response (UCR): *A response that is natural and needs no training (e.g., salivation at the smell of food)*

Figure 4-2*b* illustrates what happens during conditioning. The tuning fork is repeatedly sounded just before presentation of the meat powder. The goal of conditioning is for the tuning fork to develop into a substitute for the unconditioned stimulus (meat powder) and therefore to bring about the same sort of response as the unconditioned stimulus. During this period, salivation gradually increases each time the tuning fork is sounded until the tuning fork alone causes the dog to salivate.

When conditioning is complete, the tuning fork has evolved from a neutral stimulus to what is now called a **conditioned stimulus**, or **CS**. At this time, salivation that occurs as a response to the conditioned stimulus (tuning fork) is considered a **conditioned response**, or **CR**. This situation is depicted in Figure 4-2*c*. The conditioned stimulus evokes the conditioned response.

Conditioned stimulus (CS): *A once-neutral stimulus that has been paired with an unconditioned stimulus to bring about a response formerly caused only by the unconditioned stimulus*

Conditioned response (CR): *A response (e.g., salivation) that, after conditioning, follows a previously neutral stimulus (e.g., vibration of a tuning fork)*

The sequence and timing of the presentation of the unconditioned stimulus and the conditioned stimulus is particularly important. Analogous to the ineffectiveness of a signal light at a railroad crossing that does not operate until after a train has passed by, a neutral stimulus that follows an unconditioned stimulus has little chance of becoming a conditioned stimulus. On the other hand, just as a warning light works best if it goes on right before a train is about to go by, a neutral stimulus that is presented just before the unconditioned stimulus is most apt to result in successful conditioning. Research has shown, in fact,

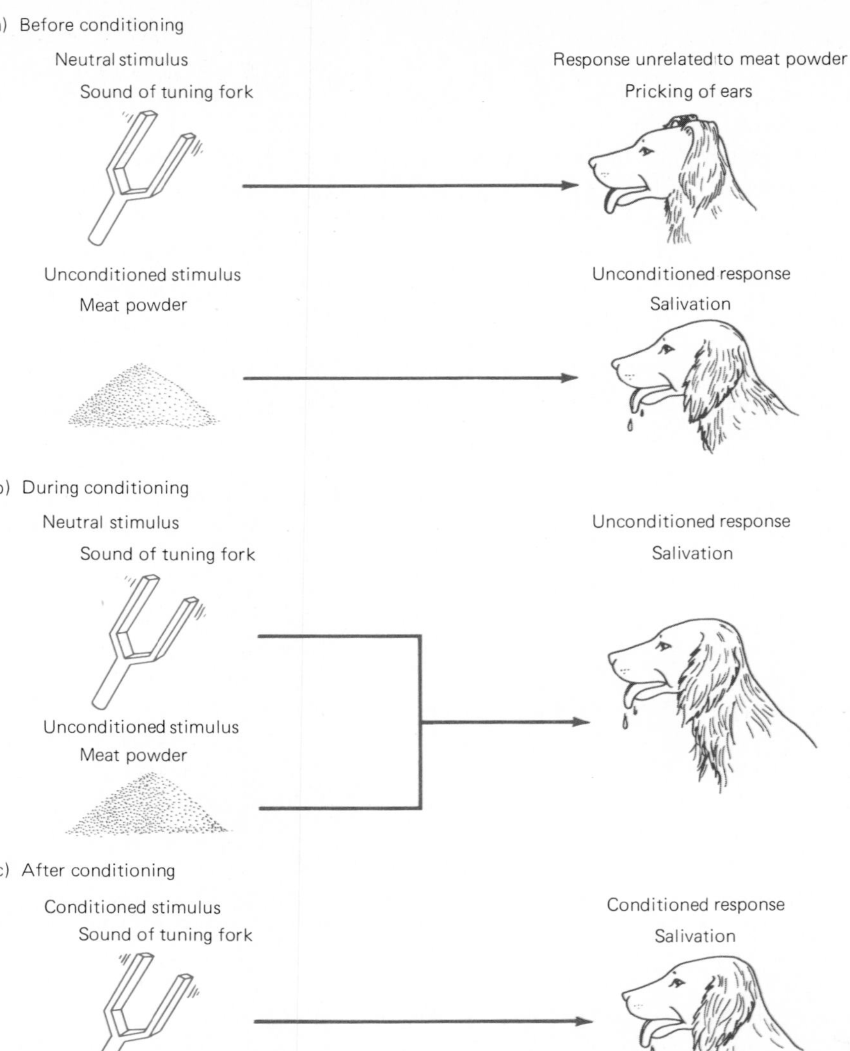

Figure 4-2
The basic process of classical conditioning: (*a*) Prior to conditioning, the sound of a tuning fork does not bring about salivation—making the tuning fork a neutral stimulus. On the other hand, meat powder naturally brings about salivation, making the meat powder an unconditioned stimulus and salivation an unconditioned response. (*b*) During conditioning, the tuning fork is sounded just before the presentation of the meat powder. (*c*) Eventually the sound of the tuning fork alone brings about salivation. We can now say that conditioning has been accomplished: The previously neutral stimulus of the tuning fork is now considered a conditioned stimulus which brings about the conditioned response of salivation.

that conditioning is most effective if the conditioned stimulus precedes the unconditioned stimulus by between a half second to several seconds, depending on what kind of response is being conditioned.

Although the terminology employed by Pavlov to describe classical conditioning may at first seem confusing, the following rules of thumb can help to make the relationships between stimuli and responses easier to understand and remember:

- *Un*conditioned stimuli lead to *un*conditioned responses, and *un*conditioned stimulus–*un*conditioned response pairings are *un*learned and *un*trained.
- Conditioned stimuli lead to conditioned responses, and conditioned stimulus–conditioned response pairings are a consequence of learning and training.
- Unconditioned responses and conditioned responses refer to similar re-

sponses (such as salivation in the example described above), but the conditioned response must be learned, while the unconditioned response occurs naturally.

Classical Conditioning Is Not Just for the Dogs: Applying Conditioning Principles to Human Behavior

While the initial classical conditioning experiments were carried out with animals, the principles that underlay the early work were soon found to influence many aspects of everyday human behavior. Consider our example of Perry, who tells his companion that his mouth begins to water whenever he sees McDonald's golden arches. Because of classical conditioning, the previously neutral arches have come to be associated with the food inside the restaurant (the unconditioned stimulus), causing the arches to become a conditioned stimulus that brings about the conditioned response of salivation.

Emotional responses are particularly apt to be learned through classical conditioning processes. For instance, how do some of us develop fears of mice, spiders, and other creatures that—if we thought about it much—do not seem intrinsically more ferocious or potentially more harmful than a pet dog or cat? In a now-famous experiment designed to show that classical conditioning was at the root of such fears, an 11-month-old infant named Albert, who initially showed no fear of rats, was exposed to a loud noise at the same time that a rat was presented to him (Watson & Rayner, 1920). The noise (the UCS) evoked fear (the UCR); after just a few pairings, Albert began to show fear of the rat by itself. The rat, then, had become a CS that brought about the CR, fear. Similarly, it is likely that the pairing of the appearance of certain species with the fearful action of an adult causes children to develop the same fears their parents have.

As an adult, learning via classical conditioning occurs a bit more subtly. You may come to know that a professor's mood is particularly menacing when her tone of voice changes; in the past you may have seen that the professor uses that tone only when she is about to criticize someone's work harshly. Likewise,

The association between pain and dentistry explains why many people develop a classically conditioned unpleasant emotional reaction to dentists. *(Walker Bros. Creations/Photo Researchers, Inc.)*

you may be afraid of dental examinations because of prior associations with dentists and pain. Or you may have a particular fondness for the color blue because that was the color of your childhood bedroom. Classical conditioning, then, explains many of the reactions we have to stimuli in the world around us.

Unlearning What You Have Learned: Extinction

As long as you can remember, you have hated broccoli. The very sight of it makes you queasy. Yet your new girlfriend's parents seem to love it—perhaps they own a broccoli farm?—serving it every time you come to visit. Being polite, you feel you must eat a little of it. The first few times it is torture; you feel as if you are about to embarrass yourself by getting sick at the table, but you steel yourself to keep the broccoli down. After a few weeks it becomes easier. In fact, after a couple months, you are surprised to realize that you no longer feel sick at the thought of eating broccoli.

Extinction (x TINK shun): *The weakening and eventual disappearance of a conditioned response, resulting from the discontinuation of the reward*

Your behavior can be explained by one of the basic phenomena of learning: extinction. **Extinction** occurs when a previously conditioned response becomes weaker and eventually disappears. To produce extinction, one needs to end the association between conditioned and unconditioned stimuli. If we had trained a dog to salivate at the sound of a bell, we could bring about extinction by ceasing to provide meat after the bell was sounded. At first the dog would continue to salivate when it heard the bell, but after a few such instances, the amount of salivation would probably decline, and the dog would eventually stop responding to the bell altogether. At that point, we could say that the response had been extinguished. In sum, extinction occurs when the conditioned stimulus is repeatedly presented without the unconditioned stimulus.

Systematic desensitization: *A form of therapy in which fears are minimized through different degrees of exposure, the patient eventually learning to feel comfortable in the presence of the object of his or her former fears*

As will be described more fully in Chapter 13, psychologists have treated people with irrational fears or phobias using a form of therapy called **systematic desensitization**, in which the goal is to bring about the extinction of the phobia. For instance,a person who has an intense fear of heights, and has been undergoing systematic desensitization therapy, might be told to climb to the first floor of a building and look out the window. When he is on the first floor, he uses relaxation procedures he has been taught by the therapist until he feels comfortable at that height. To feel truly relaxed, he may have to repeat this process several times. Next he is told to climb to a somewhat higher floor and do the same thing. By increasing the height to which he climbs each time—and discovering that there are no negative consequences—he may eventually be able to overcome his fear of high places.

The basic goal of systematic desensitization is to bring about the extinction of the phobia in question. When the treatment begins, the patient demonstrates a conditioned response to the feared object; in our example, for instance, a high place acts as a conditioned stimulus that produces the conditioned response of fear. Each time the person is exposed to the conditioned stimulus (being in a high place) without experiencing the unconditioned stimulus (negative consequences), the likelihood that the conditioned stimulus will evoke the undesirable response is weakened. Eventually, then, the conditioned response is extinguished.

The Return of the Conditioned Response: Spontaneous Recovery

Once a conditioned response has been extinguished, is it lost forever? Not necessarily. As Pavlov discovered, if he returned to his previously conditioned dog the day after the conditioned behavior had been extinguished and rang a bell, the dog would once again salivate. Similarly a person once "cured" of a phobia may find that the phobia returns after a long period of absence from the feared object.

This phenomenon is called **spontaneous recovery**—the reappearance of a previously extinguished response after time has elapsed without exposure to the conditioned stimulus. Usually, however, responses that return through spontaneous recovery are weaker than they were initially and can be extinguished more readily than before.

Spontaneous recovery: *The reappearance of a previously extinguished response after a period of time during which the conditioned stimulus has been absent*

A Rose Is a Rose Is a Rose: Generalization and Discrimination

Despite differences in color and shape, to most of us a rose is a rose is a rose: The pleasure we experience at the beauty, smell, and grace of the flower is similar for different roses. Pavlov noticed an analogous phenomenon: His dogs often salivated not only to the sound of the tuning fork that was used during their original conditioning, but to the sound of a bell or a buzzer as well.

Such behavior can be explained by the concept of stimulus generalization. **Stimulus generalization** takes place when a conditioned response follows a stimulus that is similar to the original conditioned stimulus. The greater the similarity between the two stimuli, the greater the likelihood of stimulus generalization. Baby Albert, who, as we mentioned earlier, was conditioned to be fearful of rats, was later found to be afraid of other furry white things; he was fearful of white rabbits, white fur coats, and even a white Santa Claus mask. On the other hand, according to the principle of stimulus generalization, it is unlikely that he would be afraid of a black dog, since its color would differentiate it sufficiently from the original fear-evoking stimulus.

Stimulus generalization: *Response to a stimulus that is similar to but different from a conditioned stimulus; the more similar the two stimuli, the more likely generalization is to occur*

The conditioned response that is evoked by the new stimulus is usually not as intense as the original conditioned response, although the more similar the new stimulus is to the old one, the more similar will be the new response. It is unlikely, then, that Albert's fear of the Santa Claus mask was as great as his learned fear of a rat. In contrast, stimulus generalization permits us to know that we ought to brake at all red lights, even if there are minor variations in size, shape, and shade.

If stimuli are sufficiently distinct from one another so that the presence of one evokes a conditioned response but the other does not, we can say that stimulus discrimination has occurred. **Stimulus discrimination** is the process in which an organism is trained to differentiate among different stimuli and restrict its responding to one stimulus rather than to others. Without the ability to discriminate between a red and a green traffic light, we would be mowed down by oncoming traffic; and if we could not discriminate a cat from a mountain lion, we might find ourselves in uncomfortable straits on a camping trip.

Stimulus discrimination: *The process in which an organism is trained to differentiate among stimuli, restricting response to one in particular*

When a CS Becomes a UCS: Higher-Order Conditioning

If you are knocked over a few times by your neighbor's vicious Doberman, Rover, it would not be surprising that merely hearing his name called would produce an unpleasant emotional reaction. This represents an example of higher-order conditioning. **Higher-order conditioning** occurs when a conditioned stimulus that has been established during earlier conditioning is then paired with a neutral stimulus, and the neutral stimulus comes to evoke a conditioned response

Higher-order conditioning: *A form of conditioning that occurs when an already-conditioned stimulus is paired with a neutral stimulus until the neutral stimulus evokes the same response as the conditioned stimulus*

similar to the original conditioned stimulus. The original conditioned stimulus, in effect, acts as an unconditioned stimulus.

Our example of Rover can illustrate higher-order conditioning. You have learned to associate the sight of vicious Rover, who originally was a neutral stimulus, with his rough behavior. The mere sight of Rover, then, has become a conditioned stimulus, which evokes the conditioned response of fear.

Later, however, you realize that every time you see Rover, his owner is calling his name, saying, "Here, Rover." Because of this continual pairing of the name of Rover (which was originally a neutral stimulus) with the sight of Rover (now a conditioned stimulus), you become conditioned to experience a reaction of fear and loathing whenever you hear the name Rover, even though you may be safely inside your house. The name "Rover," then, has become a conditioned stimulus because of its earlier pairing with the conditioned stimulus of the sight of Rover. Higher-order conditioning has occurred: The sound of Rover's name has become a conditioned stimulus evoking a conditioned response.

Theoretically, it ought to be possible to keep producing unlimited higher-order response chains, associating one conditioned stimulus with another, and in fact Pavlov hypothesized that all learning is nothing more than long strings of conditioned responses. However, this notion has not been supported by subsequent research, and it turns out that classical conditioning provides us with only a partial explanation of how people and animals learn. There are many instances in which learning does not build upon natural, innate responses such as salivation when exposed to food or avoidance of unpleasant stimuli (Catania, 1984). As we discuss in the section that follows, there is another major model of learning, called operant conditioning, that accounts for an individual's learning in order to obtain some reward.

RECAP AND REVIEW I

Recap

- Learning is a relatively permanent change in behavior brought about by experience.
- Classical conditioning is a kind of learning in which an initially neutral stimulus, which does not evoke a relevant response, is paired repeatedly with an unconditioned stimulus until it evokes a response similar to that brought about by the unconditioned stimulus.
- Classical conditioning underlies many sorts of everyday learning, such as the acquisition of emotional responses.
- Among the basic phenomena of classical conditioning are extinction, systematic desensitization, spontaneous recovery, stimulus generalization and discrimination, and higher-order conditioning.

Review

The last three times Theresa has visited Dr. Noble for checkups, he has administered a painful preventative injection that has left her in tears. When her mother takes her for yet another checkup, Theresa begins to sob as soon as she comes face to face with Dr. Noble, before he has even had a chance to say hello.

Referring to the above passage, answer questions 1 through 4.

1. The painful shot that Theresa received during each visit was an ____________ , which elicited the ____________ ____________, her tears.
2. Dr. Noble is upset because his presence has become a ____________ for Theresa's tears.
3. When elicited by Dr. Noble's presence alone, Theresa's crying is referred to as a ____________ ____________ ____________.
4. Fortunately, Dr. Noble will give Theresa no more shots for quite some time. Over that time she will gradually stop crying and will even come to like him. That is, ____________ will occur.
5. Systematic desensitization is based in part on the process of extinction. True or false?

6. Responses made during a spontaneous recovery are generally stronger than those made before extinction. True or false?
7. Responding to one stimulus and not to others is known as
   a. Stimulus generalization **b.** Stimulus discrimination **c.** An unconditioned response **d.** Inferred learning

(Answers to review questions are at bottom of page 138.)

THE REWARDS OF REINFORCEMENT: OPERANT CONDITIONING

When they finally reached the entrance to the porpoise show at Sea-Land, Bonnie and Joel were once again on the verge of another argument.

''I wish you could back off a bit,'' said Joel, as they bought their tickets at the entrance and went inside. ''This is supposed to be a vacation, not an opportunity for more of your complaints about what I'm doing wrong.''

''My complaints? I wouldn't have any reason to complain if you had driven a little slower and hadn't gotten that speeding ticket. That's going to cost fifty bucks, you know.''

''Yeah—I know. But if you hadn't gotten me so angry with your constant criticism and advice I might have been driving a little slower.''

''Look,'' Bonnie said, as the porpoises began to leap through hoops and walk on the water with their tails, ''don't blame your driving on me—when I criticize you it's for your own good. But let's watch the show now. I hear it's great. Phyllis Bradley, who was here last year, told me that they get these porpoises to do the most amazing things just by rewarding the animals with bits of food. In fact, I think she said they never resort to punishing the porpoises to get them to perform. But they could never get them to do all those tricks without ever using punishment, could they?''

To a confirmed critic like Bonnie, it might seem impossible that rewards alone could make animals such as porpoises move through a series of compli-

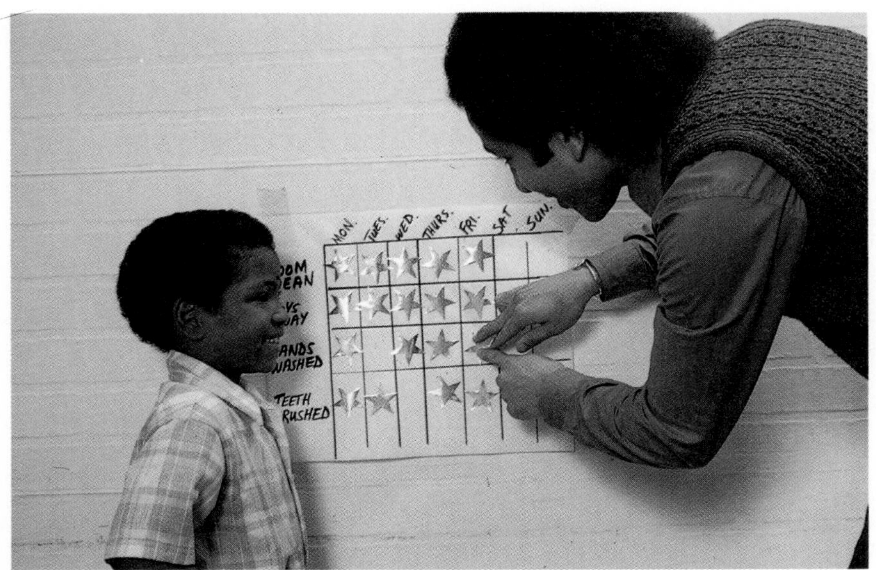

In this example of operant conditioning, a child receives rewards of gold stars for carrying out desired behavior. *(Mimi Cotter/International Stock Photo)*

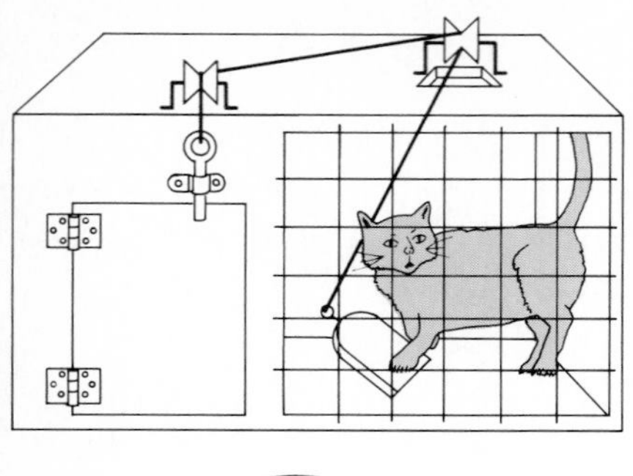

Figure 4-3
Edward L. Thorndike devised this puzzle box to study the process by which a cat learns to press a paddle to escape the box and receive food. (*Thorndike, 1932.*) (*©Sepp Seitz/Woodfin Camp. & Assoc.*)

cated tricks. Yet in reality, the most complicated of behaviors can be taught by using rewards when employing techniques of operant conditioning, the second major type of learning. Operant conditioning forms the basis for much of the most important kinds of human learning, as well.

In **operant conditioning**, the focus is on learning in which people make responses because they have learned that positive or negative consequences are contingent (or dependent) on the response. Unlike classical conditioning, in which the original responses are the natural, biological outgrowth of the presence of some stimulus such as food, water, or pain, operant conditioning applies to voluntary responses, which an organism performs willfully—in order to produce a desirable outcome. The term **operant** emphasizes this point: The organism *operates* on its environment in order to produce some desired result. Thus, working diligently to get a raise, cleaning one's room to get Mom to buy a toy truck, or studying hard to get a good grade are all examples of operant conditioning.

Opperant conditioning: *Learning that occurs as a result of certain positive or negative consequences; the organism* operates *on its environment in order to produce a desired result*

Operant: *The learning process involving one's operation of the environment (see operant conditioning)*

Cat-in-a-Box: Thorndike's Law of Effect

If you placed a hungry cat in a cage and then put a small piece of food outside, chances are the cat would eagerly search for a way out of the cage. The cat might first claw at the sides or push against an opening. Suppose, though, that you had rigged things so that the cat could escape by stepping on a small paddle that released the latch to the door of the cage (see Figure 4-3). Eventually, as it moved around the cage, the cat would happen to step on the paddle, the door would open, and the food could be eaten.

What would happen then if you returned the cat to the box? The next time, it would probably take a little less time before the cat stepped on the paddle and escaped. After a few trials, the cat would deliberately step on the paddle as soon as it was placed in the cage. What would have occurred, according to Edward L. Thorndike (1932), who studied the situation extensively, was that the cat would have learned that pressing the paddle was associated with the desirable consequence of getting food. He summarized that relationship by for-

If you respond positively to opinion statements made by an acquaintance during a conversation, you may notice an increase in the number of opinions the acquaintance offers—an example of operant conditioning. *(Jim Hamilton/The Picture Cube)*

Figure 4-4
A Skinner box, used to study operant conditioning. Laboratory animals learn to press the lever in order to obtain food, which is delivered in the tray. (© Sepp Seitz 1985/Woodfin Camp. & Assoc.)

mulating the law of effect. Basically, the **law of effect** states that responses that are satisfying are more likely to be repeated, and those that are not satisfying are less likely to be repeated.

Law of effect: *Thorndike's theory that responses which satisfy are more likely to be repeated, while those that don't satisfy will be discontinued*

From Cat-in-the-Box to Skinner Box: The Basics of Operant Conditioning

Thorndike's early research formed the foundation for the work of the most famous contemporary psychologist, B. F. Skinner. You may have heard of the "Skinner box," (shown in one form in Figure 4-4), a chamber with a highly controlled environment used to study operant-conditioning processes with laboratory animals. Whereas Thorndike's goal was to get his cats to learn to obtain food by leaving the box, animals in a Skinner box learn to obtain food by operating on their environment within the box.

Skinner, whose work goes far beyond perfecting Thorndike's earlier apparatus, is considered the father of a whole generation of psychologists studying operant conditioning. To illustrate Skinner's contribution to the understanding of operant learning, let's consider what happens to a pigeon in the typical Skinner box.

Suppose you want to teach a hungry pigeon to peck a key that is located in its box. At first the pigeon will wander around the box, exploring the environment in a relatively random fashion. At some point, however, it will probably peck the key by chance, and when it does, it will receive a food pellet. The first time this happens, the pigeon will not make the connection between pecking and receiving food and will continue to explore the box. Sooner or later the pigeon will again peck the key and receive a pellet and in time, the frequency of the pecking response will increase. Eventually, the pigeon will peck the key continually until it satisfies its hunger, thereby demonstrating that it has learned that the receipt of food is contingent on the pecking behavior.

Reinforcer: *Any stimulus that increases the probability that a preceding response will be repeated*

Reinforcing Desired Behavior In a situation such as this one, the food is called a reinforcer. A **reinforcer** is any stimulus that increases the probability that a preceding response will occur again. Here, food is a reinforcer because it increases the probability that a response—pecking the key—will occur again. In other instances, bonuses, toys, and good grades could also serve as reinforcers since they strengthen a response that comes before the introduction of the reinforcer. In each case, it is critical that the organism learn that the delivery of the reinforcer is contingent on the response occurring.

Of course, we are not born knowing that 50 cents can buy us a candy bar. Rather, through experience we learn that money is a valuable commodity because of its association with stimuli, such as food, drink, or shelter, that are naturally reinforcing. This fact suggests a distinction that can be drawn regarding whether something is a primary reinforcer or a secondary reinforcer. A **primary reinforcer** involves reinforcements that satisfy some biological need and work naturally, regardless of a person's prior experience; food for the hungry person, warmth for the cold person, and cessation of pain for a person who is hurting would all be classified as primary reinforcers. A **secondary reinforcer**, in contrast, is a stimulus that becomes reinforcing because of its association with a primary reinforcer. For instance, we know that money is valuable because it allows us to obtain other desirable objects, including primary reinforcers such as food and shelter.

Primary reinforcer: *A reward that satisfies biological needs (e.g., hunger or thirst) and works naturally*

Secondary reinforcer: *A stimulus that becomes reinforcing by its association with a primary reinforcer (e.g., money, which allows us to obtain food, a primary reinforcer)*

What makes something a reinforcer is very individualistic. While a Hershey bar may act as a reinforcer for one person, an individual who hates chocolate might find a dollar bill much more to his liking. The only way we can know if a stimulus is a reinforcer for a given organism is to observe whether the rate of response of a previously occurring behavior increases after the presentation of the stimulus. (To determine the effects of reinforcement for yourself, see the Try It! box.)

Positive Reinforcers, Negative Reinforcers, and Punishment In many respects, reinforcers can be thought of in terms of rewards; both a reinforcer and a reward increase the probability that a preceding response will occur again. But the term "reward" is limited to *positive* occurrences, and this is where it differs from a reinforcer—for it turns out that reinforcers may be positive or negative.

A **positive reinforcer** is a stimulus added to the environment that brings about an increase in a preceding response. If food, water, money, or praise is provided following a response, it is more likely that that response will occur again in the future. The paycheck I get at the end of the month, for example, increases the likelihood that I will work the following month.

Positive reinforcer: *A stimulus added to the environment that brings about an increase in the response that preceded it*

In contrast, the concept of a **negative reinforcer** refers to a stimulus whose *removal* is reinforcing, leading to an increase in the probability that a preceding response will occur in the future. For example, if you have cold symptoms that are relieved when you take medicine, you are more likely to take the medicine when you experience such symptoms again. Similarly, if the radio is too loud and hurts your ears, you are likely to find that turning it down relieves the situation; lowering the volume is negatively reinforcing and you are more apt to repeat the action in the future. Negative reinforcement, then, teaches the

Negative reinforcer: *A stimulus whose removal is reinforcing, leading to a greater probability that the response bringing about this removal will occur again*

ANSWERS TO REVIEW QUESTIONS

Review I: **1.** Unconditioned stimulus, unconditioned response **2.** Conditioned stimulus **3.** Conditioned response **4.** Extinction **5.** True **6.** False **7.** b

TRY IT!

USING POSITIVE REINFORCEMENT TO CHANGE BEHAVIOR

You can demonstrate the effects of positive reinforcement on behavior by conducting an experiment that was first carried out in the 1950s (Verplanck, 1955). Try holding a conversation about a controversial issue with an acquaintance. Every time he or she makes an opinion statement—whether you agree with it or not—nod your head and say something like, "That makes sense." If you are subtle in supplying the positive reinforcement, the rate of opinion statements that your acquaintance makes is likely to rise, demonstrating the effects of the positive reinforcement.

individual that taking an action removes a negative condition that exists in the environment prior to taking that action.

It is important to note that negative reinforcement is not the same as punishment. **Punishment** refers to unpleasant or painful stimuli or events that are *added* to the environment if a certain behavior occurs; the result is a *decrease* in the probability that that behavior will occur again. In contrast, negative reinforcement is associated with the *removal* of an unpleasant or painful stimulus, which produces an *increase* in the behavior that brought an end to the unpleasant stimulus. If we receive a shock for behaving in a particular fashion, then, we are receiving punishment; but if we are already receiving a shock and do something to stop that shock, the behavior that stops the shock is considered to be negatively reinforced. In the first case, then, a specific behavior is apt to decrease because of the punishment; in the second, we are likely to increase the behavior because of the negative reinforcement (Azrin & Holt, 1966).

Punishment: *An unpleasant or painful stimulus that is added to the environment after a certain behavior occurs, decreasing the likelihood that the behavior will occur again*

While punishment is typically considered in terms of applying some unpleasant stimulus—the back of the hand for being disobedient or ten years in jail for committing a crime—it may also consist of the removal of something positive. For instance, when a teenager is told she will no longer be able to use the family car because of her poor grades, or when an employee is told that he has been demoted with a cut in pay because of poor job evaluations, punishment in the form of the removal of a positive reinforcer is being administered.

The distinctions between the types of punishment, as well as positive and negative reinforcement, may appear confusing at first glance, but the following rules of thumb (and the summary in Table 4-1) can help you to distinguish these concepts from one another:

- Reinforcement is meant to *increase* the behavior preceding it; punishment is meant to *decrease* the behavior preceding it.
- The *application* of a *positive* stimulus is intended to bring about an increase in behavior and is referred to as positive reinforcement; the *removal* of a *positive* stimulus is meant to decrease behavior and is called punishment by removal.
- The *application* of a *negative* stimulus is intended to reduce behavior and is called punishment by application; the *removal* of a *negative* stimulus which results in an increase in behavior is termed negative reinforcement.

Why Reinforcement Beats Punishment: The Pros and Cons of Punishment Is punishment an effective means of modifying behavior? Punishment

TABLE 5-1

Types of reinforcement and punishment

Nature of Stimulus	Application	Removal or Termination
Positive	*Positive reinforcement* Example: Giving a raise for good performance Result: Increase in frequency of response of good performance	*Punishment by removal* Example: Removal of favorite toy after misbehavior Result: Decrease in frequency of response of misbehavior
Negative	*Punishment by application* Example: Giving a spanking following misbehavior Result: Decrease in frequency of response of misbehavior	*Negative reinforcement* Example: Terminating a headache by taking aspirin Result: Increase in frequency of response of taking aspirin

often presents the quickest route to changing behavior that, if allowed to continue, might be dangerous to an individual. For instance, we may not have a second chance to warn a child not to run into a busy street, so punishing the first incidence of this behavior might prove to be wise. Moreover, the use of punishment to suppress behavior, even temporarily, provides the opportunity to reinforce a person for behaving in a more desirable way.

On the other hand, several disadvantages make the routine use of punishment questionable. For one thing, it is frequently ineffective, particularly if the punishment is not delivered shortly after the behavior being suppressed or if the individual is able to withdraw from the setting in which the punishment is being given. An employee who is reprimanded by the boss may quit; a teenager who loses the use of the family car may run away from home. In such instances, then, the initial behavior that is being punished may be replaced by one that is even less desirable than the original.

Even worse, physical punishment may convey to the recipient the idea that physical aggression is permissible and perhaps even desirable. A father who yells and hits his son teaches the son that aggression is an appropriate, adult response, and the son may soon copy his father's behavior and act aggressively toward others.

Finally, punishment does not convey any information about what an alternative, more appropriate response might be. In order to be useful in bringing about more desirable behavior in the future, then, punishment must be paired with specific information about what is being punished, along with information about a more desirable behavior. To punish a child for staring out the window in school may lead her to stare at the floor instead. Unless we teach her the appropriate way to respond, we have just substituted one undesirable behavior for another. If punishment is not combined with reinforcement for alternative behavior that is more appropriate, little will be accomplished. In sum, reinforcing desired behavior is a more appropriate technique for modifying behavior than is using punishment. In the scientific arena, then, reinforcement usually beats punishment.

RECAP AND REVIEW II

Recap

- Operant conditioning is a form of learning in which a response is made because of the positive or negative consequences that follow the response or because of the negative consequences that are ended or avoided by the response.
- A reinforcer is any stimulus that increases the probability that a preceding response will occur.
- Primary reinforcers are those that satisfy a biological need and therefore are effective without prior experience; secondary reinforcers are stimuli that, because of their previous association with primary reinforcers, begin to elicit the same responses as primary reinforcers.
- A positive reinforcer is a stimulus that is added to the environment to increase the likelihood of a response. A negative reinforcer is a stimulus whose removal leads to an increase in the probability that a preceding response will occur in the future.
- Punishment is the administration of an unpleasant stimulus, following a response, which is meant to decrease or suppress behavior; it may also consist of the removal of a positive reinforcer.
- The distinction between punishment and negative reinforcement is critical: In punishment, the goal is to decrease or suppress undesired behavior by administering a stimulus; in negative reinforcement, the goal is to increase a desired behavior by removing a stimulus.

Review

1. ______________________ has its focus on responses learned as a result of the positive or negative consequences which are contingent upon the response.
2. Ms. Flifton has attempted to get one of her students to speak up more in class by praising her publicly when she does talk. Unfortunately, her student has become even more silent in class. It is clear that, in this case, positive reinforcement hasn't worked. True or false?
3. Sandy had had a rough day and his son's noisemaking is not helping him to relax. Not wanting to scold his son, Sandy lowers his tone of voice and says to him in a serious manner that he is very tired and would like him to play quietly for an hour. Sandy's strategy works. The change in his son's behavior, as a consequence of Sandy's strategy, is an example of
   a. Positive reinforcement **b.** Secondary reinforcement **c.** Punishment **d.** Negative reinforcement
4. Sandy is pleased. He had not been happy with himself last week when he yelled loudly at his son. On that occasion he had halted his son's excessive noise through the use of
   a. Removal of a reinforcer **b.** Punishment **c.** Negative reinforcement **d.** Extinction
5. Usually when a person's behavior is suppressed through punishment, the individual can be expected to spontaneously replace that suppressed behavior with a new positive alternative response. True or false?

(Answers to review questions are at bottom of page 142.)

Timing Life's Rewards: Schedules of Reinforcement

The world would be a different place if a cardplayer stopped playing as soon as he was dealt a losing hand, a fisherman stopped fishing as soon as he missed a catch, or a door-to-door salesperson stopped selling at the first house in which the occupant turned her away. The fact that such unreinforced behaviors continue, often with great frequency, illustrates that reinforcement need not be received continually in order for behavior to be learned and maintained. In fact, behavior that is reinforced only occasionally may ultimately be learned better than behavior that is always reinforced.

When we refer to the frequency and timing of reinforcement following desired behavior we are talking about **schedules of reinforcement**. Behavior that is reinforced every time it occurs is said to be on a **continuous reinforcement schedule**; if it is reinforced some but not all of the time, it is on a **partial reinforcement schedule**. Although learning occurs more rapidly under a continuous reinforcement schedule, learned behavior lasts longer after reinforcement stops when learned under a partial reinforcement schedule.

Schedules of reinforcement: *The frequency and timing of reinforcement following desired behavior*

Continuous reinforcement: *The reinforcing of a behavior every time it occurs*

Partial reinforcement: *The reinforcing of a behavior some, but not all, of the time*

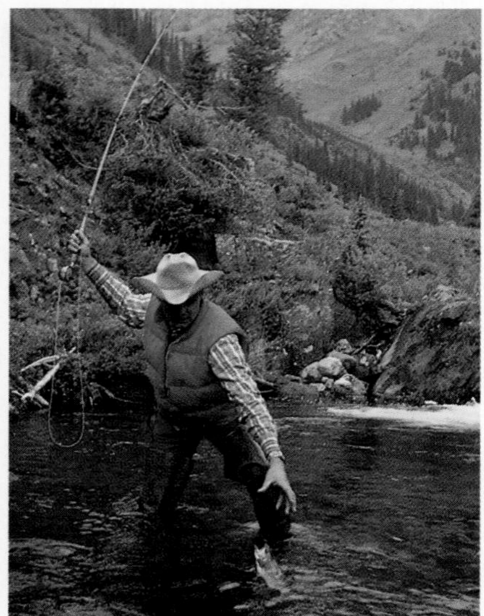

Partial reinforcement schedules—such as those experienced in fishing—may result in performance that continues for lengthy periods, even when reinforcement is rare. *(Bill Gillette/Stock, Boston)*

Why should partial reinforcement schedules result in stronger, longer-lasting learning than continuous reinforcement schedules? An answer comes from comparing the behavior of someone using a broken vending machine with that of someone using a broken slot machine. When using a vending machine, one expects the schedule of reinforcement to be continuous—every time a person puts in 50 cents, the reinforcement, a candy bar, ought to be delivered. But suppose the machine is broken and nothing comes out after the money is put in. It will not be long before the person stops depositing coins; probably the most we could expect would be one or two more tries before he leaves in disgust.

Now consider the behavior of the same person at a broken slot machine. Prior experience with other slot machines has taught him that it is unlikely that he will win money every time he puts in 50 cents. Instead, he has learned that most of the time he will not receive anything. At the same time he also has learned that occasionally he will probably win *something,* and this knowledge is sufficient to keep him standing at the broken slot machine, throwing in money for a considerably longer time than he would at the broken vending machine.

In formal terms, the two situations differ in terms of their reinforcement schedules: Correctly operating vending machines work on a continuous reinforcement schedule, while the slot machine works on a partial reinforcement schedule. These examples illustrate the general rule that partial reinforcement schedules maintain performance longer than do continuous reinforcement schedules before the behavior is extinguished.

Cumulative recorder: *A device that automatically records and graphs the pattern of responses made in reaction to a particular reinforcement schedule*

Using a **cumulative recorder**, a device that automatically records and graphs the pattern of responses made in reaction to a particular schedule (see Figure 4-5), learning psychologists have found that certain kinds of partial reinforcement schedules produce stronger and lengthier responding before extinction than do others. Although many different partial reinforcement schedules have been examined, they can be most readily classified into two categories: schedules that consider the *number of responses* made before reinforcement is given—called

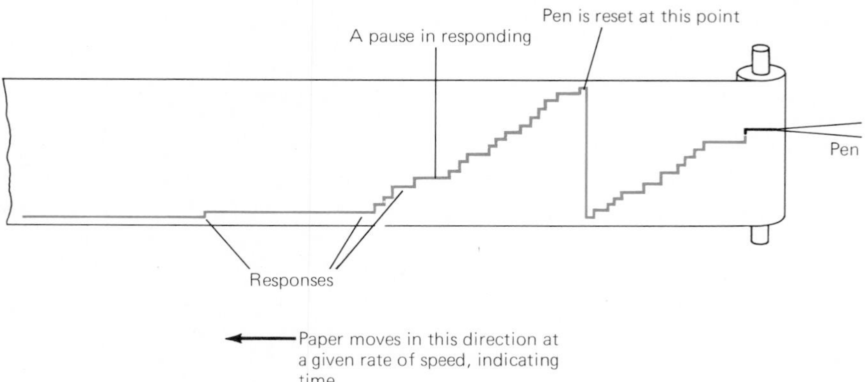

Figure 4-5
A cumulative recorder. As the paper slowly unrolls, the pen indicates when a response has been made by moving a notch upward. Pauses in responding are indicated by a lack of upward movement of the line. As is the case in this example, it is typical for the time between responses to decrease as the organism learns to make the response.

ANSWERS TO REVIEW QUESTIONS

Review II: **1.** Operant conditioning **2.** False; by definition, the public praise could not be called positive reinforcement, since it did not lead to an increase in the probability that the preceding response of speaking in class would occur again. **3.** d **4.** b **5.** False; an alternative response should be selected and reinforced.

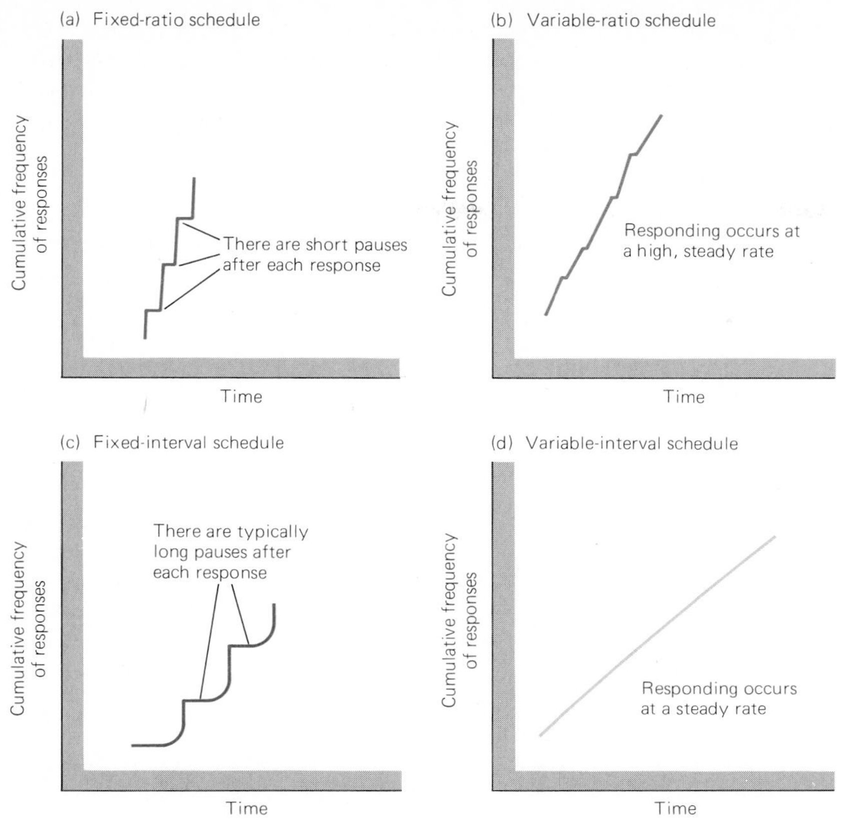

Figure 4-6
Typical outcomes of different reinforcement schedules: (*a*) In a fixed-ratio schedule, there are short pauses following each response. Because the more responses, the more reinforcement, fixed-ratio schedules produce a high rate of responding.(*b*) In a variable-ratio schedule, responding also occurs at a high rate. (*c*) A fixed-interval schedule produces lower rates of responding, especially just after reinforcement has occurred, since the organism learns that a specified time period must elapse between reinforcements. (*d*) A variable-interval schedule produces a fairly steady stream of responses.

fixed-ratio and variable-ratio schedules—and those that consider the *amount of time* that elapses before reinforcement is provided—called fixed-interval and variable-interval schedules. Figure 4-6 summarizes the distinctions and outcomes of various kinds of reinforcement schedules.

Counting Responses: Fixed- and Variable-Ratio Schedules In a **fixed-ratio schedule**, reinforcement is given only after a certain number of responses is made. For instance, a pigeon might receive a food pellet every tenth time it pecks a key; here, the ratio would be 1:10. Similarly, garment workers are generally paid using fixed-ratio schedules: They receive *x* dollars for every ten blouses they sew. Because a greater rate of production means more reinforcement, people on fixed-ratio schedules are apt to work as quickly as possible. Even when rewards are no longer offered, responding comes in bursts—although pauses between bursts of responses become longer and longer until the response peters out entirely.

Fixed-ratio schedule: *A schedule whereby reinforcement is given only after a certain number of responses is made*

In a **variable-ratio schedule**, reinforcement occurs after a varying number of responses rather than after a fixed number. Although the specific number of responses necessary to receive reinforcement varies, the number of responses usually hovers around a specific average. Probably the best example of a variable-ratio schedule is that encountered by a door-to-door salesperson. She may make a sale at the third, eighth, ninth, and twentieth houses she stops at, without being successful at any of the houses in between. Although the number of

Variable-ratio schedule: *A schedule whereby reinforcement occurs after a varying number of responses rather than after a fixed number*

responses that must be made before making a sale varies, it averages out to a 20 percent success rate. Under these circumstances, you might expect that the salesperson would try to make as many calls as possible in as short a time as possible. This is the case with all variable-ratio schedules; they promote a high rate of response and a high resistance to extinction.

Passing Time: Fixed- and Variable-Interval Schedules In contrast to fixed- and variable-ratio schedules—in which the crucial factor is the number of responses—fixed- and variable-*interval* schedules focus on the amount of *time* that has elapsed since a person or animal was rewarded. One example of a fixed-interval schedule is a weekly paycheck. For people who receive regular, weekly paychecks, it makes little difference how much they produce in a given week—as long as they show up and do *some* work.

Fixed-interval schedule: *A schedule whereby a reinforcer is given at established time intervals*

Because a **fixed-interval schedule** provides a reinforcement for a response only if a fixed time period has elapsed, overall rates of response are relatively low. This is especially true in the period just after reinforcement when the time before another reinforcement is relatively great. Students' study habits often exemplify this reality: If the periods between exams are relatively long (meaning that the opportunity for reinforcement for good performance is fairly infrequent), students often study minimally or not at all until the day of the exam draws near. Just before the exam, however, students begin to cram for it, signaling a rapid increase in their rate of their studying response (Mawhinney et al., 1971). As you might expect, just after the exam there is a rapid decline in the rate of responding, with few people opening a book the day after a test.

Variable-interval schedule: *A schedule whereby reinforcement is given at various times, usually causing a behavior to be maintained more consistently*

One way to decrease the delay in responding that occurs just after reinforcement, and to maintain the desired behavior more consistently throughout an interval, is to use a variable-interval schedule. In a **variable-interval schedule**, the time between reinforcements varies around some average rather than being fixed. For example, a professor who gives surprise quizzes that vary from one every three days to one every three weeks, averaging one every two weeks, is using a variable-interval schedule. Students' study habits would most likely be very different as a result of such an unpredictable schedule than those we observed with a fixed-interval schedule. Students would be apt to study more regularly since they would never know when the surprise quiz would be coming. Variable-interval schedules, in general, are more likely to produce relatively steady rates of responding than are fixed-interval schedules, with responses that take longer to extinguish after reinforcement ends.

Learning the Right Stimulus from the Wrong: Discrimination and Generalization in Operant Conditioning

It does not take a child long to learn that a red light at an intersection means stop, while a green light indicates that it is permissible to continue. Just as in classical conditioning, then, operant learning also involves the phenomena of discrimination and generalization.

Stimulus control training: *Training in which an organism is reinforced in the presence of a certain specific stimulus, but not in its absence*

The process by which people learn to discriminate stimuli is known as stimulus control training. In **stimulus control training**, an organism is reinforced in the presence of a certain stimulus, but not when it is absent. For example, physicians in training are reinforced by their medical school professors when they learn that the presence of certain cells in the blood indicates that a patient's fever is caused by an infection, while the absence of such cells indicates the fever is caused by some other source. In this case, the cells act as a **discrimi-**

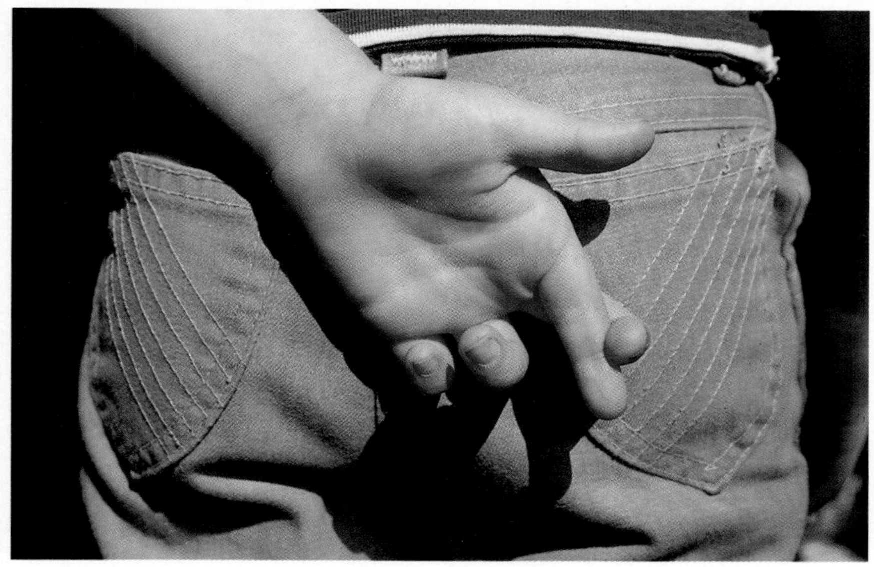

Superstitious behavior is learned because of the coincidental association between an idea, object, or behavior and subsequent reinforcement. *(Mimi Cotter/International Stock Photo)*

native stimulus, a stimulus to which an organism learns to respond during stimulus control training. A discriminative stimulus signals the likelihood that reinforcement will follow a response. For example, if you wait until your roommate is in a good mood before asking for the loan of her favorite record, your behavior can be said to be under stimulus control.

Discriminative stimulus: *A stimulus to which an organism learns to respond as part of stimulus control training*

Just as in classical conditioning, the phenomenon of stimulus generalization, in which an organism learns a response to one stimulus and then applies it to other stimuli, is also found in operant conditioning. If you have learned that being polite produces the reinforcement of getting your way in a certain situation, you are likely to generalize your response to other situations. Sometimes, though, generalization can have unfortunate consequences, such as when people behave negatively toward all members of a racial group because they have had an unpleasant experience with one member of the racial group.

Superstitious Behavior

Whenever Phil Esposito, a hockey star for eighteen years, drove to a game, he always wore a black tie and always passed through the same tollbooth he had driven through on the way to his last winning game. When he arrived at the site of the game, he would put on the black turtleneck he wore when he became the team's high scorer. He then arranged his wardrobe in a particular order (underwear, pants, skates, and laces), and was sure to include a pack of gum plus one additional stick of gum. Next, he arranged his skating paraphernalia with black tape on the bottom, then white tape, and then his gloves, which he carefully aligned and placed palms up on each side of his hockey stick. As the game was about to start he would say a Hail Mary and the Lord's Prayer and would pray that his team played well and that the game would be free of injuries. *Then* he was ready to play hockey.

While it is easy to scoff at Phil Esposito's elaborate pregame ritual of **superstitious behavior**, such behavior is relatively common among athletes (Zimmer, 1984). In fact, many of us have some superstitions of our own: wearing a special

Superstitious behavior: *The mistaken belief that particular ideas, objects, or behavior will cause certain events to occur, due to learning that is based on the coincidental association between the idea, object, or behavior and subsequent reinforcement*

shirt when we take a test or go for a job interview, saying to ourselves that if we make all the traffic lights on a certain road we'll have good luck for the rest of the day, or—an old favorite—avoiding a black cat in your path.

Where do such superstitions come from? To learning psychologists, there is a simple answer, having to do with the principles of reinforcement. As we have discussed, behavior that is followed by a reinforcer tends to be strengthened. Occasionally, however, the behavior that occurs prior to the reinforcement is entirely coincidental. Imagine, for instance, that a baseball player hits his bat against the ground three times in a row and then gets a home run. The hit is, of course, coincidental to the batter's hitting the ground, but to the player it may be seen as somehow related. Because the association is made in the player's mind, he may hit the ground three times every time he is at bat in the future. And because he will be at least partially reinforced for this behavior—batters usually get a hit around 25 percent of the time—his ground-hitting behavior will probably be maintained.

Do superstitions actually affect subsequent behavior? In fact, they do. According to some psychologists, superstitious behavior allows people to cope with anxiety by providing routines or rituals that can give one a sense of control over a situation (Zimmer, 1984). In this way, wearing a "lucky" shirt helps to calm a person—which, in fact, may lead to better performance on a test or during a stressful interview. As you can see, then, your superstitions may shape your subsequent behavior.

Reinforcing What Doesn't Come Naturally: Shaping

Consider the difficulty of using operant conditioning to teach people to repair an automobile transmission. If you had to wait until they fixed it perfectly before you provided them with the reinforcement of telling them that they were repairing it correctly, the Model T might be back in style long before they ever mastered the repair.

There are many complex behaviors, ranging from auto repair to zebra hunting, which we would not expect to occur naturally as part of anyone's spontaneous behavior. In cases such as these, in which there otherwise might be no opportunity to provide reinforcement for the particular behavior (since it never occurs in the first place), a procedure known as shaping is used.

Shaping: *The process of teaching a complex behavior by rewarding closer and closer approximations of the desired behavior*

Shaping is the process of teaching a complex behavior by rewarding closer and closer approximations of the desired behavior. In shaping, any behavior that is at all similar to the behavior you want the person to learn is reinforced at first. Later, you reinforce only closer responses to the behavior you ultimately want to teach. Finally, you reinforce only the desired response. Each step in shaping, then, moves only slightly beyond the previously learned behavior, permitting the person to link the new step to the behavior learned earlier.

Shaping allows even lower animals to learn complex responses that naturally would never occur, ranging from the example of porpoises trained to jump through hoops and walk on the water with their tails to pigeons trained to rescue people lost at sea (see the Cutting Edge box).

Shaping also underlies the learning of many complex human skills. For instance, the organization of most textbooks is based on the principles of shaping. Typically, material is presented so that new material builds on previously learned concepts or skills. For example, the concept of shaping could not be presented in this chapter until we had discussed the more basic principles of operant learning.

THE CUTTING EDGE

A PIGEON POSSE: SAVING LIVES WITH OPERANT CONDITIONING

Your sailboat has capsized in the Pacific and you have been drifting for three days. Your mouth is dry, your stomach hungers for food, and you don't know how much longer you can hang on to the side of the boat. Suddenly, you see a speck in the sky off in the distance. It gets closer and closer until it is flying directly above, and you can see on it the markings of a Coast Guard rescue helicopter. As it hovers above, you wonder how you will ever be able to repay the pilots of the helicopter who have saved your life.

Actually, if you did thank the pilots for rescuing you, you might well be thanking the wrong people—or more accurately, the wrong species. For in reality you might owe your life to three pigeons caged in the belly of the helicopter.

These pigeons, trained in Sea Hunt, a Navy program currently under development, represent a dramatic example of the use of operant-conditioning principles. The director of the Sea Hunt project, James Simmons, has taken ordinary pigeons and, using operant conditioning, trained them to peck a series of keys at the sight of an orange speck in the ocean—such as a downed sailor wearing a life jacket (Cusack, 1984).

Figure 4-7
In the Sea Hunt system, pigeons, trained by operant conditioning to identify downed sailors wearing orange life jackets, are strapped into the belly of a search helicopter. When a pigeon spots an appropriate stimulus, it pecks a key, which alerts the helicopter pilot. (*Based on Simmons, 1981.*)

Their training uses basic shaping procedures: They are first taught in a Skinner box to peck a key to receive food, and then to peck it only when an orange light is present. Next, the size of the light is decreased so the pigeons learn to peck only when an orange speck of light is present. (Lasers are used to control with exact precision the size of the light beam.) Finally the pigeons are taken out to sea and taught to peck at the key only when they see an orange stimulus in the ocean. The entire training process takes from six to ten months (Simmons, 1984).

In operation, the Sea Hunt system is simplicity itself. When the pigeons, which are strapped in the belly of a search helicopter (see Figure 4-7), peck a key to indicate the sighting of an orange stimulus, a signal is sent to the pilot. With three trained birds being used simultaneously, each in a separate chamber with a different viewing area, the pilot knows in what direction to orient the search. Because their visual acuity is far superior to that of humans, pigeons can spot a target 90 percent of the time the first time they are over an area—considerably better than the 40 percent success rates of human searchers. Moreover, they are less apt to be affected by sun glare and the problems of concentration and boredom that pilots experience during long searches.

Because the Sea Hunt system is effective, easy to use, reliable, and economical, the Navy is giving serious consideration to routinely using pigeons trained through operant conditioning as part of rescue operations. If you are ever stranded at sea, then, you should not be too surprised if you are saved not by a human search party, but by a feathered one.

Programmed instruction: *The development of learning by building gradually on basic knowledge, with review and reinforcement when appropriate*

One of the most frequent applications of shaping is in the form of programmed instruction for computers (Cherry, 1983; Skinner, 1984). **Programmed instruction** (see the example in Figure 4-8) explicitly uses the principles of learning in the design of instructional material. A student using such material is first asked to type into the computer very simple responses that are printed on the screen; then the student moves on to increasingly complex problems. Correct responses are immediately reinforced, while mistakes evoke a review of previous material. The reinforcement for correct responses may be explicit, in the form of encouragement printed on the screen (''Good,'' ''Great job, Wendy,'' ''Keep it up,'' or the like), or the user may simply be allowed to move on to the next part of the lesson, which in itself can act as a powerful reinforcer. Each correct response shapes the student's behavior to bring him or her closer to the final desired behavior—mastery of a relatively complex body of material.

Programmed or computer-assisted instruction has proved to be an effective teaching technique (Wilkinson, 1983). However, unless it is carefully constructed, programmed instruction can be worse than no instruction at all, leading students to become disinterested in the material. As we will discuss next, there are ways of distinguishing good programmed instruction from bad.

The Informed Consumer of Psychology: Using Computer-Assisted Programmed Instruction to Shape Your Own Behavior

One of the best reasons for caution when considering computer-assisted instruction is exemplified in the following headlines taken from advertisements suggesting that computer programs be purchased to teach a variety of skills: ''Learn French by computer''; ''Spelling made easy''; ''Everything there is to know about the stock market''; ''Do better on the SAT.''

As the personal computer becomes more widely used, advertisements such as these are becoming more commonplace. Consequently, consumers are faced with difficult choices concerning the purchase of instructional programs to run on their home computers. Indeed, with more than 7000 programs devoted to teaching particular skills and subject areas, the choices appear almost limitless.

Still, there are ways of sorting through the maze of programs, particularly when it comes to self-help programs designed to teach a subject area or skill. Keeping in mind the principles of learning we have discussed throughout this chapter, a number of suggestions can be made for deciding what kinds of programs to purchase:

- Look before you leap. Do not purchase instructional programs that you have not previewed. Even a quick review will tell you if the program is mainly of a drill-and-practice type, which merely presents one problem set after another without any explanation or analysis of errors. Good programmed instruction responds appropriately and individually to the level of the user's proficiency, based on the pattern of the user's responses.
- Find out whether the program's goals and objectives match yours. If the program has been designed using the principles of learning theory, it should include clearly stated goals and objectives. Beware of programs that present vague goals such as "Improve your math." Instead, look for programs that clearly spell out what they are attempting to teach (such as "Use of this program will permit you to compute percentages and to figure sales tax").
- Determine whether the program provides appropriate reinforcement for correct answers. Some programs make use of sophisticated graphics and other elaborate responses to reinforce a correct response. Although such techniques tend to maintain user motivation, there is a danger that they may detract from the information that is being conveyed. Make sure, then, that the reinforcement strategies do not overshadow the educational content of the material.
- Find out whether the program uses shaping techniques effectively. Some programs merely say, "Wrong, try again," when a mistake is made, then repeat the same question. Such an approach is clearly inferior to one in which the reply to a wrong response is "Sorry, but you're probably not ready to become a member of the New York Stock Exchange. Remember that the price-earnings ratio is figured by dividing the price of the stock by the average per-share earnings. Now try the problem again." In this example, the user's behavior is shaped more effectively toward the desired response.
- Find out whether the program has been field-tested. Good programs have been tried out on sample users before going to market. Without this crucial step, there is no guarantee that the program will teach you anything.

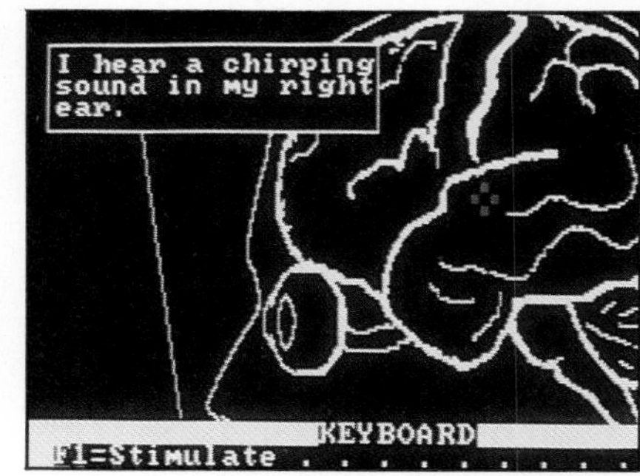

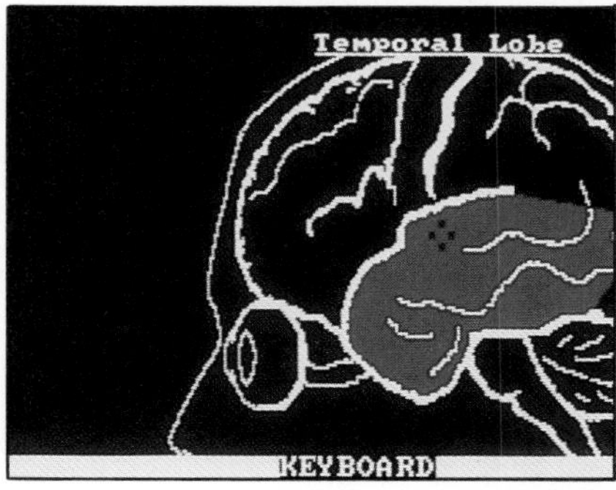

Figure 4-8
In this example of computerized programmed instruction—drawn from "PsychWorld," a set of programs designed to accompany *Understanding Psychology*—the effects of stimulating different areas of the brain are graphically illustrated. This sequence is designed to teach what happens when an electric current is passed through the temporal lobes. (*John Hay,* Psychworld, *McGraw-Hill, 1985*)

While following these guidelines does not guarantee that a program you purchase will be effective, they will provide a starting point. Moreover, it is important to remember that, like a book, a computer program is just a tool; what is made of it is as much up to the user as it is up to the program itself.

Discriminating between Classical and Operant Conditioning: The Difference Is Not Always Clear

Up to this point, we have been discussing classical and operant conditioning as though they were two entirely distinct approaches. However, these two types of conditioning share several features in common.

For example, generalization and discrimination processes are found in operant conditioning, just as they are in classical conditioning. A pigeon who has learned to peck a red key to receive food will probably do the same thing to a blue key, illustrating that generalization has occurred. Similarly, discrimination processes are also present in operant conditioning. When a child learns from the reinforcers his parent provides that he ought to stay away from strangers but be polite and friendly to acquaintances, we can see an example of discrimination.

The fact that generalization and discrimination are present in both classical and operant conditioning suggests that the distinction between these two types of learning is not always clear-cut. Consider, for instance, what happens when you are called into the house for dinner. As you hear the call for dinner, you begin to salivate, and the smells of the food get stronger as you walk toward the kitchen. You quickly reach the table and receive your reward for coming: a big helping of roast beef, potatoes, and salad.

Is your behavior due to classical conditioning or operant conditioning? Actually, it is both. Your salivation reflects classical conditioning; you have learned to associate your being called in to dinner with the food that follows it. But the footsteps taking you to the table, which actually allow you to receive the reinforcement of food, reflect a behavioral pattern learned through operant conditioning; you have purposefully responded in a way that gets you a reward.

As you see, the distinction between classical and operant conditioning is not always clear when we consider specific instances of behavior, since both processes are often at work in terms of a particular sequence of behavior. Moreover, even some of the most basic differences between operant and classical conditioning have been called into question. For example, as we discussed in Chapter 2, people are able to learn to control ''involuntary'' responses, such as blood pressure and heart rate, through biofeedback. What would typically be thought of as a response involving classical conditioning, then, can be viewed in terms of operant conditioning.

Still, the essential distinctions between classical and operant conditioning are evident in most of the cases of behavior that we analyze: In classical conditioning, the unconditioned stimulus precedes the response; the response is elicited by the unconditioned stimulus. In operant conditioning, in contrast, the response is made prior to the reinforcement and is therefore performed intentionally—i.e., the response is made to obtain the reward. In classical conditioning, then, the response is basically involuntary, while in operant conditioning the response is voluntary.

RECAP AND REVIEW III

Recap

- Reinforcement need not be constant in order for behavior to be learned and maintained; partial schedules of reinforcement, in fact, lead to greater resistance to extinction than continuous schedules of reinforcement.
- In fixed-ratio schedules, reinforcement is given only after a set number of responses is made. In variable-ratio schedules, reinforcement is given after a varying number of responses.
- In fixed-interval schedules, reinforcement is given after a desired response only if a specified period of time has elapsed since the last reinforcement. In contrast, in variable-interval schedules, the time between delivery of reinforcement varies around some average period of time.
- Generalization, discrimination, and shaping are among the basic phenomena of operant conditioning.
- Although the difference between classical and operant conditioning is usually clear, there may be overlap in certain kinds of behavior.

Review

1. Carl decides to reward himself for studying by allowing himself to listen to music after each hour of studying. What kind of reinforcement schedule has he arranged?

a. Fixed ratio **b.** Variable interval **c.** Fixed interval **d.** Variable ratio

2. It just isn't working! Carl finds himself staring at one or two pages for an hour. Then he comes up with a great idea. He will listen to music only after reading fifteen pages. His reinforcement schedule would now be termed a

a. Fixed ratio **b.** Variable interval **c.** Fixed interval **d.** Variable ratio

3. Feeling even more inquisitive, Carl decides to have his roommate, Jim, provide him access to music contingent upon differing numbers of pages read. Carl instructs Jim to provide access to music sometimes after, say, eight or so pages, but at other times after perhaps thirty pages, choosing the number randomly but keeping the average around fifteen pages. This new arrangement would be called a ____________ schedule.

a. Fixed-ratio **b.** Variable-interval **c.** Fixed-interval **d.** Variable-ratio

4. One day Cathy decided to alter her path to work. She crossed the street to look at storefront displays. As she passed a flower cart, the vendor reached out and gave her a free rose. Cathy thereafter established a new route to work, even though the vendor was rarely stationed across the street. This could be termed an example of ____________.

5. What are two distinctions between operant and classical conditioning?

(Answers to review questions are at bottom of page 152.)

THE THINKING PERSON'S LEARNING THEORY: COGNITIVE APPROACHES TO LEARNING

The criminal in the television movie hits a policeman's head against a brick wall. By knocking the policeman out, the criminal manages to escape. He smiles triumphantly and cooly steps on the policeman's body as he runs away.

* * *

An 8-year-old boy, who has seen the movie the previous evening, gets into a fight with his brother. Although in the past the fights have never involved physical violence, this time the boy knocks his brother into a wall, and tries to step on him.

The source of the boy's new behavior is clear: It is the television movie. But the underlying process cannot easily be explained using either classical or operant conditioning. Knocking people into a wall would not seem to be an unconditioned or conditioned response, nor, given the fact that the boy had never had fights of this sort in the past, would there have been the opportunity for him to be reinforced for such behavior. Instances such as these suggest that some kinds of learning involve higher-order thinking processes in which people's thoughts, memories, and the way they process information account for their responses.

Some psychologists have concentrated on the thought processes that underlie learning—an approach known as **cognitive learning theory**. Although psychologists using cognitive learning theory do not deny the importance of classical and operant conditioning, these psychologists have developed approaches that focus on the unseen mental processes that occur during the learning process, rather than concentrating solely on external stimuli, responses, and reinforcements.

Cognitive learning theory: *The study of the thought processes that underlie learning*

In its most basic formulation, cognitive learning theory suggests that it is not enough to say that people make responses because there is a hypothetical link between a stimulus and a response due to a past history of reinforcement for the response. Instead, according to this point of view, people—and even animals—develop an *expectation* that they will receive a reinforcer upon making a response.

Evidence for cognitive learning comes from a famous series of experiments that revealed a phenomenon called **latent learning**. In latent learning, a new

Latent learning: *Learning in which a new behavior is acquired but not readily demonstrated until reinforcement is provided*

behavior is learned but is not demonstrated until reinforcement is provided for displaying it (Tolman & Honzik, 1930). In the studies, some rats were allowed to wander around a maze without receiving a reward, while others always received a reward for reaching the end of the maze. When the unrewarded rats—who had earlier seemed to wander about aimlessly—were later given a reward for running the maze, their running time and error rate almost immediately matched those of the other group. To cognitive learning theorists, it seemed clear that the unrewarded rats had learned the layout of the maze early on in their explorations, developing what was called a **cognitive map** of the maze. They just never displayed their knowledge until the reinforcement was offered.

Cognitive map: *A mental "picture" of locations and directions*

Learning by Copying: Observational Learning

Although latent learning suggests how a behavior may be learned but not demonstrated, it does not explain the case of the boy who imitates a response that he has earlier observed on a television show. How does a person who has no direct experience in carrying out a particular behavior acquire it?

Psychologist Albert Bandura (1977) carried out research that led him to conclude that a major part of human learning consists of **observational learning**: learning through observing the behavior of another person, a **model** (Bandura, 1977). Bandura and his colleagues demonstrated rather dramatically the ability of models to elicit learning. In what is now considered a classic experiment, young children saw a movie of an adult wildly hitting a 5-foot-tall inflatable punching toy called a Bobo doll (Bandura, Ross, & Ross, 1963). Later the children were given the opportunity to play with the Bobo doll themselves, and, sure enough, they displayed the same kind of behavior, in some cases mimicking the aggressive behavior almost identically.

Observational learning: *Learning through observation of others (models)*
Model: *A person serving as an example to an observer; if a model's behavior is rewarded, the observer may imitate that behavior*

According to Bandura, observational learning takes place in four steps: (1) paying attention and perceiving the most critical features of another person's behavior; (2) remembering the behavior; (3) reproducing the action; and (4) being motivated to learn and carry out the behavior. Instead of learning occurring through trial and error, then, with successes being reinforced and failures punished, many important skills are learned through observational processes.

Observational learning is particularly important in acquiring skills in which shaping is inappropriate. Piloting an airplane and brain surgery, for example, would hardly be behaviors that could be learned using trial-and-error methods without grave cost—literally—to those involved in the learning.

Not all behavior that we witness is learned or carried out, of course. One crucial factor that determines whether we later imitate a model depends on the consequences of the model's behavior. If we observe a friend being rewarded for putting more time into her studies by receiving higher grades, we are more likely to model her behavior than if her behavior results in no increase in grades but rather greater fatigue and less social life. Models who are rewarded for behaving in a particular way are more apt to be mimicked, then, than models

ANSWERS TO REVIEW QUESTIONS

Review III: **1.** c **2.** a **3.** d **4.** Superstitious behavior **5.** Classical: (1) Unconditioned stimulus occurs before the response, and (2) the response is involuntary. Operant: (1) The response is made before reinforcement, and (2) The response is voluntary.

Observational learning, which is based on the observation of the behavior of others, is an important source of learning. (In this case, the skill is one which the child may someday come to regret!) *(Eric Roth/The Picture Cube)*

who receive punishment. Interestingly, though, observing the punishment of a model does not necessarily stop observers from learning the behavior. Observers can still recount the model's behavior—they are just less apt to perform it (Bandura, 1977).

Accepting the Unacceptable: Learned Helplessness

Have you ever heard someone say, "You can't fight city hall"; "No matter how hard I study I'll never pass this course"; or "I'll never learn to play tennis, regardless of how much I practice"? According to psychologist Martin Seligman, each of these statements may represent an example of **learned helplessness**, the learned belief of a person or animal that no control can be exerted over the environment (Seligman, 1975).

Learned helplessness: *An organism's learned belief that it has no control of the environment*

Learned helplessness was first demonstrated in experiments in which dogs were exposed to a series of moderately painful but not physically damaging shocks that they could not avoid. Although at first the dogs tried desperately to escape, they eventually accepted the shocks. But the next phase of the experiment was the most revealing: The dogs were placed in a box with two compartments, separated by a low barrier that they could easily jump over. By jumping the barrier, they could avoid any shock administered in the first compartment. In comparison with dogs who had not received shocks previously and who quickly learned to jump into the next compartment, the dogs who had received the inescapable shocks earlier tended to give up rapidly, lie down, and wait for the shock to be over.

The conclusion drawn by Seligman was that the dogs had learned to be helpless. They expected that nothing they did would be useful in preventing the shocks and therefore simply accepted them. As will be discussed in Chapter 12, this same process may underlie cases of severe human depression in which people may come to feel that they are victims of events beyond their control and are helpless in their environment.

The Unresolved Controversy: Cognitive Learning Theory in Perspective

The degree to which a person's learning is based on unseen internal factors, rather than on external factors, remains one of the major issues dividing learning theorists today. Both classical conditioning and operant conditioning consider learning in terms of external stimuli and responses—a kind of "black-box" analysis in which all that matters are the observable features of the environment, not what goes on inside a person's head. To the cognitive learning theorists, such an analysis misses the mark; what is crucial is the mental activity—in the form of thoughts and expectations—that takes place.

Still, while the controversy surrounding different approaches to learning rages on as a major issue of psychology, tremendous advances are taking place in the practical application of principles derived from the various theories, as we shall see in the remainder of this chapter.

BEHAVIOR ANALYSIS AND BEHAVIOR MODIFICATION

A couple who had been married for three years began to fight more and more frequently. Their arguments ranged from the seemingly petty, such as who was going to do the dishes, to the more profound, such as the quality of their love life and whether they found each other interesting. Disturbed about this increasingly unpleasant pattern of interaction, they went to a behavior analyst, a psychologist who specialized in behavior-modification techniques. After interviewing each of them alone and then speaking to them together, he asked them to keep a detailed written record of their interactions over the next two weeks—focusing, in particular, on the events that preceded their arguments.

When they returned two weeks later, he carefully went over the records with them. In doing so, he noticed a pattern that the couple themselves had observed after they had started keeping their records: Each of their arguments had occurred just after one or the other had left some household chore undone. For instance, the wife would go into a fury when she came home from work and found that her husband, a student, had left his dirty lunch dishes on the table and had not even started dinner preparations. The husband would get angry when he found his wife's clothes draped on the only chair in the bedroom; he insisted it was her responsibility to pick up after herself.

Using the data that had been collected, the behavior analyst devised a system for the couple to try out. He asked them to list all of the chores that could possibly arise and assign each one a point value depending on how long it took to complete. Then he had them divide the chores equally and agree in a written contract to fulfill the ones assigned to them. If either failed to carry out one of the assigned chores, he or she would have to place $1 per point in a fund for the other to spend. They also agreed to a program of verbal praise, promising to verbally reward each other for completing each chore.

Although skeptical about the value of such a program, the couple agreed to try it for a month, and to keep careful records of the number of arguments they had during this period. To their surprise, the number declined rapidly, and even the more basic issues in their marriage seemed on their way to being resolved.

PSYCHOLOGY AT WORK

SAFETY ON THE JOB:

Preventing Accidents by Changing Human Behavior

When they first visited the paper manufacturing plant in which they were studying safety, behavior analysts Beth Sulzer-Azaroff and Denise Fellner observed an environment that could readily lead to accidents: stacks of boxes piled up to the ceiling, careless handling of hazardous materials, failure to use machine guards on dangerous equipment, and a host of other unsafe conditions and practices. It came as no surprise to these psychologists, then, that the plant's employees had an unacceptably high rate of accidents and injuries.

The challenge was to find a way to modify the behavior of the workers in the interest of creating a safer environment. After spending some time observing the situation at the plant, they concluded that one reason the workers allowed these unsafe conditions to develop and continue was because they lacked feedback about their behavior. In other words, they simply were unaware of any link between their own behavior and consequent reinforcers or punishments. It seemed essential, then, to develop a system whereby feedback for safe behavior could be provided.

To remedy the situation, the two psychologists devised a feedback system (Fellner & Sulzer-Azaroff, 1984). Each week, a group of observers systematically monitored safety conditions and practices in different divisions of the paper plant. They then provided written feedback on their findings, which was posted throughout the plant. Workers could see the improvement (or, on occasion, the decline) of safe practices and conditions in their own division as well as in others. In addition, once a month data were collected on the number of injuries that had occurred.

The results were promising. After receiving feedback on safe and unsafe conditions within the plant for a six-month period, most of the divisions that were monitored demonstrated an improvement. Moreover, just two months after feedback began, the workers' personal observance of safe practices showed a significant improvement. Most important, the number of injuries in the plant declined significantly.

Because of the prevalence of accidents throughout industry—there are more than 2 million disabling injuries each year—the implications of Sulzer-Azaroff and Fellner's work are important. Not only will industry benefit in economic terms from a decrease in time lost because of injuries, but, far more important, the quality of work life for employees will improve.

Behavior modification: *A formalized technique for promoting the frequency of desirable behaviors and decreasing the incidence of unwanted ones*

The case described above provides an illustration of **behavior modification**, a formalized technique for promoting the frequency of desirable behaviors and decreasing the incidence of unwanted ones. Using the basic principles of learning theory, behavior-modification techniques have proved to be helpful in a variety of situations (Wielkiewicz, 1985). Severely retarded people have learned the rudiments of language and, for the first time in their lives, have started dressing and feeding themselves. Behavior modification has also helped people to lose weight, give up smoking, and, as we discuss in the Psychology at Work box, behave more safely.

The variety of techniques used by behavior analysts is as varied as the list of processes that modify behavior—including the use of reinforcement scheduling, shaping, generalization training, discrimination training, and extinction. Behavioral approaches do, however, typically follow a series of similar basic steps in a behavior-change program (Royer & Feldman, 1984). These steps include:

■ Identifying goals and target behaviors. The first step is to define "desired behavior." Is it an increase in time spent studying? A decrease in weight? An increase in the use of language? A reduction in the amount of aggression displayed by a child? The goals must be stated in observable terms and lead to specific targets. For instance, a goal might be "to increase study time," while the target behavior would be "to study at least two hours per day on weekdays and an hour on Saturdays."

■ Designing a data-recording system and recording preliminary data. In order to determine whether behavior has changed, it is necessary to collect data before any changes are made in the situation. This provides a baseline against which future changes can be measured.

■ Selecting a behavior-change strategy. The most crucial step is to select an appropriate strategy. Since all the principles of learning can be employed to bring about behavior change, a "package" of treatments is normally used. This package might include the systematic use of positive reinforcement for desired behavior (verbal praise or something more tangible, such as food), as well as a program of extinction for undesirable behavior (ignoring a child who throws a tantrum).

■ Implementing the program. The next step is to institute the program. Probably the most important aspect of program implementation is consistency; if the program is not consistently applied, the chances for success are greatly reduced. Another crucial task is record keeping; if the target behaviors are not monitored, there is no way of knowing whether the program has actually been successful.

■ Evaluating and altering the ongoing program. Finally, the results of the program should be compared with preimplementation data to determine its effectiveness. If the program seems successful, the procedures employed can be gradually phased out. For instance, if the program called for reinforcing every instance of picking up one's clothes from the bedroom floor, the reinforcement schedule could be modified to a fixed-ratio schedule in which every third instance was reinforced. On the other hand, if the program has not been successful in bringing about the desired behavior change, consideration of other approaches might be advisable.

The Informed Consumer of Psychology: Using Behavior-Modification Techniques to Manage Your Time

Do you ever feel that you don't have enough time for everything you want to accomplish? Most of us, at one time or another, have such feelings, especially during our college years when numerous courses make separate and equally important demands on us—not to mention our extracurricular activities, social lives, and a host of other tasks that we want to accomplish. And such demands do not cease once one leaves college; life is filled with competing demands on our time. How can one manage to meet these demands successfully?

Time management: *A method of planning our time to make the most efficient use of it*

Psychologists specializing in learning have devised a technique—called **time management**—that can teach us to use our time most effectively. Although the specifics vary, it is generally agreed that tasks must be broken down into their most basic components and that these components must be scheduled on a day-by-day basis. One system, designed specifically for use by college students in scheduling their study time, includes the following steps (Chase & Schulze, 1984):

■ Buy two calendars that have spaces to write in activities and events for each day. One calendar should be reserved for long-term events; a calendar that displays the semester on one page might be appropriate here. The second should permit you to pencil in daily events. Having two calendars allows you to hold both a long-term focus, giving you an idea of when you should begin more ambitious projects, such as papers and studying for major exams, and a short-term focus for the day-to-day details. Put the calendars where you can see them every time you come into your room—don't hide them behind a door or in a desk drawer. The object is to see them often enough so that they act as a stimulus for an appropriate response.

■ Collect every schedule, syllabus, and school calendar that will affect you over the semester, and use them to record on your calendars all pertinent deadlines, tests, papers due, social activities, athletic events, and the like. Also list your regular classes, meetings, jobs, and so forth.

■ A very general rule of thumb—which varies widely, but at least gives you a start—is to allow yourself *at least* two hours of study time for each hour you spend in the classroom. For instance, if your introductory psychology course is a three-credit course that meets three hours per week, it is wise to leave at least six hours per week for studying. Include additional study time for special projects, such as a term paper due at the end of the semester. If after scheduling your other classes and activities you find you do not have sufficient study time available to meet this goal, it is probably wise to cut back on some nonacademic activity or perhaps to enroll in one less course.

■ Mark your study time on your calendar, considering what time of day you work best. The time you schedule for yourself to study should be as important—and free from interruption—as the events that others schedule for you. Guard it, and don't be tempted to fill it up with activities that come up on the spur of the moment.

■ As any good learning theorist would say, be sure to build some rewards into your schedule. Give yourself breaks during your study time, perhaps saving a candy bar or soda until after you have studied for a certain period. It is also important to reinforce yourself by scheduling some "time off" every once in a while, particularly after very busy periods of the semester. And don't over-schedule yourself—leave time for the unexpected.

■ Finally, review your schedule each day and revise it according to the demands of the school term. Reviewing will enable you to make out a daily list of tasks you intend to accomplish—and, most rewarding of all, check off the accomplishments of the previous day.

As you can see from the preceding suggestions, the key to time management is specifying your goals and structuring the situation so that you are most apt to meet those goals—and are reinforced for reaching them. Because time management is so rewarding, it is a behavior that is likely to be maintained and generalized beyond the college years, giving you continuing control over one of life's most precious commodities—time.

RECAP AND REVIEW IV

Recap

- Cognitive learning theory focuses on the unseen, internal mental processes that are occurring within a person.
- Modeling consists of learning from the observation of others' behavior. The rewards that a model receives contribute to the imitation of the model.
- Learned helplessness is the learned belief of a person or animal that no control can be exerted over the environment.
- Behavior modification, a formal technique for promoting desirable behaviors and reducing undesirable ones, has been used successfully in changing both one's own and others' behavior.

Review

1. Six-year-old Judy unexpectedly performs a break-dancing maneuver similar to the one she had observed at the break-dancing show she had attended last week. Her parents find it charming and let Judy know it through their laughter and hugs. Cognitive learning theorists might refer to Judy's behavior as an example of
   a. Cognitive mapping **b.** Expectation **c.** Latent learning **d.** Negative reinforcement
2. Higher-order thinking and unseen mental processes are focused on in cognitive learning theory. True or false?
3. According to cognitive learning theorists, a rat comes to display a response such as pressing a bar because it has developed a(n) ____________ about the reinforcement that will follow.
4. In Tolman's maze experiment, the rat's perception of the layout of the maze is called a ____________ ____________.
5. Fill in the key steps missing in the behavior-analysis model:
   a. Identify goals and target behaviors. **b.** ____________
   c. Select a behavior-change strategy. **d.** Implement the program. **e.** ____________

(Answers to review questions are at bottom of page 161.)

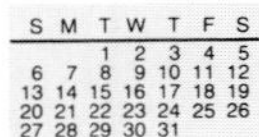

Psychology Looks Toward the 1990s
Computers Learn to Learn

> A computer is teaching itself to read out loud. Initially, its attempts sound like gibberish, since it has not been given any rules about what the sounds of particular letters are. However, it receives corrective feedback following each mistake it makes, and fairly soon it begins to make baby-like babbling sounds as it learns to distinguish between vowels and consonants. After an evening of computing, it reads with only minor errors. (Pollack, 1987)

New computer programs, such as this one developed by Terrence Sejnowski of Johns Hopkins University, are demonstrating that computers can learn how to learn—and in the process, are illuminating the manner in which human beings themselves learn. These new programs employ a technology called "neural networks" and hold the promise of a generation of computers that in essence program themselves, without requiring a person to produce a set of rules and procedures for the computer to follow (Ballard, Hinton, & Sejnowski, 1983).

Computers using a neural network approach operate in a manner that is analogous to the way in which neurons in the brain operate during learning. A computer using a neural network has many processing units (called "nodes") that operate simultaneously on a problem, similar to the way in the which the brain has billions of neurons. Each of these nodes is connected to many others, again analogous to the way in which the brain's neurons are connected via synapses to other neurons, with the strength of the connections varying.

Each node has a particular activation level which determines whether or not it will "fire," thereby sending information to another node. Moreover, not only does the strength of the activation level vary, but the magnitude of the connection between two nodes may differ. The strength of the activation level required for "firing," as well as the magnitude of the connection between the two nodes, may be set by the computer programmer in advance, or the computer itself can, through trial and error, set its own levels, according to the nature of the problem on which it is working (Ackley, Hinton, & Sejnowski, 1985).

When faced with a problem, the computer network processes information simultaneously on many levels. Unlike traditional computers, in which the rules must be completely specified in advance (for example, that the letter "t" is pronounced differently when it is followed by an "h" than when it is followed by a vowel), neural network computers can develop their own rules based on the feedback they receive.

What is particularly interesting is how closely the feedback process employed by the computers mimics shaping procedures developed by psychologists to teach complex information. Neural network computers are helping to unravel the question of how much learning is due to the mere application of rules, and under what conditions classical conditioning, operant conditioning, and cognitive learning theories are most pertinent.

Still, computers have yet to approach the learning capabilities of human beings. Given the fact there are literally billions of neurons in the human brain, the likelihood that any computer will soon reach the level of human learning is low. Ultimately, however, the day may come when a computer can be made to effectively learn—and in the process, help us to better understand how humans learn.

LOOKING BACK

1. Learning, a relatively permanent change in behavior due to experience, is a basic topic of psychology. Although it is a process that must be assessed indirectly (we can only assume that learning has occurred by observing performance, which is susceptible to such factors as lack of effort or fatigue), learning theories explain such diverse phenomena as emotional responses and school performance.

2. One major form of learning is known as classical conditioning. First studied by Ivan Pavlov, classical conditioning occurs when a neutral stimulus—one that brings about no relevant response—is repeatedly paired with a stimulus (called an unconditioned stimulus) that brings about a natural, untrained response. For instance, a neutral stimulus might be a buzzer; an unconditioned stimulus might be a dish of ice cream. The response ice cream might bring about in a hungry person—salivation—is called an unconditioned response; it occurs naturally, due to the physical makeup of the individual being trained.

3. The actual conditioning occurs when the neutral stimulus is repeatedly presented just before the unconditioned stimulus. After repeated pairings, the neutral stimulus begins to bring about the same response as the unconditioned stimulus. When this occurs, we can say that the neutral stimulus is now a conditioned stimulus, and the response made to it is the conditioned response. For example, after a person has learned to salivate to the sound of the buzzer, we say the buzzer is a conditioned stimulus, and the salivation is a conditioned response. Classical conditioning underlies many important types of learning, including the learning of many types of emotional responses.

4. Learning is not always permanent, however. Extinction occurs when a previously learned response weakens and eventually disappears. Extinction provides the basis for systematic desensitization, a treatment designed to decrease people's strong, irrational fears. Extinction may be temporary, though; spontaneous recovery sometimes occurs, whereby a previously extinguished response reappears after a period of time has elapsed without exposure to a stimulus.

5. Stimulus generalization occurs when a conditioned response follows a stimulus that is similar to the original conditioned stimulus. The greater the similarity between the two stimuli, the greater the likelihood of stimulus generalization; and the closer the new stimulus to the old one, the more similar will be the new response. The converse phenomenon, stimulus discrimination, occurs when an organism responds to one stimulus but not to another.

6. Higher-order conditioning occurs when an established conditioned stimulus is paired with a neutral stimulus, and the new neutral stimulus comes to evoke the same conditioned response as the original conditioned stimulus. The neutral stimulus changes, then, into another conditioned stimulus.

7. The second major form of learning is operant conditioning. Moving beyond Edward Thorndike's original work on the law of effect, which states that responses producing satisfying results are more likely to be repeated than those that do not, B. F. Skinner carried out pioneering work on operant learning.

8. According to Skinner, the major factor underlying learning is the reinforcer—any stimulus which increases the probability that the preceding response will occur again. We can know whether a stimulus is a reinforcer only by observing its effects upon behavior. If behavior increases, the stimulus is, by definition, a reinforcer. Primary reinforcers involve rewards that are naturally effective without prior exposure because they satisfy a biological need. Secondary reinforcers, in contrast, begin to act as if they were primary reinforcers through frequent pairings with a primary reinforcer.

9. There are two kinds of reinforcers: positive and negative. Positive reinforcers are stimuli that are added to the environment, and lead to an increase in a preceding response. Negative reinforcers are stimuli whose removal from the environment leads to an increase in the preceding response.

10. Punishment is the administration of an unpleasant stimulus following a response in order to produce a decrease in the incidence of that response. Punishment is also characterized by the removal of a positive reinforcer. In contrast to reinforcement, in which the goal is to increase the incidence of behavior, punishment is meant to decrease or suppress behavior. Although there are a number of advantages to the use of punishment (for instance, it can work quickly in suppressing unwanted behavior), its disadvantages—it may allow even worse behaviors to appear in place of the unwanted behavior, it may teach or provoke aggression, and it fails to specify more desirable behaviors—usually outweigh its positive aspects. In sum, the use of punishment is a less preferred means of behavior change than is the use of reinforcement.

11. Schedules and patterns of reinforcement affect the strength and duration of learning. Generally, partial reinforcement schedules—in which reinforcers are not delivered on every trial—produce stronger and longer-lasting learning than do continuous reinforcement schedules, although specific kinds of partial reinforcement schedules differ in their effects.

12. Among the major categories of reinforcement schedules are fixed- and variable-ratio schedules, which are based on the number of responses made, and fixed- and variable-interval schedules, which are based on the time interval that elapses before reinforcement is provided when a desired response is made. Fixed-ratio schedules provide reinforcement only after a certain number of responses are made; variable-ratio schedules provide reinforcement after a varying number of responses are made—although the specific number typically varies around some average. In contrast, fixed-interval schedules provide reinforcement after a fixed amount of time has elapsed since the last reinforcement; variable-interval schedules provide reinforcement over varying amounts of time, although the time typically forms a specified average. The particular schedule chosen has an important effect on how often responses are made and how long responses will continue once reinforcement is discontinued.

13. Generalization and discrimination are phenomena at work in operant conditioning as well as in classical conditioning. Generalization refers to a situation in which an organism makes the same or a similar response to a new stimulus that it has learned to make in the past to a similar stimulus. Discrimination occurs when the organism responds to one stimulus, but does not respond to a similar (though different) stimulus.

14. Shaping is a process for teaching complex behaviors by rewarding closer and closer approximations of the desired final behavior. Shaping forms the basis for learning and teaching many everyday skills and is central to presenting complicated information in textbooks and in computerized programmed instruction.

15. Although there may be elements of both classical and operant conditioning present in particular situations, it is usually possible to distinguish between them. In classical conditioning, the unconditioned stimulus precedes the response and the response is elicited by the unconditioned stimulus. In operant conditioning, the response comes prior to the reinforcement. In sum, the response in classical conditioning is basically involuntary; in operant conditioning the response is voluntary.

16. Cognitive learning seeks to explain phenomena such as latent learning—in which a new behavior is learned but not performed until reinforcement is provided for its performance—and the apparent development of cognitive maps. Learning also occurs through the observation of the behavior of others, known as models. The major factor that determines whether a behavior will actually be performed is the nature of reinforcement or punishment a model receives. Learned helplessness, the learned belief of a person or animal that no control can be exerted over the environment, also suggests the importance of cognitive processes in learning.

17. Behavior modification is a method for formally using the principles of learning theory to promote the frequency of desired behaviors and to decrease or eliminate unwanted ones. In implementation of a behavior-change program, the typical steps include identifying goals and target behaviors, designing a data-recording system, recording preliminary data, selecting a behavior-change strategy, implementing the program, and evaluating and altering the ongoing program.

KEY TERMS AND CONCEPTS

learning (p. 127)
maturation (127)
classical conditioning (129)
neutral stimulus (129)
unconditioned stimulus (UCS) (129)
conditioned response (CR) (129)
extinction (132)
systematic desensitization (132)
spontaneous recovery (133)
stimulus generalization (133)
stimulus discrimination (133)
higher-order conditioning (133)
operant conditioning (136)
operant (136)
law of effect (137)
reinforcer (137)
primary reinforcer (138)
secondary reinforcer (138)
positive reinforcer (138)
negative reinforcer (138)
punishment (139)
schedules of reinforcement (141)
continuous reinforcement (141)
partial reinforcement (141)
cumulative recorder (142)
fixed-ratio schedule (143)
variable-ratio schedule (143)
fixed-interval schedule (144)
variable-interval schedule (144)
stimulus control training (144)
discriminative stimulus (145)
superstitious behavior (145)
shaping (146)

programmed instruction (148)
cognitive learning theory (151)
latent learning (151)
cognitive map (152)
observational learning (152)
model (152)
learned helplessness (153)
behavior modification (155)
time management (156)

FOR FURTHER STUDY AND APPLICATION

Domjan, M. P., & Burkhard, B. (1986). *Principles of learning and behavior.* 2nd ed., Monterey, CA: Brooks/Cole.

This is basic, well-written, understandable introduction to learning theory and its application.

Hill, W. F. (1981). *Principles of learning: A handbook of applications.* Sherman Oaks, CA: Alfred Publishing.

This book provides a practical overview of learning theories and how they may be applied to everyday problems involving the mastery of new material.

Sulzer-Azaroff, B., & Mayer, R. (1986). *Achieving educational excellence using behavioral strategies.* New York: Holt.

This interesting book is filled with insights into the use of operant conditioning to improve your scholastic performance.

Epstein, R. (Ed.). (1982). *Skinner for the classroom: Selected papers.* Champaign, IL: Research Press.

This is an excellent collection of B. F. Skinner's papers, with commentary that provides a context for the work and explains its importance in the study of operant conditioning.

Pavlov, I. P. (1927). *Conditioned reflexes.* New York: Oxford University Press.

Surprisingly readable, this volume describes Pavlov's original work—which may leave you salivating to learn more about classical conditioning.

Skinner, B. F. (1948). *Walden two.* New York: Macmillan.

A number of communities are actually trying to follow the approach laid out by Skinner in this fascinating book, which details his utopian vision, based on the principles of operant conditioning.

Ferner, J. D. (1980). *Successful time management.* New York: Wiley.

This practical volume is devoted to procedures for using one's time better. Using operant conditioning principles, the methods described are comprehensive—and the rewards of gaining more time for oneself are well worth the effort.

ANSWERS TO REVIEW QUESTIONS

Review IV: **1.** c **2.** True **3.** Expectation **4.** Cognitive map **5.** b. Designing a recording system and recording preliminary data; e. Evaluating and altering the ongoing program

CHAPTER 5

MEMORY

PROLOGUE

LOOKING AHEAD

THE THREE R'S OF REMEMBERING: RECORDING, RETAINING, AND RETRIEVING INFORMATION
The initial encounter: Sensory memory
Our working memory: Short-term memory
TRY IT! Impress Yourself with Your Own Memory
The final repository: Long-term memory
Levels of processing
Recap and review I

IT'S THERE SOMEWHERE—THE TRICK IS FINDING IT: REMEMBERING WHAT IS STORED IN LONG-TERM MEMORY
Flashbulb memories
Building memories: Constructive processes in memory
PSYCHOLOGY AT WORK. The Witness: Memory in the Courtroom
Recap and review II

WHEN MEMORY FAILS: FORGETTING WHAT YOU HAVE REMEMBERED
The before and after of forgetting: Proactive and retroactive interference
THE CUTTING EDGE. Memory Systems and the Brain
The informed consumer of psychology: Improving your memory
Recap and review III
PSYCHOLOGY LOOKS TOWARD THE 1990s. Mapping Memory: The Search for the Engram

LOOKING BACK

KEY TERMS AND CONCEPTS

FOR FURTHER STUDY AND APPLICATION

PROLOGUE

He could remember, quite literally, nothing—nothing, that is, that had happened since the loss of his temporal lobes and hippocampus during experimental surgery to reduce epileptic seizures. Until that time his memory had been quite normal. But after the operation he was unable to retain any information for more than a few minutes, and then the memory was seemingly lost forever. He did not remember his address, or the name of the person to whom he was talking. He would read the same magazine over and over again. According to his own description, his life was like waking from a dream and being unable to know where he was or how he got there (Milner, 1966).

. . .

He seemed to remember nearly everything. After reading passages of the Divine Comedy in Italian—a language he did not speak—he was able to repeat it back from memory and still do so some fifteen years later. He could memorize lists of fifty unrelated words and recall them at will more than a decade later. He could even repeat the same list of words backwards, if asked. His recall seemed nearly perfect (Luria, 1968).

LOOKING AHEAD

Most of us have memory abilities that lie somewhere between the two unusual extremes presented above. We are able to recall a vast array of information to which we have been exposed, such as the name of a friend we haven't seen or been in touch with for ten years or a picture that hung in our bedroom as a child. At the same time it is not uncommon to forget where the keys to the car are or the answer to an exam question about material studied just a few hours before.

In this chapter we address a number of questions about memory that psychologists are investigating: What is memory and how does it operate? Are there different kinds of memory? How are we able to recall material from long ago, yet forget information to which we have been exposed a few moments earlier? Can we improve our memories?

We begin the chapter by examining the issue of how information is stored and recalled in memory. We discuss evidence showing that there are actually three separate types of memory, and explain how each type operates in a somewhat different fashion to allow us to remember material we have been exposed to. Next, the problems of retrieving information from memory and the reasons information is sometimes forgotten are examined. We also consider some of the biological foundations of memory. Finally, we discuss some practical means of increasing one's memory capacity.

After reading and studying this chapter, then, you will be able to

- List and describe the three kinds of memory
- Explain the phenomena involved in retrieving what is stored in memory
- Identify and describe the major causes of forgetting
- Outline four methods for improving your memory
- Define and apply the key terms and concepts listed at the end of the chapter

THE THREE R'S OF REMEMBERING: RECORDING, RETAINING, AND RETRIEVING INFORMATION

What is memory, and why do we remember certain events and activities and forget others? Psychologists define **memory** as the capacity to record, retain, and retrieve information—the three R's of remembering. Without memory, learning would be impossible; people could not build on past experiences or adapt their knowledge to new situations.

Memory: *The capacity to record, retain, and retrieve information*

According to one influential theory, there are three kinds of memory, which vary in terms of their function and the length of time information is retained (Atkinson & Shiffrin, 1968). (See Figure 5-1.) **Sensory memory** refers to the initial, momentary storage of information, lasting only an instant; it is recorded by the person's sensory system as a raw, nonmeaningful stimulus. **Short-term memory** holds information for fifteen to twenty-five seconds; in this phase, the information is stored in terms of its meaning rather than as mere sensory stimulation. The third type of memory is **long-term memory**. Here, information is relatively permanent, although it may be difficult to retrieve.

Sensory memory: *The initial, short-lived storage of information recorded as a meaningless stimulus*
Short-term memory: *The storage of information for fifteen to twenty-five seconds (also known as working memory)*
Long-term memory: *The storage of information on a relatively permanent basis, although retrieval may be difficult*

The Initial Encounter: Sensory Memory

A momentary flash of lightning, the sound of a twig snapping, and the sting of a pinprick all represent stimulation of exceedingly brief duration, but they may nonetheless provide important information that potentially requires some response. Such stimuli are initially—and briefly—stored in sensory memory, the first repository of the information that the world presents to us. Actually, the term "sensory memory" encompasses several types of sensory memories, each related to a different source of sensory information. There is an **iconic memory,** which reflects information from our visual system, an **echoic memory**, which stores information coming from the ears, as well as corresponding memories for each of the other senses.

Iconic (i KON ik) **memory**: *The storage of visual information*
Echoic (eh KO ik) **memory**: *The storage of information obtained from the sense of hearing*

Regardless of the individual subtypes, sensory memory in general is able to store information for only a very short time, and if material does not change to another form of memory, that information is lost for good. For instance, iconic memory seems to last less than a second, and echoic memory seems to fade within four seconds of exposure to a stimulus (Darwin, Turvey, & Crowder, 1972). However, despite the brief duration of sensory memory, its precision is high: It is able to store almost an exact replica of each stimulus to which one is exposed.

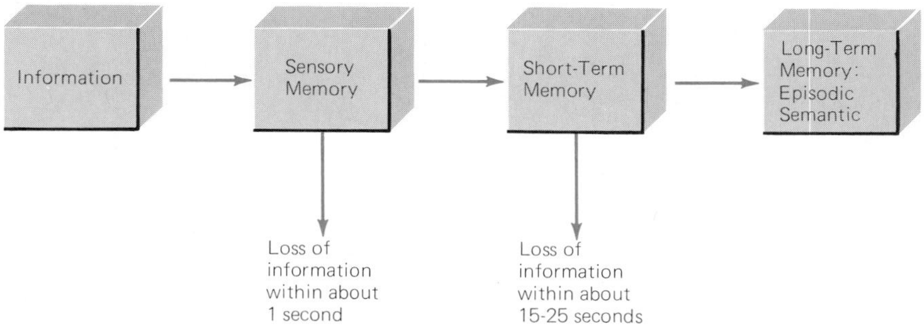

Figure 5-1
In this three-stage model of memory, information initially recorded by the person's sensory system enters sensory memory. It then immediately moves to short-term memory, which holds the information for fifteen to twenty-five seconds. Finally, the information may move into long-term memory, which is relatively permanent. (*Atkinson & Shiffrin, 1968.*)

If the storage capabilities of sensory memory are so limited and information stored within sensory memory so fleeting, it would seem almost impossible to find evidence for its existence; new information would be constantly replacing older information, even before a person could report its presence. Not until psychologist George Sperling (1960) conducted a series of clever and now-classic studies was sensory memory well understood. Sperling briefly exposed people to a series of twelve letters arranged in the following pattern:

F T Y C
K D N L
Y W B M

When exposed to this pattern for just one-twentieth of a second, most people could accurately recall only four or five of the letters. Although they knew that they had seen more, the memory had faded by the time they reported the first few letters. It was possible, then, that the information had initially been accurately stored in sensory memory, but during the time it took to verbalize the first four or five letters the memory of the other letters faded.

To test that possibility, Sperling had a high, medium, or low tone sounded just after a person had been exposed to the full pattern of letters. People were told to report the letters in the highest line if a high tone were sounded, the middle line if the medium tone occurred, or the lowest line at the sound of the low tone. Because the tone occurred after the exposure, people had to rely on their memory to report the correct row.

The results of the study showed very clearly that people had been storing the complete pattern in memory: They were quite accurate in their recollection of the letters in the line that had been indicated by the tone, regardless of whether it was the top, middle, or bottom line. Obviously, *all* the lines they had seen had been stored in sensory memory. Despite its rapid loss, then, the information in sensory memory was an accurate representation of what the people had seen.

By gradually lengthening the time between the presentation of the visual

"Well, here I sit, surrounded by my memorabilia, and I can't remember having done a damn thing."

(Drawing by Richter; © 1982 The New Yorker Magazine, Inc.)

pattern and the tone, Sperling was able to determine with some accuracy the length of time that information existed in sensory memory. The ability to recall a particular row of the pattern when a tone was sounded declined progressively as the period between visual exposure and tone lengthened, but leveled off when it reached about one second in duration. The conclusion: The entire visual image was stored in sensory memory for less than a second.

In sum, sensory memory operates as a kind of snapshot that stores information—which may be of a visual, auditory, or other sensory nature—for a brief moment in time. But it is as if each snapshot, immediately after being taken, is destroyed and replaced with a new one. Unless the information in the snapshot is transferred to some other type of memory, it is lost.

If you have ever looked up a number in a telephone directory outside a phone booth, and then forgotten the number just as you were about to begin to dial, you are aware of the limitations of short-term memory. (© Joel Gordon)

Our Working Memory: Short-Term Memory

Because the information that is stored briefly in our sensory memories consists of representations of raw sensory stimuli, it is not necessarily meaningful to us. In order for us to make sense of it and to allow for the possibility of long-term retention, the information must be transferred to the next stage of memory, short-term memory. Short-term memory, sometimes referred to as working memory, is the memory in which material initially has meaning, although the maximum length of retention is relatively short.

The specific process by which sensory memories are transformed into short-term memories is not yet clear. Some theorists suggest that the information is first translated into graphical representations or images, and others hypothesize that the transfer occurs when the sensory stimuli are changed to words (Baddeley, 1985). What is clear, however, is that unlike sensory memory, which holds a relatively full and detailed—if short-lived—representation of the world, short-term memory has incomplete representational capabilities.

In fact, the specific amount of information that can be held in short-term memory has been identified: seven bits, or "chunks," of information, with variations up to plus or minus two chunks. A **chunk** is a meaningful grouping of stimuli which can be stored as a unit in short-term memory. According to George Miller (1956), it could be individual letters, as in the following list:

Chunk: *A meaningful grouping of stimuli that can be stored as a unit in short-term memory*

C T N Q M W N

But a chunk might also consist of larger categories such as words or other meaningful units. For example, consider the following list of letters:

TWACIAABCCBSMTVUSAAAA

Clearly, because the list exceeds seven digits, it is difficult to recall them after one exposure. But suppose they were presented to you as follows:

TWA CIA ABC CBS MTV USA AAA

In this case, even though there are still twenty-one letters, it would be possible to store them in memory, since they represent only seven chunks. (For a demonstration of chunking, see the Try It! box.)

Chunks can vary in size from single letters or numbers to categories that are far more complicated, and the specific nature of what constitutes a chunk varies according to one's past experience. You can see this for yourself by trying an experiment that was first carried out comparing expert and inexperienced chess players (deGroot, 1966).

TRY IT!

IMPRESS YOURSELF WITH YOUR OWN MEMORY

Look at the following shapes for a few moments, and try to memorize them in the exact sequence in which they appear below:

An impossible task, you say? Here's a hint that will guarantee that you can easily memorize all the shapes: they are the shapes of each part of the letters in the word "PSYCHOLOGY." The reason the task suddenly became so simple was that the shapes could be grouped together into one chunk—a word that we all recognize. Rather than being nineteen separate, mysterious-looking symbols, they are recoded in memory as just one chunk.

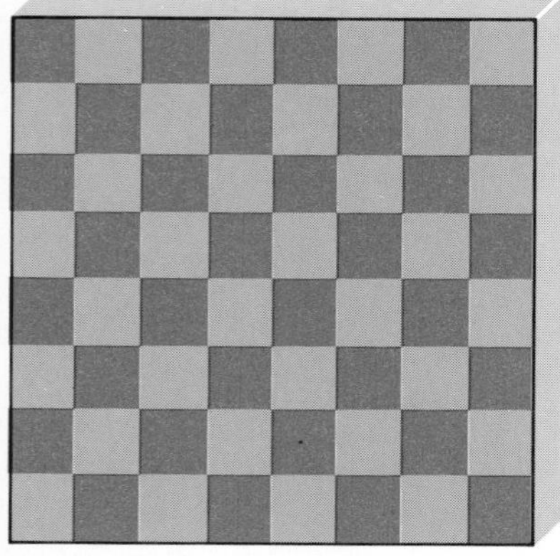

Figure 5-2
Look at the chessboard at the top for about five seconds and then cover it with your hand. Now try to recreate the placement of the chess pieces, using the blank board at the bottom. Unless you are an experienced chess player, you will probably have a good deal of difficulty in recalling the configuration and types of chess pieces. On the other hand, expert chess players have little difficulty in recreating the board at the top. (*deGroot, 1966.*)

Examine the chessboard on the top in Figure 5-2 for about five seconds, and then, after covering up the board, try to reproduce the position of the pieces on the blank chessboard on the bottom. Unless you are an experienced chess player, you will likely have great difficulty in carrying out such a task. Yet chess masters—the kind who win tournaments—do quite well: Ninety percent are able to correctly reproduce it. In comparison, inexperienced chess players typically are able to reproduce only 40 percent of the board properly.

The chess masters do not have superior memories in other respects; they test normally on other measures of memory. What they can do better than others is to chunk the board into meaningful units and reproduce the chess pieces by using these units. An analogous sort of skill is characteristic of electronics technicians, who are able to glance at a complicated circuit drawing and recall it without difficulty because of their ability to chunk it into meaningful configurations, as you can see in Figure 5-3 (Egan & Schwartz, 1979).

Although it is possible to remember seven or so relatively complicated sets of information entering short-term memory, the information cannot be held there very long. Just how short-term is short-term memory? Anyone who has looked up a telephone number at a pay phone, struggled to find coins, and forgotten the number just as the dial tone was finally heard knows that information in short-term memory does not remain there terribly long. Most psychologists believe that information in short-term memory is lost after about fifteen to twenty-five seconds—unless it is transferred to long-term memory.

The Final Repository: Long-Term Memory

Given the speed at which information is lost from short-term memory, we would never remember anything about our past if information from short-term memory were not transferred into long-term memory. Long-term memory is a relatively permanent repository for information that has been filtered through the sensory and short-term memory systems. The information is filed and catalogued in long-term memory so that it can be retrieved when we need it.

Evidence for the existence of long-term memory, as distinct from short-term memory, comes from a number of sources. Recall, for instance, the person described at the beginning of the chapter who could retain nothing new following brain surgery (Milner, 1966). After the surgery, he could remember only people or events that had been part of his experience before the operation. He reported

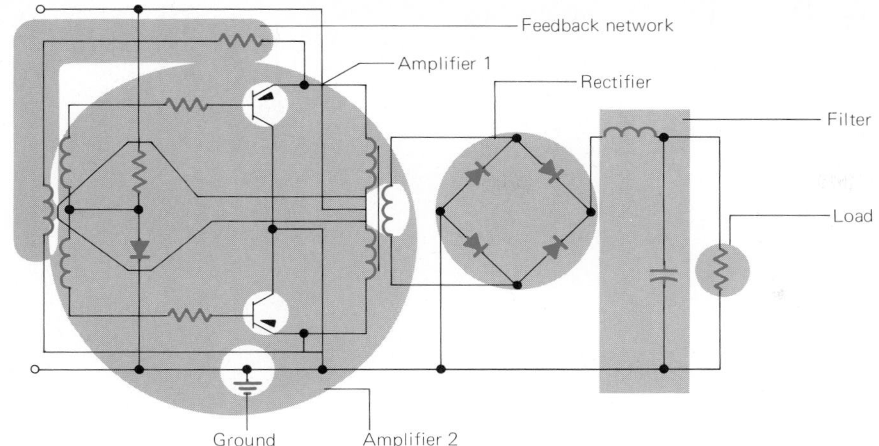

Figure 5-3
Although most of us would have difficulty in memorizing this circuit schematic, experienced electronics technicians recall it with ease because they are able to view it as a meaningful unit or chunk. (*Egan & Schwartz, 1979.*)

his age as 27 (the year he had the surgery) and his address as the one he had prior to the operation; he could not recall that his family had changed residences subsequent to the operation.

The facts of this case are consistent with the existence of a separate short- and long-term memory. This person's short-term memory seemed unimpaired, since he could recall things for brief periods following exposure to them. Yet any distraction led to an immediate and permanent loss of current memory; seemingly, nothing new could be placed in long-term storage. At the same time, information stored in his long-term memory prior to the operation was intact, allowing him to continue to draw upon memories stored before the surgery. His case, then, suggests that there are two distinct memories, one for short-term and one for long-term storage.

Evidence from laboratory experiments is also consistent with the notion of separate short- and long-term memories. For example, in one set of studies people were asked to recall a relatively small amount of information (such as a set of three letters)—but then, to prevent practice of the initial information, were required to recite some extraneous material aloud, such as counting backward by three (Brown, 1958; Peterson & Peterson, 1959). By varying the amount of time between which the initial material was first presented and its recall was required, investigators found that recall was quite good when the interval was near zero, but it declined rapidly thereafter. In fact, after fifteen seconds had gone by, recall hovered at around 10 percent of the material initially presented.

Apparently, counting backward prevented almost all the initial material from reaching long-term memory. Initial recall was good because it was coming from short-term memory, but these memories were lost at a rapid rate. Eventually, all that could be recalled was the small amount of material that had made its way into long-term storage despite the distractions of counting backward. In sum, it appears that the three letters were first stored in short-term memory but that that information was lost after about fifteen seconds. After that period, any recall that occurred was drawn from long-term memory.

Episodic and Semantic Memory There are actually two kinds of memories held in long-term memory: episodic and semantic (Tulving, 1983). **Episodic memories** relate to our individual lives, recalling what we have done and the kinds of experiences we have had. When you recall your first date, the time

Episodic memories: *Stored information relating to personal experiences*

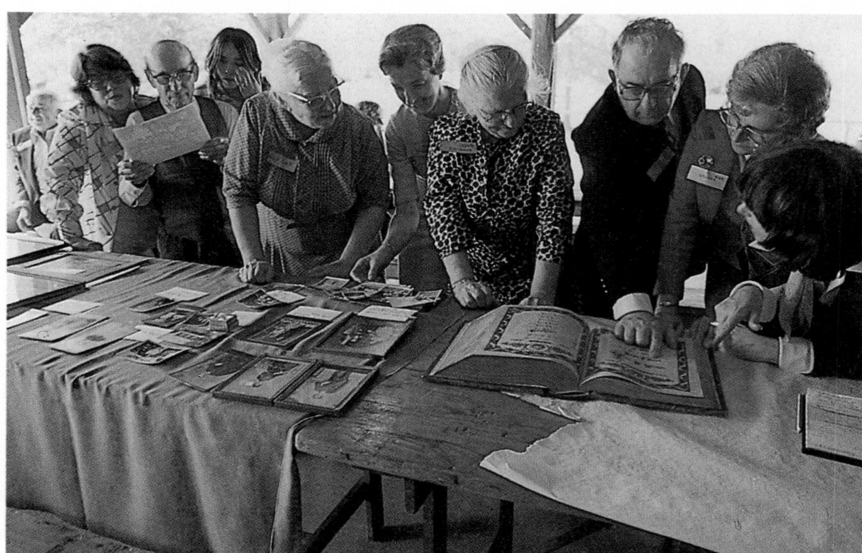

As they examine mementos of the past, these people are likely to recall episodic memories relating to their own unique experiences. (David S. Strickler/The Picture Cube)

Semantic (seh MAN tik) **memories**: *Stored, organized facts about the world (e.g., mathematical and historical data)*

you fell off your bicycle, or what you felt like when you graduated from high school, you are recalling episodic memories. The information in episodic memory is connected with specific times and places. In contrast, **semantic memories** consist of organized knowledge and facts about the world; because of semantic memory, we know that $2 \times 2 = 4$, the earth is round, and ''memoree'' is misspelled.

Episodic memories can be surprisingly detailed. Consider, for instance, what your response would be if you were asked to identify what you were doing on a specific day two years ago. An impossible task? You might think otherwise as you read the following exchange between a researcher and a subject who was asked, in a memory experiment, what he was doing ''on Monday afternoon in the third week of September two years ago.''

SUBJECT: Come on. How should I know?
EXPERIMENTER: Just try it anyhow.
SUBJECT: OK. Let's see: Two years ago . . . I would be in high school in Pittsburgh. . . . That would be my senior year. Third week in September—that's just after summer—that would be the fall term. . . . Let me see. I think I had chemistry lab on Mondays. I don't know. I was probably in chemistry lab. Wait a minute—that would be the second week of school. I remember he started off with the atomic table—a big fancy chart. I thought he was crazy trying to make us memorize that thing. You know, I think I can remember sitting. . . . (Lindsay & Norman, 1977).

Episodic memory, then, can provide information from events that happened long in the past. But semantic memory is no less impressive: By calling upon it, all of us are able to dredge up thousands of facts ranging from the date of our birthday to the knowledge that $1 is less than $5. Both individual pieces of information and the rules of logic for deducing other facts are stored in semantic memory.

Rehearsal The transfer of material from short- to long-term memory proceeds largely on the basis of rehearsal. **Rehearsal** is merely the repetition of information that has entered short-term memory. Rehearsal accomplishes two things. First, as long as the information is repeated, it is kept alive in short-term memory. More importantly, however, rehearsal allows the material to be transferred into long-term memory.

Rehearsal: *The transfer of material from short- to long-term memory via repetition*

Whether or not the transfer is made from short- to long-term memory seems to depend largely on the kind of rehearsal that is carried out. If the material is simply repeated over and over again—as we might do with a telephone number while we rush from the phone book to the telephone—it is kept current in short-term memory, but it will not necessarily be placed in long-term memory. Instead, as soon as we stop dialing, the number is likely to be replaced by other information and will be completely forgotten.

On the other hand, if the information in short-term memory is rehearsed using a process called elaborative rehearsal, it is considerably more likely to be transferred into long-term memory (Craik & Lockhart, 1972). **Elaborative rehearsal** occurs when the material is considered and organized in some fashion. The organization might include expanding the information to make it fit into a logical framework, linking it to another memory, turning it into an image, or transforming it in some other way. For example, a list of vegetables to be purchased at a store could be woven together in memory as items being used to prepare an elaborate salad, they could be linked to the items bought on an earlier shopping trip, or they could be thought of in terms of the image of a farm with rows of each item.

Elaborative rehearsal: *Organizing information to fit into a logical framework, which assists in recall*

By using organizational strategies called mnemonics, the recall of information is vastly improved (Higbee & Kunihira, 1985). **Mnemonics** are formal techniques for organizing material so that it is more likely to be remembered. For instance, when a beginning musician learns that the spaces on the music staff spell the word "FACE" or when we learn the rhyme "Thirty days hath September, April, June, and November; all the rest have . . .," we are using mnemonics.

Mnemonics (neh MON ix): *Formal techniques for organizing material to increase the likelihood of its being remembered*

Levels of Processing

One influential contemporary approach to understanding what information is forgotten and what is recalled focuses on the ways in which material is first perceived and analyzed. Rather than considering memory in terms of three stages (sensory, short-, and long-term storage), the levels-of-processing approach emphasizes the ways in which perception interacts with learning processes to promote the recall of material (Craik & Lockhart, 1972).

Levels-of-processing theory suggests that the way in which information is initially perceived and analyzed determines the success with which the information is eventually recalled. According to this approach, the depth of processing during exposure to the material is critical. At shallow levels, information is processed merely in terms of its physical and sensory aspects; for example, we may pay attention only to the shapes that make up the letters in the word "dog." At an intermediate level of processing, the shapes are translated into meaningful units—in this case, letters. These letters are considered in the context of words, and the specific sound of the word may be attached to the letters.

Levels-of-processing theory: *The theory that suggests that the way that information is initially perceived and learned determines recall*

At the deepest level of processing, information is analyzed in terms of its meaning. It may be seen in a wider context, and associations between the meaning of the information and broader networks of knowledge may be drawn. For instance, we may think of dogs in relation to cats, or we may form an image of our own dog.

According to the levels-of-processing approach, the deeper the initial level of processing involved with specific information, the longer the information will be retained. The approach suggests, then, that the way people first consider material they want to remember will have a crucial effect on whether the material will ultimately be remembered or forgotten.

The levels-of-processing theory considers memory as involving more active mental processes than the three-stages-of-memory approach. However, because neither approach can account for all phenomena relating to memory, it is too early to tell—let alone remember—which represents the most accurate representation of memory.

RECAP AND REVIEW I

Recap

- Memory is the capacity to record, retain, and retrieve information.
- Sensory memory contains a brief but accurate representation of physical stimuli to which a person is exposed. Each representation is constantly being replaced with a new one, however.
- Short-term memory has a capacity of seven (plus or minus two) chunks of information. Memories remain in short-term storage for from fifteen to twenty-five seconds, and then are either transferred to long-term memory or lost.
- Long-term memories are either episodic or semantic. Memories enter long-term storage through rehearsal.
- The levels-of-processing approach suggests that information is analyzed at different levels, with memory being better for material processed at deeper levels.

Review

1. As your friend Beth rushes off, she looks back and shouts her new phone number, 747-0190. Unless you make some effort to organize these numbers they will probably remain (for only fifteen to twenty-five seconds) in your
   a. Sensory memory **b.** Short-term memory **c.** Long-term memory **d.** Semantic memory
2. Suppose that in the above encounter you paused and thought, "Okay, 19 is my age. It's surrounded by zeros. And 747 is a type of jet." You think this through once more, before going about your business. This strategy of organization is referred to as ______________.
3. Your strategy in item 2 above would probably result in the storage of the phone number in your ______________ memory.
4. The average capacity for short-term memory is seven chunks. True or false?
5. Recalling the first time you drove a car on your own is an example of
   a. Semantic memory **b.** Echoic memory **c.** Iconic memory **d.** Episodic memory
6. Formal techniques that facilitate memory through associations are called
   a. Elaborative rehearsal **b.** Sensory memory **c.** Behavior modification **d.** Mnemonics

(Answers to review questions are at bottom of page 174.)

IT'S THERE SOMEWHERE—THE TRICK IS FINDING IT: REMEMBERING WHAT IS STORED IN LONG-TERM MEMORY

An hour after his job interview, Rich was sitting in a coffee shop, telling his friend Laura about how it went, when the woman who had interviewed him walked in. "Well, hello, Rich. How are you doing?" Trying to make a good impression, Rich began to introduce Laura, but then realized he could not remember the name of the interviewer. Stammering, he desperately searched his memory for her name, but couldn't remember. "I *know* her name," he thought to himself, "but here I am, looking like a jerk. I can kiss this job goodbye."

Have you ever tried to remember someone's name, being absolutely certain that you knew it, but unable to recall it no matter how hard you tried? This not infrequent occurrence—known as the **tip-of-the-tongue phenomenon**—exemplifies the difficulties that can occur in retrieving information stored in long-term memory (Harris & Morris, 1984). On the other hand, think of the ease with which you can recall the names of close friends, the quickest route to the grocery store, and the endless number of facts about your life and the world. Clearly, it is easier to remember some kinds of information than others.

Tip-of-the-tongue phenomenon: *The inability to recall information that one realizes one knows, a result of the difficulty of recalling information from long-term memory*

One reason recall is not perfect is because of the sheer quantity of recollections that are stored in long-term memory. Although the issue is far from settled, many psychologists have suggested that the material that makes its way there is relatively permanent (Tulving & Psotka, 1971). If they are correct, this suggests that the capacity of long-term memory is vast, given the variety of people's experiences and learning. For instance, if you are like the average college student, your vocabulary includes some 50,000 words, you know hundreds of mathematical "facts," and you are able to conjure up images—such as the way your childhood home looked—with no trouble at all. In fact, simply cataloging all your memories would probably take years of work.

How do we sort through this vast array of material and retrieve specific information at the appropriate time? One of the major ways is through the use of retrieval cues. A **retrieval cue** is a stimulus that allows us to more easily recall information which is located in long-term memory (Tulving & Thompson, 1973). It may be a word, an emotion, a sound; whatever the specific cue, a memory will suddenly come to mind when the retrieval cue is present. For

Retrieval cue: *A stimulus such as a word, smell, or sound that allows us to more easily recall information located in long-term memory*

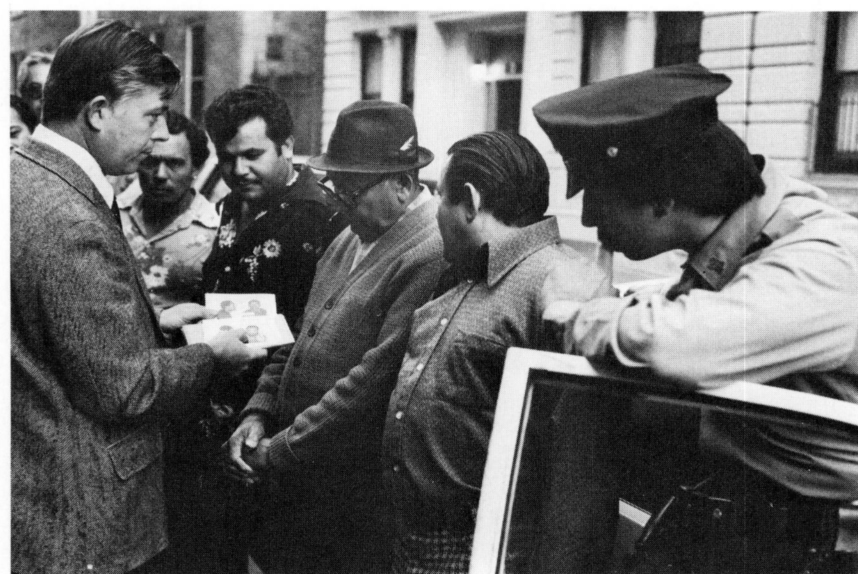

The police detective asking witnesses if they can identify the suspect in the picture he is holding is employing a recognition memory task. (Leonard Freed/Magnum)

example, the smell of roasting turkey may evoke memories of Thanksgiving or family gatherings.

Retrieval cues guide people through the vast array of information stored in long-term memory in much the same way as the cards in a card catalog guide people through a library. They are particularly important when *recalling* information, as opposed to being asked to *recognize* material stored in memory. In **recall**, a specific piece of information must be retrieved—such as that needed to fill in the blanks or write an essay on a test. In contrast, **recognition** occurs when people are presented with a stimulus and asked if they have been exposed to it previously.

Recall: *Drawing from memory a specific piece of information for a specific purpose*

Recognition: *Acknowledging prior exposure to a given stimulus, rather than recalling the information from memory*

As you might guess, recognition is considerably easier than recall. Suppose, for instance, you witnessed a robbery and were asked to describe the thief—a recall task. Clearly, this would be harder than being shown a police "mug book" and asked to pick out the robber—a recognition problem. The reason that recall is more difficult is that it consists of a series of processes: a search through memory, retrieval of potentially relevant information, and then a decision regarding whether or not the information you have found is accurate. If it appears correct, the search is over, but if it does not, the search must continue. On the other hand, recognition is simpler since it involves fewer steps (Anderson & Bower, 1972).

Flashbulb Memories

Ask anyone over the age of 35 what he or she was doing on first hearing that President John F. Kennedy was assassinated, and that person is likely to be able to provide you with a thorough description of his or her activities some twenty-five years ago.

Similarly, perhaps it is easy for you to recall events that took place last New Year's Eve. What makes this possible is a phenomenon known as flashbulb memories. **Flashbulb memories** are memories centered around a specific, important event that are so clear it is as if they represent a snapshot of the event. For example, common flashbulb memories of college students include involvement in a car accident, meeting one's roommate for the first time, and the night of high school graduation (Rubin, 1985). (See Figure 5-4.)

Flashbulb memories: *Memories of a specific event that are so clear they seem like "snapshots" of the event*

Of course, not every detail of an original scene is recalled in a flashbulb memory. While I may remember that I was sitting in Mr. Sharp's tenth-grade geometry class when I heard that President Kennedy was shot, and I remember where my seat was located and what my classmates did, I may not recall what I was wearing or what I had for lunch that day.

Still, flashbulb memories are extraordinary because of the details they do include. An analysis of people's recollections of the Kennedy assassination found that their memories tended to have a number of features in common (Brown & Kulik, 1977). Most contained information regarding where the rememberer heard the news, who told him or her about it, what was interrupted by the news, the emotions of the informant, the rememberer's own emotions, and some personal details of the event (such as seeing a robin fly by while the information was being given).

Flashbulb memories illustrate a more general phenomenon about memory:

ANSWERS TO REVIEW QUESTIONS

Review I: **1.** b **2.** Elaborative rehearsal **3.** Long-term **4.** True **5.** d **6.** d

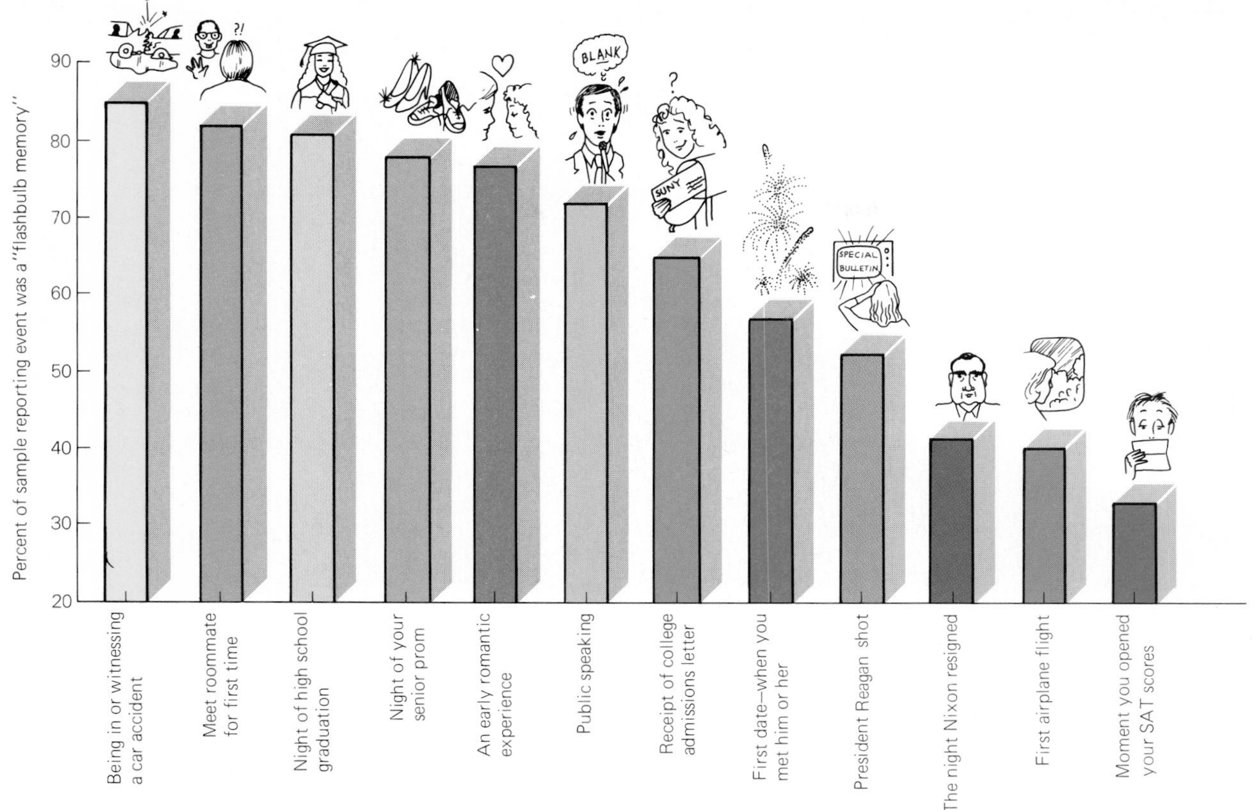

Figure 5-4
The most common flashbulb memories of a sample of college students are shown here. (*Rubin, 1985.*)

Memories that are distinctive are more easily retrieved than those relating to events that are commonplace. We are more likely, for example, to recall a particular number if it appears in a group of twenty words than if it appears in a group of twenty other numbers. The more distinctive a stimulus, then, the more likely we are to recall it later—the **von Restorff effect**, a phenomenon named after its discoverer (von Restorff, 1933).

von Restorff effect: *The phenomenon by which distinctive stimuli are recalled more readily than less distinctive ones*

Building Memories: Constructive Processes in Memory

While it is clear that we can have detailed recollections of significant and distinctive events, it is difficult to gauge the accuracy of such memories. In fact, it is apparent that our memories reflect, at least in part, **constructive processes**, processes in which memories are influenced by the meaning that we give to events. When we retrieve information, then, the memory that is produced is affected not just by the direct prior experience we have had with the stimulus, but by our guesses and inferences about its meaning as well.

Constructive processes: *Processes in which memories are influenced by the interpretation and meaning given to events*

One example underscoring the point that recall of some information is particularly susceptible to the expectations that a person holds is illustrated by the cartoon in Figure 5-5. Look at it briefly, and then try to describe it to someone else without looking back at it. Then ask that person to describe it to another, and repeat the process with still one more person. The process is known as **serial reproduction**. If you listen to the last person's report of the contents of the cartoon, you are sure to find that it differs in important respects from the cartoon itself. Many people recall the cartoon as showing a razor in the hand

Serial reproduction: *The passage of interpretive information from person to person, often resulting in inaccuracy through personal bias and misinterpretation*

PSYCHOLOGY AT WORK

THE WITNESS:
Memory in the Courtroom

It is a scene immortalized in scores of old television shows and movies: A lineup is called and a nervous but beautiful heroine picks out one of five suspects, saying with confidence, "He's the one. I'm certain of it."

Ongoing research on eyewitness memory for details of crimes suggests that most eyewitnesses should be considerably less confident than they often are in their ability to recall either the identity of a suspect or any other details of a crime. Work on eyewitness identification has shown that witnesses are apt to make substantial errors when they try to recall details of criminal activity (Kassin, 1985).

Consider the three faces shown below. As you can see, the men share certain characteristics; they are all wearing glasses and have moustaches and similar hairstyles. Their similarity led to near-tragic consequences when one of them was arrested for several rapes and another for a robbery, all crimes that the third person had actually committed. The bases of their arrests were the mistaken impressions of eyewitnesses who—before the actual criminal had been found—felt sure that they had identified the right person as the perpetrator.

This case of mistaken identification is not an isolated event, according to research on the topic; eyewitnesses are prone to frequent errors in memory (Wells & Loftus, 1984). For instance, viewers of a twelve-second film of a mugging that was shown on a New York City television news program were later given the opportunity to pick out the assailant from a six-person lineup. Of some 2000 viewers that called the station after the program, only 15 percent were able to pick out the right person—a figure just slightly higher than if they had guessed randomly (Buckhout, 1975).

Other research suggests that the mistakes witnesses make show wide variability. For example, one study found that witnesses of staged crimes disagreed by as much as 2 feet in their estimates of the height of a perpetrator and averaged a difference of 8 inches from his true height. There was a discrepancy from true age averaging eight years, hair color was recalled incorrectly 83 percent of the time, and about a quarter of all witnesses left out more than half of the details they had actually seen (Gardner, 1933).

Even the specific wording of a question posed to a witness can affect the way in which something is recalled, as a number of experiments illustrate. For example, in one experiment subjects were shown a film of two cars crashing into each other. Some were then asked the question, "About how fast were the cars going when they *smashed* into each other?" They estimated the speed to be an average of 40.8 miles per hour. In contrast, when another group of subjects were asked, "About how fast were the cars going when they *contacted* each other?" the average estimated speed was only 31.8 miles per hour (Loftus & Palmer, 1974).

In sum, our memories are far from infallible—a fact that judges and jurors must take into consideration when they weigh the evidence presented by eyewitnesses, no matter how certain those eyewitnesses may be of their own accounts.

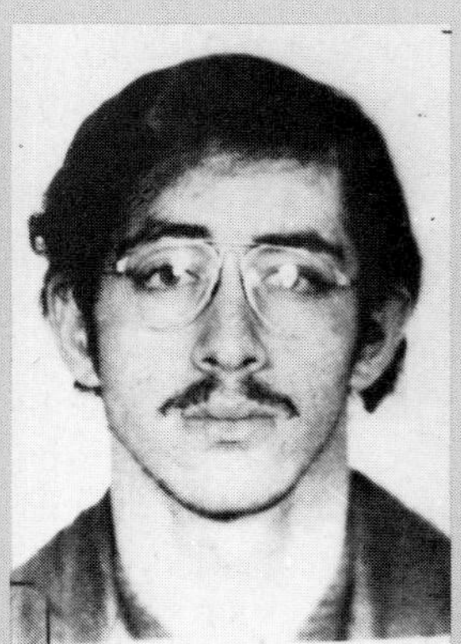

In a case of mistaken identification, the people in the photos on the left and right were arrested for crimes actually committed by the person in the center. Both of the innocent men had been identified as guilty in separate lineups by victims of the real criminal (*Buckhout, 1975.*)

Figure 5-5
When one person views this cartoon and then describes it from memory to a second person, who in turn describes it to a third, and so on—in a process known as serial reproduction—the last person to repeat the contents of the cartoon typically provides a description that differs in important respects from the original. (*Allport & Postman, 1958.*)

of the black person—obviously an incorrect recollection, given that the razor is held by the white person (Allport & Postman, 1958).

What this example, which is drawn from a classic experiment, illustrates is the role of expectations in memory. The migration of the razor from the white person's hand to the black person's hand in memory clearly indicates that expectations about the world—reflecting in this case the prejudice that blacks may be more violent than whites and thus more apt to be holding a razor—have an impact upon how events are recalled. Moreover, as we discuss in the Psychology at Work box, these inaccuracies of memory can have important consequences.

RECAP AND REVIEW II

Recap

- The tip-of-the-tongue phenomenon refers to the inability to recall something that a person is sure he or she knows.
- Retrieval cues are particularly important when recalling information—as opposed to recognizing it.
- Flashbulb memories are memories that are centered around a specific, important event and are so clear it is as if they represented a snapshot of the event.
- Memories reflect, at least in part, constructive processes, which influence the meaning that we give to events.

Review

1. A classmate asks you if you can remember that important word about memory discussed in your last psychology class. You just can't think of it, but when you glance at the glossary terms in your book, you immediately discover the word. It was "recall"! You remembered the word through the process of
a. Retention **b.** Recall **c.** Recognition **d.** Retrieval

2. Even though ten years have passed, you can remember clearly your fourth-grade teacher because of that distinctive green scarf she wore to class every day. This phenomenon is best referred to as
a. Flashbulb memory **b.** Recognition **c.** The von Restorff effect **d.** Serial reproduction

3. "Constructive processes" refers to the way in which memories vary as a function of the number of times we are exposed to an event. True or false?

4. You can easily remember the details of the moment you received your diploma during your high school graduation. This is an example of
a. Flashbulb memory **b.** von Restorff effect **c.** Figural representation **d.** Sensory memory

5. A friend witnesses a car hit a tree. Being interested in exactly what happened, you ask, "How fast was the car going when it *smashed* into the tree?" Your friend answers, "About 35 miles an hour." If you had asked instead, "How fast was the car going when it *contacted* the tree," his answer would most likely have been
a. 45 miles per hour **b.** 25 miles per hour **c.** Similar, no matter how you worded the question **d.** He would be unwilling to even guess, since witnesses rarely feel any confidence in their estimates.

(Answers to review questions are at bottom of page 180.)

WHEN MEMORY FAILS: FORGETTING WHAT YOU HAVE REMEMBERED

Recall the person described at the beginning of the chapter who could remember nearly everything. While having such a skill would at first seem to have few drawbacks, it actually presented quite a problem. His mind became a jumble of lists of words, numbers, and names, and when he tried to relax, his mind was filled with images. Even reading was difficult, since every word evoked a flood of thoughts from the past that interfered with his ability to understand the meaning of what he was reading. Partially as a consequence of his unusual memory, he appeared to psychologist A. R. Luria, who studied his case, to be a "disorganized and rather dull-witted person" (Luria, 1968, p. 65).

Forgetting, then, has its advantages, and psychologists interested in memory have investigated the processes that underlie the inability to recall information to which people have been previously exposed. Several explanations of forgetting have been suggested.

Decay: *The loss of information through nonuse*

Memory trace: *A physical change in the brain that reflects memories*

Engram (EN gram): *See memory trace*

One theory of forgetting relies on a process called **decay**, which is the loss of information through its nonuse. The theory assumes that when new material is learned, a **memory trace** or **engram**—an actual physical change in the brain—is produced. In decay, the trace simply fades away with the mere passage of time.

Although there is evidence that decay does occur, it does not seem to be the full explanation for forgetting. The difficulty with such a theory is that there is often no relationship between the time at which material was first learned and whether it can later be recalled. People who are given tests on the same material sequentially often recall more information on the second test than they did on the first. If decay were operating, we would expect the opposite to occur.

Interference: *A phenomenon in which recall is hindered by other information in memory*

It appears, then, that decay is not the only reason for forgetting. Instead, another process, interference, has been proposed to explain how we forget information stored in long-term memory. In **interference**, information in memory displaces or blocks out other information, preventing its recall.

To distinguish between decay and interference, you might think of the two processes in terms of a row of books on a library shelf. In decay, the old books are constantly crumbling and rotting away, leaving room for new arrivals. Interference processes suggest that new books knock the old ones off the shelf, where they become inaccessible.

Most research suggests interference and decay play different roles in short- and long-term memory. Interference is the main cause of forgetting from short-term memory, while decay appears to be the primary reason why people forget material stored in long-term memory. On the other hand, decay does play a minor role in short-term-memory forgetting, and interference processes are also at work in forgetting from long-term memory (Glass & Holyoak, 1985).

Figure 5-6
Proactive interference occurs when material learned earlier interferes with recall of newer material. In the example above, exposure to French prior to learning Spanish interferes with performance on a Spanish test. In contrast, retroactive interference exists when material learned after initial exposure to other material interferes with the recall of the first material—in this case, recall of French is hurt because of later exposure to Spanish.

The Before and After of Forgetting: Proactive and Retroactive Interference

There are actually two sorts of interference that influence forgetting: proactive and retroactive. In **proactive interference**, information learned earlier interferes with recall of newer material. For instance, suppose, as a student of foreign languages, you first learned French in tenth grade, and then in eleventh grade you took Spanish. When it comes time to take a college achievement test in the twelfth grade in Spanish you may find you have difficulty recalling the Spanish translation of a word because all you can think of is its French equivalent. On the other hand, **retroactive interference** refers to difficulty in recall of information because of later exposure to different material. If, for example, you have difficulty on a French achievement test because of your more recent exposure to Spanish, retroactive interference is the culprit (see Figure 5-6).

Proactive interference: *The phenomenon by which information stored in memory interferes with recall of later-learned material*

Retroactive interference: *The phenomenon by which there is difficulty in recall of information learned earlier because of later exposure to different material*

While the concepts of proactive and retroactive interference provide a description of why material may be forgotten, they do not explain whether forgetting is caused by the actual loss of information from storage because of the interference or because of problems in retrieving the information from storage. Although most research suggests that material that has apparently been lost because of interference can eventually be recalled if appropriate stimuli are presented (Tulving & Psotka, 1971), the question has not been fully answered. In an effort to resolve the issue, some psychologists have begun to study the biological bases of memory in order to better understand what is remembered and what is forgotten—an increasingly important avenue of investigation discussed in the accompanying Cutting Edge box.

THE CUTTING EDGE

MEMORY SYSTEMS AND THE BRAIN

> To a casual observer, Harold appears to be a brilliant golfer. He seems to have learned the game perfectly; his shots are almost flawless.
>
> Yet anyone accompanying him on the course is bound to notice some startling incongruities. Although he is immediately able to size up a situation and hit the ball exactly where it should go, he cannot remember where the ball has just landed. At the end of each hole, he forgets the score (Blakeslee, 1985, p. Cl).

Harold suffers from **Alzheimer's disease**, an illness that includes severe memory problems among its symptoms. His condition, while personally tragic, may help researchers to answer some important questions about memory, and it focuses on some of the enormous strides that have been made in the last decade in understanding the processes of memory.

According to Daniel Schacter, a scientist at the Memory Disorders Unit of the University of Toronto, Harold's condition provides evidence for a theory suggesting that memory, in contrast to the three-stage model discussed earlier, is made up of two distinct systems, each located in a different area of the brain. One system is concerned with **declarative knowledge**, which concerns facts: names, faces, dates, and the like. The other system relates to **procedural knowledge**, skills and habits such as riding a bike or hitting a golf ball.

People such as Harold seem to have deficits primarily in the area of the brain concerning declarative knowledge. Declarative knowledge must be consciously brought to mind, while procedural knowledge cannot be recalled in a concrete sense. People who are able to throw a basketball into a hoop have the skill stored in memory, but they are unable to describe the process they use—it is procedural knowledge.

Studies of animals and individuals who have suffered from brain disease and injury indicate that declarative memory is largely controlled by the hippocampus and amygdala of the brain (see Chapter 2). On the other hand, control of procedural memory seems to be more widespread throughout the brain (Squire & Butters, 1985).

Other work, described in the section "Psychology Looks Toward the 1990s" at the end of the chapter, has focused on the specific nature of changes that occur in the brain related to memory. For example, research with animals has shown that acquisition of information leads to modifications in the size, shape, and number of contacts and branches between and within nerve cells. Moreover, when animals are trained, there are changes in brain chemistry,

Alzheimer's (ALZ hy merz) **disease**: *An illness associated with aging that includes severe memory loss*
Declarative knowledge: *The body of knowledge that concerns facts—faces, dates, names, etc.*
Procedural knowledge: *The body of knowledge encompassing skills and habits*

People with Alzheimer's disease eventually become unable to recall the most simple facts. In the early stages of the disease, they can overcome this problem if they are given constant reminders; later, though, they are unable even to read and understand the reminders. (Ira Wyman/Sygma)

ANSWERS TO REVIEW QUESTIONS
Review II: **1.** c **2.** c **3.** False **4.** a **5.** b

particularly in terms of the increased production of chemicals such as RNA (ribonucleic acid) and of proteins (Davis & Squire, 1984; Deutsch, 1983).

Probably of greatest interest is the fact that the administration of particular kinds of drugs in animals can lead to impairment or facilitation of memory. In one study, chicks were trained to avoid pecking a bitter solution. When they were subsequently administered a drug that inhibited protein synthesis, they showed significantly poorer performance on a measure of recall than those not receiving the drug (Gibbs & Ng, 1977).

Moreover, the administration of the drug arecholine in one experiment improved verbal learning in humans—but only for those who had relatively low scores without the drug. The drug was useful, then, in leading people to show recall at their optimal level—but the results suggest that it may not be possible to improve memory if people are already operating at their maximum level of performance.

Where is research in the biology of memory leading? According to Mark Rosenzweig, a leading researcher in memory at the University of California, Berkeley, the recent advances in our understanding of memory suggest a number of possible applications. He suggests that it may be possible to help people who suffer from deficiencies of memory (such as Harold, the person with Alzheimer's disease described earlier) or people with some forms of mental retardation. According to him, "It may even be possible to aid those with 'normal' memory to perform better or at least to perform at their best level most of the time" (Rosenzweig, 1984, p. 373). Sometime in the future, then, all of our memories may benefit from research on the biological bases of memory.

The Informed Consumer of Psychology: Improving Your Memory

Given our understanding of memory, is it possible to suggest practical ways of increasing our recall of information? Most definitely; a good deal of research has revealed a number of strategies that can be used to help us develop better memories. Among the best:

■ The keyword technique. Anyone who has tried to study a foreign language knows the difficulty—and necessity—of learning long lists of vocabulary words. One way of easing this process is to use the **keyword technique**, in which a foreign word is paired with a common English word that has a similar sound. This English word is known as the keyword. For example, to learn the Spanish word for duck (*pato,* pronounced "pot o"), the keyword might be "pot"; for the Spanish word for horse (*caballo,* pronounced "cob eye yo"), the keyword might be "eye."

Keyword technique: *The pairing of a foreign word with a common, similar-sounding English word to aid in remembering the new word*

Once a keyword has been identified, a mental image of the keyword graphically "interacting" with the English translation of the word is formed. For instance, we might envision a duck taking a bath in a pot to remember the word *pato,* or a horse with a large, bulging eye in the center of its head to recall *caballo*. Results using this technique are considerably superior for learning foreign language vocabulary than more typical techniques involving memorization of the words themselves (Pressley & Levin, 1983).

■ Method of loci. When ancient Greek orators sought to memorize long speeches, they used the **method of loci** to organize their recollections of what they wanted to say. In this technique—whose name comes from the Latin word for places, *loci*—each part of a speech is imagined "residing" in a different location of a building.

Method of loci (LO sy): *Assigning words or ideas to places, thereby improving recall of the words by envisioning those places*

For instance, you might think of the preface of the speech as being in your house's entryway, the first major point being located in the living room, the next point in the dining room, and so forth, until the end of the speech is reached at the back bedroom of the house. This technique can easily be adapted for use in learning lists of words; each word on the list is imagined as being located in a series of sequential locations. The method works best by using the most outlandish images possible: If you wanted to remember a list of groceries consisting of bananas, ketchup, and milk, for instance, you might think of a banana intertwined in the leaves of your living-room begonia, the ketchup spilled over the end table, and the milk spraying from the top of a table lamp. When you got to the supermarket, you could mentally "walk" through your living room, recalling the items easily.

■ Organizing information in textbooks. Most of life's more important recall tasks do not involve lists of words, but rather remembering material that one has read. How can you facilitate recall of such material? One proven technique for improving recall of written material involves organizing the material in memory as it is being read for the first time. To do this, you should first identify any advance information about the structure and content of the material by using the table of contents, chapter outline, headings, and even the end-of-chapter summary before reading the chapter itself. By understanding the structure of the material, later recall is facilitated.

Another technique is to ask yourself questions that integrate the material you have read, and then answer them. By asking questions, you will be able to form networks between the various specific facts and promote the processing of the material at a deeper level—which, as the levels-of-processing approach to memory that we discussed earlier suggests, will aid later recall (Royer & Feldman, 1984). For example, you might at this moment ask yourself, "What are the major techniques for remembering material in textbooks?" and then try to answer the question.

■ Practice and rehearsal. Although practice does not necessarily make perfect, it does help. By studying and rehearsing material past the point of initial mastery—a process called **overlearning**—people are able to show better long-term recall than if they stop practicing after they have learned the material initially.

Overlearning: *Rehearsing material beyond the point of mastery to improve long-term recall*

Eventually, of course, practice has little or no effect; you probably already know your address so well that no amount of additional practice will make you recall it any better than you already do. But it is safe to say that, given the volume of material that is covered in most courses, academic material is rarely so securely retained, and you would generally be wise to review material a few times even after you feel the material has been learned in order to reach a true level of overlearning.

Research on the outcomes of elaborative rehearsal, discussed earlier in the chapter, also suggests that it is important that the practice be as active as possible, questioning and rehearsing the answers to possible questions. In this way, the connections between the parts of the material are likely to become explicit, aiding in its later recall by providing ample retrieval cues.

Finally, people who cram for tests should note that the best retention comes from practice that is distributed over many sessions, rather than left for one long session. Research clearly demonstrates that fatigue and other factors prevent long practice sessions from being as effective as distributed practice.

RECAP AND REVIEW III

Recap

- Decay and interference are the primary processes underlying forgetting.
- There are two kinds of interference: proactive interference (when information learned earlier interferes with recall of information learned later) and retroactive interference (when new information interferes with recall of information learned earlier).
- Some specific techniques for increasing the recall of information include the keyword technique, the method of loci, the organization of information in textbooks, and practice and rehearsal.

Review

1. It appears that decay is the major cause of forgetting from long-term memory. True or false?
2. Sue just told you yesterday the name of the new movie starring your favorite actress. But today, all you can recall are the names of the actress' earlier films. The ''culprit'' interfering with your memory is
   a. Memory trace **b.** Decay **c.** Proactive interference **d.** Retroactive interference
3. In order to help himself remember who was at the business meeting, Jim imagined each of the attendees standing in a different room in his house. His technique is known as
   a. Rehearsal **b.** The method of loci **c.** Overlearning **d.** The keyword technique
4. Research clearly shows that the best way to study before a test is to overlearn the material in one long session just before the exam. True or false?
5. ____________________ knowledge encompasses facts about names, faces, and dates, while ____________________ knowledge relates to skills and habits such as driving a car or hitting a backhand in tennis.

(Answers to review questions are at bottom of page 185.)

Psychology Looks Toward the 1990s
Mapping Memory: The Search for the Engram

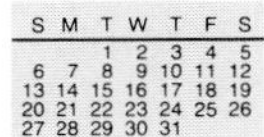

Just where is the engram, the physical, neuronal trace that represents a memory in the brain, located?

This question has proven to be a major puzzle to psychologists interested in memory, and has been the focus of a good deal of ongoing work. The search began in the 1920s, when psychologist Karl Lashley ran a series of experiments in which he removed portions of the cortex of rats. He found that rats who were made to relearn a problem involving running a maze showed learning deficits in proportion to the extent of the damage to their cortex; the more material in the cortex that had been removed, the greater the rats' learning difficulties.

More intriguing, however, was the finding that the time it took to relearn the problem was unrelated to the specific location of the injury. Regardless of what particular portion of the brain had been removed, the degree of learning deficit was fairly similar, suggesting that memory traces are fairly evenly distributed across the brain. Results of Lashley's work—summarized in a famous paper entitled ''In Search of the Engram''—led to the view held for several decades that stored memories are widely and fairly equally distributed across the brain (Lashley, 1950).

Contemporary research, however, seems to be coming to a different conclusion. Findings on the physiology of learning show that separate, distinct areas of the cortex simultaneously process information about particular dimensions of the world, including visual, auditory, and all other sensory stimuli that the world presents. Because different areas of the cortex are simultaneously involved in processing information about particular aspects of a stimulus, it seems reasonable to suppose that information storage might be linked to and localized in the specific neural systems that are used during learning.

If these assumptions are correct, then, the location of an engram is dependent on the nature of the material that is being learned and the specific neuronal system that processed the information (Squire, 1986; 1987). For example, a portion of the cortex known as the inferotemporal area is the final part of the brain involved in the visual processing of patterns. The process begins in a different area of the cortex (the striate cortex) and has passed through several stages of processing before it reaches the inferotemporal area. Consequently, it may be that the inferotemporal cortex not only provides the location of this visual processing, but is also the storage site of the visual memories that are the outcome of the processing. Traces of a specific memory, then, may be located in the area of the brain associated with how that memory was learned initially.

How can we reconcile the growing contemporary view that memory is related to specific neuronal processing employed during learning with Lashley's earlier findings that memory deficits in his rats were unrelated to the location of injury to the cortex? One answer is that the contradiction between the two findings is more apparent than real. It is likely, for example, that Lashley's procedure of having rats run through a maze actually involves several kinds of information and learning—including visual information, spatial configuration, smells, and perhaps even sounds. Given that this is the case, learning and processing of information must have been occurring in several modalities simultaneously, although presumably in different locations in the brain. If each of these processing modalities resulted in a separate memory trace, cutting out any particular portion of the cortex, then, still would leave the other memory traces intact—and cause the same apparent deficit in performance relatively independently of the location of an area of the cortex that is injured.

In sum, it appears that memory is localized to specific areas in that a particular memory trace is related to a particular brain information processing system. But in a larger sense, memory traces are distributed, since several brain processing systems are involved in any learning situation—leading to the distribution of memory traces throughout various areas of the brain (Weinberger, McGaugh, & Lynch, 1985).

LOOKING BACK

1. The term ''memory'' is defined by the three R's of remembering; it consists of the capacity to record, retain, and retrieve information. There are three basic kinds of memory storage: sensory memory, short-term memory, and long-term memory.

2. Sensory memory (made up of memories corresponding to each of the sensory systems) is the first place where information about the world is saved, although the memories are very brief. For instance, iconic memory (made up of visual sensations) lasts less than a second, and echoic memory (corresponding to auditory sensations) lasts less than four seconds. Despite their brevity, however, sensory memories are very precise, storing almost an exact replica of each stimulus to which they are exposed. Unless they are transferred to other types of memory, however, sensory memories appear to be lost.

3. Roughly seven (plus or minus two) chunks of information are capable of being transferred and held in short-term memory. A chunk is a meaningful bit of information, ranging in size from a letter or a single digit to more complicated categorizations. Information in short-term memory is held from fifteen to twenty-five seconds and, if not transferred to long-term memory, is lost.

4. If memories are transferred into long-term memory, they become relatively permanent. Long-term memories are of two types: episodic and semantic. Episodic memories relate to our individual lives (e.g., recall of what a grade school teacher looked like), while semantic memories consist of organized knowledge and facts about the world (e.g., recall of $4 \times 5 = 20$).

5. Memories are transferred into long-term storage through rehearsal. The most effective type is elaborative rehearsal, in which the material to be remembered is organized and expanded. Formal techniques for organizing material are called mnemonics.

6. The levels-of-processing approach to memory suggests that the way in which information is initially perceived and analyzed determines the success with which the information is recalled. The deeper the initial processing, the greater will be the recall of the material. Deep processing is characterized by attention to the meaning of the material and its context; shallow processing focuses on the physical aspects of the information (such as the shapes of the letters that make up the information).

7. The tip-of-the-tongue phenomenon refers to the experience of vainly trying to remember information that one is certain one knows. One major way of successfully retrieving information is through the use of retrieval cues, stimuli that permit a search through long-term memory. Retrieval cues are more useful for recall of information than for mere recognition.

8. Flashbulb memories are memories centered around a specific, important event. The memories are so clear that they appear to represent a "snapshot" of the event. Flashbulb memories illustrate the broader point that the more distinctive a memory, the more easily it can be retrieved—a phenomenon called the von Restorff effect.

9. Memory is a constructive process in which we relate memories to the meaning, guesses, and expectations that we have given to the events the memory recalls.

10. Even with the use of retrieval cues, some information appears irretrievable because of decay or interference. Interference is the main cause of forgetting from short-term memory, while decay appears to be the primary reason why people forget material stored in long-term memory.

11. There are two sorts of interference: proactive interference (when information learned earlier interferes with recall of material to which one is exposed later) and retroactive interference (when new information interferes with recall of information to which one has been exposed earlier).

12. Research on the biology underlying memory has suggested that memory is made up of two distinct systems, each located in different areas of the brain: One is related to declarative knowledge, which includes facts about names, faces, and dates, while the other concerns procedural knowledge—skills and habits such as riding a bike. Other work has found changes in brain chemistry following training of animals. Moreover, certain drugs impair or aid memory in animals, suggesting that drugs may be used to improve the memory of people in the future.

13. Psychologists have developed a number of specific techniques to improve memory. These include the keyword technique for memorizing foreign vocabulary, the method of loci for use in learning lists, organizing textbook material, and practicing enough so that overlearning—studying and rehearsing past the point of initial mastery—occurs.

KEY TERMS AND CONCEPTS

memory (p. 165)
sensory memory (165)
short-term memory (165)
long-term memory (165)
iconic memory (165)
echoic memory (165)
chunk (167)
episodic memory (169)
semantic memory (170)
rehearsal (171)
elaborative rehearsal (171)
mnemonics (171)
levels-of-processing theory (171)
tip-of-the-tongue phenomenon (173)
retrieval cue (173)
recall (174)
recognition (174)
flashbulb memories (174)
von Restorff effect (175)
constructive processes (175)
serial reproduction (175)
decay (178)
memory trace (178)
engram (178)
interference (178)
proactive interference (179)
retroactive interference (179)
Alzheimer's disease (180)
declarative knowledge (180)
procedural knowledge (180)
keyword technique (181)
method of loci (181)
overlearning (182)

FOR FURTHER STUDY AND APPLICATION

Norman, D. A. (1982). *Learning and memory.* San Francisco: Freeman.

This is a readable, useful account of memory, written by an expert in the field.

Neisser, U. (1982). *Memory observed: Remembering in natural context.* San Francisco: Freeman.

This is an excellent, comprehensive guide to remembering. You will not easily forget the fascinating phenomena reported in this volume.

Wells, G. L., & Loftus, E. A. (Eds.). (1984). *Eyewitness testimony: Psychological perspectives.* New York: Cambridge University Press.

This text provides a number of interesting, although technical, perspectives on the accuracy of, and the processes involved in, eyewitness testimony. It gives concrete suggestions for changing courtroom procedures to ensure the fairness of trials.

Luria, A. R. (1968). *The mind of a mnemonist.* New York: Basic Books.

This is the fascinating story of the person with an extraordinary memory. (The case began our chapter.) As the book makes clear, remembering so much is a mixed blessing.

Reason, J., & Mycielska, K. (1982). *Absent-minded? The psychology of mental lapses and everyday errors.* Englewood Cliffs, NJ: Prentice-Hall.

The title speaks for itself. The book contains a deft combination of laboratory and everyday examples of absent-mindedness.

ANSWERS TO REVIEW QUESTIONS

Review III: **1.** True **2.** c **3.** b **4.** False **5.** Declarative; procedural

CHAPTER 6

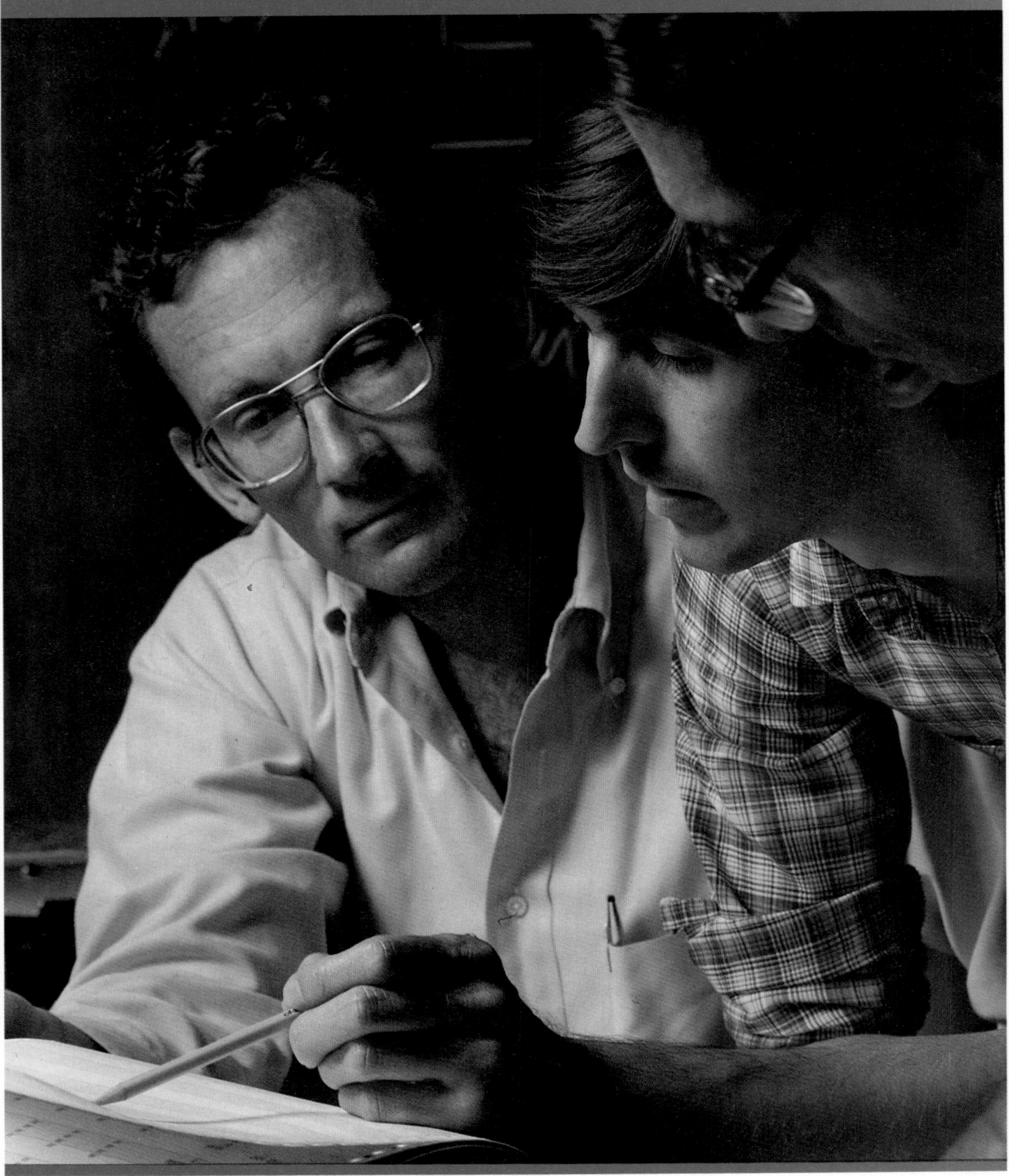

COGNITION AND LANGUAGE

PROLOGUE

LOOKING AHEAD

COGNITIVE PROCESSES IN PROBLEM SOLVING
Thinking and problem solving
Recap and review I

HINDRANCES TO PROBLEM SOLVING: BIASES IN JUDGMENT
What is obvious may not be right: Functional fixedness
When it's wrong to follow the rules: Biases in algorithms and heuristics
TRY IT! Problems to Ponder
The informed consumer of psychology: Solving problems creatively
PSYCHOLOGY AT WORK. Teaching College Students to Think
Recap and review II

COMMUNICATING OUR THOUGHTS: LANGUAGE
The language of language: Grammar
Developing a way with words: Language development
The roots of language: Understanding language acquisition
THE CUTTING EDGE. Exploring Human Language—by Communicating with Animals
Does language determine thought—or does thought determine language?
Categorizing the world: Using concepts
Recap and review III
PSYCHOLOGY LOOKS TOWARD THE 1990s. Capturing the Complexities of Common Sense

LOOKING BACK

KEY TERMS AND CONCEPTS

FOR FURTHER STUDY AND APPLICATION

PROLOGUE

Consider the lowly potato chip. Though scorned by gourmets, it is among most people's favorite snack foods, and a picnic would not be complete without a bowlful. No supermarket worth its salt (or potatoes, for that matter) would fail to have a large display devoted to the various brands.

Yet potato chips represent something of a problem to both their manufacturers and their sellers: After they are placed in the traditional cellophane packages in which they usually come, they take up too much space in warehouses and on supermarket shelves, adding greatly to their cost. Moreover, most obvious solutions to the problem—such as packing the chips more tightly—have failed; the result has typically been crushed and crumbled potato chips. Thus, the old-fashioned, cumbersome packaging devised by manufacturers early in potato-chip history has survived—that is, until a manufacturer finally devised a better way of making and packaging chips.

According to legend, the solution to the problem came when thinking turned from potato chips to nature. It was not until the manufacturers began to purposely shift their thoughts toward natural objects that were similar in size and shape to potato chips that they made any progress. One problem solver came up with a likely candidate: dry leaves that had fallen to the ground. Like potato chips, dry leaves crumble when pressed together, and in size and shape leaves and potato chips are not all that dissimilar. Moreover, the manufacturers noted another interesting characteristic of dry leaves that led to the ultimate solution to their problem: If the leaves were moistened, they could be packed tightly together, and after they had dried they were less apt to crumble.

Cognitive psychologists: *Psychologists who specialize in the study of cognition*
Cognition: *Higher mental processes by which we understand the world, process information, make judgments and decisions, and communicate knowledge to others*

In shifting their attention from potato chips to nature, then, the manufacturers had found their natural model for a new process of making potato chips. The chips could be moistened and cut into uniform shapes. They could then be neatly stacked in compact packages. The result of these efforts: Pringle's Potato Chips, which are now found on supermarket shelves across the country (Rice, 1984).

LOOKING AHEAD

Although few of us would claim that the invention of Pringle's represented a major culinary advance in the world of potato chips, it cannot be denied that the packaging process devised by the manufacturer is unique. More importantly, the processes underlying the discovery raise a number of issues of interest to psychologists: How do people use and retrieve information to devise innovative solutions to problems? How is such knowledge transformed, elaborated upon, and utilized? More basically, how do people think about, understand, and, using language, describe the world?

While gourmets may debate the gastronomic merits of Pringle's potato chips, it is clear that their unique packaging represents a creative solution to problems inherent in more traditionally shaped packages of potato chips. (Courtesy of Procter & Gamble)

These questions and others are addressed by **cognitive psychologists**, psychologists who specialize in the study of cognition. **Cognition** encompasses the higher mental processes of humans, including how people know and understand the world, process information, make judgments and decisions, and describe their knowledge and understanding to others.

In this chapter, we concentrate on the major processes of cognition: problem solving and language. We begin by examining problem solving. We discuss various ways to approach problems, means of generating solutions, and ways of making judgments about the usefulness and accuracy of solutions. We also examine some of the psychological obstacles to problem solving that decrease the probability of our developing useful solutions. Next, strategies for effectively solving problems are presented.

In the final part of the chapter we discuss language. We consider how people develop and acquire language, its basic characteristics, and whether language is a uniquely human skill. Finally, we explore the relationship between thinking and language.

After reading and studying this chapter, then, you will be able to

- Describe how people go about solving problems
- Identify the major hindrances to problem solving
- Suggest ways of improving problem-solving strategies
- Describe how language develops
- Identify the major theories of language acquisition
- Discuss the relationship between language and thought
- Describe classification systems called concepts
- Define and apply the key terms and concepts listed at the end of the chapter

COGNITIVE PROCESSES IN PROBLEM SOLVING

To an uninformed observer, it may have been a strange sight: a monkey cage in which boxes and sticks were strewn about, with a bunch of bananas hanging high in the cage, out of the monkey's reach. Yet to Wolfgang Köhler, intent on studying problem solving, the objects in the cage were carefully chosen to provide the cage's occupant, a chimp named Sultan, the tools to reach the bananas. In fact, if the experiment were to be made into a cartoon, it would probably show Sultan seeming to ponder the situation, after which a light bulb would suddenly come on above his head. It would then show him acting out his solution to the problem: He would stack the boxes on top of one another, use the stick to reach the bananas, and end up munching happily on the fruit.

Most of us have experienced a flash of awareness in which the solution to a problem suddenly becomes obvious. To understand the processes involved in this type of problem solving, Wolfgang Köhler, a German psychologist, carried out a lengthy series of experiments, starting about the time of World War I, in which he studied learning and problem-solving processes in chimps (Köhler, 1927). He exposed them to challenging situations, such as the one described above, in which the elements of the solution were all present; all that was necessary was for the chimps to put them together.

At first, the chimps would engage in a variety of trial-and-error attempts at getting to the bananas; they would throw the stick at the bananas, jump from the box, or leap wildly from the ground. Frequently, they would seem to give up in frustration, leaving the bananas dangling temptingly overhead. But then, in what looked like a sudden revelation, they would leave whatever activity they were involved in and stack the boxes so as to reach the bananas. Köhler called the cognitive processes underlying the chimps' behavior **insight**, a sudden awareness of the relationship between various elements that had previously appeared to be independent of one another.

Insight: *Sudden awareness of the relationship between various elements that had previously appeared to be independent of one another*

Although Köhler emphasized the apparent suddenness with which solutions were revealed, subsequent research showed the importance of experience and initial trial-and-error practice in problem solving. One study demonstrated that only chimps who had experience in playing with sticks could successfully solve

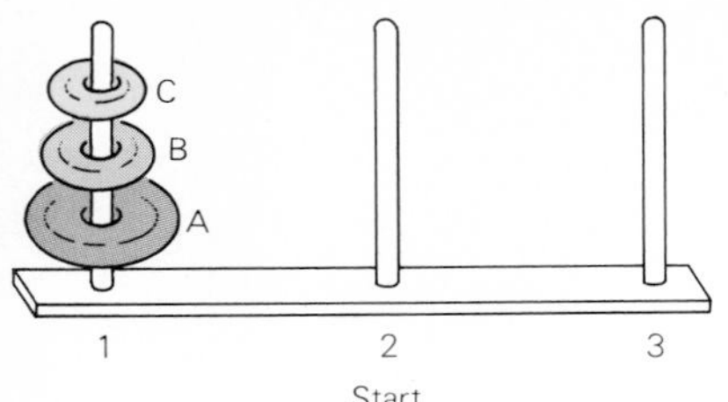

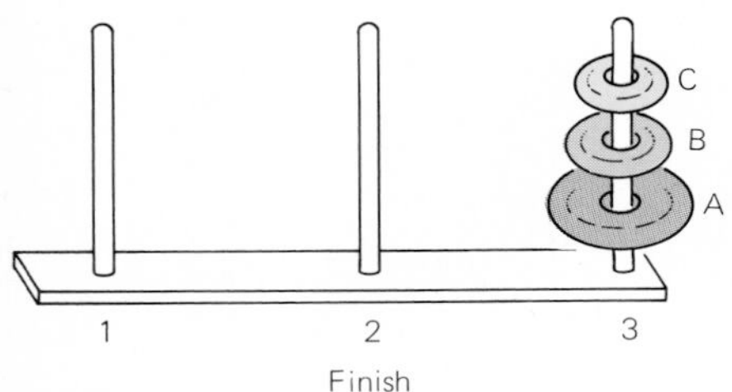

Figure 6-1
The goal of the Tower of Hanoi puzzle is to move all three disks from the first post to the last while preserving the original order of the disks, and using the smallest number of moves possible. Try it yourself before you look at the solution, which is listed according to the sequence of moves. (Solution: Move C to 3, B to 2, C to 2, A to 3, C to 1, B to 3, and C to 3.)

the problem; inexperienced monkeys never made the connection (Birch, 1945). Moreover, some researchers have suggested that the responses of the monkeys represented little more than the chaining together of previously learned responses, no different from the way that a pigeon learns, by trial and error, to peck a key (Epstein & Skinner, 1984). It is clear, then, that previous experience with the elements involved in a problem is crucial to finding its solution.

Thinking and Problem Solving

Cognitive psychologists today focus most of their attention on explicitly identifying the thinking processes underlying people's attempts to solve problems (Nickerson, Perkins, & Smith, 1985). Consider, for example, a problem known as the Tower of Hanoi puzzle—supposedly named after a group of monks in Hanoi who are working on a similar, although more complex, puzzle which, they believe, will bring an end to the world if solved (Raphael, 1976). (There is no need for immediate concern; according to one estimate, the complexity of the monk's puzzle is such that it will take about a trillion years to reach a solution.)

In the simpler version of the puzzle, illustrated in Figure 6-1, there are three posts on which three disks are to be placed in the order shown. The goal of the puzzle is to move all three disks to the third post in the same order, using the smallest number of moves possible. But there is a restriction: Only one disk can be moved at a time, and no disk can ever cover a smaller one during a move.

How do people solve this problem? Rather than waiting for a burst of insight, most people proceed using a logical, step-by-step strategy, and they are ultimately able to come up with the solution indicated in the figure caption. The process they use exemplifies the stages that people move through during problem-solving activities; these stages, summarized in Figure 6-2, include preparation, production, and judgment (Bourne, Dominowski, & Loftus, 1979).

Preparation: Understanding the Problem When presented with a problem such as the Tower of Hanoi, most people begin by trying to ensure that they thoroughly understand the problem. If the problem is novel, they will likely pay particular attention to any restrictions placed on coming to a solution and the initial status of the components of the problem. If the type of problem is familiar, they are apt to spend considerably less time in this stage.

The outcome of the preparation stage is the development of their own personal, cognitive representation of the problem in their mind. In a sense, it consists of putting a problem into a personal framework. It may be divided into subparts, or people may try to simplify the task by ignoring some of the information that has been given to them in the initial presentation of the problem.

Production: Generating Solutions If a problem is relatively simple, a direct solution may be already stored in long-term memory, and all that is necessary is to retrieve the appropriate solution. If the solution cannot be found, a process by which possible solutions are generated and compared with information in long- and short-term memory is instigated.

Algorithm (AL go rith em): *A set of rules that, if followed, guarantee a solution, though the reason they work may not be understood by the person using them*

Most complex problem solving involves the use of algorithms and heuristics. An **algorithm** is a set of rules which, if followed, guarantees a solution, even if the reason it works is not understood. For example, you may know that the length of the third side of a right triangle may be found by using the formula $a^2 + b^2 = c^2$. You may not have the foggiest notion why it works, but it is an

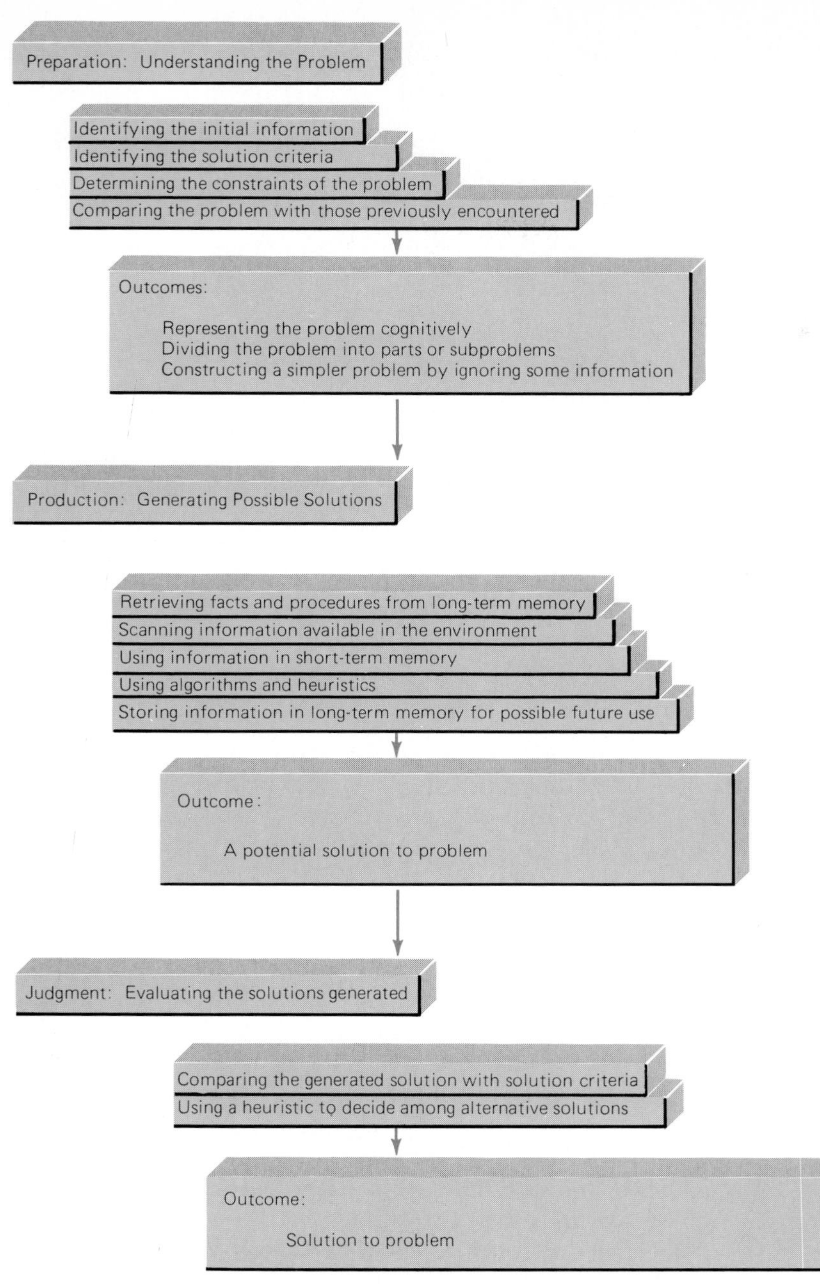

Figure 6-2
The stages of problem solving.

algorithm that is always accurate and that provides you with a solution to a particular problem.

A **heuristic**, in contrast, is a rule of thumb that may lead to a solution, but is not guaranteed to do so (Groner, Groner, & Bischof, 1983). For example, a heuristic that chess players often follow is to gain control of the center of the board. It doesn't guarantee that they will win, but it does increase their chances. Similarly, students may follow the heuristic of preparing for a test by ignoring the assigned textbook reading, and studying only their lecture notes—a strategy that may or may not pay off.

Heuristic (hyur ISS tik): *A rule of thumb that may bring about a solution to a problem but is not guaranteed to do so*

Because many problems do not have clearly applicable algorithms, people

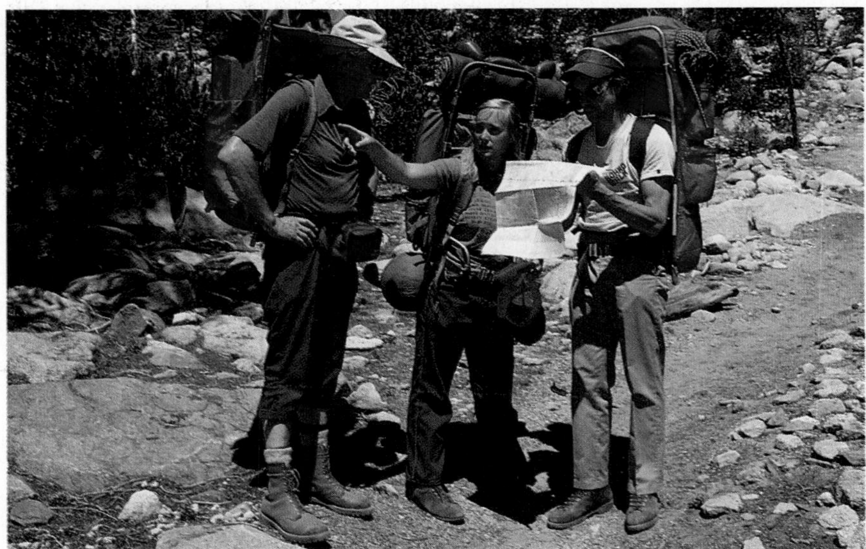

Choosing the most direct route to get to a final destination is an example of a means-ends analysis. Each choice in routing brings these people closer to their ultimate goal of arriving at their destination. (© Tim Davis/Photo Researchers, Inc.)

Means-ends analysis: *Repeated testing to determine and reduce the distance between real and desired outcomes in problem solving*

tend to fall back on heuristics during the production stage of problem solving. Probably the most frequently applied heuristic is a means-ends analysis. In a **means-ends analysis**, a person will repeatedly test for differences between the desired outcome and what currently exists, trying each time to reduce the difference between the possible solution and desired outcome. Each change, then, brings the solution closer. For example, people using a means-ends analysis to search for the correct sequence of roads to get to a city that they can see in the distance would analyze their solutions in terms of how much closer each individual choice of roadways brings them to the ultimate goal of arriving at the city. Such a strategy is effective, though, only if there is a direct solution to the problem. If the problem is such that indirect steps have to be taken that appear to *increase* the discrepancy between the current state and the solution, means-ends analyses can be counterproductive. In our example, then, if roadways are laid out in such a way that a person must temporarily move *away* from the city in order to reach it, a means-ends analysis will keep people from reaching their goal.

Judgment: Evaluating the Solutions That Have Been Generated The final step in problem solving consists of judging the adequacy of a solution. Often, this is a simple matter; if there is a clear solution—as in the Tower of Hanoi problem—a person will know immediately if he or she has been successful. On the other hand, if the solution is less concrete or if there is no single correct solution (such as with the potato-chip packaging problem that began this chapter), evaluating solutions becomes more difficult.

If there is more than one solution to a problem, people must decide which alternative is best. In making up their minds, people employ decision-making heuristics, the most common of which are the representativeness and the availability heuristics.

Representativeness heuristic (hyur ISS tik): *A rule in which people and things are judged by the degree to which they represent a certain category*

The **representativeness heuristic** is used when people base their decisions on whether a given example is a member of a particular category by evaluating how representative of that category the example is. Suppose, for instance, that as an owner of a fast-food store, you have been robbed many times by people who come into your store looking nervous and shifty. The next time someone who fits this description enters your store, it is likely that—if you employ the representativeness heuristic—you will assume that danger lurks, since your prior experience suggests that the person is likely to be a member of a class of people you have come to know as "thief."

The **availability heuristic** involves judging the probability of an event by how easily the event can be recalled from memory (Kahneman & Tversky, 1973). According to this heuristic, we assume that events we recall easily are likely to have occurred more frequently in the past, and we therefore assume that the same sort of event is more likely to occur in the future. The availability heuristic explains why, after we have heard about an airplane crash, our estimate of the likelihood of being in an airplane crash rises temporarily.

Availability heuristic (hyur ISS tik): *A rule for judging the probability that an event will occur by the ease with which it can be recalled from memory*

Theoretically, if the heuristics and information we rely on to make decisions are appropriate and valid, we can make accurate choices among problem solutions. However, as we see in the next section of the chapter, there are several kinds of hindrances and biases involved in problem solving that affect the quality of the decisions we make.

RECAP AND REVIEW I

Recap

- Cognitive psychologists specialize in the study of the higher mental processes of humans, including problem solving, knowing, reasoning, judging, and decision making.
- One major goal of cognitive psychologists is to identify the thinking processes that underlie problem solving. Typically, people pass through a series of three steps in problem solving: preparation, production, and judgment.
- People frequently use algorithms (sets of rules that, if followed, guarantee a solution will be reached) and heuristics (rules of thumb that may lead to a solution). Two major heuristics are representativeness and availability heuristics.

Review

1. "Debbie, come see if you can solve this puzzle in the newspaper. I have a general idea of how to complete it, but I just can't quite get there."
   "Let's see, Joel. Oh, I know! There's a three-step solution I know for problems like this. Watch. There, it's finished."
   Whereas Joel used a(n) ________________ to attempt to solve the problem, Debbie was successful by using a(n) ________________.
2. Ever since he was attacked by a wild boar, Gary has tried to keep his distance when he sees one. Which decision-making heuristic does Gary employ?
   a. Availability **b.** Means-end analysis **c.** Algorithm **d.** Representativeness
3. "Aha!" said Michael. Seemingly out of nowhere, he had the idea of bringing together two unrelated objects to solve the problem. Köhler would have labeled his cognitive process as ________________.
4. The three stages of problem solving include preparation, ________________, and judgment.
5. The availability heuristic involves judging problem-solving capabilities by measuring the speed with which a problem is solved. True or false?

(Answers to review questions are at bottom of page 194.)

HINDRANCES TO PROBLEM SOLVING: BIASES IN JUDGMENT

Consider the following problem-solving test (Duncker, 1945): You are presented with a set of tacks, candles, and matches in small boxes, and told your goal is

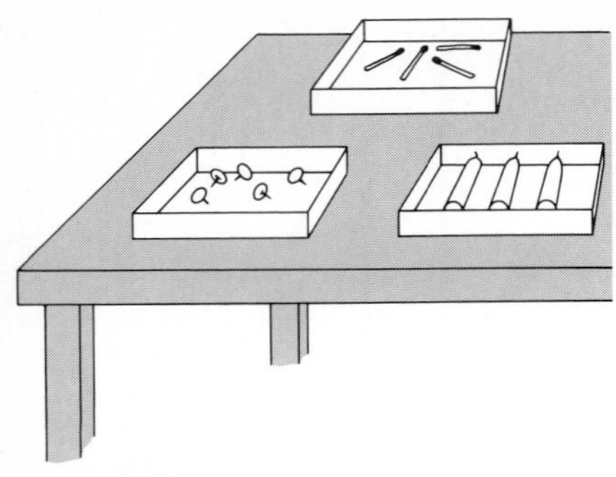

Figure 6-3
The problem here is to place three candles at eye level on a nearby door so that the wax will not drip on the floor as the candles burn—using only the materials in the figure (tacks, candles, and matches in small boxes).

to place three candles at eye level on a nearby door, so that wax will not drip on the floor as the candles burn (see Figure 6-3). How would you solve this challenge?

If you have difficulty solving the problem, you are not alone: Most people are unable to solve it if it is presented to them in the manner illustrated in the figure, in which the objects are located *inside* the boxes. On the other hand, if the objects were to be presented to you *beside* the boxes, just resting on the table, chances are you would solve the problem much more readily—which, in case you are wondering, requires tacking up the boxes, and then placing the candles on top of them. (See Figure 6-4.)

What Is Obvious May Not Be Right: Functional Fixedness

Functional fixedness (FIX ed ness): *The tendency to think of an object in terms of its most typical use*

The reason for most people's difficulty with the problem of Figure 7-3 is a phenomenon known as **functional fixedness**, the tendency to think of an object only in terms of its typical use. Functional fixedness occurs because the boxes are seen simply as containers for the objects they hold when the objects are first presented inside them, rather than as a potential part of the solution. In the same manner, the potato-chip problem we discussed at the beginning of the chapter was solved when the manufacturer overcame functional fixedness and viewed the potato chip in a new light.

Functional fixedness is illustrative of one of a number of biases in problem solving and judgment making. Although cognitive approaches to problem solving suggest that thinking proceeds along fairly rational, logical lines as a person confronts a problem and considers various solutions, there are actually a number of factors acting to hinder the development of creative, appropriate, and accurate solutions to problems.

When It's Wrong to Follow the Rules: Biases in Algorithms and Heuristics

Although algorithms and heuristics most frequently help people to solve problems, their use may sometimes backfire, illustrating another type of hindrance to problem solving. It is possible to apply algorithms and heuristics to situations in which they are not relevant, thereby leading to incorrect solutions. It is also possible to apply them incorrectly. Consider, for example, the following information:

> There are two programs in a high school. Boys are a majority (65 percent) in program A and a minority (45 percent) in program B. There are an equal number of classes in each of the two programs. You enter a class at random and observe that 55 percent of the students are boys. What is your best guess—does the class belong to program A or to program B? (Kahneman & Tversky, 1972, p. 433.)

Most people rely on the heuristic of representativeness to come up with the answer that the class belongs to program A—which is incorrect. People assume that just because there are more boys in this class, and there are more boys than

ANSWERS TO REVIEW QUESTIONS

Review I: **1.** Heuristic, algorithm **2.** d **3.** Insight **4.** Production **5.** False girls in program A, that this particular class is more likely to represent program A.

However, there are several considerations that lead to a different—and more correct—conclusion. First, recall that there are equal numbers of classes in each of the two programs, and therefore any class that one enters is equally likely to be in either program. Moreover, the specific percentage of boys found in the class (55 percent) is halfway between the percentage of boys in program A (65 percent) and the percentage of boys in program B (45 percent). In fact, then, the most reasonable answer is that it is no more likely for the class to be in either program A or B. In this case, the representativeness heuristic leads people astray.

The availability heuristic, in which judgments of the probability of an event are based on how easily the event can be recalled, is also a source of error in problem solving. For instance, suppose you were asked to choose a word of at

TRY IT!

PROBLEMS TO PONDER

In their study of problem-solving strategies, psychologists have devised a long list of problems to use in their research. Here are three (all taken from Anderson, 1980) you might want to attempt to solve:

1. In the following grid, draw four straight lines so that they pass through all nine dots—without lifting your pencil from the page.

•   •   •

•   •   •

•   •   •

2. A man climbs a mountain on Saturday, leaving at daybreak and arriving at the top near sundown. He spends the night at the top. The next day, Sunday, he leaves at daybreak and heads down the mountain, following the same path that he climbed the day before. The question is this: Will there be any time during the second day when he will be at exactly the same point on the mountain as he was at that time on the first day?

3. A couple is planning to take a plane to New York and then a boat to Greece. Three airlines fly from their hometown to New York, and five steamship lines go from New York to Greece. How many ways does this give them of getting from their home to Greece?

Answers

1. Think beyond the outlines of the figure, and you might be able to come up with this solution (Anderson, p. 145):

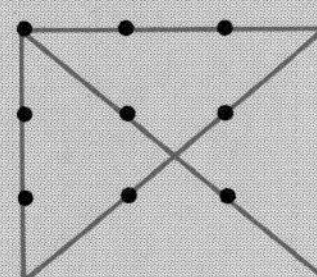

2. The way to answer this question is by drawing a graph (Anderson, p. 155). Remember, the goal is not to determine the time, but just to indicate whether there is an exact time.

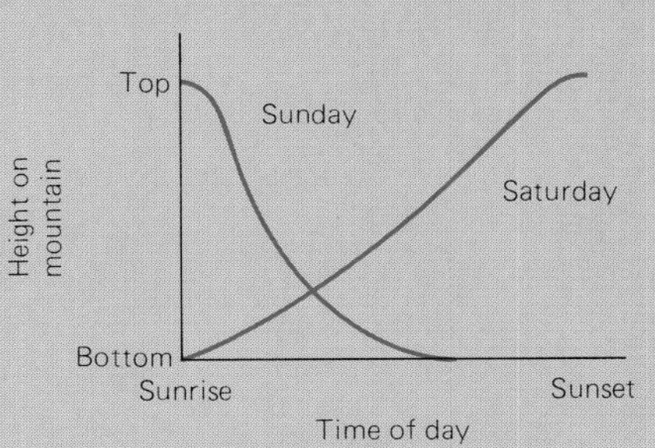

3. 15 (Anderson, p. 245). The solution can be found graphically by sorting out the possibilities:

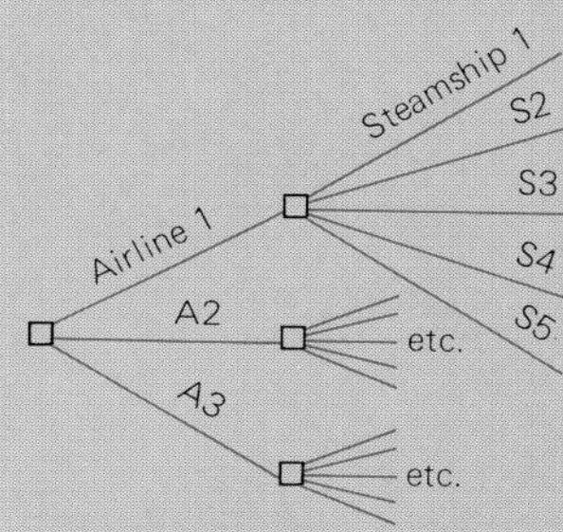

least three letters at random from a dictionary. Would you think it more likely that the first or the third letter of the chosen word would be an "r"?

Most people tend to answer that the first letter would more likely be an "r," which is erroneous ("r" actually occurs more frequently as the third letter than the first in the English language). The reason for the mistaken judgment? It is considerably easier to retrieve words from memory that start with a given letter (run, rats, root) than it is to retrieve words based on their third letter (bar, tart, purse).

The Informed Consumer of Psychology: Solving Problems Creatively

If presented with the potato-chip problem that began the chapter, do you think you would have come up with as creative a solution? While not all of us could have come up with an idea that fit the necessities of the situation, there are certain things that anyone can do to increase success and creativity in problem solving. Among them:

- Redefine a problem. When facing a difficult task, one way of finding a solution is to redefine the problem. The boundaries and assumptions that are held can be modified; the problem can be rephrased at a more abstract or more concrete level, depending on how it is initially presented; or it can be divided into separate parts (Rice, 1984).
- Use analogies. When trying to find a better way to package potato chips, the manufacturer of Pringle's turned to a natural phenomenon to come up with a solution. In fact, the use of analogies represents a good general strategy for problem solving. One particularly effective means of coming up with analogies is to look for them in the animal kingdom when the problem concerns people, and in physics or chemistry when the problem concerns inanimate objects.
- Use heuristics. As we mentioned earlier, heuristics are rules of thumb that can help bring about a solution to a problem. If the nature of the problem is such that it has a single correct answer, and a heuristic is available—or can be constructed—its use will frequently assist in developing a solution.
- Experiment with different solutions. Don't be afraid to experiment; using different routes to solutions (verbal, mathematical, graphic, even acting out a situation) can be very effective. Try coming up with every conceivable idea you can, no matter how wild or bizarre some may seem at first. After you have come up with a list of solutions, you can go back over each and try to think of ways of making what at first appeared impractical seem more feasible.

Although they vary in applicability depending on the nature of the problems, each of these approaches to problem solving has proved effective. Moreover, as we discuss in the accompanying Psychology at Work box, psychologists are devising new techniques designed to help people think more creatively in their attempts to resolve the problems they encounter.

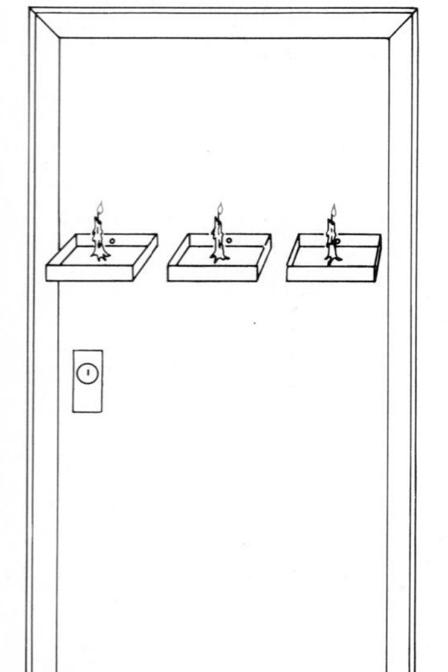

Figure 6-4
A solution to the problem posed in Figure 6-3 involves tacking the boxes to the door and placing the candles on the boxes.

PSYCHOLOGY AT WORK

TEACHING COLLEGE STUDENTS TO THINK

Can people be taught to think?

According to researchers involved in the Cognitive Processes Research Group at the University of Massachusetts at Amherst, they certainly can be. The researchers have developed a technique called Pair Problem Solving, in which two students work together on specially designed problems (Lochhead, 1985). The partners alternate in taking one of two roles: One partner reads a description of the problem and tries to reach a solution by thinking it through out loud, while the other listens. The listener is not passive, however; he or she continually checks for the partner's accuracy, and constantly urges the problem solver to think aloud. Thinking aloud is a critical part of the program, because it allows the listener to examine any erroneous assumptions and check the accuracy of the speaker, as well as making speakers themselves aware of fuzziness in their logic.

To facilitate the Pair Problem Solving process, students are sometimes given samples of problems, with illustrations of how experienced problem solvers attack and solve them (see Figure 6-5). By demonstrating how problems must be broken down into small steps, as well as how important initial assumptions are, the sample problems play an important role in the development of the participants' thinking processes.

Does the program work? Accumulating evidence from this program and others with similar aims indicate that it does (Konnold, 1985; Weinstein, 1986). The day may come, then, when cognitive psychologists routinely teach students not only to increase the success with which they are able to solve problems but to improve their basic thinking skills as well.

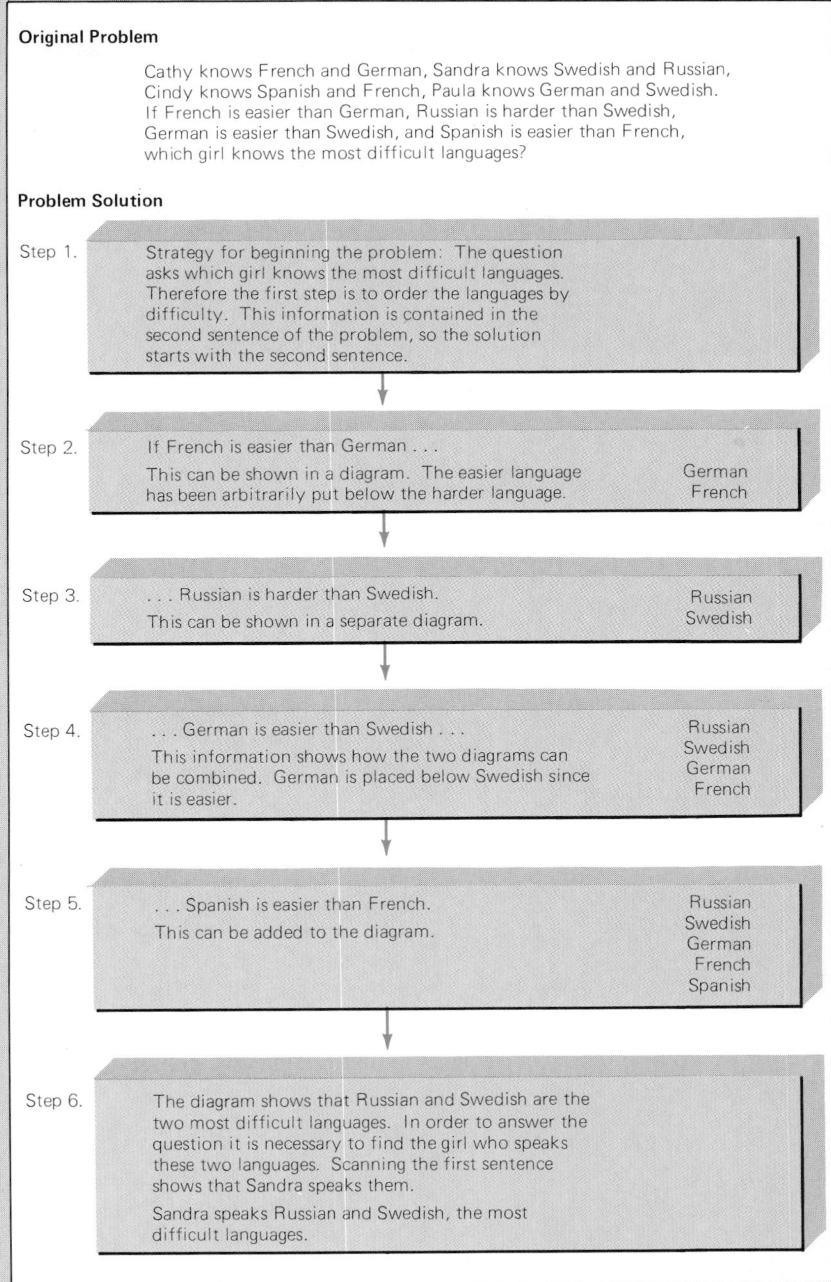

Original Problem
Cathy knows French and German, Sandra knows Swedish and Russian, Cindy knows Spanish and French, Paula knows German and Swedish. If French is easier than German, Russian is harder than Swedish, German is easier than Swedish, and Spanish is easier than French, which girl knows the most difficult languages?
Problem Solution
Step 1.
Strategy for beginning the problem: The question asks which girl knows the most difficult languages. Therefore the first step is to order the languages by difficulty. This information is contained in the second sentence of the problem, so the solution starts with the second sentence.
Step 2.
If French is easier than German . . .
This can be shown in a diagram. The easier language has been arbitrarily put below the harder language.
German
French
Step 3.
. . . Russian is harder than Swedish.
This can be shown in a separate diagram.
Russian
Swedish
Step 4.
. . . German is easier than Swedish . . .
This information shows how the two diagrams can be combined. German is placed below Swedish since it is easier.
Russian
Swedish
German
French
Step 5.
. . . Spanish is easier than French.
This can be added to the diagram.
Russian
Swedish
German
French
Spanish
Step 6.
The diagram shows that Russian and Swedish are the two most difficult languages. In order to answer the question it is necessary to find the girl who speaks these two languages. Scanning the first sentence shows that Sandra speaks them.
Sandra speaks Russian and Swedish, the most difficult languages.

Figure 6-5
A problem used in teaching thinking skills, with an illustration of the way in which experienced problem solvers work it out. (*Lochhead, 1985.*)

RECAP AND REVIEW II

Recap

- Among the hindrances to problem solving are functional fixedness, faulty use of heuristics, and method of problem presentation.
- Some methods of solving problems creatively include redefining a problem, using analogies, using heuristics, and experimenting with different solutions.

Review

1. Tom tried what he thought were all the possible ways to solve the problem, then claimed flatly that it could not be done. He was very surprised when a friend came over and solved it in a way he just hadn't considered. Tom was a victim of ______________.
2. Constructing analogies to try to solve a problem usually ends up confusing the process and should be avoided. True or false?
3. Generating an array of different solutions can be a good first step toward solving a problem. True or false?
4. Research has shown that thinking is a process that cannot be taught. True or false?

(Answers to review questions are at bottom of page 200.)

COMMUNICATING OUR THOUGHTS: LANGUAGE

'Twas brillig, and the slithy toves
  Did gyre and gimble in the wabe:
All mimsy were the borogoves,
  And the mome raths outgrabe.

Although few of us have ever come face to face with a tove, we have little difficulty in discerning that in Lewis Carroll's (1872) poem ''Jabberwocky,'' the phrase ''slithy toves'' contains an adjective, ''slithy,'' and the noun it modifies, ''toves.''

Our ability to make sense out of nonsense, if the nonsense follows typical rules of language, illustrates both the sophistication of human language capabilities and the complexity of the processes that underlie the development and use of language. The way in which people are able to use **language**—the systematic, meaningful arrangement of symbols—clearly represents an important ability, one that is indispensable for communicating with others. But language is not only central to communication, it is closely tied to the very way in which we think about and understand the world; there is a crucial link between cognition and language. It is not surprising, then, that psychologists have devoted considerable attention to studying the topic of language.

Language: *The systematic, meaningful arrangement of symbols*

The Language of Language: Grammar

In order to understand how language develops, and its relationship to cognition, we first need to discuss some of the formal elements that constitute language. The basic structure of language rests on grammar. **Grammar** is the framework of rules that determine how our thoughts can be expressed.

Grammar: *The framework of rules that determine how our thoughts can be expressed*

Grammar deals with three major components of language: phonology, syntax, and semantics. **Phonology** refers to the sounds (called **phonemes**) we make when we speak and how we use those sounds to produce meaning by placing them into the form of words. Speakers of English use just forty-six basic phonemes to produce words, while the basic phonemes of other languages range in number from a mere fifteen to as many as eighty-five. The differences in pho-

Phonology (fone OL ojee): *The study of the sounds we make when we speak and of how we use those sounds to produce meaning by forming them into words*

Phonemes (FONE eems): *The smallest units of sound used to form words* nemes underlie one reason why people have difficulty in learning other languages: For example, to the speaker of Japanese, a language that does not have an "r" phoneme, English words such as "roar" present some difficulty.

Syntax refers to the rules that indicate how words are joined together to form sentences. Every language has intricate rules that guide the order in which words may be strung together to communicate meaning. English-speakers have no difficulty in knowing that *"Radio down the turn"* is not an appropriate sequence, while *"Turn down the radio"* is. Moreover, the importance of appropriate syntax is demonstrated by the changes in meaning that stem from modifications in the order of words in the following three sentences: "John kidnapped the boy," "John, the kidnapped boy," and "The boy kidnapped John."

Syntax (SIN tax): *The rules that indicate how words are joined to form sentences*

The third major component of language is semantics. **Semantics** refers to the rules governing the meaning of words and sentences of language. Semantic rules allow us to use words to convey the most subtle of nuances. For instance, we are able to make the distinction between "The truck hit Laura" (which we would be likely to say if we had just seen the vehicle hitting Laura) and "Laura was hit by a truck" (which we would probably say if asked why Laura was missing class while she recuperated).

Semantics (seh MAN tix): *The rules governing the meaning of words and sentences*

Despite the complexities of language, most people learn its grammar effortlessly and are able to communicate without referring to a complicated set of rules. We turn now to how such sophisticated abilities are acquired.

Developing a Way with Words: Language Development

To parents, the sound of their infant babbling and cooing is music to their ears (except, perhaps, at three o'clock in the morning). These sounds also serve an important function: they mark the first step on the road to the development of language. When children **babble**—making speechlike but meaningless sounds—they actually produce, at one time or another, all the sounds found in every language, not just the one to which they are exposed. Babbling occurs from around 3 to 6 months of age, after which time the sounds begin to be more specific to the particular language the child will first speak. By the time the child is 9 or 10 months old, sounds that are not in the language are dropped. It is then a short step to the production of actual words. In English, these are typically short words that start with a consonant such as "b," "d," "m," "p," or "t"—helping to explain why "mama" and "dada" are so often among the first words to be said. Of course, even before they produce their first words, children are capable of understanding a fair amount of the language they hear. Language comprehension, then, precedes language production.

Babble: *Speechlike but meaningless sounds*

After the age of 1 year, children begin to learn more complicated forms of language. They produce two-word combinations, which become the building blocks of sentences, and there is an acceleration in the number of different words they are capable of using. For example, by the age of 2 years the average child has a vocabulary of more than fifty words. Just six months later, the vocabulary has grown to several hundred. At that time, children can produce short sentences, although they use **telegraphic speech**—sentences that literally sound as if they were part of a telegram, in which words not critical to the message are dropped. Rather than saying, "I showed you the book," a child using telegraphic speech might say, "I show book," and "I am drawing a dog" might become "Drawing dog." As the child gets older, of course, the use of telegraphic speech declines and sentences become increasingly more complex (see Table 6-1).

Telegraphic speech: *Sentences containing only the most essential words*

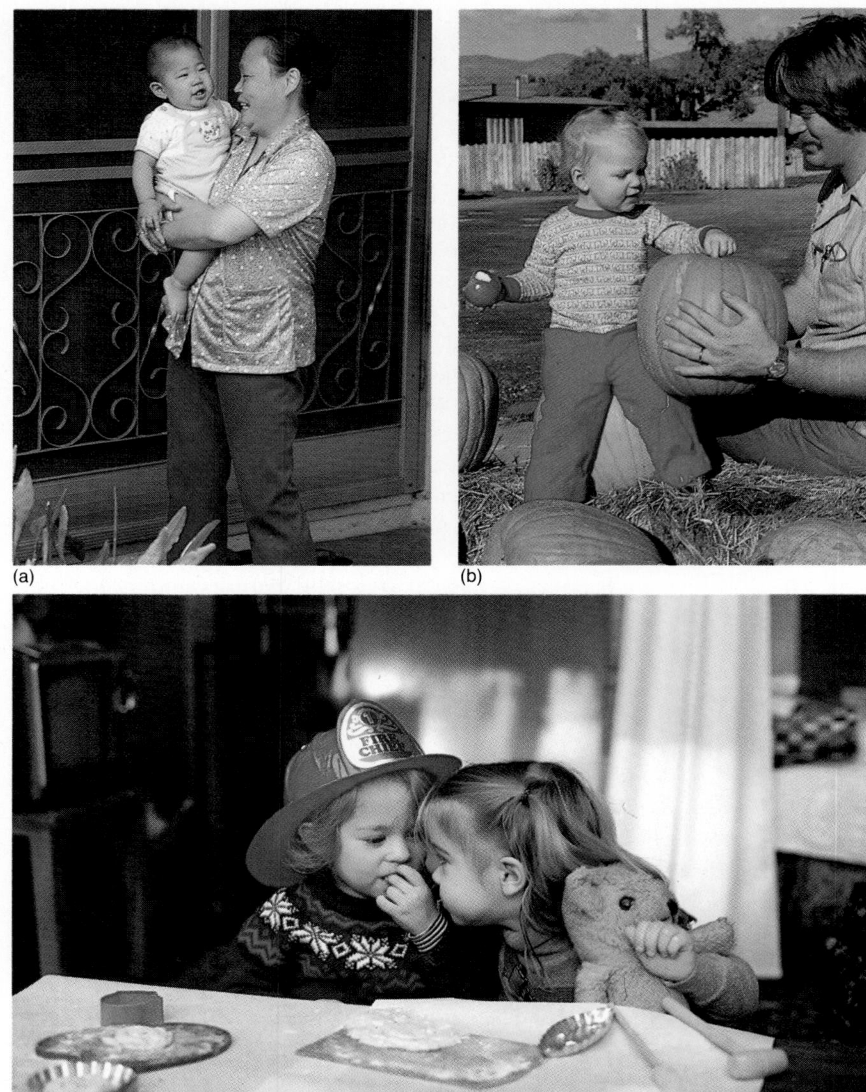

As children develop, their language becomes more and more sophisticated. (*a*) During the earliest period, children babble and begin to make the sounds appropriate to their particular language. (*b*) Later, they learn to produce specific, meaningful words. (*c*) By the time they are 5, they are able to communicate in a surprisingly sophisticated fashion, having acquired most of the basic rules of language. (*a*) (John Lei/Stock, Boston), (*b*) (David Frazier/Photo Researchers, Inc.) (*c*) (Cary Wolinsky/Stock, Boston)

Overregularization: *Applying rules of speech in instances in which they are inappropriate*

By the time children are 3 years old, they learn to make plurals by adding ''s'' to nouns, and they are able to form the past tense by adding ''ed'' to verbs. This ability also leads to errors, since children tend to apply rules indiscriminately. This phenomenon is known as **overregularization**, whereby children apply rules even when the application results in an error. Thus, although it is correct to say ''he walked'' for the past tense of ''walk,'' the ''ed'' rule doesn't work quite so well when children say ''he runned'' for the past tense of ''run.''

Although a full vocabulary and the ability to use more subtle grammatical

ANSWERS TO REVIEW QUESTIONS

Review II: **1.** Functional fixedness **2.** False **3.** True **4.** False

TABLE 7-1

Children's imitation of sentences, showing decline of telegraphic speech

	EVE, 25½ MONTHS	ADAM, 28½ MONTHS	HELEN, 30 MONTHS	IAN, 31½ MONTHS	JIMMY, 32 MONTHS	JUNE, 35½ MONTHS
I showed you the book.	I show book.	(I show) book.	C	I show you the book.	C	Show you the book.
I am very tall.	(My) tall.	I (very) tall.	I very tall.	I'm very tall.	Very tall.	I very tall.
It goes in a big box.	Big box.	Big box.	In big box.	It goes in the box.	C	C
I am drawing a dog.	Drawing dog.	I draw dog.	I drawing dog.	Dog.	C	C
I will read the book.	Read book.	I will read book.	I read the book.	I read the book.	C	C
I can see a cow.	See cow.	I want see cow.	C	Cow.	C	C
I will not do that again.	Do—again.	I will that again.	I do that.	I again.	C	C

C = correct imitation
Source: Brown & Fraser, 1963.

rules is not attained until later, much of children's acquisition of the basic rules of language is complete by the time they are 5. For example, if you showed a 5-year-old boy a blindfolded doll and asked, "Is the doll easy or hard to see," he would have great difficulty answering the question. In fact, if he were asked to make the doll easier to see, he would probably try to take off the doll's blindfold. On the other hand, 9-year-olds have little difficulty understanding the question, realizing that the doll's blindfold has nothing to do with an observer's ability to see the doll (Chomsky, 1969).

The Roots of Language: Understanding Language Acquisition

While anyone who is around children will notice the enormous strides that are made in language development throughout childhood, the reasons for this rapid growth are less obvious. Two major approaches have been put forward: one based on learning theory and the other on innate processes.

The learning-theory approach suggests that language acquisition follows the principles of reinforcement and conditioning we discussed in Chapter 4. For example, a child who utters the word "mama" is hugged and praised by her mother, thereby reinforcing the behavior and making its repetition more likely. This view suggests that children first learn to speak by being rewarded for making sounds that approximate speech. Ultimately, through a process of shaping, language becomes more and more like adult speech (Skinner, 1957).

The learning-theory approach is less successful when it comes to explaining the acquisition of language rules. The problem occurs because children are reinforced not only when they use proper language, but also when they respond incorrectly. For example, parents answer "Why the dog won't eat?" as eagerly as they do the correct "Why won't the dog eat?"; both sentences are understood equally well. Learning-theory views do not seem, then, to provide the full story of language acquisition.

Universal grammar: *An underlying structure shared by all languages, the basis of Chomsky's theory that certain language characteristics are based in the brain's structure and are, therefore, common to all people*

Language-acquisition device: *A neural system of the brain hypothesized to permit understanding of language*

An alternative model is provided by Noam Chomsky (1968, 1978), who argues that innate mechanisms play an important role in learning a language. He suggests that humans are born with an innate linguistic capability that emerges primarily as a function of maturation. According to his analysis, all the world's languages share a similar underlying structure—what he calls a **universal grammar**—which is based on the structure and functions of the human brain. The brain has a neural system, the **language-acquisition device**, which not only permits the understanding of the structure of a language, but also provides people with strategies and techniques for learning the unique characteristics of a native language. According to this view, then, language is a uniquely human phenomenon brought about by the presence of the language-acquisition device.

Chomsky's view, as you might suspect, is not without its critics, particularly among learning theorists, who contend that the fact that animals can seemingly be taught the fundamentals of human language (see the Cutting Edge box) argues against the innate view. The issue of how humans acquire language, then, remains hotly contested.

THE CUTTING EDGE

EXPLORING HUMAN LANGUAGE—BY COMMUNICATING WITH ANIMALS

Deaf, mute, and retarded since birth, 23-year-old Sandra was written off by her doctors as a hopeless case. But in the past two years the once hostile, violent young woman has been transformed. Today, she can request her favorite foods and communicate with her teachers—thanks to a computer-based language that was originally developed for the study of chimpanzees. "Sandra's learned to express herself," says Steve Watson, director of the Developmental Learning Center at Atlanta's Georgia Regional Hospital, where she lives. "That's a way of being set free" (Keerdoja, 1985, p. 66).

The language that liberated Sandra is **Yerkish**, initially developed at the Yerkes Primate Center in Atlanta to study the communicative abilities of chimpanzees. It consists of some 225 geometric symbols, each representing a common English word, that can be pressed on a computer keyboard to make sentences (Savage-Rumbaugh, Rumbaugh, & Boysen, 1980).

Yerkish was developed to investigate an enduring issue that has long puzzled psychologists: whether language is uniquely human or whether lower animals are

Yerkish: *A language system, taught to chimpanzees, that consists of about 225 geometric symbols representing English words*

Figure 6-7
Kanzi's ability to communicate in Yerkish has implications for the treatment of humans with language disabilities. (Elizabeth Robert.)

able to acquire it as well. It is clear that many animals communicate with one another in some rudimentary forms, such as fiddler crabs who wave their claws to signal, bees whose dance indicates the direction in which food will be found, or certain birds who say "zick, zick" during courtship and "kia" when they are about to fly away. However, researchers have yet to demonstrate conclusively that these animals use true language, which is characterized in part by the ability to produce and communicate new and unique meanings following a formal grammar.

Psychologists have, however, been able to teach chimps to communicate at surprisingly high levels. For instance, Kanzi, a 4-year-old pygmy chimpanzee, has Yerkish linguistic skills that are close to those of a 1- or 2-year-old human being (Keerdoja, 1985). (See Figure 6-7.) Another chimp, Washoe, was taught American Sign Language (originally developed for the deaf), and has been able to join signs together to form new meanings. For example, after learning the sign "more" in reference to tickling (which she loved), she used the sign later in terms of requesting more food and more brushing (Klima & Bellugi, 1973). Moreover, chimps can combine the signs into "sentences," can use them to express humor, to be deceptive, and even to form new words by combining different signs (Ristau & Robbins, 1982).

Despite the skills displayed by such animals, the language that they use still lacks a grammar and other sufficiently complex and novel constructions to approach human capabilities (Terrace, 1985). In fact, critics contend that the chimps are displaying skills no different from those used by a dog who learns to lie down on command in order to get a reward.

Most evidence, then, still supports the contention that humans are better equipped to produce and organize language in the form of meaningful sentences. But the question of whether animals are capable of being taught to communicate in a way that closely resembles human language remains a controversial one (Terrace, Pettito, Sanders, & Bever, 1981; Herman & Forestell, 1985). In the meantime, ongoing research into the issue promises to produce even more sophisticated techniques for improving the communication abilities of people such as Sandra.

Does Language Determine Thought—or Does Thought Determine Language?

When an Eskimo girl peers outside her igloo and sees that it is snowing, she doesn't simply announce, "It's snowing." For Eskimos have at their disposal more than twenty individual words to describe different sorts of snow. This linguistic prowess suggests an important question: Do Eskimos *think* about the snow differently than do English-speakers?

The answer to that question is controversial. According to the **linguistic-relativity hypothesis**, language shapes and, in fact, may determine the way people of a particular culture perceive and understand the world (Whorf, 1956). According to this view, Eskimos think about snow in a way that is qualitatively different from the way English-speakers think about it, since the range of linguistic categories provided by the Eskimo language permits finer discriminations than the more limited English language.

Linguistic-relativity hypothesis: *The theory claiming that language shapes and may even determine the way people perceive and understand the world*

Let us consider another possibility, however. Suppose that, instead of language being the *cause* of certain ways of thinking about the world, language is a *result* of thinking about and experiencing relevant stimuli in the environment. In this view, thought *produces* language. The only reason Eskimos have more words for "snow" than we do is because snow is considerably more relevant to them than it is to people in most other cultures. According to this point of view, if we were to move to the arctic circle (or become ski bums), we would be perfectly capable of differentiating various types of snow. Our language usage might not be particularly eloquent (we might say, "deep, crunchy, hard-packing snow that is going to be on the ground all winter"), but we would have no trouble perceiving and thinking about the differences in snow.

Most research has not supported the linguistic-relativity hypothesis, leading

According to the linguistic relativity hypothesis, Eskimos think about snow in a qualitatively different manner than people from other cultures because the Eskimo language provides more precise categorizations for different kinds of snow. (B. & C. Alexander/Black Star)

cognitive psychologists to feel that the proposition that language determines thought is inaccurate. Instead, it appears more appropriate to conclude that cognition influences language.

On the other hand, language does affect thinking and cognition in some ways. For instance, the manner in which information is stored in memory—and how well such information can subsequently be retrieved—is related to language (Cairns & Cairns, 1976). Likewise, the categories of language available in a given language affect the way that concepts (which we consider next) are formed. Although language may not determine thought, then, it certainly influences it.

Categorizing the World: Using Concepts

If someone asked you what was in your kitchen cabinet, you might answer with a detailed list of every item ("a jar of Skippy peanut butter," "three chipped dinner plates," and so forth). More likely, though, you would respond with some broader categories, such as "food" and "dishes."

Concepts: *A categorization of objects, events, or people that share common properties*

The categorization that you use reflects the operation of concepts. A **concept** is a categorization of objects, events, or people that share common properties. Through the use of concepts, we are able to distill the complexities of the world into more simplified—and therefore more easily usable—cognitive categories.

Concepts allow us to classify newly encountered objects into a form that is understandable in terms of our past experience. For example, we are able to tell that a small, four-legged creature with a wagging tail is probably a dog—even if we have never encountered that specific animal before. Concepts also influence behavior; we would assume, for instance, that it would be appropriate to pet the animal, given its canine categorization. The importance of concepts, then, lies in their ability to allow us to think about and deal with a complex, intricate world in a more manageable and successful way.

RECAP AND REVIEW III

Recap

- Language is characterized by grammar, a framework of rules that determine how our thoughts can be expressed, which contains the three major components of language: phonology, syntax, and semantics.
- Language acquisition proceeds rapidly from birth, and by the age of 5 is largely complete, although there are later increases in vocabulary and sophistication.
- Learning-theory views suggest that language is learned via the principles of reinforcement and conditioning. In contrast, Chomsky's view suggests that language capabilities are innate, centered in a language-acquisition device in the brain.
- The issue of whether language determines thought—the linguistic-relativity hypothesis—or thought determines language has been controversial, although today most people think the latter is more accurate.
- Concepts are categorizations of objects, events, or people that share common properties.

Review

1. "Pass over to me some popcorn" is a statement in need of correction for
a. Semantics **b.** Syntax **c.** Phonology **d.** Tense
2. Children generally produce words before they can comprehend language. True or false?
3. "Look, Dad. Mommy gived me an orange!" This child's grammatical error is referred to as
a. Overregularization **b.** Babbling **c.** Telegraphic speech **d.** Phonology
4. Noam Chomsky argues that language acquisition occurs through the process of positive reinforcement. True or false?
5. The view that our experience with relevant stimuli in our environment shape our language is labeled the linguistic-relativity hypothesis. True or false?
6. Categorizing academic courses such as psychology and sociology as "social science" illustrates our use of ________________.

(Answers to review questions are at bottom of page 207.)

Psychology Looks Toward the 1990s
Capturing the Complexities of Common Sense

S	M	T	W	T	F	S
		1	2	3	4	5
6	7	8	9	10	11	12
13	14	15	16	17	18	19
20	21	22	23	24	25	26
27	28	29	30	31		

As you step outside your front door heading for school, you notice that the grass is wet. Thinking about it for a moment, you decide that it must have rained during the night, and in fact you are pretty confident that your assumption is correct.

However, just as you are about to set out for school, your father calls out to you, asking that you make sure he remembered to turn off the sprinkler the previous evening. Suddenly, your confidence in your original decision dwindles, and you re-evaluate the inference you made earlier about the cause of the wet grass. You no longer are quite so sure that it has rained.

The situation described above is a simple one—but it represents one of the thorniest problems for cognitive psychologists intent on understanding commonsense reasoning. The reason for their difficulty is that the scenario represents a flagrant breach of the formal laws of logic, as developed by philosophers and mathematicians during hundreds of years of study (Waldrop, 1987).

According to conventional logic, the typical way in which conclusions are drawn is to represent a particular conclusion as a theorem, and then to go about proving that theorem through the use of facts (known to logicians as *axioms*), much as you may have done when proving theorems in geometry. To the chagrin of researchers trying to represent common sense, however, conventional logic implies that a new fact or axiom cannot change the validity of a theorem that has been proved earlier (although it can permit new theorems to be solved). In our example, then, once you have decided that the grass is wet because it rained, i.e., proven the theorem that it had rained, using the fact or axiom that the grass is wet, you would be stuck with that conclusion—which, no matter how elegant the logical reasoning that has led to such a conclusion, clearly does not make very good common sense.

There are even further difficulties using conventional logic. If we return to your front lawn once more, suppose that one morning you are walking through the grass and notice that your shoes are wet. You conclude that the grass is wet. Now suppose, as you look around some more, you notice that the grass looks shiny and is reflecting the sun. As common sense would have you believe, this additional piece of information adds to your certainty that the grass is wet.

Your conclusions are sound, but they make for problems for cognitive psychologists. The difficulty is that the additional piece of information that you received (the shininess of the grass) reinforced your original conclusion, rather than contradicting it as in our first example. When stated as axioms and theorems, however, the form of the two sets of logical arguments used in reasoning about the two situations are identical.

To solve the difficulties raised by commonsense reasoning, cognitive psychologists are turning away from formal logical models and instead developing new approaches. For example, Judea Pearl of the Cognitive Systems Laboratory of the University of California at Los Angeles suggests that the key to understanding common sense is to focus on distinctions between cause and effect (Pearl, 1987). For instance, in our first example, the wet grass could be considered an effect, while the rain and sprinkler were two competing causes. In contrast, the second example revealed the wet grass as a cause, while the wet shoes and reflective grass were effects. The logical differences between causes and effects are typified by this example: usually, causes compete with one another as explanations, while effects offer corroborative evidence.

Pearl is in the process of developing a model of commonsense logic based on beliefs people hold about causes and effects. Of course, the model is far more complex than our examples suggest, given that most events in the real world have a multiplicity of causes and produce multiple effects. Still, Pearl believes that no matter how intricate the situation, just a few basic rules of inference based on causes and effects can be employed to explain them. Ultimately, then, our models of cognitive processing may explain to us why the grass in our front lawn is wet with as much ease as our common sense is able to.

LOOKING BACK

1. In this chapter, we have discussed the work of cognitive psychologists, who study the higher mental processes of humans. Two areas of specialization were highlighted: problem solving and language.

2. Psychologists use many approaches to understanding problem-solving behavior. One approach is exemplified by Köhler's research with chimps, in which the elements of the situation had to be manipulated in a novel fashion in order for the chimps to solve the problem. Köhler called the cognitive processes underlying the chimps' behavior insight, a sudden awareness of the relationship between elements that had previously seemed independent.

3. One focus of contemporary cognitive psychologists is the thinking processes that underlie problem solving. These psychologists have found that people systematically approach problems by moving through three stages: preparation, production (including the use of algorithms and heuristics), and judgment. Depending upon the complexity and nature of a problem, this cycle may be repeated several times before the problem is solved.

4. Among the factors that hinder effective problem solving are functional fixedness (the tendency to think of an object only in terms of its most typical use) and the inappropriate use of algorithms and heuristics. However, these problems may be overcome in part by the use of a number of techniques devised by psychologists to improve problem solving. Among them are brainstorming, problem redefinition, use of analogies, and the systematic use of heuristics.

5. Language is the systematic, meaningful arrangement of symbols. Languages have a grammar—a framework of rules that determine how our thoughts can be expressed—that encompasses the three major components of language: phonology, syntax, and semantics. Phonology refers to the sounds (called phonemes) we make when we speak and to the use of those sounds to produce meaning by placing them into the form of words; syntax refers to the rules that indicate how words are joined together to form sentences; and semantics refers to the rules governing the meaning of words and sentences of language.

6. Language production, which is preceded by language comprehension, develops out of universal babbling (speechlike but meaningless sounds), which leads to the production of actual words. After one year of life, a child is generally capable of two-word combinations, and vocabulary increases thereafter. Children first use telegraphic speech, in which words not critical to the message are dropped. By the time a child is 5, acquisition of language rules is relatively complete.

7. There are two major theories of language acquisition. Learning theory suggests language is acquired simply through reinforcement and conditioning. In contrast, Chomsky suggests that there is an innate language-acquisition device which guides the development of language. The degree to which language is a uniquely human skill remains controversial.

8. The linguistic-relativity hypothesis suggests that language shapes and may determine the way people think about the world. On the other hand, it is possible that thought produces language. Most evidence suggests that although language does not determine thought, it does affect how information is stored in memory and how well it can be retrieved.

9. Concepts are categorizations of objects, events, or people that share common properties. The use of concepts allows people to reduce a complex world into more manageable and useful categories.

KEY TERMS AND CONCEPTS

cognitive psychologist (p. 188)
cognition (188)
insight (189)
algorithm (190)
heuristic (191)
means-ends analysis (192)
representativeness heuristic (192)
availability heuristic (193)
functional fixedness (194)
language (198)
grammar (198)
phonology (198)
phonemes (198)
syntax (199)
semantics (199)
babble (199)
telegraphic speech (199)
overregularization (200)
universal grammar (202)
language-acquisition device (202)
Yerkish (202)
linguistic-relativity hypothesis (203)
concept (204)

FOR FURTHER STUDY AND APPLICATION

Mayer, R. E. (1983). *Thinking, problem solving, and cognition.* New York: Freeman

This is a fine overview of research into the ways people are able to solve problems.

Glass, A., & Holyoak, K. J. (1985). *Cognition* (2nd ed.). Reading, MA: Addison-Wesley.

Applied and theoretical cognitive psychology are integrated in this updating of a basic text on cognitive psychology. The book uses interesting case reports to carefully explain memory and problem solving.

Nickerson, R. S., Perkins, D. N., & Smith, E. E. (1985). *The teaching of thinking.* Hillsdale, NJ: Erlbaum.

This volume addresses the question of whether thinking and problem solving can be taught, and comes up with an affirmative answer. It provides a theoretical and practical overview of the field of cognitive psychology, which seeks to improve human cognitive capabilities.

Clark, H. H., & Clark, E. V. (1977). *Psychology and language: An introduction to psycholinguistics.* New York: Harcourt Brace Jovanovich.

This book, well written and comprehensive, remains one of the best introductions to the area of language. You will see in detail how psychologists approach the area.

ANSWERS TO REVIEW QUESTIONS

Review III: **1.** b **2.** False **3.** a **4.** False **5.** False **6.** Concepts

CHAPTER 7

INTELLIGENCE

PROLOGUE

LOOKING AHEAD

BEING SMART ABOUT INTELLIGENT BEHAVIOR: DEFINING INTELLIGENCE

Separating the intelligent from the unintelligent: Measuring intelligence

The IQ measuring sticks: Stanford-Binet, Wechsler, et al.

IQ tests don't tell all: Alternate formulations of intelligence

Does information processing equal intelligence?: Contemporary approaches to understanding intelligence

PSYCHOLOGY AT WORK. Is Work Intelligence Different from School Intelligence?

The informed consumer of psychology: Can you learn to do better on standardized tests?

Recap and review I

ABOVE AND BELOW THE NORM: VARIATIONS IN INTELLECTUAL ABILITY

Falling below the norm: Mental retardation

The other end of the spectrum: The intellectually gifted

THE CUTTING EDGE: High Intelligence, Low Intelligence and Now, Artificial Intelligence

Recap and review II

INDIVIDUAL DIFFERENCES IN INTELLIGENCE: HEREDITY, ENVIRONMENT—OR BOTH?

TRY IT! A Culture-Unfair Intelligence Test

The basic controversy: Heredity versus environment

Neither heredity nor environment: Putting the question in perspective

Recap and review III

PSYCHOLOGY LOOKS TOWARD THE 1990s. Establishing Intelligence: The Earliest Signs of IQ.

LOOKING BACK

KEY TERMS AND CONCEPTS

FOR FURTHER STUDY AND APPLICATION

PROLOGUE

The paintings are varied. Some are landscapes, others are portraits, while still others depict the early-morning light casting its shadows on a wintry scene. All are drawn, according to one critic, with "the precision of a mechanic and the vision of a poet." They have appeared in galleries all over the world, and more than 1000 pictures have sold, ranging in price from $100 to $2000. Some observers have labeled the pictures as works of an artistic genius.

The artist 31-year-old Richard Wawro. But he is no ordinary artist. What makes him unique is that he is mentally retarded, with the mental capabilities of only a young child. Furthermore, he is legally blind, suffering from severe visual deficiencies; he has diabetes; he did not produce an understandable word until he was 11 years old, and even now can hold only the simplest of conversations. Yet despite his multiple handicaps—and the fact that by most standards he lacks so much—his contributions to the artistic world are extraordinary, far beyond the capabilities of most people with "normal" intelligence.

Savant (SAV ont) **syndrome**: *A condition in which a mentally retarded person displays unusual talent in one specific area*

Wawro's condition, called the **savant syndrome**, is a very rare one in which an individual, despite being mentally retarded, demonstrates spectacular talent in one specific area. In one case, for example, a severely retarded savant who could not do the simplest arithmetic problem could, for each year during the 1900s, name the months in which the eighteenth day fell on a Saturday. Another could compute square roots in his head, and still another could play a tune on the piano perfectly after hearing it only once.

If you asked Wawro how he is able to draw such sensitive, sophisticated pictures, he would be unable to explain it to you. What he does say in response to praise is this: "Being happy is a good idea. I am happy when my pictures make people feel good. I can see feeling good" (Blank, 1983).

LOOKING AHEAD

While the capabilities of Richard Wawro and other savants have yet to be explained satisfactorily, one thing is clear: Intelligence is an unusually complex phenomenon. It is also a major focal point for psychologists intent on understanding how people are able to adapt their behavior to the world in which they live and how individuals differ from one another in their capacity to learn about and understand the world.

This chapter begins by considering the challenges involved in defining and measuring intelligence. We examine the development and use of standardized intelligence tests and the way these tests are used to provide the measure of intelligence called IQ. The use of achievement and aptitude tests, as well as other alternative formulations of intelligence, is also examined.

Next, we consider the extremes of individual differences in intelligence: the mentally retarded and the gifted. The special challenges of each population are discussed along with special programs that have been developed to help such individuals reach their full potential. The chapter ends with a discussion of the ongoing controversy concerning the degree to which intelligence is influenced by heredity and by environment, and the issue of whether traditional tests of intelligence are biased toward the dominant cultural groups in society.

Artist Richard Wawro, shown with his father, has produced hundreds of paintings, such as the one here called "Washday in Pakistan." Critics have called him an artistic genius, and his paintings have won many awards. What makes his accomplishments particularly extraordinary, however, is that Wawro is mentally retarded, having the mental capabilities of only a young child. (*a*) (*Stanley Farrar/American Statesman*), (*b*) (*Courtesy of Dr. Laurence Becker*)

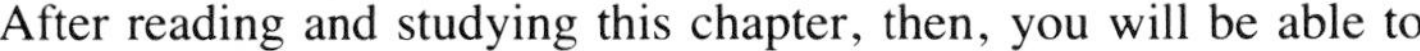

After reading and studying this chapter, then, you will be able to

- Define intelligence using alternative formulations of the concept
- Identify the major tests of intelligence
- Use the formula for IQ
- Differentiate the extremes of intelligence, including the specific types of mental retardation, and describe special programs designed to help people maximize their full potential
- Discuss the issue of the degree to which intelligence is influenced by environment and heredity, as well as the related issue of whether traditional IQ tests are culturally biased
- Define and apply the key terms and concepts listed at the end of the chapter

BEING SMART ABOUT INTELLIGENT BEHAVIOR: DEFINING INTELLIGENCE

It is typical for members of the Trukese tribe, a small Micronesian society, to sail a hundred miles in open ocean waters. Although their destination may be just a small dot of land less than a mile across, the Trukese are able to sail unerringly toward the island—without the aid of compass, chronometer, sextant, or any of the other sailing tools that are at the heart of modern western navigation. They are able to sail accurately even when prevailing winds do not allow a direct approach to the island and they must take a zig-zag course (Gladwin, 1964).

How are the Trukese able to navigate so effectively? If you asked them, they could not explain it. They might tell you that they use a process that takes into account the rising and setting of the stars and the appearance, sound, and feeling of the waves against the side of the boat. But at any given moment

The flawless Trukese navigational techniques, although primitive by western standards, are indicative of intelligence that is not easily measured on traditional intelligence tests. (*Eugenia Clark/American Museum of Natural History*)

as they are sailing along, they could not identify their position or say why they are doing what they are doing. And they certainly could not explain the navigational theory underlying their sailing technique.

Some might say the Trukese inability to explain how their sailing technique works is a sign of primitive and even unintelligent behavior—especially if we asked western sailors versed in the methods of more modern sailing procedures. In fact, if we made Trukese sailors take a standardized western test of navigational knowledge and theory, or for that matter a traditional test of intelligence, they might very well do poorly on it. Yet, as a practical matter, it is hard to accuse the Trukese of being unintelligent: Despite their inability to explain how they do so, they are able to navigate successfully through the open ocean waters.

The way in which the Trukese navigate points out the difficulty in coming to grips with what is meant by intelligence. To a westerner, traveling in a straight line along the most direct and quickest route using a sextant and other navigational tools would likely represent the most "intelligent" kind of behavior; a zigzag course, based on the "feel" of the waves, would not seem very reasonable. To the Trukese, who are used to their own system of navigation, however, the use of complicated navigational tools might well seem so overly complex and unnecessary that they might think of western navigators as lacking in intelligence. After all, the Trukese method works; it ultimately gets their sailors where they want to go, with a minimum of fuss and effort.

It is clear that the term "intelligence" can take on many different meanings. If, for instance, you lived in a remote, primitive African village, the way you differentiate between more intelligent and less intelligent people might be unlike the way someone living in the middle of New York City would distinguish individual differences. To the African, high intelligence might be represented by extraordinary hunting or other survival skills; to the New Yorker, it might be exemplified by dealing effectively with a mass-transit system, by achieving success as a member of a high-salaried, prestigious profession, or by getting good grades at a rigorous private school.

In fact, each of these conceptions of intelligence is reasonable, for each represents an instance in which more intelligent people are better able to use the resources of their environment than are less intelligent people, a distinction that we would assume to be basic to any definition of intelligence. Yet it is also clear that these conceptions represent very different views of intelligence.

That two such different sets of behavior can exemplify the same psychological concept has proved to be a problem to psychologists. They have long grappled with the issue of devising a general definition of intelligence that would remain independent of a person's specific culture and other environmental factors. Interestingly, untrained laypersons have fairly clear conceptions of intelligence (Sternberg, 1985). For example, in one survey that asked a group of people to define what they meant by intelligence, three major components of intelligence emerged (Sternberg, Conway, Ketron, & Bernstein, 1981). First, there was problem-solving ability: People who reason logically and identify more solutions to problems were seen as intelligent. Second, verbal abilities were thought to exemplify intelligence. Finally, intelligence was assumed to be indicated by social competence: the ability to show interest in others and interact effectively with them.

The French psychologist Alfred Binet developed the first intelligence test. (*Bettmann Archive*)

The definition of intelligence that psychologists employ is more focused, although it contains many of the same elements contained in the layperson's conception. To psychologists, **intelligence** is the capacity to understand the world, think with rationality, and use resources effectively when faced with challenges (Wechsler, 1975).

Intelligence: *The capacity to understand the world, think rationally, and use resources effectively when faced with challenges*

Unfortunately, neither the layperson's nor the psychologist's conception of intelligence is much help when it comes to distinguishing, with any degree of precision, more intelligent people from less intelligent. To overcome this problem, psychologists interested in intelligence have focused much of their attention on the development of batteries of tests, known, quite appropriately, as **intelligence tests**, and have relied on such tests to identify a person's level of intelligence.

Intelligence tests: *A battery of measures to determine a person's level of intelligence*

Separating the Intelligent from the Unintelligent: Measuring Intelligence

The first intelligence tests followed a simple premise: If performance on certain tasks or test items improved with age, then performance could be used to distinguish more intelligent people from less intelligent ones within a particular age group. Using this principle, Alfred Binet, a French psychologist, devised the first formal intelligence test, which was designed to identify the "dullest" students in the Paris school system in order to provide them with remedial aid.

Binet began by presenting tasks to same-age students who had been labeled "bright" or "dull" by their teachers. If a task could be completed by the bright students but not by the dull ones, he retained the task as a proper test item; otherwise it was discarded. In the end he came up with a test that distinguished between the bright and dull groups, and—with further work—one that distinguished between children in different age groups (Binet & Simon, 1916).

On the basis of the Binet test, children were assigned a score that corresponded to their **mental age**, the age of children taking the test who achieved the same score. For example, if a 10-year-old boy received a score of 45 on the test and this was the average score received by 8-year-olds, his mental age would be considered to be 8 years. Similarly, a 14-year-old girl who scored an 88 on the

Mental age: *The typical intelligence level found for people at a given chronological age*

test—matching the mean score for 16-year-olds—would be assigned a mental age of 16 years.

Although assigning a mental age to students provided an indication of whether they were performing at the same level as their peers, it did not allow for adequate comparisons between people of different **chronological**, or physical, **ages**. By using mental age alone, for instance, it would be assumed that an 18-year-old responding at a 16-year-old's level would be as bright as a 5-year-old answering at a 3-year-old's level, when actually the 5-year-old would be displaying a much greater *relative* degree of slowness.

Chronological (kron uh LOJ ih kul) **age**: *One's physical age*

A solution to the problem came in the form of the **intelligence quotient**, or **IQ score**, a measure of intelligence that takes into account an individual's mental *and* chronological ages. To calculate an IQ score, the following formula is used, in which MA stands for mental age and CA for chronological age:

Intelligence quotient (KWO shunt) **(IQ) score**: *A measure of intelligence that takes into account an individual's mental and chronological ages*

$$\text{IQ score} = \frac{\text{MA}}{\text{CA}} \times 100$$

Using this formula, we can return to the earlier example of an 18-year-old performing at a mental age of 16 and calculate an IQ score of $(16 \div 18) \times 100 = 88.9$. In contrast, the 5-year-old performing at a mental age of 3 comes out with a considerably lower IQ score: $(3 \div 5) \times 100 = 60$.

As a bit of trial and error with the formula will show you, anyone who has a mental age equal to his or her chronological age will have an IQ equal to 100. Moreover, people with a mental age that is greater than their chronological age will have IQs that exceed 100.

Although the basic principles behind the calculation of an IQ score still hold, scores are figured today in a more mathematically sophisticated manner and are known as **deviation IQ scores**. The average deviation IQ score is still considered to be 100, but tests are now designed so that the degree of deviation from this score allows one to calculate the proportion of people who have similar scores. As you can see from Figure 7-1, approximately two-thirds of all individuals fall within 15 IQ points of the average score of 100. As scores rise and fall beyond that range, the percentage of people in a category falls considerably.

Deviation IQ score: *A calculation of an IQ score that allows determination of one person's performance in relation to others'*

The IQ Measuring Sticks: Stanford-Binet, Wechsler, et al.

Just what is an IQ test like? It is probable that sometime during your academic career you have taken one; almost all of us are given IQ tests at one time or another.

The original test is still with us, although it has been revised many times and in its modern incarnation bears little resemblance to the original version. Now called the **Stanford-Binet test**, it was last revised in 1985 (Hagen, Sattler, & Thorndike, 1985). The test consists of a series of items which vary in nature according to the age of the person being tested. For example, young children are asked to copy figures or answer questions about everyday activities. Older people are asked to solve analogies, explain proverbs, and describe similarities that underlie sets of words.

Stanford-Binet (STAN ford bin AY) **test**: *A test of intelligence that includes a series of items varying in nature according to the age of the person being tested*

The test is administered orally. An examiner begins by finding a mental age level at which the person is able to answer all questions correctly and then moves on to successively difficult problems. When a mental age level is reached at which no items can be answered, the test is over. By examining the pattern of correct and incorrect responses, the examiner is able to compute an IQ score for the person being tested.

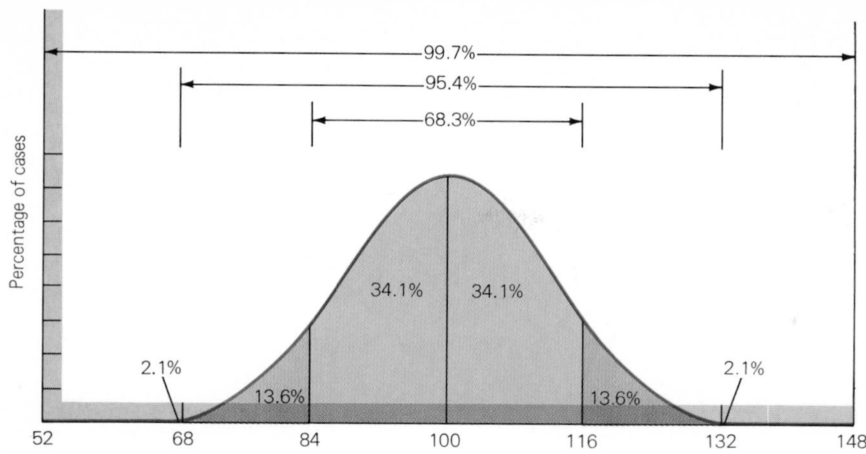

Figure 7-1
The average and most frequent IQ score is 100, and approximately 68 percent of all individuals are within a 30-point range of that score. Some 95 percent of all people have scores that are within 32 points above or below 100, and 99.7 percent of the population have scores that are between 52 and 148.

The other frequently used IQ test in America is a test devised by psychologist David Wechsler known as the **Wechsler Adult Intelligence Scale—Revised**, or, more commonly, the **WAIS-R**. There is also a children's version, the **Wechsler Intelligence Scale for Children—Revised**, or **WISC-R**. Both the WAIS-R and the WISC-R have two major parts: a verbal scale and a performance—or nonverbal—scale. As you can see from the sample questions in Figure 7-2, the two scales include questions of very different types. Whereas verbal tasks consist of more traditional kinds of problems, including vocabulary definition and comprehension of various concepts, the nonverbal part consists of assembling small objects and arranging pictures in a logical order. Although an individual's scores on the verbal and performance sections of the test are generally close to each other, the scores of a person with a language deficiency or from a background of severe cultural deprivation may show a relatively large discrepancy. By providing separate scores, then, the WAIS-R and WISC-R give a more precise picture of a person's specific abilities.

Wechsler (WEX lur) **Adult Intelligence Scale—Revised (WAIS-R) test**: *A test of intelligence consisting of verbal and nonverbal performance sections, providing a relatively precise picture of a person's specific abilities*

Wechsler (WEX lur) **Intelligence Scale for Children—Revised (WISC-R)**: *An intelligence test for children; see Wechsler Adult Intelligence Scale—Revised*

Because the Stanford-Binet, WAIS-R, and WISC-R all require individualized administration, it is relatively difficult and time-consuming to administer and score them on a wide-scale basis. Consequently, there are now a number of IQ tests that allow for group administration (Carroll, 1982). Rather than having one examiner asking one person at a time to respond to individual items, group IQ tests are strictly paper-and-pencil measures, in which those taking the tests read the questions and provide their answers in writing. The primary advantage of group tests is their ease of administration.

There are, however, sacrifices made in group testing which, in some cases, may outweigh the benefits. For instance, there is a loss of detail about a person's general behavior such as is obtained from an individual administration. Moreover, people may be more motivated to perform at their highest ability level when working on a one-to-one basis with a test administrator. Finally, in some cases, it is simply impossible to employ group tests, particularly with young children or people with unusually low IQs.

Achievement and Aptitude Tests IQ tests are not the only kind of tests that you have taken during the course of your schooling. Two other kinds of tests related to intelligence but designed to measure somewhat different phenomena are achievement tests and aptitude tests. An **achievement test** is a test meant to ascertain the level of knowledge in a given subject area; rather than

Achievement test: *A test intended to determine one's level of knowledge in a given subject*

Verbal scale

Information	Where does milk come from? Who invented the telephone?
Comprehension	Why do we put food in the refrigerator? What should you do if you see a person leave his or her groceries on a bus?
Arithmetic	Stacey had two crayons and the teacher gave her two more. How many did she have all together? How long will it take a train traveling at 80 miles an hour to reach the station 320 miles away?
Similarities	In what way are cows and horses alike? In what way are rivers and roads the same?
Digit span	Repeat the following numbers: 5, 8, 2 Repeat the following numbers in reverse order: 3, 2, 9, 7, 4, 1, 4.
Vocabulary	What is a candle? What does administer mean?

Performance scale

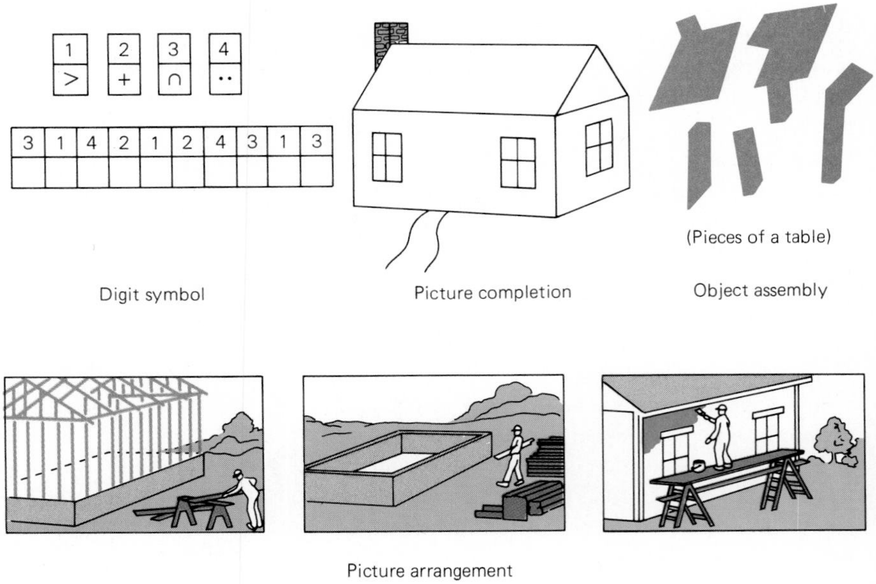

1 2 3 4
3 1 4 2 1 2 4 3 1 3

(Pieces of a table)

Digit symbol

Picture completion

Object assembly

Picture arrangement

Figure 7-2
Typical kinds of items found on the verbal and performance scales of the Wechsler Intelligence Scale for Children (WISC-R).

measuring general ability as an intelligence test does, an achievement test concentrates on the specifics of what a person has learned.

Aptitude test: *A test designed to predict one's ability in a particular line of work*

An **aptitude test** is designed to predict a person's ability in a particular area or line of work. You have probably already taken the most famous aptitude test of them all: the Scholastic Aptitude Test, or SAT. The SAT is meant to predict how well people will do in college, and has proved over the years to correlate very strongly with college grades.

Although in theory the distinction between intelligence, aptitude, and achievement tests can be precisely drawn, as a practical matter there is a good deal of overlap between them. For example, the SAT has been roundly criticized for being less of a predictive aptitude test than one that actually measures achievement. It is difficult, then, to devise tests that predict future performance but do not rely on past achievement.

IQ Tests Don't Tell All: Alternate Formulations of Intelligence

Although Binet's procedure for measuring intelligence, exemplified by the modern Stanford-Binet and WAIS-R intelligence tests, remains one of the most frequently employed, some theorists argue that it lacks an underlying conception of intelligence. To Binet and his followers, intelligence was generally conceived of as what his test measured. It was, and remains, an eminently practical approach, but it depends not on an understanding of the nature of intelligence but primarily on comparing one person's performance with those of others. For that reason, the intelligence test of Binet and his successors does little to increase our understanding of what intelligence is all about; it merely measures behavior that is assumed to exemplify intelligence.

This has not meant, however, that researchers and theoreticians have ignored the question of what intelligence really is. In fact, there are a number of alternative approaches designed to explain the nature of intelligence—particularly in terms of its subcomponents (Frederiksen, 1986). For example, some researchers believe that there are really two different kinds of intelligence: fluid intelligence and crystallized intelligence (Cattell, 1967). **Fluid intelligence** is the ability to deal with new problems and encounters. If you were asked to group a series of letters according to some criterion or to remember a set of numbers, you would be using fluid intelligence. **Crystallized intelligence** is the store of specific information, skills, and strategies that people have acquired through experience, and the ability to use such material. You would likely rely on crystallized intelligence, for instance, if you were asked to analyze financial trends or to solve a mystery, exercises in which you would be drawing upon your past unique experience.

Fluid intelligence: *The ability to deal with new problems and encounters*

Crystallized intelligence: *The store of specific information, skills, and strategies that people have acquired through experience*

Others divide intelligence into even more fine-grained subdivisions. For instance, J. P. Guilford (1968, 1982) suggested that a **structure-of-intellect model**, illustrated in Figure 7-3, provided the most accurate representation of human intelligence. On the basis of observations of performance on a wide variety of

Structure-of-intellect model: *A model of intelligence based on performance along three different dimensions: task content, task requirements, and product*

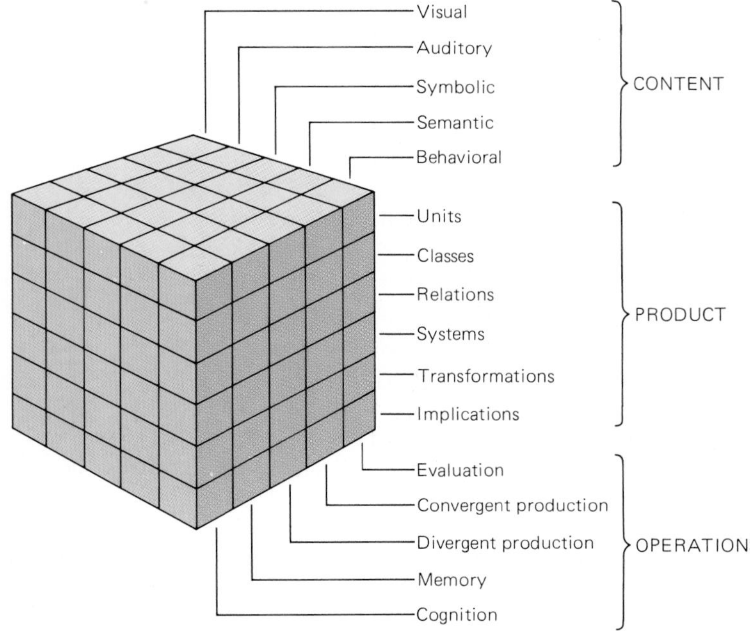

Figure 7-3
According to Guilford's structure-of-intellect model, there are 150 separate mental abilities that fall along the three major dimensions (task content, operations involved in carrying out a task, and task product) represented in this cube. (*Guilford, 1982.*)

tasks, he proposed that there are 150 separate mental abilities underlying intelligence. These abilities fall along three major dimensions: content of a task (made up of five subdivisions), the requirements—called operations—involved in carrying out the task (also made up of five subdivisions), and the product of the task (made up of six subdivisions).

Although such minute distinctions between different components of intelligence present difficulties in terms of reliable measurement, Guilford's model has led to a number of advances in our understanding of the nature of intelligence. For example, one outgrowth of the model has been tests that include items in which more than one answer can be correct, providing the opportunity for the demonstration of creative thinking. According to Guilford's approach, then, different kinds of intelligence may produce differing sorts of equally valid responses to a question.

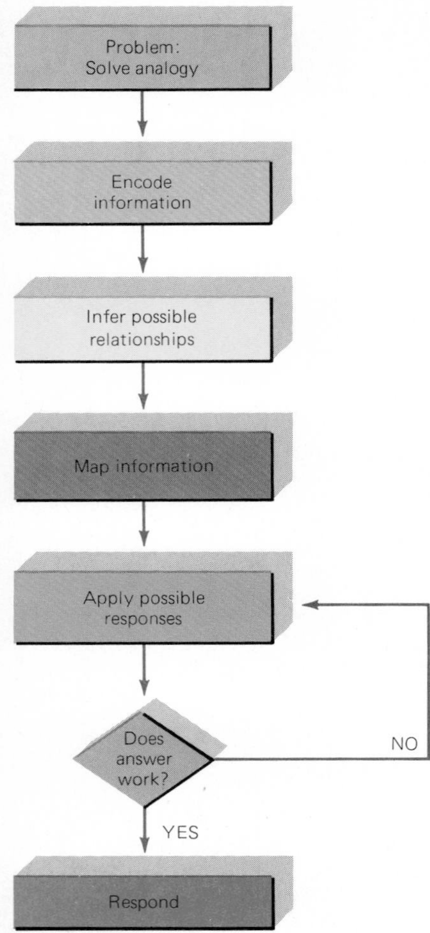

Figure 7-4
Information-processing stages in solving analogies. (*Sternberg, 1982.*)

Does Information Processing Equal Intelligence?: Contemporary Approaches to Understanding Intelligence

The most recent contribution to understanding intelligence comes from cognitive psychologists. Drawing on work that we discussed in Chapters 5 and 6, cognitive psychologists use an information-processing approach, which assumes that the way people represent material in memory and how they use that material to solve intellectual tasks provide the most accurate conception of intelligence (Sternberg, 1981). By breaking tasks and problems down into their component parts and identifying the nature and speed of problem-solving processes, researchers have noted distinct differences between those who score high on traditional IQ tests and those scoring lower.

Take, for example, a college student who is asked to solve the following analogy problem (Sternberg, 1982):

lawyer is to *client* as *doctor* is to:

(**a**) *patient* or (**b**) *medicine*

A student presented with this analogy tends to move through a series of stages in attempting to reach a solution (see Figure 7-4). First she will *encode* the initial information, which means providing each item with identifying cues that help retrieve relevant information buried in long-term memory. For instance, she may think of lawyer in terms of law school, the Supreme Court, an ambulance chaser, Perry Mason, and a courtroom. Each of the other terms will be similarly encoded. Next, she will *infer* any possible relationship between lawyer and client. She may infer that the relevant relationship is that a client employs a lawyer, or alternatively, that a lawyer gives services to a client.

Once she has inferred the relationship, she must *map* the higher-order relationship between the first half of the analogy and the second half—both deal with people who provide professional services for a fee. The crucial stage that follows is one of *application,* in which she tries out each answer option with the relationship she has inferred. She will presumably decide that a doctor provides professional services to a patient, not to medicine. Finally, the last component of solving the problem is responding.

By breaking problems into component parts in this manner, it is possible to identify systematic differences in both quantitative and qualitative aspects of problem solving, and to demonstrate that people with higher intelligence levels differ not only in the number of correct solutions they come up with, but in their method of solving problems. For instance, high scorers are apt to spend more time on the initial encoding stages of a problem, identifying the parts of the problem and retrieving relevant information from long-term memory. This initial emphasis on recalling relevant information pays off in the end; those who spend relatively less time on the initial stages tend to be less able to find a solution. People's use of such information-processing abilities, then, may underlie the differences in intelligence. (For yet another view of intelligence, see the Psychology at Work box.)

PSYCHOLOGY AT WORK

IS WORK INTELLIGENCE DIFFERENT FROM SCHOOL INTELLIGENCE?

One of the strongest claims that intelligence tests actually measure intelligence rests on the fact that there is a high correspondence between people's IQ scores and their performance in academic settings. Literally hundreds of studies have shown that students with high IQs tend to get high grades; those with low IQs tend to be less successful in school.

Yet IQ does not always relate to *career* success. Although IQ—as measured by traditional intelligence tests—is associated with the type of job a person initially attains, eventual success on the job is not. For example, while it is clear that successful business executives usually score at least moderately well on IQ tests, the rate at which they advance and their ultimate business achievement is only minimally associated with their specific IQ scores. A more significant influence, according to psychologist Siegried Streufert (1984), is the way in which people approach problems and the style of their thinking—something called **practical intelligence**.

Practical intelligence is manifested in successful business leaders through a kind of cognitive complexity in decision making. Instead of being locked into a simple pattern of thinking, successful managers are able to acquire and integrate complex sets of information and to see the interrelationships among events with clarity. Rather than viewing problems in terms of a single goal or factor—such as profit making—leaders with high practical intelligence are able to coordinate differing goals simultaneously when devising solutions to problems.

Where does someone acquire practical knowledge? Wagner and Sternberg (1985) suggest that—in contrast to more intellectual knowledge learned in a classroom—practical knowledge is obtained primarily through on-the-job experience. Because it is not directly talked about or taught, however, it is difficult to learn the specific components that make it up, and people sometimes end up making erroneous assumptions about what constitutes practical intelligence.

In sum, it is clear that there are many ways to be "intelligent." A high IQ does not guarantee success in life—especially if it accompanies low practical intelligence.

Albert Einstein is a good example of an individual whose poor academic performance during his early years in school was clearly not indicative of his intelligence. (*Wide World Photos*)

Practical intelligence: *A person's style of thought and approach to problem solving, which may differ from traditional measures of intelligence*

The Informed Consumer of Psychology: Can You Learn to Do Better on Standardized Tests?

Although psychologists may disagree about the nature of intelligence, all of us have had to cope with formal testing at some point in our lives. Many of us can probably understand the feelings expressed by one student:

> The big day had finally arrived. Weeks after signing up, it was time for Ronnie to take the SAT. Chewing on his No. 2 pencil, he turned to his friend Bill and muttered sarcastically, "Cheer up. All that hangs on this is the rest of our lives."

One outcome of the prevalence of tests, ranging from the Scholastic Aptitude Test to those that measure school achievement and intelligence, has been the development of numerous coaching services that purport to train people to raise their scores by reviewing basic skills and teaching test-taking strategies. But do they work?

Although the Educational Testing Service at one time suggested that coaching for the SAT was useless, today they take a more positive approach toward testing. While still suggesting that the SAT measures underlying competencies so fundamental that a course of a few weeks' duration will provide little advantage, they concede that practice in test taking provided during the course may have a slightly beneficial effect. But they go on to point out that the coaching required to bring about average score increases of more than 20 to 30 points is so extensive that it would be the equivalent of going to school full time (Messick & Jungeblut, 1981).

Most research carried out by psychologists verifies that coaching for the SAT exams produces small effects—usually in the range of 15-point increases in verbal and math scores (Kulik, Bangert-Drowns, & Kulik, 1984). On the other hand, research also shows that coaching on other sorts of aptitude and intelligence tests can result in more substantial increases in test scores.

Since some kinds of coaching do help raise the scores people receive on tests, one crucial concern is to determine what kind of coaching is most likely to be effective. Among the points to consider when deciding if coaching will be an effective and useful strategy for raising one's score on an upcoming test are whether the coaching provides instruction in the basic areas covered by the test, particularly those in which one is rusty and may need drill and practice; whether the instruction is geared to the specific test; whether the instructor has recent public versions of the test that can be used for practice with the mechanics of the test itself; and whether there are data to show that this particular coaching service has previously produced significant gains in the scores of students. Finally, you must ask yourself whether it is worth the cost of the course in time and money to end up with only a small gain on the test—particularly in view of the fact that most people have higher test scores the second time they take a test whether they are coached or not.

Only careful research can answer these questions, and it is wise to be skeptical of the claims of coaches. At the same time, there are certain steps you can take, without the benefit of coaching, to maximize your opportunity to score well on standardized tests. For example, these four points provide good advice for anyone taking a standardized test (Crocetti, 1983):

- Preview each section. Not only will it give you a chance to take a deep breath and prevent you from frantically rushing through the section, it will alert you to any unexpected changes in the test format. Previewing will give you a sense of what to expect as you work through each problem.

- Time yourself carefully. The computer that scores your test will not care how deeply you have thought out and considered each answer; all it notes is whether or not you have answered a problem correctly. Therefore, it is important not to spend too much time on initial problems at the expense of later ones. If you are unsure of an answer, try to narrow down the options, then guess and go on to the next problem. Perfection is not your goal; maximizing the number of correct responses is.
- Check the test-scoring policy to determine if guessing is appropriate. On the Scholastic Aptitude Test, wrong answers are subtracted from your score, making blind guessing a bad strategy. In comparison, the Graduate Record Exam, as well as many other tests, does not penalize you for wrong answers. On tests with penalties for wrong answers, guess only if you can narrow the choices down to two or three. On the other hand, for tests in which wrong answers do not lower your score, it pays to guess, even if you have no idea of the correct response.
- Complete answer sheets accurately. Although an obvious point, it is sensible to check your answer sheet when you have finished the test. It is also a good idea to write your answers in the test booklet itself, so that when you go back to review your answers you won't have to refer to the answer sheet.

While these tips won't ensure a high score on the next test you take, they will help to maximize your opportunity for better performance.

RECAP AND REVIEW I

Recap

- Intelligence is the capacity to understand the world, think rationally, and use resources effectively when faced with challenges.
- The measure of intelligence used in tests is the intelligence quotient, or IQ.
- There are a number of alternative formulations of intelligence, including models that look at the subcomponents of intelligence and those suggesting that information-processing strategies provide the most useful understanding of intelligence.
- Coaching seems to have some impact on test scores, although there is wide variability in its effectiveness.

Review

1. Ten-year-old Sharon is given an intelligence test. She achieves a mental age score of 11. Using the formula for determining intelligence quotient, calculate Sharon's IQ score.
2. Mandy has had a wide range of experiences in dealing with novel situations. Consequently, she has developed a broad set of skills and strategies for dealing with a variety of situations. Her storehouse of information and strategies is referred to as
   a. Structure of intellect **b.** Crystallized intelligence **c.** Fluid intelligence **d.** A cognitive map
3. Achievement tests are designed to predict future performance. True or false?
4. Name the model of J. P. Guilford that divides intelligence into 150 separate mental abilities.
5. Cognitive psychologists utilize an information-processing approach to understanding intelligence. Accordingly, they suggest that when breaking information into components, people with high IQ scores tend to focus on
   a. Encoding and inferring **b.** Encoding and applying **c.** Mapping and applying **d.** Applying and responding
6. You are surprised to learn that Harry Middleton, a very rich and successful builder and real-estate dealer, has only a low-to-average IQ score. It would probably not surprise you, however, to learn that his ________________ intelligence (the way he approaches problems and his style of thinking) is high.

(Answers to the review questions are at the bottom of page 222.)

People with Down's syndrome can lead productive lives as adults. (*Will McIntyre/Photo Researchers, Inc.*)

ABOVE AND BELOW THE NORM: VARIATIONS IN INTELLECTUAL ABILITY

Bill never liked school all that much. For the first few years he managed to get by, although his parents had to push hard to get him to do a minimally acceptable level of first- and second-grade work. He always seemed slower at learning things that the other kids had no trouble with, and—while he wasn't exactly a poorly behaved child—his attention span was short and he had trouble following what was going on in class. He also seemed tired much of the time, but a physical examination ruled out any medical problems. His teachers began to suspect he was simply lazy and unmotivated, though he did, on occasion, show great interest in lessons that involved working with his hands. Finally, out of desperation, his teachers and parents arranged for him to be evaluated by a psychologist. To their surprise they found out he had an IQ of 63—so far below average that his fell into the range of IQ scores classified as mentally retarded.

Bill is one of more than 6.5 million people in the United States who have been identified as having intelligence far enough below average to regard it as a serious deficit. Both those people with low IQs, known as the mentally retarded, and those with unusually high IQs, referred to as the intellectually gifted, make up classes of individuals who require special attention to reach their full potential.

Falling Below the Norm: Mental Retardation

Mental retardation: *A significantly subaverage level of intellectual functioning accompanying deficits in adaptive behavior*

Although sometimes thought of as a rare phenomenon, mental retardation occurs in 1 to 3 percent of the population. There is wide variation among those labeled as mentally retarded—in large part because of the inclusiveness of the definition by the American Association on Mental Deficiency. The association suggests that **mental retardation** exists when there is "significantly subaverage general intellectual functioning existing concurrently with deficits in adaptive behavior and manifested during the developmental period" (Grossman, 1983). What this means is that people classified as mentally retarded can range from individuals whose performance differs little in a qualitative sense from those with higher IQs, to those who virtually cannot be trained and who must receive institutional treatment throughout their lives.

Mild retardation: *Mental retardation characterized by an IQ between 55 and 69 and the ability to function independently*

Moderate retardation: *Mental retardation characterized by an IQ between 40 and 54*

Severe retardation: *Mental retardation characterized by an IQ between 25 and 39 and difficulty in functioning independently*

Profound retardation: *Mental retardation characterized by an IQ below 25 and an inability to function independently*

Most mentally retarded people have relatively low levels of deficits and are classified as **mildly retarded**. These individuals have IQ scores ranging from 55 to 69, and they constitute some 90 percent of all retarded individuals. Although their development is typically slower than that of their peers, they can function quite independently by adulthood and are able to hold jobs and have families of their own.

At greater levels of retardation—**moderate retardation** (IQs of 40 to 54), **severe retardation** (IQs of 25 to 39), and **profound retardation** (IQs below 25)—the difficulties are more pronounced. With the moderately retarded, deficits

ANSWERS TO REVIEW QUESTIONS

Review I: **1.** 110 **2.** b **3.** False **4.** Structure-of-intellect model **5.** a **6.** Practical are obvious early, with language and motor skills lagging behind those of peers. While these people can hold simple jobs, it is necessary for them to have a moderate degree of supervision throughout their lives. The severely and profoundly retarded are generally unable to function independently. Often they have no language ability, poor motor control, and even an inability to be toilet-trained. These people tend to be institutionalized for their entire lives.

What are the causes of mental retardation? In nearly one-third of the cases there is a known biological cause, the most common being Down's syndrome. **Down's syndrome**, which was once referred to as mongolism because the facial configuration of those with the disorder had an oriental appearance, is caused by the presence of an extra chromosome. Birth complications, such as a temporary lack of oxygen, may also cause retardation.

Down's syndrome: *A common cause of mental retardation, brought about by the presence of an extra chromosome*

The majority of cases of mental retardation are classified as familial retardation. In **familial retardation** there is no known biological defect but a history of retardation within the person's family. Whether that history is caused by environmental factors—such as extreme, continuous poverty—or by some underlying genetic factor inherited from one's parents is usually impossible to determine for certain. What is apparent about familial retardation is the presence of more than one retarded person in the immediate family—whether caused by environment, genetic factors, or some combination of the two.

Familial retardation: *Mental retardation in which there is a history of retardation in a family but no evidence of biological causes*

Regardless of the cause of mental retardation, important advances in the care and treatment of the mentally retarded have occurred in the last ten years. Much of this change was instigated by the Education for All Handicapped Children Act of 1975 (Public Law 94-142). In this federal law, Congress ruled that the mentally retarded are entitled to a full education and that they must be educated and trained in the "**least-restrictive environment**." The law increased the educational opportunities for the retarded, facilitating their integration into regular classrooms as much as possible—a process known as **mainstreaming**.

Least-restrictive environment: *The official phrase from PL94-142 that guarantees the right of full education for retarded people in an environment that is most similar to the educational environment of typical children*

Mainstreaming: *The integration of retarded people into regular classroom situations*

The philosophy behind mainstreaming suggests that the interaction of retarded and nonretarded students in regular classrooms will improve the educational opportunities for the mentally retarded, increase their social acceptance, and

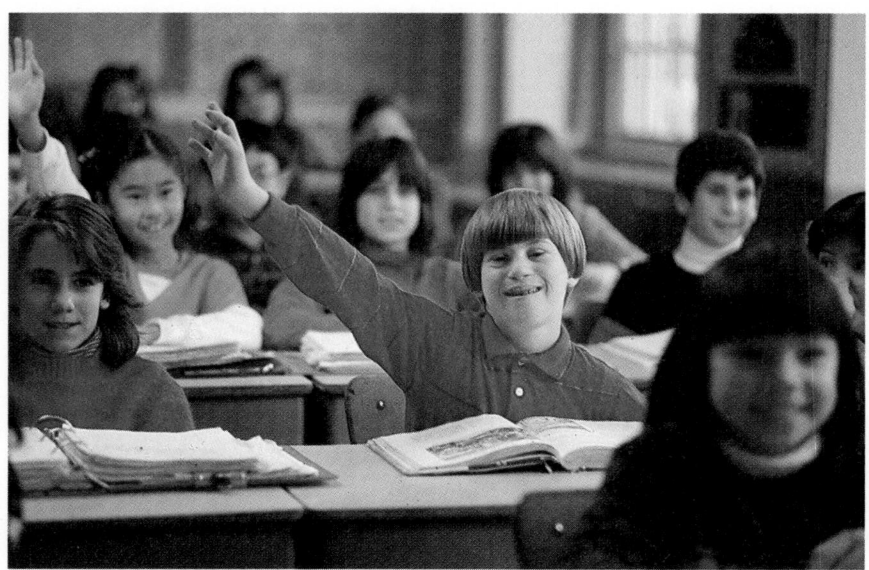

In mainstreaming, the mentally retarded are educated and trained in the least restrictive environment, which often includes their integration into regular classrooms. (*Richard Hutchings/Photo Researchers, Inc.*)

facilitate their integration into society as a whole. The philosophy was once to segregate the retarded into special-education classes where they could learn at their own pace along with other handicapped students. Mainstreaming attempts to prevent the isolation inherent in special-education classes and to reduce the social stigma of retardation by allowing the handicapped to interact with their age peers as much as possible.

Of course, there are still special-education classes; some retarded individuals function at too low a level to benefit from placement in regular classrooms. Moreover, retarded children mainstreamed into regular classes typically attend special classes for at least part of the day. Still, mainstreaming holds the promise of increasing the integration of the mentally retarded into society and allowing them to make their own contributions to the world at large.

The Other End of the Spectrum: The Intellectually Gifted

Intellectually gifted: *Individuals characterized by higher-than-average intelligence, with IQ scores above 130*

While the uniqueness of the mentally retarded is readily apparent, members of another group differ equally from the norm. Instead of having low intelligence, though, the **intellectually gifted** have higher-than-average intelligence.

Comprising 2 to 4 percent of the school-aged population, the intellectually gifted have IQ scores greater than 130. While the stereotype associated with the gifted suggests a person who is an awkward, shy, social misfit unable to get along well with peers, most research suggests just the opposite: that the intellectually gifted are outgoing, well-adjusted, popular people who are able to do most things better than the average person (Stanley, 1980).

For example, in a long-term study begun by Lewis Terman that started in the early 1920s and is still going on, 1500 children who had IQ scores above 140 were followed and examined periodically through the next 60 years (Sears, 1977; Terman & Oden, 1947). From the very start, members of this group were physically, academically, and socially more able than their nongifted peers. They were generally healthier, taller, heavier, and stronger than average. Not surprisingly, they did better in school as well. They also showed better social adjustment than average. And all these advantages paid off in terms of career success: As a group, the gifted received more awards and distinctions and higher incomes, and made more contributions in art and literature. For example, by the time the members of the group were 40 years old they had written over 90 books, 375 plays and short stories, and 2000 articles and had registered more than 200 patents. Perhaps most important, they reported greater satisfaction in life.

On the other hand, the picture of these intellectually gifted people was not unvaryingly positive. Not every member of the group Terman studied was successful, and in fact there were some notable failures. Moreover, other research suggests that high intelligence is not a homogeneous quality; a person with a high overall IQ is not necessarily gifted in every academic subject but may excel in just one or two (Stanley, 1980). A high IQ, then, does not guarantee success in everything.

While special programs attempting to overcome the deficits of the mentally retarded abound, only recently have ways of encouraging the talents of the intellectually gifted been developed. Part of this lack of special attention has been due to the persistent view that the gifted ought to be able to "make it on their own"; if they can't, then they really aren't gifted in the first place, according to this philosophy (Maeroff, 1977). More enlightened approaches, however, have acknowledged that without some form of special attention, the gifted

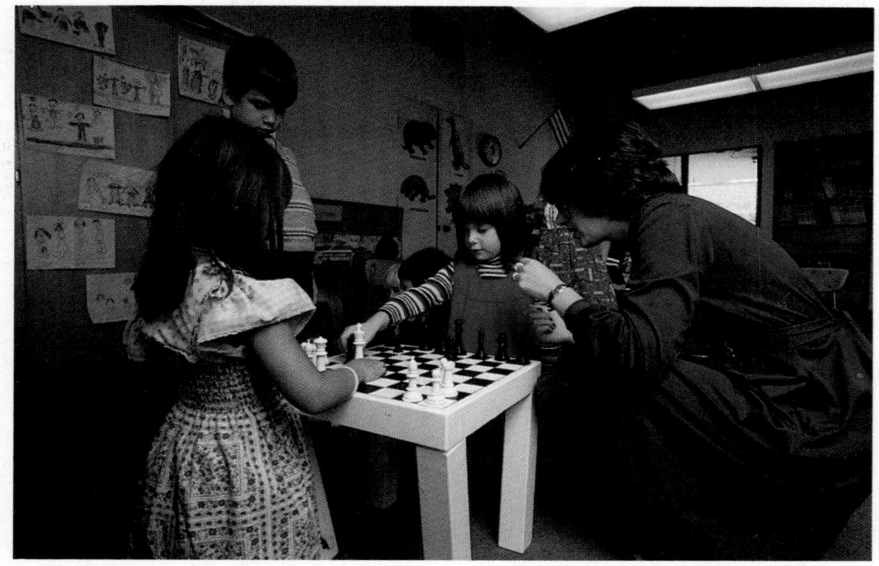

Despite stereotypes of the intellectually gifted as being socially and physically inept, the true story is different: They tend to be physically, academically, and socially more able than their nongifted peers. (*Lester Sloan/Woodfin Camp & Assoc.*)

may become bored and frustrated with the pace of their schooling and may never reach their full potential.

One particularly successful program for the intellectually gifted is a project called the Study of the Mathematically Precocious Youth (SMPY). In the program, seventh graders who have shown unusual mathematical success are enrolled in summer classes in which they are rapidly taught complex mathematical skills, culminating in college-level calculus (Stanley, 1980). In addition, they receive instruction in a variety of other subjects, including the sciences and languages. The ultimate goal of the program, and others like it, is to provide sufficient enrichment and acceleration to the gifted to allow their talents to flourish, and to increase the likelihood that they will reach their maximum potential. Although it is too early to tell if enrichment programs such as SMPY are effective—since the graduates of these programs have yet to reach adulthood—such special programs have been highly rated by participants. (For another facet of intelligence, see the accompanying Cutting Edge box.)

Artificial intelligence: *Intelligence demonstrated by computers and other machines*

THE CUTTING EDGE

HIGH INTELLIGENCE, LOW INTELLIGENCE, . . . AND NOW, ARTIFICIAL INTELLIGENCE

THERAPIST: What seems to be your problem?
PATIENT: My mother drinks too much.
THERAPIST: Who else in your family drinks too much?

A reasonable exchange between therapist and patient? Actually, the therapist is a computer program named Eliza, responding to a "patient" who has typed his problem into the computer (Weizenbaum, 1966). Although no one seriously suggests that therapy will one day be conducted via computer, this interchange represents one of the first efforts in a new area of interest to psychologists: artificial intelligence. Until now, our discussion of intelligence has concerned only that which emanates from the human brain. Probably the most important contemporary development relating to intelligence is in the area of **artificial intelligence**—intelligence that is demonstrated by computers and other machines.

The central question being asked by investigators of artificial

This "seeing-eye-robot"—a replacement for the more traditional Seeing Eye dog—uses artificial intelligence technology to help a blind person maneuver through the countryside. (*Richard Kalvar/Magnum*)

intelligence is whether a computer is capable of simulating the thinking and problem-solving capabilities of human beings. Will we one day be able to go up to our home computer and tell it our car insurance is expiring and ask what kind of new policy to buy? Or get it to tell us what courses we should register for? Or ask for advice on buying a new car, or where we left our car keys?

To Roger Schank and his colleagues at Yale University, such questions are not as farfetched as they sound. These people are working on computers that are capable of understanding, and ultimately thinking in and responding to, the English language—which is proving to be no easy task (Schank, 1985). Consider, for instance, the following sentence:

John sold Mary a book for $2.

Although seemingly simple, to a computer this sentence represents some serious problems. The computer has to know that other sentences presented to it mean the same thing, such as "John gave Mary a book and she gave him $2"; "Mary paid John $2 and received a book"; "The book that Mary bought from John cost $2." Moreover, it needs to know the implications of the act: Mary now has the book; she didn't have it before; John has $2 more than when he began the transaction. While not necessarily logical implications, most human listeners would assume them to be true—and so the computer must make these assumptions as well (Kendig, 1983).

The complexities of artificial intelligence are such that truly intelligent machines have not yet been developed, although computers are becoming increasingly sophisticated in mimicking human thinking processes. Moreover, by developing computers that are fashioned after human thinking processes, scientists are moving closer to the day when machines can respond to queries and—even more important—learn new information, thereby growing smarter and smarter.

Perhaps the reality is that some day a computer *will* be able to tell you where to look for your missing car keys. For now, though, consider what happened when one computer, programmed to translate from English to Russian and then back to English, was asked to work on the biblical phrase, "The spirit is willing, but the flesh is weak." After a series of translations, the final version read, "The wine was agreeable, but the meat was spoiled."

RECAP AND REVIEW II

Recap

- Mental retardation is defined by significantly subaverage general intellectual functioning accompanied by deficits in adaptive behavior.
- The levels of retardation include mildly retarded (IQ of 55 to 69), moderately retarded (IQ of 40 to 54), severely retarded (IQ of 25 to 39), and profoundly retarded (IQ below 25).
- The most frequent causes of mental retardation are Down's syndrome and familial influences.
- The intellectually gifted have IQs above 130 and comprise 2 to 4 percent of the school-aged population.

Review

1. Russell displays some deficits in adaptive functioning and scores 59 on a standard IQ test. By definition, he would be classified as ______________ retarded.
a. Mildly **b.** Moderately **c.** Severely **d.** Profoundly
2. In general, someone like Russell will probably never be capable of living independently. True or false?
3. Russell's younger brother is also mentally retarded. No known biological cause for either brother's retardation has been identified. Cases of retardation such as theirs are classified as ______________.
a. Down's syndrome **b.** Genetic retardation **c.** Mongolism **d.** Familial retardation
4. What are three possible advantages of mainstreaming?
5. Research generally reveals that intellectually gifted people are socially backward. True or false?

(Answers to the review questions are at the bottom of page 228.)

INDIVIDUAL DIFFERENCES IN INTELLIGENCE: HEREDITY, ENVIRONMENT—OR BOTH?

Kwanga is often considered a pleckse tied to a ______________.

(*a*) rundel

(*b*) flinke

(*c*) pove

(*d*) quirj

If you found this kind of item on an intelligence test that you were taking, you would probably complain that the test was totally absurd and had nothing to do with your intelligence or anyone else's. How could anyone be expected to respond to items presented in a language that was completely unfamiliar to them?

But suppose you found the following item, which at first glance might look equally foreign:

Which word is most out of place here?

(*a*) splib

(*b*) blood

(*c*) gray

(*d*) spook

(*e*) black

TRY IT!

A CULTURE-*UN*FAIR INTELLIGENCE TEST

If you have been raised within the dominant white culture, particularly in a suburban or rural environment, you may have difficulty in answering the following questions, which are designed to illustrate the importance of devising culture-fair intelligence tests.

1. Bird, or Yardbird, was the jacket jazz lovers from coast to coast hung on ____
(*a*) Lester Young
(*b*) Peggy Lee
(*c*) Benny Goodman
(*d*) Charlie Parker
(*e*) Birdman of Alcatraz

2. The opposite of square is ____
(*a*) round
(*b*) up
(*c*) down
(*d*) hip
(*e*) lame

3. If you throw the dice and 7 is showing on the top, what is facing down? ____
(*a*) 7
(*b*) Snake eyes
(*c*) Boxcars
(*d*) Little Joes
(*e*) 11

4. Jazz pianist Ahmad Jamal took an Arabic name after becoming really famous. Previously he had what he called his "slave name." What was his previous name? ____
(*a*) Willie Lee Jackson
(*b*) LeRoi Jones
(*c*) Wilbur McDougal
(*d*) Fritz Jones
(*e*) Andy Johnson

5. In C. C. Rider, what does "C. C." stand for? ____
(*a*) Civil Service
(*b*) Church Council
(*c*) County Circuit Preacher
(*d*) Country Club
(*e*) Cheating Charley (the "Boxcar Gunsel")

6. Cheap chitlings (not the kind you purchase at the frozen-food counter) will taste rubbery unless they are cooked long enough. How soon can you quit cooking them to eat and enjoy them? ____
(*a*) 15 minutes
(*b*) 2 hours
(*c*) 24 hours
(*d*) 1 week (on a low flame)
(*e*) 1 hour

7. A "handkerchief head" is ____________. ____
(*a*) a cool cat
(*b*) a porter
(*c*) an "Uncle Tom"
(*d*) a hoddi
(*e*) a "preacher"

Answers It is obvious how this test illustrates, in an exaggerated fashion, the difficulties that a black from an inner-city background might have in responding to items on the typical intelligence test, which mirrors the dominant middle- and upper-class white culture. The correct answers are **1.** *d;* **2.** *d;* **3.** *a;* **4.** *d;* **5.** *c;* **6.** *c;* **7.** *c.*

Just as absurd, you say? On the contrary, there is considerably more reason to use this second item on an intelligence test than the first example, which was made up of nonsense syllables. Although this second item may appear meaningless to the white population of the United States, to urban blacks the question might be a reasonable test of their knowledge.

The item is drawn from a test created by sociologist Adrian Dove, who tried to illustrate a problem that has plagued the developers of IQ tests from the beginning. By using terminology that would be familiar to urban blacks with inner-city backgrounds, but typically unfamiliar to whites (and to blacks raised within the dominant white culture), he dramatized the fact that cultural experience could play a critical role in determining intelligence-test scores. (The answer to the item presented above, by the way, is *c*. To try your hand at other items drawn from Dove's test, see the Try It! box.)

The importance of devising fair intelligence tests that measure knowledge unrelated to cultural and family background and experience would be minor if

ANSWERS TO REVIEW QUESTIONS

Review II: **1.** a **2.** False **3.** d **4.** Mainstreaming increases educational opportunities, increases social acceptance, and facilitates integration into society. **5.** False it were not for one important and persistent finding: Members of certain racial and cultural groups consistently score lower than members of other groups (MacKenzie, 1984). For example, as a group blacks tend to average about 15 IQ points lower than whites. Does this reflect a true difference in intelligence, or are the questions biased in the kinds of knowledge they test? Clearly, if whites perform better because of their greater familiarity with the kind of information that is being tested, their higher IQ scores are not necessarily an indication that they are more intelligent than members of other groups.

In fact, there is good reason to believe that some standardized IQ tests contain elements that discriminate against minority-group members whose experiences differ from those of the white majority. Consider the question: "What would you do if another child grabbed your hat and ran with it?" Most white middle-class children answer that they would tell an adult, and this response is scored as "correct." On the other hand, a reasonable response might be to chase the person and fight to get the hat back, the answer chosen by many urban black children—but one which is scored as incorrect (Albee, 1978).

The Basic Controversy: Heredity versus Environment

In an attempt to produce what has come to be called a **culture-fair IQ test**, one that does not discriminate against members of any minority cultural group, psychologists have tried to devise test items which assess experiences that are common to all cultures or which place an emphasis on questions that do not require language usage. However, test makers have found this difficult to do, and some culture-fair tests have produced even larger discrepancies between majority and minority groups than traditional tests which rely more heavily on verbal skills (Anastasi, 1982).

Culture-fair IQ test: *A test that does not discriminate against members of any minority culture group*

The efforts of psychologists to produce culture-fair measures of intelligence relates to a lingering controversy concerning differences in intelligence between members of minority and majority groups. In attempting to identify whether there are differences between such groups, psychologists have been faced with the broader issue of determining the relative contribution to intelligence of genetic factors (i.e., heredity) and experience (i.e., environment).

Arthur Jensen, an educational psychologist, fueled the fires of the debate with the 1969 publication of an article in which he argued that an analysis of IQ differences between whites and blacks suggested that, although environmental factors played a role, there were also basic genetic differences between the two races underlying the differences in measured intelligence. He based his argument on a number of findings. For instance, the finding that whites typically score about 15 points higher, on an average, than blacks on traditional IQ tests remains even when one takes socioeconomic class into account. According to Jensen, middle- and upper-class blacks score lower than middle- and upper-class whites, just as lower-class blacks score lower on average than lower-class whites. Intelligence differences between blacks and whites, then, could not be attributed to environmental differences alone.

Moreover, intelligence in general shows a high degree of **heritability**, a measure of the degree to which a characteristic is related to genetic, inherited factors. As can be seen in Figure 7-5, the closer the genetic link between two people, the greater the correspondence of IQ scores. Using data such as these, Jensen argued that fully 75 to 80 percent of the variability in IQ scores could be attributed solely to genetic factors. If we rule out environmental causes of differences between races in IQ scores, then, we are left with the conclusion—

Heritability: *A measure of the degree to which a characteristic is related to genetic, inherited factors, as opposed to environmental factors*

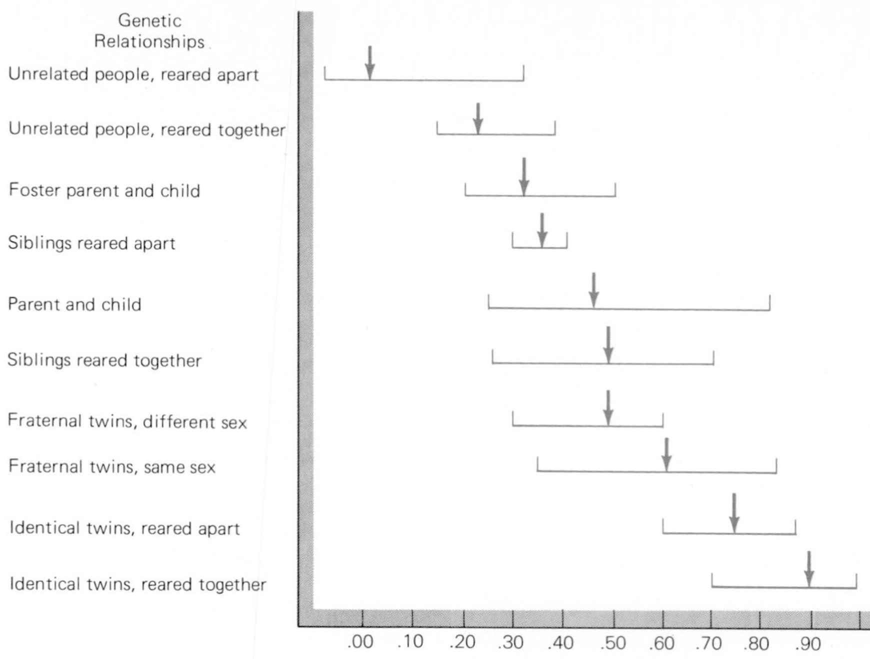

Figure 7-5
Summary findings on the correlation of IQ and genetic relationship: The length of the line indicates the range of correlations found in different studies, while the arrows show the average correlation. Note, for example, that the average correlation for unrelated people reared apart is quite low, while the correlation for identical twins, reared together, is substantially higher. The more similar the genetic and environmental background of two people, the greater the correlation.

claimed by Jensen—that these differences in IQs are caused by genetic-based differences in intelligence.

The psychology community reacted quickly to Jensen's contentions and convincingly refuted many of his claims. For one thing, even when socioeconomic conditions are supposedly held constant there remain wide variations among individual households, and no one can convincingly assert that living conditions of blacks and whites are identical even when socioeconomic status is similar. Secondly, as we discussed earlier, there is reason to believe that traditional IQ tests may discriminate against lower-class urban blacks, asking for information regarding experiences to which they are unlikely to have been exposed.

Moreover, there is direct evidence that blacks who are raised in enriched environments do not tend, as a group, to have lower IQ scores than whites in similar environments. For example, a study by Sandra Scarr and Richard Weinberg examined black children who were adopted as young children by white middle-class families of above-average intelligence (Scarr & Weinberg, 1976). The IQ scores of the children averaged 106—about 15 points above the average IQ scores of unadopted black children reared in their own homes, and above average in terms of the general population. In addition, the younger a child was when adopted, the higher his or her IQ score tended to be. The evidence that genetic factors play the major role in determining racial differences in IQ, then, is not compelling—although the question still evokes controversy (MacKenzie, 1984).

Ultimately, it is crucial to remember that IQ scores and intelligence have greatest relevance in terms of individuals, not groups, and that by far the greatest discrepancies in IQ occur not between mean *group* IQ scores but between the IQ scores of *individuals*. There are blacks who score high on IQ tests and whites who score low, just as there are whites who score high and blacks who score low. For the concept of intelligence to be useful in improving society, then, we must look at how *individuals* perform, not the groups to which they belong.

Moreover, traditional IQ scores are not always good predictors of success in school or life (as discussed earlier in the Psychology at Work box), and in fact actual school achievement differences between whites and blacks appear to be narrowing (Jones, 1984). In sum, questions concerning differences in white and black intelligence levels may prove to be less pertinent than those relating to understanding the differences in IQ between individuals, without regard to their race.

Neither Heredity nor Environment: Putting the Question in Perspective

There is no absolute resolution to the question of the degree to which intelligence is influenced by heredity and by environment, because we are dealing with an issue for which true experiments to unequivocally determine causality cannot be done. (A moment's thought about how one might experimentally assign infants to enriched or deprived environments will reveal the impossibility of devising ethically reasonable experiments!)

The more critical question to ask, then, is not so much whether it is primarily heredity or environment that underlies intelligence but whether there is anything we can do to maximize the intellectual development of each individual (Scarr & Carter-Saltzman, 1982). We then will be able to make changes in the environment—which may take the form of improvements in home and school—that can lead each person to reach his or her highest potential.

RECAP AND REVIEW III

Recap

- The issue of whether IQ tests are biased in favor of dominant groups in society has become important because blacks tend to average around 15 IQ points lower than whites on standardized tests.
- Culture-fair IQ tests have been developed in an attempt to avoid discriminating against minority groups.
- Major controversies concerning intelligence consider the degree to which IQ is determined by heredity and by environment and whether there are racial differences in intelligence.
- Probably the most important issue concerning IQ is not the degree to which it is caused by heredity and by environment, but what we can do to nurture and maximize the development of intelligence in all individuals.

Review

1. IQ tests have been criticized because of
   a. Length **b.** Scoring devices **c.** The testing environment **d.** Cultural bias
2. An argument supporting genetic differences in intelligence points out that the disparity between blacks' and whites' scores on IQ tests is consistent regardless of socioeconomic class. True or false?
3. ______________ refers to a measure of the degree to which a trait is related to genetic, inherited factors.
4. Evidence has shown that the average IQ of blacks who are raised in white middle-class homes, with parents of above-average intelligence, is higher than the average IQ of unadopted blacks raised in their own homes. True or false?

(Answers to the review questions are at the bottom of page 233.)

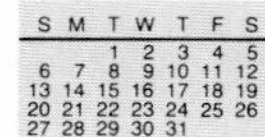

Psychology Looks Toward the 1990s
Establishing Intelligence: The Earliest Signs of IQ

How soon can we determine an individual's intelligence?

Until recently, most psychologists would have answered that it is not until a child is 3 or 4 years of age that accurate predictions can be made. However, a growing number of psychologists now feel that relatively accurate estimates of adult intelligence can be made in children as young as 6 months of age (Bornstein & Sigman, 1986).

Specifically, it appears that certain tasks that show how babies process information in the first six months of their lives are correlated with their performance on IQ tests when they reach school age. For example, according to Marc Bornstein of New York University and Susan Rose of Albert Einstein College of Medicine of New York, tests of visual attentiveness administered during the first six months correlate with IQ scores at ages 4 and 6 years of +.50 and +.60, respectively. Moreover, these results are independent of children's socioeconomic status or the educational level of their parents (Kolata, 1987).

In Bornstein's and Rose's work, a group of 6-month-old infants were shown photographs of faces or abstract patterns and geometric shapes. Next, after viewing the first picture, they were shown a new one, and the experimenters measured how long the infant spent looking at the new, as opposed to the old, picture. Overall, infants spent an average of 60 percent of their time looking at new pictures, but there were large differences between children. It was these differences that were associated with intelligence tests scores at ages 4 and 6.

The reason that such a test seems sensitive to the infants' intelligence is that the processes that are being measured seem to go beyond mere perceptual memory and instead are related to the way in which the infants are processing information. It appears that the babies not only remember the first photo, but are also discriminating the novelty of the second one, comparing it to the first.

It is still too early to judge what the practical implications of these findings are. For one thing, there are still ample possibilities for the influence of environmental factors, since the majority of school-age intelligence is not predicted by the six-month visual attentiveness measure results. Moreover, as we mentioned earlier in the chapter, IQ scores are not particularly adequate predictors of ultimate success in life.

Still, these new findings suggest the possibility that interventions can be made in the earliest years of life which might help raise the IQs of children who are at risk for poor school performance (the measure which is most closely associated with IQ scores). The task now for psychologists is not only to hone their measures more finely, but to identify the sort of interventions that would be most successful in raising children's intelligence levels.

LOOKING BACK

1. Because intelligence can take many forms, defining it presents a challenge to psychologists. One commonly accepted view is that intelligence is the capacity to understand the world, think rationally, and use resources effectively when faced with challenges.

2. Intelligence tests are used to measure intelligence. They provide a mental age which, when divided by a person's chronological age and then multiplied by 100, gives an IQ, or intelligence quotient, score. Specific tests of intelligence include the Stanford-Binet test, the Wechsler Adult Intelligence Scale—Revised (WAIS-R), and the Wechsler Intelligence Scale for Children—Revised (WISC-R). In addition to intelligence tests, other standardized tests take the form of achievement tests (which measure level of knowledge in a given area) and aptitude tests (which predict ability in a given area). The Scholastic Aptitude Test (SAT) is the best-known example of an aptitude test; it is designed to predict college performance.

3. Although intelligence tests are able to identify individual differences in intelligence, they do not increase our understanding of the underlying nature of intelligence. Among the alternative conceptions of intelligence are those suggesting that there are two kinds of intelligence: fluid intelligence and crystallized intelligence. Guilford's approach puts forward a structure-of-intellect model, which theorizes that there are 150 separate mental abilities. Finally, information-processing approaches suggest that intelligence should be conceptualized the way in which people represent and use material cognitively.

4. At the two extremes of intelligence are the mentally retarded and the intellectually gifted. The levels of mental retardation include mild retardation (IQ of 55 to 69), moderate retardation (IQ of 40 to 54), severe retardation (IQ of 25 to 39), and profound retardation (IQ below 25). About one-third of the cases of retardation have a known biological cause, with Down's syndrome being the most common type of retardation with a biological basis. Most cases, however, are classified as due to familial retardation, in which there is no known biological cause, but a history of retardation within a person's family.

5. There have been a number of recent advances in the treatment of both the mentally retarded and the intellectually gifted, particularly after federal law mandated that the mentally retarded be educated in the "least-restrictive environment." The most frequent technique used to carry out the law is mainstreaming, in which the mentally retarded are integrated into regular education classrooms as much as possible. Special programs for the intellectually gifted, such as the Study of the Mathematically Precocious Youth (SMPY), have been designed to allow the gifted to reach their fullest potential.

6. Traditional intelligence tests frequently have been criticized as being biased in favor of the white middle-class population majority. That controversy has led to attempts to devise culture-fair tests, IQ measures which avoid questions that depend on a particular cultural background.

7. Two major controversies have grown out of research on intelligence: whether there are racial differences in intelligence and the degree to which intelligence is influenced by heredity and by the environment. Although some researchers have claimed that differences in measured IQ are due primarily to heredity, equally compelling research—which notes important environmental differences between white and black households—suggests that the differences can be explained by environmental factors. The more important fact, though, is that individual IQ scores vary far more than group IQ scores. It is critical, then, to ask not whether intelligence is influenced primarily by heredity or by the environment, but what we can do to maximize the intellectual development of each individual.

KEY TERMS AND CONCEPTS

savant syndrome (p. 210)
intelligence (213)
intelligence test (213)
mental age (213)
chronological age (214)
intelligence quotient (IQ) score (214)
deviation IQ score (214)
Stanford-Binet test (214)
Wechsler Adult Intelligence Scale—Revised (WAIS-R) (215)
Wechsler Intelligence Scale for Children—Revised (WISC-R) (215)
achievement test (215)
aptitude test (216)
fluid intelligence (217)
crystallized intelligence (217)
structure-of-intellect model (217)
practical intelligence (219)
mental retardation (222)
mild retardation (222)
moderate retardation (222)
severe retardation (222)
profound retardation (222)
Down's syndrome (223)
familial retardation (223)
least-restrictive environment (223)
mainstreaming (223)
intellectually gifted (224)
artificial intelligence (225)
culture-fair IQ test (227)
heritability (227)

FOR FURTHER STUDY AND APPLICATION

Wigdor, A. K., & Garner, W. R. (Eds.) (1982). *Ability testing: Uses, consequences, and controversies.* Washington, D.C.: National Academy Press.

This is a comprehensive look at intelligence, ranging from the history of testing to such contemporary issues as the use of IQ scores by schoolteachers.

Sternberg, R. J. (Ed.). (1982). *Handbook of human intelligence.* New York: Cambridge University Press.

Written by the leading experts in the field, this book provides a state-of-the-art view of intelligence. Although technical, it is probably the best single source on intelligence available today.

Eysenck, H. J., vs. Kamin, L. (1981). *The intelligence controversy.* New York: Wiley.

This intriguing book presents widely divergent views of the nature of intelligence and covers many of the major issues raised by psychologists concerning the topic.

Sternberg, R. J. (1986). *Intelligence applied: Understanding and increasing your intellectual skills.* San Diego: Harcourt Brace Jovanovich.

A practical look at ways of improving your intellectual abilities, from a leading theoretician.

ANSWERS TO REVIEW QUESTIONS

Review III: **1.** d **2.** True **3.** Heritability **4.** True

PART FOUR

FEELING AND EXPERIENCING THE WORLD

We now move away from the realm of thought into that of feelings and inner experience. We will meet a person trapped for forty days in a canyon, and see how the motivation to live results in an amazing story of survival. And we will meet a young woman who uses daydreaming to come to an important decision about her life.

In this part of the book, we will discuss how various kinds of motivation affect our choice of behaviors. We examine how emotions influence behavior and their function in everyday life. We also focus on consciousness, considering how we experience it and how our typical state of consciousness can be altered.

In Chapter 8, then, we discuss the motivation behind behavior and the way our emotions are related to our behavior.

In Chapter 9, we turn to states of consciousness, including sleep, hypnosis, and drugs.

CHAPTER 8

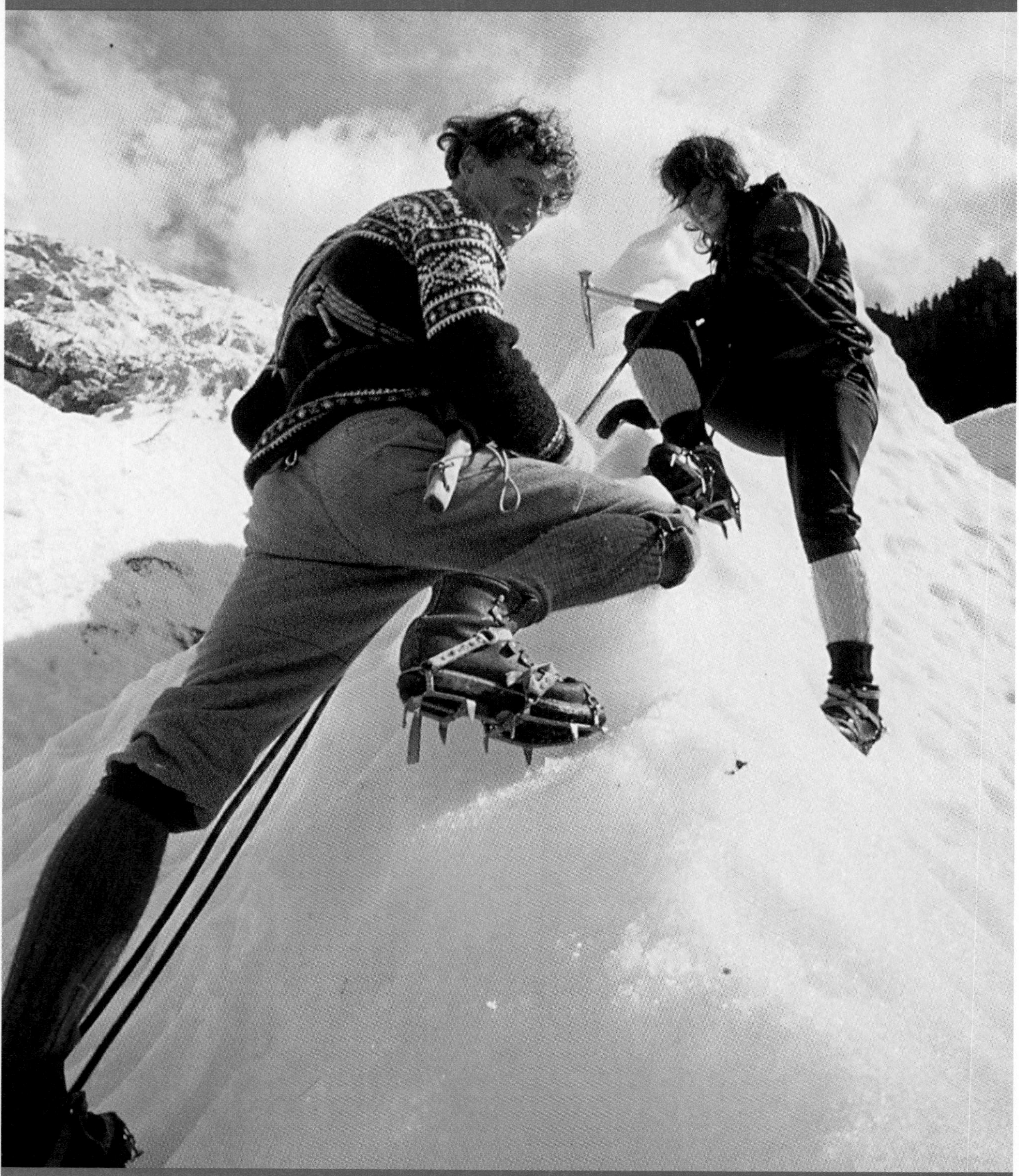

MOTIVATION AND EMOTION

PROLOGUE

LOOKING AHEAD

THE PRIMARY DRIVES
Eating your needs away: Hunger
The informed consumer of psychology: Dieting and losing weight successfully
The Facts of Life: Human Sexual Motivation
Recap and review I

HUMAN STRIVING: ACHIEVEMENT, AFFILIATION, AND POWER MOTIVATION
Striving for success: The need for achievement
Striving for friendship: The need for affiliation
Striving for impact on others: The need for power

COMBINING HUMAN MOTIVES
Homeostasis is not enough: Theories of motivation
THE CUTTING EDGE. For Money or Love?: Rewarding Intrinsic Motivation
TRY IT! Do You Seek Out Sensation?
Ordering motivational needs: Maslow's hierarchy
Recap and review II

UNDERSTANDING EMOTIONAL EXPERIENCES
What emotions do for us: Understanding the functions of emotions
Labeling our feelings: Determining the range of emotions

KNOWING HOW WE FEEL: UNDERSTANDING OUR OWN EMOTIONS
Do gut reactions equal emotions?: The James-Lange theory
Physiological reactions as the result of emotions: The Cannon-Bard theory
Emotions as labels: The Schachter-Singer theory
Summing up the theories of emotion
PSYCHOLOGY AT WORK. The Truth about Lies: Using Emotional Responses to Separate the Honest from the Dishonest
Recap and review III

EXPRESSING EMOTIONS: THE ROLE OF NONVERBAL BEHAVIOR
If you met some New Guineans, would you know what they were feeling? Universality in emotional expressivity
Smile, though you're feeling blue: The facial-feedback hypothesis
The informed consumer of psychology: Can you "read" others' nonverbal behavior?
Recap and review IV
PSYCHOLOGY LOOKS TOWARD THE 1990s. Understanding the Link between Diet and Exercise

LOOKING BACK

KEY TERMS AND CONCEPTS

FOR FURTHER STUDY AND APPLICATION

PROLOGUE

Marine Lance Cpl. Karl Bell, 22, crawled under a rock to escape the hot afternoon sun. His right ankle throbbed painfully, his arms stung where thorns had torn at his blisters.

It was the thirtieth day of his entrapment in the canyon, and he was no closer to finding a way up the sheer rock walls. Every attempt had left him weaker. Soon he would not even have the strength to try.

He smacked at an ant scurrying on his arm, and then put the half-inch black carcass into his mouth. Slowly, he chewed it, crunching the thin shell. The taste was bitter, though not repugnant. So he crushed another ant from the many on his pants. Before long, he had eaten at least twenty ants.

Lying back in the dirt and leaves, Bell felt he had crossed a line that separated living from raw, instinctive survival. *Do what you must,* he told himself. *You're too young to die* (Michelmore, 1984, pp. 116–117).

LOOKING AHEAD

After spending a total of forty days in the canyon into which he had fallen in a freak hiking accident, Bell finally managed to find a way out. He had lost 75 pounds, his ankle was fractured, his body was covered with hundreds of cuts, and his clothing was torn to shreds. He had experienced the extremes of emotion, from elation—when he thought he spotted rescuers—to the depths of despair—when he felt that he was doomed. But he had managed to stay alive, fighting day and night to save himself.

What was it that drove Karl Bell on, even in the face of seemingly insurmountable odds? Motivation and emotion, two important topics in psychology, provide an answer to the question. Motivation looks at the factors that direct and energize the behavior of humans and other organisms, while emotion deals with the feelings we experience throughout the course of our lives. Together, these topics seek to explain the internal forces producing behavior and feelings.

Motives: *Desired goals that prompt behavior*

Psychologists who study motivation seek to discover the **motives**, or desired goals, that underlie behavior. Such motives may be as fundamental as acquiring food to relieve hunger or as inconsequential as taking a walk in order to obtain exercise. To the psychologist specializing in the study of motivation, the common factor of both behaviors is the underlying motives that steer and energize the choice of both activities.

Motivation: *The factors that direct and energize behavior*

The study of **motivation**, then, basically consists of trying to identify why people do the things they do. Such questions as "Why do people choose particular goals for which to strive?" "What specific motives direct behavior?" and "What are the individual differences in motivation that account for the variability in people's behavior?" are asked by psychologists specializing in motivation.

While psychologists studying motivation are concerned with the forces that direct future behavior, the focus of the study of emotion is on the internal experience of a person at any given moment. Most of us have felt a variety of emotions: the happiness of getting an A on a difficult exam, the sadness brought about by the death of a loved one, the anger of being unfairly treated. Because emotions play such an important role in our everyday lives by acting as a crucial influence on our behavior, they have been a critical focus of study for psychologists.

In this chapter, we discuss motivation and emotion. The chapter begins with a discussion of fundamental, biologically based motives such as hunger and considers how underlying biological needs interact with social factors to influence a person's behavior. We then examine motives that are relatively unique to humans: the need for achievement, the need for affiliation, and the need for power. Focusing on the major theories of motivation, we discuss how the different motives and needs people experience jointly affect behavior.

We then turn to a discussion of the nature of emotional experience on both a physiological and a cognitive level. We consider the roles and functions that emotions play in people's lives, discussing a number of theories meant to explain how people understand what emotions they are experiencing at a given moment. Finally, the chapter ends with a discussion of how emotions are communicated to others through nonverbal behavior.

After reading and studying this chapter, then, you will be able to

- Identify and describe the primary motives
- Differentiate the biological and social factors underlying eating behavior and discuss the strategies suggested for dieting
- Describe the biological bases of human sexuality
- Discuss the major findings regarding solitary sex, premarital sex, marital sex, and sex between same-sex couples
- Describe the two major forms of nonconsenting sex: rape and sexual abuse of children
- Explain the needs for achievement, affiliation, and power, and what effects they have on behavior
- Describe the major theories of motivation and discuss how different motivational needs are related to one another
- Explain the factors leading to the experience of an emotion
- Identify the major emotions and their functions
- Describe the major theories of emotion
- Discuss the relationship between nonverbal behavior and emotional expression
- Define and apply the key terms and concepts listed at the end of the chapter

When Gabriela Andersen-Schiess determinedly continued through the last lap of her 26-mile marathon run, her behavior illustrated the limits to which motivation can push an individual. (*Focus on Sports*)

THE PRIMARY DRIVES

As she entered the stadium, it was apparent that something was seriously wrong with Swiss Olympic runner Gabriella Andersen-Schiess. A contender in the 26-mile marathon in the 1984 Olympics, she wobbled, stumbled, and almost fell as she entered the stadium for the final few laps around the field. Her gait was uneven, and her head tilted to one side, prompting Olympic officials to run to her side to determine whether she should be removed from the race for medical reasons. Yet Andersen-Schiess waved them away, and, as a stadiumful of spectators watched with a combination of admiration and horror, she made her way around the field and crossed the finish line, then collapsed. Officials, who were later widely criticized for allowing her to finish, said in their defense that her motivation to complete the race was so overwhelmingly apparent that they felt they had no right to stop her, even though it might have been in her own best long-term interests for them to have done so.

Gabriella Andersen-Schiess's behavior illustrates both the limits and strengths of human determination to reach a goal; it exemplifies an occasion in which a person's thoughts, feelings, and emotions can override the body's efficient regulation of its internal operation to attain a goal that is perceived to be important.

Drive: *A motivational tension or arousal that energizes behavior in order to fulfill a need*

To understand human motivation, one must begin with the concept of **drive**. A drive is a motivational tension or arousal that energizes behavior in order to fulfill some need. Many basic kinds of drives, such as hunger, thirst, sleepiness, and sex are related to biological requirements of the body or species. We call these **primary drives**. Primary drives contrast with **secondary drives**, drives in which no obvious biological need is being fulfilled. In secondary drives, the needs are brought about by prior experience and learning. For example, Andersen-Schiess's motivation to complete her marathon run fulfilled no biological need; instead, she was attempting to fulfill a secondary drive to succeed. Similarly, as we will discuss later, some people have strong needs to achieve academically and in their careers; we can say that their drive to achieve is motivating their behavior.

Primary drives: *Biological needs such as hunger, thirst, fatigue, and sex*

Secondary drives: *Drives in which no biological need is fulfilled (e.g., need for achievement)*

We usually try to resolve a primary drive by reducing the need underlying it: After exercising, we typically become thirsty and seek out the nearest water fountain. We become hungry after not eating for a few hours, and may raid the refrigerator if our next scheduled meal is too far away. If the weather turns cold, we put on extra clothing or raise the setting on the thermostat in order to keep warm.

The reason for such behavior is homeostasis, a basic motivational principle underlying primary drives. **Homeostasis** is the process by which an organism tries to maintain some optimal level of internal biological functioning. It does this by compensating for deviations from its usual, balanced, internal state. Although not all basic biological behaviors related to motivation fit a homeostatic model—sexual behavior is one example—the other primary drives of life, including hunger, thirst, and the need for sleep, can be explained reasonably well by such an approach.

Homeostasis (ho me o STAY sis): *The process by which an organism tries to maintain an internal biological balance, or "steady state"*

Eating Your Needs Away: Hunger

Losing unwanted weight is an American obsession. Many people spend untold time, energy, and money attempting to regulate the amount and type of food they eat in order to decrease their weight. Others, with a problem many of us would envy, are concerned with trying to *gain* weight. Yet, in most cases, people who are not monitoring their weight show only minor weight fluctuations in spite of substantial variations in how much they eat and exercise over time. Clearly, then, food intake is subject to some form of homeostasis.

Psychologists investigating eating motivation began their search for explanations with animals, which are relatively free from the problems of obesity that beset human beings. Most animals, when left in an environment in which food is readily available, do a good job regulating their intake—as anyone who leaves a dish of food constantly available for a pet knows. Cats, for instance, will eat only until their immediate hunger is satisfied; they will leave the remainder, returning to it only when internal cues tell them to eat.

Moreover, there appear to be internal mechanisms that regulate not only the quantity of food intake, but the kind of food that an animal desires. Hungry rats who have been deprived of particular foods tend to seek out alternatives that contain the specific nutrients their diet is lacking, and laboratory experiments show that animals given the choice of a wide variety of foods in cafeteria-like settings choose a fairly well balanced diet (Rozin, 1977).

The mechanisms by which organisms know if they require food or should stop eating are complex ones (Keesey & Powley, 1986). It is not just a matter

The fact that our food preferences are
The fact that our food preferences are affected by social influences and past experiences illustrates that eating is not just a function of internal, biological factors. (*Alex Webb/Magnum*)

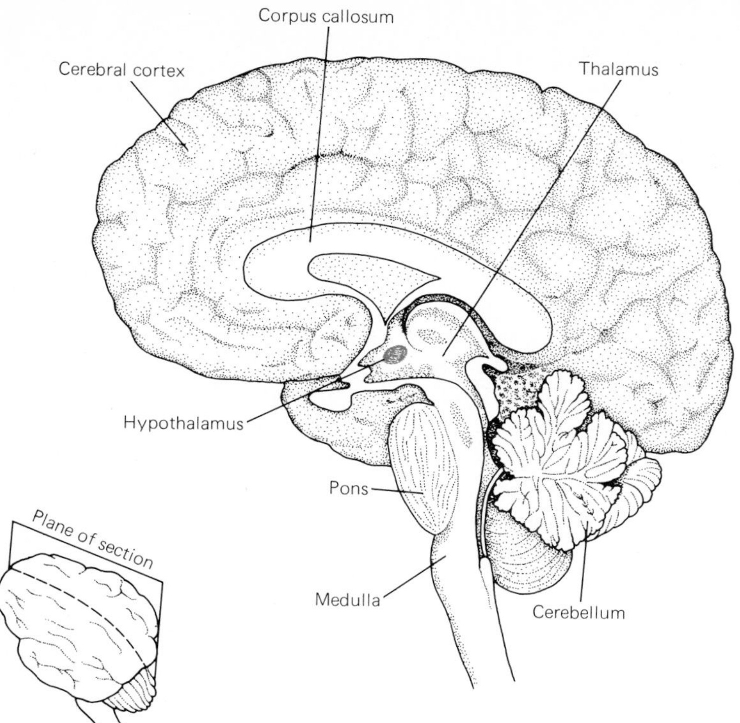

Figure 8-1
The hypothalamus acts as the brain's "feeding center," being primarily responsible for food intake.

Figure 8-2
Following an operation in which its ventromedial hypothalamus was cut, this obviously pudgy rat became hyperphagic, and tips the scales at something on the order of four times its normal weight. (Courtesy of Neal E. Miller.)

of an empty stomach causing hunger pangs and a full one alleviating hunger, since people who have had their stomachs removed still experience the sensation of hunger (Inglefinger, 1944). Similarly, laboratory animals tend to eat larger quantities when their food is low in nutrients; in contrast, when given a high-nutrient diet, they lower their food intake—regardless of the degree to which their stomachs are empty or full or the amount of time it takes to eat the food (Harte, Travers, & Savich, 1948).

It appears, then, that animals, as well as people, are sensitive to nutritional value of the foods they eat (Barker, Best, & Domjan, 1977). Some research suggests that specific cells are used to regulate the three major sources of energy derived from food: sugar, fat, and protein (Rozin, 1977). Moreover, one particular part of the brain, the **hypothalamus** (see Figure 8-1), also appears to be primarily responsible for food intake. Injury to the hypothalamus has been shown to cause radical changes in eating behavior, depending upon the site of the injury. For example, rats whose **lateral hypothalamus** is damaged may literally starve to death; they refuse food when offered, and unless they are force-fed they eventually die. In contrast, rats with an injury to the **ventromedial hypothalamus** display the opposite problem: extreme overeating. Rats with this injury can increase in weight by as much as 400 percent (see Figure 8-2). Similar phenomena occur in humans who have tumors of the hypothalamus.

Hypothalamus (hy po THAL uh muss): *Located below the thalamus of the brain, its major function is to maintain homeostasis, including food intake*

Lateral hypothalamus (hy po THAL uh muss): *The portion of the hypothalamus that signals a need for food*

Ventromedial hypothalamus (ven tro MEE dee ul hy po THAL uh muss): *The portion of the hypothalamus that signals that the body has consumed enough food*

While it is clear that the hypothalamus plays an important role in regulating food intake, the exact mechanism by which it operates is uncertain. Some researchers think it affects the experience of hunger directly, while others hypothesize that it affects the neuronal connections relating to eating behavior itself (Stricker & Zigmond, 1976).

Weight set point: *According to one theory, the specific weight a body strives to maintain*

One theory suggests that hypothalamus injury affects the weight set point by which food intake is regulated (Nisbett, 1972). The **weight set point** is the particular level of weight the body strives to maintain. Acting as a kind of internal ''weight thermostat,'' the hypothalamus calls for either more or less food intake. According to this explanation, injury to the hypothalamus drastically raises or lowers the set point, and the organism strives to meet its internal goal by increasing or decreasing its food consumption.

Social Factors in Eating Anyone who has finished a full meal, saying that he or she couldn't eat another thing, and has then proceeded to consume a huge piece of a delicious-looking pie for dessert, knows that internal biological factors are not the whole story when it comes to explaining eating behavior. External social factors related to what we have learned from past experience also plays an important role.

Take, for example, the simple fact that people customarily eat breakfast, lunch, and dinner at approximately the same times every day. Because we are accustomed to eating on schedule every day, we tend to feel hungry as the usual hour approaches—sometimes quite independently of what our internal cues are telling us. Similarly, we tend to take roughly the same amount of food on our plates every day—even though the amount of exercise we may have had, and consequently our need for energy replenishment, varies from day to day. We also tend to prefer particular foods over others; grasshoppers may be a delicacy in one culture, but few of us in western cultures find them greatly appealing—despite their potentially high nutritional value. In sum, cultural influences and our own individual habits play an important role in determining when, what, and how much we eat (Polivy & Herman, 1985).

Obesity (o BEE sih tee): *The state of being more than 20 percent above one's ideal weight*

An oversensitivity to external social cues seems to be related to **obesity** (typically defined as being more than 20 percent above the average weight for a person of a given height) in many individuals. Research has shown, for example, that obese people who are placed in a room next to an inviting bowl of crackers are apt to eat considerably more than nonobese people—even though they may have just finished a filling sandwich (Schachter, Goldman, & Gordon, 1968). In addition, obese individuals are more apt to scorn and avoid unpleasant-tasting

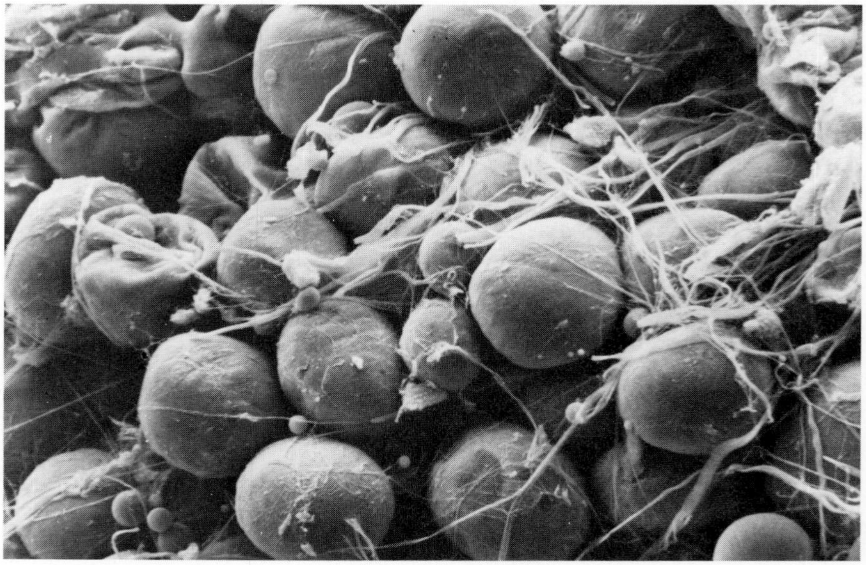

The appearance of these fat cells, magnified many times, hints at the outcome of overeating. (From *Tissues and Organs:* A Text-Atlas of Scanning Electron Microscopy by Richard G. Kessel and Randy H. Kardon. W. H. Freeman and Company. Copyright © 1979.)

food—even if they have been deprived of food for a period of time—than nonobese individuals, who tend to be less concerned with the taste of the food. Finally, the obese are less apt to eat if doing so involves any sort of work: Obese subjects in one experiment were less likely to eat nuts that had to be shelled, but ate large amounts of unshelled nuts. Nonobese people, in contrast, ate the same amount of nuts, regardless of whether it was necessary to remove the shells (Schachter, 1971).

At the same time that obese people are overly sensitive to external cues, they may be relatively insensitive to internal hunger cues. In fact, there is essentially no correspondence between reports of hunger in obese individuals and the amount of time they have been deprived of food, in contrast to a significant correlation for people of normal weight (Nisbett, 1968). It appears, then, that many obese people give undue attention to external cues and are less aware of the internal cues that help nonobese people to regulate their eating behavior.

On the other hand, many individuals who are highly reliant on external cues have never become obese, and there are quite a few obese people who are relatively unresponsive to external cues (Rodin, 1981). Other factors, then, are clearly at work in determining why a person becomes obese.

The Weight Set Point and Obesity One suspect that appears to be a plausible cause of obesity is the weight set point. Specifically, it is possible that overweight people have higher set points than people of normal weight. Because their set points are unusually high, their attempts to lose weight by eating less may make them especially sensitive to external, food-related cues, and therefore more apt to eat, perpetuating their obesity.

But why may some people's weight set points be higher than others? One factor may be the number of fat cells in the body, which rises as a function of weight increase. The set-point level may be a function of the number of fat cells a person has. Any increase in weight, then, raises the number of fat cells, consequently raising the set point. Moreover, any loss of weight after the age of 2 years does not decrease the number of fat cells in the body, although it may cause them to shrink in size (Knittle, 1975). Hence, although fat babies are sometimes considered cute, obese children may have acquired so many fat cells that their weight set point is too high—long after they have reached the age at which being chubby or fat is no longer appealing.

In sum, according to weight-set-point theory, the presence of too many fat cells may result in the set point becoming "stuck" at a higher level than is desirable. Under such circumstances, losing weight becomes a difficult proposition, since one is constantly at odds with one's own internal set point.

Other factors also work against people's efforts to lose weight. For example, there are large differences in people's **metabolism**, the rate at which energy is produced and expended by the body. Some people seem to be able to eat as much as they want without gaining weight, while others, who may eat only half as much, gain weight readily. Actually, those who gain weight easily are biologically more efficient: They have the advantage (?) of easily converting food into body tissue. In contrast, those who are able to eat large quantities without gaining weight are inefficient in using the foods they eat; much gets wasted—and they stay thin.

Metabolism (meh TAB o liz um): *The rate at which energy is produced and expended by the body*

There are still other factors that may lead to obesity. Children who are given food whenever they report to their parents that they are upset—"Here, have some cookies; you'll feel better"—may learn, through the basic mechanisms of classical and operant conditioning, that eating is associated with consolation, and so may eat whenever they experience difficulties as adults. Stress, anxiety, and depression, which are ''treated'' by parents by providing food, also may become learned responses to any emotional difficulty, leading to eating behavior that has little or nothing to do with internal hunger cues.

In the most extreme cases, eating behavior becomes so disordered that it becomes life-threatening. One major disorder, which afflicts mainly females, is **anorexia nervosa**. People who suffer from the problem may literally starve themselves to death, while denying that their appearance—which may become skeleton-like—is unusual. Their lives revolve around food, although they eat little themselves; they may cook for others, go shopping for food frequently, or collect cookbooks (Brunch, 1973).

Anorexia nervosa (an o REX ee ah ner VO sah): *An eating disorder, usually striking young women in which symptoms include self-starvation or near-starvation in an attempt to avoid obesity*

Bulimia (boo LIM ee ah): *An eating disorder characterized by vast intake of food that may be followed by self-induced vomiting*

A related problem is **bulimia**, a disorder in which a person eats incredibly large quantities of food (Sinoway, Rawpp, & Newman, 1985). An entire gallon of ice cream and a whole pie may easily be consumed in a single sitting. Following such a binge, sufferers feel guilt and may induce vomiting to rid themselves of the food. Constant vomiting, and the use of drugs to induce the vomiting, may create a chemical imbalance that can lead to death, even though the weight of a person suffering from bulimia typically remains normal.

The Informed Consumer of Psychology: Dieting and Losing Weight Successfully

In a country where obesity afflicts a significant proportion of the population—as is the case in the United States—dieting is big business. Yet dieting often represents a losing battle: Most people who diet eventually regain the weight they have lost, so they try again, and get caught in a seemingly endless cycle of weight loss and gain. Given what we know about the causes of obesity this is not entirely surprising, since there appear to be so many factors that affect eating behavior and weight.

Still, the knowledge that psychologists and other health professionals have amassed can provide us with a basis for formulating some concrete guidelines regarding the most effective methods of dieting. Among the approaches that have proved to be most successful are the following:

One proven way of losing weight is to increase one's physical exercise. (© *Joseph Nettis 1984/Photo Researchers, Inc.*)

- Exercise. When you exercise, you burn fat stored in your body, which is used as fuel for the muscles that are working. As this fat is used, you will probably lose weight. Moreover, weight-set-point theory suggests another advantage to moderate exercise: It may lower your set point. Experts recommend at least thirty consecutive minutes of moderate exercise at least three times a week.
- Lower your intake of food. In general, an overall decrease in the amount of food you eat will eventually lead to a decrease in weight. But keep in mind that you must consider the energy value of the food as well as the overall quantity, and that it is necessary to have a diet that is well balanced in different kinds of nutrients.
- Decrease the effects of external social stimuli. There are a number of things you can do to lower your susceptibility to external food cues. For example, you can give yourself smaller portions of food, or you can leave the table before you see what is available for dessert. Don't even buy snack foods such as peanuts or potato chips; if they're not readily available in the kitchen cupboard, you're not apt to eat them. Wrap foods in the refrigerator in aluminum foil so you

cannot see the contents. That way, you won't be tantalized by the sight of the food every time you open the refrigerator.

■ Avoid fad diets. They won't work over the long term.

■ When you reach your desired weight, you're not finished. You must maintain the habits you built up while dieting in order to avoid gaining back the weight you have lost.

While these techniques require commitment, willpower, and hard work, they have been proved effective. If you follow them, you are likely to lose weight.

The Facts of Life: Human Sexual Motivation

You would probably find no argument with the statement that sex is very different from hunger as a motivational drive. Unlike hunger, no one ever died from an unfulfilled sexual need. Similar to hunger, however, sex remains one of our primary motivating forces, fulfilling not only important biological needs but some crucial social ones as well.

As anyone who has seen two dogs mating knows, sexual behavior has a biological basis; it seems unlikely that anyone enrolled their pooches in a veterinarian's sex-education class. Instead, their sexual behavior appears to occur spontaneously, without much prompting on the part of others.

In fact, the sexual behavior of animals is strongly influenced by a number of genetically controlled factors. For instance, animal behavior is affected by the presence of hormones in the blood. Moreover, females are receptive to sexual advances only at certain, relatively limited periods of time during the year.

Human sexual behavior, by comparison, is more complicated, although the underlying biology is not all that different from related species. In males, for example, the **testes** secrete **androgen,** the male sex hormone, beginning at puberty. Not only does androgen produce secondary sex characteristics, such as the development of body hair and a deepening of the voice, but it increases the sex drive. Although there are long-term changes in the amount of androgen that is produced—with the greatest production occurring just after sexual maturity—its short-term production is fairly constant. Men, therefore, are capable of (and interested in) sexual activities without any regard to biological cycles. Given the proper stimuli leading to arousal, male sexual behavior can occur.

Testes (TES teez): *The male reproductive organs responsible for secreting androgens*

Androgen (AN dro jun): *The male sex hormone*

Women, on the other hand, show a different pattern. When they reach maturity at puberty, the **ovaries,** the female reproductive organs, produce **estrogen**—the female sex hormone. Estrogen, however, is not produced consistently; instead, its production follows a cyclical pattern. The greatest production occurs during **ovulation,** when an egg is released from the ovaries, making the chances of fertilization by a male sperm cell highest. Although in lower animals the period around ovulation is the only time that the female is receptive to sex, human beings are different. While there are variations in reported sex drive, women are receptive to sex throughout their cycles, depending on the kinds of external stimuli they encounter in their environment.

Ovaries (O vuh reez): *The female reproductive organs*

Estrogen (ES tro jun): *The female sex hormone*

Ovulation (ov u LAY shun): *The monthly release of an egg from an ovary*

Though biological factors "prime" people for sex, it takes more than hormones to motivate and produce sexual behavior. In animals it is the presence of a partner who provides arousing stimuli that leads to sexual activity. Humans are considerably more versatile; not only other people, but nearly any object, sight, smell, sound, or other stimulus can lead to sexual excitement. Because of prior associations, then, people may be "turned on" sexually by the smell of Chanel No. 5, the sight of lacy underwear, or the sound of a favorite song. The reaction to a specific, potentially arousing stimulus is a very individual one.

The Varieties of Sexual Experience The vast variety of sexual behavior in which people engage was largely a mystery shrouded in ignorance until the late 1930s, when Albert Kinsey, a biologist by training, began a series of surveys on the sexual behavior of Americans that was to span eighteen years. The resulting books—*Sexual Behavior in the Human Male* (1948) and *Sexual Behavior in the Human Female* (1953)—produced the first comprehensive look at sexual practices.

Kinsey's work set the stage for later surveys, which have provided us with a good understanding of the kinds of sexual activities and behaviors that people typically engage in in private. Of course, we are dealing with survey methods, which means that there is always the possibility that what people say they do does not match their actual sexual practices. Still, although these findings must be looked at with a degree of caution, the consistency of the results across many different samples of subjects suggests we now have a valid portrait of contemporary sexual behavior.

Masturbation (mass tur BAY shun): *Sexual self-stimulation*

One of the most widely practiced forms of sexual activity is **masturbation,** or sexual self-stimulation. Some 94 percent of all males and 63 percent of all females have masturbated at least once, and among college students, the frequency ranges from ''never'' to ''several times a day'' (Houston, 1981; Hunt, 1974). Males tend to begin masturbating earlier than females, and the frequency for those who do masturbate is higher for men than for women.

Although masturbation is often considered an activity to engage in only if no other sexual outlets are available, this view bears little relationship to reality. Close to three-quarters of married men surveyed (age 20 to 40) report masturbating an average of twenty-four times a year, and 68 percent of the married women in the same age group masturbate an average of ten times a year (Hunt, 1974).

Despite the high incidence of masturbation, attitudes toward it often reflect negative views. For instance, one survey found that around 10 percent of the people who masturbated experienced feelings of guilt, and 5 percent of the males and 1 percent of the females considered their behavior perverted (Arafat & Cotton, 1974). Despite these negative attitudes, however, most experts on sex view masturbation not only as a healthy, legitimate—and harmless—sexual activity, but also as a means of learning about one's own sexuality.

Heterosexuality: *Sexual behavior between a man and a woman*

Heterosexuality **Heterosexuality,** or sexual behavior between a man and a woman, is probably the most frequent of sexual activities. People often believe that the first time they have sexual intercourse represents one of life's major milestones. Although heterosexuality goes well beyond sexual intercourse (encompassing kissing, petting, caressing, massaging, and other forms of sex play), the focus of sex researchers has been on the act of intercourse, particularly in terms of its first occurrence and its frequency.

Premarital Sex Until fairly recently, premarital sex, at least for women, was considered one of the major taboos of our society. Traditionally, women have been warned by society that ''nice girls don't do it.'' Men have been told that while premarital sex is OK for them, they should make sure they marry virgins. This view, that premarital sex is permissible for males but not for females, is called the **double standard.**

Double standard: *The view that premarital sex is permissible for males but not for females*

Although as recently as the mid-1960s about 80 percent of adult Americans believed that pre-marital sex was always wrong, by the 1970s a dramatic shift had occurred: Only about one-third felt this way (Reiss, 1980). Even higher rates of approval for premarital sex are found within certain age groups; for example, 80 percent of the males and 68 percent of the females in one poll of college students agreed that sexual intercourse prior to marriage was permissible (Arena, 1984).

Changes in approval of premarital sex have been matched by changes in actual rates of premarital sexual activity. In one survey, for example, close to 80 percent of women under the age of 25 said they had experienced premarital intercourse, while just over 20 percent of those over 55 years of age reported having premarital sexual intercourse (Horn & Bachrach, 1985). Today, in fact, by the time they are in college, 59 percent of females maintain that they have already had sexual intercourse (Arena, 1984).

Males, too, have shown an increase in the rate of premarital sexual intercourse, although the increase has not been as dramatic as it has for females—probably because the rates for males were higher to begin with. For instance, the first surveys carried out in the 1940s showed a rate of 84 percent; recent surveys put the figure at closer to 95 percent. Moreover, the average age of males' first sexual experience has also been declining steadily, and some 76 percent of college-age males have already had intercourse (Arena, 1984).

What may be most interesting about these patterns is that they show a convergence of male and female attitudes and behavior in regard to premarital sex. But is the change sufficient to signal an end to the double standard?

The answer appears to be "no." Although in one survey of students, 95 percent of men and women were in favor of identical sexual standards for men and women involved in love relationships, the figure slipped to 82 percent when the man and woman were "casual acquaintances." Moreover, where differing standards remained, the attitudes were almost always more lenient toward the male than the female (Peplau, Rubin, & Hill, 1977; Sullivan, 1985). It appears, then, that the double standard, although declining, has yet to disappear.

Marital Sex To judge by the number of articles about sex in marriage, one would think that sexual behavior was the number one standard by which marital bliss is measured. Married couples are often concerned that they are having too little sex, too much sex, or the wrong kind of sex.

Although there are many different dimensions against which sex in marriage is measured, one is certainly the frequency of sexual intercourse. What is typical? As with most other types of sexual activities, there is no easy answer to the question, since there are such wide variations in patterns between individuals. We do know that the average frequency for married couples is approximately 8.2 times per month (Westoff, 1974). In addition, there are differences according to the age of the couple; younger couples tend to have sexual intercourse more frequently than older ones. The overall frequency of marital sexual intercourse is higher than in other recent historical periods.

The increase in the frequency of sexual intercourse in marriage has been accompanied by an increase in the frequency of **extramarital sex,** sexual activity that occurs between a married person and someone who is not his or her spouse. In the 1940s, some 50 percent of all married men and 25 percent of all married women admitted to having had sex at least once with a partner other than their

Extramarital sex: *Sexual activity between a married person and someone who is not his or her spouse*

husband or wife. More recent surveys have shown a slight increase for men, but a more significant rise for women. What has not changed at all are people's attitudes toward extramarital sex: There is a high, consistent rate of disapproval, with more than three-quarters of those surveyed saying the practice is wrong (Hunt, 1974).

Homosexuality: *A sexual attraction to a member of one's own sex*

Bisexuality: *A sexual attraction to members of both sexes*

Homosexuality Humans are not born with an innate attraction to the special characteristics of the opposite sex. We should not find it surprising, then, that some people, **homosexuals,** are sexually attracted to members of their own sex, while others, **bisexuals,** are sexually attracted to people of the same *and* the opposite sex. In fact, the number of people who choose same-sex sexual partners at one time or another is considerable. Estimates suggest that about 20 to 25 percent of males and about 15 percent of females have had at least one homosexual experience during adulthood, and between 5 and 10 percent of both men and women are estimated to be exclusively homosexual during extended periods of their lives (Hunt, 1974; Kinsey, Pomeroy, & Martin, 1948).

Why are people homosexual? Although there are a number of theories, none has proved completely satisfactory. Some approaches are biological in nature, suggesting that there may be a genetic or hormonal reason for the development of homosexuality (Gladue, 1984; Hutchinson, 1978). There is little conclusive evidence for such an approach, however, although it is still possible that there may be some genetic or biological factor that predisposes a person toward homosexuality, if certain environmental conditions are met.

Other theories of homosexuality have focused on the childhood and family background of homosexuals. For instance, Freud felt that homosexuality occurred as a result of inappropriate identification with the opposite-sex parent during development (Freud, 1922/1959). Similarly, other psychoanalysts suggest that the nature of the parent-child relationship can lead to homosexuality, and that homosexuals frequently have overprotective, dominant mothers and passive, ineffective fathers (Bieber, 1962).

The problem with such theories is that there are probably as many homosexuals who were not subjected to the influence of such family dynamics as who were. The evidence does not support explanations which rely on the difficulties related to child-bearing practices or on the nature of the family structure.

Another plausible explanation rests on learning theory (Masters & Johnson, 1979). According to this view, sexual orientation is learned through rewards and punishments in much the same way that we learn to prefer bananas over apples. For example, a young adolescent who had a heterosexual experience whose outcome was unpleasant might learn to link unpleasant associations with the opposite sex. If that same person had a rewarding, pleasant homosexual experience, homosexuality might be incorporated into his or her sexual fantasies. If such fantasies are then used during later sexual activities—such as masturbation—they may be positively reinforced through orgasm, and the association of homosexual behavior and sexual pleasure might eventually cause homosexuality to become the preferred form of sexual behavior.

Although we don't know at this point exactly why people become homosexual, one thing is clear: There is no relationship between psychological adjustment and sexual preference (Reiss, 1980). Bisexuals and homosexuals enjoy the same overall degree of mental and physical health as do heterosexuals, and they hold equivalent ranges and types of attitudes about themselves, independent of sexual orientation.

RECAP AND REVIEW I

Recap

- The study of motivation looks at the factors that energize and direct an organism's behavior.
- A drive is a motivational tension that energizes behavior in order to fulfill some need. Primary drives typically operate according to the principle of homeostasis, in which an organism strives to restore any deviations from a balanced, preferred internal state.
- Hunger, a primary drive, is affected by internal cues that regulate the amount and kind of food eaten. The three major sources of energy (sugar, fat, and protein) are monitored by different cells. In addition, the hypothalamus plays an important role in determining food intake.
- The weight set point, sensitivity to external social cues, number of fat cells, and a person's metabolism also affect eating patterns.
- Masturbation (sexual self-stimulation) is common among both men and women, although it is still viewed negatively by many people in the general population.
- Attitudes regarding premarital heterosexuality still show a double standard, although both a tolerance for and actual acts of premarital sex have increased greatly over the last decades.
- Homosexuals are attracted to members of their own sex, and bisexuals are attracted to people of both the same and the opposite sex. While no theory fully explains why people are homosexual, it is clear that homosexuals and bisexuals show no differences in overall degree of psychological adjustment.

Review

1. Drives that energize behavior that fulfills such needs as hunger and thirst are known as ______________________ drives.

2. An organism's preferred internal state is called

a. Motivation **b.** Homeostasis **c.** The weight set point **d.** Metabolism

3. Research on the activity of the hypothalamus, metabolism, and weight set point has clearly demonstrated that social factors do not play a significant role in people's desire to eat. True or false?

4. "Oh, come on! Julie doesn't have an eating problem!" argued Karen. "Her weight is about normal, and we all have occasional late-night binges."

"But Karen, she makes herself vomit after those binges. I think something is wrong."

Julie may be suffering from

a. A hypothalamus disorder **b.** Bulimia **c.** Anorexia nervosa **d.** An intestinal disorder

5. The traditional view that it is appropriate for males to have premarital sex, but inappropriate for females, represents a ______________________________.

6. The view described in item 5 above has, for the most part, disappeared from contemporary society. True or false?

(Answers to the review questions are at the bottom of page 250.)

HUMAN STRIVING: ACHIEVEMENT, AFFILIATION, AND POWER MOTIVATION

To Bob, doing well in college meant that he would get into a good law school, which he saw as a stepping-stone for a successful future. Consequently, he never let up academically, and so was always trying his hardest to do well in his courses. But his constant academic striving went well beyond the desire to get into law school; he tried to get not only good grades, but *better* grades than his classmates.

In fact, Bob was always trying to be the best at everything he did. He could turn the simplest activity into a competitive test. You couldn't even play poker without Bob acting as if his winning the game was essential. There were, however, some areas in which he didn't compete. He was interested only if he thought he had a fighting chance to succeed; he ignored challenges that were too difficult, as well as those that were too easy for him.

Because there is no clear biological basis for Bob's behavior, we cannot look to primary drives, such as hunger or thirst, to explain the motivation behind it. Instead, psychologists would turn to the secondary drives—those uniquely human strivings, based on learned needs and past experience—that might explain his behavior.

Secondary drives play a crucial role in human behavior of all sorts: Whether the behavior is skydiving, stamp collecting, or striving for excellence, the rich variety of behaviors expressed by humans can be viewed in motivational terms (McClelland, 1985). Although psychologists have examined a number of such secondary drives, we will focus on the ones that have received the greatest attention: the need for achievement, affiliation, and power.

Striving for Success: The Need for Achievement

Need for achievement: *A stable, learned characteristic in which satisfaction comes from striving for and achieving a level of excellence*

Bob's behavior in our example represents a classic case of someone who has a high **need for achievement**. The need for achievement is a stable, learned characteristic in which satisfaction is obtained by striving for and attaining a level of excellence (McClelland, Atkinson, Clark, & Lowell, 1953).

People with a high need for achievement seek out situations in which they can compete against some standard—be it grades, money, or winning at a game—and prove themselves successful. But they are not indiscriminate when it comes to picking their challenges: They tend to avoid situations in which success will come too easily (which would be unchallenging) or those in which success is unlikely. Instead, people high in achievement motivation are apt to choose tasks that are of intermediate difficulty.

In contrast, those with lower need for achievement tend to choose tasks that are either very easy or very hard, and avoid tasks of intermediate difficulty (Atkinson & Feather, 1966). This is because people with low achievement motivation tend to be mainly motivated by a desire to avoid failure. As a result, they seek out easy tasks, being sure to avoid failure; or they seek out very difficult tasks for which failure has no negative implications, since almost everyone will fail at them. People with a high fear of failure will stay away from tasks of intermediate difficulty, then, since they may fail where others have been successful.

The outcomes of a high need for achievement are generally positive, at least in a success-oriented society such as our own (Heckhausen, Schmalt, & Schneider, 1985; Spence, 1985). For instance, people motivated by a high need for achievement are more likely to attend college than their low-achievement counterparts, and once in college they tend to receive higher grades in classes that are related to their future careers (Atkinson & Raynor, 1974). In fact, achievement motivation has been linked to economic success, and techniques for increasing people's levels of need for achievement have actually increased subsequent business success (McClelland & Winter, 1969).

ANSWERS TO REVIEW QUESTIONS

Review I: **1.** Primary **2.** b **3.** False; social factors may play a major role **4.** b **5.** Double standard **6.** False

Measuring Achievement Motivation How can we measure a person's need for achievement? The technique used most frequently is to administer a **Thematic Apperception Test**, or **TAT**. In the TAT, people are shown a series of ambiguous pictures, such as the one shown in Figure 8-3. They are told to write a story that describes what is happening, who the people are, what led to the situation, what the people are thinking or wanting, and what will happen next. A standard scoring system is then used to determine the amount of achievement imagery in people's stories. For example, someone who writes a story in which the main character is striving to beat an opponent, studying in order to do well at some task, or working hard in order to get a promotion shows clear signs of achievement imagery. It is assumed that the inclusion of such achievement-related imagery indicates an unusually high degree of concern with—and therefore a relatively strong need for—achievement.

Figure 8-3
This ambiguous picture is similar to those used in the Thematic Apperception Test to determine a person's underlying motivation. (Harvard University Press, © 1943, 1971. All rights reserved.)

Other techniques for measuring achievement motivation have been developed, including several questionnaires. Moreover, psychologists have developed several procedures for measuring achievement motivation on a societal level (Reuman, Alwin, & Veroff, 1984). For example, a good indication of the overall level of achievement motivation in a particular society can be found by assessing achievement imagery in children's stories or folk tales. Moreover, researchers who have examined children's reading books for achievement imagery over long periods have found correlations between the amount of imagery and the economic activity over the next few decades (DeCharms & Moeller, 1962). Whether stories incorporating achievement imagery actually influence children or simply

Thematic Apperception (thee MA tik app per SEP shun) **Test (TAT)**: *A test consisting of a series of ambiguous pictures about which a person is asked to write a story. The story is taken to be a reflection of the writer's personality.*

"Well, you can stop lecturing me about my will to fail. I've failed."

Some theories of achievement motivation suggest that certain people may have a fear of success. (*Drawing by Ed Arno; © 1978 The New Yorker Magazine, Inc.*)

reflect growing economic trends cannot be determined, of course. It is clear, though, that children might be learning more from their books than how to read—they may be acquiring the level of achievement motivation that society expects from them.

There has been one major drawback to the work on achievement motivation: The findings have been considerably more consistent for men than for women, and TAT results do not correlate with actual achievement for females as strongly as they do for males. One explanation has suggested that achievement and success by women are viewed with a certain ambivalence (Horner, 1972). Because women have traditionally been raised to avoid competition and independence, success in a field typically dominated by males might be anxiety-provoking for a woman. Women, then, may actually have a **fear of success**: They are afraid that being successful may have a negative influence on the way others view them and on their definition of themselves as females.

Fear of success: *A fear that being successful will have a negative influence on the way one is perceived by one's self and by others*

While the evidence in support of the fear-of-success explanation is far from consistent, it does illustrate how complex our motivations may be (Gama, 1985). Rather than assuming that people consistently strive in varying degrees for success, we need to consider that some people may be afraid of success and actively try to avoid it.

Striving for Friendship: The Need for Affiliation

Few of us choose to lead our lives as hermits. Why?

One reason is that most people have a **need for affiliation**, a concern with establishing and maintaining relationships with other people. Individuals with a high need for affiliation write TAT stories that emphasize the desire to maintain or reinstate friendships and show concern over being rejected by friends.

Need for affiliation: *A need to establish and maintain relationships with other people*

People who are higher in affiliation needs are particularly sensitive to relationships with others. They like to work with their friends and may be more likely to pay attention to the social relationships within work settings than to getting the job done. For example, United States presidents whose inaugural addresses were high in affiliation imagery tend to be rated by historians as relatively inactive and ineffective (Winter, 1976). On the other hand, such presidents also seem to avoid war and to sign weapons-control agreements.

Striving for Impact on Others: The Need for Power

The **need for power**, a tendency to seek impact on others, represents a third major type of motivation. The basic goal of power motivation is to gain influence over others' behavior and to be seen by others as a powerful individual.

Need for power: *A tendency to want to make an impression or have an impact on others in order to be seen as a powerful individual*

As you might expect, people with a strong need for power are more apt to belong to organizations and seek office than those with less need for power. In some people, however, the need for power is expressed in less obvious ways: Men may show unusually high levels of aggression, have strong physiological reactions to conflict, be heavy drinkers, participate more frequently in competitive sports, or collect prestigious possessions, such as stereos and sports cars (Fodor, 1985; Winter, 1973).

COMBINING HUMAN MOTIVES

As he strapped his parachute onto his back, Marty Klein noticed that his hands were slippery with sweat. He wasn't too surprised: His skydiving in-

"And if I am elected President, I will be very happy."

Some motivational needs are directed toward attaining power. (*Drawing by Mort Gerberg; © 1976 The New Yorker Magazine, Inc.*)

structor said most people were nervous and scared the first time up. But his instructor hadn't said anything about the knot that Marty now felt in the pit of his stomach, or warned that he might be shaking all over. "Oh, well," he thought to himself, "I've come this far. I can't very well change my mind now." With that thought, he jumped from the plane. Trying to ignore his terror, he managed to do everything he was supposed to—and he made a perfect landing. Although dazed at first from all the excitement, he began to feel better and better, until he could hardly contain his euphoria. It was as if the extreme terror he had experienced before the dive had been transformed into an equally extreme feeling of euphoria. In fact, he couldn't wait to get up into a plane again.

When Marty Klein jumped out of the plane, he was awash with different motives directing his behavior. He clearly was motivated by the challenge and thrill of skydiving, but at the same time he had real concerns regarding personal safety needs. How did these differing motivations relate to each other?

Until now we have been considering individual motives in isolation, but it is obvious that people hold many motives simultaneously that may be vastly dissimilar in nature. We turn now to some of the broad principles underlying such differing motives, and consider how different levels of motives and needs relate to one another.

Homeostasis Is Not Enough: Theories of Motivation

If you were to ask Marty Klein why he likes to skydive, he would probably reply, "For the fun of it." Yet skydiving is clearly at odds with the notion of homeostasis, which suggests that organisms will do only what is necessary to maintain a steady, resting biological state.

Actually, there are many such behaviors—ranging from skydiving to playing chess—that are unrelated to specific biological needs, yet seem to be satisfying in and of themselves (see the Cutting Edge box). They may even raise one's level of arousal by providing a sense of danger or excitement. Moreover, such behavior is not limited to human beings: Even monkeys will learn to press a bar just to be able to peer into another room, especially if something interesting (such as a toy train moving along a track) can be glimpsed (Butler, 1954). Monkeys will also expend considerable energy solving simple mechanical puzzles, even though the behavior produces no obvious reward (Harlow, Harlow, & Meyer, 1950; Mineka & Hendersen, 1985).

Instinct: *An inborn pattern of behavior that is biologically determined*

One way of explaining such behavior is to rely on the concept of **instinct**, an inborn pattern of behavior that is biologically determined. According to

THE CUTTING EDGE

FOR MONEY OR LOVE?: Rewarding Intrinsic Motivation

Which produces the better results: offering students a high grade for good performance or reminding them of the intellectual pleasure of performing well academically?

According to work done by psychologists studying motivation, the answer is clearly to avoid offering grades and instead concentrate on the inherent satisfactions of a job well done. The reason relates to a distinction that has been drawn between two kinds of motivation: intrinsic motivation and extrinsic motivation. **Intrinsic motivation** causes people to participate in an activity for their own enjoyment, not for what it will get them. In contrast, **extrinsic motivation** causes us to do something for a tangible reward. According to research on the two types of motivation, we are most apt to persist, work harder, and produce work of higher quality when motivation for a task is intrinsic rather than extrinsic (Deci & Ryan, 1985; Lepper, 1984).

Ongoing work on intrinsic and extrinsic motivation is illustrated well by a recent experiment by Teresa Amabile (1985). She asked a group of volunteers who were involved in creative writing to write a poem. After writing their poems, some of the participants were given a list of "extrinsic" reasons for writing poetry (such as financial gain, impressing others, and becoming well known), while another group was given a list of "intrinsic" reasons for writing (such as enjoyment in using words and expressing oneself with precision). Both groups were then asked to write a second poem.

A group of poets then made judgments about the creativity of the two poems written by each of the participants. The judges found no difference between the two groups in the creativity of the first poems. However, the second poems revealed a difference. The poems of the writers who were given extrinsic reasons showed a marked decline in creativity from their first attempt—while the poems of the other group members showed no change in creativity between their first and second efforts.

Research such as this suggests the importance of promoting intrinsic motivation, and indicates that providing extrinsic rewards (or, as in this case, simply calling attention to them) may actually undermine performance effort and quality (Amabile, Hennessey, & Grossman, 1986). Teachers might think twice, then, about offering their students an A for a good composition. Instead, the work on intrinsic motivation suggests that better results would come from reminding students about the intrinsic reasons—such as the joys of producing a carefully crafted paper—for good performance.

Intrinsic (IN trin zik) **motivation**: *Motivation by which people participate in an activity for their own enjoyment, not for the reward it will get them*

Extrinsic (EX trin zik) **motivation**: *Motivation by which people participate in an activity for a tangible reward*

Arousal theory suggests that people try to maintain a characteristic level of stimulation and activity. If this level is not reached, they may seek to increase stimulation through their choice of activities. (*Galen Rowell/Peter Arnold, Inc.*)

instinct theories of motivation, people and animals are born with preprogrammed sets of behaviors that are essential to their survival. These instincts provide the energy that channels behavior in appropriate directions. Hence, exploratory behavior might be viewed as motivated by an instinct to explore.

The difficulty with such a conception, however, is that it provides little more than a label for behavior. An explanation for a particular behavior based on the concept of instincts does not go very far in explaining why a specific pattern of behavior, and not some other, has appeared in a given individual. Moreover, the variety and complexity of behavior, much of which is clearly learned, are difficult to explain if instincts are the primary motivational force. Other theories, then, have been developed to explain motivation.

Drive-Reduction Theories of Motivation In rejecting instinct theory, psychologists first proposed the simple drive-reduction theory (Hull, 1943). The **drive-reduction theory** suggests that when people lack some basic biological requirement such as water, a drive (in this case, thirst) is produced.

Drive-reduction theory of motivation: *The theory that activities are carried out in order to satisfy a need and cease when the need is fulfilled*

While the drive-reduction theory provides a good explanation of how primary drives motivate behavior, it is inadequate when it comes to explaining behaviors—such as mountain climbing—in which the goal is not to reduce a drive, but rather to maintain or even to increase a particular level of excitement or arousal. Alternate theories have therefore been proposed.

Looking for Stimulation: Arousal Theory In order to explain behavior in which the goal is the maintenance or increase in excitement, some psychologists have proposed arousal theory (Berlyne, 1967). According to the **arousal theory of motivation**, each of us tries to maintain a certain level of stimulation and

Arousal theory of motivation: *The belief that we try to maintain certain levels of stimulation and activity, increasing or reducing them as necessary*

activity. As with the drive-reduction model, if the stimulation and activity levels become too high, we try to reduce them. But the model also suggests something quite different from the drive-reduction model: It says that if the levels of stimulation and activity are too low we will try to *increase* them by seeking stimulation.

There seems to be, then, an optimal level of stimulation sought, with relatively wide variations between individuals (Mineka & Henderson, 1985). While some may aim for a high level (the mountain climbers and skydivers among us), others may opt for a relatively low level (including more sedentary exploits, such as playing chess). To get a sense of your own level of sensation-seeking, see the Try It! box.

TRY IT!

DO YOU SEEK OUT SENSATION?

How much stimulation do you crave in your everyday life? You will have an idea of how much after you complete the following questionnaire, which lists some items from a scale designed to assess your sensation-seeking tendencies (Zuckerman, 1978). Circle either A or B for each pair of statements.

1. A I would like a job that requires a lot of traveling.
B I would prefer a job in one location.

2. A I am invigorated by a brisk, cold day.
B I can't wait to get indoors on a cold day.

3. A I get bored seeing the same old faces.
B I like the comfortable familiarity of everyday friends.

4. A I would prefer living in an ideal society in which everyone is safe, secure, and happy.
B I would have preferred living in the unsettled days of our history.

5. A I sometimes like to do things that are a little frightening.
B A sensible person avoids activities that are dangerous.

6. A I would not like to be hypnotized.
B I would like to have the experience of being hypnotized.

7. A The most important goal of life is to live it to the fullest and to experience as much as possible.
B The most important goal of life is to find peace and happiness.

8. A I would like to try parachute-jumping.
B I would never want to try jumping out of a plane, with or without a parachute.

9. A I enter cold water gradually, giving myself time to get used to it.
B I like to dive or jump right into the ocean or a cold pool.

10. A When I go on a vacation, I prefer the comfort of a good room and bed.
B When I go on a vacation, I prefer the change of camping out.

11. A I prefer people who are emotionally expressive, even if they are a bit unstable.
B I prefer people who are calm and even-tempered.

12. A A good painting should shock or jolt the senses.
B A good painting should give one a feeling of peace and security.

13. A People who ride motorcycles must have some kind of unconscious need to hurt themselves.
B I would like to drive or ride a motorcycle.

Scoring Give yourself one point for each of the following responses: 1A, 2A, 3A, 4B, 5A, 6B, 7A, 8A, 9B, 10B, 11A, 12A, 13B. Find your total score by adding up the number of points and then use the following scoring key:
0-3 very low sensation-seeking
4-5 low
6-9 average
10-11 high
12-13 very high

Keep in mind, of course, that this short questionnaire, for which the scoring is based on the results of college students who have taken it, provides only a rough estimate of your sensation-seeking tendencies. Moreover, as people get older, their sensation-seeking scores tend to decrease. Still, it will give you at least an indication of where you stand when it comes to filling your life with sensation.
Source: Zuckerman, 1978.

Arousal theory is consistent with one of the oldest principles of psychology: the **Yerkes-Dodson law**. According to this law, there is a particular level of motivational arousal that produces optimal performance on a task, and, more specifically, that performance on simple tasks usually benefits from higher levels of arousal than does performance on more complex tasks. It seems as if high arousal gets in the way of successful responding with complex tasks, while it promotes better performance with more simple ones. (See Figure 8-4.)

On the other hand, both complex and simple tasks suffer when the level of arousal is *too* high. In this case, the arousal is distracting and anxiety-producing, hindering performance regardless of the task difficulty. In sum, consistent with arousal theory, there is an optimal level of arousal for task performance; arousal that is either too high or too low will result in poorer performance.

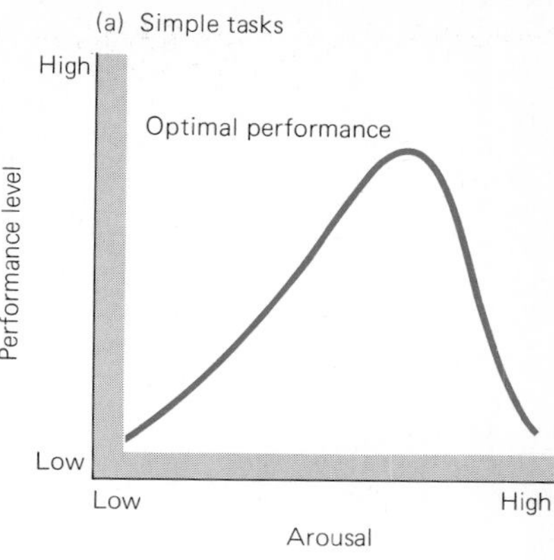

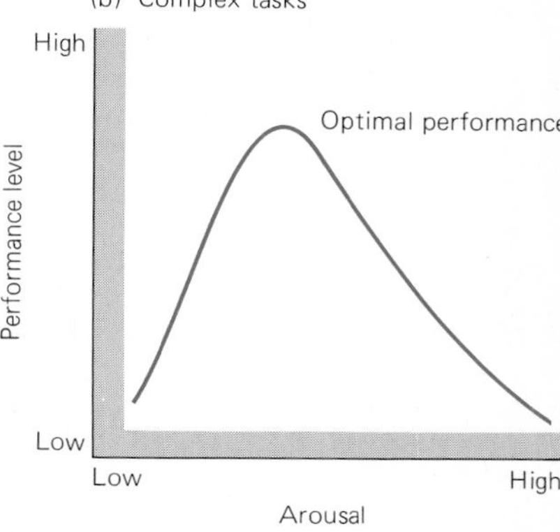

Figure 8-4
The Yerkes-Dodson law suggests that the optimal performance of a task will come from different levels of arousal, depending on whether the task is simple, as seen in (*a*), or complex, as seen in (*b*).

Pulling Behavior: Incentive Theory The **incentive theory of motivation** arose from the observation that our behavior frequently is motivated not by inner needs but by the nature of external stimuli. When a beautiful dessert is brought to the table after a filling meal, the attraction we feel has little or nothing to do with internal drives. Rather, our behavior is motivated by the external stimulus itself, which acts as an anticipated reward. This reward, in motivational terms, is called an incentive.

Many psychologists feel that the internal drives proposed by drive theory work together with the external incentives of incentive theory to "push" and "pull" behavior, respectively. Rather than the two theories contradicting each other, then, the two processes may both be at work (Hoyenga & Hoyenga, 1984).

The Yin and Yang of Motivation: Opponent-Process Theory When Chinese philosophers suggested long ago that there were two opposing forces in the universe—the yin and the yang—which influenced human behavior, they were foreshadowing the development of one further model of motivation called the **opponent-process theory** (Solomon & Corbit, 1974). Opponent-process theory helps explain the motivation behind phenomena such as drug addiction and the physiological and emotional reactions that occur as a result of extremes of physical danger, such as in skydiving.

According to the opponent-process theory, increases in arousal produce a calming reaction in the nervous system, and vice versa. Moreover, while the initial arousal response will remain fairly stable or perhaps even decline, the opponent process—the reaction to the original arousal response—will tend to grow in strength with each exposure to the stimulus (see Figure 8-5).

Some concrete examples will make the theory more understandable. Suppose that a man takes a drug that produces feelings of excitement and happiness. According to the theory, an opponent process will follow, swinging him toward fear and sadness. Initially, the drug will mask the effects of the opponent process, but after the drug wears off, the man will be left with just the opponent process—a feeling of fear and sadness. In addition, the opponent process (sadness and fear) tends to strengthen each time he takes the drug, while the initial process (happiness and excitement) tends to weaken. Therefore, his negative reaction will increase after each drug use, while the pleasure he receives from the drug will tend to decline. Ultimately, his motivation to increase the positive process will lead him to take a larger quantity of drugs—resulting in addiction.

Opponent processes work in the opposite way when the initial experience is negative. Suppose we return to the example of Marty Klein, the skydiver about

Yerkes-Dodson (YUR keez) **law**: *The theory that a particular level of motivational arousal produces optimal performance of a task*
Incentive theory of motivation: *The belief that behavior is motivated by the external stimuli of rewards and incentives*
Opponent-process theory of motivation: *The theory that suggests that increases in arousal produce a calming reaction in the nervous system, and vice versa*

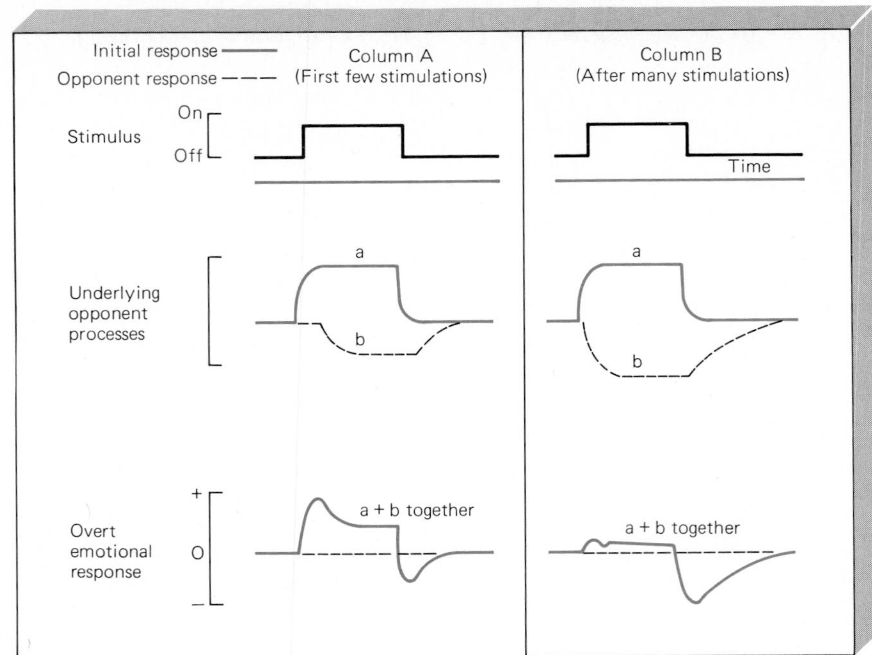

Figure 8-5
These graphs illustrate the opponent-process theory. In the left half of the figure, column A, you can see what happens the first few times a person is exposed to an arousing stimulus such as a quick-acting drug. The first row shows when the stimulus is "turned on" (when the drug produces its effects) and "off" (when the drug is no longer exerting its effects). When the drug is first taken, the initial positive arousal response, represented as *a* in the second row of the chart, occurs; this response ends as soon as the stimulus is removed or its effects are no longer felt. However, the opposite, opponent-process (an unpleasant reaction to the drug) occurs more slowly, not starting until some time has elapsed after the onset of the original stimulus. The sequence of the opponent process is indicated by the *b* line in the second row of the graph. The person, however, experiences both the initial *a* reaction and the opponent *b* reaction simultaneously, producing the combined response shown in the last row. In the combined case, it can be seen that the overall reaction is generally positive, although eventually there is a negative reaction.
The right half of the figure—column B—shows why, after many exposures to the same stimulus, the opponent process *b* comes to predominate, and the general combined reaction is negative. While the *a* response has not changed, the negative *b* response has become stronger. When the two are combined, the *b* response becomes the major determinant of the emotional reaction. In this case, a person looking for a "high" might seek to increase the initial positive reaction by increasing the dosage of the drug (*Source: After Solomon & Corbit, 1974.*)

to make his first jump. As we saw, his initial reaction was one of fear. But there was also an opponent process at work, and because of this he felt euphoric after the jump. Moreover, the theory suggests that each time he jumps, the original process resulting in terror will grow no stronger and in fact may even weaken, while the opponent process will likely increase in strength. Ultimately, then, skydiving should become almost addictive to Klein.

In sum, opponent-process theory helps explain why people hold strong mo-

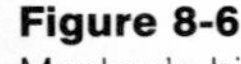

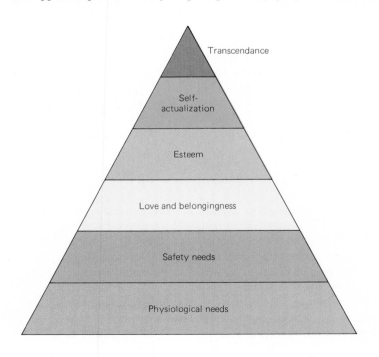

Figure 8-6
Maslow's hierarchy shows how our motivation progresses up the pyramid from a basis in the broadest, most fundamental biological needs to higher-order ones. (*Source: After Maslow, 1970.*)

According to opponent-process theory, the initial terror that pilots of hang gliders experience on their maiden voyages will probably decline in later jumps, while the excitement and euphoria will grow, thus leading to a kind of addiction to the risky sport. (*Peter Marlow/Magnum*)

tivation for behavior that on the surface has few benefits. It is frequently the opponent process, not the initial reaction, that maintains the motivation to carry out such behavior.

Thinking about Motives: Cognitive Theory One contemporary approach to motivation focuses on the role of thoughts, expectations, and understanding of the causes of people's behavior. As we discuss in some detail in Chapter 14, psychologists have developed sophisticated explanations for how we come to understand the causes of others'—and our own—behavior. Moreover, our expectations of what motivates others has an important impact on how we behave toward them. In short, each of us tries to develop and act upon our own motivational theories in an effort to explain the reasons behind our own behavior and that of others.

Ordering Motivational Needs: Maslow's Hierarchy

What do Eleanor Roosevelt, Abraham Lincoln, and Albert Einstein have in common? Quite a bit, according to a model of motivation devised by psychologist Abraham Maslow: Each of them reached and fulfilled the highest levels of motivational needs underlying human behavior.

Maslow's model considers the way different motivational needs are ordered in a hierarchy, and it suggests that before more sophisticated, higher-order needs can be met, certain primary needs must be satisfied (Maslow, 1970). The model can be thought of as a pyramid (see Figure 8-6) in which the more basic needs are at the bottom and the higher-level needs are at the top. In order for a particular need to be activated and guide a person's behavior, the more basic needs in the hierarchy must be met first.

The most basic needs are those we have described in terms of primary drives: thirst, hunger, sleep, sex, and the like. In order to move up the hierarchy, a

People are self-actualized when they are self-fulfilled and realize their highest potential. (*George Ancona/International Stock Photo*)

person must have these basic physiological needs met. Safety needs come next in the hierarchy; Maslow suggests that people need a safe, secure environment in order to function effectively. The physiological and safety needs compose the lower-order needs.

It is only when the basic lower-order needs are met that a person can consider fulfilling higher-order needs, consisting of love and belongingness, esteem, self-actualization, and transcendance. Love and belongingness needs include the need to obtain and give affection and to be a contributing member of some group or society. After these needs are fulfilled, the person strives for esteem. In Maslow's thinking, esteem relates to the need to develop a sense of self-worth by knowing that others are aware of your competence and value.

Self-actualization: *In Maslow's theory, a state of self-fulfillment in which people realize their highest potential*

Once these four sets of needs are fulfilled—no easy task—the person is ready to strive for the highest-level needs, self-actualization and transcendance. **Self-actualization** is a state of self-fulfillment in which people realize their highest potential. When Maslow first discussed the concept, he used it to describe just a few well-known individuals such as Eleanor Roosevelt, Lincoln, and Einstein. But self-actualization is not limited to the famous. A woman with excellent mothering skills who raises a family, a teacher who year after year produces successful students, or an artist who realizes her potential might all be self-actualized. The important thing is that people feel at ease with themselves and satisfied that they are using their talents to the fullest. In a sense, reaching self-actualization produces a decline in the striving and yearning for greater fulfillment that marks most people's lives and instead provides a sense of satisfaction with the current state of affairs in one's life.

Transcendance (tranz SEN danz): *In Maslow's theory, a state in which one views oneself in terms of the universe and laws of nature*

In his latest writings, Maslow added an even higher level, which he called transcendance. **Transcendance** refers to the spiritual need to view oneself from the perspective of others, considering oneself in terms of the universe and the laws of nature.

While there is little research to validate the exact ordering of the stages of the theory, and even Maslow himself acknowledges that there must be some degree of flexibility, the model does highlight the complexity of human needs. It also emphasizes the fact that until more basic biological needs are met, people are going to be relatively disinterested in higher-order needs. If people are hungry, their first interest will be in obtaining food; they will not be concerned with such things as love and self-esteem. The model helps explain, then, why individuals who are the victims of disasters such as famine or war may suffer the breakdown of normal family ties and be disinterested in the welfare of anyone other than themselves.

RECAP AND REVIEW II

Recap

- Among the major secondary drives are those relating to achievement, affiliation, and power motivation.
- Drive-reduction theory proposes that behavior is motivated by drives to reduce biological needs. However, it does not explain why people sometimes seek out stimulation.
- Arousal theory suggests that we try to maintain a certain level of stimulation and activity. Arousal theory is consistent with the Yerkes-Dodson law, which demonstrates that too much or too little arousal will result in inferior performance, depending on the nature of the talk.
- Opponent-process theory suggests that changes in arousal level in one direction lead to a reaction in the nervous system in the opposite direction. Therefore, if a person experiences extreme positive reactions, there will ultimately be extreme negative reactions, and vice versa.
- According to Maslow's motivational hierarchy, motivational needs are ordered from most basic to higher-order needs. The specific categories include physiological needs, safety, love and belongingness, esteem, self-actualization, and transcendance.

Review

1. Jim is considered to be a person with a high need for achievement. His boss would probably be correct in assuming that Jim would readily accept the challenge of completing a risky task, where success is doubtful. True or false?
2. Shelley's Thematic Apperception Test (TAT) story depicts a young girl who had been rejected by one of her peers and sought to regain her friendship with them. What major type of motivation is Shelley displaying in her story?
   a. Need for achievement **b.** Need for motivation **c.** Need for affiliation **d.** Need for power
3. Drive-reduction theory provides the best explanation of the motivation to engage in exhilerating sports activities such as hang gliding and surfing. True or false?
4. Adam was almost sick with fear before his first rock-climbing experience. However, the feelings of fear gradually diminished over time and were replaced by stronger and stronger feelings of euphoria. Which theory best explains this seemingly contradicting phenomenon?
   a. Incentive theory **b.** Drive-reduction theory **c.** Reinforcement theory **d.** Opponent-process theory
5. Which of the following is true of Maslow's hierarchy of needs?
   a. Basic needs must be met before higher-order needs can be met. **b.** Self-actualization is achieved by nearly everyone.
   c. Higher-order needs are unimportant to everyday living.
   d. Love, belongingness, and esteem are examples of lower-order needs.

(Answers to the review questions are at the bottom of page 262.)

UNDERSTANDING EMOTIONAL EXPERIENCE

As he reached into the mailbox, Karl Andrews glimpsed the envelope he had been waiting for. It could be his ticket to his future: An offer of admission to his first-choice college. But what was it going to say? He knew it could go either way; his grades were pretty good, and he had been involved in some activities; but his SAT scores had been, to put it bluntly, lousy. He had hoped that his careful explanation in the essays on his application had been strong enough to sway the admissions committee.

The emotion of happiness is characterized by positive feelings and thoughts. (*Louis Fernandez/Black Star*)

> Well, enough of this reflection, he thought to himself. At the same time, he felt so nervous—scared really—that his hands shook as he opened the thin envelope (not a good sign, he thought). Here it comes. "Dear Mr. Andrews," it read. "The President and Trustees of the University are pleased to inform you that you have been admitted. . . ."
>
> That was all he needed. With a whoop of excitement, Karl found himself gleefully jumping up and down. A rush of emotion overcame him as it sank in that he had, in fact, been accepted. He was on his way. . . .

At one time or another, all of us have felt the strong emotions that accompany both very pleasant and very negative experiences. Perhaps it was the thrill of being accepted into college, the joy of being in love, the sorrow over someone's death, or the anguish of inadvertently hurting someone. Moreover, we experience emotions on a less intense level throughout our daily lives: the pleasure of a friendship, the enjoyment of a movie, or the embarrassment of forgetting to return a borrowed item.

Despite the varied nature of all these feelings, there is a common link between them: They all represent emotions. While defining emotions seems simple to the nonexpert, finding a definition acceptable to psychologists has proved to be an elusive task. One reason is that different theories of emotion—which we will discuss later—emphasize different aspects of emotions, and therefore each theory ultimately produces its own definition. Despite these difficulties, though, we can use a general definition: **Emotions** are feelings that generally have both physiological and cognitive elements and that influence behavior.

Emotions: *Feelings (such as happiness, despair, and sorrow) that generally have both physiological and cognitive elements and that influence behavior*

Consider, for example, how it feels to be happy. First, you obviously experience a feeling of happiness, a feeling that you can differentiate from other emotions. It is likely you also experience some identifiable physical changes in your body: Perhaps your heart rate increases, or—as in our example earlier—

ANSWERS TO REVIEW QUESTIONS

Review II: **1.** False **2.** c **3.** False **4.** d **5.** a you find yourself "jumping for joy." Finally, there are likely cognitive elements to the emotion; your understanding and evaluation of the meaning of what is happening in your environment prompts your feelings of happiness.

On the other hand, it is possible to experience an emotion without the presence of cognitive elements. For instance, we may react with fear to an unusual or novel situation (such as coming into contact with a disturbed, unpredictable individual), or we may experience pleasure over sexual excitation without having cognitive awareness or understanding of what it is about the situation that is exciting.

In fact, some psychologists argue that there are entirely separate systems that govern cognitive responses and emotional responses. One controversy concerns whether the emotional response takes predominance over the cognitive response or vice versa. Specifically, some theorists suggest that we first respond to a situation with an emotional reaction, and later try to understand it (Zajonc, 1985). For example, we may enjoy a complex modern symphony without understanding it or knowing why we like it.

In contrast, other theorists suggest that people first develop cognitions about a situation and then react emotionally (Lazarus, 1984). To these people, it is necessary to first think about and understand a stimulus or situation, relating it to what they already know before reacting on an emotional level.

Both sides of this debate are supported by research, and the question is far from being resolved (Scheff, 1985). It is possible that the sequence varies from situation to situation, with emotions predominating in some instances and cognitive processes occurring first in others. Whatever the ultimate sequence, however, it is clear that our emotions play a major role in affecting our behavior.

What Emotions Do for Us: Understanding the Functions of Emotions

Imagine what it would be like if you had no emotions—no depths of despair, no depression, no feeling apologetic, but at the same time, no happiness, joy, or love. Obviously, life would be much less interesting, even dull, without the experience of emotion.

But do emotions serve any purpose beyond making life interesting? Psychologists have identified a number of important functions that emotions play in our daily lives (Scherer, 1984). Among the most important of those functions are the following:

- Preparation for action. Emotions act as a link between events in the external environment and behavioral responses that an individual makes. For example, if we saw an angry dog charging toward us, the emotional reaction (fear) would be associated with physiological arousal of the sympathetic division of the autonomic nervous system, which we discussed in Chapter 2. The role of the sympathetic division is to prepare us for emergency action, which presumably would get us moving out of the dog's way—quickly. Emotions can be seen, then, as stimuli that aid in the development of effective responses to various situations.
- Shaping future behavior. Emotions serve to promote learning of information that will assist us in making appropriate responses in the future. For example, the emotional response that occurs when a person experiences something unpleasant—such as the threatening dog—teaches that person to avoid similar circumstances in the future. Similarly, pleasant emotions act as reinforcement for prior behavior and therefore are apt to lead an individual to seek out similar

situations in the future. Thus, the feeling of satisfaction that follows giving to a charity is likely to reinforce charitable behavior and make it more likely to occur in the future.

■ Helping to regulate social interaction. As we shall discuss in detail later, the emotions we experience are frequently obvious to observers, as they are communicated through our verbal and nonverbal behaviors. These behaviors can act as a signal to observers, allowing them to better understand what we are experiencing and predict our future behavior. In turn, this promotes more effective and appropriate social interaction. For instance, a mother who sees the terror on her 2-year-old son's face when he sees a frightening picture in a book is able to comfort and reassure him, thereby helping him to deal with his environment more effectively in the future.

In sum, emotions serve to prepare us for action, shape future behavior through the learning of new responses, and act as a means of aiding and regulating social interaction. As such, they serve important functions in people's lives.

Labeling Our Feelings: Determining the Range of Emotions

If we were to try to list the words in the English language that have been used to describe emotions, we would end up with at least 500 different examples (Averill, 1975). The list would range from such obvious emotions as "happiness" and "fear" to less common ones, such as "adventurous" and "pensive."

One challenge for psychologists has been to try to sort through this list in order to identify the most important, fundamental emotions. The most comprehensive effort has been carried out by Robert Plutchik (1984). Plutchik asked people to rate twenty-two different terms relating to emotions along thirty-four different rating scales. Then he mathematically combined the results to learn which terms were related to which others.

The results were clear: Eight different fundamental emotions (joy, acceptance, fear, surprise, sadness, disgust, anger, and anticipation) emerged, and they formed the circular pattern shown in Figure 8-7. Emotions nearer one another

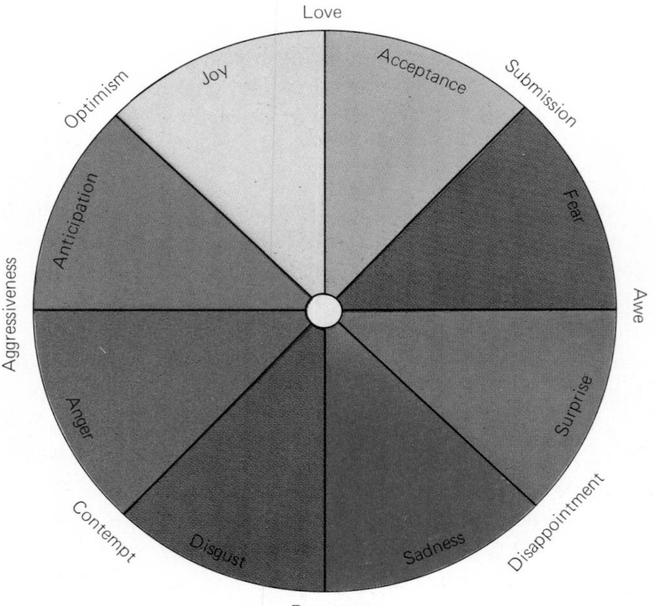

Figure 8-7
Plutchik's emotion wheel demonstrates how eight primary emotions are related to one another—as well as mirroring, in some respects, the relationships among the primary colors. (*Source: Plutchik, 1980.*)

in the circle are more closely related, while those opposite each other are conceptual opposites. For instance, sadness is opposite joy, and anticipation is opposite surprise.

One of the most surprising findings that emerged in this configuration of emotions was how closely it paralleled the way primary colors combine to form other colors. As shown in the emotion wheel, adjacent colors can be combined to form secondary colors. Similarly, by combining adjacent emotions, secondary emotions can be formed. For example, sadness and surprise form disappointment, while acceptance and joy result in love.

While Plutchik's configuration of the basic emotions is reasonable, it is not the only plausible one. Other psychologists have come up with somewhat different lists—as we shall see when we discuss the communication of emotion and nonverbal behavior later in this chapter. Still, while we may have trouble coming up with a definitive list of the primary emotions, each of us has little difficulty identifying what we are experiencing at any given moment. The process by which we come to this understanding forms the basis of a number of theories of emotion, which we discuss next.

KNOWING HOW WE FEEL: UNDERSTANDING OUR OWN EMOTIONS

> I've never been so angry before; I feel my heart pounding, and I'm trembling all over.
>
> * * *
>
> I don't know how I'll get through the performance. I feel like my stomach is filled with butterflies.
>
> * * *
>
> That was quite a mistake I made! My face must be incredibly red.
>
> * * *
>
> When I heard the footsteps in the night I was so frightened that I couldn't catch my breath.

If you examine our language, you will find that there are literally dozens of ways to describe how we feel when we are experiencing an emotion, and that the language we use to describe emotions is, for the most part, based on the physical symptoms that are associated with a particular emotional experience.

Consider, for instance, the experience of fear. Pretend that it is late one New Year's Eve. You are walking down a dark road, and you hear a stranger approaching behind you. It is clear that he is not trying to hurry by but is coming directly toward you. You think of what you will do should the stranger attempt to rob you—or worse, hurt you in some way.

While these thoughts are running through your head, it is almost certain that something rather dramatic will be happening to your body. Among the most likely physiological reactions, which are associated with activation of the autonomic nervous system (see Chapter 2), that may occur are those listed here:

- The rate and depth of your breathing will increase.
- Your heart will speed up, pumping more blood through your circulatory system.
- The pupils of your eyes will open wider, allowing more light to enter and thereby increasing your visual sensitivity.

■ Your mouth will become dry as your salivary glands, and in fact your entire digestive system, stop functioning. At the same time, though, your sweat glands may increase their activity, since increased sweating will help you rid yourself of excess heat developed by any emergency activity in which you engage.

■ As the muscles just below the surface of your skin contract, your hair may literally stand on end.

Of course, all these physiological changes are likely to occur without your awareness. At the same time, though, the emotional experience accompanying them will be obvious to you: You would most surely report being fearful.

Although it is a relatively straightforward matter to describe the general physical reactions that accompany emotions, the specific role that these physiological responses play in the experience of emotions has proved to be a major puzzle for psychologists. As we shall see, some theorists suggest that there are specific bodily reactions that *cause* us to experience a particular emotion—we experience fear, for instance, *because* our heart is pounding and we are breathing deeply. In contrast, other theorists suggest that the physiological reaction is the *result* of the experience of an emotion. In this view, we experience fear, and this emotional experience causes our heart to pound and our breathing to deepen.

Do Gut Reactions Equal Emotions?: The James-Lange Theory

To William James and Carl Lange, who were among the first researchers to explore the nature of emotions, emotional experience is, very simply, a reaction to instinctive bodily events that occurred as a response to some situation or event in the environment. This view is summarized in James's statement, ". . . we feel sorry because we cry, angry because we strike, afraid because we tremble" (James, 1890).

James and Lange took the view, then, that the instinctive response of crying at a loss leads us to feel sorrow; that striking out at someone who frustrates us results in our feeling anger; that trembling at a menacing threat causes us to feel afraid. They suggested that every major emotion has a particular physiological "gut" reaction of internal organs—called a **visceral experience**—attached to it, and it is this specific pattern of visceral response that leads us to label the emotional experience.

Visceral (VIS er al) **experience**: *The "gut" reaction experienced internally, triggering an emotion (see James-Lange theory)*

In sum, James and Lange proposed that we experience emotions as a result of physiological changes that produce specific sensations. In turn, these sensations are interpreted by the brain as particular kinds of emotional experiences (see Figure 8-8). This view has come to be called the **James-Lange theory of emotion**.

James-Lange (LANG) **theory of emotion**: *The belief that emotional experience is a reaction to bodily events occurring as a result of an external situation ("I feel sad because I am crying")*

The James-Lange theory has some serious drawbacks, however. In order for the theory to be correct, visceral changes would have to occur at a relatively rapid pace, since we experience some emotions—such as the fear upon hearing a stranger rapidly approaching on a dark night—almost instantaneously. Yet, emotional experiences frequently happen even before many physiological changes have time to be set into motion. Because of the slowness with which some visceral changes take place, then, it is hard to see how they could be the source of immediate emotional experience.

The James-Lange theory poses another difficulty: Physiological arousal does not invariably produce emotional experience. For example, a person who is jogging has an increased heartbeat and respiration rate, as well as many of the other physiological changes associated with certain emotions. Yet joggers do not typically think of such changes in terms of emotions. There cannot be a

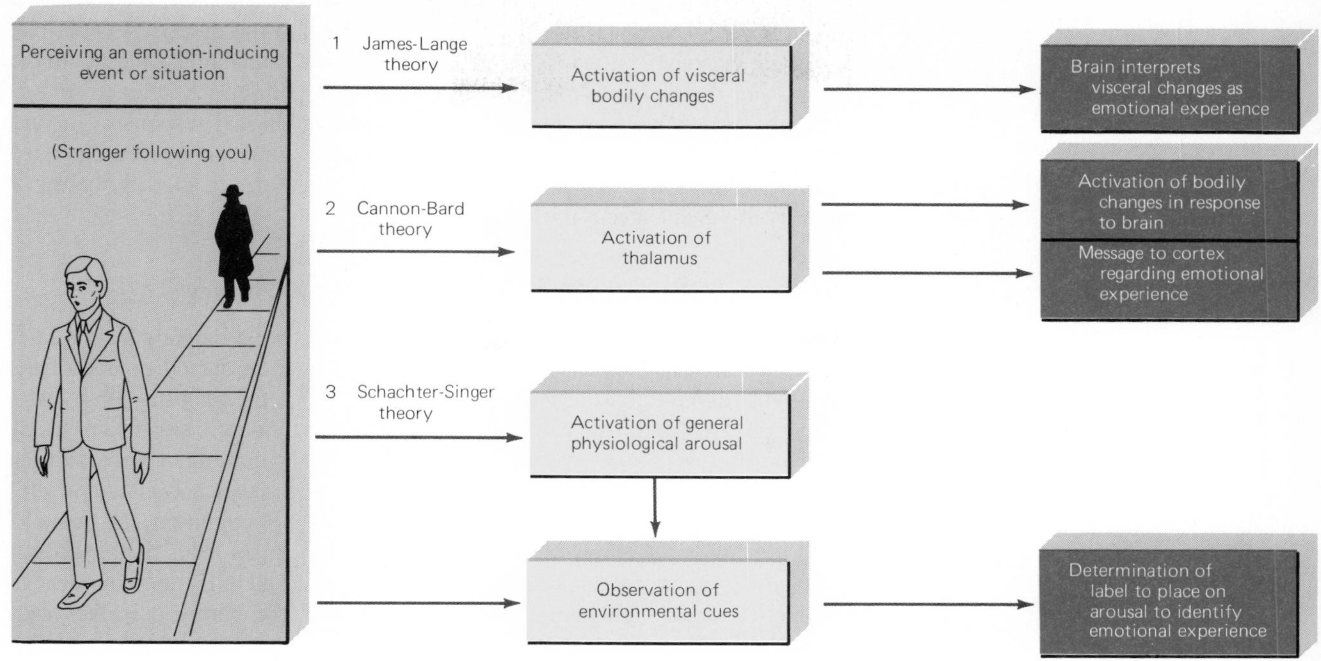

Figure 8-8
Comparison of three models of emotion.

one-to-one correspondence, then, between visceral changes and emotional experience, and visceral changes—by themselves—may not be sufficient to produce emotion.

Finally, the viscera are relatively limited in the nature of sensations they are capable of producing. It is difficult to imagine how the range of emotions that people are capable of experiencing could be the result of unique visceral changes. Many emotions are actually correlated with relatively similar sorts of visceral changes, a fact that contradicts the James-Lange theory.

Physiological Reactions as the Result of Emotions: The Cannon-Bard Theory

In response to the difficulties inherent in the James-Lange theory, Walter Cannon—and later Philip Bard—suggested an alternative view. In what has come to be known as the **Cannon-Bard theory of emotion**, they proposed the model illustrated in the second part of Figure 8-8 (Cannon, 1929). The major thrust of the theory is to reject the view that physiological arousal alone leads to the perception of emotion. Instead, it assumes that both physiological arousal *and* the emotional experience are produced simultaneously by the same nerve impulse, which Cannon and Bard suggested emanates from the brain's thalamus.

Cannon-Bard theory of emotion: *The belief that both physiological and emotional arousal are produced simultaneously by the same nerve impulse*

According to the theory, then, after an emotion-inducing stimulus is perceived, the thalamus is the initial site of the emotional response. In turn, the thalamus sends a signal to the viscera, which are then activated, and at the same time communicates a message to the cerebral cortex regarding the nature of the emotion being experienced. Hence, it is not necessary for different emotions to have unique physiological patterns associated with them—as long as the message sent to the cerebral cortex differs according to the specific emotion.

The Cannon-Bard theory seems to have been accurate in its rejection of the view that physiological arousal alone accounts for emotions. However, recent research has provided some important modifications to the theory. As you may recall from Chapter 2, it is now understood that the hypothalamus and the limbic system—not the thalamus—play a major role in emotional experience. In addition, the simultaneity of the physiological and emotional responses—a fundamental assumption of the theory—has yet to be conclusively demonstrated (Pribram, 1984). This ambiguity has allowed room for yet another theory of emotions: the Schachter-Singer theory.

Emotions as Labels: The Schachter-Singer Theory

Suppose, as you were being followed down the dark street on New Year's Eve, you noticed a man being followed by a shady figure on the other side of the street. Now assume that instead of reacting with fear, the man begins to laugh and act gleeful. Might the reactions of this other individual be sufficient to lay your fears to rest? Might you, in fact, decide there is nothing to fear, and get into the spirit of the evening by beginning to feel happiness and glee yourself?

Schachter-Singer (SHACK tur) **theory of emotion**: *The belief that emotions are determined jointly by a nonspecific kind of physiological arousal* and *its interpretation, based on environmental cues*

According to an explanation that focuses on the role of cognition, the **Schachter-Singer theory of emotion**, this might very well happen. This final approach to explaining emotions emphasizes the notion that we identify the emotion we are experiencing by observing our environment and comparing ourselves with others (Schachter & Singer, 1962).

A classic experiment found evidence for this hypothesis, indicating that the way we label our emotional experiences may be due in large part to the situation in which we find ourselves. In the study, subjects were told that they would receive a vitamin injection of a drug called Suproxin. In reality, they were given epinephrine, a drug that causes an increase in physiological arousal, including higher heart and respiration rates and a reddening of the face—responses that typically occur as part of strong emotional responses. Although one group of subjects was informed of the actual effects of the drug, another was kept in the dark.

Subjects in both groups were then individually placed in a situation whereby a confederate of the experimenter acted in one of two ways. In one condition, he acted angry and hostile, complaining that he would refuse to answer the personal questions on a questionnaire that the experimenter had asked him to complete. In the other condition, his behavior was quite the opposite: He behaved euphorically, flying paper airplanes and tossing wads of paper, in general acting quite happy with the situation.

The key purpose of the experiment was to determine how the subjects would react emotionally to the confederate's behavior. When they were asked to describe their own emotional state at the end of the experiment, subjects who had been told of the effects of the drug were relatively unaffected by the behavior of the confederate: Being informed of the effects of the epinephrine earlier, they thought their physiological arousal was due to the drug and therefore were not faced with the need to find a reason for their arousal.

On the other hand, subjects who had not been told of the drug's real effects reported being influenced by the confederate's behavior. Those subjects exposed to the angry confederate reported that they felt angry, while those exposed to the euphoric confederate reported feeling happy. In sum, the results suggest that uninformed subjects were faced with the task of explaining their physiological arousal, and they turned to the environment and the behavior of others for an explanation of the emotion they were experiencing.

The results of the Schachter-Singer experiment, then, support a cognitive view of emotions, in which emotions are determined jointly by a relatively nonspecific kind of physiological arousal *and* the labeling of the arousal based on cues from the environment (refer back to the third part of Figure 9-8). Unfortunately, however, this theory too has met with contradictory evidence (Reisenzein, 1983). There has been criticism about the way the original experiment was conducted and about the ambiguity of some of its results. Moreover, some drugs invariably produce depression as a side effect no matter what the situation or the environmental cues present. In some cases, then, physiological factors *alone* seem to account for one's emotional state without any labeling process occurring (Marshall & Zimbardo, 1979).

On the whole, however, the Schachter-Singer theory of emotions is important because it suggests that, at least under some circumstances, emotional experiences are a joint function of physiological arousal and the labeling of that arousal. When the source of physiological arousal is unclear to us, we may look to our environment to determine just what it is we are experiencing.

Summing Up the Theories of Emotion

At this point, you have good reason to ask why there are so many theories of emotion and, perhaps even more important, which is most accurate. Actually, we have only scratched the surface; there are even more explanatory theories of emotion (Scherer & Ekman, 1984; Zajonc, 1985; Foa & Kozak, 1986).

The answer to both why there are so many theories and which is the most accurate is actually the same: Emotions are such complex phenomena that none of the theories have been able to explain all facets of emotional experience with complete satisfaction. For each of the three major theories there is contradictory evidence of one sort or another, and therefore none has proved invariably accurate in its predictions. On the other hand, this is not a cause for despair—or unhappiness, fear, or any other negative emotion. It simply reflects the fact that psychology is an evolving, developing science. Presumably, as more evidence is gathered, the specific answers to questions about the nature of emotions will become more clear. Moreover, the lack of definitive knowledge about the nature of emotions has not stopped people from applying what we now know about emotional responses to some practical problems—as we discuss in the Psychology at Work box.

PSYCHOLOGY AT WORK

THE TRUTH ABOUT LIES:

Using Emotional Responses to Separate the Honest from the Dishonest

When the White House decided that there were too many leaks from its employees to the press about supposedly confidential projects, it ordered that employees with access to secret documents undergo periodic lie-detector tests.

* * *

When an accused rapist wanted to prove his innocence, he asked for, and received, a lie-detector test.

* * *

In order to get a job working for a major defense contractor, Jim Tane was told he needed to get a security clearance. The major part of the investigation into his past consisted of a lie-detector test, in which he was asked questions about his allegiance to his country, his past friends and associates, and any possible criminal activity, ranging from occasional drug use to major crimes.

The common element in each of these actual situations is the use of the lie detector, or **polygraph**, an electronic device that is designed to expose people who are telling lies. The basic assumption behind the apparatus is straightforward: The sympathetic nervous system of a person who is not being truthful becomes aroused as his or her emotionality increases, and the physiological changes that are indicative of this arousal can be detected by the polygraph.

Actually a number of separate physiological changes are measured simultaneously by a lie detector, including an irregularity in breathing pattern, an increase in heart rate and blood pressure, and an increase in sweating. In theory, the polygraph operator asks a series of questions, some of which he knows will elicit verifiable, truthful responses—such as what a person's name and address are. Then, when more critical questions are answered, the operator can observe the nature of the physiological changes that occur. Answers whose accompanying physiological responses deviate significantly from those accompanying truthful responses are assumed to be false.

Unfortunately, there is no foolproof technique for assessing the extent of the physiological changes that may indicate a lie. Moreover, even truthful responses may elicit physiological arousal—if the question is emotion-laden (Waid & Orne, 1982). How many innocent people accused of a murder, for instance, would *not* respond emotionally when asked if they had committed the crime, since they know that their future may hang in the balance?

One further drawback of lie-detector tests is that people are occasionally capable of fooling the polygraph (Barland & Raskin, 1973). For instance, biofeedback techniques (see Chapter 2) can be employed to produce emotional responses to accompany even truthful statements, meaning that the polygraph operator will be unable to distinguish any difference between honest and dishonest responses. Even biting one's tongue or hiding a tack in a shoe and pressing on it as each question is answered may be sufficient to produce physiological arousal during each response—obliterating any differences between truthful and deceptive responses (Honts, Hodes, & Raskin, 1985).

Because of these sources of error, users of lie detectors often make mistakes when trying to judge another person's honesty (Saxe, Dougherty, & Cross, 1985), and the American Psychological Association recently adopted a resolution stating that the evidence for the effectiveness of polygraphs "is still unsatisfactory" (A.P.A. Monitor, 1986). Even the major proponent of the use of polygraphs—the American Polygraph Association—admits an error rate of between 4 and 13 percent, and critics suggest that research has shown that the actual rate is closer to 30 percent (Meyer, 1982).

Despite the prevalent use of lie-detector tests in many different areas of society, then, there is good reason to doubt that such tests can determine if someone is lying. Clearly, you would not want to bet your future on the results of a lie-detector test—although someday you may be asked to do so.

Polygraph (POL ee graf): *An electronic device that measures bodily changes that may signal that a person is lying, often called a lie detector*

RECAP AND REVIEW III

Recap

- Emotions are feelings that generally have both a physiological component and a cognitive component.
- Emotions have a number of functions, including preparation for action, the shaping of future behavior by aiding in the learning of new responses, and the regulation of social interaction through the communication of emotion to observers.
- A number of physiological changes accompany strong emotion, including rapid breathing and increased heart rate, opening of the pupils, dryness in the mouth, increase in sweating, the sensation of hair "standing on end."
- The major theories of emotion are the James-Lange, Cannon-Bard, and Schachter-Singer theories.

Review

1. Evidence has clearly proved that emotional responses occur only after the cognitive process takes place. True or false?

2. a. You label as "disgust" the emotion you feel regarding sexist behavior of a person at a party you're attending. Using the emotion wheel (Figure 8-7), what emotion would you identify as the opposite of what you're experiencing? **b.** If you also felt anger in combination with disgust, how would you then label your emotional state according to the emotion wheel?

3. The ______________________ - ______________________ theory states that the thalamus triggers physiological and emotional reactions simultaneously. In contrast, the ______________________ - ______________________ theory suggests that emotions follow physiological arousal.
4. Another name for ''gut reaction'' is ______________________.
5. The Schachter-Singer theory states that emotions are determined in part by one's interpretation of the environment. True or false?

(Answers to the review questions are at the bottom of page 272.)

EXPRESSING EMOTIONS: THE ROLE OF NONVERBAL BEHAVIOR

As she asked Jason the question for the second time, Mrs. Howard was sure he didn't know the answer. In fact, she suspected he wasn't paying attention at all. But that was always the case with Jason. Since the first day of school, he had looked down at the floor every time she asked him a question. Even when he came up to ask her a question he always seemed to look away, as if he were hiding something. ''I've got to do something about this kid,'' she said to herself. ''Something is going on, but I can't put my finger on it.''

One additional fact may help explain the situation: Jason is black and Mrs. Howard is white. The significance of these racial identities has to do with the subtle differences in the nonverbal behavior of whites and blacks. In certain black subcultures, children are taught that looking an adult directly in the eye is a sign of disrespect (Byers & Byers, 1972). Moreover, even adult blacks and whites show significant differences in nonverbal behavior; whites tend to gaze at speakers quite steadily while conversing, but blacks do so considerably less (LaFrance & Mayo, 1978). Rather than lacking an understanding of the questions or having something to hide, then, Jason may simply be demonstrating learned nonverbal behavior indicating his respect for Mrs. Howard.

As this example suggests, nonverbal behavior can have important effects on social interaction. Such behavior represents the major channel through which we communicate our emotions and, therefore, has important implications for understanding how emotions operate in everyday life. In the remainder of the chapter, we consider a number of issues relating to how emotions are expressed nonverbally. We address the issue of whether emotional expression is universal and explore the differences in the ways that emotions are displayed by members of various cultures and subcultures.

If You Met Some New Guineans, Would You Know What They Were Feeling?: Universality in Emotional Expressivity

Consider, for a moment, the six photos displayed in Figure 8-9. Can you identify the emotions being expressed by the person in each of the photos?

If you are a good judge of facial expressions, you will conclude that six of the basic emotions are displayed: surprise, sadness, happiness, anger, disgust, and fear. These categories are the emotions that emerge in literally hundreds of studies of nonverbal behavior as being consistently distinct and identifiable, even by untrained observers (Wagner, MacDonald, & Manstead, 1986).

What is particularly interesting about these six categories is that they are not limited to members of western cultures; they appear to represent the basic emo-

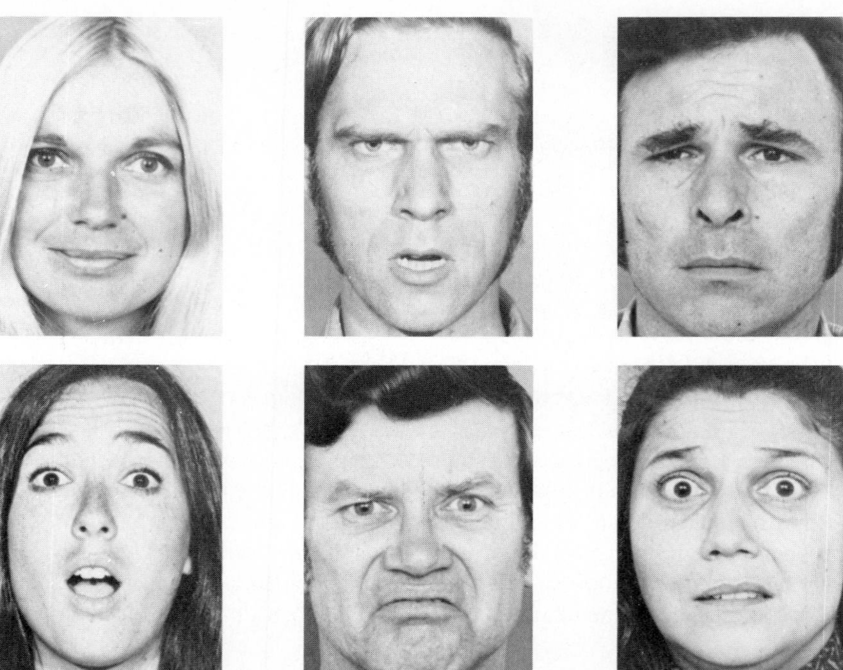

Figure 8-9
These photos demonstrate six of the primary emotions: happiness, anger, sadness, surprise, disgust, and fear. (Courtesy of Paul Ekman.)

tions expressed universally by members of the human race, regardless of where they have been raised and what learning experiences they have had. This point was demonstrated convincingly by psychologists Paul Ekman, who traveled to New Guinea to study members of an isolated jungle tribe having had almost no contact with westerners (Ekman, Friesen, & Ellsworth, 1982). The people of the tribe did not speak or understand English, they had never seen a movie, and they had had very limited experience with Caucasians before Ekman's arrival.

To learn about how the New Guineans used nonverbal behavior in emotional expression, Ekman told them a story involving an emotion, and then showed them a set of three faces of westerners, one of which was displaying an emotion appropriate for the story. The task was to choose the face showing the most reasonable expression. The results showed that the New Guineans' responses were quite similar to those of western subjects. Interestingly, the only difference occurred in identifying fearful faces, which were often confused with surprise by the tribespeople. Moreover, New Guinean children showed even greater skill in identifying the respective emotion than did the New Guinean adults.

In addition to learning whether the New Guinean natives interpreted emotional expression in the same way as westerners did, it was important to find out whether both groups showed similar nonverbal responses. To do this, other natives were told the stories that Ekman had used earlier and were asked to provide a facial expression appropriate to the subject of the story. These expressions were videotaped, and a group of subjects in the United States were asked to look at the faces and identify the emotion being expressed. The results were

ANSWERS TO REVIEW QUESTIONS

Review III: **1.** False **2.** a. Acceptance b. Contempt **3.** Cannon-Bard; James-Lange **4.** Visceral experience **5.** True clear: The western viewers—who had never before seen any New Guineans—were surprisingly accurate in their judgments, with the exception of expressions of fear and surprise.

In sum, there is convincing evidence that there is universality in the way basic emotions are displayed and interpreted across cultures. Because the New Guineans were so isolated, they could not have learned from westerners to recognize or produce similar facial expressions. Instead, their similar abilities and manner of responding emotionally appear to have been present innately. Of course, it is possible to argue that similar experiences in both cultures led to learning of similar types of nonverbal behavior, but this appears unlikely, since the two cultures are so very different. The expression of basic emotions, then, seems to be universal (Zivin, 1985).

What is the mechanism that produces similarity in the expression of basic emotions across cultures? One explanation is based on a hypothesis known as the facial-affect program (Ekman, 1982). The **facial-affect program**—which is assumed to be universally present at birth—is analogous to a computer program that is turned on when a particular emotion is experienced. When set in motion, the ''program'' activates a set of nerve impulses that make the face display an appropriate expression. Each primary emotion produces a unique set of muscular movements, forming the kind of expressions seen in Figure 8-9. For example, the emotion of happiness is universally displayed by movement of the zygomatic major, a muscle that raises the corners of the mouth—forming what we would call a smile.

Facial-affect program: *The activation of a set of nerve impulses that make the face display the ''appropriate'' expression*

Smile, Though You're Feeling Blue: The Facial-Feedback Hypothesis

If you want to feel happy, try smiling.

That is the implication of an intriguing notion known as the **facial-feedback hypothesis**. According to this hypothesis, facial expressions not only *reflect* emotional experience, they also help *determine* how people experience and label emotions (Izard, 1977). The basic idea is that ''wearing'' an emotional expression provides muscular feedback to the brain which helps produce an emotion congruent with the expression. For instance, the muscles activated when we smile may send a message to the brain indicating the experience of happiness—even if there is nothing in the environment that would produce that particular emotion. Some theoreticians have gone even further, suggesting that facial expressions are *necessary* for an emotion to be experienced (Rinn, 1984). According to this view, if there is no facial expression present, the emotion cannot be felt.

Facial-feedback hypothesis: *The notion that facial expressions are involved in determining the experience of emotions and in labeling them*

Although support for the facial-feedback hypothesis is not firm, an intriguing experiment has suggested that there is some truth to the notion (Ekman, Levenson, & Friesen, 1983). In the study, a group of professional actors was asked to follow very explicit instructions regarding movement of facial muscles (see Figure 8-10). You might try this example yourself:

> Raise your brows and pull them together; raise your upper eyelids; now stretch your lips horizontally back toward your ears.

After carrying out these directions—which, as you may have guessed, are meant to produce an expression of fear—the actors showed a rise in heart rate and a decline in body temperature, physiological reactions that are characteristic

Figure 8-10
The instructions given this actor were to (*a*) raise the brows and pull them together, (*b*) raise the upper eyelids, and (*c*) stretch the lips horizontally, back toward the ears. If you follow these directions yourself, it may well result in your experiencing fear. (*Source:* Ekman, Levenson, & Friesen, 1983.)

of fear. Overall, facial expressions representative of the primary emotions produced physiological effects similar to those accompanying the emotions in other circumstances.

So the old lyrics ''Smile, though you're feeling blue'' may just be accurate in their suggestion that you will feel better if you put a smile on your face—if, in fact, the facial-feedback hypothesis is valid.

The Informed Consumer of Psychology: Can You "Read" Others' Nonverbal Behavior

You Can Read a Person Like a Book . . . Body Talk . . . Body Language. A glance through a bookstore will reveal many titles such as these, all aimed at helping you to understand other people's nonverbal behavior. But do they work?

For a number of reasons, psychologists who study emotional expressivity would urge extreme caution in accepting advice from these books. First, cultural **display rules**—learned rules that inform us about the appropriateness of showing emotion nonverbally—operate to mask and modify emotional displays. Therefore, what we are seeing is just as likely to be nonverbal behavior brought about by adherence to a display rule as it is a result of an actual emotion.

Display rules: *Learned rules that inform us about the appropriateness of showing emotions nonverbally*

Moreover, there is not a one-to-one relationship between a particular emotion and nonverbal behavior. Just as with word homonyms, such as ''bear'' and ''bare,'' which sound the same but may have very different meanings, the same nonverbal behavior may sometimes mean one thing and, at other times, quite another. Take, for instance, a smile. A smile may, and probably most frequently does, indicate happiness. On the other hand, people who are highly fearful and preparing to defend themselves aggressively may bare their teeth, presenting an expression which at first glance is surprisingly similar to a smile. The meaning behind the expression, however, is quite different.

Finally, there is no evidence that what has been called ''body language'' actually has any of the characteristics of a language. There is no evidence for a syntax and grammar of emotional expressions and, except in sign language, people do not put various nonverbal signs and signals together to form a nonverbal equivalent of sentences. The term ''body language,'' then, is misleading.

Despite these cautions, facial expressions often are a true indication of emotions, given all the scientific evidence that nonverbal expressivity is related to emotional expression. The issue, therefore, becomes one of increasing the accuracy of understanding others' nonverbal behavior. Among the principles you can use to do this are the following:

cultural food preferences, the attractiveness of food, and other learned habits determine when and how much one eats. An oversensitivity to social cues and an insensitivity to internal cues also may be related to obesity. In addition, obesity may be caused by an unusually high weight set point—the weight at which the body attempts to maintain homeostasis—or by the rate of metabolism. Research on eating behavior suggests several strategies for losing excess weight, including changing one's weight set point, decreasing food intake, and minimizing the effects of external social stimuli, such as the presence of food.

5. Human sexuality represents a rich combination of biology and psychology. While biological factors, such as the presence of androgens (the male sex hormone) and estrogens (the female sex hormone) prime people for sex, almost any kind of stimulus can produce sexual arousal, depending on a person's prior experience. Masturbation is sexual self-stimulation. The frequency of masturbation is high, particularly for males. Although attitudes toward masturbation have become more liberal, they are still somewhat negative—even though no negative consequences have been detected.

6. Heterosexuality, or sex between a man and a woman, is the most common sexual orientation. In terms of premarital sex, there is still a double standard: It is thought to be more permissible for men than for women. However, approval for premarital sex for women has risen considerably in the last few decades, as has the incidence of the behavior.

7. Marital sex varies widely in terms of frequency. However, younger couples tend to have sexual intercourse more frequently than older ones. In addition, extramarital sex, of which most people disapprove, occurs with about half of all married men and one-quarter of married women.

8. Homosexuals are sexually attracted to members of their own sex; bisexuals are sexually attracted to people of both the same and the opposite sex. About one-quarter of males and 15 percent of females have had at least one homosexual experience, and around 5 to 10 percent of all men and women are exclusively homosexual during extended periods of their lives. No explanation for why people become homosexual has been confirmed; among the possibilities are genetic or biological factors, childhood and family influences, and prior learning experiences and conditioning. What is clear is that there is no relationship between psychological adjustment and sexual preference.

9. Need for achievement refers to the stable, learned characteristic in which a person strives to attain a level of excellence. People high in need for achievement tend to seek out tasks that are of moderate difficulty, while those low in need for achievement seek out only very easy and very difficult tasks. This is because achievement motivation combines a desire for success with a fear of failure. People high in need for achievement generally have a greater desire for success than a fear of failure, while those low in achievement orientation show the opposite pattern. However, inconsistent findings regarding females' need for achievement have led some researchers to suggest that women have a fear of success related to achievement motivation.

10. Need for achievement is usually measured through the Thematic Apperception Test (TAT). The TAT provides a series of pictures about which a person writes a story. It is assumed that the degree of achievement imagery in the story indicates the writer's need for achievement.

11. Besides need for achievement, there are two other major secondary needs: the needs for affiliation and for power. The need for affiliation is a concern with establishing and maintaining relationships with others, while the need for power is a tendency to seek impact on others.

12. There are a number of broad theories of motivation that move beyond explanations that rely on instincts. The drive-reduction theory, while useful in explaining primary drives, is inadequate for explaining behavior in which the goal is not to reduce a drive but to maintain or even increase excitement or arousal. Arousal theory suggests that we try to maintain a particular level of stimulation and activity. If the level increases, we try to reduce it; if it declines, we try to raise it. The Yerkes-Dodson law, dealing with the relationship between task difficulty and the optimal level of motivation, is consistent with arousal theory. Finally, opponent-process theory suggests that the motivating forces behind such phenomena as drug addiction are opponent forces in the nervous system that arise when initial arousal results from some stimulus. If the initial arousal is positive, the opponent forces are negative, and vice versa.

13. Maslow's hierarchy of needs suggests that needs fall into a specific sequence. The needs, in ascending order, are those for survival, safety, love and belongingness, esteem, self-actualization, and transcendance. Only after the more basic needs are fulfilled is a person able to move toward higher-order needs. The highest levels, self-actualization and transcendance, are attained when people realize their full potential, experience a sense of competence and mastery, and consider themselves a part of the universe and in tune with the laws of nature.

14. It has been difficult to devise an acceptable definition of the term "emotion." One definition that seems appropriate across differing theoretical perspectives presents emotions as feelings that may affect behavior and generally have both a physiological and a cognitive component. What this definition does not do is address the issue of whether there are separate systems that govern cognitive and emotional responses, and whether one has primacy over the other.

15. Emotions serve a number of functions. These include preparing us for action, shaping future behavior through learning, and helping to regulate social interaction. The range of emotions is wide; there are some 500 words in the English language identifying different emotional states. According to at least one system of categorizing, however, there are only eight primary emotions: joy, acceptance, fear, surprise, sadness, disgust, anger, and anticipation. These eight can be arranged in the configuration of a circle, similar to a color wheel.

16. There are a number of general physiological responses to strong emotion, including increased rates of breathing and heartbeat, increased blood pressure, opening of the pupils, dryness of the mouth, and increased sweating. These physiological changes do not provide a full explanation of emotional experience, however. This has led to the development of a number of distinct theories of emotion.

17. The James-Lange theory suggests that emotional experience is a reaction to bodily, or visceral, changes that occur as a

response to an environmental event. These visceral experiences are interpreted as an emotional response.

18. In contrast to the James-Lange theory, the Cannon-Bard theory contends that visceral movements are too slow to explain rapid shifts of emotion and that visceral changes do not always produce emotion. Instead, the Cannon-Bard theory suggests that both physiological arousal *and* an emotional experience are produced simultaneously by the same nerve impulse. Therefore, the visceral experience itself does not necessarily differ with differing emotions.

19. The third explanation, the Schachter-Singer theory, rejects the view that the physiological and emotional responses are simultaneous. Instead, it suggests that emotions are determined jointly by a relatively nonspecific physiological arousal and the subsequent labeling of that arousal. This labeling process uses cues from the environment to determine how others are behaving in the same situation.

20. Emotions can be revealed through a person's facial expression. In fact, there is universality in emotional expressivity, at least for the basic emotions, across members of different cultures. In addition, there are similarities in the way members of different cultures understand the emotional expressions of others. One explanation for this similarity rests on the existence of a facial-affect program, analogous to a computer program, which activates a set of muscle movements representing the emotion being experienced. Related to this notion is the facial-feedback hypothesis, which suggests that facial expressions are not only a reflection of emotions but can actually help determine and produce emotional experience.

KEY TERMS AND CONCEPTS

motive (238)
motivation (238)
drive (240)
primary drive (240)
secondary drive (240)
homeostasis (240)
hypothalamus (241)
lateral hypothalamus (241)
ventromedial hypothalamus (241)
weight set point (242)
obesity (242)
metabolism (243)
anorexia nervosa (244)
bulimia (244)
testes (244)
androgen (244)
ovaries (244)
estrogen (244)
ovulation (244)
masturbation (245)
heterosexuality (245)
homosexuality (246)
double standard (246)
extramarital sex (247)
homosexuals (247)
bisexuals (247)
need for achievement (250)
Thematic Apperception Test (TAT) (251)
fear of success (252)
need for affiliation (252)
need for power (252)
intrinsic motivation (254)
extrinsic motivation (254)
instinct (254)
drive-reduction theory of motivation (255)
arousal theory of motivation (255)
Yerkes-Dodson law (257)
incentive theory of motivation (257)
opponent-process theory of motivation (257)
self-actualization (260)
transcendance (260)
emotion (262)
visceral experience (266)
James-Lange theory of emotions (266)
Cannon-Bard theory of emotions (267)
Schachter-Singer theory of emotions (268)
polygraph (270)
facial-affect program (273)
facial-feedback hypothesis (273)
display rules (274)

ANSWERS TO REVIEW QUESTIONS

Review IV: **1.** Surprise, sadness, happiness, anger, disgust, and fear **2.** Facial-affect **3.** The facial-feedback hypothesis **4.** False

FOR FURTHER STUDY AND APPLICATION

Beck, R. (1983). *Motivation: Theories and principles* (2nd ed.). Englewood Cliffs, NJ: Prentice-Hall.

Franken, R. E. (1982). *Human motivation.* Monterey, CA: Brooks/Cole.

Both of these volumes provide good, general guides to motivation. Not only do they include the classic issues, but they provide information on a number of practical applications.

McClelland, D. C., & Winter, D. G. (1969). *Motivating economic achievement.* New York: Free Press.

This volume provides details of the program developed by McClelland and Winter to teach achievement motivation in India. It includes a wealth of other data on the need for achievement.

Polivy, J., & Herman, C. P. (1983). *Breaking the diet habit.* New York: Basic Books.

This is one of the few popular diet books that can be recommended. Based not on fad diets but on the kind of principles we discuss in this chapter, the book contains numerous hints for losing weight sensibly.

Ekman, P., & Friesen, W. V. (1975). *Unmasking the face.* Englewood Cliffs, NJ: Prentice-Hall.

An interesting, well-illustrated guide to human emotions, this book is coauthored by one of the most eminent authorities on the expression of emotions.

Darwin, C. (1872). *The expression of emotions in man and animals.* Chicago: University of Chicago Press. (1965 reprint.)

This classic on emotions remains surprisingly readable and fascinating more than 100 years after it was written.

Strongman, K. T. (1978). *The psychology of emotions* (2nd ed.). New York: Wiley.

This is a good, readable overview of the topic of emotions.

Ekman, P. (1985). *Telling lies.* New York: Norton.

This book is a guide to deception, detailing what psychologists know about lying, about ways of detecting lies, and about how lies are used in society.

CHAPTER 9

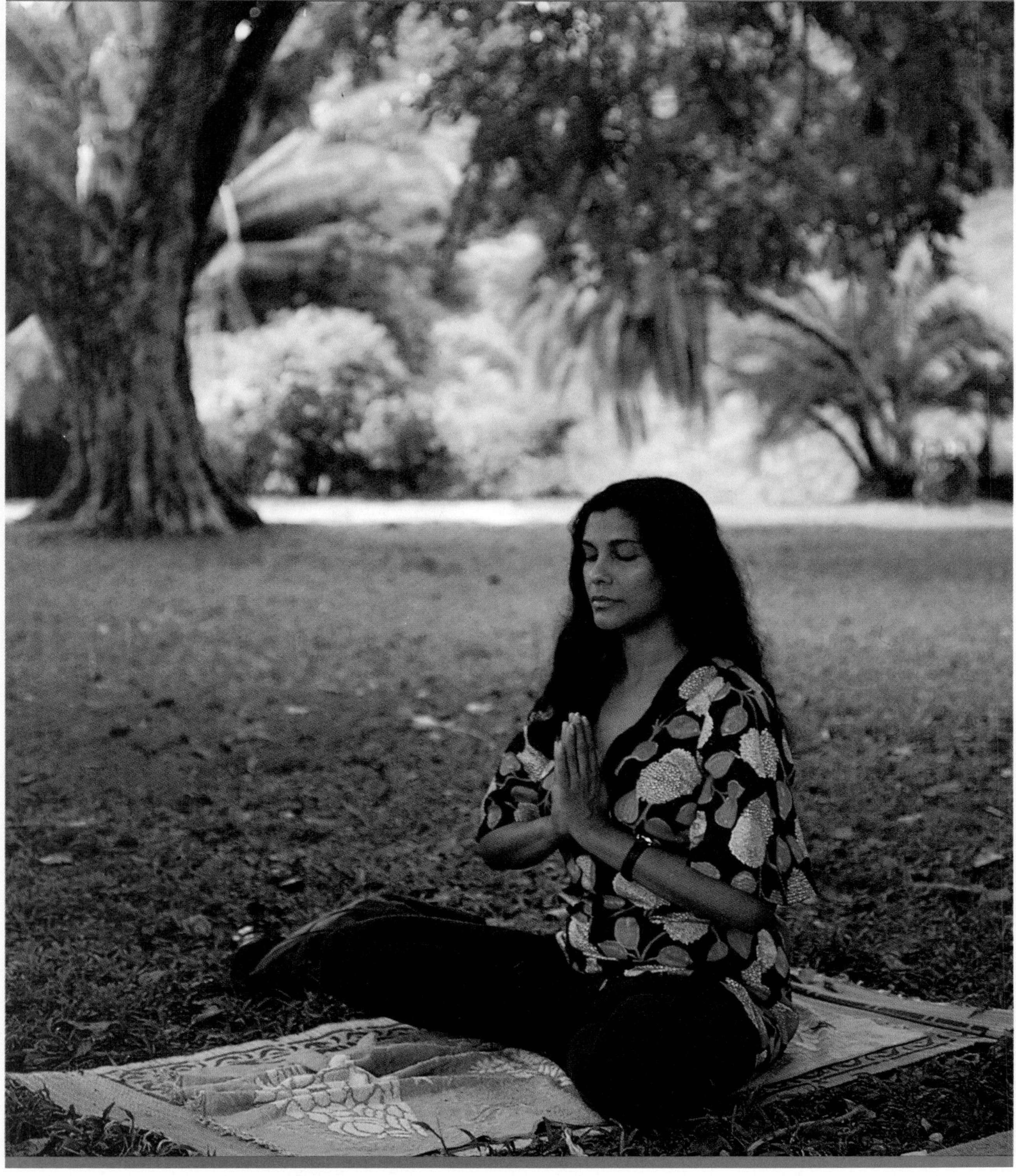

STATES OF CONSCIOUSNESS

PROLOGUE

LOOKING AHEAD

LIFE IS BUT A DREAM . . .: SLEEP AND DREAMS

TRY IT! Testing Your Knowledge of Sleep and Dreams
Awakening our knowledge of sleep: The stages of sleep
Is sleep necessary?
The reality of dreams: The function and meaning of dreaming
Dreams without sleep: Daydreams
Slumbering problems: Sleep disturbances
The informed consumer of psychology: Sleeping better
Recap and review I

ALTERED STATES OF CONSCIOUSNESS: HYPNOSIS AND MEDITATION

You are under my power—or are you?: Hypnosis
PSYCHOLOGY AT WORK. Using Hypnosis Outside the Laboratory
Regulating your own state of consciousness: Meditation
Recap and review II

THE HIGHS AND LOWS OF CONSCIOUSNESS: DRUG USE

Drug highs: Stimulants
Drug lows: Depressants
THE CUTTING EDGE. Discovering the Secrets of Alcoholism
Flying high while staying on the ground: Hallucinogens
The informed consumer of psychology: Dealing with drug and alcohol problems
Recap and review III
PSYCHOLOGY LOOKS TOWARD THE 1990s. Looking for a "Sober" Pill

LOOKING BACK

KEY TERMS AND CONCEPTS

FOR FURTHER STUDY AND APPLICATION

PROLOGUE

Carla, a straight-A high school student, found herself in a predicament. Having received a scholarship to her first-choice college, she still yearned to use her considerable musical talents and join a rock band, putting off college for the time being. Yet part of her felt that to give up the scholarship would be a mistake she would long regret.

To help resolve the question, she held a heated conversation about her future with some close acquaintances. Barb argued that Carla had no reasonable alternative other than to accept the scholarship. Kathy, on the other hand, suggested that Carla would be better off rejecting the scholarship and should instead immediately join the rock band, pursuing her musical talents. Ultimately, it was Becky who came up with a compromise position. She argued that Carla could have the best of both choices by going to college and joining a campus band when she got there. Convinced by Becky's arguments, Carla decided to begin college that fall.

On the surface, Carla had made a rational choice, guided by the helpful advice of Barb, Kathy, and Becky. Yet there was something out of the ordinary about the process: Barb, Kathy, and Becky were dolls, and their "advice" was part of an elaborate fantasy woven by Carla to help make up her mind (Lynn & Rhue, 1985).

LOOKING AHEAD

In most respects, Carla was a well-adjusted, typical teenager. However, she was unusual in one area: She was what could be called a "fantasy addict." With an intense, active imagination, she frequently produced vivid fantasies. According to her own reports, her imagination was so intense that she experienced anxiety and nausea while watching violent television shows, and she could even have an orgasm without any physical stimulation by fantasizing sexual situations.

Although almost everyone has fantasies, the extent of Carla's fantasy life is unusual. Her behavior raises a number of questions of interest to psychologists studying the nature of consciousness, the topic we discuss in this chapter. **Consciousness** is a person's awareness of the sensations, thoughts, and feelings being experienced at a given moment. It is the subjective understanding that we have regarding both the environment around us and our private internal world, unobservable to outsiders.

Consciousness (KON chus nus): *A person's awareness of the sensations, thoughts, and feelings that he or she is experiencing at a given moment.*

Because consciousness is so personal a phenomenon—who can say that your consciousness is the same as or, for that matter, different from anyone else's?—psychologists have sometimes been less than eager to study it. In fact, some early psychological theoreticians suggested that the study of consciousness was out of bounds for the psychologist, since it could be understood only by relying on the "unscientific" introspections of subjects about what they were experiencing at a given moment. Proponents of this view argued that the study of consciousness was better left to philosophers, who could speculate at their leisure on such knotty issues as whether consciousness is separate from the physical body, how people know they exist, how the body and mind are related to each other, and how we identify what state of consciousness we are in at a given moment in time.

Most contemporary psychologists reject the view that the study of conscious-

"If you ask me, all three of us are in different states of awareness."

Psychologists agree that we may experience different states of consciousness. (*Drawing by Frascino; © 1983, The New Yorker Magazine, Inc.*)

ness is improper for psychology, arguing instead that there are several approaches that allow the scientific study of consciousness. For example, new insights into the biology of the brain allow measurement of brain-wave patterns under conditions of consciousness ranging from sleep to waking to hypnotic trances. Moreover, new understandings of the effects of drugs, such as marijuana and alcohol, on behavior have provided insights into the way they produce their positive—and negative—effects. Finally, psychologists have come to understand that there are actually several kinds of consciousness that may be studied separately. By concentrating on particular **altered states of consciousness**—those that differ from a normal, waking consciousness—they have been able to study the phenomenon of consciousness scientifically, even if the more difficult questions, such as whether our consciousness exists separately from our physical bodies, remain unanswered.

Altered states of consciousness: *Experiences of sensation or thought that differ from one's normal experience.*

In this chapter, we begin with a discussion of a state of consciousness that all of us experience: sleep. We explain how sleep proceeds through a series of stages and explore the meanings and functions of dreaming during sleep. The nature of daydreams is also considered. We also offer some suggestions for sleeping better, based on what psychologists have come to understand about the nature of sleep.

Next, we turn to states of consciousness found under conditions of hypnosis and meditation. The nature of the psychological processes underlying these states is discussed, as are the ways in which they differ from normal waking consciousness. Finally the chapter ends with a section on drug-induced altered states of consciousness. We consider the major kinds of drugs, their effects on behavior, and ways of establishing if a person has a drug-related problem.

After reading and studying this chapter, then, you will be able to

- Identify different states of consciousness
- Describe the different stages of sleep
- Discuss the meaning and function of dreams

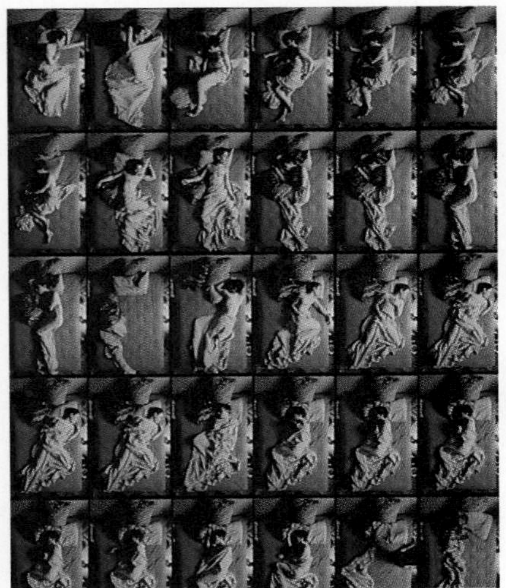

Although we generally view sleep as a period of repose and tranquility, sleep researchers have found that a considerable amount of physical and mental activity occurs during sleep, as these series of photos taken during the course of one night suggest. (*Ted Spagna*)

- Identify the nature of daydreaming
- Outline what is experienced by a person who is hypnotized or meditating, and explain the evidence that these phenomena represent altered states of consciousness
- Classify the major types of drugs and their effects
- Identify some of the clues suggesting that a person has a drug problem that requires professional help
- Define and apply the key terms and concepts listed at the end of the chapter

LIFE IS BUT A DREAM . . .: SLEEP AND DREAMS

> I was sitting at my desk thinking about the movie I was going to see that evening. Suddenly I remembered that this was the day of my chemistry final! I felt awful; I hadn't studied a bit for it. In fact, I couldn't even remember where the class was held, and I had missed every lecture all semester. What could I do? I was in a panic, and began running across campus desperately searching for the classroom so that I could beg the professor to give me another chance. But I had to stop at every classroom building, looking in one room after another, hoping to find the professor and the rest of the class. It was hopeless; I knew I was going to fail and flunk out of college.

If you have ever had a dream like this one, you are not alone: This kind of dream is common among people involved in academic pursuits.

After you have awakened, and found to your relief that the scene that moments before had seemed so real was only a dream, you may have asked yourself what such dreams mean and whether they serve any purpose—questions psychologists have themselves considered in their study of sleep and dreams. We turn now to some of the answers they have arrived at. (Before you read on, you might want to test your knowledge of sleep and dreams by answering the questions in the accompanying Try It! box.)

Awakening Our Knowledge about Sleep: The Stages of Sleep

Most of us consider sleep a time of quiet tranquility, as we peacefully set aside the tensions of the day and spend the night in uneventful slumber. However, a closer look at sleep shows that there is a good deal of activity occurring throughout the night, and what at first appears to be an undifferentiated state is, in fact, quite diverse.

Electroencephalogram (ee LEK tro en SEF uh lo gram) **(EEG)**: *A technique that records the brain's electrical activity*

Most of our knowledge of what happens during sleep comes from the **electroencephalogram** or **EEG**, which, as discussed in Chapter 2, is a measurement of electrical activity within the brain. When an EEG machine is attached to the surface of a sleeping person's scalp and face, it becomes readily apparent that instead of being dormant, the brain is active throughout the night, producing electric discharges that form regular, wavelike patterns. Moreover, instruments that measure muscle stimulation and eye movements also reveal a good deal of activity.

It turns out that there are four distinct stages of sleep through which a person progresses during a night's rest. These stages come and go, cycling approximately every ninety minutes. Each of these four stages is associated with a unique pattern of brain waves, as shown in Figure 9-1. Moreover, there is a specific pattern indicative of dreaming.

TRY IT!

Testing Your Knowledge of Sleep and Dreams

Although sleeping is something we all do for a significant part of our lives, many myths and misconceptions about the topic abound. To test your own knowledge of sleep and dreams, try answering the following true-false questions before reading further.

1. Some people never dream. True or false? ____

2. Most dreams are caused by bodily sensations such as an upset stomach. True or false? ____

3. It has been proved that eight hours of sleep is needed to maintain mental health. True or false? ____

4. When people do not recall their dreams it is probably because they are secretly trying to forget them. True or false? ____

5. Depriving someone of sleep will cause the individual to become mentally unbalanced. True or false? ____

6. If we lose some sleep, we will eventually make up all the lost sleep the next night or another night. True or false? ____

7. No one has been able to go for more than forty-eight hours without sleep. True or false? ____

8. Everyone is able to sleep and breathe at the same time. True or false? ____

9. Sleep enables the brain to rest since there is little brain activity taking place during sleep. True or false? ____

10. Drugs have been proved to provide a long-term cure for sleeping difficulties. True or false? ____

Scoring: This is an easy set of questions to score, for every item is false. But don't lose any sleep if you missed them; they were chosen to represent the most common myths regarding sleep. (Items were drawn from a questionnaire developed by Palladino & Carducci, 1984.)

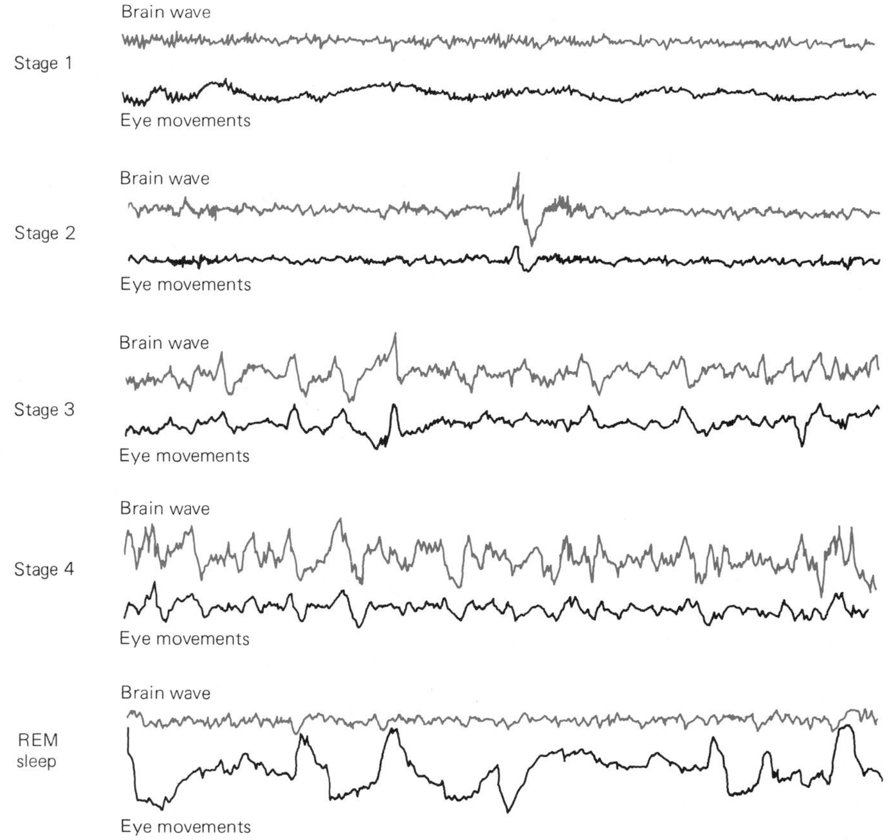

Figure 9-1
Brain-wave patterns (measured by an EEG machine) and eye movements in the different stages of sleep. (*Source: Cohen, 1979.*)

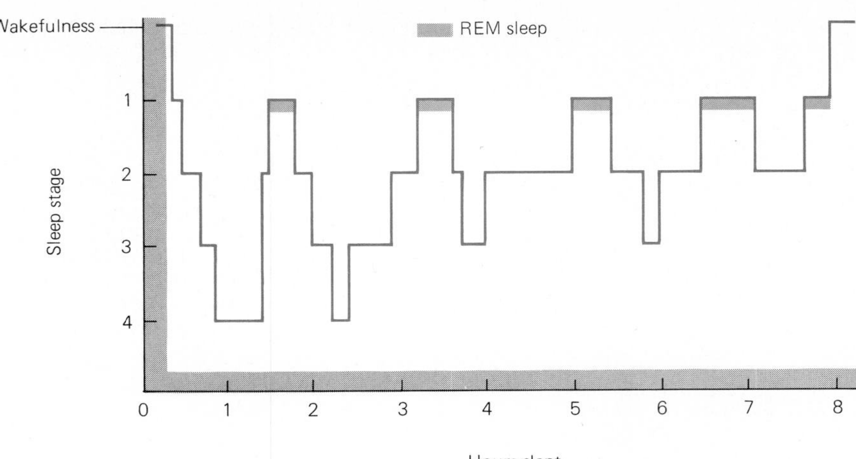

Figure 9-2
During the night, the typical sleeper passes through all four stages of sleep and several REM periods. (*Source: From E. Hartman,* The Biology of Dreaming, *1967. Courtesy of Charles C Thomas Publisher, Springfield, Illinois.*)

Stage 1 sleep: *The state of transition between wakefulness and sleep*

When people first go to sleep, they move into **stage 1 sleep**, which is characterized by relatively rapid, low-voltage waves. This is actually a stage of transition between wakefulness and sleep. During stage 1, images sometimes appear; it's as if one were viewing still photos. However, true dreaming does not occur during the initial entry into this stage of sleep.

Stage 2 sleep: *A sleep deeper than that of stage 1, characterized by sleep spindles*

Sleep spindles: *Momentary interruptions in the brain-wave pattern during stage 2 sleep*

As sleep becomes deeper, people enter **stage 2**, which is characterized by a slower, more regular wave pattern. However, there are also momentary interruptions of sharply pointed waves called **sleep spindles**. It becomes increasingly difficult to awaken a person from stage 2 sleep, which accounts for about half of a college-age person's total sleep.

Stage 3 sleep: *A sleep characterized by slow brain waves, with greater peaks and valleys in the wave pattern*

Stage 4 sleep: *The deepest stage of sleep, during which we are least responsive to outside stimulation*

As people drift into **stage 3**, the next stage of sleep, the brain waves become slower, with an appearance of higher peaks and lower valleys in the wave pattern. By the time sleepers arrive at **stage 4**, the pattern is even slower and more regular, and they are least responsive to outside stimulation.

As you can see in Figure 9-2, stage 4 sleep is most likely to occur during the early part of the night when a person has first gone to sleep. In addition to there being regular transitions between stages of sleep, then, people tend to sleep less deeply over the course of the night (Dement & Wolpert, 1958).

The Paradox of Sleep: REM Sleep Several times a night after a sleeper cycles from higher stages back into stage 1 sleep, something curious happens: The heart rate increases and becomes irregular, the blood pressure rises, the breathing rate increases, and males—even male infants—have erections. Most characteristic of this stage is the back-and-forth movement of the eyes, as if they're watching an action-filled movie. This stage of sleep is called **REM**, or **rapid eye movement**, sleep. REM sleep occupies a little over 20 percent of an adult's total sleeping time.

Rapid eye movement (REM) sleep: *Sleep occupying around 20 percent of an adult's sleeping time, characterized by increased heart rate, blood pressure, and breathing rate; erections; eye movements; and the experience of dreaming*

Paradoxically, while all this activity is occurring, the major muscles of the body act as if they are paralyzed, and it is hard to awaken the sleeper. In addition, REM sleep is usually accompanied by dreams, which—whether people remember them or not—are experienced by *everyone* during some part of the night.

One possible but still unproven explanation for the occurrence of rapid eye movements is that the eyes follow the action that is occurring in the dream

(Dement, 1979). For instance, people who have reported dreaming about watching a tennis match just before they were awakened showed regular right-left-right eye movements, as if they were observing the ball flying back and forth across the net.

There is good reason to believe that REM sleep is critical to human functioning. People deprived of REM sleep—by being awakened every time they begin to display the physiological signs of the stage—show a **rebound effect** when allowed to rest undisturbed. Under this rebound effect, REM-deprived sleepers spend significantly more time in REM sleep than they normally do. It is as if the body requires a certain amount of REM sleep in order to function properly.

Rebound effect: *An increase in REM sleep after one has been deprived of it*

Is Sleep Necessary?

Sleep, in general, seems necessary for human functioning, although surprisingly enough this fact has not been firmly established. While most people sleep between seven and eight hours each night, there is wide variability among individuals, with some people needing as little as three hours. Sleep requirements also vary over the course of a person's lifetime; as people age, they generally need less and less sleep (see Figure 9-3).

Interestingly, people who have participated in sleep deprivation experiments, in which they are kept awake for stretches of as long as 200 hours, show no lasting effects (Dement, 1976). They do experience weariness, lack of concentration, irritability, and a tendency toward hand tremors while they are being kept awake, but after being able to sleep once again they bounce back quickly. College students who worry that lack of sleep due to long hours of study is ruining their health should feel encouraged, then; there should be no long-term consequences of their sleep deprivation.

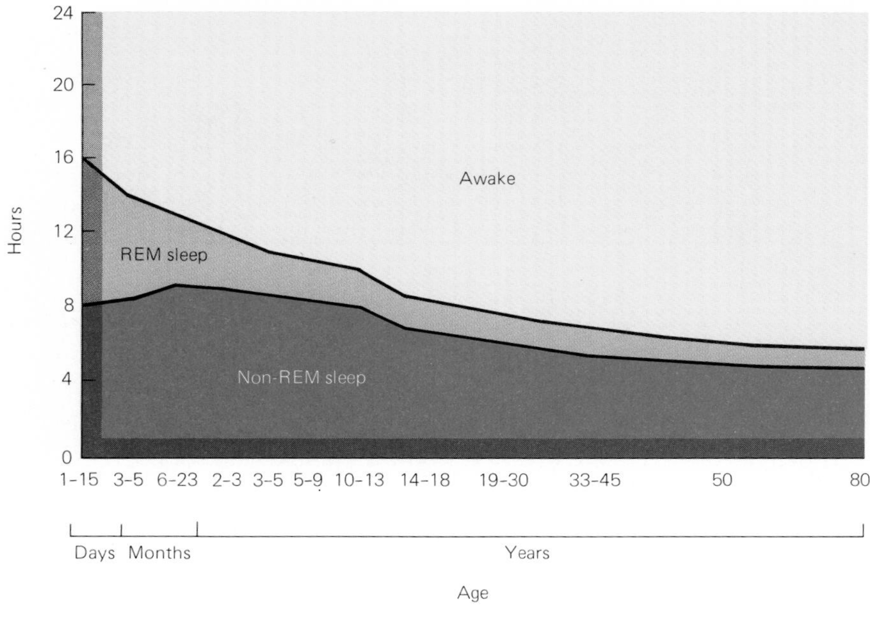

Figure 9-3
As people age, the amount of time they sleep declines. (*Source: Adapted from Roffwarg, Muzio, & Dement, 1966.*)

The Reality of Dreams: The Function and Meaning of Dreaming

If you have had a dream similar to the one described earlier about missing a final exam, you know how utterly convincing are the panic and fear that events in a dream can bring about. Some dreams could not seem more real. On the other hand, many dreams are much less dramatic, recounting such everyday events as going to the supermarket or preparing a meal; we just seem to remember the more exciting ones more readily (Webb, 1979). (The most common dreams are shown in Figure 9-4.)

The question of whether or not dreams have a specific function is one that scientists have considered for many years. Sigmund Freud, for instance, used dreams as a guide to the unconscious (Freud, 1900). He thought that dreams represented unconscious wishes that the dreamer wanted to fulfill. However, because these wishes were related to unconscious desires that were threatening to the dreamer's conscious awareness, the actual wishes—called the **latent content** of the dream—were disguised. The true subject and meaning of a dream, then, may have little to do with its overt story line, called by Freud the **manifest content**.

Latent content of dreams: *According to Freud, the "disguised" meanings of dreams, hidden by more obvious subjects*

Manifest (MAN ih fest) **content of dreams**: *According to Freud, the surface meaning of dreams*

To Freud, it was important to pierce the armor of a dream's manifest content to understand the true meaning. To do this Freud tried to get people to discuss their dreams, associating symbols in the dreams to events in the past. He also suggested that there were certain common symbols with universal meaning that appeared in dreams. For example, he suggested that dreams in which the person was flying symbolized a wish for sexual intercourse. (See Table 9-1 for other common symbols.)

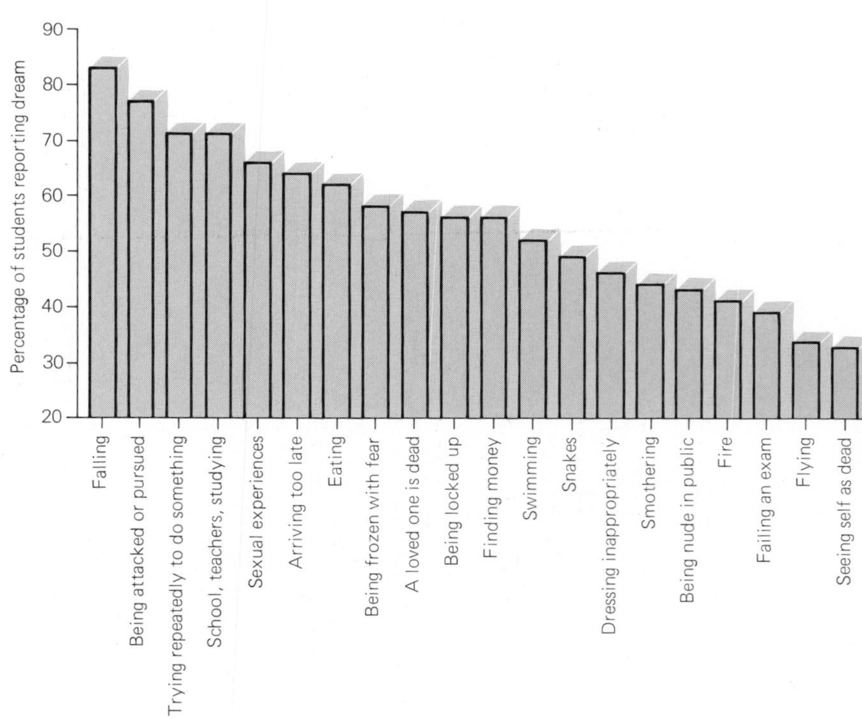

Figure 9-4
The twenty most common dreams.
(*Source: Griffith, Miyago, & Tago, 1958.*)

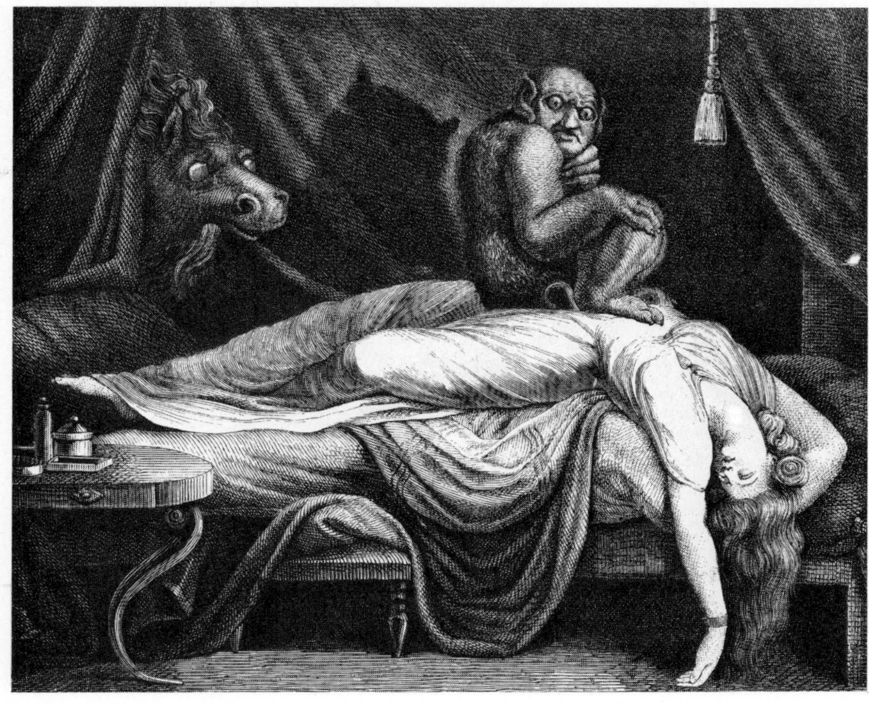

The phantoms that may inhabit our dreams are depicted in this old woodcut. (*Mary Evans Picture Library/Photo Researchers, Inc.*)

Today many psychologists reject Freud's view that dreams typically represent unconscious wishes and that particular objects and events in a dream are symbolic. Instead, the direct, overt action of a dream is considered the focal point in understanding its meaning. If we dream that we are walking down a long hallway to take an exam for which we haven't studied, for instance, it does not relate to unconscious, unacceptable wishes; rather, it simply means we are concerned about an impending test.

Moreover, we now know that some dreams reflect events occurring in the dreamer's environment as he or she is sleeping. For example, sleeping subjects in one experiment were sprayed with water while they were dreaming; these unlucky volunteers reported more dreams involving water than a comparison group who were left to sleep undisturbed (Dement & Wolpert, 1958). Similarly, it is not unusual to wake up to find that the doorbell that was being rung in a dream is actually an alarm clock telling us it is time to get up.

TABLE 9-1

Dream symbols

Sexual intercourse	Climbing up a stairway, crossing a bridge, riding an elevator, flying in an airplane, walking down a long hallway, entering a room, train traveling through a tunnel
Breasts	Apples, peaches, grapefruits
Male sex organs	Bullets, fire, snakes, sticks, umbrellas, guns, hoses, knives
Female sex organs	Ovens, boxes, tunnels, closets, caves, bottles, ships

Although the content of dreams clearly can be affected by environmental stimuli, the question of *why* we dream remains unresolved. Some psychologists suggest that dreaming represents an opportunity to resolve our problems and difficulties (Cartwright, 1978). By allowing our emotions to be brought to bear on personal issues in an uninhibited fashion, and by trying out different schemes for resolving our problems, we can safely "rehearse" different solutions during our dreams.

Other psychologists look at dreaming in terms of the more fundamental biological activity (Hobson & McCarley, 1977). According to this theory, the brain produces electric energy during REM sleep, and this energy randomly stimulates different memories lodged in various portions of the brain. The brain takes these random memories and weaves them into a logical story line, filling in the gaps to produce a scenario that makes a reasonable degree of sense. In this view, then, dreams are closer to a self-generated game of Madlibs than to significant, meaningful psychological phenomena.

Dreams without Sleep: Daydreams

It is the stuff of magic: Our past mistakes can be wiped out, and the future can be filled with noteworthy accomplishments. Fame, happiness, and wealth can be ours. In the next moment, though, the most horrible of tragedies can occur, leaving us alone, penniless, a figure of pitiful unhappiness.

Daydreams: *Fantasies people construct while awake*

The source of these scenarios is **daydreams**, fantasies that people construct while awake. Unlike dreaming that occurs while sleeping, daydreams are more under people's control, and therefore their content is often more closely related to immediate events in the environment than is the content of the dreams that occur during sleep. Although they may include sexual content, daydreams also pertain to other activities or events that are relevant to a person's life.

Daydreams are a typical part of waking consciousness, but the extent and involvement in them varies from one person to another. For example, Carla, the high school girl who used her dolls in an elaborate fantasy to make a decision about her future, engaged in daydreaming more than half her free time. Although most people daydream much less frequently, almost everyone fantasizes to some degree (Singer, 1975).

People who daydream most frequently report having had lonely childhoods and appear to have developed a pattern of fantasizing to escape a lack of stimulation. On the other hand, this pattern is not universal: Some frequent daydreamers come from rich environments and had parents who encouraged the use of imagination, sometimes to the extent of building joint fantasies about the world (Lynn & Rhue, 1985).

Although frequent daydreaming would seem to suggest psychological difficulties, there actually seems to be little relationship between psychological disturbance and daydreaming. Except in those rare cases in which a daydreamer is unable to distinguish a fantasy from reality (a mark of serious problems, as we discuss in Chapter 12), daydreaming seems to be a normal part of waking consciousness.

Slumbering Problems: Sleep Disturbances

Insomnia (in SOM nee uh): *An inability to get to sleep or stay asleep*

At one time or another, almost all of us have sleeping difficulty—a condition known as **insomnia**. It may be due to a particular situation such as the death of

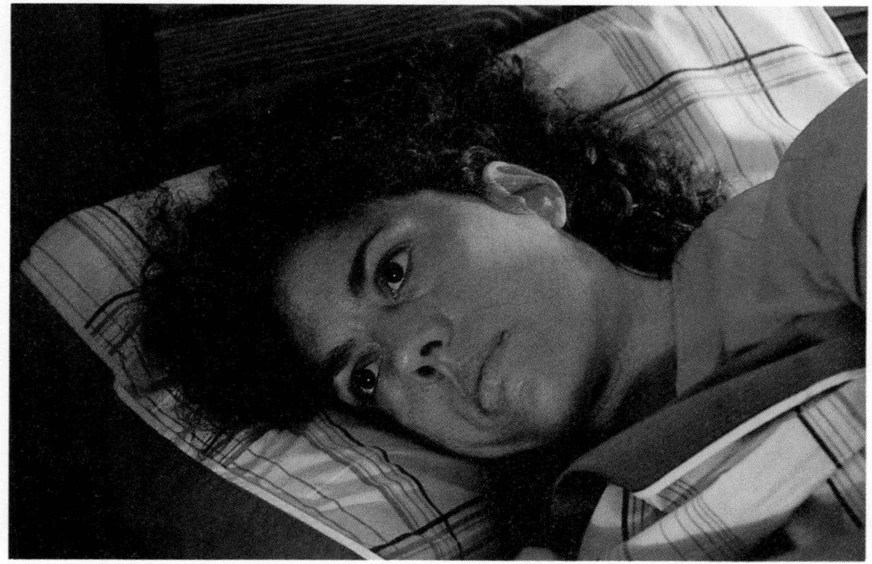

The sleeplessness of insomnia afflicts almost everyone at one time or another. (*Bill Stanton/International Stock Photo*)

a friend or close relative or concern about a test score or the loss of a job. In some cases of insomnia, however, there is no obvious reason for the problem; some people may not be able to fall asleep easily, while others may go to sleep readily but wake up frequently during the night. Insomnia is a problem that afflicts some one-quarter of the population of the United States.

Other sleep problems are less common than insomnia. **Narcolepsy** is an uncontrollable need to sleep for short periods during the day. No matter what the activity—holding a heated conversation, exercising, or driving—the narcoleptic will suddenly drift into sleep. People with **sleep apnea** have difficulty breathing and sleeping simultaneously. The result is disturbed, fitful sleep, as the person is constantly reawakened when the lack of oxygen becomes sufficiently great to trigger a waking response. Sleep apnea may account for **sudden infant death syndrome**, a mysterious killer of seemingly normal infants who die while sleeping.

Narcolepsy (NARK o lep see): *An uncontrollable need to sleep for short periods during the day*

Sleep apnea (AP nee uh): *A sleep disorder characterized by difficulty in breathing and sleeping simultaneously*

Sudden infant death syndrome: *A disorder in which seemingly healthy infants die in their sleep*

The Informed Consumer of Pyschology: Sleeping Better

Fortunately, the most severe sleep disorder most of us suffer is insomnia. Yet the fact that things could be worse provides little solace to weary insomniacs, whose difficulty in sleeping can make them feel exhausted every waking moment.

For those of us who spend hours tossing and turning in bed, psychologists studying sleep disturbances have made a number of suggestions for overcoming insomnia. These include:

- Exercise during the day; not surprisingly, it helps to be tired before going to sleep!
- Avoid drinks with caffeine (such as coffee, tea, and soft drinks) after lunch; their effects can linger for as long as eight to twelve hours after they are consumed.
- Drink a glass of warm milk at bedtime. Your grandmother was right, al-

though she probably didn't know the reason why. (Milk contains the chemical tryptophan, which helps people get to sleep.)

- Don't use your bed as an all-purpose area; leave studying, reading, eating, watching TV, and other recreational activities to some other area of your room.
- Avoid sleeping pills. Although over $100 million a year is spent on sleeping pills in the United States, most of this money is wasted. Although they can be temporarily effective, in the long run sleeping pills can cause more harm than good, since they disrupt normal sleep cycles.
- Don't *try* to go to sleep. This advice, which sounds odd at first, actually makes a good deal of sense. Psychologists have found that part of the reason people have difficulty falling asleep is that they are trying so hard. A better strategy is one suggested by Richard P. Bootzin of Northwestern University, who teaches people to recondition their sleeping habits. He tells them to go to bed only when they feel tired. They are told that if they don't get to sleep within ten minutes, they should leave the bedroom and do something else, returning to bed only when they feel tired. This process should be continued, all night if necessary. But in the morning, the patient must get up at his or her usual hour, and must not take a nap during the day. After three to four weeks on this regimen, most people become conditioned to associate their beds with sleep—and fall asleep rapidly at night (Youkilis & Bootzin, 1981).

Even if these techniques do not work to your satisfaction and you still feel that insomnia is a problem, there is one consolation: Many people who *think* they have sleeping problems are mistaken. When they enter a sleep laboratory for treatment, observers find that these patients actually sleep much more than they think they do. For example, researchers have found that some people who report being up all night actually fall asleep in thirty minutes and stay that way all night. The problem, then, is not insomnia, but people's perceptions of their sleeping patterns. In many cases, just becoming aware of how long they really do sleep—and understanding the fact that the older they become the less sleep they need—is enough to "cure" people's perception that they have a sleep disorder.

RECAP AND REVIEW I

Recap

- Consciousness refers to a person's awareness of the sensations, thoughts, and feelings being experienced at a given moment.
- There are four distinct stages of sleep, as well as REM (rapid eye movement) sleep. These stages recur in cycles during the course of a normal night's sleep.
- Dreams may have symbolic meanings, although some psychologists feel that dream content simply reflects the conscious concerns of the dreamer, an attempt to resolve problems, or a reaction to random electrical activity in the brain.
- The major sleep disorders include insomnia, narcolepsy, and sleep apnea.

Review

1. An electroencephalogram (EEG) showing a slow, regular wave pattern momentarily broken by sleep spindles characterizes stage ____ sleep.
2. Irregular heart rate, rise in blood pressure, and dreaming characterize:
   a. Stage 4 sleep **b.** The rebound effect **c.** Rapid eye movement sleep **d.** Stage 1 sleep
3. "I knew I shouldn't have picked up those two extra courses this semester," Victoria muttered wearily. "I've hardly slept at all

the past two nights. I must be ruining my health!'' Victoria's sleep deprivation will probably not affect her long-term health. True or false?

4. According to Freud, the often quizzical themes we experience in dreams actually mask the true wishes of the dreamer. The dream, as experienced, represents the ________________ content, whereas the underlying wishes are labeled the ________________ content.
5. Gabrielle abruptly fell asleep at the table during a dinner party. Her dinner guests might have considered Gabrielle's behavior a bit rude had her husband not been present to explain that Gabrielle suffered from
   a. Sleep apnea **b.** Daydreaming **c.** Insomnia **d.** Narcolepsy
6. We go through each of the four stages of sleep only once in an eight-hour night. True or false?
7. About half of college-age people's sleep is spent in
   a. Stage 1 **b.** Stage 2 **c.** Stage 3 **d.** Stage 4

(Answers to review questions are at the bottom of page 294.)

ALTERED STATES OF CONSCIOUSNESS: HYPNOSIS AND MEDITATION

You are feeling relaxed and drowsy. You are getting sleepier and sleepier. Your body is becoming limp. Now you are starting to become warm, at ease, more comfortable. Your eyelids are feeling heavier and heavier. Your eyes are closing; you can't keep them open any more. You are totally relaxed.

Now, as you listen to my voice, do exactly as I say. Place your hands above your head. You will find they are getting heavier and heavier—so heavy you can barely keep them up. In fact, although you are straining as hard as you can, you will be unable to hold them up any longer.

An observer watching the above scene would notice a curious phenomenon occurring: Many of the people listening to the voice would, one by one, drop their arms to their sides, as if they were holding heavy lead weights. The reason for this strange behavior is probably no surprise: The people have been hypnotized.

You Are Under My Power—or Are You?: Hypnosis

A person under **hypnosis** is in a state of heightened susceptibility to the suggestions of others. In some respects, it appears that a person in a hypnotic trance is asleep (although measures of brain waves show that this is not the case). Yet other aspects of behavior contradict this appearance of sleep, for the person is attentive to the hypnotist's suggestions and carries out suggestions that may be bizarre and silly.

Hypnosis: *A state of heightened susceptibility to the suggestions of others*

At the same time, people do not lose all will of their own when hypnotized: They will not perform antisocial behaviors, and they will not carry out self-destructive acts. Moreoever, people cannot be hypnotized against their will—despite the popular misconceptions.

There are wide variations in people's susceptibility to hypnosis. About 5 to 10 percent of the population cannot be hypnotized at all, while some 15 percent are very easily hypnotized. Most people fall in between. Moreover, the ease with which a person is hypnotized is related to a number of other characteristics. People who are readily hypnotized are also easily absorbed while reading books or listening to music, becoming unaware of what is happening around them,

Marvel Characters © 1981 by Marvel Comics Group. All rights reserved. Produced in conjunction with and to the standards of the Marvel Comics Group

Figure 9-5
If this comic were true to life, Spiderman would have little to fear from the evil Mesmero: Despite common misconceptions, people cannot be hypnotized against their will. (*Source: Marvel Comics Group, 1981.*)

and they often spend an unusual amount of time daydreaming (Hilgard, 1974; Lynn & Rhue, 1985). In sum, then, they show a high ability to concentrate and to become completely absorbed in what they are doing.

A Different State of Consciousness? The issue of whether hypnosis represents a state of consciousness that is qualitatively different from normal waking consciousness has long been controversial among psychologists.

Ernest Hilgard (1975) has argued convincingly that hypnosis does represent a state of consciousness that differs significantly from other states. He contends that there are particular behavioral characteristics that clearly differentiate hypnosis from other states, including higher suggestibility; increased ability to recall and construct images, including visual memories from early childhood; a lack of initiative; and the ability to accept uncritically suggestions that clearly contradict reality. Moreover, recent research has found that there are changes in electrical activity in the brain that are associated with hypnosis, supporting the position that hypnotic states represent a state of consciousness different from that of normal waking (Guzelier et al., 1984).

Still, some theorists reject the notion that hypnosis represents an altered state of consciousness. They argue that altered brain-wave patterns are not sufficient to demonstrate that a state of hypnotic trance is qualitatively different from normal waking consciousness, given that there are no other specific physiological changes that occur when a person is in a trance. Moreover, some researchers have shown that people merely pretending to be hypnotized show behaviors that are nearly identical to those of truly hypnotized individuals, suggesting that there is nothing qualitatively special about the hypnotic trance (Barber, 1975; Orne & Evans, 1965).

The jury remains out on whether hypnosis represents a state of consciousness that is truly unique. On the other hand, hypnosis has been applied in a number of important areas, as we discuss in the Psychology at Work box, and as such represents a useful therapeutic tool.

Meditation, practiced today by many westerners, has its roots in the ancient oriental religion of Zen Buddhism. (*John Launois/Black Star*)

Regulating Your Own State of Consciousness: Meditation

When traditional practitioners of the ancient eastern religion of Zen Buddhism want to achieve greater spiritual insight, they turn to a technique that has been

ANSWERS TO REVIEW QUESTIONS

Review I: **1.** 2 **2.** c **3.** True **4.** manifest, latent **5.** d **6.** False **7.** b

PSYCHOLOGY AT WORK

USING HYPNOSIS OUTSIDE THE LABORATORY

Although there is disagreement over the true nature of consciousness associated with hypnotic states, few would dispute the tremendous practical value of hypnosis in a variety of settings. Psychologists working in many disparate areas have found hypnosis to be a reliable, effective tool. Among the range of applications are the following:

- Medical care. Patients suffering from chronic pain may be given the suggestion, while hypnotized, that their pain is eliminated or reduced. Similarly, they may be taught to hypnotize themselves to relieve pain or to be given a sense of control over their symptoms. Hypnosis has proved particularly useful during childbirth and dental procedures.
- Professional sports. Athletes frequently turn to hypnosis to improve their performance. For example, Ken Norton, the championship fighter, used hypnosis prior to his fights to prepare himself for the encounter, and baseball star Rod Carew has used hypnotism to increase his concentration when batting (Udolf, 1981).

Hypnosis, then, has many potential applications. Of course, it is not invariably effective: For the significant number of people who cannot be hypnotized, it offers little help. But for people who make good hypnotic subjects, hypnosis has the potential for providing significant benefits.

used for centuries to alter their state of consciousness. This technique is called meditation.

Meditation is a learned technique for refocusing attention that brings about an altered state of consciousness. Although there is an exotic sound to it, some form of meditation is found within every major religion—including Christianity and Judaism. In the United States today, major proponents of meditation are followers of Maharishi Mahesh Yogi, who practice a form of meditation called **transcendental meditation**, or **TM**, although there are several other groups teaching various forms of meditation.

Meditation: *A learned technique for refocusing attention that brings about an altered state of consciousness*

Transcendental (tran sen DEN tul) **meditation (TM)**: *A popular type of meditation practiced by followers of Maharishi Mahesh Yogi*

Mantra (MON truh): *A sound, word, or syllable repeated over and over to take one into a meditative state*

The specific meditative technique used in TM involves repeating a **mantra**—a sound, word or syllable—over and over; in other forms of meditation, the focus is on a picture, flame, or specific part of the body (see Figure 9-6). Regardless of the nature of the particular initial stimulus, in most forms of meditation the key to the procedure is concentrating on it so thoroughly that the meditator becomes unaware of any outside stimulation and a different state of consciousness is reached. In this new state, the meditator loses conscious awareness of the environment surrounding him or her. Following meditation, people report feeling thoroughly relaxed, having sometimes gained new insights into themselves and the problems they are facing.

Studies of the physiological changes that occur during meditation indicate that *something* different is happening in that state, but whether these changes qualify as a true change in consciousness is controversial. For example, oxygen usage decreases, heart rate and blood pressure decline, and brain-wave patterns may change (Wallace & Benson, 1972). On the other hand, similar changes occur during relaxation of any sort, and so whether they indicate some special state of consciousness remains an open question (Holmes, 1985).

It *is* clear that you yourself can meditate without exotic trappings by using a few simple procedures developed by Herbert Benson, who has studied meditation extensively (Benson, Kotch, Crassweller, & Greenwood, 1977). The basics—which are similar in several respects to those developed as a part of eastern religions, but have no spiritual component—include sitting in a quiet room with

Figure 9-6
An ancient mandala that can be used to focus one's attention while meditating. A mandala is constructed so that attention is drawn to the center of the figure. (Manfred Kage/Peter Arnold, Inc.)

eyes closed, breathing deeply and rhythmically, and repeating a word or sound over and over. Although the procedure is a bit more complicated than this, most people find themselves in a deeply relaxed state after just twenty minutes. Practiced twice a day, Benson's meditative techniques seem to be just as effective in bringing about relaxation as more mystical methods (Benson & Friedman, 1985).

RECAP AND REVIEW II

Recap

- Hypnosis places people in a state of heightened susceptibility to the suggestions of others. People cannot be hypnotized against their will, and they vary in their susceptibility to hypnosis.
- One crucial question about hypnosis is whether or not it represents a separate state of consciousness. There is evidence for both sides of the issue.
- Meditation is a learned technique for refocusing attention that is meant to bring about an altered state of consciousness.

Review

1. Which of the following is *not* characteristic of someone undergoing hypnosis?
   a. Attentive to the hypnotist's suggestions **b.** Susceptibility to performance of antisocial or self-destructive acts **c.** A sleeplike trance **d.** Behavior which may be strange or silly
2. For which of the following purposes is hypnosis *not* commonly used?
   a. To sharpen memory of certain events **b.** To eliminate certain symptoms or behavior **c.** To improve performance on a chosen task **d.** To interview suspects in criminal cases
3. Almost everyone can be hypnotized, usually very easily, by an experienced hypnotist. True or false?
4. Leslie repeats a unique sound, known as a ______________, when she engages in transcendental meditation.
5. Meditation can be learned only by following procedures which include a spiritual component. True or false?

(Answers to review questions are at the bottom of page 298.)

THE HIGHS AND LOWS OF CONSCIOUSNESS: DRUG USE

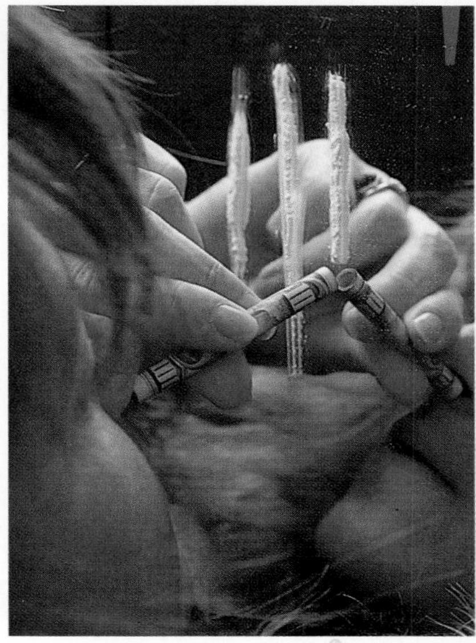

The use of the stimulant cocaine, here being inhaled or "snorted," represents one of today's major drug problems. (*Stanley Rowin/The Picture Cube*)

I experimented with cocaine in college, but it was too expensive then. When I got to the city, a lot of people in my social and business lives were doing it.

It was part of being accepted, like drinking. It was there, and I did it along with everyone else.

It was a form of release at the end of the day. It didn't trouble me because it was illegal. As long as I wasn't selling it, I didn't feel I was committing a crime. . . .

In 1982, I had a lot of business pressures. I wanted to leave the company I was with and start my own investment-consulting company. I was unhappy at work, and at the same time I became friendly with a group of people in the commodities exchange who do it in massive quantities.

I stopped buying a gram or two from friends and started to meet with real hard-core dealers. I needed larger and larger quantities—$2,000 a week. . . .

Last year, I also got married, and there was the pressure of work, and a fight with my landlord. Coke put me in a different world. I didn't care any more. I was going downhill at work. All I was looking forward to was the next high.

I thought I was concentrating, but I wasn't. I'd go to Lutece for a business luncheon and not eat a thing. There were a couple of deals that I definitely blew.

Last October, I confessed to my wife I was doing it in large quantities. I went to a psychiatrist and stopped for two months. Then it started again, worse than ever. I felt wired, but not in a frenzied condition. My hands shake, and you're always blowing your nose. . . .

Emotionally, it was tearing me apart. I was losing my temper, losing my shrewdness. I was talking too much when I should have been discreet. I tortured my wife—started fights with her just for the fun of it.

Sometimes I was so high I'm lucky I didn't kill myself by stepping in front of a bus. (*New York Times,* 1984, p. 50.)

Although few of us reach the extremes of this person—now enrolled in a rehabilitation program—almost all of us are experienced drug users. From infancy on, most people take vitamins, aspirin, cold-relief medicine, and the like. These drugs have little effect on our consciousness, operating primarily on our biological functions. When we speak of drugs that affect consciousness, we are referring instead to **psychoactive drugs**, drugs that affect a person's emotions, perceptions, and behavior. Even these drugs are common in most people's lives; if you have ever had a cup of coffee or sipped a beer, you have had a psychoactive drug. In fact, the number of people who have used more potent—and dangerous—psychoactive drugs is large, as shown in Figure 9-7.

Psychoactive (sy ko AK tiv) **drugs**: *Drugs that affect a person's emotions, perceptions, and behavior*

Obviously, drugs vary in the nature of the effects they have on users. The most dangerous are those that are addictive. **Addictive drugs** are those that produce a physical or psychological dependence in the user, and their withdrawal leads to a craving for the drug that, in some cases, may be nearly irresistible.

Addictive drugs: *Drugs that produce a physical or phychological dependence in the user*

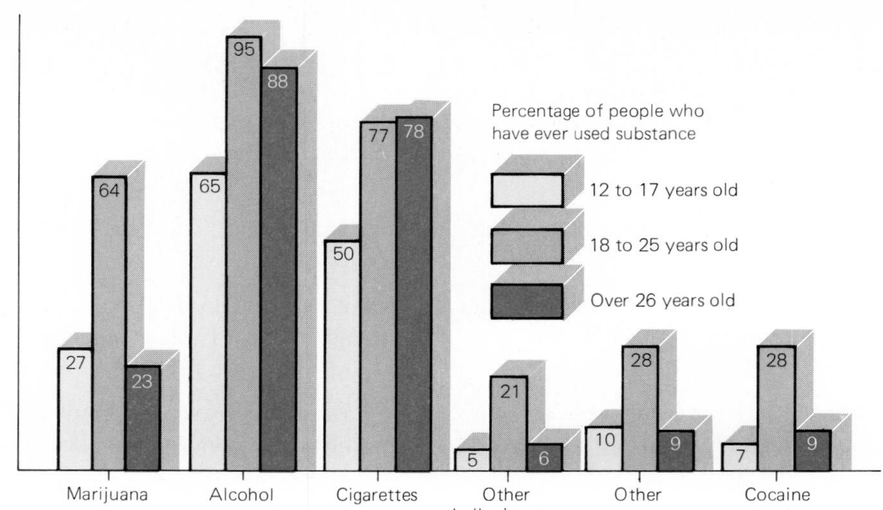

Figure 9-7
Who uses what drug? The results of a recent survey show the use of various drugs by different age groups. The "other" category includes nonmedical use of stimulants, sedatives, tranquilizers, and painkillers. (*Source: Miller, 1984.*)

Addictions may be biologically based, in which the body becomes so accustomed to functioning in the presence of a drug that it cannot function in its absence, or they may be psychological, in which case people perceive that they require the drug in order to respond to the stresses of daily living. While we generally think of addiction in terms of drugs such as heroin, everyday sorts of drugs such as caffeine (found in coffee) and nicotine (found in cigarettes) have their addictive aspects as well.

Drug High: Stimulants

Caffeine (kaf FEEN): *A stimulant found most abundantly in coffee, soda, and chocolate*

Stimulants: *Drugs that affect the central nervous system, causing increased heart rate, blood pressure, and muscle tension*

If you have ever urged someone to drink another cup of coffee in order to stay awake, you have, in reality, been urging that person to increase consumption of a major *stimulant*, caffeine. **Caffeine** is one of a number of **stimulants** that affect the central nervous system by causing a rise in heart rate, blood pressure, and muscular tension.

Caffeine is not present in coffee alone; it is an important ingredient in tea, soft drinks, and chocolate as well. The major behavioral effects of caffeine are an increase in attentiveness and a decrease in reaction time. Too much caffeine, however, can result in nervousness and insomnia. People can build up a biological dependence on the drug: If they suddenly stop drinking coffee, they may experience headaches or depression. Many people who drink large amounts of coffee on weekdays have headaches on weekends due to a sudden drop in the amount of caffeine they are consuming.

Nicotine (NIK o teen): *A stimulant present in cigarettes*

Another common stimulant is **nicotine**, found in cigarettes. The presence of nicotine helps explain why cigarette smoking is rewarding for smokers, who continue to smoke despite clear evidence of its long-term health dangers. Moreover, smoking is addictive; smokers develop a dependence on nicotine, and smokers who suddenly stop develop strong cravings for the drug.

ANSWERS TO REVIEW QUESTIONS

Review II: **1.** b **2.** d **3.** False **4.** Mantra **5.** False

"Speed Kills": Amphetamines The phrase ''speed kills'' was made popular in the late 1970s when use of **amphetamines**, strong stimulants such as Dexedrine and Benzedrine (popularly known as speed), soared. In small quantities, amphetamines bring about increased confidence, a sense of energy and alertness, and a mood ''high.'' They may also cause a loss of appetite, increased anxiety, and irritability. When taken over long periods of time, amphetamines can cause feelings of being persecuted by others, as well as a general sense of suspiciousness. If taken in too large a quantity, amphetamines cause so much stimulation of the central nervous system that convulsions and death can occur—hence the phrase, ''speed kills.'' (For a summary of the effects of amphetamines and other illegal drugs, see Table 9-2.)

Amphetamines (am FET uh meens): *Strong stimulants that cause a temporary feeling of confidence and alertness, but may increase anxiety and appetite loss, and taken over a period of time, suspiciousness and feelings of persecution*

Cocaine and its derivative crack are dangerous stimulants that have grown in popularity over the last ten years. Cocaine is inhaled or ''snorted'' through the nose and is rapidly absorbed into the bloodstream, making its effects apparent almost immediately. Although illegal and expensive, cocaine use is not uncommon, particularly among the upper and upper-middle classes, as indicated in the case history described earlier.

Cocaine (ko KANE): *A stimulant that initially creates feelings of confidence, alertness, and well-being, but eventually causes mental and physical deterioration*

When taken in relatively small quantities, cocaine has many of the same effects as amphetamines in general—euphoria, increased confidence, alertness, and a sense of well-being. It also allows people to work for long periods of time without feeling tired (although this can be followed by a ''crash'' in which the user sleeps for long periods of time).

The price paid by users for these effects is profound. The drug is pyschologically addictive, and users may grow obsessed with obtaining it (Fischman, 1985). Their lives become tied to the drug; they deteriorate mentally and physically, losing weight and growing suspicious of others. In extreme cases, cocaine can cause hallucinations; a common one is that insects are crawling over one's body.

One of the most frequently used stimulants is nicotine, a chief ingredient of cigarettes. (*Robert Jordan/International Stock Photo*)

TABLE 9-2

Illegal drugs and their effects

DRUG	STREET NAME	EFFECTS	WITHDRAWAL SYMPTOMS	ADVERSE/OVERDOSE REACTIONS
Stimulants Amphetamines Benzedrine Dexedrine Cocaine	 Speed Speed Coke, blow, toot, snow, lady, crack	Increased confidence, mood elevation, sense of energy and alertness, decreased appetite, anxiety, irritability, insomnia, transient drowsiness, delayed orgasm	Apathy, general fatigue, prolonged sleep, depression, disorientation, suicidal thoughts, agitated motor activity, irritability, bizarre dreams	Elevated blood pressure, increase in body temperature, face-picking, suspiciousness, bizarre and repetitious behavior, vivid hallucinations, convulsions, possible death
Depressants Barbiturates Nembutal Seconal Phenobarbital Quaalude	 Yellowjackets, yellows Reds Ludes, 714s	Impulsiveness, dramatic mood swings, bizarre thoughts, suicidal behavior, slurred speech, disorientation, slowed mental and physical functioning, limited attention span	Weakness, restlessness, nausea and vomiting, headaches, nightmares, irritability, depression, acute anxiety, hallucinations, seizures, possible death	Confusion, decreased response to pain, shallow respiration, dilated pupils, weak and rapid pulse, coma, possible death
Heroin Morphine	H, hombre, junk, smack, dope, horse, crap Drugstore dope, cube, first line, mud	Apathy, difficulty in concentration, slowed speech, decreased physical activity, drooling, itching, euphoria, nausea	Anxiety, vomiting, sneezing, diarrhea, lower back pain, watery eyes, runny nose, yawning, irritability, tremors, panic, chills and sweating, cramps	Depressed levels of consciousness, low blood pressure, rapid heart rate, shallow breathing, convulsions, coma, possible death
Hallucinogens Cannabis Marijuana Hashish Hash oil	 Bhang, kif, ganja, dope, grass, pot, smoke, hemp, joint, weed, bone, Mary Jane, herb, tea	Euphoria, relaxed inhibitions, increased appetite, disoriented behavior	Hyperactivity, insomnia, decreased appetite, anxiety	Severe reactions are rare, but include panic, paranoia, fatigue, bizarre and dangerous behavior, decreased production of testosterone over long term, immune system effects
LSD	Electricity, acid, quasey, blotter acid, microdot, white lightning, purple barrels	Fascination with ordinary objects; heightened esthetic responses to color, texture, spatial arrangements, contours, music; vision and depth distortion; hearing colors, seeing music; slowing of time; heightened sensitivity to faces and gestures; magnified feelings of love, lust, hate, joy, anger, pain, terror, despair, etc.; paranoia; panic; euphoria; bliss; impairment of short-term memory; projection of self into dreamlike images	Not reported	Nausea and chills; increased pulse, temperature, and blood pressure; trembling; slow, deep breathing; loss of appetite; insomnia; longer, more intense "trips"; bizarre, dangerous behavior possibly leading to injury or death

DRUG	STREET NAME	EFFECTS	WITHDRAWAL SYMPTOMS	ADVERSE/OVERDOSE REACTIONS
Hallucinogens (*continued*)				
Phencylidine (PCP)	Angel dust, hog, rocket fuel, superweed, peace pill, elephant tranquilizer, dust, bad pizza	Increased blood pressure and heart rate, sweating, nausea, numbness, floating sensation, slowed reflexes, altered body image, altered perception of time and space, impaired immediate and recent memory, decreased concentration, paranoid thoughts and delusions	Not reported	Highly variable and possibly dose-related: disorientation, loss of recent memory, lethargy/stupor, bizarre and violent behavior, rigidity and immobility, mutism, staring, hallucinations and delusions, coma

Drug Lows: Depressants

In contrast to the initial effect of stimulants, which is an increase in arousal of the central nervous system, the effect of **depressants** is to impede the nervous system by causing the neurons to fire more slowly. Small doses result in at least temporary feelings of **intoxication**—drunkenness—along with a sense of euphoria and joy. In large amounts, however, speech becomes slurred, muscle

Depressants: *Drugs that slow down the nervous system*

Intoxication: *A state of drunkenness*

TABLE 9-3

Effects of alcohol

DISTILLED SPIRITS CONSUMED IN 2 HR, OUNCES	ALCOHOL IN BLOOD, PERCENT	TYPICAL EFFECTS, AVERAGE-SIZE ADULT
3 (2 drinks)	0.05	Judgment, thought, and restraint weakened; tension release, giving carefree sensation
4½ (3 drinks)	0.08	Tensions and inhibitions of everyday life lessened
6 (4 drinks)	0.10	Voluntary motor action affected, making hand and arm movements, walk, and speech clumsy
10 (6.7 drinks)	0.20	Severe impairment–staggering, loud, incoherent, emotionally unstable; 100 times greater traffic risk
14 (9.3 drinks)	0.30	Deeper areas of brain affected, with stimulus response and understanding confused; stuporous
18 (12 drinks)	0.40	Incapable of voluntary action; sleepy, difficult to arouse; equivalent of surgical anesthesia
22 (14.7 drinks)	0.50	Comatose; centers controlling breathing and heartbeat anesthetized; death

Note: A drink refers to a typical 12-ounce glass of beer, a 1.5-ounce shot of hard liquor, or a 5-ounce glass of wine.

control becomes disjointed, causing difficulty of motion, and ultimately consciousness may be lost entirely.

The most common depressant is alcohol, although most people would probably claim that it increases their sense of sociability and well-being (Steele & Southwick, 1985). The discrepancy between the actual and perceived effects of alcohol lies in its initial effects: releasing tension and producing a breakdown in judgment. As the dose of alcohol increases, however, the depressive effects become clearer. People may feel emotionally and physically unstable; their intellectual abilities decline; and they become incoherent and may eventually fall into a stupor and pass out (Hannon et al., 1985). (See Table 11-3.) As we discuss in the Cutting Edge box, alcohol has addictive qualities that are just now beginning to be understood.

Barbiturates (bar BIH chur uts): *Depressants used to induce sleep and reduce stress, the abuse of which, especially when combined with alcohol, can be deadly*

Morphine (MOR feen): *Derived from the poppy flower, a powerful depressant that reduces pain and induces sleep*

Heroin (HAIR o in): *A powerful depressant, usually injected, that gives an initial rush of good feeling but leads eventually to anxiety and depression; extremely addictive*

Methadone (METH uh doan): *A chemical used to detoxify heroin addicts*

Hallucinogen (ha LOOS en o jen): *A drug that is capable of producing changes in perception, or hallucinations*

Barbiturates, which include such drugs as Nembutal, Seconal, and phenobarbital, are another form of depressant. Frequently prescribed by physicians to induce sleep or to reduce stress, barbiturates produce the immediate effect of a relaxant with effects similar to those of alcohol. Yet, they are psychologically and physically addictive and, when combined with alcohol, can be deadly, since such a combination relaxes the muscles of the diaphragm to such an extent that the user suffocates. The street drug known as Quaalude is closely related to the barbiturate family and has similar dangers associated with it.

It's Not Poppycock: Morphine and Heroin Two of the most powerful depressants, **morphine** and **heroin**, are derived from the poppy flower. Both reduce pain and cause sleepiness. Although morphine is used medically to control severe pain, heroin is illegal in the United States. This has not prevented its widespread use.

Heroin users usually inject the drug directly into their veins with a hypodermic needle. The immediate effect has been described as a ''rush'' of positive feeling, similar in some respects—and just as difficult to describe —as a sexual orgasm. After the rush, a heroin user experiences a sense of well-being and peacefulness that lasts three to five hours. When the effects of the drug wear off, however, the user feels extreme anxiety and a desperate desire to repeat the experience. Moreover, larger amounts of heroin are needed each time to produce the same pleasurable effect. This leads to a cycle of biological and psychological addiction: The user is constantly either shooting up or attempting to obtain ever-increasing amounts of the drug. Eventually, the life of the addict becomes centered around heroin.

Heroin, which is typically injected directly into a user's vein, is a powerful drug that produces both biological and psychological addiction. (*Dan McCoy/Black Star*)

Because of the powerful positive feelings the drug produces, heroin addiction is particularly difficult to cure. One treatment that has shown some success is the use of methadone. **Methadone** is a chemical that satisfies a heroin user's physiological cravings for the drug without providing the ''high'' that accompanies heroin. When heroin users are placed on regular doses of methadone they may be able to function relatively normally. The use of methadone has one substantial drawback, however: Although it removes the psychological dependence on heroin, it replaces the biological addiction to heroin with a biological addiction to methadone.

Flying High While Staying on the Ground: Hallucinogens

What do mushrooms, jimsonweed, and morning glories—besides being fairly common plants—have in common? Each can be a source of a powerful **hallu-**

THE CUTTING EDGE

DISCOVERING THE SECRETS OF ALCOHOLISM

It is near the end of the cocktail party. Several guests are still talkative, friendly, charming, and witty. But in one corner a woman is crying. Two men nearby are arguing, picking fights at every turn. Another guest has passed out. Yet another, who half an hour ago was happy and friendly, is now sick and depressed (Blakeslee, 1984, p. C1).

The source of these diverse behaviors is one and the same drug: alcohol. Yet only recently have scientists begun to understand how alcohol brings about its varied effects.

According to Ernest Noble, director of the Alcohol Research Center at the University of California at Los Angeles, researchers have recently learned that alcohol affects the walls of neurons by decreasing their ability to transmit messages. When most people consume alcohol, the normal pathways of the neurons become less rigid, and messages become garbled and disoriented—resulting in the depressive effects that occur in the central nervous system.

In contrast, alcoholics—people who come to rely on alcohol and continue to drink even though it causes serious problems—develop a tolerance for the drug; their cell walls remain rigid even in the presence of alcohol. In fact, when the alcohol content of the blood decreases, alcoholics suffer from withdrawal symptoms, since their cell walls are no longer able to process messages in the drug's absence (see Figure 9-8).

It is still unclear why certain people become alcoholic and develop a tolerance for alcohol, while others do not. Some evidence suggests a genetic cause; the chances of becoming alcoholic is considerably higher if alcoholics are present in earlier generations. Most researchers following this line of research think that heredity makes certain people genetically susceptible to alcoholism (Franks, 1985; Holden, 1985).

Whatever the specific cause of the increased tolerance to alcohol that is found in alcoholics, the findings pertaining to the rigidity of the cell membranes suggest some novel approaches to treating alcoholism. Because certain foods affect the density of the neuronal cell membranes, it is possible that changes in diet might help people become less susceptible to alcoholism in the same way that dietary changes are recommended to help prevent heart disease. Even more interesting is the possibility of a "sober" pill, which would prevent alcohol from affecting the cell membranes and thereby prevent the behavioral effects of alcohol from occurring.

There is even the chance that in the distant future there will be a substance that will mimic the good effects of alcohol—no drug is better able to produce decreases in anxiety—while avoiding the bad. Someday, then, people may be able to take a drink and not worry about the very real negative consequences that such an act implies today.

Nonalcoholics
Normal cell
Walls of neuron cells are believed to consist of protein icebergs afloat in seas of fat. Messages controlling emotions and behavior move through channels between these icebergs.

Alcohol-affected
When alcohol is added, the normal fluidity between the icebergs increases. They become disoriented; the channels get disrupted and messages are garbled.

Alcoholics

Alcohol-dependent
After frequent, long-term exposure to alcohol, the walls become more rigid than normal. The brain becomes less sensitive to alcohol.

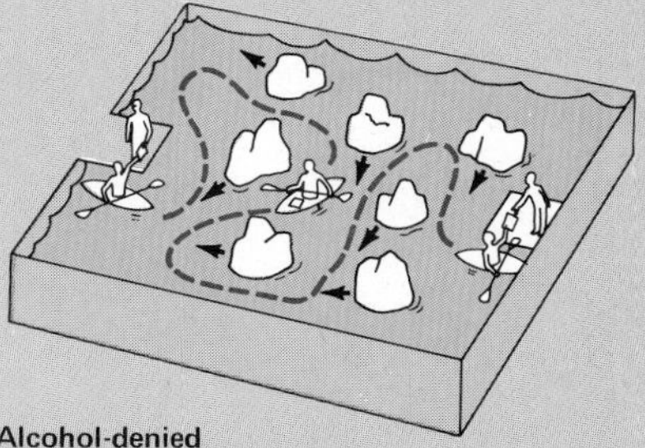

Alcohol-denied
When alcohol is removed, withdrawal symptoms occur. The channels are unable to recover normal fluidity, causing overactivity in the central nervous system.

Figure 9-8
Finding the key to alcoholism. (*Source: Adapted from Blakeslee, 1984.*)

One of the most commonly used drugs is marijuana. Although illegal, it is apt to be used by around 15 percent of the population over the age of 15 in any given week. (*Louis Fernandez/Black Star*)

cinogen, a drug that is capable of producing hallucinations, or changes in the perceptual process.

Marijuana (mare uh WAN uh): *A common hallucinogen, usually smoked*

The most common hallucinogen in widespread use today is **marijuana**, whose active ingredient—tetrahydrocannabinol (THC)—is found in a common weed, cannabis. Marijuana is typically smoked in cigarettes, although it can be cooked and eaten. At least one-third of all Americans over the age of 12 have tried it at least once, and among those people in the 18- to 25-year-old range, the figure is twice as high (National Institute of Drug Abuse, 1983). Despite its illegality, marijuana use is so prevalent that about 15 percent of the population over 15 years old are likely to use it in a given week.

The effects of marijuana vary from person to person, but they typically consist of feelings of euphoria and general well-being. Sensory experiences seem more vivid and intense, and a person's sense of self-importance seems to grow. Memory may be impaired, causing the user to feel pleasantly "spaced out." On the other hand, the effects are not universally positive: Individuals who take marijuana when feeling depressed can end up even more depressed, since the drug tends to magnify both good and bad feelings.

Marijuana has the reputation for being a "safe" drug when used in moderation, and there seems to be no scientific evidence that its use is addictive or that users "graduate" to more dangerous drugs. However, the long-term effects of marijuana use are not entirely clear. There is some evidence that heavy use decreases the production of the male sex hormone, testosterone, although not so much that it affects sexual activity (Miller, 1975). Similarly, heavy use affects the reactions of the body's immune system to germs, but once again it is unclear that the effect is great enough to cause physiological difficulties. One negative effect of smoking large quantities of marijuana is clear, though: The smoke damages the lungs much in the way cigarette smoke does, producing an increased likelihood of developing cancer and other lung diseases (Institute of Medicine, 1982).

In sum, the *short-term* effects of marijuana use appear to be relatively minor—

as long as users follow obvious cautions, such as avoiding driving or using machinery. However, it is less clear whether the long-term consequences are harmful. The case regarding the use of marijuana is far from closed, and more research is necessary before the question of its safety can be settled.

The Acid Test: LSD and PCP Two of the strongest hallucinogens are **lysergic acid diethylamide** or **LSD** (known commonly as ''acid''), and **phencyclidine**, or **PCP** (often referred to as ''angel dust''). Both of these drugs seem to affect the operation of neurotransmitters in the brain, causing an alteration in brain-cell activity and perception.

Lysergic (ly sur jik) **acid diethylamide** (dy ETH ul ah mide) **(LSD)**: *One of the most powerful hallucinogens, affecting the operation of neurotransmitters in the brain, causing brain-cell activity to be altered*

Phencyclidine (fen SY kluh dine) **(PCP)**: *A powerful hallucinogen that alters brain-cell activity*

LSD produces vivid hallucinations. Perception is altered so much that even the most mundane experience—such as looking at the knots in a wooden table—can seem exciting and moving. Objects and people may be viewed in a new way: Some users say LSD increases their understanding of the world. For others, however, the experience brought on by LSD can be terrifying, particularly if users have had emotional difficulties in the past.

One of the most recent additions to the drug scene, PCP, or ''angel dust,'' also causes strong hallucinations. However, the potential side effects associated with its use make the drug even more dangerous than LSD. Large doses may cause paranoid and destructive behavior, and in some cases users become violent toward themselves and others.

The Informed Consumer of Psychology: Dealing with Drug and Alcohol Problems

In a society that is bombarded with commercials for drugs guaranteed to do everything from curing the common cold to giving new life to tired blood, it is no wonder that drug-related problems present a major social issue. Yet, many people with drug and alcohol problems deny that they have them, and even close friends and family members may fail to realize when occasional social use of drugs or alcohol has turned into abuse.

There are certain signs, however, that indicate when use becomes abuse (Brody, 1982). Among them are the following:

- Being high more often than not
- Getting high to get oneself going
- Going to work or class while high
- Driving a car while high
- Coming in conflict with the law because of drugs
- Doing something uncharacteristic while high
- Being high in nonsocial, solitary situations
- Being unable to stop getting high
- Feeling a need for a drink or a drug to get through the day
- Becoming physically unhealthy
- Failing at school or on the job
- Thinking about liquor or drugs all the time

Any combination of these symptoms is sufficient to alert a person that he or she has a serious problem. Because drug and alcohol dependence are almost impossible to cure on one's own, people who suspect that they have a problem should get immediate attention from a psychologist, physician, or counselor.

RECAP AND REVIEW III

Recap

- Psychoactive drugs affect a person's emotions, perceptions, and behavior. The most dangerous drugs are those that are addictive—they produce a biological or psychological dependence.
- Stimulants produce an increase in the arousal of the central nervous system.
- Depressants decrease arousal in the central nervous system; they can produce intoxication.
- Hallucinogens produce hallucinations and other modifications of perception.

Review

1. Cocaine should not be considered an addictive drug because it does not seem to produce a biological dependence. True or false?

2. The drugs Benzedrine and Dexedrine are types of

a. barbiturates **b.** amphetamines **c.** depressants **d.** hallucinogens

3. The class of depressant drugs known as ____________________ can be deadly if combined with alcohol.

4. What is the major drawback of using methadone as a treatment for heroin addiction?

5. The concern over dangerous long-term effects resulting from marijuana use can be put to rest; marijuana can be considered safe. True or false?

6. Alex is somewhat concerned about his drinking. He has always drunk at parties to remove his inhibitions. He now drinks beer while studying alone and often fails to complete his work as a result. Moreover, he has begun to make a habit of having a drink in the early afternoon before his toughest class. Has Alex's alcohol use become abuse?

7. Match each substance with its description:

a. ____ Marijuana	1.	An addictive stimulant, inhaled for an immediate high
b. ____ Cocaine	2.	Present in many food and drink products
c. ____ Alcohol	3.	The most commonly used hallucinogen
d. ____ LSD	4.	Causes an addiction that is treatable by methadone
e. ____ Heroin	5.	Alters brain-cell activity, creating vivid hallucinations
f. ____ Caffeine	6.	A depressant that at first gives a feeling of well-being

(Answers to review questions are at the bottom of page 309.)

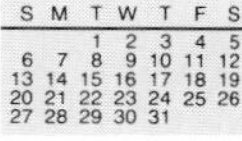

Psychology Looks Toward the 1990s
Looking for a "Sober" Pill

It has been a rowdy party, and large quantities of liquor have been consumed. As the party draws to a close, however, each of the participants is handed a small pill to swallow by the host. In a few minutes, all signs of raucous behavior have disappeared, and the party-goers appear altogether sober.

Such a curious scenario might someday become a reality if scientists are successful in perfecting a recently discovered experimental drug that makes drunk animals appear to be sober. Tentatively called Ro15-4513, the drug not only seems to reverse the effects of alcohol, but it may help to reveal the biochemical basis for alcohol's actions and holds the future promise of helping alcoholics to overcome their problems.

The effects of Ro15-4513 on experimental animals is dramatic (Paul, 1986). In one experiment, rats were given so much alcohol that they became heavily sedated; if they were put on their backs, they did not roll over, and their arms and legs flopped away from their bodies when they lay on their stomachs. But two minutes after an injection of Ro15-4513, the animals would get up and walk around, appearing completely sober. Moreover, if the rats received a dose of the drug before they were given alcohol, they never acted intoxicated in the first place.

Some scientists suggest that Ro15-4513 will aid in understanding how alcohol affects behavior—something that is not now well understood. Moreover, it may prove to be helpful in the treatment of alcoholism, allowing alcoholics to learn to live without alcohol. For example, recovering alcoholics might take the pill daily in order to prevent intoxication, even if they found themselves in situations in which they felt compelled to take a drink (Kolata, 1986).

The drug holds particular promise because of its apparent lack of side effects. Although other drugs have been found to reverse alcohol's effects, they have always proven dangerous, producing convulsions and sometimes even death in experimental animals. In contrast, Ro15-4513 is a fairly close relation of such relatively safe drugs as Valium and Librium.

On the other hand, there are important ethical issues that may preclude the widespread use of Ro15-4513 among the general population. For example, although the drug impedes the behavioral effects of alcohol, the amount of alcohol and its metabolism within the body are not affected by Ro15-4513. The harmful side effects of long-term alcohol use, then, such as the possibility of irreversible damage to the liver, would not be remedied from use of the drug.

It thus remains to be seen whether Ro15-4513 will eventually serve as the ultimate nightcap at parties, used by people to become sober when it is time to drive home after an evening of revelry. Whether or not this use of the drug would represent social progress, of course, is an open question.

LOOKING BACK

1. In this chapter, we have discussed states of consciousness. Consciousness refers to a person's awareness of the sensations, thoughts, and feeling being experienced at a given moment. It is the subjective understanding that we have regarding both the environment around us and our internal world. Although initially some psychologists felt that it was impossible to study such phenomena scientifically, today most feel that consciousness can be examined using scientific methods. These methods include the study of brain waves and functioning, controlled experiments using drugs and alcohol, and techniques for studying altered states of consciousness.

2. One state of consciousness with which we all have experience is sleep. Using the electroencephalogram, or EEG, scientists have found that the brain is active throughout the night. In fact, sleep proceeds through a series of stages, identified by unique patterns of brain waves. Stage 1 is characterized by relatively rapid, low-voltage waves, while stage 2 shows more regular, spindle patterns. In stage 3, the brain waves become slower, with higher peaks and lower valleys apparent. Finally, stage 4 sleep includes waves that are even slower and more regular.

3. There is a qualitatively different stage that sleepers enter several times each night as they return to stage 1 sleep. Called REM, or rapid eye movement sleep, it is characterized by increase in the heart rate, blood pressure, and rate of breathing and by erections in males. Most striking is the rapid movement of the eyes, which dart back and forth under closed eyelids. Because dreams occur during this stage, the hypothesis that the eyes are following the dream's action is a reasonable one. REM sleep seems to be critical to human functioning.

4. According to Freud, dreams have both a manifest content, their apparent story line, and a latent content, their true meaning. He suggested that the latent content provides a guide to a dreamer's unconscious, showing unfulfilled wishes or desires. Many psychologists disagree with this view; they suggest that the manifest content relates to the actual import of the dream. Other theorists suggest that dreaming is a result of an attempt to work out waking concerns or of random electrical activity in the brain.

5. Daydreaming is a common occurrence, although there are wide individual differences in the amount of time devoted to it. While some evidence suggests that daydreaming is related to a lack of stimulation in childhood, many people who daydream had rich environments as children.

6. Insomnia is a disorder in which a person has difficulty sleeping. In narcolepsy, an individual has an uncontrollable urge to sleep, while sleep apnea is reflected in difficulties in sleeping and breathing at the same time.

7. Psychologists and sleep researchers have devised a number of measures that help overcome insomnia, including increasing exercise during the day, avoiding caffeine and sleeping pills, drinking a glass of warm milk before bedtime, and avoiding *trying* to go to sleep.

8. In hypnosis, a person is in a state of heightened susceptibility to the suggestions of the hypnotist. Although there are no physiological indicators that distinguish hypnosis from normal waking consciousness, there are significant behavioral characteristics. These include increased concentration and suggestibility, heightened ability to recall and construct images, a lack of initiative, and the acceptance of suggestions that clearly contradict reality.

9. Meditation is a learned technique for refocusing attention that brings about an altered state of consciousness. In transcendental meditation, the most popular form practiced in the United States, a person repeats a mantra (a sound, word, or syllable) over and over, concentrating until he or she becomes unaware of any outside stimulation and reaches a different state of consciousness. The goal is to feel thoroughly relaxed and to gain new insights into oneself and the world.

10. Drugs can produce an altered state of consciousness. However, they vary in how dangerous they are and in whether or not they are addictive, producing a physical or psychological dependence.

11. Stimulants cause arousal in the central nervous system. Among common stimulants are caffeine (found in coffee, tea, and soft drinks) and nicotine (found in cigarettes). More dangerous are amphetamines, or "speed," and cocaine. Although in small quantities they bring about increased confidence, a sense of energy and alertness, and a "high," in larger quantities they may overload the central nervous system, leading to convulsions and death.

12. Depressants decrease arousal in the central nervous system, causing the neurons to fire more slowly. They may cause intoxication along with feelings of euphoria. The most common depressant is alcohol, which initially relieves tension. Other depressants, which include barbiturates, morphine, and heroin, are particularly dangerous.

13. Hallucinogens are drugs that produce hallucinations and other changes in perception. The most frequently used hallucinogen is marijuana; its use is common throughout the United States. Although occasional, short-term use of marijuana seems to be of little danger, long-term effects are less clear. The lungs may be damaged; there is the possibility that testosterone levels are lowered in males; and the immune system may be affected. Two other hallucinogens are LSD and PCP. Each of these affects the operation of neurotransmitters in the brain, causing an alteration in brain-cell activity and perception.

14. There are a number of signals that indicate when use of drugs becomes abuse. Some of these are frequent usage, getting high in order to get to class or work, driving while high, developing legal problems, and being high alone. A person who suspects that he or she has a drug problem should get professional help; people are almost never capable of solving drug problems on their own.

KEY TERMS AND CONCEPTS

consciousness (282)
altered state of consciousness (283)
electroencephalogram (EEG) (284)
stage 1 sleep (286)
stage 2 sleep (286)
sleep spindles (286)
stage 3 sleep (286)
stage 4 sleep (286)
rapid eye movement (REM) sleep (286)
rebound effect (287)
latent content of dreams (288)
manifest content of dreams (288)
daydreams (290)
insomnia (290)
narcolepsy (291)
sleep apnea (291)
sudden infant death syndrome (291)
hypnosis (293)
meditation (295)
transcendental meditation (TM) (295)
mantra (295)
psychoactive drugs (297)
addictive drugs (297)
caffeine (298)
stimulants (298)
nicotine (298)
amphetamines (299)
cocaine (299)
depressants (301)
intoxication (301)
barbiturates (302)
morphine (302)
heroin (302)
methadone (302)
hallucinogen (302)
marijuana (304)
lysergic acid diethylamide (LSD) (305)
phencyclidine (PCP) (305)

FOR FURTHER STUDY AND APPLICATION

Ornstein, R. E. (1977). *The psychology of consciousness* (2nd ed.). New York: Harcourt Brace Jovanovich.

A well-written, fascinating account of a broad range of topics associated with consciousness, this text is authored by an acknowledged expert in the field.

Hales, D. (1981). *The complete book of sleep.* Reading, MA: Addison-Wesley.

This volume provides a sound, useful guide to those interest in learning more about sleep—or getting a better night's rest each evening.

Dement, W. C. (1974). *Some must watch while some must sleep.* San Francisco: Freeman.

Written by the foremost researcher in sleep and dreams, this book gives a readable account of how research on sleep is carried out and what is known about sleep and dreams.

Udolf, R. (1981). *Handbook of hypnosis for professionals.* New York: Van Nostrand.

Although the title suggests this book is just for professionals, it provides a clear overview of hypnosis, is readable by the layperson, and provides a good foundation for the understanding of hypnosis.

Ray, O. (1983). *Drugs, society, and human behavior* (3rd ed.). St. Louis: Mosby.

This book gives a levelheaded, comprehensive view of the range of consciousness-changing drugs, including their effects on the body's sensation and functioning.

Mothner, I., & Weitz, A. (1984). *How to get off drugs.* New York: Rolling Stone Press.

This book provides sound, workable advice on how to lick a drug problem. The volume offers specific recommendations for dependence problems involving a variety of substances, including alcohol, marijuana, and cocaine.

ANSWERS TO REVIEW QUESTIONS

Review III: **1.** False, it may produce psychological dependence **2.** b **3.** Barbiturates **4.** Addiction to methadone is substituted **5.** False **6.** Certain warning signs suggest that his problem has turned to alcohol abuse. **7.** a.3; b.1; c.6; d.5; e.4; f.2

PART FIVE

THE PERSON DEVELOPS AND DIFFERENTIATES

We come now to the world of the newborn, who begins as a speck of humanity and gradually moves through the years into old age. We see the rites of passage of an adolescent, who must endure repeated beatings, multilations, and psychological indignities as he enters adulthood. And we meet an elderly person, as she contemplates the end of her own life.

In this part of the book, we consider what psychologists have discovered about the universal patterns of growth and change occurring throughout life. We will learn what has been discovered about the interaction of biologically determined patterns of behavior and the ever-changing environment. We will see the regularities in growth that occur throughout people's lifetimes. Moreover, we will consider the factors that differentiate one person from another and the consistencies in behavior that people display throughout their own lives.

In Chapter 10, the focus is on development, starting at the moment of conception and continuing through old age and death.

In Chapter 11, we turn to a consideration of personality, both in terms of the characteristics that differentiate one person from another, and in the degree of uniformity people show in their behavior as they move from one situation to another.

CHAPTER 10

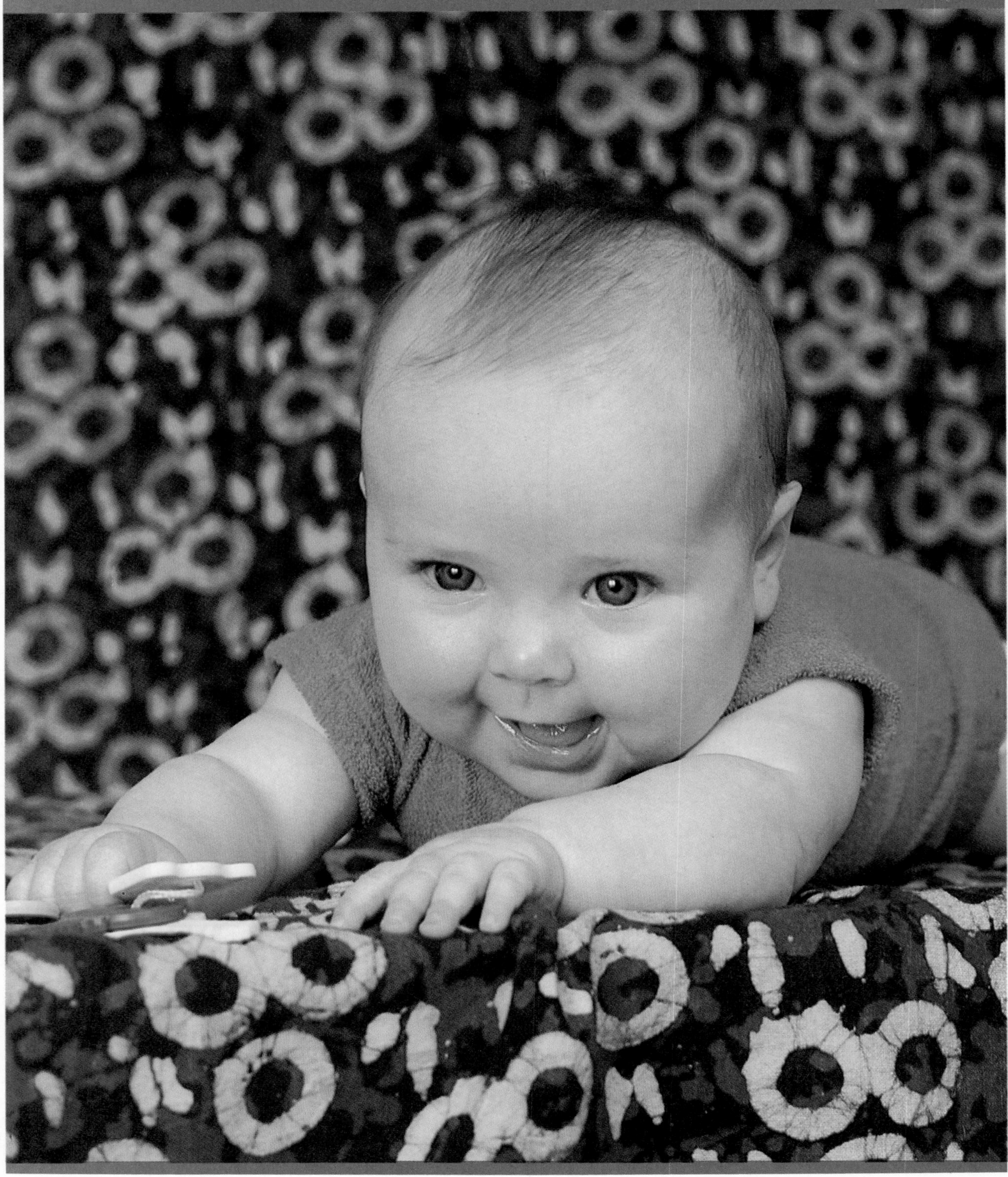

DEVELOPMENT

PROLOGUE

LOOKING AHEAD

NATURE VERSUS NURTURE: A FUNDAMENTAL DEVELOPMENTAL QUESTION
TRY IT! Nature or Nurture—That's the Question
Addressing the nature-nurture question
The start of life: Conception and beyond
Recap and review I

HOW WE DEVELOP PHYSICALLY AND SOCIALLY
Growth after birth
Taking in the world: Development of perception
Forming relationships: Social development
PSYCHOLOGY AT WORK. Who Is Taking Care of the Children?: Determining the Effects of Day-Care
Recap and review II

OUR MINDS: HOW WE DEVELOP COGNITIVELY
Stages of understanding: Piaget's theory of cognitive development
The informed consumer of psychology: Maximizing cognitive development
THE CUTTING EDGE. Raising a Superstar Child: How Is Talent Nurtured?
Recap and review III

BECOMING AN ADULT: ADOLESCENCE
The changing adolescent: Physical development
Distinguishing right from wrong: Moral and cognitive development
Searching for identity: Psychosocial development

THE MIDDLE YEARS OF LIFE: EARLY AND MIDDLE ADULTHOOD
The peak of health: Physical development
Working at life: Social development

THE LATER YEARS OF LIFE: GROWING OLD
Physical aging: Physical changes during old age
Thinking about—and during—old age: Cognitive changes in the elderly
Facing death
Recap and review IV
PSYCHOLOGY LOOKS TOWARD THE 1990s. Keeping Smart: Avoiding Intellectual Declines in Old Age

LOOKING BACK

KEY TERMS AND CONCEPTS

FOR FURTHER STUDY AND APPLICATION

PROLOGUE

There is a zest and vitality in human infancy that shows itself at every turn. Infants look with absorption, drink in their environment well before they "know how" to do anything about taking hold of it. They scout their world for every sign of what is novel and monitor not only what goes on right before them but what is happening at the edges of their world. At the start, in the opening weeks of life, babies are either alert, "turned on" and in a mood to explore, or they are "turned off" in the total way that young infants have of turning off. Gradually, alertness spreads over longer periods and infants begin on new tasks—social life, manipulation of things, and the gradual lacing together of the world of the eyes with the world of the hands. A career of self-projected travel begins early—perhaps when babies can turn from their back to their tummy—and the realm over which control extends expands as no empire ever has.

There are memorable landmarks. There is the first time children sustain their look into their mothers' eyes and begin on a career of social exchange of such complexity that no grammar has yet been devised to explicate it. There is the first smile, earlier than the books say, and a genuine expression of pleasure, in spite of early detractors who suspected gas pains. There is the first time that infants are able to go on looking at the world around them while still feeding at breast or bottle—probably the opening achievement of the art of doing two things at once, which will burgeon later on. There is the first visually guided reach for an object, hand widespread, attention long sustained, and a final capture with object delivered for inspection to the mouth—the mouth, that lighthouse in the midline, the all-purpose sense organ. And it goes on. (Bruner, 1969, pp. xiii–xiv.)

LOOKING AHEAD

. . . and on, and on. The drama and scope of the changes that occur during infancy do not stop during that period, but continue throughout each person's lifetime. And they are a source of wonder not only to proud parents, but to professionals who study how the environment and the natural endowment with which the human being is born interact to produce a unique individual.

Developmental psychology: *The branch of psychology that studies people's growth and change over the life span*

Developmental psychology is the branch of psychology that studies the patterns of growth and change occurring throughout life. In large part, developmental psychologists are concerned with the interaction between the unfolding of biologically predetermined patterns of behavior and a constantly changing, dynamic environment. They ask how our genetic background affects our behavior throughout our lives, whether our potential is limited by heredity, and how our built-in biological preprogramming affects our day-to-day development. Similarly, they are concerned with how the environment works with—or against—our genetic capabilities, how the world we live in affects our development, and how we can be encouraged to develop our full potential.

More so than other psychologists, developmental psychologists are concerned with day-to-day patterns and changes in behavior that occur across the lifespan. We thus move through the life cycle in this chapter, beginning with birth and infancy; moving through childhood, adolescence, and adulthood; and finally ending with old age and death.

We begin our discussion of development by examining the approaches that have been used to understand and delineate the factors directing a person's development—factors relating to environment and to a person's genetic endowment. Then we consider the very start of development, beginning with conception and the nine months of life prior to birth. We discuss both genetic and environmental influences on the unborn individual, and how these can affect behavior throughout the remainder of the life cycle.

Next, we examine physical development after birth, witnessing the enormous and rapid physical growth that occurs during the early stages of life, and considering how the infant develops perceptual capabilities. We also focus on the developing child's social world, indicating what draws the child into relationships with others and membership in society.

We then consider cognitive growth during infancy and childhood, tracing changes in the way children think about the world. We discuss several methods that parents can use to foster children's cognitive development and special talents.

Next, we focus on some of the major physical, emotional, and cognitive changes that occur during a person's adolescence, adulthood, and old age. We discuss the developmental changes that people undergo during these periods and their relationship to their work, families, and living patterns. Finally, in our discussion of old age, we examine the kinds of physical, intellectual, and social changes that occur as a consequence of the aging process, and we see that aging may bring about both decline and improvement in various kinds of functioning.

After reading and studying this chapter, then, you will be able to:

- Describe how and why development is a joint function of genetic and environmental factors
- Identify the periods of growth prior to birth and discuss the primary influences on development during that stage
- Outline how physical, perceptual, and social growth proceeds after birth
- Explain the principal approaches to cognitive development
- Identify the major kinds and causes of physical, social, and intellectual changes that occur in adolescence, adulthood, and old age
- Define and apply the key terms and concepts listed at the end of the chapter

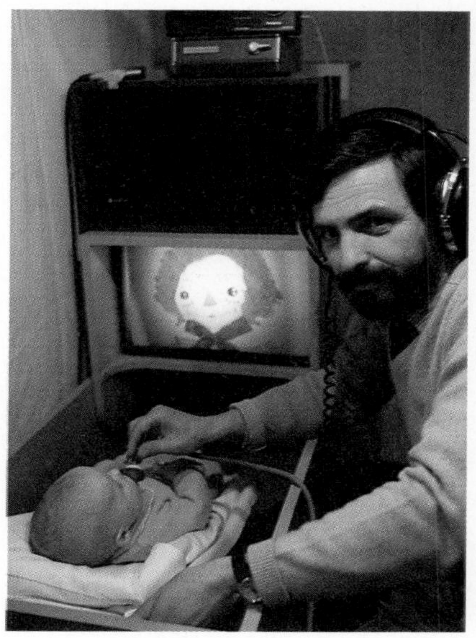

By measuring the vigor with which this baby sucks on a nipple, this developmental psychologist is able to determine the baby's interest in the picture being projected on the screen. (*Enrico Ferorelli/DOT*)

NATURE VERSUS NURTURE: A FUNDAMENTAL DEVELOPMENTAL QUESTION

They were raised in the same home, lived in the same neighborhood, had the same parents. Yet two brothers could hardly be more different: Emmanuel Torres stood accused of attempting to rape and then stabbing to death a drama student on a New York City apartment roof, while his brother, Alfredo Torres, was a well-respected, third-year resident in internal medicine. The differences between the two brothers were apparent from childhood; Emmanuel continually misbehaved and later had difficulty holding a job, whereas Alfredo showed a fierce ambition from an early age to become a physician (*New York Times,* December 9, 1984).

To the developmental psychologist, one of the central challenges to understanding human development is illustrated by the family described above: How can we identify the factors that explain why people raised in similar environments develop in such different ways?

Stated in another way, the question becomes even more basic: How can we differentiate between behavior that can be attributed to the **environment**—the influence of parents, siblings, family, friends, schooling, nutrition, and all the

Environment: *Influences on behavior that occur in the world around us, including family, friends, school, nutrition, and many other factors*

Heredity: *Influences on behavior that are transmitted biologically from parents to a child*

Nature-nurture question: *The issue of the degree to which environment and heredity influence behavior*

Genetic (jeh NEH tik): *Pertaining to the biological factors that transmit heredity information*

Maturation: *The unfolding of biologically predetermined behavior patterns*

other experiences to which a child is exposed—and behavior that can be attributed to **heredity**—the influences on behavior that are transmitted biologically from parents to children and which affect growth throughout one's life? A fundamental issue, then, is one we first discussed when we considered the determinants of intelligence in Chapter 7: the **nature-nurture question**, where nature refers to hereditary influences and nurture to environmental influences.

Although the question was first posed as the "nature *versus* nurture" question, today developmental psychologists agree that *both* nature and nurture interact to produce specific developmental patterns. No one grows up without being influenced by the environment, nor does anyone develop without being affected by his or her inherited, or **genetic**, makeup. However, the debate over the relative influence of the two factors remains an ongoing one, with different approaches and theories of development emphasizing the environment or heredity to a greater or lesser degree.

For example, some developmental theories stress the role of learning in producing changes in behavior in the developing child, relying on the basic principles of learning we discussed in Chapter 4; such theories emphasize the role of environment in accounting for development. In contrast, other approaches, grounded more closely in the biological aspects of the human being we first encountered in Chapter 2, emphasize the physiological makeup and functioning of the individual. Such theories stress the role of heredity and **maturation**—the unfolding of biologically predetermined patterns of behavior—in producing developmental change. Maturation can be seen, for instance, in the development of sex characteristics (such as breast development or growth of body hair) that occur at the start of adolescence.

On some points, however, there is good agreement among developmental psychologists of different theoretical persuasions. For example, it seems clear that inherited factors provide the potential for particular behaviors or traits to emerge by predisposing a particular level of performance and by placing limitations on such behavior or traits. For instance, heredity defines a person's general level of intelligence, setting an upper limit which—regardless of the nature of the environment—the person cannot exceed. It also provides limits on physical abilities; humans simply cannot run at a speed of 60 miles an hour, nor are they going to grow as tall as 10 feet, no matter what the nature of their

TRY IT!

NATURE OR NURTURE—THAT'S THE QUESTION

The range of behaviors that have strong genetic components is wide. You are probably familiar with some of them—tall children tend to have tall parents, and intelligence, as we discussed in Chapter 7, is linked to heredity. But consider the list below. Which of the items do you think has been shown to be strongly influenced by heredity?

1. Tone of voice ___
2. Blood pressure ___
3. Age of language acquisition ___
4. Tooth decay ___
5. Shyness ___
6. Emotionality ___
7. Neuroticism ___
8. Athletic ability ___
9. Firmness of handshake ___
10. Age of death

The answer: all of them. Each item on this list has been demonstrated to have a strong genetic component. Of course, it is crucial to keep in mind that this does not mean that they are *entirely* determined by heredity—merely that the best knowledge researchers have amassed suggests that variations in these factors are due in part to the genetic makeup of an individual (Papalia & Olds, 1986).

These twins, reunited after being separated at birth, are providing critical information regarding the relative influence of environment and heredity on development. (*Joe McNally/Wheeler Pictures*)

environment. (For a glimpse of which behaviors are most affected by heredity, see the Try It! box.)

On the other hand, environmental factors are critical in allowing people to reach the potential capabilities provided by heredity (Case, 1985). Had Albert Einstein received no intellectual stimulation as a child and not been sent to school, it is unlikely that he would have been able to reach his genetic potential. Similarly, a great athlete like baseball star Pete Rose would have been unlikely to display much physical skill had he not been raised in an environment that nurtured his native talent and allowed him the opportunity to train and perfect his natural skills.

Developmental psychologists, then, take an **interactionist** position on the nature-nurture issue, suggesting that a combination of genetic predisposition and environmental influences produce development. The challenge facing them is to identify the specific nature and relative strength of each of these influences on the individual.

Interactionist: *One who believes that a combination of genetic predisposition and environmental influences determine the course of development*

Addressing the Nature-Nurture Question

Developmental psychologists have confronted the question of determining the relative influence of genetic and environmental factors on behavior in several different ways, although no technique is foolproof. We can, for example, experimentally control the genetic makeup of laboratory animals, carefully breeding them for specific traits. Just as the people who distribute Butterball turkeys have learned to produce a breed of turkeys that grow particularly quickly (so they can be brought to the marketplace less expensively), psychologists are able to breed strains of laboratory animals who share a similar genetic makeup. By observing animals with a similar genetic background in varied environments, the effects of particular kinds of environmental stimulation can then be ascertained. (Of course, we do have the problem of generalizing the findings of research with animals to a human population.)

Human twins provide us with an important source of information about the relative effects of genetic and environmental factors. If **identical twins** (those who are genetically identical) display different patterns of development, we have

Identical twins: *Twins with identical genetic makeup*

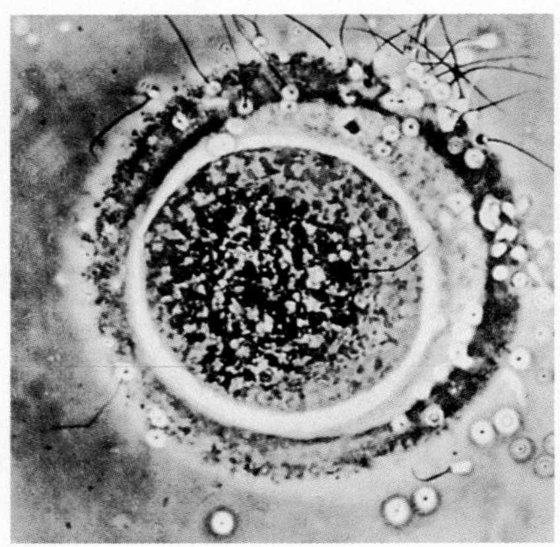

The moment—and miracle—of conception, when a male's sperm cell meets a female's egg cell. (*Dr. Landrum B. Shettles*)

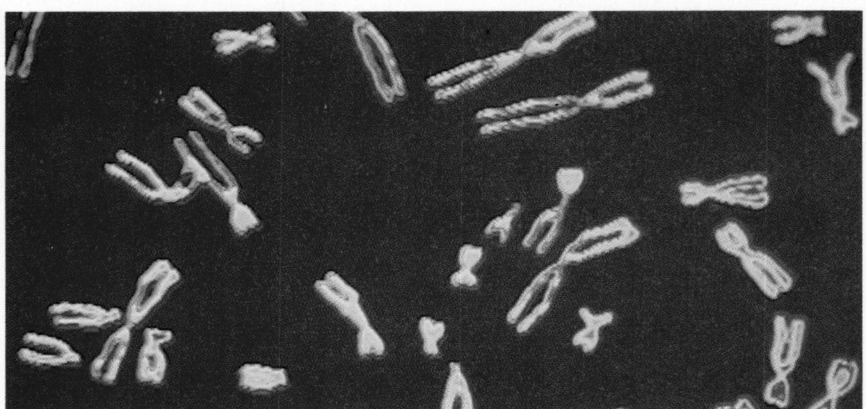

Rod-shaped chromosomes carry the basic information of heredity. Each chromosome contains thousands of genes. (*Howard Sochurek/Woodfin Camp & Assoc.*)

to attribute such differences to variations in the environment in which they were raised. The most useful data come from identical twins who are adopted at birth by different sets of foster parents and raised apart from each other in different environments. Studies of nontwin siblings who are raised in different environments also shed some light on the issue. Because they share relatively similar genetic backgrounds, siblings who show similarities as adults provide strong evidence for the importance of heredity.

It is also possible to take the opposite tack. Instead of concentrating on people with similar genetic backgrounds who are raised in different environments, we may consider people raised in similar environments who have totally dissimilar genetic backgrounds. If we find, for example, that two adopted children—who have dissimilar genetic backgrounds—raised in the same family develop similarly, we have evidence for the importance of environmental influences on development. Moreover, it is possible to carry out research with animals with dissimilar genetic backgrounds; by experimentally varying the environment in which they are raised, it is possible to determine the influence of environmental factors, independent of heredity, on development.

The Start of Life: Conception and Beyond

Conception: *The process by which an egg cell is fertilized by a sperm cell*

Zygote (ZY gote): *The one-celled product of fertilization*

Chromosomes (KROME uh soamz): *Rod-shaped structures that contain basic hereditary information*

Genes (jeenz): *The parts of a chromosome through which genetic information is transmitted*

Our understanding of the biology of the start of life—when a male's sperm cell meets a female's egg cell at the moment of **conception**—makes it no less of a miracle. At that single moment, an individual's genetic endowment is established for the rest of his or her life.

When the egg becomes fertilized by the sperm, the result is a one-celled **zygote** that immediately begins to develop. The zygote contains twenty-three pairs of **chromosomes**, rod-shaped structures that contain the basic hereditary information. One member of each pair is from the mother and the other is from the father. Each chromosome contains thousands of **genes**—smaller units through which genetic information is transmitted—that, either individually or in combination, produce particular characteristics of the individual.

While some genes are responsible for the development of systems common to all members of the human species—the heart, circulatory system, brain,

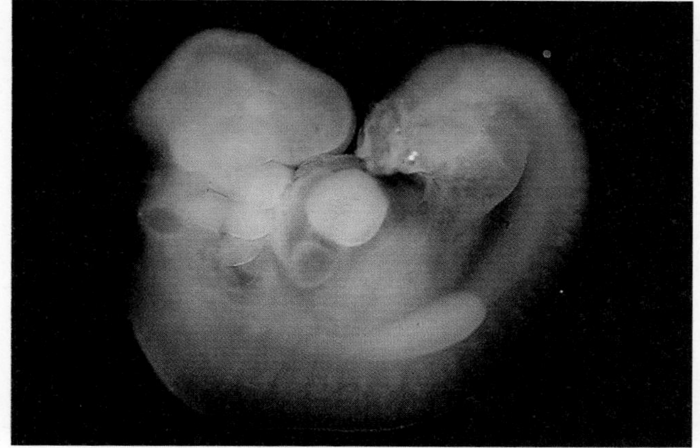

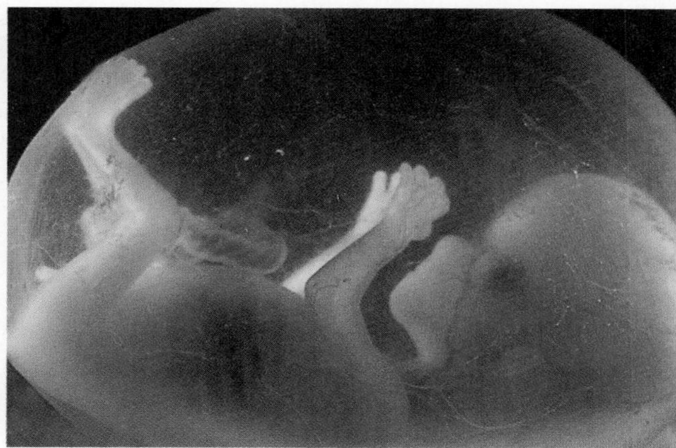

Figure 10-1
These remarkable photos of live fetuses display the degree of physical development at 4 and 15 weeks. (Left) © Lennart Nilsson: *A Child is Born*. English translation © 1966, 1977 by Dell Publishing Co., Inc. (Right) Guigoz/Petit Format/Photo Researchers, Inc.

lungs, and so forth—others control the characteristics that make each human unique—facial configuration, height, eye color, and the like. The zygote starts out as a microscopic speck, but as it divides, it grows 10,000 times larger in just four weeks, to about $\frac{1}{5}$ of an inch long. At that point it is called an **embryo** and has developed a rudimentary heart (that beats), a brain, an intestinal tract, and a number of other organs. Although all these parts are at a primitive stage of development, they are clearly recognizable. Moreover, by the eighth week, the embryo is about 1 inch long, and arms, legs, and face can be distinguished. (See Figure 10-1.)

Embryo (EM bree o): *A developed zygote that has a heart, a brain, and other organs*

Beginning in the ninth week and continuing until birth, the developing individual is called a **fetus**. At the start of this period, it begins to be responsive to touch; it bends its fingers when touched on the hand. At 16 to 18 weeks, its movements become strong enough for the mother to sense the baby. At the same time, hair may begin to grow on the baby's head, and the facial features are similar to those the child will display at birth. The major organs begin to function, although the fetus could not be kept alive outside the mother. In addition, a lifetime's worth of brain neurons are in place—although it is unclear whether the brain is capable of thinking in any real sense at this early stage.

Fetus (FEE tus): *A developing child, from nine weeks after conception until birth*

By the twenty-fourth week, a fetus has many of the characteristics it will display as a newborn. In fact, when an infant is born prematurely at this age, it can open and close its eyes; suck; cry; look up, down, and around; and even grasp things placed in its hands, although it is still unable to survive for long outside the mother.

The fetus continues to develop prior to birth. Fatty deposits appear under its skin and it gains weight. The fetus reaches the **age of viability**, the point at which it can survive if born prematurely, at about 28 weeks—a figure which, through advances in medical technology, is becoming lower. (In fact, about 50 percent of infants born between 26 and 28 weeks survive.)

Age of viability (vy uh BILL ih tee): *The point at which a fetus can survive if born prematurely*

At about 28 weeks, the fetus weighs about 3 pounds and is about 16 inches long. In the final weeks of pregnancy the fetus continues to put on weight and grow, becoming increasingly fit. At the end of the normal thirty-eight weeks of pregnancy, the fetus typically weighs around $7\frac{1}{2}$ pounds and is about 20 inches in length.

Genetic Influences on the Fetus The process of fetal growth that we have been discussing reflects normal development—something that happens in 95 to 98 percent of all pregnancies. Yet in some cases the process goes awry, for in the remaining 2 to 5 percent of the cases, children are delivered with major birth defects. One prime cause of such defects is genetic: The information in the chromosomes inherited from one or both of the parents causes a problem. Among the most common genetic disorders are the following:

Sickle-cell anemia: *A disease of the blood that affects about 10 percent of America's black population*

- *Sickle-cell anemia*. About 10 percent of the American black population have the possibility of passing on **sickle-cell anemia**, a disease that gets its name from the abnormal shape of the red blood cells. It can occur when a sufferer has an infection or is under stress. Children with the disease may have poor appetites, swollen stomachs, and yellowish eyes; they rarely live beyond childhood.

Phenylketonuria (FEEN ul kee toe NYUR ee uh) **(PKU)**: *The inability to produce an enzyme that resists certain poisons, causing profound mental retardation*

- *Phenylketonuria (PKU)*. A child born with the inherited disease **phenylketonuria** (PKU) cannot produce an enzyme that is required for normal development. This results in accumulation of poisons that eventually cause profound mental retardation. The disease is treatable, however; if it is caught early enough—and most infants today are routinely tested for PKU—children can be placed on a special diet which allows them to develop normally.

Tay-Sachs (TAY SAKS) **disease**: *A genetic defect preventing the body from breaking down fat and typically causing death by the age of 3 or 4*

Down's syndrome: *A disorder caused by the presence of an extra chromosome, resulting in mental retardation*

- *Tay-Sachs disease*. Children born with **Tay-Sachs disease**, a genetic defect found most often in Jews of eastern European ancestry, usually die by the age of 3 or 4 because of the body's inability to break down fat. If both parents carry the trait, their child has a one-in-four chance of being born with the disease.
- *Down's syndrome*. In Chapter 7, we discussed **Down's syndrome** as a cause of mental retardation. Down's syndrome is brought about not by an inherited trait passed on by the parents, but by a malfunction whereby the zygote receives an extra chromosome at the moment of conception, causing retardation and an unusual physical appearance (which led to an earlier label for the disease: mongolism). Down's syndrome is related to the mother's and father's age; mothers over 35, in particular, stand a higher risk of having a child with the problem.

Prenatal Environmental Influences Genetic factors are *not* the only causes of difficulties in fetal development; a number of environmental factors also have an important effect on the course of development. The major prenatal environmental influences include:

- The mother's nutrition and state of mind. What and how well a mother eats during her pregnancy can have important implications for the health of her baby. Mothers who are seriously undernourished cannot provide adequate nutrition to the growing baby, and they are likely to give birth to underweight babies or babies that are more susceptible to disease (Wyden, 1971). Moreover, there is some evidence that the mother's emotional state affects the baby. Mothers who are anxious and tense during the end of their pregnancies are more apt to have infants who are irritable and who sleep and eat poorly (Kagan, Kearsley, & Zelazo, 1978). The reason? One hypothesis is that the autonomic nervous system of the fetus becomes especially sensitive to the chemical changes produced by the mother's emotional state.

Rubella (roo BELL uh): *German measles that, when contracted by pregnant women, can cause severe birth defects*

- The mother's health. During 1964 and 1965 there was an epidemic of **rubella**, or German measles, in the United States. Although the disease has rel-

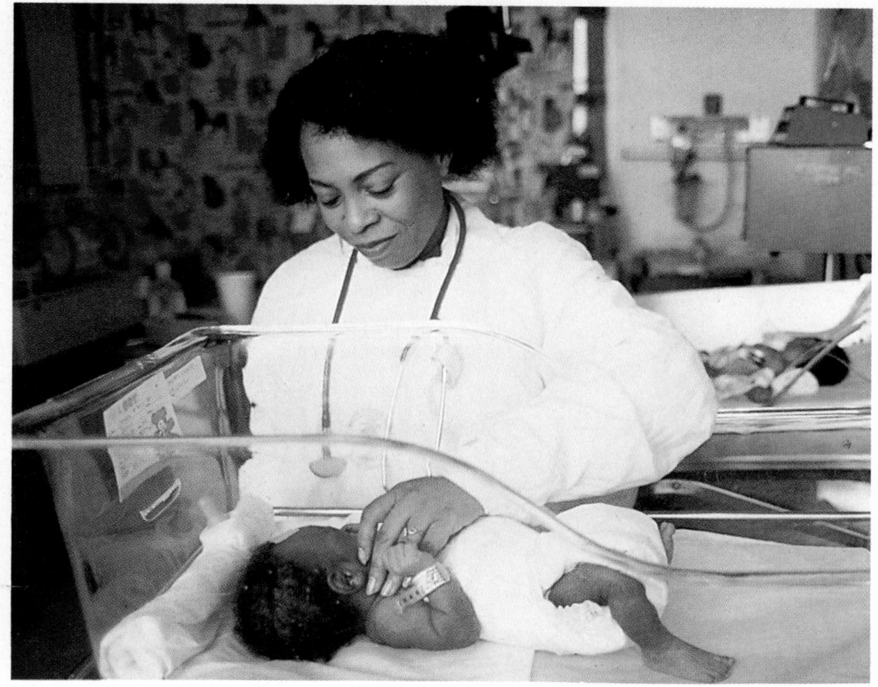

This infant, the child of a cocaine addict, was born addicted itself and is being treated for the painful symptoms of withdrawal from the drug. (*John Livzey/ Time Magazine*)

atively minor effects on pregnant women who contract it during the early part of pregnancy, this outbreak resulted in the prenatal death or malformation of close to 50,000 children born during those years. Rubella is but one of a number of diseases that can have devastating results on the prenatal child if contracted during specific parts of a pregnancy; other such illnesses include AIDS, syphilis, diabetes, and high blood pressure.

■ The mother's drug intake. Drugs taken by a pregnant woman can have a deadly effect on the unborn child. Probably the most dramatic example was the use of **thalidomide**, a tranquilizer that was prescribed during the 1960s—until it was discovered that it caused severe birth defects such as the absence of arms and legs. Alcohol and nicotine are also dangerous to fetal development. For example, **fetal alcohol syndrome**, an ailment resulting in mental and physical retardation, has been found in the children of some alcoholic mothers. Moreover, mothers who take physically addictive drugs run the risk of passing on their addiction to their newborns, who suffer painful withdrawal symptoms after they are born (Chavez, Ostren, Stryker, & Smialek, 1979).

Thalidomide (thuh LID o mide): *A tranquilizer that, when taken by pregnant women, can cause severe birth defects*

Fetal alcohol syndrome: *An ailment resulting in a baby's mental and physical retardation as a result of the mother's high alcohol intake while pregnant*

■ Birth complications. Although most births occur without complication, the process sometimes goes awry, resulting in injury to the infant. For example, the umbilical cord connecting the baby to the mother may become compressed, withholding oxygen from the child. If this occurs for too long, the child may suffer permanent brain damage.

A number of other environmental factors have an impact upon the child prior to and during birth (see Table 10-1). It is important to keep in mind, however, that the vast majority of births occur without difficulty, and development typically follows normal patterns—which we discuss next.

TABLE 10-1

Environmental factors affecting prenatal development and their possible effects

FACTOR	POSSIBLE EFFECT
Rubella (German measles)	Blindness, deafness, heart abnormalities, stillbirth
Syphilis	Mental retardation, physical deformities, miscarriage
Addictive drugs	Low birth weight, addiciton of infant to drug, with possible death after birth from withdrawal
Smoking	Premature birth, low birth weight and length
Alcohol	Mental retardation, smaller-than-average birth weight, small head, limb deformities
Radiation from x-rays	Physical deformities, mental retardation
Inadequate diet	Reduction in growth of brain, smaller-than-average weight and length at birth
Mother's age—less than age 18 at birth of child	Premature birth, increased incidence of Down's syndrome
Mother's age—older than 35 at birth of child	Increased incidence of Down's syndrome
DES (diethylstilbestrol)	Increased incidence of genital cancer in adolescents whose mothers were given DES during pregnancy to prevent miscarriage, impaired reproductive performance

Source: Adapted from Schikendanz, 1982, p. 95.

RECAP AND REVIEW I

Recap

- A fundamental issue of developmental psychology is the nature-nurture question, which seeks to determine the relative influence of environmental and genetic factors on development.
- During the course of prenatal development, the one-cell zygote evolves into an embryo and subsequently into a fetus. Birth typically occurs thirty-eight weeks after conception.
- The major difficulties caused by genetic factors are sickle-cell anemia, phenylketonuria (PKU), Tay-Sachs disease, and Down's syndrome. Among the primary environmental influences on prenatal development and newborn health are the mother's nutrition, state of health, and drug intake and the baby's delivery.

Review

1. Contemporary developmental psychologists adhere strongly to the "nature" side of the nature-nurture debate. True or false?
2. The age of viability is the stage at which
   a. A fetus can survive if born prematurely **b.** An embryo is most susceptible to developmental defects **c.** A newborn is first able to control its own movements **d.** The chromosomes of the parents first determine a baby's characteristics
3. Number the following stages of human development in the order in which they occur:
   ____ fetus ____ egg/sperm ____ embryo ____ zygote
4. Dr. Jackson described the birth of an infant who was born lacking the ability to produce an enzyme necessary for human development. Fortunately, early medical testing and intervention saved this infant from a life of profound mental retardation. The

genetic disease she described was

a. Down's syndrome **b.** Phenylketonuria (PKU) **c.** Tay-Sachs disease **d.** Sickle-cell anemia

5. Martha felt that as long as she stopped her alcohol and nicotine intake, and was careful to follow a healthy diet, she could continue to work at her high-stress job during pregnancy without creating a risk to the infant. Does evidence exist to contradict her presumption?

6. Factors such as birth complications, mother's health, mother's nutrition, and mother's state of mind are examples of

a. Prenatal genetic influences **b.** Prenatal environmental influences **c.** Factors that rarely influence development during pregnancy **d.** Factors that completely determine a child's subsequent intelligence

(Answers to review questions are at the bottom of page 324.)

HOW WE DEVELOP PHYSICALLY AND SOCIALLY

> His head was molded into a long melon shape and came to a point at the back . . . He was covered with a thick, greasy white material known as "vernix," which made him slippery to hold, and also allowed him to slip easily through the birth canal. In addition to a shock of black hair on his head, his body was covered with dark, fine hair known as "lanugo." His ears, his back, his shoulders, and even his cheeks were furry. . . . His skin was wrinkled and quite loose, ready to scale in creased places such as his feet and hands. The hair, matted with vernix, gave an odd, pasted appearance. . . . His ears were pressed to his head in unusual positions—one ear was matted firmly forward on his cheek. His nose was flattened and pushed to one side by the squeeze as he came through the pelvis (Brazelton, 1969, p. 3).

What kind of creature is this? Although the description hardly fits what we see when we look at a picture of the Gerber baby in commercials, we are in fact talking about a normal, completely developed child just after the moment of birth. Called a **neonate**, the newborn presents itself to the world in a form that hardly meets the typical standards of beauty against which we normally measure others. Yet, ask any parent: No sight is more beautiful or exciting than their first glimpse of their newborn.

Neonate (NEE o nate): *A newborn child*

The neonate's less-than-perfect appearance is brought about by a number of factors. Its travels through its mother's birth canal may have squeezed the incompletely formed bones of the skull together and squashed the nose into the head. It is covered with **vernix**, a white, greasy covering which is secreted to protect its skin prior to birth, and it may have **lanugo**, a soft fuzz, over its entire body. Its eyelids may be puffy with an accumulation of fluids because of its upside-down position during birth.

Vernix (VUR nix): *A white lubricant that covers a fetus, protecting it during birth*

Lanugo (lan OO go): *A soft fuzz covering the body of a newborn*

Reflexes: *Unlearned, involuntary responses to certain stimuli*

All this changes during the first two weeks of life, as the neonate takes on an appearance more like the one we see in commercials. Even more impressive are the capabilities that the neonate begins to display from the time it is born—capabilities that grow at an astounding rate over the ensuing months and years.

The neonate is born with a number of **reflexes**—unlearned, involuntary responses that occur automatically in the presence of certain stimuli. Many of these reflexes are critical for survival and unfold naturally as a part of an infant's ongoing maturation. The **rooting reflex**, for instance, causes neonates to turn their heads toward things that touch their cheeks—such as a nipple of a mother's breast or a bottle. Similarly, there is a **sucking reflex** which prompts the infant to suck at things that touch its lips. Among the other reflexes are a **gag reflex** (to clear its throat); the **Moro**, or **startle**, **reflex** (a series of movements in which

Rooting reflex: *A neonate's tendency to turn its head toward things that touch its cheek*

Sucking reflex: *A reflex that prompts an infant to suck at things that touch its lips*

Gag reflex: *An infant's reflex to clear its throat*

Moro (startle) reflex: *The reflex action in which an infant, in response to a sudden noise, flings its arms, arches its back, and spreads its fingers*

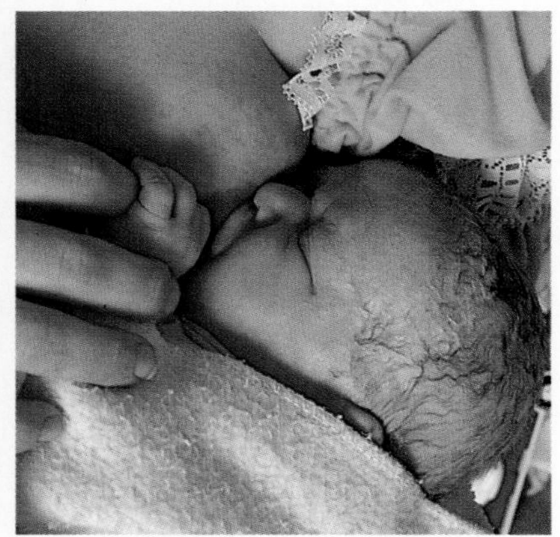

The rooting reflex causes newborns to turn their heads toward things that touch their cheeks—such as their mother's nipple. After they find the nipple, their sucking reflex makes it possible for them to obtain nourishment. (*Fred Ward/Black Star*)

Fine motor movements

25 to 50 percent complete the task

50 to 90 percent complete the task

Hands together

Reaches for object

Transfers cube from hand to hand

Bangs two cubes held in hands

Gross motor movements

Rolls over

Sits without support

Walks holding on furniture

Walks well alone

0 1 2 3 4 5 6 7 8 9 10 11 12 13 14 15

Age (months)

Figure 10-2
These landmarks of physical development illustrate the range of ages at which most infants learn various physical tasks. (*Source: Frankenburg & Dodds, 1967.*)

Babinski reflex: *The reflex action in which an infant fans out its toes in response to a stroke on the outside of its foot*

the infant flings out its arms, fans its fingers, and arches its back in response to a sudden noise); and the **Babinski reflex** (the baby's toes fan out when the outer edge of the sole of its foot is stroked).

As these primitive reflexes are lost after the first few months of life, they are replaced by more complex and organized behaviors. Although at birth the neonate is capable of only jerky, limited voluntary movement, during the first year of life the capability to move independently grows enormously. The typical baby is able to roll over by the age of 3 months; at 6 months it can sit without support; it stands alone at about $11\frac{1}{2}$ months; and by the time it is just over a year old, a baby has begun to walk. Not only does the ability to make large-scale movements improve during this time, but fine-muscle movements also become increasingly sophisticated (as illustrated in Figure 10-2).

Growth after Birth

Perhaps the most obvious sign of development is the physical growth of the child. During the first year of life, children typically triple their birth weight, and their height increases by about half. This rapid growth slows down as the

ANSWERS TO REVIEW QUESTIONS

Review I: **1.** False **2.** a **3.** 4, 1, 3, 2 **4.** b **5.** Yes; a mother's state of mind may adversely affect prenatal development. **6.** b child gets older—think how gigantic adults would be if that rate of growth were constant—and the average rate of growth from age 3 to the beginning of adolescence, around age 13, is a gain of about 5 pounds and 3 inches a year.

The physical changes that occur as children develop are not just a matter of increasing size; the proportion of the various body parts changes dramatically as children age. As you can see in Figure 10-3, the head of the fetus (and the newborn) is proportionally large. However, the head soon becomes more in proportion to the rest of the body as growth occurs mainly in the trunk and legs.

Taking in the World: Development of Perception

When proud parents pick up the neonate and peer into its eyes, is the child able to return their gaze? While it was thought for some time that newborns could see only a hazy blur, most current findings indicate that the capabilities of the neonate are much more impressive.

Although their eyes have limited capacity to modify the shape of the lens, making it difficult to focus on objects that are not within a 7- to 8-inch distance from the face, neonates are able to follow objects moving within their field of vision (Bornstein, 1984; Cohen, DeLoache, & Strauss, 1979). They also show the rudiments of depth perception, as they react by raising their hands when an object appears to be moving rapidly toward the face.

You might think that it would be hard to figure out just how well neonates are able to see, since their lack of language ability would clearly prevent them from saying what direction the E on a vision chart is facing—even if they were able to read. However, a number of ingenious methods, which rely on physiological responses and innate reflexes of the newborn, have been devised to test their perceptual skills (Hay, 1986).

One important technique relies on changes in an infant's heart rate, for heart rate is closely correlated with the baby's reaction to a stimulus that he or she is looking at—a phenomenon known as habituation. **Habituation** is a decrease in responding to repeated presentations of the same stimulus. Infants who are first shown a novel stimulus will pay close attention to it, and their heart rates will show a change in speed. But if the infant is repeatedly shown the same stimulus, his or her attention to it decreases, as indicated by the return to a normal heart rate—showing that habituation has occurred.

Habituation (ha BIH choo a shun): *A decrease in responding to repeated presentations of the same stimulus*

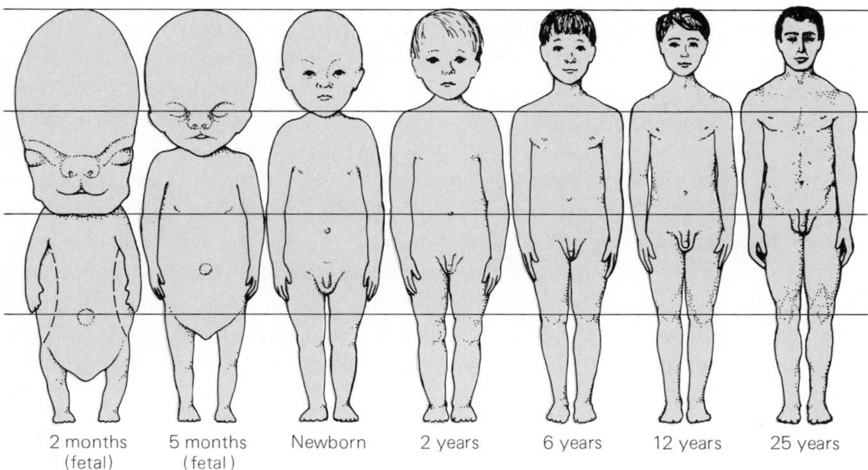

Figure 10-3
As a human develops, the relative size of the head—in relation to the rest of the body—decreases until adulthood is reached. (*Source: Adopted from Robbins*, 1929.)

However, when another new stimulus is presented, there is once again a discernible change in heart rate, although this change occurs only if the child is able to detect that the new stimulus is different from the old one. Using this technique, then, developmental psychologists can tell when a stimulus can be detected and discriminated by a child too young to speak (Bornstein, 1984).

A number of other methods of measuring neonate and infant perception have been developed. In one, for instance, a nipple is attached to a computer, and the rate and vigor with which a baby sucks are used to show that a change in a stimulus can be perceived (Milewski, 1976). In other studies, the baby's eye movements are examined (Hainline & Lemerise, 1982), while still others simply observe which way babies move their heads when presented with a visual stimulus.

Research using such techniques has shown that an infant's visual perception is remarkably sophisticated, even at birth, and that it develops rapidly during the first few months of life. At birth, babies show preferences for patterns with contours and edges, rather than for less distinct patterns. In fact, neonates have the skill to discriminate facial expressions—even to imitate them (Field, 1982). As can be seen in Figure 10-4, newborns exposed to an adult with a happy, sad, or surprised facial expression are able to produce a good imitation of the adult's expression. Even newborns, then, can be responsive to the moods that their caregivers' facial expressions reveal.

Other visual abilities grow rapidly after birth. By the end of their first month, babies can distinguish some colors from others, and after 3 months they can readily focus on near or far objects. By 4 or 5 months, they are able to recognize two- and three-dimensional objects, and they can make use of the gestalt patterns that we discussed in terms of adult perception in Chapter 3.

In addition to vision, a newborn's other sensory capabilities are quite impressive. A baby can distinguish different sounds to the point of being able to recognize its own mother's voice at an age of 3 days (DeCasper & Fifer, 1980). Moreover, babies are capable of discriminating different tastes and smells (Steiner, 1979). There even seems to be something of a built-in sweet tooth: Neonates drink larger amounts of liquids that have been sweetened with sugar than they do of unsweetened drinks.

Forming Relationships: Social Development

Attachment: *The positive emotional bond that develops between parents and their children*

As anyone who has seen an infant smiling at the sight of its mother can guess, while infants are developing physically and perceptually, they are also developing social relationships that will affect them for the rest of their lives. **Attachment**, the positive emotional bond that develops between parents and their children, is the most important form of social development that occurs during infancy.

One of the first investigators to demonstrate the importance and nature of attachment was psychologist Harry Harlow. Harlow found that infant monkeys who were given the choice of a wire "monkey" that provided food, or a soft, terry-cloth "monkey" that was warm but did not provide food clearly preferred the cloth one, although they made occasional forays to the wire monkey to nurse (Harlow & Zimmerman, 1959). (See Figure 10-5.) Clearly, the cloth monkey provided greater comfort to the infants; food alone was insufficient to foster attachment.

Building on this initial work, other researchers have suggested that attachment grows through the responsiveness of infants' caregivers to the signals the babies

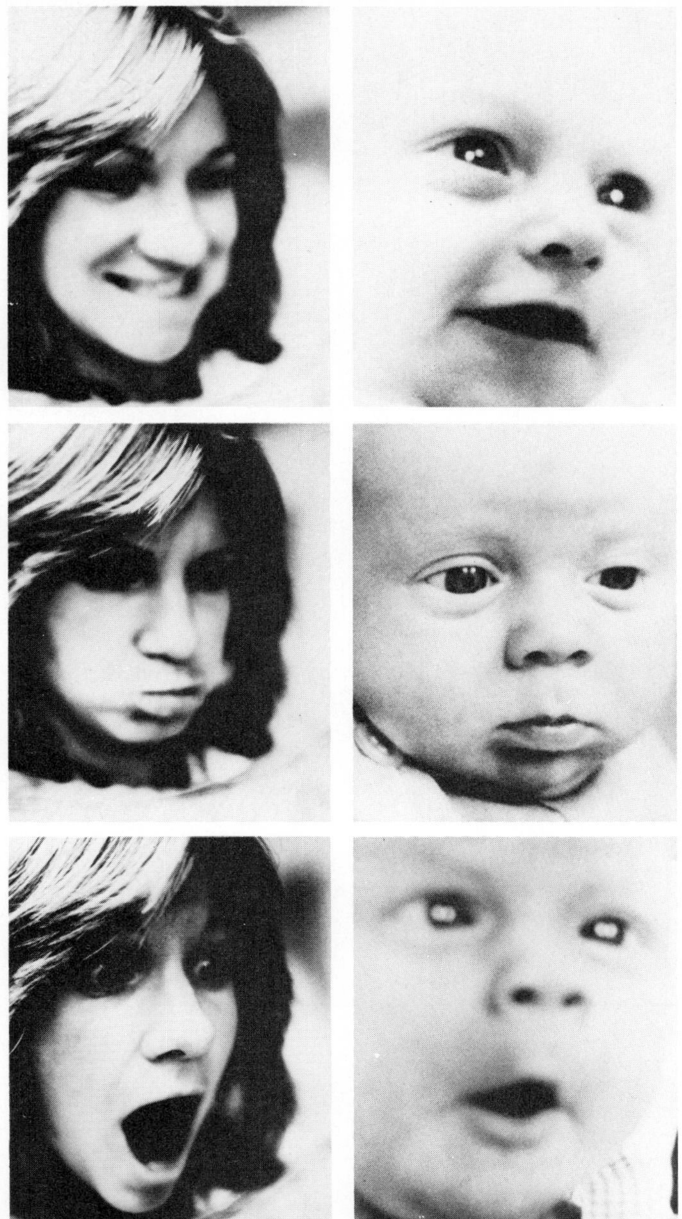

Figure 10-4
This newborn infant is clearly imitating the happy, sad, and surprised expressions of the adult model in these amazing photos. (*Source: Courtesy of Dr. Tiffany Field.*)

provide, such as cries, smiles, reaching, and clinging. The greater the responsiveness of the mother to the child's signals, the more likely it is that a secure bond will be formed. Full attachment eventually develops as a result of a complex series of interactions between caregiver and child known as the Attachment Behavioral System, illustrated in Figure 10-6 (Bell & Ainsworth, 1972; Tomlinson-Keasey, 1985). It is important to note that the infant plays as critical and active a role in the formation of an attachment bond as the caregiver.

Traditionally it was thought that the mother-infant bond was the most crucial in a child's life. However, most research today indicates that fathers and even full-time nonparental caregivers can produce bonding as strong as that between

Figure 10-5
Although the wire "monkey" dispensed milk to the hungry infant monkey, the soft, terry-cloth "monkey" was preferred. (*Source: Harry Harlow Primate Laboratory/ University of Wisconsin.*)

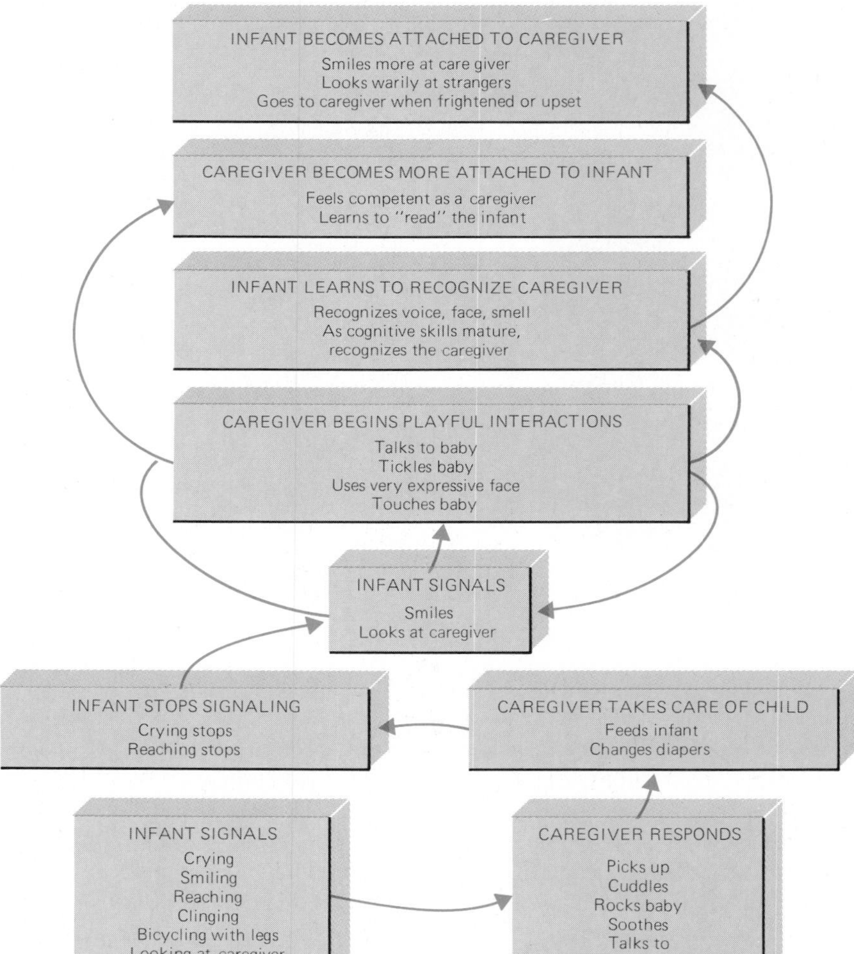

Figure 10-6
The Attachment Behavioral System shows the sequence of activities that infants employ to keep their primary caregivers physically close and to bring about attachment. Early in life, crying is the most effective behavior. Later, though, infants are able to keep the caregiver near through other, more socially appropriate behaviors such as smiling, looking, and reaching. After they are able to walk, children are able to play a more active role in staying close to the caregiver. At the same time, the caregiver's behavior interacts with the baby's activities to promote attachment. (*Source: Tomlinson-Keasey, 1985.*)

mothers and their children, and that children can be simultaneously attached to both their parents (Lamb, 1982). Such findings have important implications for the concern of parents over their use of day-care (see the Psychology at Work box).

PSYCHOLOGY AT WORK

WHO IS TAKING CARE OF THE CHILDREN?:

Determining the Effects of Day-Care

One of the biggest social changes to occur over the last decade is the upsurge in the number of day-care centers. Children as young as infants are looked after by paid child-care workers, generally outside of the home, from a couple of hours a day to all day long. To parents contemplating enrolling their children in such a center, certain questions are critical: What are the effects of day-care on children? How early can children start? What separates good day-care from bad? Because day-care is a necessity in many families with two working parents or in single-parent families, such questions take on particular urgency.

Fortunately, initial answers to these questions have begun to emerge as a result of research conducted during the last fifteen years (Bee, 1985; Vaughn & Waters, 1985). Although the research is based primarily on results derived from very good day-care centers, and therefore may not be entirely applicable to all centers, the findings are still enlightening. Among the best substantiated findings are the following:

■ Intellectual development. For children from poor or disadvantaged homes, day-care in specially enriched environments—those with many toys, books, a variety of children, and high-quality care providers—may prove to be more intellectually stimulating than the home environment. Such day-care can lead to increased intellectual achievement in terms of higher IQ scores and better language development. For instance, in one study (Ramey, 1981) children from poor families who attended a special day-care center from 2 months until 3 years of age showed higher IQ scores than those who were reared at home (see Figure 10-7). Other researchers have found similar results with children from impoverished backgrounds. The results are less positive with middle- and upper-class families; day-care does *not* seem to improve intellectual performance—nor does it hurt it. The conclusion: Children from middle- and upper-class families—who may already come from intellectually stimulating environments—will not suffer intellectually from day-care, and, because of the increased stimulation provided, children from disadvantaged homes can actually benefit intellectually from day-care.

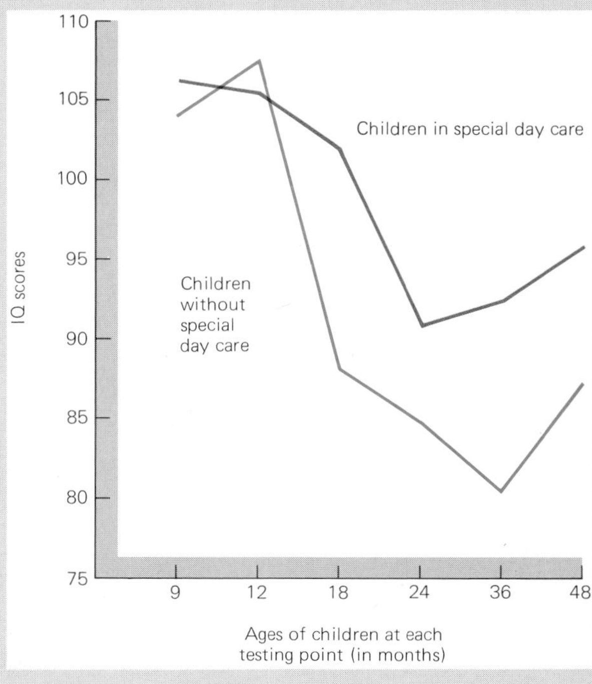

Figure 10-7
According to the results of one study, the IQ test scores of children from impoverished families in a day-care center, although they had started out at similar levels, ended up being higher than the scores of a comparison group of children raised at home during the day by their mothers. (*Source: Ramey, 1981.*)

■ Relationship with parents. Are children less attached to their mothers and fathers when they spend part of the day being cared for by others? This question—raised by many critics of day-care—is a difficult one to answer. However, most evidence suggests that there is no difference in the strength of the parental attachment bonds of infants and toddlers who have been in day-care (regardless of how long they have been there) and the bonds of those who have been raised solely by their parents. Moreover, there is no evidence that children in day-care centers are more attached to the day-care workers than to their parents; in fact, they almost always appear to be more attached to their parents (Ragozin, 1980; Rutter, 1982).

■ Peer relationships. A hint of difference between children in day-care and those who spend their days at home is revealed in the nature of their peer relationships: Although the data are inconsistent, some studies have found that day-care children are more aggressive and assertive than their peers (McKinney & Edgerton, 1983). Aside from this finding, however, no other differences in the quality of peer relationships have emerged from the research on day-care.

In sum, most research has found little evidence of negative outcomes for children who have been involved in day-care—and, in many cases, quite positive consequences emerge (Deutsch, 1985; Deutsch, Jordan, & Deutsch, 1985). Yet there are many unanswered questions: Is there an age before which day-care curriculum is used? What are the critical characteristics to consider when choosing a day-care center? These questions currently are being addressed by developmental psychologists in order to provide parents with clear guidance on the issues.

Erikson's Theory of Psychosocial Development According to Erik Erikson (1963), a psychologist who developed a comprehensive, life-span theory of social development, the developmental changes occurring throughout a person's life can be viewed as a series of eight stages of psychosocial development. **Psychosocial development** includes people's changing interactions and understanding of each other as well as their changing knowledge and understanding of themselves as members of society.

Psychosocial development: *Development of individuals' interactions and understanding of each other and of their knowledge and understanding of themselves as members of society*

Erikson suggests that passage through each of the stages necessitates resolution of a crisis or conflict. Accordingly, each of Erikson's eight stages is represented as a pairing of the most positive and most negative aspects of the crisis of the period. Although each crisis is never resolved entirely—life becomes increasingly complicated as a person grows older—it needs to be resolved enough so that a person is equipped to deal with demands that the next stage makes.

Trust-versus-mistrust stage: *According to Erikson, the first stage of psychosocial development, occurring from birth to 18 months of age, during which time infants develop feelings of trust or lack of trust*

In the first stage of psychosocial development, **trust versus mistrust** (birth to $1\frac{1}{2}$ years), infants develop feelings of trust if their physical requirements and psychological needs for attachment are consistently met and their interactions with the world are generally positive. On the other hand, inconsistent care and unpleasant interactions with others can lead to the development of mistrust, and leave the infant unable to meet the challenges required in the next stage.

Autonomy-versus-shame-and-doubt stage: *The period during which, according to Erikson, toddlers (ages 18 months to 3 years) develop independence and autonomy if exploration and freedom are encouraged, or shame and self-doubt if they are restricted and overprotected*

In the second stage, **autonomy versus shame and doubt** ($1\frac{1}{2}$ to 3 years), toddlers develop independence and autonomy if exploration and freedom are encouraged, or they experience shame, self-doubt, and unhappiness if they are overly restricted and protected. According to Erikson, the key to the development of autonomy, rather than of shame and doubt, during this period is for the child's caregivers to provide the appropriate amount of control. If parents provide too much control, children will be unable to assert themselves and develop their own sense of control over their environment; if parents provide too little control, children themselves become overly demanding and controlling.

Initiative-versus-guilt stage: *According to Erikson, the period during which children aged 3 to 6 years experience conflict between independence of actions and the sometimes negative results of that action*

The next crisis that children face concerns **initiative versus guilt** (ages 3 to 6). In this stage, the major conflict is between a child's desire to initiate activities independently and the guilt that comes from unwanted and unexpected conse-

Erik Erikson has developed a comprehensive stage theory to describe psychosocial development throughout the entire life span. (*UPI/Bettmann Newsphotos*)

Between the ages of 3 to 6, children enter the initiative versus guilt stage, according to Erikson. During this time they strive to initiate independent activities. (*Lionel Atwill/Peter Arnold, Inc.*)

quences of such activities. If parents react positively to the child's attempts at independence, they help resolve the initiative-versus-guilt crisis positively.

The last stage of childhood is **industry versus inferiority** (ages 6 to 12). During this period, successful psychosocial development is characterized by increasing adequacy in social interactions and in basic skills as well as by the development of a sense of oneself. In contrast, difficulties in this stage lead to feelings of failure and inadequacy.

Industry-versus-inferiority stage: *According to Erikson, the period during which children aged 6 to 12 years may develop positive social interactions with others or may feel inadequate and become less sociable*

Erikson's theory suggests that psychosocial development continues throughout life, and there are four more crises to face past childhood. We will discuss these later in the chapter, when we deal with adolescence through the end of life.

RECAP AND REVIEW II

Recap

- Among the major reflexes of the neonate are the rooting reflex; the sucking reflex; the Moro, or startle, reflex; and the Babinski reflex.
- Physical growth is rapid; during the first year, children typically triple their birth weight, and height increases by 50 percent. Rate of growth declines after age 3, averaging thereafter about 5 pounds and 3 inches a year until adolescence.
- Using ingenious methods such as analysis of habituation, heart rate, sucking, and eye movements, developmental psychologists have learned that visual and other sensory abilities improve rapidly after birth.
- The most critical part of social development in infancy is the development of attachment, the emotional bond that develops between parents and their children.

- Erikson's theory suggests that there are four stages of psychosocial development during childhood, with four others spanning the rest of life.

Review

1. The reflex that causes a baby to turn its head toward things that touch its cheeks is called the ______________ reflex.
2. Which of the following is true about a baby's first simple reflexes?
   a. They disappear within several hours of birth. **b.** They are replaced by more complex, voluntary movements. **c.** They evolve into complex reflexes. **d.** They continue throughout the life cycle.
3. A parent gently shakes a rattle in front of his neonatal infant's eyes. The baby's heart rate increases at first, but soon decreases to normal with repeated presentations, indicating that ______________ has occurred.
4. The method described above has been used to provide evidence that neonates have remarkably sophisticated visual perception. True or false?
5. Jerry and Christine have both been responsive to their infant's behavioral signals. As a result, they enjoy a positive emotional bond known as ______________.
6. Which of the following is *not* true about the effects of day-care centers?
   a. They weaken the attachment of a child to his or her parents. **b.** They can improve the intellectual development of lower-class children. **c.** Day-care children may be somewhat more aggressive. **d.** They do not hurt the intellectual abilities of upper- and middle-class children.

(Answers to review questions are at the bottom of page 334.)

OUR MINDS: HOW WE DEVELOP COGNITIVELY

Suppose you had two drinking glasses of different shapes—one short and broad and one tall and skinny. Now imagine that you filled the short, broad one with soda about half way and then poured the liquid from that glass into the tall one. The soda appears to fill about three-quarters of the second glass. If someone asked you whether there was more soda in the second glass than there had been in the first, what would you say?

You might think that such a simple question hardly deserves an answer; of course there is no difference in the amount of soda in the two glasses—the

It is clear to an adult that the amount of liquid being poured from one container to another remains constant, regardless of the shape of the container into which it is poured. Young children, however, have a different viewpoint: they feel certain that the amount of liquid varies depending on the shape of the container. (*Paul Fusco/Magnum*)

quantity remains the same, despite the difference in appearance when poured from one glass to the other. However, though this question may present no problem to you, most 4-year-olds would be likely to say that there is more soda in the second glass. In fact, if you then poured the soda back into the short glass, they would say there is now less soda than there was in the taller glass.

Why are young children confused by this problem? The reason is not readily apparent. Anyone who has observed preschoolers must be impressed at how far they have progressed from the early stages of development. They speak with ease, know the alphabet, count, play complex games, use a phonograph, tell stories, and communicate quite ably.

Yet, despite this outward sophistication, there are profound gaps in children's understanding of the world. Some theorists have suggested that children are incapable of understanding certain ideas about the world until they reach a particular stage of **cognitive development**—the process by which a child's understanding of the world changes as a function of age and experience.

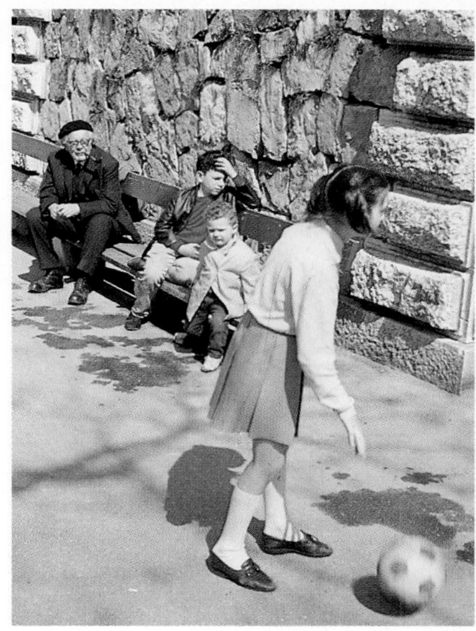

Jean Piaget, a towering figure in developmental psychology, studied children's cognitive development in part by observing them at play. (*Yves DeBraine/Black Star*)

Stages of Understanding: Piaget's Theory of Cognitive Development

No theory of cognitive development has had more impact than that of Swiss psychologist Jean Piaget. Piaget (1970) suggested that children proceed through a series of four separate stages in a fixed order that is universal across all children. He maintained that these stages differ not only in terms of the *quantity* of information acquired at each stage, but in the *quality* of knowledge and understanding as well. Taking an interactionist point of view, he suggested that movement from one stage to the next occurred when the child reached an appropriate level of maturation *and* was exposed to relevant types of experiences. Without such experiences, children were assumed to be incapable of reaching their highest level of cognitive growth.

Piaget's four stages are known as the sensorimotor, preoperational, concrete operational, and formal operational stages. (See Table 10-2.) Let's examine each of them.

Cognitive development: *The process by which a child's understanding of the world changes as a function of age and experience*

Sensorimotor (SEN sor ee MO tor) **stage**: *According to Piaget, the stage from birth to 2 years during which a child has little competence in representing the environment using images, language, or other symbols*

Sensorimotor Stage: Birth to 2 Years During the initial part of the **sensorimotor stage** the child has relatively little competence in representing the

TABLE 10-2

A summary of Piaget's stages

APPROXIMATE AGE RANGE	STAGE	MAJOR CHARACTERISTICS
Birth–2 years	Sensorimotor	Development of object performance, development of motor skills, little or no capacity for symbolic representation
2–7 years	Preoperational	Development of language and symbolic thinking, egocentric thinking
7–12 years	Concrete operational	Development of conservation, mastery of concept of reversibility
12–adulthood	Formal operational	Development of logical and abstract thinking

environment using images, language, or other kinds of symbols. Consequently, the infant has no awareness of objects or people who are not immediately present at a given moment, lacking what Piaget calls object permanence. **Object permanence** is the awareness that objects—and people—continue to exist even if they are out of sight.

Object permanence: *The awareness that objects do not cease to exist whan they are out of sight*

How can we know that children lack object permanence? Although we cannot ask infants, we can watch their reaction when a toy that they are playing with is hidden under a blanket. Until the age of about 9 months, children will make no attempt to locate the toy. However, soon after this age they will begin to actively search for the object when it is hidden, indicating that they have developed some sort of mental representation of the toy. Object permanence, then, is a critical development during the sensorimotor stage.

Preoperational Stage: 2 to 7 Years The most important development during the **preoperational stage** is the development of language, described in more detail in Chapter 6. Children develop internal representational systems of the world that allow them to describe people, events, and feelings. They even use symbols in play, pretending, for example, that a book pushed across the floor is a car.

Preoperational stage: *According to Piaget, the period from 2 to 7 years of age that is characterized by language development*

Although children's thinking is more advanced in this stage than in the earlier sensorimotor stage, it still is qualitatively inferior to that of adults. One example of this is seen in the preoperational child's **egocentric thought**, in which the world is viewed entirely from the child's own perspective. Preoperational children think that everyone shares their own perspective and knowledge. Thus, children's stories and explanations to adults can be maddeningly uninformative, as they are described without any context. For example, a preoperational child may start a story with "He wouldn't let me go," neglecting to mention who "he" is or where the storyteller wanted to go. Egocentric thinking is also seen when children at the preoperational stage play hiding games. For instance, 3-year-olds frequently hide with their faces against a wall, covering their eyes—although they are still in plain view. It seems to them that if *they* cannot see, no one else will be able to see them, since they assume that others share their view.

Egocentric (EE go SEN trik) **thought**: *Viewing the world entirely from one's own perspective*

Another deficit of the preoperational child is demonstrated by the **principle of conservation**, which is the knowledge that quantity is unrelated to the arrangement and physical appearance of objects. Children who have not mastered this principle do not know that the amount, volume, or length of an object does not change when its shape or configuration is changed. The question about the two glasses—one short and broad, the other tall and thin—with which we began our discussion of cognitive development illustrates this point quite clearly. Children who do not understand the principle of conservation invariably state that the amount of liquid changes as it is poured back and forth; they cannot comprehend that a transformation in appearance does not imply a transformation in amount. Instead, it seems just as reasonable to the child that there is a change in quantity as it does to the adult that there is no change.

Principle of conservation: *The knowledge that quantity is unrelated to the arrangement and physical appearance of objects*

There are a number of other ways in which the lack of an understanding of the principle of conservation affects children's responses, several of which are illustrated in Figure 10-8. Research on conservation illustrates that principles

ANSWERS TO REVIEW QUESTIONS

Review II: **1.** Rooting **2.** b **3.** Habituation **4.** True **5.** Attachment **6.** a

Type of conservation	Dimension	Change in physical appearance	Average age at which invariance is grasped
Number	Number of elements in a collection 	Rearranging or dislocating elements 	6–7
Substance (mass) (continuous quantity)	Amount of a malleable substance (e.g., clay or liquid) 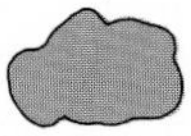	Altering shape 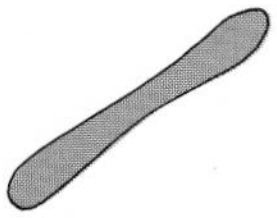	7–8
Length	Length of a line or object 	Altering shape or configuration 	7–8
Area	Amount of surface covered by a set of plane figures 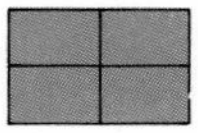	Rearranging the figures 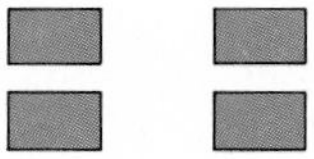	8–9
Weight	Weight of an object 	Altering its shape 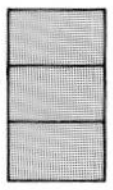	9–10
Volume	Volume of an object (in terms of water displacement) 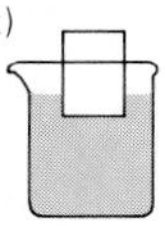	Altering its shape 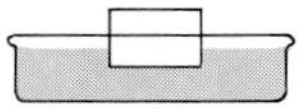	14–15

Figure 10-8
These tests are among those used most frequently to assess whether children are able to conserve across a variety of dimensions. (*Source: Schikendanz, Schikendanz, & Forsythe, 1982.*)

that are obvious and unquestioned by adults may be completely misunderstood by children during the preoperational period. However, by the end of the preoperational period, children gradually begin to learn the principle, and by the time they enter the third stage, their mastery becomes relatively complete. However, there are still aspects of conservation—such as conservation of weight and volume—that are not fully understood for a number of years.

Concrete Operational Stage: 7 to 12 Years During the **concrete operational stage**, children develop the ability to think in a more logical manner, and they begin to overcome some of the egocentrism that is characteristic of the preoperational period.

Concrete operational stage: *According to Piaget, the period from 7 to 12 years of age that is characterized by logical thought and a loss of egocentrism*

Reversibility: *The idea that some changes can be undone by reversing an earlier action*

One of the major principles that children learn during this stage is reversibility. **Reversibility** is the idea that some changes can be undone by reversing an earlier

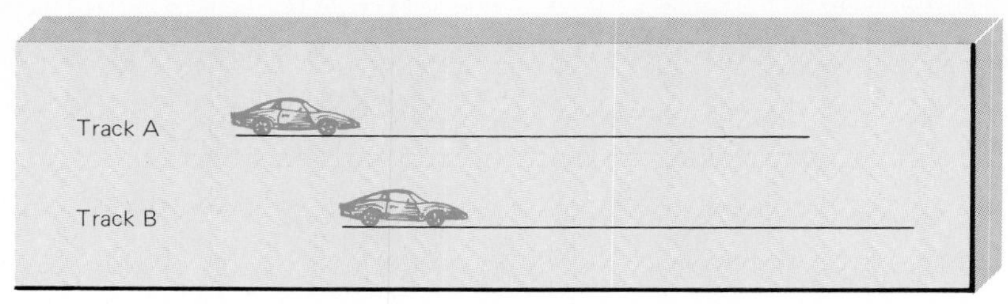

Figure 10-9
These two tracks, arranged in this way, are used to test children's understanding of space and time.

action. For example, children in the concrete operational stage can understand that when a ball of clay is rolled into a long sausage shape, it is possible to recreate the original ball by reversing the action. In fact, they can even conceptualize this principle in their heads, without having to see the action performed before them.

Another advance that occurs during the concrete operational stage is the development of a better understanding of time and space. Consider, for instance, the two tracks shown in Figure 10-9. Suppose you were told that the two cars start out at the same time and move along the tracks—which are exactly the same length—at the same speed. Would the cars take the same amount of time to reach the end of the track?

Naturally, you would say. But the answer would be different for children. To children just entering the concrete operational stage, the response would be that the car traveling along track A would stop first and take less time than the other. In fact, even after being told the contrary, children would claim that the second car started later than the first. The spatial arrangement, then, dominates their judgment.

A little later in the stage the answer might be different, though: Older children might assert that although the two cars start and stop simultaneously, the car moving along track A takes less time. It is not until the end of the concrete operational stage that children understand the problem; at that point their confusion over time and space has cleared up.

While there are important advances made in the logical capabilities of children during the concrete operational stage, there is still one major limitation to their thinking: They are largely bound to the concrete, physical reality of the world. For the most part, they have difficulty understanding questions of an abstract, hypothetical nature.

Formal operational stage: *According to Piaget, the period from age 12 to adulthood that is characterized by abstract thought*

Formal Operational Stage: 12 Years to Adulthood The **formal operational stage** produces a new kind of thinking—that which is abstract, formal, and logical. Thinking is no longer tied to events that are observed in the environment, but makes use of logical techniques to resolve problems.

The emergence of formal operational thinking is illustrated by the way in which the "pendulum problem," devised by Piaget, is attacked (Piaget & Inhelder, 1958). The problem solver is asked to figure out what determines how fast the pendulum swings. Is it the length of the string, or the weight of the pendulum, or the force with which the pendulum is pushed? (For the record, the answer is the length of the string.)

Children in the concrete operational stage approach the problem haphazardly, without a logical or rational plan of action. For example, they may simultaneously change the length of the string *and* the weight on the string *and* the force with which they push the pendulum. Naturally, since they are varying all factors at once, they are unable to tell which factor is the critical one. In contrast, people in the formal operational stage approach the problem systematically. Acting as if they were scientists conducting an experiment, they examine the effects of changes in just one variable at a time. This ability to rule out competing possibilities is characteristic of formal operational thought.

Although people begin using formal operational thought during the teenage years, this type of thinking is, in some cases, used only infrequently. Moreover, it appears that many individuals never reach this stage at all; most studies show that only between 40 and 60 percent of college students and adults fully reach this stage, with some estimates running as low as around 25 percent in the general population (Keating, 1980). In addition, in certain cultures—particularly those that are less technologically sophisticated than western society—almost no one reaches the formal operational stage (Chandler, 1976; Super, 1980).

Is Piaget Right? Stages versus Continuous Development While no other theorist has provided us with as comprehensive a theory of cognitive development as Piaget has, some contemporary theorists suggest that a better description of how children develop cognitively can be provided by approaches that do not employ a series of stages (Daehler & Bukato, 1985). Such theoreticians point to evidence of inconsistencies in the performance of various tasks, both across and within various stages (Tomlinson-Keasey, Eisert, Kahle, Hardy-Brown, & Kearsey, 1979). Moreover, some developmental psychologists suggest that cognitive development proceeds in a more continuous fashion than Piaget's stage theory would suggest, placing greater emphasis on quantitative, rather than qualitative, changes. They suggest that although there are differences in when, how, and to what extent a child is capable of using a given cognitive ability, the processes underlying the ability are assumed to be similar at different ages (Gelman & Baillargeon, 1983).

Most developmental psychologists do agree that, although the processes that underlie changes in cognitive abilities may not be those suggested by his theory, Piaget has provided us with an accurate account of age-related changes in cognitive development. Moreover, the influence of the theory has been enormous (Gholson & Rosenthal, 1984). For example, his suggestion that increases in cognitive performance cannot be attained unless there is both a cognitive readiness brought about by maturation *and* the appropriate environmental stimulation has been influential in determining the nature and structure of our educational curriculum and methods.

The Informed Consumer of Psychology: Maximizing Cognitive Development

Are there ways of maximizing a child's cognitive development? While some current work—discussed in the Cutting Edge box—is beginning to examine the backgrounds of a broad range of unusually talented people, most research to date has concentrated on identifying elements of child rearing that lead children to perform better in the specific domain of cognitive development. Such research has identified a number of general child-rearing practices that seem to be important (Bee, 1985; Gottfried, 1984). Among the most crucial of those are the following:

- Being emotionally responsive and involved with the child. Parents with high-achieving children are involved in their children's lives and encourage and reinforce their efforts. They are warm and supportive.

- Speaking to a child. Using language that is highly descriptive and accurate and avoiding "baby talk" is important.
- Providing *appropriate* play materials. The sheer quantity of toys and other play materials is less important than their appropriateness in terms of the child's age and developmental level.
- Giving children a chance to make mistakes. Parents of successful children tend to avoid harsh, arbitrary rules and highly restrictive control, and they do not use punishment frequently. Instead, while remaining firmly in control of their children's behavior and not being overly permissive, they are more likely to guide their children with a combination of firmness and warmth, providing children with a rationale for the rules they must follow.
- Holding high expectations. Parents communicate that they expect their children to do well, demonstrating to their children the importance of success and achievement.

While these guidelines do not guarantee that a child will be an intellectual genius, they will help to maximize the child's genetic potential.

THE CUTTING EDGE

RAISING A SUPERSTAR CHILD:

How Is Talent Nurtured?

How do you raise a superstar child?

Although most psychologists would be hesitant to answer a question couched in such exaggerated terms, despite the fact that there are literally hundreds of books and articles with such provocative titles, studies now under way are attempting to document child-rearing practices that are related to producing especially talented children.

Some of the clearest findings come from ongoing work by Benjamin Bloom (1985), who recently completed a five-year examination of some 120 especially talented men and women—concert pianists, Olympic swimmers, sculptors, mathematicians, and scientists. They were not necessarily geniuses in the usual sense, but rather people who had reached the top of their respective fields, most before the age of 35.

Such individuals, it turns out, are not just born winners—they have been brought up in a way that maximizes their talents. But there generally was no "master plan" for raising a superstar; instead, parents just did what seemed right at the time. Most of the parents were observant of any signs of talent in one direction or another, and nurtured that talent. If children showed talent at picking out tunes on the piano, they were given lessons; if they were interested in tennis, they were given a racket and the opportunity to play. Moreover, there was constant reinforcement for success, an emphasis on self-discipline, and enthusiasm for the philosophy that hard work brings success.

The successful children seemed to move through three basic stages. First, when learning the particular skill, they each fell in love with the pursuit. Next they viewed the skill as a technical challenge and attempted to master its intricacies, motivated by a sense of challenge and competence. Finally, they reached a stage in which they tried to develop their own personal styles.

At the same time, parents tried to match their support to the stage the child was in. At first they provided a warm, supportive teacher; then, during the second stage, they often shifted to a more demanding individual who could hone their child's skills; and finally, during the last stage, they provided a teacher who was outstanding in his or her own field and acknowledged as a teacher of extraordinary students.

Of course, as Bloom acknowledges, we cannot be sure that following these specific steps will produce successful people. As he says, "We wrote from hindsight. We picked people who were already successful. We therefore couldn't tell where things go wrong. We only looked at where things had already gone right. Much more study is needed" (Hechinger, 1985, p. C5).

RECAP AND REVIEW III

Recap

- The major theory of cognitive development—the way in which children's understanding of the world changes as a function of age and experience—is that of Piaget. He proposes four major stages: sensorimotor, preoperational, concrete operational, and formal operational.
- Among the hallmarks of cognitive development are the understanding of object permanence, a decline in egocentric thought, and an understanding of the principle of conservation.
- Although Piaget's description of what happens within the various stages of cognitive development has largely been upheld, some theorists argue that development is more continuous and due more to quantitative than to qualitative changes in cognition.

Review

1. The process by which our understanding of the world develops is called
a. Sensation **b.** Sensorimotor stage **c.** Developmental psychology **d.** Cognitive development

2. Match each developmental stage with the (hypothetical) example of behavior:

a. Sensorimotor stage	1. Sandy, who watched her parents unroll their new bathroom rug, returns later to roll it back up into its original form.
b. Preoperational stage	2. Jenny puts her hands up to her eyes and says to her friend, "You can't see me now."
c. Concrete operational stage	3. By systematically testing out his hypothesis, Randy is able to figure out the motion problem.
d. Formal operational stage	4. Jonathan does not go searching for his stuffed animal when his father slips it out of sight behind his back. Seemingly, to Jonathan, it no longer exists.

3. Now, using the same numbered examples in the right-hand column above, match them to the proper labels:
a. ____ egocentric thought
b. ____ object permanence
c. ____ logical thought
d. ____ reversibility

4. It has been suggested that cognitive development is more continuous and quantitative than Piaget proposed. True or false?

5. Which of the following child-rearing practices has *not* been identified as a means to enhance cognitive development?
a. Reinforce a child's efforts in a warm and supportive manner. **b.** Provide developmentally appropriate play materials.
c. Punish mildly a child's mistakes. **d.** Demonstrate the importance of success and achievement.

(Answers to review questions are at the bottom of page 340.)

BECOMING AN ADULT: ADOLESCENCE

> They are passionate, irascible, and apt to be carried away by their impulses. . . . Youth is the time when people are most devoted to their friends or relations or companions. . . . If the young commit a fault, it is always on the side of excess and exaggeration . . . for they carry everything too far, whether it be their love or hatred or anything else.

This view of adolescence might well sound familiar—for it has been around for more than 2000 years. Moreover, despite the exaggerated nature of these thoughts on adolescence made by the philosopher Aristotle, they do reflect the fact that for most people adolescence is a time of profound change and, sometimes, turmoil. Considerable biological changes mark the adolescent's attainment of sexual and physical maturity, and there are equally important social, emotional, and cognitive changes as adolescents strive for independence and move toward adulthood.

These punk rockers, faddishly dressed for the 1980s, bring to mind Aristotle's remark of two thousand years ago. "If the young commit a fault, it is always on the side of excess and exaggeration." (*Roger Sandler/Black Star*)

Adolescence (add o LESS ens): *The developmental stage between childhood and adulthood during which many physical, cognitive, and social changes take place*

Adolescence, which is generally thought of as a developmental stage between childhood and adulthood, represents a critical period in a person's development. Given the length of education that precedes starting work in our society, the stage is a fairly lengthy one, beginning just before the teenage years and ending just after them. No longer children, but considered by society to be not quite adults, adolescents face a period of rapid physical, cognitive, and social change that affects them for the rest of their lives.

The Changing Adolescent: Physical Development

If you think back to the start of your own adolescence, it is likely that the most dramatic changes you remember are of a physical nature. A spurt in height, growth of breasts in girls, deepening voices in boys, development of body hair, and intense sexual feelings are sources of curiosity, interest, and sometimes embarrassment for individuals entering adolescence.

Puberty (PEW bur tee): *The period during which maturation of the sexual organs occurs*

The physical changes that occur at the start of adolescence, which are largely a result of the secretion of various hormones (see Chapter 2), affect virtually every aspect of the adolescent's life; not since infancy has development been so dramatic. These changes mark the start of **puberty**, a period in which maturation of the sexual organs occurs, beginning at about age 11 or 12 for girls and 13 or 14 for boys. However, there are wide variations, and it is not too rare for a girl to begin to menstruate—the first sign of sexual maturity in females—as early as age 10 or as late as age 16. Moreover, the average age at which adolescents reach sexual maturity has been steadily decreasing over the last century, most likely due to better nutrition and medical care (Dreyer, 1982).

ANSWERS TO REVIEW QUESTIONS

Review III: **1.** d **2.** a. 4, b. 2, c. 1, d. 3 **3.** a. 2, b. 4, c. 3, d. 1 **4.** True **5.** c

Distinguishing Right from Wrong: Moral and Cognitive Development

> In Europe, a woman is near death from a special kind of cancer. There is one drug that the doctors think might save her. It is a form of radium that a druggist in the same town has recently discovered. The drug is expensive to make, and the druggist is charging ten times that cost. He paid $200 for the radium and is charging $2000 for a small dose of the drug. The sick woman's husband, Heinz, goes to everyone he knows to borrow the money, but he can get together only about $1000. He tells the druggist that his wife is dying and asks him to sell the drug more cheaply or to let him pay later. The druggist says, "No, I discovered the drug and I'm going to make money from it." Heinz is desperate and considers breaking into the man's store to steal the drug for his wife (Kohlberg, 1983).

What would you tell Heinz he should do?

According to psychologist Lawrence Kohlberg, your advice would reveal a great deal about your stage of moral development, as well as your more general level of cognitive development. Kohlberg suggests that people pass through a series of stages in the evolution of their sense of justice and in the kind of reasoning they use to make moral judgments (Kohlberg, 1984). Largely because of the kind of cognitive deficits that Piaget described, children tend to think either in terms of concrete, unvarying rules ("It is always wrong to steal" or "I'll be punished if I steal") or in terms of following the rules of society ("Good people don't steal" or "What if everyone stole?") prior to adolescence.

Adolescents, however, are capable of reasoning on a higher plane, typically having reached Piaget's formal operations stage of cognitive development. Because they are able to comprehend broad, moral principles, they can understand that morality is not always black and white and that there can be conflict between two sets of socially accepted standards. To them, then, the dilemma that Heinz faces is weighing the illegality of stealing against a human being's right to life.

Kohlberg (1984) suggests that the changes occurring in moral reasoning can be understood best by placing them in a three-level sequence, which, in turn, is divided into the six stages shown in Table 10-3. The system assumes that people move through the six stages in a fixed order, and that they are not capable of reaching the highest stage until about the age of 13—primarily because of deficits in cognitive development that are not overcome until that age. However, many people never reach the highest level of moral reasoning. In fact, Kohlberg suggests that only about 25 percent of all adults rise above stage 4 of his model.

Although Kohlberg's theory seems to be a generally accurate account of how moral *judgments* develop, such judgments are not always related to moral *behavior* (Malinowski & Smith, 1985; Snarey, 1985). Knowing right from wrong, then, does not mean that we will always act in accordance with our judgments.

Moreover, there is increasing evidence that males and females do not develop moral judgments in the same way. For instance, Carol Gilligan (1982) suggests that women may be more apt to understand morality in terms of their relationship with specific people involved in a situation and in terms of a willingness to sacrifice themselves to help a specific individual within that relationship, while men look at morality more in terms of broad, abstract principles—a fact that would account for the surprising finding that women typically score at a lower level than men on tests of moral judgments using Kohlberg's stage sequence.

TABLE 10-3

Kohlberg's sequence of moral reasoning

LEVEL	STAGE	SAMPLE MORAL REASONING: IN FAVOR OF STEALING	SAMPLE MORAL REASONING: AGAINST STEALING
Level 1 Preconventional morality: At this level, the concrete interests of the individual are considered in terms of rewards and punishments.	*Stage 1* Obedience and punishment orientation: At this stage, people stick to rules in order to avoid punishment, and there is obedience for its own sake.	If you let your wife die, you will get in trouble. You'll be blamed for not spending the money to save her and there'll be an investigation of you and the druggist for your wife's death.	You shouldn't steal the drug because you'll be caught and sent to jail if you do. If you do get away, your conscience will bother you thinking how the police will catch up with you at any minute.
	Stage 2 Reward orientation: At this stage, rules are followed only for one's own benefit. Obedience occurs because of rewards that are received.	If you do happen to get caught, you could give the drug back and you wouldn't get much of a sentence. It wouldn't bother you much to serve a little jail term, if you have your wife when you get out.	You may not get much of a jail term if you steal the drug, but your wife will probably die before you get out, so it won't do much good. If your wife dies, you shouldn't blame yourself; it wasn't your fault she has cancer.
Level 2 Conventional morality: At this level, moral problems are approached as a member of society. People are interested in pleasing others by acting as good members of society.	*Stage 3* "Good boy" morality: Individuals at this stage show an interest in maintaining the respect of others and doing what is expected of them.	No one will think you're bad if you steal the drug, but your family will think you're an inhuman husband if you don't. If you let your wife die, you'll never be able to look anybody in the face again.	It isn't just the druggist who will think you're a criminal; everyone else will too. After you steal it, you'll feel bad thinking how you've brought dishonor on your family and yourself; you won't be able to face anyone again.
	Stage 4 Authority and social-order-maintaining morality: People at this stage conform to society's rules and consider that "right" is what society defines as right.	If you have any sense of honor, you won't let your wife die just because you're afraid to do the only thing that will save her. You'll always feel guilty that you caused her death if you don't do your duty to her.	You're desperate and you may not know you're doing wrong when you steal the drug. But you'll know you did wrong after you're sent to jail. You'll always feel guilty for your dishonesty and lawbreaking.
Level 3 Postconventional morality: People at this level use moral principles which are seen as broader than any particular society.	*Stage 5* Morality of contract, individual rights, and democratically accepted law: People at this stage do what is right because of a sense of obligation to laws which are agreed upon within society. They perceive that laws can be modified as part of changes in an implicit social contract.	You'll lose other people's respect, not gain it, if you don't steal. If you let your wife die, it will be out of fear, not out of reasoning. So you'll just lose self-respect and probably the respect of others too.	You'll lose your standing and respect in the community and violate the law. You'll lose respect for yourself if you're carried away by emotion and forget the long-range point of view.
	Stage 6 Morality of individual principles and conscience: At this final stage, a person follows laws because they are based on universal ethical principles. Laws that violate the principles are disobeyed.	If you don't steal the drug, if you let your wife die, you'll always condemn yourself for it afterward. You won't be blamed and you'll have lived up to the outside rule of the law but you won't have lived up to your own standards of conscience.	If you steal the drug, you won't be blamed by other people but you'll condemn yourself because you won't have lived up to your own conscience and standards of honesty.

Source: Adapted from Kohlberg, 1969.

In Gilligan's view, then, women's morality is centered more on individual well-being than on moral abstractions, and the highest levels of morality are represented by compassionate concern for other's welfare.

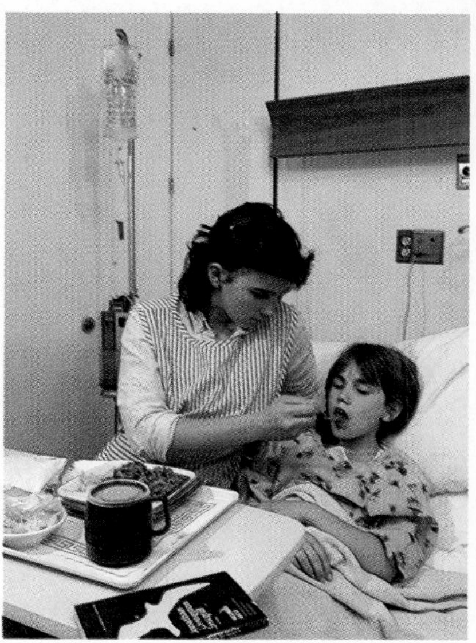

Developmental psychologists have investigated the causes of moral behavior. (*Billy E. Barnes/Stock Boston*)

Searching for Identity: Psychosocial Development

To most adolescents, answering the questions "Who am I?" and "How do I fit into the world?" is one of life's major challenges. Although these questions continue to be posed throughout a person's lifetime, they take on particular significance during the adolescent years.

Erikson's theory of psychosocial development, which we first discussed earlier in the chapter, places particular importance on this search for identity during the adolescent years. As we noted earlier, psychosocial development encompasses how people's understanding of themselves, each other, and the world around them changes as a part of development (Erikson, 1963).

The fifth stage of Erikson's theory (which is summarized, with the other stages, in Table 10-4) is labeled the **identity-versus-role-confusion** period and encompasses adolescence. This stage is a time of major testing, as people try to determine what is unique and special about themselves. They attempt to discover who they are, what their skills are, and what kinds of roles they are best suited to play for the rest of their lives—in short, their **identity**. Confusion over what is the most appropriate role to follow in life can lead to either the lack of a stable identity, the adoption of a socially unacceptable role such as that of a societal deviant, or difficulty in maintaining close personal relationships later in life (Kahn, Zimmerman, Csikszentmihalyi, & Getzels, 1985).

Identity-versus-role-confusion stage: *According to Erikson, a time in adolescence of testing to determine one's own unique qualities*

Identity: *The distinguishing character of the individual: who each of us is, what our roles are, and what we are capable of*

During the identity-versus-role-confusion period, pressures to identify what one wants to do with one's life are acutely felt. Because they come at a time

TABLE 10-4

A summary of Erikson's stages

STAGE	APPROXIMATE AGE	POSITIVE OUTCOMES	NEGATIVE OUTCOMES
1. Trust vs. mistrust	Birth–$1\frac{1}{2}$ yr	Feelings of trust from environmental support	Fear and concern regarding others
2. Autonomy vs. shame and doubt	$1\frac{1}{2}$–3 yr	Self-sufficiency if exploration is encouraged	Doubts about self, lack of independence
3. Initiative vs. guilt	3–6 yr	Discovery of ways to initiate actions	Guilt from actions and thoughts
4. Industry vs. inferiority	6–12 yr	Development of sense of competence	Feelings of inferiority, no sense of mastery
5. Identity vs. role confusion	Adolescence	Awareness of uniqueness of self, knowledge of role to be followed	Inability to identify appropriate roles in life
6. Intimacy vs. isolation	Early adulthood	Development of loving, sexual relationships and close friendships	Fear of relationships with others
7. Generativity vs. stagnation	Middle adulthood	Sense of contribution to continuity of life	Trivialization of one's activities
8. Ego-integrity vs. despair	Late adulthood	Sense of unity in life's accomplishments	Regret over lost opportunities of life

of major physical changes and important changes in what society expects of them, adolescents can find this period a particularly difficult one.

The identity-versus-role-confusion stage has another important characteristic: a decline in reliance on adults for information, and a shift toward using the peer group as a source of social judgments. The peer group becomes increasingly important, allowing adolescents to form close, adultlike relationships and helping to clarify their own personal identities.

Intimacy-versus-isolation stage: *According to Erikson, a period during early adulthood, with a focus on developing close relationships*

During the college years, most students enter the **intimacy-versus-isolation stage** (spanning the period of early adulthood, from around age 18 to 30), in which the focus is on developing close relationships with others. Difficulties during this stage result in feelings of loneliness and a fear of relationships with others, while successful resolution of the crises of the stage results in the possibility of forming relationships that are intimate on a physical, intellectual, and emotional level.

Generativity-versus-stagnation stage: *According to Erikson, a period in middle adulthood during which we take stock of our contributions to family and society*

Erikson goes on to describe the last stages of adulthood, in which development is considered to continue. During middle adulthood, people are in the **generativity-versus-stagnation** stage. Generativity refers to a people's contribution to their family, community, work, and society as a whole. Success in this stage results in positive feelings about the continuity of life, while difficulties lead to feelings of triviality regarding one's activities and a sense of stagnation or of having done nothing for upcoming generations. In fact, if a person has not successfully resolved the identity crisis of adolescence, he or she may still be floundering toward identifying an appropriate career.

Ego-integrity-versus-despair stage: *According to Erikson, a period from late adulthood until death during which we review life's accomplishments and failures*

Finally, the last stage of psychosocial development, the period of **ego-integrity versus despair**, comprises later adulthood and continues until death. Success in resolving the difficulties presented by this stage of life is signified by a sense of accomplishment; difficulties result in regret over what might have been achieved, but was not.

One of the most noteworthy aspects of Erikson's theory is its suggestion that development does not stop at adolescence, but rather continues throughout adulthood. Prior to Erikson, the prevailing view was that psychosocial development

One's peers become particularly important during adolescence. (*Peter Vandermark/ Stock, Boston*)

During early adulthood, many people experience a wealth of new responsibilities, particularly in terms of marriage and children. (*James H. Simon/ The Picture Cube*)

was largely complete after adolescence. His theory helped to establish that considerable development continues throughout our lives, as we will see next.

THE MIDDLE YEARS OF LIFE: EARLY AND MIDDLE ADULTHOOD

> At some point it just dawned on me: I'm an adult now. I've got a wife, I've got children, a mortgage, I complain about my taxes—I'm not too different from my own father, in fact. Probably the biggest change in my life that made me feel like an adult was having kids. Here were other people who were dependent on me. I couldn't just say to heck with it, walk away, and go on. . . . I had responsibilities. And I couldn't think any longer, "Someday I'll do this, someday I'll do that." Someday was *here*. If I wasn't successful, if I messed up my life, there would be no second chances.

The sentiments expressed by this young adult are common during the years of life known as early and middle adulthood. During this period, people "grow up"; they are considered both legally and socially to be full-fledged adult members of society.

Psychologists generally consider early adulthood to begin at around age 20 and last until about age 40 to 45, and middle adulthood to last from about age 40 to 45 to around 65. Despite the enormous importance of these periods of life—both in terms of the accomplishments that occur within them and their overall length (together they span some forty years)—they have been studied less than any other stages by developmental psychologists. One reason is that the physical changes during these periods are less apparent and occur more gradually than those at other times during the life span. In addition, the social changes are so diverse that they prevent simple categorization. Still, there has been a recent upsurge of interest in adulthood among developmental psychologists, with a special focus on the social changes that occur in terms of the family, marriage, divorce, and careers for women.

The Peak of Health: Physical Development

For most people, early adulthood marks the peak of physical health. From about 18 to 25 years of age, people's strength is greatest, their reflexes are quickest, and their chances of dying from disease are quite slim. Moreover, reproductive capabilities are at their highest level.

The changes that begin at age 25 are largely of a quantitative rather than a qualitative nature. The body begins to operate slightly less efficiently and becomes somewhat more prone to disease. Overall, however, ill health remains the exception; most people stay remarkably healthy. (Can you think of any machine other than the body that can operate without pause for so long a period?)

Menopause (MEN o paws): *The point at which women stop menstruating, generally at around age 45*

The major biological change that does occur pertains to reproductive capabilities during middle adulthood. On average, during their late forties or early fifties, women begin **menopause**, the point at which they stop menstruating and are no longer fertile. Because menopause is accompanied by a reduction in estrogen, a female hormone, women sometimes experience symptoms such as hot flashes, which are sudden sensations of heat. It was also once thought that menopause brought on psychological symptoms such as depression, but most research now suggests that such problems, when they do occur, are caused more by women's perceived reactions to reaching an ''old'' age in a society in which youth is so highly valued. Society's attitudes, then, more than physiological changes of menopause, may produce psychological difficulties (Ballinger, 1981).

The aging process during middle adulthood for men is more subtle, since they remain fertile. In fact, males remain capable of fathering children until well into old age. Although they may experience some decrease in fertility and frequency of orgasm, such declines come about gradually. Once again, though, psychological difficulties, when they occur, tend to be brought about not so much by physical deterioration as by the inability of the aging individual to meet the artificial standards of youthfulness held in high regard by our society.

Working at Life: Social Development

While physical changes during adulthood reflect changes of a quantitative nature, social developmental changes are more profound. It is during this period that people typically launch themselves into careers, marriage, and families.

Psychologist Daniel Levinson (1986) has proposed a model of adult development based on a comprehensive study of major events in the lives of a group of men. According to Levinson, people pass through a series of stages. After a transitional period at around age 20, the stages in early adulthood relate to leaving one's family and entering the adult world. Career choices are made, and perhaps discarded, during early adulthood, until eventually long-term choices are settled on. This leads to a period of settling down in the late thirties, during which time people establish themselves in a particular set of roles and begin to evolve and work toward a vision of their own future.

Midlife transition: *Beginning around the age of 40, a period during which one comes to the realization that life is finite*

Around the age of 40 or 45, people generally begin to question their lives as they enter a period called the **midlife transition**, and the idea that life is finite becomes paramount in their thinking. Rather than maintaining a view of life that is future-oriented, people begin to ask questions about their past accomplishments, assessing what they have done and how satisfying it has been to them (Gould, 1978). They realize that not all they had wanted to accomplish will be completed before they die.

In some cases, people's assessments of their lives are negative, and they experience what has been popularly labeled a **midlife crisis**. They face signs of physical aging, and they become aware that their careers are not going to progress considerably further. Even if they have attained the heights to which they aspired—be it company president or well-respected community leader—they find that the reality of their accomplishments is not all that they had hoped it would be. As they look at their past, they may also be motivated to try to define what went wrong and how they can remedy past dissatisfactions.

Midlife crisis: *The negative feelings that accompany the realization that one has not accomplished in life what he or she had hoped to*

In most cases, though, the passage into middle age is relatively calm. If forty-year-olds' reflections on their lives and accomplishments are generally positive, their midlife transition proceeds relatively smoothly, and the forties and fifties are a particularly rewarding period of life. Rather than looking to the future, they concentrate on the present, and their involvement with families, friends, and other social groups takes on new importance. A major developmental thrust of this period of life, then, is learning to accept that the die has been cast, and that one must come to terms with one's circumstances.

Finally, during the last stages of middle adulthood—the fifties—people generally become more accepting of others and their lives and less concerned about issues or problems which once bothered them. Rather than being driven to achieve as they were in their thirties, they come to accept the realization that death is inevitable, and they try to understand their accomplishments in terms of the broader meaning of life (Gould, 1978).

Because Levinson's work was based on the study of men's lives, it is reasonable to ask if the phases of women's lives follow the same pattern. Unfortunately, there is no easy answer to the question, since comparable work has not yet been carried out with females. It is likely, though, that there are several differences, given that women, either by choice or because of societal expectations, often play different social roles than men. Moreover, women's roles have undergone rapid change in the last decade, making generalizations about women's development during early and middle adulthood difficult. In some respects, then, developmental patterns may be different for women and men (Gilligan, 1982; Kahn et al., 1985).

THE LATER YEARS OF LIFE: GROWING OLD

I can't quite figure out where all the time went. Seventy-six years old. It sounds ancient, even to me.

The funny part is I really don't *feel* any older. Oh, my body has its share of aches and pains, and I don't move around as fast as I used to. And I forget things. But I've been forgetting things all my life.

Basically, though, I don't feel my thinking is all that different—I certainly don't wake up in the morning and think, "Well, you're old now." In fact, in those first few hazy moments just before full wakefulness comes, I could just as well be a 10-year-old again. Then I wake up and realize time has gone by, faster than I ever wanted it to, and that death cannot be too far away.

The fact that death is indeed a universal experience has not stopped it from being a source of fear and concern. And many people exhibit the same kinds of feelings toward the entire period of old age.

Developmental changes occur throughout the life span. (*Catherine Ursillo/Photo Researchers, Inc.*)

Gerontologists (jer on TALL o jists): *Specialists who study aging*

However, our understanding of old age is rapidly increasing as **gerontologists**, specialists who study aging, have begun to focus on the period starting at around age 65. The knowledge that they have acquired has made an important contribution by clarifying the capabilities of the elderly and demonstrating that developmental processes continue even during old age.

Physical Aging: Physical Changes during Old Age

Napping, eating, walking, conversing. It probably doesn't surprise you that these relatively unvigorous activities represent the typical pastimes of the elderly. But what is striking about this list is that these activities are identical to the most common leisure activities reported in a survey of college students. Although the students cited more active pursuits—such as sailing and basketball—as their favorite activities, in actuality they engaged in such sports relatively infrequently, spending most of their free time napping, eating, walking, and conversing (Harper, 1978).

Although the leisure activities in which the elderly engage may not differ all that much from those that younger people pursue, there are, of course, many physical changes that pursue, there are, of course, many physical changes that are affected by the aging process. Although the most obvious are those of appearance—hair thinning and turning gray, skin wrinkling and folding, and sometimes a slight loss of height as the size of the discs between vertebrae in the spine decreases—there are also more subtle changes in the body's biological functioning (Munnichs, Mussen, Obrich, & Coleman, 1985).

For example, sensory acuity decreases as a result of aging; vision and hearing are less sharp, and smell and taste are not as sensitive. Reaction time declines. There are changes in physical stamina. Because oxygen intake and heart-pumping ability decline, the body is unable to replenish lost nutrients as quickly—and therefore the rebound from physical activity is slower (Shock, 1962). Of course, none of these changes suddenly begins at age 65; gradual declines in some kinds of functioning start earlier. It is in old age, however, that these changes become more apparent.

Thinking About—and during—Old Age: Cognitive Changes in the Elderly

Three women were talking about the inconveniences of growing old.

"Sometimes," one of them confessed, "when I go to my refrigerator, I can't remember if I'm putting something in or taking something out."

"Oh, that's nothing," said the second woman. "There are times when I find myself at the foot of the stairs wondering if I'm going up or if I've just come down."

"Well, my goodness!" exclaimed the third woman. "I'm certainly glad I don't have any problems like that"—and she knocked on wood. "Oh," she said, starting up out of her chair, "there's someone at the door." (Dent, 1984, p. 38.)

At one time, many gerontologists would have agreed with the view—suggested by the story above—that the elderly are forgetful and confused. Today, however, most research tells us that this is far from an accurate assessment of elderly people's capabilities.

One reason for the change in view is the use of more sophisticated research techniques. For example, because the elderly are more likely than younger people to suffer from physical ill health, some studies in the past have inadvertently compared IQ scores of a group of physically healthy younger people with those of a group of elderly people who were generally less healthy—resulting in findings of significantly lower scores for the elderly group. However, when only *healthy* elderly people are observed, intellectual declines are markedly less evident (Avorn, 1985; Riegel & Riegel, 1972). Similarly, declines in the elderly may be caused by their having lower motivation to perform well on intelligence tests than younger people.

On the other hand, some declines in the intellectual functioning of the elderly have been found, even when using more sophisticated research methods (Cerella, 1985; Schaie & Willis, 1985). One decline is in terms of fluid intelligence. If you recall from Chapter 7, intelligence can be conceptualized in terms of **fluid intelligence**—the ability to deal with new problems and situations—and **crystallized intelligence**, which is based on the accumulation of particular kinds of knowledge and experience, as well as on strategies that have been acquired through the use of fluid intelligence. Tests show clear, although not substantial, declines in fluid intelligence in old age. It is noteworthy, however, that such changes actually begin to appear in early adulthood, as indicated in Figure 10-10 (Baltes & Schaie, 1974; Schaie, 1985).

Fluid intelligence: *The ability to deal with new problems and situations*

Crystallized intelligence: *Intelligence based on the store of specific information, skills, and strategies that people have acquired through experience*

Crystallized intelligence, in contrast, does not decline; it actually improves with age, as shown in Figure 10-10. For example, an elderly woman asked to solve a geometry problem (which taps fluid intelligence) might have greater difficulty than she once did, but she might be better at solving verbal problems that require reasoned conclusions.

Are the Elderly Forgetful? Memory Changes in Old Age One of the characteristics most frequently attributed to the elderly is forgetfulness. How accurate is this?

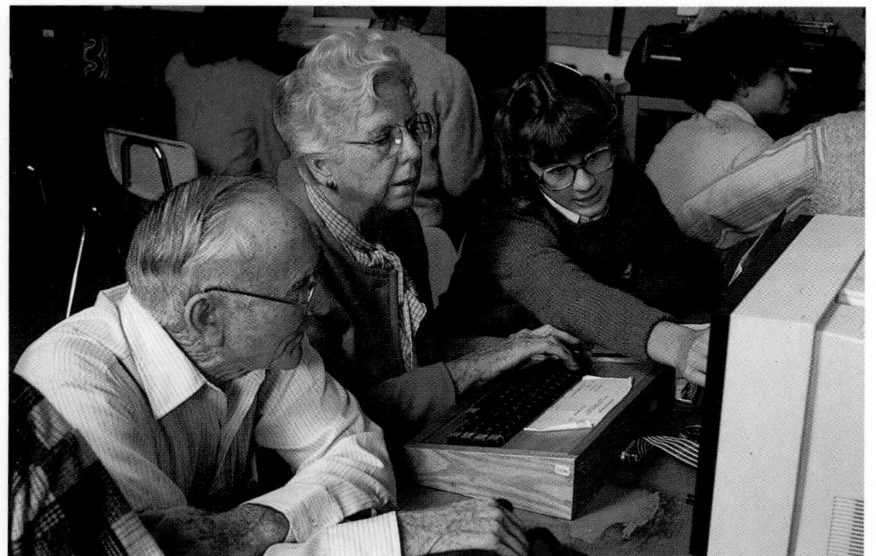

While it may take the elderly longer to learn than at earlier stages in their development, they are quite capable of learning what they want to. In fact, some intellectual capabilities actually improve during old age. (*Jim Balog/Black Star*)

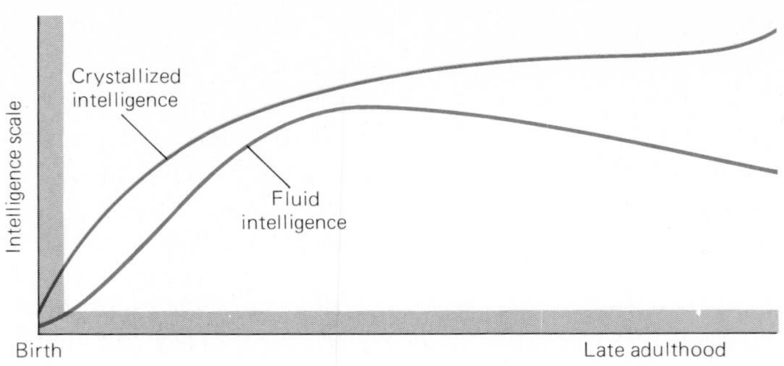

Figure 10-10
Although crystallized intelligence remains steady and even seems to increase slightly in the elderly, fluid intelligence does show a decline. (*Source: Schaie, 1984.*)

Most evidence suggests that memory change is not inevitable in the aging process, although some elderly people show declines. Moreover, when there are memory deficits, they most typically occur only in long-term memory; the capacity of short-term memory rarely declines except in cases of illness (Craik, 1977).

In severe cases of memory decline, and where the decline is accompanied by other cognitive difficulties, an elderly person may be viewed as suffering from senility. **Senility** is actually a broad, imprecise term, typically applied to elderly people who experience progressive deterioration of mental abilities, including memory loss, disorientation to time and place, and general confusion.

Senility: *A broad, imprecise term used in reference to elderly people who experience progressive deterioration of mental abilities, including memory loss, confusion of time and place, and general disorientation*

Although senility was once thought to be an inevitable state that accompanies aging, most gerontologists now view it as a label that has outlived its usefulness. Rather than viewing senility as the cause of certain symptoms, the symptoms are now viewed as being caused by some other factor. In some cases there is an actual disease, such as **Alzheimer's disease** (discussed in Chapter 5), in which progressive brain damage leads to a gradual and irreversible decline in mental abilities (Crook & Miller, 1985). In other cases, however, the symptoms of senility are caused by temporary anxiety and depression, which may be successfully treated, or may even be due to overmedication.

Alzheimer's (ALZ hy mers) **disease**: *A progressive brain disease leading to an irreversible decline in mental and physical abilities*

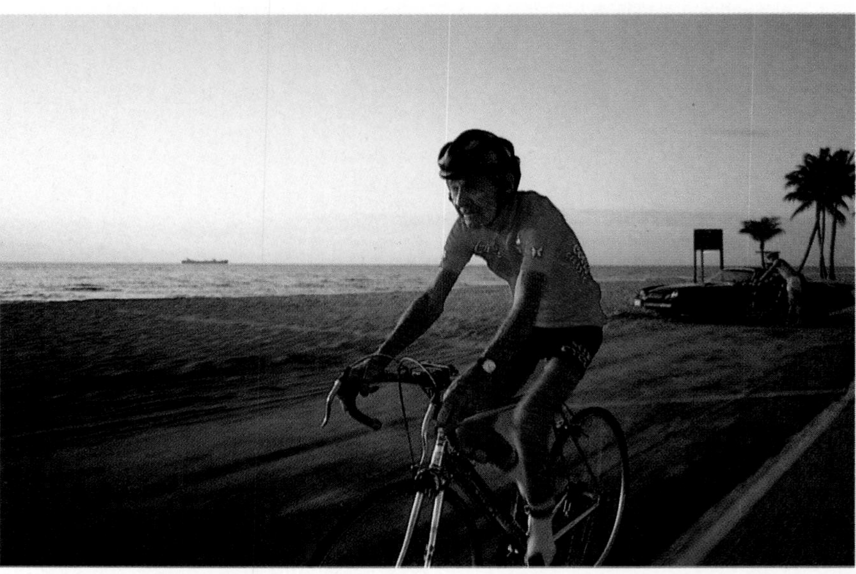

Grand master cyclist Fred Knoller, 87 years old, illustrates the view that the elderly who age the most successfully are those who maintain the activities of earlier years. (*James Kamp/Black Star*)

Facing Death

Following the death of a loved one, survivors pass through a number of stages of grief. (*Dennis Stock/Magnum*)

At some time in your life, you will face death—certainly your own, and probably the deaths of friends and loved ones. Yet, although there is nothing more inevitable in people's lives than death, it remains a frightening, emotion-laden topic. In fact, there may be nothing more stressful than the death of a loved one or the contemplation of your own imminent death, and how you prepare for death will likely represent one of your most crucial developmental tasks.

Not too long ago, talk of death was taboo. The topic of death was never mentioned to dying people, and gerontologists had little to say about it. That changed, however, with the pioneering work of Elisabeth Kübler-Ross (1969), who brought the subject out into the open with her observation that people tend to move through five stages as they face death:

- Denial. In this first stage, people resist the idea that they are dying. Even if told that their chances for survival are small, they refuse to admit that they are facing death.
- Anger. After moving beyond the denial stage, dying people are angry—angry at people around them who are in good health, angry at God, angry at medical professionals for being ineffective. They ask the question "Why me?" and are unable to answer it without feeling anger.
- Bargaining. Anger leads to bargaining, in which the dying try to think of ways to postpone death. They may decide to dedicate their lives to religion if God saves them; they may say, "If only I can live to see my son married, I will accept death then." Such bargains are rarely kept, most often because the dying person's illness keeps progressing and invalidates any "agreements."
- Depression. When dying people come to feel that bargaining is of no use, they move to the next stage: depression. They realize that the die is cast, that they are losing their loved ones and their lives really are coming to an end. They are experiencing what Kübler-Ross calls "preparatory grief" for their own death.
- Acceptance. In this last stage, people are past mourning for the loss of their own lives, and they accept impending death. Usually, they are unemotional and uncommunicative; it is as if they have made peace with themselves and are expecting death without rancor.

While not everyone experiences each of these stages in the same way, if at all, Kübler-Ross's theory remains our best description of people's reactions to their approaching death. There are, however, vast differences, depending on the specific cause of death as well as on sex, age, personality, and type of support received from family and friends (Kastenbaum, 1975).

RECAP AND REVIEW IV

Recap

- Adolescence is the developmental stage between childhood and adulthood. It includes several critical physical transitions.
- According to Kohlberg, moral development passes through a series of increasingly sophisticated levels. In Gilligan's contrasting view of moral development, women, more than men, focus on the individual rather than abstract principles.
- During adolescence, people enter the crucial identity-versus-role-diffusion stage, which may include an identity crisis. Psychosocial development continues throughout the lifespan.

- The peak of physical strength occurs approximately from the age of eighteen to twenty-five, after which there are declines in strength and general health.
- Although the leisure activities of the elderly do not differ substantially from those of younger people, there are a number of physical declines with age. For instance, fluid and crystallized intelligence and memory are affected by aging.
- People approaching death progress through a series of stages.

Review

1. The period of adolescence generally extends from:
a. early teenage years to old age **b.** late childhood to puberty **c.** just before the teenage years to just after them
d. ages eleven to twelve in girls and thirteen to fourteen in boys

2. Match each example with its corresponding stage of psychosocial development by placing the appropriate number in each blank.

a. _______ Identity vs. role confusion	1. A few years back, Paul felt that his contributions to his family, work, and commitments were insignificant. He now values his contributions and is optimistic about his future.
b. _______ Intimacy vs. isolation	2. Joni is having an emotionally trying adolescence. She finds herself grasping at different ways of behaving, trying to get a handle on who she really is.
c. _______ Generativity vs. stagnation	3. Mark has never before felt the desire for such an intimate relationship as he does now with his college classmate Alicia.

3. Forty-year-old Martin has recently found himself surveying his goals and accomplishments to date. Although he has accomplished much, he realizes that many of his goals will not be met in his lifetime. Levinson would term this stage in Martin's life the ____________________ ____________________.

4. Which of the following is *not* characteristic of midlife crisis?
a. depression over a lack of accomplishment **b.** concern about physical aging **c.** disappointment with life status
d. contentment with the present

5. The ability to deal with new problems and situations often declines in the elderly. In contrast, their ability to use past learnings and acquired strategies to solve problems often improves. In technical terms, ____________________ intelligence tends to decline with age, but ____________________ intelligence tends to improve.

6. Jackie remembers her dying grandfather saying that if he recovered from his disease, he would devote the rest of his life to helping the poor. Kübler-Ross would label this stage of dying:
a. optimism **b.** acceptance **c.** denial **d.** bargaining

(Answers to review questions are at the bottom of page 354.)

Psychology Looks Toward the 1990s
Keeping Smart: Avoiding Intellectual Declines in Old Age

Winston Churchill becomes British prime minister for the first time. Age: 65.

Grandma Moses, who began to paint in her late seventies, has her first one-person exhibit. Age: 80.

Cellist Pablo Casals receives an ovation for his brilliant concert performance. Age: 88.

While the stereotype of old age suggests inevitable senility and declines in awareness of what is happening in the world, many elderly people, such as the individuals mentioned above, clearly rebut this mistaken notion. Still, for many people the stereotype becomes reality, and there is a clear decline in cognitive abilities as they age. For example, as we discussed earlier in the chapter, reductions in fluid intelligence (the ability to deal with new problems and situations) and long-term memory deficits are common in the elderly.

On the other hand, there are large individual differences; some people keep and even increase their intellectual capabilities well into their eighties and nineties. The fact that some elderly people perform so well cognitively raises the question of whether intellectual declines are necessarily inevitable (Rowe & Kahn, 1987).

In fact, some gerontologists have argued that, with appropriate environmental stimulation, cognitive deterioration largely might be prevented—and in some cases even reversed.

In clear support of this hypothesis, K. Warner Schaie and Sherry L. Willis of Pennsylvania State University recently devised a five-hour training program involving the teaching of reasoning and spatial skills to the elderly (Schaie & Willis, 1986). Participants in the program were taught general strategies for dealing with problems, and they also completed practice test items typical of the type used to measure cognitive skills.

After completing the training program, subjects were tested on a variety of measures, and the program was demonstrated to be a success. Of those participants who had previously shown declines in reasoning and spatial skills, most began to improve, and the training enhanced the performance of participants whose abilities had remained relatively stable.

The results demonstrate quite clearly that declines in cognitive functioning in old age should not be considered unavoidable. Intellectual abilities in the elderly remain resilient, and even when reductions have occurred, it seems as if they may be reversed through training.

Apart from specific training, are there things that the elderly can do to maintain their capabilities at maximum potential? John Horn, a psychologist at the University of Denver, has begun to provide us with an understanding of the factors that allow some people to keep active in their old age (Goleman, 1984). Among the most important that he has identified are:

- Maintaining social relationships with others. By staying socially involved with other people, the elderly avoid the declines that can occur rapidly in people who withdraw from others.
- Being mentally active. The old phrase that is applied to physical exercise—"use it or lose it"—seems to apply equally well to mental agility. People who were well-educated and who maintain their intellectual interests are less apt to show declines than those who show little concern over intellectual matters. In fact, measures of verbal intelligence can actually increase in the elderly if they remain mentally active.
- Having a flexible personality. People who have had a high tolerance for ambiguity—who have not viewed the world in terms of black and white—are more apt to maintain their capabilities, as are those who have enjoyed new experiences in middle age. Rigidity works against the maintenance of intelligence in old age.

In sum, a decline in intelligence, which was once thought of as an inevitable part of old age, now appears to be something that may be largely avoidable.

LOOKING BACK

1. In this chapter we discussed developmental psychology—the branch of psychology that studies the growth and change that occurs throughout life—from the moment of conception to death.

2. One of the fundamental questions that underlies developmental psychology is how much of developmental changes are due to nature—heredity and genetic factors—and to nurture—environmental factors. Most developmental psychologists feel that heredity defines the upper limits of our growth and change, while the environment affects the degree to which the upper limits are reached. Studies of the nature-nurture question include controlling animals' genetic backgrounds and observing twins placed in different environments.

3. At the moment of conception, a male's sperm cell and a female's egg cell unite, each contributing to the new individual's genetic makeup. The new cell, a zygote, immediately begins to grow, becoming an embryo in four weeks and measuring at that time about one-fifth of an inch long. By the ninth week, the embryo is called a fetus and is responsive to touch and other stimulation. At twenty-eight weeks (and sometimes earlier) it reaches the age of viability: It can conceivably survive if born prematurely. A fetus is normally born after thirty-eight weeks of pregnancy, weighing around 7½ pounds and measuring about 20 inches in length.

4. Genetic difficulties that produce birth defects include sickle-cell anemia, phenylketonuria (PKU), Tay-Sachs disease, and Down's syndrome. Among the prenatal environmental influences on fetal growth are the mother's nutritional status, illnesses, drug intake, and birth complications.

5. The newborn, or neonate, has many capabilities. Among the reflexes are the rooting reflex, the Moro or startle reflex, and the Babinski reflex, most of which disappear in a number of months. After birth, physical development is rapid; children typically triple their birthweights after a year. Perceptual abilities also increase rapidly; infants, who are capable of perceiving patterns and facial expressions at birth, are able to distinguish color and depth after just 1 month. Their other sensory capabilities are also impressive at birth; they can distinguish sounds and discriminate tastes and smells. However, more sophisticated perceptual abilities are predicated on increased cognitive abilities.

6. Social development in infancy is marked by the development of attachment, the positive emotional bond between parents and their children, during infancy. Attachment develops according to the Attachment Behavioral System.

7. According to Erikson, there are eight stages of psychosocial development that encompass people's changing interactions and understanding of themselves and others. During childhood, there are four stages, each of which relates to a crisis that requires resolution. These stages are labeled trust versus mistrust (birth to 18 months), autonomy versus shame and doubt (18 months to 3 years), initiative versus guilt (3 to 6 years), and industry versus inferiority (6 to 12 years).

8. Piaget's theory suggests that cognitive development proceeds through four stages in which there are qualitative changes in thinking. In the sensorimotor stage (birth to two years), children develop object permanence, the awareness that objects and people continue to exist even if they are out of sight. In the preoperational stage (2 to 7 years) children display egocentric thought, and by the end of the stage they begin to understand the principle of conservation—the knowledge that quantity is unrelated to the arrangement and physical appearance of an object. This understanding of conservation is not fully grasped, however, until the concrete operational stage (7 to 12 years), in which children begin to think more logically, and to understand the concept of reversibility. In the final stage, the formal operational period (12 years to adulthood), thinking becomes abstract, formal, and fully logical.

9. Although Piaget's theory has had an enormous influence on the study of cognitive development, some theorists suggest that the stage notion is inaccurate. They say that development is more continuous, and that the changes occurring within and between stages are more reflective of changes in quantity than in quality. Moreover, they suggest that the causes underlying changes in cognitive ability are similar throughout an individual's life.

10. Because environmental factors play such an important role in cognitive development, child-rearing practices can have an important effect on the degree to which a child reaches his or her genetic potential. Parents can help by being emotionally responsive and involved with their children, being verbally interactive, providing appropriate play materials, giving children a chance to make and learn from mistakes, and holding high expectations.

11. Adolescence is the developmental stage between childhood and adulthood. The period is marked by the start of puberty, the point at which sexual maturity occurs. The age at which puberty begins has implications for the way people view themselves and are seen by others.

12. Moral judgments during adolescence increase in sophistication, according to Kohlberg's six-stage model. Although Kohlberg's stages are an adequate description of males' moral judgments, they seem not as useful when it comes to describing females' judgments. Specifically, Gilligan suggests that women view morality in terms of individual well-being rather than broad, general principles.

13. According to Erikson's model of psychosocial development, adolescence is a time when there can be an identity crisis, although this is by no means universal. This stage is followed by three subsequent stages of psychosocial development which cover the remainder of the lifespan.

14. Early adulthood marks the peak of physical health. Physical changes occur relatively gradually during adulthood, although one major change occurs at the end of middle adulthood for women: They begin menopause, the point at which they are no longer fertile. For men, the aging process is more subtle, since they remain fertile. In general, then, both men and women experience few physical changes during middle adulthood.

15. Levinson's model of adult development suggests that there are six major stages that occur beginning with the entry into early adulthood at around age 20 and ending at around age 60 to 65. One of the most critical transitions—at least for men—occurs during midlife, when people typically experience a midlife transition in which the notion that life is not infinite becomes more important. In some cases this can lead to a midlife crisis, although usually the passage into middle age is relatively calm.

16. As aging continues during middle adulthood, the focus shifts from the future to the present. Ultimately, people realize in their fifties that their lives and accomplishments are fairly well set, and they try to come to terms with their lives.

17. Old age may bring marked physical declines. Although the

ANSWERS TO REVIEW QUESTIONS

Review IV: **1.** c **2.** a.2; b.3; c.1 **3.** Midlife transition **4.** d **5.** Fluid, crystallized **6.** d activities of the elderly are not all that different from those of younger people, elderly people do experience sensory and reaction-time declines, as well as a decrease in physical stamina. **18.** Although intellectual declines were once thought to be an inevitable part of aging, most research suggests that this is not necessarily the case. Fluid intelligence does decline with age, and long-term memory abilities are sometimes impaired. In contrast, crystallized intelligence shows slight increases with age, and short-term memory remains at about the same level. Senility, then, is no longer seen as a universal outcome of old age. **19.** According to Kübler-Ross, dying people move through five stages as they face death: denial, anger, bargaining, depression, and acceptance.

KEY TERMS AND CONCEPTS

developmental psychology (p. 314)
environment (p. 315)
heredity (p. 316)
nature-nurture question (p. 316)
genetic (p. 316)
maturation (p. 316)
interactionist (p. 317)
identical twins (p. 317)
conception (p. 318)
zygote (p. 318)
chromosomes (p. 318)
genes (p. 318)
embryo (p. 319)
fetus (p. 319)
age of viability (p. 319)
sickle-cell anemia (p. 320)
phenylketonuria (PKU) (p. 320)
Tay-Sachs disease (p. 320)
Down's syndrome (p. 320)
rubella (p. 320)
thalidomide (p. 321)
fetal alcohol syndrome (p. 321)
neonate (p. 323)
vernix (p. 323)
lanugo (p. 323)
reflex (p. 323)
rooting reflex (p. 323)
sucking reflex (p. 323)
gag reflex (p. 323)
Moro (startle) reflex (p. 323)
Babinski reflex (p. 324)
habituation (p. 325)
attachment (p. 326)
psychosocial development (p. 330)
trust-versus-mistrust stage (p. 330)
autonomy-versus-shame-and-doubt stage (p. 330)
initiative-versus-guilt stage (p. 330)
industry-versus-inferiority stage (p. 331)
cognitive development (p. 333)
sensorimotor stage (p. 333)
object permanence (p. 334)
preoperational stage (p. 334)
egocentric thought (p. 334)
principle of conservation (p. 334)
concrete operational stage (p. 335)
reversibility (p. 335)
formal operational stage (p. 336)
adolescence (p. 340)
puberty (p. 340)
identity-versus-role-confusion stage (p. 343)
identity (p. 343)
intimacy-versus-isolation stage (p. 344)
generativity-versus-stagnation stage (p. 344)
ego-integrity-versus-despair stage (p. 344)
menopause (p. 346)
midlife transition (p. 347)
midlife crisis (p. 347)
gerontologists (p. 348)
fluid intelligence (p. 349)
crystallized intelligence (p. 349)
senility (p. 350)
Alzheimer's disease (p. 350)

FOR FURTHER STUDY AND APPLICATION

Tomlinson-Keasey, C. (1985). *Child development: Psychological, sociocultural, and biological factors.* Homewood, IL: Dorsey Press.

Santrock, J. W. & Yussen, S. R. (1987). *Child development: An introduction* (3rd ed.). Dubuque, IA: W. C. Brown.

These two fine, broad, introductory texts on child development cover the entire range of childhood changes.

Daehler, M., & Bukato, D. (1985). *Cognitive development.* New York: Random House.

This book provides a good, in-depth introduction to the area of cognitive development.

Brazelton, T. B. (1969). *Infants and mothers: Differences in development.* New York: Dell.

Brazelton, T. B. (1974). *Toddlers and parents.* New York: Delta.

Written by a physician who has become the "Dr. Spock of the 1980s," these books provide an anecdotal account of three infants' and three toddlers' development in the early stages of life. They give a good understanding of the complexities of child rearing and of how development differs among children with unique temperaments.

Rice, F. P. (1984). *The Adolescent: Development, relationships, and culture* (4th ed.). Boston: Allyn & Bacon.

This book provides a detailed overview of the adolescent period of development, probably the best-researched period past childhood.

Santrock, J. W. (1985). *Adult development and aging.* Dubuque, IA: W. C. Brown.

This book provides a good review of postadolescent development.

Sheehy, G. (1976). *Passages.* New York: Dutton.

Although not sophisticated in a scientific sense, this book describes patterns of development during adulthood and provides rich insights into the kinds of changes that occur during one's lifetime.

Kübler-Ross, E. (1981). *Living with death and dying.* New York: Macmillan.

A sensitive look at the end of life, written by one of the foremost experts on the psychological processes associated with death.

CHAPTER 11

CHAPTER 11

PERSONALITY

PROLOGUE

LOOKING AHEAD

EXPLAINING THE INNER LIFE: PSYCHOANALYTIC THEORIES OF PERSONALITY

What you see is *not* what you get: Freud's psychoanalytic theory

Revising Freud: The neo-Freudian psychoanalysts

Recap and review I

IN SEARCH OF PERSONALITY: TRAIT, LEARNING, AND HUMANISTIC APPROACHES

Labeling personality: Trait theories

THE CUTTING EDGE. Is Personality a Myth?: Personality versus Situational Factors

Explaining the outer life, ignoring the inner life: Learning theories of personality

Understanding the self: Humanistic theories of personality

TRY-IT! Assessing Your Real Self-Concept and Your Ideal Self-Concept

Answering the old question: Which theory is right?

Recap and review II

DETERMINING WHAT MAKES YOU SPECIAL: ASSESSING PERSONALITY

The keys to assessing personality: Reliability and validity

Asking a little to learn a lot: Self-report measures of personality

PSYCHOLOGY AT WORK. Assessment Comes to the Personnel Office

Looking into the unconscious: Projective methods

The informed consumer of psychology: Assessing personality assessments

Recap and review III

PSYCHOLOGY LOOKS TOWARD THE 1990s. The Roots of Personality: The Inheritance of Traits

LOOKING BACK

KEY TERMS AND CONCEPTS

FOR FURTHER STUDY AND APPLICATION

PROLOGUE

When she went to a party—and she generally chose not to—Michelle LeBlanc could usually be found in the most inconspicuous corner. She rarely talked to more than a few close friends, if anyone at all, and her attempts at socializing consisted mostly of asking people to pass her something she couldn't reach from the bar. If they had taken the time to notice, people who observed her behavior at social engagements would probably have called her the shyest person they had ever seen.

Yet, if they had happened to see her in her job as hostess at a local restaurant, they would have been shocked: She was witty and charming, and customers were immediately drawn to her. It was as if she were an entirely different person.

And the same observers would have been even more surprised if they had seen her with her family, for here she was like still another person, so outgoing and energetic that her brothers always referred to her as the family social director. It was clear that her family adored her lively and outgoing ways, and that in their eyes she could do no wrong.

LOOKING AHEAD

Will the real Michelle LeBlanc please stand up?

You probably know people like Michelle LeBlanc—individuals who show a certain set of characteristics in one situation, but in another display characteristics that are quite the opposite. (In fact, you might include yourself in this category.) At the same time, you probably know people whose behavior is so predictable that you can tell, almost without thinking, what they are going to do in a particular situation—people whose behavior is almost entirely consistent from one setting to the next.

Personality: *The sum total of characteristics that differentiate people or the stability in a person's behavior across different situations*

To psychologists, understanding the characteristic ways in which people behave makes up the study of what is known as **personality**. The term ''personality'' itself is actually used in two different, but related, ways: On one hand, personality refers to the characteristics that differentiate people from one another—those behaviors that make an individual unique. But the concept of personality is also used in a second way: in terms of the stability in people's behavior that may lead them to act uniformly both in different situations and over extended periods of time.

In this chapter we consider a number of theories that have been developed to explain personality. We begin with a discussion of the broadest and most comprehensive approach to personality: Freud's psychoanalytic theory. Freud maintained that every aspect of behavior is touched by underlying personality characteristics. We also discuss theorists whose work was heavily influenced by Freud's contributions.

Next we turn to more recent theories of personality. We consider approaches which concentrate on identifying the most fundamental personality traits that differentiate one person from another, theories that emphasize how personality is a set of learned behaviors, and those, known as humanistic theories, that highlight the uniquely human aspects of personality. Finally, the chapter ends with a discussion of the ways in which personality is measured and the uses to which personality tests can be applied.

(a)

(b)

According to personality theorists known as psychoanalysts, the underlying personality structure of the very neat and methodical woman in photo *a* may be quite similar to that of the unusually messy person in *b*. (*(a) Richard Pasley/Stock, Boston, (b) Jerry Berndt/Stock, Boston*)

After reading and studying this chapter, then, you will be able to

- Define the ways in which psychologists use the concept of personality
- Describe the structure and development of personality according to Freud and his successors
- Summarize and compare the major aspects of trait, learning, and humanistic theories of personality
- Outline the keys to accurate assessment of personality
- Identify the major types of personality measures, including specific, frequently employed tests
- Define and apply the key terms and concepts listed at the end of the chapter

EXPLAINING THE INNER LIFE: PSYCHOANALYTIC THEORIES OF PERSONALITY

Rick was without doubt the sloppiest person I had ever known. His dorm room was a mess. Clothes were strewn all over the place, some clean, some dirty—you never knew which, and of course, neither did he. There were piles of papers on his desk, and stacks of books cluttered the floor. If he had gone out of his way to be messy, he couldn't have done a better job.

* * *

Ben was so neat and organized it almost drove me crazy. Everything was in its place, and if you picked up a book from its shelf and then put it down somewhere else, he immediately scooped it up and put it back where it belonged. Even his writing was extremely neat and controlled. I had the impression he would go into a panic if someone happened to spill something on the furniture.

Psychoanalysts (sy ko AN uh lists): *Physicians or psychologists who specialize in psychoanalysis*

At first glance, these sound like descriptions of people with very different personalities. Yet to one group of personality theorists, **psychoanalysts**, these two young men may actually be very similar—at least in terms of the underlying aspect of their personalities that is motivating their behavior. According to psychoanalysts, behavior is caused largely by powerful forces that are shaped to a large degree by childhood experiences and about which people are unaware. The originator and most important of the theorists to hold such a view, and indeed one of the best-known figures in all of psychology, is Sigmund Freud. An Austrian physician, Freud was the originator of **psychoanalytic theory** in the early 1900s.

Psychoanalytic (sy ko an uh LIT ik) **theory**: *Freud's theory that unconscious forces act as determinants of personality*

What You See Is Not What You Get: Freud's Psychoanalytic Theory

"Did you see the picture of Arnold Schwarzenegger sexing—oops, I mean, flexing—his muscles on the cover of *People* magazine this week?" asked Debbie, as she and her friend Kathy walked home from class.

Although this may seem to be merely an embarrassing slip of the tongue, according to psychoanalytic theory mistakes such as these are not errors at all. Rather, they are indications of deeply felt emotions and thoughts that are harbored in the **unconscious**, a part of the personality of which a person is not aware. Many of life's experiences are painful, and the unconscious provides a "safe" haven for our recollections of such events, where they can remain without continually disturbing us. Similarly, the unconscious contains **instinctual drives**: infantile wishes, desires, demands, and needs that are hidden from conscious awareness because of the conflicts and pain they would cause us if they were part of our everyday lives.

Unconscious: *A part of the personality of which a person is unaware and which is a potential determinant of behavior*

Instinctual drives: *Infantile wishes, desires, demands, and needs hidden from conscious awareness*

To Freud, conscious experience is just the tip of the iceberg; just as with the unseen mass of a floating iceberg, the material found in the unconscious dwarfs the information about which we are aware. Much of people's everyday behavior, then, is viewed as being motivated by unconscious forces about which they know little. For example, a child's concern over being unable to please his strict and demanding parents may lead him to have low self-esteem as an adult, although he may never understand why his accomplishments—which may be considerable—never seem sufficient. Indeed, consciously he may recall his childhood with great pleasure; it is the unconscious, which holds the painful memories, that provokes the low self-evaluation.

According to Freud, to fully understand personality it is necessary to illuminate and expose what is in the unconscious. But because the unconscious disguises the meaning of material it holds, it cannot be observed directly. It is therefore necessary to interpret clues to the unconscious—slips of the tongue, fantasies, and dreams—in order to understand the unconscious processes di-

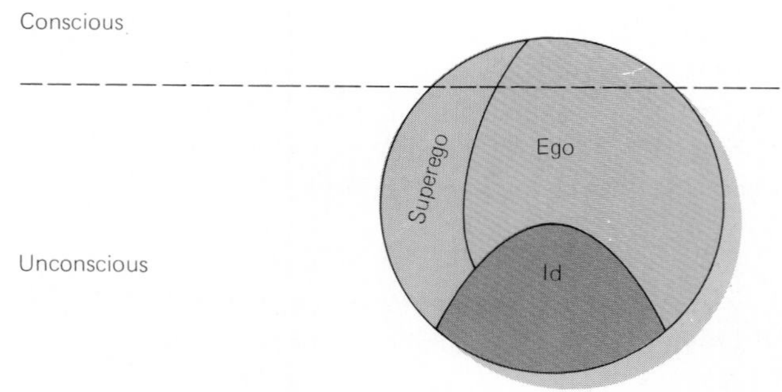

Figure 11-1
In Freud's model of personality, there are three major structures: the id, the ego, and the superego. As the schematic shows, only a small portion of personality is conscious. It is important to note that this figure should not be thought of as an actual physical structure, but rather as a model of the interrelationships between the parts of personality.

recting behavior. A slip of the tongue, such as the one we quoted earlier, might be interpreted as revealing the speaker's underlying unconscious sexual interests.

While the notion of an unconscious does not seem all that farfetched to most of us, this is only because Freudian theory has had such a widespread influence, with applications ranging from literature to religion. In Freud's day, however, the idea of an unconscious was revolutionary, and the best minds of the time rejected his ideas as without basis and even laughable. That it is so easy for us to understand theories that are based on the assumption that there is a part of personality about which people are unaware—one that is responsible for much of our behavior—is a tribute to the influence of the theory.

Structuring Personality: Id, Ego, and Superego To describe the structure of personality, Freud developed a comprehensive theory in which he said personality consisted of three separate but interacting parts, the id, the ego, and the superego. Although Freud describes these parts in very concrete terms, it is important to realize that they are not actual physical structures found in a certain part of the brain; instead, they represent parts of a general *model* of personality that describes the interaction of various processes and forces within one's personality that motivate behavior. Yet the id, ego, and superego can be represented figuratively; as we can see in Figure 11-1, Freud suggested that they can be depicted as in the diagram, which also shows how the three components of personality are related to the conscious and the unconscious.

If personality were to consist only of primitive, instinctual cravings and longings, it would need only one component: the id. The **id** is the raw, unorganized, inherited part of personality whose sole purpose is to reduce tension created by primary drives related to hunger, sex, aggression, and irrational impulses. The id operates according to the **pleasure principle**, in which the goal is the immediate reduction of tension and the maximization of satisfaction.

Id: *The raw, unorganized, inherited part of personality whose purpose is to reduce tension created by biological drives and irrational impulses*

Pleasure principle: *The principle by which the id operates, in which the person seeks the immediate reduction of tension and the maximization of satisfaction*

Unfortunately for the id—but luckily for people and society—reality prevents the demands of the pleasure principle from being fulfilled in most cases. Instead, the world produces constraints: We cannot always eat when we are hungry, and sexual drives can be discharged only when time, place—and partner—are willing. To account for this fact of life, Freud suggested a second part of personality, which he called the ego.

The **ego** provides a buffer between the id and the realities of the objective, outside world. In contrast to the pleasure-seeking nature of the id, the ego operates according to the **reality principle**, in which instinctual energy is restrained in order to maintain the safety of the individual and help integrate the person into society. In a sense, then, the ego is the "executive" of personality: It makes decisions, controls actions, and allows thinking and problem solving of a higher order than the id is capable of. The ego is also the seat of higher cognitive abilities such as intelligence, thoughtfulness, reasoning, and learning.

Ego (EE go): *The part of personality that provides a buffer between the id and the outside world*

Reality principle: *The principle by which the ego operates, in which instinctual energy is restrained in order to maintain an individual's safety and integration into society*

The **superego**, the final personality structure to develop, represents the rights and wrongs of society as handed down by a person's parents, teachers, and other important figures. It becomes a part of personality when children learn right from wrong, and continues to develop as people begin to incorporate the broad moral principles of the society in which they live into their own standards.

Superego: *The part of personality that represents the morality of society as presented by parents, teachers, etc.*

The superego actually has two parts, the **conscience** and the **ego-ideal**. The conscience *prevents* us from doing morally bad things, while the ego-ideal *motivates* us to do what is morally proper. The superego helps to control impulses coming from the id, making them less selfish and more virtuous.

Conscience: *The part of the superego that prevents us from doing what is morally wrong*

Ego-ideal: *The part of the superego that motivates us to do what is morally proper*

Although on the surface the superego appears to be the opposite of the id,

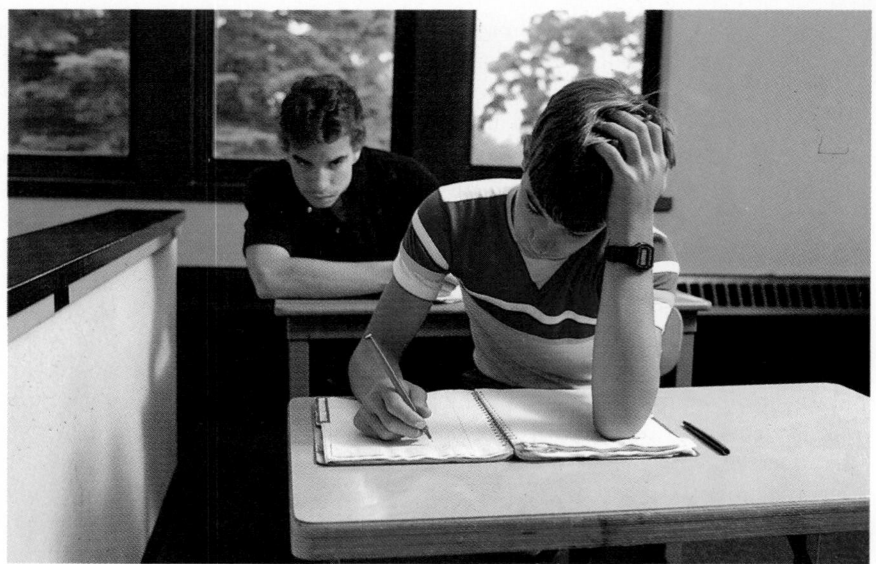

Freud theorized that the superego, the part of personality representing society's rights and wrongs, is made up of two parts, the conscience and the ego-ideal. The conscience prevents us from acting improperly—such as cheating on a test—while the ego-ideal motivates us to behave in morally appropriate ways. (*Barbara Kirk/ The Stock Market*)

the superego and the id share an important feature: They are both unrealistic in that they do not consider the constraints of society. While this lack of reality within the superego pushes the person toward greater virtue, if left unchecked it would create perfectionists who were unable to make the compromises that life requires. Similarly, an unrestrained id would create a primitive, pleasure-seeking, thoughtless individual, seeking to fulfill without delay every desire. The ego, then, must compromise between the demands of the superego and the id, permitting a person to obtain some of the gratification sought by the id while keeping the moralistic superego from preventing the gratification.

Developing Personality: A Stage Approach Freud did not stop after describing the structure of adult personality; his theory also provides a view of how personality develops throughout a series of stages during childhood. What is particularly important about the sequence, summarized in Table 11-1, is that it suggests how experiences and difficulties during a specific childhood stage may predict specific sorts of idiosyncracies in adult personality. The theory is also unique in focusing each stage on a major biological function, which is assumed to be the focus of pleasure in a given period.

Oral stage: *According to Freud, a stage from birth to 12–18 months, in which an infant's center of pleasure is the mouth*

In the first period of development, called the **oral stage**, the baby's mouth is the focal point of pleasure. During the first year of life, children suck, mouth, and bite anything that will fit into their mouths. To Freud, this behavior suggested that the mouth was the primary site of a kind of sexual pleasure, and if infants were either overly indulged (perhaps by being fed every time they cried) or were very frustrated in their search for oral gratification, they might become fixated at this stage. Displaying **fixation** means that an adult shows personality characteristics that are related to an earlier stage of development. For example, fixation at the oral stage might produce an adult who was unusually interested in overtly oral activities—eating, talking, smoking—or who showed symbolic sorts of oral interests: being "bitingly" sarcastic or being very gullible ("swallowing" anything).

Fixation: *Behavior reflecting an earlier stage of development*

Anal stage: *According to Freud, a stage, from 12–18 months to 3 years of age, in which a child's pleasure is centered on the anus*

From around 12 to 18 months until 3 years of age—where the emphasis in most cultures is on toilet training—the child enters the **anal stage**. At this point, the major source of pleasure changes from the mouth to the anal region, and children derive considerable pleasure from both retention and expulsion of feces. If the external concerns of society in the form of toilet training are particularly demanding, the result may be fixation. If fixation occurs during the anal stage, Freud suggested that adults might show unusual rigidity, orderliness, punctuality—or extreme cleanliness or sloppiness, as in our earlier examples of Rick and Ben.

At about age 3, the **phallic stage** begins, signaling another major shift in the primary source of pleasure for the child. This time, the interest focuses on the genitals and the pleasures derived from fondling them. This is also the stage of one of the most important points of development: the **Oedipal conflict**. As children focus their attention on their genitals, the differences between male and female anatomy are of more interest. Moreover, at this time the male begins to develop sexual interests in his mother and begins to see his father as a rival, and—as Oedipus did in the ancient Greek drama—wishes to kill his father. But because he views his father as too powerful, he represses his desires for his mother and instead forms an **identification** with his father, trying to be as much like him as possible.

For girls the process is a little different. Freud reasoned that girls begin to feel sexual arousal toward their fathers and—in a suggestion that was to later bring serious, and not unreasonable, accusations that he viewed women as inferior to men—that they begin to experience **penis envy**: They wish they had the anatomical part that, at least to Freud, seemed most clearly missing in girls. They blame their mothers for their lack of a penis, believing that their mothers are responsible for their castration. As with males, though, they find that in order to resolve such unacceptable feelings, they must identify with the same-sex parent. In this way, a girl's identification with her mother is completed.

At this point, the Oedipal conflict is said to be resolved, and, if things have gone smoothly, Freudian theory assumes that both males and females move on to the next stage of development. If difficulties arise during this period, however, all sorts of problems are thought to occur, including a lack of conscience and improper sex-role behavior.

An adult fixated at the oral stage of development is unusually concerned with activities such as eating and smoking. (*Charles Gupton/Stock, Boston*)

Phallic stage (FAL ik): *According to Freud, a period, beginning around age 3, during which a child's interest focuses on the genitals*

Oedipal (ED ih pul) **conflict**: *A child's sexual interest in his or her opposite-sex parent, typically resolved through identification with the same-sex parent*

Identification: *A child's attempt to be similar to his or her same-sex parent*

Penis envy: *According to Freud, a girl's wish, developing around age 3, that she had a penis*

TABLE 11-1

The stages of personality development according to Freud's psychoanalytic theory

STAGE	AGE	MAJOR CHARACTERISTICS
Oral	Birth to 12–18 months	Interest in oral gratification from sucking, eating, mouthing, biting
Anal	12–18 months to 3 years	Gratification from expelling and withholding feces; coming to terms with society's controls relating to toilet training
Phallic	3 to 5–6 years	Interest in the genitals; coming to terms with oedipal conflict, leading to identification with same-sex parent
Latency	5–6 years to adolescence	Sexual concerns largely unimportant
Genital	Adolescence to adulthood	Reemergence of sexual interest and establishment of mature sexual relationships

Latency (LAY ten see) **period**: *According to Freud, the period, between the phallic stage and puberty, during which children's sexual concerns are temporarily put aside*

Genital (JEN ih tul) **stage**: *According to Freud, a period from puberty until death, marked by mature sexual behavior, i.e., sexual intercourse*

Following the resolution of the Oedipal conflict, typically at around age 5 or 6, children move into the **latency period** which lasts until puberty. During this period, not much of interest is occurring, according to Freud; sexual concerns are more or less put to rest, even in the unconscious. Then, during adolescence, sexual feelings reemerge, marking the start of the final period, the **genital stage**, which extends until death. The focus in the genital stage is on mature, adult sexuality, which Freud defined as sexual intercourse.

Anxiety (ang ZI eh tee): *A feeling of apprehension or tension*

Neurotic (ner AH tik) **anxiety**: *Anxiety caused when irrational impulses from the id threaten to become uncontrollable*

Defense mechanisms: *Unconscious strategies people use to reduce anxiety by concealing its source from themselves and others*

Repression: *The primary defense mechanism, in which unacceptable id impulses are pushed back into the unconscious*

Dealing with the Dangers from Within: Defense Mechanisms Freud's efforts to describe and theorize about the underlying dynamics of personality and its development were motivated by very practical problems that his patients faced in dealing with **anxiety**, an intense, negative emotional experience. According to Freud, anxiety is a danger signal to the ego. Although anxiety may arise from realistic fears—such as seeing a poisonous snake about to strike—it may also occur in the form of **neurotic anxiety**, in which irrational impulses emanating from the id threaten to burst through and become uncontrollable. Because anxiety, naturally, is unpleasant, Freud suggested that people develop a range of defense mechanisms to deal with it. **Defense mechanisms** are unconscious strategies people use to reduce anxiety by concealing the source from themselves and others.

The primary defense mechanism is **repression**, in which unacceptable id impulses are pushed back into the unconscious. Repression is the most direct method of dealing with anxiety; instead of dealing with an anxiety-producing impulse on a conscious level, one simply ignores it. For example, a person who feels hatred for his father might repress these feelings: They would remain lodged within the id, since acknowledging them would be so anxiety-provoking. This does not mean, however, that they would have no effect: The true feelings might be revealed through dreams, slips of the tongue, or symbolically, in some other fashion. He might, for instance, have difficulty with authority figures, such as teachers, and do poorly in school. Alternatively, he might join the military, where he could give harsh orders to others and never have them questioned.

Regression: *Behavior reminiscent of an earlier stage of development, carried out in order to have fewer demands put upon oneself*

If repression is ineffective in keeping anxiety at bay, other defense mechanisms may be called upon. For example, **regression** might be used, whereby people behave as if they were at an earlier stage of development. By retreating to a younger age—for instance by complaining and throwing tantrums—they might succeed in having fewer demands put upon them.

Displacement: *The expression of an unwanted feeling or thought, directed toward a weaker person instead of a more powerful one*

Rationalization: *A defense mechanism whereby people justify a negative situation in a way that protects their self-esteem*

Denial: *A refusal to accept or acknowledge anxiety-producing information*

Anyone who has ever been angered by a professor and then returned to the dorm and yelled at his or her roommate knows what displacement is all about. In **displacement**, the expression of an unwanted feeling or thought is redirected from a more threatening, powerful person to a weaker one. A classic case is yelling at one's secretary after being criticized by the boss.

Rationalization, another defense mechanism, occurs when we distort reality by justifying what happens to us: We come up with explanations that allow us to protect our self-esteem. If you've ever heard someone saying that he didn't mind being stood up for a date because he really had a lot of work to do that evening, you might be seeing rationalization at work.

In **denial**, a person simply refuses to accept or acknowledge an anxiety-producing piece of information. For example, when told that his wife has died in an automobile crash, a husband may at first deny the tragedy, saying that there must be some mistake, and only gradually come to conscious acceptance

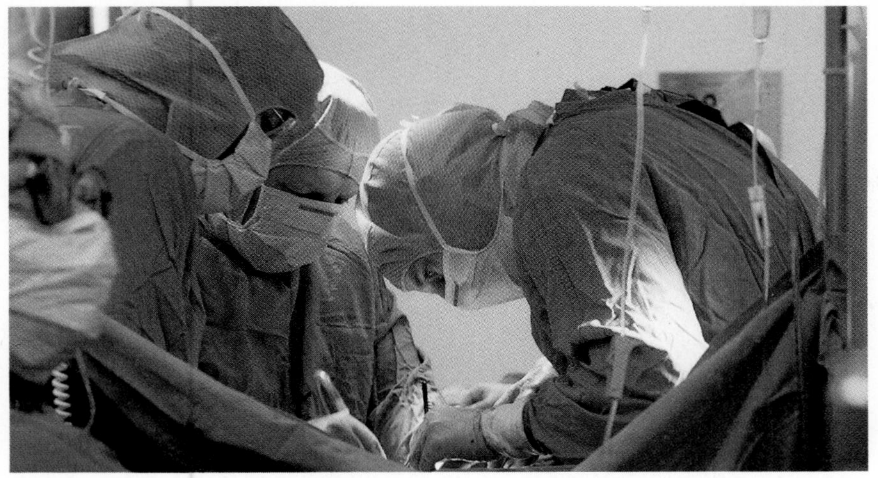

One of the healthier defense mechanisms is sublimation, in which people channel their unwanted impulses into socially approved behavior. For example, Freud might suggest that a surgeon's choice of profession is influenced by unconscious aggressive tendencies. (*M. Feinberg/The Picture Cube*)

that she actually has been killed. In extreme cases, denial may linger; the husband may continue to expect that his wife will return home.

Projection is a means of protecting oneself by attributing unwanted impulses and feelings to someone else. For example, a man who feels sexually inadequate may complain to his wife that *she* is sexually inept.

Projection: *A defense mechanism in which people attribute their own inadequacies or faults to someone else*

Finally, one defense mechanism that Freud considered to be particularly healthy and socially acceptable is **sublimation**. In sublimation, people divert unwanted impulses into socially approved thoughts, feelings, or behaviors. For example, a person with strong feelings of aggression may become a butcher—and hack away at meat instead of people. Sublimation allows the butcher the opportunity not only to release the psychic tension, but to do so in a way that is socially acceptable.

Sublimation (sub lim A shun): *A defense mechanism, considered healthy by Freud, in which a person diverts unwanted impulses into socially acceptable thoughts, feelings, or behaviors*

All of us employ defense mechanisms to some degree according to Freudian theory. Yet some people use them so much that a large amount of psychic energy must be constantly directed toward hiding and rechanneling unacceptable impulses, making everyday living difficult. In this case, the result is a neurosis, a term (referring to mental disorders produced by anxiety) which we will discuss further in the chapter on abnormal behavior.

Evaluating Freudian Theory More so than almost any other psychological theory we have discussed, Freud's personality theory presents an elaborate and complicated set of propositions—some of which are so removed from everyday explanations of behavior that they may appear difficult to accept. But laypersons are not the only ones to be concerned about the validity of Freud's theory; personality psychologists, too, have been quick to criticize its inadequacies.

Among the most compelling criticisms is the lack of scientific data to support his theory. Although there are a wealth of individual assessments of particular people that *seem* to support the theory, there is a lack of definitive evidence showing that the personality is structured and operates along the lines Freud laid-out—due, in part, to the fact that Freud's conception of personality is built on unobservable abstractions. Moreover, while we can readily employ Freudian theory in after-the-fact explanations, it is extremely difficult to predict how certain developmental difficulties will be displayed in the adult. For instance, if a person is fixated at the anal stage, he might, according to Freud, be unusually

To Jung, *Star Wars* characters Darth Vader and Luke Skywalker would represent broad archetypes of both father and son and evil and good. (*The Empire Strikes Back, © Lucasfilm Ltd. (LFL), 1980. All rights reserved. Courtesy of Lucasfilm Ltd.*)

messy—or he might be unusually neat. His theory provides no guidance for predicting which manifestation of the difficulty will occur. Freudian theory produces good history, then, but not such good science. Finally, Freud made his observations—albeit insightful ones—and derived his theory from a limited population: primarily upper-class Austrian women living in the strict, puritanical era of the early 1900s. How far can one generalize beyond this population is a matter of considerable question.

Despite these criticisms, which cannot be dismissed, Freud's theory has had an enormous impact on the field of psychology and indeed on all of western thinking. The concepts of the unconscious, anxiety, and defense mechanisms and the notion that adult psychological difficulties have their roots in childhood experiences have permeated people's views of the world and their understanding of the causes of their own behavior and that of others. Moreover, psychoanalytic theory spawned a significant method of treating psychological disturbances, as we discuss further in Chapter 13. For these reasons, then, Freud's psychoanalytic theory remains a significant contribution to our understanding of personality.

Revising Freud: The Neo-Freudian Psychoanalysts

Neo-Freudian psychoanalysts (neo-Freudians): *Theorists who place greater emphasis than did Freud on the functions of the ego and its influence on our daily activities*

One particularly important outgrowth of Freud's theorizing was the work done by a series of successors who were trained in traditional Freudian theory but who later strayed from some of the major points of the original theory. These theorists are known as **neo-Freudian psychoanalysts**.

The neo-Freudians placed greater emphasis than did Freud on the functions of the ego, suggesting that it had more control than the id over day-to-day activities. They also paid greater attention to social factors and the effects of society and culture on personality development. Carl Jung, for example, who initially adhered closely to Freud's thinking, later rejected the notion of the primary importance of unconscious sexual urges—a key notion of Freudian theory—and instead looked at the primitive urges of the unconscious more positively. He suggested that people had a **collective unconscious**, a set of influences we inherit from our own particular ancestors, the whole human race, and even animal ancestors from the distant past. This collective unconscious is shared by everyone, and is displayed by behavior that is common across diverse cultures,

Collective unconscious: *A concept developed by Jung proposing that we inherit certain personality characteristics from our ancestors and the human race as a whole*

such as love of mother, belief in a supreme being, and even behavior as specific as fear of snakes.

Jung went on to propose that the collective unconscious contained **archetypes**, universal symbolic representations of a particular person, object, or experience. For instance, there is a mother archetype, which contains both our experiences with our own mothers and reflections of our ancestors' relationship with mother figures. The existence of such an archetype is suggested by the prevalence of mothers in art, religion, literature, and mythology. (Think of the Virgin Mary, Earth Mother, wicked stepmothers of fairy tales, Mother's Day, and so forth!) To Jung, these archetypes play an important role in determining our day-to-day reactions to stimuli. Jung might, for example, attribute the popularity of such movies as *Star Wars* to their use of broad archetypes of good and evil (the Force versus the Empire), father and son (Luke Skywalker versus Darth Vader), and several others.

Archetypes (ARK eh types): *According to Jung, universal symbolic representations of a particular person, object, or experience*

To Alfred Adler, another important neo-Freudian psychoanalyst, Freudian theory's emphasis on sexual needs was misplaced. Instead, Adler proposed that the primary motivation behind human behavior was a striving for superiority, an attempt to achieve perfection. Adler used the term **inferiority complex** to describe the phenomenon in which adults have not been able to overcome the feelings of inferiority that they had as children when they were physically small and limited in their knowledge about the world. Early social relationships with parents have an important effect on how well children are able to outgrow feelings of personal inferiority and instead orient themselves toward attaining more socially useful goals of perfecting society—rather than themselves.

Inferiority complex: *A phenomenon whereby adults have continuing feelings of weakness and insecurity*

RECAP AND REVIEW I

Recap

- Psychoanalytic theory proposes that many deeply felt emotions and thoughts are found in the unconscious, the part of personality of which a person is unaware. Personality is structured into three components: the id, the ego, and the superego.
- According to psychoanalytic theory, personality develops during a series of stages in which sexual energy is centered around a particular part of the body. The stages are the oral, anal, phallic (which leads to the oedipal conflict), latency, and genital stages.
- Defense mechanisms are unconscious strategies people use to reduce anxiety by concealing its source. Among the most important are repression, regression, displacement, rationalization, denial, projection, and sublimation.
- Among the neo-Freudian psychoanalysts who built and modified psychoanalytic theory are Jung, who developed the concepts of the collective unconscious and archetypes, and Adler, who coined the term "inferiority complex."

Review

1. The part of the personality of which we are unaware is the
a. oral stage **b.** conscience **c.** animus **d.** unconscious

2. Match each of the following with its description:

a. ____ Id	1. Diverting unwanted impulses into socially accepted behaviors
b. ____ Ego	2. The personality's decision maker
c. ____ Superego	3. The distortion of reality to protect self-esteem
d. ____ Sublimation	4. Feelings of inadequacy based on one's life position
e. ____ Archetypes	5. Attachment to some form of gratification
f. ____ Inferiority complex	6. Unconscious cravings for pleasure
g. ____ Rationalization	7. Universal symbolic representations of people, objects, or experiences
h. ____ Fixation	8. The component of the personality responsible for moral behavior

3. Roger is the kind of person who is always punctual and orderly—so much so that his lifestyle is very rigid. According to Freud, Roger may have experienced fixation during the ________________ stage.
4. Theresa, still reeling from an argument with her husband, yells at her young son when he accidentally spills his juice, and sends him to his room. The defense mechanism employed by Theresa is called
   a. repression **b.** regression **c.** displacement **d.** projection
5. An intense, negative emotional experience that serves as a danger signal to the ego is ________________.
6. The idea of a collective unconscious was suggested by Alfred Adler. True or false?
7. Which of the following theorists suggested that our primary motivation is a striving for superiority?
   a. Freud **b.** Allport **c.** Jung **d.** Adler

(Answers to review questions are at the bottom of page 372.)

IN SEARCH OF PERSONALITY: TRAIT, LEARNING, AND HUMANISTIC APPROACHES

"Tell me about Roger, Sue," said Wendy.

"Oh, he's just terrific. He's the friendliest guy I know—goes out of his way to be nice to everyone. He hardly ever gets mad. He's just so even-tempered, no matter what's happening. And he's really smart, too. About the only thing I don't like is that he's always in such a hurry to get things done; he seems to have boundless energy, much more than I have."

"He sounds great to me, especially in comparison to Richard," replied Wendy. "He is so self-centered and arrogant it drives me crazy. I sometimes wonder why I ever started going out with him."

Friendly. Even-tempered. Smart. Energetic. Self-centered. Arrogant.

If we were to analyze the conversation printed above, the first thing we would notice is that it is made up of a series of trait characterizations of the two people being discussed. In fact, most of our understanding of the reasons behind others' behavior is based on the premise that people possess certain traits that are assumed to be consistent across different situations. A number of formal theories of personality employ variants of this approach. We turn now to a discussion of these and other personality theories, all of which provide alternatives to the psychoanalytic emphasis on unconscious processes in determining behavior.

Labeling Personality: Trait Theories

If someone were to ask you to characterize another person, it is probable that you—like the two people in the conversation just presented—would come up with a list of their personal qualities, as you see them. But how would you know which of these qualities were most important in determining that person's behavior?

Personality psychologists have asked similar questions themselves. In order to answer them, they have developed a sophisticated model of personality known as **trait theory**. **Traits** are relatively enduring dimensions of personality characteristics along which people differ from one another.

Trait theory: *A model that seeks to identify the basic traits necessary to describe personality*

Traits: *Enduring dimensions of personality characteristics differentiating people from one another*

Trait theorists do not assume that some people have a trait and others do not; rather, they propose that all people have certain traits, but that the degree to which the trait applies to a specific person varies and can be quantified. For instance, you might be relatively friendly, while I might be relatively unfriendly.

But we both have a "friendliness" trait, although you would be quantified with a higher score and I with a lower one. By taking this approach, the major challenge for trait theorists has been to identify the specific primary traits necessary to describe personality—and, as we shall see, different theorists have come up with surprisingly different sets.

Getting Down to Basics: Allport's Trait Theory When Gordon Allport sat down with an unabridged dictionary in the 1930s, he found some 18,000 separate terms that could be used to describe personality. But which of these were the most crucial?

Allport answered this question by suggesting that there were three basic categories of traits: cardinal, central, and secondary (Allport, 1961, 1966). A **cardinal trait** is a single characteristic that directs most of a person's activities. For instance, a Don Juan is motivated to seduce every woman he meets; another person might be totally driven by power needs. Most people, however, do not develop all-encompassing cardinal traits; instead, they possess a handful of central traits that make up the core of personality. **Central traits**, such as honesty or sociability, are the major characteristics of the individual; they usually number from five to ten in any one person. Finally, **secondary traits** are characteristics that affect behavior in fewer situations and are less influential than central or cardinal traits. For instance, a preference for ice cream or a dislike of modern art would be considered a secondary trait.

Cardinal trait: *A single personality trait that directs most of a person's activities (e.g., greed, lust, kindness)*

Central traits: *A set of major characteristics that make up the core of a person's personality*

Secondary traits: *Less important personality traits (e.g., preferences for certain clothes or movies) that do not affect behavior as much as central and cardinal traits do*

Factoring Out Personality: The Theories of Cattell and Eysenck More recent attempts at discovering the primary traits have centered on a statistical technique known as factor analysis. **Factor analysis** is a method for combining

Factor analysis: *A statistical technique for combining traits into broader, more general patterns of consistency*

TABLE 11-2

The sixteen trait dimensions in Cattell's trait theory of personality

LOW SCORES	HIGH SCORES
1. Sizia: reserved, detached, aloof	Affecta: outgoing, warmhearted
2. Low intelligence: dull	High intelligence: bright
3. Low ego strength: agitated, emotionally unstable	High ego strength: calm, emotionally stable
4. Submissiveness: humble, docile	Dominance: assertive, competitive
5. Desurgency: sober, serious	Surgency: happy-go-lucky, fun-loving
6. Weak superego: ignores rules, immoral	Strong superego: conscientious, moral
7. Threctia: shy, timid	Parmia: adventurous, bold
8. Harria: tough-minded, self-reliant	Premsia: tender-minded, sensitive
9. Alaxia: trusting, accepting	Protension: suspicious, rejecting
10. Praxernia: practical, down-to-earth	Autia: imaginative, head-in-the-clouds
11. Artlessness: forthright, socially awkward	Shrewdness: astute, socially skilled
12. Untroubled adequacy: secure, self-assured	Guilt proneness: apprehensive, self-blaming
13. Conservatism: conservative, traditional	Radicalism: liberal, free-thinking
14. Group adherence: joins groups, follows others	Self-sufficiency: independent, self reliant
15. Low self-sentiment integration: uncontrolled, impulsive	High self-sentiment integration: controlled, compulsive
16. Low ergic tension: relaxed, composed	High ergic tension: tense, frustrated

Source: Irwin, 1980.

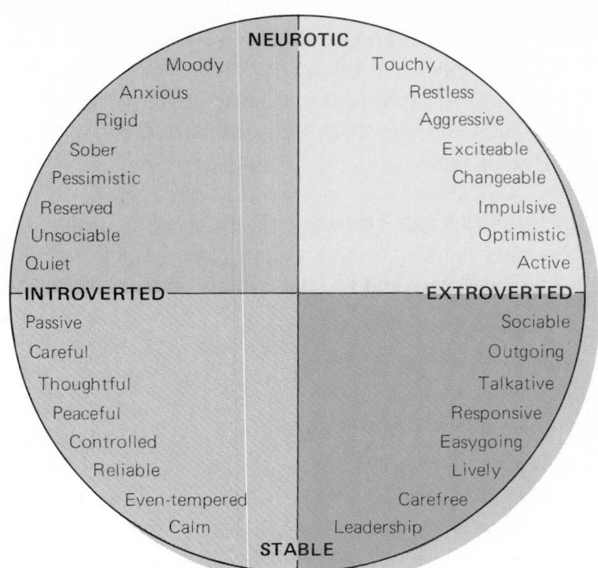

Figure 11-2
According to Eysenck, personality can be viewed as lying along two major dimensions: introversion-extroversion and neuroticism-stability. Other personality characteristics can be ordered along the circular figure depicted here. (*Source: Eysenck, 1973.*)

descriptions of many different individual traits into broad, overall patterns of consistency.

Surface traits: *According to Cattell, clusters of a person's related behaviors that can be observed in a given situation*

Source traits: *The sixteen basic dimensions of personality that Cattell identified as the root of all behavior*

Raymond Cattell (1965) suggested that the characteristics that can be observed in a given situation represent **surface traits**, clusters of related behaviors such as assertiveness or gregariousness. Yet these surface traits are merely representations of more fundamental **source traits**. Source traits are the sixteen basic dimensions of personality that Cattell identified as being at the root of all behavior. These traits are described in Table 11-2.

Introversion-extroversion: *According to Eysenck, a dimension of personality traits encompassing the shyest to the most sociable people*

Neuroticism-stability: *Eysenck's personality spectrum encompassing people from the moodiest to the most even-tempered*

Although he also used the method of factor analysis to identify patterns within traits, Hans Eysenck (1975), another trait theorist, came to a very different conclusion about the nature of personality. He found that personality could be best described in terms of two basic dimensions: **introversion-extroversion** and **neuroticism-stability**. On the one extreme of the introversion-extroversion dimension are people who are quiet, careful, thoughtful, and restrained (the introverts), and on the other are those who are outgoing, sociable, and active (the extroverts). Independently of that, people can be rated as neurotic (moody, touchy, sensitive) or stable (calm, reliable, even-tempered); see Figure 11-2. By evaluating people along these two dimensions, Eysenck has been able to make accurate predictions of behavior in a number of situations.

Which Theorist's Traits Are the Right Traits?: Evaluating Trait Theories of Personality We have seen that trait theorists describing personality have come to quite different conclusions about which traits are the most fundamental and descriptive. The difficulty in determining which of the theories is most accurate has led many psychologists to question the validity of trait conceptions of personality in general.

Actually, there is an even more fundamental difficulty with trait approaches. Even if we are able to identify a set of primary traits, we are left with little

---

ANSWERS TO REVIEW QUESTIONS

Review I: **1.** d **2.** a. 6; b. 2; c. 8; d. 1; e. 7; f. 4; g. 3; h. 5 **3.** Anal **4.** c **5.** Anxiety **6.** False **7.** d more than a label or description of personality—rather than an explanation of behavior. If we say that someone donates money to charity because he or she has the trait of "generosity," we still do not know *why* the person became generous in the first place, or the reasons for generosity being displayed in a given situation. Traits, then, provide nothing in the way of explanation of behavior, but are merely descriptive labels.

Perhaps the biggest problem with trait conceptions is one that is fundamental to the entire area of personality: Is behavior really as consistent over different situations as trait conceptions would imply? How, for instance, would a trait theorist explain Michelle LeBlanc's behavior in the three situations described at the beginning of this chapter? Trying to answer such questions has provided personality theory with one of its most vexing and controversial problems, as we discuss in the Cutting Edge box.

Explaining the Outer Life, Ignoring the Inner Life: Learning Theories of Personality

While psychoanalytic and trait theories concentrate on the inner person—the stormy fury of an unobservable but powerful id or a hypothetical but critical set

THE CUTTING EDGE

IS PERSONALITY A MYTH?:

Personality versus Situational Factors

When personality psychologist Walter Mischel began to review the literature on the strength of the relationship between people's personality traits and their behavior, he found a curious thing: Broad personality traits could be used to explain only a minor, insignificant portion of behavior. Instead, it seemed to him that most behavior could be explained primarily by the nature of the situation in which the people found themselves—not by their personalities (Mischel, 1968).

Mischel's views fanned the flames of a raging controversy that continues to be one of the major issues dividing personality theorists: the degree to which people's behavior is caused by personality versus situational factors. On one side of the controversy are traditional personality theorists who argue that traits, if measured appropriately, provide a valid explanation of behavior across diverse situations. For example, Seymour Epstein (Epstein & O'Brien, 1985) has argued that it is necessary to consider behavior over repeated settings and times to get a true picture of the degree of consistency displayed. When this has been done, by assessing a group of subjects repeatedly over a period of months, there have been strong indications of consistency, contrary to Mischel's suggestions.

In response, Mischel has argued that while his critics may have demonstrated consistency in personality over time, they have not shown consistency across situations. For instance, Jack may be verbally aggressive toward his staff day in and day out, thereby showing consistency over time, without ever being verbally aggressive toward his boss—demonstrating *in*consistency over situations—as Michelle LeBlanc was shown to do at the beginning of the chapter. It is this inconsistency across situations that makes personality-trait approaches suspect to Mischel (Mischel, 1984; Mischel & Peake, 1982).

While this controversy regarding the degree to which personality traits provide accurate predictions of behavior across different situations shows no signs of abating, it has focused attention on some of the fundamental issues surrounding personality. Moreover, as a result of the controversy, personality theorists have begun to shift their attention toward person-situation interactions—how the specific characteristics of a situation will influence the behavior of an individual with a specific type of personality (Magnusson & Endler, 1977, Pervin, 1985). By focusing attention on the nature of such person-situation interactions, personality psychologists are likely to be able to develop a more accurate portrait of the role of personality in everyday life.

of traits—learning theories of personality focus on the outer person. In fact, to a strict learning theorist, personality is simply the sum of learned responses to the external environment. Internal events such as thoughts, feelings, and motivations are ignored; while their existence is not denied, learning theorists say that personality is best understood by looking at features of a person's environment.

According to the most influential of the learning theorists, B. F. Skinner (whom we discussed first in terms of operant conditioning in Chapter 4), personality is a collection of learned behavior patterns (Skinner, 1975). Similarities in responses across different situations are caused by similar patterns of reinforcement that have been received in such situations in the past. If I am sociable both at parties and at meetings, then, it is because I have been reinforced previously for displaying social behaviors—not because I am fulfilling some unconscious wish based on experiences during my childhood or because I have an internal trait of sociability.

Strict learning theorists such as Skinner are less interested in the consistencies in behavior across situations, however, than in ways of modifying behavior. In fact, their view is that humans are infinitely changeable; if one is able to control and modify the patterns of reinforcers in a situation, behavior that other theorists would view as stable and unyielding can be changed, and ultimately improved. These learning theorists, then, are optimistic in their attitudes about the potential for resolving personal and societal problems through treatment strategies based on learning theory—methods we will discuss further in Chapter 13.

Where Freud Meets Skinner: Dollard and Miller's Stimulus-Response Theory Not all learning theories of personality take such a strict view in rejecting the importance of what is "inside" the person by focusing solely on the "outside." John Dollard and Neal Miller (1950) are two theorists who tried to meld psychoanalytic notions with traditional stimulus-response learning theory in an ambitious and influential explanation of personality.

Dollard and Miller translated Freud's notion of the pleasure principle—trying to maximize one's pleasure and minimize one's pain—into terms more suitable for learning theory by suggesting that both biological *and* learned drives energize an organism. If the consequence of a particular behavior is a reduction in drive, the drive reduction is viewed as reinforcing, which in turn increases the probability of the behavior occurring again in the future.

Learned not-thinking: *Dollard and Miller's notion that unpleasant thoughts can be repressed, eliminating negative feelings that are otherwise present*

According to Dollard and Miller, the Freudian notion of repression, in which anxiety-producing thoughts are pushed into the unconscious, can be looked at instead as an example of **learned not-thinking**. Suppose the thought of sexual intercourse makes you anxious. Freud might propose that you would deal with the anxiety by avoiding conscious thought about intercourse and instead relegating the idea to your unconscious—i.e., repressing the thought. In contrast, Dollard and Miller might suggest that "not thinking" about the topic will become reinforcing to you because you find that it leads to a reduction in the unpleasant state of anxiety that thinking about it evokes. "Not thinking," then, will become an increasingly likely behavior.

Social learning theory (of personality): *The theory that suggests that personality develops through observational learning*

Where the Inner Person Meets the Outer One: Social Learning Theories of Personality Unlike other learning theories of personality, **social learning theory** emphasizes the influence of a person's thoughts, feelings, expectations, and values in determining personality. According to Albert Bandura, the main proponent of this point of view, we are able to foresee the possible outcomes of certain behaviors in a given setting without actually having to carry them out. This takes place mainly through the mechanism of **observational learning**—viewing the actions of others and observing the consequences (Bandura, 1977).

Observational learning: *Learning that is the result of viewing the actions of others and observing the consequences*

More so than other learning theories, social learning theory considers how we can modify our own personalities through the exercise of self-reinforcement. We are constantly judging our own behavior based on our internal expectations and standards, and then providing ourselves with cognitive rewards or punishments. For instance, a person who cheats on her income tax may mentally punish herself, feeling guilty and displeased with herself. If, just before mailing her tax return, she corrects her "mistake," the positive feelings she will experience will be rewarding and will serve to reinforce her view of herself as a law-abiding citizen.

Evaluating Learning Theories of Personality By ignoring the internal processes that are uniquely human, traditional learning theorists such as Skinner have been accused of oversimplifying personality so much that the concept becomes meaningless. In fact, reducing behavior to a series of stimuli and responses and excluding thoughts and feelings from the realm of personality leaves learning theorists practicing an unrealistic and inadequate form of science, at least in the eyes of their critics.

Of course, some of these criticisms are blunted by social learning theory, which explicitly considers the role of cognitive processes in personality. Still, all learning theories share a highly deterministic view of human behavior, a view that maintains behavior is shaped primarily by external forces. In the eyes of some critics, **determinism** disregards the ability of people to take control of their behavior.

Determinism: *The view that suggests that behavior is shaped primarily by factors external to the person*

On the other hand, learning approaches have had a major impact in a variety of ways. For one thing, they have helped make the study of personality an objective, scientific venture by focusing on observable features of people and the environments in which they live. Beyond this, learning theories have produced important, successful means of treating personality disorders. The degree of success these treatments have enjoyed provides confidence that learning theory approaches have merit.

Understanding the Self: Humanistic Theories of Personality

Where, in all these theories of personality, is an explanation for the saintliness of a Mother Teresa, the creativity of a Michelangelo, the brilliance and perseverance of an Einstein? An understanding of such unique individuals—as well as more everyday sorts of people who share some of the same attributes—comes from humanistic theory.

According to humanistic theorists, the theories of personality that we have discussed share a fundamental error in their views of human nature. Instead of seeing people as controlled by unconscious, unseen forces (as does psychoanalytic theory), a set of stable traits (trait theory), or situational reinforcements and punishments (learning theory), **humanistic theory** emphasizes people's basic goodness and their tendency to grow to higher levels of functioning. It is this conscious, self-motivated ability to change and improve, along with people's unique creative impulses, that make up the core of personality.

Humanistic theory (of personality): *The theory that emphasizes people's basic goodness and their natural tendency to rise to higher levels of functioning*

The major representative of the humanistic point of view is Carl Rogers (1971). Rogers suggests that there is a need for positive regard which reflects a

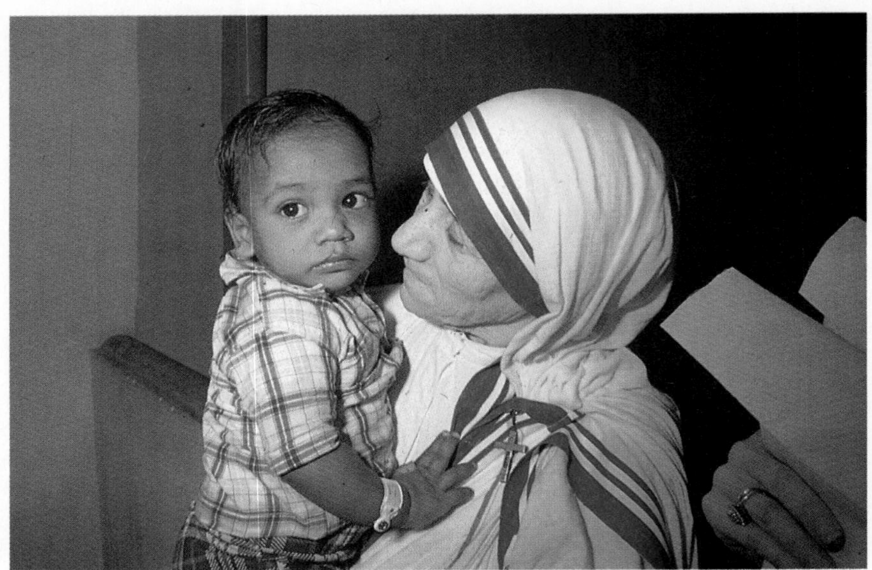

Mother Teresa's selflessness can be explained by humanistic theories of personality. (*Bettmann Newsphotos*)

universal requirement to be loved and respected. Because others provide this positive regard, we grow dependent on them. We begin to see and judge ourselves through the eyes of other people, relying on their values.

Self-concept: *The impression one holds of oneself*

According to Rogers, one outgrowth of placing import on the values of others is that there is often some degree of mismatch between a person's experiences and his or her **self-concept**, or self-impression. If the mismatch is minor, so are the consequences. But if it is great, it will lead to psychological disturbances in daily functioning, such as the experience of frequent anxiety.

Unconditional positive regard: *Supportive behavior from another individual, regardless of one's words or actions*

Rogers suggests that one way of overcoming the discrepancy between experience and self-concept is through the receipt of unconditional positive regard from others—a friend, a spouse, or a therapist. As we will discuss further in Chapter 13, **unconditional positive regard** consists of supportive behavior on the part of an observer, no matter what a person says or does. This support, says Rogers, allows people the opportunity to evolve and grow both cognitively and emotionally as they are able to develop more realistic self-concepts. (See the Try It! box.)

Self-actualization: *A state of self-fulfillment in which people realize their highest potential*

To Rogers and other humanistic personality theorists (such as Abraham Maslow, whose theory of motivation we discussed in Chapter 8), an ultimate goal of personality growth is self-actualization. **Self-actualization** is a state of self-fulfillment in which people realize their highest potential: This, Rogers would argue, occurs when their experience with the world and their self-concept are closely matched. People who are self-actualized accept themselves as they are in reality, which enables them to achieve happiness and fulfillment.

Evaluating Humanistic Theories Although humanistic theories suggest the value of providing unconditional positive regard toward people, unconditional positive regard toward humanistic theories has been less forthcoming from many personality theorists. The criticisms have centered on the difficulty of verifying the basic assumptions of the theory, as well as on the question of whether unconditional positive regard does, in fact, lead to greater personality adjustment.

Humanistic approaches have also been criticized for making the assumption

TRY IT!

ASSESSING YOUR REAL SELF-CONCEPT AND YOUR IDEAL SELF-CONCEPT

The concept of self is central to humanistic personality theory. Yet how well do most of us know ourselves? Few of us take the time to systematically assess our view of ourselves, and to determine how closely our self-concept matches the ideal self to which we aspire.

To get an idea of how well your real self-concept and ideal self-concept match up, try the following exercise. First, quickly place a check mark next to each item that describes you. (Use the first column for your checks.) Be truthful and honest! Next, go back through the list and place a check beside each item, this time in the second column, that describes your ideal self—the kind of person you would like to be. Once again work through the list quickly.

1. Absent-minded ____ ____
2. Anxious ____ ____
3. Artistic ____ ____
4. Attractive ____ ____
5. Capable ____ ____
6. Charming ____ ____
7. Clear-thinking ____ ____
8. Clever ____ ____
9. Confused ____ ____
10. Courageous ____ ____
11. Dissatisfied ____ ____
12. Dreamy ____ ____
13. Emotional ____ ____
14. Energetic ____ ____
15. Enterprising ____ ____
16. Excitable ____ ____
17. Forceful ____ ____
18. Forgetful ____ ____
19. Gentle ____ ____
20. Good-looking ____ ____
21. Handsome ____ ____
22. Hard-headed ____ ____
23. Hasty ____ ____
24. Headstrong ____ ____
25. Hurried ____ ____
26. Imaginitive ____ ____
27. Impatient ____ ____
28. Impulsive ____ ____
29. Industrious ____ ____
30. Ingenious ____ ____
31. Initiating ____ ____
32. Insightful ____ ____
33. Inventive ____ ____
34. Irritable ____ ____
35. Moody ____ ____
36. Nervous ____ ____
37. Original ____ ____
38. Persevering ____ ____
39. Pessimistic ____ ____
40. Polished ____ ____
41. Preoccupied ____ ____
42. Resourceful ____ ____
43. Restless ____ ____
44. Tactful ____ ____
45. Wise ____ ____
46. Witty ____ ____

Now make three lists. In the first, list the terms that are characteristic of your real, but not your ideal, self. In the second, list characteristics of your ideal, but not your real, self. Finally, make a list of the characteristics that apply both to your ideal self and your real self. The first list will tell you things about yourself that are inconsistent with what you would like to be like. The second list gives you a sense of the way you would like to be. Finally, the last list shows you the traits on which you already match your ideal. How well do your ideal and real self-concepts match up?

You also might want to compare yourself with the responses of a broad sample of subjects who answered these questions as part of a study (Gough, Fioravanti, & Lazzari, 1979). For those people, these items were rated as more characteristic of their real selves than their ideal selves: 1, 2, 9, 11, 12, 13, 16, 18, 22, 23, 24, 25, 27, 28, 34, 35, 36, 39, 41, and 43. In comparison, the following items were more characteristic of their ideal selves than their real selves: 3, 4, 5, 6, 7, 8, 10, 14, 15, 17, 19, 20, 21, 26, 29, 30, 31, 32, 33, 37, 38, 40, 42, 44, 45, and 46. (Source: Byrne & Kelley, 1981.)

that people are basically "good"—a notion that is not only unverifiable, but one in which nonscientific values are used to build supposedly scientific theories. Still, the humanistic theories have been important in highlighting the uniqueness of human beings and in guiding the development of a significant form of therapy designed to alleviate psychological difficulties.

Answering the Old Question: Which Theory Is Right?

By now, you have come across this question a number of times in connection with a number of diverse areas of psychology. The response, once again, is the same: This is not an appropriate question to be asking. Each theory looks at somewhat different aspects of personality and holds different premises, and in many cases personality is most reasonably viewed from a number of perspectives simultaneously. Of course, the potential exists that someday there will be a unified theory of personality, but the field has not yet reached that point, and the likelihood of it happening in the near future is slim.

In the meantime, though, it is possible to highlight and compare the major differences between each of the theories. We list below the most important dimensions along which the theories differ:

- The unconscious versus the conscious. Psychoanalytic theory emphasizes the importance of the unconscious; humanistic theory stresses the conscious; and trait and learning theories largely disregard both.
- Nature (genetic factors) versus nurture (environmental factors). Psychoanalytic theory stresses genetic factors; learning theory focuses on the environment; trait theory varies; and humanistic theory stresses the interaction between both in the development of personality.
- Freedom versus determinism. While humanistic theories stress the freedom of individuals to make choices in their lives, other theories stress determinism, the view that behavior is directed and caused by factors outside people's willful control. Determinism is particularly evident in psychoanalytic and learning theories, as well as in most trait theories; in such approaches, people's behavior is assumed to be brought about by factors largely outside of their control.

RECAP AND REVIEW II

Recap

- Traits are relatively enduring dimensions along which people differ from one another. Trait theorists have tried to identify the major traits that characterize personality.
- Allport divided traits into cardinal, central, and secondary traits. Using a statistical technique called factor analysis, Cattell identified surface traits and sixteen basic source traits, while Eysenck found just two major dimensions: introversion-extroversion and neuroticism-stability.
- Learning theories of personality concentrate on how environmental factors shape personality. Among the most important approaches are those of Skinner, Dollard and Miller's stimulus-response theory, and social learning theories.
- Humanistic theories view the core of personality as the ability to change, improve, and be creative in a uniquely human fashion. According to Rogers, personality is influenced by a need for positive regard, reflecting universal requirements for being loved and respected.
- The major characteristics along which personality theories differ include the role of the unconscious versus the conscious, nature (genetic factors) versus nurture (environmental factors), and freedom versus determinism.

Review

1. According to Allport, a ____________ trait is a single characteristic that directs most of a person's activities, while a ____________ trait makes up the core of personality.
2. One explanation of factor analysis is that it
   a. combines individuals' traits into overall patterns
   b. breaks down a personality trait into degrees of positiveness or negativeness
   c. seeks to explain the presence of certain traits
   d. determines an individual's behavior by assessing his or her self-concept
3. Raymond Cattell used surface traits and source traits to explain behaviors based on sixteen personality dimensions. True or false?
4. Laurel is quiet, pensive, and restrained in her social relationships, whereas her roomate Judy is more outgoing, talkative, and socially active. According to Hans Eysenck, Laurel and Judy would vary on the ____________ - ____________ dimension of personality.

5. Learning theorists Dollard and Miller believed that an organism is energized by
   a. a desire for pleasure **b.** the need for a positive self-concept **c.** the need for love and respect **d.** biological and learned drives
6. The notion of unconditional positive regard was proposed by B. F. Skinner in his learning theory of personality. True or false?
7. Match the theory with the appropriate description.

a. ___ Trait theory	1. Emphasizes the role of observation of others in determining personality
b. ___ Learning theory	2. Criticized for its limitations in labeling, but not explaining, personalities
c. ___ Humanistic theory	3. Focuses on observable traits, responses to environment, and behavior modification
d. ___ Social learning theory	4. Begins with the idea that people are basically good
e. ___ Psychoanalytic theory	5. Emphasizes the role of the unconscious

(Answers to review questions are at the bottom of page 380.)

DETERMINING WHAT MAKES YOU SPECIAL: ASSESSING PERSONALITY

How well does the following personality profile fit you?

> You have a need for other people to like and admire you.
>
> You have a tendency to be critical of yourself.
>
> You have a great deal of unused potential that you have not turned to your advantage.
>
> While you have some personality weaknesses, you are generally able to compensate for them.
>
> Your adjustment to the opposite sex has presented problems to you.
>
> More disciplined and self-controlled outside, you tend to be worrisome and insecure inside.
>
> At times you have serious doubts as to whether you have made the right decision or done the right thing.
>
> You prefer a certain amount of change and variety and become dissatisfied when hemmed in by restrictions and limitations.
>
> You do not accept others' statements without satisfactory proof.
>
> You have found it unwise to be too frank in revealing yourself to others.

If you think these statements provide a surprisingly accurate account of your personality, you are not alone: Most college students think that the statements are tailored just to them. In fact, though, the descriptions are intentionally designed to be so vague as to be applicable to just about anyone (Forer, 1949; Russo, 1981).

The ease with which we can agree with such imprecise statements underscores the difficulty in coming up with accurate and meaningful assessments of people's personalities (Johnson, Cain, Falke, Hayman, & Perillo, 1985). Just as trait theorists were faced with the problem of determining what were the most critical and important traits, psychologists interested in assessing personality must be able to define what are the most meaningful measures of discriminating between one person's personality and another's. To do this, they use **psychological tests**, standard measures devised to objectively assess behavior. Such tests are used by psychologists to help people make decisions about their lives and understand more about themselves; they are also employed by researchers interested in the causes and consequences of personality.

Psychological tests: *Standard measures devised to objectively assess behavior*

The Keys to Assessing Personality: Reliability and Validity

When we use a ruler, we expect to find that it measures an inch in the same way as the last time we used it. When we weigh ourselves on the bathroom scale, we hope that the variations we see on the scale are due to changes in our weight and are not errors on the part of the scale (unless the change in weight is in the wrong direction!).

In the same way, we hope that psychological tests have **reliability**—that they measure what they are trying to measure consistently. We need to be sure that each time we administer the test, a person taking the test will get the same results—assuming that nothing about the person has changed relevant to what is being measured.

Reliability: *Consistency in the measurements made by a test*

Suppose, for instance, when you first took the College Boards you scored a 300 on the verbal section of the test. Then, when taking the test again a few months later, you scored a 700. Upon receiving your new score, you might well stop celebrating for a moment to question whether the test is reliable, since it is unlikely that your abilities could have changed enough to raise your score by 400 points.

But suppose your score changed hardly at all, and both times you received a score of about 300. While you couldn't complain about a lack of reliability, if you knew your verbal skills were above average you might be concerned that the test did not adequately measure what it was supposed to measure. The question has now become one of validity rather than of reliability. A test has **validity** when it actually measures what it is supposed to measure.

Validity: *The ability of a test to measure what it is supposed to measure*

Knowing that a test is reliable is no guarantee that it is also valid. For instance, we could devise a very reliable means for measuring the circumference of the skull, if we decided that skull size is related to trustworthiness. But there is certainly no guarantee that the test is valid, since one can assume with little danger of being contradicted that skull size has nothing to do with trustworthiness. In this case, then, we have reliability without validity.

On the other hand, if a test is unreliable, it cannot be valid. Assuming that all other factors—such as a person's motivation, knowledge of the material, health, and so forth—are similar, if someone scores high the first time she takes a specific test and low the second time, the test cannot be measuring what it is supposed to measure, and is therefore both unreliable and invalid.

Test validity and reliability are prerequisites for accurate personality assessment. We turn now to some of the specific sorts of measures used by psychologists in their study of personality.

ANSWERS TO REVIEW QUESTIONS

Review II: **1.** Cardinal, central **2.** a **3.** True **4.** Introversion-extroversion **5.** d **6.** False **7.** a. 2; b. 3; c. 4; d. 1; e. 5

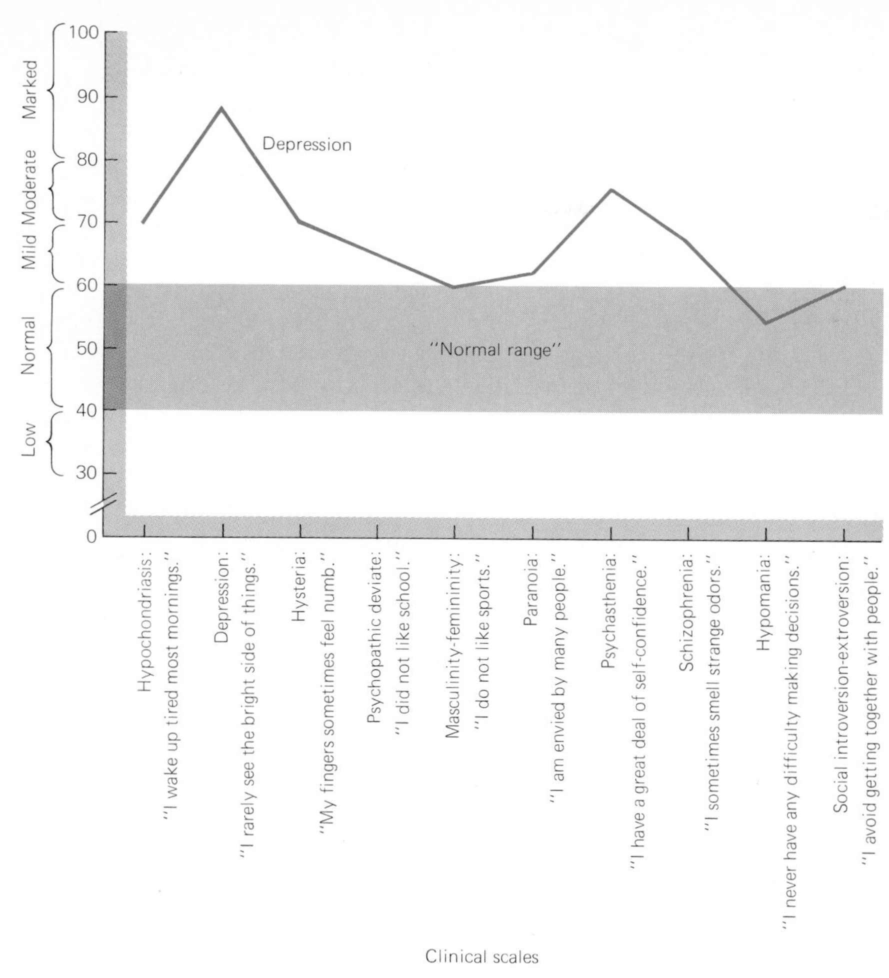

Figure 11-3
A sample profile on the MMPI of a person who has been diagnosed as suffering from severe depression. Sample items from each scale are included with the scale name on the *X* axis. (*Source: Adapted from Kleinmuntz, A67, and Rosen, 1958.*)

Asking a Little to Learn a Lot: Self-Report Measures of Personality

If someone wanted to assess your personality, one method he might use would be to carry out an extensive interview in order to determine the most important events of your childhood, your social relationships, and your successes and failures. Obviously, though, such a technique would be extraordinarily costly in terms of time and effort.

Self-report measures: *A method of gathering data about people by asking them questions about their behavior*

Minnesota Multiphasic Personality Inventory (MMPI): *A test used to identify people with psychological difficulties*

It is also unnecessary. Just as physicians do not need to drain your entire blood supply in order to test it, psychologists can utilize **self-report measures** that ask people about a sample of their range of behaviors in order to infer the presence of particular personality characteristics.

The most frequently used personality test is the **Minnesota Multiphasic Personality Inventory**, or **MMPI**, developed by a group of researchers in the 1940s and later revised (Hathaway, Monachedsi, & Salasin, 1970). Although the original purpose of this measure was to differentiate people with specific sorts of psychological difficulties from those without disturbance, it has been found to predict a variety of other behaviors. For instance, college students' MMPI scores have been shown to be good predictors of whether a person will marry within ten years and whether he or she will get an advanced degree (Dworkin & Widom, 1977).

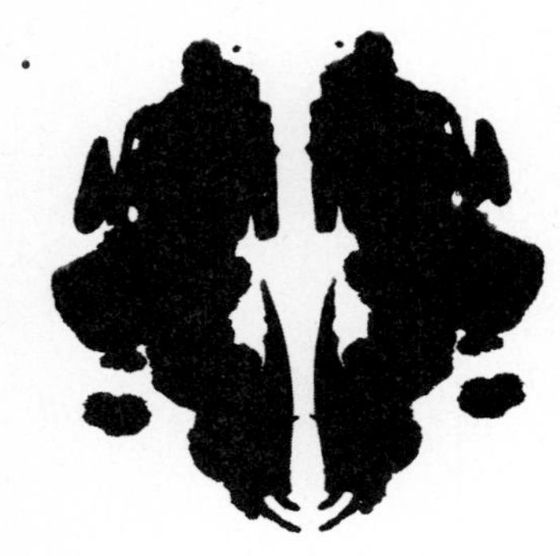

Figure 11-4
This inkblot is similar to the type used in the Rorschach personality test. What do *you* see in it?

The test itself consists of a series of 550 statements to which a person responds "true," "false," or "cannot say." The questions cover a variety of issues, ranging from mood ("I am happy most of the time") to occupational questions ("I would like to be a soldier") to physical and psychological health ("I am seldom troubled by constipation" and "Someone has control over my mind"). There are no right or wrong answers, of course. Instead, interpretation of the results rests on the pattern of responses. The test yields scores on ten separate scales (see Figure 11-3) plus three scales meant to measure the validity of the respondent's answers. For example, there is a "lie scale" that indicates, from items such as "I can't remember ever having a bad night's sleep," when people are falsifying their responses in order to present themselves more favorably.

How did the authors of the MMPI determine what was indicated by specific patterns of responses? The procedure they used is typical of personality-test construction. When the test was first devised, groups of psychiatric patients with a specific diagnosis, such as depression or schizophrenia, were asked to complete a large number of items. The authors then determined which items best differentiated members of these groups from a comparison group of normal subjects, and these specific items were included in the final version of the test. By systematically carrying out this procedure on groups with different diagnoses, they were able to devise the ten separate scales which identified different forms of abnormal behavior.

When the MMPI is used for the purposes for which it was devised—identification of personality patterns—it has proved to do a reasonably good job (Butcher & Owen, 1978). However, like other personality tests, it presents the opportunity for abuse. For example, employers who use it as a screening tool for job applicants may interpret the results improperly, relying too heavily on the results of individual scales instead of taking into account the overall patterns of results, which require skilled interpretation. Other tests, such as the **California Psychological Inventory** and the **Edwards Personal Preference Schedule** are more appropriately used in employment settings; they can also be used to provide people with information about their personalities, helping them to identify their strengths and weaknesses and to make informed career choices—as we discuss further in the Psychology at Work box.

California Psychological Inventory: *An assessment tool used to identify personality traits*

Edwards Personal Preference Schedule: *An assessment tool used in employment settings*

Looking into the Unconscious: Projective Methods

If you were shown the kind of inkblot seen in Figure 11-4 and asked what it represented to you, you might not think that your impressions would mean very much. But to a psychoanalytic theoretician, your responses to such an ambiguous figure would provide valuable clues to the state of your unconscious, and ultimately to your general personality characteristics.

The inkblot in the figure is representative of **projective personality tests**, in which a person is shown an ambiguous stimulus and asked to describe it or tell a story about it. The responses are then considered to be "projections" of what the person is like.

Projective personality test: *An ambiguous stimulus presented to a person for the purpose of determining personality characteristics*

Rorschach (ROAR shock) **test**: *A test consisting of inkblots of indefinite shapes, the interpretation of which is used to assess personality characteristics*

The best-known projective test is the **Rorschach test**. Devised by Swiss psychiatrist Hermann Rorschach (1924), the test consists of a series of symmetrical stimuli, similar to the one shown in Figure 11-4, that are shown to people who are then asked what the figures represent to them. Their responses are recorded, and through a complex set of clinical judgments on the part of the examiner, people are classified into different personality types. For instance,

PSYCHOLOGY AT WORK

ASSESSMENT COMES TO THE PERSONNEL OFFICE

When H. Parker Sharpe, Inc., a firm selling insurance, considered hiring Larry Lagerhausen, it first administered a standardized personality questionnaire. The test indicated that Lagerhausen would do well—but only if closely supervised and recognized for his achievements.

"So Mr. Sharpe put me in a plush office and treated me like a million-dollar producer," said Lagerhausen. It seems to have worked; in his first six months on the job, he sold $2.2 million worth of insurance, some ten times more than he had sold on his previous job.

The use of personality measures is growing, as employers find that they are helpful not only in selecting employees initially, but in getting the most out of them once they are on the job. Today, companies in the United States are spending about $50 million a year on testing procedures, and the amount is rising annually (*Tuller,* 1985).

One reason for the growth of such tests is the use of computerization. Before the advent of inexpensive microcomputers, many companies had to send test responses to a central scoring facility, waiting as long as two weeks for results. Today, however, scores can be determined immediately through the use of computerized scoring procedures, aiding in timely decision making.

An even more important factor in the growth of testing has been the development of more sophisticated, valid, and bias-free tests. For instance, a group of power companies developed a series of tests for a number of job categories. They now have specific tests to measure decision-making capability and electrical knowledge for systems operators, mechanical comprehension for maintenance workers, and language skills for clerical positions. The power companies estimate that they should save at least $20 million this year alone because of the improvement in employee-selection procedures (*Tuller,* 1985). Another example is provided by the armed forces, which uses personality tests to screen soldiers who work in stressful jobs involving nuclear weaponry.

Given the increasing use of personality measures in employment settings, then, you should not be surprised if the first thing you are given when you apply for a new job is not a traditional job interview, but a personality test.

---

respondents who see a bear in one form are thought to have a strong degree of emotional control, according to the rules developed by Rorschach.

The **Thematic Apperception Test**, or **TAT**, is another well-known projective test. As was described when we discussed achievement motivation in Chapter 8, the TAT consists of a series of pictures about which a person is asked to write a story. The stories are then used to draw inferences about the writer's personality characteristics.

Thematic Apperception Test (TAT): *A test consisting of a series of ambiguous pictures about which a person is asked to write a story, which is then taken to be a reflection of the writer's personality*

By definition, tests with stimuli as ambiguous as the Rorschach and TAT require particular skill and care in their interpretation. In fact, they are often criticized as requiring too much inference on the part of the examiner. However, they are widely used, particularly in clinical settings, and their proponents suggest that their reliability and validity are high.

The Informed Consumer of Psychology: Assessing Personality Assessments

It is not unusual today to be required to take a personality test before being offered a job. Likewise, there are many organizations which—for a hefty fee—will give you a battery of personality tests that purport to steer you toward a career for which your personality is particularly suited.

Before you rely on the results of such testing too heavily—as a potential employee, employer, or consumer of testing services—you should keep the following points in mind:

■ Understand what the test purports to measure. Standard personality measures are accompanied by information that discusses how the test was developed, to whom it is most applicable, and how the results should be interpreted. If possible, you should read the accompanying literature; it will help you understand the meaning of any results.

■ Remember that decisions should not be based solely on the results of any one test. Test results should be interpreted in the context of other information—academic records, social interests, and home and community activities. Without these data, individual scores are relatively uninformative at best, and may even be harmful.

■ Tests are not infallible. The results may be in error; the test may be unreliable or invalid; you may have had a "bad day" when you took the test; the person scoring and interpreting the test may have made a mistake. You should not place undue stock in the results of the single administration of any test.

In sum, it is important to keep in mind the complexity of human behavior—particularly your own. No one test can provide an understanding of the intricacies of someone's personality without considering a good deal more information than can be provided in a single testing session.

RECAP AND REVIEW III

Recap

- Psychological tests are standard measures used to objectively measure behavior. They must be reliable and valid.
- Self-report measures of personality, such as the Minnesota Multiphasic Personality Inventory (MMPI) ask people about a sampling range of their behaviors; the results are then used to infer personality characteristics.
- Projective personality tests such as the Rorschach test and Thematic Apperception Test (TAT) present an ambiguous stimulus, which the person must describe or tell a story about.
- When using the results of personality assessments, it is important to keep in mind what the test is designed to measure and the importance of not relying totally on any single measure or score.

Review

1. The primary application of personality tests is
  a. determining whether or not someone is honest **b.** analyzing someone's qualifications for a particular position
  c. providing an objective measure of behavior **d.** determining whether the taker is depressed or schizophrenic

2. ________________ refers to the consistency with which a test evaluates its takers.

3. ________________ refers to the accuracy with which a test measures the object it proposes to measure.

4. Projective tests have such high reliability and validity that confidence can be placed in a personality evaluation based on a single test. True or false?

5. The Rorschach test employs symmetrical inkblots which resemble specific objects. A subject who sees something different from the typical response is likely to have a psychological disturbance, often requiring treatment. True or false?

(Answers to review questions are at the bottom of page 386.)

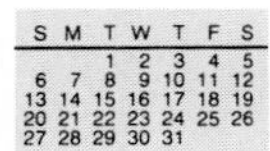

Psychology Looks Toward the 1990s
The Roots of Personality: The Inheritance of Traits

The two identical twins, separated at birth, presented an eerie sight: reunited for a study of twins raised apart, they both wore blue double-breasted shirts, had mustaches, and wire-rimmed glasses. Moreover, both had quick tempers and an unusual sense of humor, exemplified by their enjoyment of startling others by sneezing in elevators (Holden, 1987).

While most traditional theories of personality view parents and the family environment as the primary determinant of personality traits, there is increasing evidence that heredity plays an important role. In fact, a major new study of identical twins reared apart from one another suggests that more than half of the variation in people's traits is brought about by heredity, with a minority of the influence being due to the environment.

In an ongoing study, Auke Tellegen and a group of colleagues at the University of Minnesota have been examining the personality traits of some 350 pairs of twins. Forty-four pairs of the twins were genetically identical but raised apart from one another, providing the opportunity of determining the influence of genetic factors on personality (Tellegen, Lykken, Bouchard, Wilcox, Segal, & Rich, 1988).

Each of the twins was given a battery of tests, including one that measured eleven key personality traits. The results of the test, called the Multidimensional Personality Questionnaire, indicated that in major respects the twins were quite similar in personality to one another. Moreover, certain traits were more influenced by heredity than others. For example, social potency (the degree to which a person takes mastery and leadership roles in social situations) and traditionalism (the following of authority) had particularly strong genetic components, while achievement and social closeness had relatively weak genetic components.

Other studies support Tellegen's findings. For example, the expression of both altruism and aggression are affected by heredity (Rushton, Fulker, Neale, Nias, & Eysenck, 1986). Even human sexuality and political attitudes—at least in terms of basic conservatism and authoritarianism—are related to genetic factors (Eysenck, 1976; Eaves & Eysenck, 1974).

It seems, then, that genetics play an important role in determining an individual's personality. Does this mean that parental influence and other environmental factors are of only minor importance? The answer is a clear "no," since parents and other figures in the child's environment probably shape the extent to which traits produced by heredity assert themselves. It is possible, for instance, to reduce the degree of self-absorption in children who are high in that trait by exposing them to constructive experiences that involve them with other children. Similarly, highly assertive children might have their assertiveness reduced through experiences that make them more aware of the feelings of others. Still, if the current data are valid, it seems that it might be a difficult task to take children with a disposition toward timidity and turn them into unusually brave ones.

LOOKING BACK

1. In this chapter, we have examined characteristics and behaviors that make people different from one another—those that psychologists consider to be at the root of personality. More formally, personality is thought of in two different, but related, ways: First, it refers to the characteristics that differentiate one person from another. Second, it provides a means of explaining the stability in people's behavior that leads them to act uniformly both in different situations and over extended periods of time.

2. According to psychoanalysts, much of behavior is caused by parts of personality that are found in the unconscious, and of which we are unaware. According to Freud, the major psychoanalytic theorist, personality is composed of the id, the ego, and the superego. The id is the unorganized, inherited part of personality whose purpose is to immediately reduce tensions relating to hunger, sex, aggression, and other primitive impulses according to the pleasure principle. The ego operates according to the reality principle, in which instinctual energy is restrained in order to maintain the safety of the individual and to help the person be a member of society. The ego is the rational "executive" of personality, thinking and solving problems within the constraints of the world. The superego represents the rights and wrongs of society. It consists of the conscience, which prevents us from doing things that are morally wrong, and the ego-ideal, which motivates us to do what is morally correct.

3. Freud's psychoanalytic theory suggests that personality develops through a series of stages, each of which is associated with a major biological function. The oral stage is the first period, occurring during the first year of life. In this stage, the mouth is the major source of sexual pleasure. Next comes the anal stage, in which the major source of pleasure is the anus. This lasts from approximately age 1 to age 3. The phallic stage follows, with interest focusing on the genitals. At age 5 or 6, near the end of the phallic stage, children experience the Oedipal conflict, a process through which they learn to identify with the same-sex parent by acting as much like that parent as possible. Then follows a latency period lasting until puberty, after which people move into the genital stage, a period of mature sexuality.

4. Defense mechanisms provide a means for dealing with anxiety relating to impulses from the id. They provide people with unconscious strategies to reduce anxiety by concealing the source of anxiety from themselves and others. The most common defense mechanisms include repression, regression, displacement, rationalization, denial, projection, and sublimation.

5. Freud's psychoanalytic theory has provoked a number of criticisms. These include a lack of supportive scientific data, the theory's inadequacy in making predictions, and its limitations because of the restricted population on which it is based. Still, the theory remains a pivotal one for psychology, having spawned considerable research and theory. For instance, the neo-Freudian psychoanalytic theorists built on Freud's work, although they placed greater emphasis on the role of the ego, and paid greater attention to social factors in determining behavior.

6. Among the alternatives to psychoanalytic approaches to personality are trait theories, learning theories, and humanistic theories of personality. Trait theories have tried to identify the most basic and relatively enduring dimensions along which people differ from one another—dimensions known as traits. For example, Allport suggested that there were three kinds of traits—cardinal, central, and secondary. Later theorists employed a statistical technique called factor analysis to identify the most crucial traits. Using this method, Cattell identified sixteen basic traits, while Eysenck found two major dimensions: introversion-extroversion and neuroticism-stability.

7. Learning theories of personality concentrate on observable behavior. In fact, to the strict learning theorist, personality is the sum of learned responses to the external environment. In contrast, Dollard and Miller's stimulus-response theory combines psychoanalytic concepts with learning approaches, and social learning theory concentrates on the role of thoughts, feelings, expectations, and values in determining personality. Social learning theory pays particular attention to observational learning.

8. Humanistic theory emphasizes the basic goodness of people and their tendency to grow into higher levels of functioning. It considers as the core of personality a person's unique creative impulses and his or her ability to change and improve. Rogers' concept of the need for positive regard suggests that a universal requirement to be loved and respected underlies personality.

9. Each of the major personality theories speaks to somewhat different aspects of personality, and thus none can be totally accepted—or rejected, for that matter. The theories differ along a number of important dimensions, including the role of the unconscious versus the conscious, nature versus nurture, and freedom versus determinism.

10. Psychological tests are standard measures that objectively measure behavior. They must be reliable, measuring what they are trying to measure consistently, and valid, measuring what they are supposed to measure.

11. Self-report measures ask people about a sample range of their behaviors. These reports are used to infer the presence of particular personality characteristics. The most commonly used self-report measure is the Minnesota Multiphasic Personality Inventory, or MMPI, designed to differentiate people with specific sorts of psychological difficulties from normal individuals. It consists of a series of 550 statements to which a person can agree, disagree, or not respond. The MMPI is a useful test when employed to identify psychological difficulties, as are many other tests. But these test are less useful when applied to purposes for which they were not designed.

12. Projective personality tests present an ambiguous stimulus; the observer's responses are then used to infer information about the observer. The two most frequently used projective tests are the Rorschach, in which reactions to inkblots are employed to classify personality types, and the Thematic Apperception Test, or TAT, in which stories about ambiguous pictures are used to draw inferences about the storyteller's personality. Before using the results of any test, however, it is important to understand what the test is meant to measure. Moreover, decisions should not be based on the results of any single test, for the tests are not infallible.

ANSWERS TO REVIEW QUESTIONS

Review III: **1.** c **2.** Reliability **3.** Validity **4.** False **5.** False

KEY TERMS AND CONCEPTS

personality (360)
psychoanalysts (361)
psychoanalytic theory (362)
unconscious (362)
instinctual drives (362)
id (363)
pleasure principle (363)
ego (363)
reality principle (363)
superego (363)
conscience (363)
ego-ideal (363)
oral stage (364)
fixation (364)
anal stage (364)
phallic stage (365)
Oedipal conflict (365)
identification (365)
penis envy (365)
latency period (366)
genital stage (366)
anxiety (366)
neurotic anxiety (366)
defense mechanisms (366)
repression (366)
regression (366)
displacement (366)
rationalization (366)
denial (366)
projection (367)
sublimation (367)
neo-Freudian psychoanalysts (368)
collective unconscious (368)
archetypes (369)
inferiority complex (369)
trait theory (370)
trait (370)
cardinal trait (371)
central trait (371)
secondary trait (371)
factor analysis (371)
surface trait (372)
source trait (372)
introversion-extroversion (372)
neuroticism-stability (372)
learned not-thinking (374)
social learning theory (374)
observational learning (375)
determinism (375)
humanistic theory (375)
self-concept (376)
unconditional positive regard (376)
self-actualization (376)
psychological tests (380)
reliability (380)
validity (380)
self-report measures (381)
Minnesota Multiphasic Personality Inventory (MMPI) (381)
California Psychological Inventory (382)
Edwards Personal Preference Schedule (382)
projective personality test (382)
Rorschach test (382)
Thematic Apperception Test (TAT) (383)

FOR FURTHER STUDY AND APPLICATION

Feist, J. (1985). *Theories of personality*. New York: Holt.
Hall, C. S., & Lindzey, G. (1978). *Theories of personality* (3rd ed.). New York: Wiley.

Each of these provides a good, comprehensive overview of the various theories of personality.

Freud, S. (1962). *New introductory lectures on psychoanalysis*. London: Hogarth Press.

Here is Freud in an original (although translated from the German) version. It lays out his theory in an understandable fashion, using many examples and case histories.

Aiken, L. R. (1985). *Psychological testing and assessment* (5th ed.). Boston: Allyn & Bacon.

This volume includes descriptions of the frequently used tests and measurements—the number of which is bound to surprise you.

American Psychological Association. (1974). *Standards for educational and psychological tests*. Washington, DC: American Psychological Association.

If you are interested in how psychologists go about creating and using formal tests, this booklet gives you the answers.

PART SIX

ABNORMAL BEHAVIOR AND TREATMENT

We now encounter a man whose psychological difficulties are exemplified by his attempt to assassinate the President. We meet an unusual professor, who lies and cheats without guilt. We also eavesdrop on a psychologist's therapy session, in which a patient with psychological difficulties is receiving treatment.

As you will see in Part Six, psychologists have focused their attention on a variety of issues related to abnormal behavior and treatment. In this section of the book, we consider ways of defining and classifying abnormal behavior, and the methods used to treat it.

In Chapter 12, we examine psychological health, discussing the distinctions between normal and abnormal behavior, the theories of and explanations for abnormality, and the various types of abnormal behavior.

In Chapter 13, we discuss the various techniques used in the treatment of psychological disorders and the ways of distinguishing among them.

CHAPTER 12

ABNORMAL BEHAVIOR

PROLOGUE

LOOKING AHEAD

NORMAL VERSUS ABNORMAL: MAKING THE DISTINCTION

TRY IT! Separating Normal from Abnormal
Approaches to abnormality
Drawing the line on abnormality: The continuum of abnormal and normal behavior
THE CUTTING EDGE. The Mental State of the Union: A Census of Mental Disorder
Recap and review I

MODELS OF ABNORMALITY: FROM SUPERSTITION TO SCIENCE

Abnormal behavior as a biological disease: The medical model
Conflicting cases of abnormal behavior: The psychoanalytic model
When behavior itself is the problem: The behavioral model of abnormal behavior
Putting the person in control: The humanistic model of abnormal behavior
Society as the cause of abnormal behavior: The sociocultural model
Applying the models: The case of John Hinckley
PSYCHOLOGY AT WORK. When Law and Psychology Mix: The Insanity Defense
The informed consumer of psychology: Do you feel abnormal?
Recap and review II

THE ABC'S OF DSM-III: CLASSIFYING TYPES OF ABNORMAL BEHAVIOR

THE MAJOR DISORDERS

Anxiety without reason: Anxiety disorders
When the physical leads to the psychological Somatoform disorders
One becomes two (or more): Dissociative disorders
Recap and review III
The mood is wrong: Affective disorders
PSYCHOLOGY AT WORK. The Special Problems of College Students
When reality is lost: Schizophrenia
THE CUTTING EDGE. Schizophrenia: A Behavioral or a Biological Problem?
Lacking distress: Personality disorders
The informed consumer of psychology: Deciding when you need help
Recap and review IV
PSYCHOLOGY LOOKS TOWARD THE 1990s. The Psychology of Health and Stress

LOOKING BACK

KEY TERMS AND CONCEPTS

FOR FURTHER STUDY AND APPLICATION

PROLOGUE

He had what many would consider the perfect background: caring parents, the best schools, beautiful homes, wealth. Yet, when John Hinckley pulled the trigger, sending a bullet into President Ronald Reagan's chest, his act revealed publicly a troubled, desperately unhappy 26-year-old.

For most of his childhood, Hinckley seemed little different from other children of the upper-middle class. There were minor concerns, though: He rarely cracked a smile, and he was extremely quiet and shy. But when he entered sixth grade the family moved, and his behavior became more obviously unusual. His parents noticed that he made no new friends, and he spent many hours in his room playing his guitar and listening to Beatles records—alone except for two beloved cats. He dreamed of becoming a rock singer, yet never played music with others.

After graduating from high school, during which he had become increasingly uncommunicative and rebellious, he attended college intermittently for seven years. According to his mother, "John just seemed to be going downhill, downhill, downhill, and becoming more and more withdrawn, more and more antisocial, and depressed, and so down on himself. He was always alone."

Hinckley became something of a drifter, moving from place to place across the country. He became entranced with the movie *Taxi Driver* and its female lead, Jodi Foster. He fantasized about becoming president and began to think he was head of a fictitious political organization called the American Front.

In October 1980 he attempted suicide by taking an overdose of drugs. Soon after his unsuccessful attempt, he began trailing President Jimmy Carter around the country, and when Ronald Reagan was elected President, he began following him. Hinckley began to feel, according to psychiatrists, that the only way to end his inner turmoil and pain was through an act of violence—one that would simultaneously make him famous and result in his own death.

His unsuccessful assassination attempt accomplished the former goal, but his wish to end his life was not achieved: He is now residing in St. Elizabeth's Hospital in Washington, D.C., where he was committed after a court case that found him not guilty by reason of insanity.

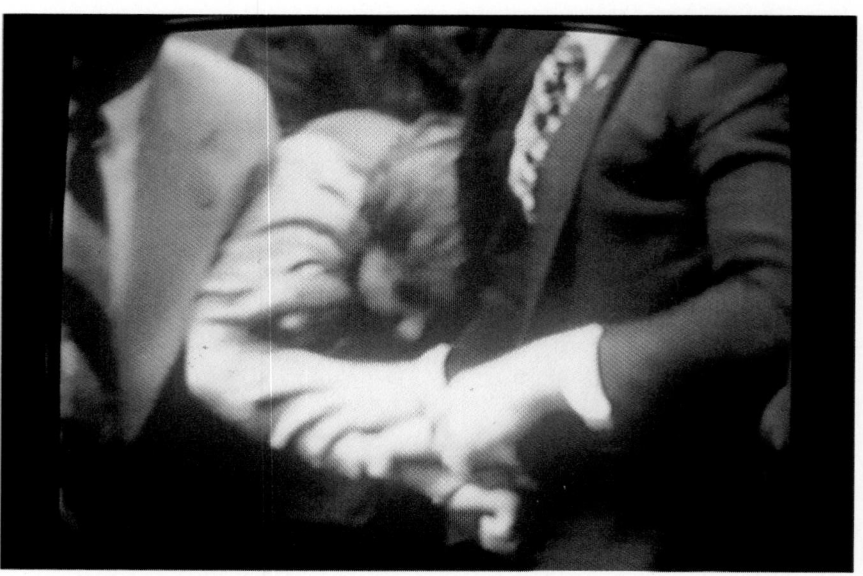

John Hinckley is shown here being seized by a Secret Service agent just after his assassination attempt on President Reagan. Explaining his abnormal behavior presents a challenge to psychologists. (*J. P. Laffont/Sygma*)

LOOKING AHEAD

When we consider the case of John Hinckley, we are faced with a series of perplexing questions. What made him shoot Reagan? When did his behavior first become abnormal? How was his abnormal behavior related to his background? Was there something medically wrong with him? Could he have been prevented from carrying out his assassination attempt by early treatment? How could his behavior be categorized and classified, and how could the specific nature of his problem be pinpointed?

While these questions cannot be answered definitively, especially with a case as complex as this, we will begin to address some of the issues raised by Hinckley's obviously atypical behavior in this and the following chapter. We begin by discussing the distinction between normal and abnormal behavior. Although in some cases—such as this one—the distinction is easy to make, in others the differences are more subtle than you might imagine.

The next section of the chapter considers various approaches that have been used to explain abnormal behavior. Starting with explanations based on superstition, we move on to more contemporary, scientific approaches—formally called models of abnormality—each of which seeks to identify the causes of abnormal behavior. Finally, we apply the models to the case of John Hinckley, showing how the various explanations complement one another.

The heart of the chapter consists of a description of the various types of abnormal behaviors. Using the classification system employed by mental-health workers, we examine the most significant kinds of disorders. By the end of the chapter you should have a good understanding of the behaviors associated with each of these broad classifications. The chapter also includes a discussion of the problems and dangers of self-diagnosis and of the signals that might make you consider seeking help from a mental health professional.

In sum, after reading and studying this chapter, you will be able to

- Describe the approaches used to distinguish normal from abnormal behavior
- Identify the models of abnormal behavior that are used by mental-health professionals
- Describe the major characteristics of each model of abnormal behavior
- Apply the models of abnormal behavior to specific cases such as that of John Hinckley
- Describe the classification system used to categorize abnormal behavior
- Outline the major mental-health disorders
- Describe the major indicators that signal the need for the help of a mental-health worker
- Define and apply the key terms and concepts found at the end of the chapter

NORMAL VERSUS ABNORMAL: MAKING THE DISTINCTION

Universally that person's acumen is esteemed very little perceptive concerning whatsoever matters are being held as most profitably by mortals with sapience endowed to be studied who is ignorant of that which the most in doctrine erudite and certainly by reason of that in them high mind's ornament deserving of veneration constantly maintain when by general consent they affirm that other circumstances being equal by no exterior splendour is the prosperity of a nation more efficaciously asserted than by the measure of how far forward may have progressed the tribute of its solicitude for that proliferent continuance which of evils the original if it be absent when fortunately present constitutes the certain sign of omnipollent nature's incorrupted benefaction.

It would be easy to conclude that these words were the musings of a madman; the passage does not seem, at least at first consideration, to make any sense at all. But literary scholars would disagree; in actuality this passage is from James Joyce's classic *Ulysses,* which has been hailed as one of the major works of twentieth-century literature (Joyce, 1934, p. 377).

As this example illustrates, a cursory examination of a person's writing is insufficient to determine the degree to which he or she is "normal." But even when we consider more extensive samples of an individual's behavior, we find that there may be only a fine line between behavior that is considered normal and that which is considered abnormal—a line that even trained professionals sometimes have difficulty drawing clearly, as a classic study by David Rosenhan (1973) illustrated dramatically.

In the study, Rosenhan and seven of his colleagues presented themselves at the doors of separate mental hospitals across the United States and sought admission. The reason, they each stated, was that they were hearing voices—"unclear voices" which said, "empty," "hollow," and "thud." Aside from changing their names and occupations, *everything* else they did and said was representative of their true behavior, including the responses they gave during extensive admission interviews and answers to the battery of tests they were asked to complete. In fact, as soon as they were admitted, they said they no longer heard any voices. In sum, each of the pseudopatients acted in the "normal" way.

One would have assumed that Rosenhan and his colleagues would have been quickly discovered as the imposters they were, but this was not the case. In fact, each of them was diagnosed as severely abnormal based on observed behavior. Most were labeled as schizophrenic, and they were kept in the hospital from three to fifty-two days, with the average stay being nineteen days. In most cases, they were not allowed to leave without some help from people outside the hospital. And even when they were discharged, most of the "patients" left with the label "schizophrenia—in remission," meaning that the abnormal behavior had only temporarily subsided and could recur at any time.

Most disturbing of all is the fact that in none of the cases were the pseudopatients identified by the staff of the hospitals as imposters. On the other hand, a number of real patients felt that the investigators were not actually suffering from a mental problem. One patient said, "You're not crazy. You're a journalist or a professor. You're checking up on the hospital" (Rosenhan, 1973, p. 252). This insight came from the fact that the pseudopatients were openly taking notes—a behavior that, when noticed by the hospital staff, was viewed as a sign of mental disorder.

The surprising results of Rosenhan's study suggest that the differences between normal and abnormal behaviors can be sufficiently subtle to elude detection even in situations where behavior is—or at least should be —the focus of attention. Clearly, then, the differences between normal and abnormal behavior are not as apprarent as we might at first think. (To get a sense of some of the difficulties involved in identifying abnormal behavior, see the Try It! box.)

TRY IT!

SEPARATING NORMAL FROM ABNORMAL

To learn firsthand the obstacles involved in distinguishing normal from abnormal behavior, read the following passages. Two were written by people diagnosed with some form of abnormal behavior, while the other two were written by well-known contemporary poets:

> Regardless of your lively life/I am still here writhing in pain/I am still reeling from the truth/Regardless of the outside sun/I remain the far side of crazy/I remain the mortal enemy of Man/Regardless of a million smiles/I can't escape this torture chamber/I can't begin to be happy/Regardless of your dream come true/I continue to grovel for normalcy/I continue to scream inside/Regardless of everyone's friends/I plot revenge in the dark/I plot escape from this asylum/Regardless of Disneyland/I follow the example of perverts/I follow the long lost swine/Regardless of Miss America's attitude/I stagger from day to day/I stagger toward the future/Regardless of the laughter of children/I cannot continue to pretend/I cannot continue to live.

> My mother's name was Bill . . . and coo? St. Valentine's Day is the start of the breedin' season of the birds. All buzzards can coo. I'd like to see it pronounced buzzards rightly. They work hard. So do parakeets.

> When the red pond fills fish appear/When the red pond dries fish disappear./Everything built on the desert crumbles to dust/Electric cable transmission wires swept down./The lizard people came out of the rock./The red Kangaroo people forgot their own song./Only a man with four sticks can cross the Simpson Desert./One rain turns red dust green with leaves./One raindrop begins the universe./When the raindrop dries, worlds come to their end.

> (Poem beginning with parenthesis:—God!)/Garver has an Aztec Hammer/To batter the tacks in/It's made of Pyramid Stone/The shape of a Knot—/Cleopatra's Knot—/The Knotty issue Marc/Brandelian Antonio/Julius Marc McAnthony/Thorny horn of hare/Propensities and hair/And disgusting to the bare./Aztec Hammer, never stop./Folded ripplefold over there nice,/Tacks went in,/"It's take an artist to do all this"/Careful man of cellophane/decks/&/sometimes/ceremonial/silver/foil/but/usually/plain pleasant paper.

Answers The first two selections were written by people diagnosed as suffering from mental disturbance. (John Hinckley, who made the assassination attempt on President Reagan, wrote the first poem.) The last two, though, are written by contemporary poets: "Ayers Rock Uluru Song" by Allen Ginsberg (1977) and "38th Chorus" by Jack Kerouac (1959). It's not easy to tell, is it?

Approaches to Abnormality

The difficulty in distinguishing normal from abnormal behavior has led to a diversity of approaches for devising a precise, scientific definition of ''abnormal behavior.'' Over the years, in fact, the definition of what consititutes normal and abnormal behavior has taken a number of twists, with four major approaches being employed at one time or another (Howells & Osborn, 1984).

Different Equals Abnormal: Deviation from the Average Perhaps the most obvious approach to defining normality revolves around the notion of deviation from the average—a statistical definition. In order to determine abnormality, we simply observe what behaviors are rare or infrequent in a given society or culture and label these deviations from the norm as abnormal (Ullman & Krasner, 1975).

Although such a definition may be appropriate in some instances, its drawback is that some behaviors that are statistically rare clearly do not lend themselves to classification as abnormal. If most people prefer to have orange juice with breakfast, but you prefer apple juice, this hardly makes your behavior abnormal. A definition of abnormality that rests on deviation from the average, then, is not sufficient by itself.

Aiming for Perfection: Deviation from the Ideal An alternate approach to defining abnormality is one that takes into account not what most people do (the average), but the standard toward which most people are striving—the ideal. Using this sort of definition, behavior is considered abnormal if it deviates a sufficient degree from some kind of ideal or standard (Jahoda, 1958). Unfortunately, this definition suffers from even more difficulties than the deviation-from-the-average definition, since society has so few standards about which people agree. Moreover, the standards that do arise tend to change over time, leaving the deviation-from-the-ideal approach inadequate.

Normal Feels Good, Abnormal Feels Bad: Abnormality as Sense of Subjective Discomfort Given the drawbacks of both the deviation-from-the-average and deviation-from-the-ideal definitions of normality, we must turn to more subjective approaches. In fact, one of the most useful definitions of abnormal behavior is one that concentrates on the psychological consequences of the behavior for the individual. In this approach, behavior is considered abnormal if it produces a sense of distress, anxiety, or guilt in an individual—or if it is harmful to others in some way. According to this view, then, behavior becomes abnormal only to the extent that it produces a sense of psychological discomfort in a person or produces discomfort in others.

Of course, even a definition that rests on subjective discomfort has its drawbacks, for in some particularly severe forms of mental disturbance people report feeling euphoric and on top of the world—yet to others, their behavior is bizarre. In this case, then, there is a subjective state of well-being, yet the behavior is clearly within the realm of what most people would consider abnormal—leading to a final approach to abnormality which considers people's ability to function effectively.

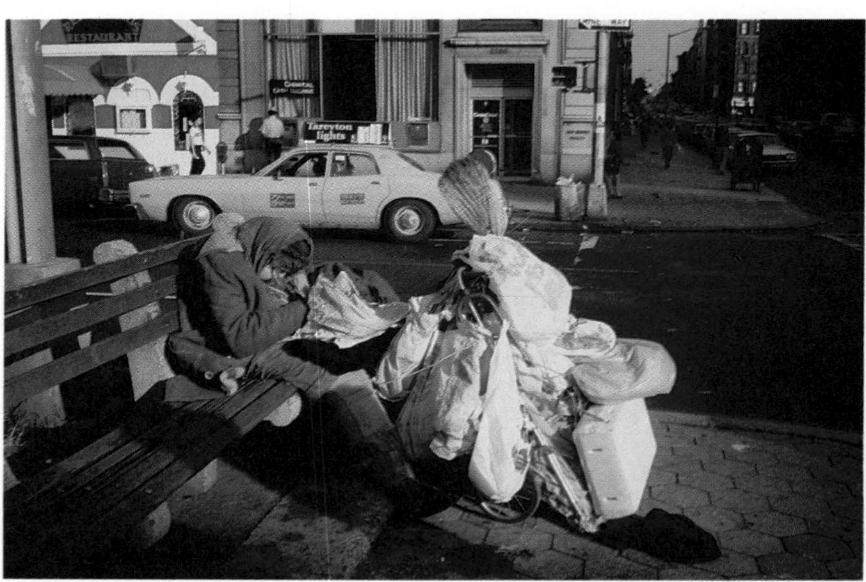

This woman, whose wordly possessions are entirely contained in her shopping bags, is an unambiguous example of an individual whose functioning as a member of society is impaired. (*Cecile Brunswick/ Peter Arnold, Inc.*)

THE CUTTING EDGE

THE MENTAL STATE OF THE UNION:
A Census of Mental Disorder

Given the difficulties in satisfactorily defining abnormality, it should come as no surprise that taking a census of people who show signs of abnormality is no simple task. But the U. S. government decided to take a stab, and the result led to some startling statistics (Reiger et al., 1984).

The survey, conducted in five communities and including about 10,000 Americans, found that close to 20 percent of the adults queried had a mental disorder and that the rates were about equal for men and women. In individual interviews that lasted two hours, each subject answered 200 questions about particular kinds of problems, such as feeling panicky upon leaving the house or losing interest in normally pleasant activities. By using standard categories of mental disturbance that we will be discussing later in the chapter, the researchers were able to produce a statistical profile of the mental state of the union.

Projecting the results to the nation as a whole indicates that over 29 million Americans have one or more mental disorders or have suffered from one within the past six months. For example, 13 million have difficulties related to anxiety, 10 million abuse alcohol or some other drug, and some 11 million have irrational fears. Surprisingly, just one in five of those with a problem seeks help for it.

These results suggest that abnormal behavior is far from rare. Moreover, in further surveys now underway, the researchers are obtaining information about which mental disorders benefit most from treatment and which ones simply go away on their own, as well as about how major life events (such as a marriage or a death in the family) influence mental disorder. This work, then, offers the promise of identifying specific events that trigger abnormal behavior and of finding ways to prevent their occurrence.

Getting Along in the World: Abnormality as the Inability to Function Effectively Most people are able to feed themselves, hold a job, get along with others, and, in general live as productive members of society. Yet there are those who are unable to adjust to the demands of society and function effectively.

According to this last view, those who are unable to function effectively and adapt to the demands of society are considered abnormal. For example, the unemployed homeless living on street corners of cities can be considered as unable to function effectively and therefore displaying abnormal behavior—even if they have chosen to live in this fashion and report being pleased with their plight. It is their inability to adapt to the requirements of society that labels their behavior as abnormal, according to this approach.

Drawing the Line on Abnormality: The Continuum of Abnormal and Normal Behavior

None of the four definitions alone is sufficiently broad to cover all instances of abnormal behavior, and the division between normal and abnormal behavior often remains indistinct. Probably the best way to deal with this definitional imprecision is to consider normal and abnormal behavior not as absolute states, but rather as marking the two ends of a **continuum** (or scale) of behavior, with completely normal functioning at one end and totally abnormal behavior at the other. Obviously behavior will often fall somewhere in between these two extremes. (For a look at how many of us fall into the abnormal range, see the Cutting Edge box.)

Continuum (kon TIN u um): *a continuous measurement scale*

RECAP AND REVIEW I

Recap

- Distinguishing normal from abnormal behavior is difficult.
- Definitions of abnormality include those based on deviation from the average, on deviation from the ideal, on the psychological consequences of the behavior for the individual, and on the ability to function effectively and adapt as a member of society.
- It is reasonable to view abnormal and normal behavior as marking the two ends of a continuum, or scale.

Review

1. David Rosehan's 1973 study that placed "normal" people in mental institutions most convincingly proved which of the following?
a. Most specialists cannot differentiate the behavior of normal people from that of the mentally ill. **b.** In an institution it is very difficult to act as you do in everyday life. **c.** The differences between normal and abnormal behavior are sometimes too subtle to be detected, even by specialists **d.** Normal and abnormal behaviors are so similar it can take several days of observation to determine a patient's classification

2. Match each theory with its description by writing the appropriate number in the blank.

a. ____ Deviation-from-the-ideal definition of abnormal behavior	1. Considers behavior causing distress, anxiety, or guilt in oneself or others as abnormal
b. ____ Nonadaptive behavior	2. Considers "unusual" behavior statistically
c. ____ Subjective-discomfort definition of abnormal behavior	3. An inability to function in society
d. ____ Deviation-from-the-average definition of abnormal behavior	4. Compares behavior against a standard for which most people strive

3. Karl has chosen to live his life in a treehouse. Because living in a treehouse is not the choice of most people, a person who lived in a treehouse would be abnormal in the eyes of most psychologists. True or false?

4. A scale of behavior ranging from "most abnormal" to "most normal" is called a ____________ .

5. Virginia's mother tells her that she is breaking the laws of nature by moving in with her boyfriend and is acting crazy because of it. Virginia's mother is using what approach to defining abnormal behavior? ____________

(Answers to review questions are at the bottom of page 400.)

MODELS OF ABNORMALITY: FROM SUPERSTITION TO SCIENCE

> The disease occurred at the height of the summer heat. People, asleep or awake, would suddenly jump up, feeling an acute pain like the sting of a bee. Some saw the spider, others did not, but they knew that it must be the tarantula. They ran out of the house into the street, to the market place, dancing in great excitement. Soon they were joined by others who like them had been bitten, or by people who had been stung in previous years. . . .
>
> Thus groups of patients would gather, dancing wildly in the queerest attire. . . . Others would tear their clothes and show their nakedness, losing all sense of modesty. . . . Some called for swords and acted like fencers, others for whips and beat each other. . . . Some of them had still stranger fancies, liked to be tossed in the air, dug holes in the ground, and rolled themselves into the dirt like swine. They all drank wine plentifully and sang and talked like drunken people. . . . (Sigerist, 1943, pp. 103,106-107.)

This description of a peculiar form of abnormal behavior that occurred during the thirteenth century—which was attributed, at the time, to the bite of a real or imagined tarantula spider—indicates that mental disturbance, and theories

Abnormal behavior is not just a twentieth-century phenomenon, as this old woodcut, showing groups of people dancing uncontrollably during the Middle Ages, illustrates. (*Bettmann Archive*)

(a)

(b)

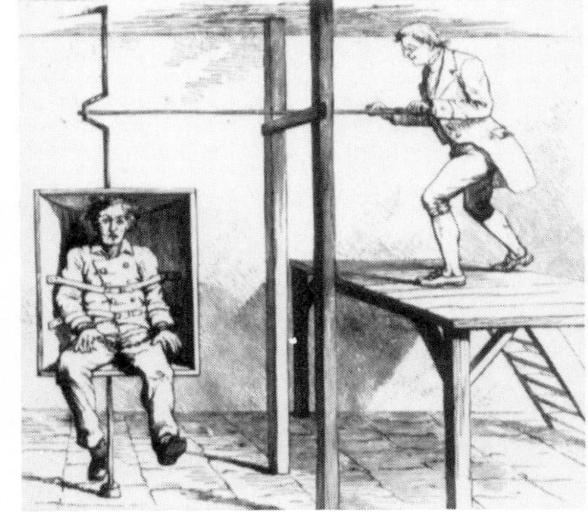

Until the twentieth century, abnormal behavior was linked to witchcraft and superstition. As a result, its treatment involved (a) religious ceremonies and (b) bizarre paraphernalia designed to drive out evil spirits. (*Bettmann Archive*)

about its causes, is nothing new. Yet our understanding of the causes of such behavior has become considerably more sophisticated.

For much of the past, abnormal behavior was linked to superstition and witchcraft; people displaying abnormal behavior were accused of being possessed by the devil or some sort of demonic god (Howells & Osborn, 1984). Given this cause, authorities felt justified in "treating" abnormal behavior by attempting to drive out the source of the problem. This typically involved whipping, immersion in hot water, starvation, or other forms of torture in which the cure was often worse than the affliction.

Contemporary approaches to abnormal behavior take a more enlightened view, and five major models of abnormal behavior tend to predominate: the medical model, the psychoanalytic model, the behavioral model, the humanistic model, and sociocultural models. These models not only suggest different causes of abnormal behavior, but—as we shall see in the next chapter—different treatment approaches as well.

Abnormal Behavior as a Biological Disease: The Medical Model

Medical model of abnormality : *The model that suggests that when an individual displays symptoms of abnormal behavior, the cause is physiological*

When a person displays the symptoms of tuberculosis, we generally find the tuberculin germ in his or her body tissue. In the same way, the **medical model of abnormality** suggests that when an individual displays the symptoms of abnormal behavior, the root cause will be found in an examination of some physical aspect of the individual, such as hormonal imbalance, a chemical deficiency, or an injury to part of the body. Indeed, when we speak of mental *illness,* the *symptoms* of abnormal behavior, and mental *hospitals,* we are using terminology related to the medical model.

Because, as we will discuss later, many sorts of abnormal behaviors have been linked to physiological causes, the medical model would seem to be a reasonable approach. In fact, the medical model does represent a major advance over explanations of abnormal behavior based on superstitions. Yet serious criticisms have been leveled against it. For one thing, there are many instances in which no physiological cause has been identified for abnormal behavior, thus negating the basic assumption of the medical model. Other criticisms have equally important, though less obvious, implications. For instance, some critics have argued that the use of the term "illness" implies that there is something "wrong" with a person, something that is in need of a cure (Szasz, 1982). Using such terms suggests that persons displaying abnormal behavior hold little control over their actions and have no responsiblity for them—and that any "cure" is entirely in the hands of someone else (who, given the assumptions of the medical model, would presumably be a physician).

Conflicting Causes of Abnormal Behavior: The Psychoanalytic Model

On the surface, John Hinckley had a model upbringing. Yet could certain aspects of his past, of which he was unaware, have brought about his assassination

---

ANSWERS TO REVIEW QUESTIONS

Review I: **1.** c **2.** a. 4, b. 3, c. 1, d. 2 **3.** False **4.** Continuum **5.** Deviation from the ideal attempt? Such a possibility is suggested by the psychoanalytic model of abnormal behavior.

While the medical model suggests that physiological causes are at the root of abnormality, the **psychoanalytic model of abnormality** holds that it stems from childhood conflicts over opposing wishes regarding sex and aggression. As we discussed in Chapter 11, Freud believed that children pass through a series of stages in which sexual and aggressive impulses take different forms that require resolution. If the conflicts of childhood are not dealt with successfully, they remain unresolved in the unconscious and eventually bring about abnormal behavior during adulthood.

Psychoanalytic model of abnormality: *The model that suggests that abnormality stems from childhood conflicts over opposing wishes*

For example, it is not unrealistic to think that aspects of John Hinckley's childhood produced unresolved conflicts. Perhaps his family's move to a new community when he was in sixth grade triggered unresolved insecurities and conflicts that he had experienced as a much younger child. Of course, this is mere speculation—and it points out one of the major difficulties with psychoanalytic theorizing. Because there is no conclusive way of linking people's childhood experiences with the abnormal behaviors they display as an adult, we can never be sure that the mechanisms suggested by psychoanalytic theory are accurate. Moreover, psychoanalytic theory, like the medical model, presents people as having little control over their actions and paints a picture of behavior guided by unconscious impulses that people do not even know about.

On the other hand, the contributions of psychoanalytic theory have been great. More than any other approach to abnormal behavior, it highlights the fact that people can have a rich, involved inner life which must be understood in order to resolve their psychological difficulties.

When Behavior Itself is the Problem: The Behavioral Model of Abnormal Behavior

The medical model and the psychoanalytic model share a common approach to abnormal behavior: They both look at abnormal behaviors as *symptoms* of some underlying problem. In contrast, the **behavioral model of abnormality** looks at the behavior itself as the problem. According to theorists using this approach, one need not look beyond a person's display of abnormal behavior or past the environment to be able to understand and ultimately change that behavior.

Behavioral model of abnormality: *The model that suggests that abnormal behavior itself is the problem to be treated, rather than viewing behavior as a symptom of some underlying medical or psychological problem*

Using the principles of learning we discussed in Chapter 4, then, one can explain why people behave abnormally—or normally. Both normal and abnormal behavior are seen as responses to a set of stimuli, responses that have been learned through past experience and are guided in the present by the stimuli that one finds in one's environment. Indeed, in its most extreme form, the behavioral model rejects the notion that it is important to understand what a person is thinking. What is critical is analyzing how an abnormal behavior has been learned and observing the circumstances in which it is displayed in order to explain why such behavior is occurring. For example, a behavioral approach would explain an individual's inability to get work done on time as due to a lack of skill in time management. This could be remedied by teaching the individual techniques for working more efficiently. Other approaches, in contrast, would try to determine the underlying causes of this inability to manage one's time.

The emphasis on overt observable behavior represents both the greatest strength and the greatest weakness of the behavioral approach to abnormal behavior. Because of its emphasis on the here and now, the behavioral approach is the most precise and objective in examining manifestations of abnormal behavior. Rather than hypothesizing elaborate, underlying, unobservable mechanisms to explain abnormal behavior, behavioral theorists concentrate on immediate behavior. They have developed many techniques (which we will discuss in the next chapter) to successfully modify such behavior.

On the other hand, the behavioral approach has received its share of criticism. For example, behavioral theories, like medical and psychoanalytic explanations, tend to view people's behavior as being caused by factors largely outside of their own control, although for different reasons. Moreover, according to critics, one cannot overlook the very real fact that people have complex unobservable thoughts that influence their behavior. This latter criticism has led some behavioral theorists to modify their position and begin to consider cognitive approaches, in which cognitions—people's thoughts and beliefs—are viewed as a reasonable behavior to change through treatment. For example, they may teach a person who, with every exam, thinks, "This exam is crucial to my future," to modify her thoughts to be more realistic: "My future is not dependent on this one exam." The basic principles of learning theory are still employed; what is different is the target behavior. Although not all behavioral theorists subscribe to these views, the behavioral model has been broadened by the addition of such cognitive approaches.

Putting the Person in Control: The Humanistic Model of Abnormal Behavior

You might be asking yourself whether there is any model of abnormal behavior that considers a person to be in complete control of his or her behavior, and in fact this is a reasonable question in light of the three models we have discussed. In each of these models the individual is seen, to a greater or lesser degree, as something of a pawn, beset by physiological difficulties, unconscious conflicts, or environmental stimuli that direct and motivate his or her behavior.

Psychologists who subscribe to the humanistic approach, in contrast, emphasize the control and responsibility that people have for their own behavior—even when such behavior is abnormal. The **humanistic model of abnormality** concentrates on what is uniquely human, viewing people as basically rational, oriented toward a social world, and motivated to get along with others (Rogers, 1980).

Humanistic model of abnormality: *The model that suggests that people are basically rational, and that abnormal behavior results from an inablity to fulfill human needs and capabilities*

Although diverse in many ways, humanistic approaches to abnormal behavior focus on the relationship of the individual to the world, the ways people view themselves in relation to others and see their place in the world in a philosophical sense. People have an awareness of life and of themselves that leads them to search for meaning and self-worth. So-called abnormal behavior is basically a sign of a person's inability to fulfill his or her human needs and capabilities. Moreover, humanistic approaches take a much less judgmental view of atypical behavior than other models. Rather than assuming that a "cure" is required, the humanistic model suggests that individuals can, by and large, set their own limits of what is acceptable behavior. As long as they are not hurting others and do not feel personal distress, people should be free to choose the behaviors they engage in. It is only if *they* feel that their behavior needs some correction that they ought to consider taking responsibility for modifying it, and the way to bring about such modification is by exploring ways to reach higher levels of self-fulfillment.

Humanistic models consider abnormal behavior, then, in a less negative light than the earlier models we discussed. Rather than assuming there is something wrong with an individual, abnormal behavior is seen as a reasonable reaction to circumstances one finds in one's daily life. Moreover, the humanistic model suggests that people have relatively high degree of control over their lives and can make informed and rational choices to overcome their difficulties.

The humanistic model is not without its detractors. For instance, it has been criticized for its reliance on unscientific, unverifiable information, as well as for its vague, almost philosophical formulation related to such concepts as "human striving" and "fulfillment of human needs." Despite these criticisms, the humanistic model offers a view of abnormal behavior that stresses the unique aspects of being human and provides a number of important suggestions for helping those with psychological problems.

Society as the Cause of Abnormal Behavior: The Sociocultural Model

Sociocultural approaches to abnormal behavior make the assumption that people's behavior—both normal and abnormal—is shaped by the kind of family group, society, and culture in which they live. We all are part of a social network of family, friends, acquaintances, and even strangers, and the kinds of relationships that evolve with others may support abnormal behaviors and even cause them to occur. According to the **sociocultural model of abnormality** then, the kinds of stresses and conflicts people experience—not in terms of unconscious processes, but as part of their daily interactions with those around them—can promote and maintain abnormal behavior.

Sociocultural model of abnormality: *The model that suggests that people's behavior, both normal and abnormal, is shaped by family, society, and cultural influences*

In fact, some proponents of this view take the extreme position that there really is no such thing as abnormal behavior. Although people who violate social rules may be labeled by society as showing abnormal behavior, in reality there is nothing wrong with such individuals. Rather, there is something wrong with a society that is unwilling to tolerate deviant behavior.

To support the position that sociocultural factors shape abnormal behavior, theorists point to statistics showing that certain kinds of abnormal behavior are far more prevalent among certain social classes than others, and poor economic times tend to be linked to general declines in psychological functioning (Pines, 1982). For instance, diagnoses of schizophrenia tend to be higher among members of lower socioeconomic classes than in members of more affluent groups (Hollingshead & Redlich, 1958). The reason may relate to the way in which abnormal behavior is interpreted by diagnosticians, who tend to be psychiatrists and psychologists from upper socioeconomic classes. Alternatively, it may be that stresses on members of lower socioeconomic classes are greater than those on people in higher classes. Whatever the reason, there is frequently a link between sociocultural factors and abnormal behavior, suggesting the possibility of a cause-and-effect sequence.

As with the other theories, the sociocultural model does not have unequivocal support. Alternate explanations abound for the association between abnormal behavior and social factors. For example, people of lower classes may be less likely than those of higher classes to seek help until their symptoms become relatively severe and warrant a more serious diagnosis (Gove, 1982). Moreover, sociocultural explanations provide relatively little in the way of direct guidance for the treatment of individuals showing mental disturbance, since the focus is on broader societal factors.

Applying the Models: The Case of John Hinckley

We began this chapter by discussing John Hinckley's assassination attempt on President Ronald Reagan. Perhaps you are wondering which of these models brings us closer to understanding the reasons for his behavior. Indeed, you may be looking for the answer to a more encompassing question: Which of these approaches provides the best model for explaining abnormal behavior in general?

The most appropriate answer to both questions is, in fact, that *all* of them can be reasonably and profitably used. For in most cases, psychologists have found that there is more than one workable approach to the problems of abnormal behavior; as we shall see, effective and worthwhile approaches to resolving psychological problems have been made using each of the different models. Indeed, it is possible to address various parts of a given problem simultaneously using each model.

Consider the case of John Hinckley. We might first use the medical model to see if Hinckley had any physical problems—such as a brain tumor, a chemical imbalance in the brain, or some disease—that might account for his unusual behavior. (In fact, an examination of his brain did show some irregularities; McKean, 1982.)

A psychoanalytic theorist would take a very different approach, seeking out information about Hinckley's past, concentrating on his childhood and probing his memories to determine the nature of conflicts residing in his unconscious. A behavioral theorist would take still another approach, concentrating on the nature of the rewards and punishments that Hinckley received for behaving the way he did, as well as the stimuli in the environment that maintained or reinforced his behavior. For instance, shooting Reagan certainly brought him attention—a reward which he had a history of seeking out. Moreover, his environment seemed to maintain his inability to sustain friendships and the consequent lack of social interaction. The problems he had allowed him to withdraw more and more into his own world.

Finally, humanistic and sociocultural approaches would concentrate on Hinckley's view of himself, in relation to other people and the world in general. Humanistic theorists would point to his drifting as a sign of his efforts to come to grips with the meaning of his life. They would also see his early desire to be a rock musician as an attempt to be part of his peer culture. Sociocultural approaches would carry such an analysis further, examining Hinckley's relationships with his peers, the effects of being considerably better off financially than most people, and the influence of his family structure and cultural background on his behavior. (For consideration of Hinckley's case from another perspective, see the Psychology at Work Box.)

As you can see, finding support for one or another of these approaches does not automatically make the others wrong; each focuses on somewhat different aspects of Hinckley's behavior and life. Of course, if we analyzed his background in depth, we might ultimately find that one model provides a better explanation than any other. But because the approaches consider abnormal be-

PSYCHOLOGY AT WORK

WHEN LAW AND PSYCHOLOGY MIX: The Insanity Defense

When John Hinckley pulled the trigger and shot Ronald Reagan, he did more than almost kill the President: Ultimately, he set into motion a series of events that almost produced a lethal blow to the legal plea of insanity. For when he was found not guilty by reason of insanity, the public outrage at the verdict was so great that Congress soon considered legislation to change the way in which that defense could be used.

Whether or not he had shot Reagan was never an issue, of course, during Hinckley's trial. Millions of people had witnessed the shooting on videotapes that were played repeatedly on television following the incident. What was at issue was Hinckley's state of mind: Was he legally insane at the time of the shooting?

According to law in twenty-two states, insanity—which is a legal, not a psychological term—means that defendants at the time they commit a criminal act cannot understand the difference between right and wrong. In twenty-six other states, however, a somewhat different definition is used; defendants are considered insane if they are substantially confused or unable to control themselves. And two other states—Idaho and Montana—do not accept insanity pleas at all.

As a defendant in a federal crime, Hinckley had to prove that he was incapable of knowing that his actions were wrong when he shot the President. To prove this, the defense called expert witness after expert witness to the stand to portray Hinckley as a man overcome by schizophrenia, as well as an assortment of other severe mental problems. On the other hand, expert witnesses for the prosecution contended that Hinckley had made a conscious and rational decision to shoot Reagan, and that while he was self-centered and manipulative, he suffered from only minor mental-health problems. To the jury, the task of determining which side was right seemed impossible; one juror, Maryland Copelin, said afterwards, "If the expert psychiatrists could not decide whether the man was sane, then how are we supposed to decide?" (*Time,* July 5, 1982, p. 25).

In the end, the jury decided that Hinckley had been legally insane. Their verdict produced rage and indignation, with a clear majority of people polled in an ABC news survey maintaining that the verdict was unjust. Some individuals called for drastic modification of the plea. For example, the *Denver Post* editorialized, "It's the system which found him innocent that's insane," while some called for the complete abolition of the insanity plea.

Most people, though, while acknowledging the drawbacks to a plea about which even experts cannot agree, let alone juries made up of people from all walks of life, believed that it was unreasonable to abolish the plea completely. Surely there was *something* wrong with Hinckley, whether or not he met the legal criteria for insanity, and abolishing the plea might prove to be like throwing out the baby with the bathwater. We might hope that, as our understanding of abnormal behavior advances sufficiently, it will be possible to provide more conclusive answers regarding the nature of a person's state of mind. Until that happens, however, we are going to have to grapple with the issues raised by Hinckley's trial.

havior at different levels, and because people's lives are made up of so many facets, a single approach may be insufficient to provide a full explanation for a person's abnormal behavior—particularly when that person is as seriously disturbed as Hinckley.

The Informed Consumer of Psychology: Do You Feel Abnormal?

As we conclude this introduction to abnormal behavior and begin to consider the specific classifications and treatments of abnormal behavior, it is important to note a phenomenon that has long been known to medical students, and one

Medical student's disease: *The feeling that symptoms and illnesses about which one studies are characteristic of oneself*

that you, too, may find yourself susceptible to—a phenomenon called **medical student's disease**. Although in the present case it might be more aptly labeled "psychology student's disease," the basic symptoms are the same: deciding that you suffer from the same sort of problems you are studying.

In most cases, of course, this will not be the case. As we have discussed, the differences between normal and abnormal behavior are often so fuzzy that it is easy to jump to the conclusion that one has the same symptoms that are involved in serious forms of mental disturbance.

Before coming to such a conclusion, though, it is important to keep in mind that from time to time we all experience a wide range of emotions and subjective experiences, and it is not unusual to feel deeply unhappy, to fantasize about bizarre situations, or to feel anxiety about life's circumstances. It is the persistence, depth, and consistency of such behavior that sets normal reactions apart from abnormal ones. If you have not previously had serious doubts about the normality of your behavior, it is unlikely that reading about others' abnormality should prompt you to reevaluate your earlier conclusion.

RECAP AND REVIEW II

Recap

- Historically, abnormal behavior was first linked to superstition and witchcraft.
- Current approaches view abnormal behavior in terms of five major models: the medical, psychoanalytic, behavioral, humanistic, and sociocultural models.
- The question of which model provides the best explanation of abnormal behavior can be answered most reasonably by noting that each model can be profitably used.
- People studying psychological disorders often begin to feel that they suffer from the problems about which they are reading, a phenomenon known as "medical (or psychology) student's disease."

Review

1. Which of the following is given as an argument against the medical model?
   a. Physiological abnormalities are almost impossible to identify. **b.** There is no conclusive way to link past experience and behavior. **c.** The medical model rests too heavily on the effects of nutrition. **d.** Blaming behavior on a physical problem removes the responsibility from the individual
2. Behavioral models focus on retraining to eliminate abnormal behaviors. True or false?
3. If we say that Tom's lingering depression is due to the fact he was raised in a poor neighborhood, we are using a __________ model.
4. Cheryl has strong feelings of inferiority. According to a humanistic psychologist, the best way to help her "abnormal" behavior would be to
   a. direct her in modifying her goals **b.** treat the underlying physical problem **c.** express a great deal of caring **d.** uncover her negative past experiences through hypnosis
5. Sigmund Freud is most closely associated with which model?
   a. Medical **b.** Psychoanalytic **c.** Behavior **d.** Humanistic
6. Imagine that a wealthy acquaintance of yours was recently arrested for shoplifting an $8.95 necktie. Briefly explain this behavior in terms of
   a. the medical model **b.** the psychoanalytic model **c.** the behavioral model **d.** the humanistic model **e.** the sociocultural model
7. Experiencing another person's problems as a result of reading about them is called __________.

(Answers to review questions are at the bottom of page 408.)

THE ABC'S OF *DSM-III:* CLASSIFYING TYPES OF ABNORMAL BEHAVIOR

Crazy. Nutty as a fruitcake. Loony. Insane. Neurotic. Strange. Demented. Odd. Possessed.

Society has long placed labels on people displaying abnormal behavior. Unfortunately, most of the time these labels have had negative connotations and they have been used without giving much thought to what the label signified.

Providing appropriate and specific names and classifications for abnormal behavior has presented a major challenge to psychologists. It is not too hard to understand why. Given the difficulties we discussed earlier in simply distinguishing normal from abnormal behavior, we might expect that the classification of different types of abnormal behavior would not be a simple matter.

Yet classification systems are necessary in order to be able to describe abnormal behavior, and over the years many different classification systems have been used with varying degrees of agreement among mental-health workers regarding their utility. Today, however, one standard system—devised by the American Psychiatric Association—has emerged and is used by most professionals to classify abnormal behavior. The classification system is known as ***DSM-III***—the ***Diagnostic and Statistical Manual of Mental Disorders***, third edition.

***Diagnostic and Statistical Manual of Mental Disorders*, third edition (*DSM-III*)**: *A manual that presents comprehensive definitions of more than 230 separate diagnostic categories for identifying problems and behaviors*

Published in 1980, *DSM-III* presents comprehensive and relatively precise definitions for more than 230 separate diagnostic categories. By following the criteria present in the system, diagnosticians can provide a clear description of the specific problem an individual is experiencing.

One particular noteworthy feature of *DSM-III* is that it is meant to be primarily descriptive and is devoid of suggestions as to the underlying causes of an individual's behavior and problems (Klerman, 1984). Hence, the term "neurotic"—a label that is commonly used by people in their everyday descriptions of abnormal behavior—is not listed as a *DSM-III* category. The reason is that "neurotic" derives directly from Freud's theory of personality (discussed in Chapter 11). Because the term refers to problems with a specific cause and theoretical approach, therefore, neurosis is no longer listed as a category.

DSM-III has the advantage, then, of providing a descriptive system that does not specify the cause or reason behind a problem. Instead, it paints a picture of the behavior that is being manifested. Why should this be important? For one thing, it allows communication between mental-health professionals of diverse backgrounds and approaches and does not immediately suggest that there is only one appropriate treatment. Another important point is that precise classification allows research to go forward and to explore the causes of a problem. If one cannot reliably describe the manifestations of an abnormal behavior, researchers will be hard-pressed to find ways of investigating the difficulties. Finally, it provides a kind of conceptual shorthand through which professionals can describe the behaviors that tend to occur in an individual.

It is also important to note that the *DSM* is designed to be periodically revised. Reflecting the fact that changes in society affect what behaviors are viewed as abnormal, *DSM-III-R* (a minor updating) was published in 1987 and *DSM-IV* (a major revision) is scheduled for completion in the early 1990s.

Of course, *DSM-III* has its drawbacks, as does any classification system (Vaillant, 1984). Perhaps the strongest criticism relates to what critics say is its overreliance on a medical model. Because it was drawn up by psychiatrists—

who are physicians—it is criticized as having a tendency to view abnormal behaviors primarily in terms of symptoms of some underlying physiological disorder. Moreover, some critics suggest that *DSM-III* pigeonholes people into inflexible categories, and that it would be more reasonable to use systems that classify people along some sort of continuum, or scale.

Other concerns with *DSM-III* are more subtle but equally important. For instance, Szasz (1961) argues that labeling an individual as a deviant provides a lifetime label that is dehumanizing. Moreover, there is a tendency for a diagnosis itself to be mistaken as an explanation for a problem. Saying, for instance, that a schizophrenic woman hears voices may seem as though schizophrenia is an *explanation* for her behavior—even though "schizophrenia" is simply a label that gives no clue as to *why* the woman hears voices (Rosehan, 1975). Furthermore, after an initial diagnosis is made, other diagnostic possibilities may be overlooked by mental-health professionals who concentrate on that diagnostic category.

Despite these drawbacks, *DSM-III* remains the major categorization system in use today. It has increased both the reliability and validity of diagnostic categorization, and it also provides a logical way to organize our examination of the major types of mental disturbance.

THE MAJOR DISORDERS

> I remember walking up the street, the moon was shining and suddenly everything around me seemed unfamiliar, as it would be in a dream. I felt panic rising inside me, but managed to push it away and carry on. I walked a quarter of a mile or so, with the panic getting worse every minute. . . . By now, I was sweating, yet trembling; my heart was pounding and my legs felt like jelly. . . . Terrified, I stood not knowing what to do. The only bit of sanity left in me told me to get home. Somehow this I did very slowly, holding onto the fence in the road. I cannot remember the actual journey back, until I was going into the house, then I broke down and cried helplessly (Melville, 1977, p. 1, 14).

Anxiety without Reason: Anxiety Disorders

Anxiety (ang ZY eh tee): *A feeling of apprehension or tension*

All of us, at one time or another, experience **anxiety**, a feeling of apprehension or tension, in reaction to stressful situations, There is nothing "wrong" with such anxiety; everyone feels it to some degree, and usually it is a reaction to stress that helps, rather than hinders, our daily functioning. Without anxiety, for instance, most of us would not be terribly motivated to study hard, to undergo physical exams, or to spend long hours at our jobs.

But some people—such as the person who wrote the passage above—experience anxiety in situations in which there is no external reason or cause. When anxiety occurs without external justification and begins to impede people's daily

ANSWERS TO REVIEW QUESTIONS

Review II: **1.** d **2.** True **3.** Sociocultural **4.** c **5.** b **6.** Possible answers, which may vary, include: a. he or she may have a physical ailment or a disease; b. unresolved experiences in his or her childhood led to the behavior; c.he or she had stolen things in the past and enjoyed the immediate rewards; d. he or she felt a need to discover himself or herself, or to impress someone else. e. stealing was caused by peer pressure; **7.** Medical (or psychology) student's disease functioning, it is considered a psychological problem known as an **anxiety disorder**. There are four main types of anxiety disorders: generalized anxiety disorder, panic disorder, phobic disorder, and obsessive-compulsive disorder.

A person with a generalized anxiety disorder experiences long-term, consistent anxiety—without knowing the reason for the anxiety. (*Edward Lettau/Photo Researchers, Inc.*)

Generalized Anxiety Disorder As the name implies, **generalized anxiety disorder** is a disorder in which an individual experiences long-term, consistent anxiety without knowing why. Such people feel afraid of *something,* but are unable to articulate what it is they fear. Because of their anxiety they are unable to function normally. They cannot concentrate, they cannot set their fears aside, and their lives become centered around their anxiety. Such anxiety may eventually result in the development of physiological problems. Because of heightened muscle tension and arousal, individuals with a generalized anxiety disorder may begin to experience headaches, dizziness, heart palpitations, or insomnia.

Panic Disorder In another type of anxiety disorder, **panic disorder**, there are instances of **panic attacks** that last from a few seconds to as much as several hours. During an attack, such as the one described at the start of this section of the chapter, the anxiety that a person has been chronically experiencing suddenly rises to a peak, and the individual feels a sense of impending, unavoidable doom. Although symptoms differ from person to person, they may include heart palpitations, shortness of breath, unusual amounts of sweating, faintness and dizziness, an urge to urinate, gastric sensations and—in extreme cases—a sense of imminent death (Lader & Matthews, 1970). After an attack such as this, it is no wonder that people tend to feel exhausted.

Anxiety disorder: *The occurrence of anxiety without obvious external cause, intruding on daily functioning*
Generalized anxiety disorder: *The experience of long-term anxiety with no explanation*
Panic disorder: *Anxiety that manifests itself in the form of panic attacks*
Panic attack: *Sudden anxiety characterized by heart palpitations, shortness of breath, sweating, faintness, and great fear*
Phobic (FOBE ik) **disorder**: *Disorders characterized by unrealistic fears (phobias) that may keep people from carrying out routine daily behaviors*
Phobias (FOBE ee ahs): *Intense, irrational fears of specific objects or situations*

Phobic Disorders Claustrophobia. Acrophobia. Xenophobia. Although these sound like characters in a Greek tragedy, they are actually members of a class of psychological disorders known as **phobias**. Phobias are intense, irrational fears of specific objects or situations. For example, claustrophobia is a fear of enclosed places, acrophobia a fear of high places, and xenophobia a fear of strangers. Although the objective danger posed by an anxiety-producing stimulus (which can be just about anything, as you can see from the list in Table 12-1) is typically small or nonexistent, to the individual suffering from the phobia it represents great danger, and a full-blown anxiety attack may follow exposure to the stimulus. Phobic disorders differ from generalized anxiety disorders and panic disorders in that there is a specific, identifiable stimulus that sets off the anxiety reaction.

Phobias may have only a minor impact on people's lives if the people who suffer from them can avoid the things they fear. Unless one is a professional firefighter or tightrope walker, for example, a fear of heights may have little impact on one's daily life. On the other hand, a fear of strangers presents a more debilitating problem. In one extreme case, a Washington housewife left her home just three times in thirty years—once to visit her family, once for an operation, and once to purchase ice cream for a dying companion (Adler, 1984).

Obsessive-compulsive (ob SESS iv kom PULS iv) **disorder**: *A disorder characterized by obsessions or compulsions*
Obsession (ob SEH shun): *A thought or idea that keeps recurring*

Obsessive-Compulsive Disorder An **obsession** is a thought or idea that keeps recurring in one's mind. For example, a student may not be able to stop feeling that he has neglected to put his name on a test and may think about it constantly for the two weeks it takes to get it back; a man may go on vacation and wonder the whole time if he locked his front door; or a woman may hear the same tune running through her head over and over again. In each case, the thought or idea is unwanted and is difficult to put out of mind. Of course, many

To a person suffering from acrophobia—a fear of heights—climbing even a short stairway may present major difficulties. (*James Wilson/Woodfin Camp & Assoc.*)

Compulsion (kom PUL shun): *An urge to repeatedly carry out an act that even the sufferer realizes is unreasonable*

of us suffer from mild obsessions from time to time, but usually such thoughts persist for a short time only. For those with serious obsessions, however, the thoughts persist for days or months, and may consist of bizarre, troubling images. In one classic case of an obsession, the patient

> complained of having "terrible thoughts." When she thought of her boyfriend she wished he were dead; when her mother went down the stairs, she "wished she'd fall and break her neck"; when her sister spoke of going to the beach with her infant daughter, the patient "hoped that they would both drown." These thoughts "make me hysterical. I love them; why should I wish such terrible things to happen? It drives me wild, makes me feel I'm crazy and don't belong to society" (Kraines, 1948, p. 199).

As part of an obsessive-compulsive disorder, people may also experience **compulsions**, urges to repeatedly carry out some act that seems strange and unreasonable, even to them. Whatever the compulsive behavior, people experience extreme anxiety if they cannot carry it out, even if it is something they want to stop. The acts involved may be relatively trivial, such as repeatedly checking the stove to make sure all the burners are turned off, or more unusual, such as a continuous need to wash oneself (Rachman & Hodgson, 1980). For example, consider this case report of a 27-year-old woman with a cleaning ritual:

> Bess would first remove all of her clothing in a pre-established sequence. She would lay out each article of clothing at specific spots on her bed, and examine each one for any indications of "contamination." She would then thoroughly scrub her body, starting at her feet and working meticulously up to the top of her head, using certain washcloths for certain areas of her body. Any articles of clothing that appeared to have been "contaminated" were thrown into the laundry. Clean clothing was put in the spots that were vacant. She would then dress herself in the opposite order from which she took the clothes off. If there were any deviations from this order, or if Bess began to wonder if she had missed some contamination, she would go through the entire se-

TABLE 12-1

Giving fear a proper name

PHOBIA	STIMULUS	PHOBIA	STIMULUS
Acrophobia	Heights	Herpetophobia	Reptiles
Aerophobia	Flying	Hydrophobia	Water
Agoraphobia	Open spaces	Mikrophobia	Germs
Ailurophobia	Cats	Murophobia	Mice
Amaxophobia	Vehicles, driving	Mysophobia	Dirt or germs
Anthophobia	Flowers	Numerophobia	Numbers
Anthrophobia	People	Nyctophobia	Darkness
Aquaphobia	Water	Ochlophobia	Crowds
Arachrophobia	Spiders	Ophidiophobia	Snakes
Astraphobia	Lightning	Ornithophobia	Birds
Brontophobia	Thunder	Phonophobia	Speaking out loud
Claustrophobia	Closed spaces	Pyrophobia	Fire
Cynophobia	Dogs	Thanatophobia	Death
Dementophobia	Insanity	Trichophobia	Hair
Gephyrophobia	Bridges	Xenophobia	Strangers

quence again. It was not rare for her to do this four or five times in a row on certain evenings (Meyer & Osborne, 1982, p. 156).

Unfortunately for people experiencing an obsessive-compulsive disorder, there is no reduction of anxiety from carrying out a compulsive ritual. They tend to lead lives, then, filled with unrelenting tension.

When the Physical Leads to the Psychological: Somatoform Disorders

Most of us know people who cannot wait to regale us with their latest physical problems; even an innocent "How are you?" brings a long list of complaints in response. People who consistently report physical problems, have a preoccupation with their health, and have unrealistic fears of disease may be experiencing a problem known as **hypochondriasis**. In hypochondriasis there is a constant fear of illness, and physical sensations are misinterpreted as signs of disease. It is not that the "symptoms" are faked; hypochondriacs actually experience the aches and pains that most of us feel as we go through an active existence (Costa & McCrae, 1985). It is the misinterpretation of these sensations as symptoms of some dread disease—often in the face of unarguable medical evidence to the contrary—that characterizes hypochondriasis.

Hypochondriasis (HY po kon DRY a sis): *A constant fear of illness and misinterpretation of normal aches and pains*

Hypochondriasis is just one example of a class of disorders known as **somatoform disorders**—psychological difficulties that take on a physical (or somatic) form of one sort or another. Even though an individual reports physical symptoms, there is no underlying physical problem. Only when a physical examination rules out actual physiological difficulties can a diagnosis of somatoform disorder be made.

Somatoform (so MAT ah form) **disorders**: *Psychological difficulties that take on physical (somatic) forms*

In addition to hypochondriasis, the other major somatoform disorder is conversion disorder. In contrast to hypochondriasis, where there is no actual physical problem, **conversion disorders** involve an actual physical disturbance such as the inability to use a sensory organ or the complete or partial inability to move an arm or a leg. The *cause* of such physical disturbance is purely psychological; there is no biological reason for the problem.

Conversion disorder: *Psychological disturbances characterized by actual physical disturbances, such as the inability to speak or move one's arms*

Some of Freud's classic cases involved conversion disorders. For instance, one patient of Freud's was unable to use her arm—but suddenly, quite dramatically, regained its use. Conversion disorders are often characterized by the sudden onset of such difficulties as blindness, deafness, or numbness that is restricted to a certain part of the body.

Interestingly, one of the characteristics of conversion disorders is a surprising lack of concern over the symptoms that one would expect to be highly anxiety-producing. For instance, a person in good health who wakes up blind might react in a bland, matter-of-fact way. Considering how most people would feel if it happened to them, this reaction hardly seems appropriate.

Most conversion disorders occur when an individual is under some sort of emotional stress that can be alleviated by the appearance of a physical symptom. The physical condition allows the person to avoid accepting responsibility for the stress-induced problem. An emotional problem is turned, then, into a physical ailment that acts to relieve the original emotional problem.

In one large-scale example of conversion disorder, Mucha and Reinhardt (1970) found that some 16 percent of the student aviators at the U.S. Naval Aerospace Medical Institute suffered symptoms for which there was no underlying physical problem. The difficulties most frequently included blurred vision,

Although in reality quite rare, the disorder of multiple personality has been featured in many novels and films. For instance, movie buffs will recall *The Three Faces of Eve*, a famous film that describes the case of a woman with three separate personalities. (*Movie Star News*)

double vision, or the development of blind spots and focusing trouble. Investigation revealed that the students found outright quitting an unacceptable response to the stress they were experiencing and instead developed physical responses that allowed them to avoid the demands of the program. Their stress was thus relieved through a face-saving physical problem.

One Becomes Two (or More): Dissociative Disorders

Dissociative (dis SO see ah tiv) **disorders**: *The splitting apart of critical personality facets, allowing stress avoidance by escape*

The most dramatic and celebrated cases of psychological dysfunctioning—although they are actually quite rare—have been **dissociative disorders**. The movie *The Three Faces of Eve,* the book *Sybil,* about a girl with sixteen personalities, and cases of people found wandering the streets with no notion of who they are or where they came from exemplify dissociative disorders. The key factor in such problems is the splitting apart (or dissociation) of critical parts of personality that are normally integrated and work together. This lack of integration acts to allow certain parts of a personality to avoid stress—since another part can be made to face it. By dissociating themselves from key parts of their personality, then, such individuals can eliminate anxiety.

Multiple personality: *A disorder in which a person displays characteristics of two or more distinct personalities*

There are three major types of dissociative disorders: multiple personality, psychogenic amnesia, and psychogenic fugue. A person with a **multiple personality** displays characteristics of two or more distinct personalities. Each personality has a unique set of likes and dislikes and its own reactions to situations, In fact, some people with multiple personalities carry several pairs of glasses because their vision changes with each personality (Braun, 1985). Moreover, each individual personality can be well adjusted, when considered on its own.

The problem, of course, is that there is only one body available to the various personalities, forcing the personalities to take turns. Because there can be strong variations in personalities, the person's behavior—considered as a whole—can appear very inconsistent. For instance, in the famous case portrayed in *The*

Three Faces of Eve, the meek, bland Eve White provided a stunning contrast to the dominant and carefree Eve Black (Nunes, 1975).

Psychogenic amnesia, another dissociative disorder, is a failure or an inability to remember past experiences. In the most severe forms, individuals cannot recall their names, are unable to recognize parents and other relatives, and do not know their addresses. In other respects they appear quite normal: Apart from an inability to remember certain facts about themselves, amnesiacs are able to recall skills and abilities that they developed earlier. For instance, even though a chef may not remember where he grew up and received training, he may still be able to prepare gourmet meals.

Psychogenic amnesia (sy ko JEN ik am NEE zee ah): *A failure to remember past experience*

A more unusual form of amnesia is a condition known as **psychogenic fugue**. In this state people will take an impulsive, sudden trip, often assuming a new identity. After a period of time—days, months, or sometimes even years—they suddenly realize that they are in a strange place and completely forget the time that they have spent wandering. Their last memories are those just before they entered the fugue state.

Psychogenic fugue (sy ko JEN ik FEWG): *An amnesiac condition in which people take sudden, impulsive trips, sometimes assuming a new identity*

What the dissociative disorders have in common is that they allow people to escape from some anxiety-producing situation. Either the person produces a new personality to deal with stress or the situation that caused the stress is forgotten or left behind as the individual journeys to some new—and hopefully less anxiety-ridden—situation.

RECAP AND REVIEW III

Recap

- Although they have their drawbacks, classification systems are necessary to describe and ultimately understand abnormal behavior.
- The *Diagnostic and Statistical Manual of Mental Disorders, third edition* (*DSM-III*), provides a description of some 230 separate diagnostic categories of abnormal behavior.
- Anxiety disorders occur when anxiety is so great that it impedes a person's everyday functioning.
- Somatoform disorders are psychological problems that take on a physical form.
- Dissociative disorders occur when there is a splitting apart of personality.

Review

1. *DSM-III* is intended to both describe abnormal behaviors and suggest their underlying causes. True or false?
2. The cause of anxiety in a generalized anxiety disorder is usually known and understood by the person with the disorder. True or false?
3. Kathy is terrified by elevators. She is likely to be suffering from a(n)
   a. obsessive-compulsive disorder **b.** phobic disorder **c.** panic disorder **d.** generalized anxiety disorder
4. John described an incident where his anxiety rose suddenly to a peak and he felt a sense of impending doom. He had experienced a(n) ____________ ____________.
5. Troubling thoughts which persist for days or months are known as
   a. obsessions **b.** compulsions **c.** rituals **d.** panic attacks
6. A physical examination to rule out actual physiological difficulties is necessary before a diagnosis of a somatoform disorder can be made. True or false?
7. In what major way does a conversion disorder differ from hypochondriasis?
8. The splitting apart of the personality is the key factor in ____________ disorders.
9. Sue Ann displays two entirely separate and inconsistent personalities. She probably suffers from
   a. psychogenic fugue **b.** psychogenic amnesia **c.** variable personality **d.** multiple personality

(Answers to review questions are at the bottom of page 414.)

While temporary depression is a normal outcome following one of life's disappointments, in some cases depression is so severe and lingering that it represents a major psychological disorder. (*Norman Mosallem/Medichrome*)

Affective disorders: *Mood disturbances severe enough to interfere with normal living*

Major depression: *A severe form of depression that interferes with concentration, decision making, and sociability*

The Mood Is Wrong: Affective Disorders

> I do not care for anything. I do not care to ride, for the exercise is too violent. I do not care to walk, walking is too strenuous. I do not care to lie down, for I should either have to remain lying, and I do not care to do that, or I should have to get up again, and I do not care to do that either. . . . I do not care at all.

Have you ever studied days and days for a big test, walked in confident that you knew the material, and found the test so difficult that you knew from the first moment you were going to fail? Although the feelings you experienced as you left the examination room were probably not as strong as those felt by the Danish philosopher Søren Kierkegaard, who wrote the passage above, it is likely that you experienced a feeling of depression, an emotional reaction of sadness and melancholy. More than likely, however, you soon returned to a more pleasant frame of mind.

We all experience mood swings. Sometimes we are happy, perhaps even euphoric; at other times we feel upset, saddened, or depressed. Such changes in mood are a normal part of everyday life. In some people, however, moods are so pronounced and so long-lasting that they interfere with the ability to function effectively. In extreme cases, a mood may become life-threatening and in others it may cause the person to lose touch with reality. Moods such as these represent **affective disorders**, mood disturbances strong enough to intrude on everyday living.

Feeling Down: Major Depression When Menachem Begin resigned as prime minister of Israel in 1983, his behavior was already a source of speculation in the world press. He was said to be unable to concentrate on events, unable to make decisions, and incapable of socializing even with old friends and family. The general opinion of those close enough to him to observe his behavior was that he was suffering from **major depression**, one of the most common forms of affective disorders. In fact, the percentage of people who are likely to experience major depression during their lifetimes is 8 to 12 percent for men and 20 to 26 percent for women (Boyd & Weissman, 1981). Moreover, depression is the most frequent problem diagnosed in outpatient clinics, affecting about one-third of the patients (Winokur, 1983; Woodruff, Clayton, & Guze, 1975).

When psychologists speak of major depression they do not mean the sadness that comes from experiencing one of life's disappointments. Some depression is normal following the break-up of a long-term relationship, the death of a loved one, or the loss of a job. It is even normal for less serious problems: doing badly in school or not getting into the college of one's first choice. In fact, many college students experience some form of ''normal'' depression during their years in school. Blatt, D'Afflitti, and Quinlan (1976) studied cases of ''normal''depression in college students and found that depression tended to be characterized by three sets of factors: dependency on others' help and support, exaggeration of one's faults, and the sense that one is not in control of one's life. (For more information on the kinds of psychological difficulties college students experience, see the Psychology at Work box.)

ANSWERS TO REVIEW QUESTIONS

Review III: **1.** False **2.** False **3.** b **4.** Panic attack **5.** a **6.** True **7.** There is an actual physical disturbance present with a conversion disorder. **8.** Dissociative **9.** d

PSYCHOLOGY AT WORK

THE SPECIAL PROBLEMS OF COLLEGE STUDENTS

> I remember my first week at college. My parents drove me to the campus. It was rainy and dark. I felt sort of scared 'cause I'd come from a small town. All my high school teachers said I'd do great at college. I wasn't so sure. What if they were wrong? What if I was really just a "big fish in a little pond?" Well, the day was rainy, the other students walked around aimlessly as did I. I remember the sick feeling I had when my parents drove off and left me. I was left to grow up. Even with all the fighting and hate that went on in our house over the previous two years, and even though I couldn't wait to get away, I was scared, sad, unbelievably lonely (Duke & Nowicki, 1979, p. 517).

Have you experienced similar feelings during your college career? In fact, such thoughts are relatively common, and represent one of the special psychological difficulties of college students—the freshman adjustment reaction. Students with this problem are depressed, severely homesick, and may be anxious and withdrawn from others. It often is most severe in students who had perceived themselves as particularly successful high school seniors—either socially or academically—and suddenly find themselves without status or authority and looked down upon by upperclassmen. The cure? Often just the passage of time is enough, especially since time passing by inevitably brings the next class of freshmen to campus. In severe cases, however, counseling may be appropriate.

Duke and Nowicki (1979) have identified other problems that can create psychological difficulties and are of particular concern to college students.

- For male students:
  - Grades
  - Social life
  - Vocational decisions
  - The future
  - Sexual relationships
  - Peer pressures
  - Adjusting to new environment
  - Leaving family for first time
  - Competition
  - Depression
- For female students:
  - What to do with their lives
  - Developing sexual and emotional relationships
  - Strain from too much work
  - Grades
  - Adjustment
  - Gaining independence
  - Identity
  - Pressure from parents
  - Peer pressures
  - Morals

As you can see from this list, many of the problems students experience are unique to the specific demands of college and the particular stage of a student's life. In fact, knowing that others are going through the same sorts of problems is often a step in alleviating some of the stress involved in the difficulties, which tend to be fairly universal among college students.

Individuals who suffer from major depression experience similar sorts of feelings, but the severity tends to be considerably greater. They may feel useless, worthless, and lonely, and feel despair over the future—feelings that may continue for months and years. They may have uncontrollable crying jags and disrupted sleep. It is the depth and the length of time such behavior lasts, then, that is the hallmark of major depression.

Because it represents a major mental-health problem, depression has received a good deal of study, and a number of approaches have been used to explain its occurrence (Clayton & Barrett, 1983). Psychoanalytic approaches, for example, see depression as the result of anger at oneself. In this view, people feel responsible for the bad things that happen to them and direct their anger inward. On the other hand, there is convincing evidence that heredity plays a role in depression, since major depression seems to run in certain families (Rosenthal, 1970). Moreover, some researchers have found a chemical imbalance in the brains of depressive patients. There appear to be abnormalities in the chemical substance involved in the transmission of electric charges across the gaps between nerve cells (Wender & Klein, 1981). The genetic and chemical evidence suggests that people's moods may be determined in part by biological factors rather than the psychological factors suggested by psychoanalytic approaches (McNeal & Cimbolic, 1986).

There are still other explanations for depression. For instance, Seligman (1975) suggests that depression is a response to learned helplessness, a state in which a person preceives and eventually learns that there is no way to escape or cope with stress and simply gives up fighting it. Whatever the specific approach used to explain depression, each suggests that somewhat different treatment strategies be taken.

Ups and Downs: Mania and Bipolar Disorders While some people are sinking into the depths of depression, others are emotionally soaring high, experiencing what is called mania. **Mania** refers to an extended state of intense euphoria and elation. People experiencing mania feel intense happiness, power, invulnerability, and energy. They may become involved in wild schemes, believing that they will succeed at anything they attempt. There are many cases on record of people squandering all their money while in a state of mania; consider, for example, the following description of an individual who experienced a manic episode:

Mania (MAY nee ah): *An extended state of intense euphoria and elation*

> Mr. O'Reilly took a leave of absence from his civil service job, purchased a large number of cuckoo clocks and then an expensive car which he planned to use as a mobile showroom for his wares, anticipating that he would make a great deal of money. He proceeded to "tear around town" buying and selling clocks and other merchandise, and when he was not out, he was continuously on the phone making "deals." He rarely slept and, uncharacteristically, spent every evening in neighborhood bars drinking heavily and, according to him, "wheeling and dealing". . . . He was $3,000 in debt and had driven his family to exhaustion with his excessive activity and overtalkativeness. He said however that he felt "on top of the world" (Spitzer, Skodol, Gibbon, & Williams, 1983, p. 115).

Mania is typically paired with bouts of depression. This alternation of mania and depression is called **bipolar disorder** (or, as it used to be known, manic-depressive disorder). The swings between highs and lows may occur as frequently as a few days apart or they may alternate over a period of years. In addition, the periods of depression tend to be longer in most individuals than the periods of mania, although this pattern is reversed in some.

Bipolar disorder: *A disorder in which a person alternates between euphoric feelings of mania and bouts of depression*

Interestingly, it has been suggested that some of society's most creative individuals may suffer from a mild form of bipolar disorder (Fieve, 1975). The imagination, drive, excitement, and energy that they display during manic stages allows them to make unusually creative contributions. On the other hand, most people who display mania go beyond the bounds of what would generally be considered normal, and their behavior clearly causes self-harm.

When Reality Is Lost: Schizophrenia

> For many years she has heard voices, which insult her and cast suspicion on her chastity. They mention a number of names she knows, and tell her she will be stripped and abused. The voices are very distinct, and, in her opinion, they must be carried by a telescope or a machine from her home. Her thoughts

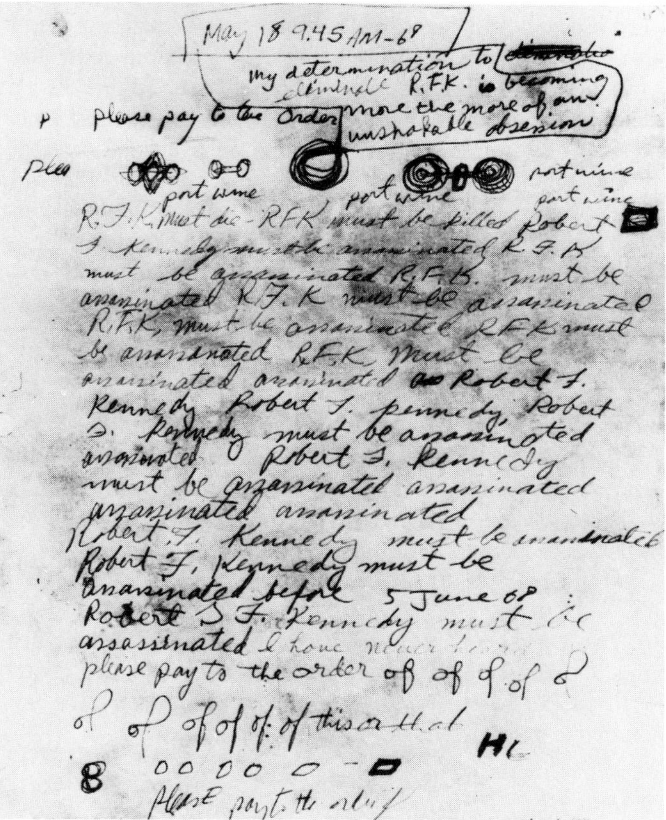

May 18 9.45 AM-68

my determination to eliminate R.F.K. is becoming more the more of an unshakable obsession

please pay to the order

port wine port wine port wine port wine

R.F.K. must die - RFK must be killed Robert F. Kennedy must be assassinated R.F.K. must be assassinated R.F.K. must be assassinated R.F.K. must be assassinated R.F.K. must be assassinated RFK must be assassinated R.F.K. Must be assassinated assassinated Robert F. Kennedy Robert F. Kennedy Robert F. Kennedy must be assassinated assassinated Robert F. Kennedy must be assassinated assassinated assassinated assassinated Robert F. Kennedy must be assassinated Robert F. Kennedy must be assassinated before 5 June 68 Robert F. Kennedy must be assassinated I have never heard please pay to the order of of of of of of of of of of this or that

8 00000

please pay to the

Figure 12-1
This excerpt from the diary of Sirhan Sirhan, the killer of Robert F. Kennedy, shows the disturbances of thought and language characteristic of schizophrenia. (Wide World Photos)

are dictated to her; she is obliged to think them, and hears them repeated after her. She is interrupted in her work, and has all kinds of uncomfortable sensations in her body, to which something is "done." In particular, her "mother parts" are turned inside out, and people send a pain through her back, lay ice-water on her heart, squeeze her neck, injure her spine, and violate her (Kraepelin, 1904).

The label given to the most severe forms of mental disturbance, such as that described in the famous case study above, is **schizophrenia**. People suffering from schizophrenia make up by far the largest percentage of those hospitalized for mental disorders, and in most respects are the least likely to recover from their difficulties.

Schizophrenia (skits uh FREN ee ah): *A class of disorders characterized by a severe distortion of reality, resulting in antisocial behavior, silly or obscene behavior, hallucinations, and disturbances in movement*

Schizophrenia refers to a class of disorders in which there is severe distortion of reality. Thinking, perception, and emotion may deteriorate; there may be a withdrawal from social interaction; and there may be displays of bizarre behavior. Although there is no one absolute pattern to displays of schizophrenia (see Table 12-2), there are a number of characteristics that reliably distinguish it:

- Decline from a previous level of functioning. An individual can no longer carry out activities he or she was once able to do.
- Disturbances of thought and language. Schizophrenics use logic and language in a peculiar way: Their thinking does not make sense and they do not

Figure 12-2
This haunting art was created by an individual suffering from severe mental disturbance. (Prinzhorn, H., *Artistry of the Mentally Ill.* © 1972 Springer-Verlag Berlin-Heidelberg-New York-Tokyo)

Delusions (dee LU jhuns): *Firmly held beliefs with no basis in reality*
Hallucinations (hah loos in A shuns): *Perceptions of things that do not actually exist*

follow conventional linguistic rules. Schizophrenics often have **delusions**—firmly held, unshakable beliefs with no basis in reality—that they are being controlled by someone else or that they are being persecuted by others (see Figure 12-1).

- Perceptual disorders. Schizophrenics do not perceive the world as most other people do. They may see, hear, or smell things differently from other people (see Figure 12-2). They do not even have a sense of their bodies in the way that others do. Some reports suggest that schizophrenics have difficulty determining where their own bodies stop and the rest of the world begins (Ritzler & Rosenbaum, 1974). They may also have **hallucinations**, the experience of perceiving things that do not actually exist.
- Emotional disturbances. Schizophrenics sometimes show a bland lack of emotion, or, conversely, emotion that is inappropriate to a situation. For example, a schizophrenic might laugh at a funeral or may react with anger when being helped by someone.
- Withdrawal. Schizophrenics tend to have little interest in others. They tend not to socialize or hold real conversations with others, although they may talk *at* another person. In the most extreme cases they do not even acknowledge the presence of other people, appearing to be in their own isolated world.

Solving the Puzzle: The Causes of Schizophrenia. While it is clear that schizophrenic behavior departs radically from normal behavior, its causes are less apparent. It does appear, however, that schizophrenia has genetic, biochemical, and environmental components at its roots (Mirsky & Duncan, 1986; Watt, 1985).

TABLE 12-2

The major types of schizophrenia

TYPE	SYMPTOMS
Disorganized (hebephrenic) schizophrenia	Inappropriate laughter and giggling, silliness, incoherent speech, infantile behavior, strange and sometimes obscene behavior
Paranoid schizophrenia	Delusions and hallucinations of persecution or of greatness, loss of judgment, erratic and unpredictable behavior
Catatonic schizophrenia	Major disturbances in movement; in some phases, loss of all motion, with patient frozen into a single position, remaining that way for hours and sometimes even days; in other phases, hyperactivity and wild, sometimes violent, movement
Undifferentiated schizophrenia	Variable mixture of major symptoms of schizophrenia; classification used for patients who cannot be typed into any of the more specific categories
Residual schizophrenia	Minor signs of schizophrenia following a more serious episode.

GENETIC COMPONENTS. Because schizophrenia is more common in some families than in others, genetic factors seem to be involved in producing at least a susceptibility or readiness for developing schizophrenia (Faraone & Tsuang, 1985). For example, some studies show that people who have been classified as suffering from schizophrenia have about a 25 percent chance of having children with severe psychological problems. Furthermore if one of a pair of identical twins has schizophrenia, the other has as much as a 42 percent chance of developing it (Gottesman & Schields, 1972; Kringlen, 1978). However, if genetics alone were entirely accountable, the chance of the other identical twin having schizophrenia would be 100 percent, since identical twins share the same genetic makeup. The development of schizophrenia, then, is due to more than just genetic factors.

BIOCHEMICAL COMPONENTS. One of the most intriguing hypotheses to explain schizophrenia is that there is some sort of biochemical imbalance in the brains of people with the disorder (Asnis & Ryan, 1983; Noll & Davis, 1983). One form of this theory suggests that schizophrenia occurs when a person's body in a condition of stress produces chemicals that cause hallucinations or disorganized thought—similar to the effects of ingesting drugs such as LSD—in a sort of self-induced chemical overdose (Carson, 1983).

On the other hand, alternate theories resting on the notion of a biochemical imbalance are also plausible. For instance, the **dopamine hypothesis** suggests that schizophrenia occurs when there is excess activity in those areas of the brain that use the chemical dopamine to transmit impulses across nerve cells (Snyder, 1978). This hypothesis came to light after the discovery that drugs which block dopamine action in brain pathways can be highly effective in reducing the symptoms of schizophrenia. (Further biological evidence is discussed in the Cutting Edge box.)

Dopamine (DOPE uh meen) **hypothesis**: *A theory that suggests that schizophrenia occurs when there is excess activity in those areas of the brain using dopamine to transmit nerve impulses*

Unfortunately, the dopamine hypothesis does not provide the whole story. Drugs that block dopamine action produce a biological reaction in just a few hours after they're taken—yet the symptoms of schizophrenia don't subside for weeks. If the hypothesis were entirely correct, we would expect an immediate improvement in schizophrenic symptoms. Moreover, these drugs are not only effective in reducing symptoms in schizophrenics but in those suffering from very different sorts of psychological problems such as mania and depression (Carson, 1983). Nevertheless, the dopamine hypothesis provides a starting point in understanding biochemical factors in schizophrenia.

ENVIRONMENTAL COMPONENTS. Given that genetic and biochemical factors do not provide a full explanation for schizophrenia, we need to consider environmental factors (Keith & Matthews, 1983). Psychoanalytic approaches suggest that schizophrenia is a form of regression to earlier experiences and stages of life. Freud says, for instance, that people with schizophrenia lack strong enough egos to cope with their unacceptable impulses. They regress to the oral stage—a time in which the id and ego are not yet separated. Therefore, individuals suffering from schizophrenia essentially lack an ego and act out impulses without concern for reality.

Although theoretically reasonable, there is little evidence to support psychoanalytic explanations. More compelling are theories that look toward the family and other major figures in the lives of people with schizophrenia. One influential theory, known as the **double-bind hypothesis**, states that individuals with

Double-bind hypothesis: *A theory that suggests that people suffering from schizophrenia may have received simultaneous contradictory messages from their mothers and never learned what behavior was appropriate*

THE CUTTING EDGE

SCHIZOPHRENIA

A Behavioral or a Biological Problem?

While diagnoses of schizophrenia are typically made on the basis of an individual's behavior, an exciting new approach to diagnosis—as well as an important advance in understanding the causes of schizophrenia—suggests that the brains of schizophrenics have structural abnormalities that someday could be used to predict when a person will show behaviors typical of schizophrenia.

The notion that there are abnormalities in the brains of people with schizophrenia is based on research being done in the laboratories of Arnold Scheibel and Joyce Kovelman of the University of California's Brain Research Institute in Los Angeles. They have found that they are able to distinguish between the brains of schizophrenics and normal individuals by examining microscopic photographs of brain samples taken from the hippocampus, an area of the brain related to the expression of emotions.

In their initial work, they took specimens from ten long-term schizophrenics and eight normal people who had died when they were between the ages of 25 and 67. They later studied the samples—without knowing from which population they came—and were able to distinguish between the two groups. The major difference was in the organization of cells: In normal people, the nerve cells were arranged in orderly rows, while the cells of those with schizophrenia were in disarray. Not only were some of the cells of those with schizophrenia rotated some 90 degrees from their proper orientation, but some of the dendrites of the nerve cells were disorganized. Moreover, further research has revealed that there is a rough correlation between the severity of cell disorganization and schizophrenia symptoms: The greater the disorganization, the more severe are the schizophrenic symptoms (Scheibel, 1984).

This work is the first demonstration that there are clear structural problems in the brains of people with schizophrenia. In an interview for this book, Dr. Scheibel suggested that the problems associated with schizophrenia may have their origin as early as the first three months of pregnancy, when the nerve cells of the developing embryo are supposed to align themselves appropriately.

When this research is added to other current work that uses CAT and PET scans (discussed in Chapter 2) to assess the brains of schizophrenics, it becomes increasingly clear that someday biological techniques may be developed to accurately and reliably diagnose schizophrenia—and perhaps, in addition, other forms of mental disturbance. Ultimately, it may be possible to do genetic screening in unborn infants to test for schizophrenia. Just as today we take blood tests for granted, diagnosticians in the not-so-distant future may make routine use of brain-cell tests.

schizophrenia may have received simultaneous messages from their mothers that contradict one another (Bateson, 1960). Consider, for example, how you would react if someone told you to "come here," and then, as you approached, waved you away. According to the hypothesis, this is essentially what happens in some families: The mother is warm and loving on a verbal level but anxious and rejecting on an emotional and nonverbal level. The results are so devastating to the child that eventually he or she develops schizophrenia.

Although the details of the double-bind hypothesis have not received considerable support, there is firm evidence that families with members who have schizophrenia often have abnormal communication patterns (Wynne, Singer, Bartko, & Toohey, 1975). These families may differ on a number of other dimensions as well, including socioeconomic status, anxiety level, and general degree of stress present (Lidz, 1973). Theorists taking a behavioral perspective believe these differences support a **learned-inattention theory of schizophrenia** (Ullman & Krasner, 1975).

Learned-inattention theory of schizophrenia: *A theory that suggests that schizophrenia is a learned behavior consisting of a set of inappropriate responses to social stimuli*

According to the learned-inattention view, schizophrenia is a learned behavior consisting of a set of inappropriate responses to social stimuli. Instead of responding to others, people with schizophrenia have learned to ignore appropriate stimuli and pay attention instead to stimuli that are not related to normal social interaction. Because this results in bizarre behavior, others respond to them in a negative way, leading to social rejection and unpleasant interactions and ultimately to an even less appropriate response by the individual. Eventually the individual begins to ''tune out'' appropriate stimuli and develops schizophrenic characteristics.

THE CAUSES OF SCHIZOPHRENIA: NOT ONE, BUT MANY? As we have seen, there is research supporting genetic, biochemical, and environmental causes of schizophrenia. It is likely, then, that not just one but several causes jointly explain the onset of the problem. The predominant approach used today is one that considers a number of factors simultaneously: the **predisposition model of schizophrenia** (Zubin and Spring, 1977). This model suggests that individuals may inherit a predisposition or an inborn sensitivity to schizophrenia which makes them particularly vulnerable to stressful factors in the environment (Faraone & Tsuang, 1985). The stressors may vary—a poor family environment, social rejection, or dysfunctional communication patterns—but if they are sufficiently strong and are coupled with the specific genetic predisposition, this model suggests that the result will be the onset of schizophrenia. In sum, the predisposition model suggests that schizophrenia is not produced by any single factor but is an amalgamation of interrelated problems.

Predisposition model of schizophrenia: *A model that suggests that individuals may inherit a predisposition toward schizophrenia that makes them particularly vulnerable to stressful factors in the environment*

Lacking Distress: Personality Disorders

I had always wanted lots of things; as a child I can remember wanting a bullet that a friend of mine had brought in to show the class. I took it and put it into my school bag and when my friend noticed it was missing, I was the one who stayed after school with him and searched the room, and I was the one who sat with him and bitched about the other kids and how one of them took his bullet. I even went home with him to help him break the news to his uncle, who had brought it home from the war for him.

But that was petty compared to the stuff I did later. I wanted a Ph.D. very badly, but I didn't want to work very hard—just enough to get by. I never did the experiments I reported; hell, I was smart enough to make up the results. I knew enough about statistics to make anything look plausible. I got my master's degree without even spending one hour in a laboratory. I mean, the professors believed anything. I'd stay out all night drinking and being with my friends and the next day I'd get in just before them and tell'em I'd been in the lab all night. They'd actually feel sorry for me. I did my doctoral research the same way, except it got published and there was some excitement about my findings. The research helped me get my first college teaching job. There my goal was tenure.

The rules at my university were about the same as at any other. You had to publish and you had to be an effective teacher. ''Gathering'' data and publishing it was never any problem for me, so that was fine. But teaching was evaluated on the basis of forms completed by students at the end of each semester. I'm a fair-to-good teacher, but I had to be sure that my record showed me as excellent. The task was simple. Each semester, I collected the evaluation forms, took out all the fair-to-bad ones and replaced them with doctored ones. It would take me a whole evening, but I'd sit down with a bunch of different colored pens and pencils and would fill in as many as 300 of the forms. Needless to say, I was awarded tenure (Duke & Nowicki, 1979, pp. 309-310).

Personality disorder: *A mental disorder characterized by a set of inflexible, maladaptive personality traits that keep a person from functioning properly in society*

Before you think that all college professors are like the one describing himself above, it should be stated that this person represents a clear example of someone with a **personality disorder**. Personality disorders are different from the other problems that we have discussed in this chapter, because there is often little sense of personal distress associated with the psychological maladjustment of those affected. In fact, people with personality disorders frequently lead seemingly normal lives—until one looks just below the surface. There one finds a set of inflexible, maladaptive personality traits that do not permit the individual to function appropriately as a member of society.

Antisocial (sociopathic) (an TIE so shul so she o PATH ik) **personality disorder**: *A disorder in which individuals display no regard for moral and ethical rules or for the rights of others*

The best-known type of personality disorder is the **antisocial** or **sociopathic personality disorder**. Individuals with this disorder tend to display no regard for the moral and ethical rules of society or for the rights of others. Although they appear intelligent and are usually likeable at first, they can be seen as manipulative and deceptive upon closer examination. Moreover, they tend to share certain other characteristics (Coleman, Butcher, & Carson, 1984):

- A lack of conscience, guilt, or anxiety over transgressions. When those with an antisocial personality behave in a way that injures someone else, they understand intellectually that they have caused the harm, but feel no remorse.
- An inability to withstand frustration and impulsive behavior. Antisocial personalities are unable to withstand frustration without reacting in some way—which may include violating the rights of others, if doing so allows them to remove the frustration.
- Manipulation of others. Antisocial personalities frequently have very good interpersonal skills: They are charming, engaging, and able to convince others to do what they want. In fact, some of the best con men have antisocial personalities and are able to get people to hand over their life savings without a second thought. The misery that follows in the wake of such activities is not cause for concern to the antisocial personality.

What causes such an unusual constellation of problems? A variety of factors have been suggested, ranging from a biological inability to experience emotions to problems in family relationships. For example, in many cases of antisocial behavior, the individual has come from a home in which a parent has died or left, one in which there is a lack of affection, a lack of consistency in discipline, or outright rejection. Other explanations concentrate on sociocultural factors, since an unusually high proportion of antisocial personalities come from lower socioeconomic groups. Some researchers have suggested that the breakdown of societal rules, norms and regulations that may be found in severely deprived economic environments may encourage the development of antisocial personalities (Melges & Bowlby, 1969). Still, no one has been able to pinpoint the specific causes of antisocial personalities, and it is likely that some combination of factors is responsible.

The Informed Consumer of Psychology: Deciding When You Need Help

After considering the range and variety of psychological disturbances that can afflict people, it would not be surprising if you were to feel that you are suffering from one (or more) of the problems we have discussed. This would be a perfectly natural reaction, for, as we mentioned earlier, people often conclude that they have the same problems that they are studying—the classic medical student's disease. Because this is such a common phenomenon, it is important that you be well aware of the pitfalls of self-diagnosis.

One of the truisms of the legal profession is that a lawyer who defends himself has a fool for a client. Similarly we might say that people who try to categorize their own mental disorders are making a foolish mistake. With categories that are subjective under the best of circumstances, and with problems that can be elusive and fleeting even to well-trained,experienced mental-health professionals, it is unreasonable to expect that after reading a chapter in an introductory psychology book anyone could make a valid diagnosis.

On the other hand, there are guidelines you can use to determine when some kind of professional help is warranted. The following signals suggest the possible necessity of some outside intervention:

- Long-term feelings of psychological distress that interfere with your sense of well-being, competence, and ability to function effectively in daily activities
- Occasions in which there is overwhelmingly high stress, accompanied by feelings of inability to cope with the situation
- Prolonged depression or feelings of hopelessness, particularly when you do not have any clear cause such as the death of someone close
- A chronic physical problem for which no physical cause can be determined
- A fear, or phobia, that prevents you from engaging in normal everyday activities
- Feeling that other people are out to get you or are talking about and plotting against you
- The inability to interact effectively with others, preventing the development of friendships and loving relationships

The above criteria can serve as a rough set of guidelines for determining when the normal problems of everyday living are beyond the point that you are capable of dealing with them yourself. In such situations, the least reasonable approach would be to pour over the psychological disorders we have discussed in an attempt to pigeonhole yourself into a specific category. A more reasonable strategy is to consider seeking professional help—a possibility that we discuss in the next chapter.

RECAP AND REVIEW IV

Recap

- Affective disorders are characterized by mood disturbances that are so great they impede daily living.
- Schizophrenia represents the most common diagnosis for those hospitalized for mental disturbance.
- People with personality disorders do not feel the personal distress associated with other disorders, although they have maladaptive traits that prevent them from functioning as normal members of society.

Review

1. Henry's feeling of deep despair, worthlessness, and loneliness have persisted for months. His symptoms are indicative of
   a. an adjustment reaction **b.** normal depression **c.** major depression **d.** affective depression
2. The experience of intense euphoria and elation is called ________________. When such euphoria and elation are paired with bouts of depression, this state is known as a ________________ disorder.

3. If you were to go into an institution for people hospitalized with mental disorders, you would be likely to find only a small percentage of people diagnosed as schizophrenics. True or false?
4. List five characteristics that reliably distinguish schizophrenia from other mental disturbances.
5. What are the five major types of schizophrenia?
6. Because of support for the notion that several factors cause schizophrenia, the predominant approach used today is the
   a. double-bind hypothesis **b.** regression theory **c.** predisposition model **d.** learned-inattention theory
7. The maladaptive traits of people with personality disorders cause them a great deal of personal distress. True or false?
8. A disregard for the moral and ethical rules governing society and the rights of others characterizes the ____________ ______________________________, or ____________, personality disorder.

(Answers to review questions are at the bottom of page 426.)

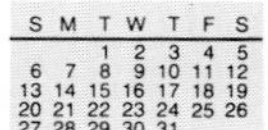

Psychology Looks Toward the 1990s
The Psychology of Health and Stress

As an enterprising businessman, Harry Everett led a life filled with stress and tension. His schedule allowed him little time to exercise, he smoked heavily, and he matched his coworkers drink for drink. He wouldn't eat an egg unless it was fried in bacon grease. By the time he learned that his cholesterol level was dangerously high, it was too late for simple remedies, and a few months later he underwent a quadruple coronary bypass operation.

Now Everett's life is radically different. With the help of a psychologist, he modified his reactions to situations that previously would have produced stress. He also gave up smoking, exercises four or five days a week, and sticks to a careful diet. He feels physically—and psychologically—better than he ever has before.

Traditionally, psychologists have focused on psychological health, leaving issues relating to physical health to the medical profession. However, it is now clear that illnesses that were once considered purely biological in character—such as Harry Everett's heart disease—have significant psychological components. This realization has spawned a new specialty area within psychology, known as health psychology. **Health psychology** explores the relationship between physical and psychological factors, focusing on the prevention, diagnosis, and treatment of medical problems.

Health psychology: *The branch of psychology that explores the relationship between physical and psychological factors*

Health psychology considers questions about how illness is influenced and, in some cases, caused by psychological factors and how psychological principles and findings can provide a basis for treating disease and illness. It is also concerned with issues of prevention, such as how problems like heart disease and stress can be avoided by more healthful behavior.

Stress: *The response to events that are threatening or challenging*

Stressors: *Circumstances that produce threats to our well-being*

One of the major areas of interest to health psychologists is that of **stress,** the response to events that are threatening or challenging. Life is filled with circumstances, known as **stressors,** that produce threats to our well-being. These stressors are not always of a negative nature; even pleasant events, such as planning a wedding or starting a sought-after job can produce stress.

Everyone's life contains stress, and in fact some health psychologists believe that our daily lives involve a series of repeated sequences of perceiving a threat, coping with that threat (with greater or lesser success), and ultimately responding to the threat (Gatchel & Baum, 1983). While the response is often minor and occurs without our being aware of it, in those cases where the stress is more severe and longer-lasting, responding requires a major adaptation effort and can result in physiological and psychological responses that lead to health problems.

Psychologists are finding that stress can take its toll in many ways. Generally, it provokes an immediate physiological reaction. Stress induces a rise in certain hormones secreted by the adrenal glands, a rise in heart rate and blood pressure, and changes in how well the skin conducts electrical impulses (Mason, 1975; Selye, 1976). On a short-term basis, these responses may provide an adaptive response because they can produce an "emergency reaction"—the reaction of the sympathetic nervous system discussed in Chapter 2.

However, continued exposure to stress results in a decline in the body's overall level of biological functioning due to the continued secretion of the stress-related hormones. Over time, in fact, stressful reactions can promote actual deterioration of body tissues such as the blood vessels and the heart (Schneiderman, 1983). Ultimately, we become more susceptible to disease as our ability to fight off germs is lowered.

In addition to major health difficulties, many of the minor aches and pains that we experience may be caused or worsened by stress. These include headaches, backaches, skin rashes, indigestion, fatigue, and constipation (Brown, 1984). Moreover, a whole class of medical problems, known as **psychosomatic disorders,** often result from stress. These medical problems are caused by an interaction of psychological, emotional, and physical difficulties. Among the most common psychosomatic disorders are ulcers, asthma, high blood pressure, and eczema. In fact, the greater the number of stressful events a person experiences, the more likely it is they will suffer from a major illness.

Psychosomatic (psy ko so MAT ik) **disorders**: *Medical problems caused by an interaction of psychological, emotional, and physical difficulties*

On a psychological level, stress prevents people from coping with life adequately. Their view of the environment can become clouded (a minor criticism made by a teacher is blown out of proportion), and—with high levels of stress—emotional responses may be so severe that people are unable to act at all. Moreover, people become less able to deal with new stressors. The ability to contend with future stress, then, declines as a result of past stress (Eckenrode, 1984).

The efforts to control, reduce, or learn to tolerate the threats that lead to stress are known as **coping.** For example, one means of dealing with stress that occurs on an unconscious level is the use of **defense mechanisms.** As we discussed in Chapter 11, defense mechanisms are reactions that maintain a person's sense of control and self-worth by distorting or denying the true nature of the situation; people may simply deny the existence of an unpleasant circumstance. For instance, you may know people who can ignore the fact that they have failed several courses and are in danger of being thrown out of college; they just continue with their lives, making no attempt to face up to or change the situation. Other defense mechanisms sometimes used to "cope" with stress include repression, the blocking of unpleasant thoughts from conscious awareness, and emotional insulation, in which a person stops experiencing any emotions at all, thereby remaining unaffected and unmoved by both positive and negative experiences. The problem with defense mechanisms is that they do not deal with reality but merely hide the problem.

Coping: *The efforts to control, reduce, or learn to tolerate the threats that lead to stress*

Defense mechanisms: *Unconscious strategies people use to reduce anxiety by concealing its source from themselves and others*

Of course, people use other, more direct and potentially more positive means for coping with stress. For example, a large-scale field study being carried out by researchers at the University of California at Berkeley has focused on the factors that lead to more effective coping. In one part of the study, the researchers found that coping was associated with seeking out the social support of others (Dunkel-Schetter, Folkman, & Lazarus, 1987). In another experiment, 100 men and women were asked to record how they coped with a number of different stressors in their lives over a seven-month period. The results showed that people used two major sorts of techniques for dealing with stress: the conscious regulation of emotions, called *emotion-focused coping,* and the management of the stressful problem or stimulus, called *problem-focused coping.* Examples of emotion-focused coping included such strategies as "accepted sympathy and understanding from someone" and "tried to look on the bright side," while examples of problem-focused strategies included "got the person responsible to change his or her mind" and "made a plan of action and followed it." In over 98 percent of the stressful incidents reported, *both* emotion-focused and problem-focused strategies were employed. However, emotion-focused strategies were used more frequently in circumstances perceived as being unchangeable, while problem-focused approaches were used more readily in situations seen as relatively changeable (Folkman & Lazarus, 1980).

The work on stress being carried out by psychologists exemplifies how the borders between physical and mental health are being broken down. As psychologists expand their efforts to understand the impact of psychological factors on health, we are likely to find new answers to questions about the causes and cures of both psychological and physical disorders.

LOOKING BACK

1. We examined abnormal behavior in this chapter, beginning by considering its definition. Two proved inadequate: the deviation-from-the-average and the deviation-from-the-ideal approaches to defining abnormality.

2. A more satisfactory definition is one based on the psychological consequences of abnormal behavior, in which the individual's behavior is thought of as abnormal if it produces a sense of distress, anxiety, or guilt, or if it is harmful to others. Another useful definition is one in which people who cannot adapt to society and are unable to function effectively are considered abnormal. Still, no single definition is totally adequate, and therefore it is reasonable to consider abnormal and normal behavior as marking two ends of a continuum, or scale, with completely normal functioning at one end and completely abnormal behavior at the other.

3. The medical model of abnormal behavior views abnormality as a symptom of an underlying disease—a disease that requires a cure, typically by some expert practitioner. The psychoanalytic model suggests that abnormal behavior is caused by conflicts in the unconscious stemming from past experience. In order to resolve psychological problems, then, it is necessary to resolve the unconscious conflicts.

4. In contrast to the medical and psychoanalytic models, behavioral approaches view abnormal behavior not as a symptom of some underlying problem, but as the problem itself. To resolve the problem, then, one must change the behavior. While traditional behavioral models ignore a person's inner life and focus instead on overt behavior, some behavioral theorists suggest it is appropriate to take a cognitive approach in which the modification of cognitions (thoughts and beliefs) is carried out.

5. Humanistic approaches view people as rational and motivated to get along with others; abnormal behavior is seen as a difficulty in fulfilling one's needs. People are seen as being in control of their lives and able to resolve their own problems.

6. Sociocultural approaches view abnormal behavior in terms of difficulties due to family and other social relationships, concentrating on such factors as socioeconomic status and the rules society creates to define normal and abnormal behavior.

7. Each of these models is helpful in understanding particular aspects of abnormal behavior, and all suggest specific treatments to help resolve psychological difficulties.

8. Students of psychology are susceptible to the same sort of "disease" that afflicts medical students: the perception that they suffer from the problems about which they are studying. Unless their psychological difficulties are persistent, have depth, and are consistent, however, it is unlikely that their concerns are valid.

9. The system to classify abnormal behaviors that is used most widely today is that presented in *DSM-III—Diagnostic and Statistical Manual of Mental Disorders*, third edition.

10. Anxiety disorders are present when a person experiences so much anxiety that it impedes daily functioning. Among the specific sorts of anxiety disorders are generalized anxiety disorder, panic disorder, phobic disorder, and obsessive-compulsive disorder. Generalized anxiety disorder occurs when a person experiences long-term anxiety with no apparent cause. Panic dis-

ANSWERS TO REVIEW QUESTIONS

Review IV: **1.** c **2.** Mania, bipolar **3.** False **4.** Decline from a previous level of functioning; disturbances of thought and language; perception disorders; emotional disturbances; withdrawal **5.** Disorganized (hebephrenic) type; paranoid type; catatonic type; undifferentiated type; residual type **6.** c **7.** False **8.** Antisocial, sociopathic orders are marked by panic attacks, which are sudden, intense feelings of anxiety. Phobic disorders are characterized by intense, irrational fears of specific objects or situations, while those with obsessive-compulsive disorders display obsessions, recurring thoughts or ideas, or compulsions, which are repetitious, unwanted behaviors.

11. Somatoform disorders refer to psychological difficulties that are displayed through physical problems. One example is hypochondriasis, in which there is a constant fear of illness and a preoccupation with disease. Another somatoform disorder is conversion disorder, in which there is an actual physical difficulty that occurs without a physiological cause.

12. Dissociative disorders are marked by the splitting apart, or dissociation, of crucial parts of personality that are usually integrated with one another. The three major kinds of dissociative disorders are multiple personality, psychogenic amnesia, and psychogenic fugue. In multiple-personality disorder, a person shows characteristics of two or more distinct personalities. Psychogenic amnesia is a failure or an inability to remember certain past experiences, and psychogenic fugue occurs when people take sudden, impulsive trips, often taking on new identities.

13. Affective disorders are characterized by moods of depression or euphoria that are so strong they intrude on everyday living. In major depression, people experience such deep sorrow that it may threaten their lives. In mania, there is an extended sense of elation and powerfulness. Sometimes the two moods alternate; this is an example of bipolar disorder.

14. Schizophrenia is one of the most severe forms of mental disorder. The manifestations of schizophrenia include declines in functioning, thought and language disturbances, perception disorders, emotional disturbances, and withdrawal from others. There is strong evidence linking schizophrenia to genetic, biochemical, and environmental factors. According to the predisposition model, there is likely to be an interaction among various factors.

15. Personality disorders are the last classification of mental disorder that we discussed in this chapter. Personality disorders produce little or no sense of personal distress, but they do cause an inability to function as a normal member of society. The best-known type of personality disorder is the antisocial, or sociopathic, personality disorder in which there is no regard paid to the moral and ethical rules of society.

16. There are a number of signals that indicate a need for professional help. These include long-term feelings of psychological distress, feelings of inability to cope with stress, prolonged feelings of hopelessness, chronic physcial problems with no apparent causes, phobias and compulsions, paranoia, and an inability to interact with others.

KEY TERMS AND CONCEPTS

continuum (397)
medical model of abnormality (400)
psychoanalytic model of abnormality (401)
behavioral model of abnormality (401)
humanistic model of abnormality (402)
sociocultural model of abnormality (403)
medical student's disease (406)
DSM-III (407)
anxiety (408)
anxiety disorder (408)
generalized anxiety disorder (409)
panic disorder (409)
panic attack (409)
phobic disorder (409)
phobia (409)
obsessive-compulsive disorder (409)
obsession (409)
compulsion (410)
hypochondriasis (411)
somatoform disorder (412)
conversion disorder (412)
dissociative disorder (412)
multiple personality (412)
psychogenic amnesia (413)
psychogenic fugue (413)
affective disorder (414)
major depression (414)
mania (416)
bipolar disorder (416)
schizophrenia (417)
delusions (418)
hallucinations (418)
disorganized (hebephrenic) schizophrenia (418)
paranoid schizophrenia (418)
catatonic schizophrenia (418)
undifferentiated schizophrenia (418)
residual schizophrenia (418)
dopamine hypothesis (419)
double-bind hypothesis (419)
learned-inattention theory of schizophrenia (420)
predisposition model of schizophrenia (421)
personality disorder (422)
antisocial (sociopathic) personality disorder (422)
health psychology (424)
stress (424)
stressors (424)
psychosomatic disorders (425)
coping (425)
defense mechanisms (425)

FOR FURTHER STUDY AND APPLICATION

Coleman, J. C., Butcher, J. N., & Carson, R. C. (1984). *Abnormal psychology and modern life.* Glenview, IL: Scott, Foresman.

A classic overview of abnormal behavior, now in its seventh edition, this volume provides the full sweep and depth of abnormal psychology.

Sutherland, N. S. (1976). *Breakdown.* New York: Stein & Day.

If you have ever wondered what it is like to experience a mental breakdown, read this book. Written by a psychologist, it is an autobiographical narration of the author's breakdown and subsequent recovery.

Hinckley, J., Hinckley, J., & Sherrill, E. (1985). *Breaking points.* Grand Rapids, MI: Zondervan.

An account of John Hinckley's life and times as seen through the eyes of his parents, this book provides insight into the development of Hinckley's abnormal behavior.

Meyer, R., & Osborne, Y. (1982). *Case studies in abnormal behavior.* Boston: Allyn & Bacon.

This book presents some fascinating case studies of individuals who suffer from many of the problems discussed in this chapter, along with explanations for the disorders.

Thigpen, C. H., & Cleckley, H. M. (1954). *The three faces of Eve.* Kingsport, TN: Kingsport Press.

This is a fascinating account of a woman with three—and actually more—separate personalities. You may also want to see the film that was based on the book.

CHAPTER 13

CHAPTER 13

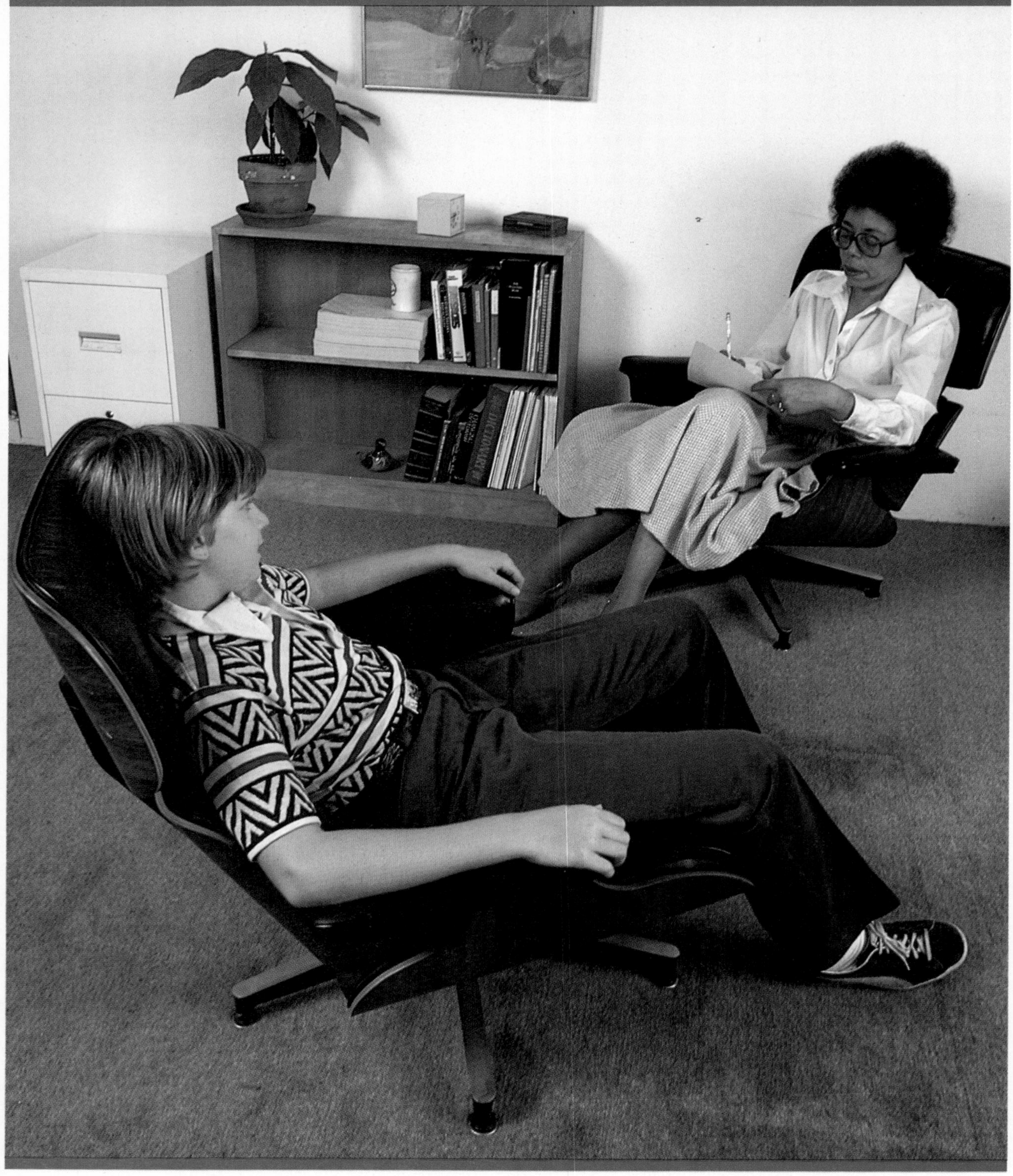

TREATMENT OF ABNORMAL BEHAVIOR

PROLOGUE

LOOKING AHEAD

PSYCHOTHERAPY: PSYCHOLOGICAL APPROACHES TO TREATMENT

Beyond the therapy-room couch: Psychodynamic treatment

Learning the good and unlearning the bad: Behavioral approaches to treatment

TRY IT! Learning to Relax

PSYCHOLOGY AT WORK. When Being Your Own Therapist Works: Self-Management through Behavior Modification

Recap and review I

Helping people to help themselves: Humanistic approaches to therapy

Evaluating psychotherapy

Recap and review II

THE MEDICAL MODEL AT WORK: BIOLOGICAL TREATMENT APPROACHES

Medicine for mental disturbances: Drug therapy

Shocking abnormal behavior away: Electroconvulsive therapy (ECT)

Cutting out the bad: Psychosurgery

Can abnormal behavior be cured?: Biological treatment in perspective

The informed consumer of psychology: Choosing the right therapist

THE CUTTING EDGE. Focus on Prevention: The Campus Crisis Center

Recap and review III

PSYCHOLOGY LOOKS TOWARD THE 1990s. In Search of New Treatments

LOOKING BACK

KEY TERMS AND CONCEPTS

FOR FURTHER STUDY AND APPLICATION

PROLOGUE

CLIENT: I just feel nervous a lot of the time.
THERAPIST: What is the feeling like?
CLIENT: I don't know. It's hard to describe . . . I just feel nervous.
THERAPIST: So you know what the feeling is like, but it's kind of difficult to describe it in words.
CLIENT: Yes, it is. You know, it's just a feeling of uneasiness and apprehension. Like when you know something bad may happen, or at least you're afraid that it might.
THERAPIST: So emotionally, and perhaps physically, there's a fear that something might happen, although you may not be certain exactly what.
CLIENT: Yes.
THERAPIST: When you're feeling that way, what do you experience physically?
CLIENT: Well, my heart starts pounding and I feel myself tense up all over. It's not always that bad; sometimes it's only mild.
THERAPIST: In other words, depending upon the circumstances, you may feel more or less anxious.
CLIENT: Yes.
THERAPIST: Tell me something about the situations that make you *most* anxious.
CLIENT: Well, it's usually when I deal with other people.
THERAPIST: I would find it particularly helpful to hear about some typical situations that may upset you.
CLIENT: It's hard to come up with something specific.
THERAPIST: I can understand how it may be hard to come up with specific examples right on the spot. That's not at all uncommon. Let me see if I can help to make it a little easier for you. Let's take the past week or so. Think of what went on either at work, at home, or when you were out socially that might have upset you.
CLIENT: O.K. Something just occurred to me. We went out to a party last weekend, and as we were driving to the place where the party was being held, I felt myself starting to panic.
THERAPIST: Can you tell me more about that situation?
CLIENT: Well, the party was at . . . (Goldfried and Davison, 1976, 40–42).

LOOKING AHEAD

The transcript reproduced above represents the view that most people have of what treatment for psychological disorders is all about. Popularized by the media, the notion that treatment always involves a therapist asking a series of probing questions and a client searching for answers to a difficult problem has come to represent society's general idea of the nature of therapy.

In fact—although many kinds of therapy do encompass the kind of situation described by the transcript—treatment approaches are much broader than this example of an initial interview with a person experiencing anxiety. There are over 250 different kinds of treatments used by therapists today, ranging from one-session informal discussions to long-term treatments involving powerful drugs. However, no matter what type of therapy is employed, all share a common goal: the relief of psychological disorder, ultimately enabling individuals to achieve richer, more meaningful, and more fulfilling lives.

In this chapter we discuss a number of important issues related to abnormal behavior: How do we treat individuals with psychological disorders? Who is the most appropriate kind of person to provide treatment? What is the future like for people with severe disturbances? Is one form of therapy better than others? Does any therapy *really* work? How do you choose the "right" kind of therapy?

These questions and others are addressed in this chapter, which considers the treatment of abnormal behavior. Most of the chapter focuses on the various approaches used by providers of treatment for psychological disturbances, which, despite their diversity, basically boil down to two main categories: psychologically based and biologically based therapy.

Psychologically based therapy, or **psychotherapy**, is the process in which a patient (often referred to as the client) and a professional attempt to remedy psychological difficulties. In psychotherapy, the emphasis is on change as a result of discussions and interactions between therapist and client. In contrast, biologically based therapy uses drugs and other medical procedures to improve psychological functioning.

Psychotherapy (sy ko THARE uh pee): *The process in which a patient (client) and a professional attempt to remedy the client's psychological difficulties*

The chapter first examines the psychologically based forms of treatment. These include Freud's psychoanalysis and more contemporary psychodynamic approaches, behavioral approaches, and humanistic approaches to psychotherapy. We also discuss how each of these forms of therapy—and psychotherapy in general—stacks up when they are formally evaluated. Next, the chapter examines biological approaches to treatment, including drug, electroconvulsive shock, and surgical therapies. Finally, the chapter concludes with a section that offers advice on how to be an informed consumer of psychological services.

As we discuss the various approaches to therapy, it is important to keep in mind that, although the distinctions may seem clear-cut, there is a good deal of overlap between the classifications, procedures employed, and even the titles and training of various kinds of therapists (see Table 13-1). In fact, many therapists today use a variety of methods with a given person, in what is referred to as an **eclectic approach to therapy** (Karasu, 1982).

Eclectic (ek LEK tik) **approach to therapy**: *An approach to therapy that uses a variety of treatment methods rather than just one*

After reading and studying this chapter, then, you will be able to

- Differentiate between psychologically and biologically based treatment approaches
- Describe psychodynamic, behavioral, and humanistic psychotherapy
- Evaluate and compare the different types of psychotherapies
- Describe biological treatment approaches, including drug, electroconvulsive, and psychosurgical techniques
- Recognize important factors in choosing the right therapist
- Define and apply the key terms and concepts listed at the end of the chapter

PSYCHOTHERAPY: PSYCHOLOGICAL APPROACHES TO TREATMENT

Although diverse in many respects, all psychological approaches see treatment as a way of solving psychological problems by modifying people's behavior, and helping them gain a better understanding of themselves and their past, present, and future. We will consider three major kinds of psychotherapies: psychodynamic, behavioral, and humanistic, all of which are based on the different models of abnormal behavior we discussed in Chapter 12.

TABLE 13-1

Getting help from the right person

Clinical psychologist	Ph.D. who specializes in assessment and treatment of psychological difficulties
Counseling psychologist	Psychologist with Ph.D. or master's who usually treats day-to-day adjustment problems in a counseling setting such as a university mental-health clinic
Psychiatrist	M.D. with postgraduate training in abnormal behavior, can prescribe medication as part of treatment.
Psychoanalyst	Either an M.D. or psychologist who specializes in psychoanalysis, a treatment technique first developed by Freud
Psychiatric social worker	Professional with a master's degree and specialized training in treating people in home and community settings

Each of these trained professionals could be expected to give helpful advice and direction, although the nature of the problem a person is experiencing may make one or the other more appropriate. For example, a person who is suffering from severe disturbance and has lost touch with reality will typically require some sort of biologically based drug therapy. In that case, a psychiatrist—who is a physician—would clearly be the professional of choice. On the other hand, those suffering from milder disorders, such as difficulty in adjusting to the death of a family member, have a broader choice that might include any of the professionals listed above. The decision can be made easier because mental-health facilities in communities, colleges, and health organizations often provide guidance, during an initial consultation, in selecting an appropriate therapist.

Beyond the Therapy-Room Couch: Psychodynamic Treatment

If you have a notion of what psychotherapy is like, it is probably based on a psychodynamic model: a hushed room, a patient lying on a couch baring his or her soul about a difficult childhood to an elderly, bearded psychotherapist who sits upright, taking notes and occasionally making an insightful comment. Actually, while such an image has been reinforced by Hollywood films, psychodynamic therapy is considerably more complex and varied than this stereotype leads us to believe.

Psychodynamic (sy ko dy NAM ik) **therapy**: *Therapy based on the notion that the basic sources of abnormal behavior are unresolved past conflicts and anxiety*

Defense mechanisms: *Psychological strategies that protect people from unconscious impulses*

Neurotic (nur RAH tik) **symptoms**: *According to Freud, abnormal behavior brought about by anxiety associated with unwanted conflicts and impulses*

Psychodynamic therapy is based on the premise, first suggested by Freud, that the basic sources of abnormal behavior are unresolved past conflicts and anxiety over the possibility that unacceptable unconscious impulses will enter the conscious part of a person's mind. To guard against this undesirable possibility, individuals employ **defense mechanisms**—psychological strategies that protect them from these unconscious impulses (see Chapter 11). Even though repression, the most common defense mechanism (in which threatening conflicts and impulses are pushed back into the unconscious) typically occurs, our unacceptable conflicts and impulses can never be completely buried. Therefore, some of the anxiety associated with them can produce abnormal behavior in the form of what Freud called **neurotic symptoms.**

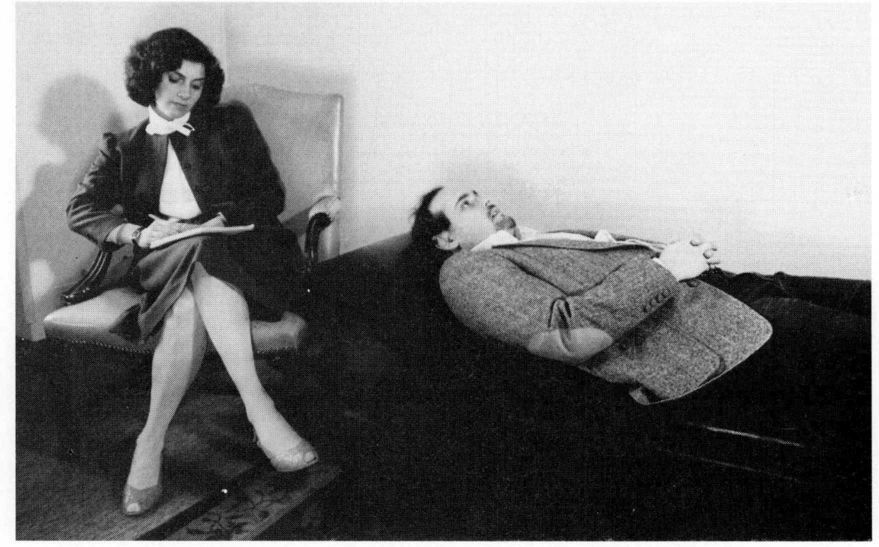

In psychodynamic therapy, through a consideration of their past experiences, people attempt to identify and confront the hidden conflicts and impulses residing in the unconscious. (*Susan Rosenberg/Photo Researchers, Inc.*)

How does one rid oneself of the anxiety caused by the repression of unconscious, unwanted impulses and drives? To Freud, the answer was to confront the conflicts and impulses by bringing them out of the unconscious part of the mind and into the conscious part. Freud assumed that, by doing this, anxiety over the past would be reduced and the patient could participate in his or her daily life more effectively.

The challenge facing a psychodynamic therapist, then, is how to facilitate patients' attempts to explore and understand their unconscious. The technique that has evolved has a number of components, but basically it consists of leading patients to consider and discuss their past experiences, from the time of their first memories, in explicit detail. Through this process, it is assumed that patients will eventually stumble upon long-hidden crises, traumas, and conflicts that are producing anxiety in their adult lives. They will then be able to "work through" these difficulties.

Freud's Therapy: Psychoanalysis Classic Freudian psychodynamic therapy—called **psychoanalysis**—tends to be a lengthy and expensive affair. Patients typically meet with their therapists an hour a day, four to six days a week, for several years. In each session, they often use a technique developed by Freud called **free association**. In free association, patients are told to say whatever comes to mind, regardless of its apparent irrelevance or senselessness. In fact, they are urged *not* to try to make sense of things or impose logic upon what they are saying, since it is assumed that the ramblings evoked during free association actually represent important clues to the unconscious, which has its own logic. It is the analyst's job to recognize and label the connections between what is being said and the patient's unconscious.

Psychoanalysis (sy ko an AL uh sis): *Psychodynamic therapy that involves frequent sessions and often lasts for many years*

Free association: *A Freudian therapeutic technique in which patients say everything that comes to mind to give the therapist a clue to the workings of the patient's unconscious*

Another important tool of the therapist is **dream interpretation.** As we discussed in Chapter 9, this is an examination of the patients' dreams to find clues to the unconscious conflicts and problems being experienced. According to Freud, dreams provide a closer look at the unconscious because people's defenses tend

Dream interpretation: *An examination of a patient's dreams to find clues to the unconscious conflicts and problems being experienced*

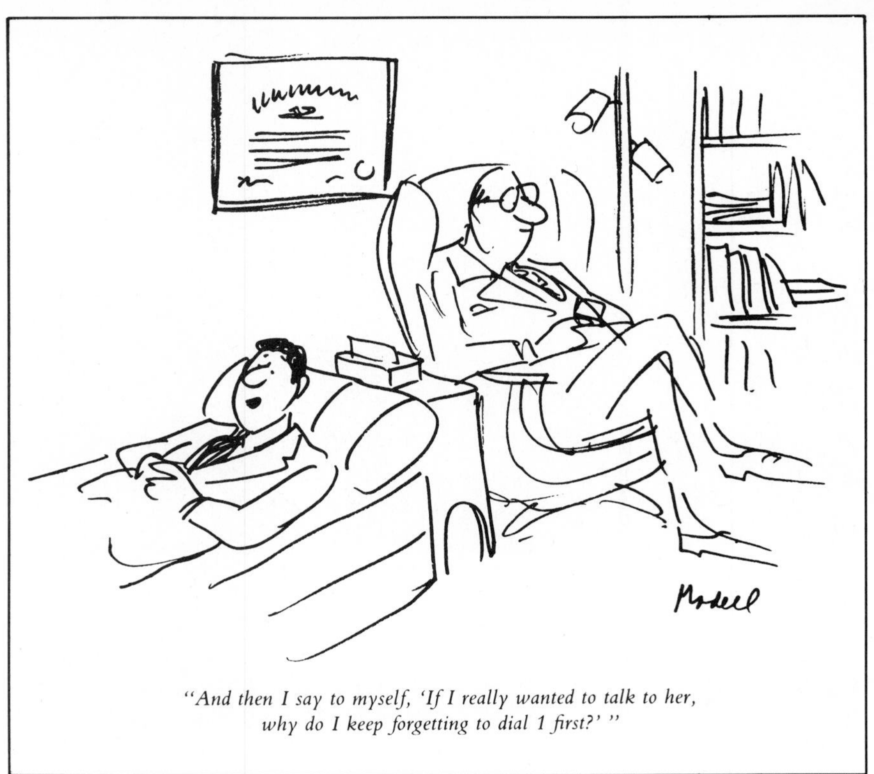

"And then I say to myself, 'If I really wanted to talk to her, why do I keep forgetting to dial 1 first?' "

(Drawing by Modell; © 1981 The New Yorker Magazine, Inc.)

to be lowered when they are asleep. But even in dreaming there is a censoring of thoughts; events and people in dreams are usually represented by symbols. Because of this, one must move beyond the surface description of the dream—the **manifest content**—and consider its underlying meaning—the **latent content**—which reveals the true message of the dream.

Manifest content: *The surface description and interpretation of a dream*

Latent content: *The "true" message hidden within a dream*

The processes of free association and dream interpretation do not always move easily forward. The same unconscious forces that initially produced repression may work to keep past difficulties out of the conscious, producing resistance. **Resistance** is an inability or unwillingness to discuss or reveal particular memories, thoughts, or motivations. Resistance can be expressed in a number of ways. For instance, a patient may be discussing a childhood memory and suddenly forget what he was saying, or he may completely change the subject. It is the therapist's job to pick up instances of resistance and to interpret their meaning, as well as to ensure that the patient returns to the subject—which is likely to hold difficult or painful memories for him.

Resistance: *An inability or unwillingness to discuss or reveal particular memories, thoughts, or motivations*

Because of the close, almost intimate interaction between patient and psychoanalyst, the relationship between the two often becomes emotionally charged and takes on a complexity unlike most others. In fact, patients may come to see the analyst as symbolic of significant others in their past, perhaps a parent or a lover, and apply some of their feelings for that person to the analyst—a phenomenon known as **transference.**

Transference: *A patient's transferal of certain strong feelings for others to the analyst*

Transference can be used by a therapist to help the patient recreate past relationships that were psychologically difficult. For instance, if a patient undergoing transference views his therapist as symbolic of his father—with whom he had a difficult relationship—the patient and therapist may "redo" an earlier interaction, this time including more positive aspects. Through this process, conflicts regarding the real father may be resolved.

Contemporary Alternatives to Psychoanalysis: Is Freud Dead? If time is money, patients in psychoanalysis need a lot of both. As you can imagine, few people have the time, money, or patience that participating in years of traditional psychoanalysis requires. Moreover, there is no conclusive evidence that psychoanalysis, as originally conceived by Freud, works better than other, more contemporary versions of psychodynamic therapy. Today, for instance, psychodynamic therapy tends to be shorter, usually lasting no longer than three months or twenty sessions. Moreover, the therapist takes a more active role than Freud would have liked, controlling the course of therapy and prodding and advising the patient with considerable directness. Finally, there is less emphasis on a patient's past history and childhood. Instead, a more here-and-now approach is used, in which the therapist concentrates on an individual's current relationships and level of functioning (Parloff, 1976; Reppen, 1981; Strupp, 1981).

Even with its current modifications, psychodynamic therapy has its critics. It is still relatively time-consuming and expensive, especially in comparison with other forms of psychotherapy that we will discuss later. Moreover, only certain kinds of patients tend to be well suited for this method: those who suffer from anxiety disorders and those who are highly articulate—characteristics enshrined in a (facetious) acronym, YAVIS, for the perfect patient: young, attractive, verbal, intelligent, and successful (Schofield, 1964).

Ultimately, the most important concern about psychodynamic treatment is whether it actually works, and here we find no pat answer. Psychodynamic treatment techniques have been controversial since Freud introduced them. Part of the problem is the difficulty in establishing whether or not a patient has improved following psychodynamic therapy. One must depend on reports from the therapist or the patients themselves, reports that are obviously open to bias and subjective interpretation (Luborsky & Spence, 1978; Peterfreund, 1984).

Others have questioned the entire theoretical basis of psychodynamic theory, maintaining that there is no proof that such constructs as the unconscious exist. Despite the considerable criticism, though, the psychodynamic treatment approach has remained a viable technique, not only providing effective treatment in many cases of psychological disturbances but permitting the potential development of an unusual degree of insight and understanding in people's lives.

Learning the Good and Unlearning the Bad: Behavioral Approaches to Treatment

Remember how your mother would reward you with an ice cream cone if you were especially good . . . or send you to your room if you misbehaved? As we saw in Chapter 4, the principles behind such thinking are quite valid: Good behavior is maintained by rewards, and unwanted behavior can be eliminated by punishment.

These principles represent the basic underpinnings of behavioral treatment approaches. Building upon the basic processes of learning—classical and operant conditioning—**behavioral treatment approaches** make a fundamental assumption: both abnormal and normal behavior is *learned* (Craighead, Kazdin, & Mahoney, 1981; Karoly & Kanfer, 1982). People who display abnormal behavior have either failed to learn the skills needed to cope with the problems of

Behavioral treatment approach: *Approaches to abnormal behavior that assume that both normal and abnormal behaviors are learned and that treatment consists of learning new behavior or unlearning maladaptive behavior*

One treatment for people who want to stop smoking involves aversive conditioning, in which smoking and cues relating to smoking are repeatedly paired with unpleasant stimuli. (*Lester Sloan/Woodfin Camp & Assoc.*)

everyday living or they have acquired faulty skills and patterns that are being maintained through some form of reinforcement. To modify abnormal behavior, then, people must do one or both of two things: learn new behavior to replace the faulty skills they have developed or unlearn their maladaptive behavior patterns.

To behavioral psychologists, it is not necessary to delve into people's pasts or dig into their psyches; rather than viewing abnormal behavior as a symptom of some underlying problem, they consider the abnormal behavior itself as the problem in need of modification. Changing people's behavior to allow them to function more effectively solves the problem—with no need for concern about the underlying cause. In this view, then, if you can change abnormal behavior, you've cured it.

Learning to Hate What You Love and Love What You Hate: Classical Conditioning Approaches Suppose you bite into your favorite candy bar and find that it is infested with ants and that you've swallowed a bunch of them. You immediately become sick to your stomach and throw up. Your long-term reaction? You never eat that kind of candy bar again; in fact, it may be months before you eat any type of candy.

This simple example hints at how classical conditioning might be used to modify behavior. You might remember from our discussion in Chapter 4 that by pairing a stimulus that naturally evokes a negative response (such as an unpleasant taste or a puff of air in the face) with a previously neutral stimulus (such as the sound of a bell), the negative stimulus can bring about a similar negative reaction to the neutral stimulus by itself. By using this procedure, first developed by Ivan Pavlov, it is likewise possible to produce unpleasant reactions to stimuli that previously were enjoyed—possibly to excess—by an individual. Such a technique, known as **aversive conditioning**, has been used in cases of alcoholism, drug abuse, and smoking.

Aversive conditioning: *A technique used to help people break unwanted habits by associating the habits with very unpleasant stimuli*

The basic procedure in aversive conditioning is relatively straightforward. For example, a person with a drinking problem might be given an alcoholic drink along with a drug that causes severe nausea and vomiting. After these two are paired a few times, the alcohol alone becomes associated with the vomiting and loses its appeal. In fact, what typically happens is that just the sight or smell of alcohol triggers the aversive reaction.

Although aversion therapy works reasonably well to inhibit certain problems, such as alcoholism and certain kinds of sexual deviation, its effectiveness in other cases is short-lived. Moreover, there are important ethical drawbacks to the use of aversion techniques employing such potent stimuli as electric shock—used only in the most extreme cases, such as self-mutilation—instead of drugs that merely induce gastric discomfort (Russo, Carr, & Lovaas, 1980; Sulzer-Azaroff & Mayer, 1986).

The most successful treatment based on classical conditioning is known as systematic desensitization. In **systematic desensitization**, a stimulus that evokes pleasant feelings is repeatedly paired with a stimulus that evokes anxiety in the hope that the positive feelings will eventually become associated with the anxiety-producing stimulus, thereby alleviating the anxiety (Rachman & Hodgson, 1980; Wolpe, 1969).

Systematic desensitization: *A procedure in which a stimulus that evokes pleasant feelings is repeatedly paired with a stimulus that evokes anxiety in the hope that the anxiety will be alleviated*

Suppose, for instance, you were afraid of flying. In fact, the very thought of being in an airplane made you begin to sweat and shake, and you'd never even been able to get yourself near enough to an airport to know how you'd react if you actually had to fly somewhere. Using systematic desensitization to treat your problem, you would first be trained in muscle-relaxation techniques by a behavior therapist (see the Try It! box), learning to relax your body fully—a highly pleasant state, as you might imagine. The next step would involve the construction of a **hierarchy of fears**—a list, in order of increasing severity, of the things that are associated with your fears. For instance, your hierarchy might resemble this one:

Hierarchy (HIRE ar kee) **of fears**: *A list, in order of increasing severity, of the things that are associated with one's fears*

- Watching a plane fly overhead
- Going to an airport
- Buying a ticket
- Stepping into the plane
- Seeing the plane door close
- Having the plane taxi down the runway
- Taking off
- Being in the air

Once this hierarchy had been developed and you had learned relaxation techniques, the two sets of responses would be associated with each other. To do this, you might be asked by your therapist to put yourself into a relaxed state and then to imagine yourself in the first situation identified in your hierarchy. After you were able to consider that first step while remaining relaxed, you would move on to the next situation, eventually moving up the hierarchy in gradual stages until you could imagine yourself being in the air without experiencing anxiety. In some cases, all this would take place in a psychologist's office, while in others people are actually placed in the fear-evoking situation. Thus, it would not be surprising if you were brought, finally, to an airplane to use your relaxation techniques.

Systematic desensitization has proved to be an effective treatment for a number of problems, including phobias, anxiety disorders, and even impotence and fear of sexual contact (Karoly & Kanfer, 1982; Kennedy & Kimura, 1974). As you see, you *can* learn to enjoy the things you once feared.

TRY IT

LEARNING TO RELAX

To get a sense of how behavior therapists train people to relax, try this procedure developed by Herbert Benson (1975):

1. Sit quietly in a comfortable position.
2. Close your eyes.
3. Deeply relax all your muscles, beginning at your feet and progressing to your face—keep them relaxed.
4. Breathe through your nose. Become aware of your breathing. As you breathe out, say the word "one" silently to yourself. For example, breathe in . . . out, "one"; in . . . out, "one"; etc. Breathe easily and naturally.
5. Continue for ten to twenty minutes. You may open your eyes to check the time, but do not use an alarm. When you finish, sit quietly for several minutes, at first with your eyes closed and later with your eyes open. Do not stand up for a few minutes.
6. Do not worry about whether you are successful in achieving a deep level of relaxation. Maintain a passive attitude and permit relaxation to occur at its own pace. When distracting thoughts occur, try to ignore them by not dwelling upon them, and return to repeating "one."

With practice, the response should come with little effort. Practice the techniques once or twice daily, but not within two hours after any meal, since the digestive processes seem to interfere with the elicitation of the relaxation response (Benson, 1975, pp. 114–115).

Following the "Fearless Peer": Observational Learning and Modeling If we had to be hit by a car in order to learn the importance of looking both ways before we crossed the street, the world would likely be suffering from a serious underpopulation problem. Fortunately, this is not necessary, for we learn a significant amount through **observational learning**, by **modeling** the behavior of other people.

Observational learning: *Learning by watching others' behavior and the consequences of that behavior*
Modeling: *Imitating the behavior of others (models)*

Behavior therapists have used modeling to systematically teach people new skills and ways of handling their fears and anxieties. For example, some people have never learned fundamental social skills such as maintaining eye contact with those they are speaking to. A therapist can model the appropriate behavior and thereby teach it to someone deficient in such skills (Sarason, 1976). Similarly, children with dog phobias have been able to lose their fears by watching another child—called the "Fearless Peer"—repeatedly walk up to a dog, touch it, pet it, and finally play with it (Bandura, Grusec, & Menlove, 1967). Modeling, then, can play an effective role in resolving some kinds of behavior difficulties, particularly if the model is rewarded for his or her behavior.

Reward the Good, Extinguish the Bad: Operant Conditioning Approaches Consider the A you get for a good paper . . . the raise for fine on-the-job performance . . . the pat on the head for helping an old lady cross the street. Such rewards for your behavior produce a greater likelihood that you will repeat such behavior in the future. Similarly, behavioral approaches using operant conditioning techniques (which demonstrate the effects of rewards and punishments on future behavior) are based on the straightforward notion that we should reward people for carrying out desirable behavior, and extinguish behavior that we wish to eliminate.

WHERE NORMAL IS RICH AND ABNORMAL IS POOR: TOKEN SYSTEMS Probably the best example of the systematic application of operant conditioning principles is the **token system**, whereby a person is rewarded with tokens such as a poker chip or some kind of play money for desired behavior. The behavior may range from such simple things as keeping one's room neat to personal grooming to interacting with other people. The tokens that are earned for such behavior can then be exchanged for some desired object or activity, such as snacks, new clothes, or in extreme cases, being able to sleep in one's own bed (as opposed to the floor).

Token system: *A procedure whereby a person is rewarded for performing certain desired behaviors*

Although it is most frequently employed in institutional settings for individuals with relatively serious problems, the system is not unlike what parents do when they give children money for being well behaved—money that they can later exchange for something they want. In fact, a variant of the more extensive token system, a variant known as **contingency contracting**, has proved quite effective in producing behavior modification. In contingency contracting, a written agreement is drawn up between a therapist and patient (or teacher and student or parent and child). The contract states a series of behavioral goals that the patient hopes to attain. It also specifies the consequences for the patient if the goals are reached—usually some explicit reward such as money or additional privileges. Finally, contracts frequently state negative consequences if the goals are not reached.

Contingency contracting: *Acting upon a written contract between a therapist and a patient (or parent and child, etc.) that sets behavioral goals, with rewards for achievement*

For instance, suppose a person is having difficulty quitting smoking. He and his therapist might devise a contract in which he would pledge that for every day he went without a cigarette he would receive a reward. On the other hand, the contract could include punishments for failure. If, for instance, the patient smoked on a given day, the therapist would send a check—written out in advance by the patient and given to the therapist to hold—to a cause the patient had no interest in supporting (the American Nazi Party, for instance).

Where Thinking Better Leads to Feeling Better: Cognitive-Behavioral Approaches and Rational-Emotive Therapy Consider the following assumptions:

- It is necessary to be loved or approved by virtually every significant other person for everything we do.
- We should be thoroughly competent, adequate, and successful in all possible respects if we are to consider ourselves worthwhile.
- It is horrible when things don't turn out the way we want them to.

Although each of these statements verges on the absurd, psychologist Albert Ellis suggests that many people lead unhappy and sometimes even psychologically disordered lives because they harbor these very kinds of irrational, unrealistic ideas about themselves and the world (Ellis, 1962, 1975). In developing a treatment approach based on this premise—called **rational-emotive therapy**—he has suggested that the goal of therapy should be to restructure a person's belief system into a more realistic, rational, and logical set of views of the world. To do this, a therapist might bluntly dispute the logic employed by a person in treatment by saying, "Why does the fact that your girlfriend left you mean that *you* are a bad person?" or "How does failing an exam indicate that you have *no* good qualities?" By pointing out the problems in logic, therapists employing this form of treatment believe that people can adopt a more realistic view of themselves and their circumstances (Bernard & Joyce, 1985).

Rational-emotive therapy: *Psychotherapy based on Ellis's suggestion that the goal of therapy should be to restructure one's belief system into a more realistic, rational, and logical system*

Rational-emotive therapy exemplifies a **cognitive-behavioral approach** to

Cognitive-behavioral therapy: *A process by which people's faulty cognitions about themselves and the world are changed to more accurate ones*

PSYCHOLOGY AT WORK

WHEN BEING YOUR OWN THERAPIST WORKS:

Self-Management through Behavior Modification

A fellow student, whom you don't know all that well, asks if you attended class the previous morning. When you say that you did, he asks to borrow your notes. This is the fourth time this semester he has asked you, and you feel that it is grossly unfair that you go to class and take notes and then he asks to borrow them. You're beginning to feel like his personal secretary. But, feeling that he might become angry at you if you refuse his request, you quietly hand over your notebook.

This is not the first time you've felt that others take advantage of you, and you begin to wonder if you have a serious problem with your lack of assertiveness. In fact, you begin to feel so bad about your inability to be assertive that you think about entering therapy. One day, though, a friend mentions that she was able to become more assertive entirely on her own, without professional assistance, through a technique known as behavioral self-management—and she assures you that you can do the same thing on your own.

Although the dangers of self-diagnosis and treatment have been emphasized a number of times—and caution should indeed always be used—there is one treatment approach that specifically allows people suffering from minor problems to "cure" themselves: behavioral self-management. In **behavioral self-management** people are taught to identify their problems and design their own ways of resolving them by using behavioral techniques. (Initially, of course, *someone* must teach the technique to the person; but once that process has been completed, people are primarily on their own.)

Using techniques derived from behavioral treatment approaches, self-management techniques have been shown to be effective in many cases for a variety of problems, including alcoholism, drug dependence, high blood pressure, stress control, poor study habits, and insomnia. Although many different strategies have been employed, they basically consist of altering the cues that promote an undesirable behavior, directly modifying a response that should be changed, and/or providing reinforcement or punishment for desirable or undesirable behavior.

The problems associated with self-assertion provide an excellent illustration of a problem that is responsive to self-management techniques. In a typical procedure, people are first asked to identify the cues and circumstances associated with a lack of assertiveness. For a student named Jim, such cues included being unable to refuse when asked for a favor and being unable to talk to strangers at a party.

To remedy his lack of assertiveness, the general strategy employed was to find some way to modify his reaction to cues that had become associated with unassertiveness. To do this, a number of goals and "rules" were set up about when, where, and how Jim should be assertive. For example, he set a goal of initiating conversations with at least two strangers at any party he went to. To accomplish this, he made a list of ways of initiating conversations, such as asking a question or making a comment on the situation, complimenting a person, or asking for help, advice, information, or an opinion.

Jim also used role-playing to learn strategies for dealing with situations in which he was asked a favor. For example, he practiced scenarios in his mind—and sometimes out loud with a close friend—in which, when asked a favor, he asked for time to think it over, asked for more information before agreeing or disagreeing, or simply said "no" to the person asking the favor.

Jim also developed a system of self-reinforcement, in which he would reward himself after acting assertively by treating himself to a movie. Moreover, he used self-punishment; when he hadn't acted assertively, he forced himself to send a check for $5 to a political party whose views he completely opposed.

By using such self-management procedures, Jim was able to become more assertive. Behavioral self-management techniques, then, provide a means by which people can, in a sense, be their own therapists.

Behavioral self-management: *A procedure in which people learn to identify and resolve their problems using techniques based on learning theory* therapy (Beck, 1983). Rather than relying exclusively on overt behaviors as indicators of psychological disorder, cognitive-behavioral therapists attempt to change faulty cognitions that people hold about the world and themselves. Cognitive-behavioral therapists, then, bring an eclectic point of view to behavioral therapy, combining ideas derived from cognitive psychology with a behavioral approach.

Albert Ellis developed a treatment approach known as rational-emotive therapy. (*Institute for Rational Living*)

The Crucial Question: How Does Behavior Therapy Stack Up? Behavior therapy is quite good for certain kinds of problems. Depending on the specific problem being addressed, the success rate can range from 50 to as high as 90 percent (Kazdin & Wilson, 1978). For instance, behavior therapy works well for phobias and compulsions, for establishing control over impulses, and for learning complex social skills to replace maladaptive behavior. It also has, more than any of the other therapeutic techniques, produced methods that can be employed by nonprofessionals to change their own behavior (see the Psychology at Work box). Moreover, it tends to be economical in terms of time, since it is directed toward the solution of carefully defined problems (Marks, 1982).

Nonetheless, behavior therapy has its critics. The most serious concerns revolve around the notion that by treating the surface symptoms of a problem, one ignores the deeper—and, according to the critics, more important—underlying causes that produced the symptoms in the first place. According to these critics, the symptoms may disappear but the real problem remains, and so does the potential for future psychological disturbances in which new symptoms are substituted for old ones—a phenomenon called **symptom substitution**. While the evidence for symptom substitution is not extensive, there is an increasing use of nonbehavioral methods of therapy in conjunction with behavior therapy. This eclectic approach has been helpful in ensuring that improvements in behavior last.

Symptom substitution: *The phenomenon by which new symptoms of psychological disturbance replace old symptoms when the underlying cause of the disturbance has not been eliminated*

RECAP AND REVIEW I

Recap

- Psychotherapy is psychologically based therapy in which the emphasis is on change based on discussion and interaction between client and therapist. Biologically based therapy uses drugs and other medical procedures.
- Psychodynamic therapy is based on Freud's notions that abnormal behavior is caused by unconscious conflicts and anxiety. To treat psychological problems, it is necessary to probe the unconscious and bring old difficulties to the surface through free association and dream interpretation.
- Behavioral approaches to therapy are built on the premise that people who display abnormal behavior either have failed to acquire appropriate skills or have learned faulty or maladaptive skills. To remedy the problem, it is necessary to learn new, more adaptive behaviors or to unlearn old faulty patterns of behavior.
- Among the approaches used by behavioral therapists are classical conditioning, including aversive conditioning and systematic desensitization; modeling; operant conditioning; and rational-emotive therapy, a cognitive-behavioral approach. Behavioral approaches have a relatively high success rate, particularly for certain kinds of problems.

Review

1. Freud called anxiety associated with unacceptable conflicts and impulses __________ __________.
2. The main purpose of psychoanalysis is to uncover repressed experiences that are causing abnormal behavior or anxiety. True or false?
3. Systematic desensitization is used to
   a. combat anxiety through positive associations with other stimuli **b.** teach control by alternating pleasure with anxiety
   c. break down the components of past anxiety **d.** replace pain with pleasure
4. Learning by imitating others is called __________.

5. The development of a system of rewards and punishments is part of rational-emotive therapy. True or false?
6. To overcome your habit of biting your nails, you develop a program to monitor and control the habit. This is an example of
a. free association **b.** resistance **c.** aversive conditioning **d.** self-management

(Answers to review questions are at the bottom of page 446.)

Helping People to Help Themselves: Humanistic Approaches to Therapy

As you know from your own experience, it is impossible to master the material covered in a course without some hard work, no matter how good the teacher and the textbook are. It is *you* who must take the time to study, to memorize the vocabulary, to learn the concepts. Nobody else can do it for you. If you choose to put in the effort, you'll succeed; if you don't, you'll fail. The responsibility is primarily yours.

Humanistic therapy: *Therapy in which the underlying assumption is that people have control of their behavior, they can make choices about their lives, and they are essentially responsible for solving their own problems*

Humanistic therapy draws upon this philosophical point of view in developing treatment techniques. Although many different types of therapy fit into this category, the basic notions that underlie them are the same: We have control of our own behavior; we can make choices about the kinds of lives we want to live, and it is up to us to solve the difficulties that we encounter in our daily existence. Instead of therapists being the directive figures they are in some psychodynamic and behavioral approaches, humanistic therapists view themselves as guides or facilitators, leading people to realizations about themselves and to ways of changing in order to come closer to the ideal they hold for themselves. In this view, abnormal behavior is one result of people's inability to find meaning in life, in feeling lonely and unconnected with others, and in believing that they are pawns in a world that acts upon them without their being able to respond adequately.

Client, Heal Thyself: Client-Centered Therapy Consider the following dialogue between a therapist and a client named Alice who is seeking treatment:

ALICE: I was thinking about this business of standards. I somehow developed a sort of a knack, I guess, of—well—habit—of trying to make people feel at ease around me, or to make things go along smoothly. . . .
COUNSELOR: In other words, what you did was always in the direction of trying to keep things smooth and to make other people feel better and to smooth the situation.
ALICE: Yes. I think that's what it was. Now the reason why I did it probably was—I mean, not that I was a good little Samaritan going around making other people happy, but that was probably the role that felt easiest for me to play. I'd been doing it around home so much. I just didn't stand up for my own convictions, until I don't know whether I have any convictions to stand up for.
COUNSELOR: You feel that for a long time you've been playing the role of kind of smoothing out the frictions or differences or what not. . . .
ALICE: M-hm.
COUNSELOR: Rather than having any opinion or reaction of your own in the situation. Is that it?
ALICE: That's it. Or that I haven't been really honest being myself, or actually knowing what my real self is, and that I've been just playing a sort of false role . . . (Rogers, 1951, pp. 151–153).

"Of course you have strengths, dear. It's just that you don't communicate them."

(Drawing by Lorenz; © 1977 The New Yorker Magazine, Inc.)

If you carefully consider the responses of the counselor, you will see that they are not interpretations or answers to questions that the client has raised. Instead, they tend to clarify or reflect back in some way what the client has said. This therapeutic technique is known as **nondirective counseling**, and it is at the heart of client-centered therapy. First practiced by Carl Rogers (1951, 1980), client-centered therapy is the best-known and most frequently used type of humanistic therapy.

Nondirective counseling: *A therapeutic technique in which the therapist creates a warm, supportive environment to allow the client to better understand and work out his or her problems*

Client-centered therapy: *Therapy in which the therapist reflects back the patient's statements in a way that causes the patient to find his or her own solutions*

The goal of **client-centered therapy** is to enable people to better reach the potential for self-actualization (a state of self-fulfillment) that is assumed to be inherent in everyone. By providing a warm and accepting environment, therapists hope to motivate clients to air their problems and feelings, which, in turn, will allow them to make realistic and constructive choices and decisions about the things that bother them in their current lives. Instead of directing the choices clients make, then, the therapist provides what Rogers calls **unconditional positive regard**—expressing acceptance regardless of what the client says or does—thereby creating an atmosphere in which clients are able to come to decisions that can improve their lives.

Unconditional positive regard: *Supportive behavior from another individual, regardless of one's words or actions*

Freeing the Fear of Freedom: Existential Therapy What is the meaning of life? While we have probably all pondered this thought at one time or another, for some people it is a central issue in their daily existence. For those individuals who experience psychological problems as a result of difficulty in finding a satisfactory answer, existential therapy is often the treatment of choice because this question is central to existential therapeutic techniques.

Existential (ex ih STEN chul) **therapy**: *A humanistic approach that addresses the meaning of life, allowing a client to devise a system of values that gives purpose to his or her life*

In contrast to other humanistic approaches that view a person's unique freedom and potential as a positive force, **existential therapy** is based on the premise that such freedom can produce anguish, fear, and concern (May, 1969). In existential therapy, then, the goal is to allow individuals to come to grips with

In Gestalt therapy, people closely examine, and sometimes try to recreate, experiences from their childhood. (*Alex Webb/Magnum*)

the freedom they have, to begin to understand how they fit in with the rest of the world, and to devise a system of values that permits them to give meaning to their lives.

The specific processes used in existential therapy are more varied than in client-centered approaches. The therapist is considerably more directive in existential therapy, probing and challenging the client's views of the world. In addition, therapists will try to establish a deep and binding relationship with their clients, attempting to be as open with them about their own feelings and points of view as possible. Their objective is to allow clients to see that they share in the difficulties and experiences that arise in trying to deal with the freedom that is part of being human.

Making People Whole in a Fragmented World: Gestalt Therapy Have you ever thought back to some childhood incident in which you were treated unfairly, and again felt the rage that you had experienced at that time? To therapists working in a gestalt perspective, the healthiest thing for you to do psychologically might be to act out that rage—by hitting a pillow, kicking a chair, or yelling in frustration. In fact, this sort of activity represents an important part of what goes on in gestalt therapy sessions, in which the client is encouraged to act out past conflicts and difficulties.

The rationale for this approach to treatment is that it is necessary for people to integrate their thoughts, feelings, and behaviors into a gestalt, the German term for ''whole'' (as we discussed in reference to perception in Chapter 3). According to Fritz Perls (1967, 1970), who developed **gestalt therapy**, the way to do this is for people to examine their earlier experience and complete any ''unfinished business'' from their past that still affects and colors present-day relationships. Specifically, Perls assumed that people should reenact the specific conflicts that they experienced earlier. For instance, a client might first play the

Gestalt therapy: *An approach that attempts to integrate thoughts, feelings, and behavior into a whole*

ANSWERS TO REVIEW QUESTIONS

Review I: **1.** Neurotic symptoms **2.** True **3.** a **4.** Modeling **5.** False **6.** d part of his angry father, and then play himself when his father yelled at him, in order to experience the different parts of a conflict. By increasing their perspectives on a situation, clients are better able to understand their problems and to experience life in a more unified, honest, and complete way.

Can You Become More Human in the Consulting Room?: Humanistic Approaches in Perspective You may be bothered by the lack of specificity of the humanistic treatments, and this is a problem that has also troubled its critics. Humanistic approaches are, in fact, not very precise, and are probably the least scientifically and theoretically sophisticated. Moreover, this form of treatment is best suited for the same type of highly verbal client who profits most from psychoanalytic treatment.

On the other hand, the emphasis of humanistic approaches on what is uniquely human and their acknowledgment that the freedom we possess can lead to psychological difficulties work to provide an unusually supportive environment for therapy. In turn, this atmosphere can aid in finding solutions to difficult psychological problems.

Evaluating Psychotherapy

> Your best friend at school, Colette, comes to you because she just hasn't been feeling right about things lately. She's upset because she and her boyfriend aren't getting along, but her difficulties go beyond that. She can't concentrate on her studies, has a lot of trouble getting to sleep, and—this is what really bothers her—she's begun to think that people are ganging up on her, talking about her behind her back. It just seems that no one really cares about or understands her, or makes any effort to see why she's become so miserable.
>
> Colette is aware, though, that she ought to get *some* kind of help, but she is not sure where to turn. She is fairly skeptical of psychologists and psychiatrists, thinking that a lot of what they say is just mumbo-jumbo, but she's willing to put her doubts aside and try anything to feel better. She also knows there are many different types of therapy, and she doesn't have a clue as to which would be best for her. She turns to you for advice, since she knows you are taking a psychology course. She asks, "Which kind of therapy works best?"

If you were to reply honestly to Colette's question, your response would have to be complex, for there is no easy answer. In fact, before considering whether any one form of therapy works better than any other, you would have to determine whether therapy in *any* form is effective in alleviating psychological disturbances.

How Effective Is Psychotherapy in General? Until the 1950s most people simply assumed that therapy, on the face of it, was an effective strategy for resolving psychological difficulties. But in 1952 psychologist Hans Eysenck published an influential article, reviewing the published literature on the subject, which challenged this commonly held assumption. He claimed that people who received psychodynamic treatment and related therapies were no better off at the end of treatment than those people who were placed on a waiting list for treatment—but who had never received it. According to his analysis, about two-

Spontaneous remission: *Recovery without treatment*

thirds of the people who reported suffering from "neurotic" symptoms believed that those symptoms had disappeared after two years, regardless of whether or not they had been in therapy. Eysenck concluded that people suffering from neurotic symptoms would go into **spontaneous remission**, recovery without treatment, if they were simply left alone—certainly a cheaper and more efficient process.

As you can imagine, Eysenck's review was controversial from the start, and its conclusions were quickly challenged. Critics pointed to the inadequacy of the data he reviewed, suggesting that he was basing his conclusions on studies that contained a number of flaws. There are many potential sources of error in such studies. Most often the data involved are based on therapist and patient self-reports, which may be biased and unreliable. All of the parties involved are motivated to see themselves as successful, so all may report an improvement in psychological functioning where none really exists. Only when independent judges are used to determine how much progress a person has made can one be assured that the self-report is accurate. Even the use of judges has its drawbacks, however, since no well-agreed-upon set of criteria exists to determine what constitutes good and bad mental health. For all of these reasons, then, critics of Eysenck's review rejected his findings.

Eysenck's early review did serve, however, to stimulate a continuing stream of better-controlled, carefully crafted studies on the effectiveness of psychotherapy, and today it appears that we can say, with some confidence, that psychotherapy *is* effective. For example, recent comprehensive reviews suggest that therapy results in greater improvement than does no treatment at all (Casey & Berman, 1985; Garfield, 1983; Landman & Dawes, 1984; Luborsky, Singer, & Luborsky, 1974; Smith, Glass & Miller, 1980) and that the rate of spontaneous remission is around 43 percent, considerably lower than Eysenck had initially estimated (Bergin & Lambert, 1978).

Which Kind of Therapy Works Best?: A Harder Question While most people agree that psychotherapeutic treatment *in general* is more effective than no treatment at all, there is little agreement on the question of whether any specific form of treatment is superior to any other (Orwin & Condray, 1984; Stiles, Shapiro, & Elliott, 1986). In part, this is due to methodological issues. For instance, it is difficult to equate the "cures" that various forms of treatment produce, because they may be qualitatively very different. Is the reduction of depression-related anxiety obtained from psychodynamic treatment equivalent to the reduction of phobia-related anxiety brought about by behavior therapy? In both cases the problems are alleviated—but, if we were keeping a tally of cures versus noncures for the two forms of treatment, would they each receive one point? You can see the difficulties involved in comparing types of treatment.

The problems, however, are not insurmountable. One solution has been to compare the "cure" rate for a particular form of treatment with the "cure" rate for a group of untreated controls. Next, we could do the same thing with another type of treatment and compare this cure rate with its own untreated control. Finally, we could see which of the two forms of therapy produced a higher cure rate. For instance, we could take a sample of people who, because of the nature of their problems, would be "eligible" for psychodynamic treatment, treat half of them, and compare their results to the untreated half. By following the same procedure with a group of people "eligible" for another form of treatment, we could infer which kind of treatment was most successful.

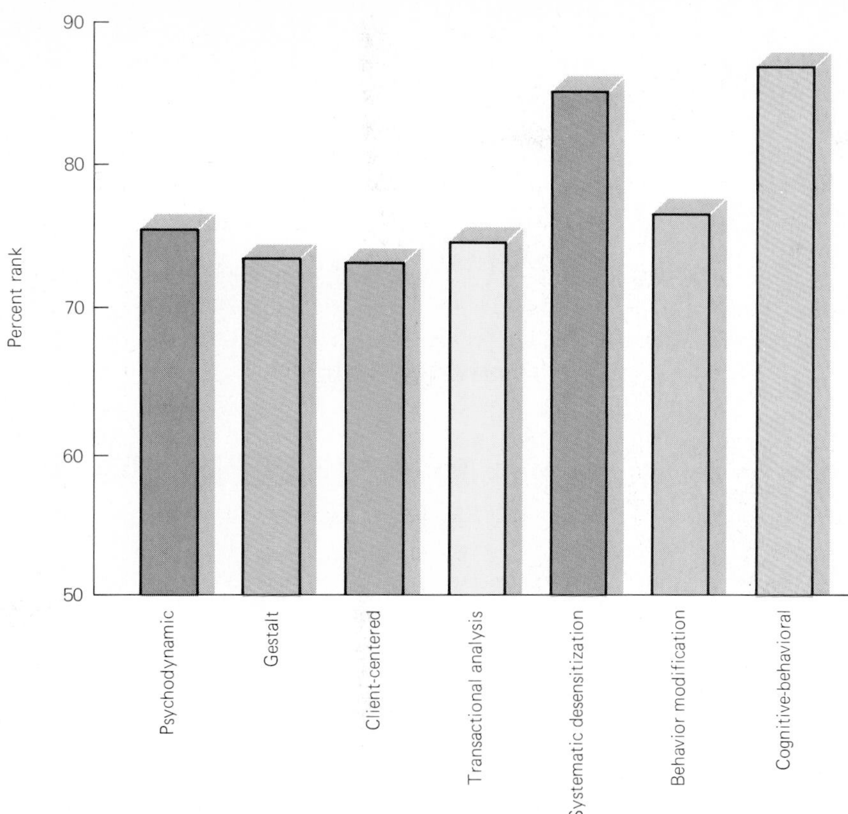

Figure 13-1
Estimates of the effectiveness of different types of treatment in comparison with control groups of untreated people. The percentile score shows how much more effective a particular type of treatment is for the average patient than is no treatment. For example, people given psychodynamic treatment score, on average, more positively on outcome measures than about 75 percent of untreated people. (*Adapted from Smith, Glass, & Miller, 1980.*)

Using this kind of procedure, Smith, Glass, & Miller (1980) came to the conclusions displayed in Figure 13-1. As you can see, although there is one variation between the success rates of the various treatment forms, most are fairly close to one another, ranging from about 70 to 85 percent greater success for treated than for untreated individuals. There is a slight tendency for behavioral approaches and cognitive-behavioral approaches to be a bit more successful, although this may be due to differences in the severity of cases treated (Orwin & Cordroy, 1984). In sum, research generally finds that the differences are only minor between the success rates for various types of therapy (Berman, Miller, & Massman, 1985).

On the other hand, this does not mean that every problem will be resolved equally well by different sorts of therapy. Recall the way that therapy-comparison studies are typically carried out: They initially consider only problems appropriate for a given treatment approach, and then compare treated versus untreated people within that specific approach to see which group of people does better. Such studies say little about whether specific sorts of problems are better treated by one approach or another (Garfield, 1983).

Clearly, however, particular kinds of therapies are more appropriate for some problems than for others—a point made earlier when we considered each of the specific treatment approaches individually (Klerman, 1983). For example, if someone is suffering from the kind of general unhappiness and anxiety described by Colette in the earlier scenario, psychodynamic or humanistic approaches, which emphasize gaining insight into one's problems, would probably be most appropriate. On the other hand, if Colette's problems had been more focused on a particular set of circumstances that brought about her anxiety—such as a phobia or a lack of good study skills that was preventing her from doing well in school—then a behavioral approach might be more reasonable.

Finally, there are an increasing number of eclectic therapy approaches, in which a therapist uses a variety of techniques taken from different approaches to treat a person's problems. By using eclectic procedures, the therapist is able to choose the appropriate mix in accordance with the specific needs of the individual.

The question of which therapy works best, then, cannot be answered without reference to the specific type of psychological problem that is being treated. The accuracy of the match between the problem and the method best determines the likelihood of success in resolving psychological difficulties.

RECAP AND REVIEW II

Recap

- Humanistic approaches view therapy as a way to help people solve their own problems; the therapist merely acts as a guide or facilitator.
- Among the types of humanistic therapies are client-centered therapy, existential therapy, and gestalt therapy.
- A long-standing issue is whether psychotherapy is effective, and, if it is, whether one kind is superior to others. Although there is a good deal of agreement that therapy—in general—is effective, it is less clear whether one kind works better than others.

Review

1. Which of the following would a client be most likely to hear from a humanistic therapist?
   a. "Remember the anger you felt and scream until you feel better." **b.** "When you have gone without a drink for a week, go buy something new." **c.** "There's nothing wrong with feeling that way, but how would you like to change it?" **d.** "That's not appropriate behavior. Let's work on replacing it with something else."
2. Unconditional positive regard is the acceptance of a client's words and deeds, no matter how unpleasant. True or false?
3. ____________ therapy emphasizes the integration of thoughts, feelings, and behaviors.
4. Hans Eysenck's conclusions about the effectiveness of psychotherapy suggested that
   a. no method is superior to the others **b.** people receiving no treatment fare as well as those receiving treatment **c.** the humanistic approach is the most client-sensitive kind of therapy **d.** the humanistic approach results in longer-lasting results
5. Treatments that combine methodology from all theoretical approaches are called ____________ procedures.

(Answers to review questions are at the bottom of page 452.)

THE MEDICAL MODEL AT WORK: BIOLOGICAL TREATMENT APPROACHES

If you get a kidney infection, you're given some penicillin and, with luck, about a week later your kidney is as good as new. If your appendix becomes inflamed, a surgeon removes it. Again—the result is that your body functions normally once more. Could a similar approach be taken with psychological disturbances?

According to biological approaches to treatment, the answer is affirmative. In fact, biologically based treatments are used routinely for certain kinds of problems. The basic model suggests that rather than focusing on a patient's psychological conflicts, past traumas, or environmental factors that may support abnormal behavior, it is more appropriate in certain cases to treat brain chemistry

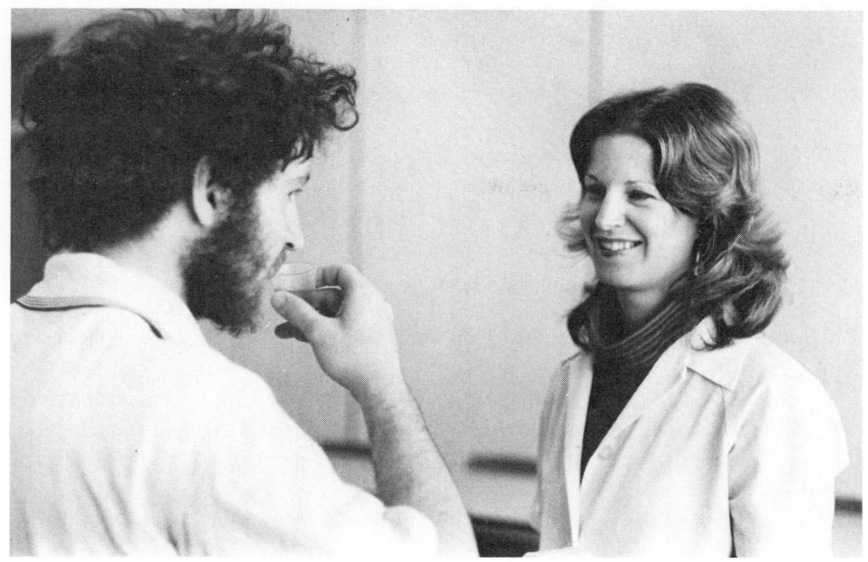

Antipsychotic drugs have alleviated the symptoms of several different types of serious mental disturbance. (*Kenneth Karp*)

and other neurological factors directly. This can be done through the use of drugs, electric shock, or surgery.

Medicine for Mental Disturbances: Drug Therapy

Are we close to the day when we take a pill each morning to maintain good psychological health, in the same way that we now take a vitamin pill to help us stay physically healthy? Although that day has not yet arrived, there are quite a few forms of **drug therapy** that successfully alleviate symptoms of a number of psychological disturbances.

Drug therapy: *Control of psychological problems through drugs*

Antipsychotic Drugs Probably no greater change has occurred in mental hospitals than the successful introduction in the mid-1950s of **antipsychotic drugs**—drugs used to alleviate psychotic symptoms such as agitation and overactivity. Previously, mental hospitals typically fulfilled all the stereotypes of the insane asylum—with screaming, moaning, clawing patients displaying the most bizarre behaviors. Suddenly, in just a matter of months, the hospital wards became considerably calmer environments in which professionals could do more than just try to get the patients through the day without serious harm to themselves or others.

Antipsychotic drugs: *Drugs that temporarily alleviate psychotic symptoms such as agitation and overactivity*

This dramatic change was brought about by the introduction of a drug from the phenothiazine family called **chlorpromazine**. This drug, and others of similar type, rapidly became the most popular—and successful—treatment for schizophrenia. Today drug therapy is the preferred treatment for most cases of severely abnormal behavior, used for almost 90 percent of all hospitalized patients (Carson, 1983; MacDonald & Tobias, 1976).

Chlorpromazine (klor PRO mah zeen): *An antipsychotic drug that is used in the treatment of schizophrenia*

How do antipsychotic drugs work? They seem to function by blocking the production of dopamine at the sites where electric impulses travel across nerve receptors, a process we discussed in Chapter 12 (Kane, 1983). Unfortunately, they do not produce a ''cure'' in the same way that, say, penicillin cures an infection—because as soon as the drug is withdrawn, the original symptoms tend to reappear. Moreover, there can be long-term side effects of such drugs, such as dryness of the mouth and throat, dizziness, and even the development of tremors and loss of muscle control that may continue even after drug treatments are stopped (Kane & Siris, 1983).

Perhaps even more devastating than these physical side effects are the numbing effects of antipsychotic drugs on the emotional responses of patients. For example, Mark Vonnegut (son of author Kurt Vonnegut) describes his reactions to the use of the antipsychotic drug Thorazine while he was institutionalized for schizophrenia:

> The side effects were bad enough, but I liked what the drug was supposed to do even less. It's supposed to keep you calm, dull, uninterested, and uninteresting. No doctor or nurse ever came out and said so in so many words, but what it was was an antihero drug. . . . What the drug is supposed to do is keep away hallucinations. What I think it does is just fog up your mind so badly you don't notice the hallucinations or much else. . . . On Thorazine everything's a bore. Not a bore, exactly. Boredom implies impatience. You can read comic books . . . you can tolerate talking to jerks forever. . . . The weather is dull, the flowers are dull, nothing's very impressive (Vonnegut, 1975, pp. 196–197).

Antidepressant drugs: *Medication that improves a patient's mood and feeling of well-being*

Antidepressant Drugs As you might guess from the name, **antidepressant drugs** are a class of medications used in cases of severe depression to improve the moods of patients. They were discovered quite by accident: It was found that patients suffering from tuberculosis who were given the drug iproniazid suddenly became happier and more optimistic. When the same drug was tested on people suffering from depression, a similar result occurred, and drugs became an accepted form of treatment for depression (McNeal & Cimbolic, 1986).

Antidepressant drugs work by creating an increase in the concentration of certain neurotransmitters within the brain, and although there may be side effects such as drowsiness and faintness, the overall success rate is quite good (Prien, 1983; Siris & Rifkin, 1983). In fact, unlike antipsychotic drugs, antidepressants can produce lasting, long-term recoveries from depression; in many cases, even after the drugs are no longer being taken, the depression does not return.

Lithium (LITH ee um): *A drug used in the treatment of bipolar disorders*

Lithium, a form of simple mineral salts, is another drug that has been used very successfully in cases of bipolar disorders. Although no one knows why it works (it has no known psychological function), it is very effective in reducing manic episodes, ending manic behavior some 70 percent of the time. On the other hand, its effectiveness in resolving depression is not as impressive. It works only in certain cases, and, like other antidepressants, it can produce a number of side effects (Coopen, Metcalfe, & Wood, 1982).

Lithium has a quality that sets it apart from other drug treatments: It represents, more than any other drug, a *preventive* treatment. People who have been subject to manic-depressive episodes in the past often can, after returning to a normal state, take a daily dose of lithium that prevents a recurrence of their symptoms. Lithium, then, presents one thought-provoking vision of the future, suggested by medical-model approaches to abnormal behavior: a future where people take drugs daily to make them psychologically healthier. The reality, though, is that for better or for worse, such a future is far away.

ANSWERS TO REVIEW QUESTIONS

Review II: **1.** c **2.** True **3.** Gestalt **4.** b **5.** Eclectic

The Minor Tranquilizers: Antianxiety Drugs Valium, Miltown, Librium—perhaps you are familiar with these drug names, which are among the most common of all the drugs physicians prescribe. A cure for infection? Relief of the common cold? On the contrary, these drugs have nothing to do with physical symptoms. Instead, they are members of a class of drugs known as **antianxiety drugs** (sometimes known as **minor tranquilizers**) which are prescribed—often by family physicians—to alleviate the stress and anxiety experienced by patients during particularly difficult periods of their lives. In fact, more than half of all Americans have had a family member who is taking such a drug at one time or another.

Antianxiety drugs: *Drugs that alleviate stress and anxiety*
Minor tranquilizers: *See antianxiety drugs*

As their name implies, antianxiety drugs reduce the level of anxiety experienced, essentially by reducing excitability and in part by increasing drowsiness. They are used not only to reduce general tension in people who are experiencing temporary difficulties, but can be employed as part of the treatment for more serious anxiety disorders.

Although the popularity of antianxiety drugs suggests that they are relatively risk-free, in fact they can produce a number of potentially serious side effects. For instance, they can cause fatigue, and long-term use can lead to dependence. Moreover, taken in combination with alcohol, some antianxiety drugs can become lethal. But a more important question concerns their use to suppress anxiety. Since almost every theoretical approach to psychological disturbance views continuing anxiety as a symptom of some sort of problem, drugs that mask anxiety may simply be hiding difficulties that might be more appropriately faced and solved—rather than simply being glossed over.

Shocking Abnormal Behavior Away: Electroconvulsive Therapy (ECT)

If you thought that people who have epilepsy—a disorder characterized by seizures and convulsions—were immune to schizophrenia, what might you conclude? A number of psychiatrists in the 1930s, who mistakenly believed that this relationship did exist, concluded that if some way could be found to actually induce convulsions in patients with schizophrenia, they might be cured. To this end, two Italian physicians, Cerletti and Bini (Bini, 1938) tried to induce convulsions by administering shocks to the heads of patients suffering from schizophrenia—and reported some success in alleviating its symptoms.

The use of **electroconvulsive therapy (ECT)** has continued to the present, although the way in which it is administered has been improved. An electric current of 70 to 150 volts is passed through the head of a patient for about a second and a half, causing the patient to lose consciousness and often experience a seizure. The typical patient receives about ten such treatments in the course of a month (Breggin, 1979; Weiner, 1982).

Electroconvulsive (ee LEK tro kon VUL siv) **therapy**: *Treatment involving the administration of an electric current to a patient's head to treat depression*

As you might expect, ECT is a controversial technique. Apart from the obvious distastefulness of a treatment that evokes images of capital punishment, there are several frequent side effects. For instance, following treatment, patients often experience disorientation, confusion, and sometimes memory loss that may remain for months. Moreover, many patients fear ECT, even though they are anesthetized during the actual treatment and thus experience no pain. Finally, we still do not know how or why ECT works, and although it has never been proved, there is the reasonable fear that the treatment may produce permanent neurological damage to the brain (Fisher, 1985).

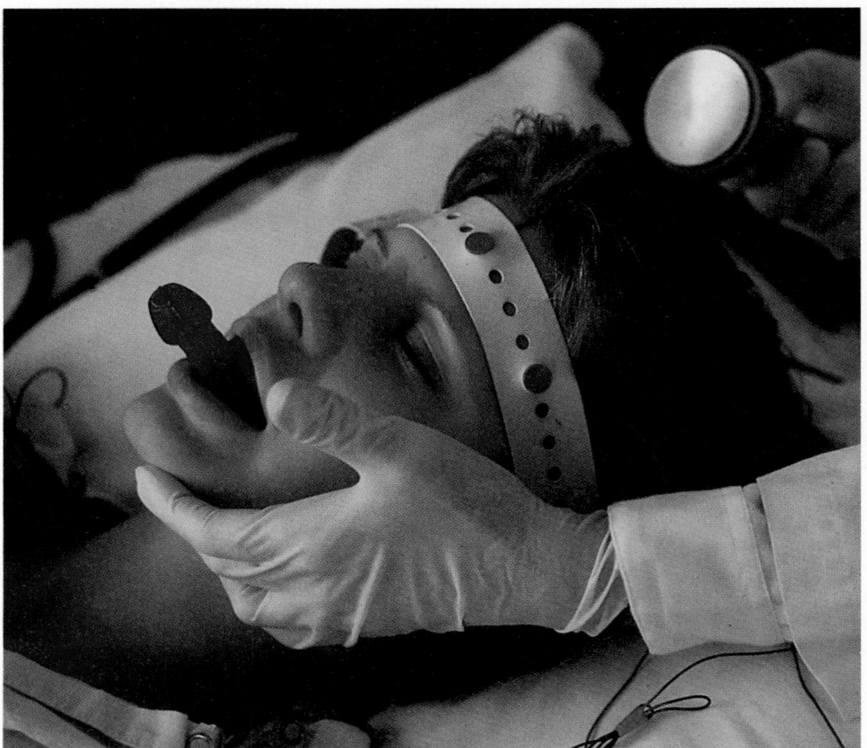

Electroconvulsive therapy (ECT), sometimes used in the treatment of severe depression, involves administering an electric current through a patient's head. (*Will McIntyre/Photo Researchers, Inc.*)

Given the drawbacks to ECT, why is it used at all? The basic reason is that in many cases it still seems to be an effective treatment for severe cases of depression (Sackheim, 1985). Still, it is used much less today than it once was, as drug treatments without the problems of ECT have been proved to alleviate such psychological disturbances.

Cutting Out the Bad: Psychosurgery

Psychosurgery: *Brain surgery, once used to alleviate symptoms of mental disorder but rarely used today*

Prefrontal lobotomy: *The surgical destruction of certain areas of a patient's frontal lobes to improve the control of emotionality*

If ECT strikes you as a questionable procedure, the use of **psychosurgery**—brain surgery in which the object is to alleviate symptoms of mental disorder—will likely appear even more suspect. A treatment technique that has largely disappeared, psychosurgery was first introduced as a treatment of "last resort" in the 1930s. The procedure—specifically, a **prefrontal lobotomy**—consists of surgically destroying or removing certain parts of a patient's frontal lobes, which control emotionality. The rationale for such a procedure was that by destroying the connections between various parts of the brain, patients would be less subject to emotional impulses, and their general behavior would improve.

In fact, psychosurgery often did improve a patient's behavior—but not without drastic side effects. For along with remission of symptoms of mental disorder, patients sometimes suffered personality changes, becoming bland, colorless, and unemotional. In other cases, patients became aggressive and unable to control their impulses; in the worst cases, the patients died from treatment.

However, despite these problems—and the obvious ethical questions regarding the appropriateness of forever altering someone's personality—psychosurgery was used in thousands of cases in the 1930s and 1940s. In fact, the treatment became so routine that in some places fifty patients a day received psychosurgery (Freeman, 1959).

With the advent of effective drug treatments, psychosurgery became practically obsolete. It is still used, in modified form, in very rare cases when all other procedures have failed and the patient's behavior presents a high risk to self and others or when there is severe, uncontrollable pain in terminal cases. When psychosurgery is used today, more precise techniques are employed, and only extremely small areas of brain tissue are destroyed. Still, even in these cases, important ethical issues are raised, and psychosurgery remains a highly controversial treatment (Valenstein, 1980).

Can Abnormal Behavior be Cured?: Biological Treatment in Perspective

In some respects, there has been no greater revolution in the field of mental health than that represented by the biological treatment approaches. Mental-hospital personnel have been able to concentrate more on actually helping patients and less on custodial functions as previously violent, uncontrollable patients have been calmed by the use of drugs. Similarly, patients whose lives have been disrupted by depression or manic-depressive episodes have been able to function normally, and other forms of drug therapies in particular have shown remarkable results.

On the other hand, biological therapies can be criticized. For one thing, in many cases they merely provide relief of the *symptoms* of mental disorder; as soon as the drugs are withdrawn, the symptoms return. While considered a major step in the right direction, such treatment does not invariably solve the underlying problem that may continue to haunt a patient even while he or she is undergoing treatment. Moreover, as we have seen, biological treatments can have numerous side effects, ranging from physical reactions to the development of *new* symptoms of abnormal behavior. Finally, there is recent evidence that drugs may be no better than psychotherapy in the treatment of certain forms of mental disturbance. For instance, one major study recently found that two forms of psychotherapy were as effective as the use of standard drug treatment in alleviating depression (Elkin, 1986). For these reasons, then, biologically based treatment approaches do not represent a cure-all for psychological disorders.

The Informed Consumer of Psychology: Choosing the Right Therapist

Suppose your friend Colette, after reviewing the various treatment approaches, decides on the general nature of the treatment that she wants and begins therapy. How does she know that she has chosen the right therapist?

Once again, there is no simple answer. There are, however, a number of factors that informed consumers of psychological services can and should take into consideration to determine if they have made the right choice. Among those factors are the following:

- The relationship between client and therapist should be a comfortable one; the client should not be afraid or in awe of the therapist, but should trust the therapist and feel free to discuss the most personal issues without fearing a negative reaction.

THE CUTTING EDGE

FOCUS ON PREVENTION:

The Campus Crisis Center

I need some help . . . I just can't seem to get things together . . . I'm behind in all my classes, and every time I sit down to work, my mind wanders off and I don't accomplish anything. But the thing that's really getting me down is my girlfriend. I think we've just about had it. She doesn't seem to care at all about how I feel, she's so wrapped up in herself . . . I've begun to think about suicide . . . I've got no one to turn to. . . .

Giving college students someone to whom to turn in times of psychological crisis is the idea behind one of the newest innovations on many college campuses: the college crisis center. Modeled after suicide-prevention hot-line centers, campus crisis centers provide callers with the opportunity to discuss life crisis with a sympathetic listener who is most often a student volunteer.

Although not professionals, the volunteers receive careful training in telephone counseling. They role-play particular problems and are told how to respond to the difficulties they may confront with callers. The volunteers also hold group meetings to discuss the kinds of problems they are encountering and to share experiences about the kinds of strategies that are most effective.

Callers to campus crisis centers have a range of problems, but most center on dating relationships and family problems. Others include rape, feelings of loneliness, unwanted pregnancy, academic difficulties, marital problems, and drug and alcohol difficulties (Orzek, 1983; Tucker, Megenity, & Virgil, 1970). In fact, the problems are essentially no different from those found at noncollege crisis centers except for a higher incidence of school-related problems.

Because they are not professionals, the staff of college crisis centers do not, of course, offer long-term therapy to those who contact them. But they are able to provide a supportive, constructive response to callers—often when it is most needed. They are also able to refer callers to appropriate agencies on and off campus to get the help they need on a long-term basis.

What is the future for campus crisis centers? One guess is that crisis counseling will become more integrated into the student's own everyday environment. For instance, Texas A & M University set up a program in which dormitory resident advisors are taught crisis intervention and stress-management techniques (Brunson & McKee, 1982). This program provides the resident advisors with an opportunity to identify psychological problems early on, in the hope of preventing them from developing into more serious ones.

■ The therapist should have appropriate training and credentials for the type of therapy that he or she is conducting and should be licensed by appropriate state and local agencies. Far from being a breach of etiquette to ask a therapist on an initial visit about the kind of training that he or she received, it behooves a wise consumer of psychological services to make such inquiries.

■ Clients should feel that they are making progress toward resolving their psychological difficulties after therapy has begun, despite occasional setbacks. If, after repeated visits, they sense no improvement, this issue should be discussed, with an eye toward the possibility of making a change. Most therapy that is done today is of fairly brief duration, especially that involving college students—who average just five therapy sessions (Nowicki & Duke, 1978).

■ Finally, clients should be aware that they will have to put in a great deal of effort in therapy. They should be committed to making therapy work and should know that it is they, and not the therapist, who must do most of the work to resolve their problems. The potential is there for the effort to pay off handsomely—as people experience more positive, fulfilling, and meaningful lives.

RECAP AND REVIEW III

Recap

- Biological-treatment approaches encompass drug therapy, electoconvulsive (shock) therapy, and surgical therapy.
- Drug therapy has produced dramatic reductions in psychotic behavior. Among the medications used are antipsychotic drugs, antidepressant drugs, and antianxiety drugs.
- Electroconvulsive therapy (ECT) consists of passing an electric current through the brain of a patient suffering from severe psychological disturbance, particularly schizophrenia or depression.
- The most extreme form of biological therapy is psychosurgery, in which patients undergo brain surgery. Although rarely used today, prefrontal lobotomies were a common earlier form of treatment.

Review

1. Like penicillin, antipsychotic drugs have provided effective, long-term, and complete cures for psychologtical problems. True or false?
2. Which of the following is most like a vitamin, acting as a preventive drug for psychological disorders?
   a. chlorpromazine **b.** lithium **c.** Librium **d.** Valium
3. A treatment of schizophrenia started in the 1930s in which electric current is administered to a patient's head is called ________ therapy.
4. Psychosurgery has grown in popularity as a method of treatment as surgical techniques have become more precise. True or false?

(Answers to review questions are at the bottom of page 458.)

Psychology Looks Toward the 1990s
In Search of New Treatments

In treatment for severe depression, the patient lay down on a bed in a small room in the early morning hours. As she comfortably reclined on the bed, a series of bright lights were lit. For two hours, the patient stayed in the room, bathed in the artificial light. Then, her therapy over for the day, she left, knowing that the next morning she would return for another treatment.

Experimental evidence has begun to accumulate suggesting a new treatment for certain kinds of depression: exposure to light. In a study reported by a team of researchers at the Oregon Health Sciences University, a group of patients who regularly suffered from depression in the winter—when the length of the days shortens—were exposed to bright lights at various times of the day. The results showed that when the patients were exposed to two hours of bright light in the early morning, their depression improved. In contrast, bright light exposure in the evening had no effect (Lewy, Sack, Miller, & Hoban, 1987).

The antidepressive effects of morning exposure to bright light were accompanied by a shift in the timing of the patients' production of the chemical melatonin, which typically follows a predictable pattern during the day. It appears, then, that the exposure to light produced a change in the patients' natural biological rhythms, and suggests that the depression of the subjects may have stemmed originally from disorders in their natural biological rhythms, which exposure to light—at the appropriate time—corrected.

If the potential of light exposure as a treatment for certain kinds of depression becomes realized—and it should be stressed that the treatment is purely experimental at this point—it will join several other new forms of therapies that are being devised for the treatment of psychological disorders. Of course, the implementation of new therapies raises the issue, once more, of which type of therapy is the most effective in treating abnormal behavior, an issue which is being addressed continually by researchers.

For example, one recent study examined the question of which type of therapy is optimal for the treatment of depression, and the results were immediately controversial. In a major study presented at a meeting of the American Psychiatric Association, a team of researchers found that two forms of psychotherapy are as effective as a standard drug regimen in treating depression (Boffey, 1986; Elkin, Shea, Imber, Pilkonis, Stotsky, Glass, Watkins, Leber, Collins, 1986). The study found that both cognitive behavior therapy and a type of therapy labeled "interpersonal" psychotherapy—which focuses on patients' interpersonal problems and social functioning—were at least as effective as drug therapy in reducing the symptoms of depression and improving the functioning of patients.

In the study, a group of 250 patients who were either moderately or severely depressed were divided randomly into three experimental groups, plus an untreated control group. The patients assigned to the two psychotherapy groups were given sixteen weeks of treatment, while a third group was given an antidepressant drug. The control group received a biologically inactive placebo, plus informal weekly support consultations with a therapist.

Approximately 50 to 60 percent of the patients in the three treatment groups became fully recovered, in contrast to the untreated control, in which less than 30 percent recovered. No significant differences in recovery rates were found between the different treatment groups.

The study is continuing, with an eighteen-month follow-up planned. It is clear from even these preliminary results, however, that the question of which therapy approach is most effective is far from being answered with certainty, and that new techniques will continue to be developed.

LOOKING BACK

1. This chapter has examined the treatment of abnormal behavior. It began by discussing the two major categories of treatment types: psychologically based therapy, known as psychotherapy, and biologically based therapy. Although the specific treatment types are diverse, they generally share the goal of resolving psychological problems by modifying people's thoughts, feelings, expectations, evaluations, and ultimately, their behavior.
2. Psychoanalytic treatment is based on Freud's psychodynamic theory. It seeks to bring unresolved past conflicts and unacceptable impulses from the unconscious into the conscious, where the problems may be dealt with more effectively. To do this, patients meet frequently with their therapists and use techniques such as free association and dream interpretation. It can be a difficult process, because of patient resistance and transference, and there is no unquestioned evidence that the process works.
3. Behavioral approaches to treatment view abnormal behavior itself as the problem, rather than viewing the behavior as a symptom of some underlying cause. In order to bring about a "cure," then, this view suggests that one must change the outward behavior. Behavioral psychologists have developed a number of ways of doing this. In aversive conditioning, unpleasant stimuli are linked to a behavior that the patient enjoys but wants to stop—such as alcohol or drug intake. Systematic desensitization uses the opposite procedure: A stimulus that evokes pleasant feelings is repeatedly paired with a stimulus that evokes anxiety in order to reduce that anxiety.
4. Observational learning is another behavioral treatment used to teach new, more appropriate behavior, as are techniques such as token systems, in which desired behavior is directly rewarded. Finally, rational-emotive therapy is an example of a class of behavioral therapy known as cognitive-behavioral therapy. It suggests that the goal of therapy should be a restructuring of a person's belief system into a more realistic, rational, and logical view of the world. Behavior therapy in general has been shown

ANSWERS TO REVIEW QUESTIONS

Review III: **1.** False **2.** b **3.** Electroconvulsive (electric shock) **4.** False to be relatively successful, although critics argue that behavioral approaches may overlook the underlying problem, producing the possibility of symptom substitution.

5. Humanistic therapy is based on the premise that people have control of their behavior, that they can make choices about their lives, and that it is up to them to solve their own problems. To follow this philosophy, humanistic therapists take a nondirective approach, acting more as guides who facilitate a client's search for answers. One example of humanistic therapy is client-centered therapy, developed by Carl Rogers, in which the goal is to allow people to reach the potential good assumed to be characteristic of each of us. Existential therapy helps people cope with the unique freedom and potential that human existence offers, while gestalt therapy is directed toward aiding people in the integration of their thoughts, feelings, and behavior.

6. Most research suggests that, in general, therapy is more effective than no therapy, although how much more effective is not known. Moreover, the answer to the more difficult question—which therapy works best—is even less clear, in part because the therapies are so qualitatively different and in part because the definition of "cure" is so vague. It is clear, though, that particular kinds of therapy are more appropriate for some problems than for others.

7. Biological treatment approaches suggest that one ought to treat the physiological causes of abnormal behavior, rather than considering psychological factors. Drug therapy is the best example of biological therapy; it has been effective in bringing about dramatic reductions in the appearance of severe signs of mental disturbance.

8. Antipsychotic drugs such as chlorpromazine are very effective in reducing psychotic symptoms, although they can produce serious side effects. Antidepressant drugs such as lithium are useful in reducing depression; more than any other drug, lithium has been used as a part of a preventive treatment. The antianxiety drugs or minor tranquilizers are among the most frequently prescribed medications of any sort; they act to reduce the experience of anxiety.

9. Electroconvulsive therapy (ECT) consists of passing an electric current of 70 to 150 volts through the head of a patient, who loses consciousness and has a strong seizure. Although the reason is unknown, this procedure has been shown to be an effective treatment for severe cases of schizophrenia and depression. Another biological treatment is psychosurgery. The typical procedure consists of surgically destroying certain parts of a patient's brain in an operation known as a prefrontal lobotomy. Given the grave ethical problems and possible adverse side effects, the procedure is rarely used today.

KEY TERMS AND CONCEPTS

psychotherapy (p. 433)
eclectic approach to therapy (p. 433)
clinical psychologist (p. 434)
counseling psychologist (p. 434)
psychiatrist (p. 434)
psychoanalyst (p. 434)
psychiatric social worker (p. 434)
psychodynamic therapy (p. 434)
defense mechanisms (p. 434)
neurotic symptoms (p. 434)
psychoanalysis (p. 435)
free association (p. 435)
dream interpretation (p. 435)
manifest content (p. 436)
latent content (p. 436)
resistance (p. 436)
transference (p. 436)
behavioral treatment approaches (p. 437)
aversive conditioning (p. 438)
systematic desensitization (p. 439)
hierarchy of fears (p. 439)
observational learning (p. 440)
modeling (p. 440)
token system (p. 441)
contingency contracting (p. 441)
rational-emotive therapy (p. 441)
cognitive-behavioral therapy (p. 441)
behavioral self-management (p. 442)
symptom substitution (p. 443)
humanistic therapy (p. 444)
client-centered therapy (p. 445)
nondirective counseling (p. 445)
unconditional positive regard (p. 445)
existential therapy (p. 445)
gestalt therapy (p. 446)
spontaneous remission (p. 448)
drug therapy (p. 451)
antipsychotic drugs (p. 451)
chlorpromazine (p. 451)
antidepressant drugs (p. 452)
lithium (p. 452)
antianxiety drugs (p. 453)
minor tranquilizers (p. 453)
electroconvulsive therapy (ECT) (p. 453)
psychosurgery (p. 454)
prefrontal lobotomy (p. 454)

FOR FURTHER STUDY AND APPLICATION

Karoly, P., & Kanfer, F. H. (1982). *Self-management and behavior change.* New York: Pergamon Press.

This is an excellent guide to behavior-modification techniques that you can apply to yourself, with step-by-step instructions.

Bootzin, R. R., & Acocella, J. R. (1984). *Abnormal psychology: Current perspectives* (4th ed.). New York: Random House.

A well-written introduction to treatment approaches, this book features current findings and theories.

Moos, R. H. (1976). *Human adaptation: Coping with life crisis*. Lexington, MA: Heath.

In a series of articles, various sorts of life crises are discussed, and ways of coping with the stress and anxiety they bring about are presented.

Williams, J. B. W., & Spitzer, R. L. (1983). *Psychotherapy research: Where are we and where should we go?* New York: Guilford Press.

In a series of technical but readable chapters written by experts, this book provides an excellent overview of the kinds of psychotherapy and the research findings that support them. Of particular interest are chapters discussing the issue of how well psychotherapy works.

Kanfer, F. H., & Goldstein, A. P. (Eds.). (1983). *Helping people change.* (3rd ed.). New York: Pergamon Press.

This book provides a clear overview of the various techniques that are currently used to treat people with psychological difficulties.

PART SEVEN

PART SEVEN

THE SOCIAL FOUNDATIONS OF BEHAVIOR

We turn now to a consideration of the social world of which all of us are a part. We come to a hotly contested election in which the participants make a concerted effort to influence the votes of their friends. We view a jungle scene, in which hundreds of people line up to drink from a cauldron filled with poison that they know will bring them, and their children, an agonizing death. And we consider a scientist who asks people to give electric shocks to others—and finds ready acceptance of his request.

In this part of the book, we turn to the social world and how it affects people's behavior. We will consider how we decide what other people are like and how we determine why they behave as they do. We will see what psychologists have learned about social influence, how our everyday activities are affected by the behavior of others. Finally, we will explore the reasons why we like and fall in love with particular people, and we will consider two opposite forms of human behavior: aggression and helping behavior.

In Chapter 14, we consider attitudes and persuasion: how we understand what others are like and how we understand the causes behind others'—and our own—behavior.

In Chapter 15, the focus is on the ways in which we interact with others in a social world, as we discuss conformity, liking and loving, aggression, and helping behavior.

CHAPTER 14

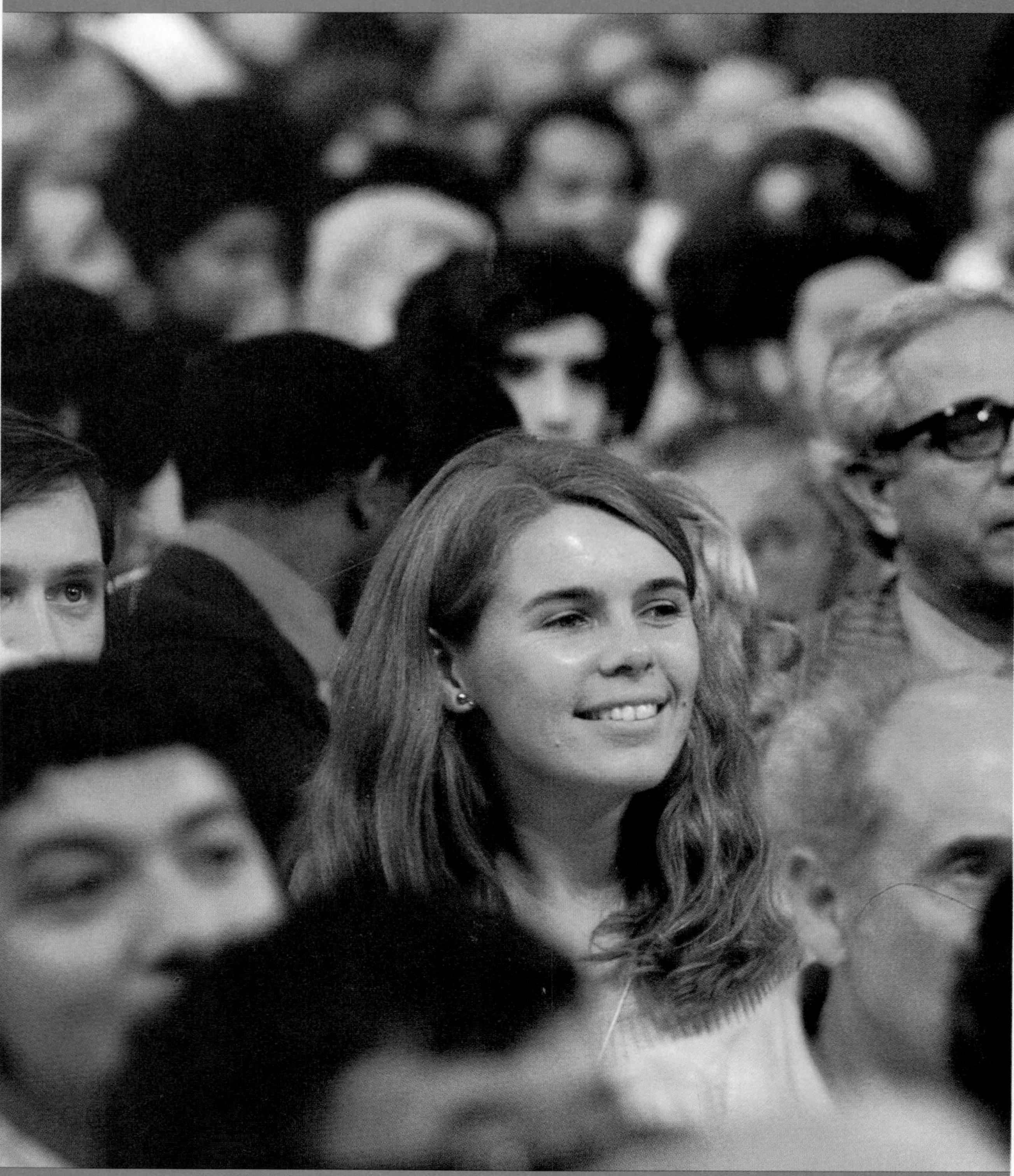

SOCIAL PSYCHOLOGY: THE INDIVIDUAL IN A SOCIAL WORLD

PROLOGUE

LOOKING AHEAD

ATTITUDES, BEHAVIOR, AND PERSUASION
Forming and maintaining attitudes
PSYCHOLOGY AT WORK. Professional Persuasion: The Rules Advertisers Follow
Fitting attitudes and behavior together: Cognitive consistency approaches
Recap and review I

UNDERSTANDING OTHERS: SOCIAL COGNITION
Understanding what others are like: Social Cognition
TRY IT! Are You Susceptible by Stereotyping?
Recap and review II

UNDERSTANDING THE CAUSES OF BEHAVIOR: ATTRIBUTION PROCESSES
We all make mistakes: Biases in attribution
Understanding our own behavior: Self-perception theory
THE CUTTING EDGE. Improving Your Grades by Improving Your Attributions
The informed consumer of psychology: Forming more accurate impressions
Recap and review III
PSYCHOLOGY LOOKS TOWARD THE 1990s. Imitating the Japanese: Changing Attitudes on the Job

LOOKING BACK

KEY TERMS AND CONCEPTS

FOR FURTHER STUDY AND APPLICATION

PROLOGUE

Jolette Berkman knew the vote would be close, but she thought she had won the battle. She was fairly certain that most members of the undergraduate Student Senate had finally come around to her position on banning the sale of beer and liquor at college concerts and sporting events. Of course, you could never tell for sure; sometimes people said one thing in private but did another in public. But she had pulled out all the stops in her campaign—making signs, passing out leaflets, placing advertisements in the school newspaper. One of the best ideas was getting Jill Costin, the movie star, to come to campus and speak in favor of the idea; her arguments—as well as her mere presence—seemed to sway a lot of people's attitudes. Of course, the other side had put together *its* own campaign, getting those lawyers to lecture on freedom and the rights of the individual. In some respects, though, it seemed to just boil down to who was the most persuasive. In fact, at times Jolette felt no different from someone selling Jell-o.

LOOKING AHEAD

Social psychology: *The branch of psychology concerned with how people's thoughts, feelings, and actions are affected by others*

To Jolette Berkman, what mattered most was whether her side eventually won the vote. But to a social psychologist observing the situation, the critical factor would be the importance of persuasion and social influence in determining the outcome. These topics are central to the field of **social psychology**, which is concerned with how people's thoughts, feelings, and actions are affected by others.

The broad scope of social psychology is conveyed by the kinds of questions social psychologists ask, such as: How can we convince people to agree with a new point of view, to change their attitudees, or to adopt new ideas and values? How do we understand what others are like? How are we influenced by what others do and think? Why do people sometimes display such violence, aggression, and cruelty toward others that people throughout the world live in fear of annihilation? Yet why, at other times, do people place their own lives at risk to help others?

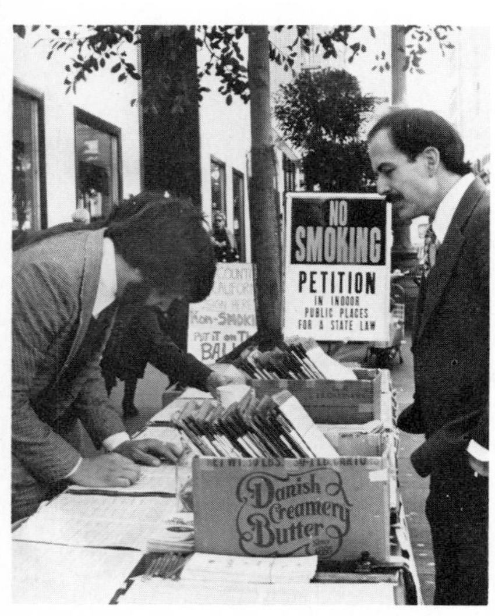

Social psychologists study issues involving persuasion and social influence. (*Christine Jakobs*)

In this chapter and the next one, we explore social psychological approaches to these and other issues. Not only do we examine those processes that underlie social behavior, we discuss solutions and approaches to a variety of problems and issues facing all of us—problems and issues that range from understanding persuasive tactics to forming more accurate impressions of others.

In the first section, we begin with a look at attitudes, our evaluations of people and other stimuli. We see how those attitudes can be influenced and changed by the behavior of others and by the kinds of information to which we are exposed.

Next, we discuss the ways we form judgments about others. We discover that our impressions of others are not formed in a haphazard manner, but follow regular, predictable patterns.

In the last part of the chapter, we examine the ways in which we determine the meaning of other people's behavior, and the kinds of biases that affect our impressions. We see how our understanding of the causes of other people's behavior affects the way we treat those people. Finally, we discuss how we can form more accurate impressions of others.

After reading and studying this chapter, then, you will be able to

- Define what is meant by the term "attitudes" and describe how they develop
- Identify ways of modifying attitudes
- Understand how people form impressions of others
- Explain how people determine the meaning of others' behavior
- Describe the common biases that color the way in which people view the behavior of others
- Identify techniques for enhancing the accuracy of our judgments about others
- Define and apply the key terms and concepts listed at the end of the chapter

ATTITUDES, BEHAVIOR, AND PERSUASION

"Where's the beef?" "How do you spell relief?" "Coke is it."

You've heard it all before, and you know you'll hear it over and over again. We are constantly bombarded with advertisements designed to persuade us to purchase specific products. In fact, these attempts illustrate basic principles that have been articulated by social psychologists who study **attitudes**, learned predispositions to respond in a favorable or unfavorable manner to a particular object (Fishbein & Ajzen, 1975).

Attitudes: *Learned predispositions to respond in a favorable or unfavorable manner to a particular object*

Attitudes, of course, are not restricted to consumer products; they also relate to specific individuals, as well as to more abstract issues—such as Jolette Berkman's position on drinking at college affairs. For example, you, no doubt, hold vastly differing attitudes about the various people in your life, depending on the nature of your interactions with them. These attitudes may range from highly positive, as in the case of a lover, to extremely negative, as with a despised rival. Attitudes are also likely to vary in importance. While our attitudes toward friends, family, and peers are generally central to our interactions in our social world, our attitudes toward, say, television newscasters may be relatively insignificant. Whatever the specific attitudes we consider, however, they are likely to develop according to the general principles that social psychologists have discovered about how they are formed, maintained, and changed—principles that we discuss in this part of the chapter.

Forming and Maintaining Attitudes

Although we do not enter the world holding well-defined attitudes toward any particular person or object, anyone who has seen an infant smile at its parents knows that at least certain attitudes develop quickly. Interestingly, some of the same principles governing how attitudes in the youngest of children are acquired and developed continue to operate throughout one's life.

Smile When You Think of Dog Food: Classical Conditioning and Attitudes One of the basic processes that underlies attitude formation and development relates to learning principles (McGuire, 1985). Research has shown that the same classical conditioning processes that made Pavlov's dogs salivate at the sound of a bell (see Chapter 4) can explain how attitudes are acquired. In one experiment, for example, subjects were exposed to paired auditory and visual stimuli in which the names of particular countries were paired with words that had either positive connotations (such as "gift" or "happy"), neutral connotations, or negative connotations. For example, when the name of a country toward which the experimenter wanted the subjects to form a positive attitude was flashed on a screen, the experimenter said a word with a positive connotation (such as "happy"). After repeated trials in which each nationality appeared eighteen times, the subjects' attitudes toward each of the nationalities were assessed. In general, the results showed that subjects held more positive attitudes toward the nationalities associated with positive words, and more negative attitudes toward nationalities that had been associated with negative words (Staats, 1967; Staats & Staats, 1958).

Advertisers are well aware of results such as these, and often try to link a product they want consumers to buy with a positive feeling or event. For instance, many advertisements feature young, attractive, healthy men and women using a product—even if it is one as uninteresting as dog food. The goal behind such advertisements is to create a classically conditioned reaction to the product, so that just seeing a can of Alpo makes you feel good. (See the accompanying Psychology at Work box.)

Reinforcers and attitude formation.

Praising You for the "Right" Attitude: Reinforcement Approaches to Attitude Acquisition Another basic learning process, operant conditioning, underlies attitude acquisition. Attitudes that are reinforced, either verbally or nonverbally, tend to be maintained, whereas a person who states an attitude that elicits ridicule from others may modify or abandon the attitude. But it is not only direct reinforcement or punishment that can influence attitudes. **Vicarious learning**, in which a person learns something through the observation of others, also accounts for attitude development—particularly when the individual has no direct experience with the object about which the attitude is held. It is through vicarious learning processes that children pick up the prejudices of their parents. For example, even if they have never met a blind person, children whose parents say that "blind people are incompetent" may adopt such attitudes themselves.

Vicarious (vy CARE ee us) **learning**: *Learning by observing others*

Fitting Attitudes and Behavior Together: Cognitive Consistency Approaches

If Jolette Berkman were to be successful in her attempt to ban liquor from college concerts and sports events, she might be surprised to find that some of the same student senators who expressed support for the ban were still sneaking flasks of rum into football games.

What would be the result of such incongruence between an attitude and the behavior related to that attitude? One prediction—that their attitude might later change to become less supportive of the liquor ban—comes from work examining the degree of consistency among the attitudes people hold and their behavior relating to the attitudes.

Most social psychologists interested in the nature of the consistency between attitudes, and between attitudes and behavior, suggest that people strive to fit their attitudes and behavior together in a logical framework. For instance, consider the following incident:

> You've just spent what you feel is the most boring hour of your life, turning pegs for a psychological experiment. Just as you're finally finished and about to leave, the experimenter asks you to do him a favor. He tells you that he needs a confederate to tell subsequent subjects about the task. All you have to do is tell them how interesting it was. For this, you'll be paid $1.

PSYCHOLOGY AT WORK

PROFESSIONAL PERSUASION:

The Rules Advertisers Follow

What is it about Bill Cosby that leads people to buy more Jell-o, or about Michael Jackson that makes people want to drink more Pepsi?

According to David Berger, each of these people represents a carefully selected match between the particular product and the individual chosen to represent it. It is not just a matter of finding a well-known celebrity; the person must also be believable, trustworthy, and representative of the qualities that advertisers want their particular product to project. Berger should know. As director of research at Foote, Cone and Belding—one of the largest advertising companies in the world—he has been involved in advertising for literally hundreds of products over the last twenty-five years.

Berger says that contemporary advertising relies on a careful blend of scientific research and creativity to influence people's attitudes and, at the bottom line, to convince them to purchase products. According to him, advertising agencies formulate an overall marketing strategy that describes what it is they want to achieve, and then they identify the target consumers according to particular needs and wants.

The work of Berger and other advertisers draws heavily upon findings from social psychology regarding persuasion (Alwitt, Barnet, & Mitchell, 1985). This research has identified a number of factors (see Figure 14-1) that promote effective persuasion—many of which you will recognize if you consider for a moment some of the advertisements with which you are most familiar:

- Message source. The individual who provides a persuasive message has a major impact on the effectiveness of that message. Communicators who are both physically and socially attractive seem to produce greater attitude change (Chaiken, 1979). Moreover, the expertise and trustworthiness of a communicator are related to the impact of a message (Hovland, Janis, & Kelly, 1953)—unless the communicator is believed to have an ulterior motive. If a prestigious communicator seems to be benefiting from the persuasion of others, the message may be discounted (Eagly, Wood, & Chaiken, 1978).
- Characteristics of the message. As you might expect, it is not just *who* delivers a message, but *what* the message is like that affects attitude and behavior change. One-sided arguments—in which only the communicator's side is presented—are probably best if the communicator is initially viewed favorably by the audience. But if the audience receives a message presenting an unpopular viewpoint, then two-sided messages—which include both the communicator's position and the one he or she is arguing against—are more effective, probably because they are seen as more precise and thoughtful (Karlins & Abelson, 1979). In addition, fear-producing messages ("If you don't use our dental floss, your teeth are sure to fall out") are effective only if they include precise recommendations for actions to avoid danger. Otherwise, messages that are fear-arousing tend to evoke people's defense mechanisms and may be ignored (Leventhal, 1970).
- Characteristics of the recipient or target. Once a message has been communicated, the manner in which it is interpreted by the target determines whether or not it is accepted. One important factor is the nature of information processing carried out by the recipient.

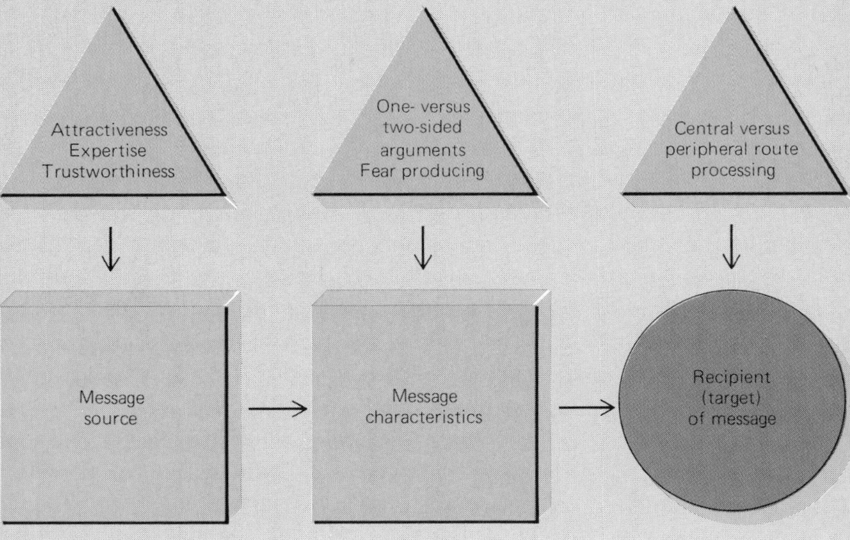

Figure 14-1
In this model of the critical factors affecting persuasion, the message source and message characteristics are shown to influence the recipient or target of a persuasive message.

There are two routes to persuasion: central and peripheral (Cialdini, 1984; Petty & Cacioppo, 1981). **Central route processing** means that the recipient thoughtfully considers the issues and arguments involved in persuasion. **Peripheral route processing,** in contrast, occurs when the recipient uses more easily understood information that requires less thought, such as the nature of the source or other information less central to the issues involved in the message itself.

In general, central route processing results in the most lasting attitude change. However, if central route processing cannot be employed (for instance, if the target is inattentive, bored, or distracted), then the nature of the message becomes less important and peripheral factors more critical (Petty & Cacioppo, 1984). Advertising that uses celebrities to sell a product, then, tends to produce change along the peripheral route. In fact, it is possible that well-reasoned, carefully crafted messages might well be *less* effective when delivered by a celebrity than by an anonymous source—if the target pays greater attention to the source (leading to peripheral route processing) than the message (leading to central route processing). On the other hand, since recipients of advertising messages are often in a fairly inattentive state, the use of celebrities is probably an excellent strategy. Advertisers such as David Berger are correct, then, in their assumption that well-known individuals can have a significant persuasive impact.

Central route processing: *Message interpretation characterized by thoughtful consideration of the issues and arguments used to persuade*

Peripheral (pur IF er ul) **route processing**: *Message interpretation characterized by consideration of the source and related general information rather than of the message itself*

Cognitive dissonance: *The conflict that arises when a person holds contrasting cognitions*

Cognitions: *Attitudes, thoughts, or beliefs*

If you agree to such a request, you may be setting yourself up for a state of psychological tension that is known as **cognitive dissonance**. According to Leon Festinger, a major social psychologist who formulated the theory in 1957, cognitive dissonance occurs when a person holds two attitudes or thoughts (referred to as **cognitions**) that contradict each other. For example, a smoker who knows that smoking leads to lung cancer holds contradictory cognitions: (1) I smoke; and (2) smoking leads to lung cancer. The theory predicts that these two thoughts will lead to a state of cognitive dissonance. More importantly, it predicts that the individual will be motivated to reduce such dissonance by one of the following methods: (1) modifying one or both of the cognitions; (2) changing the perceived importance of one cognition; (3) adding additional cognitions; or (4) denying that the two cognitions are related to each other. Hence, the smoker might decide that he really doesn't smoke all that much (modifying the cognition), that the evidence linking smoking to cancer is weak (changing the importance of a cognition), that the amount of exercise he gets compensates for the smoking (adding cognitions), or that there is no evidence linking smoking and cancer (denial). Whatever technique is used, the result is a reduction in dissonance.

If we consider the situation in which a subject in an experiment is paid just $1 to tell someone else that a boring task was interesting, as in the situation described above, we have set up classic dissonance-producing circumstances. A subject in such a situation is left with two contradictory thoughts: (1) I believe the task is boring; but (2) I said it was interesting with only a dollar's worth of justification—which is not a very good reason.

According to the theory, dissonance should be aroused. But how can such dissonance be reduced? One can't very well deny having said that the task was interesting without making a fairly strong break with reality. But, relatively speaking, it is easy to change one's attitude toward the task—and thus the theory predicts that dissonance will be reduced as the subjects change their attitudes to be more positive.

This prediction was confirmed by a classic dissonance experiment (Festinger

"Nothing there appeals to me."

As this cartoon aptly illustrates, cognitive dissonance arising from the two contradictory cognitions of "I want a drink" and "I can't afford a drink" may be reduced by deciding that one really doesn't want a drink after all. (*Drawing by B. Tobey; © 1978 The New Yorker Magazine, Inc.*)

& Carlsmith, 1959). The experiment followed essentially the same procedure described earlier, in which a subject was offered a dollar to describe a boring task as interesting. In addition, as a control, a condition was included in which subjects were offered $20 to say that the task was interesting. The reasoning behind this condition was that $20 was so much money that subjects in this condition had a good reason to be telling something that was incorrect; dissonance would *not* be aroused, and *less* attitude change would be expected. The results supported this notion: Subjects changed their attitudes more (becoming more positive toward the peg-turning task) when they were paid $1 than subjects who were paid $20.

We now know that dissonance explains a number of everyday occurrences involving attitudes and behavior. For example, consider what happens when you decide to make a major purchase, such as a new car. First you will probably get as much information as possible about a range of models by talking to people and reading about different cars. But after you make your decision, what happens? Most people experience some degree of dissonance because the car they've chosen has some undesirable characteristics, while those models that were rejected have some positive features. What typically happens to reduce such dissonance, after a decision has been reached, is that people's attitudes toward the rejected models become *more* negative, while their attitudes toward the chosen model become *more* positive (Converse & Cooper, 1979). Moreover, a **selective exposure** phenomenon occurs: In order to minimize dissonance, people selectively expose themselves to information that supports their own choice, and attempt to avoid information that is contrary to their choice (Sears, 1968; Sweeney & Gruber, 1984).

Selective exposure: *An attempt to minimize dissonance by exposing oneself only to information that supports one's choice*

Since its development in the late 1950s, dissonance theory has generated a tremendous amount of research, most of which has supported the theory. Research continues today, with investigators examining the specific physiological reactions induced by the state of dissonance (Croyle & Cooper, 1983). However, the theory has not been without its critics. Some psychologists have criticized the methodology used in dissonance experiments, while others have suggested alternative theoretical explanations.

Self-perception theory: *Bem's theory that people form attitudes by observing their own behavior and applying the same principles to themselves as they do to others*

One of the most plausible alternatives was suggested by Darryl Bem (1967, 1972) in his **self-perception theory**. He put forth the idea that people form attitudes by observing their own behavior, using the same principles that they use when they observe *others'* behavior to draw conclusions about the others' attitudes. In other words, people are sometimes unclear about the reasons for which they have just demonstrated a certain behavior. In those instances, they will look at their behavior and try to figure out just why they did what they did.

For example, if I were the subject who received $1 for saying that a task I hated was actually very interesting, I might look at what I said and try to figure out why I said it. The most likely explanation is "Well, if I agreed to say I liked the task for a paltry $1, then I probably didn't dislike it all that much. In fact, I probably liked it." Therefore, when asked by the experimenter to indicate my attitude, I might respond with a relatively positive attitude toward the task. Of course, this is the same result that dissonance theory would predict—more positive attitude change in the lower-incentive condition ($1) than in the higher-incentive condition ($20)—but the underlying reason is different. Whereas the dissonance explanation suggests that attitude change is due to the presence (in the $1 condition) of the unpleasant state of dissonance that a subject tries to overcome, the self-perception theory suggests it is due to an active search for understanding one's behavior.

Although we cannot be sure whether dissonance or self-perception theory provides the more accurate description of how people react to inconsistencies between their attitudes and their behavior, it is clear most of us try to make sense of our own attitudes and behavior and maintain consistency between them. When we behave in a way that is inconsistent with our attitudes, we tend to change our attitudes to make them fit better with our behavior.

RECAP AND REVIEW I

Recap

- Attitudes are learned predispositions to respond in a favorable or unfavorable manner to a particular object.
- Classical conditioning and operant conditioning both underlie some attitude formation and development.
- People strive to fit their attitudes and behavior together in a logical framework and to overcome any inconsistencies that they perceive.
- Cognitive dissonance, a state of psychological tension, occurs when a person holds two attitudes or thoughts (known as cognitions) that contradict each other. A person will try to reduce the dissonance by modifying one or both of the cognitions, changing the perceived importance of a cognition, adding additional cognitions, or denying that the two cognitions are related to each other.
- Self-perception theory provides an alternate explanation to dissonance theory. It suggests that people form and change attitudes through the observation of their own behavior.

Review

1. How do social psychologists define "attitudes"?
2. Gus finds that his fellow workers usually laugh at his racial jokes, so he tells even more. Unfortunately, he finds himself acquiring prejudicial attitudes he didn't seem to have before. What process has caused his attitude change?
   a. Classical conditioning **b.** Negative reinforcement **c.** Operant conditioning **d.** Stimulus pairing

3. Jim firmly believes what his doctor said about his need to lose weight and reduce his cholesterol intake. The tension he feels as he finishes his second bowl of ice cream is known as ______ ______.
4. Name four methods that Jim might be expected to use to reduce the inconsistency between his behavior and his attitudes concerning his health.
5. The theory which suggests that people form attitudes by observing and trying to understand their *own* behavior is called
   a. operant conditioning theory **b.** cognitive dissonance theory **c.** vicarious learning theory **d.** self-perception theory

(Answers to review questions are at the bottom of page 474.)

UNDERSTANDING OTHERS: SOCIAL COGNITION

Over and over, the results of national polls show that whether or not they agree with his specific policies, most Americans genuinely *like* President Ronald Reagan. Seen as a "nice guy," he remains one of the most popular Presidents of the century (Weisman, 1984).

Whether you liked his politics or not, it was a fact: Throughout the Reagan presidency, survey results showed that the majority of people in the United States had a clear, positive impression of the man himself—although they frequently disagreed profoundly with how he ran the country.

Phenomena such as these illustrate the power of our impressions and suggest the importance of determining how people develop an understanding of others. In fact, one of the dominant areas of study in social psychology during the last few years has focused on learning how people come to understand what others are like and to explain the reasons underlying others' behavior (Ross & Fletcher, 1985).

Understanding What Others Are Like: Social Cognition

Consider for a moment the enormous amount of information about other people to which we are exposed. How are we able to decide what is important and what is not, and to make judgments about the characteristics of others? Social

Regardless of whether they agree or disagree with President Reagan's specific policies, most people have a positive impression of him as a person. (*Bill Nation/Sygma*)

Social cognition: *The processes that underlie our understanding of the social world*

Schemas (SKEEM uhs): *Sets of cognitions about people and social experiences*

psychologists interested in this question study **social cognition**—the processes that underlie our understanding of the social world. They have learned that individuals have highly developed **schemas**, sets of cognitions about people and social experiences. These schemas organize information stored in memory, represent in our minds the way the social world operates, and give us a framework to categorize and interpret information relating to social stimuli (Fiske & Taylor, 1983).

We typically hold schemas for particular types of people in our environments. Our schema for "teacher," for instance, generally consists of a number of characteristics: knowledge of the subject matter he or she is teaching, a desire to impart that knowledge, and an awareness of the student's need to understand what is being said. Or, we may hold a schema for "mother" that includes the characteristics of warmth, nurturance, and caring. Regardless of the accuracy of such schemas—and, as we shall see, very often there are inaccuracies—they are important because they organize the way in which we recall, recognize, and categorize information about others. Moreover, they allow us to make predictions of what others are like on the basis of relatively little information, since we tend to fit people into schemas even when there is not much concrete evidence to go on (Smith, 1984; Snyder & Cantor, 1979).

Impression formation: *The process by which an individual organizes information about another individual to form an overall impression of that person*

Impression Formation: Constructing What Others Are Like How do we decide that Gail is a flirt, or Andy is a jerk, or Jon is a really nice guy? The earliest work on social cognition was designed to examine **impression formation**, the process by which an individual organizes information about another individual to form an overall impression of that person. In one classic study, for instance, a group of students was told that they were about to hear a guest lecturer (Kelley, 1950). One group of students was told that the lecturer was "a rather warm person, industrious, critical, practical, and determined," while a second group was told that he was "a rather cold person, industrious, critical, practical, and determined." The difference in the descriptions, of course, lay in the use of the words "cold" and "warm."

This simple substitution was responsible for drastic differences in the way the students in each group perceived the lecturer, even though he gave the same talk in the same style in each condition. Students who had been told he was "warm" rated him considerably more positively than students who had been told he was "cold."

Central traits: *The major traits considered in forming impressions of others*

The findings from this experiment led to a good deal of research on impression formation that focused on the way people pay particular attention to certain unusually important traits—known as **central traits**—to help them form an overall impression of others. According to this work, the presence of a central trait alters the meaning of other traits (Asch, 1946). Hence, the description of the lecturer as "industrious" presumably meant something different according to whether it was associated with the central trait "warm" or "cold."

Other research on impression formation has made use of approaches derived from cognitive psychology (see Chapter 6) to develop more mathematically oriented models of how individual personality traits are combined to create an

ANSWERS TO REVIEW QUESTIONS

Review I: **1.** Attitudes are learned predispositions to respond in a favorable or unfavorable manner to a particular object. **2.** c. **3.** Cognitive dissonance **4.** He may modify one or both cognitions; change the perceived importance of one cognition; add additional cognitions; or deny that the two cognitions are related to each other. **5.** d.

overall impression (Anderson, 1974). Generally, the results of this work suggest that we tend to form a mathematical average of the individual traits we see in people when we form an overall judgment (Kaplan, 1975).

Of course, as we gain more experience with people and see them exhibiting behavior in a variety of situations, our impressions of them become more complex. Still, because there are usually gaps in our knowledge of others, we tend to fit them into personality schemas we have developed that represent particular "types" of people. For instance, we might hold a "gregarious person" schema, made up of the traits of friendliness, assertiveness, and openness. The presence of just one or two of these traits might be sufficient to make us assign a person to a particular schema. These schemas allow us to develop expectations about how others will behave, permitting us to plan our interactions with others more easily, and ultimately serve to simplify a complex social world.

Stereotypes: The Negative Side of Social Cognition What do we think of when someone says, "He's black," or "She's Chinese," or "He's a *real* man"? If we're honest, most of us would have to admit we tend to form some sort of immediate impression of what that person is like. (See the Try It! box.) This fact illustrates an important point: While schemas can be helpful in organizing the social world, they also have their negative side—particularly when they promote an oversimplified understanding of other people. A **stereotype** is a kind of schema in which beliefs and expectations about members of a group are held simply on the basis of their membership in that group. Stereotypes represent one particularly damaging consequence of our tendency to form general impressions of others.

Stereotype: *A kind of schema in which beliefs and expectations about members of a group are held simply on the basis of their membership in that group*

TRY IT!

ARE YOU SUSCEPTIBLE TO STEREOTYPING?

To understand the subtleties of stereotyping, try to answer the following riddle:

> A father and his son were driving along the interstate highway when the father lost control of the car, swerved off the road, and crashed into a telephone pole. The father died instantly, and his son was critically injured. An ambulance rushed the boy to a nearby hospital. A prominent surgeon was summoned to provide immediate treatment. When the surgeon arrived and entered the operating room to examine the boy, a loud gasp was heard. "I can't operate on this boy," the surgeon said. "He is my son."

How could this be, if the father had died in the crash? Try to write down as many explanations as you can think of. If you still don't think you've come up with a satisfactory explanation, try this riddle:

> A father and his son were driving along the interstate highway when the father lost control of the car, swerved off the road, and crashed into a telephone pole. The father died instantly, and his son was critically injured. An ambulance rushed the boy to a nearby hospital. A prominent surgeon was summoned to provide immediate treatment. When the surgeon arrived and entered the operating room to examine the boy, the surgeon burst into tears and became hysterical. "I can't operate on this boy," the surgeon sobbed. "He is my son!" (Byrne & Kelley, 1981, pp. 304–305).

Now do you get it? The answer to both riddles is the same: The surgeon is the boy's *mother*. If you had difficulty with the first, it is due to stereotyping: Most of us tend to assume that surgeons are male. And if you were able to answer the second one more easily, it is also a consequence of stereotyping, because the surgeon was given characteristics that our society labels as more common in women than men: crying and hysteria. The pervasiveness and subtlety of stereotypes are clearly illustrated by these two riddles.

Some of the most prevalent stereotypes have to do with racial and ethnic categorizations. Over the years, various groups have been called, for example, ''lazy'' or ''shrewd'' or ''cruel'' with varying degrees of regularity by nongroup members (Katz & Brayly, 1933; Weber & Crocker, 1983). But stereotypes are by no means confined to racial and ethnic groups. For example, age stereotyping is all too common as well. The stereotype for the elderly tends to include the traits of passivity, unsociability, and senility (Rodin & Langer, 1980). There is even a general stereotype relating to members of *any* group to which we do not belong, known as the **ingroup-outgroup bias** (Brewer, 1979; Evans & Dovido, 1983). We tend to hold less favorable opinions regarding members of groups of which we are not a part (**outgroups**) and more favorable opinions about members of groups to which we belong (**ingroups**).

Ingroup-outgroup bias: *The tendency to hold less favorable opinions about groups to which we do not belong (outgroups), while holding more favorable opinions about groups to which we do belong (ingroups)*

Outgroups: *Groups to which an individual does not belong*

Ingroups: *Groups to which an individual belongs*

SEX-ROLE STEREOTYPES Although there is little evidence to support the accuracy of most stereotypes, they can have potentially damaging effects. One of the most clear-cut examples of this is in terms of sex-role stereotypes, the notion that men and women typically have, and ought to have, particular charcteristics. For instance, society's traditional expectations regarding appropriate male behavior—that a man be aggressive, competitive, and ambitious—differ markedly from what is typically seen as appropriate female behavior—meek, nurturant, and passive (Broverman, Vogel, Broverman, Clarkson, & Rosenkrantz, 1972; Spence, Deaux, & Helmreich, 1985).

The pervasiveness of such sex-role stereotypes is illustrated by the fact that even in nursery school, boys generally report that they will have active, nonfamily-oriented careers, while girls tend to predict that they will be mothers, teachers, or nurses (Papalia & Tennent, 1975). Such stereotyping may help to account for the finding, discussed first in the chapter on motivation and emotion, that women's levels of achievement motivation are typically lower than those of males.

Because of the potentially damaging effects of stereotyping, some psychologists have suggested a new standard for psychological health, based on sex-role traits, called androgyny (Bem, 1976). An **androgynous** person is one who incorporates traits which are traditionally considered ''feminine,'' such as compassion and sensitivity, with those traditionally viewed as ''masculine,'' such as competitveness and aggressiveness. According to this view, men and women who learn to display both traditionally masculine and feminine traits can overcome the restrictions that society's sex roles would otherwise place on them.

Androgynous (an DROJ un us): *Having a combination of traits typically considered to be ''masculine'' and ''feminine''*

Still, sex-role stereotypes remain commonplace in our society—as the difficulties some people have in answering the Try It! box riddles makes evident. Moreover, what makes stereotypes particularly damaging is the subtle way in which they operate (Frable & Bem, 1985). For instance, they can actually *cause* members of groups to behave in ways that correspond to the stereotype through a phenomenon known as a self-fulfilling prophecy (Archibald, 1974). A **self-fulfilling prophecy** is an expectation about the occurrence of a future event or behavior that acts to increase the likelihood that the event or behavior *will* occur. For example, if people think that members of a particular group are lazy, they may treat them in a way that actually brings about laziness on the part of the group being stereotyped (Skrypnek & Snyder, 1982).

Self-fulfilling prophecy: *An expectation about the occurrence of an event or behavior that increases the likelihood that the event or behavior will happen*

Moreover, the knowledge that others hold a stereotype can cause behavior representative of that stereotype in an effort to make a positive impression on those holding the stereotype—even if the behavior is not typical of the person.

"Welcome aboard. This is your captain, Margaret Williamson, speaking."

Our stereotypes might lead us to be as startled as the people in this cartoon upon hearing an announcement such as this. (*Drawing by Richter; © 1973 The New Yorker Magazine, Inc.*)

For example, researchers found that women interacting with an attractive, desirable male, who they thought stereotyped women as passive and dependent, tended to espouse views that were more passive and dependent than women who thought the attractive male held an untraditional view of women. In contrast, when the male was unattractive, the women's behavior was not affected by the nature of the stereotype they thought he held. In sum, only when they felt motivated to make a good impression did they behave according to the stereotype (Zanna and Pack, 1975).

It is clear from research on stereotyping, then, that the processes of social cognition leading to the creation of schemas both help and hinder social interaction. While schemas allow us to simplify an otherwise complex social world, they can also lead to oversimplification; we may assume that individuals possess certain traits associated with a group—just because of their membership in that group.

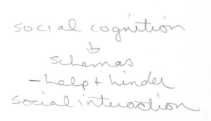

RECAP AND REVIEW II

Recap

- The topic of social cognition is concerned with the processes that underlie our understanding of the social world. This understanding can be held in the form of schemas, sets of cognitions about people and our social experience.
- One way that we form impressions of others is by combining individual traits into overall impressions. This may be done by relying on basic, central traits or by mathematically averaging individual traits into a general impression.
- Stereotypes, a kind of schema, are beliefs and expectations about members of a group formed simply on the basis of their membership in that group.
- Stereotypes are frequently held regarding members of racial, ethnic, sex, and age groups. Such stereotypes—although showing little validity—can produce difficulties in social interaction due in part to the phenomenon of the self-fulfilling prophecy.

Review

1. Lawyers, secretaries, football players. The set of characteristics we hold for particular types of people such as those mentioned are called ______________________.

2. Our overall impression of a person is sometimes formed by our paying attention to certain unusually important characteristics which are known as
   a. social cognitions **b.** central traits **c.** schemas **d.** stereotypes
3. Having stereotypes about members of any group to which we do not belong is called
   a. ingroup-outgroup bias **b.** racial stereotyping **c.** schematic stereotyping **d.** ethnic bias
4. What are self-fulfilling prophecies?
5. The creation of schemas, which allow us to organize our complex social world, can only help to enhance our social interactions. True or false?

(Answers to review questions are at the bottom of page 480.)

UNDERSTANDING THE CAUSES OF BEHAVIOR: ATTRIBUTION PROCESSES

When Leesa, a new employee at the Staditron Computer Company, completed a major staffing project two weeks early, her boss, Marian, was delighted. At the next staff meeting, she announced how pleased she was with Leesa and explained that *this* was an example of the kind of performance she was looking for in her staff. The other staff members looked on resentfully, trying to figure out why Leesa had worked night and day to finish the project not just on time, but two weeks early. She must be an awfully compulsive person, they decided.

Attribution theory: *The theory that seeks to explain how we decide, on the basis of samples of an individual's behavior, what the specific causes of that behavior are*

Most of us have, at one time or another, puzzled over the reasons behind someone's behavior. In contrast to work on social cognition, which describes how people develop an overall impression about others' personality traits, **attribution theory** seeks to explain how we decide, on the basis of samples of an individual's behavior, what the specific causes of that behavior are (Harvey & Weary, 1985; Weiner, 1985).

Situational causes of behavior: *Causes of behavior that are based on environmental factors*

Dispositional causes of behavior: *Causes of behavior that are based on internal traits or personality factors*

When trying to understand the causes underlying a given behavior, individuals typically try first to determine whether the cause is situational or dispositional (Heider, 1958). **Situational causes** are those brought about by something in the environment. For instance, someone who knocks over a quart of milk and then cleans it up is probably doing so not because he or she is a terribly neat person, but because the *situation* is one that requires it. In contrast, a person who spends hours shining the kitchen floor is probably doing so because he or she *is* a neat person—hence, the behavior has a **dispositional cause**, prompted by the person's disposition (his or her internal traits or personality characteristics).

In our example involving Leesa, her fellow employees, in trying to attribute her behavior to either the situation or her disposition, assumed that her disposition was the cause. But from a logical standpoint, it is equally plausible that there was something about the situation that caused the behavior. If asked, Leesa might attribute her accomplishments to situational factors, explaining that she had so much other work to do that she just had to get the project out of the way. To her, then, the reason for her behavior might not be dispositional at all; it could be situational.

Consensus information: *The degree to which people behave similarly in the same situation*

How do we determine whether Leesa's behavior is motivated by situational or dispositional factors? Harold Kelley (1967) suggested that people use three types of information to answer this question. First, there is **consensus information**—the degree to which people behave similarly in the same situation. For instance, if most people would have completed the project two weeks early, Leesa's behavior would be high in consensus; but if most would have procrastinated, her behavior is low in consensus. Second, there is **consistency information**—the degree to which an individual behaves similarly in a similar situation. If Leesa always gets her work in early on the job, no matter what the project, she is high in consistency. Finally, there is **distinctiveness information**, the extent to which the behavior occurs across other situations. If Leesa gets her work done early only on her job, but procrastinates everywhere else, her behavior is high in distinctiveness.

Consistency information: *The degree to which an individual behaves similarly in similar situations*

Distinctiveness information: *The extent to which a given behavior occurs across different situations*

By simultaneously considering all three kinds of information, people are able to make an attribution that is primarily based on dispositional factors or on situational factors. As shown in Figure 14-2, information that is high in consensus, high in consistency, and high in distinctiveness leads to attributions that are situational: In our example, Leesa's behavior would be attributed to the demands of the job. But with situations in which consensus and distinctiveness are low and consistency is high, people tend to make dispositional attributions, assuming the behavior is related to one's personality.

We All Make Mistakes: Biases in Attribution

If we always processed information in the rational manner that Kelley's model suggests, the world might run a lot more smoothly. Unfortunately, although Kelley's attribution formulation generally makes accurate predictions—at least for cases in which people have concrete, firsthand knowledge regading consensus, consistency, and distinctiveness (Orvis, 1982; Wells & Harvey, 1978)—people do not always process information about others in as logical a fashion as the theory seems to suggest. In fact, research shows that there tend to be certain consistent biases in our attributions.

Behavior	Type of Information	Attribution
Leesa is the only one who gets her work in on time.	Low consensus	Dispositional attribution: Leesa's behavior is characteristic of her personality.
Leesa always gets her work in on time.	High consistency	
Leesa does everything early.	Low distinctiveness	
All employees finish their work early.	High consensus	Situational attribution: Leesa's behavior is due to the situation.
Leesa always gets her work in on time.	High consistency	
Leesa gets her work in on time, but is late in other situations.	High distinctiveness	

Figure 14-2
An illustration of Kelley's model of attribution. Learning that Leesa's behavior represents low consensus, high consistency, and low distinctiveness leads to a dispositional attribution. In contrast, determining that Leesa's behavior represents high consensus, high consistency, and high distinctiveness leads to a situational attribution.

Fundamental attribution bias: *A tendency to attribute others' behavior to dispositional causes but to attribute one's own behavior to situational causes*

One particularly noteworthy bias in the attributions that people make is a tendency to attribute others' behavior to dispositional causes—but to attribute their own behavior to situational causes. Known as the **fundamental attribution bias**, this tendency is quite common (Watson, 1982). For example, an analysis of letters and advice in newspaper columns such as "Dear Abby" and "Ann Landers" showed that writers tended to attribute their own problems to situational factors, while they describe the problems of others as due to dispositional causes (Schoeneman & Rubanowitz, 1985). In our own example, we saw how Leesa attributed her behavior to constraints of the environment (situational) factors, while Leesa's colleagues thought her behavior was due to her personality characteristics (dispositional factors).

Why should the fundamental attribution bias be so prevalent? One reason has to do with the nature of information that is available to the people making an attribution. When we view the behavior of another person, the information that is most perceptually obvious is the person's behavior itself. The individual's environment is relatively stable and invariant. As a result, the person is the center of our attention. But when we consider our own behavior, changes in the environment are going to be more obvious, and we are more likely to make attributions based on situational factors.

What this suggests, then, is that we may excuse our own failures by attributing them to extenuating circumstances ("I couldn't finish my paper because the library didn't have the book I needed"), while we blame others for their personality flaws when *they* have a problem ("He's just too lazy to finish his paper on time").

Understanding Our Own Behavior: Self-Perception Theory

The fundamental attribution bias illustrates an important point about attributional processes: People not only make attributions about others, they can sometimes act as observers of their *own* behavior and make attributions based on what they see themselves doing. As we discussed earlier in the chapter in reference to attitudes, Bem's theory of self-perception suggests that people monitor their own behavior and make judgments about themselves based on what they see themselves doing (Bem, 1967). The theory suggests, then, that when situational cues are weak or past experience does not provide relevant information, people will look to their own behavior to make attributions about themselves.

How does the theory work? An illustration of self-perception theory can clarify what Bem meant. Suppose, for instance, you are called and asked to join the board of directors of the campus drama club. You are pleased to be asked, but are not too sure you can spare the time, so you tell the person who called you will get back to him with your decision in a few days. As the days drag on, though, you never seem to have the time to call him back, and you just can't make up your mind. After a few weeks have gone by, you begin to wonder why you can't reach a decision. As you ponder the question, you conclude that

ANSWERS TO REVIEW QUESTIONS

Review II: **1.** Schemas **2.** b **3.** a **4.** Self-fulfilling prophecies are expectations about the occurrence of future events or behaviors that act to increase the likelihood that the event or behavior will occur. **5.** False

THE CUTTING EDGE

IMPROVING YOUR GRADES BY IMPROVING YOUR ATTRIBUTIONS

If you are like most people, when you first began college, you were concerned about whether you'd be able to make the grade. Could you do well enough to compete effectively with your classmates? Would you be able to meet the standards set by your professors? Would you, in short, be smart enough to do well?

For some college freshmen, these concerns become so great that they produce anxiety that interferes with their work. Moreover, any difficulties that they experience early in their college careers are viewed as confirmation that they are ill-equipped to do college-level work. This attribution leads to further disruption of their studying, leading ultimately to even poorer performance.

In actuality, statistics show that *most* students' performance improves over the course of their college careers, so it is not unusual to expect that freshman-year performance will be less than optimal. This finding led social psychologists Timothy Wilson and Patricia Linville (1982, 1985) to devise a program to change the way first-year college students concerned about their grades attributed the causes of their academic performance. By exposing them to information that showed that poor first-year performance was likely caused by temporary factors that were susceptible to change, rather than by permanent, unchangeable causes, these psychologists hypothesized that student performance would improve.

To test this reasoning, Wilson and Linville carried out a series of simple experiments. In them, university freshmen who had expressed concern about their first-year grades viewed videotapes of interviews with juniors and seniors who stated that their grades had improved since they had started college. In addition, the freshmen were given statistical information indicating that grades typically improve among college students in general.

The program showed clear success. In contrast to a control group of students who received no treatment, students who viewed the videotapes and were exposed to the information that the causes of low grades are usually temporary showed an improvement in their actual grades in the semester following the study, as well as having a lower dropout rate.

In sum, exposure to a one-time program designed to change attributions regarding the causes of people's own behavior was sufficient to produce better performance. These results are promising, as are those for similar programs (Försterling, 1985), for other everyday problems may be solved simply by changing people's attributions regarding the causes of their behavior (Baumgardner, Heppner, & Arkin, 1986).

your avoidance of calling him back must mean that you are unenthusiastic and really don't want to join the board of directors. In sum, you use your own behavior as an indicator of its underlying motivation—and come to the same conclusion you would have if you had been looking at someone else's behavior. (For another look at self-perception theory, see the Cutting Edge box.)

The Informed Consumer of Psychology: Forming More Accurate Impressions

At one time or another, we've all been guilty of forming an impression of someone and later finding out we were completely off base. For although people try to use the information available to them to construct a meaningful, orderly social world for themselves, there is ample opportunity in both the development of schemas and in attributional processes to make errors, to oversimplify, and thereby to misperceive other people. This would not be of much concern were it not for the fact that once individuals make decisions about others, they act upon these decisions—sometimes with very undesirable consequences. As a result, social psychologists have designed a number of techniques to increase the accuracy with which people can make judgments about others. They have paid particular attention to strategies for reducing the negative effects of stereotyping. Among the most useful of those strategies are the following:

- Increasing contact between the target of stereotyping and the holder of the stereotype. A good deal of research has shown that increasing the amount of interaction between people can reduce negative stereotyping (Amir, 1976; Miller & Brewer, 1984). But certain kinds of contact are more likely than others to lead to the development of more accurate schemas: Situations where there is relatively intimate contact, where the individuals are of equal status, or where participants are dependent upon one another are most likely to bring about a reduction in stereotyping. The explanation for the effectiveness of contact seems to be that schemas regarding stereotyped groups become more detailed, individualized, and accurate as the amount of interaction increases. This finding provides part of the basis for such social practices as school integration and fair housing laws.
- Making the values of negatively stereotyped groups more salient. Rather than relying on contact to change the nature of schemas and stereotypes, this approach suggests that people be shown the inconsistencies between values they hold regarding equality and fair treatment of others on one hand, and negative stereotyping on the other. Rokeach (1971) found that if people were simply made to see that the values they held regarding equality and freedom were inconsistent with some of their perceptions of minority group members, the people were more likely to later join a group organized to further minorities and to register for a class in ethnic relations.
- Providing information about the objects of stereotyping. Probably the most direct means of changing schemas about the objects of stereotyping is through education, by teaching people to be more aware of the positive characteristics of objects of stereotyping (Langer, Bashner, & Chanowitz, in press). For instance, if the meaning behind puzzling behavior that is quite common to members of a stereotyped group is pointed out to people who hold the stereotypes, they may come to understand the significance of the behavior—although it may still appear foreign and perhaps even threatening (Fiedler, Mitchell, & Triandis, 1971; Landis, Day, McGrew, Thomas & Miller, 1976).

Cultural assimilator: *A teaching aid designed to minimize racial prejudice through understanding of others' behavior*

For example, Figure 14-3 shows an example of a teaching aid—called a **cultural assimilator**—devised to decrease racial prejudice among military personnel through better understanding the meaning of others' behavior. In the procedure, trainees read about an incident and are then presented with four explanations for the behavior that occurred, only one of which is accurate. The assimilator provides a rationale for both right and wrong choices, and by going through a large number of such incidents, the trainee develops a more accurate understanding of the causes behind behavior of minority group members. Ultimately, this results in a more precise schema pertaining to members of different groups.

Each of these techniques—while not invariably effective—serves to illustrate a major approach taken by social psychologists to foster more accurate impression formation and social cognition. The ultimate goal of this work, of course, is to increase the quality of social interaction—something that should follow after people develop a more accurate understanding of each other.

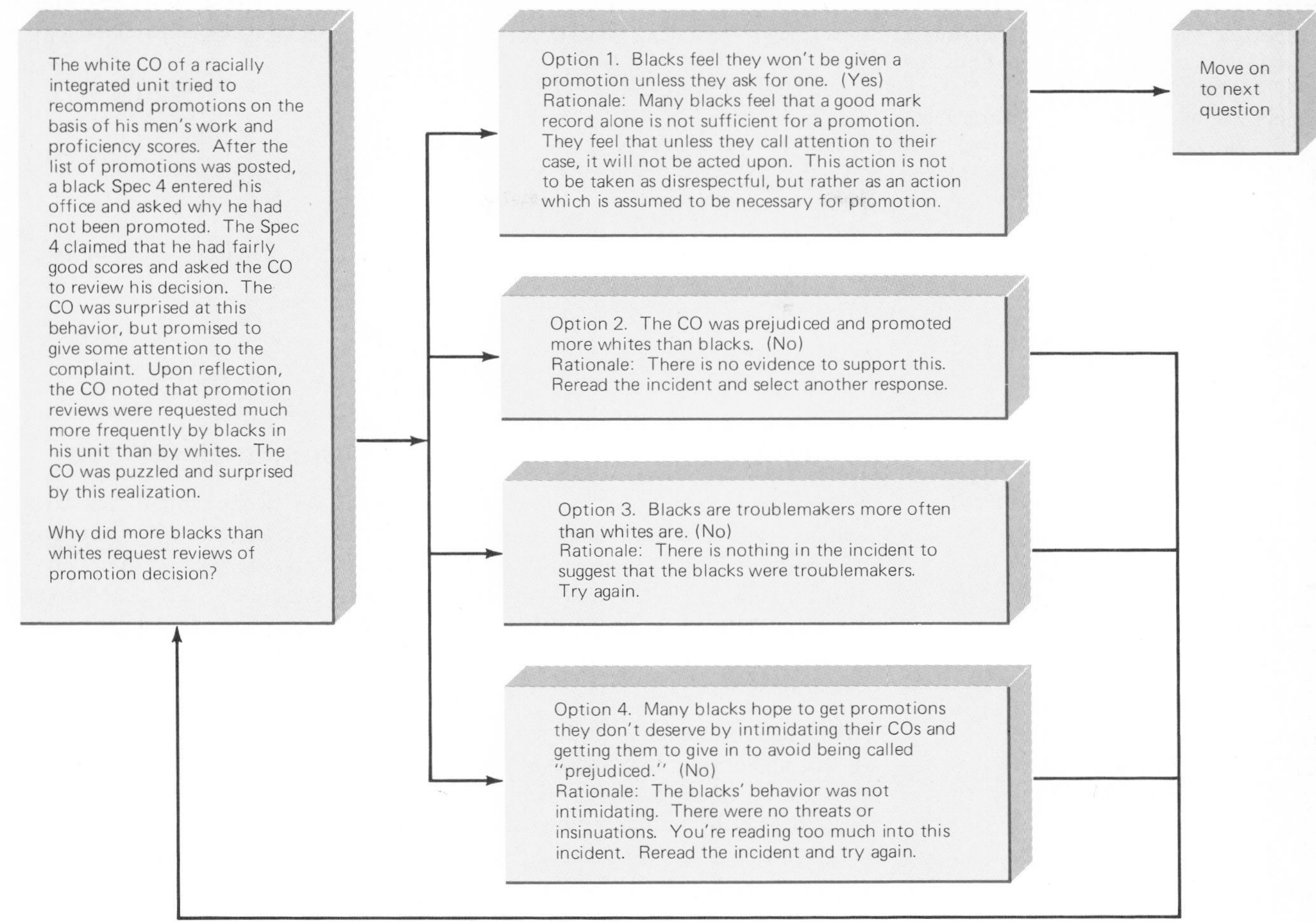

The white CO of a racially integrated unit tried to recommend promotions on the basis of his men's work and proficiency scores. After the list of promotions was posted, a black Spec 4 entered his office and asked why he had not been promoted. The Spec 4 claimed that he had fairly good scores and asked the CO to review his decision. The CO was surprised at this behavior, but promised to give some attention to the complaint. Upon reflection, the CO noted that promotion reviews were requested much more frequently by blacks in his unit than by whites. The CO was puzzled and surprised by this realization.
Why did more blacks than whites request reviews of promotion decision?
Option 1. Blacks feel they won't be given a promotion unless they ask for one. (Yes) Rationale: Many blacks feel that a good mark record alone is not sufficient for a promotion. They feel that unless they call attention to their case, it will not be acted upon. This action is not to be taken as disrespectful, but rather as an action which is assumed to be necessary for promotion.
Move on to next question
Option 2. The CO was prejudiced and promoted more whites than blacks. (No) Rationale: There is no evidence to support this. Reread the incident and select another response.
Option 3. Blacks are troublemakers more often than whites are. (No) Rationale: There is nothing in the incident to suggest that the blacks were troublemakers. Try again.
Option 4. Many blacks hope to get promotions they don't deserve by intimidating their COs and getting them to give in to avoid being called "prejudiced." (No) Rationale: The blacks' behavior was not intimidating. There were no threats or insinuations. You're reading too much into this incident. Reread the incident and try again.

Figure 14-3
An example of a cultural assimilator used to decrease racial prejudice. (*Landis, Day, McGrew, Thomas, & Miller, 1976.*)

RECAP AND REVIEW III

Recap

- Attribution theory explains the processes that underlie how we attribute the causes of others' behavior, particularly in terms of situational versus dispositional causes. This is typically done using consensus, consistency, and distinctiveness information.
- Attribution processes are affected by a number of biases, including the fundamental attribution bias, which leads us to view situational factors as the cause of our own behavior and dispositional factors as the cause of others' behavior.
- Self-perception theory suggests that we monitor our own behavior to identify its causes, similar to the way in which we make attributions about others' behavior.
- There are several ways to increase the accuracy of impressions and to reduce stereotyping; they include increasing contact, making relevant values salient, and providing information about the targets of stereotyping.

Review

1. "Chris is always exactly on time for our study group meeting," Ann remarked to her colleague Doug. "It makes me feel guilty when I'm five minutes late." "Me, too!" Doug replied. "What do you suppose causes him to be so prompt?" he asked. "I think he's just compulsive,'' Ann suggested, as Doug nodded in agreement. Was the cause of Chris's promptness, as suggested by Ann and Doug, situational or dispositional?

2. If Ann and Doug discover that Chris is quite often late for every meeting other than the study group meeting, what type of information would they have received?
   a. Consensus **b.** Dispositional **c.** Situational **d.** Distinctiveness
3. With their new information, would Ann and Doug change their original explanation?
4. Attributing our own failures to situational circumstances while attributing the shortcomings of others to personality flaws is an example of __________ __________ __________.
5. Social psychologists have designed several techniques to increase the accuracy with which people make judgments about others and thereby reduce negative stereotyping. Name three such techniques.

(Answers to review questions are at the bottom of page 486.)

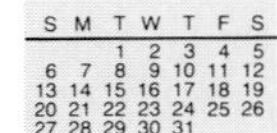

Psychology Looks Toward the 1990s
Imitating the Japanese: Changing Attitudes on the Job

The scene was not one that you would expect to see in the typical American factory: On a bright, sunny afternoon, some 500 workers wearing company T-shirts shouted ''Good morning'' to the company president, and then began an afternoon of relay races, tug-of-war, and other games. With executives and workers participating side by side, the afternoon was devoted to celebrating the success of their plant, which only seven years earlier had been near bankruptcy.

How had the company managed to turn its fortunes around? The major reason was the implementation of a set of changes designed to foster changes in worker attitudes, based on a management system similar to that found in the typical Japanese industrial organization. Seven years earlier, the Arkansas plant, which made television sets for Sears, was losing money and on the verge of closing. At that time, however, the factory was bought by the Sanyo Manufacturing Corporation, and it adopted a Japanese management system in which concern for the company employees became a dominant focus.

Heralded by some as the wave of the future, and by others as dictatorial and paternalistic, the Japanese management style has become a topic of much debate in this country. The major reason for this interest is that the Japanese economy has witnessed an enormous growth in the last two decades—a rate of growth that has outpaced that in the United States. According to advocates, the success of Japanese technology is due in no small measure to the attitudes of Japanese workers and management, which differ measureably from those of their American counterparts.

What are the attitudinal differences between Japanese and American workers, and how were attitudes more similar to those in Japanese plants fostered in the Sanyo plant in America? Several general strategies were employed (Hatvany and Pucik, 1981; Holden, 1986; Szilagyi & Wallace, 1987):

■ Providing a unique philosophy and set of attitudes for workers. A conscious effort is made to create a cohesive, family-like atmosphere among employees. Workers are encouraged to live together in company housing, to take vacations together, and to socialize with one another during their spare time. Such group activity acts to foster a strong sense of attraction to the organization and motivates workers to adopt the attitudes desired by management. Rather than giving allegiance to informal groups within the organization, a worker will adopt the rules and attitudes of the company as a whole. The high attraction to the group serves in this case to increase the influence of the organization over the individual.

■ Encouraging strong socialization into the organization. **Socialization** is the process by which an individual learns the rules and norms of appropriate behavior during development. Similarly, **organizational socialization** occurs when a worker learns to behave and adopt attitudes similar to others in the organization. Japanese organizations tend to promote socialization through intensive training programs that may last as long as six months. In these programs, employees are exposed to all aspects of the company, not just the jobs for which they were hired. The result, again, is to build loyalty to the company as a whole rather than to a small subunit of the organization. Moreover, socialization begins on one level even before the official training program: potential employees are probed during job interviews to determine if they hold initial attitudes that are compatible with those the organization wants to see in its employees.

Socialization (SO shul i ZAY shun): *The development process by which an individual learns the rules and norms of appropriate behavior*

Organizational socialization: *The process by which a worker learns to behave like others in the organization and to adopt similar attitudes*

■ Developing a stable internal labor pool. Employees are hired right after graduation, and it is assumed that they will stay with the same company until retirement. Consequently, companies develop their own labor pool, which remains stable and becomes well-trained in the particular operations of the company. Moreover, Japanese companies tend to have relatively rapid job rotation, whereby an employee is placed in numerous different specific jobs within the company. This is coupled with a slow promotion policy—most job changes do not result in a change in status—so that the majority of employees gain wide experience in a number of positions. In contrast, employees in the United States typically feel little loyalty to their employer and frequently move from one company to another.

The use of these three strategies fosters employee attitudes that are very different from those of employees in typical American companies. Instead of developing an individualistic orientation (following their own personal goals and being concerned with their own career advancement), employees of firms using Japanese management strategies tend to be committed to the workplace and *its* goals. Of course, this does not mean that the Japanese management style will work universally in the United States, as there are vast differences between the two cultures. It does suggest, however, that the Japanese management style is worth considering when looking for ways to improve the functioning of industrial organizations in this country.

LOOKING BACK

1. The way in which people's thoughts, feelings, and actions are affected by others—the subject matter of social psychology—has been discussed in this chapter.

2. Attitudes, a central area of study of social psychology, are learned predispositions to respond in a favorable or unfavorable manner to a particular object. We acquire attitudes through classical conditioning processes (in which a previously neutral object begins to evoke the attitudes associated with another object because of repeated pairings) and through operant conditioning (in which there is positive reinforcement of attitudes).

3. A number of theories suggest that people try to maintain consistency between attitudes. Cognitive dissonance occurs when two cognitions—attitudes or thoughts—contradict each other and are held simultaneously by an individual. To resolve the contradiction, the person may modify the cognition, change its importance, add additional cognitions, or deny it, thereby bringing about a reduction in dissonance. However, alternate explanations based on self-perception theory, have been proposed to explain dissonance phenomena.

4. Impressions of others are formed through social cognition, which is the study of the processes that underlie our understanding of the social world. People develop schemas, which organize information about people and social experiences in memory. Such schemas represent our social life and allow us to interpret and categorize information about others.

5. One of the ways in which people form impressions of others is through the use of central traits, traits which are given unusually heavy weighting when an impression is formed. Cognitive approaches have found that we tend to average sets of traits to form an overall impression.

6. Stereotypes are beliefs and expectations about members of groups held on the basis of membership in those groups. Although they most frequently are used for racial and ethnic groups, stereotypes are also found in categorizations of sex- and age-group membership. Stereotyping can lead to self-fulfilling prophecies, expectations about the occurrence of future events or behaviors that act to increase the likelihood that the event or behavior will actually occur.

7. Attribution theory tries to explain how we understand the causes of behavior, particularly with respect to situational or dispositional factors. To determine causes, people use consensus, consistency, and distinctiveness information. Moreover, self-perception theory suggests that attribution processes similar to those we use with others may be used to understand the causes of our own behavior.

8. Even though logical processes are involved, however, attribution is still prone to error, as the fundamental attribution bias and the prevalence of stereotyping demonstrate. Among the ways of increasing the accuracy of attributions and impressions are increasing contact, making values salient, and providing information about the target of the attribution or stereotype.

KEY TERMS AND CONCEPTS

social psychology (p. 466)
attitudes (p. 467)
vicarious learning (p. 468)
central route processing (p. 470)
peripheral route processing (p. 470)
cognitive dissonance (p. 470)
cognitions (p. 470)
selective exposure (p. 471)
self-perception theory (p. 472)
social cognition (p. 474)
schemas (p. 474)
impression formation (p. 474)
central traits (p. 474)
stereotype (p. 475)
ingroup-outgroup bias (p. 476)
outgroups (p. 476)
ingroups (p. 476)
androgynous (p. 476)
self-fulfilling prophecy (p. 476)
attribution theory (p. 478)
situational causes of behavior (p. 478)
dispositional causes of behavior (p. 478)
consensus information (p. 478)
consistency information (p. 479)
distinctiveness information (p. 479)
fundamental attribution bias (p. 480)
cultural assimilator (p. 482)

FOR FURTHER STUDY AND APPLICATION

Rajecki, D. W. (1982). *Attitudes: Themes and advances.* Sunderland, MA: Sinauer Associates.

This volume provides a readable, interesting overview of the field of attitudes. It does a fine job of integrating various theories, as well as of providing practical applications of the work in a number of areas.

Shaver, P. (1984). *An introduction to attribution processes.* Hillsdale, NJ: Erlbaum.

This is an excellent guide to attribution theory, written in a way that makes this complex theory clear and lucid.

Fiske, S. T., & Taylor, S. E. (1983). *Social cognition.* Reading, MA: Addison-Wesley.

This book provides a good overview of the latest work on social cognition, particularly in terms of implications for future research.

Feldman, R. S. (1985). *Social psychology: Theory, research, and applications.* New York: McGraw-Hill.

This is a comprehensive overview of the field, emphasizing the applications drawn from social psychological theories.

ANSWERS TO REVIEW QUESTIONS

Review III: **1.** Dispositional **2.** d **3.** Yes; they would be more likely to attribute Chris's promptness at study group meetings to situational causes. **4.** Fundamental attribution bias **5.** Increasing contact between the target of stereotyping and the holder of the stereotype; making values relevant to the target of stereotyping more salient; and providing information/education about the objects of stereotyping.

CHAPTER 15

CHAPTER 15

SOCIAL PSYCHOLOGY: INTERACTING WITH OTHERS

PROLOGUE

LOOKING AHEAD

SOCIAL INFLUENCE
Doing what others do: Conformity
Doing what others tell us to do: Compliance
The informed consumer of psychology: Strategies for maintaining your own point of view
Recap and review I

LIKING AND LOVING: INTERPERSONAL ATTRACTION AND THE DEVELOPMENT OF RELATIONSHIPS
How do I like thee? Let me count the ways
How do I love thee? Let me count the ways
The rise and fall of liking and loving: Understanding the course of relationships
Recap and review II

HURTING AND HELPING OTHERS: AGGRESSION AND PROSOCIAL BEHAVIOR
Hurting others: Aggression
TRY IT! Is This Aggression?
THE CUTTING EDGE. Does It Hurt to Watch TV?: Media Aggression
PSYCHOLOGY AT WORK. Should Pornography Be Banned?: The Link between Pornography and Violence toward Women
Helping others: The brighter side of human nature
The informed consumer of psychology: Learning to be helpful
Recap and review III
PSYCHOLOGY LOOKS TOWARD THE 1990s. Hot Flashes: Environmental Psychology

LOOKING BACK

KEY TERMS AND CONCEPTS

FOR FURTHER STUDY AND APPLICATION

PROLOGUE

The scene was from another world. Amidst the vast beauty of the dense South American jungle, a group of people stood in line to reach a cauldron of soda laced with cyanide. As they neared, they could see the people who had preceded them writhing in agony on the ground as the poison began its deadly work. Reverend Jim Jones, the leader of the religious cult that made its home in the settlement, urged people forward, assuring them that the mass suicide was the only reasonable action to take and that they should step forward and meet their deaths with eagerness. Whole families moved through the line together, with mothers feeding the poison to their children. Jones's exhortations were effective: When it was all over, some 900 people—the entire population of the settlement—were dead.

LOOKING AHEAD

When we consider the bizarre event depicted above, it is tempting to conclude that the mass suicide was a unique, chance occurrence unrelated to everyday life. Yet it provides a disturbing example of the power of one individual to influence the behavior of others—different in magnitude but similar in kind to many everyday situations.

For instance, how often have we followed the orders of a parent, teacher, or boss, doing things that we thought were incorrect but going along with it anyway, since the requests came from someone with authority? How often have we purchased and worn clothing because "everybody else" was wearing the same sort of clothes? And how often have we come away from a store having spent more than we intended because of the influence of a persuasive salesperson?

Social influence: *The area of social psychology concerned with situations in which the action of an individual or group affects the behavior of others*

This chapter begins with a discussion of **social influence**, the area of social psychology concerned with situations in which the actions of an individual (or a group) affect the behavior of others. We discuss how our everyday activities, from the products we buy to the music groups we like, are affected by what others do and say. We also consider some techniques identified by social psychologists that can help us to maintain our independence from the social pressures that affect us all.

Next, we discuss another, more special, form of social relationship between people: liking and loving. We examine what social psychologists have learned about the ways in which people become attracted to one another, form relationships, and fall in love with each other.

The chapter ends with a look at the factors that underlie some of the most negative and positive social behaviors. We talk about aggressive behavior, exploring the degree to which aggression may be innate and to what degree it is learned. Then we examine helping behavior and try to explain the factors that motivate it—as well as the factors that keep people from helping one another. Finally, we consider techniques developed by social psychologists to decrease the incidence of aggression and to increase helping behavior.

After reading and studying this chapter, then, you will be able to

- Identify the major sources of social influence and the tactics that are used to bring it about
- Discuss strategies for remaining independent from social pressure

The grim aftermath of the Jonestown mass suicide illustrates the power of one individual to influence the behavior of others. (*Tim Chapman/Black Star*)

- Describe the factors that produce interpersonal attraction, including liking and loving
- Explain the factors underlying aggression and prosocial behavior
- Define and apply the key terms and concepts listed at the end of the chapter

SOCIAL INFLUENCE

You have just transferred to a new college and are attending your first class. When the professor enters, you find that your fellow classmates all rise, bow down, and then face the back of the room. You have no understanding of this behavior. Even so, is it more likely that you will (1) jump up to join the rest of the class or (2) remain seated?

Based on what research has told us about social influence, the answer to such a question would almost always be (1). As you undoubtedly know from your own experience, pressures to conform can be painfully strong, and they can bring about changes in behavior that, when considered in perspective, would never have otherwise occurred.

Doing What Others Do: Conformity

Conformity is a change in behavior due to a desire to follow the beliefs or standards of other people. The classic demonstration of pressure to conform comes from a series of studies carried out in the 1950s by Solomon Asch (Asch, 1951). In the experiments, subjects thought they were participating in a test of perceptual skills with a group of six other subjects. The subjects were shown one card with three lines of varying length and a second card which had a fourth line that matched one of the first three (see Figure 15-1). The task was seemingly straightforward: All the subjects had to do was to announce aloud which of the

Conformity: *A change in behavior due to a desire to follow the beliefs or standards of other people*

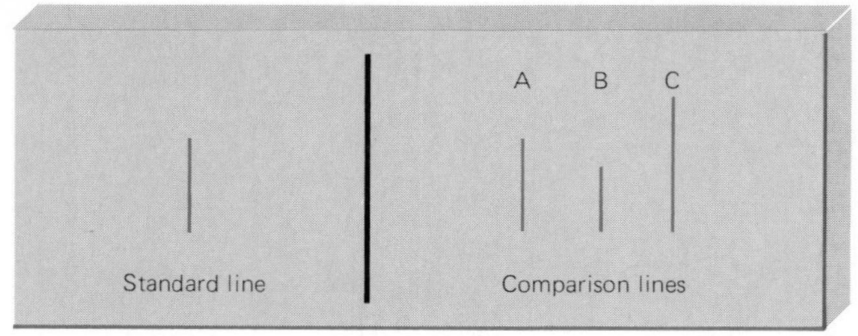

Figure 15-1
Subjects in Asch's conformity experiment were first shown a "standard" line and then asked to identify which of the three comparison lines was identical in length. As this example illustrates, there was always an obvious answer.

first three lines was identical in length to the fourth. Because there was always an obvious answer, the task seemed easy to the participants.

Indeed, since the subjects all agreed on the first few trials, the procedure was quite a simple one. But then something odd began to happen. From the perspective of the subject in the group who got to answer last, all of the first six subjects' answers seemed to be wrong—in fact, unanimously wrong. And this continued: Over and over again, the first subjects provided answers that unanimously contradicted what the last subject felt was the correct one. The dilemma that this situation posed for the last subject was whether to follow his or her own perceptions or to follow the group and repeat the answer that everyone else was giving.

As you might have guessed, the situation in the experiment was more contrived than it first appeared. The first six subjects were actually confederates of the experimenter and had been instructed to give unanimously erroneous answers in many of the trials. And the study had nothing to do with perceptual skills. Instead, the issue under investigation was that of conformity.

What Asch found was that in about one-third of the trials subjects conformed to the unanimous but erroneous group answer. However, there were strong individual differences; some subjects remained totally independent, while others conformed nearly all the time. Overall, some 75 percent of all subjects conformed at least once.

Since Asch's pioneering work, literally hundreds of studies have examined the factors affecting conformity, and we now know a great deal about the phenomenon (Moscovici, 1985; Tanford & Penrod, 1984). Among the most important variables producing conformity are the following:

Status: *The social rank held within a group*

- The nature of the group. The more attractive the group, the greater its ability to produce conformity; the lower the **status**—the social rank held within a group—of a person, the greater the similarity of the individual to the group, the greater the group's influence.
- The nature of the individual's response. Conformity is considerably higher when people must make a response publicly than when they can respond privately, as our founding fathers noted when they authorized secret ballots in voting.
- The kind of task. People working on tasks and questions that are ambiguous (having no clear answer) are more susceptible to social pressure. Giving an opinion, then, such as what is fashionable in clothing, is more apt to produce conformity than answering a question of fact. Moreover, tasks at which an individual is less competent relative to the group create conditions in which conformity is more likely.
- Unanimity of the group. Conformity pressures are most pronounced in groups that are unanimous in their support of a position. But what of the case in which

persons with dissenting views have an ally in the group—known as a **social supporter**—who agrees with them? It turns out that having just a single person present who shares the unpopular point of view is sufficient to reduce conformity pressures (Allen, 1975).

Social supporter: *A person who shares an unpopular opinion or attitude of another group member, thereby encouraging nonconformity*

Doing What Others Tell You to Do: Compliance

When we discuss conformity, we are usually talking about a phenomenon in which the social pressure is not overt or in the form of a direct order. But in some situations the social pressure is much more obvious, and there is direct, explicit pressure to endorse a certain point of view or to behave in a particular way. Social psychologists call this behavior that occurs in response to direct social pressure **compliance**.

Compliance: *Behavior that occurs in response to direct social pressure*

To begin our discussion of compliance, stop for a minute and think how you might respond if you were asked by a stranger to help him out. Suppose he said to you:

> I've devised a new way of improving memory. All I need is for you to teach people a list of words and then give them a test. The test procedure requires only that you give learners a shock each time they make a mistake on the test. To administer the shocks you will use a ''shock generator'' that gives shocks ranging from 30 to 450 volts. You can see that the switches are labeled from ''slight shock'' through ''danger: severe shock'' at the top level, where there are three red X's. But don't worry; although the shocks may be painful, they will cause no permanent damage.

Presented with this situation, you would likely think that neither you, nor anyone else, would go along with the stranger's unusual request. Clearly, it lies outside the bounds of what we consider good sense.

Or does it? Suppose the stranger asking for your help was a psychologist conducting an experiment. Or suppose it were your teacher, your employer, or your military commander—all people in authority and with some seemingly legitimate reason for their request.

If you still think it unlikely that you would comply, you might reconsider. For the situation represented above describes a now-classic experiment conducted by social psychologist Stanley Milgram in the 1960s (Milgram, 1974). In the study, subjects were placed in a situation in which they were told by an experimenter to give increasingly strong shocks to another person as part of a study on learning (see Figure 15-2). In reality, the experiment had nothing to do with learning; the real issue under consideration was the degree to which subjects would comply with the experimenter's requests. In fact, the person supposedly receiving the shocks was actually a confederate who never really received any punishment at all.

Most people who hear a description of the experiment feel that it is unlikely that *any* subject would give the maximum level of shock—or, for that matter, any shock at all. Even a group of psychiatrists who had the situation described to them predicted that fewer than 2 percent of the subjects would comply completely. However, the actual results contradicted both experts' and nonexperts' predictions: Almost two-thirds of the subjects eventually used the highest setting on the shock generator to ''electrocute'' the learner.

Why did so many individuals comply fully with the experimenter's demands? Extensive interviews carried out with subjects following the experiment showed

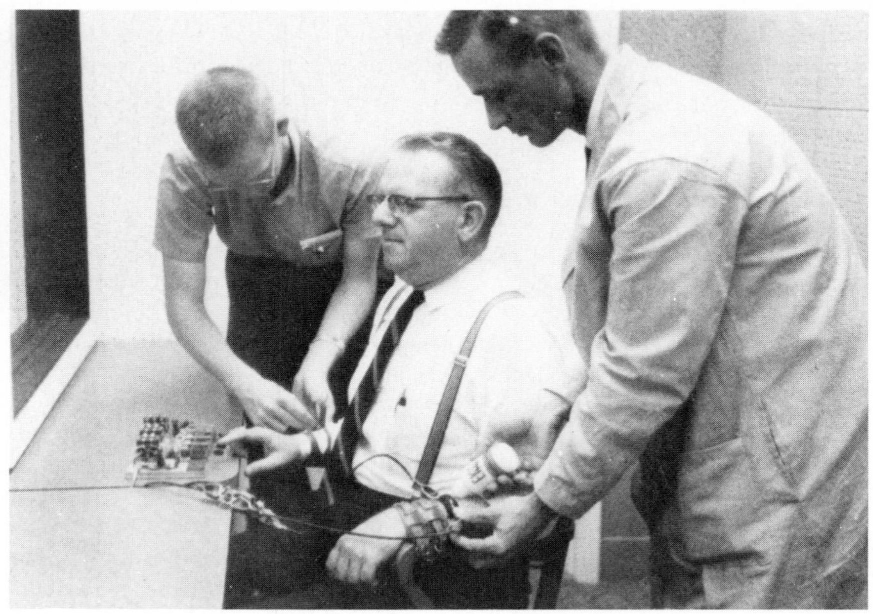

Figure 15-2
This impressive-looking "shock generator" was used to lead participants to believe they were administering electric shocks to another person, who was connected with the generator by electrodes that were attached to the skin. (*Copyright © 1965 by Stanley Milgram. From the film* Obedience, *distributed by the New York Film Division and the Pennsylvania State University.*)

that they were obedient primarily because they believed that the experimenter would be responsible for any potential ill effects that befell the learner. The experimenter's orders were accepted, then, because the subjects thought that they personally could not be held accountable for their actions—they could always blame the experimenter.

Although the Milgram experiment has been criticized for creating an extremely trying set of circumstances for the subjects—thereby raising serious ethical questions—and on methodological grounds (Orne & Holland, 1968), it remains one of the strongest laboratory demonstrations of compliance. We need only consider actual instances of compliance to authority to witness some frightening real-life parallels. A major defense of German officers after World War II, for instance, was that they were "only following orders." Moreover, Jim Jones's cult members uniformly complied with his orders—though it meant their own deaths. Milgram's results, then, force each of us to consider how able we would be to withstand the potent power of authority.

The Informed Consumer of Psychology: Strategies for Maintaining Your Own Point of View

We have seen how susceptible people are to the pressures of others, whether they be relatively indirect, as with pressures to conform, or direct, as with compliance with orders. How can one remain independent in the face of these sorts of pressures? Social psychological theory and research have suggested a number of techniques for helping one to remain faithful to one's own point of view:

■ Inoculation. To avoid smallpox, people receive a shot containing a small dose of smallpox germs. This injection produces antibodies in the body that can repel a major invasion of smallpox germs, should the individual be exposed to the disease in the future. Analogously, one procedure for helping people to remain independent of future attempts at persuasion is for people to expose themselves to a sample of counterarguments to which they might be subjected in the future. In an example of this technique, William McGuire (1964) showed that subjects could be made more resistant to persuasion if they were first exposed to a sample of opposing arguments along with information that refuted those arguments. Exposure to the opposing arguments—**inoculation**, as he called it—led to less subsequent change in beliefs than simply exposing subjects to information that bolstered their own initial views.

Inoculation (in ok u LAY shun): *Exposure to arguments opposing one's beliefs, making the subject more resistant to later attempts to change those beliefs*

■ Forewarning. Telling people that a persuasive message is coming and what that message involves, a strategy called **forewarning**, is sometimes sufficient to reduce social influence, even if counterarguments are not provided. This is particularly true if the issues are important and the target of influence has a large amount of information available (Cacioppo & Petty, 1979; Petty & Cacioppo, 1977). Knowing simply that a persuasive message is likely to be received without knowing the specific content of the upcoming message can reduce subsequent attitude change. The reason? When people are aware that they are going to receive counterattitudinal information they tend to develop their own arguments in support of their attitudes. Forewarned is thus forearmed.

Forewarning: *A procedure in which a subject is told in advance that a persuasive message is forthcoming, sometimes reducing the effects of social influence since the subject is prepared to stand firm*

■ Consistency. One technique that is not only effective in reducing persuadability but that can actually change the attitude of the persuader is **consistency**. Under certain conditions, particularly in group settings where a majority is attempting to influence a minority, the unyielding persistence of the minority in its point of view can actually bring about a change in the majority's attitudes (Moscovici & Mugny, 1983; Tanford & Penrod, 1984). Apparently, the unyielding repetition of one's own point of view can cause others to rethink their position and, ultimately, to be persuaded by the minority's opinion.

Consistency: *The persistence of those holding an unpopular view, eventually bringing about a change in the attitude of the majority*

On the other hand, some evidence suggests that a somewhat different approach is more appropriate. Hollander (1980) addresses situations in which a minority is attempting to remain independent of a majority position. He suggests a strat-

The proximity of neighbors is one factor that leads us to like them: We tend to be attracted to those who are geographically close to us. (*Jim Anderson/Woodfin Camp & Assoc.*)

egy in which individuals should conform initially to the views of the source of influence. After doing so in order to establish themselves as competent and reasonable group members, they can behave more independently and espouse views that are contrary to the majority's views. Instead of remaining consistently adamant in a deviant position, as Moscovici's consistency approach suggests, Hollander's theory suggests that people should first conform—but that after establishing their "credentials," they should then press their minority views.

Experimental evidence supports both approaches (Maass & Clark, 1984; Wold, 1985). Consequently, it is clear that social influence is not a one-way street; when we are the targets of social influence, we have a fighting chance to remain independent.

Recap and Review I

Recap

- Social influence is concerned with situations in which the actions of one individual or group affect the behavior of another.
- The most important types of social influence are conformity and compliance. Conformity is a change in behavior due to a desire to follow the beliefs or standards of other people, while compliance reflects a change in behavior made in response to direct, explicit social pressure.
- Among the primary techniques for remaining independent from group pressure are inoculation, forewarning, and consistency.

Review

1. When social psychologists discuss ____________, they are referring to a change in behavior resulting from a desire to follow the beliefs or standards of others. However, when a change in behavior occurs in response to more direct social pressure, such as in the form of a direct order, the change is called ____________.

2. List four of the most important variables producing conformity.

3. Deb's long debate with Chris over certain moral beliefs both exposed her to, and gave her the chance to respond to, various opposing arguments. Interestingly, when later in the week a group of her friends unanimously presented similar opposing arguments on the same topic she remained independent and was not persuaded to accept their beliefs. Deb had unknowingly practiced with Chris what technique for maintaining her point of view?
a. Consistency **b.** Persuasion **c.** Forewarning **d.** Inoculation

4. Research has demonstrated that when one holds the minority point of view, the only way to change the attitude of the majority is to consistently repeat your point of view right from the start. True or false?

(Answers to review questions are at the bottom of page 498.)

LIKING AND LOVING: INTERPERSONAL ATTRACTION AND THE DEVELOPMENT OF RELATIONSHIPS

Interpersonal attraction: *Positive feelings for others*

Close relationships: *See interpersonal attraction*

When nineteenth-century poet Elizabeth Barrett Browning wrote, "How do I love thee? Let me count the ways," she was expressing feelings about a topic that is central to most people's lives—and one that has developed into a major subject of investigation by social psychologists: loving and liking. Known more formally as the study of **interpersonal attraction** or **close relationships**, this topic encompasses the factors that lead to positive feelings for others.

How Do I Like Thee? Let Me Count the Ways

By far the greatest amount of research has focused on liking, probably because it has always proved easier for investigators conducting short-term experiments

Love is a state of interpersonal attraction that can be clearly differentiated from mere liking. (*Edward L. Miller/Stock, Boston*)

to produce states of liking in strangers who have just met than to promote and observe loving relationships over long periods of time. Hence, traditional studies have given us a good deal of knowledge about the factors that attract two people to each other (Berscheid, 1985). Among the most important factors discovered are the following:

- Proximity. If you live in a dormitory or an apartment, consider the friends you made when you first moved in. Chances are, you became friendliest with those who lived geographically closest to you. In fact, this is one of the best-established findings in the interpersonal attraction literature; **proximity** leads to liking (Festinger, Schachter, & Back, 1950; Nahome & Lawton, 1976).

Proximity (prox IM ih tee): *One's nearness to another, one cause for liking*

- Mere exposure. Repeated exposure to a person is often sufficient to produce attraction. Interestingly, repeated exposure to *any* stimulus—be it a person, picture, record, or what have you—most frequently makes us like the stimulus more (Birnbaum & Mellers, 1979; Zajonc, 1968). Becoming familiar with a stimulus can evoke positive feelings; these positive feelings due to familiarity are then transferred to the stimulus itself. There are exceptions, though: In cases in which the initial interactions are strongly negative, repeated exposure is unlikely to cause us to like another person more; instead, we may end up disliking such an individual more the more we are exposed to him or her.
- Similarity. We tend to like those who are similar to us; discovering that others are similar in terms of attitudes, values, or traits promotes liking for them (Byrne, 1969; Hill & Stull, 1981; Meyer & Pepper, 1971). Moreover, the more similar they are, the more we like them. There is also a strong **reciprocity-of-liking effect**, a tendency to like those who like us—as well as the converse: we assume that when we like someone else, they like us in return (Metee & Aronson, 1974; Tagiuri, 1958).

Reciprocity-of-liking effect: *A tendency to like those who like us*

- Physical attractiveness. For most people, the equation "beautiful = good" is a very real one. As a result, people who are physically attractive are more popular than those who are physically unattractive, if all other factors are equal. This finding, which contradicts the values that most people would profess, is apparent even in childhood—with nursery-school-age children rating popularity

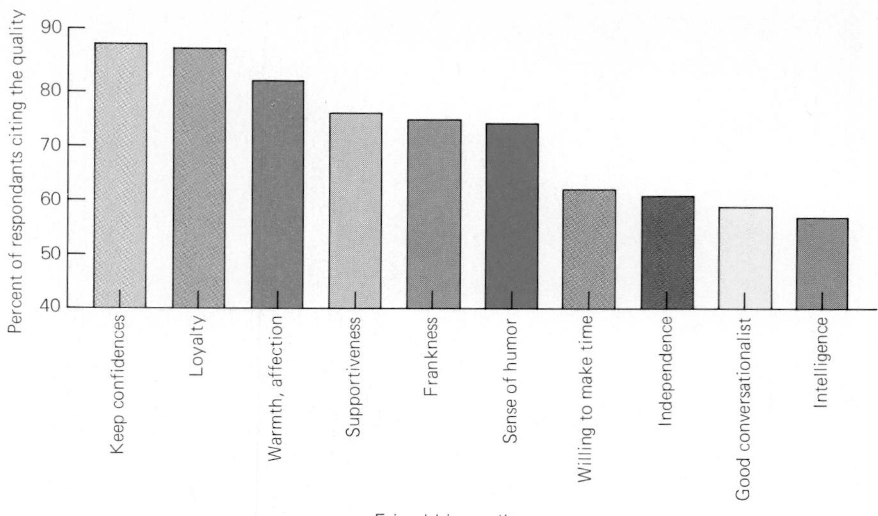

Figure 15-3
These are the key qualities people look for in a friend according to some 40,000 respondents to a questionnaire. (*Adapted from Parlee, 1979.*)

on the basis of attractiveness (Dion & Berscheid, 1974)—and continues into adulthood. Indeed, physical attractiveness may be the single most important element promoting initial liking in college dating situations, although its influence decreases when people get to know each other better (Berscheid & Walster, 1974). Moreover, there are some cases in which physical attractiveness is a drawback: Although good looks lead to more positive impressions of men in job-related situations, beauty can work against women in managerial positions, since a common (although totally unfounded) stereotype holds that attractive women attain their position due to looks rather than ability (Heilman & Stopek, 1985). Physical attractiveness, then, is generally a powerful factor in determining who people are attracted to and the kind of social life one has (Reis, Wheeler, Spiegel, Kerris, Nezlek, & Perri, 1982).

Proximity, mere exposure, similarity, and physical attractiveness are not, of course, the only factors that are important in liking. For example, survey research has sought to determine the factors that are critical in friendships. In one questionnaire that was answered by some 40,000 respondents, the qualities that were most valued in a friend were identified (Parlee, 1979). (See Figure 15-3.) The key factors were the ability to keep confidences, loyalty, and warmth and affection, followed closely by supportiveness, frankness, and a sense of humor.

How Do I Love Thee? Let Me Count the Ways

While our knowledge of what makes people like each other is extensive, our understanding of love is a more limited and relatively recent phenomenon. Many social psychologists believed for a long time that love represents a phenomenon too difficult to observe and study in a controlled, scientific way. However, love is such a central issue in most people's lives that, in time, social psychologists

ANSWERS TO REVIEW QUESTIONS

Review I: **1.** Conformity, compliance **2.** The nature of the group, the nature of the individual's response, the kind of task, and unanimity of the group **3.** d **4.** False

TABLE 15-1

Loving and liking

Sample love items:
- I feel that I can confide in ________________ about virtually everything.
- I would do almost anything for ________________.
- I feel responsible for ________________'s well-being.

Sample liking items:
- I think that ________________ is unusually well-adjusted.
- I think that ________________ is one of those people who quickly wins respect.
- ________________ is one of the most likable people I know.

Source: Rubin, 1973

could not resist its allure and became infatuated with the topic (Sternberg & Grajek, 1984).

As a first step, researchers have tried to identify the distinguishing characteristics between mere liking and full-blown love. Using this approach, they have discovered that love is not simply liking of a greater quantity, but a qualitatively different psychological state (Walster & Walster, 1978). For instance, at least in its early stages, love includes relatively intense physiological arousal, an all-encompassing interest in another individual, fantasizing about the other, and relatively rapid swings of emotion. Similarly, Davis (1985) suggests that love has elements of fascination, exclusiveness, sexual desire, and intense caring that liking lacks.

Social psychologist Zick Rubin (1970, 1973) has tried to differentiate between love and liking using a paper-and-pencil scale. As can be seen from the sample items in Table 15-1, each question refers to the person to whom the individual is attracted.

Researchers have found that couples scoring high on the love scale differ considerably from those with low scores. They gaze at each other more, and their relationships are more likely to be intact six months later than are the relationships of those who score low on the scale.

Other experiments have found evidence suggesting that the heightened physiological arousal hypothesized to be characteristic of loving is indeed present when a person reports being in love. Interestingly, though, it may not be just arousal of a sexual nature. Berscheid & Walster (1974) have theorized that when we are exposed to *any* stimulus that increases physiological arousal—such as danger, fear, or anger—our feelings for another person present at the time of the arousal may be labeled as love, if there are situational cues that suggest that "love" is an appropriate label for the feelings being experienced. In sum, we say we are in love when general physiological arousal is coupled with the thought that the cause of the arousal is most likely love.

This theory explains, then, why a person who keeps being rejected or hurt by another could still feel "in love" with that person. If the rejection leads to physiological arousal, but the arousal still happens to be attributed to love—and not to rejection—then a person will still feel "in love".

Other researchers have theorized that there are actually several kinds of love (Hendrick & Hendrick, 1986). For example, Robert Sternberg (1986) suggests that love is made up of three components: an intimacy component, encompassing feelings of closeness and connectedness; a passion component made up of the

TABLE 15-2

The kinds of love

	Component*		
	INTIMACY	PASSION	DECISION/COMMITMENT
Nonlove	−	−	−
Liking	+	−	−
Infatuated love	−	+	−
Empty love	−	−	+
Romantic love	+	+	−
Companionate love	+	−	+
Fatuous love	−	+	+
Consummate love	+	+	+

*+ = component present; − = component absent.
Source: Sternberg, 1986, Table 2.

motivational drives relating to sex, physical closeness, and romance; and a decision/commitment component encompassing the cognition that one loves someone (in the short term) and longer-term feelings of commitment to maintain love. As can be seen in Table 15-2, particular combinations of the three components produce several different kinds of love.

The Rise and Fall of Liking and Loving: Understanding the Course of Relationships

With one out of two marriages ending in divorce and broken love affairs a common phenomenon, it is not surprising that social psychologists have begun to turn their attention increasingly toward understanding what makes some relationships last and others fail (Hays, 1985; Ickes, 1984; Snyder, Berscheid, & Glick, 1985).

Social psychologist George Levinger (1983) has speculated on the reasons behind the deterioration of relationships. One important factor appears to be a change in judgments about the meaning of a partner's behavior. Behavior that was once viewed as "charming forgetfulness" comes to be seen as "boorish indifference," and the partner becomes less valued. In addition, communications may be disrupted; rather than listening to what the other person is saying, each partner becomes bent on justifying himself or herself, and communication deteriorates. Eventually, a partner may begin to invite and agree with criticism of the other partner from people outside of the relationship and look to others for the fulfillment of basic needs that were previously met by the partner.

Not all relationships deteriorate, of course. What characterizes successful ones? Some answers to this question come from a study by Jeanette and Robert Lauer (1985), who surveyed couples who reported being happily married for fifteen years or more. When asked to indicate what it was that had made their marriages last, both the husbands and wives gave remarkably similar responses. As you can see in Table 15-3, the most frequently named reason was perceiving one's spouse as one's best friend and liking him or her "as a person." There was also a strong belief in marriage as a commitment and a desire to make the relationship work, as well as agreement about aims and goals. On the other

"When I fell in love with you, suddenly your eyes didn't seem close together. Now they seem close together again."

When relationships begin to deteriorate, flaws that were previously viewed as charming come to be perceived in a more negative light. (*Drawing by Wm. Hamilton; © The New Yorker Magazine, Inc.*)

hand, there was not blind commitment to the other person: People acknowledged their partner's flaws, but they tended to overlook them. As one husband said, "She isn't perfect. But I don't worry about her weak points, which are very few. Her stong points overcome them too much" (Lauer & Lauer, 1985).

Another factor affecting the long-term success of loving relationships concerns the rate at which the various components of love develop. According to Sternberg's (1986) theory of love, the three individual components of love—intimacy, passion, and decision/commitment—vary in their influence over time and follow distinct courses, as illustrated in Figure 15-4. In strong loving relationships, the level of commitment peaks and then remains stable, while intimacy continues to grow over the course of a relationship. Passion, on the other hand, shows a marked decline over time, reaching a plateau fairly early on in a relationship. Still, it remains an important component of loving relationships.

The emerging work on relationships has led to the development of a number of programs designed for couples who are about to be married (Goleman,1985). These programs, which concentrate on communication skills between husband and wife, most often include these elements:

- The couples are told to focus on one topic at a time and to provide rationales and explanations for their behavior (for instance, "I'm acting angry because I got stuck in a traffic jam on the way home, not because of anything you did.").
- The couples learn to "stop the action" and enter "cooling-off" periods

TABLE 15-3

Most-often-cited reasons* for success in marriage

CITED BY HUSBANDS	CITED BY WIVES
My spouse is my best friend.	My spouse is my best friend.
I like my spouse as a person.	I like my spouse as a person.
Marriage is a long-term commitment.	Marriage is a long-term commitment.
Marriage is sacred.	Marriage is sacred.
We agree on aims and goals.	We agree on aims and goals.
My spouse has grown more interesting.	My spouse has grown more interesting.
I want the relationship to succeed.	I want the relationship to succeed.
An enduring marriage is important to social stability.	We laugh together.
We laugh together.	We agree on a philosophy of life.
I am proud of my spouse's achievements.	We agree on how and how often to show affection.
We agree on a philosophy of life.	An enduring marriage is important to social stability.
We agree about our sex life.	We have a stimulating exchange of ideas.
We agree on how and how often to show affection.	We discuss things calmly.
I confide in my spouse.	We agree about our sex life.
We share outside hobbies and interests.	I am proud of my spouse's achievements.

*In order of frequency.
Source: Lauer & Lauer, 1985.

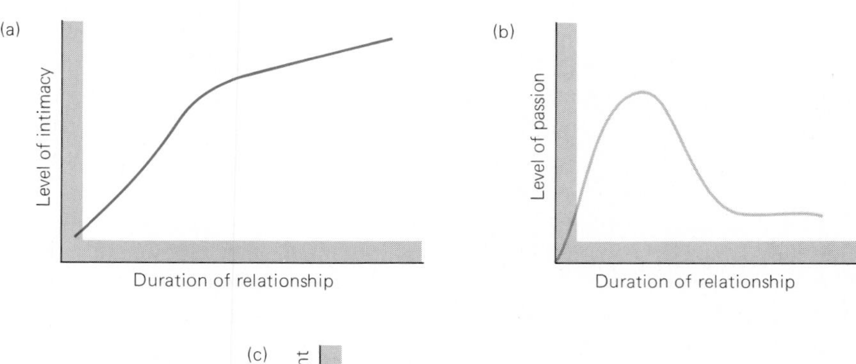

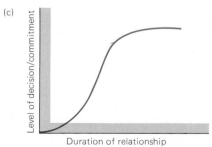

Figure 15-4
The changing ingredients of love. The three components of love vary in strength over the course of a relationship. (*Sternberg, 1986.*)

during a conflict. This "stop-the-action" maneuver allows both partners to become less engrossed in the conflict and in so doing lessens the chances that the conflict will escalate into a major battle.

- Another fundamental strategy is to avoid criticizing the partner and to make an active effort not to open old wounds from the past.
- Finally, couples are taught to talk in terms of specific changes in behavior they would like to see in each other, rather than to simply label the unattractive behavior in a way that is bound to cause offense. For instance, a spouse who is told, "Having to pick up your laundry at the cleaners makes me feel like I am being taken advantage of" is likely to react more positively than if he or she is told, "You're too lazy to pick up your own laundry, so I have to do it."

While these behaviors cannot guarantee that a relationship will be a lasting one, they do increase its chances of enduring.

RECAP AND REVIEW II

Recap

- The study of interpersonal attraction, or close relationships, is concerned with the phenomena of liking and loving.
- Among the most important elements that affect liking are proximity, mere exposure, similarity, and physical attractiveness.
- Love is assumed to be differentiated from liking in qualitative, as well as quantitative, respects. Paper-and-pencil measures have been used to distinguish love from liking, and some theories suggest that love is related to general physiological arousal.
- Social psychologists have begun to pay increasing attention to the factors relating to the maintenance and decline of relationships.

Review

1. What four factors are among the most important with regard to attracting two people to each other?
2. In differentiating between loving and liking, theories suggesting that love is related to physiological arousal generally stipulate that the physiological arousal must be tied to
   a. Fear arousal **b.** The cognition that sexual arousal is occurring **c.** The attribution that the cause of the arousal is love **d.** Situational constraints
3. Research conducted by Lauer and Lauer (1985) found that partners in successful marriages had surprisingly different perceptions of what made their marriages endure. True or false?
4. Programs designed to focus on communication skills for couples about to be married include teaching partners how to discuss specific changes in behavior they would like each other to make. True or false?

(Answers to review questions are at the bottom of page 504.)

HURTING AND HELPING OTHERS: AGGRESSION AND PROSOCIAL BEHAVIOR

A 22-year-old woman who stopped in a bar for a drink late one evening was sexually assaulted and repeatedly raped on a pool table by a group of four men. Despite her desperate pleas to at least nine bystanders, no one came to her aid. In fact, instead of helping her, the other people in the bar simply stood by, and some even cheered.

While the circumstances facing the woman described above were unusually extreme, the phenomenon illustrated by the event, unfortunately, is not. Psychologists have long pondered the issues of what motivates helping behavior and its counterpart, aggression. Much of the work was inspired by an incident—described in Chapter 1—that occurred some twenty years ago when a young woman named Kitty Genovese was heard screaming, "Oh, my God, he stabbed me," and "Please help me," by no fewer than thirty-eight of her neighbors. Not one witness came forward to help; and it was not until thirty minutes had gone by that even one person bothered to call the police. Genovese subsequently died in an alleyway before the police arrived—the victim of a vicious attack by a mugger.

Just as events such as these permit only a negative, pessimistic interpretation of human capacities, there are other, equally dramatic incidents that promote a more optimistic view of humankind. Consider the case of Reginald Andrews, an unemployed father of eight who jumped onto the tracks at a subway station to save a 75-year-old blind man who had fallen between two cars of a train that was about to pull out ("Subway Altruism," 1982). Or ponder the cases in which people in German-occupied countries during World War II risked death to help Jews escape from the Nazis. Clearly, these instances of helping behavior are no less characteristic of human behavior than the less savory examples. In this part of the chapter we explore the work that social psychologists have done in an effort to explain instances of both aggressive and helping behavior.

Hurting Others: Aggression

We need look no further than our daily paper or the nightly news to be bombarded with examples of aggression, both on a societal level (war, invasion, assassination) and on an individual level (crime, child abuse, and the many petty cruelties that humans are capable of inflicting on one another). Is such aggression an inevitable part of the human condition, or is aggression primarily a function of particular circumstances that might potentially be alleviated by changing the conditions that cause it?

Social psychologists investigating this issue have begun by attempting to define the term "aggression" (Krebs & Miller, 1985). This is not as simple as it may at first appear, since there are many examples of pain or injury being inflicted that may or may not qualify as aggression, depending upon one's definition. While it is clear, for instance, that a rapist is acting aggressively toward his victim, it is less certain that a physician carrying out an emergency medical procedure without an anesthetic, thereby causing incredible pain to the patient, should be considered aggressive. (See the accompanying Try It! box.)

Aggression: *Intentional injury or harm to another person*

Most social psychologists, then, define aggression in terms of the intent and purpose behind the behavior: **Aggression** is the intentional injury or harm to another person (Berkowitz, 1974). Using this definition, it is clear that the rapist in our example is acting aggressively, while the physician causing pain during a medical procedure is not.

Aggression as a Release: Instinct Approaches If you have ever punched an adversary in the nose, you may have experienced a certain satisfaction, despite your better judgment. Instinct theories, noting the prevalence of aggres-

ANSWERS TO REVIEW QUESTIONS

Review II: **1.** Proximity, mere exposure, similarity, and physical attractiveness **2.** c **3.** False **4.** True

TRY IT!

IS THIS AGGRESSION?

To see for yourself the difficulties involved in defining aggression, consider each of the following instances and determine whether it represents aggressive behavior according to your own definition of the term "aggression."

1. A spider eats a fly. ____
2. Two wolves fight for the leadership of the pack. ____
3. A soldier shoots an enemy at the front line. ____
4. The warden of a prison executes a convicted criminal. ____
5. A juvenile gang attacks members of another gang. ____
6. Two men fight for a piece of bread. ____
7. A man viciously kicks a cat. ____
8. A man, while cleaning a window, knocks over a flowerpot, which, in falling, injures a pedestrian. ____
9. A girl kicks a wastebasket. ____
10. Mr. X, a notorious gossip, speaks disparagingly of many people of his acquaintance. ____
11. A man mentally rehearses a murder he is about to commit. ____
12. An angry son purposely fails to write to his mother, who is expecting a letter and will be hurt if none arrives. ____
13. An enraged boy tries with all his might to inflict injury on his antagonist, a bigger boy, but is not successful in doing so. His efforts simply amuse the bigger boy. ____
14. A man daydreams of harming his antagonist, but has no hope of doing so. ____
15. A senator does not protest the escalation of bombing to which he is morally opposed. ____
16. A farmer beheads a chicken and prepares it for supper. ____
17. A hunter kills an animal and mounts it as a trophy. ____
18. A dog snarls at a mail carrier, but does not bite. ____
19. A physician gives a flu shot to a screaming child. ____
20. A boxer gives his opponent a bloody nose. ____
21. A Girl Scout tries to assist an elderly woman, but trips her by accident. ____
22. A bank robber is shot in the back while trying to escape. ____
23. A tennis player smashes his racket after missing a volley. ____
24. A person commits suicide. ____
25. A cat kills a mouse, parades around with it, and then discards it. ____

Now, go back over each instance, and consider whether it represents aggression according to the definition used by social psychologists: "the intentional injury or harm to another person." You are likely to find some differences the second time through the list. Note how the kind of definition you use affects whether or not you see aggression in a situation (Benjamin, 1985, p. 41).

sion not only in humans but in animals as well, propose that aggression is primarily the outcome of **innate**—or inborn—urges.

Innate (in ATE): *Inborn, biologically determined*

The major proponent of the instinct approach is Konrad Lorenz, an ethologist (a scientist who studies animal behavior) who suggested that humans, along with members of other species, have a fighting instinct, which in earlier times ensured protection of food supplies and weeded out the weaker of the species (Lorenz, 1966, 1974). The controversial notion arising from Lorenz's instinct approach is the idea that aggressive energy is constantly being built up within an individual until it is finally discharged. The longer it is built up, says Lorenz, the greater will be the magnitude of the aggression displayed when it is discharged.

Probably the most controversial idea to come out of instinct theories of aggression is Lorenz's proposal that society ought to provide acceptable means of aggression release through, for instance, participation in sports and games, in order to prevent its discharge in less socially desirable ways. However, while making logical sense, there is no way of devising an adequate experiment to test the notion. In fact, there is relatively little support for instinct theories in general because of the difficulty in finding evidence for any kind of pent-up reservoir of aggression (Berkowitz,

1974; Green & Donnerstein, 1983). Most social psychologists, then, suggest that we should look to other approaches to explain aggression.

Frustration: *A state produced by the thwarting or blocking of some ongoing, goal-directed behavior*

Aggressive cues: *Stimuli that have been associated with aggression in the past*

Aggression as a Reaction to Frustration: Frustration-Aggression Approaches Have you ever worked painstakingly on a model or puzzle, only to have someone clumsily knock it over and ruin it just as you were about to complete it? The feelings you experienced toward the person who destroyed your work probably placed you on the verge of real aggression, and you no doubt seethed inside.

Frustration-aggression theory tries to explain aggression in terms of events such as the one described above. When first put forward, the theory said flatly that frustration *always* led to aggression of some sort, and that aggression was *always* the result of some frustration, where **frustration** is defined as the thwarting or blocking of some ongoing, goal-directed behavior (Dollard, Doob, Miller, Mowrer, & Sears, 1939). More recent formulations, however, have modified the original one, suggesting instead that frustration produces anger, leading to a *readiness* to act aggressively. Whether or not actual aggression occurs depends on the presence of **aggressive cues**, stimuli that have been associated in the past with actual aggression or violence and that will trigger aggression again (Berkowitz, 1984).

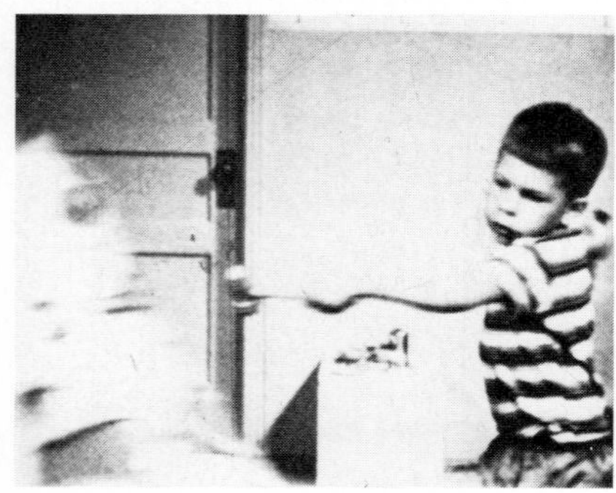

After observing an adult model behaving aggressively, angered children carried out behaviors remarkably similar to those they had seen earlier. (*Courtesy of Albert Bandura*)

What kinds of stimuli can act as aggressive cues? They can range from the most overt, such as the presence of weapons, to the most subtle, such as the mere mention of the name of an individual who has behaved violently in the past. For example, in one experiment, angered subjects behaved significantly more aggressively when in the presence of a rifle and revolver than in a comparable situation in which the guns were not present (Berkowitz & LePage, 1967). Similarly, frustrated subjects in an experiment who had viewed a violent movie were more aggressive to a confederate with the same name as the star of the movie than to a confederate with a different name (Berkowitz & Geen, 1966). It appears, then, that frustration does lead to aggression, at least when aggressive cues are present.

Learning to Hurt Others: Observational Learning Approaches Do we learn to be aggressive? The observational learning (sometimes called "social learning") approach to aggression says we do. Taking an almost opposite view from the instinct theories, which focus on the innate aspects of aggression, observational learning theory, which we discussed first in Chapter 4, emphasizes how social and environmental conditions can teach individuals to be aggressive. Aggressive is not seen as inevitable, but rather as a learned response that can be understood in terms of rewards and punishments (Bandura, 1973; Zillman, 1978).

Suppose, for instance, that a young girl hits her younger brother when he damages a new toy of hers. While instinct theories would suggest that the aggression had been pent up and was now being discharged, and frustration-aggression theory would examine the girl's frustration at no longer being able to use her new toy, observational learning theory would look for a previous reinforcement that the girl had received for being aggressive. Perhaps she had learned that aggression resulted in her getting attention from her parents, or perhaps in the past her brother had apologized after being hit. In either case, observational learning theory views the aggression as a result of past rewards the girl had obtained for such behavior.

THE CUTTING EDGE

DOES IT HURT TO WATCH TV?

Media Aggression

Since the average American child between the ages of 5 and 15 is exposed to no fewer than 13,000 violent deaths on television, one of the most important questions being addressed by social psychologists concern the effects of viewing media violence (Berkowitz, 1984; Freedman, 1984; Gerbner, Gross, Jackson-Beeck, Jeffries-Fox, & Signorelli, 1978). With observational learning research on modeling showing that observers frequently imitate aggression, are we headed toward a world that is destined to become even more violent than it already is?

Most research conducted on the effects of media violence on viewers suggests that there is, in fact, a significant association between watching violent television programs and aggressive behavior (Eron, 1982). For example, one experiment showed that people who had watched a lot of television as third graders became more aggressive adults than those who hadn't watched so much (Eron, Huesmann, Lefkowitz, & Walden, 1972). Of course, these results cannot prove that viewing television was the *cause* of the adult aggression; some other factor, such as socioeconomic status, may have led to both higher levels of television viewing *and* increased aggression.

Still, most experts agree that watching media violence can lead to a greater readiness to act aggressively, if not invariably toward direct aggression. This conclusion has led social psychologist L. Rowell Huesmann and his colleagues at the University of Illinois to develop an innovative program designed to help limit the effects of media violence. In the program, the emphasis is on viewers' interpretations of the aggressive behaviors they see on television. By teaching viewers explicitly that television violence is unrealistic, that aggressive behavior is less acceptable in the real world than it appears to be on television, and that modeling television aggression is inappropriate, Huesmann hopes to reduce the impact of the observation of aggression (Eron & Huesmann, 1985; Huesmann, Eron, Klein, Brice, & Fischer, 1983).

Findings from the program are encouraging. In a field test, a sample of first and third graders participated in three training sessions intended to demonstrate that the behavior of television characters was not representative of the way that most people behaved, and that people generally resolved their problems without resorting to aggression. Moreover, they were told how special effects and camera techniques were used to create the illusion that aggression was occurring. Finally, nine months later, the children were explicitly taught that watching television violence was undesirable and that they should refrain from imitating what they saw on television.

In comparison to a control group of children who did not receive the special training, the children participating in the lessons were rated by their classmates as showing significantly less aggression. In addition, the children's attitudes toward media aggression became less favorable.

It seems, then, that Huesmann's procedure was effective. The effects of exposure to media aggression can be reduced by changing people's understanding of the meaning of aggression. The question remaining is how long-lasting the effects of the program are—a question that will be addressed in future research.

Huesmann and colleague Eric Dubrow are currently considering other techniques for reducing aggression (Huesmann, 1985). In one study, for instance, they are teaching behavior-disordered children nonaggressive techniques for solving social problems. The ultimate goal of such research, according to Huesmann, is to develop effective strategies that can be used to produce reliable declines in children's aggression.

Observational learning theory pays particular attention not only to direct rewards and punishments that individuals themselves receive, but to the rewards and punishments that models—individuals who provide a guide to appropriate behavior—receive for their aggressive behavior. According to observational learning theory, people observe the behavior of models and the subsequent consequences of the behavior. If the consequences are positive, the behavior is likely to be imitated when the observer finds himself or herself in a similar situation.

This basic formulation of observational learning theory has received wide support. For example, nursery-school-age children who have watched an adult behave aggressively display the same behavior themselves if they have been previously angered (Bandura, Ross, & Ross, 1963). It turns out, though, that exposure to models typically leads to spontaneous aggression only if the observer has first been angered, insulted, or frustrated (Bandura, 1973). The strong research support for observational learning explanations of aggression has important implications for understanding the effects of media aggression. (See the Cutting Edge box.)

Reducing and Preventing Aggression Billy, a seventh grader, gets into fights almost weekly on the school playground. His teacher thinks he ought to get involved in football in order to, as she says, "get rid of his aggression." His father thinks he's frustrated over his inability to read very well. His mother thinks they ought to withhold his allowance until he has gone without a fight for two weeks. The school counselor suggests still another approach: Every week that Billy displays no aggression, he should receive a $5 reward.

Who is right? Looking back at the different explanations of aggression, we find that each of these approaches may have some merit. Instinct theories of aggression suggest that aggression builds up until it is discharged; this hypothesis—termed the **catharsis hypothesis** and expressed by the teacher's point of view that Billy should play football—suggests that by behaving aggressively in socially acceptable ways we can relieve aggressiveness that would otherwise be expressed in less desirable ways. Unfortunately, the scientific evidence in support of the theory is quite inconsistent (Ebbesen, Duncan, & Koněcni, 1975), and the only case in which catharsis is seemingly effective is when a person's aggression is directed toward an individual who initially caused that person to be angry (Doob & Wood, 1972). Moreover, as we discussed in the Cutting Edge box earlier, exposure to aggression in media forms can actually lead to an increase in aggression. In sum, instinct approaches have not garnered much scientific support.

Catharsis (cuh THAR sis) **hypothesis**: *The notion that aggression is built up and must be discharged through violent acts*

More promising approaches to reducing aggression are provided by frustration-aggression and observational learning theories. As suggested by the father's point that Billy's inability to read leads to frustration, removing frustration is effective in reducing aggression. However, the difficulty with such a technique is that life is full of all sorts of frustrations, and removing them all is an impossibility. One cannot create an environment completely free of frustration, and techniques for reducing aggression that are based on frustration-aggression theory may not be practical.

To date, the most promising approach to reducing aggression comes from learning theory, which deals with the modification of the rewards and punishments that follow aggression. The mother's suggestion to withhold Billy's allowance is an example of the most frequently used technique to control aggression and is built on observational-learning-theory approaches: the use of punishment following aggressive behavior. Interestingly, though, the use of punishment turns out to be a relatively ineffective technique for reducing aggression. One reason is that the people who do the punishing, especially when they use physical punishment, can actually serve as aggressive models themselves and thereby increase the likelihood of future aggression. Moreover, research shows that the effects of punishment tend to be relatively transitory (Sulzer-Azaroff & Mayer, 1986).

The research evidence is clear, however, in supporting the school counselor's strategy of reinforcing Billy's nonaggressive behavior, for research demonstrates that providing rewards for nonaggressive behavior can lead to a reduction in aggression. In fact, even exposure to nonaggressive models leads to reduced aggression, at least in laboratory studies (Baron & Kepner, 1970). Moreover, the recent work on changing people's interpretations of models' behavior (see the Cutting Edge box) has shown that aggression can be minimized (Huesmann, Eron, Klein, Brice, & Fischer, 1983). In sum, most research seems to suggest that approaches to reducing aggression based on observational learning theory, and particularly those employing rewards for nonaggressive behavior, are most successful. (For further discussion of the effects of observing aggression, see the Psychology at Work box.)

PSYCHOLOGY AT WORK

SHOULD PORNOGRAPHY BE BANNED?

The Link between Pornography and Violence toward Women

Does viewing pornography lead to violence toward women? This question is a complex one, but recent evidence suggests that there may, in fact, be a link between erotic material and aggression.

In an experiment examining this issue, angered male subjects who had viewed an erotic movie that contained violence toward a woman showed significantly more subsequent aggression toward a female than if they had viewed an erotic movie that contained no violence (Donnerstein & Berkowitz, 1981). Moreover, other studies have shown that people exposed to pornographic materials that include aggressive content are more likely to report a willingness to rape a woman than those who see nonaggressive pornographic materials (Malamuth & Donnerstein, 1982).

Overall, research in this area suggests that the viewing of media pornography does lead, under certain conditions, to the increased likelihood of aggression toward women (Check & Malamuth, 1986; Malamuth & Donnerstein, 1984). What appears to be particularly critical, though, is whether the pornography contains violence toward women; aggressive content in erotic materials clearly raises the level of aggression subsequently displayed by those exposed to it.

Whether these findings mean that pornography should be banned is an open question—but they do alert us to the danger of exposure to pornography depicting aggression against women.

The link between erotic material containing violence toward women and subsequent aggression by those exposed to the material has led some people to argue that pornographic literature and films ought to be banned. (*Mark Mellet/Taurus Photos*)

Helping Others: The Brighter Side of Human Nature

Prosocial behavior: *Helping behavior*

Turning away from aggression, we move now to the opposite—and brighter—side of the coin of human nature: helping behavior. Helping behavior, or **prosocial behavior** as it is more formally known, has been investigated using many different approaches, but the question that has been looked at most closely is one relating to bystander intervention in emergency situations. What are the factors that lead someone to give help to a person who is in need of aid?

Diffusion of responsibility: *The tendency for people to feel that responsibility for helping is shared among those present*

As we noted in Chapter 1, one critical factor relates to the number of others present. When there is more than one witness to an emergency situation, there can be a sense of diffusion of responsibility among bystanders. **Diffusion of responsibility** is the tendency for people to feel that responsibility for acting is shared or diffused among those present. The more people present in an emergency, then, the less personally responsible each individual feels—and therefore the less help provided (Latané & Nida, 1981).

Rewards-costs approach: *The notion that, in a situation requiring help, a bystander's perceived rewards must outweigh the costs if helping is to occur*

Although the majority of research on helping behavior supports the diffusion-of-responsibility formulation, other factors clearly are involved in helping behavior. According to a model developed by Latané and Darley (1970), the process of helping involves four basic steps (see Figure 15-5):

1. Noticing a person, event, or situation that may require help.
2. Interpreting the event as one that requires help. Even if an event is noticed, it may be sufficiently ambiguous to be interpreted as a nonemergency situation (Shotland, 1985). It is here that the presence of others first affects helping behavior: The presence of inactive others may indicate to the observer that a situation does not require help—a judgment not necessarily made if the observer is alone.
3. Assuming responsibility for taking action. It is at this point that diffusion of responsibility is likely to occur if others are present. Moreover, a bystander's particular expertise is apt to play a role in whether helping occurs. For instance, if people with training in medical aid or lifesaving techniques are present, untrained bystanders are less apt to intervene because they feel they have less expertise. This point was well illustrated in a study by Jane and Irving Piliavin (1972), who conducted a field experiment in which an individual seemed to collapse in a subway car with blood trickling out of the corner of his mouth. The results of the experiment showed that bystanders were less likely to help when a person (actually a confederate) appearing to be an intern was present than when the ''intern'' was not present.
4. Deciding on and implementing the form of assistance. After an individual assumes responsibility for helping, then the decision must be made as to how assistance will be provided. Helping can range from very indirect forms of intervention, such as calling the police, to more direct forms, such as giving first aid or bringing the victim to a hospital. Most social psychologists use a **rewards-costs approach** for helping to predict the nature of assistance that a bystander will choose to provide. The general notion is that the rewards of helping, as perceived by the bystander, must outweigh the costs if helping is to occur (Lynch & Cohen, 1978), and most research tends to support this notion.

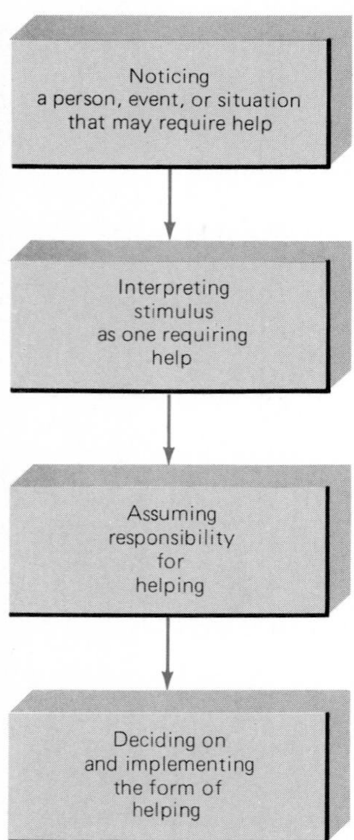

Figure 15-5
The basic steps of helping. (*Based on a model of Latané & Darley, 1970.*)

After the nature of assistance is determined, there is still one step remaining: the actual implementation of the assistance. A rewards-costs analysis suggests that the least costly form of implementation is the most likely to be used. However, this is not the whole story: In some cases, people behave altruistically. **Altruism** is helping behavior that is beneficial to others but clearly requires self-sacrifice. For example, an instance in which a person runs into a burning house to rescue a stranger's child might be considered altruistic, particularly when compared to the alternative of calling the fire department.

Altruism (AL tru iz um): *Helping behavior that is beneficial to others while requiring sacrifice on the part of the helper*

Some research suggests that individuals who intervene in emergency situations tend to have certain personality characteristics that differentiate them from nonhelpers. For example, Shotland (1984) suggests that helpers tend to be more self-assured, and other research suggests that individuals who are characteristically high in **empathy**—a personality trait in which an individual observing another person experiences the emotions of that person—are more likely to respond to others' needs (Eisenberg-Berg & Mussen, 1978). Still, most social psychologists agree that there is no single set of attributes that differentiate helpers from nonhelpers; situational factors play the predominant role in determining whether or not an individual intervenes in a situation requiring aid.

Empathy (EM pah thee): *One person's experiencing of another's emotions, leading to an increased likelihood of responding to the other's needs*

The Informed Consumer of Psychology: Learning to Be Helpful

Our earlier description of the Kitty Genovese attack and the reluctance of bystanders to help raises a crucial question. Are there ways in which our society can promote prosocial behavior to prevent the recurrence of such episodes?

Social psychologists specializing in helping behavior have suggested a number of approaches to teaching the virtues of helping. Among the most important of those approaches are the following:

■ Providing helpful models. One approach emphasizes the importance of providing models who behave in a prosocial manner. Growing out of work on

The model provided by this person placing money in the basket is likely to lead other bystanders to act more generously. (*Jan Lukas/Photo Researchers, Inc.*)

observational learning theory, it suggests that the presence of models who are rewarded for their prosocial behavior can lead to increased prosocial behavior on the part of observers. For example, research shows that viewing another person behaving generously will lead to increased generosity on the part of the observer. Similarly, viewing a selfish model results in more selfish behavior (Rushton, 1975; Staub, 1971).

A now-classic experiment demonstrated quite directly the effects of modeling on helping. In the study, subjects in one condition passed by a man helping a woman change a flat tire on a busy highway. A quarter mile later, they came across another woman with a flat tire, but this time she was alone and appeared to be in need of assistance. The experimental question was how many people would stop to help, in comparison with a condition in which the passersby had not first seen a helpful model. The results showed that the model was effective in producing helping behavior. In the no-model condition, only 35 of 4,000 passersby stopped, while more than double that figure stopped to offer aid to the second woman in the model condition (Bryan & Test, 1967).

- Using moral admonitions. Another approach to promoting prosocial behavior involves the use of moral admonitions. When parents teach their children the golden rule, or politicians say, "Do what is best for your country, not for yourselves," they are providing a form of moral education. How effective are such moral admonitions? Unfortunately, most research suggests that they do not work particularly well. In fact, most work shows that compared with individuals who actually behave helpfully, models who just *preach* prosocial behavior are considerably less effective in eliciting helping behavior in observers (Grusec & Skubiski, 1970).
- Teaching moral reasoning. One further approach to promoting prosocial behavior is to try to actually teach moral reasoning. Based on Kohlberg's model of moral reasoning (see Chapter 10), the technique involves presenting moral dilemmas, creating conflicts between various solutions to the dilemmas, and helping people to take the perspective of those involved in the dilemma in order to illustrate that many points of view must be considered simultaneously (Hersh, Paolitto, & Reimer, 1979).

Each of these techniques is promising, although there is as yet no definitive data indicating their effectiveness in actually raising the incidence of prosocial behavior (Kaplan, 1983). Still, considered together, they do appear to be reasonable approaches to bringing about a society in which helping behavior is the rule instead of the exception.

RECAP AND REVIEW III

Recap

- Aggression refers to intentional injury or harm to another person. Some theories view aggression as instinctual, while others view it as a reaction to frustration. Another approach, based on observational learning theory, concentrates on the way in which aggression is learned and modeled from others.
- There is strong evidence linking aggression viewed in media—both from television programs and in pornography—to subsequent aggression, although a cause-and-effect link has yet to be established.
- Each of the major approaches to aggression suggests ways of reducing aggression and observational learning theories suggest removing frustration, employing nonaggressive models, and rewarding nonaggressive behavior.

- Diffusion of responsibility is the tendency for people to feel that responsibility is shared among bystanders at an emergency. The more people present, then, the greater the diffusion of responsibility, and, consequently, the less helping behavior that will occur.
- Helping involves four steps: (1) Noticing a person, event, or situation that may require help; (2) interpreting the event as one that requires help; (3) assuming responsibility for taking action; and (4) deciding on and implementing the form of assistance.
- Helping behavior can be increased through providing helpful models, moral admonitions, and teaching moral reasoning.

Review

1.
   a. A model **b.** Aggressive cues **c.** Pent-up aggressive urges **d.** Innate urges
2. Observational learning theorists state that a person is most likely to imitate the aggressive behavior of a model if the consequences of the model's behavior are
   a. Positive **b.** Negative **c.** Expected **d.** Neutral
3. Michael has been hitting his younger brother frequently. His parents have asked him to stop it, but he persists. Based on research on reducing aggression, their best approach would be to
   a. Punish Michael by spanking him **b.** Reward him for nonaggressive behavior **c.** Provide him with a punching bag to vent his aggression **d.** Remove as many of the aggressive cues as possible in his environment
4. Diffusion of responsibility predicts that, in general, the more people who are present in an emergency, the more apt each will be to join with others and help out. True or false?
5. Helping behavior which is beneficial to others but requires self-sacrifice is known as ____________________.
6. List three promising approaches suggested by social psychologists to teach the virtues of prosocial behavior.

(Answers to review questions are at the bottom of page 514.)

Psychology Looks Toward the 1990s
Hot Flashes: Environmental Psychology

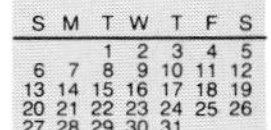

Earthquake. Overcrowding. Volcanic eruption. Landslide. Avalanche. Chemical waste spill. Acid rain. Famine.

We are all aware of the fragility of our environment. What is less obvious is the degree to which our behavior is influenced by the physical environment in which we live. In fact, it is only relatively recently that psychologists have recognized the impact of the environment by developing a relatively new branch of the field, known as environmental psychology. **Environmental psychology** considers the relationship between the environment and people's behavior and sense of well-being.

Environmental psychology: *The branch of psychology that studies the relationship between people and the environment*

One of the major areas of interest of environmental psychologists has been the study of **crowding,** the unpleasant psychological and subjective state relating to how a person reacts to the density of the environment (Baum & Paulhus, 1986). Crowding has wide-ranging effects upon our behavior in a variety of ways—some of which are surprisingly powerful. For example, higher rates of illness are related to crowding in several kinds of settings. Thus, one study showed that college students who live in dormitories of higher density pay more visits to the student health center than those living in low-density housing (Baron, Mandel, Adams, & Griffen, 1976). Even more striking are findings showing that the death rates for inmates in a state psychiatric prison were related to the population density. As the prison population grew, so did the per capita death rate; and as it fell, the death rate followed suit (Paulus & McCain, 1983; Paulus, McCain, & Cox, 1978).

Crowding: *An unpleasant psychological and subjective state involving people's reaction to the density of their environment*

Crowding has similar—although not as deadly—effects on interpersonal attraction: People are less likely to like one another under conditions of high density than when the density is lower. For instance, college students housed in rooms built for two who were forced to cram in a third person liked their roommates less and viewed one another as less cooperative than those in less crowded conditions (Baron, Mandel, Adams, & Greiffen, 1976). Even when density is lower, people prefer double rooms over triple rooms; in triples, there is a tendency for two of the roommates to form a close relationship, isolating the third one and leaving all three less satisfied with the situation (Aiello, Baum, & Gormley, 1980).

Finally, crowding leads to decreases in helping behavior, increases in aggression, and declines in the level of performance on various tasks (Holahan, 1982). Despite the seemingly unrelentingly negative view of crowding, however, the picture is not universally gloomy. For instance, field studies of residential areas in which social density is extremely high—such as in Hong Kong, one of the most densely populated areas of the world—show little or no negative effects that could be attributed to housing density (Mitchell, 1971). It may be that people eventually adapt to crowded conditions, particularly when their neighbors are living under the same circumstances.

Other aspects of the physical environment are also being shown to have broad effects on human behavior. For example, the incidence of aggressive crime is related to the temperature of the air. According to a comprehensive, two-year analysis of rapes and murders in the Houston, Texas, metropolitan area, as well as an examination of national crime data, the number of violent crimes tends to rise sharply as the temperature increases (Anderson & Anderson, 1984; Anderson, 1987).

These findings are consistent with other research findings suggesting that air temperature is related to the incidence of riots—a common explanation for the large-scale urban rioting that occurred during the 1960s. Indeed, laboratory research supports the view that aggression is related to air temperature, although the relationship is complex (Baron & Ransberger, 1978). Specifically, aggression seems to rise as air temperature increases, but only up to a certain level. When it gets *too* hot, people may prefer flight over fight and leave the situation.

The results of work showing a relationship between heat and aggression suggest several mechanisms which might help to reduce the level of violent crime associated with high temperature. For one thing, institutions that are prone to relatively high levels of violence, such as prisons, might be air-conditioned. Moreover, we might attempt to reduce the major frustrations that are found in people's lives—through such measures as providing job training for those who live in poorer, unair-conditioned areas of cities. Finally, it might be possible to make people more aware of the propensity of heat to increase aggression, allowing them to identify when the heat is producing negative affective states and making them better able to combat its affects.

ANSWERS TO REVIEW QUESTIONS

Review III: **1.** b **2.** a **3.** b **4.** False **5.** Altruism **6.** Providing helpful models, using moral admonitions, and teaching moral reasoning

LOOKING BACK

1. Social influence is the area of social psychology concerned with situations in which the actions of an individual or group affect the behavior of others.

2. Conformity refers to changes in behavior that occur as the result of a desire to follow the beliefs or standards of others. Among the factors affecting conformity are the nature of the group, the nature of the response required, the kind of task, and the unanimity of the group.

3. Compliance occurs when there is direct, explicit pressure to obey someone else. Among the ways to remain independent are through innoculation, forewarning, and consistency.

4. The study of interpersonal attraction, or close relationships, considers liking and loving. Among the primary determinants of liking are proximity, mere exposure, similarity, and physical attractiveness.

5. Love is distinguished from liking by the presence of intense physiological arousal, an all-encompassing interest in another, fantasies about the other, rapid swings of emotion, fascination, sexual desire, exclusiveness, and strong feelings of caring. According to Sternberg, love is made up of three components: intimacy, passion, and decision/commitment.

6. Recent work has examined the maintenance and deterioration of relationships. Partners in lasting marriages tend to be remarkably similar in their perceptions of what made their marriage endure. Several programs have been developed to teach couples techniques to prevent the deterioration of their relationship.

7. Aggression is the intentional injury or harm to another person. Instinct approaches suggest that humans have an innate drive to behave aggressively and that if aggression is not released through socially desirable ways, it will be discharged in some other form—a belief for which there is relatively little support. Frustration-aggression theory suggests that frustration produces a readiness to be aggressive—if there are aggressive cues present. Finally, observational learning theory hypothesizes that aggression is learned through reinforcement—particularly reinforcement that is given to models. Each of the approaches suggests means of reducing aggressive behavior.

8. Helping behavior in emergencies is influenced by the phenomenon of diffusion of responsibility, which results in a lower likelihood that helping will occur when more people are present. Deciding to help is the outcome of a four-stage process, which consists of noticing a possible need for help, interpreting the situation as one that requires help, assuming responsibility for taking action, and deciding on and implementing the form of assistance. Techniques for promoting prosocial behavior include providing helpful models, using moral admonitions, and teaching moral reasoning.

KEY TERMS AND CONCEPTS

social influence (p. 490)
conformity (p. 491)
status (p. 492)
social supporter (p. 493)
compliance (p. 493)
inoculation (p. 495)
forewarning (p. 495)
consistency (p. 495)
interpersonal attraction (p. 496)
close relationships (p. 496)
proximity (p. 497)
reciprocity-of-liking effect (p. 497)
aggression (p. 504)
innate (p. 505)
frustration (p. 506)
aggressive cues (p. 506)
catharsis hypothesis (p. 508)
prosocial behavior (p. 510)
diffusion of responsibility (p. 510)
rewards-costs approach (p. 510)
altruism (p. 511)
empathy (p. 511)
environmental psychology (p. 513)
crowding (p. 513)

FOR FURTHER STUDY AND APPLICATION

Cialdini, R. (1984). *Social influence.* New York: Morrow.

A very readable, informative, and enjoyable book, this text is filled with practical insights regarding persuasion and other forms of social influence.

Hendrick, C., & Hendrick, S. (1983). *Liking, loving, and relating.* Monterey, CA: Brooks/Cole.

This is an excellent overview of the topics of liking and loving, written in an open and accessible fashion. The rise and fall of relationships are clearly described.

Nadler, A., Fisher, J. D., & DePaulo, B. M. (1983). *Applied research in help-seeking and reactions to aid.* New York: Acedemic Press.

This volume contains a number of applications relating to helping behavior, especially in field settings. Although there are many technical details, the layperson can get a good sense of the work.

Malamuth, N. M., & Donnerstein, E. (1984). *Pornography and sexual aggression.* New York: Academic Press.

Readers interested in the current state of knowledge regarding the relationship between pornography and aggression should refer to this book, which provides the most up-to-date information about the topic.

APPENDIX

GOING BY THE NUMBERS: STATISTICS IN PSYCHOLOGY

PROLOGUE

LOOKING AHEAD

DESCRIPTIVE STATISTICS
Finding the average: The mean
Finding the middle: The median
Finding what is most frequent: The mode
Comparing the three M's:
  Mean versus median versus mode
Recap and review I

MEASURES OF VARIABILITY
Highest to lowest: The range
Differences from the mean: The standard deviation
Recap and review II

USING STATISTICS TO ANSWER QUESTIONS: INFERENTIAL STATISTICS AND CORRELATION
Measuring relationships: The correlation coefficient
The informed consumer of psychology:
  Evaluating statistics
Recap and review III

LOOKING BACK

KEY TERMS AND CONCEPTS

FOR FURTHER STUDY AND APPLICATION

PROLOGUE

As the boat moved closer to shore, the outline of the Statue of Liberty was plainly visible in the distance. Closer and closer it came, sending a chill down the spine of Ampelio Carucci. A symbol of America, the statue represented the hopes he carried from his native Sicily in this year of 1908—hopes of liberty, of success, of a life free of economic and social concern.

Yet as the boat moved closer to Ellis Island, the first point of debarkation in the United States, Carucci did not realize that his very presence—and that of the other thousands of immigrants seeking their fortune in a land of opportunity—was threatened. A strong political movement was growing in the country on which he was pinning his hopes. This movement sought, by using information collected by psychologists, to stem the flow of immigrants through "scientific" analysis of data.

The major assertion of this group was that a flood of mentally deficient immigrants was poisoning the intellectual capacity of the United States. To proponents of this view, unless drastic measures were taken, it would not be too many years before western civilization collapsed from a lack of collective intelligence.

To support this assertion, Lathrop Stoddard, a member of the anti-immigration movement, reported the results of a study of intelligence in which tests were administered to a group of 82 children and 400 adults. On the basis of these test results, he concluded that the average mental age of Americans was only 14 years—proof to him that unlimited immigration had already seriously eroded American mental capacity.

LOOKING AHEAD

Fortunately for immigrants such as Ampelio Carucci, observers in favor of immigration pointed out the fallacy of using data from a relatively small sample—when a considerably larger set of intelligence test data was available. Specifically, the Army had been collecting intelligence data for years and had the test scores of 1.7 million men available. When these scores were analyzed, it was immediately apparent that the claim that the average mental age of American adults was 14 years was completely without merit.

A debate reminiscent of this earlier one rages today, as some observers suggest that an unrestrained flow of immigrants—this time from Latin America and Asia—would seriously damage the United States. This time, though, the debate is based more on analyses of social and economic statistics, with opponents of immigration suggesting that the social fabric of the country will be changed and that jobs are being taken away from longer-term residents because of the influx of immigrants. Equally vehement proponents of immigration suggest that the relevant statistics are being misinterpreted, and that *their* analyses of the situation result in a quite different conclusion.

Statistics: *The branch of mathematics concerned with collecting, organizing, analyzing, and drawing conclusions from numerical data*

Statistics, the branch of mathematics concerned with collecting, organizing, analyzing, and drawing conclusions from numerical data, is a part of all our lives. For instance, all of us are familiar with the claims and counterclaims regarding the effects of smoking. The U.S. government requires that cigarette manuracturers include a warning that smoking is dangerous to people's health on every package of cigarettes and in their advertisements; the government's data show clear statistical links between smoking and disease. At the same time, the American Tobacco Institute questions in its advertisements that there is any scientific validity to the claim that smoking is dangerous, for, according to its statistics, the data are inconclusive.

Statistics also lie at the heart of a considerable number of debates within the field of psychology. How do we determine the nature and strength of the effects of heredity on behavior? What is the relationship between learning and schedules of reinforcement? How do we know if the "double standard" of male and female sexual practices has shifted over time? These questions, and most others of interest to psychologists, cannot be answered without a reliance on statistics.

In this appendix, we consider the basic approaches to statistical measurement. We first discuss approaches to summarizing data that allow us to describe sets of observations. Next, we consider techniques for deciding how different one set of scores is from another. Finally, we examine approaches to measuring the relationship between two sets of scores.

After reading and studying this material, then, you will be able to

- Identify and describe measures that are used to summarize sets of data
- Calculate the basic statistical measures
- Describe the strengths and weaknesses of the basic statistical procedures
- Describe techniques for determining the nature of a relationship and the significance of differences between two sets of scores
- Define and apply the key terms and concepts listed at the end of the appendix

DESCRIPTIVE STATISTICS

Suppose, as a teacher of college psychology, you wanted to evaluate your class's performance on its initial exam. Where might you begin?

You would probably start by using **descriptive statistics**, the branch of statistics that provides a means of summarizing data. For instance, you might first simply list the scores the pupils had received on the test:

Descriptive statistics: *The branch of statistics that provides a means of summarizing data*

72 78 78 92 69 73

85 49 86 86 72 59

58 85 89 80 83 69

78 90 90 96 83

Viewed in this way, the scores are a jumble of numbers that are difficult to make any sense of. However, there are several methods by which you could begin to organize the scores in a more meaningful way. For example, you might sort them in order of highest to lowest score, as is done in Table A-1. By indicating the number of people who obtained each score, you would have produced what is called a **frequency distribution**, an arrangement of scores from a sample that indicates how often a particular score is present.

Frequency distribution: *An arrangement of scores from a sample that indicates how often a particular score is present*

Another way of summarizing the scores is to consider them visually. For example, you could construct a **histogram** or bar graph, shown in Figure A-1. In the histogram, the number of people obtaining a given score is represented pictorially. The scores are ordered along one dimension of the graph, and the number of people obtaining each score along the other dimension.

Histogram (HISS toe gram): *A bar graph used to represent data graphically*

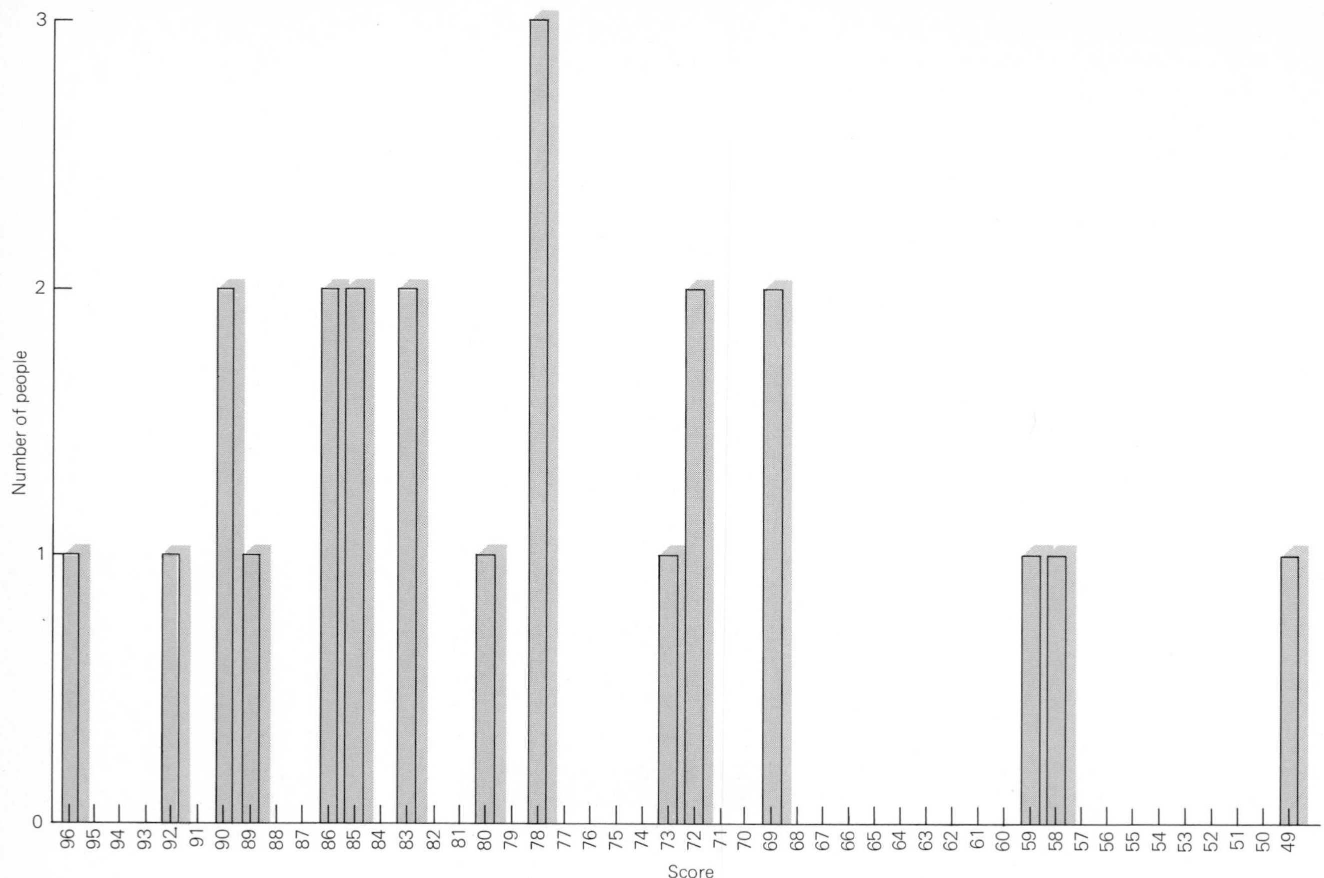

Figure A-1
In this histogram, the number of people obtaining each score is represented by a bar.

TABLE A-1

A sample frequency distribution

SCORE	NUMBER OF PEOPLE ATTAINING THAT SCORE
96	1
92	1
90	2
89	1
86	2
85	2
83	2
80	1
78	3
73	1
72	2
69	2
59	1
58	1
49	1

Arranging the scores from highest to lowest allows us to visually interpret the data. Most often, however, visual inspection is insufficient. For one thing, there may be so many scores in a sample that it is impossible to construct a meaningful visual representation. For another, as the research that we discussed in Chapter 4 suggests, our perceptions of the meaning of stimuli are often biased and inaccurate; more precise, mathematically based measures would seem to be preferable. In cases in which a precise means of summarizing the data is desirable, then, psychologists turn to measures of **central tendency**, the most representative score in a distribution of scores. There are three major measures of central tendency: the mean, the median, and the mode.

Central tendency: *The most representative score in a distribution of scores (the mean, median, and mode are measures of central tendency)*

Finding the Average: The Mean

The most familiar measure of central tendency is the mean. A **mean** is the technical term for an average, which is simply the sum of all the scores in a set, divided by the number of scores making up the set. For example, to calculate the mean of the sample we have been using, begin by adding each of the numbers (96 + 92 + 90 + 90 + 89 + . . . and so forth). When you have the total, divide this sum by the number of cases, which is 23. This calculation, 1800 ÷ 23 = 78.26, produces a mean score, or average, for our sample, then, of 78.26.

Mean: *The average of all scores, arrived at by adding scores together and dividing by the number of scores*

In general, the mean is an accurate reflection of the central score in a set of scores; as you can see from the histogram in Figure A-1, our mean of 78.26 falls roughly in the center of the distribution of scores. Yet the mean does not always provide the best measure of central tendency. For one thing, the mean is very sensitive to extreme scores. As an example, imagine that we added two additional scores of 20 and 22 to our sample of scores. The mean would now become 1842 ÷ 25, or 73.68, a drop of almost 5 points. Because of its sensitivity to extreme scores, then, the mean can sometimes present a deceptive picture of a set of scores, especially where the mean is based on a relatively small number of scores.

Finding the Middle: The Median

A measure of central tendency that is less sensitive to extreme scores than the mean is the median. The **median** is the point in a distribution of scores that divides the distribution exactly in half. For example, consider a distribution of five scores 10, 8, 7, 4, and 3. The point that divides the distribution exactly in half is the score 7: Two scores in the distribution lie above the 7 score, while two scores lie below it. If there are an even number of scores in a distribution—in which case there would be no score lying in the middle—the two middle scores would be averaged. If our distribution consisted of scores of 10, 8, 7, 6, 4, and 3, then, we would average the two middle scores of 7 and 6 to form a median of 7 + 6 divided by 2, or 13 ÷ 2 = 6.5.

Median: *The point in a distribution of scores that divides the distribution exactly in half when the scores are listed in numerical order*

In our original sample test scores, there are twenty-three scores. The score that divides the distribution exactly in half will be the twelfth score in the frequency distribution of scores, since the twelfth score has eleven scores above it and eleven below it. If you count down to the twelfth score in the distribution depicted in Table A-1 you will see the score is 80. Therefore, the median of the distribution is 80.

One advantage of the median as a measure of central tendency is that it is insensitive to extreme scores. For example, adding the scores of 20 and 22 to our distribution would change the median no more than adding scores of 48 and

47 to the distribution. The reason is clear: The median divides a set of scores in half, and the magnitude of the scores is of no consequence in this process.

The median is often used instead of the mean when extreme scores might be misleading. For example, government statistics on income are typically presented using the median as the measure of central tendency, since the median corrects for the small number of extreme cases of very wealthy individuals, whose high incomes might otherwise inflate the mean income.

Finding What Is Most Frequent: The Mode

Mode: *The most frequently occurring score in a set of scores*

The final measure of central tendency is the mode. The **mode** is the most frequently occurring score in a set of scores. If you return to the distribution in Table A-1, you can see that three people scored 78, and the frequency of all of the other scores is either 2 or 1. The mode for the distribution, then, is 78.

Some distributions, of course, might have more than one score occurring most frequently. For instance, we could imagine that if the distribution had an additional score of 86 added to the two that are already there, there would be two most frequently occurring categories: 78 and now 86. In this instance, we would say there are two modes—a case known as a **bimodal distribution.**

Bimodal distribution: *Cases in which a frequency distribution includes two modes*

The mode is often used as a measure of preference or popularity. For instance, if teachers wanted to know who was the most popular child in their elementary school classrooms, they might develop a questionnaire which asked the students to choose someone with whom they would like to participate in some activity. After the choices were tallied, the mode would probably provide the best indication of which child was most popular.

Comparing the Three M's: Mean versus Median versus Mode

If a sample is sufficiently large, there is generally little difference between the mean, median, and mode. The reason is that with large samples, scores typically form what is called a normal distribution. A **normal distribution** is a distribution of scores that produces the bell-shaped curve displayed in Figure A-2, in which the right half mirrors the left half.

Normal distribution: *A distribution of scores that produces a bell-shaped, symmetrical curve*

Most large distributions, those containing many scores, produce a normal curve. For instance, if you asked a large number of students how many hours a week they studied, you might expect to find that most studied within a similar range of hours, while there would be a few who studied many, many hours, and some very few who studied not at all. There would be many scores in the center of the distribution of scores, then, and only a few at the extremes—producing a normal distribution. Many phenomena of interest to psychologists

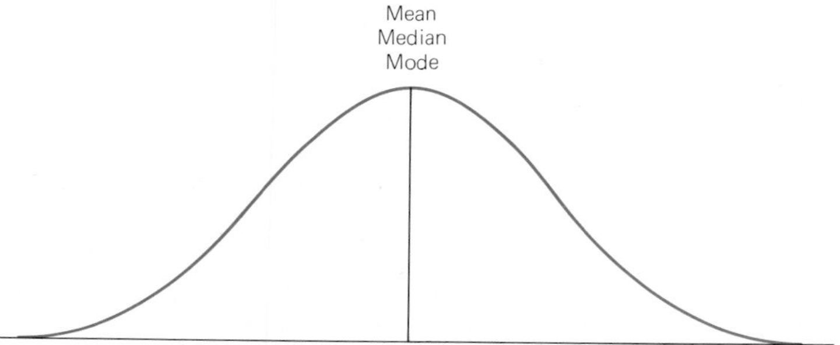

Figure A-2
In a normal distribution, the mean, median, and mode are identical, falling at the center of the distribution.

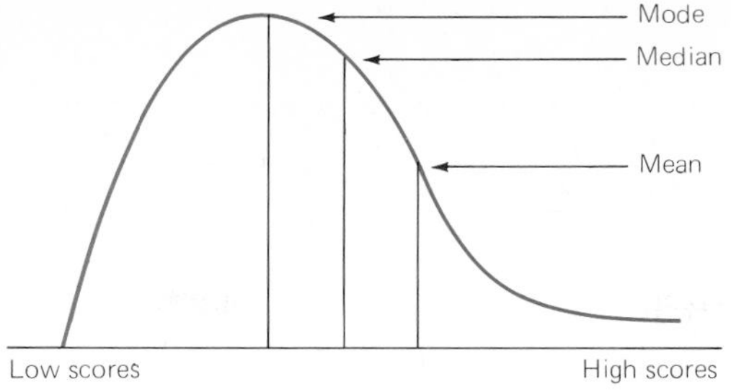

Figure A-3
In this skewed distribution, most scores are low.

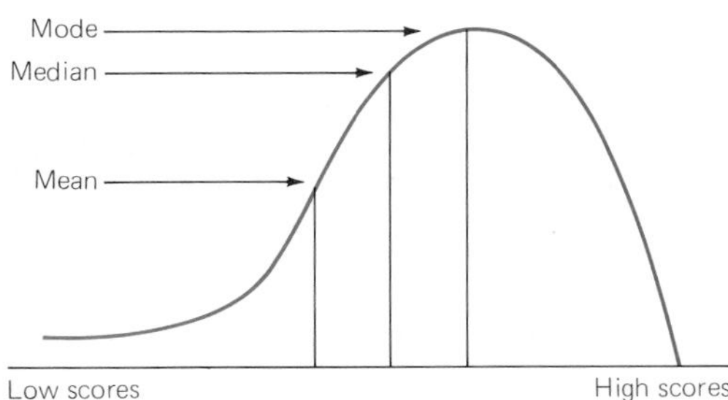

Figure A-4
In this example of a skewed distribution, there tend to be more high scores than low ones.

produce a normal curve when graphed. For example, if you turn to Figure 8-1 in Chapter 8, where the distribution of intelligence scores is given, you can see the pattern of scores falls into a normal distribution.

The mean, median, and the mode fall at exactly the same point in a normal distribution. This means that in a normal distribution of scores, the mean score will divide the distribution exactly in half (the median), and it will be the most frequently occurring score in the distribution (the mode).

The mean, median, and mode differ, however, when distributions are not normal. In cases in which the distributions are **skewed**, or not symmetrical, there is a ''hump'' at one end or the other (see Figures A-3 and A-4). For instance, if we gave a calculus exam to a group of students enrolled in an elementary algebra class, we would expect that most students would fail the test, leading to low scores being overrepresented in the distribution, as in Figure A-3. On the other hand, if we gave the same students a test of elementary addition problems, the scores would probably form a distribution in which high scores predominated, such as in Figure A-4. Both distributions are skewed, although in opposite directions, and the mean, median, and mode are different from one another.

Skewed distribution: *A distribution that is not normal and therefore creates a curve that is not symmetrical*

RECAP AND REVIEW I

Recap

- Statistics is the branch of mathematics concerned with collecting, organizing, analyzing, and drawing conclusions from numerical data.
- Descriptive statistics is the branch of statistics that provides a means of summarizing data.
- Measures of central tendency provide an index of where the centermost point in a distribution of scores lies. The most common measures of central tendency are the mean, median, and mode.

Review

1. A frequency distribution of numbers could be displayed pictorially by constructing a bar graph, or ______________ .
2. Match each item in the left-hand column with the corresponding item in the right-hand column.
   a. ____ Mean = 10.0 (1.) 2, 8, 10, 12, 13, 18
   b. ____ Median = 11 (2.) 4, 5, 10, 10, 15, 16
   c. ____ Mode = 12 (3.) 4, 5, 12, 12, 12, 16
3. The mean, median, and mode are measures of ______________ ______________ .
4. Professor Peters explains to the class that most of the forty exam scores fell within a B range, but there were two extremely high scores. Should she report the median or the mean as a measure of central tendency?
5. The mean, median, and mode will differ in a normal distribution. True or false?

(Answers to review questions are at the bottom of page 526.)

MEASURES OF VARIABILITY

Although measures of central tendency provide us with information about where the center of a distribution lies, often this information is insufficient. For example, suppose a psychologist was interested in determining the nature of people's eye movements while they were reading in order to perfect a new method of teaching reading. It would not be enough to know how *most* people moved their eyes (information that a measure of central tendency would provide); it would also be important to know how much individual people's eye movements differed or varied from one another.

Variability: *The spread or dispersion, of scores in a distribution*

A second important characteristic of a set of scores provides this information: variability. **Variability** is a term that refers to the spread of scores in a distribution. Figure A-5 contains two distributions of scores that have identical means, but which differ in variability. Measures of variability provide a means of describing the spread of scores in a distribution.

Highest to Lowest: The Range

Range: *The highest score in a distribution minus the lowest score*

The simplest measure of variability is the range. A **range** is the highest score in a distribution minus the lowest score. In the set of scores, presented in Table A-1 the distribution has a range of 47 (96 − 49 = 47).

The fact that a range is simple to calculate is about the only virtue it has. The problem with this particular measure of variability is that it is based entirely on extreme scores, and a single score that is very different from the others in a distribution can distort the picture of the distribution as a whole. For example, the addition of a score of 20 to the test score distribution in Table A-1 would almost double the range measure, even though the variability of the remaining scores in the distribution has not changed at all.

Differences from the Mean: The Standard Deviation

Standard deviation: *An index of how far an average score in a distribution of scores deviates from the distribution's center*

The most frequently used method of characterizing the variability of a distribution of scores is the **standard deviation**. The standard deviation bears a conceptual relationship to a mean. You will recall that the mean is the average score in a distribution of scores. A standard deviation is related to the mean in that it provides an index of how far an average score in a distribution of scores deviates from the center of the distribution.

Consider, for instance, the distributions in Figure A-5. The distribution on the left is widely dispersed and on the average an individual score in the distri-

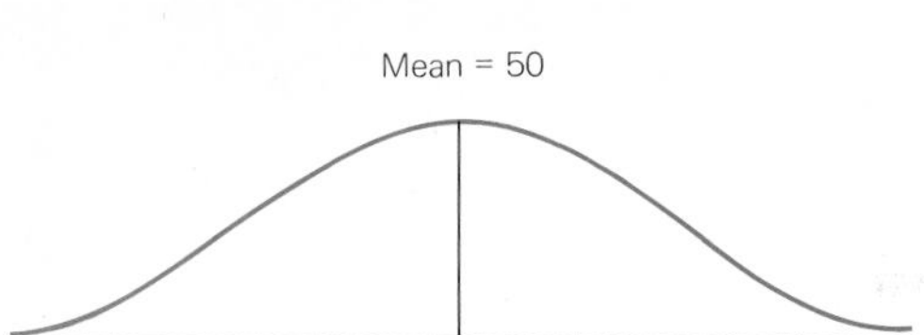

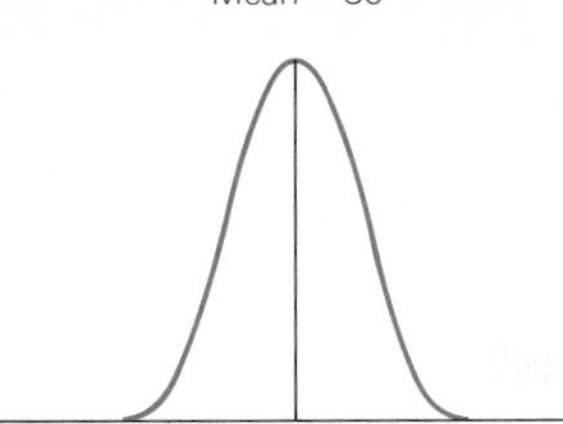

Figure A-5
Although the mean is identical in these two distributions, the variability, or spread of scores, is very different.

bution can be thought of as deviating quite a bit from the center of the distribution. Certainly the scores in the distribution on the left are going to deviate more from the center of the distribution than those in the distribution on the right.

On the other hand, in the distribution on the right, the scores are closely packed together and there is little deviation of a typical score from the center of the distribution. Based on this analysis, then, it would be expected that a good measure of variability would yield a larger value for the distribution on the left than it would for the one on the right—and, in fact, a standard deviation would do exactly this by indicating how far away a typical score lies from the center of the distribution.

TABLE A-2

Calculating a standard deviation

1. The calculation of a standard deviation begins with the calculation of the mean of distribution. In the following distribution of scores on a psychology student's weekly quizzes, the mean is 84.5: 82, 88, 71, 86, 96, 84. (As you recall, the mean is the sum of the scores divided by the number of scores in the distribution, or 507 ÷ 6 = 84.5.)
2. The next step is to produce a deviation score for each score in the distribution. A deviation score is simply an original score minus the mean of all the scores in a distribution. This has been done in the second column below:

ORIGINAL SCORE	DEVIATION SCORE*	DEVIATION SCORE SQUARED
82	−2.5	6.25
88	3.5	12.25
71	−13.5	182.25
86	1.5	2.25
96	11.5	132.25
84	−.5	.25

*Original score minus the mean of 84.5.

3. In the third step, the deviation scores are squared (multiplied by themselves) to eliminate negative numbers. This has been carried out in the third column above.
4. The squared deviation scores are then added together, and this sum is divided by the number of scores. In the example above, the sum of the deviation scores is 6.25 + 12.25 + 182.25 + 2.25 + 132.25 + .25 = 335.50, and 335.50 ÷ 6 = 55.916.
5. The final step is to take the square root of the resulting number. The square root of 55.916 is 7.4777—which is the standard deviation of the distribution of scores.

The calculation of the standard deviation follows the logic of calculating the difference of individual scores from the mean of the distribution, and the exact technique is presented in Table A-2. It provides an excellent indicator of the variability of a set of scores because it is based on all of the scores within a set and because it is not highly sensitive to extreme scores. Moreover, the standard deviation provides a means for converting initial scores on standardized tests such as the Scholastic Aptitude Test (SAT) into the scales used to report results. In this way, it is possible to make a score of 585 on the verbal section of the SAT exam, for example, equivalent from one year to the next, even though the specific test items differ from year to year.

RECAP AND REVIEW II

Recap

- Measures of variability provide an index of the dispersion, or spread, of a distribution of scores.
- The range and standard deviation are the most commonly used measures of variability.

Review

1. A measure of variability based solely on the distance between the most extreme scores is the
   a. Spread **b.** Standard deviation **c.** Deviation score **d.** Range
2. By simply eyeing the following sets of numbers, predict which will have a higher standard deviation:
   a. 6, 8, 10, 10, 11, 12, 13
   b. 2, 5, 8, 11, 16, 17, 18
3. Calculate the mean and standard deviation for set **a** and **b** in the previous question.
4. The standard deviation is highly sensitive to extreme scores. True or false?

(Answers to review questions are at the bottom of page 528.)

USING STATISTICS TO ANSWER QUESTIONS: INFERENTIAL STATISTICS AND CORRELATION

Suppose you were a psychologist who was interested in whether there was a relationship between smoking and anxiety. Would it be reasonable to simply look at a group of smokers and measure their anxiety using some rating scale? Probably not, since—as we discussed in Chapter 1—it would clearly be more informative if you compared their anxiety to the anxiety exhibited by a group of nonsmokers.

Once you had decided to observe anxiety in two groups of people, you would have to determine just who would be your subjects. In an ideal world with unlimited resources, you might contact *every* smoker and nonsmoker, since these are the two populations with which you are concerned. A **population** consists of all the members of a group of interest. Obviously, however, this would be impossible, given the all-encompassing size of the two groups; instead, you

Population: *All the members of the group being studied*

ANSWERS TO REVIEW QUESTIONS

Review I: **1.** Histogram **2.** a.2; b.1; c.3 **3.** Central tendency **4.** The median; the mean is too sensitive to extreme scores. **5.** False; they will be equal.

would limit your subjects to a sample of smokers and nonsmokers. A **sample**, in formal statistical terms, is a subgroup of a population of interest that is representative of the larger population. Once you had identified samples representative of the population of interest to you, it would be possible to carry out your study, yielding two distributions of scores—one from the smokers and one from the nonsmokers.

Sample: *A subgroup of a population of interest*

The obvious question is whether the two samples differ in the degree of anxiety displayed by their members. The statistical procedures that we have been discussing earlier are helpful in answering this question, since each of the two samples can be examined in terms of central tendency and variability. The more important question, though, is whether the magnitude of difference between the two distributions is sufficient to conclude that the distributions truly differ from one another, or if, instead, the differences are attributable merely to chance. To answer this question, one must turn to a different sort of statistical technique.

To answer the question of whether samples are truly different from one another, psychologists use **inferential statistics**, the branch of statistics that uses data from samples to make predictions about a larger population. To take a simple example, suppose you had two coins that were each flipped 100 times. Suppose further that one coin came up heads forty-one times and the other came up heads sixty-five times. Are both coins fair? We know that a fair coin should come up heads about fifty times in 100 flips. But a little thought would also suggest that it is unlikely that even a fair coin would come up heads exactly fifty times in 100 flips. The question is, then, how far could a coin deviate from fifty heads before the coin would be considered unfair?

Inferential statistics: *The branch of statistics that uses data from samples to make predictions about the larger population from which the sample is drawn*

Questions such as this—as well as whether the results found are due to chance or represent unexpected, nonchance findings—revolve around how "probable" certain events are. Using coin flipping as an example, fifty-three heads in a hundred flips would be a highly probable outcome since it departs only slightly from the expected outcome of fifty heads. In contrast, if a coin was flipped 100 times and 90 of those times it came up heads, it would be a highly improbable outcome. In fact, 90 heads out of 100 flips should occur by chance only one time in 2 million trials of 100 flips of a fair coin. Ninety heads in a hundred flips, then, is an extremely improbable outcome; if ninety heads did appear, the odds would be that the coin or the flipping process was rigged.

Inferential statistics are used to mathematically determine the probability of observed events. Using inferential statistics to evaluate the result of an experiment, psychologists are able to calculate the likelihood of whether the difference is a reflection of a true difference between populations. For example, suppose we find that the mean on an anxiety scale is 68 for smokers, and 48 for nonsmokers. Inferential statistical procedures allow us to determine whether this difference is really meaningful, or whether we might expect the same difference to occur merely because of chance factors.

Results of inferential statistical procedures are described in terms of measures of significance. To a psychologist, a **significant outcome** is one in which the observed outcome would be expected to occur by chance less than five times out of a hundred. Put another way, a significant difference between two means says that there is a 95 percent or better probability that the difference an experimenter has found is due to real differences between two groups rather than to chance.

Significant outcome: *An outcome expected to occur by chance less than 5 percent of the time*

Measuring Relationships: The Correlation Coefficient

How do we know if television viewing is related to aggression, if reading romance novels is related to sexual behavior, or if mothers' IQs are related to their daughters'?

Scatterplot: *A means of graphically illustrating the relationship between two variables*

Each of these questions revolves around the issue of the degree of relationship between two variables. One way of answering them is to draw a **scatterplot**, a means of graphically illustrating the relationship between two variables. We would first collect two sets of paired measures and assign one score to the horizontal axis (variable X) and the other score to the vertical axis (variable Y). Then we would draw a dot at the place where the two scores meet on the graph.

Positive relationship: *A relationship established by data that shows high values of one variable corresponding with high values of another, and low values of the first variable corresponding with low values of the other*

Negative relationship: *A relationship established by data that shows high values of one variable corresponding with low values of the other*

The three scatterplots illustrated in Figure A-6 present typical situations. In the first, there is a **positive relationship**, in which high values of variable X are associated with high values of variable Y and low values of X are associated with low values of Y. In the second, there is a **negative relationship**: As values of variable X increase, the values of variable Y decrease. The third panel of the figure illustrates a situation in which no clear relationship betwen variable X and variable Y exists.

It is also possible to consider scores in terms of their mathematical relationship to one another, rather than simply the way they appear on a scatterplot. Suppose, for example, a psychologist was interested in the degree to which a daughter's IQ was related to the mother's IQ—specifically, if a mother with a high IQ tended to have a daughter who also had a high IQ, and whether a mother with a low IQ tended to have a daughter with a low IQ. The psychologist then went out and measured the IQs of ten mothers and daughters and arranged their IQs as presented in Table A-3.

An inspection of the data present in the table indicates that the mothers and daughters obviously do not have the same IQs. Moreover, they do not even have IQs that are rank-ordered the same in the two columns. For example, the mother with the highest IQ does not have the daughter with the highest IQ, and the mother with the lowest IQ does not have the daughter with the lowest IQ. It is apparent, then, that there is not a *perfect* relationship between the IQ of the mother and the IQ of the daughter. However, it would be a mistake to conclude that there is a *zero,* or no, relationship betwen the IQs of the mothers and daughters, since it is clear that there is a tendency for mothers who have high IQs to have daughters with high IQs, and that mothers with low IQs tend to have daughters with low IQs.

Correlation coefficient (kor eh LAY shun ko ef FISH ent): *A number that indicates the relationship between two variables*

The statistic that provides a precise mathematical index of the degree to which two variables are related is the correlation coefficient. A **correlation coefficient** is a number that indicates the extent of the relationship between two variables. It ranges in value from $+1.00$ to -1.00. A value of $+1.00$ would indicate that two variables had a perfect positive relationship with one another, meaning that the highest score on one variable would be associated with the highest score on the other variable, the second highest score on the first variable would be associated with the second highest score on the second variable, and so on. A value of -1.00 would indicate that there was a perfect negative relationship between the two variables; the highest score on the first variable would be

ANSWERS TO REVIEW QUESTIONS

Review II: **1.** d **2.** b, because the numbers are more widely dispersed **3.** Mean = 10; standard deviation = 2.20; mean = 11, standard deviation = 5.80 **4.** False

TABLE A-3

IQ scores of mothers and daughters

MOTHER'S IQ	DAUGHTER'S IQ
135	122
128	130
125	110
120	132
114	100
110	116
102	108
96	89
90	84
86	92

associated with the lowest score on the second variable, the second highest score would be associated with the second lowest score, and so forth.

Correlation coefficients around zero indicate that there is no relationship between the two variables. In such cases, there is no tendency for high values on one variable to be associated with either high or low values on the second variable.

Correlation coefficients that range between zero and +1.00 and −1.00 reflect varying degrees of relationship between the two variables. For instance, a value of +.20 or −.20 would indicate that there was a slight relationship between the two variables, a value of around +.50 and −.50 would indicate a moderate relationship, and a value of +.80 or −.80 would indicate a relatively strong relationship between the variables. As an example, if we were to calculate the correlation of the two sets of variables in Table A-3, we would find a correlation which is quite strong: The coefficient is +.86.

It is important to note that finding a positive correlation between two variables does *not* in any way indicate that one variable *causes* changes in another—only that they are associated with one another. While it might seem plausible to us, for example, that it is the mother's intelligence that causes higher intelligence in a daughter, it is just as possible that a daughter's intelligence affects how the mother performs on an IQ test. (Perhaps the daughter's behavior affects the general home environment, affecting the mother's performance on IQ tests.) It is even plausible that some other unmeasured—and previously unconsidered—third variable is causing both mother's and daughter's IQs to increase or decrease simultaneously. In a clear example of this possibility, even if we found that ice cream sales and violent crimes are correlated with one another (as they happen to be), we would not presume that they were causally related. In this case, it is likely they are both influenced by a third factor—the weather.

The crucial point is that even if we find a perfect correlation between two sets of variables, we would not be able to say that the two variables were linked causally—only that they were strongly related to one another.

The Informed Consumer of Psychology: Evaluating Statistics

It has been said that statisticians can sit with their heads in a refrigerator and their feet in an oven and report that, on the average, they feel fine. Yet despite

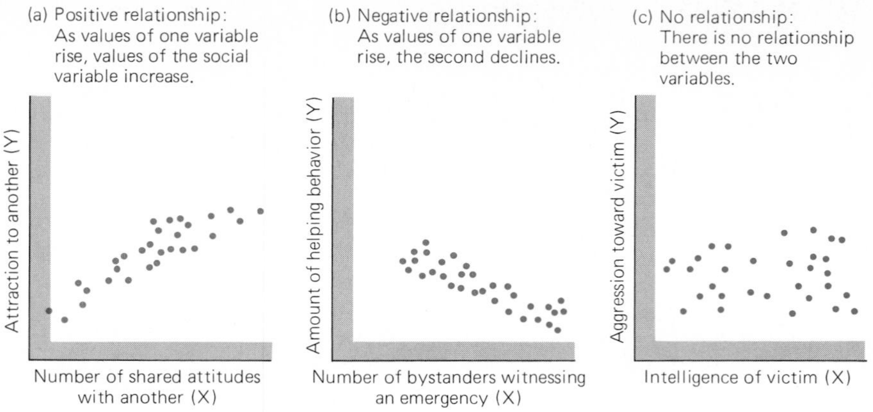

Figure A-6
Scatterplots representing (*a*) a positive relationship between two variables; (*b*) a negative relationship, and (*c*) no clear relationship between two variables.

(a) Positive relationship: As values of one variable rise, values of the social variable increase.

(b) Negative relationship: As values of one variable rise, the second declines.

(c) No relationship: There is no relationship between the two variables.

Attraction to another (Y) / Number of shared attitudes with another (X)

Amount of helping behavior (Y) / Number of bystanders witnessing an emergency (X)

Aggression toward victim (Y) / Intelligence of victim (X)

many people's personal feelings regarding statistics, the science of psychology is built on a statistical foundation. A glance at any report of research in the psychology literature will confirm that analysis of data represents an indispensable element in the advance of the science.

Just because someone publishes a statistical result, however, does not mean that either the statistic or the conclusions based on it are necessarily appropriate. Although it is difficult for a person who is not well versed in statistics to argue effectively with the kind of sophisticated mathematics that you are likely to see in published research articles, there are certain basic questions that you can ask yourself when considering the results of research that are based on statistical tests. Among the most important are the following:

- Is the sample appropriate? The sample should be representative of the population for which conclusions are being made. The results of an experiment that uses only college sophomores as subjects might well be considered inapplicable to poor, unemployed, unskilled workers. Moreover, it is important to consider the size of the sample; very small samples may produce results that are not representative of the population at large.
- Are the measures used in the study appropriate? Statistics are only as good as the measures on which they are based, and no statistical machinations can produce something useful if the measures are not initially valid and reliable.
- Are the conclusions made from the statistical analyses drawn directly from the statistical tests? Research reports vary in terms of how closely the conclusions are built upon the results of tests. Investigators who are eager to distance their conclusions from their analyses should be treated with suspicion.
- Do results have practical, as well as statistical, meaning? It is possible to find a statistically significant difference between two means that are mathematically very close if a sufficiently large sample is used. At the same time, the practical significance of such differences may be relatively minor. It is crucial to attempt to determine the practical, as well as statistical, meaning of experimental results.

Statistical procedures represent important weapons in the arsenal of psychologists. As such, they should be treated with respect. At the same time, it is important to remember that statistics are no more infallible than the people who use them. The better informed you are about statistics and the way that they are employed, the better able you will be to make use of the findings of the science of psychology.

RECAP AND REVIEW III

Recap

- Inferential statistical analysis is a technique that uses data from samples to make predictions about a larger population.
- Statistical significance occurs when the probability that a difference between means is due to chance is less than 5 in 100.
- Measures of relationship provide an index of the degree to which two variables are related. The most frequently used measure is the correlation coefficient.

Review

1. Researchers would like to estimate the level of stress for college freshmen for a given year at a large university. A stress index is given to a randomly assigned group of 500 freshmen. The class size is 6000 for that year. In this example the group of 500 is known as a ____________________, and the entire class of freshmen is known as the ____________________.
2. Dr. Sanders states that the results of his experiment show a difference between the two groups, and that there is a 90 percent probability that the results are due to a true difference between the groups and not by chance. Are his results statistically significant?
3. A hypothetical set of data for college freshmen at a university might indicate that as rate of caffeine consumption increases, amount of sleep decreases. The scatterplot for this data is apt to show a ____________________ relationship.
4. What would the value of the correlation coefficient be for
   a. A perfect negative relationship **b.** A perfect positive relationship **c.** No relationship?
5. If we observed a correlation coefficient of −.90 in item 3, we would probably be safe in saying that caffeine consumption *causes* lack of sleep in college students. True or false?
6. The researchers in item 3 want to extend their findings to include all college students. As an informed consumer, would you accept their generalization? Why or why not?

(Answers to review questions are at the bottom of page 532.)

LOOKING BACK

1. Statistics is concerned with collecting, organizing, analyzing, and drawing conclusions from numerical data. One branch of statistics, descriptive statistics, provides a means of summarizing data.

2. A frequency distribution arranges scores from a sample by indicating how often a particular score is presented. A histogram, or bar graph, presents the same data pictorially.

3. There are three major measures of central tendency, which is the most representative score in a distribution of scores. The mean (or average) is generally the best measure of central tendency. It is calculated by summing the scores in a distribution and dividing by the number of scores. The median is the point or score in a distribution that divides the distribution in half, so that half the scores are higher and half are lower. The third measure of central tendency is the mode. The mode is the most frequently occurring score in a distribution of scores. Distributions sometimes have more than one mode.

4. The range and standard deviation are two measures of variability, which is the spread of scores in a distribution. The range is the highest score in a distribution minus the lowest score. The standard deviation is an index of the extent to which the average score in a distribution deviates from the center of the distribution. The range is a very limited measure of variability because of its sensitivity to extreme scores. The standard deviation, however, is an excellent measure of variability.

5. Inferential statistics, techniques that use data from samples to make predictions about a larger population, are useful in deciding whether differences between distributions of data are attributable to real differences or to chance variation. Usually, if a difference would occur by chance more than 5 times in 100, the difference is attributed to chance. On the other hand, if the difference would occur by chance fewer than 5 times in 100, it is attributed to a true difference brought about by an experimental manipulation.

6. Measures of relationship provide a numerical index of the extent to which two variables are related. The correlation coefficient ranges in value from +1.00 to −1.00, with +1.00 indicating a perfect positive relationship and −1.00 a perfect negative relationship. Correlations close to or at zero indicate there is little or no relationship between two variables. It is critical to realize that even when correlations are close to perfect one cannot assume that two variables are related in a causal sense.

KEY TERMS AND CONCEPTS

statistics (518)
descriptive statistics (519)
frequency distribution (519)
histogram (519)
central tendency (521)
mean (521)
median (521)
mode (522)
bimodal distribution (522)
normal distribution (522)
skewed distribution (523)
variability (524)
range (524)
standard deviation (524)
population (526)
sample (527)
inferential statistics (527)
significant outcome (527)
scatterplot (528)
positive relationship (528)
negative relationship (528)
correlation coefficient (528)

FOR FURTHER STUDY AND APPLICATION

Runyon, R. P. & Haber, A. (1984). *Fundamentals of behavioral statistics.* Reading, MA: Addison-Wesley.

If your statistical appetite has been whetted by the material discussed in this appendix, you might want to look at this volume, which provides a more in-depth overview of statistics.

Kimble, G. (1978). *How to use (and misuse) statistics.* Englewood Cliffs, NJ: Prentice-Hall.

This book is filled with practical advice on how to make use of statistics. It is particularly useful in terms of how to evaluate the statistics presented to you by others.

Pagano. R. R. (1982). *Understanding statistics in the behavioral sciences.* St. Paul: West.

A clear overview of how scientists in psychology and related fields use statistics to interpret research findings.

ANSWERS TO REVIEW QUESTIONS

Review III: **1.** Sample; population **2.** No, at least not at the .05 level. **3.** Negative **4.** a. −1.00; b. +1.00; c. 0 **5.** False; we cannot assume a causal relation, only an association. **6.** No, the sample (freshmen) does not represent the population (all college students at the university).

ACKNOWLEDGMENTS

Figure 1-5 from Darley, B. J., & Latane, B., Bystander intervention in emergencies: Diffusion of responsibilities. *Journal of Personality and Social Psychology, 8,* 184. Copyright © 1968 by the American Psychological Association. Reprinted by permission of the authors.

Try It! box in Chapter 1 from Lamal, P. A., College students' common beliefs about psychology. *Teaching of Psychology*, 1979, *6*, 155–158.

Figure 2-14 from Rosenzweig, M. R., & Lehman, A. L. *Physiological Psychology* by Mark Rosenzweig and Arnold Lehman. Copyright © 1982 by D. C. Health and Company. Reprinted by permission of the publisher.

Figure 2-16. Reprinted with permission of Macmillian Publishing Company from *The Cerebral Cortex of Man* by Wilden Penfield and Theodore Rasmussen. Copyright © 1950 by Macmillian Publishing Company, renewed 1978 by Theodore Rasmussen.

Quotation in Chapter 3. Wallis, *Unlocking Pain's Secrets*. Copyright © 1984 Time, Inc. All rights reserved. Reprinted by permission of Time, Inc.

Figure 3-7 from Coren, S., Coren, C., & Ward, L. M., *Sensation and Perception,* 1979. New York: Harcourt Brace Jovanovich.

Figure 3-9 from Lindsey, P. H., & Norman, D. A. *Human Information Processing*, 2nd ed. 1977. New York, Harcourt Brace Jovanovich.

Figure 3-10 from Cornsweet, T. N., *Visual Perception*. Copyright ©1970 by Academic Press, Inc. Reproduced by permission of Harcourt Brace Jovanovich.

Figure 3-15 Copyright © 1984 by the New York Times Company. Reprinted by permission.

Figure 3-17 from Meilgaard, M. C., Dalgliesh, C. E., and Clapperton, J. F., Beer Flavor Terminology, *Journal of American Society of Brewing Chemists, 37* (1), 47–52.

Figure 3-19 from Mednick, S. A., Higgins, S., Kirshman, J. Copyright © 1975 John Wiley & Sons, Inc. Reprinted by permission.

Figure 4-10 from G. Kaniza, Subjective contours. Copyright © 1976 by Scientific American, Inc. All rights reserved.

Figure 5-2 in B. Kleimnuntz, *Problem Solving: Research Method and Theory,* 1966. New York: John Wiley and Sons.

Figure 5-4 in D. C. Rubin, Recalling our past, *Psychology Today,* September, 1985, 39–46. Reprinted with permission from *Psychology Today Magazine*. Copyright © 1985 (APA).

Figure 6-5 from J. Lochhead. Teaching analytic reasoning skills through pair problem solving. In J. W. Segal, S. F. Chapman, & R. Glazer (Eds.), *Thinking and Learning Skills* (1985, vol. 1). Hillsdale, NJ: Erlbaum.

Try It! box problems in Chapter 6. From the book *The Complete Thinker* by Barry F. Anderson, © 1980 by Prentice-Hall, Inc., Englewood Cliffs, NJ. Reprinted by permission of the publisher, Prentice-Hall, Inc.

Quotation in Chapter 7 from Meyer, R. G., and Osborne, Y. U. H., *Case Studies in Abnormal Behavior,* 1982. Boston: Allyn & Bacon.

Figure 7-4. Taking the Chitling Test. Copyright © 1968 by Newsweek, Inc. All rights reserved. Reprinted by permission.

Try It! box in Chapter 7. Copyright © 1968 by Newsweek, Inc. All rights reserved. Reprinted by permission.

Figure 8-5 from Solomon R. L., & Corbit J. D. An opponent process theory of motivation: In temporal dynamics of affect. *Psychological Review, 81,* 1974. Reprinted with permission by the American Psychological Association. Copyright © 1978.

Try It! box, questionnaire in Chapter 8 from Zuckerman, M. Abridged sensation seeking questionnaire. *Psychology To-*

day, 11, 38–46. Reprinted with permission from *Psychology Today Magazine*. Copyright © 1978 (APA).

Quotation in Chapter 9 from Michelmore, P., "You're too young to die." *Readers Digest*, March 1984. Reprinted with permission.

Table 9-2 Adapted with permission of the Free Press, a division of Macmillan, Inc., from *Alcoholism and Substance Abuse: Strategies for Clinical Intervention,* edited by Thomas E. Bratter and Gary G. Forrest, copyright © 1985 by the Free Press.

Table 9-3, adapted from Chafetz, M., *Why Drinking Can Be Good for You*. Copyright © 1976 Stein and Day.

Figure 9-4 from Griffith, R. M., Miyago, O., & Tago, A., Universality of typical dreams Japanese versus American. Reproduced by permission of the American Anthropological Association from *American Anthropologist, 60*(6), 1958. Not for further reproduction.

Figure 9-7 from Miller, J. D., George Washington University, U. S. Department of Health and Human Services, *Psychology Today,* June, 1984. Reprinted with permission from *Psychology Today Magazine*. Copyright © 1984 (APA).

Figure 9-8. © 1984 by The New York Times Company. Reprinted by permission.

Questionnaire in Chapter 9 Try It! Box from Palladino, J. J., & Carducci, B. J., Students' knowledge of sleep and dreams. *Teaching of Psychology, 11,* 1984, 189–191.

Table 10-1 from Schickedanz, J., Schickedanz, D., and Forsyth, P., *Toward Understanding Children,* p. 95. Copyright © 1982 by Judith A. Schickedanz, David I. Schickedanz, and Peggy Forsyth. Reprinted by permission of Little, Brown and Company.

Figure 10-2 from Frankenburg, W. K., and Dodds, J. B., The Denver Developmental Screening Test, 1967. *Journal of Pediatrics, 71,* 181–191.

Figure 10-6 from Tomlinson-Keasey, C., *Child Development,* 1985. Homewood, IL: Dorsey Publishers.

Figure 10-7 from Ramey, C. T., Consequences of Infant Daycare in *Infants: Their Social Environments* (1981). Copyright © 1985 by the National Association for the Education of Young Children.

Quote in Chapter 10 from Bruner, adapted from Brazelton, T. (1969), Excerpted from the book *Infants and Mothers: Differences in Development* by T. Berry Brazelton, M. D. Reprinted by permission of Delacorte Press/Seymour Lawrence.

Figure 10-10 From Tanner, J. M., *Education and Physical Growth* (2nd ed), 1978. New York: International Universities Press.

Figure 10-5 adapted from a drawing by Barbara Maslin, February 21, 1984, from article, The aging mind proves capable. Copyright © 1984 by The New York Times Company. Reprinted by permission.

Table 10-2 from Kohlberg, L., Stage and sequence: The cognitive development approach to socialization, in *Handbook of Socialization theory and Research,* David A. Goslin, Editor. Copyright © 1969 by Houghton Mifflin Company. Reprinted with permission.

Figure 11-1 from Eysenck, H. J., *Eysenck on Extraversion*. Collins Professional and Technical Books, Ltd., 1973.

Try It! box questionnaire. Byrne, D., and Kelley, K. *An Introduction to Personality* (3rd ed). Englewood Cliffs, NJ: Prentice-Hall, 1981.

Quotation in Chapter 12 from Joyce, James, *Ulysses*. NY: Random House (1934).

Quote from Sigerist, H. E., *Civilization and Disease*. Ithaca, NY; Cornell University Press (1943).

Quotation in Try It! box in Chapter 12 from Kerouac, J., *Mexico City Blues* (1959). New York: Grove Press.

Quote from Duke, M., & Nowicki, J. R., *Abnormal psychology: Perspectives on Being Different*. Monterey, CA: Brooks/Cole Publishing Co. (1979).

G. V., and Miller, T. S., *The Benefits*

Quote from Melville, J., *Phobias and Obsessions*. Copyright © 1977 A. D. Peters & Co., Ltd.

Figure 13-1 from Smith, M. H., Glass, *of Psychotherapy*. Baltimore: Johns Hopkins (1980).

Quote from *Clinical Behavior Therapy* by Goldfried, M. R., & Davison, G. C. Copyright ©1976 by Holt, Rinehart and Winston. Reprinted by permission of CBS College Publishing.

Quote from Benson, H., Eliciting the relaxation response, from *The Relaxation Response* by Herbert Benson, M. D., with Miriam Z. Klipper. Copyright © 1975 by William Morrow and Company, Inc. Reprinted by permission of the publisher.

Quote in Chapter 13 from Rogers, C. R., (1951). *Carl Rogers' Cleint-Centered Therapy*. Copyright © 1951 by Carl R. Rogers, Renewed 1979 by Houghton Mifflin Company. Reprinted with permission.

Figure 14-3 from Landis, D., Day, H., McGrew, P. L., Thomas, J., & Miller A., Can a black culture assimilator increase racial understanding? *Journal of Social Issues, 2*(2) 169–183.

Figure 15-3 from Parlee, M. B., The friendship bond. *Psychology Today,* October 13, 1979. Reprinted from *Psychology Today Magazine*. Copyright © 1979 (APA).

Table 15-3 from Lauer, J., & Lauer, R., Marriages made to last. *Psychology Today, 19*(16), 22–26. Reprinted with permission from *Psychology Today Magazine*. Copyright © 1985 (APA).

Figure 15-4 from Sternberg, R. J., Triangular theory of love. *Psychological Review* (1986). Copyright © 1986 by the American Psychological Association. Adapted by permission of the publisher and the author.

Table 15-1 from *Liking and Loving: An Invitation to Social Psychology* by Zick Rubin. Copyright © 1973 by Holt, Rinehart and Winston, Inc. Reprinted by permission of CBS College Publishing.

Part-Opening Photographs

One Steve Niedorf/The Image Bank
Two Roy Schneider/The Stock Market
Three Steve Dunwell/The Image Bank
Four © Peter B. Kaplan/Photo Researchers, Inc.
Five © Richard Hutchings/Photo Researchers, Inc.
Six © Day Williams/Photo Researchers, Inc.
Seven John Launois/Black Star

Chapter-Opening Photographs

1. © John Earle 1982/The Stock Market
2. Dan McCoy/Black Star
3. © Lanny Johnson 1984/Woodfin Camp & Assoc.
4. © Dan Bernstein/Photo Researchers, Inc.
5. © Jeffry W. Myers 1985/Stock, Boston
6. © Jay Freis/The Image Bank
7. © Joel Gordon 1983
8. © Chris Bonington/Woodfin Camp & Assoc.
9. © Carl Frank/Photo Researchers, Inc.
10. © Erika Stone/Peter Arnold, Inc.
11. Jeff Perkell/The Stock Market
12. Ted Russell/The Image Bank
13. Robin Forbes/The Image Bank
14. © Burt Glinn/Magnum Photos
15. © M. Courtney-Clarke/Photo Researchers, Inc.

GLOSSARY

(Numbers in parentheses indicate the chapters where the terms are discussed. *A* indicates the Appendix.)

absolute refractory period The period following the triggering of a neuron in which the neuron recovers and prepares for another impulse (2)

absolute threshold The smallest amount of physical intensity by which a stimulus can be detected (3)

accommodation The ability of the lens to vary its shape in order to focus incoming images on the retina (3)

acetylcholine (uh see tul KO leen) **(ACH)** A common neurotransmitter that produces contractions of skeletal muscles (2)

achievement test A test intended to determine one's level of knowledge in a given subject (7)

action potential An electric nerve impulse that travels through a neuron when it is set off by a "trigger," changing the cell's charge from negative to positive (2)

activity theory of aging A theory that suggests that the elderly who age most successfully are those who maintain the interests and activities they had during middle age (10)

acupuncture (a kew PUNK shur) A Chinese technique of relieving pain through specific placement of needles in the body (3)

adaptation An adjustment in sensory capacity following prolonged exposure to stimuli (3)

addictive drugs Drugs that produce a physical or psychological dependence in the user (9)

adolescence (add o LESS ens) The developmental stage between childhood and adulthood during which many physical, cognitive, and social changes take place (10)

affective disorders Mood disturbances severe enough to interfere with normal living (12)

afterimage The image appearing when you move your eyes from a certain image to a blank object (3)

age of viability (vy uh BILL ih tee) The point at which a fetus can survive if born prematurely (10)

aggression Intentional injury or harm to another person (15)

aggressive cues Stimuli that have been associated with aggression in the past (15)

algorithm (AL go rith em) A set of rules that, if followed, guarantee a solution, though the reason they work may not be understood by the person using them (6)

all-or-nothing law The principle governing the state of neurons, which are either on (firing) or off (resting) (2)

altered states of consciousness Experiences of sensation thought that differ from one's normal experience (9)

altruism (AL tru iz um) Helping behavior that is beneficial to others while requiring sacrifice on the part of the helper (15)

Alzheimer's (ALZ hy merz) **disease** An illness associated with aging that includes severe memory loss. (5, 10)

amphetamine (am FET uh meen) Strong stimulant that causes a temporary feeling of confidence and alertness, but may increase anxiety and appetite loss and, taken over a period of time, suspiciousness and feelings of persecution (9)

anal stage According to Freud, a stage, from 12–18 months to 3 years of age, in which a child's pleasure is centered on the anus (11)

androgen (AN dro jun) The male sex hormone (8)

androgynous (an DROJ un us) Having a combination of traits typically considered to be "masculine" and "feminine" (14)

anorexia nervosa (an o REX ee ah ner VO sah) An eating disorder, usually striking young women, in which symptoms include self-starvation or near-starvation in an attempt to avoid obesity (8)

antianxiety drugs Drugs that alleviate stress and anxiety (13)

antidepressant drugs Medication that improves a patient's mood and feeling of well-being (13)

antipsychotic drugs Drugs that temporarily alleviate psychotic symptoms such as agitation and overactivity (13)

antisocial (sociopathic) (an TIE so shul, so sheo PATH ik) **personality disorder** A disorder in which individuals display no regard for moral and ethical rules or for the rights of others (12)

anvil A tiny bone in the middle ear that transfers vibrations to the stirrup (3)

anxiety (ang ZY eh tee) A feeling of apprehension or tension (11, 12)

anxiety disorder The occurrence of anxiety without obvious external cause, intruding on daily functioning (12)

aphasia (uh FAYZH ee uh) Problems with verbal expression due to brain injury (2)

apraxia (uh PRAX ee uh) The inability to perform activities in a logical way (2)

aptitude test A test designed to predict one's ability in a particular line of work (7)

archetypes (ark eh types) According to Jung, universal symbolic representations of a particular person, object, or experience (11)

archival (ar KY vul) **research** The examination of written records for the purpose of understanding behavior (1)

arousal theory of motivation The belief that we try to maintain certain levels of stimulation and activity, increasing or reducing them as "necessary" (8)

artificial intelligence Intelligence demonstrated by computers and other machines (7)

association area One of the major areas of the brain, the site of the higher mental processes such as thought, language, memory, and speech (2)

attachment The positive emotional bond that develops between parents and their children (10)

attitudes Learned predispositions to respond in a favorable or unfavorable manner to a particular object (14)

attribution theory The theory that seeks to explain how we decide, on the basis of samples of an individual's behavior, what the specific causes of that behavior are (14)

auditory canal A tubelike passage in the ear through which sound moves to the eardrum (3)

autonomic (ott uh NOM ik) **division** The part of the nervous system that controls involuntary movement (the actions of the heart, glands, lungs, etc.) (2)

autonomy-versus-shame-and-doubt stage The period during which, according to Erikson, toddlers (ages 18 months to 3 years) develop independence and autonomy if exploration and freedom are encouraged, or shame and self-doubt if they are restricted and overprotected (10)

availability heuristic (hyur ISS tik) A rule for judging the probability that an event will occur by the ease with which it can be recalled from memory (6)

aversive conditioning A technique used to help people break unwanted habits by associating the habits with very unpleasant stimuli (13)

axon A long, slim, tubelike extension from the end of a neuron that carries messages (2)

babble Speechlike but meaningless sounds (6)

Babinski reflex The reflex action in which an infant fans out its toes in response to a stroke on the outside of its foot (10)

barbiturates (bar BIH chur uts) Depressants used to induce sleep and reduce stress, the abuse of which, especially when combined with alcohol, can be deadly (9)

basilar (BAZ ih lar) **membrane** A structure dividing the cochlea into an upper and a lower chamber (3)

behavior modification A formalized technique for promoting desirable behaviors and decreasing the incidence of unwanted ones (4)

behavioral model The psychological model that suggests that observable behavior should be the focus of study (1)

behavioral model of abnormality The model that suggests that abnormal behavior itself is the problem to be treated, rather than viewing behavior as a symptom of some underlying medical or psychological problem (12)

behavioral self-management A procedure in which people learn to identify and resolve their problems using techniques based on learning theory (13)

behavioral treatment approaches Approaches to abnormal behavior that assume that both normal and abnormal behaviors are learned and that treatment consists of learning new behavior or unlearning maladaptive behavior (13)

bimodal distribution A distribution of scores that produces a bell-shaped, symmetrical curve (A)

binocular disparity (by NOCK you lur dis PAIR ih tee) The difference between the images that reach the retina of each eye; this disparity allows the brain to estimate distance (13)

biofeedback The control of internal physiological processes through conscious thought (2)

biological model The psychological model that views behavior in terms of biological functioning (1)

biopsychology The branch of psychology that studies the biological basis of behavior (1)

biopsychologists Psychologists who study the ways biological structures and body functions affect behavior (2)

bipolar (by PO lur) **cells** Nerve cells leading to the brain that are triggered by nerve cells in the eye (3)

bipolar disorder A disorder in which a person alternates between the euphoric feeling of mania and bouts of depression (12)

bisexuals People who are attracted to members of both sexes (8)

brain electrical activity mapping (BEAM) A computerized scan technique that indicates electrical activity within the brain (2)

brain scan A method of "photographing" the brain without actually opening the skull (2)

Broca's aphasia (BRO kaz uh FAYZH ee uh) A specific syndrome involving problems with verbal expression (2)

bulimia (boo LIM ee ah) An eating disorder characterized by vast intake of food that may be followed by self-induced vomiting (8)

caffeine (kaf FEEN) A stimulant found most abundantly in coffee, soda, and chocolate (9)

California Psychological Inventory An assessment tool used to identify personality traits (11)

Cannon-Bard theory of emotion The belief that both physiological and emotional arousal are produced simultaneously by the same nerve impulse (8)

cardinal trait A single personality trait that directs most of a person's activities (e.g., greed, lust, kindness) (11)

case study An in-depth interview of an individual in order to better understand that individual and to make inferences about people in general (1)

catatonic (cat ah TON ik) **schizophrenia** Mental disorder characterized by major disturbances in movement (12)

catharsis (kuh THAR sis) **hypothesis** The notion that aggression is built up and must be discharged through violent acts (15)

central core The "old brain," which controls breathing, eating, sleeping, etc., and is common to all vertebrates (2)

central nervous system (CNS) The system that includes the brain and the spinal cord (2)

central tendency The most representalive score in a distribution of scores (the mean, median, and mode are measures of central tendency) (A)

central traits A set of major characteristics that make up the core of a person's personality (11); the major traits considered in forming impressions of others (14)

cerebellum (cer rah BELL um) The part of the brain that controls bodily balance (2)

cerebral cortex (suh REE brul KOR tex) The "new brain," responsible for the most sophisticated information processing in the brain; contains the lobes (2)

chlorpromazine (klor PRO mah zeen) An antipsychotic drug that is used in the treatment of schizophrenia (13)

chromosomes (KROME uh soamz) Rod-shaped structures that contain basic hereditary information (10)

chronological (kron uh LOJ ih kul) **age** One's physical age (7)

chunk A meaningful grouping of stimuli that can be stored as a unit in short-term memory (5)

classical conditioning A kind of learning in which a response is made to a previously neutral stimulus that would not naturally bring about that response (4)

client-centered therapy Therapy in which the therapist reflects back the patient's statements in a way that causes the patient to find his or her own solutions (13)

clinical psychology The branch of psychology that studies diagnosis and treatment of abnormal behavior (1)

close relationships See interpersonal attraction (15)

closure (KLO zhur) Tendency to group according to enclosed or complete figures rather than open or incomplete ones (3)

cocaine (ko KANE) A stimulant that initially creates feelings of confidence, alertness, and well-being, but eventually causes mental and physical deterioration (9)

cochlea (KOKE lee uh) A coiled tube filled with fluid that receives sound via the oval window or through bone conduction (3)

cognition (cog NIH shun) Higher mental processes by which we understand the world, process information, make judgments and decisions, and communicate knowledge to others (6)

cognitions Attitudes, thoughts, or beliefs (14)

cognitive-behavioral therapy A process by which people's faulty cognitions about themselves and the world are changed to more accurate ones (13)

cognitive development The process by which a child's understanding of the world changes as a function of age and experience (10)

cognitive dissonance (COG nih tiv DIS o nuns) The conflict that arises when a person holds contrasting attitudes (14)

cognitive learning theory The study of the thought processes that underlie learning (4)

cognitive map A mental "picture" of locations and directions (4)

cognitive model The psychological model that focuses on how people know, understand, and think about the world (1)

cognitive psychologists Psychologists who specialize in the study of cognition (6)

cognitive psychology The branch of psychology that considers higher mental processes including thinking, language, memory, problem solving, knowing, reasoning, judging, and decision making (1)

collective unconscious A concept developed by Jung proposing that we inherit certain personality characteristics from our ancestors and the human race as a whole (11)

compliance Behavior that occurs in response to direct social pressure (15)

compulsion (kom PUL shun) An urge to repeatedly carry out an act that even the sufferer realizes is unreasonable (12)

computerized axial tomography (AX ee ul toe MOG rah fee) **(CAT) scan** A scanning procedure that shows the structures within the brain (2)

concept A categorization of objects, events, or people that share common properties (6)

conception The process by which an egg cell is fertilized by a sperm cell (10)

concrete operational stage According to Piaget, the period from 7 to 12 years of age that is characterized by logical thought and a loss of egocentrism (10)

conditioned response (CR) A response (e.g., salivation) that, after conditioning, follows a previously neutral stimulus (e.g., vibration of a tuning fork) (4)

conditioned stimulus (CS) A once-neutral stimulus that has been paired with an unconditioned stimulus to bring about a response formerly caused only by the unconditioned stimulus (4)

cones Cone-shaped, light-sensitive receptor cells in the retina that are responsible for sharp focus and color perception, particularly in bright light (3)

confederate (kon FED er it) A participant in an experiment who has been instructed to behave in ways that will affect the responses of other subjects (1)

conformity A change in behavior due to a desire to follow the beliefs or standards of other people (15)

conscience The part of the superego that prevents us from doing what is morally wrong (11)

consciousness (KON chus nes) A person's awareness of the sensations, thoughts and feelings that he or she is experiencing at a given moment (9)

consensus information The degree to which people behave similarly in the same situation (14)

conservation, the principle of The knowledge that quantity is unrelated to the arrangement and physical appearance of objects (10)

consistency The persistence of those holding an unpopular view, eventually bringing about a change in the attitude of the majority (15)

consistency information The degree to which an individual behaves similarly in similar situations (14)

constructive processes Processes in which memories are influenced by the interpretation and meaning given to events (5)

consumer psychology The branch of psychology that considers our buying habits and the effects of advertising on buyer behavior (1)

contingency contracting Acting upon a written contract between a therapist and a patient (or parent and child, etc.) that sets behavioral goals, with rewards for achievement (13)

continuous reinforcement The reinforcing of a behavior every time it occurs (4)

continuum (kon TIN u um) A continuous measurement scale (12)

control group The experimental group receiving no treatment (1)

conversion disorder Psychological disturbances characterized by actual physical disturbances, such as the inability to speak or move one's arms (12)

cornea (CORN ee uh) A transparent, protective window in the eyeball (3)

correlation coefficient (Kor eh LAY shun ko ef FISH ent) A number that indicates the relationship between two variables (A)

correlational research Research to determine whether there is a relationship between certain behaviors and responses (1)

counseling psychologist A psychologist who specializes in treatment of day-to-day adjustment problems (13)

counseling psychology The branch of psychology that focuses on educational, social, and career adjustment issues (1)

crowding An unpleasant psychological and subjective state involving people's reaction to the density of their environment (15)

crystallized intelligence The store of specific information, skills, and strategies that people have acquired through experience (7, 10)

cultural assimilator A teaching aid designed to minimize racial prejudice through understanding of others' behavior (14)

culture-fair IQ test A test that does not discriminate against members of any minority culture group (7)

cumulative recorder A device that automatically records and graphs the patterns of responses made in reaction to a particular reinforcement schedule (4)

dark adaptation A heightened sensitivity to light resulting from being in low-level light (3)

daydreams Fantasies people construct while awake (9)

decay The loss of information through nonuse (5)

decibels (DES ih bells) Individual measures of sound intensity (3)

declarative knowledge The body of knowledge that concerns facts—faces, dates, names, etc. (5)

defense mechanisms Unconscious strategies people use to reduce anxiety by concealing its source from themselves and others (11, 13)

delusions (dee LU jhuns) Firmly held beliefs with no basis in reality (12)

dendrites Fibers at one end of a neuron that receive messages from other neurons (2)

denial A refusal to accept or acknowledge anxiety-producing information (11)

dependent variable The variable that is measured and is expected to change as a result of experimenter manipulation (1)

depressants Drugs that slow down the nervous system (9)

depth perception The ability to view the world in three dimensions and to perceive distance (3)

descriptive statistics The branch of statistics that provides a means of summarizing data (A)

determinism The view that suggests that behavior is shaped primarily by factors external to the person (11)

developmental psychology The branch of psychology that studies patterns of growth and change throughout life (1, 10)

deviation IQ score A calculation of an IQ score that allows determination of one person's performance in relation to others (7)

***Diagnostic and Statistical Manual of Mental Disorders*, third edition (*DSM-III*)** A manual that presents comprehensive definitions of more than 230 separate diagnostic categories for identifying problems and behaviors (12)

dichotic (dy KOT ik) **listening** A procedure in which an individual wears earphones through which different messages are sent to each ear at the same time (3)

difference threshold The smallest detectable difference between two stimuli, or the just noticeable difference (3)

diffusion of responsibilty The tendency for people to feel that responsibility for helping is shared among those present (15)

discriminative stimulus A stimulus to which an organism learns to respond as part of stimulus control training (4)

disengagement theory of aging A theory that suggests that aging is a gradual withdrawal from the world on physical, psychological, and social levels (10)

disorganized (hebephrenic) schizophrenia (hee bah FREN ik) Mental disorder characterized by inappropriate giggling, incoherent speech, and other strange behavior (12)

displacement The expression of an unwanted feeling or thought, directed toward a weaker person instead of a more powerful one (11)

display rules Learned rules that inform us about the appropriateness of showing emotion nonverbally (8)

dispositional causes of behavior Causes of behavior that are based on internal traits or personality factors (14)

dissociative (dis SO see ah tiv) **disorders** The splitting apart of critical personality facets, allowing stress avoidance by escape (12)

distinctiveness information The extent to which a given behavior occurs across different situations (14)

dopamine (DOPE uh meen) A common neurotransmitter that inhibits certain neurons and excites others (2)

dopamine (DOPE uh meen) **hypothesis** A theory that suggests that schizophrenia occurs when there is excess activity in those areas of the brain using dopamine to transmit nerve impulses (12)

double-bind hypothesis A theory that suggests that people suffering from schizophrenia may have received simultaneous contradictory messages from their mothers and never learned what behavior was appropriate (12)

double-blind procedure The technique by which both the experimenter and the subjects are kept from knowing which subjects received a drug, making any observed behavior variations more reliable (1)

double standard The view that premarital sex is permissible for males but not for females (8)

Downs's syndrome A common cause of mental retardation, brought about by the presence of an extra chromosome (7, 10)

dream interpretation An examination of a patient's dreams to find clues to the unconscious conflicts and problems being experienced (13)

drive A motivational tension or arousal that energizes behavior in order to fulfill a need (8)

drive-reduction theory The theory, as opposed to instinct theory, that activities are carried out in order to satisfy a need and cease when the need is fulfilled (8)

drug therapy Control of psychological problems through drugs (13)

dyslexia (dis LEX ee uh) A disability with a perceptual basis that can result in the reversal of letters during reading and writing, confusion between left and right, and difficulties in spelling (3)

eardrum The part of the ear that vibrates when sound waves hit it (3)

echoic (eh KO ik) **memory** The storage of information obtained from the sense of hearing (5)

eclectic (ek LEK tik) **approach to therapy** An approach to therapy that uses a variety of treatment methods rather than just one (13)

educational psychology The branch of psychology that considers how the educational process affects students (1)

Edwards Personal Preference Schedule An assessment tool used in employment settings (11)

ego (EE go) The part of personality that provides a buffer between the id and the outside world (11)

ego-ideal The part of the superego that motivates us to do what is morally proper (11)

ego-integrity-versus-despair stage According to Erikson's theory, a period from late adulthood until death, during which we review life's accomplishments and failures (10)

elaborative rehearsal Organizing information to fit into a logical framework, which assists in recall (5)

electroconvulsive (ee LEK tro kon VUL siv) **therapy (ECT)** Treatment involving the administration of an electric current to a patient's head to treat depression (13)

electroencephalogram (ee LEK tro en SEF uh lo gram) **(EEG)** A technique that records the brain's electrical activity (2, 9)

embryo (EM bree o) A developed zygote that has a heart, a brain, and other organs (10)

emotions Feelings (such as happiness, despair, and sorrow) that generally have both physiological and cognitive elements and that influence behavior (8)

empathy (EM pah thee) One person's experiencing of another's emotions, leading to an increased likelihood of responding to the other's needs (15)

endocrine (EN doe krin) **system** A chemical communication network that sends messages throughout the nervous system and secretes hormones that affect body growth and functioning (2)

endorphins (en DOR fins) Chemicals produced by the body that interact with an opiate receptor to reduce pain (2)

engram (EN gram) See memory trace (5)

environment Influences on behavior that occur in the world around us, including family, friends, school, nutrition, and many other factors (10)

environmental psychology The branch of psychology that studies the relationship between people and their physical environment (1)

episodic memories Stored information relating to personal experiences (5)

estrogen (ES tro jun) The female sex hormone (8)

excitatory message A chemical secretion that "tells" a receiving neuron to fire (2)

existential (ex is STEN chul) **therapy** A humanistic approach that addresses the meaning of life, allowing a client to devise a system of values that gives purpose to his or her life (13)

experiment A study carried out to investigate the relationship between two or more factors in order to determine causality (1)

experimental bias Factors that could lead an experimenter to an erroneous conclusion about the effect of the independent variable on the dependent variable (1)

experimental manipulation The intentional alteration of factors in an experiment to affect responses or behaviors (1)

experimental psychology The branch of psychology that studies the processes of sensing, perceiving, learning, and thinking about the world (1)

experimenter expectations An experimenter's unintentional message to a subject about results expected from the experiment (1)

extinction (ex TINK shun) The weakening and eventual disappearance of a conditioned response, resulting from the discontinuation of reinforcement (4)

extramarital sex Sexual activity between a married person and someone who is not his or her spouse (10)

extrinsic (ex TRIN zik) **motivation** Motivation by which people participate in an activity for a tangible reward (9)

facial-affect program The activation of a set of nerve impulses that make the face display the "appropriate" expression (8)

facial-feedback hypothesis The notion that facial expressions are involved in determining the experience of emotions and in labeling them (8)

factor analysis A statistical technique for combining traits into broader, more general patterns of consistency (11)

familial retardation Mental retardation in which there is a history of retardation in a family but no evidence of biological causes (7)

fear of success A fear that being successful will have a negative influence on the way one is perceived by one's self and others (8)

fetal (FEE tul) **alcohol syndrome** An ailment resulting in a baby's mental and physical retardation as a result of the mother's high alcohol intake while pregnant (2, 10)

fetus (FEE tus) A developing child, from nine weeks after conception until birth (10)

figure/ground Figure refers to the object being perceived, whereas ground refers to the background or spaces within the object (3)

fixation Behavior reflecting an earlier stage of development (11)

fixed-interval schedule A schedule whereby a reinforcer is given at established time intervals (such as a weekly paycheck) (4)

fixed-ratio schedule A schedule whereby reinforcement is given only after a certain number of responses is made (4)

flashbulb memories Memories of a specific event that are so clear they seem like "snapshots" of the event (5)

fluid intelligence The ability to deal with new problems and situations (7, 10)

forensic (for EN sik) **psychology** The branch of psychology that studies insanity and other legal issues related to psychology (1)

forewarning A procedure in which a subject is told in advance that a persuasive message is forthcoming, sometimes reducing the effects of social influence since the subject is prepared to stand firm (15)

formal operational stage According to Piaget, the period from age 12 to adulthood that is characterized by abstract thought (10)

fovea (FOV ee uh) A very sensitive region of the retina that aids in focusing (3)

free association A Freudian therapeutic technique in which patients say everything that comes to mind to give the therapist a clue to the workings of the patient's unconscious (13)

free will The human ability to make decisions about one's own life (1)

frequency The number of wave crests occurring each second in any particular sound (3)

frequency distribution An arrangement of scores from a sample that indicates how often a particular score is present (A)

frequency theory of hearing The theory that suggests that the entire basilar membrane acts like a microphone, vibrating in response to sound (3)

frontal lobes The brain structure, located at the front center of the cortex, that contains major motor and speech and reasoning centers (2)

frustration A state produced by the thwarting or blocking of some ongoing, goal-directed behavior (15)

functional fixedness (FIX ed ness) The tendency to think of an object in terms of its most typical use (6)

fundamental attribution bias A tendency to attribute others' behavior to dispositional causes but to attribute one's own behavior to situational causes (14)

gag reflex An infant's reflex to clear its throat (10)

ganglion (GANG lee yon) **cells** Nerve cells that collect and summarize information from the rods and carry it to the brain (3)

gate-control theory of pain The theory that suggests that particular nerve receptors lead to specific areas of the brain that are related to pain; when these receptors are activated by an injury or bodily malfunction, a "gate" to the brain is opened and pain is sensed (3)

genes (jeens) The parts of a chromosome through which genetic information is transmitted (10)

generalized anxiety disorder The experience of long-term anxiety with no explanation (12)

generativity-versus-stagnation stage According to Erikson, a period in middle adulthood during which we take stock of our contributions to family and society (10)

genetic (jeh NEH tik) Pertaining to the biological factors that transmit hereditary information (10)

genetic preprogramming theories of aging Theories that suggest that there is a built-in time limit to the reproduction of human cells (10)

gerontologists (jer on TALL o jists) Psychologists who study aging (10)

gestalt (geh SHTALLT) **laws of organization** A series of principles which describe how we organize pieces of information into meaningful wholes; they include closure, proximity, similarity, and simplicity (3)

gestalt (geh SHTALLT) **psychology** An approach to psychology that focuses on the organization of perception and thinking in a "whole" sense, rather than on the individual elements of perception (1)

gestalt therapy An approach that attempts to integrate thoughts, feelings, and behavior into a whole (13)

gestalts Patterns studied by the gestalt psychologists (3)

glaucoma (glaw KO muh) A dysfunction of the eye in which fluid pressure builds up and causes a decline in visual acuity (3)

grammar The framework of rules that determine how our thoughts can be expressed (6)

habituation (ha BIH choo a shun) A decrease in responding to repeated presentations of the same stimulus (10)

hair cells Tiny cells covering the basilar membrane that, when bent by vibrations entering the cochlea, activate sensory receptor cells (3)

hallucinations (hah loos in A shuns) Perceptions of things that do not actually exist (12)

hallucinogen (ha LOOS en o jen) A drug that is capable of producing changes in perception, or hallucinations (9)

hammer A tiny bone in the middle ear that transfers vibrations to the anvil (3)

health psychology The branch of psychology that explores the relationship of physical and psychological factors (1, 15)

hemispheres Symmetrical left and right halves of the brain (2)

heredity Influences on behavior that are transmitted biologically from parents to a child (10)

heritability A measure of the degree to which a characteristic is related to genetic, inherited factors, as opposed to environmental factors (7)

heroin (HARE o in) A powerful depressant, usually injected, that gives an initial rush of good feeling but leads eventually to anxiety and depression; extremely addictive (9)

heterosexuality Sexual behavior or attraction between a man and a woman (8)

heuristic (hyur ISS tik) A rule of thumb that may bring about a solution to a problem but is not guaranteed to do so (6)

hierarchy (HIRE ar kee) **of fears** A list, in order of increasing severity, of the things that are associated with one's fears (13)

higher-order conditioning A form of conditioning that occurs when an already-conditioned stimulus is paired with a neutral stimulus until the neutral stimulus evokes the same response as the conditioned stimulus (4)

histogram (HISS toe gram) A bar graph used to represent data graphically (A)

homeostasis (ho mee o STAY sis) The process by which an organism tries to maintain an internal biological balance, or "steady state" (8)

homosexuals People who are sexually attracted to members of their own sex (8)

hormones Chemicals that circulate throughout the blood and affect the functioning and growth of parts of the body (2)

humanistic model The psychological model that suggests that people are in control of their lives (1)

humanistic model of abnormality The model that suggests that people are basically rational and that abnormal behavior results from an inability to fulfill human needs and capabilities (12)

humanistic theory (of personality) The theory that emphasizes people's basic goodness and their natural tendency to rise to higher levels of functioning (11)

humanistic therapy Therapy in which the underlying assumption is that people have control of their behavior, they can make choices about their lives, and they are essentially responsible for solving their own problems (13)

hypnosis A state of heightened susceptibility to the suggestions of others (9)

hypochondriasis (HY po kon DRY a sis) A constant fear of illness and misinterpretation of normal aches and pains (12)

hypothalamus (hy po THAL uh muss) Located below the thalamus of the brain, its major function is to maintain homeostasis, including food intake (8)

hypotheses Predictions to be tested experimentally (1)

iconic (i KON ik) **memory** The storage of visual information (5)

id The raw, unorganized, inherited part of personality whose purpose is to reduce tension created by biological drives and irrational impulses (11)

identical twins Twins with identical genetic makeups (10)

identification A child's attempt to be similar to his or her same-sex parent (11)

identity The distinguishing characteristics of the individual: who each of us is, what our roles are, and what we are capable of (10)

identity-versus-role confusion stage According to Erikson, a time in adolescence of testing to determine one's own unique qualities (10)

impression formation The process by which an individual organizes information about another individual to form an overall impression of that person (14)

incentive theory of motivation The belief that behavior is motivated by the external stimuli of rewards and incentives (8)

independent variable The variable that is manipulated in an experiment (1)

industrial-organizational psychology The branch that studies the psychology of the workplace, considering productivity, job satisfaction, and related issues (1)

industry-versus-inferiority stage According to Erikson, the period during which children aged 6 to 12 years may develop positive social interactions with others or may feel inadequate and become less sociable (10)

inferential statistics The branch of statistics that uses data from samples to make predictions about the larger population from which the sample is drawn (A)

inferiority complex A phenomenon whereby adults have continuing feelings of weakness and insecurity (11)

informal groups Groups that develop as a result of the interests and needs of the individuals making up an organization (20)

ingroup-outgroup bias The tendency to hold less favorable opinions about groups to which we do not belong (outgroups), while holding more favorable opinions about groups to which we do belong (ingroups) (14)

ingroup Groups to which an individual belongs (14)

inhibitory message A chemical secretion that prevents a receiving neuron from firing (2)

initiative-versus-guilt stage According to Erikson, the period during which children aged 3 to 6 years experience conflict between independence of action and the sometimes negative results of that action (10)

innate (in ATE) Inborn, biologically determined (15)

inner ear The interior structure that changes sound vibrations into a form that can be transmitted to the brain (3)

inoculation (in ok u LAY shun) Exposure to arguments opposing one's beliefs, making the subject more resistant to later attempts to change those beliefs (15)

insight A sudden awareness of the relationship between various elements that had previously appeared to be independent of one another (6)

insomnia (in SOM nee uh) An inability to get to sleep or stay asleep, often due to the presence of an unpleasant situation in our lives (9)

instinct An inborn pattern of behavior that is biologically determined (8)

instinctual drives Infantile wishes, desires, and needs hidden from conscious awareness (11)

intellectually gifted Individuals characterized by higher-than-average intelligence, with IQ scores above 130 (7)

intelligence The capacity to understand the world, think rationally, and use resources effectively when faced with challenges (7)

intelligence quotient (KWO shunt) **(IQ) score** A measure of intelligence that takes into account an individual's mental and chronological ages (7)

intelligence tests A battery of measures to determine a person's level of intelligence (7)

intensity A feature of wave patterns that allows us to distinguish between loud and soft passages (3)

interference A phenomenon in which recall is hindered by other information in memory (5)

interactionist One who believes that a combination of genetic predisposition and environmental influences produces development (10)

interpersonal attraction Positive feelings for others (15)

intimacy-versus-isolation stage According to Erikson, a period during early adulthood, with a focus on developing close relationships (10)

intoxication A state of drunkenness (9)

intrinsic (IN trin zic) **motivation** Motivation by which people participate in an activity for their own enjoyment, not for the rewards it will get them (8)

introversion-extroversion According to Eysenck, a dimension of personality traits encompassing the shyest to the most social people (11)

iris The colored part of the eye located behind the pupil that bends rays of light to focus them on the retina (3)

James-Lange (LANG) **theory of emotion** The belief that emotional experience is a reaction to bodily events occurring as a result of an external situation ("I feel sad because I am crying") (8)

just noticeable difference See difference threshold (3)

keyword technique The pairing of a foreign word with a common, similar-sounding English word to aid in remembering the new word (5)

language The systematic, meaningful arrangement of symbols (6)

language acquisition device A neural system of the brain hypothesized to permit understanding of language (6)

lanugo (lan OO go) A soft fuzz covering the body of a newborn (10)

latent content of dreams According to Freud, the true meaning of dreams, hidden by more obvious subjects (9)

latent learning Learning in which a new behavior is acquired but not readily demonstrated until reinforcement is provided (4)

latency (LAY ten see) **period** According to Freud, the period, between the phallic stage and puberty, during which children's sexual concerns are temporarily put aside (11)

lateral hypothalamus The portion of the hypothalamus that signals a need for food (8)

lateralization The dominance of one hemisphere of the brain in specific functions (2)

law of effect Thorndike's theory that responses which satisfy are more likely to be repeated, while those that don't satisfy will be discontinued (4)

learned helplessness An organism's learned belief that it has no control over the environment (4)

learned-inattention theory of schizophrenia The theory that suggests that schizophrenia is a learned behavior consisting of a set of inappropriate responses to social stimuli (12)

learned not-thinking Dollard and Miller's notion that unpleasant thoughts can be repressed, eliminating negative feelings that are otherwise present (11)

learning A relatively permanent change in behavior brought about by experience (4)

least-restrictive environment The official phrase from PL94-142 that guarantees the right of full education for retarded people in an environment that is most similar to the educational environment of typical children (7)

lens The part of the eye located behind the pupil that bends rays of light to focus them on the retina (3)

levels-of-processing theory The theory that suggests that the way that information is initially perceived and learned determines recall (5)

light The stimulus that produces vision (3)

light adaptation The eye's temporary insensitivity to light dimmer than that to which it has become accustomed (as when entering a movie theater) (3)

limbic system The part of the brain located outside the "new brain" that controls eating and reproduction (2)

linear perspective The phenomenon by which distant objects appear to be closer together than nearer objects (3)

linguistic-relativity hypothesis The theory claiming that language shapes and may even determine the way people perceive the world (6)

lithium (LITH ee um) A drug used in the treatment of bipolar disorders (13)

long-term memory The storage of information on a relatively permanent basis, although retrieval may be difficult (5)

lysergic (ly sur jik) **acid diethylamide** (dy ETH ul ah mide) **(LSD)** One of the most powerful hallucinogens, affecting the operation of neurotransmitters in the brain, causing brain-cell activity to be altered (9)

magnitude The strength of a stimulus (3)

mainstreaming The integration of retarded people into regular classroom situations (7)

major depression A severe form of depression that interferes with concentration, decision making, and sociability (12)

mania (MAY nee ah) An extended state of intense euphoria and elation (12)

manifest (MAN ih fest) **content of dreams** According to Freud, the surface meaning of dreams (9, 13)

mantra (MON truh) A sound, word, or syllable repeated over and over to take one into a meditative state (9)

marijuana (mare uh WAN uh) A common hallucinogen, usually smoked (9)

masturbation (mass tur BAY shun) Sexual self-stimulation (8)

maturation The unfolding of biologically predetermined patterns of behavior due to aging (4, 10)

mean The average of all scores, arrived at by adding scores together and dividing by the number of scores (A)

means-ends analysis Repeated testing to determine and reduce the distance between real and desired outcomes in problem solving (6)

median The point in a distribution of scores that divides the distribution exactly in half when the scores are listed in numerical order (A)

medical model of abnormality The model that suggests that when an individual displays symptoms of abnormal behavior, the cause is physiological (12)

medical student's disease The feeling that symptoms and illnesses about which one studies are characteristic of oneself (12)

meditation A learned technique for refocusing attention that brings about an altered state of consciousness (9)

medulla (meh DOO lah) The part of the central core of the brain that controls many important body functions such as breathing and heartbeat (2)

memory The capacity to record, retain, and retrieve information (5)

memory trace A physical change in the brain that reflects memories (5)

menopause (MEN o paws) The point at

which women stop menstruating, generally at around age 45 (10)

mental age The typical intelligence level found for people at a given chronological age (7)

mental retardation A significantly subaverage level of intellectual functioning accompanying deficits in adaptive behavior (7)

metabolism (meh TABO lizum) The rate at which energy is produced and expended by the body (8)

methadone (METH uh doan) A chemical used to detoxify heroin addicts (9)

method of loci (LO sy) Assigning words or ideas to places, thereby improving recall of the words by envisioning those places (5)

middle ear A tiny chamber containing three bones—the hammer, the anvil, and the stirrup—which transmit vibrations to the oval window (3)

midlife crisis The negative feelings that accompany the realization that one has not accomplished in life what he or she had hoped to (10)

midlife transition Beginning around the age of 40, a period during which one comes to the realization that life is finite (10)

mild retardation Mental retardation characterized by an IQ between 55 and 69 and the ability to function independently (7)

Minnesota Multiphasic Personality Inventory (MMPI) A test meant to identify people with psychological difficulties (11)

minor tranquilizers See antianxiety drugs (13)

mnemonics (neh MON ix) Formal techniques for organizing material to increase the likelihood of its being remembered (5)

mode The most frequently occurring score in a set of scores (A)

model A person serving as an example to an observer; if a model's behavior is rewarded, the observer may imitate that behavior (4)

modeling Imitating the behavior of others (models) (13)

models Systems of interrelated ideas and concepts used to explain phenomena (1)

moderate retardation Mental retardation characterized by an IQ between 40 and 54 (7)

monocular (mon OCK u lar) **cues** Signals that allow us to perceive distance and depth with just one eye (3)

moro (startle) reflex The reflex action in which an infant, in response to a sudden noise, flings its arms, arches its back, and spreads its fingers (10)

morphine (MOR feen) Derived from the poppy flower, a powerful depressant that reduces pain and induces sleep (9)

motion parallax (MO shun PAIR uh lax) The relative movement of objects as your head moves (3)

motivation The factors that direct and energize behavior (8)

motives Desired goals that prompt behavior (8)

motor area One of the major areas of the brain, responsible for voluntary movement of particular parts of the body (2)

Muller-Lyer (MEW lur LY ur) **illusion** An illusion where two lines of the same length appear to be of different lengths because of the direction of the arrows at the ends of each line; the line with arrows pointing out appears shorter than the line with arrows pointing in (3)

multiple personality A disorder in which a person displays characteristics of two or more distinct personalities (12)

myelin sheath (MY uh lin SHEETH) An axon's protective coating, made of fat and protein (2)

narcolepsy (NARK o lep see) An uncontrollable need to sleep for short periods during the day (9)

naturalistic observation Observation without interference, in which the researcher records information in a naturally occurring situation in a way that does not influence the situation (1)

nature-nurture question The issue of the degree to which environment and heredity influence behavior (10)

need for achievement A stable, learned characteristic in which satisfaction comes from striving for and achieving a level of excellence (8)

need for affiliation A need to establish and maintain relationships with other people (8)

need for power A tendency to want to make an impression or have an impact on others in order to be seen as a powerful individual (8)

negative reinforcer A stimulus whose removal is reinforcing, leading to a greater probability that the response bringing about this removal will occur again (4)

negative relationship A relationship established by data that shows high values of one variable corresponding with low values of the other (A)

neo-Freudian psychoanalysts (neo Freudians) Theorists who place greater emphasis than did Freud on the functions of the ego and its influence on our daily activities (11)

neonate (NEE o nate) A newborn child (10)

nervous system The brain and its pathways extending throughout the body (2)

neurons (noor onz) The basic elements of the nervous system that carry messages (2)

neurotic (nyur RAH tik) **anxiety** Anxiety that occurs when irrational impulses from the id threaten to become uncontrollable (11)

neurotic (nyur RAH tik) **symptoms** According to Freud, abnormal behavior brought about by anxiety associated with unwanted conflicts and impulses (13)

neuroticism-stability Eysenck's personality continuum encompassing people from the moodiest to the most even-tempered (11)

neurotransmitter (noor o TRANZ mittur) A chemical secreted when a nerve impulse comes to the end of an axon, that carries messages between neurons (2)

neutral stimulus A stimulus that, before conditioning, has no effect on the desired response (4)

nicotine (NIK o teen) A stimulant present in cigarettes (9)

noise Background stimulation that interferes with the perception of other stimuli (3)

nondirective counseling A therapeutic technique in which the therapist creates a warm, supportive environment to allow the client to better understand and work out his or her problems (13)

normal distribution A distribution of scores that produces a bell-shaped, symmetrical curve (A)

nuclear magnetic resonance (NMR) scan A scan produced by a magnetic field which shows brain structures in great detail (2)

obesity (o BEE sih tee) The state of being more than 20 percent above one's ideal weight (8)

object permanence The awareness that objects do not cease to exist when they are out of sight (10)

observational learning Learning that is the result of viewing the actions of others (models) and observing the consequences (4, 10, 13)

obsession (ob SEH shun) A thought or idea that keeps recurring (12)

obsessive-compulsive (ob SESS iv kom PULS iv) **disorder** A disorder characterized by obsessions or compulsions (12)

occipital (ox SIP ih tul) **lobes** The structures of the brain lying behind the temporal lobes; the major visual center (2)

oedipal (ED ih pul) **conflict** A child's sexual interest in his or her opposite-sex parent, typically resolved through identification with the same-sex parent (11)

olfactory (all FAK tor ee) **cells** The receptor cells of the nose (3)

operant The learning process involving one's operation of the environment (see operant conditioning) (4)

operant conditioning Learning that occurs as a result of certain positive or negative consequences; the organism operates on its environment in order to produce a desired result (usually a reward) (4)

operationalization The process of translating a hypothesis into experimental procedures (1)

opiate (O pee ut) **receptor** A neuron that acts to reduce the experience of pain (2)

opponent-process theory of color vision The theory that suggests that members of pairs of different receptor cells are linked together to work in opposition of each other (3)

opponent-process theory of motivation The theory which maintains that increases in arousal produce a calming reaction in the nervous system, and vice versa (8)

optic chiasma (ky AZ muh) A point between and behind the eyes at which nerve impulses from the optic nerve are reversed and "righted" in the brain (3)

optic nerve A bundle of ganglion axons in the back of the eyeball that carry visual information to the brain (3)

oral stage According to Freud, a stage, from birth to 12–18 months in which an infant's center of pleasure is the mouth (11)

otoliths Structures in the semicircular canals that sense body acceleration (3)

outer ear The visible part of the ear that acts as a sound collector (3)

outgroups Groups to which an individual does not belong (14)

oval window A thin membrane between the middle ear and the inner ear that transmits vibrations while increasing their strength (3)

ovaries (O vuh reez) The female reproductive organs (8)

overlearning Rehearsing material beyond the point of mastery to improve long-term recall (5)

overregularization Applying rules of speech in instances in which they are inappropriate (6)

ovulation (ov u LAY shun) The monthly release of an egg from an ovary (8)

panic attack Sudden anxiety characterized by heart palpitations, shortness of breath, sweating, faintness, and great fear (12)

panic disorder Anxiety that manifests itself in the form of panic attacks (12)

paraplegia (pair u PLEE ja) The inability, as a result of injury to the spinal cord, to move any muscles in the lower half of the body (2)

parasympathetic (pair uh SIMP uh thet ik) **division** The part of the autonomic division of the peripheral nervous system that calms the body, bringing functions back to normal after an emergency has passed (2)

parietal (puh RY uh tul) **lobes** The brain structure to the rear of the frontal lobes; the center for bodily sensations (2)

partial reinforcement The reinforcing of a behavior some, but not all, of the time (4)

penis envy According to Freud, a girl's wish, developing around age 3, that she had a penis (11)

perception The sorting out, interpretation, analysis, and integration of stimuli from our sensory organs (3)

perceptual constancy The phenomenon by which physical objects are perceived as unvarying despite changes in the appearance of the object or the surrounding environment (3)

peripheral (pur IF er ul) **nervous system** All parts of the nervous system *except* the brain and the spinal cord (includes somatic and autonomic divisions) (2)

peripheral (pur IF er ul) **vision** The ability to see objects behind the eyes' main center of focus (3)

personality The sum total of characteristics that differentiate people, or the stability in a person's behavior across different situations (11)

personality disorder A mental disorder characterized by a set of inflexible, maladaptive personality traits that keep a person from functioning properly in society (12)

personality psychology The branch of psychology that studies consistency and change in people's behavior and characteristics that differentiate people (1)

phallic (FAL ik) **stage** According to Freud, a period, beginning around age 3, during which a child's interest focuses on the genitals (11)

phencyclidine (fen SY kluh dine) **(PCP)** A powerful hallucinogen that alters brain-cell activity (9)

phenylketonuria (FEEN ul kee toe NYUR ee uh) **(PKU)** The inability to produce an enzyme that resists certain poisons, causing profound mental retardation (10)

phobias (FOBE ee ahs) Intense, irrational fears of specific objects, places, or situations (12)

phobic (FOBE ik) **disorders** Disorders characterized by unrealistic fears (phobias) that may keep people from carrying out routine daily behaviors (12)

phonemes (FONE eemz) The smallest units of sound that are used to form words (6)

phonology (fone OL o jee) The study of the sounds we make when we speak and of how we use these sounds by forming them into words (6)

pitch The "highs" or "lows" in sound (3)

pituitary (pih TOO ih tair ee) **gland** The "master gland," the major component of the endocrine system, which secretes hormones that control growth (2)

place theory of hearing The theory that states that different frequencies are responded to by different areas of the basilar membrane (3)

placebo (pla SEE bo) A biologically ineffective pill used in an experiment to keep subjects, and sometimes experimenters, from knowing whether or not the subjects have received a behavior-altering drug (1)

pleasure principle The principle by which the id operates, in which the person seeks the immediate reduction of tension and the maximization of satisfaction (11)

poggendorf (POG en dorf) **illusion** An illusion involving a line that passes diagonally through two parallel lines (3)

polygraph (POL ee graf) An electronic device that measures bodily changes that may signal that a person is lying; often called a lie detector (8)

pons The part of the brain that joins the halves of the cerebellum, transmitting motor information to coordinate muscles and integrate movement between the right and left sides of the body (2)

population All members of the group being studied (A)

positive reinforcer A stimulus added to the environment that brings about an increase in the response that preceded it (4)

positive relationship A relationship established by data that shows high values of one variable corresponding with high values of another, and low values of the first variable corresponding with low values of the other (A)

practical intelligence A person's style of thought and approach to problem solving, which may differ from traditional measures of intelligence (8)

predisposition model of schizophrenia A model that suggests that individuals may inherit a predisposition toward schizophrenia that makes them particularly vulnerable to stressful factors in the environment (12)

prefrontal lobotomy The surgical destruction of certain areas of a patient's frontal lobes to improve the control of emotionality (13)

preoperational stage According to Piaget, the period from 2 to 7 years of age that is characterized by language development (10)

primary drives Biological needs such as hunger, thirst, fatigue, and sex (8)

primary reinforcer A reward that satisfies biological needs (e.g., hunger or thirst) and works naturally (4)

proactive interference The phenomenon by which information stored in memory interferes with recall of later-learned material (5)

procedural knowledge The body of knowledge encompassing skills and habits (5)

profound retardation Mental retardation characterized by an IQ below 25 and an inability to function independently (7)

program evaluation The assessment of large-scale programs to determine their effectiveness in meeting their goals (1)

programmed instruction The development of learning by building gradually on basic knowledge, with review and reinforcement when appropriate (4)

projection A defense mechanism in which people attribute their own inadequacies or faults to someone else (11)

projective personality test An ambiguous stimulus presented to a person for the purpose of determining personality characteristics (11)

prosocial behavior Helping behavior (15)

proximity (prox IM ih tee) In Gestalt psychology, the tendency to group together those elements that are close together (4); one's nearness to another, one cause for liking (3, 15)

psychiatric (sy kee AT rik) **social worker** A social worker with specialized training in working with people in home and community settings (13)

psychoactive (SY ko ak tiv) **drugs** Drugs that affect a person's emotions, perceptions, and behavior (9)

psychoanalysis (sy ko an AL uh sis) Psychodynamic therapy that involves frequent sessions and often lasts for many years (13)

psychoanalysts (sy ko AN uh lists) Physicians or psychologists who specialize in psychoanalysis (11)

psychoanalytic (sy ko an uh LIT ik) **model of abnormality** The model that suggests that abnormality stems from childhood conflicts over opposing wishes (12)

psychoanalytic (sy ko an uh LIT ik) **theory** Freud's theory that unconscious forces act as determinants of personality (11)

psychodynamic (sy ko dy NAM ik) **model** The psychological model based on the belief that behavior is brought about by unconscious inner forces over which an individual has little control (1)

psychodynamic (sy ko dy NAM ik) **therapy** Therapy based on the notion that the basic sources of abnormal behavior are unresolved past conflicts and anxiety (13)

psychogenic amnesia (sy ko JEN ik am NEE zee ah) A failure to remember past experiences (12)

psychogenic fugue (sy ko JEN ik FEWG) An amnesiac condition in which people take sudden, impulsive trips, sometimes assuming a new identity (12)

psychological tests Standard measures devised to objectively assess behavior (11)

psychology The scientific study of behavior and mental processes (1)

psychophysics The study of the relationship between the physical nature of stimuli and a person's sensory responses to them (3)

psychosocial development Development of individuals' interactions and understanding of each other, and of their knowledge and understanding of themselves as members of society (10)

psychosurgery Brain surgery, once used to alleviate symptoms of mental disorder but rarely used today (13)

psychotherapy (sy ko THARE uh pee) The process in which a patient (client) and a professional attempt to remedy the client's psychological difficulties (13)

puberty (PEW bur tee) The period during which maturation of the sexual organs occurs (10)

punishment An unpleasant or painful stimulus that is *added* to the environment after a certain behavior occurs, decreasing the likelihood that the behavior will occur again (4)

pupil A dark hole in the center of the eye's iris which changes size as the amount of incoming light changes (3)

random assignment to condition The assignment of subjects to given conditions on a chance basis alone (1)

range The highest score in a distribution minus the lowest score (A)

rape The act whereby one person forces another to submit to sexual activity (8)

rapid-eye-movement (REM) sleep Sleep occupying around 20 percent of an adult's sleeping time, characterized by increased heart rate, blood pressure, and breathing rate; erections; eye movements; and the experience of dreaming (9)

rational-emotive therapy Psychotherapy based on Ellis's suggestion that the goal of therapy should be to restructure one's belief system into a more realistic, rational, and logical one (13)

rationalization A defense mechanism whereby people justify a negative situation in a way that protects their self-esteem (11)

reality principle The principle by which the ego operates, in which instinctual energy is restrained in order to maintain an individual's safety and integration into society (11)

rebound effect An increase in REM sleep after one has been deprived of it (9)

recall Drawing from memory a specific piece of information for a specific purpose (5)

receptive aphasia A specific syndrome involving problems with understanding language, resulting in fluent but nonsensical speech (2)

reciprocity-of-liking effect A tendency to like those who like us (15)

recognition Acknowledging prior exposure to a given stimulus, rather than recalling the information from memory (5)

reflexes Unlearned, involuntary responses to certain stimuli (10)

regression Behavior reminiscent of an earlier stage of development, carried out in order to have fewer demands put upon oneself (11)

rehearsal The transfer of material from short- to long-term memory via repetition (5)

reinforcer (ree in FORS er) Any stimulus that increases the probability that a preceding response will be repeated (4)

relative refractory period The period during which a neuron, not yet returned to a normal resting stage, requires more than the normal stimulus to be set off (2)

relative size The phenomenon by which, if two objects are the same size, the one that makes a smaller image on the retina is perceived to be farther away (3)

reliability Consistency in the measurements made by a test (11)

replication The repetition of an experiment in order to verify the results of the original experiment (1)

representativeness heuristic (hyur ISS tik) A rule in which people and things are judged by the degree to which they represent a certain category (6)

repression The primary defense mechanism, in which unacceptable id impulses are pushed back into the unconscious (11)

research Systematic inquiry aimed at discovering knowledge (1)

residual (rih ZIH ju al) **schizophrenia** Mental disorder characterized by minor symptoms of schizophrenia following a severe case or episode of schizophrenia (12)

resistance An inability or unwillingness to discuss or reveal particular memories, thoughts, or motivations (13)

resting state The nonfiring state of a neuron when the charge equals about −70 millivolts (2)

reticular (reh TIK u lar) **formation** A group of nerve cells in the brain that arouses the body to prepare it for appropriate action and screens out background stimuli (2)

retina (RET in uh) The part of the eye that converts the electromagnetic energy into useful information for the brain (3)

retrieval cue A stimulus such as a word, smell, or sound that allows us to more easily recall information located in long-term memory (5)

retroactive interference The phenomenon by which there is difficulty in recall of information learned earlier because of later exposure to different material (5)

reversibility The idea that some changes can be undone by reversing an earlier action (10)

rewards-costs approach The notion that, in a situation requiring help, a bystander's perceived rewards must outweigh the costs if helping is to occur (15)

rhodopsin (ro DOP sin) A complex, reddish-purple substance that changes when energized by light, causing a chemical reaction (3)

rods Long, cylindrical, light-sensitive receptors in the retina that perform well in poor light but are largely insensitive to color and small details (3)

rooting reflex A neonate's tendency to turn its head toward things that touch its cheek (10)

Rorschach (ROAR shock) **test** A test consisting of inkblots of indefinite shapes, the interpretation of which is used to assess personality characteristics (11)

rubella (roo BELL uh) German measles that, when contracted by pregnant women, can cause prenatal death or fetal malformation (10)

sample A subgroup of a population of interest (A)

savant syndrome (SAV ont SIN drome) A condition in which a mentally retarded person displays unusual talent in one specific area (7)

scatterplot A means of graphically illustrating the relationship between two variables (A)

Schachter-Singer (SHACK tur) **theory of emotion** The belief that emotions are determined jointly by a nonspecific kind of physiological arousal *and* its interpretation, based on environmental cues (8)

schedules of reinforcement The frequency and timing of reinforcement following desired behavior (4)

schemas (SKEEM uhs) Sets of cognitions about people and social experiences (14)

schizophrenia (skits uh FREN ee uh) A class of disorders characterized by a severe distortion of reality, resulting in antisocial behavior, silly or obsene behavior, hallucinations, and disturbances in movement (12)

school psychology The branch of psychology that considers the academic and emotional problems of elementary and secondary school students (1)

secondary drives Drives in which no biological need is fulfilled (e.g., need for achievement) (8)

secondary reinforcers A stimulus that becomes reinforcing by its association with a primary reinforcer (e.g., money, which allows us to obtain food, a primary reinforcer) (4)

secondary traits Less important personality traits (e.g., preferences for certain clothes or movies) that do not affect behavior as much as central and cardinal traits do (11)

selective attention The perceptual process of choosing a stimulus to attend to (3)

selective exposure An attempt to minimize dissonance by exposing oneself only to information that supports one's choice (14)

self-actualization In Maslow's theory, a state of self-fulfillment in which people realize their highest potential (8, 10)

self-concept The impression one holds of oneself (11)

self-fulfilling prophecy An expectation about the occurrence of an event or behavior that increases the likelihood that the event or behavior will happen (14)

self-perception theory Bem's theory that people form attitudes by observing their own behavior and applying the same principles to themselves as they do to others (14)

self-report measures A method of gathering data about people by asking them questions about their behavior (11)

semantic (seh MAN tik) **memories** Stored, organized facts about the world (e.g., mathematics, historical data) (5)

semantics The rules governing the meaning of words and sentences (6)

semicircular canals Parts of the inner ear containing fluid that moves when the body moves to control balance (3)

senility A broad imprecise term used in reference to elderly people who experience progressive deterioration of mental abilities, including memory loss, confusion of time and place, and general disorientation (10)

sensation The process by which an organism responds to a stimulus (3)

sensorimotor (SEN sor ee MO tor) **stage** According to Piaget, the stage from birth to 2 years during which a child has little competence in representing the environment using images, language, or other symbols (10)

sensory area The site in the brain of the tissue that corresponds to each of the senses, the degree of sensitivity relating to amount of tissue, also called the somatosensory area (2)

sensory memory The initial, short-lived storage of information recorded as a meaningless stimulus (5)

serial reproduction The passage of interpretive information from person to person, often resulting in inaccuracy through personal bias and misinterpretation (5)

severe retardation Mental retardation characterized by an IQ between 25 and 39 and difficulty in functioning independently (7)

shadowing A technique used during dichotic listening in which a subject is asked to repeat one of the messages aloud as it comes into one ear (3)

shaping The process of teaching a complex behavior by rewarding closer and closer approximations of the desired behavior (4)

short-term memory The storage of information for fifteen to twenty-five seconds; also known as working memory (5)

sickle-cell anemia A disease of the blood that affects about 10 percent of America's black population (10)

signal detection theory The theory that addresses the questions of whether a person can detect a stimulus and whether a stimulus is actually present at all (3)

significant outcome An outcome expected to occur by chance less than 5 percent of the time (A)

similarity The tendency to group together those elements that are similar in appearance (3)

simplicity The tendency to perceive a pattern in the most basic, straightforward, organized manner possible—the overriding gestalt principle (3)

situational causes of behavior Causes of behavior that are based on environmental factors (14)

skewed distribution A distribution that is not normal and therefore creates a curve that is not symmetrical (A)

skin senses The senses that include touch, pressure, temperature, and pain (3)

sleep apnea (AP nee uh) A sleep disorder characterized by difficulty in breathing and sleeping simultaneously (9)

sleep spindles Momentary interruptions in the brain-wave pattern during stage 2 sleep (9)

social cognition The processes that underlie our understanding of the social world (14)

social influence The area of social psychology concerned with situations in which the actions of an individual or group affect the behavior of others (15)

social learning theory (of personality) The theory that suggests that personality develops through observational learning (11)

social psychology The branch of psychology that studies how people's thoughts, feelings, and actions are affected by others (1, 14)

social supporter A person who shares an unpopular opinion or attitude of another group member, thereby encouraging nonconformity (15)

sociocultural model of abnormality The model that suggests that people's behavior, both normal and abnormal, is shaped by family, society, and cultural influences (12)

somatic (so MA tik) **division** The part of the nervous system that controls voluntary movements of the skeletal muscles (2)

somatoform (so MAT ah form) **disorders** Psychological difficulties that take on physical (somatic forms) (12)

somatosensory (so mat o SEN sor ee) **area** See sensory area (2)

sound The movement of air molecules brought about by the vibration of an object (3)

source traits The sixteen basic dimensions of personality that Catell identified as the root of all behavior (11)

spinal cord A bundle of nerves running along the spine, carrying messages between the brain and the body (2)

spinal reflexes Simple reflex movements carried out by the spinal cord without input from the brain (2)

split-brain patient A person who suffers from independent functioning of the two halves of the brain, as a result of which the sides of the body work in disharmony (2)

spontaneous recovery The reappearance of a previously extinguished response after a period of time during which the conditioned stimulus has been absent (4)

spontaneous remission Recovery without treatment (13)

stage 1 sleep The state of transition between wakefulness and sleep (9)

stage 2 sleep A sleep deeper than stage 1, which is characterized by sleep spindles (9)

stage 3 sleep A sleep characterized by slow brain waves, with greater peaks and valleys in the wave pattern (9)

stage 4 sleep The deepest stage of sleep, during which we are least responsible to outside stimulation (9)

standard deviation An index for how far an average score in a distribution of scores deviates from the distribution's center (A)

Stanford-Binet test A test of intelligence that includes a series of items varying in nature according to the age of the person being treated (7)

startle reflex See Moro reflex (12)

statistics The branch of mathematics concerned with collecting, organizing, analyzing, and drawing conclusions from numerical data (A)

status The social rank held within a group (15)

stereotypes A kind of schema in which beliefs and expectations about members of a group are held simply on the basis of their membership in that group (14)

stimulants Drugs that affect the central nervous system, causing increased heart rate, blood pressure, and muscle tension (9)

stimulus A source of physical energy that activates a sense organ (3)

stimulus control training Training in which an organism is reinforced in the presence of a certain specific stimulus, but not in its absence (4)

stimulus discrimination The process in which an organism is trained to differentiate among stimuli, restricting response to one in particular (4)

stimulus generalization Response to a stimulus that is similar to but different from a conditioned stimulus; the more similar the two stimuli, the more likely generalization is to occur (4)

stirrup A tiny bone in the middle ear that transfers vibrations to the oval window (3)

structuralism An early approach to psychology which focused on the fundamental elements underlying thoughts and ideas (1)

structure-of-intellect model A model of intelligence based on performance along three different dimensions: task content, task requirements, and product (7)

subcortex See central core (2)

subject expectations A subject's interpretation of what behaviors or responses are expected in an experiment (1)

sublimation (sub lim A shun) A defense mechanism, considered healthy by Freud, in which a person diverts unwanted impulses into socially acceptable thoughts, feelings, or behaviors (11)

sucking reflex A reflex that prompts an infant to suck at things that touch its lips (10)

sudden infant death syndrome A disorder in which seemingly healthy infants die in their sleep (9)

superego The part of personality that represents the morality of society as presented by parents, teachers, etc. (11)

superstitious behavior The mistaken belief that particular ideas, objects, or behavior will cause certain events to occur, due to learning that is based on the coincidental association between the idea, object, or behavior and subsequent reinforcement (4)

surface traits The sixteen basic dimensions of personality that Catell identified as the root of all behavior (11)

survey research Sampling a group of people by assessing their behavior, thoughts, or attitudes, then generalizing the findings to a larger population (1)

sympathetic division The part of the autonomic division of the peripheral nervous system that prepares the body to respond in stressful emergency situations (2)

symptom substitution The phenomenon by which new symptoms of psychological disturbance replace old symptoms when the underlying cause of the disturbance has not been eliminated (13)

syntax (SIN tax) The rules that indicate how words are joined to form sentences (6)

systematic desensitization A procedure in which a stimulus that evokes pleasant feelings is repeatedly paired with a stimulus that evokes anxiety in the hope that the anxiety will be alleviated (4, 13)

taste buds The receptor cells of the tongue (3)

Tay-Sachs (TAY SAKS) **disease** A genetic defect preventing the body from breaking down fat and typically causing death by the age of 3 or 4 (10)

telegraphic speech Sentences containing only the most essential words (6)

temporal lobes The portion of the brain located on either side of the cortex, the center for hearing (2)

terminal buttons Small branches at the end of an axon that relay messages to other cells (2)

testes (TES teez) The male reproductive organs responsible for secreting androgens (8)

thalamus (THAL uh muss) The part of the brain's central core that transmits messages from the sense organs to the cerebral cortex and from the cerebral cortex to the cerebellum and medulla (2)

thalidomide (thuh LID o mide) A tranquilizer that, when taken by pregnant women, can cause severe birth defects (10)

Thematic Apperception (thee MA tik ap per SEP shun) **Test (TAT)** A test consisting of a series of ambiguous pictures about which a person is asked to write a story, which is then taken to be a reflection of the writer's personality (8, 10)

theories Broad explanations and predictions concerning phenomena of interest (1)

time management A method of planning our time to make the most efficient use of it (4)

tip-of-the-tongue phenomenon The inability to recall information that one realizes one knows, a result of the difficulty of recalling information from long-term memory (5)

token system A procedure whereby a person is rewarded for performing certain desired behaviors (13)

trait theory A model that seeks to identify the basic traits necessary to describe personality (11)

traits Enduring dimensions of personality characteristics differentiating people from one another (11)

transcendance (tranz SEN danz) In Maslow's theory, a state in which one views onself in terms of the universe and laws of nature (8)

transcendental (trans sen DEN tul) **meditation (TM)** A popular type of meditation practiced by followers of Maharishi Mahesh Yogi (9)

transcutaneous (trans kew TANE ee us) **electrical nerve stimulation** A method of providing relief from pain by passing a low-voltage electric current through parts of the body (3)

transference A patient's transferal of certain strong feelings for others to the analyst (13)

treatment The manipulation implemented

by the experimenter to influence results in a segment of the experimental population (1)

treatment group The experimental group receiving the treatment, or manipulation (1)

trichromatic (try kro MAT ik) **theory of color vision** The theory that suggests that the retina has three kinds of cones, each responding to a specific range of wavelengths, perception of color being influenced by the relative strength with which each is activated (3)

trust-versus-mistrust stage According to Erikson, the first stage of psychosocial development, occurring from birth to 18 months of age, during which time infants develop feelings of trust or lack of trust (10)

tunnel vision An advanced stae of glaucoma in which vision is reduced to the narrow circle directly in front of the eye (3)

unconditional positive regard Supportive behavior from another individual, regardless of one's words or actions (11, 13)

unconditioned response (UCR) A natural response that needs no training (e.g., salivation at the smell of food) (4)

unconditioned stimulus (UCS) A stimulus that is paired with a neutral stimulus to condition a natural response that would otherwise not occur (4)

unconscious A part of the personality of which a person is unaware and which is a potential determinant of behavior (11)

undifferentiated schizophrenia Mental disorder characterized by a mixture of symptoms of schizophrenia (12)

universal grammar An underlying structure shared by all languages, the basis of Chomsky's theory that certain language characteristics are based on the brain's structure and are, therefore, common to all people (6)

validity The ability of a test to measure what it is supposed to measure (11)

variability The spread or dispersion of scores in a distribution (A)

variable A behavior or event that can be changed (1)

variable-interval schedule A schedule whereby reinforcement is given at various times, usually causing a behavior to be maintained more consistently (4)

variable-ratio schedule A schedule whereby reinforcement occurs after a varying number of responses rather than after a fixed number (4)

ventromedial (ven tro MEE dee ul) **hypothalamus** The portion of the hypothalamus that signals that the body has consumed enough food and that eating should cease (8)

vernix (VUR nix) A white lubrication that covers a fetus, protecting it during birth (10)

vicarious (vy CARE ee us) **learning** Learning by observing others (14)

visceral (VIS er al) **experience** The "gut" reaction experienced internally, triggering an emotion (see James-Lange theory) (8)

visual illusion A physical stimulus that consistently produces errors in perception (often called an optical illusion) (3)

visual spectrum (SPEK trum) The range of wavelengths to which humans are sensitive (3)

von Restorff effect The phenomenon by which distinctive stimuli are recalled more readily than less distinctive ones (5)

wear-and-tear theories of aging Theories that suggest that the body's mechanical functions cease efficient activity and, in effect, wear out (10)

Weber's law The principle that states that the just noticeable difference is a constant proportion of the magnitude of an initial stimulus (3)

Wechsler Adult Intelligence Scale—Revised (WAIS-R) test A test of intelligence consisting of verbal and nonverbal performance sections, providing a relatively precise picture of a person's specific abilities (7)

Wechsler Intelligence Scale for Children—Revised (WISC-R) An intelligence test for children; see Wechsler Adult Intelligence Scale—Revised (7)

weight set point According to one theory, the specific weight a body strives to maintain (8)

Yerkes-Dodson (YUR keez) **law** The theory that a particular level of motivational arousal produces optimal performance of a task (8)

Yerkish A language system, taught to chimpanzees, that consists of about 225 geometric symbols representing English words (6)

zygote (ZY gote) The one-celled product of fertilization (10)

REFERENCES

Adams, P. R., & Adams, G. R. (1984). Mount Saint Helen's ashfall: Evidence for a disaster stress reaction. *American Psychologist, 39,* pp. 252–260.

Aiello, J. R., Baum, A., & Gormley, F. P. (1980). *Social determinants of residential crowding.* Unpublished manuscript, Rutgers University, New Brunswick, NJ.

Albee, G. W. (1978, February 12). I.Q. tests on trial. *The New York Times,* p.E-13.

Allen, V. L. (1965). Situational factors in conformity. In L. Berkowitz (Ed.), *Advances in experimental social psychology,* Vol. 1. New York: Academic Press.

Allen, V. L. (1975). Social support for nonconformity. In L. Berkowitz (Ed.), *Advances in experimental social psychology,* Vol. 8, New York: Academic Press.

Allport, G. W., & Postman, L. J. (1958). The basic psychology of rumor. In E. E. Maccoby, T. M. Newcomb, & E. L. Hartley (Eds.), *Readings in social psychology (3rd ed.).* New York: Holt, Rinehart and Winston.

Allport, G. W. (1961). *Pattern and growth in personality.* New York: Holt, Rinehart and Winston.

Allport, G. W. (1966). Traits revisited. *American Psychologist, 21,* 1–10.

Alwitt, L., & Mitchell, A. A. (1985). *Psychological processes and advertising effects: Theory, research, and applications.* Hillsdale, NJ: Erlbaum.

Amabile, T. (1985). *The creativity maze.* Address presented at the annual meeting of the American Psychological Association, Los Angeles.

Amabile, T. M. (1985). Motivation and creativity: Effects of motivational orientation on creative writers. *Journal of Personality and Social Psychology, 48,* 393–399.

Amabile, T. M, Hennessey, B. A., & Grossman, B. S. (1986). Social influences on creativity: The effects of contracted for reward. *Journal of Personality and Social Psychology, 50,* 14–23.

American Psychological Association. (1980). *Careers in psychology.* Washington, DC

American Psychological Association. (1986, March). Council resolution on polygraph tests. *APA Monitor.*

American Psychological Association. (1981). *Ethical principles of psychologists.* Washington, DC: American Psychological Association.

Amir, Y. (1976). The role of intergroup contact in change of prejudice and ethnic relations. In P. Katz (Ed.), *Towards the elimination of racism.* New York: Pergamon.

Anastasi, A. (1982). *Psychological testing (5th ed.).* New York: Macmillan.

Anderson, C. A. (1987). Temperature and aggression: Effects on quarterly, yearly, and city rates of violent and nonviolent crime. *Journal of Personality and Social Psychology, 52,* 1161–1173.

Anderson, C. A., & Anderson, D. C. (1984). Ambient temperature and violent crime: Tests of the linear and curvilinear hypotheses. *Journal of Personality and Social Psychology, 46,* 91–97.

Anderson, J. R., & Bower, G. H. (1972). Recognition and retrieval processes in free recall. *Psychological Review, 79,* 97–123.

Anderson, J. R., & Bower, G. H. (1973). *Human associative memory.* Washington, DC: Winston.

Anderson, N. H. (1974). Cognitive algebra integration theory applied to social attribution. In L. Berkowitz (Ed.), *Advances in experimental social psychology* (Vol. 7, pp. 1–101). New York: Academic Press.

Annett, M. (1985). *Left, right, hand, and brain: The right shift theory.* Hillsdale, NJ: Erlbaum.

Apter, A., Galatzer, A., Beth-Halachmi, N., & Laron, Z. (1981). Self-image in adolescents with delayed puberty and growth retardation. *Journal of Youth and Adolescence, 10,* 501–505.

Arafat, I., & Cotton, W. L. (1974). Masturbation practices of males and females. *Journal of Sex Research, 10,* 293–307.

Archibald, W. P. (1974). Alternative explanations for the self-fulfilling prophecy. *Psychological Bulletin, 81,* 74–84.

Arena, J. M. (1984, April). A look at the opposite sex. *Newsweek on campus,* 21.

Asch, S. E. (1946). Forming impressions of personality. *Journal of Abnormal and Social Psychology, 41,* 258–290.

Asch, S. E. (1951). Effects of group pressure upon the modification and distortion of judgments. In H. Guetzkow (Ed.), *Groups, leadership, and men.* Pittsburgh: Carnegie Press.

Asch, S. E., & Zukier, H. (1984). Thinking about persons. *Journal of Personality and Social Psychology, 46,* 1230–1240.

Asnis, G., & Ryan, N. D. (1983). The psychoneuroendocrinology of schizophrenia. In A. Rifkin (Ed.), *Schizophrenia and effective disorders: Biology and drug treatment* (pp. 205–236). Boston: John Wright.

Atkinson, J. W., & Litwin, G. H. (1960). Achievement motive and test anxiety conceived as motive to approach success and motive to avoid failure. *Journal of Abnormal and Social Psychology, 60,* 52–63.

Atkinson, J. W., & Raynor, J. O. (Eds.). (1974). *Motivation and achievement.* Washington, DC: Winston.

Atkinson, R. C., & Shiffrin, R. M. (1968). Human memory: A proposed system and its control processes. In K. W. Spence and J. T. Spence (Eds.), *The psychology of learning and motivation: Advances in research and theory* (Vol. 2, pp. 80–195). New York: Academic Press.

Atwater, E. (1983). *Adolescence.* Englewood Cliffs, NJ: Prentice-Hall.

Averill, J. R. (1975). A semantic atlas of emotional concepts. *Catalog of selected documents in psychology, 5,* 330.

Axelrod, R., & Scarr, S. (in press). Human intelligence and public policy. *Scientific American.*

Azrin, N. H., & Holt, N. C. (1966). Punishment. In W. A. Honig (Ed.), *Operant behavior: Areas of research and application* (pp. 380–447). New York: Appleton.

Azrin, N. H., & Foxx, R. M. (1974). *Toilet training in less than a day.* New York: Simon and Schuster.

Bahill, T. A., & Laritz, T. (1984). Why can't batters keep their eyes on the ball? *American Scientist, 72,* pp. 249–253.

Ballinger, C. B. (1981). The menopause and its syndromes. In J. G. Howells (Ed.), *Modern perspectives in the psychiatry of middle age* (pp. 279–303). New York: Brunner/Mazel.

Baltes, P. B., & Schaie, K. W. (1974, March). The myth of the twilight years. *Psychology Today, 7,* pp. 35–38f.

Bandura, A. (1973). *Aggression: A social learning analysis.* Englewood Cliffs, NJ: Prentice-Hall.

Bandura, A. (1981). In search of pure unidirectional determinants. *Behavior Therapy, 12,* 30–40.

Bandura, A. (1977). *Social learning theory.* Englewood Cliffs, NJ: Prentice-Hall.

Bandura, A., Grusec, J. E., & Menlove, F. L. (1967). Vicarious extinction of avoidance behavior. *Journal of Personality and Social Psychology, 5,* 16–23.

Bandura, A., Ross, D., & Ross, S. (1963). Imitation of film-mediated aggressive models. *Journal of Abnormal and Social Psychology, 66,* 3–11.

Bandura, A., Ross, D., & Ross, S. (1963). Vicarious reinforcement and imitative learning. *Journal of Abnormal and Social Psychology, 67,* 601–607.

Bannatyne, A. (1971). *Language, reading, and learning disabilities.* Springfield, IL: Thomas.

Barber, T. X. (1970). Who believes in hypnosis? *Psychology Today, 4,* pp. 20; 24–27; 84.

Barber, T. X. (1975). Responding to "hypnotic" suggestions: An introspective report. *American Journal of Clinical Hypnosis, 18,* 6–22.

Barber, T. X. (1981). *Hypnosis: A scientific approach.* South Orange, NJ: Power.

Barker, L. M., Best, M. E., Domjan, M. (Eds.) (1977). *Learning mechanisms in food selection.* Waco, TX: Baylor University Press.

Barland, G. H., & Raskin, D. C. (1975). An evaluation of field techniques in defection of deception. *Psychophysiology, 12,* 321–330.

Baron, R. A., & Kepner, C. R. (1970). Model's behavior and attraction toward the model as determinants of adult aggressive behavior. *Journal of Personality and Social Psychology, 14,* 335–344.

Baron, R. A., & Ransberger, V. M. (1978). Ambient temperature and the occurrence of collective violence: The long, hot summer revisited. *Journal of Personality and Social Psychology, 36,* 351–360.

Baron, R. A., Russell, G. W., & Arms, R. L. (1985). Negative ions and behavior: Impact on mood, memory, and aggression among Type A and Type B persons. *Journal of Personality and Social Psychology, 48,* 746–754.

Baron, R. M., Mandel, D. R., Adams, C. A., & Greiffen, L. M. (1976). Effects of social density in university residential environments. *Journal of Personality and Social Psychology, 34,* 434–446.

Bartoshuk, L. M. (1971). The chemical senser: I. Taste. In J. N. Kling and L. A. Riggs (Eds.), *Experimental psychology* (3rd ed.). New York: Holt, Rinehart and Winston.

Baruch, G. K., & Barnett, R. C. (1980). On the well-being of adult women. In L. A. Bond & J. C. Rosen (Eds.), *Competence and coping during adulthood.*

Hanover, NH: University Press of New England.

Bateson, G. (1960). Minimal requirements for a theory of schizophrenia. *Archives of General Psychiatry, 2,* 477–491.

Baum, A., Fleming, R., & Singer, J. E. (1983). Coping with technological disaster. *Journal of Social Issues, 39,* 117–138.

Baum, A., Gatchel, R. J., & Schaeffer, M. A. (1983). Emotional, behavioral, and physiological effects of chronic stress at Three Mile Island. *Journal of Consulting and Clinical Psychology, 51,* 565–572.

Baum, A., & Paulus, P. (1986). Crowding. In D. Stokols & I. Altman (Eds.), *Handbook of Environmental Psychology.* New York: Wiley.

Baumgardner, A. H., Heppner, P. P., & Arkin, R. M. (1986). Role of causal attribution in personal problem solving. *Journal of Personality and Social Psychology, 50,* 636–643.

Beaton, A. (1986). *Left side, right side: A review of laterality research.* New Haven: Yale University Press.

Beck, A. T. (1985). Cognitive therapy of depression: New perspectives. In P. J. Clayton and J. E. Barret (Eds.), *Treatment of depression: Old controversies and new approaches* (pp. 265–290). New York: Raven Press.

Beck, A. T., Rush, A. J., Shaw, B., & Emery, G. (1979). *Cognitive therapy of depression: A treatment manual.* New York: Guilford Press.

Beck, J., Hope, B., & Rosenfeld, A. (Eds.). (1983). *Human and machine vision.* New York: Academic Press.

Bednar, R. L., & Kaul, T. J. (1978). Experimental group research: Current perspectives. *Handbook of Psychotherapy and Behavior Change: An empirical analysis* (2nd ed.). New York: Wiley.

Bee, H. L. (1985). *The developing child* (4th ed.). New York: Harper & Row.

Bell, S. M., & Ainsworth, M. D. S. (1972). Infant crying and maternal responsiveness. *Child Development, 43,* pp. 1171–1190.

Bem, D. J. (1967). Self-perception: An alternative interpretation of cognitive dissonance phenomena. *Psychological Review, 74,* pp. 183–200.

Bem, D. (1972). Self-perception theory. In L. Berkowitz (Ed.), *Advances in experimental social psychology* (Vol. 6, pp. 1–62). New York: Academic Press.

Benjamin, L. T., Jr. (1985, February). Defining aggression: An exercise for classroom discussion. *Teaching of Psychology, 12* (1), 40–42.

Benson, H. (1975). *The relaxation response.* New York: William Morrow.

Benson, H., & Friedman, R. (1985). A rebuttal to the conclusions of Davis S. Holme's article, "Meditation and somatic arousal reduction." *American Psychologist,* 725–726.

Benson, H., Kotch, J. B., Crassweller, K. D., & Greenwood, M. (1977). Historical and clinical considerations of the relaxation response. *American Scientist, 65,* pp. 441–445.

Berg, J. H. (1984). Development of friendship between roommates. *Journal of Personality and Social Psychology, 46,* 346–356.

Bergener, M., Ermini, M., & Stahelin, H. B. (Eds.). (1985, February). *Thresholds in aging.* The 1984 Sandoz Lectures in Gerontology. Basle, Switzerland.

Berger, J. (1984, December 12). Two Bronx brothers, two different lives. *New York Times.*

Bergin, A. E., & Lambert, M. J. (1978). The evaluation of therapeutic outcomes. *Handbook of psychotherapy and behavior change: An empirical analysis* (2nd ed.). New York: Wiley.

Berkowitz, L. (1954). Group standards, cohesiveness and productivity. *Human Relations, 7,* pp. 509–519.

Berkowitz, L. (1974). Some determinants of impulsive aggression: The role of mediated associations with reinforcements for aggression. *Psychological Review, 81,* 165–176.

Berkowitz, L. (1979). *A survey of social psychology* (2nd ed.). New York: Holt, Rinehart and Winston.

Berkowitz, L. (1983). Some parallels and differences in research with animals and humans. *American Psychologist, 38,* 1135–1144.

Berkowitz, L. (1984). Aversive conditioning as stimuli to aggression. In R. J. Blanchard and C. Blanchard (Eds.), *Advances in the study of aggression* (Vol. 1). New York: Academic Press.

Berkowitz, L., & Geen, R. G. (1966). Film violence and the cue properties of available targets. *Journal of Personality and Social Psychology, 3,* 525–530.

Berkowitz, L., & LePage, A. (1967). Weapons as aggression-eliciting stimuli. *Journal of Personality and Social Psychology, 7,* 202–207.

Berlyne, D. (1967). Arousal and reinforcement. In D. Levine (Ed.), *Nebraska symposium on motivation.* Lincoln: University of Nebraska Press.

Berman, J. S., Miller, R. C., & Massman, P. J. (1985). Cognitive therapy versus systematic desensitization: Is one treatment superior? *Psychological Bulletin, 97,* 451–461.

Bernard, M. E., & Joyce, M. R. (1984). *Rational-emotive therapy with children and adolescents.* Somerset, NJ: Wiley.

Berscheid, E. (1985). Interpersonal attraction. In G. Lindzey & E. Aronson (Eds.), *Handbook of social psychology* (3rd ed.). New York: Random House.

Berscheid, E., & Walster E. (1974). Physical attractiveness. In L. Berkowitz (Ed.), *Advances in experimental social psychology* (Vol. 7, pp. 157–215). New York: Academic Press.

Best, C. T. (Ed.).(1985). *Hemispheric function and collaboration in the child.* New York: Academic Press.

Bieber, I., et al. (1962). *Homosexuality: A psychoanalytic study.* New York: Basic Books.

Binet, A., & Simon, T. (1916). *The development of intelligence in children* (The Binet-Simon Scale). Baltimore, MD: Williams & Wilkins.

Bini, L. (1938). Experimental research on epileptic attacks induced by the electric current. *American Journal of Psychiatry,* Supplement 94, 172–183.

Birch, H. G. (1945). The role of motivation factors in insightful problem-solving. *Journal of Comparative Psychology, 38,* 295–317.

Birnbaum, M. H., & Mellers, B. A. (1979). Stimulus recognition may mediate exposure effects. *Journal of Personality and Social Psychology, 37,* 391–394.

Blakeslee, S. (1984, August 14). Scientists find key biological causes of alcoholism. *New York Times,* p. C1.

Blanchard, R. J., & Blanchard, L. (1984). *Advances in the study of aggression*. Vol. 1. New York: Academic Press.

Blank, J. P. (1983, October). "I can see feeling good." *Readers Digest, 123,* pp. 98–104.

Blatt, S. J., D'Afflitti, J. P., & Quinlan, D. M. (1976). Experiences of depression in normal young adults. *Journal of Abnormal Psychology, 85,* pp. 383–389.

Blau, Z. S. (1973). *Old age in a changing society*. New York: New Viewpoints.

Bloom, B. (1985). *Developing talent in young people*. New York: Ballantine.

Blusztajn, J. K., & Wurtman, R. J. (1983). Choline and cholinergic neurons. *Science 221,* 614–620.

Blyle, C. M. (1970). Differences between patient's and doctor's interpretations of some common medical terms. *British Medical Journal, 2,* 286–289.

Boffey, P. M. (1986, May 14). Psychotherapy is as good as drug in curing depression, study finds. *New York Times,* A1, A17.

Bolles, R. C., & Fanselow, M. S. (1982). Endorphins and behavior. *Annual Review of Psychology, 33,* 87–101.

Bootzin, R. R. (1975). *Behavior modification and therapy: An introduction*. Cambridge, MA: Winthrop Press.

Boring, E. G., Langfeld, H. S., & Weld, H. P. (1948). *Foundations of psychology*. NY: John Wiley.

Bornstein, M. H. (1984). Habituation of attention as a measure of visual information processing in human infants: Summary, systematization, and synthesis. In G. Gottleib & N. A. Krasnegor (Eds.), *Measurement of audition and vision in the first year of postnatal life: A methodological overview*. Norwood, NJ: Ablex.

Bornstein, M. H. (1984). Perceptual development. In M. H. Bornstein & M. E. Lamb (Eds.), *Developmental psychology: An advanced textbook*. Hillsdale, NJ: Erlbaum.

Bornstein, M. H. & Sigman, M. D. (1986). Continuity in mental development from infancy. *Child Development, 57,* 251–274.

Botwinick, J. (1978). *Aging and behavior: A comprehensive integration of research findings* (2nd ed.). New York: Springer.

Bourne, L. E., Dominowski, R. L., and Loftus, E. F. (1979). *Cognitive processes*. Englewood Cliffs, NJ: Prentice Hall.

Boyd, J. H., & Weissman, M. M. (1981). Epidemiology of affective disorders: A re-examination and future directions. *Archives of General Psychiatry, 38,* pp. 1039–1045.

Brady, J. V. (1958, October). Ulcers in "executive monkeys." *Scientific American*.

Braun, B. (1985, May 21). Interview by D. Goleman: New focus on multiple personality. *New York Times,* p. C1.

Brazelton, B. (1969). *Infants and mothers: Differences in development*. New York: Dell.

Breggin, P. R. (1979). *Electroshock: Its brain disabling effects*. New York: Springer.

Breisacher, P. (1971). Neuropsychological effects of air pollution. *American Behavioral Scientist, 14,* 837–864.

Breskin (1984, November 8). *Rolling Stone Magazine,* p. 26.

Brewer, M. B. (1979). Ingroup bias in the minimal intergroup situation: A cognitive motivational analysis. *Psychological Bulletin, 86,* 307–324.

Broad, N. J. (1984, January 10). Pentagon is said to focus on ESP for wartime use. *New York Times,* pp. C1, C7.

Broad, N. J. (1984, September 25). *New York Times,* p. C1.

Brody, J. (1982). *New York Times guide to personal health*. NY: Times Books.

Brody, N. (1983). *Human motivation*. New York: Academic Press.

Broverman, I. K., Vogel, S. R., Broverman, D. M., Clarkson, F. E., & Rosenkrantz, P. S. (1972). Sex-role stereotypes: A current appraisal. *Journal of Social Issues, 28,* 59–78.

Brown, B. (1984). *Between health and illness*. Boston: Houghton Mifflin.

Brown, B. B. (1977). *Stress and the art of biofeedback*. New York: Harper & Row.

Brown, P. K., & Wald, G. (1964). Visual pigments in single rod and cones of the human retina. *Science, 144,* pp. 45–52.

Brown, R. (1958). How shall a thing be called? *Psychological Review, 65,* 14–21.

Brown, R., & Fraser, C. (1963). The acquisition of syntax. In C. N. Cofer & B. Musgrave (Eds.), *Verbal behavior and learning: Problems and processes*. NY: McGraw-Hill, pp. 158–201.

Brown, R., & Kulik, J. (1977). Flashbulb memories. *Cognition, 5,* 73–99.

Bruce, V., & Green, P. (1984). *Visual perception: Physiology, psychology, and ecology*. Hillsdale, NJ: Erlbaum.

Bruch, H. (1973). *Eating disorders*. New York: Basic Books.

Bruner, J. S. (1969). Foreword. In T. B. Brazelton, *Infants and mothers: Differences in development*. New York: Dell.

Bronson, B. I., & McKee, K. D. (1982). Crisis intervention and stress management: Giving resident advisors what they need. *Journal of College Student Personnel, 23,* 547–548.

Bryan, J. H., & Test, M. A. (1967). Models and helping: Naturalistic studies in aiding behavior. *Journal of Personality and Social Psychology, 6,* 400–407.

Buckhout, R. (1975). Eyewitness testimony. *Scientific American,* pp. 23–31.

Burnham, D. K. (1983). Apparent relative size in the judgment of apparent distance. *Perception, 12,* 683–700.

Butcher, J. N., & Owen, P. L. (1978). Objective personality inventories: Recent research and some contemporary issues. In B. B. Wolman (Ed.), *Clinical diagnosis of mental disorders: A handbook*. New York: Plenum Press.

Butler, R. A. (1954). Incentive conditions which influence visual exploration. *Journal of Experimental Psychology, 48,* 19–23.

Byers, P., and Byers, H. (1972). Nonverbal communication and the education of children. In C. B. Cazden, V. P. John, and D. Hynes (Eds.), *Functions of language in the classroom*. New York: Teachers College Press.

Byrne, D. (1969). Attitudes and attraction. In L. Berkowitz (Ed.), *Advances in experimental social psychology* (Vol. 4, pp. 35–89). New York: Academic Press.

Byrne, D. & Kelley, L. (1981). *An introduction to personality* (3rd ed.). Englewood Cliffs, NJ: Prentice-Hall.

Cacioppo, J. T., & Petty, R. E. (1979). Attitudes and cognitive response: An electrophysiological approach. *Journal of Personality and Social Psychology, 37,* 2181–2199.

Cairns, H. S., & Cairns, C. E. (1976). *Psycholinguistics: A cognitive view of language*. New York: Holt, Rinehart and Winston.

Cannon, W. B. (1929). Organization for physiological homeostatics. *Physiological Review, 9,* 280–289.

Caroll, J. B. (1982). The measurement of intelligence. In R. J. Sternberg (Ed.), *The handbook of human intelligence* (pp. 29–120). Cambridge, MA: Cambridge University Press.

Carson, R. C. (1983). The schizophrenias. In H. E. Adams & P. B. Sutker (Eds.), *Handbook of clinical behavior therapy*. New York: Plenum Press.

Cartwright, D. (1968). The nature of group cohesiveness. In D. Cartwright & A. Zandu (Eds.), *Group dynamics: Research and theory* (3rd ed.). New York: Harper & Row.

Cartwright, R. D. (1978). *A primer on sleep and dreaming*. Reading, MA: Addision-Wesley.

Casey, K. L., & Morrow, T. J. (1983). Ventral posterior thalamic neurons differentially responsive to noxious stimulation of the awake monkey. *Science, 223,* pp. 675–677.

Casey, R. J., & Berman, J. S. (1985). The outcome of psychotherapy with children. *Psychological Bulletin, 98,* 388–400.

Catania, A. C. (1984). *Learning* (2nd ed.). Englewood Cliffs, NJ: Prentice-Hall.

Cattell, R. B. (1963). Theory of fluid and crystallized intelligence: A critical experiment. *Journal of Educational Psychology, 54,* 1–22.

Cattell, R. B. (1967). *The scientific analysis of personality*. Baltimore: Penguin.

Ceci, S. J., Peters, D., & Plotkin, J. (1985). Human subjects review: Personal values and the regulation of social science research. *American Psychologist, 40,* 994–1002.

Cerella, J. (1985). Information processing rates in the elderly. *Psychological Bulletin, 98,* 67–83.

Chafetz, M. (1976). *Why drinking can be good for you*. New York: Stein and Day.

Chaiken, S. (1979). Communicator physical attractiveness and persuasion. *Journal of Personality and Social Psychology, 37,* 1387–1397.

Chandler, M. J. (1976). Social cognition and life-span approaches to the study of child development. In H. W. Reese & L. P. Lipsitt (Eds.), *Advances in child development and behavior* (Vol. 11). New York: Academic Press.

Chavez, C. J., Ostrea, E. M., Stryker, J. C., & Smialek, Z. (1979). Sudden infant death syndrome among infants of drug-dependent mothers. *Journal of Pediatrics, 95,* 407–409.

Check, J. V. P., & Malamuth, N. M. (1986). Pornography and sexual aggression: A social learning theory analysis. In M. L. McLaughlin (Ed.), *Communication yearbook 9*. Beverly Hills, CA: Sage.

Check, J. V. P., Malamuth, N. M., Elias, B., & Barton, S. A. (1985, April). On hostile ground. *Psychology Today, 19,* pp. 56–61.

Cherry, E. C. (1953). Some experiments on the recognition of speech with one and two ears. *Journal of the Acoustical Society of America, 25,* 975–979.

Chomsky, N. (1968). *Language and mind*. New York: Harcourt Brace Jovanovich.

Chomsky, N. (1969). *The acquisition of syntax in children from five to ten*. Cambridge, MA: MIT Press.

Chomsky, N. (1978). On the biological basis of language capacities. In G. A. Miller & E. Lennenberg (Eds.), *Psychology and biology of language and thought* (pp. 199–220). New York: Academic Press.

Cialdini, R. B. (1984). *Social influence*. New York: William Morrow.

Cohen, D. B. (1979). *Sleep and dreaming: Origins, nature, and functioning*. New York: Pergamon.

Cohen, L. B., DeLoache, J. S., & Strauss, M. S. (1979). Infant visual perception. In J. D. Osopsky (Ed.), *Handbook of infant development* (pp. 393–438). New York: Wiley-Interscience.

Cohen, T. E., & Lasley, D. J. (1986). Visual sensitivity. In Rosenweig & Porter (Eds.), *Annual Review of Psychology, 37*. Palo Alto, CA: Annual Reviews.

Colby, A., Kohlberg, L., Gibbs, J., & Lieberman, M. (1983). A longitudinal study of moral judgement. *Monographs of the Society for Research in Child Development, 48,* 77.

Coleman, J. C., Butcher, J. N., & Carson, R. C. (1984). *Abnormal psychology and modern life*. Glenview, IL: Scott, Foresman.

Coleman, J., George, R., & Holt, G. (1977). Adolescents and their parents: A study of attitudes. *Journal of Genetic Psychology, 130,* 239–245.

Coleman, J., et. al. (1977). Adolescents and their parents: A study of attitudes. *Journal of Genetic Psychology, 130,* 239–245.

Converse, J., Jr., & Cooper, J. (1979). The importance of decisions and free-choice attitude change: A curvilinear finding. *Journal of Experimental Social Psychology, 15,* 48–61.

Cooper, A. M. (1984). Psychoanalysis at one hundred: Beginnings of maturity. *Journal of American Psychoanalytical Association, 32,* 245–268.

Cooper, C., & Payne, R. (1978). *Stress at work*. London: Wiley.

Cooper, I. S. (1981). *Living with chronic neurological disease*. New York: Norton.

Coppen, A., Metcalfe, M., & Wood, K. (1982). Lithium. In E. S. Paykel (Ed.), *Handbook of affective disorders*. New York: Guilford Press.

Corballis, M. C., & Beale, I. L. (1976). *The psychology of left and right*. Hillsdale, NJ: Erlbaum.

Corballis, M. C., & Beale, I. L. (1983). *The ambivalent mind: The neuro-psychology of left and right*. Chicago: Nelson-Hall.

Coren, S., & Porac, C. (1983). The creation and reversal of the Muller-Lyer illusion through attentional manipulation. *Perception, 12,* pp. 49–54.

Coren, S., Porac, C., & Ward, L. M. (1984). *Sensation and perception* (2nd ed.). New York: Academic Press.

Cornsweet, T. N. (1970). *Visual perception*. New York: Academic Press.

Coryell, W., & Winokur, G. (1982). Course and outcome. In E. S. Paykel (Ed.), *Handbook of affective disorders*. New York: Guilford Press.

Costa, P. T., Jr., & McCrae, R. R. (1985). Hypochondriasis, neuroticism, and aging. *American Psychologist, 40,* 19–28.

Council of Scientific Affairs (1985, April 5). Scientific status of refreshing recollection by the use of hypnosis. *Journal of the American Medical Association, 253*(13).

Craighead, W. E., Kazdin, A. E., & Mahoney, M. J. (1981). *Behavior modification: Principles, issues, and applications*. Boston: Houghton Mifflin.

Craik, F. I. M. (1977). Age differences in human memory. In J. E. Birren & K. W. Schaie (Eds.), *Handbook of the psychology of aging*. New York: Van Nostrand Reinhold.

Craik, F. I., & Lockhart, R. S. (1972). Levels of processing: A framework for memory research. *Journal of Verbal Behavior, 11,* 671–684.

Crapo, L. (1985). Hormones: Messengers of life.

Crocetti, G. (1983). *GRE: Graduate record examination general aptitude test*. New York: Arco.

Crook, T. H., & Miller, N. E. (1985). The challenge of Alzheimer's disease. *American Psychologist, 40*(11), 1245–1250.

Croyle, R. T., & Cooper, J. (1983). Dissonance arousal: Physiological evidence. *Journal of Personality and Social Psychology, 45,* 782–791.

Cummings, E., & Henry, W. E. (1961). *Growing old*. New York: Basic Books.

Cummings, L. L., & Berger, C. J. (1976). Organization structure: How does it influence attitudes and performance? *Organizational Dynamics, 5,* 34–49.

Cusack, O. (1984, April), Pigeon posses. *Omni, 6,* p. 34.

Cyert, R., & March, J. G. (1963). *A behavioral theory of the firm*. Englewood Cliffs, NJ: Prentice-Hall.

Daehler, M., & Bukato, D. (1985). *Cognitive development*. New York: Random House.

Darley, J. M., & Latané, B. (1968). Bystander intervention in emergencies: Diffusion of responsibility. *Journal of Personality and Social Psychology, 8,* 377–383.

Darwin, C. J., Turvey, M. T., & Crowder, R. G. (1972). An auditory analogue of the Sperling partial-report procedure: Evidence for brief auditory storage. *Cognitive Psychology, 3,* 255–267.

Davidson, R. J. (1984). Hemispheric asymmetry and emotion. In K. R. Scherer & P. Ekman (Eds.), *Approaches to emotion* (pp. 39–57). Hillsdale, NJ: Erlbaum.

Davis, H. P., & Squire, L. R. (1984). Protein synthesis and memory: A review. *Psychological Bulletin, 96,* pp. 518–559.

Deane, V. K., & Waters, E. (1985). *Monograph for the society for research in child development, 50,* 110–135.

DeCarlo, N. A. (1983). *Psychological games*. New York: Facts on File.

DeCasper, A. J., & Fifer, W. D. (1980). Of human bonding: Newborns prefer their mothers' voices. *Science, 208,* pp. 1174–1176.

DeCharms, R., & Moeller, G. H. (1962). Values expressed in American children's readers, 1800–1950. *Journal of Abnormal and Social Psychology, 64,* 136–142.

Deci, E. L., & Ryan, R. M. (1985). *Intrinsic motivation and self-determination in human behavior*. New York: Plenum Press.

deGroot, A. D. (1966). Perception and memory versus thought: Some old ideas and recent findings. In B. Kleinmuntz (Ed.), *Problem solving: Research, method, and theory*. New York: Wiley.

Dehn, N., & Shank, R. (1982). Artificial and human intelligence. In R. J. Sternbert (Ed.), *Handbook of human intelligence* (pp. 352–391). Cambridge, MA: Cambridge University Press.

Dement, W. C. (1976). *Some must watch while some must sleep*. New York: Norton.

Dement, W. C. (1979). Two kinds of sleep. In D. Goleman & R. J. Davisdon (Eds.), *Consciousness: Brain, states of awareness, and mysticism* (pp. 72–75). New York: Harper & Row.

Dement, W. C., & Wolpert, E. A. (1958). The relation of eye movements, body mobility, and external stimuli to dream content. *Journal of Experimental Psychology, 55,* 543–553.

Dent, J. (1984, March). *Readers Digest, 124,* p. 38.

DePaulo, B. M., & Fisher, J. (1980). The costs of asking for help. *Basic and Applied Social Psychology, 1,* 23–35.

Deregowski, J. B. (1973). Illusion and culture. In R. L. Gregory & G. H. Combrich (Eds.), *Illusion in nature and art* (pp. 161–192). New York: Scribner.

Deutsch, M. (1985). *The historical context and the challenge of Head Start*. Keynote presentation for the 20th anniversary celebration of Head Start. New York: Loeb Student Center.

Deutsch, M., Jordan, T. J., & Deutsch, C. (1985). *Long-term effects of early intervention: Summary of selected findings*. Unpublished manuscript. NYU Institute for Developmental Studies, New York.

Diaconis, P. (1978). Statistical problems in ESP research. *Science, 201,* 131–136.

Dion, K. K., & Berscheid, E. (1974). Physical attractiveness and peer perception among children. *Sociometry, 37,* 1–12.

Dolce, J. J., & Raczynski, J. M. (1985). Neuromuscular activity and electromyography in painful backs: Psychological and biomechanical models in assessment and treatment. *Psychological Bulletin, 97,* 502–520.

Dollard, J., Doob, L., Miller, N., Mower, O. H., & Sears, R. R. (1939). *Frustration and aggression*. New Haven, CT: Yale University Press.

Dollard, J., & Miller, N. E. (1950). *Personality and psychotherapy: An analysis in terms of learning, thinking and culture*. New York: McGraw-Hill.

Donnerstein, E., & Berkowitz, L. (1981). Victim reactions in aggressive erotic films as a factor in violence against women. *Journal of Personality and Social Psychology, 41,* 710–724.

Doob, A. N., & Wood, L. (1972). Catharsis and aggression: The effects of annoyance and retaliation on aggressive behavior. *Journal of Personality and Social Psychology, 22,* 156–162.

Doty, R. L. (1986). Development and age-related changes in human olfactory function. In W. Breipohl & R. Apfelbach (Eds.), *Ontogeny of olfaction in vertebrates*. Berlin: Springer-Verlag.

Dove, A. (1968, July 15). Taking the chitling test. *Newsweek*.

Dreyer, P. H. (1982). Sexuality during adolescence. In B. B. Wolman (Ed.), *Handbook of developmental psychology*. Englewood Cliffs, NJ: Prentice-Hall.

Duke, M., & Nowicki, S., Jr. (1979). *Abnormal psychology: Perspectives on* *being different*. Monterey, Ca: Brooks/Cole.

Duncker, K. (1945). On problem solving. *Psychological Monographs, 58,* (5, whole no. 270).

Dunkel-Schetter, C., Folkman, S., & Lazarus, R. S. (1987). Correlates of social support. *Journal of Personality and Social Psychology, 53,* 71–80.

Dworkin, R. H., & Widom, C. S. (1977). Undergraduate MMPI profiles and the longitudinal prediction of adult social outcome. *Journal of Consulting and Clinical Psychology, 45,* 620–625.

Eagly, A. H. (1983). Gender and social influence: A social psychological analysis. *American Psychologist,* 971–981.

Eagly, A. H., Wood, W., & Chaiken, S. (1978). Causal inferences about communicators and their effect on opinion change. *Journal of Personality and Social Psychology, 36,* 424–435.

Eaves, L. J. & Eysenck, H. J. (1974). Genetics and the development of social attitudes. *Nature, 249,* 288–289.

Ebbesen, E. B., Duncan, B., & Konečni, V. J. (1975). Effects of content of verbal aggression on future verbal aggression: A field experiment. *Journal of Experimental Social Psychology, 11,* 192–204.

Eckenrode, J. (1984). Impact of chronic and acute stressors on daily reports of mood. *Journal of Personality and Social Psychology, 46,* 907–918.

Eckholm, E. (1987, March 10). AIDS, an unknown disease before 1981, grows into a worldwide scourge. *New York Times,* A1.

Egan, D. E., & Schwartz, B. J. (1979). Chunking in recall of symbolic drawings. *Memory and Cognition, 7,* 149–158.

Egan, J. P. (1975). *Signal detection theory and ROC-analysis*. New York: Academic Press.

Eisenberg-Berg, N., & Mussen, P. (1978). Empathy and moral development in adolescence. *Developmental Psychology, 14,* 185–186.

Ekman, P. (1985). *Telling lies*. New York: Norton.

Ekman, P. (1972). Universals and cultural differences in facial expressions of emotions. In J. Cole (Ed.), *Nebraska symposium on motivation* (Vol. 19). Lincoln: University of Nebraska Press.

Ekman, P., Friesen, W. V., & Ellsworth, P. (1972). *Emotion in the human face*. Elmsford, NY: Pergamon Press.

Ekman, P., Levenson, R. W., & Friesen, W. V. (1983, September 16). Autonomic nervous system activity distinguishes among emotions. *Science, 223,* pp. 1208–1210.

Elkin, I. (1986, May). *NIMH treatment of depression: Collaborative research program*. Paper presented at the annual meeting of the American Psychiatric Association, Washington, D.C.

Elkin, I., Shea, T., Imber, S., Pilkonis, P., Sotsky, S., Glass, D., Watkins, J., Leber, W., & Collins, J. (1986, May). NIMH treatment of depression collaborative research program: Initial outcome findings. Paper presented at the annual meeting of the American Association for the Advancement of Science.

Ellis, A. (1962). *Reason and emotion in psychotherapy*. New York: Lyle Stuart.

Ellis, A. (1975). Creative job and happiness: The humanistic way. *The Humanist, 35* (1), pp. 11–13.

Epstein, A. N., Fitzsimons, J. T., & Roys, B. J. (1970). Drinking induced by injection of angiotensin into the brain of the rat. *Journal of Physiology, 210,* pp. 457–474.

Epstein, S., & O'Brien, E. J. (1985). The person-situation debate in historical and current perspective. *Psychological Bulletin, 98,* 513–537.

Erickson, E. H. (1963). *Childhood and society* (2nd ed.). New York: Norton.

Eron, L. D. (1982). Parent-child interaction, television violence, and aggression of children. *American Psychologist, 37,* 197–211.

Eron, L. D., & Huesmann, L. R. (1985). The control of aggressive behavior by changes in attitude, values, and the conditions of learning. In R. J. Blanchard and C. Blanchard (Eds.), *Advances in the study of aggression*. New York: Academic Press.

Eron, L. D., Huesmann, L. R., Lefkowitz, M. M., & Walden, L. O. (1972). Does television cause aggression? *American Psychologist, 27,* 253–263.

Evans, N. J., & Dovido, J. F. (1983, April). *Evaluation processing of racial stereotypes*. Paper presented at the 54th Annual Meeting of the Eastern Psychological Association, Philadelphia, PA.

Ewen, R. B. (1980). *An introduction to theories of personality*. New York: Academic Press.

Eysenck, H. J. (1952). The effects of psychotherapy: An evaluation. *Journal of Consulting Psychology, 16,* 319–324.

Eysenck, H. J. (1973). *Eysenck on extraversion*. New York: Wiley.

Eysenck, H. J. (1976). *Sex and personality*. London: Open Books.

Eysenck, H. J. (1985). Race, social-class, and individual-differences in IQ. *Personality and Individual Differences, 6,* 287.

Eysenck, H. J., & Eysenck, S. B. G. (1975). *Manual of the Eysenck personality questionnaire*. San Diego, CA: Educational and Industrial Testing Service.

Fanelli, R. J., Burright, R. G., & Donovick, P. J. (1983). A multi-variate approach to the analysis of genetic and septal lesion effects on maze performance in mice. *Behavioral Neuroscience, 97,* 354–369.

Faraone, S. V., & Tsuang, M. T. (1985). Quantitative models of the genetic transmission of schizophrenia. *Psychological Bulletin, 98,* 41–66.

Fayol, H. (1949). *General and industrial management*. London: Pitman.

Fazio, R. H., Zanna, M. P., & Cooper, J. (1977). Dissonance and self-perception: An integrative view of each theory's proper domain of application. *Journal of Experimental Social Psychology, 13,* 464–479.

Fellner, D. J., & Sulzer-Azaroff, B. (1984). Increasing industrial safety practices and conditions through posted feedback. *Journal of Safety Research, 15,* 7–21.

Festinger, L. (1957). *A theory of cognitive dissonance*. Stanford, CA: Stanford University Press.

Festinger, L., & Carlsmith, J. M. (1959). Cognitive consequences of forced compliance. *Journal of Abnormal and Social Psychology, 58,* 203–210.

Festinger, L., Schachter, S., & Back, K. W. (1950). *Social pressure in informal groups*. New York: Harper.

Fiedler, F. E., Mitchell, R., & Triandis, H. C. (1971). The culture assimilator:

An approach to cross-cultural training. *Journal of Applied Psychology, 55,* 95–102.

Field, T. (1982). Individual differences in the expressivity of neonates and young infants. In R. S. Feldman (Ed.), *Development of nonverbal behavior in children*. New York: Springer-Verlag.

Fieve, R. R. (1975). *Moodswing*. New York: William Morrow.

Fink, A., & Kosecoff, J. (1985). *How to conduct surveys: A step-by-step guide*. Beverly Hills, CA: Sage.

Fischman, M. (1985, August). *Cocaine use: Laboratory perspective on a growing health problem*. Paper presented at the annual meeting of the American Psychological Association, Los Angeles.

Fishbein, M., & Ajzen, I. (1975). *Belief, attitude, intention, and behavior: An introduction to theory and research*. Reading, MA: Addison-Wesley.

Fisher, K. (1985, March). ECT: New studies on how, why, who. *APA Monitor,* 18–19.

Fiske, E. B. (1984, November 11). Learning Disabled: A New Awareness. *New York Times*. Section 12, pp. 1, 44, 58.

Fiske, S. T., & Taylor, S. E. (1983). *Social cognition*. Reading, MA: Addison-Wesley.

Foa, E. B., & Kozak, M. S. (1986). Emotional processing of fear: Exposure to corrective information. *Psychological Bulletin, 99,* 20–35.

Fodor, E. M. (1985). The power motive, group conflict, and physiological arousal. *Journal of Personality and Social Psychology, 49,* 1408–1415.

Folkman, S., & Lazarus, R. S. (1980). An analysis of coping in a middle-aged community sample. *Journal of Health and Social Behavior, 21,* 219–239.

Folkman, S., Lazarus, R. S., Dunkel-Schetter, C., DeLongis, A., & Green, R. J. (1986). Dynamics of a stressful encounter: Cognitive appraisal, coping, and encounter outcome. *Journal of Personality and Social Psychology, 50,* 992–1003.

Forer, B. (1949). The fallacy of personal validation: A classroom demonstration of gullibility. *Journal of Abnormal and Social Psychology, 44,* 118–123.

Försterling, F. (1985). Attributional retraining: A review. *Psychological Bulletin, 98,* 495–512.

Frable, D. E. S., & Bem, S. L. (1985). If you are gender schematic, all members of the opposite sex look alike. *Journal of Personality and Social Psychology, 49,* 459–468.

Frankenburg, W. K., & Dodds, J. B. (1967). The Denver developmental screening test. *Journal of Pediatrics, 71,* 181–191.

Franks, L. (1985, October 20). A new attack on alcoholism. *The New York Times Magazine,* pp. 47–50; 61–65; 69.

Frauk, B. M., & Noble, J. P. (1984). Field independence-dependence and cognitive restructuring. *Journal of Personality and Social Psychology, 47,* 1129–1135.

Frederikson, N. (1986). Toward a broader conception of human intelligence. *American Psychologist, 41,* 445–452.

Freedman, J. L. (1979). Reconciling apparent differences between responses to humans and other animals to crowding. *Psychological Review, 86,* 80–85.

Freedman, J. L. (1984). Effect of television violence on aggressiveness. *Psychological Bulletin, 96,* 227–246.

Freeman, W. (1959). Psychosurgery. In *American handbook of psychiatry* (Vol. 2, pp. 1521–1540). New York: Basic Books.

Freeman, F. R. (1981). *Organic mental disease*. New York: Spectrum.

French, J. R. P. (1976, September). *Job demands and worker health*. Paper presented at the 84th Annual Convention of the American Psychological Association.

French, J. R. P., & Caplan, R. D. (1972). Organizational stress and individual strain. In *The failure of success*. New York: Amacom.

Freud, S. (1900). *The interpretation of dreams*. New York: Basic Books.

Freud, S. (1922/1959). *Group psychology and the analysis of the ego*. London: Hogarth.

Frey, D., & Wicklund, R. A. (1978). A clarification of selective exposure: The impact of choice. *Journal of Experimental Social Psychology, 14,* 132–139.

Friedman, H. S., & DiMatteo, M. R. (1982). *Interpersonal issues in health care*. New York: Academic Press.

Galanter, E. (1962). Contemporary psychophysics. In R. Brown, E. Galanter, E. Hess, & G. Maroler (Eds.), *New directions in psychology*. NY: Holt, 87–157.

Gallup, G. G., Jr., & Suarez, S. D. (1985). Alternatives to the use of animals in psychological research. *American Psychologist, 40,* 1104–1111.

Gama, E. M. P. (1985). Achievement motivation of women: Effects of achievement and affiliation arousal. *Psychology of Women, 9,* 89–103.

Gardell, G. (1976). *Arbetsinnehall och livskvalitet*. Stockholm: Prisma.

Garfield, S. L. (1983). Psychotherapy: Efficacy, generality, and specificity. In J. B. N. Williams & R. L. Spitzer (Eds.), *Psychotherapy research: Where are we and where should we go?* (pp. 295–305). New York: Guilford Press.

Gatchel, R. J., & Baum, A. (1983). *An introduction to health psychology*. Reading, MA: Addison-Wesley.

Gazzaniga, M. S. (1967). The split brain in man. *Scientific American, 217,* 24–29.

Gazzaniga, M. S. (1970). *The bisected brain*. New York: Plenum Press.

Gazzaniga, M. S. (1983). Right hemisphere language following brain bisection: A 20-year perspective. *American Psychologist, 38,* 525–537.

Gazzaniga, M. S. (1985, November). The social brain. *Psychology Today, 19,* 29–38.

Geen, R. G., & Donnerstein, E. (1983). *Aggression: Theoretical and empirical reviews*. New York: Academic Press.

Geller, E. S., & Streff, F. M. (1984, October). *Promoting safety belt use in the U.S.: The role of applied behavior analysis*. Paper presented at the U.S.-Japan workshop on risk management. Tsukuba Science City, Japan.

Geller, E. S., Winnett, R. A., & Everett, P. B. (1982). *Preserving the environment: New strategies for behavior change*. New York: Pergamon.

Gelman, R., & Baillargeon, R. (1983). A review of some Piagetian concepts. In J. H. Flavell & E. M. Markman (Eds.), *Handbook of child psychology: Vol. 3, Cognitive development* (4th ed.). New York: Wiley.

Gerbner, G., Gross, L., Jackson-Beeck, M., Jeffries-Fox, S., & Signorielli, N.

(1978). Cultural indicators: Violence profile No. 9. *Journal of Communication, 28,* 176–207.

Gholson, J. B., & Rosenthal, T. L. (Eds.). (1984). *Application of cognitive development theory.* New York: Academic Press.

Gibbs, M. E., & Ng, K. T. (1977). Psychobiology of memory: Towards a model of memory formation. *Behavioral Reviews, 1,* 113–136.

Gilligan, C. (1982). *In a different voice.* Cambridge, MA: Harvard University Press.

Ginsberg, A. (1977). *Mind breaths.* San Francisco: City Lights.

Gladue, B. (1984). Hormone markers for homosexuality. *Science, 225,* 198.

Gladwin, T. (1964). Culture and logical process. In N. Goodenough (Ed.), *Explorations in cultural anthropology: Essays in honor of George Peter Murdoch.* New York: McGraw-Hill.

Glass, A., & Holyoak, K. J. (1985). *Cognition* (2nd ed.). Reading, MA: Addison-Wesley.

Goldfried, M., & Davison, G. (1976). *Clinical behavior therapy.* New York: Holt, Rinehart and Winston.

Goleman, D. (1984, February 21). The aging mind proves capable of lifelong growth. *New York Times,* pp. C1–C3.

Goleman, D. (1985, February 5). Mourning: New studies affirm its benefits. *New York Times,* pp. C1–C2.

Gorenstein, E. E. (1984). Debating mental illness. *American Psychologist, 39,* 50–56.

Gottesman, I. I. & Shields, J. (1972). *Schizophrenia and genetics.* New York: Academic Press.

Gottfried, A. W. (Ed.). (1984). *Home environment and early cognitive development.* New York: Academic Press.

Gough, H. G., Fioravanti, M., & Lazzari, R. (1979). A cross-cultural unisex ideal self scale for the adjective checklist. *Journal of Clinical Psychology, 35,* 314–319.

Gould, R. L. (1978). *Transformations.* New York: Simon and Schuster.

Gove, W. R. (1982). Labelling theory's explanation of mental illness: An update of recent evidence. *Deviant Behavior, 3,* 307–327.

Greenberg, P. T. (1977, April). The thrill seekers. *Human Behavior, 6,* 17–21.

Greenblatt, M. (1978). The grieving spouse. *American Journal of Psychiatry, 135,* 43–47.

Gregory, R. L. (1978). *The psychology of seeing* (3rd ed.). New York: McGraw-Hill.

Griffit, N., & Veitch, R. (1971). Hot and crowded: Influences of population density on interpersonal affective behavior. *Journal of Personality and Social Psychology, 17,* 92–98.

Griffith, R. M., Miyago, O., & Tago, A. (1958). The universality of typical dreams: Japanese vs Americans. *American Anthropologist, 60,* 1173–1179.

Groner, R., Groner, M., & Bischof, W. F. (Eds.) (1983). *Methods of heuristics.* Hillsdale, NJ: Erlbaum.

Grossberg, S. & Stone, G. (1986). Neural dynamics of word recognition and recall: Attentional priming, learning, and resonance. *Psychological Review, 93,* 46–74.

Grossberg, S., & Mingolla, E. (1985). Neural dynamics of form perception: Boundary completion, illusory figures, and neon color spreading. *Psychological Review, 92,* 173–211.

Grossman, H. J. (Ed.) *Classification in mental retardation.* Washington, DC: American Associations on Mental Deficiency.

Gruenberg, B. (1980). The happy workers: An analysis of educational and occupational differences in determinants of job satisfaction. *American Journal of Sociology, 86,* 247–271.

Grusec, J. E., & Skubiski, S. L. (1970). Model nurturance, demand characteristics of the modeling experiment, and altruism. *Journal of Personality and Social Psychology, 14,* 352–359.

Gubrium, J. G. (1973). *The myth of the golden years: A socio-environmental theory of aging.* Springfield, IL: Thomas.

Guilford, J. P. (1968). The structure of intelligence. In D. K. White (Ed.), *Handbook of measurement and assessment in behavioral sciences.* Reading, MA: Addison-Wesley.

Guilford, J. P. (1982). Cognitive psychology's ambiguities: Some remedies. *Psychological Review, 89,* 48–59.

Gur, R. C., Gur, R. E., Obrist, W. D., Hungerbuhler, J. P., Younkin, D., Rosen, A. D., Skilnick, B. E., & Reivich, M. (1982,). Sex and handedness differences in cerebral blood flow during rest and cognitive activity. *Science, 217,* 659–661.

Haber, R. N. (1983). Stimulus information processing mechanisms in visual space perception. In J. Beck, B. Hope, & A. Rosenfeld (Eds.), *Human and machine vision.* New York: Academic Press.

Hagen, E., Sattler, J. M., & Thorndike, R. L. (1985). *Stanford-Binet test.* Chicago: Riverside.

Hainline, L., & Lemerise, E. (1982). Infants' scanning of geometric forms varying in size. *Journal of Experimental Child Psychology, 33,* 235–256.

Hamburg, D. A., Elliott, G. R., & Parion, D. L. (1980). *Health and behavior: Frontiers of research in the biobehavioral sciences.* Washington, DC: National Academy Press.

Hannon, R., Butler, C. P., Day, C. L., Khan, S. A., Quitoriano, L. A., Butler, A. M., & Meredith, L. A. (1985). Alcohol use and cognitive functioning in men and women college students. In M. Galanter (Ed.), *Recent developments in alcoholism* (Vol. 3, pp. 241–252). New York: Plenum Press.

Harlow, H. F., Harlow, M. K., & Meyer, D. R. (1950). Learning motivated by a manipulation drive. *Journal of Experimental Psychology, 40,* 228–234.

Harlow, H. F., & Zimmerman, R. R. (1959). Affectional responses in the infant monkey. *Science, 130,* pp. 421–432.

Harlow, J. M. (1869). Recovery from the passage of an iron bar through the head. *Massachusetts Medical Society Publication, 2,* 329–347.

Harris, G. M., & Johnson, S. B. (1983). Coping imagery and relaxation instructions in a covert modeling treatment for test anxiety. *Behavior Therapy, 14,* 144–159.

Harris Poll: National Council on the Aging (1975). *The myth and reality of aging in America.* Washington, DC: National Council on the Aging.

Hart, N. A., & Keidel, G. C. (1979). The suicidal adolescent. *American Journal of Nursing,* 80–84.

Harte, R. A., Travers, J. A., & Savich, P. (1948). Voluntary caloric intake of the growing rat. *Journal of Nutrition, 36,* 667–679.

Hartmann, E. (1967). *The biology of dreaming*. Springfield, IL: Thomas.

Hartmen, W., & Fithian, M. (1984). *Any man can*. New York: St. Martin's.

Harvey, J. G., & Weary, G. (Eds.). (1985). *Attribution: Basic issues and applications*. Orlando, FL: Academic Press.

Hathaway, B. (1984, July). Running to ruin. *Psychology Today, 18,* 14–15.

Hathaway, S. R., Monachesi, E., & Salasin, S. (1970). A follow-up study of MMPI high 8, schizoid children. In M. Roff & D. F. Ricks (Eds.), *Life history research in psychopathology*. Minneapolis: University of Minnesota Press.

Hatvany, N., & Pucik, V. (1981). An integrated management system: Lessons from the Japanese experience. *Academy of Management Review, 6,* 469–480.

Havighurst, R. J. (1973). Social roles, work, leisure, and education. In C. Eisdorfer & M. P. Lawton (Eds.), *The psychology of adult development and aging*. Washington, DC: American Psychological Association.

Hay, D. F. (1986). Infancy. *Annual Review of Psychology, 37*.

Hayduk, L. A. (1983). Personal space: Where we now stand. *Psychological Bulletin, 94,* 293–335.

Hayflick, L. (1974). The strategy of senescence. *Journal of Gerontology, 14,* 37–45.

Hays, R. B. (1985). A longitudinal study of friendship development. *Journal of Personality and Social Psychology, 48,* 909–924.

Hechinger, F. M. (1985, February 12). How talent can be nurtured. *New York Times,* p. C5.

Heckhausen, H., Schmalt, H. D., & Schneider, K. (1985). *Achievement motivation in perspective*. (M. Woodruff & R. Wicklund, Trans.). Orlando, FL: Academic Press.

Heider, F. (1958). *The psychology of interpersonal relations*. New York: Wiley.

Heilman, M. E., & Stopeck, M. H. (1985). Attractiveness and corporate success: Different causal attributions for men and women. *Journal of Applied Psychology, 70,* 379–388.

Helmreich, R. L. (1983). Applying psychology in outer space: Unfulfilled promise revisited. *American Psychologist, 38,* 445–450.

Helmreich, R. L. (in press). Social psychology in space. *Discovery*.

Hendrick, C., & Hendrick, S. (1986). A theory and method of love. *Journal of personality and social psychology, 50,* 392–402.

Herink, R. (Ed.). *The psychotherapy handbook*. New York: New American Library.

Herman, L. M., & Forestell, P. H. (1985). Reporting presence or absence of named objects by a language-trained dolphin. *Neuroscience & Biobehavioral Reviews, 9,* 667–681.

Hersh, R. H., Paolitto, D. P., & Reimer, J. (1979). *Promoting moral growth*. New York: Longmans.

Hetherington, E. M., Cox, M., & Cox, R. (1978). The aftermath of divorce. In J. H. Stevens, Jr., & M. Matthews (Eds.), *Mother-child, father-child relations*. Washington, D. C.: National Association for the Education of Young Children.

Higbee, K. L., & Kunihira, S. (1985). Cross-cultural applications of Yodni mnemonics in education. *Educational Psychologist, 20,* 57–64.

Hilgard, J. R. (1974). Imaginative involvement: Some characteristics of the highly hypnotizable and the nonhypnotizable. *International Journal of Clinical and Experimental Hypnosis, 22,* 138–156.

Hilgard, E. R. (1975). Hypnosis. *Annual Review of Psychology, 26,* 19–44.

Hobson, J. A., & McCarley, R. W. (1977). The brain as a dream state generator: An activation-synthesis hypothesis of the dream process. *The American Journal of Psychiatry, 134,* 1335–1348.

Hochberg, J. E. (1978). *Perception*. Englewood Cliffs, NJ: Prentice-Hall.

Holahan, C. J. (1982). *Environmental psychology*. New York: Random House.

Holden, C. (1985, January). Genes, personality, and alcoholism. *Psychology Today, 19,* 38–44.

Holden, C. (1987, August). The genetics of personality. *Science, 237,* 598–601.

Holden, C. (1986, July). New Toyota-GM plant is U.S. model for Japanese management. *Science, 233,* 273–277.

Hollander, E. P. (1980). Leadership and social exchange processes. In K. J. Gargon, M. Greenberg, & R. Willis (Eds.), *Social exchange: Advances in theory and research*. New York: Plenum Press.

Hollingshead, A. B., & Redich, F. C. (1958). *Social class and mental illness*. New York: Wiley.

Holmes, D. S. (1985). To meditate or rest?: The answer is rest. *American Psychologist, 40,* 728–731.

Holmes, T. S., & Holmes, T. H. (1970). Short-term intrusions into the life style routine. *Journal of Psychosomatic Research, 14,* 121–132.

Holzman, A. D., & Turk, D. C. (1985). *Pain management: A handbook of psychological treatment approaches*. New York: Pergamon.

Honts, C. R., Hodes, R. L. & Raskin, D. C. (1985). Effects of physical countermeasures on the physiological detection of deception. *Journal of Applied Psychology, 70,* 177–187.

Horn, J. L. (1980). Concepts of intellect in relation to learning and adult development. *Intelligence, 4,* 285–317.

Horn, M. C., & Bachrach, C. A. (1985). *1982 National Survey of Family Growth*. Washington, DC: National Center for Health Statistics.

Horner, M. (1972). Toward an understanding of achievement-related conflicts in women. *Journal of Social Issues, 28,* 157–175.

Houston, L. N. (1981). Romanticism and eroticism among black and white college students. *Adolescence, 16,* 263–272.

Hovland, C., Janis, I., & Kelly, H. H. (1953). *Communication and persuasion*. New Haven, CT: Yale University Press.

Howells, J. G., & Osborn, M. L. (1984). *A reference companion to the history of abnormal psychology*. Westport, CT: Greenwood Press.

Hubel, D. H., & Wiesel, T. N. (1979). Brain mechanisms of vision. *Scientific American, 241,* 150–162.

Hudson, W. (1960). Pictorial depth perception in subcultural groups in Africa. *Journal of Social Psychology, 52,* 183–208.

Huesmann, L. R. (1985). Personal communication.

Huesmann, L. R., Eron, L. D., Klein, R., Brice, P., & Fischer, P. (1983). Mitigating the imitation of aggressive behaviors by changing children's attitudes about media violence. *Journal of Personality and Social Psychology, 5,* 899–910.

Hull, C. L. (1943). *Principles of behavior.* New York: Appleton-Century-Crofts.

Hunt, M. (1974). *Sexual behaviors in the 1970s.* New York: Dell.

Hunt, W. A., & Matarazzo, J. A. (1982). Changing smoking behavior. In R. J. Gatchel, A. Baum, & J. E. Singer (Eds.), *Behavioral medicine and clinical psychology: Overlapping areas.* Hillsdale, NJ: Erlbaum.

Hurvich, L., & Jameson, D. (1974). Opponent processes as a model of neural organization. *American Psychologist, 29,* 88–102.

Hutchison, J. B. (Ed.). (1978). *Biological determinants of sexual behavior.* New York: Wiley.

Ickes, W. (Ed.). (1984). *Compatible and incompatible relationships.* New York: Springer-Verlag.

Ingelfinger, F. J. (1944). The late effects of total and subtotal gastrectomy. *New England Journal of Medicine, 231,* 321–377.

Institute of Medicine. (1982). *Marijuana and health.* Washington, DC: National Academy Press.

Izard, C. E. (1977). *Human emotions.* New York: Plenum.

Jacobs, J. (1971). *Adolescent suicide.* New York: Wiley.

James, W. (1890). *The principles of psychology.* New York: Holt.

Janis, I. (1972). *Victims of groupthink: A psychological study of foreign-policy decisions and fiascoes.* Boston: Houghton Mifflin.

Janis, I. (1984). Improving adherence to medical recommendations: Descriptive hypothesis derived from recent research in social psychology. In A. Baum, J. E. Singer, & S. E. Taylor (Eds.), *Handbook of medical psychology* (Vol. 4). Hillsdale, NJ: Erlbaum.

Janis, I. L., & Mann, L. (1976). *Decision making.* New York: Holt, Rinehart and Winston.

Janis, I. L., & Rodin, J. (1979). Attribution, control, and decision making: Social psychology and health care. In *Health psychology: A handbook.* San Francisco: Jossey-Bass.

Johnson, J. T., Cain, L. M., Falke, T. L., Hayman, J., & Perillo, E. (1985). The "Barnum Effect" revisited: Cognitive and motivational factors in the acceptance of personality descriptions. *Journal of Personality and Social Psychology, 49,* 1378–1391.

Jones, L. V. (1984). White-black achievement differences: The narrowing gap. *American Psychologist, 39,* 1207–1213.

Joyce, C. (1984, May). Space travel is no joyride. *Psychology Today, 18,* 30–37.

Joyce, J. (1934). *Ulysses.* New York: Random House.

Kagan, J., Kearsley, R. B., & Zelazo, P. R. (1978). *Infancy: Its place in human development.* Cambridge, MA: Harvard University Press.

Kahn, S., Zimmerman, G., Csikszentmihalyi, M., & Getzels, J. W. (1985). Relations between identity in young adulthood and intimacy at midlife. *Journal of Personality and Social Psychology, 49,* 1316–1322.

Kahneman, D., & Tversky, A. (1973). On the psychology of prediction. *Psychology Review, 80,* 237–251.

Kahneman, D., & Tversky, A. (1972). Subjective probability: A judgment of representativeness. *Cognitive Psychology, 3,* 430–454.

Kandel, E. R., & Schwartz, J. H. (1982). Molecular biology of learning: Modulation or transmitter release. *Science, 218, pp. 433–442.*

Kane, J. M. (1983). Hypotheses regarding the mechanism of action of antidepressant drugs: Neurotransmitters in affective disorders. In A. Rifkin (Ed.), *Schizophrenia and affective disorders: Biology and drug treatment* (pp. 19–34). Boston: John Wright.

Kanfer, F. H., & Goldstein, A. P. (Eds.). (1985). *Helping people change: A textbook of methods* (3rd ed.). New York: Pergamon.

Kaplan, M. F. (1975). Information integration in social judgment: Interaction of judge and informational components. In M. Kaplan & S. Schwartz (Eds.), *Human development and decision processes.* New York: Academic Press.

Kaplan, M. F. (1983, May). *Effect of training on reasoning in moral choice.* Paper presented at the meeting of the Midwestern Psychological Association.

Karasu, T. B. (1982). Psychotherapy and psychopharmacology: Toward an integrative model. *American Journal of Psychiatry, 139,* 1102–1113.

Karlins, M., & Abelson, H. I. (1979). *How opinions and attitudes are changed.* New York: Springer.

Karoly, P., & Kanfer, F. H. (1982). *Self management and behavior change.* New York: Pergamon.

Kassin, S. M. (1985). Eyewitness identification: Retrospective self awareness and the accuracy-confidence correlation. *Journal of Personality and Social Psychology, 41,* 878–893.

Kastenbaum, R. (1975). Is death a life crisis? On the confrontation with death in theory and practice. In N. Datan & L. H. Ginsberg (Eds.), *Life-span developmental psychology: Normative life crisis.* New York: Academic Press.

Katz, D., & Braly, K. W. (1933). Racial stereotypes of 100 college students. *Journal of Abnormal and Social Psychology, 4,* 280–290.

Katz, D., & Kahn, R. (1978). *The social psychology of organizations* (2nd ed.). New York: Wiley.

Kaufman, J., Schaffer, H., & Burglass, M. E. (1983). The clinical assessment and diagnosis of addiction. In T. Bratter & G. Forrest (Eds.), *Current treatment of substance abuse and alcoholism.* New York: Macmillan.

Kazdin, A. E. (1983). Treatment of conduct disorders. In J. B. W. Williams & R. L. Spitzer (Eds.), *Psychotherapy research: Where are we and where should we go?* (pp. 3–28). New York: Guilford Press.

Kazdin, A. E., & Wilson, G. T. (1978). *Evaluation of behavior therapy: Issues, evidence, and research strategies.* Cambridge, MA: Ballinger.

Keating, D. P., & Clark, L. V. (1980). Development of physical and social reasoning in adolescence. *Developmental Psychology, 16,* 23–30.

Keerdoja, E. (1985, July 8). Scaling the walls of silence. *Newsweek,* p. 66.

Keesey, R. E., & Powley, T. L. (1986). The regulation of body weight. *Annual Review of Psychology,* 37.

Keith, S. J., & Matthews, S. M. (1983). Scizophrenia: A review of psychosocial treatment strategies. In J. W. W. Williams & R. L. Spitzer (Eds.), *Psychotherapy research: Where are we and where should we go?* (pp. 70–88). New York: Guilford Press.

Keith-Spiegel, P., & Koocher, G. P. (1985). *Ethics in psychology*. San Francisco: Random House-Knopf.

Kelley, H. (1950). The warm-cold variable in first impressions of persons. *Journal of Personality and Social Psychology, 18,* 431–439.

Kelley, H. H. (1967). Attribution theory in social psychology. In D. Levine (Ed.), *Nebraska Symposium on Motivation*. Lincoln: University of Nebraska Press.

Kelley, H. H. (1979). *Close relationships: Their structures and processes*. Hillsdale, NJ: Erlbaum.

Kendig, F. (1983, April). A conversation with Roger Schank. *Psychology Today,17,* pp. 28–36.

Kennedy, T. D., & Kumura, H. K. (1974). Transfer, behavioral improvement and anxiety reduction in systematic desensitization. *Journal of Consulting and Clinical Psychology, 42,* 720–728.

Kerouac, J. (1959). *Mexico City blues*. New York: Grove Press.

Kertesz, A. E. (1983). Cyclofusion and stereopsis. *Perception and Psychophysics, 33,* 99–101.

Kiester, E., Jr. (1986, March). Spare parts for damaged brains. *Science 86, 7,* 33–38.

Kinsey, A. C., Pomeroy, W. B., & Martin, C. E. (1948). *Sexual behavior in the human male*. Philadelphia: Saunders.

Kinsey, A. C., Pomeroy, W. B., Martin, C. E., & Gebhard, P. H. (1953). *Sexual behavior in the human female*. Philadelphia: Saunders.

Klein, G. S. (1970). *Perception, motives, and personality*. New York: Knopf.

Kleinmuntz, B. (1967). *Personality measurement: An introduction*. Homewood, IL: Dorsey Press.

Klerman, G. L. (1983). Evaluating the efficacy of psychotherapy. In P. J. Clayton & J. E. Barret (Eds.), *Treatment of depression: Old controversies and new approaches* (pp. 291–298). New York: Raven Press.

Klerman, G. L. (1984). The advantages of DSM-III. *American Journal of Psychiatry, 141,* 539–542.

Klima, E. S., & Bellugi, U. (1973). Teaching apes to communicate. In G. A. Miller (Ed.), *Communication, language and meaning: Psychological perspectives* (pp. 76–106). New York: Basic Books.

Kloos, P. (1971). *The Maroni River caribs of Surinam*. Assen, The Netherlands: Van Gorcum.

Knittle, J. L. (1975). Early influences on development of adipose tissue. In G. A. Bray (Ed.), *Obesity in perspective*. Washington, DC: U.S. Government Printing Office.

Kohlberg, L. (1969). Stage and sequence: The cognitive-developmental approach to socialization. In D. Goslin (Ed.), *Handbook of socialization theory and research*. Chicago: Rand McNally.

Kohlberg, L. (1976). Stages and moralization: the cognitive-developmental approach. In T. Liskona (Ed.), *Moral development and behavior: Theory, research and social issues*. New York: Holt, Rinehart and Winston.

Kohlberg, L. (1984). *The psychology of moral development: Essays on moral development*. Vol. 2. San Francisco: Harper & Row.

Köhler, W. (1927). *The mentality of apes*. London: Routledge and Kegan Paul.

Kolata, G. (1987, May). Early signs of school age IQ. *Science, 236,* 774–775.

Kolata, G. (1987, April). Metabolic catch-22 of exercise regimens. *Science, 236,* 146–147.

Kolata, G. (1986, December). New drug counters alcohol intoxication. *Science, 234,* 1198–1199.

Kraepelin, E. (1904/1968). *Lectures on clinical psychiatry*. New York: Hafner.

Kraft, C. L., & Elworth, C. L. (1969). Measurement of aircrew performance: The flight deck workload and its relation to pilot performance. (NTIS70-19779/A; 699934-DTIC)

Kraines, S. H. (1948). *The therapy of the neuroses and psychoses* (3rd ed.). Philadelphia: Lea and Febiger.

Krebs, D. L., & Miller, D. T. (1985). Altruism and aggression. In G. Lindzey & E. Aronson (Eds.), *Handbook of social psychology,* (3rd ed.). New York: Random House.

Kringlen, E. (1978). Adult offspring of two psychotic parents, with special reference to schizophrenia. In L. C. Wynne, R. L. Cromwell, & S. Matthysee (Eds.), *The nature of schizophrenia: New epidemiological-clinical twin study*. Oslo: Univesitsforlaget.

Krippner, S. (Ed.). (1982). *Advances in parapsychological research*. Vol. 3. New York: Plenum Press.

Kroger, W. S., & Fexler, W. D. (1976). *Hypnosis and behavior modification: Imagery conditioning*. Philadelphia: Lippincott.

Kübler-Ross, E. (1969). *On death and dying*. New York: Macmillan.

Kulik, J. A., Bangert-Drowns, R. L., & Kulik, C. C. (1984). Effectiveness of coaching for aptitude tests. *Psychological Bulletin, 95,* 179–188.

Lader, M., & Matthews, A. (1970). Physiological changes during spontaneous panic attacks. *Journal of Psychosomatic Research, 14,* 377–382.

LaFrance, M., & Mayo, C. (1978). *Moving bodies: Nonverbal communication in social relationships*. Monterey, CA: Brooks/Cole.

Lamal, P. A. (1979). College students' common beliefs about psychology. *Teaching of Psychology, 6,* 155–158.

Lamb, M. F. (1982). Paternal influences on early socio-emotional development. *Journal of Child Psychology and Psychiatry and Allied Disciplines, 23,* 185–190.

Landis, D., Day, H. R., McGrew, P. L., Thomas, J. A., & Miller, A. B. (1976). Can a black "culture assimilator" increase racial understanding? *Journal of Social Issues, 32,* 169–183.

Landman, J., & Dawes, R. M. (1984). Reply to Orwin and Cordray. *American Consulting Psychologist, 39,* 72–73.

Landro, L. (1984, April 5). RCA will quit making players for videodisks. *Wall Street Journal*.

Langer, E. J. (1983). *The psychology of control*. Beverly Hills, CA: Sage.

Langer, E., Bashner, R. S., & Chanowitz, B. (1985). Decreasing prejudice by increasing discrimination. *Journal of Personality and Social Psychology, 49,* 113–120.

Langer, E., Janis, I. L., & Wolfer, J. A. (1975). Reduction of psychological stress in surgical patients. *Journal of Experimental Social Psychology, 11,* 155–165.

Lashley, K. S. (1950). In search of the engram. Symposia of the Society for Experimental Biology, *4,* 454–482.

Latané, B., & Darley, J. M. (1970). *The unresponsive bystander: Why doesn't he help?* New York: Appleton-Crofts.

Latané, B., & Nida, S. (1981). Ten years of research on group size and helping. *Psychological Bulletin, 89,* 308–324.

Lauer, J., & Lauer, R. (1985, June). Marriages made to last. *Psychology Today, 19,* 22–26.

Layton, B. D., & Turnbull, B. (1975). Belief, evaluation, and performance in an ESP task. *Journal of Experimental Social Psychology, 11,* 166–179.

Lazarus, A. A. (1961). Group therapy of phobic disorders by systematic desensitization. *Journal of Abnormal and Social Psychology, 63,* 504–510.

Lazarus, R. S., DeLongis, A., Folkman, S., & Gruen, R. (1985). Stress and adaptational outcomes: The problem of confounded measures. *American Psychologist, 40,* 770–779.

Lechtenberg, R. (1982). *The psychiatrist's guide to diseases of the nervous system.* New York: Wiley.

Lepper, M. R. (1985). Microcomputers in education: Motivational and social issues. *American Psychologist, 40,* 1–18.

Lepper, M. R., Greene, D., & Nisbett, R. E. (1973). Undermining children's intrinsic interest with extrinsic reward: A test of the overjustification hypothesis. *Journal of Personality and Social Psychology, 23,* 129–137.

Levin, R. J. (1975, October). The Redbook report on premarital and extramarital sex: The end of the double standard? *Redbook,* pp. 38–44; 190–192.

Levinson, D. J. (1986). A conception of adult development. *American Psychologist, 41,* 3–13.

Levinson, D. J., Darrow, C. N., Klein, E. B., Levinson, M. H., & McKee, B. (1978). *The seasons of a man's life.* New York: Knopf.

Levy, J. (1980). Cerebral asymmetry and the psychology of man. In M. C. Wittrock (Ed.), *The brain and psychology.* New York: Academic Press.

Levy, J. (1985). Language, cognition, and the right hemisphere: A response to Gazzaniga. *American Psychologist, 38,* 538–541.

Levy, W. B., Anderson, J. A., & Lehmkuhle, S. (1984). *Synaptic modification, neuron selectivity, and nervous system organization.* Hillsdale, NJ: Erlbaum.

Lewy, A. J., Sack, R. L., Miller, L. S., & Hoban, T. M. (1987, January). Antidepressant and circadian phase-shifting effects of light. *Science, 235,* 352–353.

Lichtenstein, E., & Penner, M. D. (1977). Long-term effects of rapid smoking treatment for dependent cigarette smokers. *Addictive Behaviors, 2,* 109–112.

Lidz, T. (1973). *The origin and treatment of schizophrenic disorders.* New York: Basic Books.

Lieberman, M. A., & Bond, G. R. (1978). Self-help groups: Problems of measuring outcome. *Small Group Behavior, 9,* 222–241.

Lindsay, P. H., & Norman, D. A. (1977). *Human information processing* (2nd ed.). New York: Academic Press.

Lobsenz, M. M. (1975). *Sex after sixty-five.* Public Affairs Pamphlet #519, New York Public Affairs Committee.

Lochhead, J. (1985). Teaching analytic reasoning skills through pair problem solving. In J. W. Segal, S. F. Chipman, & R. Glaser (Eds.), *Thinking and learning skills* (Vol. 1). Hillsdale, NJ: Erlbaum.

Loeb, G. E. (1985, February). The functional replacement of the ear. *Scientific American, 252,* pp. 104–111.

Loftus, E. F., & Palmer, J. C. (1974). Reconstruction of automobile destruction: An example of the interface between language and memory. *Journal of Verbal Learning and Verbal Behavior, 13,* 585–589.

Lorenz, K. (1966). *On aggression.* New York: Harcourt Brace Jovanovich.

Lorenz, K. (1974). *Civilized man's eight deadly sins.* New York: Harcourt Brace Jovanovich.

Luborsky, L., Singer, B., & Luborsky, L. (1975). Comparative studies of psychotherapies: Is it true that everyone has won and all must have prizes? *Archives of General Psychiatry, 32,* 995–1008.

Luborsky, L., & Spence, D. P. (1978). Quantitative research on psychoanalytic therapy. In S. L. Garfield & A. E. Bergin (Eds.), *Handbook of psychotherapy and behavior change: An empirical analysis* (2nd ed.). New York: Wiley.

Luria, A. R. (1968). *The mind of a mnemonist.* New York: Basic Books.

Lynch, J. G., Jr., & Cohen, J. L. (1978). The use of subjective expected utility theory as an aid to understanding variables that influence helping behavior. *Journal of Personality and Social Psychology, 36,* 1138–1151.

Lynn, S. J., & Rhue, J. (1985, September). Daydream believers. *Psychology Today, 19,* 14–15.

Lyons, R. D. (1984, June 12). Take your eye off the ball, scientist coaches sluggers. *New York Times,* p. C3.

Maass, A., & Clark, R. D., III (1984). Hidden impact of minorities: Fifteen years of minority influence research. *Psychological Bulletin, 95,* 428–450.

MacDonald, M. L., & Tobias, L. L. (1976). Withdrawal causes relapse? Our response. *Psychological Bulletin, 83,* 448–451.

Mackenzie, B. (1984). Explaining race differences in IQ: The logic, the methodology, and the evidence. *American Psychologist, 39,* 1214–1233.

Maeroff, G. I. (1977, August 21). The unfavored gifted few. *New York Times Magazine.*

Magnusson, D., & Endler, N. S. (1977). Interactional psychology: Present status and future prospects. In D. Magnusson & N. S. Endler (Eds.), *Personality at the crossroads: Current issues in interactional psychology.* Hillsdale, NJ: Erlbaum.

Malamuth, N. M. (1981). Rape proclivity among males. *Journal of Social Issues, 37,* 138–157.

Malamuth, N., & Donnerstein, E. (1982). The effects of aggressive-pornographic mass media stimuli. In L. Berkowitz (Ed.), *Advances in experimental social psychology* (Vol. 15). New York: Academic Press.

Malamuth, N. M., & Donnerstein, E. (1984). *Pornography and sexual aggression.* New York: Academic Press.

Malinak, D. P., Hoyt, M. F., & Patterson, V. (1979). Adults' reactions to the death of a parent: A preliminary study. *American Journal of Psychiatry, 136,* 1152–1156.

Malinowski, C. I., & Smith, C. P. (1985). Moral reasoning and moral conduct: An investigation prompted by Kohlberg's theory. *Journal of Personality and Social Issues, 49,* 1016–1027.

Marks, I. M. (1982). Toward an empirical clinical science: Behavioral psychotherapy in the 1980's. *Behavioral Therapies, 13,* 63–81.

Marr, D. C. (1982). *Vision.* NY: Freeman.

Marshall, G., & P. Zimbardo. (1979). The affective consequences of "inadequately explained" physiological arousal. *Journal of Personality and Social Psychology, 37,* 970–988.

Marvel Comics Group (1981). *See no evil.* New York: Marvel.

Masland, R. L., Sorason, S. B., & Gladwyn, T. (1958). *Mental subnormality.* New York: Basic Books.

Maslow, A. (1970). *Motivation and personality.* New York: Harper & Row.

Mason, J. W. (1975). A historical view of the stress field. *Journal of Human Stress, 1,* 22–36.

Masters, W. H., & Johnson, V. E. (1979). *Homosexuality in perspective.* Boston: Little, Brown.

Mathes, E. W. (1975). The effects of physical attractiveness and anxiety on heterosexual attraction over a series of five encounters. *Journal of Marriage and the Family,* 769–773.

Mawhinney, V. T., Boston, D. E., Loaws, O. R., Blumenfeld, G. T., & Hopkins, B. L. (1971). A comparison of students' studying behavior produced by daily, weekly, and three-week testing schedules. *Journal of Applied Behavior Analysis, 4,* 257–264.

May, R. (1969). *Love and will.* New York: Norton.

McAlister, A., Puska, P., Koskela, K., Pallonen, U., & Maccoby, N. (1980). Mass communication and community organization for public health education. *American Psychologist, 35,* 375–379.

McClelland, D. C. (1985). How motives, skills, and values determine what people do. *American Psychologist, 40,* 812–825.

McClelland, D. C., Atkinson, J. W., Clark, R. A., & Lowell, E. L. (1953). *The achievement motive.* New York: Appleton-Century-Crofts.

McClelland, D. C., & Winter, D. G. (1969). *Motivating economic achievement.* New York: The Free Press.

McConnell, J. V. (1985). On Gazzaniga and right hemisphere language. *American Psychologist, 40,* 1273.

McGlone, J. (1980). Sex differences in human brain asymetry: A critical survey. *The Behavioral and Brain Sciences, 3,* 215–263.

McGuire, W. J. (1985). Attitudes and attitude change. In G. Lindzey & E. Aronson (Eds.), *Handbook of social psychology* (Vol. II, 3rd ed.). New York: Random House.

McGuire, W. T. (1964). Inducing resistance to persuasion. In L. Berkowitz (Ed.), *Advances in experimental social psychology* (Vol. I). New York: Academic Press.

McKean, K. (1982, April). Anatomy of an air crash. *Discover,* 19–21.

McKusick, L., Horstman, W., & Coates, T. J. (1985). AIDS and sexual behavior reported by gay men in San Francisco. *American Journal of Public Health, 75,* 493–496.

McNeal, E. T., & Cimbolic, P. (1986). Antidepressants and biochemical theories of depression. *Psychological Bulletin, 99,* 361–374.

Mednick, S. A., Higgins, J., & Kirschbaum, J. (1974). *Psychology: Explorations in behavior and experiences.* New York: Wiley.

Melges, F. T., & Bowlby, J. (1969). Types of hopelessness in psychopathological process. *Archives of General Psychiatry, 70,* 690–699.

Melville, J. (1977). *Phobias and obsessions.* New York: Coward, McCann.

Melzack, R., & Wall, P. D. (1965). Pain mechanisms: A new theory. *Science, 150,* pp. 971–979.

Messick, S., & Jungeblut, A. (1981). Time and method in coaching for the SAT. *Psychological Bulletin, 89,* 191–216.

Metee, D. R., & Aronson, E. (1974). Affective reactions to appraisal from others. In T. L. Huston (Ed.), *Foundations of interpersonal attraction* (pp. 235–283). New York: Academic Press.

Meyer, J. P., & Pepper, S. (1977). Need compatibility and marital adjustment in young married couples. *Journal of Personality and Social Psychology, 35,* 331–342.

Meyer, R. G., & Osborne, Y. V. H. (1982). *Case studies in abnormal behavior.* Boston: Allyn & Bacon.

Michelmore, P. (1984, March). You're too young to die. *Readers Digest,* pp. 117–121.

Mihal, W. L., & Barrett, G. V. (1976). Individual differences in perceptual information processing and their relation to automobile accident involvement. *Journal of Applied Psychology, 61,* 229–233.

Miles, R. H., & Perreault, W. D. (1976). Organizational role conflict: Its antecedents and consequences. *Organizational Behavior and Human Performance, 17,* 19–44.

Milewski, A. E. (1976). Infants' discrimination of internal and external pattern elements. *Journal of Experimental Child Psychology, 22,* 229–246.

Milgram, J. (1974). *Obedience to authority.* New York: Harper & Row.

Miller, D., & Starr, M. (1967). *The structure of human decisions.* Englewood Cliffs, NJ: Prentice-Hall.

Miller, G. A. (1956). The magical number seven, plus or minus two: Some limits on our capacity for processing information. *Psychology Review, 63,* 81–97.

Miller, J. D. (1984, June). *Psychology Today,* p. 18.

Miller, L. L. (Ed.). (1975). *Marijuana: Current research.* New York: Academic Press.

Miller, N., & Brewer, M. B. (1984). *Groups in contact: The psychology of desegregation.* New York: Academic Press.

Miller, N. E. (1980). Applications of learning and biofeedback to psychiatry and medicine. In H. I. Kaplan, A. M. Freedman, & B. J. Sadock (Eds.), *Comprehensive textbook of psychiatry III.* Baltimore: Williams & Wilkins.

Miller, N. E. (1985a, February). Rx: Biofeedback. *Psychology Today, 19,* pp. 54–59.

Miller, N. E. (1985b). The value of behavioral research on animals. *American Psychologist, 40,* 423–440.

Milner, B. (1966). Amnesia following operation on temporal lobes. In C. W. M.

Whitty & P. Zangwill (Eds.), *Amnesia*. London: Butterworth.

Mineka, S., & Henderson, R. W. (1985). Controllability and predictability in acquired motivation. *Annual Review of Psychology, 36*, 495–529.

Mirsky, A. F., & Duncan, C. C. (1986). Etiology and expression of schizophrenia: Neurological and psychosocial factors. *Annual Review of Psychology*, 37.

Mischel, W. (1968). *Personality and assessment*. New York: Wiley.

Mischel, W. (1984). Convergences and challenges in the search for consistency. *American Psychologist, 39*, 351–364.

Mischel, W., & Peake, P. K. (1982). Analyzing the construction of consistency in personality. *Nebraska Symposium on Motivation*, 233–262.

Mischel, W., & Peake, P. K. (1982). Beyond deja vu in the search for cross-situational consistency. *Psychological Review, 89*, 730–755.

Mitchell, R. E. (1971). Some social implications of high-density housing. *American Sociological Review, 36*, 18–29.

Mobley, W. H. (1982). *Employee turnover: Causes, consequences and control*. Reading, MA: Addison-Wesley.

Mollon, J. D., & Sharpe, L. T. (Eds.). (1983). *Colour vision: Physiology and psychophysics*. New York: Academic Press.

Molotsky, I. (1984, November 30). Implant to aid the totally deaf is approved. *New York Times*, pp. 1, B10.

Morse, N., & Skinner, B. F. (1957). A second type of "superstition" in the pigeon. *American Journal of Psychology, 70*, 308–311.

Moscovici, S. (1985). Social influence and conformity. In G. Lindzey & E. Aronson (Eds.), *Handbook of social psychology* (3rd ed.). New York: Random House.

Moscovici, S., & Mugny, G. (1983). Minority influence. In P. B. Paulus (Ed.), *Basic group processes*. New York: Springer-Verlag.

Mucha, T. F., & Reinhardt, R. F. (1970). Conversion reactions in student aviators. *American Journal of Psychiatry, 127*, 493–497.

Munnichs, U., Mussen, P., Olbrich, E., & Coleman, P. (Eds.). (1985). *Life-span and change in a gerontological perspective*. New York: Academic Press.

Nahome, L., & Lawton, M. P. (1975). Similarity and propinquity in friendship formation. *Journal of Personality and Social Psychology, 32*, 205–213.

Nathans, J., Piantanidu, T. P., Eddy, R. L., Shows, T. B., & Hogness, D. S. (1986, April 11). Molecular genetics of inherited variation in human color vision. *Science, 232*, pp. 203–210.

Nauta, W. J. H., & Feirtag, M. (1979, September). The organization of the brain. *Scientific American*, p. 102.

Nelson, B. (1983, April 2). Despair among jobless is on rise, studies find. *The New York Times*, p. 22.

New York Times. (1984, May 20). The new addicts. *New York Times*, p. 50.

Nickerson, R. S., Perkins, D. N., & Smith, E. E. (1985). *Teaching thinking*. Hillsdale, NJ: Erlbaum.

Ninokur, G. (1983). Controversies in depression, or do clinicians know something after all? In P. J. Clayton & J. E. Barret (Eds.), *Treatment of depression: Old controversies and new approaches* (pp. 153–168). New York: Raven Press.

Nisbett, R. E. (1968). Taste, deprivation, and weight determinants of eating behavior. *Journal of Personality and Social Psychology, 10*, 107–116.

Nisbett, R. E. (1972). Hunger, obesity and the ventromedial hypothalamus. *Psychological Review, 79*, 433–453.

Noll, K. M., & Davis, J. M. (1983). Biological theories in schizophrenia. In A. Rifkin (Ed.), *Schizophrenia and affective disorders: Biology and drug treatment* (pp. 139–204). Boston: John Wright.

Norvell, N., & Worchel, S. (1981). A reexamination of the relation between equal status contact and intergroup attraction. *Journal of Personality and Social Psychology, 41*, 902–908.

Nowicki, S., & Duke, M. (1978). An examination of counseling variables within a social learning framework. *Journal of Counseling Psychology, 25*, 1–7.

Olds, J., & Milner, P. (1954). Positive reinforcement produced by electrical stimulation of septal area and other regions of rat brain. *Journal of Comparative and Physiological Psychology, 47*, 411–427.

Orlafsky, J., Marcia, J., & Lasser, I. (1973). Ego identity status and intimacy vs. isolation crisis of young adulthood. *Journal of Personality and Social Psychology, 27*, 211–219.

Orne, M. T., & Holland, C. C. (1968). On the ecological validity of laboratory deceptions. *International Journal of Psychiatry, 6*, 282–293.

Ornstein, R. E. (1977). *The psychology of consciousness* (2nd ed.). New York: Harcourt Brace Jovanovich.

Orwin, R. G., & Condray, D. S. (1984). Smith and Glass' psychotherapy conclusions need further probing: On Landman and Dawes' re-analysis. *American Psychologist, 39*, 71–72.

Orzek, A. M. (1983). Use of rape crisis center services by a university community. *Journal of College Student Personnel, 24*, 465–466.

Ouchi, W. (1981). *Theory* Z. Reading, MA: Addison-Wesley.

Packer, J., & Bain, J. D. (1978). Cognitive style and teacher student compatibility. *Journal of Educational Psychology, 70*, 864–871.

Paivio, A. (1971). *Imagery and verbal processes*. New York: Holt, Rinehart and Winston.

Palladino, J. J., & Carducci, B. J. (1984). Students' knowledge of sleep and dreams. *Teaching of Psychology, 11*, 189–191.

Panek, P. E. (1982). Do beginning psychology of aging students believe 10 common myths about aging? *Teaching of Psychology, 9*, 104–105.

Papalia, D., & Olds, S. (1986). *Human development* (3rd ed.). New York: McGraw-Hill.

Papalia, D., & Tennent, S. S. (1975). Vocational aspirations in preschoolers: A manifestation of early sex-role stereotyping. *Sex Rules, 1*, 197–199.

Parlee, M. B. (1979, October). The friendship bond. *Psychology Today, 13*, pp. 43–45.

Parloff, M. B. (1976, February 21). Shopping for the right therapy. *Saturday Review, 14–20*.

Paulus, P. B., & McCain, G. (1983). Crowding in jails. *Basic and Applied Social Psychology, 4*, 89–107.

Paulus, P. B., McCain, G., & Cox, V. C. (1978). Death rates, psychiatric commitments, blood pressure, perceived crowding as a function of institutional crowding. *Environmental Psychology and Nonverbal Behavior, 3,* 107–116.

Pavlov, I. P. (1927). *Conditioned reflexes.* London: Oxford University Press.

Pearl, J. (1987). Embracing causality in formal reasoning. Proceedings of AAAI-87. The Sixth National Conference on Artificial Intelligence, 369.

Pechacek, T. F. (1979). Modification of smoking behavior. In *Smoking and health: A report of the surgeon general.* Washington, DC: U.S. Department of Health, Education, and Welfare, Public Health Service.

Peck, J. W. (1978). Rats defend different body weights depending on palatability and accessibility of their food. *Journal of Comparative and Physiological Psychology, 91,* 555–570.

Penfield, W., & Rasmussen, T. (1950). *The cerebral cortex of man.* New York: Macmillan.

Peplau, L. A., Rubin, Z., & Hill, C. T. (1977). Sexual intimacy in dating relationships. *Journal of Social Issues, 2,* 86–109.

Perkins, D. N. (1983). Why the human perceiver is a bad machine. In J. Beck, B. Hope, & A. Rosenfeld (Eds.), *Human and machine vision.* New York: Academic Press.

Perlmutter, M. (1979). Age differences in adults' free recall, cued recall, and recognition. *Journal of Gerontology, 34,* 533–539.

Perlmutter, M., & Mitchell, D. B. (1986). The appearance and disappearance of age differences in adult memory. In I. M. Craik & S. Trehub (Eds.), *Aging and cognitive processes.* New York: Plenum Press.

Perls, F. S. (1967). Group vs. individual therapy. *ETC: A review of general semantics, 34,* 306–312.

Perls, F. S. (1970). *Gestalt therapy now: Therapy, techniques, applications.* Palo Alto, CA: Science and Behavior Books.

Pervin, L. A. (1985). Personality: Current controversies, issues and directions. *Annual Review of Psychology,* 36.

Peterson, L. R., & Peterson, M. J. (1959). Short-term retention of individual items. *Journal of Experimental Psychology, 58,* 193–198.

Petty, R. E., & Cacioppo, J. T. (1977). Cognitive responding and resistance to persuasion. *Journal of Personality and Social Psychology, 35,* 645–655.

Petty, R. E., & Cacioppo, J. T. (1981). *Attitudes and persuasion: Classic and contemporary approaches.* Dubuque, IA: Brown.

Petty, R. E., & Cacioppo, J. T. (1984). The effects of involvement on responses to argument quantity and quality: Central and peripheral routes to persuasion. *Journal of Personality and Social Psychology, 46, 69–81.*

Piaget, J. (1970). Piaget's theory. In P. H. Mussen (Ed.), *Carmichael's manual of child psychology (Vol. I, 3rd ed.). New York: John Wiley.*

Piaget, J., & Inhelder, B. (1958). *The growth of logical thinking from childhood to adolescence.* Translated by A. Parsons & S. Seagrin. New York: Basic Books.

Piliavin, J. A., & Piliavin, I. M. (1972). Effect of blood on reactions to a victim. *Journal of Personality and Social Psychology, 23,* 353–362.

Pion, G. M., & Lipsey, M. W. (1984). Psychology and society: The challenge of change. *American Psychologist, 39,* 739–754.

Plutchik, R. (1984). Emotion. In K. Scherer & P. Ekman, (Eds.), *Approaches to emotion.* Hillsdale, NJ: Erlbaum.

Polivy, J., & Herman, L. P. (1985). Dieting and binging: A causal analysis. *American Psychologist, 40,* 193–201.

Pribram, K. H. (1986). The cognitive revolution and mind/brain issues. *American Psychologist, 41,* 507–520.

Pribram, K. H. (1984). Emotion: A neurobehavioral analysis. In K. R. Scherer & P. Ekman (Eds.), *Approaches to emotion.* Hillsdale, NJ: Erlbaum.

Prien, R. F. (1983). Lithium and the long-term maintenance treatment of tricyclic antidepressant drugs and therapeutic response. In P. J. Clayton & J. E. Barret (Eds.), *Treatment of depression: Old controversies and new approaches* (pp. 105–114). New York: Raven Press.

Proxmire, W. (1975). Press release, U.S. Senate.

Rachman, S., & Hodgson, R. (1980). *Obsessions and compulsions.* Englewood Cliffs, NJ: Prentice-Hall.

Ragozin, A. S. (1980). Attachment behavior of day care children: Naturalistic and laboratory observations. *Child Development, 51,* 409–415.

Ramey, C. T. (1981). Consequences of infant day care. In B. Weissbound & J. Musick (Eds.), *Infants: Their social environments.* Washington, DC: National Association for the Education of Young Children.

Rand, J. (1978, January). The psychology of conjuring. *Technology Review, 80,* 56–63.

Raphael, B. (1976). *The thinking computer.* San Francisco: Freeman.

Reed, S. K. (1982). *Cognition: Theory and applications.* Monterey, CA: Brooks/Cole.

Reiger, D.A., Myers, J. K., Kramer, M., Robins, L. N., Blazer, D. G., Hough, R. L., Eaton, W. W., & Lock, B. Z. (1984). The NIMH epidemiological catchment area program. *Archives of General Psychiatry, 41,* 934–941.

Reinke, B. J., Holmes, D. S., & Harris, R. L. (1985). The timing of psychosocial changes in women's lives: The years 25 to 45. *Journal of Personality and Social Psychology, 48,* 1353–1364.

Reis, H. T., Wheeler, L., Spiegel, N., Kerris, M. H., Nezlek, J., & Perri, M. (1982). Physical attractiveness in social interaction: II. Why does appearance affect social experience? *Journal of Personality and Social Psychology, 43,* 979–996.

Reisenzein, R. (1983). The Schachter theory of emotion: Two decades later. *Psychological Bulletin, 94,* 239–264.

Reuman, D. A., Alwin, D. F., & Veroff, J. (1984). Assessing the validity of the achievement motive in the presence of random measurement error. *Journal of Personality and Social Psychology, 47,* 1347–1362.

Reyner, A. (1984, April). The nose knows. *Science, 224,* p. 26.

Rice, A. (1984, May). Imagination to go. *Psychology Today, 18,* pp. 48–52.

Rice, B. (1981, December). Call-in therapy: Reach out and shrink someone. *Psychology Today, 15,* pp. 39–47; 87.

Riegel, K. F., & Riegel, R. M. (1972). Development, drop, and death. *Developmental Psychology, 6,* 306–319.

Rifkin, A., & Siris, S. G. (1983). Long-term drug treatment of schizophrenia. In A. Rifkin (Ed.), *Schizophrenia and affective disorders: Biology and drug treatment* (pp. 299–322). Boston: John Wright.

Rinn, W. E. (1984). The neuropsychology of facial expression: A review of neurological and psychological mechanisms for producing facial expressions. *Psychological Bulletin, 95,* 52–77.

Ristau, C. A., & Robbins, D. (1982). Language in the great apes. In J. S. Rosenblatt, R. A. Hinde, C. Beer, & M. Busnel (Eds.), *Advances in the study of behavior*. New York: Academic Press.

Ritzler, B., & Rosenbaum, G. (1974). Proprioception in schizophrenics and normals: Effects of stimulus intensity and interstimulus interval. *Journal of Abnormal Psychology, 83,* 106–111.

Robbins, W. J. (1929). *Growth*. New Haven, CT: Yale University Press.

Roberts, A. H. (1985). Biofeedback: Research, training, and clinical roles. *American Psychologist, 40,* 938–941.

Rodin, J. (1981). Current status of the internal-external hypothesis of obesity: What went wrong? *American Psychologist, 34,* 361–372.

Rodin, J., & Janis, I. L. (1979). The social power of health care practitioners as agents of change. *The Journal of Social Issues, 35,* 60–81.

Rodin, J., & Langer, E. (1980). Aging labels: The decline of control and the fall of self-esteem. *Journal of Social Issues, 36,* 12–29.

Rodin, J., & Langer, E. (1977). Long-term effects of a control-relevant intervention with the institutionalized aged. *Journal of Personality and Social Psychology, 35,* 897–902.

Roffwarg, H. F., Muzio, J. N., & Dement, W. C. (1966). Ontogenetic development of the human sleep-dream cycle. *Science, 152,* 604–619.

Rogers, C. R. (1951). *Client centered therapy*. Boston: Houghton Mifflin.

Rogers, C. R. (1971). A theory of personality. In S. Maddi (Ed.), *Perspectives on personality*. Boston: Little, Brown.

Rogers, C. R. (1980). *A way of being*. Boston: Houghton Mifflin.

Rogers, E. M., & Rogers, R. A. (1976). *Communication in organizations*. New York: The Free Press.

Rokeach, M. (1971). Long-range experimental modification of values, attitudes, and behavior. *American Psychologist, 26,* 453–459.

Rorschach,H. (1921). *Psychodiagnosis*. Berne: Hans Huber.

Rorschach, H. (1924). *Psychodiagnosis: A diagnostic test based on perception*. New York: Grune and Stratton.

Rosen, A. (1958). Differentiation of diagnostic groups by individual MMPI scales. *Journal of Consulting Psychology, 22,* 453–457.

Rosenhan, D. L. (1973). On being sane in insane places. *Science, 179,* 250–258.

Rosenthal, D. (1970). *Genetic theory and abnormal behavior*. New York: McGraw-Hill.

Rosenweig, M. R. (1984). Experience, memory, and the brain. *American Psychologist, 39,* 365–376.

Rosenweig, M. R., & Leiman, A. L. (1982). *Physiological psychology*. Lexington, MA: Heath.

Ross, M., & Fletcher, G. J. O. (1985). Attribution and social perception. In G. Lindzy & E. Aronson (Eds.), *Handbook of social psychology* (3rd ed.). New York: Random House.

Routtenberg, A., & Lindy, J. (1965). Effects of the availability of rewarding septal and hypothalmic stimulation on bar pressing for food under conditions of deprivation. *Journal of Comparative and Physiological Psychology, 60,* 158–161.

Rowe, J. W., & Kahn, R. L. (1987, July). Human aging: Usual and successful. *Science, 237,* 143–149.

Rozin, P. (1977). The significance of learning mechanisms in food selection: Some biology, psychology and sociology of science. In L. M. Barker, M. R. Best, & M. Donijan (Eds.), *Learning mechanisms in food selection*. Waco, TX: Baylor University Press.

Rubin, D. C. (1985, September). The subtle deceiver: Recalling our past. *Psychology Today, 19,* pp. 39–46.

Rubin, Z. (1970). Measurement of romantic love. *Journal of Personality and Social Psychology, 16,* 265–273.

Rubin, Z. (1973). *Liking and loving*. New York: Holt, Rinehart and Winston.

Rudd, J. R., & Geller, E. S. (1985). A university-based incentive program to increase safety belt use: Toward cost-effective institutionalization. *Journal of Applied Behavior Analysis, 18,* 215–226.

Rushton, J. P. (1975). Generosity in children: Immediate and long-term effects of modeling, preaching, and moral judgment. *Journal of Personality and Social Psychology, 31,* 459–466.

Russo, D. C., Carr, E. G., & Lovaas, O. I. (1980). Self injury in pediatric populations. *Comprehensive handbook of behavioral medicine* (Vol. 3: Extended applications and issues). Holliswood, NY: Spectrum.

Russo, N. (1981). In L. T. Benjamin, Jr., & K. D. Lowman (Eds.), *Activities handbook for the teaching of psychology*. Washington, DC: American Psychological Association.

Rutter, M. (1982). Social-emotional consequences of day care for preschool children. In E. F. Zigler & E. W. Gordon (Eds.), *Day care: Scientific and social policy issues*. Boston: Auburn House.

Sackheim, H. A. (1985, June). The case for E.C.T. *Psychology Today, 19,* pp. 36–40.

Sanders, D. H. (1983). *Computers today*. New York: McGraw-Hill.

Sank, L. T. (1979). Community disasters: Primary prevention and Tx in a health maintenance organization. *American Psychologist, 34,* 334–338.

Sarafino, E. P. (1979). An estimate of nationwide incidence of sexual offenses against children. *Child Welfare, 58,* 127–134.

Sarason, I. G. (1976). A modeling and informational approach to delinquency. In E. Ribes-Inesta & A. Bandura (Eds.), *Analysis of Delinquency and Aggression*. Hillsdale, NJ: Erlbaum.

Savage-Rumbaugh, E. S., Rumbaugh, D. M., & Boysen, S. (1980). Do apes use language? *American Scientist, 68,* 49–61.

Saxe, L., Dougherty, D., & Cross, T. (1985). The validity of polygraph testing. *American Psychologist, 40,* 355–366.

Scarr, S. (1984). *Mother care/other care*. New York: Basic Books.

Scarr, S., & Carter-Saltzman, L. (1982). Genetics and intelligence. In R. J. Sternberg (Ed.), *Handbook of human intelli-*

gence (pp. 792–896). Cambridge: Cambridge University Press.

Scarr, S., & Weinberg, R. A. (1976). I.Q. test performance of black children adopted by white families. *American Psychologist, 3,* 726–739.

Schachter, S. (1971). Some extraordinary facts about obese humans and rats. *American Psychologist, 26,* 129–144.

Schachter, S., Ellertson, N., McBride, D., & Gregory,D. (1951). An experimental study of cohesiveness and productivity. *Human Relations, 4,* 229–238.

Schachter, S., Goldman, R., & Gordon, A. (1968). Effects of fear, food deprivation, and obesity on eating. *Journal of Personality and Social Psychology, 10,* 91–97.

Schachter, S., & Singer, J. E. (1962). Cognitive, social, and physiological determinants of emotional state. *Psychological Review, 69,* 379–399.

Schaie, K. W. (1985). *Longitudinal studies of psychological development.* New York: Guilford Press.

Schaie, K. W., & Willis, S. L. (1986). Can decline in adult intellectual functioning be reversed? *Developmental Psychology, 22,* 223–232.

Schaie, K. W., & Willis, S. L. (1985, August). *Differential ability decline and its remediation in late adulthood.* Paper presented at annual meeting of the American Psychological Association, Los Angeles.

Schank, R. (1985). *The cognitive computer.* New York: McGraw-Hill.

Scheff, T. J. (1985). The primacy of affect. *American Psychologist, 40,* 849–850.

Scheibel, A. (1984). Personal communication.

Scherer, K. R. (1984). Les émotions: Fonctions et composantes. [Emotions: Functions and Components.] *Cahiers de psychologie cognitive, 4,* 9–39.

Scherer, K. R., & Ekman, P. (Eds.). (1984). *Approaches to emotion.* Hillsdale, NJ: Erlbaum.

Schickedanz, J. A., Schickedanz, D. I., & Forsyth, P. D. (1982). *Toward understanding children.* Boston: Little, Brown.

Schiffman, H. R. (1982). *Sensation and perception: An integrated approach* (2nd ed.). NY: John Wiley.

Schmeck, H. M., Jr. (1984, March 6). Explosion of data on brain cell reveals its great complexity. *New York Times,* pp. C1–C2.

Schneiderman, N. (1983). Animal behavior models of coronary heart disease. In D. S. Krantz, A. Baum, & J. E. Singer (Eds.), *Handbook of psychology and health,* Vol. III. Hillsdale, NJ: Erlbaum.

Schoeneman, T. J., & Rubanowitz, D. E. (1985). Attributions in the advice columns: Actors and observers, causes and reasons. *Journal of Personality and Social Psychology, 11,* 315–325.

Schofield, W. (1964). *Psychotherapy: The purchase of friendship.* Englewood Cliffs, NJ: Prentice-Hall.

Schonche, D.A. (1974, August). The emotional aftermath of "the largest tornado ever." *Today's Health, pp. 16–19; 61–63.*

Schwartz, G. E., Davidson, R., & Maer, F. (1975,). Right hemisphere lateralization for emotion in the human brain: Interactions with cognition. *Science,* 286–288.

Sears, D. D. (1968). The paradox of de facto selective exposure without preferences for supportive information. In R. P. Abelson (Ed.), *Theories of cognitive consistency.* Chicago: Rand McNally.

Sears, R. R. (1977). Sources of life satisfaction of the Terman gifted men. *American Psychologist, 32,* 119–128.

Segall, M. H., Campbell, D. T., & Herskovits, M. J. (1966). *The influence of culture on visual perception.* New York: Bobbs-Merrill.

Seligman, M. E. P. (1975). *Helplessness: On depression, development, and death.* San Francisco: Freeman.

Selye, H. (1976). *The stress of life.* New York: McGraw-Hill.

Shaw, M. E. (1954). Some effects of problem complexity upon problem solution efficiency in different communication nets. *Journal of Experimental Psychology, 48,* 211–217.

Shaw, M. E. (1964). Communication networks. In L. Berkowitz (Ed.), *Advances in experimental social psychology* (Vol. 1, pp. 111–147). New York: Academic Press.

Shaw, M. E. (1981). *Group dynamics: The psychology of small group behavior* (3rd ed.). New York: McGraw-Hill.

Shock, N. W. (1962, January). The physiology of aging. *Scientific American,* 100–110.

Shotland, R. L. (1984, March). Paper presented at the Catherine Genovese Memorial Conference on Bad Samaritanism, Fordham University.

Shotland, R. L. (1985, June). When bystanders just stand by. *Psychology Today, 19,* pp. 50–55.

Simmons, J. V., Jr. (1981). U.S. patent document #4, 261, 284.

Simmons, J., & Mares, W. (1985). *Working together: Employee participation in action.* New York: University Press.

Simon, H. A. (1957). *Administrative behavior* (2nd ed.). New York: The Free Press.

Singer, J. L. (1975). *The inner world of daydreaming.* New York: Harper & Row.

Sinoway, C. G., Raupp, C. D., & Newman, J. (1985). *Binge eating and bulimia: Comparing incidence and characteristics across universities.* Paper presented at annual meeting of the American Psychological Association, Los Angeles.

Siris, S. G., & Rifkin, A. (1983). Side effects of drugs used in the treatment of affective disorders. In A. Rifkin (Ed.), *Schizophrenia and affective disorders: Biology and drug treatment* (pp. 117–138). Boston: John Wright.

Skeels, H. M. (1966). Adult status of children with contrasting early life experiences: A follow-up study. *Monographs of the Society for Research in Child Development, 31,* (3, whole No. 105).

Skinner, B. F. (1948). *Walden Two.* New York: Macmillan.

Skinner, B. F. (1957). *Verbal behavior.* New York: Appleton-Century-Crofts.

Skinner, B. F. (1975). The steep and thorny road to a science of behavior. *American Psychologist, 30,* 42–49.

Skinner, B. F., & Krakower, S. A. (1968). *Handwriting with write and see.* Chicago: Lyons and Carnahan.

Skrypnek, B. J., & Snyder, M. (1982). On the self-perpetuating nature of stereotypes about women and men. *Journal of Experimental Social Psychology, 18,* 277–291.

Sloane, R. B., Staples, F. R., Criostal, A. H., Yorkston, W. J., & Whipple,

K. (1975). *Psychotherapy vs. behavior therapy*. Cambridge, MA: Harvard University Press.

Smith, E. R. (1984). Attributions and other inferences: Processing information about the self versus others. *Journal of Experimental Social Psychology, 20,* 97–115.

Smith, M. L., Glass, G. V., & Miller, T. J. (1980). *The benefits of psychotherapy*. Baltimore: John Hopkins.

Snarey, J. R. (1985). Cross-cultural universality of social-moral development: A critical review of Kohlbergian research. *Psychological Bulletin, 97,* 202–232.

Snyder, C. R., & Shenk, R. J. (1975). The P. T. Barnum effect. *Psychology Today, 8,* pp. 52–54.

Snyder, M., Berscheid, E., & Glick, P. (1985). Focusing on the exterior and the interior: The investigations of the initiation of personal relations. *Journal of Personality and Social Psychology, 48,* 1427–1439.

Snyder, M., & Cantor, N. (1979). Testing hypotheses about other people: The use of historical knowledge, *Journal of Experimental Social Psychology, 15,* 330–343.

Snyder, S. H. (1978). Dopamine and schizophrenia. In L. C. Wynne, R. L. Cromwell, & S. Matthysse (Eds.), *The nature of schizophrenia: New approaches to research and treatment* (pp. 87–94). New York: Wiley.

Snyder, S. H. (1984). Drug and neurotransmitter receptors in the brain. *Science, 224,* pp. 22–31.

Soelberg, P. O. (1967). Unprogrammed decision making. *Industrial Management Review,* 19–29.

Solomon, R. L., & Corbit, J. D. (1974). An opponent-process theory of motivation: I. Temporal dynamics of affect. *Psychological Review, 81,* 119–145.

Spence, J. T. (1985, August). *Achievement American style: The rewards and costs of individualism*. Presidential address, 93rd Annual Convention of the American Psychological Association, Los Angeles.

Spence, J. T., Deaux, K., & Helmreich, R. L. (1985). Sex roles in contemporary American society. In G. Lindzey & E. Aronson (Eds.), *Handbook of social psychology:* Vol. II (3rd ed.). New York: Random House.

Sperling, G. (1960). The information available in brief visual presentation. *Psych Monographs, 74,* Whole no. 498.

Sperry, R. (1982). Some effects of disconnecting the cerebral hemispheres. *Science, 217,* pp. 1223–1226.

Spitzer, R. L., Skodol, A. E., Gibbon, M., & Williams, J. B. W. (1983). *Psychopathology: A case book*. New York: McGraw-Hill.

Sproull, L. S., & Kiesler, S. B. (1983). *Encounters with the alien culture*. Paper presented at the American Psychological Association annual meeting, Berkeley, CA.

Squire, L. (1986, June). Mechanisms of memory. *Science, 232,* 1612–1619.

Squire, L. (1987). *Memory and brain*. New York: Oxford University Press.

Squire, L., & Butters, N. (Eds.). (1985). *Neuropsychology of memory*. New York: Guilford Press.

Staats, A. W. (1967). Outline of an integrated learning theory of attitude formation and function. In M. Fishbein (Ed.), *Attitude theory and measurement*. New York: Wiley.

Staats, A. W., & Staats, C. K. (1958). Attitudes established by classical conditioning. *Journal of Abnormal and Social Psychology, 57,* 37–40.

Stanley, J. C. (1980). On educating the gifted. *Educational Researcher, 9,* 8–12.

Stapp, J., Fulcher, R., & Wicherski, M. (1984). The employment of 1981 and 1982 doctorate recipients in psychology. *American Psychologist, 39,* 1408–1423.

Stapp, J., Tucker, A. M., & VandenBos, G. R. (1985). Census of psychology personnel. *American Psychologist, 40,* 1317–1351.

Stark, E. (1985, May). Breaking the pain habit. *Psychology Today,* pp. 31–36.

Staub, E. (1971). A child in distress: The influence of nurturance and modeling on children's attempts to help. *Developmental Psychology, 5,* 124–133.

Steele, C. M., & Southwick, L. (1985). Alcohol and social behavior I: The psychology of drunken excess. *Journal of Personality and Social Psychology, 48,* 18–34.

Stein, A. H., & Bailey, M. M. (1973). The socialization of achievement orientation in females. *Psychological Bulletin, 80,* 345–366.

Steiner, J. E. (1979). Human facial expressions in response to taste and smell stimulation. In H. Reese & L. P. Lipsitt (Eds.), *Advances in child development and behavior* (Vol. 13). New York: Academic Press.

Sternberg, R. J. (1981). Testing and cognitive psychology. *American Psychologist, 36,* 1181–1189.

Sternberg, R. J. (1982). Reasoning, problem solving, and intelligence. In R. J. Sternberg (Ed.), *Handbook of human intelligence* (pp. 225–307). Cambridge, MA: Cambridge University Press.

Sternberg, R. J. (1985). Implicit theories of intelligence, creativity, and wisdom. *Journal of Personality and Social Psychology, 49,* 607–627.

Sternberg, R. J. (1986). Triangular theory of love. *Psychological Review, 93,* 119–135.

Sternberg, R. J., Conway, B. E., Ketron, J. L., & Bernstein, M. (1981). Peoples' conceptions of intelligence. *Journal of Personality and Social Psychology, 41,* 37–55).

Sternberg, R. J., & Grajek, S. (1984). The nature of love. *Journal of Personality and Social Psychology, 47,* 312–329.

Stevens, C. F. (1979, September). The neuron. *Scientific American,* p. 56.

Stiles, W. B., Shapiro, D. A., & Elliot, R. (1986). Are all psychotherapies equivalent? *American Psychologist, 41,* 165–180.

Stricker, E. M., & Zigmond, M. J. (1976). Recovery of function after damage to catecholamine-containing neurons: A neurochemical model for hypothalmic syndrome. In J. M. Sprague & A. N. Epstein (Eds.), *Progress in psychobiology and physiological psychology* (Vol. 6). New York: Academic Press.

Stoller, S., & Field, T. (1982). Alteration of mother and infant behavior and heart rate during a still-face perturbation of face-to-face interaction. In T. Field & A. Fogel (Eds.), *Emotion and interactions*. New York: Erlbaum.

Storandt, M. et al. (1984). Psychometric differentiation of mild senile dementia of the Alzheimer type. *Archives of Neurology, 41,* 497–499.

Streufert, S. (1984, October). The stress of excellence. *Across the Board,* 9–16.

Strong, L. D. (1978). Alternative marital and family forms: Their relative attractiveness to college students and correlates of willingness to participate in nontraditional forms. *Journal of Marriage and the Family, 40,* 493–503.

Strupp, H. H. (1981). Clinical research, practice, and the crisis of confidence. *Journal of Consulting and Clinical Psychology, 49,* 216–219.

Strupp, H. H. (1981). Toward a refinement of time-limited dynamic psychotherapy. *Forms of brief therapy.* New York: Guilford Press.

Stunkard, A. J. (1980). *Obesity.* Philadelphia: Saunders.

Sullivan, B. (1985). *Double standard.* Paper presented at the annual meeting of the Society for the Scientific Study of Sex, San Diego.

Sullivan, W. (1984, September). Transplanting cells into brain offers promise of therapy. *New York Times,* pp. C1–C2.

Sulzer-Azaroff, B., & Mayer, G. R. (1986). *Achieving educational excellence with behavioral strategies.* New York: Holt, Rinehart and Winston.

Super, C. M. (1980). Cognitive development: Looking across at growing up. In C. M. Super & S. Harakness (Eds.), *New directions for child development: Anthropological Perspectives on child development* (pp. 59–69). San Francisco: Jossey-Bass.

Svanum, S., Bringle, R. G., & McLaughlin, J. E. (1982). Father absence and cognitive performance in a large sample of six- to eleven-year-old children. *Child Development, 53,* 136–143.

Svengali squad: L. A. police (1976, September 13). *Time,* p. 76.

Sweeney, P. D., & Gruber, L. L. (1984). Selective exposure: Voter information preferences and the Watergate affair. *Journal of Personality and Social Psychology, 46,* 1208–1221.

Sweet, E. (1985, October). Date rape: The story of an epidemic and those who deny it. *Ms/Campus Times,* pp. 56–59.

Szasz, T. S. (1961). *The myth of mental illness.* New York: Harper & Row.

Szasz, T. S. (1970). *The manufacture of madness.* New York: Harper & Row.

Szasz, T. (1977). *Psychiatric slavery.* New York: Free Press.

Szasz, T. (1982). The psychiatric will: A new mechanism for protecting persons against "psychosis" and psychiatry. *American Psychologist, 37,* 762–770.

Szilagyi, A. D. (1981). *Management and performance.* Glenview, IL: Scott, Foresman.

Szilagyi, A. D., Jr., & Wallace, M. J., Jr. (1987). *Organizational behavior and performance* (4th ed.). Glenview, IL: Scott, Foresman.

Tagiuri, R. (1958). Social preference and its perception. In R. Tagiuri & L. Petrullo (Eds.), *Person, perception, and interpersonal behavior* (pp. 316–336). Stanford, CA: Stanford University Press.

Tanford, S., & Penrod, S. (1984). Social influence model: A formal integration of research on majority and minority influence processes. *Psychological Bulletin, 95,* 189–225.

Tanner, J. M. (1978). *Education and physical growth* (2nd ed.). New York: International Universities Press.

Terman, L. M., & Oden, M. H. (1947). *Genetic studies of genius, IV: The gifted child grows up.* Stanford, CA: Stanford University Press.

Terrace, H. S. (1985). In the beginning was the "name." *American Psychologist, 40,* 1011–1028.

Terrace, H. S., Petitto, L. A., Sanders, R. J., & Bever, T. G. (1981). Commentary on ape language. *Science, 221,* pp. 87–88.

Thigpen, C., & Cleckley, H. M. (1985). *Three faces of eve.* Augusta, GA: Cleckley-Thigpen.

Thorndike, E. L. (1932). *The fundamentals of learning.* New York: Teacher's College.

Tjosvold, D., & Deemer, D. K. (1980). Effects of controversy within a cooperative or competitive context on organizational decision making. *Journal of Applied Psychology, 65,* 590–595.

Tolman, E. C., & Honzik, C. H. (1930). Introduction and removal of reward and maze performance in rats. *University of California Publications in Psychology, 4,* 257–275.

Tomlinson-Keasey, C. (1985). *Child development: Psychological, sociological, and biological factors.* Homewood, IL: Dorsey.

Tomlinson-Keasey, C., Eisert, D. C., Kahle, L. R., Hardy-Brown, K., & Keasey, B. (1979). The structure of concrete operations. *Child Development,* 1153–1163.

Treisman, M. (1960,). Motion sickness: An evolutionary hypothesis. *Science,* pp. 493–495.

Tuller, D. (1985, February 24). What's new in employment testing. *New York Times* (Sunday edition), 17.

Tucker, B. J., Megenity, D., & Virgil, L. (1970). Anatomy of a campus crisis center. *Personnel and Guidance Journal, 48,* 343–348.

Tulving, E. (1972). Episodic and semantic memory. In E. Tulving and W. Donaldson (Eds.), *Organization of memory.* New York: Academic Press.

Tulving, E. (1983). *Elements of episodic memory.* New York: Oxford University Press.

Tulving, E., & Psotka, J. (1971). Retroactive inhibition in free recall: Inaccessibility of information available in the memory store. *Journal of Experimental Psychology, 87,* 1–8.

Tulving, E., & Thompson, D. M. (1973). Encoding specificity and retrieval processes in episodic memory. *Psychological Review, 80,* 352–373.

Turkington, C. (1985, September). Computer unlocks secrets in folds, functions of brain. *APA Monitor.*

Udolf, R. (1981). *Handbook of hypnosis for professionals.* New York: Van Nostrand.

Udolf, R. (1983). *Drugs, society, and human behavior* (3rd ed.). St. Louis: Mosby.

Ullman, L. P., & Krasner, L. (1975). *A psychological approach to abnormal behavior* (2nd ed.). Englewood Cliffs, NJ: Prentice-Hall.

Ungson, G., & Braunstein, D. (1982). *Design making.* Boston: Kent.

U.S. Census Bureau. (1985). *Marital status and living arrangement.* Washington, DC: Government Printing Office.

U.S. Department of Health, Education, and Welfare. (1979). *Smoking and health: A report of the Surgeon General* (DHEW Publication No. (PHS) 79-50066). Washington, DC: Public Health Service.

U.S. Department of Labor. (1985, February). *Employment and earnings.* Washington, DC: U.S. Government.

Uttal, W. R. (1983). *Visual form detection in three-dimensional space.* Hillsdale, NJ: Erlbaum.

Vaillant, G. E. (1984). The disadvantages of DSM-III outweigh its advantages. *American Journal of Psychiatry, 141,* 542–545.

Valenstein, E. S. (Ed.). (1980). *The psychosurgery debate: Scientific, legal, and ethical perspectives.* San Francisco: Freeman.

Verplanck, W. S. (1955). The control of the content of conversation: Reinforcement of statements of opinion. *Journal of Abnormal and Social Psychology, 51,* 668–676.

Vonnegut, M. (1975). *The Eden express.* New York: Bantam.

VonRestorff, H. (1933). Uber die wirking von bereichsbildumgen im Spurenfeld. In W. Kohler & H. VonRestorff, *Analyse von vorgangen in Spurenfeld. I. Psychologische forschung, 18,* 299–342.

Wagner, H. L., MacDonald, C. J., & Manstead, A. S. R. (1986). Communication of individual emotions by spontaneous facial expressions. *Journal of Personality and Social Psychology, 50,* 737–743.

Wagner, R., & Sternberg, R. (1985). Alternate conceptions of intelligence and their implications for education. *Review of Educational Research, 54,* 179–223.

Waid, W. M., & Orne, M. T. (1982). The physiological detection of deception. *American Scientist, 70,* pp. 402–409.

Waldrop, M. M. (1987, September). Causality, structure, and common sense. *Science, 237,* 1297–1299.

Wallace, R. K., & Benson, H. (1972, February). The physiology of meditation. *Scientific American,* pp. 84–90.

Wallis, C. (1984, June 11). Unlocking pain's secrets. *Time,* pp. 58–60.

Walster, E., & Walster, G. W. (1978). *Love.* Reading, MA: Addison-Wesley.

Watkins, L. R., & Mayer, D. J. (1982). Organization of endogenous opiate and non-opiate pain control systems. *Science, 216,* pp. 1185–1192.

Watson, D. (1982). The actor and the observer: How are their perceptions of causality divergent? *Psychological Bulletin, 92,* 682–700.

Watson, J. B. (1924). *Behaviorism.* New York: Norton.

Watson, J. B., & Rayner, R. (1920). Conditioned emotional reactions. *Journal of Experimental Psychology, 3,* 1–14.

Watt, N. (Ed.). (1985). *Children at risk for schizophrenia.* Cambridge, England: Cambridge University Press.

Webb, W. B. (1979). Sleep and dreams. In B. B. Wolman (Ed.), *Handbook of general psychology* (pp. 734–748). Englewood Cliffs, NJ: Prentice-Hall.

Weber, R., & Crocker, J. (1983). Cognitive processes in the revision of stereotypic beliefs. *Journal of Personality and Social Psychology, 45,* 961–977.

Wechsler, D. (1975). Intelligence defined and undefined. *American Psychologist, 30,* 135–139.

Weinberg, S. (1984). *Cyberphobia.* Unpublished manuscript, St. John's College.

Weinberger, N. M., McGaugh, J. L., Lynch, G. (Eds.). (1985). *Memory systems of the brain.* New York: Guilford.

Weiner, B. (1985). *Human motivation.* New York: Springer-Verlag.

Weiner, B. (1985). "Spontaneous" causal thinking. *Psychological Bulletin, 97,* 74–84.

Weiner, R. (1982). Another look at an old controversy. *Contemporary Psychiatry, 1,* 61–62.

Weinstein, C. E. (1986). Assessment and training of student learning strategies. In R. R. Schmeck (Ed.), *Learning styles and learning strategies.* New York: Plenum Press.

Weisman, S. R. (1984, April 29). Will the magic prevail? *New York Times Magazine,* pp. 39–56.

Weiss, L. (1985). *Dream analysis in psychotherapy.* New York: Pergamon.

Weizenbaum, J. (1966). ELIZA--a computer program for the study of natural language communication between man and machine. *Communications of the ACM, 9,* 36–45.

Wells, G. L., & Harvey, J. H. (1978). Naive attributors' attributions and predictions: What is informative and when is an effect an effect? *Journal of Personality and Social Psychology, 36,* 483–490.

Wells, G. L., & Loftus, E. A. (Eds.). (1984). *Eyewitness testimony: Psychological perspectives.* New York: Cambridge University Press.

Wender, P. H., & Klein, D. F. (1981, February). The promise of biological psychiatry. *Psychology Today, 15,* pp. 25–41.

Wertheimer, M. (1923). Untersuchuugen zur lehre von der Gestalt. II. *Psychol. Forsch., 5,* pp. 301–350. In Beardsley and M. Wertheimer (Eds.) (1958), *Readings in perception.* New York: Van Nostrand.

West, S. G., Higginbotham, H. N., & Forsyth, D. R. (1985). *Psychotherapy and behavior change: Social and cultural perspectives.* New York: Pergamon.

Westoff, C. F. (1974). Coital frequency and contraception. *Family Planning Perspectives, 8,* 54–57.

Wheeler, D., & Janis, J. L. (1980). *A practical guide for making decisions.* New York: Free Press.

Whitaker, M. (1984, December 17). It was like breathing fire. *Newsweek,* pp. 26–32.

Whorf, B. L. (1956). *Language, thought, and reality.* New York: Wiley.

Wiederhold, W. C. (Ed.). (1982). *Neurology for non-neurologists.* New York: Academic Press.

Wielkiewicz, R. M. (1985). *Behavior management in the schools: Principles and procedures.* New York: Pergamon.

Wilkinson, A. C. (Ed.) (1983). *Classroom computers and cognitive science.* New York: Academic Press.

Wilson, T. D., & Linville, P. N. (1982). Improving academic performance of college freshmen: Attribution therapy revisited. *Journal of Personality and Social Psychology, 42,* 367–376.

Wilson, T. D., & Linville, P. W. (1985). Improving the performance of college freshmen with attributional techniques. *Journal of Personality and Social Psychology, 49,* 287–293.

Winokur, G. (1983). Alcoholism and depression. *Substance and Alcohol Actions/Misuse, 4,* 111–119.

Winter, D. G. (1973). *The power motive.* New York: Free Press.

Winter, D. G. (1976, July). What makes the candidate run? *Psychology Today, 10,* pp. 45–92.

Witkin, H. A., Moore, C. A., Goodenough, D. R., & Cox, P. N. (1977). Field-dependent and field-independent cognitive styles and their educational implications. *Review of Educational Research, 47,* 1–64.

Wolf, S. (1985). Manifest and latent influence of majorities and minorities. *Journal of Personality and Social Psychology, 48,* 899–908.

Wolman, B. (1968). *The unconscious mind: The meaning of Freudian psychology.* Englewood Cliffs, NJ: Prentice-Hall.

Wolpe, J. (1969). *The practice of behavior therapy.* New York: Pergamon.

Woodruff, R. A., Clayton, P. J., & Guze, S. B. (1975). Is everyone depressed? *American Journal of Psychiatry, 132,* 627–628.

Woolfolk, R. L. (1975, October). Psychophysiological correlates of meditation. *Archives of General Psychiatry, 32,* 1326–1333.

Wright, J. D. (1978). Are working women really more satisfied?: Evidence from several national surveys. *Journal of Marriage and the Family, 40,* 301–313.

Wyden, B. (1971, December). Growth: 45 crucial months. *Life,* pp. 93–95.

Wynne, L. C., Singer, M. T., Bartko, J. J., & Toohey, M. L. (1975). Schizophrenics and their families: Recent research on parental communication. *Psychiatric Research: The Widening Perspective.* New York: International Universities Press.

Yalom, I. D. (1975). *The theory and practice of group psychotherapy* (2nd ed.). New York: Basic Books.

Yates, A. J. (1980). *Biofeedback and the modification of behavior.* New York: Plenum Press.

Youkilis, H., & Bootzin, R. R. (1981). A psychophysiological perspective on the etiology and treatment of insomnia. In S. M. Haynes & L. A. Gannon (Eds.), *Psychosomatic disorders: A psychophysiological approach to etiology and treatment.* New York: Praeger.

Yukl, G. (1974). Effects of the opponent's initial offer, concession magnitude, and concession frequency on bargaining behavior. *Journal of Personality and Social Psychology, 30,* 323–335.

Yussen, S. R. (1984). *Intellectual development: Birth to adulthood.* New York: Academic Press.

Zajonc, R. B. (1968). The attitudinal effects of mere exposure. *Journal of Personality and Social Psychology, 9,* 1–27.

Zajonc, R. B. (1985). Emotion and facial efference: A theory reclaimed. *Science, 228,* pp. 15–21.

Zajonc, R. B. (1984). On the primacy of affect. *American Psychologist, 39,* 117–123.

Zanna, M. P., & Pack, S. J. (1974). On the self-fulfilling nature of apparent sex differences in behavior. *Journal of Experimental Social Psychology, 11,* 583–591.

Zillman, D. (1978). *Hostility and aggression.* Hillsdale, NJ: Erlbaum.

Zimmer, J. (1984). Courting the Gods of sport: Athletes use superstition to ward off the devils of injury and bad luck. *Psychology Today, 18,* pp. 36–39.

Zivin, G. (Ed.) (1985). *The development of expressive behavior: Biology-environmental interactions.* New York: Academic Press.

Zubin, J., & Spring, B. (1977). Vulnerability: New view of schizophrenia. *Journal of Abnormal Psychology, 86,* 103–126.

Zuckerman, M., & Wheeler, L. (1975). To dispel fantasy about the fantasy-based measure of fear of success. *Psychological Bulletin, 82,* 932–946.

NAME INDEX

Abelson, H. I., 469
Ackley, D. H., 158
Adams, C. A., 513, 514
Adler, A., 369
Aiello, J. R., 514
Ainsworth, M. D. S., 327
Ajzen, I., 467
Albee, G. W., 229
Allen, V. L., 493
Allport, G. W., 177, 371
Alwin, D. F., 251
Alwitt, L., 469
Amabile, T. M., 254
American Psychological Association, 7, 31, 270
Amir, Y., 482
Anastasi, A., 229
Anderson, C. A., 514
Anderson, D. C., 514
Anderson, J. A., 46
Anderson, J. R., 174
Anderson, N. H., 475
Annett, M., 68
Arafat, I., 245
Archibald, W. P., 476
Arena, J. M., 246
Arkin, R. M., 481
Aronson, E., 497
Asch, S. E., 491–492
Asnis, G., 419
Atkinson, J. W., 250
Atkinson, R. C., 165
Averill, J. R., 264
Azrin, N. H., 139

Bachrach, C. A., 246
Back, K. W., 497
Baillargeon, R., 337
Ballard, D. H., 158
Ballinger, C. B., 346
Baltes, P. B., 349
Bandura, A., 152, 153, 374–375, 440, 506, 508
Bangert-Drowns, R. L., 220
Barber, T. X., 294
Bard, P., 267
Barker, L. M., 241
Barland, G. H., 270
Baron, R. A., 509, 514
Baron, R. M., 513, 514
Bartko, J. J., 420
Bartoshuk, L. M., 103
Bashner, R. S., 482
Bateson, G., 420
Baum, A., 8, 424, 513, 514
Baumgardner, A. H., 481
Beale, I. L., 67
Beaton, A., 68
Beck, A. T., 443
Beck, J., 95
Bee, H. L., 329, 337
Bell, S. M., 327
Bellugi, U., 203
Bem, D. J., 472, 476, 480
Bem, S. L., 476
Benjamin, L. T., Jr., 505
Benson, H., 295, 296, 440
Bergin, A. E., 448
Berkowitz, L., 504–507, 509
Berlyne, D., 255
Berman, J. S., 448, 449
Bernard, M. E., 441
Bernstein, M., 213
Berscheid, E., 497–500
Best, C. T., 68
Best, M. E., 241
Bever, T. G., 203
Bieber, I., 247
Binet, A., 213
Bini, L., 453
Birch, H. G., 190
Birnbaum, M. H., 497
Bischof, W. F., 191
Blakeslee, S., 180, 303
Blank, J. P., 210
Blatt, S. J., 414
Blazer, D. G., 397
Bloom, B., 338
Blumenfeld, G. T., 144
Blusztajn, J. K., 51
Boffey, P. M., 458
Bolles, R. C., 52
Bootzin, R. R., 292
Boring, E. G., 111
Bornstein, M. H., 232, 325, 326
Boston, D. E., 144
Bourne, L. E., 190
Bower, G. H., 174
Bowlby, J., 422
Boyd, J. H., 414
Boysen, S., 202
Braly, K. W., 476
Braun, B., 412
Brazelton, B., 323
Breggin, P. R., 453
Brewer, M. B., 476, 482
Brice, P., 507, 509
Broad, N. J., 117
Brody, J., 305
Broverman, D. M., 476
Broverman, I. K., 476
Brown, B., 425
Brown, B. B., 72
Brown, P. K., 95
Brown, R., 169, 174, 201
Bruce, V., 93, 109
Bruch, H., 244
Bruner, J. S., 314
Brunson, B. I., 456
Bryan, J. H., 512
Buckhout, R., 176
Bukato, D., 337
Burglass, M. E., 301
Burnham, D. K., 109
Burright, R. G., 62
Butcher, J. N., 382, 422
Butler, A. M., 302
Butler, C. P., 302
Butler, R. A., 254
Butters, N., 180
Byers, H., 271
Byers, P., 271
Byrne, D., 377, 475, 479

Cacioppo, J. T., 470, 495
Cain, L. M., 379
Cairns, C. E., 204
Cairns, H. S., 204
Campbell, D. T., 114
Cannon, W. B., 267–268
Cantor, N., 474
Carducci, B. J., 285
Carlsmith, J. M., 470–471
Caroll, J. B., 215
Carr, E. G., 439
Carson, R. C., 419, 422, 451
Carter-Saltzman, L., 231
Cartwright, R. D., 290
Casey, K. L., 60
Casey, R. J., 448
Catania, A. C., 134
Cattell, R. B., 217, 371–372
Ceci, S. J., 31
Cerella, J., 349
Chaiken, S., 469
Chandler, M. J., 337
Chanowitz, B., 482
Chase, P., 156
Chavez, C. J., 321
Check, J. V. P., 509
Cherry, E. C., 111, 148
Chomsky, N., 201, 202
Cialdini, R. B., 470

Cimbolic, P., 416, 432
Clark, R. A., 250
Clark, R. D., III, 496
Clarkson, F. E., 476
Clayton, P. J., 414, 415
Coates, T. J., 35
Cohen, L. B., 325
Cohen, T. E., 90
Coleman, J. C., 422
Coleman, P., 348
Collins, J., 458
Condray, D. S., 448, 449
Converse, J., Jr., 471
Conway, B. E., 213
Cooper, I. S., 44
Cooper, J., 471, 472
Coppen, A., 452
Corballis, M. C., 67
Corbit, J. D., 257, 258
Coren, S., 85, 111–115
Costa, P. T., Jr., 411
Cotton, W. L., 245
Cox, V. C., 513
Craighead, W. E., 437
Craik, F. I. M., 171, 350
Crapo, L., 61
Crocetti, G., 220
Crocker, J., 476
Crook, T. H., 350
Cross, T., 270
Crowder, R. G., 165
Croyle, R. T., 472
Csikszentmihalyi, M., 343, 347
Cusack, O., 147

Daehler, M., 337
D'Afflitti, J. P., 414
Darley, J. M., 22, 26–27, 30, 31, 510
Darwin, C. J., 165
Davidson, R., 68
Davis, H. P., 181
Davis, J. M., 419
Davison, G., 437
Dawes, R. M., 448
Day, C. L., 302
Day, H. R., 482, 483
Deaux, K., 476
DeCasper, A. J., 326
DeCharms, R., 251
Deci, E. L., 254
deGroot, A. D., 167
DeLoache, J. S., 325
Dement, W. C., 286, 287, 289
Dent, J., 348
Deregowski, J. B., 115
Deutsch, C., 330
Deutsch, M., 181, 330
Dion, K. K., 498
Dodds, J. B., 324
Dolce, J. J., 105
Dollard, J., 374, 506
Dominowski, R. L., 190
Domjan, M., 241
Donnerstein, E., 506, 509
Donovick, P. J., 62
Doob, A. N., 508
Doob, L., 506
Doty, R. L., 103
Dougherty, D., 270
Dove, A., 228
Dovido, J. F., 476
Dreyer, P. H., 340
Duke, M., 415, 422
Duncan, B., 508
Duncan, C. C., 418
Duncker, K., 193
Dunkel-Schetter, C., 425
Dworkin, R. H., 381

Eagly, A. H., 469
Eaton, W. W., 397
Eaves, L. J., 385
Ebbesen, E. B., 508
Eckenrode, J., 425
Eckholm, E., 35
Eddy, R. L., 93
Egan, D. E., 168, 169
Eisenberg-Berg, N., 511
Eisert, D. C., 337
Ekman, P., 272–274
Elkin, I., 455, 458
Elliot, R., 448
Ellis, A., 441, 443
Ellsworth, P., 272
Elworth, C. L., 114
Endler, N. S., 373
Epstein, S., 373
Erikson, E. H., 330–331, 343–344
Eron, L. D., 507, 509
Evans, N. J., 476
Eysenck, H. J., 372, 385, 448

Falke, T. L., 379
Fanelli, R. J., 62
Fanselow, M. S., 52
Faraone, S. V., 419, 421
Fellner, D. J., 155
Festinger, L., 470–471, 497
Fiedler, F. E., 482
Field, T., 326
Fieve, R. R., 416
Fifer, W. D., 326
Fink, A., 24
Fioravanti, M., 377
Fischer, P., 507, 509
Fischman, M., 299
Fishbein, M., 467
Fisher, K., 453
Fiske, S. T., 474
Fletcher, G. J. O., 473
Foa, E. B., 269
Fodor, E. M., 252
Folkman, S., 425, 426
Forer, B., 379
Forestell, P. H., 203
Försterling, F., 481
Forsyth, P. D., 322, 335
Frable, D. E. S., 476
Frankenburg, W. K., 324
Franks, L., 303
Fraser, C., 201
Frederikson, N., 217
Freeman, W., 455
Freud, S., 16–17, 247, 288–289, 360–368, 411
Friedman, J. L., 507
Friedman, R., 296
Friesen, W. V., 272–274

Galanter, E., 82
Gallup, G. G., Jr., 31
Gama, E. M. P., 252
Garfield, S. L., 448, 449
Gatchel, R. J., 8, 424
Gazzaniga, M. S., 67–69
Gebhard, P. H., 245
Gebner, G., 507
Geen, R. G., 506
Geller, E. S., 19, 20
Gelman, R., 337
Getzels, J. W., 343, 347
Gholson, J. B., 337
Gibbon, M., 416
Gibbs, M. E., 181
Gilligan, C., 341, 343, 347
Ginsberg, A., 395
Gladue, B., 247
Gladwin, T., 211
Glass, A., 178
Glass, D., 458
Glass, G. V., 448, 449
Glick, P., 500
Goldfried, M., 437
Goldman, R., 242
Goleman, D., 69, 353, 501
Gordon, A., 242
Gormley, F. P., 514
Gottesman, I. I., 419
Gottfried, A. W., 337
Gough, H. G., 377
Gould, R. L., 346, 347
Gove, W. R., 404
Grajek, S., 499
Green, P., 93, 109
Gregory, R. L., 114
Greiffen, L. M., 513, 514
Groner, M., 191
Groner, R., 191
Gross, L., 507
Grossberg, S., 116, 118
Grossman, B. S., 254
Grossman, H. J., 222
Grusec, J. E., 440, 512
Guilford, J. P., 217
Guze, S. B., 414

Haber, R. N., 110
Hagen, E., 214
Hainline, L., 326
Hannon, R., 302
Hardy-Brown, K., 337
Harlow, H. F., 254, 326
Harlow, J. M., 65
Harlow, M. K., 254
Harte, R. A., 241
Hartmann, E., 286
Harvey, J. G., 478
Harvey, J. H., 479

Hathaway, B., 52
Hatvany, N., 484
Hay, D. F., 325
Hayman, J., 379
Hays, R. B., 500
Hechinger, F. M., 338
Heckhausen, H., 250
Heider, F., 478
Heilman, M. E., 498
Helmreich, R. L., 12, 476
Henderson, R. W., 254, 256
Hendrick, C., 499
Hendrick, S., 499
Hennessey, B. A., 254
Heppner, P. P., 481
Herman, L. M., 203
Herman, L. P., 242
Hersh, R. H., 512
Herskovits, M. J., 114
Higbee, K. L., 171
Higgins, J., 107
Hilgard, E. R., 294
Hilgard, J. R., 294
Hill, C. T., 246
Hinton, G. E., 158
Hoban, T. M., 457
Hobson, J. A., 290
Hochberg, J. E., 107
Hodes, R. L., 270
Hodgson, R., 410, 439
Hogness, D., 93
Holahan, C. J., 514
Holden, C., 303, 385, 484
Holland, C. C., 494
Hollander, E. P., 495–496
Hollingshead, A. B., 403
Holmes, D. S., 295
Holt, N. C., 139
Holyoak, K. J., 178
Holzman, A. D., 104
Honts, C. R., 270
Honzik, C. H., 152
Hope, B., 95
Hopkins, B. L., 144
Horn, M. C., 246
Horner, M., 252
Hortsman, W., 35
Hough, R. L., 397
Houston, L. N., 245
Hovland, C., 469
Howells, J. G., 395, 400
Hudson, W., 115
Huesmann, L. R., 507, 509
Hull, C. L., 255
Hunt, M., 245, 247
Hutchison, J. B., 247

Ickes, W., 500
Imber, S., 458
Ingelfinger, F. J., 241
Inhelder, B., 336
Institute of Medicine, 304
Izard, C. E., 273

Jackson-Beeck, M., 507
James, W., 15, 16, 266
Janis, I. L., 12, 469
Jeffries-Fox, S., 507
Jensen, A., 229
Johnson, J. T., 379
Johnson, V. E., 247
Jones, L. V., 231
Jordan, T. J., 330
Joyce, C., 99
Joyce, J., 394
Joyce, M. R., 441
Jung, C., 368–369
Jungeblut, A., 220

Kagan, J., 320
Kahle, L. R., 337
Kahn, R. L., 353
Kahn, S., 343, 347
Kahneman, D., 193, 194
Kane, J. M., 451, 452
Kanfer, F. H., 437, 439
Kaplan, M. F., 475, 512
Karasu, T. B., 433
Karlins, M., 469
Karoly, P., 437, 439
Kassin, S. M., 176
Kastenbaum, R., 351
Katz, D., 476
Kaufman, J., 301
Kazdin, A. E., 437, 443
Kearsley, R. B., 320
Keasey, B., 337
Keating, D. P., 337
Keerdoja, E., 202, 203
Keesey, R. E., 240
Keith, S. J., 419
Keith-Spiegel, P., 31
Kelley, H., 474, 478–479
Kelley, L., 377, 475
Kelly, H. H., 469
Kendig, F., 226
Kennedy, T. D., 439
Kentron, J. L., 213
Kepner, C. R., 509
Kerouac, J., 395
Kerris, M. H., 498
Kertesz, A. E., 64
Khan, S. A., 302
Kinsey, A. C., 245, 247
Kirschbaum, J., 107
Klein, D. F., 415
Klein, R., 507, 509
Kleinmuntz, B., 381
Klerman, G. L., 407, 409
Klima, E. S., 203
Knittle, J. L., 243
Kohlberg, L., 341, 342, 512
Köhler, W., 189
Kolata, G., 232, 276, 307
Konecni, V. J., 508
Koocher, G. P., 31
Kosecoff, J., 24
Kozak, M. S., 269
Kraepelin, E., 417
Kraft, C. L., 114
Kraines, S. H., 410
Kramer, M., 397
Krasner, L., 395, 420
Krebs, D. L., 504
Kringlen, E., 419
Kübler-Ross, E., 351
Kulik, C. C., 220
Kulik, J. A., 174, 220
Kumura, H. K., 439

Lader, M., 409
LaFrance, M., 271
Lamal, P. A., 5
Lamb, M. F., 379
Lambert, M. J., 448
Landis, D., 482, 483
Landman, J., 448
Langer, E., 476, 482
Langfeld, H. S., 111
Lashley, K. S., 183, 184
Lasley, D. J., 90
Latané, B., 22, 26–27, 30, 31, 510
Lauer, J., 500–502
Lauer, R., 500–502
Lawton, M. P., 497
Lazari, R., 377
Lazarus, A. A., 263
Lazarus, R. S., 425, 426
Leber, W., 458
Lechtenberg, R., 66–67
Lefkowitz, M. M., 507
Lehmkuhle, S., 46
Leiman, A. L., 61
Lemerise, E., 326
LePage, A., 506
Lepper, M. R., 254
Levenson, R. W., 273, 274
Levinger, G., 500
Levinson, D. J., 346
Levy, J., 67
Levy, W. B., 46
Lewy, A. J., 457
Lindsay, P. H., 91, 170
Lindy, J., 62
Linville, P. W., 481
Loaws, O. R., 144
Lochhead, J., 197
Lock, B. Z., 397
Lockhart, R. S., 171
Loeb, G. E., 101
Loftus, E. A., 176
Loftus, E. F., 176, 190
Lorenz, K., 505
Lovaas, O. I., 439
Lowell, E. L., 250
Luborsky, L., 437, 448
Luria, A. R., 164, 178
Lynch, G., 184
Lynn, S. J., 282, 290, 294

Maass, A., 496
McCain, G., 513
McCarley, R. W., 290
McClelland, D. C., 250
McConnell, J. V., 668
McCrae, R. R., 411
MacDonald, C. J., 271
MacDonald, M. L., 451
McGaugh, J. L., 184

McGrew, P. L., 482, 483
McGuire, W. J., 567
McGuire, W. T., 495
McKean, K., 404
McKee, K. D., 456
MacKenzie, B., 228
McKusick, L., 35
McNeal, E. T., 416, 432
Maer, F., 68
Maeroff, G. I., 224
Magnusson, D., 373
Mahoney, M. J., 437
Malamuth, N. M., 509
Malinowski, C. I., 341
Mandel, D. R., 513, 514
Mann, L., 12
Manstead, A. S. R., 271
Marks, I. M., 443
Marr, D. C., 118
Marshall, G., 269
Martin, C. E., 247
Maslow, A., 258–260, 376
Mason, J. W., 425
Massman, P. J., 449
Masters, W. H., 247
Matthews, A., 409
Matthews, S. M., 419
Mawhinney, V. T., 144
May, R., 445
Mayer, D. J., 52
Mayer, G. R., 439, 508
Mayo, C., 271
Mednick, S. A., 107
Megenity, D., 456
Melges, F. T., 422
Mellers, B. A., 497
Melville, J., 408
Melzack, R., 104
Menlove, F. L., 440
Meredith, L. A., 302
Messick, S., 220
Metcalfe, M., 452
Metee, D. R., 497
Meyer, D. R., 254
Meyer, J. P., 497
Meyer, R. G., 411
Michelmore, P., 238
Milewski, A. E., 326
Milgram, J., 493–494
Miller, A. B., 482, 483
Miller, D. T., 504
Miller, G. A., 167
Miller, J. D., 298
Miller, L. L., 304
Miller, L. S., 457
Miller, N., 482
Miller, N. E., 31, 350, 374, 506
Miller, R. C., 449
Miller, T. J., 448, 449
Milner, B., 164
Milner, P., 62
Mineka, S., 254, 256
Mingolla, E., 118
Mirsky, A. F., 418
Mischel, W., 373
Mitchell, A. A., 469
Mitchell, R., 482
Mitchell, R. E., 514

Moeller, G. H., 251
Molotsky, I., 101
Moscovici, S., 492, 495, 496
Mowrer, O. H., 506
Mucha, T. F., 411
Mugny, G., 495, 496
Munnichs, U., 348
Mussen, P., 348, 511
Muzio, J. N., 287
Myers, J. K., 397

Nahome, L., 497
Nathans, J., 93
National Institute of Drug Abuse, 304
Newman, J., 244
New York Times, 101, 297, 315
Nezlek, J., 498
Ng, K. T., 181
Nickerson, R. S., 190
Nida, S., 31, 510
Nisbett, R. E., 242, 243
Noble, E., 303
Noll, K. M., 419
Norman, D. A., 91, 170
Nowicki, S., 415, 422, 456

O'Brien, E. J., 373
Oden, M. H., 224
Olbricht, E., 348
Olds, J., 62
Olds, S., 316
Orne, M. T., 270, 294, 494
Ornstein, R. E., 72
Orwin, R. G., 448, 449
Orzek, A. M., 456
Osborn, M. L., 395, 400
Osborne, Y. V. H., 411
Owen, P. L., 382

Pack, S. J., 477
Palladino, J. J., 285
Palmer, J. C., 176
Paolitto, D. P., 512
Papalia, D., 316, 476
Parlee, M. B., 498
Parloff, M. B., 437
Paulus, P. B., 513
Pavlov, I. P., 128–131
Peake, P. K., 373
Pearl, J., 206
Penfield, W., 64
Penrod, S., 492, 495
Peplau, L. A., 246
Pepper, S., 497
Perillo, E., 379
Perkins, D. N., 114, 190
Perls, F. S., 446
Perri, M., 498
Pervin, L. A., 373
Peters, D., 31
Peterson, L. R., 169
Peterson, M. J., 169
Pettitto, L. A., 203
Petty, R. E., 470, 495

Piaget, J., 330–337, 341
Piantanidu, T. P., 93
Piliavin, I. M., 510
Piliavin, J. A., 510
Pilkonis, P., 458
Plotkin, J., 31
Plutchik, R., 264–265
Polivy, J., 242
Pomeroy, W. B., 245, 247
Porac, C., 85, 111–115
Postman, L. J., 177
Powley, T. L., 240
Pribram, K. H., 66, 268
Prien, R. F., 452
Prinzhorn, H., 418
Psotka, J., 173, 179
Pucik, V., 484

Quinlan, D. M., 414
Quitoriano, L. A., 302

Rachman, S., 410, 439
Raczynski, J. M., 105
Ragozin, A. S., 330
Ramey, C. T., 329
Ransberger, V. M., 514
Raphael, B., 190
Raskin, D. C., 270
Rasmussen, T., 64
Raupp, C. D., 244
Rayner, R., 131
Raynor, J. O., 250
Redich, F. C., 403
Reiger, D. A., 397
Reimer, J., 512
Reinhardt, R. F., 411
Reis, H. T., 498
Reisenzein, R., 269
Reuman, D. A., 251
Rhue, J., 282, 290, 294
Rice, A., 188, 196
Rice, B., 32
Riegel, K. F., 349
Riegel, R. M., 349
Rifkin, A., 452
Rinn, W. E., 273
Ristau, C. A., 203
Ritzler, B., 418
Robbins, D., 203
Robbins, W. J., 325
Roberts, A. H., 71
Robins, L. N., 397
Rodin, J., 243, 476
Roffwarg, H. F., 287
Rogers, C. R., 375–376, 402, 444–445
Rokeach, M., 482
Rorschach, H., 382
Rosen, A., 381
Rosenbaum, G., 418
Rosenfeld, A., 95
Rosenhan, D. L., 394
Rosenkrantz, P. S., 476
Rosenthal, D., 415
Rosenthal, T. L., 337
Rosenzweig, M. R., 61, 181
Ross, D., 152, 508

Ross, M., 473
Ross, S., 152, 508
Routtenberg, A., 62
Rowe, J. W., 353
Rozin, P., 240, 241
Rubanowitz, D. E., 480
Rubin, D. C., 174–175
Rubin, Z., 246, 499
Rudd, J. R., 20
Rumbaugh, D. M., 202
Rushton, J. P., 512
Russo, D. C., 439
Russo, N., 379
Rutter, M., 330
Ryan, N. D., 419
Ryan, R. M., 254

Sack, R. L., 457
Sackheim, H. A., 454
Sanders, R. J., 203
Sarason, I. G., 440
Sattler, J. M., 214
Savage-Rumbaugh, E. S., 202
Savich, P., 241
Saxe, L., 270
Scarr, S., 230, 231
Schachter, S., 242, 243, 268, 497
Schacter, D., 180
Schaeffer, M. A., 8
Schaffer, H., 301
Schaie, K. W., 349, 350, 353
Schank, R., 226
Scheff, T. J., 263
Scheibel, A., 420
Scherer, K. R., 269
Schickedanz, D. I., 322, 335
Schickedanz, J. A., 322, 335
Schiffman, H. R., 83, 114
Schmalt, H. D., 250
Schmeck, H. M., Jr., 49
Schneider, K., 250
Schneiderman, N., 424
Schoeneman, T. J., 480
Schofield, W., 437
Schwartz, B. J., 168, 169
Schwartz, G. E., 68
Sears, D. D., 471
Sears, R. R., 224, 506
Segall, M. H., 114
Sejnowski, T. J., 158
Seligman, M. E. P., 153, 416
Selye, H., 425
Shapiro, D. A., 448
Shea, T., 458
Shields, J., 419
Shiffrin, R. M., 165
Shock, N. W., 348
Shotland, R. L., 510, 511
Shows, T. B., 93
Sigman, M. D., 232
Signorielli, N., 507
Simmons, J. V., Jr., 147–148
Simon, T., 213
Singer, B., 448
Singer, J. E., 268
Singer, J. L., 290
Singer, M. T., 420
Sinoway, C. G., 244
Siris, S. G., 452
Skinner, B. F., 137, 148, 190, 201, 374
Skodol, A. E., 416
Skrypnek, B. J., 476
Skubiski, S. L., 512
Smialek, Z., 321
Smith, C. P., 341
Smith, E. E., 190
Smith, E. R., 474
Smith, M. L., 448, 449
Snarey, J. R., 341
Snyder, M., 474, 476, 500
Snyder, S. H., 419
Solomon, R. L., 257, 258
Sotsky, S., 458
Southwick, L., 302
Spence, D. P., 437
Spence, J. T., 250, 476
Sperling, G., 166
Sperry, R., 69–70
Spiegel, N., 498
Spitzer, R. L., 416
Spring, B., 421
Squire, L. R., 180, 181, 184
Staats, A. W., 468
Staats, C. K., 468
Stanley, J. C., 224, 225
Stapp, J., 7, 11
Stark, E., 106
Staub, E., 512
Steele, C. M., 302
Steiner, J. E., 326
Sternberg, R. J., 213, 218, 219, 499–502
Stevens, C. F., 63
Stiles, W. B., 448
Stone, G., 116
Stopeck, M. H., 498
Strauss, M. S., 325
Streufert, S., 219
Stricker, E. M., 241
Strupp, H. H., 437
Stryker, J. C., 321
Stull, D. E., 497
Suarez, S. D., 31
Sullivan, B., 246
Sullivan, W., 66
Sulzer-Azaroff, B., 155, 439, 508
Sweeney, P. D., 471
Szasz, T. S., 400, 408
Szilagyi, A. D., Jr., 484

Tagiuri, R., 497
Tanford, S., 492, 495
Taylor, S. E., 474
Tennent, S. S., 476
Terman, L. M., 224
Terrace, H. S., 203
Test, M. A., 512
Thomas, J. A., 482, 483
Thompson, D. M., 173
Thorndike, E. L., 136–137
Thorndike, R. L., 214
Tobias, L. L., 451
Tolman, E. C., 152
Tomlinson-Keasey, C., 327, 328, 337
Toohey, M. L., 420
Travers, J. A., 241
Treisman, M., 112
Triandis, H. C., 482
Tsuang, M. T., 419, 421
Tucker, A. M., 7, 11
Tucker, B. J., 456
Tuller, D., 383
Tulving, E., 169, 173, 179
Turk, D. C., 104
Turkington, C., 57
Turvey, M. T., 165
Tversky, A., 193, 194

Udolf, R., 295
Ullman, L. P., 395, 420

Vaillant, G. E., 407
Valenstein, E. S., 455
VandenBos, G. R., 7, 11
Veroff, J., 251
Verplanck, W. S., 139
Virgil, L., 456
Vogel, S. R., 476
Vonnegut, M., 452
von Restorff, H., 175

Wagner, H. L., 271
Wagner, R., 219
Waid, W. M., 270
Wald, G., 95
Walden, L. O., 507
Waldrop, M. M., 205
Wall, P. D., 104
Wallace, M. J., Jr., 484
Wallace, R. K., 295
Wallis, C., 78
Walster, E., 498, 499
Walster, G. W., 499
Ward, L. M., 85, 111–114
Watkins, J., 458
Watkins, L. R., 52
Watson, D., 480
Watson, J. B., 18, 131
Watt, N., 418
Weary, G., 478
Webb, W. B., 288
Weber, R., 476
Wechsler, D., 213
Weinberg, R. A., 230
Weinberger, N. M., 184
Weiner, B., 478
Weiner, R., 453
Weinstein, C. E., 69, 197
Weisman, S. R., 473
Weissman, M. M., 414
Weizenbaum, J., 225
Weld, H. P., 111
Wells, G. L., 176, 479
Wender, P. H., 415
Wertheimer, M., 107
Westoff, C. F., 247
Wheeler, L., 498

Whorf, B. L., 203
Widom, C. S., 381
Wilkinson, A. C., 148
Williams, J. B. W., 416
Willis, S. L., 349, 353
Wilson, G. T., 443
Wilson, T. D., 481
Winokur, G., 414
Winter, D. G., 250, 252
Wolpe, J., 439
Wolpert, E. A., 286, 289
Wood, K., 452
Wood, L., 508
Wood, W., 469
Woodruff, R. A., 414
Worchel, S., 456
Wurtman, R. J., 51
Wyden, B., 320
Wynne, L. C., 420

Yates, A. J., 71
Youkilis, H., 292

Zajonc, R. B., 263, 269, 497
Zanna, M. P., 477
Zelazo, P. R., 320
Zigmond, M. J., 241
Zillman, D., 506
Zimbardo, P., 269
Zimmer, J., 145–146
Zimmerman, G., 343, 347
Zimmerman, R. R., 326
Zivin, G., 273
Zubin, J., 421

SUBJECT INDEX

Abnormal behavior, 391–428
affective disorders, 414–416
anxiety disorders, 408–411
approaches to, 395–397
behavioral approaches to treatment for, 437–443
behavioral model of, 401–402
biological treatment approaches to, 450–456
census of mental disorder, 397
choosing right therapist for, 455–456
continuum of normal behavior and, 397
deciding to seek help, 422–423
as deviation from average, 395–396
as deviation from ideal, 396
dissociative disorders, 412–413
distinguishing normal from, 393–397
drug therapy for, 451–453
DSM-III classification of, 407–408
electroconvulsive therapy for, 453–454
humanistic approaches to treatment for, 444–447
humanistic model of, 402–403
as inability to function effectively, 397
insanity defense, 405
medical model of, 400
models of, 398–406
personality disorders, 421–422
psychoanalytic model of, 400–401
psychodynamic treatment for, 434–437
psychological approaches to treatment for, 433–450
psychology of health and stress, 424–426
psychosurgery for, 454–455
psychotherapy for, 433–450
schizophrenia, 416–421
search for new treatments, 457–458
as sense of subjective discomfort, 396
sociocultural model of, 403–404
somatoform disorders, 411–412
treatment of, 431–460
Absolute refractory period, 49
Absolute threshold, 81–82
Accident prevention programs, 155
Accommodation, 89
Acetylcholine (ACh), 51
Achievement, need for, 250–252
Achievement test, 215–216
''Acid,'' 300, 305
Acquired immune deficiency syndrome (AIDS), psychology and, 34–36
Action potential, 49
Acupuncture, 104
Adaptation, 84
dark, 92
light, 92
Addictive drugs, 297
fetal development effects of, 322
Adler, Alfred, 369
Adolescence, 339–345
definition of, 340
moral and cognitive development in, 341–343
physical development in, 340
psychosocial development in, 343–345
Adulthood:
early and middle, 345–347
late, 347–352
Advertisements:
and brain hemispheric specialization, 69
professional persuasion, 469–470
Affective disorders, 414–416
bipolar disorders, 416
definition of, 414
major depression, 414–416
mania, 416
Affiliation, need for, 252
Afterimage, 95
Age:
chronological, 214
mental, 213
Age of viability, 319
Aggression, 504–514
crowding and, 513–514
definition of, 504
frustration-aggression approaches to, 504–506
identifying, 505
instinct approaches to, 504–506
media, 507
observational learning approaches to, 506–508
reducing and preventing, 508
temperature and, 514
Aggressive cues, 506
Aging, 347–352
avoiding intellectual decline with, 352–353
cognitive changes with, 348–350
physical, 348
AIDS (acquired immune deficiency syndrome), psychology and, 34–36
Albert, classical conditioning experiment with, 131, 133
Alcohol use, 301, 303, 305, 322
Alcoholism, 303
fetal alcohol syndrome, 321
Algorithm, 190
bias in, 194–195
All-or-nothing law, 49
Allport's trait theory, 371
ALS (amyotrophic lateral sclerosis), 49
Altered states of consciousness, 283
hypnosis, 293–295
meditation, 294–296
Altruism, 511
Alzheimer's disease, 180, 350
Amphetamines, 299, 300
Amyotrophic lateral sclerosis (ALS), 49
Anal stage, 364
Andersen-Schiess, Gabriella, 239
Andrews, Reginald, 504
Androgen, 244
Androgynous, 476
''Angel dust,'' 301, 305
Anorexia nervosa, 244
Antianxiety drugs, 453
Antidepressant drugs, 452
Antipsychotic drugs, 451–452
Antisocial personality disorder, 422
Anvil, 97
Anxiety, 366, 408
Anxiety disorders, 408–411
generalized, 409
obsessive-compulsive disorder, 409–411
panic disorder, 409
phobic disorder, 409
Aphasia, 66
Apraxia, 66
Aptitude test, 216
Archetypes, 369
Archival research, 23
Aristotle, 339
Arousal theory of motivation, 255–257
Artificial intelligence, 225–226
Association area of brain, 64–67
definition of, 65
Attachment, 326
Attachment Behavioral System, 328
Attitudes, 467–468
changing job, 484–485
classical conditioning and, 467–468
definition of, 467
forming and maintaining, 467–468
reinforcement approaches to acquisition of, 468
Attribution biases, 479–480
Attribution processes, 478–482
Attribution theory, 478
Auditory canal, 97
Autonomic division, 54
Autonomic nervous system, 55
Autonomy-versus-shame-and-doubt stage, 330, 343
Availability heuristic, 193
Average, abnormality as deviation from, 395–396

Aversive conditioning, 438
Axon, 47

Babble, 199
Babinski reflex, 324
Barbiturates, 300, 302
Basilar membrane, 98
BEAM (brain electrical activity mapping), 57, 58, 73
Begin, Menachem, 414
Behavior analysis, 154–157
Behavior modification, 155
Behavioral model, 16–18
of abnormality, 401–402
Behavioral self-management, 442
Behavioral treatment approaches, 437–443
Bell, Lance Cpl. Karl, 238
Benzedrine, 299, 300
Bimodal distribution, 522
Binet, Alfred, 213
Binocular disparity, 109
Biofeedback, 71
brain and, 70–72
for pain, 105
Biological model, 16–17
Biology:
and behavior, 43–75
of memory, 180–181
Biopsychologists, 45
models used by, 19
Biopsychology, 8
Bipolar cells, 91
Bipolar disorder, 416
Bisexuality, 247
Blind spot, 90
Blindness, color, 93–95
Brain, 56–62
association area of, 64–67
biofeedback and, 70–72
cerebral cortex, 63–67
hemispherical specialization, 67–72
motor area of, 63–64
sensory area of, 64
split-brain patients, 69–70
transplanting, 66
Brain electrical activity mapping (BEAM), 57, 58, 73
Brain scan, 57, 284
Broca, Paul, 66
Broca's aphasia, 66
Bulimia, 244

Caffeine, 298
California Psychological Inventory, 382
Campus crisis centers, 456
Cannon-Bard theory of emotion, 267–268
Cardinal trait, 371
Casals, Pablo, 352
Case study, 23
CAT (computerized axial tomography), 57, 58
CAT scans, 57, 58
Catatonic schizophrenia, 418
Catharsis hypothesis, 508
Cattell and Eysenck's trait theory, 371–372
Central core, 58
Central nervous system (CNS), 53
Central route processing, 470
Central tendency, 521
Central traits, 371, 474
Cerebellum, 59
Cerebral cortex, 63–67
definition of, 63
Chlorpromazine, 451
Chromosomes, 318
Chronological age, 214
Chunk, 167
Churchill, Winston, 352
Classical conditioning, 128–134
applied to human behavior, 131–132
and attitudes, 467–468
definition of, 129
discriminating between operant conditioning and, 149–150
extinction, 132
generalization and discrimination, 133
higher-order conditioning, 133–134
Pavlov and, 128–131
spontaneous recovery, 132–133
in therapy, 438–439
Client-centered therapy, 444–445
Clinical psychologists, models used by, 19
Clinical psychology, 9
Close relationships, 496
Closure, 107
CNS (central nervous system), 53
Cocaine, 297, 299, 300
Cochlea, 98
Cognition(s), 188, 470
Cognitive-behavioral therapy, 441–442
Cognitive consistency approach to attitudes, 468–472
Cognitive development, 332–338, 341–343, 348–350
in adolescence, 341–343
definition of, 333
maximizing, 337–338
Piaget's theory of, 333–337
Cognitive dissonance, 470
Cognitive learning theory, 151
Cognitive map, 152
Cognitive model, 16, 17
Cognitive psychologists, 188
models used by, 19
Cognitive psychology, 8
Cognitive theory of motivation, 259
Collective unconscious, 368
College students:
campus crisis centers, 456
grade improvement by attribution improvement, 481
psychological problems among, 415
teaching thinking to, 197
Color blindness, 93–95
Color vision, 93–95
Common sense, complexities of, 205–206
Compliance, 493–494
Compulsions, 410
Computer-assisted programmed instruction, 148–149
Computer learning capabilities, 158–159
Computerized axial tomography (CAT), 57, 58
Concept, 204
Conception, 318
Concrete operational stage, 335–336
Conditioned response (CR), 129
Conditioned stimulus (CS), 129
Cones, 90
Confederate, 30
Conformity, 491–493
Conscience, 363
Consciousness, 283
(*See also* States of consciousness)
Consensus information, 478
Consistency, 495
Consistency information, 479
Constructive processes, 175, 177
Consumer psychology, 10
Contingency contracting, 441
Continuous reinforcement schedule, 141
Continuum, 397
Control group, 26
Conversion disorders, 411
Coping, 425
emotion-focused, 426
problem-focused, 426
Cornea, 88
Correlation coefficient, 528–530
definition of, 528
Correlational research, 24–26
Counseling psychologists, models used by, 19
Counseling psychology, 10
Cowings, Patricia, 99
CR (conditioned response), 129
Crowding, 513–514
Crystallized intelligence, 217, 349
Cultural assimilator, 482
Culture-fair IQ test, 229
Cumulative recorder, 142

DA (dopamine), 51
Dark adaptation, 92
Day-care, effects of, 329–330
Daydreams, 290
Deaf, electronic ear implants for, 101
Death, stages in facing, 351
Decay, 178
Decibels, 100
Declarative knowledge, 180
Defense mechanisms, 366–367, 425, 434
Delusions, 418
Dendrites, 47
Denial, 366
Dependent variable, 27
Depressants, 301–302
Depression, major, 416
Depth perception, 109
DES (diethylstilbestrol), 322
Descartes, René, 14
Descriptive statistics, 519
Determinism, 375
Development, 313–356
adolescent, 339–345
aging, 347–352
cognitive, 332–338, 341–343, 348–350
conception and prenatal, 318–321
early and middle adulthood, 345–347
Erikson's psychosocial theory of, 330–331, 343–344
moral, 341–343
of perception, 325–326
physical, 323–326, 340, 346, 348

Development (*Cont.*):
Piaget's theory of cognitive, 333–337
postnatal, 323–325
social, 326–331, 343–347
Developmental psychologists, models used by, 19
Developmental psychology, 8, 314
Deviation IQ score, 214
Dexedrine, 299, 300
Diagnostic and Statistical Manual of Mental Disorders, third edition (*DSM-III*), 407–408
Dichotic listening, 111
Diet, fetal development and, 322
Diethylstilbestrol (DES), 322
Dieting, 248
and exercise, 275–276
Difference threshold, 83
Diffusion of responsibility, 510
Discriminative stimulus, 144–145
Disorganized (hebephrenic) schizophrenia, 418
Displacement, 366
Display rules, 274
Dispositional causes of behavior, 478
Dissociative disorders, 412–413
Distinctiveness information, 479
Dollard and Miller's stimulus-response theory of personality, 374
Dopamine (DA), 51
Dopamine hypothesis, 419
Double-bind hypothesis, 419
Double-blind procedure, 29
Double standard, 246
Down's syndrome, 223, 320, 322
Dream interpretation, 435
Dreams, 288–291
daydreams, 290
Freudian theory and, 288–289
function and meaning of, 288–291
latent content of, 288, 436
manifest content of, 288, 436
Drive-reduction theory of motivation, 255
Drives, 240
primary, 240
secondary, 240
Drug therapy, 451–453
antianxiety drugs, 453
antidepressant drugs, 452
antipsychotic drugs, 451–452
definition of, 451
minor tranquilizers, 453
Drug use and abuse, 297–307
addictive drugs, 297
alcohol, 301, 303, 305
dealing with, 305
depressants, 301–302
hallucinogens, 302–305
for pain, 105
psychoactive drugs, 297
"sober" pill, search for, 301, 303, 305
stimulants, 298–300
DSM-III (Diagnostic and Statistical Manual for Mental Disorders, third edition), 407–408

Ear, 97–98
electronic implants for deaf, 101
Ear (*Cont.*):
inner, 98
middle, 97
outer, 97
structure of, 97–98
Eardrum, 97
Eating:
dieting and weight loss, 248, 275–276
disorders of, 243–244
social factors in, 242–243
(*See also* Hunger)
Echoic memory, 165
Eclectic approach to therapy, 433
ECT (electroconvulsive therapy), 453–454
Education for All Handicapped Children Act of 1975 (Public Law 94-142), 223
Educational psychologists, models used by, 19
Educational psychology, 10
Edwards Personal Preference Schedule, 382
EEG (electroencephalogram), 57, 58, 284
EEG imaging, 57, 58, 284
Ego, 363
Ego-ideal, 363
Ego-integrity-versus-despair stage, 343, 344
Egocentric thought, 334
Einstein, Albert, 219, 259, 260, 317
Elaborative rehearsal, 171
Elderly (*see* Aging)
Electroconvulsive therapy (ECT), 453–454
Electroencephalogram (EEG), 57, 58, 284
Eliza computer program, 225–226
Ellis, Albert, 443
Embryo, 319
Emotion-focused coping, 426
Emotions, 261–275
Cannon-Bard theory of, 267–268
definition of, 262
expressing, 271–275
facial-feedback hypothesis, 273–274
functions of, 263–264
James-Lange theory of, 266–267
nonverbal behavior of expression of, 271–275
range of, 264–265
Schachter-Singer theory of, 268–269
understanding, 261–269
universality in emotional expressivity, 271–273
Empathy, 511
Endocrine system, 60–61
Endorphins, 52
Engram (memory trace), 178, 183–184
Environment, 315
and intelligence, 227–231
nature-nurture question, 315–318
prenatal influences, 320–322
and schizophrenia, 419–420
Environmental psychologists, models used by, 19
Environmental psychology, 10, 513
Episodic memories, 169
Erikson's theory of psychosocial development, 330–331, 343–344
Escher, M. C., 110
Eskimos, 203
Esposito, Phil, 145
Estrogen, 244
Ethics in research, 31
Excitatory message, 51
Exercise, dieting and, 275–276
Existential therapy, 445–446
Experiment, 26
Experimental bias, 28
Experimental manipulation, 26
Experimental psychologists, models used by, 19
Experimental psychology, 8
Experimental research, 26–31
Experimenter expectations, 28
Extinction, 132
Extramarital sex, 247
Extrinsic motivation, 254
Eye, 87–95
adaptation, 92
color vision and color blindness, 93–95
message to brain from, 91–93
structure of, 88–91

Facial-affect program, 273
Facial-feedback hypothesis, 273–274
Factor analysis, 371
Familial retardation, 223
Fear of success, 252
Fears, hierarchy of, 439
Fetal alcohol syndrome, 321
Fetus, 319
environmental influences on, 320–322
genetic influences on, 320
Figure/ground, 110
Fixation, 364
Fixed-interval schedule, 144
Fixed-ratio schedule, 143
Flashbulb memories, 174–175
Fluid intelligence, 217, 349
Forensic psychology, 10
Forewarning, 495
Forgetfulness:
in aging, 349–350
(*See also* Memory)
Formal operational stage, 336–337
Fovea, 90
Free association, 435
Free will, 18
Frequency, 99
Frequency distribution, 519
Frequency theory of hearing, 101
Freud, Sigmund:
and conversion disorders, 411
psychoanalytic theory of, 360, 362–368
psychoanalytic therapy of, 435–437
on schizophrenia, 419
views on dreams, 288–289
Friendship, 496–498
need for, 252
Frontal lobes, 63
Frustration, 506
Frustration-aggression approach, 506
Functional fixedness, 194
Functionalism, 15
Fundamental attribution bias, 480

Gag reflex, 323
Gage, Phineas, 64–65
Ganglion cells, 91

Gate-control theory of pain, 104
Generalized anxiety disorder, 409
Generativity-versus-stagnation stage, 343, 344
Genes, 318
Genetic influences:
on fetus, 320
(*See also* Heredity)
Genetic makeup, 316
Genital stage, 366
Genovese, Kitty, 21, 22, 504, 511
German measles, 320–321
fetal development effects of, 322
Gerontologists, 348
Gestalt laws of organization, 107–108
Gestalt psychology, 15–16
Gestalt therapy, 446–447
Gestalts, 107
Glaucoma, 92
Grade improvement by attribution improvement, 481
Grammar, 198–199
universal, 202
Grandma Moses, 352
Ground, distinguishing figure from, 110

Habituation, 325
Hair cells, 98
Hallucinations, 418
Hallucinogens, 302–305
Hammer, 97
Hashish, 300, 304
Health psychologists, models used by, 19
Health psychology, 9, 424–426
Hearing, 97–102
frequency theory of, 101
physical aspects of, 98–102
place theory of, 101
structure of ear, 97–98
Hebephrenic schizophrenia, 418
Helping behavior (*see* Prosocial behavior)
Hemispheres of brain, 67
Heredity, 316
and intelligence, 227–231
nature-nurture question, 315–318
and schizophrenia, 419
of traits, 384–385
Heritability, 229
Heroin, 300, 302
Heterosexuality, 245–246
Heuristic, 191
availability, 193
bias in, 194–195
representativeness, 192
Hierarchy of fears, 439
Higher-order conditioning, 133–134
Hinckley, John, 392, 393, 395, 400, 401, 404–405
Histogram, 519
Homeostasis, 60, 240
Homosexuality, 247
Hormones, 60
Humanistic model, 16, 18
of abnormality, 402–403
Humanistic theories of personality, 375–377
Humanistic therapy, 444–447
definition of, 444
Hunger, 240–244

Hypnosis, 293–294
outside laboratory, 295
for pain, 105
Hypochondriasis, 441
Hypothalamus, 60, 241
lateral, 241
ventromedial, 241
Hypotheses, 22

Iconic memory, 165
Id, 363
Ideal, abnormality as deviation from, 396
Identical twins, 317–318
Identification, 365
Identity, 343
Identity-versus-role-confusion stage, 343
Impression formation, 474
Incentive theory of motivation, 257
Independent variable, 27
Industrial-organizational psychologists, models used by, 19
Industrial-organizational psychology, 10
Industry-versus-inferiority stage, 331, 343
Inferential statistics, 526–527
Inferiority complex, 369
Information:
consensus, 478
consistency, 479
distinctiveness, 479
Ingroup-outgroup bias, 476
Ingroups, 476
Inhibitory message, 51
Initiative-versus-guilt stage, 330, 343
Innate, 505
Inner ear, 98
Inoculation, 495
Insanity defense, 405
Insight, 189
Insomnia, 290
Instinct, 254
Instinct approach to aggression, 504–506
Instinctual drives, 362
Intellectually gifted, 224
Intelligence, 209–233
above normal, 224–225
artificial, 225–226
below normal, 222–224
contemporary approaches to understanding, 218–219
crystallized, 217, 349
defining, 211–221
environment and, 227–231
fluid, 217, 349
heredity and, 227–231
individual difference in, 227–231
measuring, 213–218
practical, 219
psychological definition of, 213
variations in, 222–225
work versus school, 219
Intelligence quotient (IQ), 214
Intelligence tests, 213–218
culturally-fair, 229
definition of, 213
improving performance on, 220–221
Intensity, 100

Interactionist, 317
Interference, 178
proactive, 179
retroactive, 179
Interpersonal attraction, 496–503
definition of, 496
friendships, 496–498
love, 498–503
Intimacy-versus-isolation stage, 343, 344
Intoxication, 301
Intrinsic motivation, 254
Introspection, 15
Introversion-extroversion, 372
IQ (intelligence quotient), 214
IQ score, 214
culture-fair testing, 229
deviation, 214
Iris, 88

James, William, 14–16
James-Lange theory of emotion, 266–267
Japanese job attitudes, 484–485
Job safety programs, 155
Jonestown mass suicide, 490, 491
Judgment biases, 193–197
Jung, Carl, 368–369
Just noticeable difference, 83

Keyword technique, 181
Kierkegaard, Søren, 414
Knoller, Fred, 349
Knowledge:
declarative, 180
procedural, 180
Kohlberg's sequence of moral reasoning, 341, 342
Krugman, Herbert, 69

Language, 198–206
acquisition of, 201–202
definition of, 198
development of, 199–201
grammar, 198–199
and thought, relationship between, 203–204
Language-acquisition device, 202
Lanugo, 323
Latency period, 366
Latent content of dreams, 288, 436
Latent learning, 151
Lateral hypothalamus, 241
Lateralization, 67
Law of effect, 136–137
Learned helplessness, 153
Learned-inattention theory of schizophrenia, 420
Learned not-thinking, 374
Learning, 125–161
behavior analysis and behavior modification, 154–157
classical conditioning, 128–134
cognitive approaches to, 151–154
definition of, 127
latent, 151
observational, 152, 440

Learning (*Cont.*):
operant conditioning, 135–150
vicarious, 468
Learning theories of personality, 373–375
of Dollard and Miller, 374
social learning theories, 374–375
Least-restrictive environment, 223
Lens of eye, 89
Levels-of-processing theory, 171–172
Lie detector, 269–270
Light, 87
Light adaptation, 92
Limbic system, 61–62
Lincoln, Abraham, 259, 260
Linear perspective, 109
Linguistic-relativity hypothesis, 203
Listening:
dichotic, 111
(*See also* Hearing)
Long-term memory, 168–171
definition of, 165
retrieval from, 172–177
Lou Gehrig's disease, 49
Louganis, Greg, 126, 127
Love relationships, 498–500
course of, 500–503
kinds of, 500
Lysergic acid diethylamide (LSD), 300, 305

Magnitude, 81
Mainstreaming, 223
Major depression, 416
Mania, 416
Manic-depressive disorder, 416
Manifest content of dreams, 288, 436
Mantra, 295
Marijuana, 300, 304
Marital sex, 246–247
Marital success, reasons for, 502
Martin, Steve, 67
Maslow's hierarchy of motivation, 259–261
Masturbation, 245
Maturation, 127, 316
Mean, 521
versus median versus mode, 522–523
Means-ends analysis, 192
Media aggression, 507
Median, 521–522
Medical model of abnormality, 400
Medical student's disease, 406
Meditation, 294–296
transcendental (TM), 295
Medulla, 58
Memory, 163–185
biological basis of, 180–181
changes in old age, 349–350
constructive processes in, 175, 177
in courtroom, 176
definition of, 165
echoic, 165
episodic, 169
failure in (forgetting), 178–182
flashbulb, 174–175
iconic, 165
improving, 181–182
Memory (*Cont.*):
long-term, 165, 168–177
mapping, 183–184
semantic, 170
sensory, 165–167
short-term, 165, 167–168
Memory trace (engram), 178, 183–184
Menopause, 346
Mental age, 213
Mental retardation, 222–224
Metabolism, 243
Methadone, 302
Method of loci, 181
Middle ear, 97
Midlife crisis, 347
Midlife transition, 346
Mild retardation, 222
Minnesota Multiphasic Personality Inventory (MMPI), 381–382
Minor tranquilizers, 453
MMPI (Minnesota Multiphasic Personality Inventory), 381–382
Mnemonics, 171
Mode, 522
Model in learning, 152
Modeling, 440
Models of psychology, 14–19
definition of, 14
types used by different psychologists, 19
Moderate retardation, 222
Monocular cues, 109
Moral development, 341–343
Moro (startle) reflex, 323
Morphine, 300, 302
Motion parallax, 109
Motivation, 239–260
arousal theory of, 255–257
cognitive theory of, 259
combining motives, 252–261
definition of, 238
drive-reduction theory of, 255
extrinsic, 254
hunger, 240–244
incentive theory of, 257
intrinsic, 254
Maslow's hierarchy, 259–261
need:
for achievement, 250–252
for affiliation, 252
for power, 252
opponent-process theory of, 257–259
primary drives, 239–249
sexual, 244–248
theories of, 253–259
Motives, 238
Motor area of brain, 63–64
Muller-Lyer illusion, 114
Multiple personality, 412
Myelin sheath, 48

Narcolepsy, 291
NASA, 99
Naturalistic observation, 23
Nature-nurture question, 315–318
definition of, 316
(*See also* Environment; Heredity)
Need:
for achievement, 250–252
for affiliation, 252
for power, 252
Negative reinforcer, 138, 140
Negative relationship, 528
Neo-Freudian psychoanalysts, 368–369
Neonate, 323
Nervous sytem, 45, 52–55
autonomic, 55
central, 53
peripheral, 53–54
Neural networks, 158
Neurometrics, 73–74
Neurons, 46–52
definition of, 46
firing of, 49
Neurotic anxiety, 366
Neurotic symptoms, 434
Neuroticism-stability, 372
Neurotransmitter, 51
Neutral stimulus, 129
New Guineans, emotional expression among, 271–273
Nicotine, 298
NMR imaging, 57, 58
NMR (nuclear magnetic resonance) scan, 57, 58
Noise, 82
Nondirective counseling, 445
Nonverbal behavior in expression of emotions, 271–275
Normal, distinguishing abnormal from, 393–397
Normal distribution, 522
Nuclear magnetic resonance (NMR) scan, 57, 58

Obesity, 242
weight set point and, 243–244
Object permanence, 334
Observational learning, 152, 375, 440
approaches to aggression, 506–508
Obsession, 409
Obsessive-compulsive disorder, 409–411
Occipital lobes, 63
Oedipal conflict, 365
Old age (*see* Aging)
Olfactory cells, 103
Oman, Charles, 99
Operant, 136
Operant conditioning, 135–150
basics of, 137–140
computer-assisted programmed instruction, 148–149
definition of, 136
discriminating between classical conditioning and, 149–150
discrimination and generalization in, 144–145
saving lives with, 147–148
schedules of reinforcement, 141–144
shaping, 146, 148
superstitious behavior, 145–146
in therapy, 440
Thorndike's law of effect, 136–137
Operationalization, 23

Opiate receptors, 52
Opponent-process theory:
of color vision, 95
of motivation, 257–259
Optic chiasma, 92
Optic nerve, 91
Oral stage, 364
Organizational socialization, 485
Otoliths, 98
Outer ear, 97
Outgroups, 476
Oval window, 97
Ovaries, 244
Overlearning, 182
Overregularization, 200
Ovulation, 244

Pain:
relief from, 104–106
sense of, 103–106
Pain clinic, 104–106
Pair Problem Solving, 197
Panic attacks, 409
Panic disorder, 409
Paranoid schizophrenia, 418
Paraplegia, 53
Parasympathetic division, 55
Parietal lobes, 63
Parthenon, visual illusion in, 112, 113
Partial reinforcement schedule, 141
Pavlov, Ivan, 128–130, 132, 134
PCP (phenylcyclidine), 301, 305
Penis envy, 365
Perception, 78, 106–115
depth, 109
development of, 325–326
in everyday life, 112–118
figure/ground differentiation, 109–110
gestalt law of organization, 107–108
perceptual constancy, 108–109
selective attention, 111–112
visual illusions, 112, 114–115
Perceptual constancy, 108–109
Perceptual style, 114–115
Peripheral nervous system, 53–54
Peripheral route processing, 470
Peripheral vision, 90
Personality, 359–387
assessing, 379–384
definition of, 360
humanistic theories of, 375–378
learning theories of, 373–375
psychoanalytic theories of, 361–369
self-report measures of, 381–382
versus situational factors, 373
social learning theories of, 374–375
stages of (Freudian), 364–366
trait theories of, 370–373
Personality disorders, 421–422
antisocial (sociopathic), 422
definition of, 422
Personality psychologists, models used by , 19
Personality psychology, 9
Persuasion, professional, 469–470
PET (positron emission tomography), 57, 58
PET scans, 57, 58
Phallic stage, 365
Phenylcyclidine (PCP), 301, 305
Phenylketonuria (PKU), 320
Phobias, 409
names of, 410
Phobic disorder, 409
Phonemes, 198
Phonology, 198
Physical attractiveness and relationships, 497–498
Physical development, 323–326, 340, 346, 348
in adolescence, 341–343
in early and middle adulthood, 346
Piaget's theory of cognitive development, 333–337
Pitch, 100
Pituitary gland, 61
PKU (phenylketonuria), 320
Place theory of hearing, 101
Placebo, 29
Pleasure principle, 363
Poggendorf illusion, 114
Polygraph, 269–270
Pons, 58
Population, 526
Pornography, violence and, 509
Positive reinforcer, 138, 140
Positive relationship, 528
Positron emission tomography (PET), 57, 58
Postnatal development, 324–325
Power, need for, 252
Practical intelligence, 219
Predisposition model of schizophrenia, 421
Prefrontal lobotomy, 454
Premarital sex, 246
Preoperational stage, 334–335
Pressure, sense of, 103
Primary drives, 240
Primary reinforcer, 138
Principle of conservation, 334
Proactive interference, 179
Problem-focused coping, 426
Problem solving, 189–197
cognitive processes in, 189–193
creative, 196
hindrances to, 193–197
strategies for, 195
thinking and, 190–193
Procedural knowledge, 180
Profound retardation, 222
Program evaluation, 11
Programmed instruction, 148
Projection, 367
Projective personality tests, 382
Prosocial behavior, 510–511
definition of, 510
learning, 511–512
Proximity, 107, 497
Psychoactive drugs, 297
Psychoanalysis, 435–437
Psychoanalysts, 361
neo-Freudian, 368–369
Psychoanalytic model of abnormality, 400–401
Psychoanalytic theories of personality, 361–369
Psychodynamic model, 16, 17
Psychodynamic therapy, 434–437
definition of, 434
Psychogenic amnesia, 413
Psychogenic fugue, 413
Psychological counseling for pain, 105
Psychological tests, 380
Psychology, 4
careers and specializations in, 7–11
distinguishing good from bad, 32–33
future of, 20
historical perspectives on, 15–16
theory and research in, 21–33
Psychophysics, 81
Psychosocial development, Erikson's theory of, 330–331, 343–344
Psychosomatic disorders, 425
Psychosurgery, 454–455
Psychotherapy, 433–450
behavioral approaches to, 437–443
definition of, 433
evaluating, 447–450
humanistic approaches to, 444–447
psychodynamic approaches to, 434–437
Puberty, 340
Punishment, 139
pros and cons of, 139–140
Pupil, 88

Racial prejudice, 483
Random assignment to condition, 27
Range, 525
Rape, pornography and, 509
Rapid eye movement (REM) sleep, 286
Rational-emotive therapy, 441
Rationalization, 366
Reagan, Ronald, assassination attempt against (*see* Hinckley, John)
Reality principle, 363
Rebound effect, 287
Recall, 174
Receptive aphasia, 67
Reciprocity-of-liking effect, 497
Recognition, 174
Reflexes, 323–324
Regression, 366
Rehearsal, 171
elaborative, 171
Reinforcement versus punishment, 139–140
Reinforcement schedules, 141–144
continuous, 141
fixed-interval, 144
fixed-ratio, 143
partial, 141
variable-interval, 144
variable-ratio, 143
Reinforcer, 137
negative, 138, 140
positive, 138, 140
primary, 138
secondary, 138
Relative refractory period, 49
Relative size, 109
Relaxation techniques for pain, 105
Reliability, 380
REM (rapid eye movement) sleep, 286
Replication, 31
Representativeness heuristic, 193